Statistics for the Behavioral Sciences

5e

Susan A. Nolan
Seton Hall University

Thomas E. Heinzen
William Paterson University

worth publishers
Macmillan Learning
New York

Senior Vice President, Content Strategy: Charles Linsmeier
Director of Content and Assessment: Shani Fisher
Executive Program Manager: Matt Wright
Developmental Editor: Michael Kimball
Assistant Editor: Nick Rizzuti
Marketing Manager: Clay Bolton
Marketing Assistant: Chelsea Simens
Director of Content Management Enhancement: Tracey Kuehn
Senior Managing Editor: Lisa Kinne
Executive Media Editor: Laura Burden
Associate Media Editor: Stephanie Matamoros
Media Project Manager: Joseph Tomasso
Senior Workflow Manager: Paul Rohloff
Senior Content Project Manager: Harold Chester
Senior Project Manager: Vanavan Jayaraman, Lumina Datamatics, Inc.
Senior Photo Editor: Sheena Goldstein
Director of Design, Content Management: Diana Blume
Design Services Manager: Natasha Wolfe
Interior Designer: Lumina Datamatics, Inc.
Cover Designer: John Callahan
Illustrations: MPS Limited, Evelyn Pence
Composition: Lumina Datamatics, Inc.
Printing & Binding: LSC Communications
Cover Painting: *Blue Lagoon*, oil on wood, 2016, by Leslie Wayne

Library of Congress Control Number: 2018968567

ISBN-13: 978-1-319-19074-3
ISBN-10: 1-319-19074-X

Printed in the United States of America

1 2 3 4 5 6   24 23 22 21 20 19

Worth Publishers
One New York Plaza
Suite 4600
New York, NY 10004-1562
www.macmillanlearning.com

For Liam, Nolan, and your menagerie
(yes, even Igor and Gojko),
with love from Aunt Susan

Susan Nolan

Susan Nolan

To the person who had
the best idea that anyone ever had:
Charles Darwin

Tom Heinzen

ABOUT THE AUTHORS

SUSAN NOLAN turned to psychology after suffering a career-ending accident on her second workday as a bicycle messenger. Susan graduated from the College of Holy Cross and earned her PhD in clinical psychology from Northwestern University. She studies mental health stigma as well as the role of gender in the fields of science, technology, engineering, and mathematics; her research has been funded by the National Science Foundation. Susan is a professor of psychology at Seton Hall University. She served as a representative from the American Psychological Association (APA) to the United Nations and chaired the 2012 Society for the Teaching of Psychology (STP) Presidential Task Force on Statistical Literacy. Susan is a past president of the Eastern Psychological Association (EPA) was a 2015–2016 U.S. Fulbright scholar, and will be president of STP in 2021. She is a fellow of the EPA, the APA, and the Association for Psychological Science.

Susan's academic schedule allows her to pursue her love of travel. She has ridden her bicycle across the United States (despite her earlier crash), swapped apartments to live in Montréal, and explored the Adriatic coast in a 1985 Volkswagen Scirocco. She writes much of the book on her annual trip to Bosnia and Herzegovina, where she and her husband, Ivan Bojanic, own a small house on the Vrbas River in the city of Banja Luka.

TOM HEINZEN was a 29-year-old college freshman and a magna cum laude graduate of Rockford College. He earned his PhD in social psychology at the State University of New York at Albany in just 3 years.

He published his first book on frustration and creativity in government 2 years later; was a research associate in public policy until he was fired for arguing over the shape of a graph; and then began a teaching career at William Paterson University of New Jersey. He founded the psychology club, established an undergraduate research conference, and has been awarded various teaching honors while continuing to write journal articles, books, plays, and two novels that support the teaching of general psychology and statistics. He is also the editor of *Many Things to Tell You*, a volume of poetry by elderly writers.

Tom is a member of numerous professional societies, and is a Fellow of the APA, the EPA, the APS, and the New York Academy of Science.

His wife, Donna, is a physician assistant who has volunteered her time in relief work following hurricanes Mitch and Katrina; and their daughters work in public health, teaching, and medicine.

BRIEF CONTENTS

CONTENTS

PREFACE

Statistics is hotter than ever. This is the era of big data. According to an article in *The New York Times*, statistics is perhaps the most promising, adventurous career option you can choose right now—and the field has been expanding significantly, thanks to the large amounts of information (called *big data*) available to us in this digital age. Glassdoor recently named "data scientist" as the best job in the United States for 2019, the fourth straight year. And data science jobs pay almost $9000 per year more than the average salary for all bachelor's level jobs (Sigelman, 2018). Gone is the stereotype of boring (but influential) statistics geeks hiding behind their glowing screens. The new reality requires smart, reflective people who have been trained to explore big data, transforming them into something useful, while not losing sight of the people behind the numbers. This book trains you to find and create data, ask tough questions about a data set, interpret the feedback coming from data analysis, and display data in ways that reveal a precise, coherent, data-driven story. Statistical reasoning is not *at* the cutting edge of information; statistical reasoning *is* the cutting edge of information.

At the same time, the field is undergoing revolutionary change. As a result of the situation—often called a crisis—in which researchers have been unable to replicate the findings of many earlier studies, ethical researchers are questioning everything. How should we collect and analyze data? How can we share our research methods, our statistical analyses, and even our actual data? And how might we foster critical thinking about approaches to research and data on an ongoing basis? The practices resulting from this revolution, often called "open science," are increasingly part of the undergraduate curriculum in the behavioral sciences (Chopik, Bremner, Defever, & Keller, 2018). The open science movement makes it an incredibly exciting time to be a behavioral science researcher!

VIPERR: Principles for Teaching Statistics

In their classic and persuasive article, Marsha Lovett and Joel Greenhouse (2000) present principles to teach statistics more effectively (all based on empirical research from cognitive psychology). And other researchers continue to build on their helpful work (see Benassi, Overson, & Hakala, 2014). We look to this body of research as we create every edition of this statistics text, from designing the pedagogy to deciding which specific examples to include. Six principles emerge from this research on teaching statistics and drive our text. We remember the six principles by the acronym VIPERR. (The second "R" is for repetition!)

1. **Vivid examples.** Researchers have found that students are most likely to remember concepts illustrated with a vivid instructional tool (VanderStoep, Fagerlin, & Feenstra, 2000). So, whenever possible, we use striking, vivid examples to make statistical concepts memorable, including the lengths of great white sharks to explain samples, destructive hurricanes in the discussion

The VIPERR approach to learning statistics We like to remember the cognitive psychology research on the teaching and learning of psychology by the acronym VIPERR: **V**ivid examples, **I**ntegration of new knowledge with existing knowledge, **P**ractice and participation, **E**xamination of misconceptions, **R**eal-time feedback, and **R**epetition. These research-backed techniques guide our teaching and writing.

of confounding variables, a Chipotle burrito hack to teach about control groups, a Damien Hirst dot painting to explain randomness, and a supposed link between tattooed engagement rings and a lasting marriage to highlight the concepts of illusory correlation and confirmation bias. Vivid examples are often accompanied by photos to enhance their memorability. When such examples are drawn from outside the academic literature, we follow with engaging research examples from the behavioral sciences to increase the memorability of important concepts.

2. **Integrating new knowledge with previous knowledge.** When connecting new material to existing student knowledge, students can more easily embed that new material into "a framework that will enable them to learn, retrieve, and use new knowledge when they need it" (Ambrose & Lovett, 2014, p. 7). Throughout the text, we illustrate new concepts with examples that connect to things most students already know. In Chapter 1, an example of behavioral tests to determine whether shelter dogs are adoptable highlights the difficulties in operationalizing variables. In Chapter 5, we use students' understanding of the potential fallibility of pregnancy tests to teach the

difference between Type I and Type II errors. Chapter 16 teaches regression by exploring police use of algorithms to predict the locations of future crimes. And Chapter 18 presents research on characteristics of Airbnb listings to teach students how to choose the right statistical test. Learning in different contexts helps students to transfer knowledge to new situations, so we use multiple examples for each concept—typically an initial one that is easier to grasp followed by more traditional behavioral science research examples.

3. **Practice and participation.** Recent research has shown that active learning, broadly defined, increases student performance and reduces the failure rate in science courses, including psychology courses (Freeman et al., 2013). This principle pertains to work outside the classroom as well (Lovett & Greenhouse, 2000). Based on these findings, we encourage students to actively participate in their learning throughout the text. Students can practice their knowledge through the many applied exercises, especially in the Applying the Concepts and Putting It All Together sections. In these sections, as well as in the examples integrated into the chapters, the source of the original data is often supplied, whether it is YouTube data on viral videos or statistics from the blog of online dating company OkCupid, encouraging students to dig deeper. We also endorse a number of free online tools to gain extra practice understanding important concepts: tools such as the excellent *p*-hacking simulator at FiveThirtyEight.com (fivethirtyeight.com/features/science-isnt-broken/#part1) or the cool—even disruptive—statcheck tool

AJ Mast/The New York Times/Redux

A Valid Test for Shelter Dogs?
Many animal shelters use a brief behavior test to determine which rescue dogs are adoptable and which are too aggressive to place in adoptions (Hoffman, 2017). Researchers have questioned the validity of these behavior tests, however. For example, some dangerous dogs pass the test, and some friendly dogs are less friendly in the artificial situations of the behavior test, responding more aggressively, for example, to a fake dog than to a real dog (Shabelanskya, Dowling-Guyer, Quist, Segurson D'Arpino, & McCobb, 2015). Here, veterinary behaviorist Dr. Sara Bennett, left, tests a shelter dog named Bacon. Bacon failed part of the test, but was determined to be adoptable anyway, and now has a home.

(statcheck.io) that verifies the internal consistency of the statistics within any particular manuscript. Moreover, in the online supplements for this book, students can practice choosing the right statistical test in the Which Test Is Best? digital activities and can practice interpreting statistical findings in the new Interpreting Results interactive feature.

4. **Examining misconceptions.** Usually, prior knowledge can provide a foundation for new knowledge, but some kinds of prior knowledge can slow students down (Lovett & Greenhouse, 2000). Students know many statistical words—from independent to variability to significant. But they know the "everyday" definitions of these words, and this prior knowledge can impede their learning of the statistical definitions. Throughout the book, we point out students' likely prior understanding of these key terms, and contrast that with the newer statistical definitions. We also include exercises aimed at having students explain the various ways a given word can be understood. Plus, in Chapter 5, we introduce ways in which other types of misconceptions can emerge through illusory correlation, confirmation bias, and coincidence. Throughout the rest of the book, we highlight these types of flawed thinking with examples, and show how statistics can be the antidote to misconceptions—whether it's a belief that holiday weight gain is a serious problem, that cheating is associated with better grades, or that people swear a lot because they have an otherwise limited vocabulary. This is in line with an idea that Andrew Hacker (2016) calls "citizen statistics," a life skill he describes as "a facility for sensing symptoms of bias, questionable samples and dubious sources of data."

5. **Real-time feedback.** It's not uncommon—in fact, it's actually expected—for students to make mistakes when they first try their hand at a new statistical technique. Research demonstrates that one of the best ways to get past these errors is to provide students with immediate feedback (Kornell & Metcalfe, 2014). For this reason, we include solutions at the back of the book for all Check Your Learning exercises that fall after each section of a chapter and for the odd-numbered exercises at the end of each chapter. Importantly, we don't just provide final answers. We offer fully worked-out solutions that show students all of the steps and calculations to arrive at the final answers. That way, students can figure out exactly where they went astray. Learning is simply more efficient when students can immediately correct their mistakes or receive validation that they answered correctly. This learning is also bolstered by other types of feedback embedded in the book that students can use as models. These include worked-out examples in the chapters and additional "How It Works" worked-out examples at the end of each chapter, a tool demonstrated to boost learning (Atkinson, Derry, Renkl, & Wortham, 2000; Renkl, 2014). As Lovett and Greenhouse (2000) explain, "seeing worked examples before solving new problems makes the subsequent problem solving an easier task" (p. 201). Finally, students can gain additional practice by using the LearningCurve adaptive quizzing system in LaunchPad, as well as the Which Test Is Best? and Interpreting Results interactive digital features.

6. Repetition. A growing literature focuses on the role of "desirable difficulty" in learning—that is, students learn better when they struggle with new material but have support (Clark & Bjork, 2014). The three techniques of spacing, interleaving, and testing—all based on the central idea of repetition—help to create the right level of difficulty to help students learn more efficiently.

- *Spacing* involves repeated practice sessions with the same material with delays in between. Our book is set up to encourage spacing. For example, the Before You Go On sections at the beginning of each chapter offer students a chance to review previous material. Several sets of Check Your Learning questions are included across each chapter, and more exercises are included at the end of each chapter.

- *Interleaving* refers to the practice of mixing the types of exercises that the student is practicing. Rather than practicing each new task in one block of exercises, students mix exercises on a new topic with repeats of exercises on earlier topics. This repetition of practice with earlier concepts increases retention of material. We build in exercises that encourage interleaving in the Putting It All Together sections, which ask students to return to concepts learned in earlier chapters.

- *Testing* is possibly the best way to learn new material. Simply studying does not introduce the desirable difficulty that enhances learning, but testing forces errors and drives efficient retention of new material. The tiered exercises throughout the chapter and at the end of the chapter provide numerous opportunities for testing—and then more testing. The LearningCurve adaptive quizzing system in LaunchPad provides even more opportunities for students to test themselves throughout the course, as do the online exercises—that is, the Which Test Is Best? and Interpreting Results interactive digital features. We encourage students to aim for repeated practice, completing more exercises than assigned, rather than by studying in more traditional, but less effective, ways.

The Power of Narratives

In addition to the evidence-based techniques outlined in VIPERR, one of our most important teaching tools is stories—as counterintuitive as that may seem for people who swear by statistics. We tell a story at the beginning of each chapter that highlights the value of the chapter's main statistical concept. Throughout each chapter, we don't just offer examples to set up a statistical problem; instead, we tell the story of each study so that the numbers come to life.

Why? First, stories are memorable. In the words of scientist Maryam Zaringhalam (2019), stories "ameliorate the acquisition of . . . new ideas and skills. Teaching science through narrative underscores the fact that knowledge is not fixed, but rather always emerging through active questioning of the unknown."

Second, stories provide scaffolding for learning the language of statistics by embedding this language in narratives and examples. In fact, Brinthaupt and Ananth (2018) liken learning statistics to learning a new language. If you learn statistical language in the context of a story about how Florence Nightingale invented a graph or how a sexist statement by Teen Talk Barbie led to a decade-long debate about girls and math, you're more likely to successfully acquire a new way of talking—and thinking.

What's New in the Fifth Edition: New Expertise and an Emphasis on Open Science and Data Ethics

The field of statistics might seem stable, even staid. But there is an exciting statistical revolution afoot and it is taking place on a number of fronts.

We're at the forefront of this revolution in several concrete ways. We have a new consultant, a new recurring feature, and a whole new chapter!

New Consultant

We've brought on a fantastic consultant, Kelly Goedert, who is obsessed, in the best possible way, with what we should all be doing as behavioral scientists and statisticians, as well as what we should be teaching our students. Her idea of a fun vacation is a week-long Bayesian workshop in the Netherlands. (OK, she likes other, more relaxing vacations, too!) But we're thrilled to have Kelly contribute her vast and deep statistical expertise—as well as her skills as a patient, engaging instructor—to this edition of the book.

Kelly graduated from Western Kentucky University with an undergraduate degree in psychology and an MA in applied experimental psychology. After spending one year working in market research, she returned to school to earn a PhD in cognitive psychology from the University of Virginia. Kelly studies spatial attention in healthy human populations and in individuals with stroke-induced attentional impairments. She also studies how individuals make causal inferences about events (e.g., "What's causing my stomach upsets?"). Kelly especially enjoys answering questions with numbers and relishes opportunities to apply statistics to solve real-life problems. Her research has been funded by the National Institutes of Health and the National Science Foundation. She is a fellow of the Eastern Psychological Association and the Association for Psychological Science. Currently, she is professor of psychology at Seton Hall University, where she is also a faculty member in the Data Visualization and Analysis program. In her spare time, she enjoys reading, cooking, and swimming.

Data Ethics Feature

There's a crisis in the behavioral sciences. Researchers have failed to repeat—that is, *replicate*—many findings, and it has become clear that many old standards of research practice are deeply flawed. The good news is that researchers have responded to this crisis by developing new guidelines that encourage transparent, ethical research. These guidelines are part of what is often called data ethics, a set of principles related to all stages of working with data—research design, data collection, statistical analyses, interpretation of analyses, and reporting of outcomes. The push toward a more ethical and transparent approach to data is often termed "open science." This set of practices encourages collaboration and includes the sharing of research methodology, data, and statistical analyses in ways that allow others to question and to try to re-create the findings.

This new edition of *Statistics for the Behavioral Sciences* addresses the crisis—and the response to it—head-on via a Data Ethics feature in every chapter. In these features, we dig into contemporary problems with statistical research, including sneaky maneuvers such as HARKing and *p*-hacking. We describe several ways to manage problematic traditional methods of data analysis, such as preregistration and new statistical approaches (some of which are actually called the "new statistics"). In addition, we outline how to be truthful when interpreting and describing data, how to be honest with graphs, and even how to identify when someone is being sneaky with the presentation of data. When relevant, we share tips on using technology—often available for free—that can help us to become more ethical creators and interpreters of statistics.

Data Ethics | Open Data Practices

Besides preregistering studies, researchers should report any ethical data practices that they used *after* they collected their data. Are the researchers willing to share their data with other scientists who want to reanalyze it? Do the researchers share enough details of the statistical analyses that others can re-create what they did? These kinds of details are often included in a note at the end of the manuscript. In some journals, that note is labeled "Open Practices" and can include badges like the ones depicted here that indicate the manuscript has met certain criteria.

Badges That Reward Transparency in Science The Open Science Framework developed badges that journals can use to provide an incentive for researchers to practice ethical and transparent science. The blue badge for "Open Data" indicates that the researchers have made their data available for others to analyze. The yellow badge for "Open Materials" indicates that the researchers have made their experimental materials available to help others replicate their work. The red badge indicates that the study was preregistered.

New Chapter on Choosing and Interpreting Results

Perhaps most importantly, we've added an entire new chapter (Chapter 18) that outlines how to choose the correct statistical test and how to report (and interpret) findings in light of all of the revolutionary changes sweeping through the field. We cover everything from why you should preregister your study to what open-science badges tell us about the findings in a published paper. We also introduce helpful resources, including the APA's Journal Article Reporting Standards (JARS; Appelbaum et al., 2018). The entire chapter is guided by the understanding that data ethics and open science should be foundational principles of behavioral sciences research. Like the rest of the textbook, this new material is anchored in current, real-world research examples.

Importantly, the new Data Ethics features and the new Chapter 18 are embedded in our current structure for teaching statistics, so that instructors can shift their courses as they wish, introducing one, a few, or all of the new topics. We are also careful to indicate that newly popular practices aren't necessarily perfect. In revising this edition, we took the words of psychologists James Friedrich, Julia Childress, and David Cheng (2018) to heart: Reforming how we teach undergraduate statistics, including "innovations in textbooks," is not about specific procedures, but rather "the need to blend statistics reform content with common goals of promoting critical thinking, preparing students to read current literature, and enabling them to conduct and report on basic APA-style analyses" (p. 320).

Finally, we hope that our updates highlight how ethical researchers need good critical thinking skills to evaluate the current best practices in the field and understand these changes in the behavioral sciences (Chopik et al., 2018; Friedrich et al., 2018). The behavioral sciences are moving toward more ethical data practices, a sign that they are adaptive and strong—and more important than ever. Through these features, we aim to demonstrate what an exciting time it is in the behavioral sciences and give you the tools to become a more ethical researcher and statistician.

Beyond the new consultant, new Data Ethics feature, and new chapter, there are lots of additional changes in every chapter. We outline many of them here:

Changes and Updates by Chapter

Chapter 1

- In the "How to Transform Observations into Variables" section, new example about great white sharks for discrete observations.

- In the "Discrete Variables" section, new example for nominal variables using Australians and New Zealanders.

- In the "Reliability and Validity" section, new example and photo for validity using behavioral tests for shelter dogs.

- In the "Introduction to Hypothesis Testing" section, new example and photo of operational definitions with Nicki Minaj and Travis Scott going head to head on the *Billboard* album sales charts.

- In the "Correlational Studies and Confounding Variables" section, new example of correlational studies of employee wellness programs.

- In the "Conducting Experiments to Control for Confounding Variables" section, new example of an experiment on the effectiveness of employee wellness programs.

- New section that introduces the new recurring Data Ethics feature, introducing and defining the terms "data ethics" and "open science."

- New Data Ethics feature on preregistration that introduces and defines the terms "preregistration" and "HARKing."

- Six new end-of-chapter exercises concerning data ethics, open science, preregistration, and HARKing.

Chapter 2

- New chapter opener involving time spent on social media globally.

- Deleted section on frequency polygons.

- New example about distributions of course grades for the "Shapes of Distributions" section.

- New Data Ethics feature concerning dot plots and the value of understanding individual data points.

- New SPSS example and screenshot using data on numbers of volcanoes per country.

- New How It Works 2.1, "Creating a Grouped Frequency Table," using time spent on social media globally as an example.

- New example for How It Works 2.2, "Creating a Grouped Histogram," using time spent on social media globally as an example.

- Eight new end-of-chapter exercises concerning dot plots, histograms, and distributions.

Chapter 3

- New Data Ethics feature that reworks material on lying with graphs.

- New example on the relation between lifetime hours of deliberate practice and athletes' performance in sports for the descriptions of and graphs for scatterplots and line graphs.

- Example for "how to read a graph" has been updated to the numbers of tattoos and arrest history study.

- New geographic information systems (GIS) example on check-ins on the use of the social media tool Foursquare as a means to understanding how gentrification happens.

- New key term: bubble graph.

- New section on innovative ways to display variability, particularly in terms of visualizing the full variability of a data set. This material includes a new graph that demonstrates why bar graphs may obscure the underlying story of the data and a new graph depicting a violin plot.

- New key term: violin plot.

- Mention of pirate plots, including the open software used to create them, YaRrr.

- New SPSS example and screenshot using the data on deliberative practice and athletic performance.

- New exercise on a visualization of the huge increase in record album sales.

- New exercise on identifying the best graph using the following examples: listening to the audio version versus watching the TV/film version of popular fictional stories; typical hours of sleep per night across countries; the relation between money and happiness globally; and the tipping point for when a frequent overnight guest should contribute to rent.

Chapter 4

- New example using Charity Navigator scores of charitable organizations to demonstrate central tendency, range, and interquartile range.

- New photo example of a mode using the example of the modal name among contestants on *The Bachelor.*

- Discussion of the ethical presentation of central tendency reframed as a Data Ethics feature.

- Interquartile range material integrated into the main text after the introduction of the range.
- New SPSS example and screenshot using the Charity Navigator data.

Chapter 5

- Markedly streamlined instructions on how to create a list of random numbers using a random numbers table.
- Introduction of randomizer.org as a particularly useful tool for creating lists of random numbers to use for random selection and random assignment, and instructions on how to use it.
- Expanded discussion of the increasing use of and drawbacks of crowdsourced data, as well as a list of additional resources for collecting data in this manner.
- New photo example of illusory correlation and confirmation bias, involving tattooed engagement rings and a lasting marriage.
- New Check Your Learning exercise involving probability and a real-life coincidence involving online dating and reunited shelter cats.
- Discussion of the prevalence of Type I errors reframed as a Data Ethics feature.
- New SPSS example and screenshot using data on numbers of volcanoes per country.
- Exercises on how to use a random numbers table now instruct students to use an online random numbers generator.
- New end-of-chapter exercise on Mozak, a game that recruits players who, by playing, help conduct crowdsourced research on neurologic disorders.
- New end-of-chapter exercise on crowdsourced research on fake news that uses Amazon Mechanical Turk.

Chapter 6

- New chapter opener using the example of catching cheaters in sports—tennis and sumo wrestling—using the normal curve.
- New photo example of (possibly) cheating sumo wrestlers.
- Height examples that previously ran through the chapter replaced with new data from the World Happiness Report for 157 countries.
- New photo example using tiny and giant Buddhas to represent the effects of outliers on distributions.
- New Data Ethics feature on using z scores to keep researchers honest updates the existing discussion of this topic.
- New SPSS example and screenshot using the World Happiness Report data.
- New end-of-chapter exercise about comparing scores on two English language learner tests, TOEFL and IELTS, using z scores.
- New end-of-chapter exercise using the example of catching online gaming cheaters using the normal curve.

Chapter 7

- New chapter opener with an example of the difference between the portrayal of trauma injuries on TV hospital dramas and in real life.
- Added encouragement for students to learn by drawing distributions, with cited research on the powerful effects of drawing on memory and learning.
- Updated research findings on the effects of calorie counts on menus.
- New Data Ethics feature on HARKing and p-hacking.
- New SPSS example and screenshot using data on numbers of volcanoes per country.
- New end-of-chapter exercises on HARKing and p-hacking.

Chapter 8

- New photo example on puppy training methods illustrating how larger samples give us more confidence in our conclusions.
- New example on adult versus teen screen time for illustrating calculation of the confidence interval.
- Updated explanation of effect size.
- Updated explanation of statistical power and its relation to both effect size and sample size.
- Removed material on calculating statistical power by hand.
- New Data Ethics feature on sample size planning.
- New end-of-chapter exercises on power analysis, Type I and Type II errors, and the relation between sample size and effect size.

Chapter 9

- New Data Ethics feature on replication and reproducibility with updated coverage of these topics.
- New photo example of Amy Cuddy's controversial research on power posing that discusses a recent call for civility in the open-science movement.
- New and updated end-of-chapter exercises on replication and reproducibility, including an exercise on the possible role of culture in failures to replicate.
- New end-of-chapter exercise on single-sample t tests and a study on whether signing your name makes you less likely to cheat.

Chapter 10

- Inclusion of kilograms (in addition to pounds) in the holiday weight-gain example.
- New paired-samples t test example using data from an experiment on the stereotyping of people with schizophrenia as violent.
- New photo example related to the stereotyping of people with mental illnesses as violent.
- New confidence interval and effect size examples using data from an experiment on the stereotyping of people with schizophrenia as violent.
- New Data Ethics feature that updates material on avoiding order effects through counterbalancing.
- New SPSS example and screenshot on the data from an experiment on the stereotyping of people with schizophrenia as violent.

Chapter 11

- New example for the development of a distribution of differences between means using global happiness data.
- New opener for the independent-samples t test on a Payless shoe store prank that involves perceptions of shoes marketed as discount versus luxury items. New photo related to this example.
- New Data Ethics section on Bayesian analysis, which updates the existing material and adds a new example on beliefs about crime suspect culpability.
- New How It Works examples for the independent-samples t test, confidence interval, effect size, and reporting statistics using data from an experiment on Facebook use and stress.
- Repurposed (from How It Works) end-of-chapter exercises on gender and humor.
- New end-of-chapter exercise on graphic warnings, sugary beverages, the independent-samples t test, preregistration, and open science.

Chapter 12

- New figure highlighting the differences between between-groups variability and within-groups variability for the fairness-study example.

- New material introducing omega squared and its calculation as a less-biased estimate of effect size for ANOVA.

- The section on the Bonferroni test repurposed as a Data Ethics feature, with additional information on its use by researchers conducting multiple tests and by readers of research.

- New end-of-chapter exercises regarding additional uses of the Bonferroni test.

- New end-of-chapter exercises for the calculation of the effect size estimates, R^2 and ω^2.

Chapter 13

- New Data Ethics feature on ethical reporting standards in behavioral research, including noting when the sample is from a WEIRD (Western, educated, industrial, rich, and democratic) population. Includes a discussion of the benefits of including a constraints on generality (COG) statement in reports of research results.

- New exercises related to WEIRD samples and COG statements.

- New Putting It All Together exercise on interpreting the results of a within-groups ANOVA on weekly data from a smartphone app that monitors alcohol intake.

Chapter 14

- New Data Ethics feature on tools for "fact checking" statistics in your own and others' research, including discussion of the statcheck consistency-checking tool.

- New end-of-chapter exercises on checking for consistency in statistics (e.g., using statcheck).

- New end-of-chapter exercises on other data ethics topics, including WEIRD populations, constraints on generality, severe testing, and the open science movement.

Chapter 15

- New example of correlation versus causation: group sports and longevity.

- Introduction of the term "spurious correlation" with examples.

- Added mention of measures of internal consistency reliability that are more accurate than coefficient alpha, including omega total and coefficient H.

- New example of a test lacking in validity, the Myers–Briggs Type Inventory (MBTI).

- Streamlining of the partial correlation material, and addition of a new partial-correlation example on group sports and longevity.

- New Data Ethics feature on the perils of big data, including the risks of unwarranted conclusions stemming from spurious correlations.

- New How It Works example on the relation between temperature and numbers of homicides.

- New exercises on correlation versus causation with the examples of correlations between online hate speech and real-life violence and between iPhone use and the trend of millennials moving home.

- New exercises on spurious correlation.

- New exercise on reliability and Big Five personality tests.

Chapter 16

- New chapter opener on the use of predictive policing tools for predicting crime locations.

- New example running through the chapter for illustrating calculations: using the number of stressful life events to predict depression levels.

- New material on the calculation of adjusted r^2.

- New coverage of calculating the standard error of the estimate.
- New Data Ethics feature on ethical problems associated with predicting individual behavior, including racial and other biases that can emerge from the use of computer algorithms.
- New exercises on ethical problems with predictive policing.
- New exercises with calculations of the standard error of the estimate and adjusted r^2.

Chapter 17

- New Check Your Learning exercises on *The New York Times* rankings of the "50 Places to Go in 2019."
- New experimental research on whether identification with an object (a paper cup with one's name spelled correctly versus spelled incorrectly or with a name) increases recycling rates as new example for the chi-square test for independence, adjusted standardized residual, Cramér's V, and relative risk.
- Adjusted standardized residual material integrated with the chi-square test for independence.
- Relative risk material updated with new examples and reframed as a Data Ethics feature.
- New SPSS example using the recycling study.
- New exercise on types of variables using the example that sexual minorities are more likely than heterosexual people to become activists for various causes.
- New exercises on relative risk: one on the risk of drinking one alcohol beverage per day and one on drunk driving.

Chapter 18

- Entirely new chapter on choosing the right statistical test and reporting statistical results.
- Appendix on choosing the right statistical test moved to this chapter and expanded using several new examples related to understanding behavior through research based on online vacation rentals (e.g., Airbnb).
- Section on reporting statistics that includes a discussion of helpful resources, an overview of what should be included in APA-style Methods and Results sections, and an exploration of ethical practices—all using research examples on the benefits of giving versus receiving advice.
- New Data Ethics feature on additional ethical considerations for reporting data, including a discussion of Open Practice badges.

How the Fifth Edition Helps Students to Learn

In this new edition of *Statistics for the Behavioral Sciences*, we highlight innovations in statistics, especially those related to data ethics, open science, and the ethical interpretation of results. In addition, throughout the text, we connect students to statistical concepts as efficiently and memorably as possible. We've sharpened the focus of the book on the core concepts and introduce each topic with a vivid, real-world example. Our pedagogy first emphasizes mastering concepts, and then gives students multiple step-by-step examples of the process of each statistical method, including the mathematical calculations. The extensive Check Your Learning exercises at the end of each section of the chapter, along with the end-of-chapter exercises and the new LaunchPad Web site, give students lots of opportunities to practice. Indeed, there are more than twice as many exercises in the fifth edition as in the first. In the current edition, we've added even more exercises that allow students to interpret statistical findings. We've also clarified our approach by fine-tuning the following features throughout the book. Finally, we have added a new interactive feature to the current set of Which Test Is Best? modules. The Interpreting Results interactive digital feature introduces real-world research and gives students an opportunity to interpret the findings—both traditional and new statistics—as presented in an APA-style journal article.

Before You Go On

Each chapter opens with a Before You Go On section that highlights the concepts students need to have mastered before they move on to the next chapter.

> **BEFORE YOU GO ON**
>
> ■ You should be able to create histograms and frequency polygons (Chapter 2).
>
> ■ You should be able to describe distributions of scores using measures of central tendency, variability, and skewness (Chapters 2 and 4).
>
> ■ You should understand that there are distributions of scores based on samples, as well as distributions of scores based on populations (Chapter 5).

Mastering the Formulas and Mastering the Concepts

Some of the most difficult tasks for students new to statistics are identifying the key points and connecting this new knowledge to what they have covered in previous chapters. The unique Mastering the Formula and Mastering the Concept marginal notes provide students with helpful explanations that identify each formula when it is first introduced and each important concept at its point of relevance. Figure 18-1 ("Choosing the Appropriate Hypothesis Test") in Chapter 18 is a terrific summary that shows students how to apply statistical techniques to their research. It's the entire text summarized on a single page; students will learn it quickly and use it for the rest of their careers in statistics.

> **MASTERING THE FORMULA**
>
> **10-2:** The formula for Cohen's d for a paired-samples t statistic is:
>
> $$\text{Cohen's } d = \frac{(M - \mu)}{s}$$
>
> It is the same formula as for the single-sample t statistic, except that the mean and standard deviation are for difference scores rather than individual scores.

> **MASTERING THE CONCEPT**
>
> **18-5:** In the Methods section, we indicate whether the study has been preregistered, how we planned the sample size, the data analysis plan, and any relevant psychometric statistics.

Illustrative, Step-by-Step Examples

The text is filled with real-world examples from a wide variety of sources in the behavioral sciences. Many of these examples are new to the current edition of this text. We outline statistical techniques in a step-by-step fashion, guiding students through each concept by applying the material creatively and effectively.

EXAMPLE 12.2

Let's apply this to the ANOVA we conducted on fairness across different types of societies. We can use the statistics in the source table we created earlier to calculate R^2:

$$R^2 = \frac{SS_{between}}{SS_{total}} = \frac{461.643}{629.074} = 0.73$$

Table 12-12 displays Jacob Cohen's conventions for R^2 that, like Cohen's d, indicate whether the effect size is small, medium, or large. This R^2 of 0.73 is large. This is not surprising; if we can reject the null hypothesis when the sample size is small, then the effect size must be large.

We can also turn the proportion into the more familiar language of percentages by multiplying by 100. We can then say that a specific percentage of the variance in the dependent variable is accounted for by the independent variable. In this case, we

● R^2 is an estimate of the proportion of variance in the dependent variable that is accounted for by the independent variable.

Photos and Data Visualizations

As avid fans of using visualizations to teach statistics, we incorporate compelling photos and graphs, all in full color, throughout the book to emphasize important points, provide additional vivid examples, and add to the repetition of key concepts.

Preregistering Figure-Skating Routines Competitive figure skaters must submit the specifics of their routines before a competition so that the announcers and judges know what to expect. So, skaters like Nathan Chen, shown here, get lower scores when they switch out a jump in the middle of their routines. There's a move for researchers to do the same—to preregister the specifics of their studies so they can't change things along the way to get the result they want.

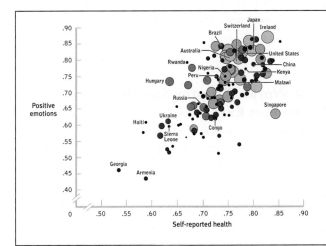

FIGURE 3-14

A Multivariable Graph

Increasingly sophisticated technology allows us to create increasingly sophisticated graphs. This bubble graph from a study by Sarah Pressman and her colleagues (2013) depicts four variables: country (each bubble), self-reported health (x-axis), positive emotions (y-axis), and gross domestic product (size and color of bubbles). The researchers could have had five variables if they had not used both the size and the color of the bubbles to represent GDP.

SPSS

For instructors who integrate SPSS into their course, each chapter includes outlined instructions and screenshots of SPSS output to help students master the program using data from the text.

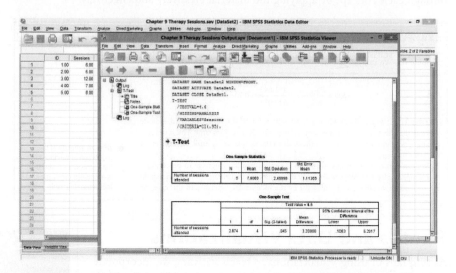

Select Analyze → Compare Means → One-Sample T Test. Highlight the dependent variable (Number of sessions attended) and click the arrow in the center to choose it. We have now told SPSS that we're interested in looking at the sample mean for this variable, number of sessions attended. We also need to tell SPSS the population to which we are comparing the sample mean. To do that, type the population mean to which we're comparing the sample, 4.6, next to "Test Value," and click "OK."

If we conduct this test using SPSS, we'll notice that the output presented includes two tables: a table with descriptive statistics for the dependent variable and a table that includes information used to calculate *t*. Both tables are in the screenshot here. In the second table, we should pay attention to three

things: the *t* statistic in the first column, the *p* value in the significance column (in the third column), and the confidence interval (in the fifth and sixth columns). Notice that the *t* statistic, 2.874, is almost identical to the one we calculated earlier, 2.873. The difference is due solely to rounding decisions.

We can also see that the confidence interval is different from the one we calculated previously. This is an interval around the difference between the two means, rather than around the mean of the sample. The *p* value is under "Sig (2-tailed)." The *p* value of .045 is less than the chosen alpha level of .05, an indication that this is a statistically significant finding. All the information we used to hand calculate the *t* statistic should be the same as the information presented in these two SPSS output tables.

HOW IT WORKS

17.1 CONDUCTING A CHI-SQUARE TEST FOR GOODNESS OF FIT

Have you heard of the Bechdel Test? Allison Bechdel developed a simple rubric to determine if a movie (or other fictional work) was at least trying for gender equality. The test: You have to be able to answer "yes" to three questions: (1) Are there at least two women in the film? (2) Who talk to each other? (3) About something other than a man? It's surprisingly hard to find films that meet these criteria. Researchers examined the effect of the screenwriters' genders on films' gender equality (Friedman, Daniels, & Blinderman, 2016). Of high-earning films written entirely by men, 53% failed the Bechdel Test. What about similarly successful films with at least one female writer? In a sample of 61 top films that had at least one woman on the writing team, 23 failed the Bechdel Test and 38 passed. (For fun, check out the researchers' Bechdel Test simulator on poly-graph.co/bechdel. You can see the likelihood that a film will pass the Bechdel Test given a particular director, producer, and writer. For example, a film directed by Tina Fey, produced by Judd Apatow, and written by Shonda Rimes would only have an 11% chance of failing.) How can we use the Bechdel Test to conduct the six steps of hypothesis testing for a chi-square test for goodness of fit for the films with at least one female writer?

Step 1: Population 1: High-earning films with at least one woman on the writing team. Population 2: High-earning films written entirely by men.

How It Works: Chapter-Specific Worked-Out Exercises

Many students have anxiety as they approach end-of-chapter exercises. To ease that anxiety, the How It Works section provides students with step-by-step worked-out exercises representative of those they will see at the end of the chapter. This section appears just before the end-of-chapter exercises and acts as a model for the more challenging Applying the Concepts and Putting It All Together questions. This edition includes a number of new exercises based on actual behavioral sciences findings.

Game Design and Practice

Like a computer game that uses repetition and small changes to lift its players to higher levels of achievement, *Statistics for the Behavioral Sciences* has increasingly difficult challenges, beginning with confidence-building Check Your Learning sections within each chapter. Many of the more than 1000 exercises in the text, most written by the authors, are based on real data, so professors and students can choose from among the most engaging exercises. Students can develop the ability to conduct, interpret, understand, and report statistics used in scientific journals by selecting from four tiers of exercises:

- **Clarifying the Concepts** questions help students to master the general concepts, the statistical terminology, and the conceptual assumptions of each topic.

- **Calculating the Statistics** exercises provide students with a way to practice making the basic calculations for each formula and statistic.

- **Applying the Concepts** exercises apply statistical questions to real-world situations across the behavioral sciences and require students to bridge their knowledge of concepts and calculations.

- **Putting It All Together** exercises encourage interleaving by asking students both to apply the concepts from the chapter to a real-world situation and to connect the chapter's concepts to ideas from previous chapters.

In addition to the exercises in the chapters, two sets of digital interactive features are available, both developed by the authors.

- **Which Test Is Best?** exercises guide students through a series of questions to determine the correct statistical test for a variety of real-world situations.

- The **Interpreting Results** feature presents results—both traditional and new statistics—from peer-reviewed journal articles. Students are provided with the opportunity to interpret the findings as they would see them in a published article.

Media and Supplements

LaunchPad with LearningCurve Quizzing

A comprehensive Web resource for teaching and learning statistics

LaunchPad combines Macmillan/Worth Publishers' award-winning media with an innovative platform for easy navigation. For students, it is the ultimate online study guide, with rich interactive tutorials, videos, an e-book, and the LearningCurve adaptive quizzing system. Students may also practice selecting the correct statistical test using the Which Test Is Best? feature, developed by the authors. And they can practice interpreting published statistical results—both traditional and new statistics—in the new Interpreting Results feature, also developed by the authors. For instructors, LaunchPad is a full course space where class documents can be posted, quizzes can be easily assigned and graded, and students' progress can be assessed and recorded. Whether you are looking for the most effective study tools or a robust platform for an online course, LaunchPad is a powerful way to enhance your class.

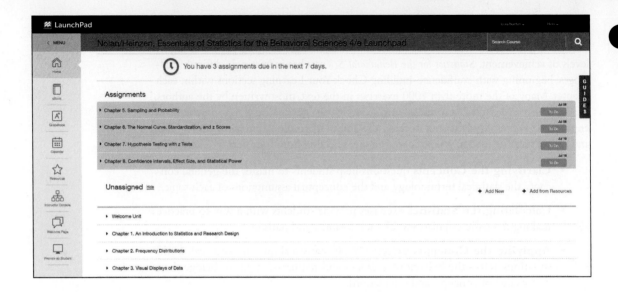

LaunchPad to accompany *Statistics for the Behavioral Sciences*, Fifth Edition, can be previewed and purchased at **launchpadworks.com**.

Statistics for the Behavioral Sciences, Fifth Edition, and LaunchPad can be ordered together (ISBN-10: 1-319-24245-6/ISBN-13: 978-1-319-24245-9).

LaunchPad for *Statistics for the Behavioral Sciences*, Fifth Edition, includes all the following resources:

- The **Which Test Is Best?** interactive feature. Developed by the authors, guides students through a series of questions to determine the correct statistical test for a variety of real-world situations.

- The **Interpreting Results** feature presents results—both traditional and new statistics—from peer-reviewed journal articles. Developed by the authors, it provides students with the opportunity to interpret research findings as they would see them in a published article.

- The **LearningCurve** quizzing system was designed using the latest findings from learning and memory research. It combines adaptive question selection, immediate and valuable feedback, and a gamelike interface to engage students in a learning experience that is unique to them. Each LearningCurve quiz is fully integrated with other resources in LaunchPad through the Personalized Study Plan, so students can review Macmillan/Worth's library of videos and activities. State-of-the-art question analysis reports allow instructors to track the progress of individual students as well as their class as a whole.

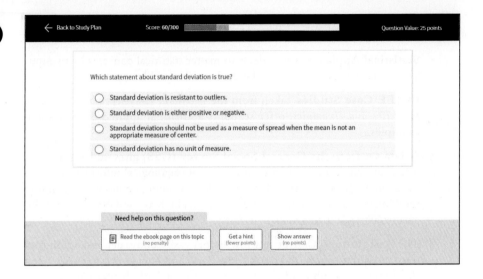

- An **interactive e-book** allows students to highlight, bookmark, and make their own notes, just as they would with a printed textbook. Students can use Google-style searching and take advantage of in-text glossary definitions.

- The **Statistical Video Series** consists of StatClips, StatClips Examples, and Statistically Speaking "Snapshots." The videos can be used to view animated lecture videos, whiteboard lessons, and documentary-style footage that illustrate key statistical concepts and help students visualize statistics in real-world scenarios.

- **StatClips lecture videos,** created and presented by Alan Dabney, PhD, Texas A&M University, are innovative visual tutorials that illustrate key statistical concepts. In 3 to 5 minutes, each StatClips video combines dynamic animation, data sets, and interesting scenarios to help students understand the concepts in an introductory statistics course.

- In **StatClips Examples,** Alan Dabney walks students through step-by-step examples related to the StatClips lecture videos to reinforce the concepts through problem solving.

- **SnapShots** videos are abbreviated, student-friendly versions of the Statistically Speaking video series, and they bring the world of statistics into the classroom. In the same vein as the successful PBS series *Against All Odds: Inside Statistics*, Statistically Speaking uses new and updated documentary footage and interviews that show real people using data analysis to make important decisions in their careers and in their daily lives. From business to medicine, from the environment to understanding the census, SnapShots help students see why statistics is important for their careers and how statistics can be a powerful tool for understanding their world.

- **Statistical Applets** allow students to master statistical concepts by manipulating data. The applets also can be used to solve problems.

- **EESEE Case Studies**, taken from the *Electronic Encyclopedia of Statistical Exercises and Examples*, offer students additional applied exercises and examples.

- A **data set from the General Social Survey (GSS)** gives students access to data from one of the most trusted sources of sociological information. Since 1972, the GSS has collected data that reflect changing opinions and trends in the United States. A number of exercises in the text use GSS data, and this data set allows students to explore further.

- The **Assignment Center** lets instructors easily construct and administer tests and quizzes from the book's Test Bank and course materials. The Test Bank includes a subset of questions from the end-of-chapter exercises and uses algorithmically generated values so that each student can be assigned a unique version of the question. Assignments can be automatically graded, and the results can be recorded in a customizable gradebook.

Additional Student Supplements

SPSS: A User-Friendly Approach by Jeffery Aspelmeier and Thomas Pierce of Radford University is an accessible introduction to using SPSS. The book uses a proven teaching method, building each section of the text around the storyline from a popular cartoon. Easing anxiety and giving students the necessary support to learn the material, *SPSS: A User-Friendly Approach* provides instructors and students with an informative guide to the basics of SPSS.

- The **iClicker** Classroom Response System is a versatile polling system developed by educators for educators that makes class time more efficient and interactive. iClicker allows instructors to ask questions and instantly record students' responses, gauge students' understanding and opinions, and take attendance. It can help instructors gather data on students that can be used to teach statistics, connecting the concepts to students' lives. iClicker is available at a 10% discount when packaged with *Statistics for the Behavioral Sciences*, Fifth Edition.

Take Advantage of Our Most Popular Combinations!

Macmillan/Worth Publishers is pleased to offer cost-saving packages of *Statistics for the Behavioral Sciences*, Fifth Edition, with our most popular supplements. In addition to LaunchPad access listed here, contact your sales representative for more combinations available for order through your local bookstore.

Statistics for the Behavioral Sciences, Fifth Edition, and LaunchPad Access Card (ISBN-10: 1-319-24245-6/ ISBN-13: 978-1-319-24245-9)

Instructor Supplements

We understand that one book alone cannot possibly meet the educational needs and teaching expectations of the modern classroom. Therefore, we have engaged our colleagues to create a comprehensive supplements package that makes both teaching and learning statistics much easier.

- **Instructor's Resources** by Jeffrey Henriques, University of Wisconsin–Madison, with contributions by Katherine Makarec, William Paterson University. The contents include "Teaching Tips" and sample course outlines. Each chapter includes a brief overview, discussion questions, classroom activities, handouts, additional reading suggestions, and online resources.

- **Downloadable Test Bank for Diploma** Available for Windows or Macintosh, the Test Bank includes multiple-choice, true/false, fill-in-the-blank, and critical thinking/problem-solving questions for each chapter. Developed by Jennifer Coleman, Western New Mexico University; Kelly M. Goedert, Seton Hall University; and Daniel Cruz, Caldwell College, the downloadable Test Bank allows instructors to add an unlimited number of new questions; edit questions; format a test; scramble questions; and include figures, graphs, and pictures. The downloadable Test Bank also allows instructors to export into a variety of formats compatible with many Internet-based testing products. **macmillanhighered.com/Catalog/**

- Macmillan/Worth Publishers supports multiple **Course Management Systems** with enhanced cartridges that include Test Bank questions and other resources. Cartridges are provided free upon adoption of *Statistics for the Behavioral Sciences*, Fifth Edition, and can be requested through Macmillan/Worth's online catalog at **macmillanhighered.com/Catalog/**.

Acknowledgments

We would like to thank the many people who have contributed directly and indirectly to the writing of this text. We want to thank our students at Seton Hall University and William Paterson University for teaching us how to teach statistics in a way that makes sense and for calling our attention to some of the more fun examples you'll now find in these pages.

Tom: The family members who know me on a daily basis and decide to love me anyway deserve more thanks than words can convey: Donna, Rebekah, Nagesh, Debbie, Anthony, Amy, Elizabeth, Mollie, Jodah, and Benjamin. The close friends, artists, and colleagues who voiced encouragement and timely support also deserve my deep appreciation: Beth, Army, Culley, and Miran Schultz; Laura Cramer-Berness; Ariana DeSimone; J. Allen Suddeth; Nancy Vail; Gerry Esposito; and Sally Ellyson.

My students have always provided a reality check on my teaching methods with the kind of candor that only students engaged in the learning process can bring. And in recent years, our psychology department has made enormous strides by following the "always hire people who are better than you" rule. Some of those "better than you" colleagues have been a steady source of helpful conversation: Michael Gordon,

Amy Learmonth, and Natalie Obrecht. Thank you. And Susan, of course, has been as fine a colleague and friend as I could ever have hoped for.

I also want to thank the people at Macmillan/Worth, all of them. They have a vision for quality textbook publishing that is different from that of many publishers. I know I speak for Susan as well when I say how deeply we appreciate their level of close cooperation, timely support, and determination to get every detail right. People with those values are what have made Macmillan/Worth's textbooks so special.

Susan: I am grateful to my Northwestern University professors and classmates for convincing me that statistics can truly be fun. I am also eternally thankful to Beatrix Mellauner for bringing Tom Heinzen and me together as coauthors; it has been a privilege and a pleasure to collaborate with Tom for so many years.

I owe thanks as well to my Seton Hall colleagues and students who are the sources for an endless stream of engaging examples. I owe a huge thank you to Seton Hall graduate student Kaylise Algrim, who contributed ideas, calculations, and accuracy checks. Kaylise also spearheaded our new interactive feature on interpreting results with her relentless search for fascinating research examples, and her careful insistence on perfection in interpretation. Thanks, too, to Seton Hall graduate student Vincent Medina, for his meticulous tracking of our sources and references. The fifth edition is better for their work on it. Finally, and as always, Seton Hall Department of Psychology secretary, Willie Yaylaci, has contributed in so many ways through her help, support, and friendship; thank you.

Much of the writing of this book took place during two sabbaticals and numerous summers in Bosnia and Herzegovina; I thank my Bosnian friends and colleagues for their warmth and hospitality every time I visit. I'm particularly grateful to have been welcomed into the Department of Psychology at the University of Banja Luka during my time there in 2015–2016 as a U.S. Fulbright Scholar.

A special thank you to the members of the Bojanic and Nolan clans—especially my parents, Diane and Jim, who have patiently endured the barrage of statistics I often inject into everyday conversation. Finally, I am most grateful to my husband, Ivan Bojanic, for the memorable adventures we've had (and the statistical observations that have grown out of many of them); Ivan has experienced the evolution of this book through countless road-trip conversations and late-night editorial sessions.

Tom and I would like to take a moment to highlight the impressive cast of instructors who have joined our team. First, we are grateful to our new consultant, Kelly Goedert, whose expertise and engaging style have contributed much to the book, and especially to the Data Ethics features. In addition, the contributions of the supplements authors are innumerable, and Katherine Makarec, Robert Weathersby, and Robin Freyberg are all professionals with a deep interest in creating successful classrooms. We appreciate the opportunity to work with people of such commitment.

Throughout the writing of the five editions of this textbook, we relied on the criticism, corrections, encouragement, and thoughtful contributions from reviewers, focus group attendees, survey respondents, and class-testers. We thank them for their expertise and for the time they set aside to help us develop this textbook. We also are grateful to the professors who have used our book and then provided specific and valuable feedback; in particular, we thank Jon Grahe, Harvey H. C. Marmurek, and Patricia A. Smiley. Special thanks go to Jennifer Coleman and Byron Reischl at

Western New Mexico University and to Kelly Goedert at Seton Hall University for their tireless work in developing the pedagogy with us, providing a responsible accuracy check, and contributing numerous ideas for us to consider as we continue to make this book even better. Special thanks also go to Melanie Maggard at the University of the Rockies, Sherry L. Serdikoff at James Madison University, Emily A. A. Dow at Loyola University in Maryland, Kurt Norlin of the Bittner Development Group, and Katerina Karaivanova at University of New Hampshire for their invaluable efforts checking the text and exercises.

Caitlin Abar
State University of New York, Brockport

Tsippa Ackerman
John Jay College

Anthony Albano
University of Nebraska

Melissa Atkins
Marshall University

Elizabeth Bauer
New York University

Taunjah Bell
Jackson State University

Kenneth Bonanno
Merrimack College

Danuta Bukatko
College of the Holy Cross

Kate Burns
University of Wisconsin, Green Bay

Heidi Burross
Pima Community College

Mary Jo Carnot
Chadron State College

Wilson Chu
*California State University,
Long Beach*

Emily Cohen-Shikora
Washington University in St. Louis

Jennifer Coleman
Western New Mexico University

Melanie Conti
College of Saint Elizabeth

Ken Cramer
University of Windsor

Maria Czyzewska
Texas State University, San Marcos

Melvin Davis
Jackson State University

Betty Dorr
Fort Lewis College

Nancy Dorr
The College of St. Rose

Kevin Eames
Covenant College

Laszlo Erdodi
University of Windsor

Warren Fass
University of Pittsburgh, Bradford

Michael Frank
Richard Stockton College of New Jersey

Nancy Gee
State University of New York, Fredonia

Shahram Ghiasinejad
*University of Central Florida, Sanford/
Lake Mary*

Marilyn Gibbons
Texas State University

Nuria Giralt
California State University, Long Beach

Anthony Greene
University of Wisconsin, Milwaukee

Tammy Greer
University of Southern Mississippi

Elizabeth Haines
William Paterson University

Leslie Hawley
University of Nebraska

Roberto Heredia
Texas A&M University

Michael Hurley
George Mason University

Cynthia Ingle
*Bluegrass Community and Technical
College*

E. Jean Johnson
Governors State University

Lauriann Jones-Moore
University of South Florida

Min Ju
State University of New York, New Paltz

Donald Keller
George Washington University

Karl Kelley
North Central College

Shelley Kilpatrick
Southwest Baptist University

Megan Knowles
University of Georgia

Paul Koch
Saint Ambrose University

Marika Lamoreaux
Georgia State University

Jennifer Lancaster
St. Francis College

Monica Levine-Sauberman
Kean University

Jarrod Lewis-Peacock
The University of Texas

Christine MacDonald
Indiana State University

Mike Mangan
University of New Hampshire

Suzanne Mannes
Widener University

Walter Marcantoni
Bishop's University

Kelly Marin
Manhattan College

Marsha McCartney
University of Kansas

Connie Meinholdt
Ferris State University

William Merriman
Kent State University

Chris Molnar
LaSalle University

Matthew Mulvaney
State University of New York, Brockport

Erin Murdoch
George Mason University

Angela K. Murray
University of Kansas

Aminda O'Hare
University of Kansas

Sue Oliver
Glendale Community College of Arizona

Kristin J. Olson-Pupek
Lake Superior State University

Stephen O'Rourke
The College of New Rochelle

Debra Oswald
Marquette University

Mark Otten
California State University, Northridge

Alison Papdakis
Loyola College in Maryland

John Poggio
University of Kansas

Laura Rabin
City University of New York, Brooklyn

Byron Reischl
Western New Mexico University

Lorena Ruci
Carleton University

Michelle Samuel
Mount St. Mary's College, Chalon

Ken Savitsky
Williams College

Heidi Shaw
Yakima Valley Community College

Julian Smit
College of Southern Nevada, Henderson

Ross B. Steinman
Widener University

Sarah Strand
*California State University,
Sacramento*

Colleen Sullivan
Worcester University

Brian Stults
Florida State University

Donald G. Sweeny
College of DuPage

Melanie Tabak
William Penn University

Mark Tengler
University of Houston, Clear Lake

Cheryl Terrance
University of North Dakota

Patricia Tomich
Kent State University

Bethany Van Vleet
Arizona State University

Alex Varakin
Eastern Kentucky University

Noe Vargas
Grand Canyon University

Laurel Wainwright
University of Massachusetts, Boston

David Wallace
Fayetteville State University

Elizabeth Weiss
The Ohio State University

Erika Wells
Boston University

Charles Woods
Austin Peay State University

Alison Young
Olivet Nazarene University

Tiffany Yip
Fordham University

Widaad Zaman
University of Central Florida, Valencia/Osceola

Accuracy Reviewers

Verne Bacharach
Appalachian State University

Jeffrey Berman
University of Memphis

Dennis Goff
Randolph College

Linda Henkel
Fairfield University

Katerina Karaivanova
University of New Hampshire

Melanie Maggard
University of the Rockies

Kurt Norlin
Bittner Development Group

Kathy Oleson
Reed College

Christy Porter
College of William and Mary

Sherry L. Serdikoff
James Madison University

Alexander Wilson
University of New Brunswick

Emily A. A. Dow
Loyola University Maryland

It has truly been a pleasure for us to work with everyone at Macmillan/Worth Publishers. From the moment we signed there, we have been impressed with the passionate commitment of everyone we have encountered at Macmillan/Worth at every stage of the publishing process. Charles Linsmeier, senior vice president, content strategy, and Catherine Woods, vice president, content management, foster that commitment to quality in the Macmillan/Worth culture.

Our developmental editor, Michael Kimball, has been with us from the beginning and could probably write most of the book without us at this point. As someone without a statistics background who nevertheless "gets" statistics, Michael helps us shape our language in ways that make it more accessible to students; he is an irreplaceable part of our team—and a friend. Director of content management enhancement Tracey Kuehn has been enormously important in shaping this edition; we rely heavily on her expert guidance and eternally good-humored encouragement. We are grateful to executive program manager Matt Wright for his humor, skill, and patience in guiding the revision process. Thanks also go to editorial assistant Nick Rizzuti who expertly and effortlessly kept track of countless details and electronic files.

Senior content project manager Harold Chester, senior project manager Vanavan Jayaraman, senior managing editor Lisa Kinne, and senior workflow project manager Paul Rohloff managed the production of the text and worked tirelessly to bring the book to fruition. The designers at Lumina united beauty with clarity and content in the interior design. John Callahan designed another stunning cover. Copyeditor Jill Hobbs and her hawk's eye made our prose more consistent, more accurate, and easier to read. Senior photo editor Sheena Goldstein helped us to select photos that told the stories of statistics. Thanks to each of you for fulfilling Macmillan/Worth's promise to create a book whose aesthetics so beautifully support the specific pedagogical demands of teaching statistics.

Associate media editor Stephanie Matamoros guided the development and creation of the supplements package, making life so much better for so many students and instructors. Marketing manager Clay Bolton quickly understood why we believe so deeply in this book, and contributed unstinting effort to advocate for this fifth edition with our colleagues across the country.

We also want to thank the tremendously dedicated Macmillan/Worth team that consistently champions our book while garnering invaluable accolades and critiques from their professor contacts—information that directly leads to a better book.

An Introduction to Statistics and Research Design

BEFORE YOU GO ON

■ **You should be familiar with basic mathematics (see Reference for Basic Mathematics in Appendix A).**

Source: Map 1. Published by C.F. Cheffins, Lith, Southampton Buildings, London, England, 1854 in Snow, John. On the Mode of Communication of Cholera, 2nd ed., John Churchill, New Burlington Street, London.

John Snow's Famous Map By mapping cholera deaths in relation to the Broad Street water well, Dr. John Snow solved the urgent mystery of how cholera could infect so many people so suddenly. The Xs are all neighborhood wells. The X in the red circle is the Broad Street well. Each dot indicates that a person living at this address died of cholera, and a cluster of cases is clearly seen around the Broad Street well (but not around the other wells). Snow was careful to include the other Xs to demonstrate that the deaths were closer to one specific source of water.

Statistics saves lives.

The London cholera epidemic of 1854 hit with terrifying swiftness and apparent randomness. Some 500 people died during the first 10 days and no one could figure out why. Everyone involved only knew that the disease dehydrated its victims in gruesome ways no matter how much water the sufferer drank. It was as if an angel of death had decided, during that late summer of 1854, to take a random stroll through London's Golden Square neighborhood. A workhouse with 535 inmates had only a few mortalities and a nearby brewery with 70 employees was untouched by the epidemic, yet another nearby factory suffered 18 deaths.

Dr. John Snow had spent years trying to determine how cholera was communicated from one person to another (Vinten-Johansen, Brody, Paneth, Rachman, & Rip, 2003). He was searching for a pattern behind the apparent randomness. He marked the location of each cholera victim's home on a map and then added an X for each neighborhood's water well. The visual presentation of these data revealed a relation between distance from the well and numbers of deaths! The closer a home was to the well on Broad Street (see the red X circled in the accompanying image), the more likely it was that a death from cholera had occurred.

Snow proposed a simple solution: Remove the pump handle—a health intervention that startled the Board of Guardians of St. James's parish. Surprisingly, when the authorities finally removed the Broad Street pump handle, cholera deaths declined dramatically. Nevertheless, Snow still had a statistical problem: The rate of deaths from cholera had started to decline before the handle was removed! How could this happen? Did Snow's intervention really make a difference? The answer is both disturbing and insightful: So many people had died or fled the neighborhood around the Broad Street well that there were fewer people left to be infected.

The Two Branches of Statistics

The statistical genius and research of Dr. Snow not only saved lives, but also anticipated the two main branches of modern statistics: descriptive statistics and inferential statistics. Learning about these, and other statistical techniques, will help you develop an essential skill—and maybe even a career. As of 2018, Glassdoor listed "data scientist" as its top job, at least in the United States, with a median salary of $110,000 and more than 4000 available positions. Ready to learn?

Descriptive Statistics

Descriptive statistics organize, summarize, and communicate a group of numerical observations. Descriptive statistics describe large amounts of data in a single number or in just a few numbers. Here's an illustration using a familiar measure: length in feet (or meters). *National Geographic* (2019) reported on its Web site that the average adult great white shark is 15 feet long, or 4.6 meters. And that's just the average. Some great white sharks grow to 20 feet, or 6 meters, long! Most dorm rooms aren't even that big. The average length of great white sharks is a descriptive statistic because it *describes* the lengths of many sharks in just one number. A single number reporting the average communicates observations more clearly than would a long list of lengths for every shark that researchers have ever studied.

● A **descriptive statistic** organizes, summarizes, and communicates a group of numerical observations.

MASTERING THE CONCEPT

1-1: Descriptive statistics summarize numerical information about a sample. Inferential statistics draw conclusions about the broader population based on numerical information from a sample.

Inferential Statistics

Inferential statistics use sample data to make estimates about the larger population. Inferential statistics infer, or make an intelligent guess about, the population. For example, the researchers from whom *National Geographic* got their data made inferences about shark length even though they did not actually measure *every* great white shark in the world. Instead, researchers studied a smaller representative group of sharks to make an intelligent guess about the entire population.

● An **inferential statistic** uses sample data to make estimates about the larger population.

● A **sample** is a set of observations drawn from the population of interest.

● The **population** includes all possible observations about which we would like to know something.

Distinguishing Between a Sample and a Population

*A **sample** is a set of observations drawn from the population of interest.* Researchers usually study a sample, but they are really interested in the ***population***, which *includes all possible observations about which we would like to know something.* For example, the average length of the researchers' sample of great white sharks was used to estimate the average length for the entire world population of great white sharks, which was *National Geographic*'s interest.

Samples are used most often because researchers are rarely able to study every person (or shark or organization or laboratory rat) in a population. For one thing, it's far too expensive. In addition, it would take too long. Snow did not want to interview every family in the Broad Street neighborhood—people were dying too fast! Fortunately, what he learned from his sample also applied to the larger population.

Cat Gennaro/CatPix: The Art of Nature/Moment/Getty Images

Descriptive Statistics Summarize Information It is more useful to use a single number to summarize the lengths of many great white sharks than to provide a long, overwhelming list of every shark's length.

CHECK YOUR LEARNING

Reviewing the Concepts	>	Descriptive statistics organize, summarize, and communicate large amounts of numerical information.
	>	Researchers working with sample data use inferential statistics to draw conclusions about larger populations.
	>	Samples, or selected observations of a population, are intended to be representative of the larger population.
Clarifying the Concepts	1-1	Which are used in inferential statistics: samples or populations?
Calculating the Statistics	1-2a	If your professor calculated the average grade for your statistics class, would that be considered a descriptive statistic or an inferential statistic?
	1-2b	If that same class average is used to predict something about how future students might do in statistics, would it be considered a descriptive statistic or an inferential statistic?
Applying the Concepts	1-3	Columbia University researcher Andrew Gelman wrote about his research in *The New York Times* (2013): "The average American knows about 600 people. How do we know this? Researchers led by my Columbia colleague Tian Zheng posed a series of questions to a representative sample of 1,500 Americans."
		a. What is the sample?
		b. What is the population?
		c. What is the descriptive statistic?
		d. What is the inferential statistic?

Solutions to these Check Your Learning questions can be found in Appendix D.

How to Transform Observations into Variables

Like John Snow, we begin the research process by making observations and transforming them into a useful format. For example, Snow observed the locations of people who had died of cholera and placed these locations on a map that also showed wells in the area. The numbers of cholera deaths and their distances from the Broad Street well are both variables. *Variables are observations of physical, attitudinal, and behavioral characteristics that can take on different values.* Behavioral scientists often study abstract variables such as motivation and self-esteem; they typically begin the research process by transforming their observations into numbers.

Researchers use both discrete and continuous numerical observations to quantify variables. *Discrete observations can take on only specific values (e.g., whole numbers); no other values can exist between these numbers.* For example, if we assessed the number of great white shark sightings in a year, the only possible values would be whole numbers. Spotters might report 6 or 95 sharks, but not 1.6 or 5.92 sharks.

Continuous observations can take on a full range of values (e.g., numbers out to several decimal places); an infinite number of potential values exists. For example, a person might complete a task in 12.83912 seconds, or a shark might be 5.27 meters long. The possible values are continuous, limited only by the number of decimal places we choose to use.

- A **variable** is any observation of a physical, attitudinal, or behavioral characteristic that can take on different values.

- A **discrete observation** can take on only specific values (e.g., whole numbers); no other values can exist between these numbers.

- A **continuous observation** can take on a full range of values (e.g., numbers out to several decimal places); an infinite number of potential values exists.

Discrete Observations

Two types of observations are always discrete: nominal variables and ordinal variables. *Nominal variables are used for observations that have categories or names as their values.* For example, when entering data into a statistics program, a researcher might code Australians, for example, with the number 1 and New Zealanders with the number 2. In this case, the numbers only identify the category, citizenship, for each participant. They do not imply any other meaning. For instance, Australians aren't better than New Zealanders because they get the first number and New Zealanders aren't twice as good as Australians because they happen to be coded as a 2. Note that nominal variables are always discrete (whole numbers).

    Ordinal variables are used for observations that have rankings (i.e., 1st, 2nd, 3rd,...) as their values. In reality television shows, like *Britain's Got Talent* or *American Idol*, for example, a performer finishes the season in a particular place, or rank. It doesn't matter if the performer was first because she was slightly more talented than the next performer or much more talented. And it doesn't matter if the winning performer was ahead of the next one by one vote or by a million votes. Like nominal variables, ordinal variables are always discrete. A singer could be 1st or 3rd or 12th, but could not be ranked 1.563.

Continuous Observations

Two types of observations can be continuous: interval variables and ratio variables. *Interval variables are used for observations that have numbers as their values; the distance (or interval) between pairs of consecutive numbers is assumed to be equal.* For example, temperature is an interval variable because the interval from one degree to the next is always the same. Some interval variables are also discrete variables, such as the number of times one has to get up early each week. This is an interval variable because the distance between numerical observations is assumed to be equal. The difference between 1 and 2 times is the same as the difference between 5 and 6 times. However, this observation is also discrete because, as noted earlier, the number of days in a week cannot be anything but a whole number. Several behavioral science measures are treated as interval measures but also can be discrete, such as some personality measures and attitude measures.

    Sometimes discrete interval observations, such as the number of times a person has to get up early each week, are also *ratio variables, variables that meet the criteria for interval variables but also have meaningful zero points.* For example, if someone never has to get up early, then zero is a meaningful observation and could represent a variety of life circumstances. Perhaps the person is unemployed, retired, ill, or merely on vacation. Another example of a discrete ratio variable is the number of times a rat pushes a lever to receive food. This also has a true zero point—the rat might never push the bar (and go hungry). Ratio observations that are not discrete include time running out in a basketball game and crossing the finish line in a race.

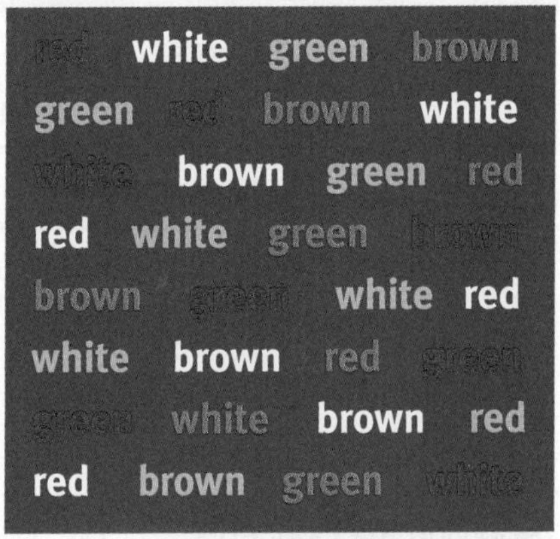

    Many cognitive studies use the ratio variable of reaction time to measure how quickly people process difficult information. For example, the Stroop task is a ratio measure that assesses how long it takes to name the color of the ink for a color word (Figure 1-1). For example, a participant should say "green" when the word *red* is printed in green or say "brown" when the word *green* is printed in brown. If it takes you 1.264 seconds to press a computer key that accurately identifies that the word *red* is actually printed in green ink, then your reaction time is a ratio variable; time always implies a meaningful zero.

- A **nominal variable** is a variable used for observations that have categories or names as their values.
- An **ordinal variable** is a variable used for observations that have rankings (i.e., 1st, 2nd, 3rd,...) as their values.
- An **interval variable** is a variable used for observations that have numbers as their values; the distance (or interval) between pairs of consecutive numbers is assumed to be equal.
- A **ratio variable** is a variable that meets the criteria for an interval variable but also has a meaningful zero point.

FIGURE 1-1

Reaction Time and the Stroop Task

Name the ink color of these color words out loud to yourself as quickly as possible. Notice what happens in the third line. Your reaction time (how long it takes to name the ink colors) is a ratio variable (also called a *scale variable*). The Stroop task assesses how long it takes to name the ink colors of color words printed in the wrong color, such as the word *red* printed in the color white.

Statistics programs often refer to both interval numbers and ratio numbers as *scale observations* because both interval observations and ratio observations are analyzed with the same statistical tests. Specifically, *a **scale variable** is a variable that meets the criteria for an interval variable or a ratio variable.* Throughout this text, we use the term *scale variable* to refer to variables that are interval or ratio, but it is important to remember the distinction between interval variables and ratio variables. Table 1-1 summarizes the four types of variables.

TABLE 1-1 Quantifying Observations

Researchers can use four types of variables to quantify their observations. Two of them, nominal and ordinal, are always discrete. Interval variables can be discrete or continuous; ratio variables are almost always continuous. (Interval variables and ratio variables are often referred to as "scale variables.")

Variable	Discrete	Continuous
Nominal	Always	Never
Ordinal	Always	Never
Interval	Sometimes	Sometimes
Ratio	Seldom	Almost always

CHECK YOUR LEARNING

Reviewing the Concepts

> Variables are quantified with discrete or continuous observations.

> Depending on the study, statisticians select nominal, ordinal, or scale (interval or ratio) variables.

Clarifying the Concepts **1-4** What is the difference between discrete observations and continuous observations?

Calculating the Statistics **1-5** Three students complete a Stroop task. Lorna finishes in 12.67 seconds, Desiree finishes in 14.87 seconds, and Marianne finishes in 9.88 seconds.

    a. Are these data discrete or continuous?

    b. Is the variable an interval or a ratio observation?

    c. On an ordinal scale, what is Lorna's score?

Applying the Concepts **1-6** Uber, the company that offers on-demand car service, measures the performance of its drivers in a variety of ways (Rosenblat, 2015). Below are several ways in which performance is measured. For each, state whether the variable is nominal, ordinal, or scale, and explain your answer.

    a. Uber drivers receive ratings from their passengers on a scale of 1–5 stars.

    b. Uber notes whether drivers have received a warning from the company regarding their performance.

    c. Uber measures hours spent logged into the Uber app during which a driver is available for passengers.

    d. Drivers are sometimes given feedback that they are, for example, among the top Uber drivers.

    e. Uber sometimes refers drivers to take a particular class to improve their performance, and tracks who has and has not taken the class.

Solutions to these Check Your Learning questions can be found in Appendix D.

Variables and Research

A major aim of research is to understand the relations among variables with many different values. It is helpful to remember that variables vary. For example, when studying a discrete nominal variable such as gender, we refer to gender as the variable because it can vary—female, male, and non-binary, for example. The term *level*, along with the terms *value* and *condition*, all refer to the same idea. *Levels are the discrete values or conditions that variables can take on.* For example, male is a level of the variable gender. Non-binary is another level of the variable gender. In both cases, gender is the variable. Similarly, when studying a continuous, scale variable, such as how fast a runner completes a marathon, we refer to time as the variable. For example, 3 hours, 42 minutes, 27 seconds is one of an infinite number of possible times it would take to complete a marathon. With this in mind, let's explore the three types of variables: independent, dependent, and confounding.

Independent, Dependent, and Confounding Variables

The three types of variables that we consider in research are independent, dependent, and confounding. Two of these, independent variables and dependent variables, are necessary for good research. But the third type, a confounding variable, is the enemy of good research. We usually conduct research to determine if one or more independent variables predict a dependent variable. *An **independent variable** has at least two levels that we either manipulate or observe to determine its effects on the dependent variable.* For example, if we are studying whether gender predicts a person's attitude about politics, then the independent variable is gender.

The **dependent variable** *is the outcome variable that we hypothesize to be related to or caused by changes in the independent variable.* For example, we hypothesize that the dependent variable (attitudes about politics) depends on the independent variable (gender). If in doubt as to which is the independent variable and which is the dependent variable, ask yourself which one depends on the other; that one is the dependent variable.

By contrast, a **confounding variable** *is any variable that systematically varies with the independent variable so that we cannot logically determine which variable is at work.* So how do we decide which is the independent variable and which might be a confounding variable (also called a *confound*)? Well, it all comes down to what *you* decide to study. Let's use an example. Suppose you want to lose weight, so you start eating fewer calories *and* begin exercising at the same time. The diet and exercise are confounded because you cannot logically tell which one is responsible for any weight loss. On the one hand, if we hypothesize that a particular diet leads to weight loss, then whether someone eats fewer calories becomes the independent variable, and exercise becomes the potentially confounding variable that we would try to control. On the other hand, if we hypothesize that exercise leads to weight loss, then whether someone exercises or not becomes the independent variable and the number of

- A **level** is a discrete value or condition that a variable can take on.

- An **independent variable** has at least two levels that we either manipulate or observe to determine its effects on the dependent variable.

- A **dependent variable** is the outcome variable that we hypothesize to be related to or caused by changes in the independent variable.

- A **confounding variable** is any variable that systematically varies with the independent variable so that we cannot logically determine which variable is at work; also called a *confound*.

Was the Damage from Wind or Water? Here, Sherwan Webber stands in what is left of his destroyed home on the Caribbean island of Barbuda after Hurricane Irma in December 2017. During hurricanes, including Hurricane Irma, high winds are often confounded with high water so it is not always possible to determine whether property damage was due to wind (often insured) or to water (often not insured).

Spencer Platt/Getty Images

calories that person eats becomes the potentially confounding variable that we would try to control. In both of these cases, the dependent variable would be weight loss. But the researcher has to make some decisions about which variables to treat as independent variables, which variables must be controlled, and which variables to treat as dependent. You, the experimenter, are in control of the experiment.

Reliability and Validity

You probably have a lot of experience in assessing variables—at least on the receiving end. You've taken standardized tests when applying to your university; you've taken short surveys to choose the right product for you, whether jeans or smartphones; and you've taken online quizzes (perhaps sent through social networking sites) such as the "What Dog Breed Are You?" quiz that uses a 10-item scale to assess the breed of dog you are most like (playbuzz.com/toddbriscoelittlethings10/what-dog-breed-are-you, 2018).

How good is this quiz? One of the authors took the quiz—answering a question about what she would prefer to do on a Saturday morning by choosing "hiking, biking, or jogging, or anything else that helps me get out some energy." She was declared to be a golden retriever. To determine whether a measure is a good one, we need to know if it is both reliable and valid.

*A **reliable** measure is consistent.* If you were to weigh yourself on your bathroom scale now, and then again in an hour, you would expect your weight to be almost exactly the same. If your weight, as shown on the scale, remains the same when you haven't done anything to change it, then your bathroom scale is reliable. As for the "What Dog Breed Are You?" quiz, the golden retriever author took it twice several months apart and was a golden retriever the second time as well, one indication of reliability.

But a reliable measure is not necessarily a valid measure. *A **valid** measure is one that measures what it was intended to measure.* Your bathroom scale could be incorrect but consistently incorrect—that is, reliable but not valid. A more extreme example is using a ruler when you want to know your weight. You would get a number, and that number might be reliable, but it would not be a valid measure of your weight.

And the "What Dog Breed Are You?" quiz? It's probably not an accurate measure of personality. We're guessing that no one has done the statistical work to determine whether it is valid. When you take such online quizzes, our advice is to view the results as entertaining rather than enlightening.

A measure with poor reliability cannot have high validity. It is not possible to measure what we intend to measure when the test itself produces varying results. The well-known Rorschach inkblot test is one example of a test whose reliability

- **Reliability** refers to the consistency of a measure.
- **Validity** refers to the extent to which a test actually measures what it was intended to measure.

A Valid Test for Shelter Dogs? Many animal shelters use a brief behavior test to determine which rescue dogs are adoptable and which are too aggressive to place in adoptions (Hoffman, 2017). Researchers have questioned the validity of these behavior tests, however. For example, some dangerous dogs pass the test, and some friendly dogs are less friendly in the artificial situations of the behavior test, responding more aggressively, for example, to a fake dog than to a real dog (Shabelanskya, Dowling-Guyer, Quist, Segurson D'Arpino, & McCobb, 2015). Here, veterinary behaviorist Dr. Sara Bennett, left, tests a shelter dog named Bacon. Bacon failed part of the test, but was determined to be adoptable anyway, and now has a home.

AJ Mast/The New York Times/Redux

is questionable, so the validity of the information it produces is difficult to inter-pret (Wood, Nezworski, Lilienfeld, & Garb, 2003). For instance, two clinicians might analyze the identical set of responses to a Rorschach test and develop quite different interpretations of those responses—meaning the test lacks reliability. Reliability can be increased with scoring guidelines, but that doesn't mean validity is increased. Just because two clinicians scoring a Rorschach test designate a per-son as psychotic, it doesn't necessarily mean the person *is* psychotic. Reliability is necessary, but not sufficient, to create a valid measure. Nevertheless, the idea that ambiguous images somehow invite revealing information remains attractive to many people; as a result, tests such as the Rorschach are still used frequently, even though there is much controversy about them (Wood et al., 2003).

> **MASTERING THE CONCEPT**
>
> **1-4:** A good measure is both reliable and valid.

CHECK YOUR LEARNING

Reviewing the Concepts
> Independent variables are manipulated or observed by the experimenter.
> Dependent variables are outcomes that occur in response to changes or differences in the independent variable.
> Confounding variables systematically vary with the independent variable, so we cannot logically tell which variable may have influenced the dependent variable.
> Researchers control factors that are not of interest to explore the relation between an independent variable and a dependent variable.
> A measure is useful only if it is both reliable (consistent over time) and valid (assesses what it is intended to assess).

Clarifying the Concepts   **1-7**   The _____ variable predicts the _____ variable.

Calculating the Statistics   **1-8**   A researcher examines the effects of two variables on memory. One variable is beverage (caffeine or no caffeine) and the other variable is the subject to be remembered (numbers, word lists, aspects of a story).

a. Identify the independent and dependent variables.

b. How many levels do the variables "beverage" and "subject to be remembered" have?

Applying the Concepts   **1-9**   Kiho Kim and Stevia Morawski (2012) studied 360 students in a university cafeteria, measuring how much food students wasted. The researchers compared waste among students when trays were available to waste among students when trays were not avail-able. They found that students wasted 32% less food when trays were not available.

a. What is the independent variable in this study?

b. What are the levels of the independent variable?

c. What is the dependent variable? Suggest at least one way in which Kim and Morawski might have measured this.

Solutions to these Check Your Learning questions can be found in Appendix D.

d. What would it mean for the food waste measure to be reliable?

e. What would it mean for the food waste measure to be valid?

Introduction to Hypothesis Testing

When John Snow suggested that the pump handle be removed from the Broad Street well, he was testing his idea that an independent variable (contaminated well water) led to a dependent variable (deaths from cholera). Behavioral scientists use research to test ideas through a specific statistics-based process called *hypothesis testing, the process of drawing conclusions about whether a particular relation between variables is supported by the evidence.* Typically, researchers examine data from a sample to draw conclusions about a population, but there are many ways to conduct research. In this section, we discuss the process of determining the variables, two ways to approach research, and two experimental designs.

- **Hypothesis testing** is the process of drawing conclusions about whether a particular relation between variables is supported by the evidence.

Determining which breed of dog you most resemble might seem silly; however, there are lots of instances in which measuring a particular variable is important. For example, we may want to know who is the most popular recording artist in a particular country, the United States, for example. One week in 2018, Nicki Minaj, furious that her album *Queen* was bested by Travis Scott's *Astroworld* on the *Billboard* charts for album sales, tweeted her dismay (Caramanica, 2018). Minaj claimed that her album was really the number 1 album, and that Scott won out only because he sold his album along with concert tickets and had help from his famous girlfriend Kylie Jenner's Instagram posts. Amid Minaj's Twitter storm, music reviewer Jon Caramanica pointed out that the *Billboard* charts are "a metric that's becoming increasingly irrelevant." Defining artist popularity, then, may not be best served by the charts.

- An **operational definition** specifies the operations or procedures used to measure or manipulate a variable.

*An **operational definition** specifies the operations or procedures used to measure or manipulate a variable.* The *Billboard* album sales charts are one way to operationalize artist popularity. You can probably think of a lot of other ways as well, including measures of concert attendance and Internet streaming. Indeed, Caramanica believes that both Minaj and Scott would be hugely popular even if they did not release traditional albums.

Our world increasingly revolves around data and metrics, and we all naturally develop hypotheses about the things we can measure in our world. Maybe you believe that true music celebrity comes from concert ticket sales. Or, with respect to the behavioral sciences, perhaps you believe that pet owners are happier than other people or that smokers simply lack the willpower to stop. Maybe you are convinced that the biggest users of social media are actually less caring than others.

In each of these behavioral science examples as shown in Table 1-2, we frame a hypothesis in terms of an independent variable and a dependent variable. The best way to learn about operationalizing a variable is to experience it for yourself. So propose a way to measure each of the variables identified in Table 1-2. We've given you a start with "pet ownership"—owns a pet versus doesn't own a pet (easy to operationalize)—and "how caring people are" (more difficult to operationalize).

Jacopo Raule/Getty Images

Operationalizing Popularity Can album sales, as measured by the Billboard chart, determine who is the most popular recording artist in the U.S.? Nicki Minaj, depicted here, and Travis Scott battled for the number one slot, even though many music reviewers see the Billboard charts as an outdated operational definition of popularity. Can you think of some better ways to define the popularity of recording artists?

TABLE 1-2	Operationalized Variables

The Independent Variable . . .	Predicts . . .	the Dependent Variable
Pet ownership ◄	─────────────►	level of happiness
Amount of willpower ◄	─────────────►	level of cigarette smoking
Social media use ◄	─────────────►	how caring people are

Conceptual Variable	Operationalized Variable
Pet ownership	Owns a pet versus doesn't own a pet
Level of happiness	_____
Amount of willpower	_____
Level of cigarette smoking	_____
Social media use	_____
How caring people are	Ask five classmates to rate how caring each person is on a scale from 1 to 5.

Correlational Studies and the Danger of Confounding Variables

Once we have decided how to operationalize the variables, we can conduct a study and collect data. There are several ways to approach research, including experiments and correlational research. *A **correlation** is an association between two or more variables.* In Snow's cholera research, it was the idea of a systematic co-relation between two variables (the proximity to the Broad Street well and the number of deaths) that saved so many lives. A correlation is one way to test a hypothesis, but it is not the only way. Researchers usually prefer to conduct an experiment rather than a correlational study because it is easier to interpret the results of experiments. Here, we'll introduce correlational research that explored whether employee wellness programs are effective, and then we'll show how an experiment is a better way to answer this question.

Around the world, 71% of workplaces have wellness programs that offer everything from nutrition advice to yoga classes, from exercise facilities to antismoking initiatives (Benefits Canada, 2018). Despite their widespread availability, most workers don't take advantage of wellness programs. In Canada, for example, only 23% of employees use their wellness programs even occasionally, so many employers try to boost usage (Murphy, 2018). Are these efforts worth it?

Over the years, a number of correlational studies have examined whether participation in wellness programs was associated—that is, correlated—with better health. The verdict: yes. One group of researchers examined a huge data set of employees from many different workplaces. They concluded that "workplace wellness programs can reduce risk factors, such as smoking, and increase healthy behaviors, such as exercise" (Mattke et al., 2013). (You can see what such a correlation might look like in Figure 1-2 on the next page.) Their findings matched those obtained in many previous studies, so employers should develop wellness programs and urge employees to participate, right?

Not so fast. In correlational studies like this one, researchers observed what employees were doing naturally—whether they were using wellness programs or not. They did

● A **correlation** is an association between two or more variables.

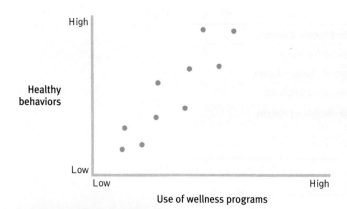

FIGURE 1-2

Correlation Between the Use of Wellness Programs and Healthy Behaviors

This graph depicts a relation between the use of wellness programs and healthy behaviors for a study of 10 fictional participants. The more a person uses wellness programs at work, the more that individual engages in healthy behaviors.

● With **random assignment**, every participant in a study has an equal chance of being assigned to any of the groups, or experimental conditions, in the study.

● An **experiment** is a study in which participants are randomly assigned to a condition or level of one or more independent variables.

not assign some people to participate in the wellness programs and other people to avoid them. Can you spot the confounding variable? It is possible that people who take advantage of wellness programs—who sign up for nutrition training and go to the office gym—are those who already tend to be healthier than others and practice many of these behaviors anyway. So, the effect of participation in wellness programs on health may be confounded by the influence of other existing behaviors, such as exercise, that also improve health. As we will discuss in Chapter 15, there are always alternative explanations in a correlational study. Don't be too eager to infer causality just because two variables are correlated.

If we want to draw a causal conclusion, we have to use an experiment. In the next section, we'll look at an experimental investigation of how effective wellness programs are.

Conducting Experiments to Control for Confounding Variables

The hallmark of experimental research is random assignment. *With **random assignment**, every participant in the study has an equal chance of being assigned to any of the groups, or experimental conditions, in the study.* And an **experiment** *is a study in which participants are randomly assigned to a condition or level of one or more independent variables.* Random assignment means that neither the participants nor the researchers get to choose the condition. Experiments are the gold standard of hypothesis testing because they are the best way to control confounding variables. Controlling confounding variables allows researchers to infer a cause–effect relation between variables, rather than merely a systematic association between variables. The critical feature that makes a study worthy of being called an *experiment* is random assignment to groups.

When researchers conduct experiments, they create approximately equivalent groups by randomly assigning participants to different levels, or conditions, of the independent variable. Random assignment controls the effects of personality traits, life experiences, personal biases, and other potential confounds by distributing them evenly across each condition of the experiment. So, if you wanted to study the effects of pet ownership on happiness using an experiment, you would have to randomly assign people to own a pet or not own a pet. This would be tricky from a practical perspective (and potentially unethical to both the humans and the pets), but it would eliminate possible confounds, such as the fact that pet owners might be more likely to have certain personality traits that lead them to be happier (or unhappier). Let's look at a real-life experiment that examined the effectiveness of wellness programs.

EXAMPLE 1.1

In the previous section on correlational studies, we saw that many employers are convinced that wellness programs lead to positive health outcomes like increased exercise and lower health care costs (Murphy, 2018). But correlational studies just demonstrate relations between variables. Without experimental research, we cannot conclude that wellness programs actually *cause* these positive health outcomes. Perhaps people who choose to participate in wellness programs do so *because* they already engage in healthier behaviors than their peers. Researchers can only conclude that wellness programs are causing positive health outcomes if they conduct an experiment and use random assignment.

Of course, from an ethical perspective, we can't actually force people to participate in wellness programs. But we can set up an experiment that randomly assigns employees to one of two levels of an independent variable: (1) to have access to a wellness program or (2) to have no access to a wellness program. Random assignment assures us that two groups are roughly equal, on average, concerning possible confounding variables that might contribute to success in wellness programs, such as eating nutritious meals, exercising frequently, (not) smoking, and being in good general health.

Random assignment diminishes the effects of all potential confounds. So random assignment to groups increases researchers' confidence that the two groups are similar, on average, *prior* to the experiment. (Figure 1-3 visually clarifies the difference between self-selection and random assignment; in Chapter 5, we explore more specifically how random assignment is implemented.) If we use random assignment, and if the "access to wellness programs" group has better health outcomes after the experiment, on average, than the "no access to wellness programs" group, then we are more confident in the conclusion that wellness programs cause better health outcomes for employees.

One research group used exactly such an experimental design to explore the causal effects of access to wellness programs. In the impressively large Illinois

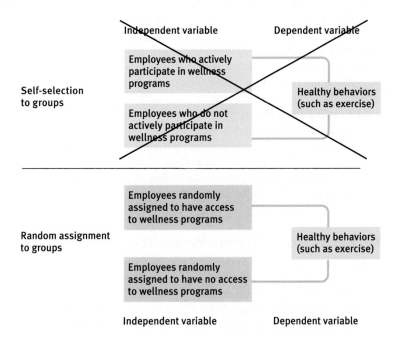

FIGURE 1-3

Self-Selected into or Randomly Assigned to One of Two Groups: Access to Wellness Programs or No Access to Wellness Programs

This figure visually clarifies the difference between self-selection and random assignment. The design of the first study does not answer the question "Do wellness programs cause increases in healthy behaviors (such as regular exercise)?"

Workplace Wellness Study, more than 12,000 employees of the University of Illinois at Urbana–Champaign were invited to participate in a study of the university's new, extensive workplace wellness programs (Jones, Molitor, & Rief, 2018). Almost 5000 employees signed up. The researchers then created two groups. In the first group, which included about two-thirds of the sign-ups, participants were randomly assigned to have access to the new wellness program, which included stopping smoking, stress management, and exercise classes. They were offered financial incentives to take part in the wellness program, including paid time off to participate and cash awards for those who completed the program. The remaining one-third of sign-ups were randomly assigned to a second group that was not allowed to join the wellness program. The researchers compared the two groups on 39 dependent variables, and failed to find effects on 37 of them! There were no statistical differences between the two groups, on average, for dependent variables such as health care spending, days absent from work, visits to the campus gym, work productivity, and a number of health behaviors.

What is particularly intriguing about this data set is that the researchers analyzed it in two ways. First, they conducted the analysis of the experimental data that we just described. Second, they analyzed just a part of the overall data as a correlational study, a twist that one journalist called "the nerdy fun part" (Carroll, 2018). In the fun part, researchers pulled out the data for just the approximately 3300 participants who had access to the wellness program. From that smaller set of participants, researchers compared two groups: (1) those who chose to actively engage with the wellness programs and (2) those who chose not to. Note that this smaller analysis is a correlational study much like the one we discussed in previous section, so confounds could be involved.

The results of that smaller data set matched those of previous correlational studies. Employees who chose to participate in wellness programs had better health outcomes, on average, than those who did not choose to participate. The bottom line: It doesn't seem to be the wellness programs that are *causing* improved health outcomes. Rather, it is the employees' preexisting behaviors that lead them to take advantage of what the wellness programs offer. Those sorts of employees find ways to get healthier even without formal wellness programs.

The finding about the ineffectiveness of wellness programs highlights the need for ongoing research. Future studies may shed light on whether different wellness options prove effective, or whether other interventions improve employee health. Regardless, as more research unfolds, an understanding of both research design and statistical analyses is essential for policy makers—including those in the workplace—as they craft programs aimed to change behaviors. ●

Between-Groups Design Versus Within-Groups Design

● With a **between-groups research design**, participants experience one and only one level of the independent variable.

Experimenters can create meaningful comparison groups in several ways. However, most studies have either a *between-groups* research design or a *within-groups* (also called a *repeated-measures*) research design.

*A **between-groups research design** is an experiment in which participants experience one and only one level of the independent variable.* An experiment that compares a control group (such as people randomly assigned to have no access to wellness programs) with an experimental group (such as people randomly assigned to have access to wellness programs) is an example of a between-groups design.

A **within-groups research design** *is an experiment in which all participants in the study experience the different levels of the independent variable.* An experiment that compares the same group of people before and after they experience a level of an independent variable, such as access to a wellness program, is an example of a within-groups design. The word *within* emphasizes that if you experience one condition of a study, then you remain within the study until you experience all conditions of the study.

Many applied questions in the behavioral sciences are best studied using a within-groups design. This is particularly true of long-term (often called *longitudinal*) studies that examine how individuals and organizations change over time, or studies involving a naturally occurring event that cannot be duplicated in the laboratory. If you participated in a study at your university that followed you over time—say, once a year—then you participated in a longitudinal study. Within-groups studies are useful in other contexts. For example, researchers obviously cannot randomly assign people to either experience or not experience a hurricane. However, researchers could use nature's predictability to anticipate hurricane season, collect "before" data, and then collect data once again "after" people experience a hurricane.

Introduction to Data Ethics

"Whipsaw literature" is how Barnett Kramer, director of disease prevention for the U.S. National Cancer Institute, described the back-and-forth motion of research studies that contradict each other (Kolata, 2016). Barnett echoes a common complaint, "One week drinking coffee is good for you, and the next week it is lethal." We've all had this experience. Should I stretch before jogging or can I skip it? Red wine—healthy or dangerous? Do brain games make us smarter, or not so much? It is clear there is a problem with data, and this challenge crosses the behavioral and biological sciences, as well as medicine.

The good news is that researchers are developing guidelines that encourage transparent, ethical research. These guidelines are part of what is often called *data ethics, a set of principles related to all stages of working with data—research design, data collection, statistical analyses, interpretation of analyses, and reporting of outcomes.* The push toward a more ethical and transparent approach to data is often termed "open science." More specifically, **open science** *is an approach to research that encourages collaboration, and includes the sharing of research methodology, data, and statistical analyses in ways that allow others to question and even to try to recreate findings.* Psychology researcher Barbara Spellman (2015) calls it a revolution, "not about the content of our science" but "about the values we hold as we conceptualize, implement, analyze, and share our science" (p. 886). Spellman describes the revolution as a response to the current crisis in psychological science—a crisis that has resulted from a number of sources:

- *Replication failures:* Researchers have not been able to reproduce or replicate the findings of a number of important studies. When some studies were repeated by other researchers, the outcomes were different.

- With a **within-groups research design**, all participants in the study experience the different levels of the independent variable; also called a *repeated-measures design*.

- **Data ethics** is a set of principles related to all stages of working with data—research design, data collection, statistical analyses, interpretation of analyses, and reporting of outcomes.

- **Open science** is an approach to research that encourages collaboration, and includes the sharing of research methodology, data, and statistical analyses in ways that allow others to question and even to try to recreate findings.

- *Problems with data collection:* Some researchers designed studies and collected data in ways that allowed them to analyze their data in multiple ways, increasing the chances of finding a result they want.
- *Old-fashioned statistics:* Researchers are starting to realize that traditional ways of analyzing data can lead to inaccurate outcomes and misinterpretations, which increases the chances that any particular finding cannot be replicated.

These three data-related problems are sometimes intentional and sometimes unintentional. They underscore bad conduct that compounds more mainstream unethical data practices of picking and choosing statistics that make a particular point, misapplying statistical techniques in pursuit of a goal, and creating misleading graphs.

Philosophy professor Deborah Mayo writes about "severe testing" as a solution to the data crisis (2018). What's severe testing? To answer that, let's first consider the opposite of a severe test—a weak test—from the blockbuster book *The Rules.* It is a terrible book (in your authors' opinions) first published in the 90s, which suggested that heterosexual women should act in specific, old-school ways to find a heterosexual man to marry. Rules like . . . don't get back to him quickly, let him take the lead, don't have strong opinions or even talk much, and so on. If he likes you back, you score! Yes, this was real, and it was best-selling. But *The Rules* offer a weak test of whether a guy truly likes a woman. The strong—or severe—test was whether he would like her when she was completely herself—when she was smart, ambitious, funny, loud, and opinionated. If he liked her then, well, then he liked her! (Spoiler alert: One of *The Rules* authors got divorced!) *The Rules* authors, by definition, hated a severe test.

The term "severity" with respect to statistics was coined by the late philosopher of science Karl Popper, but Mayo developed the concept more fully. To Mayo, severe testing is subjecting a hypothesis to rigorous statistical scrutiny aimed at uncovering any flaws in that hypothesis. The severe tester is an ethical researcher, someone who aggressively attempts to uncover the weaknesses in their data analyses and claims. In ethical research, the data should have to pass a difficult, or severe, test.

Throughout this book, we will explore the ways in which behavioral scientists develop best practices for ethical data collection, analysis, interpretation, and reporting. In each chapter, we will present a new aspect of data ethics in a featured section. We'll describe several ways to manage problematic traditional methods of data analysis, some of which are actually called the "new statistics." In addition, we'll outline how to be truthful when interpreting and describing data, how to be honest with graphs, and even how to identify when someone is being sneaky with their presentation of data. When relevant, we'll share tips on using technology—often available for free—that can help us become more ethical creators and interpreters of statistics.

It is an exciting time in the behavioral sciences. The field of statistics is moving toward more ethical data practices, and more severe tests, a sign that science is adaptive and strong.

Preregistration

Figure skating star Nathan Chen competed in the 2018 Olympics, but underperformed in his short program, in part because he changed his planned jump (a quadruple flip) to an easier jump (a double flip) in the middle of his routine (Crouse, 2018). How do we know this? All competitive skaters submit their routines in advance for the benefit of the announcers and the judges (Hill, 2018).

Lately, behavioral science researchers have tried a similar tactic, dubbed preregistration, to fix problems in the field. *Preregistration is a recommended open-science practice in which researchers outline their research design and analysis plan before conducting a study.* More specifically, preregistration details the design of the study—including all of the variables that will be measured, the methods by which data will be collected, and the statistical analyses that will be conducted. When the results of a study are reported, researchers can then show that they preregistered the methods and analyses before conducting the study, demonstrating that they did exactly what they said they would do. Importantly, researchers can keep their preregistered details hidden until they report their findings, so other researchers can't steal their ideas.

Preregistration works because it leaves no room for sketchy tactics. It ensures a more severe test of their hypotheses (Mayo, 2018). For example, researchers can't pretend that they intended to exclude participants who responded in certain ways. They can't secretly try four different statistical approaches until they find the one that works. And they certainly can't alter their hypotheses after the fact to reflect what they actually found, a trick called HARKing. *HARKing, or "(H)ypothesizing (A)fter the (R)esults are (K)nown," is an unethical practice in which researchers change their hypotheses to match their findings.* "Of course we expected these bizarre results," a HARKer might suggest. So, preregistration helps researchers, too, by reducing the chances that they will be accused of sketchy tactics.

Preregistration is now strongly encouraged by many research journals in which scientists publish findings. The Association for Psychological Science hosts perhaps the most comprehensive list of online preregistration platforms (psychologicalscience.org /publications/psychological_science/preregistration). For clear directions on how to preregister a study, the Open Science Framework (OSF) provides helpful step-by-step instructions for preregistering on its site (osf.io/sgrk6/). You may never have to preregister a study yourself, but "preregistration" is a word you should look for when reading surprising research results. "Did the researchers preregister their hypotheses, research design, and statistical analyses?"

- **Preregistration** is a recommended open-science practice in which researchers outline their research design and analysis plan before conducting a study.

- **HARKing**, or "(H)ypothesizing (A)fter the (R)esults are (K)nown," is an unethical practice in which researchers change their hypotheses to match their findings.

Preregistering Figure-Skating Routines Competitive figure skaters must submit the specifics of their routines before a competition so that the announcers and judges know what to expect. So, skaters like Nathan Chen, shown here, get lower scores when they switch out a jump in the middle of their routines. There's a move for researchers to do the same—to preregister the specifics of their studies so they can't change things along the way to get the result they want.

Some researchers have pushed back against this new tool, arguing that it prevents researchers from fully exploring their data. Others argue that researchers are already ethically free to play with their data, but only in pursuit of new hypotheses for future research. Interesting findings from data explorations can lead to new hypotheses and new studies that can then be preregistered themselves, ensuring that a surprising finding is tested in an honest way.

CHECK YOUR LEARNING

Reviewing the Concepts

> Hypothesis testing is the process of drawing conclusions about whether a particular relation between variables (the hypothesis) is supported by the evidence.

> All variables must be operationalized—that is, we need to specify how they are to be measured or manipulated.

> Correlational studies assess whether there are associations between naturally occurring variables. They do not explore whether one variable causes the other.

> Experiments attempt to explain a cause–effect relation between an independent variable and a dependent variable.

> Random assignment to groups to control for confounding variables is the hallmark of an experiment.

> Most studies have either a between-groups design or a within-groups design.

> Researchers are increasingly concerned with data ethics, principles that promote transparent and honest research, and that help prevent problematic data collection practices and statistical techniques. The use of such transparent practices is often called open science.

> Unethical practices can lead to inaccurate or misleading findings, as well as failures to reproduce the findings of previous studies.

> In the open-science practice known as preregistration, researchers record their research design and analysis plan before they conduct a study.

> Preregistration can prevent HARKing, or "hypothesizing after the results are known," an unethical practice in which researchers change their hypotheses to match their findings.

Clarifying the Concepts

1-10 How do the two types of research discussed in this chapter—experimental and correlational—differ?

1-11 How does random assignment help to address confounding variables?

Calculating the Statistics

1-12 In Check Your Learning 1-6, you saw several ways in which Uber measured the performance of its drivers (Rosenblat, 2015).

    a. Define the term *operational definition* in your own words, using one or more of these examples in your answer. What is Uber trying to operationally define?

    b. Another operational definition that Uber uses is a high cancellation rate; that is, drivers who cancel rides a lot are viewed negatively. Rosenblat (2015) points out, however, that "the contexts of . . . a high cancellation rate are not taken into account. There's no flexibility for when accepting a ride would mean the driver actually loses money, let alone a mechanism for indicating when passengers are behaving badly." In your own words, explain why "cancellation rate" might be a bad operational definition in this case.

Applying the Concepts   1-13   Expectations matter. Many researchers have examined how expectations based on stereotypes influence women's math performance (see Steele, 2011). In some studies, women were told that a gender difference was found on a certain math test and that women tended to receive lower scores than men did. Other women were told that no gender differences were evident on the test. In studies like this, women in the first group tend to perform more poorly than men do, on average, whereas women in the second group do not.

a. Briefly outline how researchers could conduct this study as a true experiment using a between-groups design.

b. Why would researchers want to use random assignment?

c. If researchers did not use random assignment but rather chose people who were *already* in those conditions (i.e., who already either believed or did not believe the stereotypes), what might be the possible confounds? Name at least two.

d. How is math performance operationalized here?

e. Briefly outline how researchers could conduct this study using a within-groups design.

Solutions to these Check Your Learning questions can be found in Appendix D.

REVIEW OF CONCEPTS

The Two Branches of Statistics

Statistics is divided into two branches: descriptive statistics and inferential statistics. *Descriptive statistics* organize, summarize, and communicate large amounts of numerical information. *Inferential statistics* draw conclusions about larger populations based on smaller samples of that population. *Samples* are intended to be representative of larger *populations*.

 **LaunchPad**
macmillan learning
Visit LaunchPad to access the e-book and to test your knowledge with LearningCurve.

How to Transform Observations into Variables

Observations may be described as either discrete or continuous. *Discrete observations* are those that can take on only certain numbers (e.g., whole numbers, such as 1), and *continuous observations* are those that can take on all possible numbers in a range (e.g., 1.68792). Two types of *variables*, nominal and ordinal, can only be discrete. *Nominal variables* use numbers simply to give names to scores. *Ordinal variables* are rank-ordered. Two types of variables can be continuous (although both can also be discrete in some cases): interval and ratio. *Interval variables* are those in which the distances between numerical values are assumed to be equal. *Ratio variables* are those that meet the criteria for interval variables but also have a meaningful zero point. *Scale variable* is a term used for both interval variables and ratio variables, particularly in statistical computer programs.

Variables and Research

Independent variables can be manipulated or observed by the experimenter, and they have at least two *levels*, or conditions. *Dependent variables* are outcomes in response to changes or differences in the independent variable. *Confounding variables* systematically vary with the independent variable, so we cannot logically determine which variable may have influenced the dependent variable. The independent and dependent variables allow researchers to test and explore the relations between variables. A measure is useful only if it is both *reliable* and *valid*. A reliable measure is one that is consistent, and a valid measure is one that assesses what it is intended to assess.

Introduction to Hypothesis Testing

Hypothesis testing is the process of drawing conclusions about whether a particular relation between variables is supported by the evidence. *Operational definitions* of the independent variable and the dependent variable are necessary to test a hypothesis. Correlational studies allow us to determine whether there is a predictable relation between two naturally occurring variables; however, correlational studies cannot tell us whether one variable causes the other variable. *Experiments* attempt to identify a cause–effect relation between an independent variable and a dependent variable. *Random assignment* to groups to control for confounding variables is the hallmark of an experiment. Most experiments have either a *between-groups design* or a *within-groups design*.

Researchers are increasingly concerned with data ethics. *Data ethics* refers to principles for data collection and statistical analyses that can help researchers avoid inaccurate or misleading findings. These principles promote *open science*, best practices that increase transparency in research.

Preregistration, in which researchers report the details of their planned study before they begin, is one of the open-science practices that ethical researchers can use. Preregistration can help prevent *HARKing*, short for "hypothesizing after the results are known," whereby researchers alter their hypotheses to match their findings.

SPSS

SPSS is divided into two main screens. The easiest way to move back and forth between these two screens is by using the two tabs located at the lower left labeled "Variable View" and "Data View." When data are collected, each data point should be connected with an identifier unique to each participant. This variable is often noted as the "ID." Every variable that is measured needs to have its own Name and Label, and SPSS needs to know how the variable was measured.

To name the variables, go to "Variable View" (see screenshot A on the next page) and select:

> **Name.** Type in a short version of the variable name—for example, BDI for the Beck Depression Inventory, a common measure of depressive symptoms. A second variable to add could be BAI, short

for the Beck Anxiety Inventory. Note that SPSS will not allow spaces in the "Name" of the variable.

To tell SPSS what the variable name means, select:

> **Label.** Type in the full name of the variable, such as Beck Depression Inventory and Beck Anxiety Inventory.

Now tell SPSS what kind of variables these are by selecting:

> **Measure.** Highlight the type of variable by clicking on the cell in the column labeled "Measure" next to each variable, then clicking on the arrow to access the tool that allows you to identify whether the variable is scale, ordinal, or nominal.

After describing all of the variables in the study in "Variable View," switch over to "Data View" (remember, at the lower left corner of the screen; see screenshot B). The information you entered was automatically transferred to that screen, but now the variables are displayed across the tops of the columns instead of along the left-hand side of the rows. You can now enter the data in "Data View" under the appropriate heading; each participant's data are entered across one row.

A

B

EXERCISES

The solutions to the odd-numbered exercises can be found in Appendix C.

Clarifying the Concepts

1.1 What is the difference between descriptive statistics and inferential statistics?

1.2 What is the difference between a sample and a population?

1.3 Identify and define the four types of variables that researchers use to quantify their observations.

1.4 Describe two ways that statisticians might use the word *scale*.

1.5 Distinguish between discrete variables and continuous variables.

1.6 What is the relation between an independent variable and a dependent variable?

1.7 What are confounding variables (or simply *confounds*), and how are they controlled using random assignment?

1.8 What is the difference between reliability and validity, and how are the two concepts related?

1.9 To test a hypothesis, we need operational definitions of the independent and dependent variables. What is an operational definition?

1.10 In your own words, define the word *experiment*—first as you would use it in everyday conversation and then as a researcher would use it.

1.11 What is the difference between experimental research and correlational research?

1.12 What is the difference between a between-groups research design and a within-groups research design?

1.13 In statistics, it is important to pay close attention to language. The following statements are wrong but can be corrected by substituting one word or phrase. For example, the sentence "Only correlational studies can tell us something about causality" could be corrected by changing "correlational studies" to "experiments." Identify the incorrect word or phrase in each of the following statements and supply the correct word.

    a. In a study on exam preparation, every participant had an equal chance of being assigned to study alone or with a group. This was a correlational study.

    b. A psychologist was interested in studying the effects of the dependent variable of caffeine on hours of sleep, and she used a scale measure for sleep.

    c. A university assessed the reliability of a commonly used scale—a mathematics placement test—to determine whether it truly measures math ability.

    d. In a within-groups experiment on calcium and osteoporosis, participants were assigned to one of two levels of the independent variable: no change in diet or supplementing the diet with calcium.

1.14 The following statements are wrong but can be corrected by substituting one word or phrase. (See the instructions in Exercise 1.13.) Identify the incorrect word or phrase in each of the following statements and supply the correct word.

    a. A researcher examined the effect of the ordinal variable "gender" on the scale variable "hours of reality television watched per week."

    b. A psychologist used a between-groups design to study the effects of an independent variable (a workout video) on the dependent variable (the weight) of a group of undergraduate students before and after viewing the video.

    c. In a study on the effects of the confounding variable of noise level on the dependent variable of memory, researchers were concerned that the memory measure was not valid.

    d. A researcher studied a population of 20 rats to determine whether changes in exposure to light would lead to changes in the dependent variable of amount of sleep.

1.15 What do researchers mean by data ethics?

1.16 Describe the kinds of unethical practices that researchers might be concerned with.

1.17 What is preregistration and why is it important?

1.18 What is HARKing and how can preregistration help to eliminate this practice?

Calculating the Statistics

1.19 A researcher studies the number of hours 2500 Canadians work out every week. Identify the sample and the population for this example.

1.20 University bookstore employees asked 225 students to complete a customer satisfaction survey after these customers bought their books. The bookstore manager wanted to find ways to improve the customer experience. Identify the sample and population for this example.

1.21 Over the course of 1 week, a grocery store randomly selected 100 customers to complete a survey about their favorite products. Identify the sample and population for this example.

1.22 A researcher studies the average distance that 130 people living in urban areas in India walk each week.

   a. What is the size of the sample?

   b. Identify the population.

   c. Is this "average" a descriptive statistic or an inferential statistic if it is used to describe the 130 people studied?

   d. How might you operationalize the average distance walked in 1 week as an ordinal measure?

   e. How might you operationalize the average distance walked in 1 week as a scale measure?

1.23 As they leave a popular grocery store, 73 people are stopped and the number of fruit and vegetable items they purchased is counted.

   a. What is the size of the sample?

   b. Identify the population.

   c. If this number of items counted is used to estimate the diets of all shoppers, is it a descriptive statistic or an inferential statistic?

   d. How might you operationalize the amount of fruit and vegetable items purchased as a nominal measure?

   e. How might you operationalize the amount of fruit and vegetable items purchased as an ordinal measure?

   f. How might you operationalize the amount of fruit and vegetable items purchased as a scale measure?

1.24 In the fall of 2008, the stock market plummeted several times, with grave consequences for the world economy. A researcher might assess the economic effect this situation had by seeing how much money people saved in 2009. That amount could be compared to the amount people saved in more economically stable years. How might you operationalize the economic implications at a national level—that is, across countries?

1.25 Suppose a researcher is interested in evaluating how pet ownership and social activity affect loneliness.

   a. Identify the independent variables and the dependent variable.

   b. Imagine that pet ownership is assessed as either owning no pets or owning at least one pet, and that social activity is assessed as went out with friends or family either not at all or at least once over the past week. How many levels do the independent variables have?

   c. How might you operationalize the dependent variable that you identified in part (a)?

1.26 A study of the effects of skin tone (light, medium, and dark) on the severity of facial wrinkles in middle age might be of interest to dermatologists.

   a. What would the independent variable be in this study?

   b. What would the dependent variable be in this study?

   c. How many levels would the independent variable have?

Applying the Concepts

1.27 **Increase in depression globally:** According to the World Health Organization (2018), more than 300 million people suffer from depression globally.

   a. Do you think the research behind this statistic is based on a sample or a population? Explain.

   b. Is 300 million a descriptive statistic or an inferential statistic? Explain.

1.28 **Sample versus population in Norway:** The Nord-Trøndelag health study surveyed more than 60,000 people in a Norwegian county and reported that gastrointestinal symptoms, depression, and anxiety disorders are strongly related (Haug, Mykletun, & Dahl, 2002).

   a. What is the sample used by these researchers?

   b. What is the population to which the researchers would like to extend their findings?

1.29 **Types of variables and Olympic swimming:** At the 2012 London Summer Olympics, American Michael Phelps won 4 gold medals, bringing his overall Olympic career total to 18 gold medals, the all-time career record for Olympic gold medals in any sport. One of the events he won was the 100-meter butterfly. For each of the following examples, identify the type of variable—nominal, ordinal, or scale.

   a. Phelps of the United States came in first, and Chad le Clos of South Africa and Evgeny Korotyshkin of Russia tied for second place.

   b. Phelps finished in 51.21 seconds, and le Clos and Korotyshkin finished in 51.44 seconds.

   c. Phelps and Korotyshkin live in the Northern Hemisphere, whereas le Clos lives in the Southern Hemisphere.

1.30 Types of variables and the Kentucky Derby: The Kentucky Derby is perhaps the premier event in U.S. horse racing. For each of the following examples from the derby, identify the type of variable—nominal, ordinal, or scale.

a. As racing fans, we would be very interested in the variable finishing position. One year, a horse called Orb won, followed by Golden Soul in second and Revolutionary in third.

b. We also might be interested in the variable finishing time. Orb won in 2 minutes, 2.89 seconds.

c. Derby attendance was 151,616 the year that Orb won, not as high as the record of 165,307 people.

d. If we were the betting type, we might examine the variable payoffs. For each $2.00 bet on Orb, a gambler won $12.80.

e. We might be interested in the history of the derby and the demographic variables of jockeys, such as gender or race. For example, in the first 28 runnings of the Kentucky Derby, 15 of the winning jockeys were African American.

f. In the luxury boxes, high fashion reigns; we might be curious about the variable of hat wearing, observing how many women wear hats and how many do not.

1.31 Discrete versus continuous variables: For each of the following examples, state whether the scale variable is discrete or continuous.

a. The capacity, in terms of songs, of a smartphone

b. The playing time of an individual song

c. The cost to download a song legally

d. The number of posted reviews that an album has on Amazon.com

1.32 Reliability and validity: Go online and take the personality test found at outofservice.com/starwars. This test assesses your personality in terms of the characters from the original *Star Wars* movies.

a. What does it mean for a test to be reliable? Take the test a second time. Does it seem to be reliable?

b. What does it mean for a test to be valid? Does this test seem to be valid? Explain.

c. The test asks a number of demographic questions at the end, including "In what country did you spend most of your youth?" Can you think of a

hypothesis that might have led the developers of this Web site to ask this question?

d. For your hypothesis in part (c), identify the independent and dependent variables.

1.33 Reliability, validity, and wine ratings: You may have been in a wine store and wondered just how useful those posted wine ratings are. (They are usually rated on a scale from 50 to 100, with 100 being the top score.) After all, aren't ratings subjective? Corsi and Ashenfelter (2001) studied whether wine experts are consistent. Knowing that the weather is the best predictor of price, the researchers wondered how well weather predicted experts' ratings. The variables used for weather included temperature and rainfall, and the variable used for wine experts' ratings was the number they assigned to each wine.

a. Name one independent variable. What type of variable is it? Is it discrete or continuous?

b. Name the dependent variable. What type of variable is it? Is it discrete or continuous?

c. How does this study reflect the concept of reliability?

d. Let's say that you frequently drink wine that has been rated highly by Robert Parker, one of this study's wine experts. His ratings were determined to be reliable, and you find that you usually agree with Parker. How does this observation reflect the concept of validity?

1.34 Operationalizing variables and rap statistics: The Web site Rap Genius (now just Genius) analyzes rap music using what it calls RapMetrics (rapgenius .com/posts/63-Introducing-rapmetricstm-the-birth-of-statistical-analysis-of-rap-lyrics). It developed a measure called rhyme density, which is the proportion of all syllables that rhyme with another syllable. Eminem's *Without Me*, for example, has a rhyme density of 0.49 (49%) because almost half of the lyrics rhyme with another syllable, whereas Notorious B.I.G.'s *Juicy* only has a rhyme density of 0.23 (23%). The people behind Rap Genius say, "Over the course of a career, the rappers with the highest rhyme densities are basically the best technical rappers."

a. How does Rap Genius operationalize the best rapper?

b. List at least three other variables that might be considered in determining the best rapper.

c. Across all songs, MF Doom came in first with an overall rhyme density of 0.44, and Cam'ron came in second with a rhyme density of 0.41. What kind of variable is the ranking, and what kind of variable is the rhyme density?

d. Rap Genius summarized its rhyme density discussion by saying: "MF Doom surprised us a little. First the big *New Yorker* profile and now this . . . it's too much! Cam'ron is much more culturally relevant and interesting (plus he doesn't need to wear a mask, he's naturally silly), so we at RapMetrics™ consider *him* the G.O.A.T. [greatest of all time] MC [rapper] overall." Rap Genius, therefore, changed its operational definition a bit. What has it added to its operational definition of the overall G.O.A.T. MC?

1.35 **Operationalizing the earnings of comedians:** In 2013, *Forbes* reported the 10 top-earning comedians, and all 10 were men—Daniel Tosh, Kevin Hart, and Larry the Cable Guy among them. A number of online journalists wanted to know why there were no women on the list. Erin Gloria Ryan of *Jezebel*, for example, wondered where women like Ellen DeGeneres and Amy Poehler were. Under a "methodology" heading, *Forbes* explained the process of gathering these data. "To compile our earnings numbers, which consist of pretax gross income, we talked to agents, lawyers and other industry insiders to come up with an estimate for what each comedian earned." *Forbes* added a caveat: "In order for comics to make the cut, their primary source of income had to come from concert ticket sales." In response to that caveat, Ryan wrote: "Okay, guys? That's a super weird definition of what constitutes a comedian."

a. Explain how *Forbes* is operationalizing the earnings of comedians.

b. Explain why *Jezebel's* Ryan might have a problem with this definition.

c. Ryan wrote: "If Dr. Dre doesn't have to record an album or perform a concert to be considered a real 'hip hop artist,' then why does Mindy Kaling need to hold a mic in front of a brick wall to be a real 'comedian'?" Based on Ryan's critique, offer at least one different way of operationalizing the earnings of comedians.

1.36 **Between-groups versus within-groups and exercise:** Noting marked increases in weight across the population, researchers, nutritionists, and physicians have struggled to find ways to stem the tide of obesity in many Western countries. They have advocated a number of exercise programs, and there has been a flurry of research to determine the effectiveness of these programs. Pretend that you are in charge of a research study to examine the effects of an exercise program on weight loss in comparison with a program that does not involve exercise.

a. Describe how you could study the exercise program using a between-groups research design.

b. Describe how you could study the exercise program using a within-groups design.

c. What is a potential confound of a within-groups design?

1.37 **Correlational research and vaping:** As the use of e-cigarettes, or vaping, becomes more popular, researchers are exploring the potential negative effects from this behavior. According to *Scientific American* (2018), researchers have investigated the harmful effects of nicotine, including its links to heart disease, as well as the dangers of several carcinogens inhaled while vaping.

a. Why was this research necessarily correlational in nature?

b. What confounding variables might make it difficult to isolate the health effects of vaping?

c. How might the nature of this research and these confounds buy time for the e-cigarette industry with regard to acknowledging the hazardous effects of smoking?

d. All ethics aside, how could you study the relation between vaping and health problems using a between-groups experiment?

1.38 **Experimental versus correlational research and culture:** A researcher interested in the cultural values of individualistic and collectivist societies collects data on the rate of relationship conflict experienced by 32 people who test high for individualism and 37 people who test high for collectivism.

a. Is this research experimental or correlational? Explain.

b. What is the sample?

c. Write a possible hypothesis for this researcher.

d. How might we operationalize relationship conflict?

1.39 **Experimental versus correlational research and recycling:** A study in Argentina concluded that grocery store customers were more likely to bring their own bags when stores charged for plastic bags than when stores did not charge (Jakovcevic et al., 2014).

Imagine that you want to design a follow-up study on this topic in a country other than Argentina.

a. Write a hypothesis for this researcher.

b. Describe how you could design a correlational study to test this hypothesis.

c. Describe how you could design an experiment to test this hypothesis.

1.40 **Data ethics and "eat your peas":** *New York Times* reporter Anahad O'Connor (2018) reported on a scandal in the field of psychology. A well-known researcher of food-related behaviors, Brian Wansink, resigned from his position at Cornell University after university investigators discovered "academic misconduct in his research and scholarship, including misreporting of research data." (For example, some have suggested that Wansink may have analyzed his data in different ways in an effort to attain the results he desired.) Several journals retracted papers that Wansink had co-authored because of questions about the research. Wansink generally defends his work, but even he acknowledges some mistakes, including in his statistics.

a. Wansink is an extreme example, but how does it highlight the need for a focus on data ethics in the behavioral sciences?

b. How might "open science" and transparency help to identify problematic research findings, such as those in Wansink's papers, sooner?

c. Among other possibly inaccurate findings, Wansink reported that children were more excited to eat their vegetables when they had exciting names like "power peas" (O'Connor, 2018). How might the media play a role in exaggerating fun findings like this one?

1.41 **HARKing, a Texas sharpshooter, and preregistration:** Australian psychologist Mark Rubin (2017) likened the unethical practice of HARKing to the tale of the Texas sharpshooter. Rubin explains that the sharpshooter "aims and fires his gun at [a] target on a barn wall but misses. He then walks up to the wall, rubs out the initial target, and draws a second target around his bullet hole in order to make it appear as if he is a good shot" (p. 309).

a. Why is this a good analogy for HARKing in research?

b. How could preregistration help with the problem of HARKing in research?

Putting It All Together

1.42 **Romantic relationships:** Goodman and Greaves (2010) reported findings from the Millennium Cohort Study, a large research project in the United Kingdom. They stated that "while it is true that cohabiting parents are more likely to split up than married ones, there is very little evidence to suggest that this is due to a causal effect of marriage. Instead, it seems simply that different sorts of people choose to get married and have children, rather than to have children as a cohabiting couple, and that those relationships with the best prospects of lasting are the ones that are most likely to lead to marriage" (p. 1).

a. What is the sample in this study?

b. What is the likely population?

c. Is this a correlational study or an experiment? Explain.

d. What is the independent variable?

e. What is the dependent variable?

f. What is one possible confounding variable? Suggest at least one way in which the confounding variable might be operationalized.

1.43 **Experiments, HIV, and cholera:** Several studies have documented that people who are HIV-positive are susceptible to cholera (likely because of having a weakened immune system). Researchers in Mozambique (Lucas et al., 2005), a country where an estimated 20% to 30% of the population is HIV-positive, wondered whether an oral vaccine for cholera would work among people who are HIV-positive. Cholera immunization was administered to 14,000 people in Mozambique who tested positive for HIV. Soon thereafter, an epidemic of cholera spread through the region, giving the researchers an opportunity to test their hypothesis.

a. Describe a way in which the researchers could have conducted an experiment to examine the effectiveness of the cholera vaccine among people who are HIV-positive.

b. If the researchers did conduct an experiment, would this have been a between-groups or a within-groups experiment? Explain.

c. The researchers did not randomly assign participants to vaccine or no-vaccine conditions; rather, they conducted a general mass immunization. Why does this limit their ability to draw causal conclusions? Include at least one possible confounding variable.

d. The researchers did not use random assignment when conducting this study. List at least one practical reason and at least one ethical reason that they might not have used random assignment.

e. Let's say that the researchers said that they had preregistered their study. In your own words, what would that mean?

1.44 Ability and wages: Arcidiacono, Bayer, and Hizmo (2008) analyzed data from a national longitudinal survey called NLSY79, which includes data from more than 12,000 men and women in the United States who were in the 14- to 22-year age range in 1979. The researchers reported that ability is related to wages in early career jobs for university graduates but not for high school graduates. In line with this finding, research has found that racial discrimination with respect to wages is more prevalent against high school graduates than college graduates, because when ability is not the primary reason for determining wages, other factors irrelevant to ability, such as race, come into play. The researchers suggest that their findings might explain why, on average, a black person is more likely to earn a college degree than is a white person of the same ability level.

a. List any independent variables.

b. List any dependent variables.

c. What is the sample in this study?

d. What is the population about which researchers want to draw conclusions?

e. What do the authors mean by "longitudinal" in this study?

f. The researchers used the Armed Forces Qualification Test (AFQT) as their measure of ability. The AFQT combines scores on word knowledge, paragraph comprehension, arithmetic reasoning, and mathematics knowledge subscales. Can you suggest at least one confounding variable in the relation between ability and wages when comparing college graduates to high school graduates?

g. Suggest at least two other ways in which the researchers might have operationalized ability.

1.45 Assessing charitable organizations: Many people do research on charitable organizations before deciding where to donate their money. Tina Rosenberg (2012) reported that traditionally many people have used sources such as Charity Navigator or the Better Business Bureau's Web sites. Both of these sites rate organizations more highly if the organizations use less of their donation money for fundraising or administration and more of it for the cause they are supporting. On Charity Navigator, for example, Doctors Without Borders, a nonprofit focused on health and medical needs, gets a rating of 57.11 out of 70 based on its financial practices, accountability, and transparency; this puts that organization in the second of Charity Navigator's five tiers (charitynavigator.org).

a. How does Charity Navigator operationalize a good charity?

b. What kind of variable is the score of 57.11 out of 70—nominal, ordinal, or scale? Explain your answer.

c. What kind of variable is the tier, second out of five—nominal, ordinal, or scale? Explain your answer.

d. There are many types of charities. Doctors Without Borders focuses on health and medical needs. What kind of variable is its type of charity—nominal, ordinal, or scale? Explain your answer.

e. According to Rosenberg (2012), Toby Ord, a moral philosopher from Oxford University, thinks the traditional operational definition of what constitutes a good charity is too limited. He has five criteria that he sees as important for a good charity: It targets the most serious problems (disease over art, for example). It uses evidence-based practices. It uses cost-effective interventions. It is competent and honest. And it "can make good use of each additional dollar." Ord touts an organization called GiveWell as a source for ratings that incorporates many of his criteria (www.givewell.org). Doctors Without Borders fares less well on GiveWell; the site reports: "We believe that the overall cost-effectiveness of [Doctors Without Borders'] activities are unlikely to compare well with those of our top charities." Explain why Web sites like Charity Navigator might look just at measures relating to finances, as opposed to a fuller definition such as that described by Ord.

f. Which is more likely to be reliable, the rating by Charity Navigator or that by GiveWell? Explain your answer.

g. Which is more likely to be valid, the rating by Charity Navigator or that by GiveWell? Explain your answer.

h. If you were to monitor whether increased donation funds led to a lower death rate in a country, would that be an experiment or a correlational study? Explain your answer.

i. If you were to randomly assign some regions to receive more donation funds and other regions to receive fewer funds, and then track the death rate in both sets of regions, would that be an experiment or a correlational study? Explain your answer.

LaunchPad
macmillan learning

Visit LaunchPad to access the e-book and to
test your knowledge with LearningCurve.

TERMS

descriptive statistic (p. 3)

inferential statistic (p. 3)

sample (p. 3)

population (p. 3)

variable (p. 4)

discrete observation (p. 4)

continuous observation (p. 4)

nominal variable (p. 5)

ordinal variable (p. 5)

interval variable (p. 5)

ratio variable (p. 5)

scale variable (p. 6)

level (p. 7)

independent variable (p. 7)

dependent variable (p. 7)

confounding variable (p. 7)

reliability (p. 8)

validity (p. 8)

hypothesis testing (p. 10)

operational definition (p. 10)

correlation (p. 11)

random assignment (p. 12)

experiment (p. 12)

between-groups research design (p. 14)

within-groups research design (p. 15)

data ethics (p. 15)

open science (p. 15)

preregistration (p. 17)

HARKing (p. 17)

Frequency Distributions

BEFORE YOU GO ON

■ **You should understand the different types of variables—nominal, ordinal, and scale (Chapter 1).**

■ **You should understand the difference between a discrete variable and a continuous variable (Chapter 1).**

John Snow didn't need an algebraic formula to think like a statistician. In fact, counting is the main mathematical skill you will need to understand frequency distributions. But don't let the simplicity of the mathematics fool you: Statistical reasoning is powerful stuff. Counting and then rearranging those numerical observations from the highest to the lowest number (or vice versa) can reveal all sorts of hidden patterns.

Let's look at an example. Think about your last time on Instagram. Did it make you happy, or did you find yourself feeling down or becoming anxious after comparing yourself with your friends? If it wasn't all fun, then you're not alone. Researchers have found links, for example, between some kinds of social media use and symptoms of depression or anxiety (Baker & Algorta, 2016; Primack et al., 2017). In fact, many behavioral science researchers are alarmed by the rise in social media use around the world, and its implications for our psychological well-being. People who use social media now spend almost 2 hours a day, on average, on these sites (Asano, 2017). U.S. teens can spend an average of 9 hours a day on social media (Robb, 2015).

As more and more people join social media platforms, an understanding of the patterns of usage of social media can help researchers to map its effects. More than 3 billion people use social media, almost half the world's population (Kemp, 2018). But how does that break down? Table 2-1 depicts the average numbers of hours spent on social media sites for people in 28 countries (Kemp, 2016).

TABLE 2-1 Average Hours per Day Spent on Social Media

Country	Hours	Country	Hours
Argentina	3.2	Philippines	3.7
Australia	1.2	Poland	1.3
Brazil	3.3	Russia	1.9
Canada	1.4	Saudi Arabia	2.9
China	1.5	Singapore	1.6
France	1.3	South Africa	2.7
Germany	1.1	South Korea	1.1
Hong Kong	1.5	Spain	1.6
India	2.3	Thailand	2.9
Indonesia	2.9	Turkey	2.5
Italy	2.0	United Arab Emirates	3.0
Japan	0.3	United Kingdom	1.5
Malaysia	3.0	United States	1.7
Mexico	3.2	Vietnam	2.3

Data from Kemp, 2016.

Rearranging the data from the fewest to the most hours (see Table 2-2) allows us to see geographic patterns that we could not see in the original data set. All of the East Asian countries, such as China, and most of the European countries, such as France, are among the half of these countries where people spend less average time on social media. All of the Latin American countries, such as Brazil, and all of the countries in South or Southeast Asia, such as Thailand, are among the half of these countries where people spend more average time on social media. Of course, we still don't know whether there is something about where people live that drives social media usage, but we may be a little closer to developing hypotheses about possible connections between region of the world and online habits. And any summary from these data is only a descriptive statistic. We would need to calculate inferential statistics to know if this is true across all countries.

In this chapter, we learn how to organize individual data points in a table. Then we go one step further and learn how to use a graph called a histogram to show the overall pattern of data. Finally, we learn to use these graphs to understand the shape of the distribution of the data points. These tools are important steps for using statistics in the behavioral sciences.

TABLE 2-2	Average Hours per Day Spent on Social Media, Ranked from Least to Most		
Country	Hours	Country	Hours
Japan	0.3	Italy	2.0
Germany	1.1	Vietnam	2.3
South Korea	1.1	India	2.3
Australia	1.2	Turkey	2.5
Poland	1.3	South Africa	2.7
France	1.3	Saudi Arabia	2.9
Canada	1.4	Thailand	2.9
Hong Kong	1.5	Indonesia	2.9
United Kingdom	1.5	United Arab Emirates	3.0
China	1.5	Malaysia	3.0
Singapore	1.6	Mexico	3.2
Spain	1.6	Argentina	3.2
United States	1.7	Brazil	3.3
Russia	1.9	Philippines	3.7

Data from Kemp, 2016.

Frequency Distributions

Researchers are usually most interested in the relations between two or more variables, such as the effect of geographic region (the independent variable) on social media usage (the dependent variable). But to understand the relation between variables, we must first understand each individual variable's data points. The basic ingredients of a data set are called *raw scores*, *data that have not yet been transformed or analyzed*. In statistics, we organize raw scores into a *frequency distribution*, which *describes the pattern of a set of numbers by displaying a count or proportion for each possible value of a variable.* For example, a frequency distribution can display the pattern of the scores—average hours spent on social media—from the list in Table 2-2.

- A **raw score** is a data point that has not yet been transformed or analyzed.

- A **frequency distribution** describes the pattern of a set of numbers by displaying a count or proportion for each possible value of a variable.

Frequency Tables

There are several different ways to organize the data in terms of a frequency distribution. The first approach, the frequency table, is also the starting point for each of the three other approaches that we will explore. A *frequency table is a visual depiction of data that shows how often each value occurred—that is, how many scores were at each value.* Once organized into a frequency table, data can be displayed as a grouped frequency table or a histogram.

EXAMPLE 2.1

Lake Kivu, one of the world's so-called killer lakes, sits between the African countries of Rwanda and the Democratic Republic of the Congo (DRC). Activity from the nearby chain of volcanoes causes dangerous gases, including highly explosive methane, to seep into the lake. The upside: The methane is harnessed to power the region. The downside: The methane might lead the lake to explode, something that occurs about every 1000 years and could kill hundreds of thousands of people (Bressan, 2018; Turner, 2015).

So what do volcanoes have to do with psychology and statistics? Clinical and environmental psychologists have focused on responses to natural disasters (see Norris, Stevens, Pfefferbaum, Wyche, & Pfefferbaum, 2008). Psychologists are interested not only in the psychological toll in the aftermath of a disaster but also how people react when a hypothetical disaster quietly, but incessantly, threatens a community.

Imagine that you lived in such a place. Or maybe you already do. The Northwest United States and the southwest of Canada up through Vancouver Island, for example, are overdue for a devastating earthquake (Schulz, 2015). What would you feel? How would you cope? Maybe you'd try to ignore it. When a reporter expressed that Lake Kivu would be better without the methane, Emanuel, a local waiter, responded, "We do not think about that too much," and quickly walked away (Turner, 2015). Maybe you'd become anxious. As lava flow threatened a town in Hawaii, one resident acknowledged the psychological impact: "I didn't expect things to get so close," she said. "It's been pretty scary. I'm afraid of ending up homeless" (Hughes, 2018).

Volcanoes are perhaps the most visible of these quiet, ongoing environmental threats because they are literally looming over the people who live near them. A psychologist interested in the human psychological damage from the threat of volcanoes might be interested in examining how this threat is dispersed around the world. Oregon State University publishes a fairly comprehensive list of the world's volcanoes (Volcanoes by country, 2018).

Table 2-3 lists the numbers of volcanoes for each of the 55 countries that has at least one volcano. We can use these data to create a frequency table.

Stressful Volcanoes Psychology researchers study the chronic stress experienced by people living under the threat of a possible natural disaster. Here, people living in Goma, a city on Lake Kivu in the Democratic Republic of the Congo, watch the aftermath of a volcanic eruption. People living along the shores of Lake Kivu may experience the stress of two environmental dangers—the potential for a volcanic eruption and the possibility that the lake itself might explode due to the build-up of volcano-induced explosive gases.

PEDRO UGARTE/AFP/Getty Images

At first glance, it is not easy to find a pattern in most lists of numbers. But when we reorder those numbers, a pattern begins to emerge. A frequency table is the best way to create an easy-to-understand distribution of data. In this example, we simply organize the data into a table with two columns, one for the range of responses (the values) and one for the frequencies of each response (the scores).

There are specific steps to create a frequency table. First, we determine the range of raw scores. For each country, we can count how many volcanoes it has. We see that the lowest score is 1 and the highest is 81. Remember, we are only including countries with at least one volcano. Also, for the purposes of this example, we won't use the four outliers—Indonesia, Japan, Russia, and the United States. *An outlier is an extreme score that is either very high or very low in comparison with the rest of the scores in the sample.* Their data would make our frequency table too long. We'll learn how to deal with this situation in the next section. So, for now the top score is 17. Simply noting that the scores range from 1 to 17 brings some clarity to the data set. But we can do even better.

After we identify the lowest and highest scores, we create the two columns that we see in Table 2-4. We examine the raw scores and determine how many countries fall at each value in the range. The appropriate number for each value is recorded in the table. For example, there is one country with 17 volcanoes, so a 1 is marked there. It is important to note that we include *all* numbers in the range; there are no countries with 11, 14, 15, or 16 volcanoes, so we put a 0 next to each one.

Here is a recap of the steps to create a frequency table:

1. Determine the highest score and the lowest score.
2. Create two columns; label the first with the variable name, and label the second "Frequency."

- A **frequency table** is a visual depiction of data that shows how often each value occurred—that is, how many scores were at each value. Values are listed in the first column, and the numbers of individuals with scores at that value are listed in the second column.

- An **outlier** is an extreme score that is either very high or very low in comparison with the rest of the scores in the sample.

TABLE 2-3 Volcanoes Around the World

This table shows the number of volcanoes in each country that has at least one volcano. The data were compiled by researchers at Oregon State University.

Country	Number	Country	Number	Country	Number	Country	Number
Antarctica	1	DRC	2	Italy	6	Portugal	3
Argentina	1	Ecuador	12	Japan	40	Russia	55
Australia	4	El Salvador	5	Kenya	7	Solomon Islands	2
Azores	3	Eritrea	2	Lesser Sunda Islands	1	Spain	5
Cameroon	2	Ethiopia	10	Libya	1	St. Kitts and Nevis	2
Canary Islands	1	France	4	Mariana Islands	4	St. Vincent	1
Cape Verde Islands	2	Galápagos Islands	1	Mexico	7	Tanzania	3
Chad	1	Greece	5	Netherlands	2	Tonga	1
Chile	10	Grenada	1	New Zealand	8	Turkey	2
China	1	Guatemala	7	Nicaragua	9	Uganda	1
Colombia	3	Iceland	5	Norway	1	United Kingdom	4
Comoros	1	India	2	Papua New Guinea	17	United States	81
Congo	2	Indonesia	45	Peru	2	Vanuatu	9
Costa Rica	4	Iran	2	Philippines	13		

Data from volcano.oregonstate.edu/volcanoes_by_country (2018)

TABLE 2-4	Frequency Tables and Volcanoes

This frequency table depicts the numbers of volcanoes per country for the 51 countries that have between 1 and 17 volcanoes. The four outliers—Indonesia, Japan, Russia, and the United States—have between 40 and 81 volcanoes and would make this frequency table too long to be of much use.

Number of Volcanoes	Frequency
17	1
16	0
15	0
14	0
13	1
12	1
11	0
10	2
9	2
8	1
7	3
6	1
5	4
4	5
3	4
2	12
1	14

Data from volcano.oregonstate.edu/volcanoes_by_country (2018)

3. List the full range of values that encompasses all the scores in the data set, from highest to lowest. Include *all* values in the range, even those for which the frequency is 0.

4. Count the number of scores at each value, and write those numbers in the frequency column.

As shown in Table 2-5, we can add a column for percentages. To calculate a percentage, we divide the number of countries at a certain value by the total number of countries, and then multiply by 100. As we observed earlier, 1 out of 51 countries had 17 volcanoes.

$$\frac{1}{51}(100) = 1.961$$

So, for countries with 17 volcanoes, the percentage for 1 of 51 countries is 1.96%. We can see from Table 2-5 that more than 50% of countries have either one or two volcanoes.

Note that when we calculate statistics, we can come up with different answers depending on the number of steps and how we decide to round numbers. In this book, we round off to three decimal places throughout the calculations, but we report the final answers to two decimal places, rounding up or down as appropriate. Sometimes the numbers don't add up to 100% exactly, due to rounding. But if you follow this guideline, then you should get the same answers that we get.

| TABLE 2-5 | Frequencies and Percentages for Volcanoes by Country |

This frequency table is an expansion of Table 2-4, which depicts the number of countries that have varying numbers of volcanoes. Again, it includes only the 51 countries that have between 1 and 17 volcanoes. It now includes percentages, which are often more descriptive than actual counts.

Number of Volcanoes	Frequency	Percentage
17	1	1.96
16	0	0
15	0	0
14	0	0
13	1	1.96
12	1	1.96
11	0	0
10	2	3.92
9	2	3.92
8	1	1.96
7	3	5.88
6	1	1.96
5	4	7.84
4	5	9.80
3	4	7.84
2	12	23.53
1	14	27.45

Data from volcano.oregonstate.edu/volcanoes_by_country (2018)

Creating a frequency table for the data gives us more insight into the set of numbers. We can see that countries with volcanoes are most likely to have just one or two, and only a few have dozens. In the next section, we'll see how to handle a data set like this with some outliers, values that are far from the others. ●

Grouped Frequency Tables

In the previous example, we used data that counted the numbers of countries, which are whole numbers. In addition, we limited our range to 1–17. But often data are not so easily understood. Consider these two situations:

1. When data can go to many decimal places, such as in reaction times
2. When data cover a wider range, such as the full set of volcano data

In both of these situations, the frequency table could go on for pages and pages. For example, if someone completed a task 0.00003 seconds faster than the next

● A **grouped frequency table** is a visual depiction of data that reports frequencies within a given interval rather than the frequencies for a specific value.

person, that first person would belong to a distinctive, unique category. Using such specific values would lead to two problems: We would create an enormous amount of unnecessary work for ourselves, and we wouldn't see trends in the data. Fortunately, we have a technique to deal with these situations: *A **grouped frequency table** allows researchers to depict data visually by reporting the frequencies within a given interval rather than the frequencies for a specific value.*

Language Alert! The word *interval* is used in more than one way by statisticians. Here, it refers to a range of values (as opposed to an interval variable, the type of variable that has equal distances between values).

EXAMPLE 2.2

The following data exemplify the second of these two situations in which the data aren't easily conveyed in a standard frequency table. This is the full set of volcano data as depicted in Table 2-3.

1	1	4	3	2	1	2	1
10	1	3	1	2	4	2	12
5	2	10	4	1	5	1	7
5	2	45	2	6	40	7	1
1	4	7	2	8	9	1	17
2	13	3	55	2	5	2	1
3	1	2	1	4	81	9	

You may remember that we omitted four outliers when we created a frequency table. If we included all of these data points, the table would go from 1 to 81. Such a table would be longer than the list of the original raw data.

Instead of reporting every single value in the range, we can report intervals, or ranges of values. Here are the five steps to generate a standard grouped frequency table:

> **STEP 1: Find the lowest and highest scores in the frequency distribution.**

In the volcano example, these scores are 1 and 81.

> **STEP 2: Get the full range of data.**

If there are decimal places, round both the highest and the lowest scores down to the nearest whole numbers. If they already are whole numbers, such as with the volcano example, use those. Subtract the lowest whole number from the highest whole number and add 1 to get the full range of the data. (Why do we add 1? Try it yourself). If we subtract 1 from 81, we get 80—but there are actually 81 values. This seems obvious when the first number is 1, but try it with a range of

3 to 10: $10 - 3 = 7$, but there are 8 values. Count them. When in doubt, always count the individual values.

In the volcano example, $81 - 1 = 80$, and $80 + 1 = 81$. The scores fall within a range of size 81.

STEP 3: Determine the number of intervals and the best interval size.

There is no consensus about the ideal number of intervals, but most researchers recommend between 5 and 10 intervals, unless the data set is enormous and has a huge range. To find the best interval size, we divide the range by the number of intervals we want, then round to the nearest whole number (as long as the numbers are not too small—that is, as long as there are not too many decimal places). For ranges that are wide, the size of intervals could be a multiple of 10 or 100 or 1000; for smaller ranges, it could be as small as 2, 3, or 5, or even less than 1, if the numbers go to many decimal places. Try several interval sizes to determine the best one.

In the volcanoes example, we might choose to have intervals of size 10, which would mean we would have 9 intervals.

STEP 4: Figure out the number that will be the bottom of the lowest interval.

We want the bottom of the lowest interval to be a multiple of the interval size. For example, if we have 9 intervals of size 10, then we want the bottom interval to start at a multiple of 10. It could start at 0, 10, 80, or 1050, depending on the data. We select the multiple of 10 that is below the lowest score.

In the volcano example, there are 9 intervals of size 10, so the bottom of the lowest interval would be 0. If the lowest score had been, say, 12, we would choose 10. (Note that this process sometimes leads to one more interval than we had planned for; this is perfectly fine.)

STEP 5: Finish the table by listing the intervals from highest to lowest and then counting the numbers of scores in each.

This step is much like creating a frequency table (without intervals), which we discussed earlier. If we decide on intervals of size 10 and the first one begins at 0, then we add 10 to get the bottom of the next interval. So, the first interval runs from 0 to 9.9999, the next one from 10 to 19.9999, and so on. With whole numbers, we can just say 0 to 9, 10 to 19, and so on. A good rule of thumb is that the *bottom* of the intervals should jump by the chosen interval size, in this case 10.

TABLE 2-6	Grouped Frequency Table of Number of Volcanoes by Country Around the World

Grouped frequency tables make sense of data sets in which there are many possible values. This grouped frequency table depicts nine intervals that summarize the numbers of volcanoes in 55 countries—the countries summarized in Table 2-4 along with the four outlier countries. (As before, these are only the countries with at least one volcano.)

Interval	Frequency
80–89	1
70–79	0
60–69	0
50–59	1
40–49	2
30–39	0
20–29	0
10–19	5
0–9	46

Data from volcano.oregonstate.edu/volcanoes_by_country (2018)

In the volcano example, the lowest interval would be 0 to 9 (technically 0.00 to 9.99). The next would be 10 to 19, and so on.

Compared to the long list of raw data or a frequency distribution, the grouped frequency table in Table 2-6 is much easier to understand. ●

Histograms

Even more than tables, graphs help us to see data at a glance. The most common method for graphing scale data for one variable is the histogram. Here we learn to construct and interpret the histogram.

● A **histogram** is a graph that looks like a bar graph but depicts just one variable, usually based on scale data, with the values of the variable on the *x*-axis and the frequencies on the *y*-axis.

*A **histogram** is a graph that looks like a bar graph but depicts just one variable, usually based on scale data, with the values of the variable on the x-axis and the frequencies on the y-axis.* Each bar reflects the frequency for a value or an interval. The difference between histograms and bar graphs is that bar graphs typically provide scores for nominal data (e.g., men and women) relative to another variable (e.g., height), whereas histograms typically provide frequencies for one scale variable (e.g., levels of pacing indices). We can construct histograms from frequency tables or from grouped frequency tables. Histograms allow for the many intervals that typically occur with scale data. The bars are stacked one against the next, with the intervals meaningfully arranged from lower numbers (on the left) to higher numbers (on the right). With bar graphs, the categories do not need to be arranged in one particular order and the bars should not touch.

MASTERING THE CONCEPT

2-2: The data in a frequency table can be viewed in graph form. In a histogram, bars are used to depict frequencies at each score or interval.

EXAMPLE 2.3

Let's start by constructing a histogram from a frequency table. Table 2-4 depicts a frequency table of countries' numbers of volcanoes, for countries with 17 or fewer volcanoes. We construct a histogram by drawing the *x*-axis (horizontal) and *y*-axis (vertical)

(vertical) of a graph. We label the x-axis with the variable of interest—in our case, "Number of volcanoes"—and we label the y-axis "Frequency." As with most graphs, the lowest numbers start where the axes intersect and the numbers go up as we go to the right on the x-axis and as we go up on the y-axis. Ideally, the lowest number on each axis is 0, so that the graphs are not misleading. However, if the range of numbers on either axis is far from 0, histograms sometimes use a number other than 0 as the lowest number. Further, if there are negative numbers among the scores (as can be the case in scores for air temperature, for example), the x-axis could have negative numbers.

Once we've created the graph, we draw a bar for each value. Each bar is *centered on* the value for which it provides the frequency. The height of the bars represents the numbers of scores that fall at each value—the frequencies. If no country had a score at a particular value, then we would not draw a bar for that value. So, for the value of 2 on the x-axis, a bar centers on 2 with a height of 12 on the y-axis, indicating that 12 countries had two volcanoes. Figure 2-1 shows the histogram for the volcano data.

Here is a recap of the steps to construct a histogram from a frequency table:

1. Draw the x-axis and label it with the variable of interest and the full range of values for this variable. (Include 0 unless all of the scores are so far from 0 that this would be impractical.)

2. Draw the y-axis, label it "Frequency," and include the full range of frequencies for this variable. (Include 0 unless it's impractical.)

3. Draw a bar for each value, centering the bar on that value on the x-axis and drawing the bar as high as the frequency for that value, as represented on the y-axis.

Grouped frequency tables can also be depicted as histograms. Instead of listing values on the x-axis, we list the midpoints of intervals. Students commonly make mistakes in determining midpoints. If an interval ranges from 0 to 4, what is the midpoint? If you said 2, you're making a *very* common mistake. Remember, this interval really goes

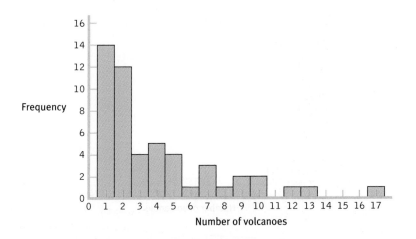

FIGURE 2-1

Histogram for the Frequency Table of Number of Volcanoes by Country Around the World

Histograms are graphic depictions of the information in frequency tables or grouped frequency tables. This histogram shows the number of volcanoes in the 51 countries that have between 1 and 17 volcanoes. Data from volcano .oregonstate.edu/volcanoes_by_country (2018)

from 0.000000 to 4.999999, or as close as you can get to 5, the bottom of the next interval, without actually being 5. Given that there are 5 numbers in this range (0, 1, 2, 3, and 4), the midpoint would be 2.5 from the bottom. So the midpoint for 0 to 4 is 2.5. A good rule: When determining a midpoint, look at the bottom of the interval that you're interested in and then the bottom of the next interval; then, determine the midpoint of these two numbers. ●

EXAMPLE 2.4

Let's look at the volcano data for which we constructed a grouped frequency table. What are the midpoints of the 9 intervals? Let's calculate the midpoint for the lowest interval, 0 to 9. We should look at the bottom of this interval, 0, and the bottom of the next interval, 10. The midpoint of these numbers is 5, so that is the midpoint of this interval. The remaining midpoints can be calculated the same way. For the highest interval, 80 to 89, it helps to imagine that we had one more interval. If we did, it would start at 90. The midpoint of 80 and 90 is 85. Using these guidelines, we calculate the midpoints as 5, 15, 25, 35, 45, 55, 65, 75, and 85. (A good check is to see if the midpoints jump by the interval size—in this case, 10.) We now can construct the histogram by placing these midpoints on the *x*-axis and drawing bars that center on them and are as high as the frequency for each interval. The histogram for these data is shown in Figure 2-2.

Here is a recap of the steps to construct a histogram from a grouped frequency table:

1. Determine the midpoint for every interval.
2. Draw the *x*-axis and label it with the variable of interest and with the midpoint for each interval on this variable. (Include 0 unless it's impractical.)
3. Draw the *y*-axis, label it "Frequency," and include the full range of frequencies for this variable. (Include 0 unless it's impractical.)
4. Draw a bar for each midpoint, centering the bar on that midpoint on the *x*-axis and drawing the bar as high as the frequency for that interval, as represented on the *y*-axis.

FIGURE 2-2

Histogram for the Grouped Frequency Table of Number of Volcanoes by Country Around the World

Histograms can also depict the data in a grouped frequency table. This histogram depicts the data seen in the grouped frequency table for volcanoes in countries that have at least one volcano. Data from volcano.oregonstate.edu/volcanoes_by_country (2018)

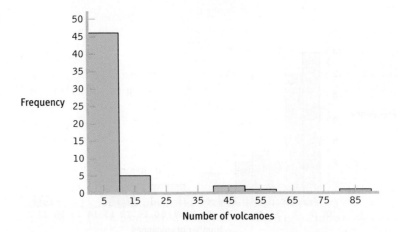

CHECK YOUR LEARNING

Reviewing the Concepts	>	The first steps in organizing data for a single variable are to list all the values in order of magnitude and then to count how many times each value occurs.
	>	There are three techniques for organizing information about a single variable: frequency tables, grouped frequency tables, and histograms.

Clarifying the Concepts

2-1 Name three different ways to organize raw scores visually.

2-2 What is the difference between frequencies and grouped frequencies?

Calculating the Statistics

2-3 In 2013, *U.S. News & World Report* published a list of the citations per faculty member score for the 400 best universities in the world. As examples, the Massachusetts Institute of Technology was number 1 on the list of best universities and McGill University in Montreal was number 18. The citation score tells us how many times a faculty member's research had been cited by other researchers over the previous 5 years, and is an indicator of research productivity. Here are the data for the top 50 institutions:

100.0	100.0	100.0	100.0	99.8	99.5	99.5	99.3	99.1	98.8
97.9	97.9	97.8	97.2	97.0	96.9	96.4	96.3	94.0	93.3
92.4	92.1	90.7	90.0	89.4	87.3	87.3	86.5	81.6	80.2
79.9	78.3	77.3	77.1	75.7	75.6	74.9	74.8	74.7	73.1
70.8	70.0	69.1	68.9	68.0	64.3	63.1	62.2	62.1	60.2

a. Construct a grouped frequency table of these data.

b. Construct a histogram for this grouped frequency table.

Applying the Concepts

2-4 Consider the data from Check Your Learning 2-3, as well as the table and graph that you constructed.

a. What can we tell from the graph and table that we cannot tell from a quick glance at the list of scores?

b. What issues might arise in considering data across countries with a wide range of academic systems?

Solutions to these Check Your Learning questions can be found in Appendix D.

Shapes of Distributions

We learned how to organize data so that we can better understand the concept of a distribution, a major building block for statistical analysis. We can't get a sense of the overall pattern of data by looking at a list of numbers, but we *can* get a sense of the pattern by looking at a frequency table. We can get an even better sense by creating a graph. Histograms allow us to see the overall pattern, or shape, of the distribution of data.

The shape of a distribution provides distinctive information. Amara Shaikh (2018), a reporter from the University of Michigan's student-run newspaper, *The Michigan Daily*, explored the distributions of grades within the university's psychology courses. She highlighted the course with the lowest average grade, Psychology of Human Sexuality. The most common grade was a C+, which translated into a grade-point

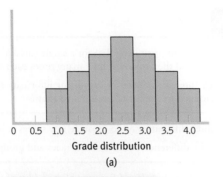 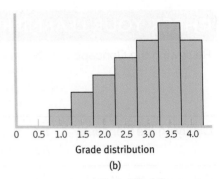

Grade distribution	Grade distribution
(a)	(b)

FIGURE 2-3

Distributions of Course Grades

These two histograms depict very different grade distributions, both approximations of actual grade distributions (Shaikh, 2018). The first histogram (a) describes the grades in one of the toughest courses at the University of Michigan, the Psychology of Human Sexuality, with a mean GPA of about 2.5 (C+); the second histogram (b) describes the grades in the typical psychology course, with a mean GPA of about 3.6 (A−). Data from Shaikh (2018)

● A **normal distribution** is a specific frequency distribution that is a bell-shaped, symmetric, unimodal curve.

● A **skewed distribution** is a distribution in which one of the tails of the distribution is pulled away from the center.

FIGURE 2-4

The Normal Distribution

The normal distribution, shown here for IQ scores, is a frequency distribution that is bell-shaped, symmetric, and unimodal. It is central to many calculations in statistics.

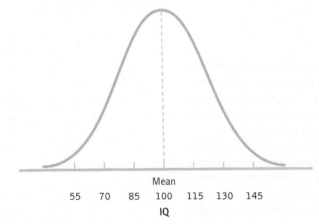

average (GPA) of about 2.5. The grades for this course looked like the distribution in Figure 2-3a. For psychology courses overall, the most common grade was around an A−, which translated to a GPA of about 3.6. The grades for courses like this looked like the distribution in Figure 2-3b.

In this section, we provide you with language that expresses the differences between these patterns. Specifically, you'll learn to describe different shapes of distributions, including normal distributions and skewed distributions.

Normal Distributions

Many, but not all, distributions of variables form a bell-shaped, or *normal*, curve. Statisticians use the word *normal* to describe distributions in a very particular way. *A **normal distribution** is a specific frequency distribution that is a bell-shaped, symmetric, unimodal curve* (Figure 2-4). Student grades in the Psychology of Human Sexuality course provide an example of a distribution that approaches a normal distribution. In fact, the professor of that course told *The Michigan Daily* reporter that she aims for her students' grades to form a normal distribution. There are fewer scores at values that are farther from the center and even fewer scores at the most extreme values (as can be seen in the bar graph in Figure 2-3a). Most scores cluster around the score of 2.5 in the middle of the distribution, which would be at the top of the bell.

Skewed Distributions

Reality is often—but not always—normally distributed, which means that the distributions describing some observations are not shaped normally. So we need a new term to help us describe some of the distributions that are not normal—*skew*. **Skewed distributions** *are distributions in*

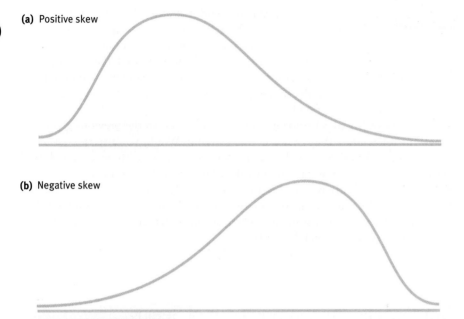

(a) Positive skew

(b) Negative skew

FIGURE 2-5

Two Kinds of Skew

The mnemonic "the tail tells the tale" means that the distribution with the long, thin tail to the right is positively skewed and the distribution with the long, thin tail to the left is negatively skewed.

which one of the tails of the distribution is pulled away from the center. Although the technical term for such data is *skewed*, a skewed distribution may also be described as lopsided, off-center, or simply nonsymmetric. Skewed data have an ever-thinning tail in one direction or the other. The distribution of grades in the typical psychology course at the University of Michigan (see Figure 2-3b) is an example of a skewed distribution. The scores cluster to the right side of the distribution around the highest GPAs, and the tail extends to the left.

When a distribution is ***positively skewed***, as in Figure 2-5a, *the tail of the distribution extends to the right, in a positive direction.* Positive skew sometimes occurs when there is a ***floor effect***, *a situation in which a constraint prevents a variable from taking values below a certain point.* For example, in the "volcano" data, scores indicating how many countries had particular numbers of volcanoes is an example of a positively skewed distribution with a floor effect. We only included countries with at least 1 volcano, which means that the data were constrained at the lower end of the distribution, 1 (i.e., they can't go below 1).

The distribution in Figure 2-5b shows ***negatively skewed*** *data, which have a distribution with a tail that extends to the left, in a negative direction.* The distribution of grades in the typical psychology course at the University of Michigan, as shown in Figure 2-40b, is favorable because it is clustered around a grade of 3.6 (an A−), but we describe the shape of that distribution as negatively skewed because the

- With **positively skewed** data, the distribution's tail extends to the right, in a positive direction.

- A **floor effect** is a situation in which a constraint prevents a variable from taking values below a certain point.

- **Negatively skewed** data have a distribution with a tail that extends to the left, in a negative direction.

2-3: If a histogram indicates that the data are symmetric and bell-shaped, then the data are normally distributed. If the data are not symmetric and the tail extends to the right, the data are positively skewed; if the tail extends to the left, the data are negatively skewed.

● A **ceiling effect** is a situation in which a constraint prevents a variable from taking on values above a given number.

thin tail is to the left side of the distribution. Not surprisingly, negative skew is sometimes the result of a *ceiling effect, a situation in which a constraint prevents a variable from taking on values above a given number.* If students in a class tend to do very well, then their grades might show a ceiling effect. A number of students would cluster close to 4.0, the highest possible score, with a few stragglers down in the lower end.

University of Michigan students actually have access to the previous grade distributions for courses they're considering taking. Would you use this information to select courses? You might register for only courses with negatively skewed grades and avoid those with a normal distribution. In fact, some students complained about the difficulty of the Psychology of Human Sexuality course, but others praised the interesting content and the emphasis on critical thinking. And the professor encouraged students to "be up for a challenge . . . even if it's not going to be an easy A" (Shaikh, 2018).

Data Ethics	Dot Plots and the Importance of Seeing the Individual Data Points

In the campy 2018 movie *The Meg,* a 75-foot (23-meter) megalodon shark terrorizes deep-sea divers and vacationing beachgoers. Fortunately, sharks the size of the megalodon do not actually exist. As we learned in Chapter 1, the largest great white sharks grow to be approximately 20 feet (6 meters) long. But if a megalodon did exist, and we had data for a sample of sharks, you would want to know if one was part of the sample.

In behavioral science research, ethical researchers want to know if there are any unusual data points. The summary data represented by descriptive statistics could be misleading if researchers don't address extreme data points. Even more problematic, any conclusions drawn from inferential statistics could be wrong.

For all these reasons, researchers concerned with data ethics examine *each* individual data point, usually by looking at a graph, before analyzing their data. In this chapter, we have explored frequency tables and histograms, both of which show us the overall pattern of data. Another technique that provides even more transparency is a dot plot. *A dot plot is a graph that displays each data point in a sample, with the range of scores along the x-axis and a dot for each data point above the appropriate value.* Dot plots are like histograms, showing us the overall shape of the data. However, dot plots are even clearer because they actually show each individual data point.

Dot plots do not have a *y*-axis, so the *y*-axis does not have a "count" or "frequency" as the histogram does. Instead, a dot plot stacks an additional dot for each data point at the same value on the *x*-axis. Dot plots are even easier to interpret than histograms because the count of observations can be read directly from

● A **dot plot** is a graph that displays each data point in a sample, with the range of scores along the *x*-axis and a dot for each data point above the appropriate value.

the graph without referencing a *y*-axis. In fact, the human brain is built to immediately and quickly apprehend quantities of four or fewer, making dot plots especially intuitive for representing small quantities of numbers (Demeyere, Rotshtein, & Humphreys, 2012; Vuokko, Niemivirta, & Helenius, 2013).

Let's look at a dot plot for data from the United Nations on average years of education per country. Every year, the United Nations publishes its Human Development Report, which includes various indicators of well-being. In 2018, the report included data for 189 countries, including the average number of years of education for individuals in that country. Here, we'll look at 28 countries randomly selected from the complete list of 189 countries (Table 2-7).

To create a dot plot, there are three basic steps.

STEP 1: Order the scores from lowest to highest.

Here we've done this for the data from Table 2-7:

2, 3, 4, 5, 6, 7, 7, 7, 8, 8, 9, 10, 10, 10, 10, 11, 11, 12, 12, 12, 12, 12, 12, 13, 13, 13, 13, 13

STEP 2: Draw an *x*-axis and label it, including the values from the lowest through highest scores. If possible, include 0. If it doesn't make sense, include cut marks to indicate that the *x*-axis does not start at 0.

STEP 3: Place a dot above the appropriate value for every score (Figure 2-6).

Here we looked at a dot plot representing one sample of data. Dot plots can also be used to compare samples. With two samples, for example, the dot plot for one sample would be placed directly above the one for the other sample, with the numbers on both dot plots lined up. Such a visual comparison would allow us to view the two samples simultaneously—a useful feature when we compare two samples in later chapters.

TABLE 2-7	Mean Years of Education Globally		
Country	Years of Education	Country	Years of Education
Argentina	10	Grenada	9
Azerbaijan	11	Guyana	8
Belarus	12	Honduras	7
Belgium	12	Ireland	13
Belize	11	Micronesia	8
Botswana	10	Palau	12
Bulgaria	12	Panama	10
Canada	13	Papua New Guinea	5
Chad	2	Samoa	10
Congo	7	Sao Tome and Principe	6
Cuba	12	Sudan	4
Czechia	13	Switzerland	13
El Salvador	7	United States	13
Finland	12	Yemen	3

Note: Each data point is rounded to nearest whole number.

Source: United Nations Human Development Program (2018, hdr.undp.org/en/2018-update)

FIGURE 2-6

Dot Plot for Mean Years of Education Globally

From this dot plot we can see that most countries average between 10 and 13 years of education. But a number of countries have low average for years of education, giving the distribution its negative skew.

Years of education

CHECK YOUR LEARNING

Reviewing the Concepts	>	A normal distribution is a specific distribution that is unimodal, symmetric, and bell-shaped.
	>	A skewed distribution "leans" either to the left or to the right. A tail to the right indicates positive skew; a tail to the left indicates negative skew.
	>	Dot plots are graphs that show the overall shape of the data, but also each individual data point.

Clarifying the Concepts	2-5	Distinguish a normal distribution from a skewed distribution.
	2-6	When the bulk of data cluster together but the data trail off to the left, the skew is _____; when data trail off to the right, the skew is _____.

Calculating the Statistics	2-7	In Check Your Learning 2-3, you constructed a histogram of the distribution of citations per faculty at top universities around the world. How would you describe this distribution? Is there skew evident in your graphs? If there is, what kind of skew is it?
	2-8	Alzheimer's disease is typically diagnosed in adults older than the age of 70; cases diagnosed sooner are called "early onset."
		a. Assuming that these early-onset cases represent unique trailing off of data on one side, would the skew be positive or negative?
		b. Do these data represent a floor effect or a ceiling effect?

Applying the Concepts	2-9	Referring to Check Your Learning 2-8, what implication would identifying such skew have in the screening and treatment process for Alzheimer's disease?
Solutions to these Check Your Learning questions can be found in Appendix D.		

REVIEW OF CONCEPTS

LaunchPad
macmillan learning
Visit LaunchPad to access the e-book and to test your knowledge with LearningCurve.

Frequency Distributions

There are several ways in which we can depict a *frequency distribution* of a set of *raw scores*. *Frequency tables* are composed of two columns, one with all possible values and one with a count of how often each value occurs. *Grouped frequency tables* allow us to work with more complicated data. Instead of containing values, the first column consists of intervals. *Histograms* display bars of different heights indicating the frequency of each value (or interval) that the variable can take on.

Shapes of Distributions

The *normal distribution* is a specific distribution that is unimodal, symmetric, and bell-shaped. Data can also display *skewness*. A distribution that is *positively skewed* has a tail in a positive direction (to the right), indicating more extreme scores above the center. It sometimes results from a *floor effect*, in which scores are constrained and cannot be below a certain number. A distribution that is *negatively skewed* has a tail in a negative direction (to the left), indicating more extreme scores below the center. It sometimes results from a *ceiling effect*, in which scores are constrained and cannot be above a certain number. Dot plots help researchers to be more ethical by allowing us to view the shape of a sample's distribution, as well as every single data point in that sample.

SPSS

As discussed in the SPSS section of Chapter 1, at the bottom left of your screen, you may choose between "Data View" and "Variable View." The left-hand column in Data View is prenumbered, beginning with 1. Each column to the right of that number contains information about a particular variable; each row represents a unique observation—that is, the data for an individual, whether it's a person, video, or country. The Variable View provides information about the name of the variable, the label for the variable, and the type of variable (e.g., nominal, ordinal, scale).

In this example, the volcano data discussed earlier in this chapter have been entered into an SPSS datafile. When entering the data, be sure to start with Variable View first, and then move to Data View. In Variable View, for the first row, Country, the "Type" of variable in the second column should be "String" and the "Measure" in the tenth column should be "Nominal." You may change these by clicking on the current selection, clicking on the small box with three dots in it, and clicking the new selection. For the second row, Volcanoes, the "Type" of variable should be "Numeric" and the "Measure" should be "Scale." We also added a more descriptive label, "Number of volcanoes," in the fifth column. Now return to Data View. Enter the data from Table 2-3 on page 33, and then, from the

menu at the top of the screen, select Analyze → Descriptive Statistics → Frequencies. Select the variables you want SPSS to describe by highlighting them and clicking the arrow in the middle. In this case, we'll select the number of volcanoes. We also want to visualize each variable, so after selecting any variables, select Charts → Histograms (click the box next to "show normal curve on histogram") → Continue → OK.

For all of the SPSS functions, an "output" file automatically appears after "OK" is clicked. You can save your output file, and even convert it to a PDF or Word document for access at a later time. The screenshot shown here depicts the part of the SPSS output that includes the histogram. Double-click on the graph to enter the SPSS Chart Editor, and then double-click on each feature to make the graph look the way you want it to. For example, you might choose to change the text of the title to be more specific (e.g., Histogram of Number of Volcanoes). You can do this by single-clicking twice to edit the title. Additionally, you may want to change the color of the bars in the chart. You can do this by double-clicking on a bar; a dialogue box will appear. Under the "Fill & Border" tab, you may choose from a variety of colors. Click and change any feature of the graph to let the data speak more clearly.

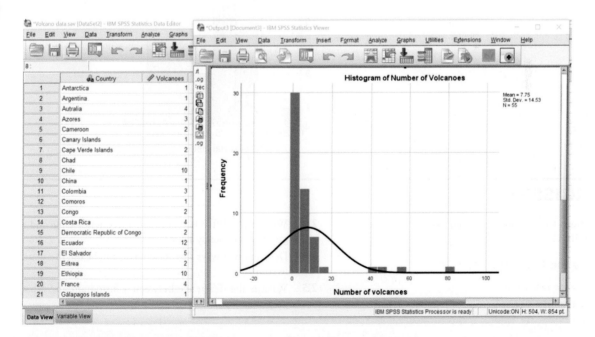

HOW IT WORKS

2.1 CREATING A GROUPED FREQUENCY TABLE

On page 31 of this chapter, we presented Table 2-2 that included average hours spent on social media use for people in 28 countries. Here is how we create a grouped frequency table for these data.

Hours	Frequency
3.5–3.9	1
3.0–3.4	5
2.5–2.9	5
2.0–2.4	3
1.5–1.9	7
1.0–1.4	6
0.5–0.9	0
0–0.4	1

2.2 CREATING A GROUPED HISTOGRAM

How can we use these same data to create a grouped histogram? First, we put the intervals for hours of social media use on the x-axis and the frequencies on the y-axis. The bar for each frequency is centered at the midpoint of each interval. The figure below shows the histogram for these data.

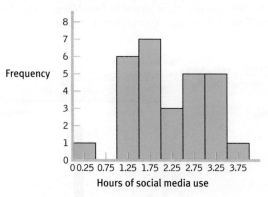

EXERCISES

The solutions to the odd-numbered exercises can be found in Appendix C.

Clarifying the Concepts

2.1 What are raw scores?

2.2 What are the steps to create a frequency table?

2.3 What is the difference between a frequency table and a grouped frequency table?

2.4 Describe two ways that statisticians might use the word *interval*.

2.5 What is the difference between a histogram and a bar graph?

2.6 What are the typical labels for the *x*-axis and the *y*-axis in a histogram?

2.7 Describe what a histogram looks like, including what goes on the *x*-axis and the *y*-axis.

2.8 What is the benefit of creating a visual distribution of data rather than simply looking at a list of the data?

2.9 In your own words, define the word *distribution*, first as you would use it in everyday conversation and then as a statistician would use it.

2.10 What is a normal distribution?

2.11 How do positively skewed distributions and negatively skewed distributions deviate from a normal distribution?

2.12 What is a floor effect and how does it affect a distribution?

2.13 What is a ceiling effect and how does it affect a distribution?

2.14 What are potential benefits of using a dot plot instead of a histogram?

2.15 In what way are dot plots similar to histograms?

Calculating the Statistics

2.16 Convert the following to percentages: 63 out of 1264; 2 out of 88.

2.17 Convert the following to percentages: 7 out of 39; 122 out of 300.

2.18 Counts are often converted to percentages. Convert 817 out of 22,140 into a percentage. Now convert 4009 out of 22,140 into a percentage. What type of variable (nominal, ordinal, or scale) are these data as counts? What kind of variable are they as percentages?

2.19 Convert 2 out of 2000 into a percentage. Now convert 60 out of 62 into a percentage.

2.20 Throughout this book, final answers are reported to two decimal places. Report the following numbers this way: 1888.999, 2.6454, and 0.0833.

2.21 Report the following numbers to two decimal places: 0.0391, 198.2219, and 17.886.

2.22 On a test of marital satisfaction, scores could range from 0 to 27.

    a. What is the full range of data, according to the calculation procedure described in this chapter?

    b. What would the interval size be if we wanted six intervals?

    c. List the six intervals.

2.23 If you have data that range from 2 to 68 and you want seven intervals in a grouped frequency table, what would the intervals be?

2.24 A grouped frequency table has the following intervals: 30–44, 45–59, and 60–74. If converted into a histogram, what would the midpoints be?

2.25 Referring to the grouped frequency table in Table 2-6, how many countries had at least 30 volcanoes?

2.26 Referring to the histogram in Figure 2-1, how many countries had 1 or 2 volcanoes?

2.27 If the average person convicted of murder killed only one person, serial killers would create what kind of skew?

2.28 Would the data for number of murders by those convicted of the crime be an example of a floor effect or a ceiling effect?

2.29 A researcher collects data on the ages of university students. As you have probably observed, the distribution of age clusters around 19 to 22 years, but there are extremes on both the low end (high school prodigies) and the high end (nontraditional students returning to school).

    a. What type of skew might you expect for such data?

    b. Do the skewed data represent a floor effect or a ceiling effect?

2.30 If you have an Instagram account, you are allowed to follow up to 7500 other accounts. At that point, Instagram cuts you off, and you have to "unfollow" people to add more. Imagine you collected data from Instagram users at your university about the number of accounts each one follows.

    a. What type of skew might you expect for such data?

    b. Do the skewed data represent a floor effect or ceiling effect?

2.31 a. Using the following set of data, construct a dot plot. Follow the steps in the Data Ethics box of the chapter to set up the dot plot.

3.5	2.0	4.0	3.5	2.0	2.5	4.5
4.0	3.0	3.5	3.0	3.0	4.0	4.5
2.5	3.5	3.5	3.0	2.5	3.5	3.5

    b. Refer to the dot plot created for part (a). Does it depict a symmetric or a skewed distribution?

2.32 Students in a statistics course reported the number of hours of sleep they get on a typical weeknight. These data appear below.

$$5 \quad 6.5 \quad 6 \quad \quad 8 \quad 6 \quad 6 \quad 6 \quad 7 \quad 5$$
$$7 \quad 6 \quad \quad 6.5 \quad 7 \quad 6 \quad 7 \quad 4 \quad 8 \quad 6$$

a. Create a dot plot of these data.

b. Use the dot plot to describe the distribution of the set of scores.

Applying the Concepts

2.33 **Frequency tables, histograms, and the National Survey of Student Engagement:** The National Survey of Student Engagement (NSSE) surveys U.S. first-year university students and seniors about their level of engagement in campus and classroom activities that enhance learning. Hundreds of thousands of students at almost 1000 schools have completed surveys since 1999, when the NSSE was first administered. Among the many questions, students are asked how often they have been assigned a paper of 20 pages or more during the academic year. For a sample of 19 institutions classified as national universities that made their data publicly available through the *U.S. News & World Report* Web site, here are the percentages of students who said they were assigned between 5 and 10 twenty-page papers:

$$0 \quad 5 \quad 3 \quad 3 \quad 1 \quad 10 \quad 2$$
$$2 \quad 3 \quad 1 \quad 2 \quad 4 \quad 2 \quad 1$$
$$1 \quad 1 \quad 4 \quad 3 \quad 5$$

a. Create a frequency table for these data. Include a third column for percentages.

b. For what percentage of these schools did exactly 4% of the students report that they wrote between 5 and 10 twenty-page papers that year?

c. Is this a random sample? Explain your answer.

d. Create a histogram of grouped data, using six intervals.

e. In how many schools did 6% or more of the students report that they wrote between 5 and 10 twenty-page papers that year?

f. How are the data distributed?

2.34 **Frequency tables, histograms, and the Survey of Earned Doctorates:** The Survey of Earned Doctorates provides data on the length of time in years that it takes to complete a doctorate. Each data point is the mean time for one university. Below is a modified list of this completion-time data, truncated to whole numbers and shortened to make your analysis easier. These data have been collected every 5 years since 1982.

$$8 \quad 8 \quad 8 \quad 8 \quad \quad 8 \quad 7 \quad 6 \quad \quad 7 \quad 7 \quad \quad 7 \quad 7 \quad 7$$
$$6 \quad 6 \quad 6 \quad 6 \quad \quad 6 \quad 6 \quad 7 \quad 8 \quad 8 \quad \quad 8 \quad 8 \quad 7$$
$$6 \quad 6 \quad 7 \quad 7 \quad \quad 7 \quad 6 \quad 11 \quad 13 \quad 15 \quad 15$$
$$14 \quad 12 \quad 9 \quad 10 \quad 10 \quad 9 \quad 9 \quad 9$$

a. Create a frequency table for these data.

b. How many schools have an average completion time of 8 years or less?

c. Is a grouped frequency table necessary? Why or why not?

d. Describe how these data are distributed.

e. Create a histogram for these data.

f. At how many universities did students take, on average, 10 or more years to complete their doctorates?

2.35 **Frequency tables, histograms, and life expectancy rates:** The United Nations Development Programme (2015b) published life expectancy rates—the number of years an adult can expect to live—for 195 countries around the world. Below is a randomly selected sample of 30 of them.

Country	Life Expectancy
Afghanistan	60.95
Armenia	74.56
Australia	82.50
Belarus	69.93
Bosnia and Herzegovina	76.37
Burkina Faso	56.34
Canada	81.48
Côte d'Ivoire	50.72
Cuba	79.26
Ecuador	76.47
Ghana	61.13
Guyana	66.30
Indonesia	70.83
Japan	83.58
Jordan	73.85
Lebanon	80.01

Country	Life Expectancy
Malaysia	75.02
Mexico	77.50
Namibia	64.48
New Zealand	81.13
Panama	77.56
Saint Lucia	74.80
Slovakia	75.40
Sweden	81.82
Tonga	72.67
Trinidad and Tobago	69.87
Tunisia	75.87
United Kingdom	80.55
United States	78.94
Zimbabwe	59.87

a. Create a grouped frequency table for these data.

b. The data have quite a range, with the lowest life expectancy of 50.72 in Côte d'Ivoire and the highest life expectancy of 83.58 in Japan. What research hypotheses come to mind when you examine these data? State at least one research question that these data suggest to you.

c. Create a grouped histogram for these data. As always, be careful when determining the midpoints of the intervals.

d. Examine the histogram and give a brief description of the distribution. Are there unusual scores? Are the data symmetric, or are they skewed? If they are skewed, in which direction?

2.36 **Frequency tables, histograms, and basketball wins:** Here are the number of wins for the 30 U.S. National Basketball Association (NBA) teams for the 2012–2013 NBA season.

$$
\begin{array}{cccccccccc}
60 & 44 & 39 & 29 & 23 & 57 & 50 & 43 & 37 & 27 \\
49 & 42 & 37 & 29 & 19 & 56 & 51 & 40 & 33 & 26 \\
48 & 42 & 31 & 25 & 18 & 53 & 44 & 40 & 29 & 23
\end{array}
$$

a. Create a grouped frequency table for these data.

b. Create a histogram based on the grouped frequency table.

c. Write a summary describing the distribution of these data with respect to shape and direction of any skew.

d. Here are the numbers of wins for the 8 teams in the National Basketball League (NBL) of Canada. Explain why we would not necessarily need a grouped frequency table for these data.

$$
\begin{array}{cc}
26 & 33 \\
20 & 22 \\
20 & 18 \\
19 & 2
\end{array}
$$

2.37 **Types of distributions:** Consider these three variables: finishing times in a marathon, number of university dining hall meals eaten in a semester on a three-meal-a-day plan, and scores on a scale of extroversion.

a. Which of these variables is most likely to have a normal distribution? Explain your answer.

b. Which of these variables is most likely to have a positively skewed distribution? Explain your answer, stating the possible contribution of a floor effect.

c. Which of these variables is most likely to have a negatively skewed distribution? Explain your answer, stating the possible contribution of a ceiling effect.

2.38 **Type of frequency distribution and type of graph:** For each of the types of data described below, first state how you would present individual data values or grouped data when creating a frequency distribution. Then, state which visual display(s) of data would be most appropriate to use. Explain your answers clearly.

a. Eye color observed for 87 people

b. Minutes used on a mobile phone by 240 teenagers

c. Time to complete the London Marathon for the more than 35,000 runners who participate

d. Number of siblings for 64 college students

2.39 **Number of televisions and a grouped frequency distribution:** The Canadian Radio-Television and Communications Commission (crtc.gc.ca/eng/publications) gathered data on the numbers of television sets in Canadian homes. Two percent of homes had no television; 28% had one television; 32% had two televisions; 20% had three televisions; and 18% had four or more televisions. Create a histogram for these percentages. (Treat "four or more televisions" as four for the purposes of this exercise.)

2.40 **Skew and surname frequencies:** Researchers published a summary of the frequency of surnames based on U.S. Census data (Word, Coleman, Nunziata, & Kominski, 2008). The table lists the frequencies of last names in the left column, the number of last names with that level of frequency in the next column, and then the cumulative number and cumulative percentage in the next two columns. For example, 2.3 million people have the last name Smith, the most common name in this data set. So, Smith would be one of the seven names listed in the top row—last names that occur more than 1,000,000 times in the population. In another example, more than 72,000 people have the last name Singh. So, Singh is one of the 3012 surnames in the third row—names that occur between 10,000 and 99,999 times in the population.

a. Is this a frequency table or a grouped frequency table? Explain your answer.

b. How is this table different from the tables you created in this chapter? Why do you think the researchers constructed this table differently?

c. Based on this table, does this distribution seem to be normal, negatively skewed, or positively skewed? Explain your answer.

d. Is there a floor effect or a ceiling effect? Explain your answer.

Last Names			
Frequency of Occurrence	Number	Cumulative Number	Cumulative Percentage
1,000,000+	7	7	0.0
100,000–999,999	268	275	0.0
10,000–99,999	3012	3287	0.1
1000–9999	20,369	23,656	0.4
100–999	128,015	151,671	2.4
50–99	105,609	257,280	4.1
25–49	166,059	423,339	6.8
10–24	331,518	754,857	12.1
5–9	395,600	1,150,457	18.4
2–4	1,056,992	2,207,449	35.3
1	4,040,966	6,248,415	100.0

2.41 Skew and movie ratings: IMDb (Internet Movie Database) publishes average ratings of movies worldwide. Anyone can log on and rate a film. What's the worst-rated film of the more than 235,000 that are listed on IMDb? The Bollywood action-romance *Gunday*, which earned a rating of 1.4 on a scale of 1–10 (Goldenburg, 2014). Hardly any other movies even came close to that low rating. In fact, the average film is rated 6.3, and most of the movies garnered ratings between 5.5 and 7.2. Even though *Gunday* got pretty good critical reviews, it tanked on the crowd-sourced IMDb. Why? Activists in Bangladesh harnessed social media to give it a bad rating. One posted, "If you're a Bangladeshi and care enough to not let some Indian crappy movie distort our history of independence, let's unite and boycott this movie!!!"

a. Based on what you know about the typical ratings on IMDb, is a histogram based on these data likely to be normally distributed, negatively skewed, or positively skewed? Explain your answer.

b. Is there more likely to be a floor effect or a ceiling effect for these data? Explain your answer.

c. Based on this story, are audience-generated IMDb ratings a good way to operationalize the quality of a movie? What might be a better way?

2.42 Consideration of Future Consequences and a dot plot: The following data are Consideration of Future Consequences (CFC) scores for 20 students, already arranged in order from lowest to highest:

> 2.0, 2.0, 2.5, 2.5, 3.0, 3.0, 3.0, 3.0, 3.5, 3.5,
> 3.5, 3.5, 3.5, 3.5, 3.5, 4.0, 4.0, 4.0, 4.5, 4.5

a. Construct a dot plot for these data.

b. What can you learn about the shape of this distribution from this plot?

2.43 Survey of Earned Doctorates and a dot plot: Use the data from Exercise 2.34 on the average number of years it takes students to complete a doctorate at 41 different universities.

a. Construct a dot plot for these data.

b. What can you learn about the shape of this distribution from this dot plot?

Putting It All Together

2.44 Frequencies, distributions, and numbers of friends: A college student is interested in how many friends the average person has. She decides to count the number of people who appear in photographs on display in dorm rooms and offices across campus. She collects data on 84 students and 33 faculty members. The data are presented below.

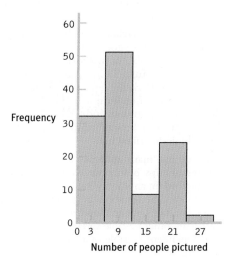

a. What kind of visual display is this?

b. Estimate how many people have fewer than 6 people pictured.

c. Estimate how many people have more than 18 people pictured.

d. Can you think of additional questions you might ask after reviewing the data displayed here?

e. Below is a subset of the data described here. Create a grouped frequency table for these data, using seven groupings.

1	5	3	9	13	0	18	15
3	3	5	7	7	7	11	3
12	20	16	4	17	15	16	10
6	8	8	7	3	17		

f. Create a histogram of the grouped data from part (e).

g. Describe how the data depicted in the original graph and the histogram you created in part (f) are distributed.

h. Refer to the histogram you created in (h). Do these data reflect a floor effect or a ceiling effect? Explain your answer.

2.45 Frequencies, distributions, and obesity around the world: The World Happiness Report publishes a number of indicators related to physical and psychological well-being (Helliwell, Layard, & Sachs, 2018). For example, it publishes adult obesity rates for more than 30 countries, with those percentages ranging from 3.7%

in Japan to 38.2% in the United States. Percentages for 20 of these countries are presented below.

30.7	32.4	12.3	12.8	10.3
22.6	9.8	24.8	16.6	38.2
17.8	3.7	27.9	15.3	21.3
19.0	23.6	14.7	25.8	19.2

a. Create a grouped frequency table for these data. Include a third column for percentages.

b. Create a histogram of these data.

c. Write a summary describing the distribution of these data with respect to shape and direction of any skew.

d. If you wanted the data to be positively skewed, how would the data have to shift to fit that goal? How could you use knowledge about the current distribution to target certain countries?

e. Are these data from correlational or experimental research? Explain your answer.

2.46 Developing research ideas from frequency distributions: Below are frequency distributions for two sets of the friends data described in Exercise 2.44, one for the students and one for the faculty members studied.

Interval	Faculty Frequency	Student Frequency
24–27	0	2
20–23	0	37
16–19	0	27
12–15	0	2
8–11	1	24
4–7	11	26
0–3	21	0

a. How would you describe the distribution for faculty members?

b. How would you describe the distribution for students?

c. If you were to conduct a study comparing the numbers of friends that faculty members and students have, what would the independent variable be and what would be the levels of the independent variable?

d. In the study described in part (c), what would the dependent variable be?

e. What is a confounding variable that might be present in the study described in part (c)?

f. Suggest at least two additional ways to operationalize the dependent variable. Would either of these ways reduce the impact of the confounding variable described in part (e)?

2.47 Frequencies, distributions, and graduate advising: In a study of mentoring in chemistry fields, a team of chemists and social scientists identified the most successful U.S. mentors—professors whose students were hired by the top 50 chemistry departments in the United States (Kuck et al., 2007). Fifty-four professors had at least 3 students go on to such jobs. Here are the data for the 54 professors. Each number indicates the number of students successfully mentored by each different professor.

```
3  3  3  4  5   9  5  3  3  5   6
3  4  8  6  3   3  3  4  4  4   7
6  3  5  5  7  13  3  3  3  3   3
4  4  4  5  6   7  6  7  8  8   3
3  3  5  3  3   5  3  5  3  3
```

a. Construct a frequency table for these data. Include a third column for percentages.

b. Construct a histogram for these data.

c. Describe the shape of this distribution.

d. How did the researchers operationalize the variable of mentoring success? Suggest at least two other ways in which they might have operationalized mentoring success.

e. Imagine that researchers hypothesized that an independent variable—good mentoring—predicts the dependent variable of mentoring job success. One professor, Dr. Yuan T. Lee from the University of California at Berkeley, trained 13 future top faculty members. Dr. Lee won a Nobel Prize. Explain how such a prestigious and public accomplishment might present a confounding variable to the hypothesis described here.

f. Dr. Lee had many students who went on to top professorships before he won his Nobel Prize. Several other chemistry Nobel Prize winners in the United States serve as graduate advisors but have not had Dr. Lee's level of success as mentors. What are other possible variables that might predict the dependent variable of attaining a top professor position?

 **LaunchPad**
macmillan learning

Visit LaunchPad to access the e-book and to test your knowledge with LearningCurve.

TERMS

raw score (p. 31)
frequency distribution (p. 31)
frequency table (p. 32)
outlier (p. 33)
grouped frequency table (p. 36)

histogram (p. 38)
normal distribution (p. 42)
skewed distribution (p. 42)
positively skewed (p. 43)
floor effect (p. 43)

negatively skewed (p. 43)
ceiling effect (p. 44)
dot plot (p. 44)

Visual Displays of Data

BEFORE YOU GO ON

- You should understand the different types of variables—nominal, ordinal, and scale (Chapter 1).

- You should understand the difference between independent variables and dependent variables (Chapter 1).

- You should know how to construct a histogram (Chapter 2).

The legendary nineteenth-century nurse Florence Nightingale was also known as the "passionate statistician" (Diamond & Stone, 1981). The lens of time has softened the image of this sarcastic, sharp-elbowed infighter (Gill, 2005) who created trouble simply by counting things. She counted supplies in a closet and discovered corruption; she counted physicians' diagnoses and discovered incompetence. She created the visual display in Figure 3-1 after counting the causes of death of British soldiers in Bulgaria and the Crimea. The British army was killing more of its own soldiers through poor hygiene than were dying due to wounds of war—and an outraged public demanded change. That is one powerful graph!

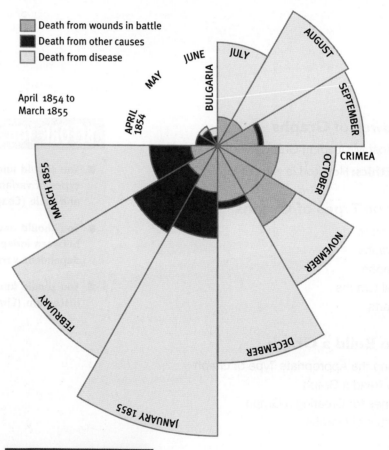

FIGURE 3-1

Graphs That Persuade

This coxcomb graph, based on Florence Nightingale's original coxcomb graph, "Diagram of the Causes of Mortality in the Army in the East," addresses the period from April 1854 to March 1855. It is called a *coxcomb graph* because the data arrangement resembles the shape of a rooster's head. The 12 sections represent the ordinal variable of a year broken into 12 months. The size of the sections representing each month indicates the scale variable of how many people died in that particular month. The colors represent the nominal variable of cause of death.

Graphs continue to save lives. Recent research documents the power of graphs to guide decisions about health care and even to reduce risky health-related behaviors (Garcia-Retamero & Cokely, 2013).

This chapter shows you how to create graphs, called *figures* in APA-speak, that tell data stories. The checklist on p. 69 will answer most of your questions about how to create graphs.

The Power of Graphs

Visual displays of data can be powerfully illuminating, like Florence Nightingale's coxcomb graph. But they also can be confusing, misleading, or even downright dishonest. Later, in the Data Ethics feature, we'll explore some of the ways people can lie with graphs. Here, we introduce an image that Michael Friendly, a psychology professor at York University in Toronto, described as possibly "the most misleading graph ever published" (see Figure 3-2).

"The Most Misleading Graph Ever Published"

The *Ithaca Times* graph in Figure 3-2 appears to answer a simple question: "Why does college have to cost so much?" This graph is chock-full of lies.

- Lie 1. The two lines cover different periods of time. The rising line represents rising tuition costs over *35 years*; the falling line represents the ranking of Cornell University over only *11 years*.
- Lie 2. The *y*-axis compares an ordinal observation (university rank) to a scale observation (tuition). These should be two different graphs.
- Lie 3. Cornell's rank arbitrarily begins at a lower point on the *y*-axis than tuition costs, suggesting that an institution already failing to deliver what students are paying for has become dramatically worse.
- Lie 4. The graph *reverses* the implied meaning of up and down. A low number in the world of rankings is a good thing. Over this 11-year period, Cornell's ranking *improved* from 15th place to 6th place!

There are many more ways to lie with graphs, and as you build your skills as an ethical statistician, we hope you'll keep watch for them. Researchers categorize lies like these into two groups: (1) lies that exaggerate and (2) lies that reverse the finding (Pandey, Rall, Satterthwaite, Nov, & Bertini, 2015). Lies that exaggerate lead us to think a given difference is bigger or smaller than it really is. Lies that reverse the finding make us think that the opposite finding is occurring—that Cornell is doing worse when it is really doing better. Researcher Anshul Vikram Pandey and his colleagues (2015) even conducted a series of studies that demonstrated that visual distortions can affect our perceptions and responses. In one example, only 7 of 38 people who saw a deceptive graph were able to interpret it correctly, whereas 39 out of 40 who saw a clearly designed version were right. For students of psychology and statistics, it is important to learn to create clear graphs and to be alert for visual lies.

MASTERING THE CONCEPT

3-1: Graphs can be misleading. As critical thinkers, we want to know whether a sample represents a population, how the variables were actually measured, and whether a graph tells an accurate data story.

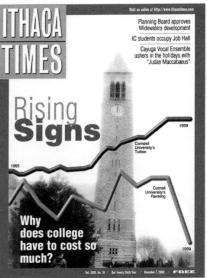

FIGURE 3-2

Graphs That Lie

Michael Friendly describes this graph as a "spectacular example of more graphical sins than I have ever seen in one image" and possibly "the most misleading graph ever published."

Data Ethics | How to Lie with Graphs

Ethical researchers develop graphs that clarify, rather than confuse. The best data visualizations avoid misleading tricks, including the following:

1. The biased-scale lie. *New York* magazine's (see nymag.com) reviewers use five stars to indicate that a restaurant's food, service, and ambience are "almost perfect" and one star means "good." There's no option for bad! Apparently, you can't buy a bad meal in New York City if a *New York* magazine reviewer has eaten there.

2. The sneaky-sample lie. You might pick up some useful information from Web sites that rate professors, but be cautious. The students most likely to supply ratings are those who strongly dislike or strongly approve of a particular professor. A self-selected sample means that the information might not apply to you.

3. The interpolation lie. Interpolation involves assuming that some value between the data points lies on a straight line between those data points. For example, *Statistics Canada* reported that in 2006, Canada had its lowest rate of break-ins (property crime) since the 1970s (see the figure below on the left), but you cannot assume a gradual decline over 30 years. In the years leading up to 1991, there was a dramatic increase in property crime. Make sure that a reasonable number of in-between data points have been reported.

4. The extrapolation lie. This lie assumes that values beyond the data points will continue indefinitely. In 1976, *The Complete CB Handbook* assumed that U.S. elementary schools would soon have to teach students how to communicate

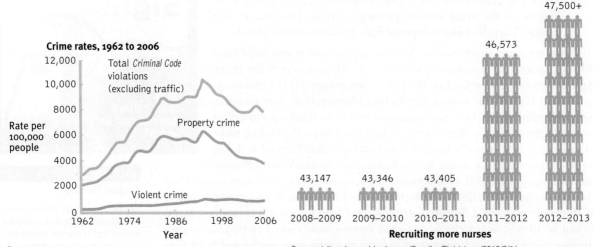

Crime rates, 1962 to 2006

Source: statcan.gc.ca

Recruiting more nurses

Source: static.guim.co.uk/sysimages/Guardian/Pix/pictures/2013/8/1/1375343461201/misleading.jpg

with CB radios, their popularity then growing exponentially. They are now used mostly by long-distance truckers. What happened? Mobile phones. Do not assume that a pattern will continue indefinitely.

5. The inaccurate values lie. This lie tells the truth in one part of the data but visually distorts it in another place. Notice in the figure at the bottom of the previous page on the right that just four stick figures are meant to represent more than 43,000 nurses in the first three columns. But when only a few thousand more nurses are included, as in the last column, 40 stick figures are used. The proportional change in the number of stick figures is much larger than the proportional change in the size of the data.

Watch out for these lies when you see graphs, and be careful not to lie, even inadvertently, when you create graphs.

CHECK YOUR LEARNING

Reviewing the Concepts	> Creating and understanding graphs are critical skills in our data-filled society.
	> Graphs can reveal or obscure information. To understand what a graph actually conveys, we must examine it and ask critical questions about it.

Clarifying the Concepts	**3-1**	What is the purpose of a graph?

Calculating the Statistics	**3-2**	Referring to the second figure in the Data Ethics feature, the inaccurate values lie, calculate how many more nurses there were in 2011–2012 than in 2010–2011. Explain why this is an example of a graphing lie.

Applying the Concepts	**3-3**	Which of the two following graphs is misleading? Which seems to be a more accurate depiction of the data? Explain your answer.

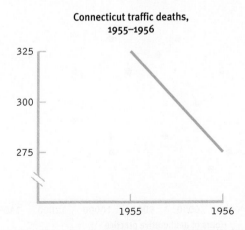

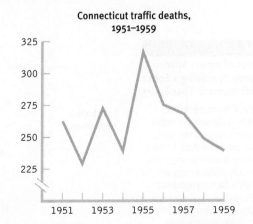

Solutions to these Check Your Learning questions can be found in Appendix D.

Common Types of Graphs

Graphs are powerful because they can display the *relation* between two or more variables in just one image. We first show you how to create scatterplots and line graphs—types of graphs that have two scale variables. Then we learn how to create—and criticize—graphs with one nominal (or sometimes ordinal) independent variable and a scale dependent variable: bar graphs, pictorial graphs, and pie charts.

Scatterplots

● A **scatterplot** is a graph that depicts the relation between two scale variables.

*A **scatterplot** is a graph that depicts the relation between two scale variables.* The values of each variable are marked along the two axes, and a mark is made to indicate the intersection of the two scores for each participant. The mark is above the participant's score on the *x*-axis and across from the score on the *y*-axis. We suggest that you think through your graph by sketching it by hand before creating it on a computer.

EXAMPLE 3.1

What makes a sports superstar? Practice or innate talent? Figure 3-3 describes the relation between lifetime hours of deliberative practice and athletes' performance in sports like field hockey, cricket, basketball, or even darts (Macnamara, Moreau, & Hambrick, 2016). In this study, the researchers' operational definition of deliberative practice was hours of participation in "activities created specifically to improve performance" (p. 334). In this example, the independent variable (*x*, on the horizontal axis) is the number of hours spent in deliberative practice, which ranged from a low of 4 hours to a high of almost 13,000 hours, and the dependent variable (*y*, on the vertical axis) is the performance for everyone from people who engaged in after-work pick-up volleyball games to Olympic athletes.

The scatterplot in Figure 3-3 suggests that more hours spent in deliberative practice is associated with better athletic performance; it includes each participant's two

MASTERING THE CONCEPT

3-2: Scatterplots and line graphs are used to depict relations between two scale variables.

FIGURE 3-3

Scatterplot of Hours Spent Deliberately Practicing a Sport and Performance in That Sport

This scatterplot depicts the relation between hours of deliberative practice and sports performance. It represents the actual relation in the study, but for a smaller number of fictional participants, and includes a hypothetical range of 0–10 for performance. Each dot represents one athlete's score on the independent variable along the *x*-axis and on the dependent variable along the *y*-axis.

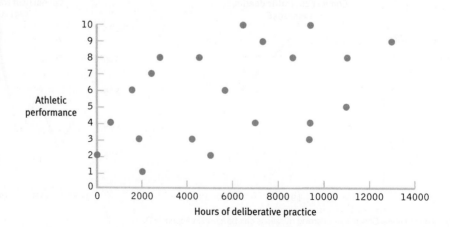

scores (one for hours engaged in deliberative practice and the other for athletic performance) that reveal the overall pattern of scores. In this scatterplot, the values on both axes go down to 0, but they don't have to. Sometimes the scores are clustered and the pattern in the data might be clearer by adjusting the range on one or both axes. (If it's not practical for the scores to go down to 0, be sure to indicate this with cut marks. Cut marks are breaks in the axis indicating that the axis starts at a value other than 0.)

To create a scatterplot:

1. Organize the data by participant; each participant will have two scores, one on each scale variable.

2. Label the horizontal *x*-axis with the name of the independent variable and its possible values, starting with 0 if practical.

3. Label the vertical *y*-axis with the name of the dependent variable and its possible values, starting with 0 if practical.

4. Make a mark on the graph above each study participant's score on the *x*-axis and next to his or her score on the *y*-axis.

A scatterplot between two scale variables can tell three possible stories. First, there may be no relation at all; in this case, the scatterplot looks like a jumble of random dots. This is an important scientific story if we previously believed that there was a systematic pattern between the two variables.

Second, *a **linear relation** between variables means that the relation between variables is best described by a straight line.* When the linear relation is positive, the pattern of data points flows upward and to the right. When the linear relation is negative, the pattern of data points flows downward and to the right. The data story about hours spent in deliberative practice and athletic performance in Figure 3-3 indicates a positive, linear relation. ●

*A **nonlinear relation** between variables means that the relation between variables is best described by a line that breaks or curves in some way.* Nonlinear simply means "not straight," so there are many possible nonlinear relations between variables, including the one depicted in Figure 3-4. For example, the Yerkes–Dodson law described in Figure 3-4 predicts the relation between level of arousal and test performance. As professors, we don't want you so relaxed that you don't even show up for the test, but we also don't want you so stressed out that you have a panic attack. You will maximize your performance somewhere in the happy middle described by a nonlinear relation (in this case, an upside-down U-curve).

Line Graphs

*A **line graph** is used to illustrate the relation between two scale variables.* One type of line graph is based on a scatterplot and allows us to construct a line of best fit that represents the predicted *y* score for each *x* value. A second type of line graph allows us to visualize changes in the values on the *y*-axis over time.

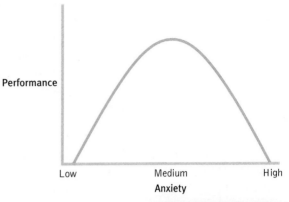

Performance — Low / Medium / High — Anxiety

FIGURE 3-4

Nonlinear Relations

The Yerkes–Dodson law predicts that stress/anxiety improves test performance—but only to a point. Too much anxiety leads to an inability to perform at one's best. This inverted U-curve illustrates the concept, but a scatterplot would better clarify the particular relation between these two variables.

● A **linear relation** between variables means that the relation between variables is best described by a straight line.

● A **nonlinear relation** between variables means that the relation between variables is best described by a line that breaks or curves in some way.

● A **line graph** is used to illustrate the relation between two scale variables.

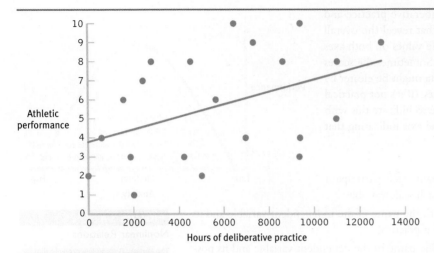

EXAMPLE 3.2

The first type of line graph, based on a scatterplot, is especially useful because the line of best fit minimizes the distances between all the data points from that line. That allows us to use the x value to predict the y value and make predictions based on only one piece of information. For example, we can use the line of best fit in Figure 3-5 to predict that an athlete will perform at about a 5 on our hypothetical 0–10 scale if she engages in deliberative practice for about 4000 hours. For now, we can sim-

FIGURE 3-5

The Line of Best Fit

The line of best fit allows us to make predictions about a person's value on the *y* variable from his or her value on the *x* variable.

ply eyeball the scatterplot and draw a line of best fit; in Chapter 16, you will learn how to calculate a line of best fit.

To create a scatterplot with a line of best fit, follow the four steps for creating a scatterplot on p. 61 and the fifth step here:

5. Visually estimate and sketch the line of best fit through the points on the scatterplot. (In Chapter 16, you'll learn how to calculate the exact line of best fit.) •

• A **time plot**, or **time series plot**, is a graph that plots a scale variable on the *y*-axis as it changes over an increment of time (e.g., second, day, century) labeled on the *x*-axis.

A second situation in which a line graph is more useful than just a scatterplot involves time-related data. *A **time plot**, or **time series plot**, is a graph that plots a scale variable on the y-axis as it changes over an increment of time (e.g., hour, day, century) labeled on the x-axis.* As with a scatterplot, marks are placed above each value on the *x*-axis (e.g., at a given hour) at the value for that particular time on the *y*-axis (i.e., the score on the dependent variable). These marks are then connected with a line. It is possible to graph several lines on the same graph in a time plot, as long as the lines use the same scale variable on the *y*-axis. With multiple lines, the viewer can compare the trends for different levels of another variable.

EXAMPLE 3.3

Figure 3-6, for example, shows a time plot for positive attitudes and negative attitudes around the world, as expressed on Twitter. The researchers analyzed more than half a billion tweets over the course of 24 hours (Golder & Macy, 2011) and plotted separate lines for each day of the week. These fascinating data tell many stories. For example, people tend to express more positive attitudes and fewer negative attitudes in the morning than later in the day; people express more positive attitudes on the weekends than during the week; and the weekend morning peak in positive attitudes is later than during the week, perhaps an indication that people are sleeping in.

Here is a recap of the steps to create a time plot:

1. Label the *x*-axis with the name of the independent variable and its possible values. The independent variable should be an increment of time (e.g., hour, month, year).

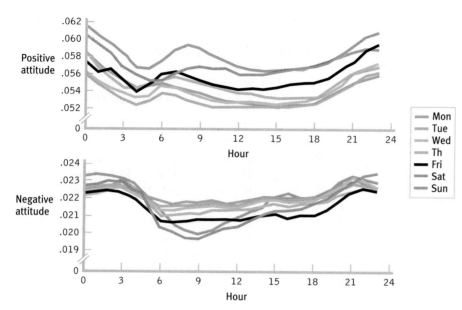

FIGURE 3-6

Time Plots Show Mood Changes on Twitter

Researchers tracked positive attitudes and negative attitudes expressed through Twitter over the course of a day and from around the globe (Golder & Macy, 2011). Time plots allow for multiple scale variables on one graph. In this case, there are separate lines for each day of the week, allowing us to see, for example, that the lines for Saturday and Sunday tend to be highest for positive attitudes and lowest for negative attitudes across the day.

2. Label the *y*-axis with the name of the dependent variable and its possible values, starting with 0 if practical.

3. Make a mark above each value on the *x*-axis at the value for that time on the *y*-axis.

4. Connect the dots. ●

Bar Graphs

*A **bar graph** is a visual depiction of data in which the independent variable is nominal or ordinal and the dependent variable is scale. The height of each bar typically represents the average value of the dependent variable for each category.* The independent variable on the *x*-axis could be either nominal (such as country) or ordinal (such as Olympic medal winners who won gold, silver, or bronze medals). We could even combine two independent variables in a single graph by drawing two separate clusters of bars to compare finishing times of the gold, silver, and bronze medalists from the northern hemisphere versus the southern hemisphere.

Here is a recap of the variables used to create a bar graph:

1. The *x*-axis of a bar graph indicates discrete levels of a nominal variable or an ordinal variable.

2. The *y*-axis of a bar graph may represent counts or percentages. But the *y*-axis of a bar graph can also indicate many other scale variables, such as average running speeds, scores on a memory task, or reaction times.

Bar graphs are flexible tools for presenting data visually. For example, if there are many categories to be displayed along the horizontal *x*-axis, researchers sometimes create a ***Pareto chart**, a type of bar graph in which the categories along the x-axis are ordered from highest bar on the left to lowest bar on the right.* This ordering allows easier comparisons and easier identification of the most common and least common categories.

● A **bar graph** is a visual depiction of data in which the independent variable is nominal or ordinal and the dependent variable is scale. The height of each bar typically represents the average value of the dependent variable for each category.

MASTERING THE CONCEPT

3-3: Bar graphs depict data for two or more categories. They tell a data story more precisely than do either pictorial graphs or pie charts.

● A **Pareto chart** is a type of bar graph in which the categories along the *x*-axis are ordered from highest bar on the left to lowest bar on the right.

EXAMPLE 3.4

Figure 3-7 shows two different ways of depicting the percentage of Internet users in a given country who visited Twitter.com over 1 month. One graph is an alphabetized bar graph; the other is a Pareto chart. Where does Canada's usage fit relative to that of other countries? Which graph makes it is easier to answer that question?

FIGURE 3-7

Pareto Charts Are Easier to Understand

The standard bar graph provides a comparison of Twitter usage among 14 levels of a nominal dependent variable, country. The Pareto chart, a version of a bar graph, orders the countries from highest to lowest along the horizontal axis, which allows us to more easily pick out the highest and lowest bars. We can more easily see that Canada places in the middle of these countries, and that the United States and the United Kingdom are toward the bottom. We have to do more work to draw these conclusions from the original bar graph.

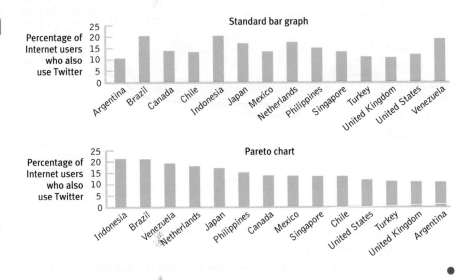

EXAMPLE 3.5

Bar graphs can help us understand the answers to interesting questions. For example, researchers wondered whether piercings and tattoos, once seen as indicators of a "deviant" worldview, had become mainstream (Koch, Roberts, Armstrong, & Owen, 2010). They surveyed 1753 college students with respect to numbers of piercings and tattoos, as well as about a range of destructive behaviors including academic cheating, illegal drug use, and number of arrests (not including traffic arrests). The bar graph in Figure 3-8 depicts one finding: The likelihood of having been arrested was fairly similar among all groups, except among those with four or more tattoos, 70.6% of whom reported having been arrested at least once. A magazine article about this research advised parents, "So, that butterfly on your sophomore's ankle is not a sign she is hanging out with the wrong crowd. But if she comes home for spring break covered from head to toe, start worrying" (Jacobs, 2010).

Liars' Alert! The small differences among the students with no tattoos, one tattoo, and two or three tattoos could be exaggerated if a reporter wanted to scare parents. Compare Figure 3-9 to the first three bars of Figure 3-8. Notice what happens when the fourth bar for four or more tattoos is eliminated: The values on the y-axis do not begin at 0, the intervals change from 10 to 2, and the y-axis ends

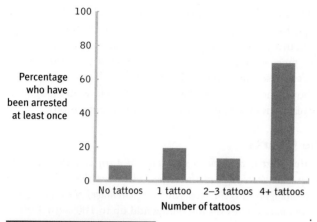

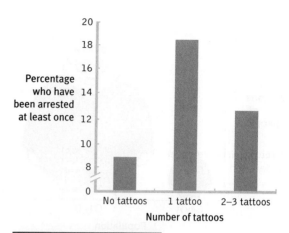

FIGURE 3-8

Bar Graphs Highlight Differences Between Averages or Percentages

This bar graph depicts the percentages of university students who have been arrested at least once (other than in a traffic arrest). The researchers measured four groups: those with no tattoos, one tattoo, two to three tattoos, and four or more tattoos. A bar graph can more vividly depict differences between percentages than just a list of the numbers themselves can: 8.5, 18.7, 12.7, and 70.6.

FIGURE 3-9

Deceiving with the Scale

To exaggerate a difference between means, graphmakers sometimes compress the rating scale that they show on their graphs. When possible, label the axis beginning with 0, and when displaying percentages, include all values up to 100%.

at 20%. The exact same data leave a very different impression. (*Note:* If the data are very far from 0, and it does not make sense to have the axis go down to 0, indicate this on the graph by including double slashes—called cut marks—like those shown in Figure 3-9.)

Here is a recap of the steps to create a bar graph. The critical choice for you, the graph creator, is in step 2.

1. Label the *x*-axis with the name and levels (i.e., categories) of the nominal or ordinal independent variable.

2. Label the *y*-axis with the name of the scale dependent variable and its possible values, starting with 0 if practical.

3. For every level of the independent variable, draw a bar with the height of that level's value on the dependent variable. ●

Pictorial Graphs

Occasionally, a pictorial graph is acceptable, but such a graph should be used sparingly and only if carefully created. *A **pictorial graph** is a visual depiction of data typically used for an independent variable with very few levels (categories) and a scale dependent variable. Each level uses a picture or symbol to represent its value on the scale dependent variable.* Eye-catching pictorial graphs are far more common in the popular media than in research journals. They tend to direct attention to the clever artwork rather than to the story that the data tell.

● A **pictorial graph** is a visual depiction of data typically used for an independent variable with very few levels (categories) and a scale dependent variable. Each level uses a picture or symbol to represent its value on the scale dependent variable.

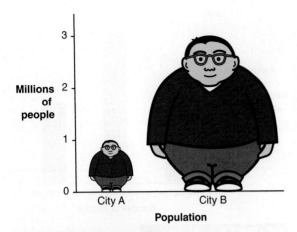

FIGURE 3-10

Distorting the Data with Pictures

In a pictorial graph, tripling the height of a picture is often coupled with tripling the width—which is multiplying by 3 twice. Instead of being three times as big, the picture is *nine times* as big!

● A **pie chart** is a graph in the shape of a circle, with a slice for every level (category) of the independent variable. The size of each slice represents the proportion (or percentage) of each level.

For example, a graphmaker might use stylized drawings of people to indicate population size. Figure 3-10 demonstrates one problem with pictorial graphs. The picture makes the person three times as tall *and* three times as wide (so that the taller person won't look so stretched out). But then the total area of the picture is about nine times larger than the shorter one, even though the population is only three times as big—a false impression.

Pie Charts

*A **pie chart** is a graph in the shape of a circle, with a slice for every level (category) of the independent variable. The size of each slice represents the proportion (or percentage) of each category.* A pie chart's slices should *always* add up to 100% (or 1.00, if using proportions). Figure 3-11 demonstrates the difficulty in making comparisons from a pair of pie charts. As suggested by this graph, data can almost always be presented more clearly in a table or bar graph than in a pie chart. Edward R. Tufte is well known for his beautiful books that demonstrate simple ways to create clearer graphs (1997/2005, 2001/2006b, 2006a). Regarding pie charts, Tufte (2006b) bluntly advises: "A table is nearly always better than a dumb pie chart" (p. 178). Because of the limitations of pie charts and the ready alternatives, we do not outline the steps for creating a pie chart here.

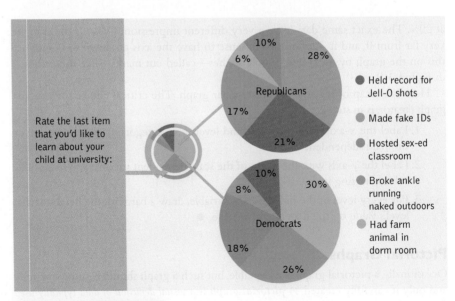

FIGURE 3-11

The Perils of a Pie Chart

Pie charts make it difficult to make comparisons. It takes some effort to determine that 6% of Republicans and 30% of Democrats in the United States would be most upset if their children had a farm animal in their university dormitory rooms. It would be far easier to make this comparison from a bar graph or even a table. Data from vanityfair.com/magazine/2013/05/60-minutes-poll-college-locations

CHECK YOUR LEARNING

Reviewing the Concepts	> Scatterplots and line graphs allow us to see relations between two scale variables.
	> When examining the relations between variables, it is important to consider linear and nonlinear relations, as well as the possibility that no relation is present.
	> Bar graphs, pictorial graphs, and pie charts depict summary values (such as means or percentages) on a scale variable for various levels of a nominal or ordinal variable.
	> Bar graphs are preferred; pictorial graphs and pie charts can be misleading.

Clarifying the Concepts	3-4	How are scatterplots and line graphs similar?
	3-5	Why should we typically avoid using pictorial graphs and pie charts?

Calculating the Statistics	3-6	What type of visual display of data allows us to calculate or evaluate how a variable changes over time?

Applying the Concepts	3-7	What is the best type of common graph to depict each of the following data sets and research questions? Explain your answers.

  a. Depression severity and amount of stress for 150 university students. Is depression related to stress level?

  b. Number of inpatient mental health facilities in Canada as measured every 10 years between 1890 and 2000. Has the number of facilities declined in recent years?

  c. Number of siblings reported by 100 people. What size family is most common?

  d. Mean years of education for six regions of the United States. Are education levels higher in some regions than in others?

  e. Calories consumed in a day and hours slept that night for 85 people. Does the amount of food a person eats predict how long he or she sleeps at night?

Solutions to these Check Your Learning questions can be found in Appendix D.

How to Build a Graph

In this section, you will learn how to choose the most appropriate type of graph and then use a checklist to ensure that the graph conforms to APA style. We also discuss innovative graphs that highlight the exciting future of graphing. Innovations in graphing can help us to deliver a persuasive message, much like that conveyed by Florence Nightingale's coxcomb graph.

Choosing the Appropriate Type of Graph

When deciding what type of graph to use, first examine the variables. Decide which is the independent variable and which is the dependent variable. Also, identify which type of variable—nominal, ordinal, or scale (interval/ratio)—each is. Most of the time, the independent variable belongs on the horizontal *x*-axis and the dependent variable goes on the vertical *y*-axis.

After assessing the types of variables that are in the study, use the following guidelines to select the appropriate graph:

1. If there is one scale variable (with frequencies), use a histogram (Chapter 2).

2. If there is one scale independent variable and one scale dependent variable, use a scatterplot or a line graph. (Figure 3-6 on page 63 provides an example of how to use more than one line on a time plot.)

3. If there is one nominal or ordinal independent variable and one scale dependent variable, use a bar graph. Consider using a Pareto chart if the independent variable has many levels.

4. If there are two or more nominal or ordinal independent variables and one scale dependent variable, use a bar graph.

How to Read a Graph

Let's use the graph of numbers of tattoos and percentages of people in each category who have been arrested in Figure 3-8 to confirm your understanding of independent and dependent variables. This study included one independent variable: number of tattoos (zero; one; two or three; four or more). The dependent variable was the percentage of people in that category who had been arrested.

Here are the critical questions you need to ask to understand the graph of the findings of the tattoos study. A well-designed graph makes it easy to see the answers; a graph intended to mislead or lie will obscure the answers.

1. What variable are the researchers trying to predict? That is, what is the *dependent variable*?

2. Is the dependent variable nominal, ordinal, or scale?

3. What are the units of measurement on the dependent variable? For example, if the dependent variable is IQ as measured by the Wechsler Adult Intelligence Scale, then the possible scores are the IQ scores themselves, ranging from 0 to 145.

4. What variables did the researchers use to predict this dependent variable? That is, what are the *independent variables*?

5. Are these two independent variables nominal, ordinal, or scale?

6. What are the levels for each of these independent variables?

Now check your answers:

1. The dependent variable (on the *y*-axis) is percentage who have been arrested.

2. Percentage is a scale variable.

3. Percentage can range from 0 to 100.

4. The independent variable (on the *x*-axis) is number of tattoos.

5. Number of tattoos is an ordinal variable, but it can be treated as a nominal variable in the graph.

6. The levels for number of tattoos are zero; one; two or three; and four or more.

Because there is one ordinal independent variable that can be treated as nominal, and one scale dependent variable, we used a bar graph to depict these data.

Guidelines for Creating a Graph

Here is a helpful checklist of questions to ask when you encounter a graph or when you're creating a graph. Some we've mentioned previously, and all are wise to follow.

❑ Does the graph have a clear, specific title?

❑ Are both axes labeled with the names of the variables? Do all labels read left to right—even the one on the *y*-axis?

❑ Are all terms on the graph the same terms that are used in the text that the graph is to accompany? Have all unnecessary abbreviations been eliminated?

❑ Are the units of measurement (e.g., minutes, percentages) included in the labels?

❑ Do the values on the axes either go down to 0 or have cut marks (double slashes) to indicate that they do not go down to 0?

❑ Are colors used in a simple, clear way—ideally, shades of gray instead of other colors?

❑ Has all chartjunk been eliminated?

The last of these guidelines involves a new term, the graph-corrupting fluff called *chartjunk*, a term coined by Tufte (2001), whom we introduced in the context of pie charts. According to Tufte, **chartjunk** *is any unnecessary information or feature in a graph that detracts from a viewer's ability to understand the data.* Chartjunk can take the form of any of three unnecessary features, all demonstrated in the rather frightening graph in Figure 3-12.

1. *Moiré vibrations* *are any visual patterns that create a distracting impression of vibration and movement.* Unfortunately, they are sometimes the default settings for bar graphs in statistical software. Tufte recommends using shades of gray instead of patterns.

2. *A* *grid* *is a background pattern, almost like graph paper, on which the data representations, such as bars, are superimposed.* Tufte recommends the use of grids only for hand-drawn drafts of graphs. In final versions of graphs, use only very light lines, if necessary.

3. *Ducks* *are features of the data that have been dressed up to be something other than merely data.* Think of ducks as data in costume. Named for the Big Duck, a store in Flanders, New York, that was built in the form of a very large duck, graphic ducks can be three-dimensional effects, cutesy pictures, fancy fonts, or any other flawed design features. Avoid chartjunk!

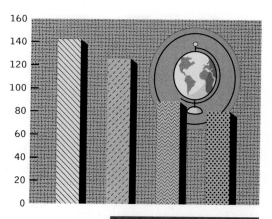

FIGURE 3-12

Chartjunk Run Amok

Moiré vibrations, such as those seen in the patterns on these bars, might be fun to use, but they detract from the viewer's ability to glean the story of the data. Moreover, the grid pattern behind the bars might appear scientific, but it serves only to distract. Ducks—like the 3-D shadow effect on the bars and the globe clip-art—add nothing to the data, and the colors are absurdly eye straining. Don't laugh; we've had students submit carefully written research papers accompanied by graphs even more garish than this!

MASTERING THE CONCEPT

3-5: Avoid chartjunk—any unnecessary aspect of a graph that detracts from its clarity.

● **Chartjunk** is any unnecessary information or feature in a graph that detracts from a viewer's ability to understand the data.

● **Moiré vibrations** are any visual patterns that create a distracting impression of vibration and movement.

● **Grids** are chartjunk that take the form of a background pattern, almost like graph paper, on which the data representations, such as bars, are superimposed.

Franck Fotos/Alamy Stock Photo

Edward Tufte's Big Duck The graphics theorist Edward Tufte was fascinated by the Big Duck, a store in the form of a duck for which he named a type of chartjunk (graphic clutter). In graphs, ducks are any aspects of the graphed data that are "overdressed," obscuring the message of the data. Think of ducks as data in a ridiculous costume.

- A **duck** is a form of chartjunk in which a feature of the data has been dressed up to be something other than merely data.

- Computer **defaults** are the options that the software designer has preselected; they are the built-in decisions that the software will implement if you do not instruct it otherwise.

Several computer-generated graphing programs have defaults that correspond to many—but not all—of these guidelines. Computer **defaults** *are the options that the software designer has preselected; they are the built-in decisions that the software will implement if you do not instruct it otherwise.* You cannot assume that these defaults represent the APA guidelines for your particular situation. To make changes, you can usually point the cursor at a part of the graph and click to view the available options.

The Future of Graphs

Thanks to computer technology, we have entered a second golden age of scientific graphing. We mention only four categories here: geographic information systems, word clouds, multivariable graphs (which are often interactive), and graphs that use innovative methods to display variability.

Geographic Information Systems (GIS) Many companies have published software that enables computer programmers to link Internet-based data to Internet-based maps (Markoff, 2005). These visual tools are all variations on geographic information systems (GIS).

Behavioral scientists can use GIS to organize workflow, assess group dynamics, study the design of classrooms, and much more. For example, U.K. researcher Desislava Hristova and her colleagues connected geographic locations in London to social networks using more than a half million check-ins on the social media tool Foursquare to understand how gentrification happens (Hristova, Williams, Musolesi, Panzarasa, & Mascolo, 2016). They learned that gentrification doesn't start when newcomers move in; it starts even earlier, with visits to cafés, bars, restaurants, and other locations by visitors who are wealthier than the typical neighborhood residents. Ironically, this advance in computerized mapping is pretty much what John Snow did without a computer in 1854 when he studied the Broad Street cholera outbreak.

Word Clouds Word clouds, an increasingly common type of graph, provide information on the most popular words used in a specific text (Figure 3-13; McKee, 2014). When creating a word cloud, the researcher defines what "most popular" means—the top 50 most frequently used words, the top 25 most frequently used words, or some other quantity. The size of the word in the graph usually indicates the frequency of the word (the larger the word, the more frequent).

For example, the Columbus Metropolitan Library in Ohio used data from the library's Facebook followers, who were asked to describe the library of their childhood (word cloud on the left, Figure 3-13a) and a library 20 years from now (word cloud on the right, Figure 3-13b). Clearly, the perceptions of the uses and purposes of libraries have changed over the past 50 years—especially with increased access to technology and the Internet—and these two word clouds demonstrate this kind of data. We can also visualize consistent trends in perceptions of libraries, with the use of the words *research*, *information*, and *books* being fairly prominent in both word clouds.

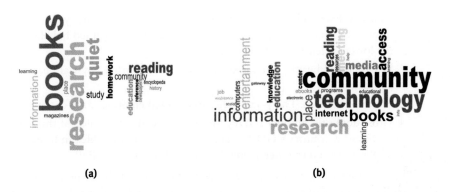

(a)   (b)

FIGURE 3-13

Word Clouds

Word clouds provide information on the most popular words used in a specific text. The bigger the word, the more commonly it was used. These two word clouds describe people's perceptions of libraries of the past (a) and libraries of the future (b). Source: theatlantic.com/national/archive/2014/10/not-your-mothers-library/381119/

Multivariable Graphs As graphing technologies become more advanced, there are increasingly elegant ways to depict multiple variables on a single graph. In fact, we've already seen one in this chapter. The two line graphs in Figure 3-6 include three variables: time of day on the *x*-axis, positive attitudes expressed on Twitter on the *y*-axis, and day of the week as different colored lines. Using the bubble graph option under "Other Charts" on Microsoft Excel (or even better, downloading Excel templates from sites such as juiceanalytics.com/chartchooser), we can create a bubble graph that depicts multiple variables. *A **bubble graph** is a graph that resembles a scatterplot, but the dots are replaced by bubbles that can represent additional variables through their color and size.*

In an article titled "Is the Emotion-Health Connection a 'First-World Problem'?", Sarah Pressman and her colleagues used a more sophisticated version of a bubble graph to display four variables (Figure 3-14; Pressman, Gallagher, & Lopez, 2013):

● A **bubble graph** is a graph that resembles a scatterplot, but the dots are replaced by bubbles that can represent additional variables through their color and size.

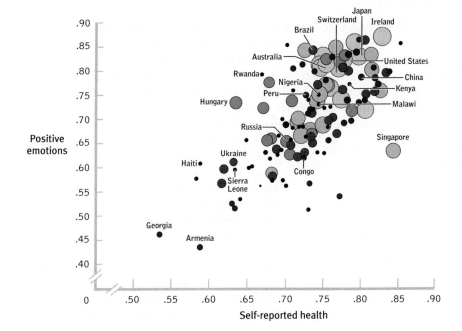

FIGURE 3-14

A Multivariable Graph

Increasingly sophisticated technology allows us to create increasingly sophisticated graphs. This bubble graph from a study by Sarah Pressman and her colleagues (2013) depicts four variables: country (each bubble), self-reported health (*x*-axis), positive emotions (*y*-axis), and gross domestic product (size and color of bubbles). The researchers could have had five variables if they had not used both the size and the color of the bubbles to represent GDP.

1. Country. Each bubble is one country. For example, the large yellow bubble toward the upper right corner represents Ireland; the small red bubble toward the lower far left represents Georgia.
2. Self-reported health. The *x*-axis indicates self-reported physical health for a country.
3. Positive emotions. The *y*-axis indicates reported emotions for a country.
4. Gross domestic product (GDP). Both the size and the color of the bubbles represent a country's GDP. Smaller and darker red bubbles indicate lower GDP; larger and brighter yellow bubbles indicate higher GDP.

The researchers could have chosen to add a fifth variable by using either size or color to represent GDP, rather than both. They might have used size, for example, to represent GDP, and color to represent the continent for each country.

From this graph, we can see a strong relation between physical health and positive emotions for countries with varying GDPs. For countries with higher GDP (larger, brighter yellow dots) and lower GDP (smaller, darker red dots), there is a link between emotions and health.

Some interactive versions of a bubble graph have, amazingly, added a sixth variable to the five that are possible on a printed page. For instance, gapminder .org/tools has fascinating bubble graphs with data on countries around the world. The graphs look like Pressman's but they are interactive. The viewer may choose which variables to include on the *x*-axis and on the *y*-axis. But Gapminder goes a step beyond Pressman's graph. The site allows you to add the variable year by clicking "Play" in the lower left corner; the graph is then animated and can show the movement of countries with respect to a range of variables since 1800!

Innovative Ways to Display Variability In the Data Ethics feature in Chapter 2, we introduced the dot plot as a way for ethical researchers to understand all of their data, not just the information from the summary statistics. Increasingly, behavioral scientists are using inventive techniques to display the variability in their data visually (McCabe, Kim, & King, 2018). Actually seeing the full variability of a data set can help us understand stories in the data that would otherwise be hidden (Weissgerber, Milic, Winham, & Garovic, 2015). Consider the bar graph in Figure 3-15a, which shows a difference between means but provides no additional information about the underlying distribution of scores. Did these data form a normal distribution, were they skewed, or is there some other deviation from what is expected? With a bar graph, we just can't know. Figure 3-15b demonstrates, for example, that we could have these exact means with an extreme score, and researchers would certainly want to know more about why this outlier exists. Figure 3-15c demonstrates that the two bars might have these

FIGURE 3-15

Uncovering Hidden Stories by Displaying Variability

Physiologist Tracey Weissgerber and her colleagues (2015) demonstrate the importance of using displays of variability to uncover hidden stories in the data. The bar graph on the left (a) shows a difference between means, but the data could take many forms. The middle graph (b) demonstrates that data with these exact means could include an extreme score. The graph on the right (c) shows that the sizes of the samples in each group might be very different and yet stlil have the same means.

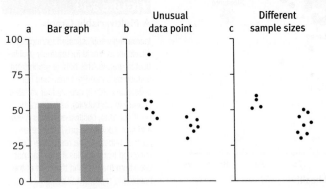

exact means and yet represent groups that vary greatly in size. Researchers would want to know about this difference in sample size. They may not trust the summary statistics from the group with just four scores as much as they trust the data from the group with 11 scores.

In Figure 3-15, graphs (b) and (c) are more illuminating than the bar graph (a). But many researchers, including Weissberger and her colleagues, use far more sophisticated graphs than these simple forms. One type of graph that displays the complexity of a distribution is the violin plot, named because of the similarity of its shape to the instrument (Pastore, Lionetti, & Altoè, 2017). Violin plots aren't new, but their popularity with behavioral scientists is (Hintze & Nelson, 1998). *Violin plots are graphs that are shaped like a violin, and include information about a distribution's middle score and overall variability.* Specifically, violin plots, like the one in Figure 3-16, show the middle score of the data as a white dot, the middle 50% of scores as a thick black vertical line, and the middle 95% of scores as a thin black vertical line. The blue violin shape around the vertical line gives us a sense of the distribution. More scores fall where the shape is thicker, and fewer scores fall where it is thinner.

The future of graphing is bright, especially because researchers now share more of their ideas through open source software. Violin plots, for example, aren't even close to the most informative ones that exist. If you want to explore more, you can create a pirate plot using a free plug-in package for the free statistics program R (Phillips, 2017). Appropriately for a pirate plot, the package, developed by Swiss cognitive scientist Nathaniel Phillips, is called *yaRrr*. YaRrr provides even more details about a data set, and even lets you choose colors from a favorite retro TV show like the kid cartoons *X-Men* and *My Little Pony*. The future of graphing is not just bright, but also fun.

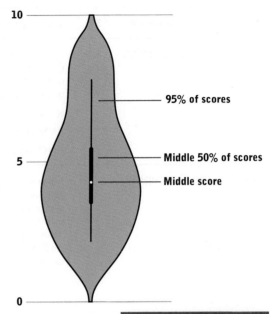

FIGURE 3-16

The Nuanced Violin Plot

Violin plots, like the one here, show the middle score, the middle 50% of the scores, and the range of most of the data. The blue shape shows the variability. More scores fall where it is thicker and fewer scores fall where it is thinner.

● **Violin plots** are graphs that are shaped like a violin, and include information about a distribution's middle score and overall variability.

CHECK YOUR LEARNING

Reviewing the Concepts

> Graphs should be used when they add information to written text or help to clarify difficult material.

> To decide what kind of graph to use, determine whether the independent variable and the dependent variable are nominal, ordinal, or scale variables.

> A brief checklist will help you create an understandable graph. Label graphs precisely and avoid chartjunk.

> The future of graphs is now! Computerized mapping, word clouds, multivariable graphs, and graphs that show the full variability of a data set are becoming increasingly common.

continued on next page

Clarifying the Concepts	3-8	What is chartjunk?
Calculating the Statistics	3-9	Decisions about which kind of graph to use depend largely on how variables are measured. Imagine a researcher is interested in how "quality of sleep" is related to statistics exam grade (measured by the number of errors made). For each of the measures of sleep below, decide which kind of graph to use.

a. Total minutes slept

b. Sleep assessed as sufficient or insufficient

c. Using a scale from 1 (low-quality sleep) to 7 (excellent sleep)

Applying the Concepts	3-10	Imagine that the graph in Figure 3-12 represents data testing the hypothesis that exposure to the sun can impair IQ. Further imagine that the researcher has recruited groups of people and randomly assigned them to different levels of exposure to the sun: 0, 1, 6, and 12 hours per day (enhanced, in all cases, by artificial sunlight when natural light is not available). The mean IQ scores are 142, 125, 88, and 80, respectively. Redesign this chartjunk graph, either by hand or by using software, paying careful attention to the dos and don'ts outlined in this section.

Solutions to these Check Your Learning questions can be found in Appendix D.

REVIEW OF CONCEPTS

LaunchPad
macmillan learning
Visit LaunchPad to access the e-book and to test your knowledge with LearningCurve.

The Power of Graphs

Graphs have enormous power. They can clarify the story in a data set, or confuse, mislead, or even lie. Learning how visual displays of statistics can lead us astray will empower you to spot lies for yourself. Visual displays of data are easily manipulated, so it is important to pay close attention to a graph's details to make sure they aren't conveying false information.

Common Types of Graphs

When developing graphing skills, it is important to begin with the basics. Several types of graphs are commonly used by social scientists. *Scatterplots* depict the relation between two scale variables. They are useful when determining whether the relation between the variables is *linear* or *nonlinear*. Some *line graphs* expand on scatterplots by including a line of best fit. Others, called *time plots* or *time series plots*, show the change in a scale variable over time.

Bar graphs are used to compare two or more categories of a nominal or ordinal independent variable with respect to a scale dependent variable. A bar graph on which the levels of the independent variable are organized from the highest bar to the lowest bar, called a *Pareto chart*, allows for easy comparison of levels. *Pictorial graphs* are like bar graphs except that pictures are used in place of bars. *Pie charts* are used to depict proportions or percentages on one nominal or ordinal variable with just a few levels. Because both pictorial graphs and pie charts are frequently constructed in a misleading way or are misperceived, bar graphs are almost always preferred to pictorial graphs and pie charts.

How to Build a Graph

We first decide which type of graph to create by examining the independent and dependent variables and by identifying each as nominal, ordinal, or scale. We then consider a number of guidelines to develop a clear, persuasive graph. It is important that all graphs be labeled appropriately and given a title that allows the graph to tell its story without additional text. For an unambiguous graph, it is imperative that graph creators avoid *chartjunk*: unnecessary information, such as *moiré vibrations*, *grids*, and *ducks*, that clutters a graph and makes it difficult to interpret. When using software to create graphs, it is important to question the *defaults* built into the software and to override them when necessary to adhere to these guidelines.

Finally, keeping an eye to the future of graphing—including computer-generated maps, word clouds, multivariable graphs, and graphs that emphasize the variability within a distribution—helps us stay at the forefront of graph-making in the behavioral sciences. New techniques allow us to make increasingly complex graphs: Bubble graphs, for example, allow us to include as many as five variables in a single graph. And violin plots show both middle scores and variability in clever, eye-catching ways.

SPSS

We can request visual displays of data from both the "Data View" screen and the "Variable View" screen. Most graphing is done in SPSS using the Chart Builder. This section walks you through the general steps to create a graph, using a scatterplot as an example. But first, enter the data in the screenshot for hours spent in deliberative practice and athletic performance that were used to create the scatterplot in Figure 3-3. You can see the data for those 21 pairs of scores here in the screenshot on the next page.

Select Graphs → Chart Builder. Under the "Gallery" tab, select the type of graph under "Choose From" by clicking on it. For example, to create a scatterplot, click on "Scatter/Dot." Drag a sample graph from the right to the large box above. Usually you'll want the simplest graph, which tends to be the upper-left sample graph.

Drag the appropriate variables from the "Variables" box to the appropriate places on the sample graph (e.g., "*x*-axis"). For a scatterplot, drag "Hours" to the *x*-axis and "Performance" to the *y*-axis. Chart Builder then looks like the screenshot shown here. Click "OK;" SPSS then creates the graph. [Note that what you see in this screenshot is the Chart Builder, not the final graph using the actual data.]

Remember: You should not rely on the default choices of the software; you are the designer of the graph. Once the graph is created, you can change its appearance by double-clicking on the graph to open the Chart Editor, the tool that allows you to make changes. Then click or double-click on the particular feature of the graph that you want to modify. Clicking once on part of the graph allows you to make some changes. For example, clicking the label of the *y*-axis allows you to change the font using the drop-down menu above; double-clicking allows you to make other changes, such as setting the label horizontal (after double-clicking, select the orientation "Horizontal" under "Text Layout").

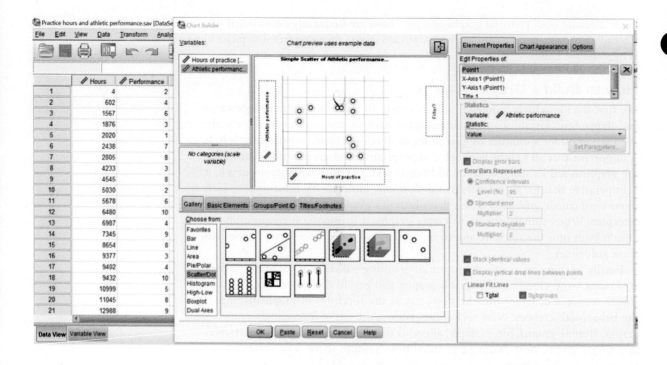

HOW IT WORKS

3.1 CREATING A SCATTERPLOT

As mentioned at the end of the chapter, gapminder.org/tools/ is a wonderful Web site that allows people to play with a graph and explore the relations between variables over time. We used Gapminder World to find scores for 10 countries on two variables.

Country	Children per woman (total fertility)	Life expectancy at birth (years)
Afghanistan	7.15	43.00
India	2.87	64.00
China	1.72	73.00
Hong Kong	0.96	82.00
France	1.89	80.00
Bolivia	3.59	65.00
Ethiopia	5.39	53.00
Iraq	4.38	59.00
Mali	6.55	54.00
Honduras	3.39	70.00

How can we create a scatterplot to show the relation between these two variables? To create a scatterplot, we put total fertility on the x-axis and life expectancy in years on the *y*-axis. We then add a dot for each country at the intersection of its fertility rate and life expectancy. The scatterplot is shown in the figure below.

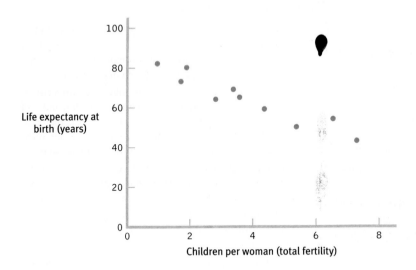

3.2 CREATING A BAR GRAPH

The International Monetary Fund listed the 2012 gross domestic product (GDP) per capita, in U.S. dollars (USD), for each of the world economic powers that make up what is called the Group of Eight, or G8, nations. (Note that Russia was kicked out in 2014 after it annexed Crimea, so this group is now the G7.)

Canada: $52,232	Italy: $33,115	United Kingdom: $38,589
France: $41,141	Japan: $46,736	United States: $49,922
Germany: $41,513	Russia: $14,247	

How can we create a bar graph for these data? First, we put the countries on the *x*-axis. Then, for each country, we draw a bar in which height corresponds to the country's GDP per capita. The following figure shows a bar graph with bars ordered from the country with the highest GDP per capita to the country with the lowest GDP per capita. This form of a bar graph is called a Pareto chart.

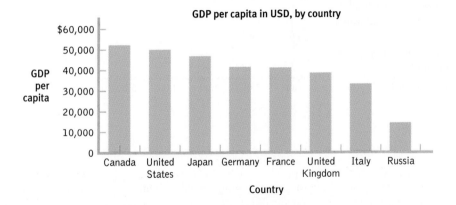

EXERCISES

The solutions to the odd-numbered exercises can be found in Appendix C.

Clarifying the Concepts

3.1 What are the five techniques discussed in this chapter for misleading with graphs?

3.2 What are the steps to create a scatterplot?

3.3 What does an individual dot on a scatterplot represent?

3.4 What does it mean for two variables to be linearly related?

3.5 How can we tell whether two variables are linearly or nonlinearly related?

3.6 What is the difference between a line graph and a time plot?

3.7 What is the difference between a bar graph and a Pareto chart?

3.8 Bar graphs and histograms look very similar. In your own words, what is the difference between the two?

3.9 What are pictorial graphs and pie charts?

3.10 Why are bar graphs preferred over pictorial graphs and pie charts?

3.11 Why is it important to identify the independent variable and the dependent variable before creating a visual display?

3.12 Under what circumstances would the x-axis and y-axis not start at 0?

3.13 Chartjunk comes in many forms. What specifically are moiré vibrations, grids, and ducks?

3.14 Geographic information systems (GIS), such as those provided by computerized graphing technologies, are particularly powerful tools for answering what kinds of research questions?

3.15 How is a bubble graph similar to a traditional scatterplot?

3.16 How does a bubble graph differ from a traditional scatterplot?

3.17 Why is it important to show variability on a graph, rather than just presenting a bar graph?

3.18 What information does a violin plot depict?

Calculating the Statistics

3.19 Alumni giving rates, calculated as the total dollars donated per year from 2010 to 2020, represent which kind of variable—nominal, ordinal, or scale? What would be an appropriate graph to depict these data?

3.20 Alumni giving rates for a number of universities, calculated as the number of alumni who donated and the number who did not donate in a given year, represent which kind of variable—nominal, ordinal, or scale? What would be an appropriate graph to depict these data?

3.21 You are exploring the relation between news source (online news Web sites versus social media) and knowledge about current affairs, as measured by scores on a test about world news.

  a. In this study, what are the independent and dependent variables?

  b. Is news source a nominal, ordinal, or scale variable?

  c. Is score a nominal, ordinal, or scale variable?

  d. Which graph or graphs would be appropriate to depict the data? Explain why.

3.22 Do the data in the graph below show a linear relation, a nonlinear relation, or no relation? Explain.

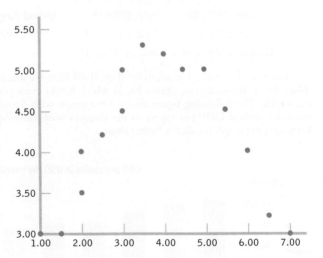

3.23 Do the data in the graph below show a linear relation, a nonlinear relation, or no relation? Explain.

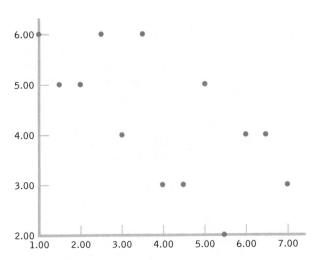

3.24 What elements are missing from the graphs in Exercises 3.22 and 3.23?

3.25 The following figure presents the enrollment of graduate students at a university, across six fall terms, as a percentage of the total student population.

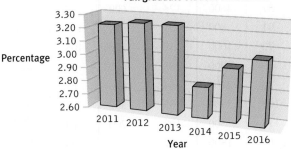

a. What kind of visual display is this?

b. What other type of visual display could have been used?

c. What is missing from the axes?

d. What chartjunk is present?

e. Using this graph, estimate graduate student enrollment, as a percentage of the total student population, in the fall terms of 2011, 2012, and 2014.

f. How would the comparisons between bars change if the y-axis started at 0?

3.26 When creating a graph, we need to make a decision about the numbering of the axes. If you had the following range of data for one variable, how might you label the relevant axis?

337   280   279   311   294   301   342   273

3.27 If you had the following range of data for one variable, how might you label the relevant axis?

0.10   0.31   0.27   0.04   0.09   0.22   0.36   0.18

3.28 The scatterplot in How It Works 3.1 depicts the relation between fertility and life expectancy. Each dot represents a country.

a. Approximately, what is the highest life expectancy in years? Approximately, what fertility rate (children per woman) is associated with the highest life expectancy?

b. Does this seem to be a linear relation? Explain why or why not, and explain the relation in plain English.

3.29 Based on the data in the bubble graph in Figure 3-14, what is the relation between physical health and positive emotions?

3.30 The colors and sizes of the bubbles in the bubble graph in Figure 3-14 represent the gross domestic product (GDP) for each country. Using this information, explain what the relation is between positive emotions and GDP.

Applying the Concepts

3.31 **Graphing the relation between international researchers and the impact of research:** Does research from international teams make a bigger splash? Researchers explored whether research conducted by multinational research teams had a bigger impact than

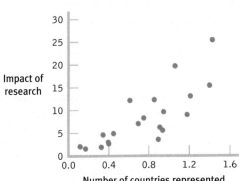

research from teams with less international representation (Hsiehchen, Espinoza, & Hsieh, 2015). The graph here shows the relation between two measures: (1) the average number of authors of articles in each journal who are from a different country than the first author, and (2) a measure that assesses the scientific impact of the journal with a higher score, indicating more influential research.

a. In this study, are the independent and dependent variables nominal, ordinal, or scale?

b. What type of graph is this? Why did the researchers choose this type of graph?

c. In your own words, explain what the researchers found.

3.32 Type of graph for the effects of cognitive-behavioral therapy on depression: A social worker tracked the depression levels of clients being treated with cognitive-behavioral therapy for depression. For each client, depression was assessed at weeks 1 to 20 of therapy. She calculated a mean for all of her clients at week 1, week 2, and so on, all the way through week 20.

a. What are the independent and dependent variables in this study?

b. Are the variables nominal, ordinal, or scale?

c. Which graph or graphs would be most appropriate to depict the data? Explain why.

3.33 Type of graph for comparative suicide rates: The World Health Organization tracks suicide rates by gender across countries. For example, in one year, the rate of suicide per 100,000 men was 17.3 in Canada, 17.7 in the United States, 44.6 in Sri Lanka, 53.9 in the Russian Federation, 1.4 in South Africa, and 2.5 in the Philippines.

a. What are the variables in this study?

b. Are the variables nominal, ordinal, or scale?

c. Which graph would be most appropriate to depict the data? Explain why.

d. If you wanted to track the suicide rates for three of these countries over 50 years, what type of graph might you use to show these data?

3.34 Scatterplot of daily cycling distances and type of climb: Every summer, the touring company America by Bicycle conducts the "Cross Country Challenge," a 7-week bicycle journey across the United States from San Francisco, California, to Portsmouth, New Hampshire. At some point during the trip, the exhausted cyclists usually start to complain that the organizers are purposely planning for days with lots of hill and mountain climbing to coincide with longer distances. The tour staff counter that no relation exists between climbs and mileage and that the route is organized based on practical issues, such as the location of towns in which riders can stay. The organizers who planned the route (these are the company owners who are not on the tour) say that they actually tried to reduce the mileage on the days with the worst climbs. Here are the approximate daily mileages and climbs (in vertical feet), as estimated from one rider's bicycle computer.

a. Construct a scatterplot of the cycling data, putting mileage on the x-axis. Be sure to label everything and include a title.

b. We haven't yet learned to calculate inferential statistics on these data, so we can't estimate what's really going on, but do you think that the amount of vertical climb is related to a day's mileage? If yes, explain the relation in your own words. If no, explain why you think there is no relation.

Mileage	Climb	Mileage	Climb	Mileage	Climb
83	600	69	2500	102	2600
57	600	63	5100	103	1000
51	2000	66	4200	80	1000
76	8500	96	900	72	900
51	4600	124	600	68	900
91	800	104	600	107	1900
73	1000	52	1300	105	4000
55	2000	85	600	90	1600
72	2500	64	300	87	1100
108	3900	65	300	94	4000
118	300	108	4200	64	1500
65	1800	97	3500	84	1500
76	4100	91	3500	70	1500
66	1200	82	4500	80	5200
97	3200	77	1000	63	5200
92	3900	53	2500		

c. It turns out that inferential statistics do not support the existence of a relation between these variables and that the staff seems to be the most accurate in their appraisal. Why do you think the cyclists and organizers are wrong in opposite directions? What does this say about people's biases and the need for data?

3.35 Scatterplot of gross domestic product and education levels: The Group of Seven (G7) consists of many of the major world economic powers. It meets annually to discuss pressing world problems. Here are one year's data for gross domestic product (GDP) and a measure of education. The measure of education is the percentage of the population between the ages of 25 and 64 that had at least one university degree (Sherman, Honegger, & McGivern, 2003).

a. Create a scatterplot of these data, with university degree percentages on the x-axis. Be sure to label everything and to give it a title. Later, we'll use statistical tools to determine the equation for the line of best fit. For now, draw a line of best fit that represents your best guess as to where it would go.

Country	GDP (in trillions of USD)	Percentage with university degree
Canada	0.98	19
France	2.00	11
Germany	2.71	13
Italy	1.67	9
Japan	4.62	18
United Kingdom	2.14	17
United States	11.67	27

b. In your own words, describe the relation between the variables that you see in the scatterplot.

c. Education is on the x-axis, indicating that education is the independent variable. Explain why it is possible that education predicts GDP. Now reverse your explanation of the direction of prediction, explaining why it is possible that GDP predicts education.

3.36 Time series plot of organ donations: The Canadian Institute for Health Information (CIHI) is a non-profit organization that compiles data from a range of institutions—from governmental organizations to hospitals to universities. Among the many topics that interest public health specialists is the problem of low levels of organ donation. Medical advances have led to ever-increasing rates of transplantation, but organ donation has not kept up with doctors' ability to perform more sophisticated and more complicated surgeries. Data reported by CIHI (secure.

cihi.ca/free_products/2011_CORR_Annua_Report_EN.pdf, 2015) provide Canadian transplantation and donation rates for 2001 to 2010. Here are the donor rates per million in the population; these numbers include only deceased donors.

Year	Donor rate per million people	Year	Donor rate per million people
2001	13.4	2006	14.1
2002	12.9	2007	14.7
2003	13.3	2008	14.4
2004	12.9	2009	14.4
2005	12.7	2010	13.6

a. Construct a time series plot from these data. Be sure to label and title your graph.

b. What story are these data telling?

c. If you worked in public health and were studying the likelihood that families would agree to donate after a loved one's death, what research question might you ask about the possible reasons for the trend suggested by these data?

3.37 Bar graph of acceptance rates for different types of psychology doctoral programs: The American Psychological Association (2015) gathered data from almost 1000 psychology doctoral programs in the United States. (*Note:* If a school offered, say, four different psychology doctorates, each would be counted separately.) The table below includes overall acceptance rates for each of 10 different types of psychology doctorates.

Psychology subfield	Acceptance rate
Clinical psychology	12.0%
Cognitive psychology	10.9%
Counseling psychology	11.0%
Developmental psychology	14.1%
Experimental psychology	12.7%
Industrial/organizational psychology	14.6%
Neuroscience	10.7%
School psychology	29.0%
Social psychology	7.0%
Other applied psychology	25.2%

a. What is the independent variable in this example? Is it nominal or scale? If nominal, what are the levels? If scale, what are the units and what are the minimum and maximum values?

b. What is the dependent variable in this example? Is it nominal or scale? If nominal, what are the levels? If scale, what are the units and what are the minimum and maximum values?

c. Construct a bar graph of these data, with one bar for each of the types of psychology doctoral programs, using the default options in your computer software.

d. Construct a second bar graph of these data, but change the defaults to satisfy the guidelines for graphs discussed in this chapter. Aim for simplicity and clarity.

e. Cite at least one research question that you might want to explore next. Your research question should grow out of these data.

f. Explain how these data could be presented as a pictorial graph. (Note that you do not have to construct such a graph.) What kind of picture could you use? What would it look like?

g. What are the potential pitfalls of a pictorial graph? Why is a bar chart usually a better choice?

3.38 Bar graph versus Pareto chart of countries' gross domestic product: In How It Works 3.2, we created a bar graph for the 2012 GDP, in U.S. dollars per capita, for each of the G8 nations. More specifically, we created a Pareto chart.

a. Explain the difference between a Pareto chart and a standard bar graph in which the countries would have been in alphabetical order along the x-axis.

b. What is the benefit of the Pareto chart over a standard bar graph?

3.39 Bar graph versus time series plot of graduate school mentoring: Johnson, Koch, Fallow, and Huwe (2000) conducted a study of mentoring in two types of psychology doctoral programs: experimental and clinical. Students who graduated from the two types of programs were asked whether they had a faculty mentor while in graduate school. In response, 48% of clinical psychology students who graduated between 1945 and 1950 and 62.31% who graduated between 1996 and 1998 reported having had a mentor; 78.26% of experimental psychology students who graduated between 1945 and 1950 and 78.79% who graduated between 1996 and 1998 reported having had a mentor.

a. What are the two independent variables in this study, and what are their levels?

b. What is the dependent variable?

c. Create a bar graph that depicts the percentages for the two independent variables simultaneously.

d. What story is this graph telling us?

e. Was this a true experiment? Explain your answer.

f. Why would a time series plot be inappropriate for these data? What would a time series plot suggest about the mentoring trend for clinical psychology graduate students and for experimental psychology graduate students?

g. For four time points—1945–1950, 1965, 1985, and 1996–1998—the mentoring rates for clinical psychology graduate students were 48.00, 56.63, 47.50, and 62.31, respectively. For experimental psychology graduate students, the rates were 78.26, 57.14, 57.14, and 78.79, respectively. How does the story we see here conflict with the one that we developed based on just two time points?

3.40 Bar graph versus pie chart and perceptions of health care advice: The company that makes Fitbit, the wristband that tracks exercise and sleep, commissioned a report that included the pie chart shown here (2013).

a. Explain why a bar graph would be more suitable for these data than a pie chart.

b. What statistical lie appears to be present in these data?

How overwhelmed do people get by the vast array of available advice on health care?

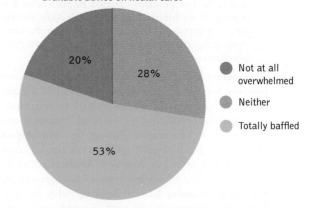

- Not at all overwhelmed
- Neither
- Totally baffled

3.41 Software defaults of graphing programs and perceptions of health care advice: For this exercise, use the data in the pie chart from the Fitbit report in the previous exercise.

   a. Create a bar graph for these data. Play with the options available to you and make changes so that the graph meets the guidelines in this chapter.

   b. List the aspects of the bar graph that you changed when creating your graph in part (a). Be specific.

3.42 Software defaults of graphing programs for depicting the "world's deepest" trash bin: The car company Volkswagen has sponsored a "fun theory" campaign in recent years in which ordinary behaviors are given game-like incentives to promote prosocial behaviors such as recycling or obeying the speed limit. In one example, Volkswagen placed a seemingly super-deep trash bin in a park in Sweden; when a person would throw something out, a high-pitched whistling sound played for 7 seconds, culminating in a far-off-sounding boom, as if the item had fallen for hundreds of feet! The fun-theory people collected data; in a single day, 72 kilograms of trash was thrown out in their "deep" bin, versus just 31 kilograms in a nearby trash bin.

   a. Use a software program that produces graphs (e.g., Excel, SPSS, Minitab) to create a bar graph for these data, using the default options.

   b. Play with the options available to you. List aspects of the bar graph that you are able to change to make your graph meet the guidelines listed in this chapter. Be specific, and include the revised graph.

3.43 Multivariable graphs and college rankings by academics and sexiness: Buzzfeed.com published a multivariable graph that purported to rank colleges by academics and "hotness." The data from this graph are represented to the right.

   a. What kind of graph is this? Explain.

   b. List the variables that are included in this graph.

   c. List at least three ways in which this graph could be redesigned in light of the guidelines in this chapter.

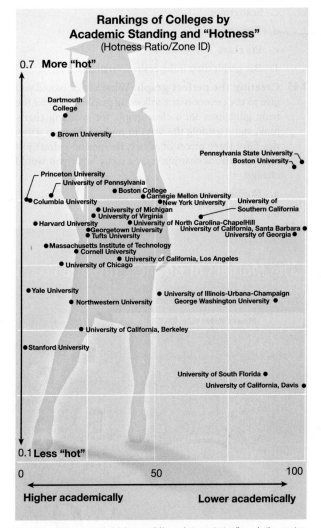

Source: buzzfeednews.com/article/annanorth/the-sexiest-smartest-colleges-in-the-country

3.44 Types of graph appropriate for behavioral science research: Give an example of a study—real or hypothetical—in the behavioral sciences for which the researchers could use each type of graph. State the independent variable(s) and dependent variable, including levels for any nominal variables.

   a. Line graph (line of best fit)

   b. Bar graph (one independent variable)

c. Scatterplot

d. Time series plot

e. Pie chart

f. Bar graph (two independent variables)

3.45 Creating the perfect graph: What advice would you give to the creator of the following graph? Consider the basic guidelines for a clear graph, for avoiding chart-junk, and regarding the ways to mislead through statistics. Give three pieces of advice. Be specific—don't just say that there is chartjunk; say exactly what you would change.

a. Business and women:

Source: womenonbusiness.com/countdown-to-equal-pay-day-2013-the-gender-pay-gap-from-1970-2013-infographic/

b. A boom in record album sales:

Source: Bernasek, 2014

3.46 Graphs in the popular media: Find an article in the popular media (newspaper, magazine, Web site) that includes a graph in addition to the text.

a. Briefly summarize the main point of the article and graph.

b. What are the independent and dependent variables depicted in the graph? What kinds of variables are they? If nominal, what are the levels?

c. What descriptive statistics are included in the article or on the graph?

d. In one or two sentences, what story is the graph (rather than the article) trying to tell?

e. How well do the text and graph match up? Are they telling the same story? Are they using the same terms? Explain.

f. Write a paragraph to the graph's creator with advice for improving the graph. Be specific, citing the guidelines from this chapter.

g. Redo the graph, either by hand or by computer, in line with your suggestions.

3.47 Interpreting a graph about two kinds of career regrets: The Yerkes–Dodson graph demonstrates that graphs can be used to describe theoretical relations that can be tested. In a study that could be applied to the career decisions made during college, Gilovich and Medvec (1995) identified two types of regrets— regrets of action and regrets of inaction—and proposed that their intensity changes over time. You can think of these as Type I regrets—things you have done that you wish you had not done (regrets of action)—and Type II regrets—things you have not done that you wish you had done (regrets of inaction). The researchers suggested a theoretical relation between the variables that might look something like the graph below.

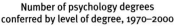

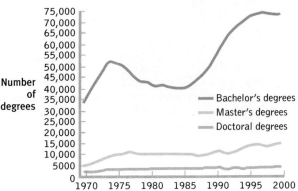

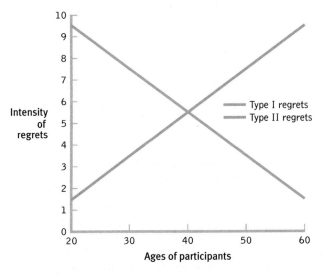

a. Briefly summarize the theoretical relations proposed by the graph.

b. What are the independent and dependent variables depicted in the graph? What kinds of variables are they? If nominal or ordinal, what are the levels?

c. What descriptive statistics are included in the text or on the graph?

d. In one or two sentences, what story is the graph trying to tell?

3.48 Thinking critically about a graph of the frequency of psychology degrees: The American Psychological Association (APA) compiles many statistics about training and careers in the field of psychology. The accompanying graph tracks the number of bachelor's, master's,

and doctoral degrees conferred between the years 1970 and 2000.

a. What kind of graph is this? Why did the researchers choose this type of graph?

b. Briefly summarize the overall story being told by this graph.

c. What are the independent and dependent variables depicted in the graph? What kind of variables are they? If nominal or ordinal, what are the levels?

d. List at least three things that the graph creators did well (i.e., in line with the guidelines for graph construction).

e. List at least one thing that the graph creators should have done differently (i.e., not in line with the guidelines for graph construction).

f. Name at least one variable other than number that might be used to track the prevalence of psychology bachelor's, master's, and doctoral degrees over time.

g. The increase in bachelor's degrees over the years is not matched by an increase in doctoral degrees. List at least one research question that this finding suggests to you.

3.49 Thinking critically about a graph about international students: Researchers surveyed Canadian students on their perceptions of the globalization of their campuses (Lambert & Usher, 2013). The 13,000 participants were domestic undergraduate and graduate students—that is, they were not recently from countries outside of Canada. The pie chart here shows the responses to one survey item: "The increasing number

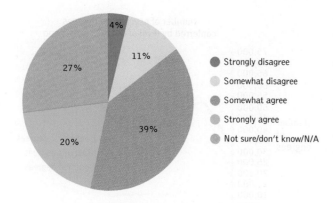

- Strongly disagree
- Somewhat disagree
- Somewhat agree
- Strongly agree
- Not sure/don't know/N/A

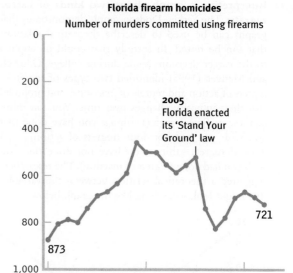

Florida firearm homicides
Number of murders committed using firearms

2005
Florida enacted
its 'Stand Your
Ground' law

873

721

Source: io9.gizmodo.com/11-most-useless-and-misleading-infographics-on-the-inte-1688239674

of international students attending my institution has led to improvements in the university's reputation and image."

a. What is the story that these data are telling?

b. Why would a bar graph of these data tell this story better than a pie chart does?

c. Create a bar graph of these data, keeping the bars in the order of the labels here—from "Strongly disagree" on the left to "Not sure/don't know/N/A" on the right.

d. Why would it not make sense to create a Pareto chart in this case?

3.50 Interpreting a graph about traffic flow: Go to maps.google.com. On a map of your country, select "Traffic" from the drop-down menu in the upper left corner.

a. How is the density and flow of traffic represented in this graph?

b. Describe traffic patterns in different regions of your country.

c. What are the benefits of this interactive graph?

3.51 Critiquing a graph about gun deaths: In this chapter, we learned about graphs that include statistical lies and graphs designed to be unclear. Think about the problems in the graph shown here.

a. What is the primary flaw in the presentation of these data?

b. How would you redesign this graph? Be specific and cite at least three ways in which you would change it.

3.52 Word clouds and statistics textbooks: The Web site Wordle lets you create your own word clouds (wordle.net/create). (There are a number of other online tools to create word clouds, including TagCrowd and WordItOut.) Here's a word cloud we made with the main text from this chapter. In your own words, explain why 10 or so of the most popular words are showing up here. That is, why are these words so important when learning how to create excellent, clear graphs?

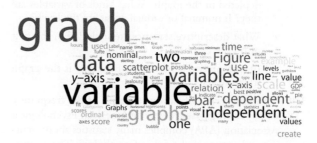

3.53 Comparing word clouds and subjective well-being: Social science researchers are increasingly using word clouds to convey their results. A research team from the Netherlands asked 66 older adults to generate a list of what they perceive to be important to their well-being (Douma, Steverink, Hutter, & Meijering, 2015). Based on these lists, the researchers identified 15 general areas perceived to be related to well-being. They created a version of the word cloud shown here to visualize the frequency that each of these areas was mentioned.

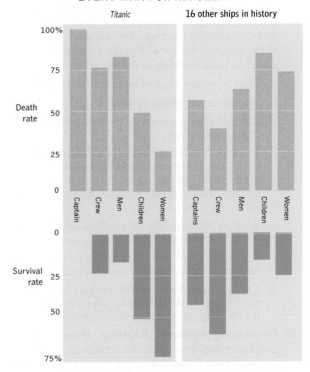

EVERY MAN FOR HIMSELF?

A review of 18 large shipwrecks from 1852 to 2011 suggests that crew members and male passengers survive at higher rates than women and children. Shipwrecks like the *Titanic*, in which the captain ordered "women and children first," are famous exceptions.

Source: nytimes.com/imagepages/2012/08/07/health/07ship.html

a. In your own words, summarize what the researchers found.

b. What research questions might these findings suggest for psychologists working in communities for older adults?

3.54 Multivariable graphs and shipwrecks: The cliché "women and children first" originated in part because of the *Titanic* captain's famous directive as his ship was sinking. Yet, the cliché is not grounded in reality. See the following multivariable graph.

a. What kind of graph is this?

b. List the variables that are included in this graph.

c. Are the data on the top and the bottom necessary to tell this story? Explain. Why do you think both sides are included?

d. In your own words, tell the story that this graph is visualizing.

Putting It All Together

3.55 Type of graph describing the effect of romantic songs on ratings of attractiveness: Guéguen, Jacob, and Lamy (2010) wondered if listening to romantic songs would affect the dating behavior of the French heterosexual women who participated in their study. The women were randomly assigned to listen to either a romantic song ("Je l'aime à Mourir," or "I Love Her to Death") or a nonromantic song ("L'heure du Thé," or "Tea Time") while waiting for the study to begin.

Later in the study, an attractive male researcher asked each participant for her phone number. Of the women who listened to the romantic song, 52.2% gave their phone number to the researcher, whereas only 27.9% of the women who listened to the nonromantic song gave their phone number to the researcher.

a. What is the independent variable in this study?

b. What is the dependent variable?

c. Is this a between-groups or a within-groups study? Explain your answer.

d. Think back to our discussion of variables in Chapter 1. How did the researcher operationalize "dating behavior" in this study? Do you think this is a valid measure of dating behavior? Explain your answer.

e. What is the best type of graph to depict these results? Explain your answer.

f. Create the graph you described in part (e) using software without changing any of the defaults.

g. Create the graph you described in part (e) a second time, changing the defaults to meet the criteria in the checklist introduced in this chapter.

3.56 Developing research questions from graphs: Graphs not only answer research questions, but can also spur new ones. Figure 3-6 on p. 63 depicts the pattern of changing attitudes, as expressed through Twitter.

a. On what day and at what time is the highest average positive attitude expressed?

b. On what day and at what time is the lowest average negative attitude expressed?

c. What research question(s) do these observations suggest to you with respect to weekdays versus weekends? (Remember, 0 on Sunday is midnight— or late Saturday night.) Name the independent and dependent variables.

d. How do the researchers operationalize mood? Do you think this is a valid measure of mood? Explain your answer.

e. One of the highest average negative attitudes occurs at midnight on Sunday. How does this fit with the research hypothesis you developed in part (c)? Does this suggest a new research hypothesis?

3.57 Identifying variables and the best graph: For each of the following studies, list (i) the independent variable or variables and how they were operationalized, (ii) the dependent variable or variables and how they were operationalized, and (iii) the ideal type of graph that would depict these data.

a. For your favorite story, is it better to listen to the audiobook or watch it in all its cinematic glory? British researchers asked participants to either listen to an audio version or watch the TV or film version of popular stories, including *The Da Vinci Code*, *The Girl on the Train*, and *Game of Thrones* (Richardson et al., 2018). As participants listened or watched excerpts of about one minute, the researchers measured their physiological response every few seconds, including heart rate and body temperature, which tend to increase when people are absorbed in the story. These measures were higher among those who listened than among those who watched, perhaps an indication of the importance of leaving the visuals to the imagination.

b. Lamenting the lack of sleep that plagues so many people around the globe, a reporter outlined the data on this issue (Barron, 2016). Specifically, he shared data from the National Sleep Foundation on participants' typical hours of sleep per night from samples of people in six countries. Here are the data:

Britain: 6 hours, 49 minutes

Canada: 7 hours, 3 minutes

Germany: 7 hours, 1 minute

Japan: 6 hours, 22 minutes

Mexico: 7 hours, 6 minutes

United States: 6 hours, 31 minutes

c. Are money and happiness related? Researcher Jeff Desjardins (2018) explored the link between average income and happiness for countries around the world. For income, he divided World Bank data on gross domestic product (GDP) in U.S. dollars by the number of people living in that country. For happiness, he used data from the World Happiness Report, which includes the average of residents' happiness scores. Desjardins found a relatively reliable increase in happiness as average GDP per person increased from $10,000 to $20,000 in U.S. dollars. From $30,000 to $60,000, there was an increase for some, but not all, countries. Beyond a certain point, though, more money didn't seem to increase happiness.

d. Suppose your roommate has a new romantic partner who starts staying overnight a lot—in your opinion, far too often. At what point do you insist that the new partner contribute to the cost of your place? Jon Bittner, a *Forbes* reporter, tackled this question, noting that the hypothetical new girlfriend "starts hanging around nearly every night, eating on the couch, watching TV, and taking showers in the morning" (Bittner, 2011). He conducted a survey, asking participants whether the new partner should chip in, depending on how often the partner stays over, from once a month to six times a week. He created a graph that depicted these data, including percentages of people who said that the partner should contribute for each frequency of sleeping over.

Visit LaunchPad to access the e-book and to test your knowledge with LearningCurve.

TERMS

Central Tendency and Variability

BEFORE YOU GO ON

- You should understand what a distribution is (Chapter 2).

- You should be able to interpret histograms and frequency polygons (Chapter 2).

Mark Collinson/Alamy Stock Photo

High-Quality Zippers The Japanese company YKK is known for its high-quality zippers. The key is low variability. The company has figured out how to ensure that just about every zipper is a good one.

There is big money in understanding statistical variability. Just ask YKK, the Japanese company that runs "the largest zipper factory in the world" and dominates the zipper market (Balzar, 1998; Stevenson, 2004).

You read that right: zippers. How do you feel when a zipper snags on material, malfunctions at the bottom, or catches unpredictably? At best, a stuck zipper is annoying, but it could be socially embarrassing or even life threatening. YKK limits product variability by controlling everything about the manufacturing process, from smelting its own brass to fabricating its own cardboard boxes for shipping. The company even builds the machines that make its products (see Balzar, 1998). Controlling every part of the manufacturing process helps YKK create and sell exceptionally consistent zippers. This low variability leads to a high-quality product, which in turn gives clothing manufacturers great confidence in YKK zippers. This is all part of a larger YKK corporate philosophy called "the cycle of goodness" (YKK, 2018).

YKK understands that no retailer wants an expensive dress, bag, or suit to fail because one of the least expensive components, the zipper, did not operate properly. YKK hopes that none of its zippers ever fails, but perfection in manufacturing is essentially impossible. So YKK wants the next best thing: low variability (or deviation) from that standard of perfection. In this chapter, you will learn three common ways to measure how much a distribution varies from its central tendency: range, variance, and standard deviation. But to fully understand variability, we first have to know how to identify the middle, or central tendency of a distribution.

Central Tendency

● **Central tendency** refers to the descriptive statistic that best represents the center of a data set, the particular value that all the other data seem to be gathering around.

Central tendency *refers to the descriptive statistic that best represents the center of a data set, the particular value that all the other data seem to be gathering around*—the "typical" score. Creating a visual representation of the distribution, as we did in Chapter 2, reveals its central tendency. The central tendency is usually at (or near) the highest point in the histogram or the polygon. The way data cluster around their central tendency can be measured in three different ways: mean, median, and mode. Let's look at an example. In keeping with the growing open-science movement, data.world is a Web site that allows users to create data sets that are then shared for free with the entire data.world community. It's a fun place to explore! One user, Rashedul Haque (2018), created a spreadsheet of openly available data from Charity Navigator, the organization that assesses large U.S.-based charities on their financial health, transparency, and accountability. Scores range from 0 to 100. Figure 4-1 shows the histogram for the largest

MASTERING THE CONCEPT

4-1: Central tendency refers to three slightly different ways to describe what is happening in the center of a distribution of data: the mean, the median, and the mode.

40 charities rated by Charity Navigator. These include international development organizations like World Vision, health and medical groups like the Alzheimer's Association, and arts organizations like the Museum of Modern Art in New York.

Mean: The Arithmetic Average

The mean is simple to calculate and is the gateway to understanding statistical formulas. The mean is such an important concept in statistics that we provide you with four distinct ways to think about it: verbally, arithmetically, visually, and symbolically (using statistical notation).

The Mean in Plain English The most commonly reported measure of central tendency is *the **mean**, the arithmetic average of a group of scores.* The mean, often called the *average*, is used to represent the "typical" score in a distribution. This is different from the way we sometimes use the word *average* in everyday conversation, noting that someone is "just" average in athletic ability or that a movie was "only" average. We need to define the mean arithmetically to determine a precise calculation.

The Mean in Plain Arithmetic The mean is calculated by summing all the scores in a data set and then dividing this sum by the total number of scores. You likely have calculated means many times in your life.

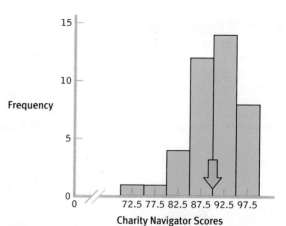

FIGURE 4-1

Estimating Central Tendency with Histograms

Histograms and frequency polygons allow us to see the likely center of a sample's distribution. The arrow points to our guess as to the center of the distribution of the Charity Navigator scores for the largest 40 charities (Haque, 2018). (Note: For clarity, we included the one perfect score of 100 in the bar that ranges from 95 to 99.9.)

EXAMPLE 4.1

For example, the mean Charity Navigator score for the 40 largest charities is calculated by (1) adding the scores for each of the 40 charities in the sample, then (2) dividing by the total number of charities. The scores in the calculations that follow are the actual Charity Navigator scores, rounded to the first decimal place, that were included in the histogram in Figure 4-1. They are arranged in order of largest to smallest charities among the top 40.

- The **mean** is the arithmetic average of a group of scores. It is calculated by summing all the scores in a data set and then dividing this sum by the total number of scores.

> **STEP 1: Add all of the scores together.**

$$97.9 + 94.1 + 90.9 + 88.8 + 88.0 + 90.9 + 85.4 + 71.5 + 100 + 92.9$$
$$+ 83.6 + 84.1 + 91.3 + 88.3 + 98.2 + 84.4 + 89.9 + 92.2 + 98.2 + 86.4$$
$$+ 92.6 + 90.1 + 97.2 + 97.2 + 89.4 + 88.5 + 89.9 + 94.7 + 87.6 + 81.5$$
$$+ 97.9 + 88.7 + 90.1 + 86.4 + 76.3 + 94.5 + 92.9 + 93.9 + 96.7 + 90.2$$

> **STEP 2: Divide the sum of all scores by the total number of scores.**

In this case, we divide 3613.3, the sum of all scores, by 40, the number of scores in this sample:

$$3613.3/40 = 90.333 \quad ●$$

FIGURE 4-2

The Mean as the Fulcrum of the Data

The mean 90.33 is the balancing point for all the scores for the 40 largest organizations rated by Charity Navigator. Mathematically, the scores always balance around the mean for any sample.

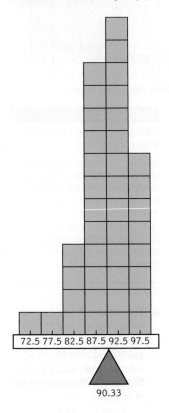

Visual Representations of the Mean Think of the mean as the visual point that perfectly balances two sides of a distribution. For example, the mean score of 90.33 is represented visually as the point that perfectly balances that distribution, as you can see in the Figure 4-2 histogram.

The Mean Expressed by Symbolic Notation Symbolic notation may sound more difficult than it really is. After all, you just calculated a mean without symbolic notation and without a formula. Fortunately, we need to understand only a handful of symbols to express the ideas necessary to understand statistics.

Here are the several symbols that represent the mean. For the mean of a sample, statisticians typically use M or $\overline{X}$. In this text, we use M; many other texts also use M, but some use $\overline{X}$ (pronounced "X bar"). For a population, statisticians use the Greek letter μ (pronounced "mew") to symbolize the mean. (Latin letters such as M tend to refer to numbers based on samples; Greek letters such as μ tend to refer to numbers based on populations.) *The numbers based on samples taken from a population are called* **statistics***; M is a statistic. The numbers based on whole populations are called* **parameters***; μ is a parameter.* Table 4-1 summarizes how these terms are used, and Figure 4-3 presents a mnemonic, or memory aid, for these terms to help you grow accustomed to using them.

TABLE 4-1	The Mean in Symbols

The mean of a sample is an example of a statistic, whereas the mean of a population is an example of a parameter. The symbols we use depend on whether we are referring to the mean of a sample or a population.

Number	Used for	Symbol	Pronounced
Statistic	Sample	M or $\overline{X}$	"M" or "X bar"
Parameter	Population	μ	"Mew"

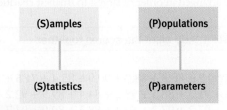

FIGURE 4-3

Samples and Parameters

Use this memory trick to remember the distinction between samples and parameters. The letter *s* means that numbers based on (*s*)amples are called (*s*)tatistics. The letter *p* means that numbers based on (*p*)opulations are called (*p*)arameters.

- A **statistic** is a number based on a sample taken from a population; statistics are usually symbolized by Latin letters.

- A **parameter** is a number based on the whole population; parameters are usually symbolized by Greek letters.

The formula to calculate the mean of a sample uses the symbol M on the left side of the equation; the right side describes how to perform the calculation. A single score is typically symbolized as X. We know that we're summing all the scores—all the Xs—so the first step is to use the summation sign, Σ (pronounced "sigma"), to indicate that we're summing a list of scores. As you might guess, the full expression for summing all the scores would be ΣX or "the sum of X." This symbol combination instructs us to add up all of the Xs in the sample.

Here are step-by-step instructions for constructing the equations:

Step 1: Add up all of the scores in the sample. In statistical notation, this is ΣX.
Step 2: Divide the total of all of the scores by the total number of scores.

The total number of scores in a sample is typically represented by N. (Note that the capital letter N is typically used when we refer to the number of scores in the entire data set; if we break the sample down into smaller parts, as we'll see in later chapters, we typically use the lowercase letter n.) The full equation would be:

$$M = \frac{\Sigma X}{N}$$

MASTERING THE FORMULA

4-1: The formula for the mean is: $M = \dfrac{\Sigma X}{N}$. To calculate the mean, we add up every score and then divide by the total number of scores.

EXAMPLE 4.2

Let's look at the mean for the Charity Navigator data that we considered earlier in Example 4.1.

> STEP 1: Add up every score.

The sum of all scores, as we calculated previously, is 3613.3.

> STEP 2: Divide the sum of all scores by the total number of scores.

In this case, we divide the sum of all scores, 3613.3, by the total number of scores, 40. The result is 90.33, rounded to two decimal places from 90.333.

Here's how it would look as a formula:

$$M = \frac{\Sigma X}{N} = \frac{3613.3}{40} = 90.33$$

Language Alert! As demonstrated here, almost all symbols are italicized, but the actual numerical values of the statistics are not italicized. In addition, changing a symbol from uppercase to lowercase often indicates a change in meaning. When you practice calculating means using this formula, be sure to italicize the symbols and use capital letters for M, X, and N. ●

Median: The Middle Score

● The **median** is the middle score of all the scores in a sample when the scores are arranged in ascending order. If there is no single middle score, the median is the mean of the two middle scores.

The second most common measure of central tendency is the median. *The **median** is the middle score of all the scores in a sample when the scores are arranged in ascending order.* We can think of the median as the 50th percentile. The American Psychological Association (APA) suggests abbreviating *median* by writing *Mdn*. APA style, by the way, is used across the social and behavioral sciences in many countries, so this would be a good time to get used to it.

To determine the median, follow these steps:

Step 1: Line up all the scores in ascending order.

Step 2: Find the middle score. With an odd number of scores, there will be an actual middle score. With an even number of scores, there will be no actual middle score. In this case, calculate the mean of the two middle scores.

Don't bother with a formula when a distribution has only a few data points. Just list the numbers from lowest to highest and note which score has the same number of scores above it and below it. The calculation is easy even when a distribution has many data points. Divide the number of scores (N) by 2 and add 1/2—that is, 0.5. That number is the ordinal position (rank) of the median, or middle score. As illustrated below, simply count that many places over from the start of the scores and report that number.

EXAMPLE 4.3

Here is an example with an odd number of scores (representing the Charity Navigator scores for the 40 largest charities plus one extreme score, the lowest score in the whole data set, 14.5). Here are the 41 scores:

> 97.9 94.1 90.9 88.8 88.0 90.9 85.4 71.5 100   92.9
> 83.6 84.1 91.3 88.3 98.2 84.4 89.9 92.2 98.2 86.4
> 92.6 90.1 97.2 97.2 89.4 88.5 89.9 94.7 87.6 81.5
> 97.9 88.7 90.1 86.4 76.3 94.5 92.9 93.9 96.7 90.2 14.5

> **STEP 1: Arrange the scores in ascending order:**

> 14.5 71.5 76.3 81.5 83.6 84.1 84.4 85.4 86.4 86.4
> 87.6 88.0 88.3 88.5 88.7 88.8 89.4 89.9 89.9 90.1
> 90.1 90.2 90.9 90.9 91.3 92.2 92.6 92.9 92.9 93.9
> 94.1 94.5 94.7 96.7 97.2 97.2 97.9 97.9 98.2 98.2 100

> **STEP 2: Find the middle score.**

To do this, first we count. There are 41 scores: $41/2 = 20.5$. If we add 0.5 to this result, we get 21. Therefore, the median is the 21st score. We now count across to the 21st score. The median is 90.1. ●

EXAMPLE 4.4

Here is an example with an even number of scores. We omitted the extreme score of 14.5.

> STEP 1: Arrange the scores in ascending order.

The data are now:

71.5 76.3 81.5 83.6 84.1 84.4 85.4 86.4 86.4 87.6
88.0 88.3 88.5 88.7 88.8 89.4 89.9 89.9 90.1 90.1
90.2 90.9 90.9 91.3 92.2 92.6 92.9 92.9 93.9 94.1
94.5 94.7 96.7 97.2 97.2 97.9 97.9 98.2 98.2 100

> STEP 2: Find the middle score.

First, we count the scores. There are 40. We then divide the number of scores by 2: 40/2 = 20. If we add 0.5 to this result, we get 20.5; therefore, the median is the average of the 20th and 21st scores. The 20th and 21st scores are 90.1 and 90.2. The median is their mean—the mean of 90.1 and 90.2 is 90.15. ●

Mode: The Most Common Score

The *mode* is perhaps the easiest of the three measures of central tendency to calculate. *The **mode** is the most common score of all the scores in a sample.* It is readily picked out on a frequency table, a histogram, or a frequency polygon. Like the median, the APA style for the mode does not have a symbol—in fact, it doesn't even have an abbreviation. When reporting modes, just write: "The mode is . . . ."

Mean, Median, Mode, and Four Laurens on *The Bachelor* In a recent season of *The Bachelor*, there were lots of interesting data points, including the fact that one contestant vying for Ben Higgins's heart listed her job as "chicken enthusiast" (Shechet, 2015). But what's wrong with this headline: "Average Age of the New Bachelor Cast Is 25, Median Name Is 'Lauren'"? It makes sense to calculate a mean for this younger-than-usual cast. But name is a categorical variable, so it wouldn't make sense to determine a "median" name. The four Laurens actually represent the mode among the 28 names. Perhaps it was inevitable that a Lauren won. (It didn't last.)

● The **mode** is the most common score of all the scores in a sample.

EXAMPLE 4.5

Let's determine the mode for the Charity Navigator data. Remember that each score represents the charity's financial health, transparency, and accountability. The mode can be found by looking through the ordered list of scores to see if some scores occur more than once. Here, we have circled scores that occur more than once. There are eight scores that occur twice, so technically there are eight modes.

71.5 76.3 81.5 83.6 84.1 84.4 85.4 (86.4 86.4) 87.6
88.0 88.3 88.5 88.7 88.8 89.4 (89.9 89.9)(90.1 90.1)
90.2 (90.9 90.9) 91.3 92.2 92.6 (92.9 92.9) 93.9 94.1
94.5 94.7 96.7 (97.2 97.2)(97.9 97.9)(98.2 98.2) 100

But this is not very useful. In cases with multiple modes across a range of scores or when there is no mode, it is more helpful to look at a grouped frequency distribution like the one in Figure 4-1 on p. 93. You can see that the bar for the scores between 90 and 94.9 includes the most scores, a total of 14 scores. So, in this case the mode is 90–94.9. ●

In the example above we reported the most common interval as the mode. When there is more than one mode, whether a single score or an interval, we report both, or all, of the most common scores. *When a distribution of scores has one mode, we refer to it as **unimodal.** When a distribution has two modes, we call it **bimodal.** When a distribution has more than two modes, we call it **multimodal.*** For example, the distribution of Charity Navigator scores is unimodal and the distribution of ages of girls and women named Violet in the United States is bimodal, as illustrated in Figure 4-4.

As demonstrated in the Charity Navigator and baby name examples, the mode can be used with scale data; however, it is more commonly used with nominal data. For example, the British newspaper *The Guardian* (Rogers, 2013) published maps based on census data that showed how residents of England and Wales typically commute to work. It reported that 3.5% work at home; 10.5% use public transportation; 40.4% commute by car; 0.5% ride a motorcycle; 1.9% ride a bicycle; 0.3% take a taxi; and 6.9% walk. In this data set, the modal commute is by car. (Note that this doesn't add up to 100 because the remaining people were not employed.)

- A **unimodal** distribution has one mode, or most common score.
- A **bimodal** distribution has two modes, or most common scores.
- A **multimodal** distribution has more than two modes, or most common scores.

FIGURE 4-4

The Bimodal Ages of Women Named Violet

With a bimodal or multimodal distribution, neither the mean nor the median is representative of the data. The ages of girls and women named Violet form a bimodal distribution (Silver & McCann, 2014). If your name is Violet, you're likely to be elderly or a child. One quarter of Violets were born before 1936, and another quarter have been born since 2010. In the intervening years, far fewer babies were named Violet each year, with almost none in the 1970s and 1980s. So, the median age for women named Violet is just over 50, but there are almost no 50-year-old women with that name.

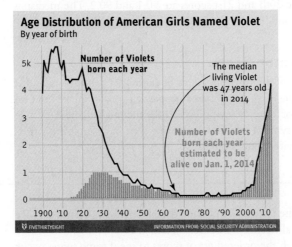

Age Distribution of American Girls Named Violet
By year of birth

How Outliers Affect Measures of Central Tendency

The mean is not the best measure of central tendency when the data are skewed by one or a few statistical outliers—extreme scores that are either very high or very low in comparison with the other scores. You may remember that we calculated two medians for the Charity Navigator. One median, 90.15, was for an even number of scores, the original 40 scores for the top 40 largest organizations. One median, 90.1,

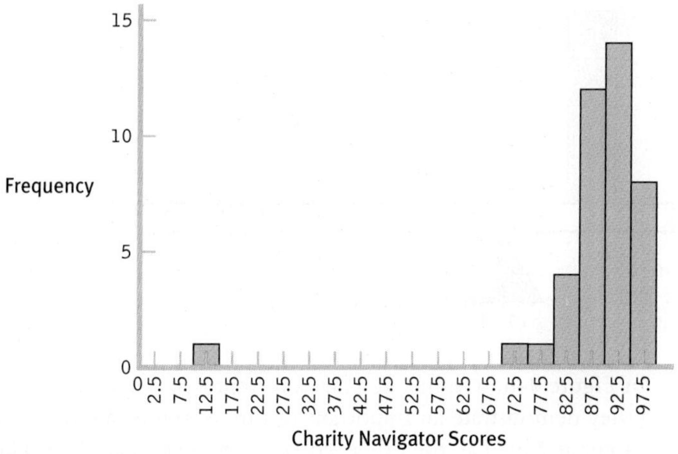

FIGURE 4-5

Histogram of the Charity Navigator Data with the Lowest-Rated Charity Included

Charity Navigator gave its lowest rating, 14.5, to an organization that supports medical patients and their families. As you can see from this histogram, in the context of the data from the largest 40 organizations, 14.5 can be considered an extreme score, an outlier.

was for an odd number of scores, the 40 original scores plus the lowest score in the entire data set, 14.5. Extreme scores like 14.5 are called outliers. The median—the middle score of the distribution—is not affected by outliers in such a drastic way. In this example, the median decreases from 90.15 without the outlier to 90.1 with the outlier—a tiny difference. But with the addition of the outlier, the mean decreases from 90.33 to 88.48. The outlier led to a decrease of 0.05 in the median, but a drop of almost 2 in the mean. The medians for the two distributions are almost identical, whereas the means have a noticeable gap between them.

EXAMPLE 4.6

To demonstrate the effect of outliers on the mean, as well as the median's resistance to the effect of outliers, let's take a look at a more extreme example. The Mundi Index estimates compare how many physicians there are per 1000 people in different countries (a statistic called *physician density*). We'll focus on the top five cases.

San Marino	47.35
Cuba	6.40
Greece	6.04
Monaco	5.81
Belarus	4.87

To get a sense of overall physician density, we might want to calculate a measure of central tendency for these five countries. We'll use the formula to get a little more practice with the symbols of statistics.

$$M = \frac{\Sigma X}{N} = \frac{(47.35 + 6.40 + 6.04 + 5.81 + 4.87)}{5} = \frac{70.47}{5} = 14.09$$

FIGURE 4-6

Outliers and the Mean

With the physician density data, the mean of 14.09 is far above the lowest four scores yet well below the highest. San Marino's score, an outlier, pulls the mean higher, even among the other countries with a high physician density. With such an extreme outlier, the mean does not do a good job of representing the story that these data tell.

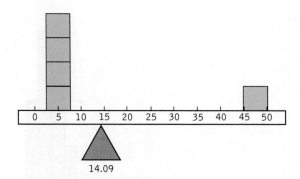

In Figure 4-6, weights are placed to represent each of the scores in the sample, and they demonstrate an important feature of the mean. Like a seesaw, the mean is the point at which all the other scores are perfectly balanced. The physician density scores range from 4.87 to 47.35 and demonstrate the problem with using the mean when there is an outlier: The mean is not typical for any of the five countries in this sample, even though the seesaw is perfectly balanced if we put its fulcrum at the mean of 14.09.

We can't help but notice that the tiny country of San Marino (an enclave within Italy; population 33,000) is very different from the other countries. Four of the scores are between 4.87 and 6.40 physicians per 1000 people, a much smaller range. But San Marino enjoys 47.35 physicians per 1000 people. When there is an outlier like San Marino, it is important to consider what this score does to the mean, especially if we have only a few observations. ●

EXAMPLE 4.7

When we eliminate San Marino's score, the data are now 6.40, 6.04, 5.81, and 4.87, and the new mean is:

$$M = \frac{\Sigma X}{N} = \frac{23.12}{4} = 5.78$$

MASTERING THE CONCEPT

4-2: The mean is the most common indicator of central tendency, but it is not always the best. When there is an outlier or there are few observations, it is usually better to use the median.

The new mean of these scores, 5.78, is a good deal lower than the original mean of the scores that included San Marino's outlier. We see from Figure 4-7 that this new mean, like the original mean, marks the point at which all other scores are perfectly balanced around it. However, this new mean is more representative of the scores: 5.78 is a more typical score for these four countries. Pay attention to outliers; they usually tell an interesting story!

FIGURE 4-7

The Mean Without the Outlier

When the outlier—San Marino—is omitted from the physician density data, the mean becomes more representative of the actual scores in the sample.

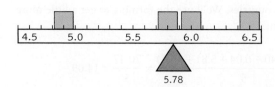

Being Fair with Central Tendency

An ethical researcher thinks carefully about the best way to report the center of her or his data. Different measures of central tendency can lead to different conclusions, but when a decision needs to be made, the choice is usually between the mean and the median. The mean usually wins, especially when there are many observations—but it doesn't always. When distributions are skewed by outliers such as San Marino in the physician density example, or when there are only a handful of available observations, the median may provide a better sense of a distribution's central tendency.

The mode is generally used in three situations: (1) when one particular score dominates a distribution; (2) when the distribution is bimodal or multimodal; and (3) when the data are nominal. When you are uncertain as to which measure is the best indicator of central tendency, be transparent and report all three.

Central tendency communicates an enormous amount of information with a single number, so it is not surprising that measures of central tendency are among the most widely reported descriptive statistics. Unfortunately, consumers can be tricked by reports that use the mean instead of the median. When you hear a report about the central tendency of housing prices, for example, first notice whether it is reporting an average (mean) or a median. You can see an example of a celebrity outlier in the housing market in the photograph on the right.

Kevin Mazur/WireImage/GettyImages

Celebrity Outliers Reports of the cost of a typical home depend on whether the mean or the median is reported. For example, performing artist Beyoncé bought a $5.9 million home in Houston, Texas, for her mother, Tina Knowles. The 23,562 square foot mansion has 8 bedrooms and 12 bathrooms! According to the real estate Web site Trulia.com, the median home price in Houston around the time Beyoncé bought the house was $88,693 and the mean was $318,377. Beyoncé's purchase was an outlier for Houston; such a purchase explains why the mean is much higher than the median for home prices in most cities. Extreme outlier purchases boost the mean, but do not affect the median.

CHECK YOUR LEARNING

Reviewing the Concepts

> The central tendency of a distribution is the one number that best describes what is typical in that distribution (often its high point).

> The three measures of central tendency are the mean (arithmetic average), the median (middle score), and the mode (most frequently occurring score).

> The mean is the most commonly used measure of central tendency, but the median is preferred when the distribution is skewed.

> The symbols used in statistics have very specific meanings; changing a symbol even slightly can change its meaning a great deal.

> Ethical researchers report the median rather than the mean in cases in which there is an extreme outlier.

continued on next page

| Clarifying the Concepts | **4-1** | What is the difference between statistics and parameters? |
| | **4-2** | Does an outlier have the greatest effect on the mean, the median, or the mode? Explain your answer. |

Calculating the Statistics	**4-3**	Calculate the mean, median, and mode of the following sets of numbers.
		a. 10 8 22 5 6 1 19 8 13 12 8
		b. 122.5 123.8 121.2 125.8 120.2 123.8 120.5 119.8 126.3 123.6
		c. 0.100 0.866 0.781 0.555 0.222 0.245 0.234

| Applying the Concepts | **4-4** | Let's examine fictional data for 20 seniors in college. Each score represents the number of nights a student spends socializing in 1 week: |

1 0 1 2 5 3 2 3 1 3 1 7 2 3 2 2 2 0 4 6

a. Using the formula, calculate the mean of these scores.

b. If the researcher reported the mean of these scores as an estimate for the whole university population, what symbol would she use for the mean? Why?

c. If the researcher were interested only in the scores of these 20 students, what symbol would she use for the mean? Why?

d. What is the median of these scores?

e. What is the mode of these scores?

f. Are the median and mean similar to or different from each other? What does this similarity or difference tell you about the distribution of scores?

4-5 Savvy companies can use their knowledge of outliers to trick consumers. For example, television networks need high average ratings to attract advertising dollars; the U.S. network NBC aired the Republican presidential primary debate in January 2012, a show that should have been categorized as "special programming." A *New York Times* article explained the trickery: "Careful viewers noticed that the debate was labeled a regular edition of the network's ratings-challenged newsmagazine program, 'Rock Center with Brian Williams'—one that, as it turned out, just happened to double the show's usual audience to just over 7.1 million viewers" (Carter, 2012). In your own words, explain why this labeling would be useful to NBC.

Solutions to these Check Your Learning questions can be found in Appendix D.

Measures of Variability

The zipper company YKK understands that a high-quality product requires low variability. Low variability lets you trust that your car will start, your computer won't crash, and your zipper will work. *Variability is a numerical way of describing how much spread there is in a distribution.* One way to numerically describe the variability of a distribution is by computing its *range*. A second and more common way to describe variability is by computing *variance* and its square root, known as *standard deviation*.

- **Variability** is a numerical way of describing how much spread there is in a distribution.

- The **range** is a measure of variability calculated by subtracting the lowest score (the minimum) from the highest score (the maximum).

Range

The range is the easiest measure of variability to calculate. *The **range** is a measure of variability calculated by subtracting the lowest score (the minimum) from the highest score (the maximum). Maximum and minimum* are sometimes substituted in this formula to describe the highest and lowest scores, and some statistical computer programs abbreviate these as *max* and *min*. The range is represented in a formula as:

$$\text{range} = X_{highest} - X_{lowest}$$

Here are scores for the lengths of the 40 Charity Navigator scores that we discussed earlier in the chapter:

71.5	76.3	81.5	83.6	84.1	84.4	85.4	86.4	86.4	87.6
88.0	88.3	88.5	88.7	88.8	89.4	89.9	89.9	90.1	90.1
90.2	90.9	90.9	91.3	92.2	92.6	92.9	92.9	93.9	94.1
94.5	94.7	96.7	97.2	97.2	97.9	97.9	98.2	98.2	100

EXAMPLE 4.8

We can determine the highest and lowest scores either by reading through the data or, more easily, by glancing at the frequency table for these data.

> **STEP 1: Determine the highest score.**

In this case, the highest score is 100.

> **STEP 2: Determine the lowest score.**

In this case, the lowest score is 71.5.

> **STEP 3: Calculate the range by subtracting the lowest score from the highest score:**

$$\text{range} = X_{highest} - X_{lowest} = 100 - 71.5 = 28.5$$

The range can be a useful first indicator of variability, but it is influenced only by the highest and lowest scores. All the other scores in between could be clustered near the highest score, huddled near the center, spread out evenly, or have some other unexpected pattern. We can't know based only on the range. In addition, the range is highly sensitive to outliers. If we included the extreme Charity Navigator score of 14.5, the range increases drastically from 28.5 to 85.5. ●

The Interquartile Range

The range is completely dependent on the maximum and minimum scores. For example, the $17 million home at the high end or the shack at the low end of the

- The **interquartile range** is a measure of the distance between the first and third quartiles.

- The **first quartile** marks the 25th percentile of a data set.

- The **third quartile** marks the 75th percentile of a data set.

distribution will skew a distribution of home prices. Whenever there are outliers, the range will be an exaggerated measure of the variability. Fortunately, we have an alternative to the range: the interquartile range.

*The **interquartile range** is a measure of the distance between the first and third quartiles.* As we learned earlier, the median marks the 50th percentile of a data set. Similarly, *the **first** quartile marks the 25th percentile of a data set,* and *the **third quartile** marks the 75th percentile of a data set.* Essentially, the first and third quartiles are the medians of the two halves of the data—the half below the median and the half above the median. We calculate the first quartile and the third quartile in a similar manner to how we calculate the median. Here are the steps for finding the interquartile range:

Step 1: Calculate the median.

Step 2: Look at all of the scores below the median. The median of these scores, the lower half of the scores, is the first quartile, often called Q1 for short.

Step 3: Look at all of the scores above the median. The median of these scores, the upper half of the scores, is the third quartile, often called Q3 for short.

Step 4: Subtract Q1 from Q3. The interquartile range, often abbreviated as *IQR*, is the difference between the first and third quartiles: $IQR = Q3 - Q1$.

Because the interquartile range is the distance between the 25th and 75th percentile of the data, it can be thought of as the range of the middle 50% of the data.

Many graphs are based on the interquartile range. Remember when we introduced violin plots in Chapter 3? We described the thick vertical line as representing the middle 50% of scores. This middle 50% is the interquartile range.

The interquartile range has an important advantage over the range. Because it is not based on the minimum and maximum—the most extreme scores—it is less susceptible to outliers. Let's look at an example.

EXAMPLE 4.9

Here are the data for the Charity Navigator example.

71.5	76.3	81.5	83.6	84.1	84.4	85.4	86.4	86.4	87.6
88.0	88.3	88.5	88.7	88.8	89.4	89.9	89.9	90.1	90.1
90.2	90.9	90.9	91.3	92.2	92.6	92.9	92.9	93.9	94.1
94.5	94.7	96.7	97.2	97.2	97.9	97.9	98.2	98.2	100

Earlier we calculated the median of these 40 scores as the mean of the 20th and 21st scores, 90.15. We now take the first 20 scores: 71.5, 76.3, 81.5, 83.6, 84.1, 84.4, 85.4, 86.4, 86.4, 87.6, 88.0, 88.3, 88.5, 88.7, 88.8, 89.4, 89.9, 89.9, 90.1, and 90.1. If we divide the number of scores, 20, by 2 and add 1/2, we get 10.5. The median of these 20 scores—the first quartile—is the mean of the 10th and 11th scores, 87.6 and 88.0, respectively. So, the first quartile is 87.8.

We'll do the same with the second half of the scores: 90.2, 90.9, 90.9, 91.3, 92.2, 92.6, 92.9, 92.9, 93.9, 94.1, 94.5, 94.7, 96.7, 97.2, 97.2, 97.9, 97.9, 98.2, 98.2, and 100. Again, there are 20 scores, so the median of these scores—the third quartile— is also the mean of the 10th and 11th scores. This time the 10th and 11th scores are 94.1 and 94.5, respectively, so the third quartile is 94.3. Earlier we calculated the range, the maximum minus the minimum: range $X_{highest} - X_{lowest} = 100 - 71.5 = 28.5$. However, the interquartile range is the third quartile minus the first quartile: $IQR = Q3 - Q1 = 94.3 - 87.8 = 6.5$.

The interquartile range is not influenced by the most extreme scores (like the minimum and maximum values), so it is a more valid measure of variability for these data than is the range. The interquartile range, unlike the range, is resistant to outliers. Imagine if we included the extreme score for the lowest-rated charity, 14.5. The range would increase dramatically from 28.5 to 85.5, but the interquartile range would be rather unaffected. ●

Variance

Variance is the average of the squared deviations from the mean. When something varies, it must vary from (or be different from) some standard. That standard is the mean. So when we compute variance, that number describes how far a distribution varies around the mean. A small number indicates a small amount of spread or deviation around the mean, and a larger number indicates a great deal of spread or deviation around the mean. The YKK zipper company, for example, was always aiming at a lower number because it meant high reliability—products you can trust.

● **Variance** is the average of the squared deviations from the mean.

EXAMPLE 4.10

Students who seek therapy at university counseling centers often do not attend many sessions. For example, in one study, the median number of therapy sessions was 3 and the mean was 4.6 (Hatchett, 2003). Let's examine the spread of scores for a sample of five fictional students: 1, 2, 4, 4, and 10 therapy sessions, with a mean of 4.2. We find out how far each score deviates from the mean by subtracting the mean from every score. First, we label with an X the column that lists the scores. Here, the second column includes the results we get when we subtract the mean from each score, or $X - M$. We call each of these a **deviation from the mean** (or just a *deviation*)—*the amount that a score in a sample differs from the mean of the sample.*

● A **deviation from the mean** is the amount that a score in a sample differs from the mean of the sample; also called a *deviation*.

X	$X - M$
1	−3.2
2	−2.2
4	−0.2
4	−0.2
10	5.8

But we can't just take the mean of the deviations. If we do (and if you try this, don't forget the signs—negative and positive), we get 0—every time. Are you surprised? Remember, the mean is the point at which all scores are perfectly balanced. Mathematically, the scores *have* to balance out. Yet we know that there *is* variability among these scores. The number representing the amount of variability is certainly not 0!

When we ask students for ways to eliminate the negative signs, two suggestions typically come up: (1) Take the absolute value of the deviations, thus making them all positive, or (2) square all the scores, again making them all positive. It turns out that the latter, squaring all the deviations, is how statisticians solve this problem. Once we square the deviations, we can take their average and get a measure of variability. Later (using a beautifully descriptive term created by our students), we will "*unsquare*" those deviations to calculate the standard deviation.

To recap:

> **STEP 1: Subtract the mean from every score.**

We call these *deviations from the mean*.

> **STEP 2: Square every deviation from the mean.**

We call these *squared deviations*.

> **STEP 3: Sum all of the squared deviations.**

This is often called the *sum of squared deviations,* or the *sum of squares* for short.

> **STEP 4: Divide the sum of squares by the total number in the sample (*N*).**

This number represents the mathematical definition of variance—the average of the squared deviations from the mean.

Let's try it. To calculate the variance for the therapy session data, we add a third column to record the squares of each of the deviations. Then we add all of these numbers up to compute the ***sum of squares*** *(symbolized as* SS*), the sum of each score's squared deviation from the mean.* In this case, the sum of the squared deviations is 48.80, so the average squared deviation is 48.80/5 = 9.76. Thus, the variance equals 9.76.

● The **sum of squares**, symbolized as *SS*, is the sum of each score's squared deviation from the mean.

X	$X - M$	$(X - M)^2$
1	−3.20	10.24
2	−2.20	4.84
4	−0.20	0.04
4	−0.20	0.04
10	5.80	33.64
		48.80

TABLE 4-2 Variance and Standard Deviation in Symbols

The variance or standard deviation of a sample is an example of a statistic, whereas the variance or standard deviation of a population is an example of a parameter. The symbols we use depend on whether we are referring to the spread of a sample or of a population.

Number	Used for . . .	Standard Deviation Symbol	Pronounced	Variance Symbol	Pronounced
Statistic	Sample	SD or s	As written	SD^2, s^2, or MS	Letters as written; if there is a superscript 2, the term is followed by "squared" (e.g., "ess squared")
Parameter	Population	σ	"Sigma"	σ^2	"Sigma squared"

Language Alert! We need a few more symbols to use symbolic notation to represent the idea of variance. Each of these symbols represents the same idea (variance) applied to slightly different situations. The symbols that represent the variance of a *sample* include SD^2, s^2, and MS. The first two symbols, SD^2 and s^2, both represent the words *standard deviation squared*. The symbolic notation MS comes from the words *mean square* (referring to the average of the squared deviations). We'll use SD^2 at this point, but we will alert you when we switch to other symbols for variance later. The variance of the *sample* uses all three symbolic notations; however, the variance of a *population* uses just one symbol: σ^2 (pronounced "sigma squared"). Table 4-2 summarizes the symbols and language used to describe different versions of the mean and variance, but we will keep reminding you as we go along.

We already know all the other symbols needed to calculate variance: X to indicate the individual scores, M to indicate the mean, and N to indicate the sample size.

$$SD^2 = \frac{\Sigma(X - M)^2}{N}$$

As you can see, variance is really just a mean—the mean of squared deviations. ●

Standard Deviation

Language Alert! Variance and standard deviation refer to the same core idea. The standard deviation is more useful because it *is the typical amount that each score varies from the mean.* Mathematically, the **standard deviation** *is the square root of the average of the squared deviations from the mean, or, more simply, the square root of the variance.* The beauty of the standard deviation—compared to the variance—is that we can understand it at a glance.

MASTERING THE FORMULA

4-4: The formula for variance is: $SD^2 = \frac{\Sigma(X - M)^2}{N}$. To calculate variance, subtract the mean (M) from every score (X) to calculate deviations from the mean; then square these deviations, sum them, and divide by the sample size (N). By summing the squared deviations and dividing by sample size, we are taking their mean.

● The **standard deviation** is the square root of the average of the squared deviations from the mean; it is the typical amount that each score varies, or deviates, from the mean.

EXAMPLE 4.11

The numbers of therapy sessions for the five students were 1, 2, 4, 4, and 10, with a mean of 4.2. The typical score does not vary from the mean by 9.76. The variance is based on squared deviations, not deviations, so it is too large. When we ask our students how to solve this problem, they invariably say, "Unsquare it," and that's just what we do. We take the square root of variance to come up with a much more useful number, the standard deviation. The square root of 9.76 is 3.12. Now we have a number that "makes sense" to us. We can now say that the typical number of therapy sessions for students in this sample is 4.2 and the typical amount a student varies from that is 3.12.

As you read journal articles, you often will see the mean and standard deviation reported as: ($M = 4.2$, $SD = 3.12$). A glance at the original data (1, 2, 4, 4, 10) tells us that these numbers make sense: 4.2 does seem to be approximately in the center, and scores do seem to vary from 4.2 by roughly 3.12. The score of 10 is a bit of an outlier—but not so much of one; the mean and the standard deviation are still somewhat representative of the typical score and typical deviation.

We didn't actually need a formula to get the standard deviation. We just took the square root of the variance. Perhaps you guessed the symbols for standard deviation by just taking the square root of those for variance. With a sample, standard deviation is either SD or s. With a population, standard deviation is σ. Table 4-2 presents this information concisely. We can write the formula showing how standard deviation is calculated from variance:

$$SD = \sqrt{SD^2}$$

We can also write the formula showing how standard deviation is calculated from the original Xs, M, and N:

$$SD = \sqrt{\frac{\Sigma(X - M)^2}{N}}$$

MASTERING THE FORMULA

4-5: The most basic formula for standard deviation is: $SD = \sqrt{SD^2}$. We simply take the square root of the variance.

MASTERING THE FORMULA

4-6: The full formula for standard deviation is: $SD = \sqrt{\dfrac{\Sigma(X - M)^2}{N}}$. To determine standard deviation, subtract the mean from every score to calculate deviations from the mean. Then, square the deviations from the mean. Sum the squared deviations, then divide by the sample size. Finally, take the square root of the mean of the squared deviations.

CHECK YOUR LEARNING

Reviewing the Concepts

> The simplest way to measure variability is to use the range, which is calculated by subtracting the lowest score from the highest score.

> The interquartile range is calculated by subtracting the score at the 25th percentile from the score at the 75th percentile. It communicates the width of the middle 50% of the data.

> Variance and standard deviation both measure the degree to which scores in a distribution vary from the mean. The standard deviation is simply the square root of the variance: It represents the typical deviation of a score from the mean.

Clarifying the Concepts

4-6 In your own words, what is variability?

4-7 Distinguish the range from the standard deviation. What does each tell us about the distribution?

| Calculating the Statistics | 4-8 | Calculate the range, variance, and standard deviation for the following data sets (the same ones from the section on central tendency). |

a. 10 8 22 5 6 1 19 8 13 12 8

b. 122.5 123.8 121.2 125.8 120.2 123.8 120.5 119.8 126.3 123.6

c. 0.100 0.866 0.781 0.555 0.222 0.245 0.234

| Applying the Concepts | 4-9 | Final exam week is approaching, and students are not eating as well as usual. Four students were asked how many calories of junk food they had consumed between noon and 10:00 P.M. on the day before an exam. The estimated numbers of empty calories, calculated with the help of a nutritional software program, were 450, 670, 1130, and 1460. |

a. Using the formula, calculate the range for these scores.

b. What information can't you glean from the range?

c. Using the formula, calculate the variance for these scores.

d. Using the formula, calculate the standard deviation for these scores.

e. If a researcher were interested only in these four students, which symbols would he use for variance and standard deviation, respectively?

Solutions to these Check Your Learning questions can be found in Appendix D.

f. If another researcher hoped to generalize from these four students to all students at the university, which symbols would she use for variance and standard deviation?

REVIEW OF CONCEPTS

Central Tendency

Three measures of *central tendency* are commonly used in research. When a numeric description, such as a measure of central tendency, describes a sample, it is a *statistic*; when it describes a population, it is a *parameter*. The *mean* is the arithmetic average of the data. The *median* is the midpoint of the data set; 50% of scores fall on either side of the median. The *mode* is the most common score in the data set. When there's one mode, the distribution is *unimodal*; when there are two modes, it's *bimodal*; and when there are three or more modes, it's *multimodal*. The mean is highly influenced by outliers, whereas the median and mode are resistant to outliers. Ethical researchers report the median rather than the mean in cases in which there is an extreme outlier.

Measures of Variability

The *range* is the simplest measure of *variability* to calculate. It is calculated by subtracting the minimum score in a data set from the maximum score. When the median is the preferred measure of central tendency, the interquartile range (IQR) is used, as it provides a better measure of variability than does the range. The IQR is the third quartile, or 75th percentile, minus the first quartile, or 25th percentile. The IQR is the width of the middle 50% of the data set and, unlike the range, is resistant to outliers.

 **LaunchPad**
macmillan learning
Visit LaunchPad to access the e-book and to test your knowledge with LearningCurve.

Variance and standard deviation are much more common measures of variability than the range and interquartile range. They are used when the preferred measure of central tendency is the mean. *Variance* is the average of the squared deviations from the mean. It is calculated by subtracting the mean from every score to get *deviations from the mean*, then squaring each of the deviations. (In future chapters, we will use the *sum of squares* of the deviations when making inferences about a population based on a sample.) *Standard deviation* is the square root of variance. It is the typical amount that a score deviates from the mean.

SPSS

Using the Charity Navigator data, we can use SPSS to identify the descriptive statistics discussed in this chapter. First, enter the data for the 40 scores as seen on the left of the screenshot here (although you won't have the names of the charities beyond the first 20). The full list is on page 93.

To get a numerical description of a variable—in this case, length of video—select: Analyze → Descriptive Statistics → Frequencies. Then select the variable of interest, "Charity Navigator rating," by highlighting it and then

clicking the arrow to move it from the left side to the right side. Then select: Statistics → Mean, Median, Mode, Std deviation, Variance, Range → Continue → OK. As you might have noticed, there are several other descriptive statistics that SPSS can provide (e.g., quartiles, minimum, maximum).

The data and output will look like those on the right side of the screenshot shown here. By default, SPSS will also provide a frequency table in the output.

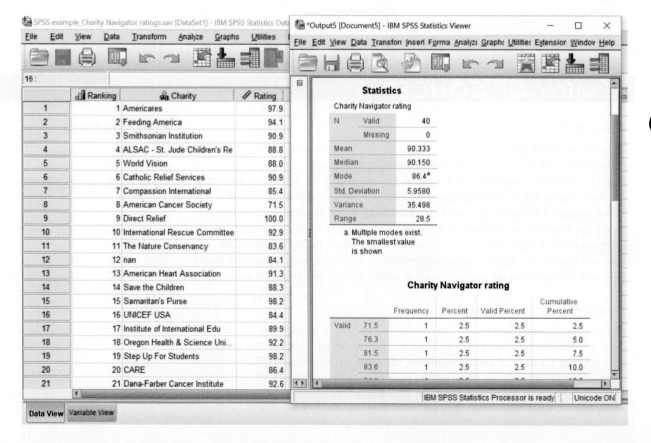

HOW IT WORKS

4.1 CALCULATING THE MEAN

How do we calculate a mean? We looked up the top 15 Vietnamese restaurants in Vancouver on yelp.com. All of these restaurants received very high overall ratings, but from different numbers of reviewers. (Why are these data useful? Well, we might decide that we trust an overall rating more for restaurants with more reviewers who agree that it's great. But of course, we must be cautious because Yelp reviewers are probably not a representative sample.) Below are the numbers of people who reviewed each of these 15 restaurants on Yelp—from Cafe Xu Hue, which has the fewest reviews among these top Vietnamese places, to Phnom Penh, which has the most:

$$423 \quad 123 \quad 50 \quad 78 \quad 43 \quad 98 \quad 139 \quad 53 \quad 78 \quad 69 \quad 112 \quad 120 \quad 74 \quad 39 \quad 130$$

How can we calculate the mean? First, we add up all of the scores:

$$423+123+50+78+43+98+139+53+78+69+112+120+74+39+130=1629$$

Then we divide by 15, the number of scores:

$$1629/15 = 108.60$$

With the formula, we calculate:

$$M = \frac{(423+123+50+78+43+98+139+53+78+69+112+120+74+39+130)}{15} = 108.60$$

4.2 CALCULATING THE MEDIAN

Using the data for numbers of Yelp reviewers for Vietnamese restaurants in Vancouver, how can we calculate the median? The median is either the middle score (for odd numbers of scores) or the average of the two middle scores (for even numbers of scores). We first arrange the data from lowest score to highest score:

$$39 \quad 43 \quad 50 \quad 53 \quad 69 \quad 74 \quad 78 \quad 78 \quad 98 \quad 112 \quad 120 \quad 123 \quad 130 \quad 139 \quad 423$$

With 15 scores (an odd number), there is one middle score, the 8th score. The 8th score is 78. The median is 78.

4.3 CALCULATING THE MODE

How can we calculate the mode for the "numbers of Yelp reviewers" data? The mode is the most common score. We can determine the mode for these data by looking at the frequency distribution. Two restaurants had 78 reviewers. The mode is 78.

4.4 CALCULATING VARIANCE

How can we calculate variance for the "numbers of Yelp reviewers" data? To calculate variance for these data, we first subtract the mean, 108.60, from every score. We then square these deviations. These calculations are shown in the table on the next page.

Score	$(X - M)$	$(X - M)^2$
39	−69.6	4844.16
43	−65.6	4303.36
50	−58.6	3433.96
53	−55.6	3091.36
69	−39.6	1568.16
74	−34.6	1197.16
78	−30.6	936.36
78	−30.6	936.36
98	−10.6	112.36
112	3.4	11.56
120	11.4	129.96
123	14.4	207.36
130	21.4	457.96
139	30.4	924.16
423	314.4	98847.36

We then add all of the scores in the third column to get the sum of squared deviations, or the sum of squares. This sum is 121,001.60.

We can use the formula to complete the calculations:

$$SD^2 = \frac{\Sigma(X - M)^2}{N} = \frac{121,001.60}{15} = 8066.773$$

The variance is 8066.773.

4.5 CALCULATING STANDARD DEVIATION

How can we calculate standard deviation for the data on the number of Yelp reviews per restaurant? The standard deviation is the square root of the variance. For these data, we calculate standard deviation directly from the variance we calculated above using this formula:

$$SD = \sqrt{SD^2} = \sqrt{8066.773} = 89.815$$

The standard deviation is 89.82.

EXERCISES

The solutions to the odd-numbered exercises can be found in Appendix C.

Clarifying the Concepts

4.1   Define the three measures of central tendency: mean, median, and mode.

4.2   The mean can be assessed visually and arithmetically. Describe each method.

4.3   Explain how the mean mathematically balances the distribution.

4.4   Explain what is meant by unimodal, bimodal, and multimodal distributions.

4.5   Explain why the mean might not be useful for a bimodal or multimodal distribution.

4.6   What is an outlier?

4.7 How do outliers affect the mean and the median?

4.8 In which situations is the mode typically used?

4.9 How does the interquartile range differ from the range?

4.10 Using your knowledge of how to calculate the median, describe how to calculate the first and third quartiles of your data.

4.11 At what percentile is the first quartile?

4.12 At what percentile is the third quartile?

4.13 Explain the concept of standard deviation in your own words.

4.14 Define the symbols used in the equation for variance:

$$SD^2 = \sqrt{\frac{\Sigma(X-M)^2}{N}}$$

4.15 Why is the standard deviation typically reported, rather than the variance?

4.16 Find the incorrectly used symbol or symbols in each of the following statements or formulas. For each statement or formula, (1) state which symbol(s) is/are used incorrectly, (2) explain why the symbol(s) in the original statement is/are incorrect, and (3) state which symbol(s) *should* be used.

    a. The mean and standard deviation of the sample of reaction times were calculated ($m = 54.2$, $SD^2 = 9.87$).

    b. The mean of the sample of high school student GPAs was $\mu = 3.08$.

    c. range $= X_{highest} - X_{lowest}$

Calculating the Statistics

4.17 Use the following data for this exercise:

    15 34 32 46 22 36 34 28 52 28

    a. Calculate the mean, the median, and the mode.

    b. Add another data point, 112. Calculate the mean, median, and mode again. How does this new data point affect the calculations?

    c. Calculate the range, variance, and standard deviation for the original data.

4.18 Use the following salary data for this exercise:

$44,751	$38,862
$52,000	$51,380
$41,500	$61,774

    a. Calculate the mean, the median, and the mode.

    b. Add another salary, $97,582. Calculate the mean, median, and mode again. How does this new salary affect the calculations?

    c. Calculate the range, variance, and standard deviation for the original salary data.

    d. How does the range change when you include the outlier salary, $97,582?

4.19 The Mount Washington Observatory (MWO) in New Hampshire claims to have the world's worst weather. Below are some data on the weather extremes recorded at the MWO.

Month	Normal Daily Maximum (°F)	Normal Daily Minimum (°F)	Record Low in °F (year)	Peak Wind Gust in Miles per Hour (year)
January	14.0	−3.7	−47 (1934)	173 (1985)
February	14.8	−1.7	−46 (1943)	166 (1972)
March	21.3	5.9	−38 (1950)	180 (1942)
April	29.4	16.4	−20 (1995)	231 (1934)
May	41.6	29.5	−2 (1966)	164 (1945)
June	50.3	38.5	8 (1945)	136 (1949)
July	54.1	43.3	24 (2001)	154 (1996)
August	53.0	42.1	20 (1986)	142 (1954)
September	46.1	34.6	9 (1992)	174 (1979)
October	36.4	24.0	−5 (1939)	161 (1943)
November	27.6	13.6	−20 (1958)	163 (1983)
December	18.5	1.7	−46 (1933)	178 (1980)

    a. Calculate the mean and median normal daily minimum temperature across the year.

    b. Calculate the mean, median, and mode for the record low temperatures.

    c. Calculate the mean, median, and mode for the peak wind-gust data.

    d. When no mode appears in the raw data, we can compute a mode by breaking the data into intervals. How might you do this for the peak wind-gust data?

    e. Calculate the range, variance, and standard deviation for the normal daily minimum temperature across the year.

    f. Calculate the range, variance, and standard deviation for the record low temperatures.

    g. Calculate the range, variance, and standard deviation for the peak wind-gust data.

4.20 Calculate the range and the interquartile range for the following set of data. Explain why they are so different.

> 83 99 103 65 66 77 55 82
>
> 93 93 108 543 72 109 115 85
>
> 92 74 101 98 84

4.21 Calculate the interquartile range for the following set of data:

> 2 5 1 3 3 4 3 6 7 1 4 3 7 2 2 2 8 3 3 12 1

4.22 Using the data presented in Exercise 4.19, calculate the interquartile range for peak wind gust.

4.23 Why is the interquartile range you calculated for the previous exercise so much smaller than the range you calculated in Exercise 4.19?

4.24 Here are recent *U.S. News & World Report* data on acceptance rates at the top 70 national universities. These are the percentages of accepted students out of all students who applied.

> 6.3 14.0 8.9 21.6 40.6 51.2 50.5 69.4 42.4 68.3
>
> 8.5 12.4 18.0 30.4 31.4 51.3 47.5 49.4 54.6 63.5
>
> 7.7 12.8 18.8 25.5 28.0 33.4 38.3 25.0 49.4 56.7
>
> 7.0 10.1 24.3 23.0 32.7 46.0 52.4 31.6 44.7 62.8
>
> 16.3 18.0 16.4 33.3 40.0 35.5 67.6 43.2 57.9 63.3
>
> 9.7 18.4 26.7 39.9 34.6 39.6 46.6 34.5 47.3 61.1
>
> 7.1 16.5 18.1 21.9 34.1 45.7 58.4 63.4 63.0 46.6

a. Calculate the mean of these data, showing that you know how to use the symbols and formula.

b. Determine the median of these data.

c. Describe the variability in these data by computing the range.

Applying the Concepts

4.25 **Mean versus median for salary data:** In Exercises 4.17 and 4.18, we saw how the mean and median changed when an outlier was included in the computations. If you were reporting the "average" salary at a company, how might the mean and the median give different impressions to potential applicants?

4.26 **Mean versus median for temperature data:** For the data in Exercise 4.19, the "normal" daily maximum and minimum temperatures recorded at the Mount Washington Observatory are presented for each month. These are likely to be measures of central tendency for each month over time. Explain why these "normal" temperatures might be calculated as means or medians. What would be the reasoning for using one type of statistic over the other?

4.27 **Mean versus median for depression scores:** A depression research unit recently assessed seven participants chosen at random from the university population. Is the mean or the median a better indicator of the central tendency of these seven participants? Explain your answer.

4.28 **Measures of central tendency for weather data:** The "normal" weather data from the Mount Washington Observatory are broken down by month. Why might you not want to average across all months in a year? How else could you summarize the year?

4.29 **Outliers, central tendency, and data on wind gusts:** There appears to be an outlier in the data for peak wind gust recorded on top of Mount Washington (see the data in Exercise 4.19). Where do you see an outlier and how does excluding this data point affect the different calculations of central tendency?

4.30 **Measures of central tendency for measures of baseball performance:** Here are winning percentages for 11 baseball players for their best 4-year pitching performances:

> 0.755 0.721 0.708 0.773 0.782 0.747
>
> 0.477 0.817 0.617 0.650 0.651

a. What is the mean of these scores?

b. What is the median of these scores?

c. Compare the mean and the median. Does the difference between them suggest that the data are skewed very much?

4.31 **Mean versus median in "real life":** Briefly describe a real-life situation in which the median is preferable to the mean. Give hypothetical numbers for the mean and median in your explanation. Be original! (Don't use home prices or another example from the chapter.)

4.32 **Descriptive statistics in the media:** Find an advertisement for an anti-aging product either online or in the print media—the more unbelievable the claims, the better!

a. What does the ad promise that this product will do for the consumer?

b. What data does it offer for its promised benefits? Does it offer any descriptive statistics or merely testimonials? If it offers descriptive statistics, what are the limitations of what they report?

c. If you were considering this product, what measures of central tendency would you most like to see? Explain your answer, noting why not all measures of central tendency would be helpful.

d. If a friend with no statistical background were considering this product, what would you tell him or her?

4.33 Descriptive statistics in the media: When there is an ad on TV for a body-shaping product (e.g., an abdominal muscle machine), often a person with a wonderful success story is featured in the ad. The statement "Individual results may vary" hints at what kind of data the advertisement may be presenting.

a. What kind of data is being presented in these ads?

b. What statistics could be presented to help inform the public about how much "individual results might vary"?

4.34 Range of data for Canadian TV ratings: Numeris (formerly BBM Canada) collects Canadian television ratings data (en.numeris.ca). The following are the average number of viewers per minute (in thousands) for the top 30 English-language shows for 1 week. The NHL playoffs are listed at 1198, which indicates that an average of 1,198,000 viewers watched per minute. When these data were collected, *Big Bang Theory* was in the number 1 position, with *2 Broke Girls* at number 30.

3117 2935 2216 2128 1785 1735 1616 1602 1548 1519
1513 1476 1462 1263 1201 1198 1193 1189 1186 1155
1117 1102 1079 1057 1036 1034 1008 925 902 887

a. What is the range of these data?

b. What is the interquartile range of these data?

c. How does the IQR you calculated in part (b) differ from the range you calculated in part (a), and why is it different?

4.35 Descriptive statistics for data from the National Survey of Student Engagement: Every year, the National Survey of Student Engagement (NSSE) asks U.S. university students how many 20-page papers they had been assigned. Here are the percentages, for 1 year, of students who said they had been assigned between 5 and 10 twenty-page papers for a sample of 19 universities.

0 5 3 3 1 10 2
2 3 1 2 4   2 1
1 1 4 3 5

a. Calculate the mean of these data using the symbols and formula.

b. Calculate the variance of these data using the symbols and formula; also use columns to show all calculations.

c. Calculate the standard deviation using the symbols and formula.

d. In your own words, describe what the mean and standard deviation of these data tell us about these scores.

4.36 Statistics versus parameters: For each of the following situations, state whether the mean or median would be a statistic or a parameter. Explain your answer.

a. According to Canadian census data, the median family income in British Columbia was $66,970, lower than the national median of $69,860.

b. The stadiums of teams in the English Premier League had a mean capacity of 38,391 fans.

c. The General Social Survey (GSS) includes a vocabulary test in which participants in the U.S. are asked to choose the appropriate synonym from a multiple-choice list of five words (e.g., *beast* with the choices *afraid*, *words*, *large*, *animal*, and *separate*). The mean vocabulary test score was 5.98.

d. The National Survey of Student Engagement (NSSE) asks students at participating U.S. institutions how often they discuss ideas or readings with professors outside of class. Among the 19 universities that made their data public, the mean percentage of students who responded "Very often" was 8%.

4.37 Central tendency and the shapes of distributions: Consider the many possible distributions of grades on a quiz in a statistics class; imagine that the grades could range from 0 to 100. For each of the following situations, give a hypothetical mean and median (i.e., make up a mean and a median that might occur with a distribution that has this shape). Explain your answer.

a. Normal distribution

b. Positively skewed distribution

c. Negatively skewed distribution

4.38 Shapes of distributions, chemistry grades, and first-generation college students: David Laude was a chemistry professor at the University of Texas at Austin (and a former underprepared college student) who developed an intervention that led underprepared students to perform at the same average level as others (Tough, 2014). He started this program because he observed a bimodal distribution of grades, rather than a unimodal distribution with a peak in the middle.

Specifically, "in each class of 500 students, there would be 400 or so who did quite well, clustered around the A and high-B range. They got it. Then there would be a second cluster of perhaps 100 students whose grades were way down at the bottom—Ds and Fs. They didn't get it."

a. Draw a distribution that ranges from F on the left to A on the right and shows what the chemistry grades would look like if the distribution were unimodal with a peak in the center.

b. Draw the distribution that Laude observed in his chemistry classes.

c. Take a guess as to what the mean would be—in terms of a letter grade—for the distribution in part (a) and the distribution in part (b).

d. For which distribution—the one in part (a) or the one in part (b)—is the mean likely to be a better measure of central tendency? Explain your answer.

e. Based on the outcome mentioned above, describe in words what you think the distribution looked like after Laude's intervention.

4.39 Outliers, Hurricane Sandy, and a rat infestation: In a *New York Times* article, reporter Cara Buckley (2013) described the influx of rats inland from the New York City shoreline following the flooding caused by Hurricane Sandy. Buckley interviewed pest-control expert Timothy Wong, who noted that rat infestations could lead to citations for buildings that did not address the problem; yet, she reported, violations had decreased across the city in the wake of the hurricane—just 1996 violations versus 2750 for the same time period a year before. Why? Buckley explained: "After Hurricane Sandy, as of Nov. 1, the Health Department said it stopped issuing violations for rodents in Zone A," the parts of New York City most vulnerable to flooding.

a. If you were to create a monthly average of rat violations over the course of the year before and after Hurricane Sandy, why would you not be able to make comparisons?

b. Explain how the removal of Zone A violations led both to the removal of an outlier and to inaccurate data.

4.40 Outliers, H&M, and designer collaborations: The relatively low-cost Swedish fashion retailer H&M occasionally partners with high-end designers. For example, it collaborated with the Italian designer brand Moschino, and the line quickly sold out. If H&M were to report the average number of sales per item of clothing, why would the designer partnerships, like that with Moschino, inflate the mean number of sales but not the median?

4.41 Central tendency and outliers from growth–chart data: When the average height or average weight of children is plotted to create growth charts, do you think it would be appropriate to use the mean for these data? There are often outliers for height, but why might we not have to be concerned with their effect on these data?

4.42 Teaching assistants, race, and standard deviations: Researchers reported that the race of the teaching assistants (TAs) for a class had an effect on student outcome (Lusher, Campbell, & Carrell, 2015). They reported that "Asian students receive a 2.3% of a standard deviation increase in course grade when the racial composition of the TAs is entirely Asian. Similarly, non-Asian students see a 3.7% of a standard deviation increase in course grade when enrolled in a class with all non-Asian TAs." They hypothesized several reasons for this effect, including that students may see TAs of a similar race as inspiring or may simply be more comfortable learning from someone of the same race. Knowing what you know about standard deviations, explain this finding in your own words. Also, state whether this is a large effect, and explain your answer.

4.43 Mean versus median for age at first marriage: The mean age at first marriage was 31.1 years for men and 29.1 years for women in Canada in 2008 (open.canada.ca/en/open-data). The median age at first marriage was 28.9 years for men and 26.9 years for women in the United States in 2011 (factfinder .census.gov/faces/tableservices/jsf/pages/productview .xhtml?pid=ACS_11_1YR_B12007&prodType=table). Beyond the fact that these data are from slightly different years, explain why we cannot directly compare these measures of central tendency to make cross-national comparisons.

4.44 Median ages and technology companies: In an article titled "Technology Workers Are Young (Really Young)," *The New York Times* reported median ages for a number of companies (Hardy, 2013). The reporter wrote: "The seven companies with the youngest workers, ranked from youngest to highest in median age, were Epic Games (26); Facebook (28); Zynga (28); Google (29); and AOL, Blizzard Entertainment, InfoSys, and Monster.com (all 30). According to the Bureau of Labor Statistics, only shoe stores and restaurants have workers with a median age less than 30."

a. Explain why the reporter provided medians rather than means for employee ages.

b. Why might it be easier to use medians rather than means to compare ages across companies?

4.45 Standard deviation and a texting intervention for parents of preschoolers: Researchers investigated READY4K, a program in which parents received text messages over an 8-month period (York & Loeb, 2014). The goal of the text messages was to help parents prepare their preschool-aged children for reading. The children of parents who received the text messages were compared to a second group of children whose parents did not receive text messages. The researchers reported that the text messages led to "student learning gains in some areas of early literacy, ranging from approximately 0.21 to 0.34 standard deviations."

a. Based on your knowledge of means and standard deviations, explain what this finding means.

b. Did the researchers use a between-groups design or a within-groups design? Explain your answer.

4.46 Range, world records, and a long chain of friendship bracelets: Guinness World Records reported that, as part of an anti-bullying campaign, elementary school students in Pennsylvania created a chain of friendship bracelets that was a world-record 2678 feet long (guinnessworldrecords.com /news/2013/5/fan-choice-record-may-17-48702/). Guinness relies on what kind of data for amazing claims like this one? How does this relate to the calculation of ranges?

Putting It All Together

4.47 Descriptive statistics and basketball wins: Here are the numbers of wins for the 30 National Basketball Association teams in one season.

60 44 39 29 23 57 50 43 37 27

49 42 37 29 19 56 51 40 33 26

48 42 31 25 18 53 44 40 29 23

a. Create a grouped frequency table for these data.

b. Create a histogram based on the grouped frequency table.

c. Determine the mean, median, and mode of these data. Use symbols and the formula when showing your calculation of the mean.

d. Using software, calculate the range and standard deviation of these data.

e. Write a one- to two-paragraph summary describing the distribution of these data. Mention center, variability, and shape. Be sure to discuss the number of modes (i.e., unimodal, bimodal, multimodal), any possible outliers, and the presence and direction of any skew.

f. State one research question that might arise from this data set.

4.48 Central tendency and outliers for data on traffic deaths: Below are estimated numbers of annual road traffic deaths for 12 countries based on data from the World Health Organization (apps.who.int/gho/data /view.main.51310):

Country	Number of Deaths
United States	35,490
Australia	1363
Canada	2296
Denmark	258
Finland	272
Germany	3830
Italy	4371
Japan	6625
Malaysia	7085
Portugal	1257
Spain	2478
Turkey	8758

a. Compute the mean and the median across these 12 data points.

b. Compute the range for these 12 data points.

c. Recalculate the statistics in part (a) and part (b) without the data point for the United States. How are these statistics affected by including or excluding the United States?

d. How might these numbers be affected by using traffic deaths per 100,000 people instead of using the number of traffic deaths overall?

e. Do you think that traffic deaths might vary by other personal or national characteristics? Could these represent confounds (as discussed in Chapter 1)?

Visit LaunchPad to access the e-book and to
test your knowledge with LearningCurve.

TERMS

central tendency (p. 92)

mean (p. 93)

statistic (p. 94)

parameter (p. 94)

median (p. 96)

mode (p. 97)

unimodal (p. 98)

bimodal (p. 98)

multimodal (p. 98)

variability (p. 102)

range (p. 102)

interquartile range (p. 104)

first quartile (p. 104)

third quartile (p. 104)

variance (p. 105)

deviation from the mean (p. 105)

sum of squares (p. 106)

standard deviation (p. 107)

FORMULAS

$$M = \frac{\Sigma X}{N} \qquad \text{(p. 95)}$$

$$IQR = Q3 - Q1 \qquad \text{(p. 104)}$$

$$SD = \sqrt{SD^2} \qquad \text{(p. 108)}$$

$$\text{range} = X_{highest} - X_{lowest} \qquad \text{(p. 103)}$$

$$SD^2 = \frac{\Sigma (X - M)^2}{N} \qquad \text{(p. 107)}$$

$$SD = \sqrt{\frac{\Sigma (X - M)^2}{N}} \qquad \text{(p. 108)}$$

SYMBOLS

M	(p. 94)	Mdn	(p. 96)	s^2	(p. 107)
$\bar{X}$	(p. 94)	Q1	(p. 104)	MS	(p. 107)
μ	(p. 94)	Q3	(p. 104)	σ^2	(p. 107)
X	(p. 94)	IQR	(p. 104)	SD	(p. 107)
Σ	(p. 95)	SS	(p. 106)	s	(p. 107)
N	(p. 95)	SD^2	(p. 107)	σ	(p. 107)

Sampling and Probability

BEFORE YOU GO ON

- **You should understand the difference between a sample and a population (Chapter 1).**

- **You should know how to measure central tendency, especially the mean (Chapter 4).**

Bettmann/Getty Images

Work Smarter, Not Harder! Sampling is a way to do things more efficiently, based on principles that Lillian Gilbreth—a pioneer in the field of industrial and organizational psychology—and her husband Frank applied to raising a happy, if occasionally chaotic, family. Eleven of their 12 children are pictured here. Frank is on the far left and Lillian is on the far right.

Lillian Gilbreth, a pioneer in the field of industrial and organizational psychology (Held, 2010), was such an introverted little girl that her parents homeschooled her until she was 9 years old. That home was a busy place, and little Lillian, the eldest of 9 children, often filled in for her ill mother. The hectic pace of life that had begun during Lillian's childhood kept up for the rest of her life. She and her husband Frank Gilbreth, both of them efficiency experts, created a consulting business and had 12 children. The couple pioneered the use of filming people at work to analyze the motions needed to perform a task more efficiently, and applied those same principles to helping their children manage their lives more effectively. The family's lifestyle inspired two of the children to later write the book *Cheaper By the Dozen*, which also became a popular film.

After Frank died at a relatively young age, Lillian continued to support her family as an industrial consultant (Association for Psychological Science [APS], 2017). She did this in an era that allowed only her husband's name to appear on the books they wrote together, out of fear of losing credibility if publishers advertised a female author! Frank had never earned a degree, but Lillian had a master's degree from the University of California, Berkeley, and a PhD from Brown University.

California Monthly described Lillian Gilbreth as "a genius in the art of living" (Maisel & Smart, 1997). Her ability to think scientifically also helped her create small and large innovations for the home and workplace (Graham, 1999). Foot pedals on garbage cans and shelves in refrigerator doors (APS, 2017)? Thank Lillian Gilbreth. The "work triangle" in efficiency kitchens? Thank Lillian Gilbreth. The driving idea behind all these ideas was human efficiency. Efficiency is the driving idea behind sampling as well. Why work harder when an easier way is readily available? Why study 400,000 people if 400 people, sampled properly, will yield the same information?

Samples and Their Populations

Almost everything worth evaluating requires a sample, from voting trends to sales patterns to the effectiveness of flu vaccines. The goal of sampling is simple: Collect a sample that represents the population. As Lillian Gilbreth reminds us, efficient living and efficient sampling are both possible—and far easier in theory than they are in practice.

There are two main types of samples: random samples and convenience samples. *A **random sample** is one in which every member of the population has an equal chance of being selected into the study. A **convenience sample** is one that uses participants who are readily available,* such as college students. A random sample remains the ideal and is far more likely to lead to a representative sample, but it is usually expensive and can

5-1: There are two main types of samples in social science research. In the ideal type (a random sample), every member of the population has an equal chance of being selected to participate in a study. In the less ideal but more common type (a convenience sample), researchers use participants who are readily available.

- A **random sample** is one in which every member of the population has an equal chance of being selected into the study.

- A **convenience sample** is one that uses participants who are readily available.

present a lot of practical problems. It is often almost impossible to get access to every member of the population so as to choose a random sample from among them. But we'll also explore technologies such as Amazon Mechanical Turk and other Internet tools that offer new ways to obtain convenience samples from a more diverse sample of participants.

Random Sampling

Imagine that there has recently been a traumatic mass murder in a town, and that there are exactly 80 officers in the town's police department. You have been hired to determine whether peer counseling or professional counseling is the more effective way to address the department's concerns in the aftermath of this trauma. Unfortunately, budget constraints dictate that the sample you can recruit must be very small—just 10 people. How do you maximize the probability that 10 officers will accurately represent the larger population of 80 officers?

The best way is to randomly sample, or randomly select, 10 officers out of the 80 officers. We don't think randomly, so we can't just pick 10 ourselves. The old-fashioned way is to number the officers from 1 to 80, and use a random numbers table like the one in Appendix B-7. Just pick a spot to start and follow a row or column, noting pairs of numbers between 01 and 80 until you have 10 officers.

More commonly, researchers use technology to choose a random sample. You can search online for a "random numbers generator," or you can just go to our favorite, randomizer.org (Urbaniak & Plous, 2013). Now in its fourth version, randomizer.org has been used over the years to generate almost 3 billion random numbers! We generated a list of 10 numbers by telling the site that we wanted one set of numbers, 10 numbers per set, numbers ranging from 1 to 80, each number in the set being unique, and numbers sorted from least to greatest. We then clicked "RANDOMIZE

Random Dots? True randomness often does not seem random. British artist Damien Hirst farms out the actual painting of many of his works, such as his famous dot paintings, to assistants. He provides his assistants with instructions, including to arrange the color dots randomly. One assistant painted a series of yellow dots next to each other, which led to a fight with Hirst, who said, "I told him those aren't random. . . . Now I realize he was right, and I was wrong" (Vogel, 2011).

Matthew Lloyd/Getty Images

NOW!" and received the following numbers: 10, 23, 27, 34, 36, 67, 70, 74, 77, and 78. You might be surprised that 4 of the 10 numbers were in the 70s. Don't be. Random numbers are truly random, even if they don't look random.

Random samples are almost never used in the social sciences because we almost never have access to the whole population. For example, if we were interested in studying the effect of video games on the attention span of teenagers in the United Kingdom, we could never identify all U.K. teenagers from whom to choose a random sample.

Convenience Sampling

It is far more convenient (faster, easier, and cheaper) to gather teenagers from the local school than to take the time to recruit a representative sample—but there is a significant downside. A convenience sample might not represent the larger population. *Generalizability refers to researchers' ability to apply findings from one sample or in one context to other samples or contexts.* This principle is also called *external validity*, and it is extremely important—why bother doing the study if it doesn't apply to anyone else? (We'll dig deeper into issues related to generalizability in the Data Ethics feature in Chapter 13.)

Fortunately, we can increase external validity through **replication**, *the duplication of scientific results, ideally in a different context or with a sample that has different characteristics* (sometimes called *reproducibility*). In other words, do the study again. And again. Then ask someone else to replicate it, too. That's the slow but trustworthy process by which science creates knowledge that is both reliable and valid, and you'll learn more about it in the Data Ethics feature in Chapter 9.

Liars' Alert! We must be even more cautious when we use a **volunteer sample** (also called a *self-selected sample*), *a convenience sample in which participants actively choose to participate in a study.* Participants volunteer, or self-select, when they respond to recruitment flyers or choose to complete an online survey, such as polls that recruit people to vote for a favorite reality show contestant or hockey team. We see volunteer samples in psychology research more and more as crowdsourcing becomes more popular. **Crowdsourcing** *in research occurs when a research team solicits input from a very large group of people, usually recruited online.* In one example, researchers collected data from those who played an online game called Airport Scanner (learn about the app here: airportscannergame.com; Mitroff, Biggs, Adamo, Dowd, Winkle, & Clark, 2015). In this study, literally millions of participants searched for dangerous items, like dynamite, that only rarely showed up. The billions—yes, billions—of data points that resulted allowed researchers to understand what affects our ability to visually search for rare occurrences. On the one hand, only with the Internet can we have so many participants and data points. On the other hand, we must be cautious because, as summarized by a journalist, these researchers explained that "collecting data through crowdsourcing means researchers have no control over who is playing" (APA, 2014).

There is a growing number of outlets for online data collection, including companies like Prolific Academic (prolific.ac), FindParticipants (findparticipants.com), and Call for Participants (callforparticipants.com), as well as some free sites, including ever-changing Reddit subthreads (Buhrmester, Talaifar, & Gosling, 2018). Perhaps the most popular—and controversial—online tool, however, is Amazon Mechanical

---

● **Generalizability** refers to researchers' ability to apply findings from one sample or in one context to other samples or contexts; also called *external validity*.

● **Replication** refers to the duplication of scientific results, ideally in a different context or with a sample that has different characteristics (sometimes called *reproducibility*).

● A **volunteer sample**, or *self-selected sample*, is a special kind of convenience sample in which participants actively choose to participate in a study.

● **Crowdsourcing** refers to when a researcher solicits input from a very large group of people, usually recruited online.

Turk (MTurk.com), an online network where anyone can recruit people to complete tasks for a small fee. For psychology, MTurk has become a common place for researchers to sample a more representative group of research participants and to collect data much more quickly than is possible with traditional samples (Bohannon, 2016). Anyone can sign up for a free account, provide basic demographic information, and participate in online surveys for monetary payment. Behavioral scientists' use of MTurk to recruit participants has grown so rapidly that in some journals, particularly in social psychology, almost half of published papers included at least one MTurk sample (Buhrmester et al., 2018).

There has been ongoing discussion about the validity and reliability of sampling participants in this way (e.g., Buhrmester, Kwang, & Gosling, 2011). For many studies, it seems as though sampling using MTurk eliminates the bias of sampling only college students, which is often the convenience sampling option for many psychological researchers. Despite this apparent advantage, MTurk and other tools like it are still volunteer sampling procedures. Likewise, the limitations of using an online volunteer sample remain, and ethical researchers must use caution. Volunteer samples may be very different from a randomly selected sample. The information that volunteer participants provide may not represent the larger population in which we are really interested. Think about the crowdsourcing example. How might people who play Airport Scanner online be different from the general population?

In addition, these tools are subject to fraud. Researchers have noticed an increase in random responses from MTurk participants, including apparently randomly selected numbers and responses to open-ended questions that don't make sense, such as "NICE!" (Bai, 2018). These responses are likely from bots—that is, web "robot" software that responds automatically. Indeed, GPS coordinates sometimes indicate that many responses come from the same location.

Finally, ethical concerns arise with respect to the participants, often called Turkers. Some note that their hourly pay amounts to far less than study participants who are paid through other means, and is less than the minimum wage in countries such as the United States and Canada (DeSoto, 2016). Others point out that the online nature of MTurk may not completely protect Turkers' privacy and anonymity (Bohannon, 2016). For those who use Turkers for their work, there are now guidelines for being an ethical researcher, including a wiki that outlines the "basics of how to be a good requester" when recruiting participants (wiki.wearedynamo.org/index.php?title=Basics_of_how_to_be_a_good_requester). It is clear that stronger and clearer expectations for the ethical treatment of online participants will increase in the future.

The Problem with a Biased Sample

Let's be blunt: If you don't understand sampling, then you make it easy for others to take advantage of you. For example, the Web site Viewpoint provides a forum for consumer reviews of products ranging from laundry detergent to cameras. Viewpoint has a page devoted to Sephora by OPI nail polish, a brand that offers colors with clever names like "I'm with Brad," "Read My Palm," and "Never Enough Shoes." A reviewer from Beverly Hills, California, called catdoganimal, recommended the polish and wrote, "It lasts for more than a week without chipping. Made my nails

Photo by Rebecca Sapp/Getty Images for Sephora

Are Testimonials Trustworthy Evidence? Does one person's positive experience with Sephora by OPI nail polish—"made my nails stronger"—provide evidence that this product actually strengthens nails? Testimonials use a volunteer sample of one person, usually a biased person. Data from a larger, representative sample are always more reliable than a sample of one.

stronger." Let's examine the flaws in this sample of "evidence"—a brief testimonial—for the supposed long-lasting, nail-strengthening nature of the Sephora by OPI polish.

The population of interest is people who use Sephora by OPI nail polish. The sample is the one person who posted a review. But there are two major problems with this sample. First, one person is not a trustworthy sample size. Second, this is a volunteer sample. The customer who had this experience chose to post a review. Would someone be likely to do so if that person did not feel very strongly about this product? The nail polish may be amazing and catdoganimal likely truly loves it, but a single testimonial from a probable animal lover from California doesn't provide trustworthy evidence. In fact, when we scouted out other testimonials for this product, there was much disagreement about the pros and cons of Sephora by OPI polish.

Self-selection is a major problem, but all is not lost! We could randomly assign a certain number of people to use Sephora by OPI nail polish and an equal number of people to use another product, then see which group had longer-lasting color as well as which group had stronger nails over time. Which do you find more persuasive: a dubious testimonial or a well-designed experiment? If our honest answer is a dubious testimonial, then statistical reasoning once again leads us to ask a better question (nicely answered by social psychologists, by the way) about why anecdotes are sometimes more persuasive than science.

Random Assignment

Random assignment is the distinctive signature of a scientific study. Why? Because it levels the playing field when every participant has an equal chance of being assigned to any level of the independent variable. Random assignment is different from random sampling (or random selection). Random sampling is the ideal way to gather a sample from a population; random assignment is what we do with participants once they have been recruited into a study, regardless of how they got there. Practical problems related to getting access to an entire population mean that random *sampling* is almost never used; however, random *assignment* is used whenever possible—and solves many of the problems associated with a convenience sample.

Random assignment involves procedures similar to those used for random sampling. If a study has two levels of the independent variable, as in the study of police officers, then you would need to assign participants to one of two groups. You could decide, arbitrarily, to number the groups 0 and 1 for the "peer counseling" and "therapist counseling" groups, respectively. Then, you could use an online random numbers generator like randomizer.org to provide one set of 10 numbers that range from 0 to 1. You would instruct the program that the numbers should *not* remain unique because we want multiple 0's and multiple 1's. In addition, you would request that the numbers *not* be sorted because you want to assign participants in the order in which the numbers are generated. When we used an online random numbers generator, the 10 numbers were 1110100001. In an experiment, we usually want equal numbers in the groups. If the numbers were not exactly half 1's and half 0's, as they are in this case, we could decide in advance to use only the first five 1's or the first five 0's. Just be sure to establish your rule for random assignment ahead of time and then stick to it!

CHECK YOUR LEARNING

Reviewing the Concepts

> Data from a sample are used to draw conclusions about the larger population.

> In random sampling, every member of the population has an equal chance of being selected for the sample.

> In the behavioral sciences, convenience samples are far more common than random samples.

> Random numbers may not always appear to be all that random; there may appear to be patterns.

> In random assignment, every participant has an equal chance of being assigned to one of the experimental conditions.

> If a study that uses random assignment is replicated in several contexts, we can start to generalize the findings.

Clarifying the Concepts

5-1 What are the risks of sampling?

Calculating the Statistics

5-2 Use an online random numbers generator like randomizer.org to select 6 people out of a sample of 80.

5-3 Use an online random numbers generator like randomizer.org to randomly assign these six people to one of two experimental conditions, numbered 0 and 1.

Applying the Concepts

5-4 For each of the following scenarios, state whether, from a practical standpoint, random sampling could have been used. Explain your answer, including in it a description of the population to which the researcher likely wants to generalize. Then state whether random assignment could have been used, and explain your answer.

a. A health psychologist examined whether postoperative recovery time was shorter among patients who received counseling prior to surgery than among those who did not.

b. The head of a school board asked a research psychologist to examine whether children perform better in history classes if they use an online textbook as opposed to a printed textbook.

c. A clinical psychologist studied whether people with diagnosed personality disorders were more likely to miss therapy appointments than were people without diagnosed personality disorders.

Solutions to these Check Your Learning questions can be found in Appendix D.

Probability

You have probably heard phrases such as "the margin of error" or "plus or minus 3 percentage points," especially during an election season. These are another way of saying, "We're not 100% sure that we can believe our own results." This could make you cynical about statistics—you do all this work, and then you still don't know if you can trust your data.

You would be more justified, however, in celebrating statistics for being so truthful—statistics allows us to quantify the uncertainty. And let's be honest—most of life is filled with uncertainty, whether it's the quality of the jacket that has the high-quality YKK zipper, the number of days your nail polish lasts without chipping, or the most efficient way for a worker to perform a task. Probability is central to inferential statistics because our conclusions about a population are based on data collected from a sample rather than on anecdotes and testimonials.

Coincidence and Probability

Probability and statistical reasoning can save us from ourselves when, for example, we are confronted with eerie coincidences. Two personal biases get intertwined in our thinking so that we say with genuine astonishment, "Wow! What are the chances of that?" *Confirmation bias is our usually unintentional tendency to pay attention to evidence that confirms what we already believe and to ignore evidence that would disconfirm our beliefs.* It is a confirmation bias when an athlete attributes her team's wins to her lucky earrings, ignoring any losses while wearing them or any wins while wearing other earrings. Confirmation biases often lead to illusory correlations. *Illusory correlation is the phenomenon of believing one sees an association between variables when no such association exists.* An athlete with a confirmation bias attributing wins to her lucky earrings now believes an illusory correlation. We invite illusory correlations into our lives whenever we ignore the gentle, restraining logic of statistical reasoning.

For example, the science show *Radiolab* told a remarkable story of coincidence (Abumrad & Krulwich, 2009). A 10-year-old girl named Laura Buxton released a red balloon from her hometown in the north of England. "Almost 10," Laura corrected the host. Laura had written her address on the balloon as well as an entreaty: "Please return to Laura Buxton." The balloon traveled 140 miles to the south of England and was found by a neighbor of another 10-year-old girl, also named Laura Buxton! The second Laura wrote to the first, and they arranged to meet. They both showed up to their meeting wearing jeans and pink sweaters. They were both the same height, had brown hair, and owned a black Labrador retriever, a gray rabbit, and a brown guinea pig with an orange spot. In fact, each brought her guinea pig to the meeting. At the time of the radio broadcast, they were 18 years old and friends.

- **Confirmation bias** is our usually unintentional tendency to pay attention to evidence that confirms what we already believe and to ignore evidence that would disconfirm our beliefs.

- **Illusory correlation** is the phenomenon of believing one sees an association between variables when no such association exists.

Amy Lombard for The New York Times

Marriage Is Forever? Or is it just the tattoos? Illusory correlations occur when people perceive a link between variables where there is likely none—like tattooed rings and a lasting marriage. In an article about the supposed trend of tattooed engagement rings, one bride explained that she and her groom "want to be married forever, and [the tattooed engagement rings] cement that" (Strauss, 2016). Why? She noted the high rates of divorce among couples who chose actual rings. This illusory correlation probably arose from confirmation bias, with the bride noticing evidence to support her belief that those couples with actual rings get divorced, but ignoring evidence about similar divorce rates occurring among couples with inked rings.

"Maybe we were meant to meet," one of the Laura Buxtons speculated. "If it was just the wind, it was a very, very lucky wind," said the other.

The chances seem unbelievably slim, but confirmation bias and illusory correlations both play a role here—and probability helps us understand why such coincidences happen. The thing is, coincidences are *not* unlikely. We notice and remember strange coincidences, but do not notice the uncountable times in which there are not unlikely occurrences—the background, so to speak. We remember unusual stories of coincidences and luck, like that of the great-grandmother who won the lottery by playing the numbers in the fortune cookie that came with her Chinese take-out (Rosario & Sutherland, 2014). But we forget the many times we bought lottery tickets and lost—and the millions of people who did the same.

The *Radiolab* story described this phenomenon as the "blade of grass paradox." Imagine a golfer hitting a ball that flies way down the fairway and lands on a blade of grass. The radio show imagines the blade of grass saying: "Wow. What are the odds that that ball, out of all the billions of blades of grass . . . just landed on me?" Yet we know that there's almost a 100% chance that some blade of grass was going to be crushed by that ball. It just seems miraculous to the individual blade of grass—or to the lottery winner.

Let's go back to our story about the Laura Buxtons. A statistician pointed out that the details were "manipulated" to make for a better story. The host had remembered that they were both 10 years old, yet the first Laura reminded him she was still 9 at the time ("almost 10"). The host also admitted there were many discrepancies—one's favorite color was pink and one's was blue, and they had opposite academic interests—biology, chemistry, and geography for one and English, history, and classical civilization for the other. Further, it was not the second Laura Buxton who found the balloon; rather, it was her neighbor. The similarities make a better story. When you add probability to confirmation bias and illusory correlation, they become the WOW! details that we remember—but it's still just another blade of grass. Still not convinced? Read on.

Expected Relative-Frequency Probability

When we discuss probability in everyday conversation, we tend to think of what statisticians call *personal probability*: *a person's own judgment about the likelihood that an event will occur*; also called *subjective probability*. We might say something like "There's a 75% chance I'll finish my paper and go out tonight." We don't mean that the chance we'll go out is precisely 75%. Rather, this is our rating of our confidence that this event will occur. It's really just our best guess.

Mathematicians and statisticians, however, use the word *probability* a bit differently. Statisticians are concerned with a different type of probability, one that is more objective. In a general sense, *probability* is *the likelihood that a particular outcome—out of all possible outcomes—will occur*. For example, we might talk about the likelihood of getting heads (a particular outcome) if we flip a coin 10 times (all possible outcomes). We use probability because we usually have access only to a sample (10 flips of a coin) when we want to know about an entire population (all possible flips of a coin).

- The **expected relative-frequency probability** is the likelihood of an event occurring based on the actual outcome of many, many trials.

- In reference to probability, a **trial** refers to each occasion that a given procedure is carried out.

- In reference to probability, **outcome** refers to the result of a trial.

- In reference to probability, **success** refers to the outcome for which we're trying to determine the probability.

Language Alert! In statistics, we are interested in an even more specific definition of probability—*expected relative-frequency probability, the likelihood of an event occurring, based on the actual outcome of many, many trials.* When flipping a coin, the expected relative-frequency probability of heads, in the long run, is 0.50. Probability refers to the likelihood that something would take place, and frequency refers to how often a given outcome (e.g., heads or tails) occurs out of a certain number of trials (e.g., coin flips). *Relative* indicates that this number is relative to the overall number of trials, and *expected* indicates that it's what we would anticipate, which might be different from what actually happens.

In reference to probability, the term ***trial*** *refers to each occasion that a given procedure is carried out.* For example, each time we flip a coin, it is a trial. ***Outcome*** *refers to the result of a trial.* For coin-flip trials, the outcome is either heads or tails. ***Success*** *refers to the outcome for which we're trying to determine the probability.* If we are testing for the probability of heads, then success is heads.

EXAMPLE 5.1

We can think of probability in terms of a formula. We calculate probability by dividing the total number of successes by the total number of trials. So the formula would look like this:

$$\text{probability} = \frac{\text{successes}}{\text{trials}}$$

If we flip a coin 2000 times and get 1000 heads, then:

$$\text{probability} = \frac{1000}{2000} = 0.50$$

Here is a recap of the steps to calculate probability:

> **STEP 1:** Determine the total number of trials.

> **STEP 2:** Determine the number of these trials that are considered successful outcomes.

> **STEP 3:** Divide the number of successful outcomes by the number of trials.

People often confuse the terms *probability*, *proportion*, and *percentage*. Probability, the concept of most interest to us right now, is the proportion that we expect to see in the long run. Proportion is the number of successes divided by the number of trials. In the short run, in just a few trials, the proportion might not reflect the underlying probability. A coin flipped six times might come up heads more or fewer than three times, leading to a proportion of heads that does not parallel the underlying probability of heads. Both proportions and probabilities are written as decimals.

Percentage is simply probability or proportion multiplied by 100. A flipped coin has a 0.50 probability of coming up heads and a 50% chance of coming up heads. You are probably already familiar with percentages, so simply keep in mind that probabilities are what we would expect in the long run, whereas proportions are what we observe.

One of the central characteristics of expected relative-frequency probability is that it only works in the long run. This is an important aspect of probability, and it is referred to as the *law of large numbers*. Think of the earlier discussion of random assignment in which we used a random numbers generator to create a series of 0's and 1's to assign participants to levels of the independent variable. In the short run, over just a few trials, we can get strings of 0's and 1's and often do not end up with half 0's and half 1's, even though that is the underlying probability. With many trials, however, we're much more likely to get close to 0.50, or 50%, of each, although many strings of 0's or 1's would be generated along the way. In the long run, the results are quite predictable. ●

Independence and Probability

Language Alert! To avoid bias, statistical probability requires that the individual trials be *independent*, one of the favorite words of statisticians. Here we use *independent* to mean that the outcome of each trial must not depend in any way on the outcome of previous trials. If we're flipping a coin, then each coin flip is independent of every other coin flip. If we're generating a random numbers list to select participants, each number must be generated without thought to the previous numbers. In fact, this is exactly why humans can't think randomly. We automatically glance at the previous numbers we have generated in an effort to best make the next one "random." Chance has no memory, and randomness is, therefore, the only way to ensure that there is no bias.

Gambling and Misperceptions of Probability Many people falsely believe that a slot machine that has not paid off in a long time is "due." A person may continue to feed coins into it, expecting an imminent payout. Of course, the slot machine itself, unless rigged, has no memory of its previous outcomes. Each trial is independent of the others.

Sylvia Serrado/Photolibrary/Getty Images

CHECK YOUR LEARNING

Reviewing the Concepts

> Probability theory helps us understand that coincidences might not have an underlying meaning; coincidences *are* probable when we think of the vast number of occurrences in the world (billions of interactions between people daily).

> An illusory correlation refers to perceiving a connection where none exists. It often follows a confirmation bias, whereby we notice occurrences that fit with our preconceived ideas and fail to notice those that do not.

> Personal probability refers to a person's own judgment about the likelihood that an event will occur (also called subjective probability).

> Expected relative-frequency probability is the likelihood of an event occurring, based on the actual outcome of many, many trials.

> The probability of an event occurring is defined as the expected number of successes (the number of times the event occurred) out of the total number of trials (or attempts) over the long run.

> Proportions over the short run might have many different outcomes, whereas proportions over the long run are more indicative of the underlying probabilities.

continued on next page

Clarifying the Concepts	5-5	Distinguish the personal probability assessments we perform on a daily basis from the objective probability that statisticians use.

Calculating the Statistics	5-6	Calculate the probability for each of the following instances.
		a. 100 trials, 5 successes
		b. 50 trials, 8 successes
		c. 1044 trials, 130 successes

Applying the Concepts	5-7	Cathleen Cavin and her daughter, Cali, adopted a kitten named Ozzy from a Petaluma, California, animal shelter, but could not adopt his brother, Butter, because their rental lease would not allow more than one animal (Bojo, 2017). But they never stopped thinking about Butter. More than a year later, Cathleen joined an online dating site and soon fell in love with Brian Herrera, who also owned one cat. Cathleen was shocked to discover that Brian's cat was Butter, whom he had adopted four days after they took Ozzy home. The couple—with Cali and their cats—now live together. Explain how a statistician would explain this coincidence. How does probability fit in to this explanation?

Solutions to these Check Your Learning questions can be found in Appendix D.

- A **control group** is a level of the independent variable that does not receive the treatment of interest in a study. It is designed to match an experimental group in all ways but the experimental manipulation itself.

- An **experimental group** is a level of the independent variable that receives the treatment or intervention of interest in an experiment.

- The **null hypothesis** is a statement that postulates that there is no difference between populations or that the difference is in a direction opposite of that anticipated by the researcher.

MASTERING THE CONCEPT

5-5: Many experiments have an experimental group in which participants receive the treatment or intervention of interest and a control group in which participants do not receive the treatment or intervention of interest. Aside from the intervention with the experimental group, the two groups are treated identically.

Inferential Statistics

In Chapter 1, we introduced the two main branches of statistics—descriptive statistics and inferential statistics. The link that connects the two branches is probability. Descriptive statistics allow us to summarize characteristics of the sample, but we must use probability with inferential statistics when we apply what we've learned from the sample, such as in an exit poll, to the larger population. Inferential statistics, calculated through a process called hypothesis testing, help us to determine the probability of a given outcome. We'll outline the logic of hypothesis testing here—but Spoiler Alert! Hypothesis testing is flawed in many ways. Throughout this text (and particularly in the Data Ethics features), we'll explore the problems with inferential statistics and offer some solutions.

Developing Hypotheses

We informally develop and test hypotheses all the time. I hypothesize that the traffic will be heavy on Western Avenue, for example, so I take a parallel street to work and keep looking down each block to see if my hypothesis is being supported. In a science blog, *TierneyLab*, reporter John Tierney and his collaborators asked people to estimate the number of calories in a meal pictured in a photograph (Tierney, 2008a, b). One group was shown a photo of an Applebee's Oriental Chicken Salad and a Pepsi. Another group was shown a photo of the same salad and Pepsi, but it also included a third item—Fortt's crackers, with a label that clearly stated "Trans Fat Free." The researchers hypothesized that the addition of the "healthy" food item would affect people's calorie estimates of the entire meal. They tested a sample and used probability to apply their findings from the sample to the population.

Let's put this study in the language of sampling and probability. The sample comprised people living in the Park Slope neighborhood of Brooklyn in New York City, an area that Tierney terms "nutritionally correct" because of the abundance of organic food in local stores. The population would include all the residents of Park Slope who could have been part of this study. The driving concern behind this research was the increasing levels of obesity in many wealthier countries (something that Tierney explored in a follow-up study). For now, however, we can only infer that the results may apply to the residents of Park Slope and similar neighborhoods. The independent variable in this case is the presence or absence of the healthy crackers in the photo of the meal. The dependent variable is the number of calories estimated.

The group that viewed the photo *without* the healthy crackers is the **control group**, *a level of the independent variable that does not receive the treatment of interest in a study*. It is designed to match *the* **experimental group**—*a level of the independent variable that receives the treatment or intervention of interest*— in all ways but the experimental manipulation itself. In this example, the experimental group would be those viewing the photo that included the healthy crackers.

The next step is the development of the hypotheses to be tested. Ethically, researchers must do this before the data from the sample are actually collected; you will see this pattern of developing hypotheses and then collecting data repeated throughout this book. When we calculate inferential statistics, we're actually comparing two hypotheses. One is *the* **null hypothesis**—*a statement that postulates that there is no difference between populations or that the difference is in a direction opposite to that anticipated by the researcher*. In most circumstances, we can think of the null hypothesis as the boring hypothesis because it proposes that nothing will happen. In the healthy food study, the null hypothesis is that the average (mean) calorie estimate is the same for both populations, which consist of all the people in Park Slope who either view or do not view the photo with the healthy crackers.

In contrast to the null hypothesis, the research hypothesis is usually the exciting hypothesis. *The* **research hypothesis** (also called the *alternative hypothesis*) *is a statement that postulates a difference between populations*. In the healthy food study, the research hypothesis would be that, on average, the calorie estimate is different for those viewing the photo with the healthy crackers than for those viewing the photo without the healthy crackers. It also could specify a direction—that the mean calorie estimate is higher (or lower) for those viewing the photo with the healthy crackers than for those viewing the photo with just the salad and Pepsi. Notice that, for all hypotheses, we are very careful to state the comparison group. We do not say merely that the group viewing the photo with the healthy crackers has a higher (or lower) average calorie estimate. We say that it has a higher (or lower) average calorie estimate *than* the group that views the photo without the healthy crackers.

Craig Warga/Bloomberg via Getty Images

The Control Burrito You can spot control groups in everyday life. Intern Dylan Grosz describes heaven as "one big Chipotle restaurant where the guac and chips are ALWAYS free" (2015). On a budget, he made it his mission to figure out how to get the most Chipotle for the money. He started by identifying his "control burrito." It included rice, beans, chicken, salsa, and cheese. He then ordered 35 burritos over 2 weeks—five each of seven different variations— and compared these experimental groups to his control burrito. He identified six tricks that, together, increased the average burrito weight by 86%! Among the tricks, order both kinds of rice and both kinds of beans.

● The **research hypothesis** is a statement that postulates that there is a difference between populations or sometimes, more specifically, that there is a difference in a certain direction, positive or negative; also called an *alternative hypothesis*.

5-6: Hypothesis testing allows us to examine two competing hypotheses. The first, the null hypothesis, posits that there is no difference between populations or that any difference is in the opposite direction from what is predicted. The second, the research hypothesis, posits that there is a difference between populations (or that the difference between populations is in a predicted direction—either higher or lower).

We formulate the null hypothesis and the research hypothesis to set them up against each other. We use statistics to determine the probability that there is a large enough difference between the means of the samples that we can conclude there's likely a difference between the means of the underlying populations. So, probability plays into the decision we make about the hypotheses.

Making a Decision About a Hypothesis

When we make a conclusion at the end of a study, the data lead us to conclude one of two things:

1. We decide to *reject* the null hypothesis.
2. We decide to *fail to reject* the null hypothesis.

We always begin our reasoning about the outcome of an experiment by reminding ourselves that we are testing the (boring) null hypothesis. In terms of the healthy food study, the null hypothesis is that there is no mean difference between groups. In hypothesis testing, we determine the probability that we would see a difference between the means of the samples, given that there is no actual difference between the underlying population means.

EXAMPLE 5.2

After we analyze the data, we do one of two things:

1. *Reject the null hypothesis.* "I reject the idea that there is no mean difference between populations." When we reject the null hypothesis that there is *no mean difference*, we can even assert what we believe the difference to be, based on the actual findings. We can say that it seems that people who view a photo of a salad, Pepsi, and healthy crackers estimate a lower (or higher, depending on what we found in our study) number of calories, on average, than those who view a photo with only the salad and Pepsi.

2. *Fail to reject the null hypothesis.* "I do not reject the idea that there is no mean difference between populations." In this case, we can only say that we do not have evidence to support our hypothesis.

Let's take the first possible conclusion, to reject the null hypothesis. If the group that viewed the photo that included the healthy crackers has a mean calorie estimate that is a good deal higher (or lower) than the control group's mean calorie estimate, then we might be tempted to say that we *accept* the research hypothesis that there is such a mean difference in the populations—that the addition of the healthy crackers makes a difference. Probability plays a central role in determining that the mean difference is large enough that we're willing to say it's real. But rather than *accept* the *research* hypothesis in this case, we *reject* the *null* hypothesis, the one that suggests there is nothing going on. We repeat: When the data suggest that there *is* a mean difference, we *reject* the idea that there is no mean difference.

The second possible conclusion is failing to reject the null hypothesis. There's a very good reason for thinking about this in terms of failing to reject the null hypothesis rather than accepting the null hypothesis. Let's say there's a small mean difference, and we conclude that we cannot reject the null hypothesis (remember, rejecting the null hypothesis is what we want to do!). We determine that it's just not likely enough—or probable enough—that the difference between means is real. It could be that a real difference between means didn't show up in this particular sample just by chance. There are many ways in which a real mean difference in the population might not get picked up by a sample. We repeat: When the data do not suggest a difference, we *fail to reject* the null hypothesis, which is that there is no mean difference.

Think of it in terms of your latest post on social media. Imagine that the null hypothesis is that a particular friend does *not* like the cat video you just posted. If she "likes" it, then you can reject the null hypothesis; you have evidence that she does like it. But if she does not "like" it, then you can't conclude anything. Maybe she doesn't like it, but she may also have been offline that day or your post didn't show up in her feed.

The way we decide whether to reject the null hypothesis is based directly on probability. We calculate the probability that the data would produce a difference between means this large and in a sample of this size *if* there was nothing going on.

We will be giving you many more opportunities to get comfortable with the logic of formal hypothesis testing before we start applying numbers to it, but here are three easy rules and a table (Table 5-1) that will help keep you on track.

1. Remember: The null hypothesis is that there is no difference between groups, and usually the hypotheses explore the possibility of a *mean* difference.
2. We either *reject* or *fail to reject* the null hypothesis. There are no other options.
3. We never use the word *accept* in reference to formal hypothesis testing.

Hypothesis testing is exciting when you care about the results. You may wonder what happened in Tierney's study. Well, people who saw the photo with just the salad and the Pepsi estimated, on average, that the 934-calorie meal contained 1011 calories. When the 100-calorie crackers were added, the meal actually increased from 934 calories to 1034 calories; however, those who viewed this photo estimated, on average, that the meal contained only 835 calories! Tierney referred to this effect as "a health halo that magically subtracted calories from the rest of the meal." Interestingly, he replicated this study with mostly foreign tourists in New York's Times Square and did not find this effect. He concluded that health-conscious people like those living in Park Slope were more susceptible to the magical health halo bias than were other people.

TABLE 5-1	Hypothesis Testing: Hypotheses and Decisions

The null hypothesis posits no difference, on average, whereas the research hypothesis posits a difference of some kind. There are only two decisions we can make. We can fail to reject the null hypothesis if the research hypothesis is *not* supported, or we can reject the null hypothesis if the research hypothesis *is* supported.

	Hypothesis	Decision
Null hypothesis	No change or difference	Fail to reject the null hypothesis (if research hypothesis is not supported)
Research hypothesis	Change or difference	Reject the null hypothesis (if research hypothesis is supported)

CHECK YOUR LEARNING

Reviewing the Concepts

> In experiments, we typically compare the average of the responses of those who receive the treatment or manipulation (the experimental group) with the average of the responses of similar people who do not receive the manipulation (the control group).

> Researchers develop two hypotheses: a null hypothesis, which theorizes that there is no average difference between levels of an independent variable in the population, and a research hypothesis, which theorizes that there is an average difference of some kind in the population.

> Researchers can draw two conclusions: They can reject the null hypothesis and conclude that they have supported the research hypothesis or they can fail to reject the null hypothesis and conclude that they have not supported the research hypothesis.

Clarifying the Concepts   5-8   At the end of a study, what does it mean to reject the null hypothesis?

Calculating the Statistics   5-9   State the difference that might be expected, based on the null hypothesis, between the average test grades of students who attend review sessions versus those who do not.

Applying the Concepts   5-10   A university lowers the heat during the winter to save money, and professors wonder whether students will perform more poorly, on average, under cold conditions.

    a. Cite the likely null hypothesis for this study.

    b. Cite the likely research hypothesis.

    c. If the cold temperature appears to decrease academic performance, on average, what will the researchers conclude in terms of formal hypothesis-testing language?

Solutions to these Check Your Learning questions can be found in Appendix D.

    d. If the researchers do not gather sufficient evidence to conclude that the cold temperature leads to decreased academic performance, on average, what will they conclude in terms of formal hypothesis-testing language?

Type I and Type II Errors

Wrong decisions can be the result of unrepresentative samples. However, even when sampling has been properly conducted, there are still two ways to make a wrong decision: (1) We can reject the null hypothesis when we *should not* have rejected it, or (2) we can fail to reject the null hypothesis when we *should* have rejected it. So let's consider the two types of errors using statistical language.

Type I Errors

- A **Type I error** involves rejecting the null hypothesis when the null hypothesis is correct.

If we reject the null hypothesis, but it was a mistake to do so, then we have made a Type I error. Specifically, *we commit a **Type I error** when we reject the null hypothesis but the null hypothesis is correct.* A Type I error is like a false positive in a medical test. For example, if a woman believes she might be pregnant, then she might buy a home pregnancy test. In this case, the null hypothesis would be that she is not pregnant, and the research hypothesis would be that she is pregnant. If the test is positive, the woman rejects the null hypothesis—the one in which she theorizes that she is not pregnant. Based on the test, the woman believes she is pregnant. Pregnancy tests, however, are not perfect. If the woman tests positive and rejects the null hypothesis, it is possible that she is wrong and it is a false positive. Based on the test, the woman believes she is pregnant even though she is not pregnant. A false positive is equivalent to a Type I error.

A Type I error indicates that we rejected the null hypothesis falsely. As you might imagine, the rejection of the null hypothesis typically leads to action, at least until we discover that it is an error. For example, the woman with a false-positive pregnancy test might announce the news to her family and start buying baby clothes. Many researchers consider the consequences of a Type I error to be particularly detrimental because people often take action based on a mistaken finding.

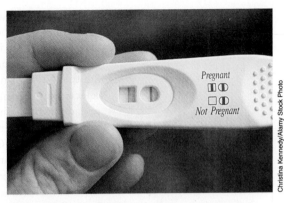

Christina Kennedy/Alamy Stock Photo

Type I and Type II Errors The results of a home pregnancy test are either positive (indicating pregnancy) or negative (indicating no pregnancy). If the test is positive, but the woman *is not* pregnant, this would be a Type I error. If the test is negative, but the woman *is* pregnant, this would be a Type II error. With pregnancy tests, as with hypothesis testing, people are more likely to act on a Type I error than on a Type II error. In the photo, the pregnancy test seems to indicate that this woman is pregnant, which could be a Type I error.

Type II Errors

If we fail to reject the null hypothesis but it was a mistake to fail to do so, then we have made a Type II error. Specifically, *we commit a **Type II error** when we fail to reject the null hypothesis but the null hypothesis is false.* A Type II error is like a false negative in medical testing. In the pregnancy example earlier, the woman might get a negative result on the test and fail to reject the null hypothesis, the one that says she's not pregnant. In this case, she would conclude that she's not pregnant when she really is. A false negative is equivalent to a Type II error.

We commit a Type II error when we incorrectly fail to reject the null hypothesis. A failure to reject the null hypothesis typically results in a failure to take action—for instance, a research intervention is not performed or a diagnosis is not given—which is generally less dangerous than incorrectly rejecting the null hypothesis. Yet there are cases in which a Type II error can have serious consequences. For example, the pregnant woman who does not believe she is pregnant because of a Type II error may drink alcohol in a way that unintentionally harms her fetus.

● A **Type II error** involves failing to reject the null hypothesis when the null hypothesis is false.

MASTERING THE CONCEPT

5-7: In hypothesis testing, there are two types of errors that we risk making. Type I errors, in which we reject the null hypothesis when the null hypothesis is true, are like false positives on a medical test; we think someone has a disease, but they really don't. Type II errors, in which we fail to reject the null hypothesis when the null hypothesis is not true, are like false negatives on a medical test; we think someone does not have a disease, but they really do.

The Shocking Prevalence of Type I Errors　　　Data Ethics

Ethical researchers are aware that Type I errors are all too common for a number of reasons. But many behavioral scientists aren't aware of how common (Gigerenzer, 2018). In the *British Medical Journal*, researchers reported that positive outcomes are more likely to be reported than null results (Sterne & Smith, 2001). First, researchers are less likely to want to publish null results, particularly if those results mean that a sponsoring pharmaceutical company's favored drug did not receive support; as one doctor described: "If I toss a coin, but hide the result every time it comes up tails, it looks as if I always throw heads" (Goldacre, 2013). Second, journals tend to publish "exciting" results, rather than "boring" ones (Sterne & Smith, 2001). To translate this into the terms of hypothesis testing, if a researcher rejects the "boring" null hypothesis, thus garnering support for the "exciting" research hypothesis, the editor of a journal is more likely to want to publish these results. Third, the mass media—abetted by us, the general public—compound this problem. As John Oliver, host of *Last Week Tonight*, explained: "We like fun, poppy science that we can share like gossip, and TV news producers know it" (2016).

Using educated estimations, researchers calculated probabilities for 1000 hypothetical studies (Sterne & Smith, 2001). Based on the literature on coronary heart disease, they assumed that the null hypothesis was false 10% of the time; so, 100 out of 1000 studies would be based on medical techniques that actually work. Based on the sometimes-flawed methods of inferential statistics, researchers would correctly reject the null hypothesis in about half of these 100 studies, missing about 50 effective techniques. But researchers also would inaccurately reject the null hypothesis—a Type I error—in approximately 50 of the 900 studies on ineffective techniques. To recap, researchers would reject the null hypothesis correctly about 50 times out of 1000 and would reject the null hypothesis incorrectly about 50 times out of 1000. Of course, researchers never know whether they are correct or incorrect. So, these numbers suggest that about half of the time that researchers reject the null hypothesis, it is a mistake! These numbers suggest that about half of published medical studies may be Type I errors.

Let's consider an example. In recent years, there has been a spate of claims about the health benefits of natural substances, which are often perceived to be healthy even though they are not necessarily risk-free. (Remember, rattlesnake venom and arsenic are natural substances!) Previous research has supported the use of vitamin E to prevent various maladies, and echinacea has been championed for its alleged ability to prevent the common cold. Yet studies that implemented rigorous research designs have largely discredited early, highly publicized accounts of the effectiveness of vitamin E and echinacea.

When the general public reads first of the value of vitamin E or echinacea and then of the health care establishment's dismissal of these treatments, we wonder what to believe and often, sadly, rely even more on our own biased common sense. It would be far better for scientists to insist on more ethical practices, such as pre-registration, that increase transparency and help avoid the temptation of sneaky maneuvers like HARKing (Nosek & Lindsay, 2018). (We will dig deeper into some of these sneaky maneuvers in the Chapter 6 Data Ethics feature.) Another solution is replication—repeating studies that have important implications for society. You'll learn more about the importance of replication in the Chapter 7 Data Ethics feature.

CHECK YOUR LEARNING

Reviewing the Concepts > When we draw a conclusion from inferential statistics, there is always a chance that we are wrong.

> When we reject the null hypothesis, but the null hypothesis is true, we have committed a Type I error.

> When we fail to reject the null hypothesis, but the null hypothesis is not true, we have committed a Type II error.

> Because of the flaws inherent in research, numerous null hypotheses are rejected falsely, resulting in Type I errors.

> The ethical researcher and the educated consumer of research are aware of their own biases and how they might affect their tendency to abandon critical thinking in favor of illusory correlations and the confirmation bias.

Clarifying the Concepts 5-11 Explain how Type I and Type II errors both relate to the null hypothesis.

Calculating the Statistics 5-12 If 7 out of every 280 innocent people are convicted of a crime, what is the rate of Type I error?

5-13 If the court system fails to convict 11 out of every 35 guilty people, what is the rate of Type II errors?

Applying the Concepts 5-14 Researchers conduct a study on perception by having participants throw a ball at a target first while wearing virtual-reality glasses and then while wearing glasses that allow normal viewing. The null hypothesis is that there is no difference in performance when wearing the virtual-reality glasses versus when wearing the glasses that allow normal viewing.

a. The researchers reject the null hypothesis, concluding that the virtual-reality glasses lead to a worse performance than do the normal glasses. What error might the researchers have made? Explain.

b. The researchers fail to reject the null hypothesis, concluding that it is possible that the virtual-reality glasses have no effect on performance. What error might the researchers have made? Explain.

Solutions to these Check Your Learning questions can be found in Appendix D.

REVIEW OF CONCEPTS

Samples and Their Populations

The gold standard of sample selection is *random sampling*, a procedure in which every member of the population has an equal chance of being chosen for study participation. A computer-based random numbers generator is used to ensure randomness. For practical reasons, random sampling is uncommon in social science research. Many behavioral scientists use a *convenience sample*, a sample that is readily available to them. One kind of convenience sample is a *volunteer sample* (also called a *self-selected sample*), in which participants themselves actively choose to participate in a study. With random assignment, every participant in a study has an equal chance of being assigned

LaunchPad
macmillan learning
Visit LaunchPad to access the e-book and to test your knowledge with LearningCurve.

to any of the experimental conditions. In conjunction with random assignment, *replication*—the duplication of scientific results—can go a long way toward increasing *generalizability*, the ability to generalize findings beyond a given sample.

Probability

Calculating probabilities is essential because human thinking is dangerously biased. Because of *confirmation bias*—the tendency to see patterns that we expect to see—we often see meaning in mere coincidence. A confirmation bias often leads to an *illusory correlation*, a relation that appears to be present but does not exist. When we think of probability, many of us think of *personal probability*, a person's own judgment about the likelihood that an event will occur. Statisticians, however, are referring to *expected relative-frequency probability*, or the long-run expected outcome if an experiment or trial were repeated many, many times. A *trial* refers to each occasion that a procedure is carried out, and an *outcome* is the result of a trial. A *success* refers to the outcome for which we're trying to determine the probability. *Probability* is a basic building block of inferential statistics. When we draw a conclusion about a population based on a sample, we can only say that it is probable that our conclusion is accurate, not that it is certain.

Inferential Statistics

Inferential statistics, based on probability, start with a hypothesis. The *null hypothesis* is a statement that usually postulates that there is no average difference between populations. The *research*, or *alternative*, *hypothesis* is a statement that postulates that there is an average difference between populations. After conducting a hypothesis test, we have only two possible conclusions. We can either reject or fail to reject the null hypothesis. When we conduct inferential statistics, we are often comparing an *experimental group*, the group subjected to an intervention, with a *control group*, the group that is the same as the experimental group in every way except the intervention. We use probability to draw conclusions about a population by estimating the probability that we would find a given difference between sample means if there is no underlying difference between population means.

Type I and Type II Errors

Statisticians must always be aware that their conclusions may be wrong. If a researcher rejects the null hypothesis, but the null hypothesis is correct, the researcher is making a *Type I error*. If a researcher fails to reject the null hypothesis, but the null hypothesis is false, the researcher is making a *Type II error*. Scientific and medical journals tend to publish, and the media tend to report on, the most exciting and surprising findings. As such, Type I errors are often overrepresented among reported findings.

SPSS

There are many ways to look more closely at the independent and dependent variables. You can request a variety of case summaries by selecting Analyze → Reports → Case Summaries. You can then highlight the variable of interest and click the arrow to move it under "Variables."

You also can break down one variable with a second "grouping" variable. For example, you could use the deliberative practice and athletic performance data from the SPSS section of Chapter 3. Select "Hours" under "Variables" and "Performance" under "Grouping Variable(s)." Then, click

"OK" to see the output screen. The output, part of which is shown in the screenshot here, tells you all the hours practiced for athletes who attained a given performance score. This summary, for instance, tells you that the three athletes who had a performance score of 3 had practiced for 1876, 4233, and 9377 hours, respectively.

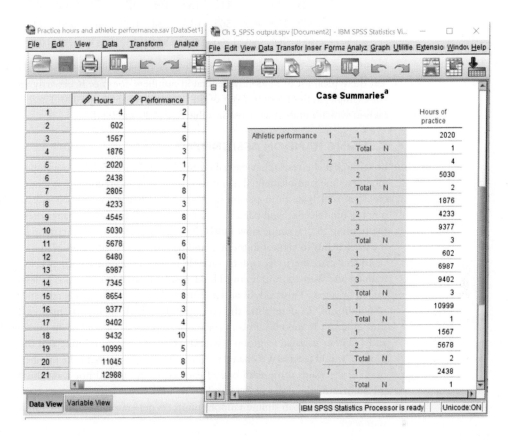

HOW IT WORKS

5.1 UNDERSTANDING RANDOM SAMPLING

There are approximately 2000 school psychologists in Australia. A researcher has developed a new diagnostic tool to identify conduct disorder in children and wants to study ways to train school psychologists to administer the tool. How can she recruit a random sample of 30 school psychologists to participate in her study?

She could use an online random numbers generator to randomly select a sample of 30 school psychologists for this study from among the target population of 2000 Australian school psychologists. Let's try it. (You can search for "random numbers generator" on the Internet or use randomizer.org.) To do so, she would tell the random numbers generator to produce one set of 30 numbers between 0001 and 2000. She would specify that she wants unique numbers, because no school psychologist can be in the study more than once. She can ask the program to sort the numbers, if she wishes, to more easily identify the participants who will be part of her sample. When we generated a set of 30 random numbers, we got the following result:

25	48	84	113	159	165	220	312	319	330
337	452	493	562	613	734	822	860	920	924
931	960	983	1290	1305	1462	1502	1515	1675	1994

Of course, each time we generate a list of random numbers, the list is different. Notice that the typical list of randomly generated numbers does not necessarily appear random. For example, in this list only 7 out of the 30 numbers are over 1000. There are also several cases in which numbers are close in value (e.g., 920 and 924).

5.2 USING RANDOM ASSIGNMENT

Imagine that the researcher described in How It Works 5.1 has developed two training modules. One is implemented in a classroom setting and requires that school psychologists travel to participate in in-person training. The other is a more cost-effective Web-based training module. She will administer a test to the 30 participants after they have received the training to determine how much they learned. How can she randomly assign half of the participants to classroom training and half to Web-based training?

In this case, the independent variable is type of training with two levels: classroom training and Web-based training. The dependent variable is amount of learning as determined by a test. This study is an experiment because participants are randomly assigned to conditions. To determine the condition to which each participant will be assigned, she could use a random numbers generator to produce one set of 30 numbers between 0 and 1. Those assigned to group 0 would receive in-person training and those assigned to group 1 would receive Web-based training. She would not want the numbers to be unique because she wants more than one of each type. She would not want the numbers to be sorted because the order of the numbers matters.

When we used an online random numbers generator, we got the following set of 30 numbers:

11000	01110
01000	00011
01110	01100

Based on these random numbers, the first two participants would be in group 1, and would receive Web-based training. The next four would be in group 0, and receive in-person training. And so on. This set contains 13 ones and 17 zeros. If we wanted exactly 15 in each group, we could stop assigning people to the 0 condition when we reached 15 zeros. Everyone else would then be assigned to the 1 condition.

5.3 CALCULATING PROBABILITY

Let's say that a university provides every student with a laptop computer, but students complain that their computers always crash when they are on the Internet and have at least three other applications open. One student thought this was an exaggeration and decided to calculate the probability that the campus computers would crash under these circumstances. How could he do this?

He could start by randomly selecting 100 different students to participate in his study. On the 100 students' computers, he could open three applications, go online, and record whether each computer crashed.

In this case, the trials would be the 100 instances (one trial on each of the 100 different laptops) in which the student opened three programs and then went online. The outcome would be whether the computer crashed. A success in this case would be a computer that crashed, and let's say that happened 55 times. (You might not consider a crashed computer a success, but in probability theory, a success refers to the outcome for which we want to determine the probability.) The researcher could then take the number of successes (55) and divide by the number of trials:

$$55/100 = 0.55$$

So the probability of a computer crashing when three programs are open and the student goes online is 0.55. Of course, to determine the true expected relative-frequency probability, he'd have to conduct many, many more trials.

EXERCISES

The solutions to the odd-numbered exercises can be found in Appendix C.

Clarifying the Concepts

5.1 Why do we study samples rather than populations?

5.2 What is the difference between a random sample and a convenience sample?

5.3 What is generalizability?

5.4 What is a volunteer sample, and what is the main risk associated with it?

5.5 What is crowdsourcing in research?

5.6 What are some of the pros and cons of crowdsourced data?

5.7 What is the difference between random sampling and random assignment?

5.8 What does it mean to replicate research, and how does replication affect our confidence in the findings?

5.9 Ideally, an experiment would use random sampling so that the data would accurately reflect the larger population. For practical reasons, this is difficult to do. How does random assignment help make up for a lack of random sampling?

5.10 What is the confirmation bias?

5.11 What is an illusory correlation?

5.12 How does the confirmation bias lead to the perpetuation of an illusory correlation?

5.13 In your own words, what is personal probability?

5.14 In your own words, what is expected relative-frequency probability?

5.15 Statisticians use terms like *trial*, *outcome*, and *success* in a particular way in reference to probability. What do each of these three terms mean in the context of flipping a coin?

5.16 We distinguish between probabilities and proportions. How does each capture the likelihood of an outcome?

5.17 What are the ways the term *independent* is used by statisticians?

5.18 One step in hypothesis testing is to randomly assign some members of the sample to the control group and some to the experimental group. What is the difference between these two groups?

5.19 What is the difference between a null hypothesis and a research hypothesis?

5.20 What are the two decisions or conclusions we can make about our hypotheses, based on the data?

5.21 What is the difference between a Type I error and a Type II error?

Calculating the Statistics

5.22 Forty-three tractor-trailers are parked for the night in a rest stop along a major highway. You assign each truck a number from 1 to 43. Use an online random numbers generator to select four trucks to weigh as they leave the rest stop in the morning.

5.23 Airport security makes random checks of passenger bags every day. If 1 in every 10 passengers is checked, use an online random numbers generator to determine the first 6 people to be checked—that is, which one of the first 10 people, which one of the second set of 10 people, and so on?

5.24 Randomly assign eight people to three conditions of a study, numbered 1, 2, and 3 using an online random numbers generator. (*Note:* Assign people to conditions without concern for having an equal number of people in each condition.)

5.25 You are running a study with five conditions, numbered 1 through 5. Using an online random numbers generator, assign the first seven participants who arrive at your lab to conditions, not worrying about equal assignment across conditions.

5.26 Explain why, given the general tendency people have of exhibiting the confirmation bias, it is important to collect objective data.

5.27 Explain why, given the general tendency people have of perceiving illusory correlations, it is important to collect objective data.

5.28 What is the probability of hitting a target if, in the long run, 71 out of every 489 attempts actually hit the target?

5.29 On a game show, 8 people have won the grand prize and a total of 266 people have competed. Estimate the probability of winning the grand prize.

5.30 Convert the following proportions to percentages:

  a. 0.0173

  b. 0.8

  c. 0.3719

5.31 Convert the following percentages to proportions:

  a. 62.7%

  b. 0.3%

  c. 4.2%

5.32 Convert the following percentages to proportions:

  a. 87.3%

  b. 14.2%

  c. 1%

5.33 Indicate whether each of the following statements refers to personal probability or to expected relative-frequency probability. Explain your answers.

  a. The chance of a die showing an even number is 50%.

  b. There is a 1 in 4 chance that I'll be late for class tomorrow.

  c. The likelihood that I'll break down and eat ice cream while studying is 80%.

  d. PlaneCrashInfo.com reported that the odds of being killed on a single flight on 1 of the top 25 safest airlines is 1 in 9.2 million.

Applying the Concepts

5.34 **Coincidence and the lottery:** "Woman wins millions from Texas lottery for 4th time" read the headline about Joan Ginther's amazing luck (Wetenhall, 2010). Two of the tickets were from the same store, whose owner, Bob Solis, said, "This is a very lucky store." Citing concepts from the chapter, what would you tell Ginther and Solis about the roles that probability and coincidence played in their fortunate circumstances?

5.35 **Random numbers and PINs:** How random is your personal identification number or PIN? Your PIN is one of the most important safeguards for the accounts that hold your money and valuable information about you. The BBC reported that, when choosing a four-digit PIN, "people drift towards a small subset of the 10,000 available. In some cases, up to 80% of choices come from just 100 different numbers" (Ward, 2013). Based on what you know about our ability to think randomly, explain this finding.

5.36 **Random sampling and a school psychologist career survey:** The Canadian government reported that there are 7550 psychologists working in Canada (2013). A researcher wants to randomly sample 100 of the Canadian psychologists for a survey study regarding aspects of their jobs.

  a. What is the population targeted by this study? How large is it?

  b. What is the sample desired by this researcher? How large is it?

  c. Describe how the researcher would select the sample by using an online random numbers generator.

  d. Using an online random numbers generator, list the first 10 participants that this researcher would select for the study.

5.37 **Hypotheses and the school psychologist career survey:** Continuing with the study described in Exercise 5.36, once the researcher had randomly selected the sample of 100 Canadian psychologists, she decided to randomly assign 50 of them to receive, as part of their survey materials, a (fictional) newspaper article about the improving job market. She assigned the other 50 to receive a (fictional) newspaper article about the declining job market. The participants then responded to questions about their attitudes toward their careers.

a. What is the independent variable in this experiment, and what are its levels?

b. What is the dependent variable in this experiment?

c. Write a null hypothesis and a research hypothesis for this study.

5.38 Random assignment and the school psychologist career survey: Refer to Exercise 5.37 when responding to the following questions.

a. Describe how the researcher would randomly assign the participants to the levels of the independent variable. Be sure to explain how the levels of the independent variable would be numbered and how the researcher would use an online random numbers generator.

b. How would the researcher use an online random numbers generator to list the levels of the independent variable to which the first 10 participants would be assigned? Use 0 and 1 to represent the two conditions.

c. Why is it possible that these numbers do not appear to be random? Discuss the difference between short-run and long-run proportions.

5.39 Random sampling and a survey of psychology majors: Imagine that you have been hired by the psychology department at your school to administer a survey to psychology majors about their experiences in the department. You have been asked to randomly select 60 of these majors from the overall pool of 300. You are working on this project in your dorm room using a random numbers table because the server is down and you cannot use an online random numbers generator. Your roommate offers to write down a list of 60 random numbers between 001 and 300 for you so you can be done quickly. In three to four sentences, explain to your roommate why she is not likely to create a list of random numbers.

5.40 Random sampling and random assignment: For each of the following studies, state (1) whether random sampling was likely to have been used, and explain whether it would have been possible to use it. Also, describe the population to which the researcher wanted to and could generalize, and state (2) whether random assignment was likely to have been used, and whether it would have been possible to use it.

a. A developmental psychologist wondered whether children born preterm (prematurely) had different social skills at age 5 than children born full term.

b. A counseling center director wanted to compare the length of therapy in weeks for students who came in for treatment for depression versus students who came in for treatment for anxiety. She wanted to report these data to the university administrators to help develop the next year's budget.

c. An industrial-organizational psychologist wondered whether a new laptop design would affect people's response time when using the computer. He wanted to compare response times when using the new laptop with response times when using two standard versions of laptops, a Mac and a PC.

5.41 Online sampling and visualizing neurons: Researcher Zoran Popović has developed a video game called Mozak (Serbo-Croatian for "brain") for the Allen Institute for Brain Science that enlists players—research participants, actually—to trace lines over images of neurons (Wingfield, 2017). The goal: to create three-dimensional models that other researchers can use to study what happens when the nervous system goes awry, such as with Parkinson's disease. Because there are so many variations of neurons—more than 100 million neurons in the human brain—Popović and his colleagues need help. They have managed to entice about 200 users to play the game daily, garnering points and attaining levels as in any video game. This work has enabled the researchers to work 10 times as fast as without the Mozak players.

a. Which method of sampling is Popović's team using to collect data?

b. What is the primary benefit of this method?

c. What is a possible ethical problem with this method?

5.42 Samples and *Cosmo* quizzes: *Cosmopolitan* magazine (*Cosmo*, as it's known popularly) publishes many of its well-known quizzes on its Web site. One quiz, aimed at heterosexual women, is titled "Are You Way Too Obsessed with Your Ex?" A question about "your rebound guy" offers these three choices: "Any random guy who will take your mind off the split," "A doppelgänger of your ex," and "The polar opposite of the last guy you dated." Consider whether you want to use the quiz data to determine how obsessed women are with their exes.

a. Describe the typical person who might respond to this quiz. How might data from such a sample be biased, even with respect to the overall *Cosmo* readership?

b. What is the danger of relying on volunteer samples in general?

c. What other problems do you see with this quiz? Comment on the types of questions and responses.

5.43 Samples and a survey on sex education: The Gizmodo blog *Throb,* a Web site focused on the science of sex, released its own sex education survey (Kelly, 2015). The journalist who developed the survey wrote: "I hope that with enough of your answers, we can start to build a picture of what sex ed actually looks like in [the United States]. And then maybe we can start to figure out how it actually affects the students who take it."

a. Do you think the journalist's results are likely to be representative of the U.S. population? Why or why not?

b. Describe the people most likely to volunteer for this sample. Why might this group be biased in comparison to the overall U.S. population?

c. The blogger says, "Five minutes poking around online forums where teens ask questions about sex can make me weep with rage and despair," an indication that she believes that misinformation is common. How might her perspective, likely one reflected in the blog *Throb* generally, lead to a particular type of survey respondent?

d. Because this survey is posted online, it's likely to get a large number of respondents. Why is it not enough to have a large sample to conduct a study with high external validity? What would we need to change about this sample to increase external validity?

5.44 Random sampling or random assignment: For each of the following hypothetical scenarios, state whether sampling or assignment is being described. Is the method of sampling or assignment random? Explain your answer.

a. A study of the services offered by counseling centers at Canadian universities studied 20 universities; every Canadian university had an equal chance of being in this study.

b. In a study of phobias, 30 rhesus monkeys were either exposed to fearful stimuli or not exposed to fearful stimuli. Every monkey had an equal chance of being placed in either of the exposure conditions.

c. In a study of cell phone usage, participants were recruited by including along with their cell phone bill an invitation to participate in the study.

d. In a study of visual perception, 120 Introduction to Psychology students were recruited to participate.

5.45 Confirmation bias and negative thought patterns: Explain how the general tendency of a confirmation bias might make it difficult to change negative thought patterns that accompany major depressive disorder.

5.46 Probability and coin flips: Short-run proportions are often quite different from long-run probabilities.

a. In your own words, explain why we would expect proportions to fluctuate in the short run, but why long-run probabilities are more predictable.

b. What is the expected long-run probability of heads if a person flips a coin many, many times? Why?

c. Flip a coin 10 times in a row. What proportion is heads? Do this 5 times. *Note:* You will learn more by actually doing it, so don't just write down numbers!

    Proportion for the first 10 flips:

    Proportion for the second 10 flips:

    Proportion for the third 10 flips:

    Proportion for the fourth 10 flips:

    Proportion for the fifth 10 flips:

d. Do the proportions in part (c) match the expected long-run probability in part (b)? Why or why not?

e. Imagine that a friend flipped a coin 10 times, got 9 out of 10 heads, and complained that the coin was biased. How would you explain to your friend the difference between short-term and long-term probability?

5.47 Probability, proportion, percentage, and *Where's Waldo?*: Salon.com reporter Ben Blatt analyzed the location of Waldo in the game in which you must find Waldo, a cartoon man who always wears a red-and-white-striped sweater and hat, in a highly detailed illustration (2013). Blatt reported that "53 percent of the time Waldo is hiding within one of two 1.5-inch tall bands, one starting three inches from the bottom of the page and another one starting seven inches from the bottom, stretching across the spread." One of Blatt's colleagues used this trick to find Waldo more quickly than another colleague who did not have this information across 11 illustrations.

a. What does the term *probability* refer to? What is the probability of finding Waldo in one of the two 1.5-inch bands that Blatt identified?

b. What does the term *proportion* refer to? What is the proportion of Waldos in one of these two 1.5-inch bands?

c. What does the term *percentage* refer to? What is the percentage of Waldos in one of these two bands?

d. Based on these data, do you have enough information to determine whether the *Where's Waldo?* game is fixed? Why or why not? (*Note:* Blatt reported that the "probability of any two 1.5-inch bands containing at least 50 percent of all Waldo's is remarkably slim, less than 0.3 percent.")

5.48 Independent trials and Eurovision Song Contest bias: As reported in the *Telegraph* (Highfield, 2005), Oxford University researchers investigated allegations of voting bias in the annual Eurovision Song Contest, which pits pop music acts from across Europe, one per country, against each other. The research team found that neighboring countries tended to vote as a block— Norway with Sweden, Belarus with Russia, and Greece with Cyprus, for example. Explain why one could not consider the votes to be independent of each other in this case.

5.49 Independent trials and the U.S. presidential election: Nate Silver is a statistician and journalist who uses statistics to create prediction tools. In an article leading up to the 2012 U.S. presidential election in which Barack Obama bested Mitt Romney, Silver (2012) explained his prediction methods as "principally, an Electoral College simulation, [which] therefore relies more heavily on state-by-state polls." Consider Silver's consolidation of data from polls across the 50 states. In what way are these polls likely to be independent trials? Why could someone argue that they are not truly independent trials?

5.50 Independent or dependent trials and probability: Gamblers often falsely predict the outcome of a future trial based on the outcome of previous trials. When trials are independent, the outcome of a future trial cannot be predicted based on the outcomes of previous trials. For each of the following examples, (1) state whether the trials are independent or dependent and (2) explain why. In addition, (3) state whether it is possible that the quote is accurate or whether it is definitely fallacious, explaining how the independence or dependence of trials influences accuracy.

a. You are playing Monopoly and have rolled a pair of sixes in 4 out of your last 10 rolls of the dice. You say, "Cool. I'm on a roll and will get sixes again."

b. You are an Ohio State University football fan and are sad because the team has lost two games in a row. You say, "That is really unusual; the Buckeyes are doomed this season. That's what happens with lots of early-season injuries."

c. You have a 20-year-old car that has trouble starting from time to time. It has started every day this week, and now it's Friday. You say, "I'm doomed. It's been reliable all week, and even though I did

get a tune-up last week, today is bound to be the day it fails me."

5.51 Null hypotheses and research hypotheses: For each of the following studies, cite the likely null hypothesis and the likely research hypothesis.

a. A forensic cognitive psychologist wondered whether repetition of false information (versus no repetition) would increase the tendency to develop false memories, on average.

b. A clinical psychologist studied whether ongoing structured assessments of the therapy process (versus no assessment) would lead to better outcomes, on average, among outpatient therapy clients with depression.

c. A corporation recruited an industrial-organizational psychologist to explore the effects of cubicles (versus enclosed offices) on employee morale.

d. A team of developmental cognitive psychologists studied whether teaching a second language to children from birth affects children's ability to speak their native language.

5.52 Decision about null hypotheses: For each of the following fictional conclusions, state whether the researcher seems to have rejected or failed to reject the null hypothesis (contingent, of course, on inferential statistics having backed up the statement). Explain the rationale for your decision.

a. When false information is repeated several times, people seem to be more likely, on average, to develop false memories than when the information is not repeated.

b. Therapy clients with major depressive disorder who have ongoing structured assessments of therapy seem to have lower post-therapy depression levels, on average, than do clients who do not have ongoing structured assessments.

c. Employee morale does not seem to be different, on average, whether employees work in cubicles or in enclosed offices.

d. A child's native language does not seem to be different in strength, on average, whether the child is raised to be bilingual or not.

5.53 Type I versus Type II errors: Examine the statements from Exercise 5.52 repeated here. For each, if this conclusion were incorrect, what type of error would the researcher have made? Explain your answer.

a. When false information is repeated several times, people seem to be more likely, on average, to develop false memories than when the information is not repeated.

b. Therapy clients with major depressive disorder who have ongoing structured assessments of therapy seem to have lower post-therapy depression levels, on average, than do clients who do not have ongoing structured assessments.

c. Employee morale does not seem to be different, on average, whether employees work in cubicles or enclosed offices.

d. A child's native language does not seem to be different in strength, on average, whether the child is raised to be bilingual or not.

5.54 Rejecting versus failing to reject an invitation: Imagine you have found a new study partner in your statistics class. One day, your study partner asks you to go on a date. This invitation takes you completely by surprise, and you have no idea what to say. You are not attracted to the person in a romantic way, but at the same time you do not want to hurt his or her feelings.

a. Create two possible responses to the person, one in which you *fail to reject the invitation* and another in which you *reject the invitation*.

b. How is your failure to reject the invitation different from rejecting or accepting the invitation?

5.55 Confirmation bias, errors, replication, and horoscopes: A horoscope on Astrology.com stated: "A big improvement is in the works, one that you may know nothing about, and today is the day for the big unveiling." A job-seeking recent college graduate might spot some new listings for interesting positions and decide the horoscope was right. If you look for an association, you're likely to find it. Yet, over and over again, careful researchers have failed to find evidence to support the accuracy of astrology (e.g., Dean & Kelly, 2003).

a. Explain to the college graduate how confirmation bias guides his logic in deciding the horoscope was right.

b. If Dean and Kelly and other researchers were wrong, what kind of error would they have made?

c. Explain why replication (i.e., "over and over again") means that this finding is not likely to be an error.

5.56 Probability and sumo wrestling: In their book *Freakonomics*, Levitt and Dubner (2005) describe a study conducted by Duggan and Levitt (2002) that broached the question: Do sumo wrestlers cheat? Sumo wrestlers garner enormous respect in Japan, where sumo wrestling is considered the national sport. The researchers examined the results of 32,000 wrestling matches over

an 11-year time span. If a wrestler finishes a tournament with a losing record (7 or fewer wins out of 15 matches), his ranking goes down, as do the money and prestige that come with winning. The researchers wondered whether, going into the last match of the tournament, wrestlers with 7-7 records (needing only 1 more win to rise in the rankings) would have a better-than-expected win record against wrestlers with 8-6 records (those who already are guaranteed to rise in the rankings). Such a phenomenon might indicate cheating. One 7-7 wrestler (wrestler A), based on *past* matches against a given 8-6 opponent (wrestler B), was calculated to have won 48.7% of the time.

a. If there is no cheating, what is the probability that wrestler A will beat wrestler B in any situation, including the one in which A is 7-7 and B is 8-6?

b. If matches tend to be rigged so that 8-6 wrestlers frequently throw matches to help other wrestlers maintain their rankings (and to get payback from 7-7 wrestlers in future matches), what would you expect to happen to the winning percentage when these two wrestlers meet under these exact conditions—that is, the first is 7-7 in the tournament and the second is 8-6?

c. State the null hypothesis and the research hypothesis for the study examining whether sumo wrestlers cheat.

d. In this particular real-life example, wrestler A was found to have beaten wrestler B 79.6% of the time when A had a 7-7 record and B had an 8-6 record. If inferential statistics determined that it was very unlikely that this would happen by chance, what would your decision be? Use the language of hypothesis testing.

5.57 Testimonials and Harry Potter: Amazon and other online bookstores offer readers the opportunity to write their own book reviews, and many potential readers scour these reviews to decide which books to buy. Harry Potter books attract a great deal of these reader reviews. One Amazon reviewer, "bel 78," submitted her review of *Harry Potter and the Half-Blood Prince* from Argentina. Of the book, she said, "It's simply outstandingly good," and suggested that readers of her review "run to get your copy." Do these reviews have an impact? In this case, more than 900 people had read bel 78's review, and close to 700 indicated that the review was helpful to them.

a. Imagine that you're deciding whether to buy *Harry Potter and the Half-Blood Prince*, and you want to know what people who had already read the book thought before you invest the money and time.

What is the population whose opinion you're interested in?

b. If you read only bel 78's review, what is the sample from which you're gathering your data? What are some of the problems in relying on just this one review?

c. About 5500 readers had reviewed this book on Amazon by 2016. What if all reviewers agreed that this book was amazing? What is the problem with this sample?

d. Given no practical or financial limitations, what would be the best way to gather a sample of Amazon users who had read this Harry Potter book?

e. A friend plans to order a book online to take on spring break. She is reading online reviews of several books to make her decision. Explain to her in just a few sentences why her reliance on testimonials is not likely to provide her with objective information.

Putting It All Together

5.58 **Horoscopes and predictions:** People remember when their horoscopes had an uncanny prediction—say, the prediction of a problem in love on the exact day of the breakup of a romantic relationship—and decide that horoscopes are accurate. Munro and Munro (2000) are among those who have challenged such a conclusion. They reported that 34% of students chose their own horoscope as the best match for them when the horoscopes were labeled with the signs of the zodiac, whereas only 13% chose their own horoscope when the predictions were labeled only with numbers and in a random order. Thirteen percent is not statistically significantly different from 8.3%, which is the percentage we'd expect by chance.

a. What is the population of interest, and what is the sample in this study?

b. Was random sampling used? Explain your answer.

c. Was random assignment used? Explain your answer.

d. What is the independent variable and what are its levels? What is the dependent variable? What type of variables are these?

e. What is the null hypothesis and what is the research hypothesis?

f. What decision did the researchers make? (Respond using the language of inferential statistics.)

g. If the researchers were incorrect in their decision, what kind of error did they make? Explain your

answer. What are the consequences of this type of error, both in general and in this situation?

5.59 **Alcohol abuse interventions:** Sixty-four male students were ordered, after they had violated university alcohol rules, to meet with a school counselor. Borsari and Carey (2005) randomly assigned these students to one of two conditions. Those in the first condition were assigned to undergo a newly developed brief motivational interview (BMI), an intervention in which educational material relates to the students' own experiences; those in the second condition were assigned to attend a standard alcohol education session (AE) in which educational material is presented with no link to students' experiences. Based on inferential statistics, the researchers concluded that those in the BMI group had fewer alcohol-related problems at follow-up, on average, than did those in the AE group.

a. What is the population of interest, and what is the sample in this study?

b. Was random sampling likely used? Explain your answer.

c. Was random assignment likely used? Explain your answer.

d. What is the independent variable and what are its levels? What is the dependent variable?

e. What is the null hypothesis and what is the research hypothesis?

f. What decision did the researchers make? (Respond using the language of inferential statistics.)

g. If the researchers were incorrect in their decision, what kind of error did they make? Explain your answer. What are the consequences of this type of error, both in general and in this situation?

5.60 **Treatment for depression:** Researchers conducted a study of 18 patients whose depression had not responded to treatment (Zarate, 2006). Half received one intravenous dose of ketamine, a hypothesized quick fix for depression; half received one intravenous dose of placebo. Far more of the patients who received ketamine improved, as measured by the Hamilton Depression Rating Scale, usually in less than 2 hours, than patients on placebo.

a. What is the population of interest, and what is the sample in this study?

b. Was random sampling likely used? Explain your answer.

c. Was random assignment likely used? Explain your answer.

d. What is the independent variable and what are its levels? What is the dependent variable?

e. What is the null hypothesis and what is the research hypothesis?

f. What decision did the researchers make? (Respond using the language of inferential statistics.)

g. If the researchers were incorrect in their decision, what kind of error did they make? Explain your answer. What are the consequences of this type of error, both in general and in this situation?

5.61 Preregistration, crowdsourcing, and fake news: Ethical researchers are increasingly using the Internet to modernize their research and conduct it in a more ethical way. In one study, not yet peer-reviewed, Yale researchers found that increased exposure to fake news headlines led to increased perceptions that these headlines were accurate (Pennycook, Cannon, & Rand, 2018). The researchers described their methods as follows: "All data are available online (https://osf .io/txf46/). We preregistered our hypotheses, primary analyses, and sample size (https://osf.io/txf46/)....All participants were recruited from Amazon's Mechanical Turk (Horton, Rand, & Zeckhauser, 2011)."

a. Describe two ways in which the researchers are using ethical, transparent practices. Explain why these practices are ethical.

b. What is HARKing, and how does one of the practices described here make it impossible for the researchers to HARK?

c. What do the researchers mean when they say that they recruited participants from Amazon's Mechanical Turk? What kind of a sample is this?

d. What are some of the benefits of collecting data in this way?

e. What are some of the drawbacks of collecting data in this way?

Visit LaunchPad to access the e-book and to test your knowledge with LearningCurve.

TERMS

random sample (p. 120)

convenience sample (p. 120)

generalizability (p. 122)

replication (p. 122)

volunteer sample (p. 122)

crowdsourcing (p. 122)

confirmation bias (p. 126)

illusory correlation (p. 126)

personal probability (p. 127)

probability (p. 127)

expected relative-frequency probability (p. 128)

trial (p. 128)

outcome (p. 128)

success (p. 128)

control group (p. 130)

experimental group (p. 130)

null hypothesis (p. 130)

research hypothesis (p. 131)

Type I error (p. 134)

Type II error (p. 135)

The Normal Curve, Standardization, and z Scores

BEFORE YOU GO ON

- You should be able to create histograms and frequency polygons (Chapter 2).

- You should be able to describe distributions of scores using measures of central tendency, variability, and skewness (Chapters 2 and 4).

- You should understand that there are distributions of scores based on samples, as well as distributions of scores based on populations (Chapter 5).

Dallas and John Heaton/SCPhotos/Alamy Stock Photo

Cheating in Sumo Wrestling? The normal curve can help us identify unusual data points, including sumo wrestling matches that have an unlikely outcome. Do sumo wrestlers sometimes throw matches to help each other achieve an overall winning record?

- A **normal curve** is a specific bell-shaped curve that is unimodal, symmetric, and defined mathematically.

Cheaters beware! Statisticians can apply principles based on the normal curve to identify patterns of cheating, usually in the form of extreme scores. *A **normal curve** is a specific bell-shaped curve that is unimodal, symmetric, and defined mathematically.* (We introduced the concept of a normal curve when we described a normal distribution in Chapter 2; see Figure 2-4 or see Figure 6-8 on p. 163 in this chapter.) If a score falls in the extreme tails of the normal curve, it can raise a red flag that there may be cheating. One Australian Open doubles tennis match, for example, received lots of attention for extreme gambling on an otherwise obscure contest (Rothenberg & Glanz, 2016). The bets were overwhelmingly in favor of the Czech Andrea Hlavackova and her Polish partner Lukasz Kubot, who beat their Spanish competitors, Lara Arruabarrena and David Marrero. It wasn't even close; indeed, the first match was an exceptionally quick 20 minutes.

Cases like this one, with extreme betting, are referred to the International Tennis Federation's watchdog group. Of course, one suspicious data point doesn't mean that Arruabarrena and Marrero cheated. In fact, Marrero had a knee injury. Someone probably noticed and spread the word to gamblers. Often, though, it means that something unusual is going on.

Similar cases have occurred in other contexts. For example, unusual patterns of wins led to the discovery of cheating among Japanese sumo wrestlers (Duggan & Levitt, 2002). A season-long winning record garners money and prestige for a sumo wrestler. It turns out that sumo wrestlers who are one match away from a winning record are more likely to win against a competitor who already has a winning record. Did some sumo wrestlers who had already achieved this lucrative status throw matches to help an opponent who might return the favor one day?

As these cases highlight, the identification of cheating, and the implementation of reforms that might prevent it, can start with an understanding of the normal, bell-shaped curve. In this chapter, we learn about the building blocks of inferential statistics: (1) the characteristics of the normal curve; (2) how to use the normal curve to standardize any variable by using a tool called the z score; and (3) the central limit theorem, which, when coupled with a grasp of standardization, allows us to make comparisons between means.

The Normal Curve

As these examples of cheating in sports illustrate, the normal curve is a powerful tool in statistics. It allows us to determine probabilities about data and then draw conclusions that we can apply beyond the data. In this section, we learn more about the normal curve through a real-life example.

EXAMPLE 6.1

The World Happiness Report presents an overview of well-being around the globe (Helliwell, Layard, & Sachs, 2017). Individuals in 157 countries were asked to provide an overall rating of their current quality of life on a scale ranging from 0 to 10. Each of the 157 countries received a score that was the mean of the ratings for participants from that country. Countries like Denmark and Canada fell on the high end, whereas countries like Yemen and Syria fell on the low end. Here is a randomly selected sample of 5 of the 157 scores:

Japan:	5.921
Mexico:	6.778
Nigeria:	4.875
Peru:	5.743
Rwanda:	3.515

Figure 6-1 shows a histogram of those countries' scores, with a normal curve superimposed on the histogram. With so few scores, we can only begin to guess whether, after more observations, it will begin to look like a normal distribution.

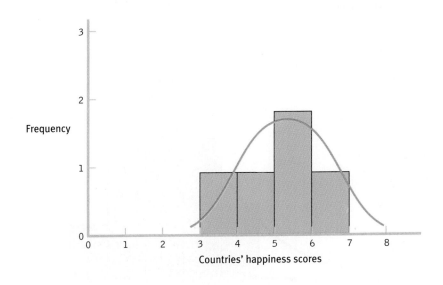

FIGURE 6-1

Sample of 5

Here is a histogram of the happiness scores for 5 countries. With so few countries, the data are unlikely to closely resemble the normal curve that we would see for an entire population of scores. Source: Helliwell, Layard, & Sachs, 2017

Now, here are the heights in inches from a sample of 30 countries:

7.413	5.771	3.069	6.005	6.078	6.705	5.822	4.219	7.039	5.768
7.291	4.276	3.763	5.977	4.356	5.856	3.866	4.201	6.929	4.513
3.622	5.291	4.139	4.871	5.177	5.546	6.596	3.974	5.151	5.045

Figure 6-2 shows the histogram for these data. Notice that the scores for 30 countries resemble a normal curve more so than do the scores of just 5 countries, although certainly they don't match it perfectly.

Now let's look at the entire population. Figure 6-3 shows the histogram for the scores from all 157 countries.

These three figures demonstrate why the number of scores is so important in relation to the normal curve. As the size of the data set increases, the distribution more and more closely resembles a normal curve (as long as the underlying population distribution is normal). Imagine even larger samples or populations—of 1000 or of 1 million. As the size of the sample approaches the size of the population, the shape of the distribution tends to be normally distributed. ●

MASTERING THE CONCEPT

6-1: The distributions of many variables approximate a normal curve, a mathematically defined, bell-shaped curve that is unimodal and symmetric.

CHECK YOUR LEARNING

Reviewing the Concepts

> The normal curve is a specific, mathematically defined curve that is bell-shaped, unimodal, and symmetric.

> The normal curve describes the distributions of many variables.

> As the size of a sample approaches the size of the population, the distribution resembles a normal curve (as long as the population is normally distributed).

Clarifying the Concepts   **6-1**   What does it mean to say that the normal curve is unimodal and symmetric?

Calculating the Statistics   **6-2**   A sample of 225 students completed the Consideration of Future Consequences (CFC) scale, a measure that assesses how much people think about the degree to which their current actions affect their future (Petrocelli, 2003). The scores are means of responses to 12 items. Overall CFC scores range from 1 to 5.

a. Here are CFC scores for 5 students, rounded to the nearest whole or half number: 3.5, 3.5, 3.0, 4.0, and 2.0. Create a histogram for these data, either by hand or by using software.

b. Now create a histogram for these scores of 30 students:

3.5 3.5 3.0 4.0 2.0 4.0 2.0 4.0 3.5 4.5

4.5 4.0 3.5 2.5 3.5 3.5 4.0 3.0 3.0 2.5

3.0 3.5 4.0 3.5 3.5 2.0 3.5 3.0 3.0 2.5

Applying the Concepts   **6-3**   The histogram below uses the actual (not rounded) CFC scores for all 225 students described in Check Your Learning 6-2. What do you notice about the shape of this distribution of scores as the size of the sample increases?

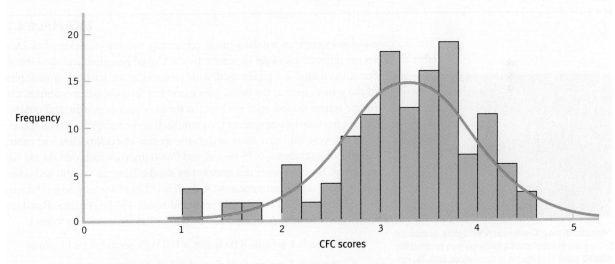

Solutions to these Check Your Learning questions can be found in Appendix D.

Standardization, z Scores, and the Normal Curve

The normal curve also means that scientists can make meaningful comparisons. Why? When data are normally distributed, we can compare one particular score to an entire distribution of scores. To do this, we convert a raw score to a standardized score (for which percentiles are already known). *Standardization is a way to convert individual scores from different normal distributions to a shared normal distribution with a known mean, standard deviation, and percentiles.*

In this section, we explain the importance of standardization and introduce the tool that helps us standardize, the *z* score. We show how we can convert raw scores to *z* scores and *z* scores to raw scores. We demonstrate how the distribution of *z* scores allows us to know what percentage of the population falls above or below a given *z* score.

- **Standardization** is a way to convert individual scores from different normal distributions to a shared normal distribution with a known mean, standard deviation, and percentiles.

- A **z score** is the number of standard deviations a particular score is from the mean.

The Need for Standardization

One of the first problems with making meaningful comparisons is that variables are measured on different scales. For example, we might measure height in inches but measure weight in kilograms. To compare heights and weights, we need a way to put different variables on the same standardized scale. Fortunately, we can standardize different variables by using their means and standard deviations to convert any raw score into a *z* score. *A **z score** is the number of standard deviations a particular score is from the mean.* A *z* score is part of its own distribution, the *z* distribution, just as a raw score, such as a person's height, is part of its own distribution, a distribution of heights. (Note that as with all statistical symbols, the *z* is italicized.)

EXAMPLE 6.2

Here is a memorable example of standardization: comparing weights of cockroaches. Different countries use different measures of weight. In the United Kingdom and the United States, the pound is typically used, with variants that are fractions or multiples of the pound, such as the dram, ounce, and ton. In most other countries, the metric system is used, with the gram as the basic unit of weight, and variants that are fractions or multiples of the gram, such as the milligram and kilogram.

If we were told that three imaginary species of cockroaches had mean weights of 8.00 drams, 0.25 pound, and 98.00 grams, which one should we most fear? We can answer this question by standardizing the weights and comparing them on the same measure. A dram is 1/256 of a pound, so 8.00 drams is 1/32 = 0.03125 of a pound. One pound equals 453.5924 grams. Based on these conversions, the weights could be standardized into grams as follows:

Cockroach 1 weighs 8.00 drams = 0.03125 pound = 14.17 grams

Cockroach 2 weighs 0.25 pound = 113.40 grams

Cockroach 3 weighs 98.00 grams

Standardizing Cockroach Weights Standardization is a way to create meaningful comparisons by converting different scales to a common, or standardized, scale. We can compare the weights of these cockroaches using different measures of weights—including drams, pounds, and grams.

Rosanne Tackaberry/Alamy Stock Photo

Standardizing allows us to determine that the second cockroach species tends to weigh the most: 113.40 grams. Fortunately, the biggest cockroach in the world weighs only about 35 grams and is about 80 millimeters (3.15 inches) long. Cockroaches 2 and 3 exist only in our imaginations. However, not all conversions are as easy as standardizing weights from different units into grams. That's why statisticians developed the z distribution. ●

Transforming Raw Scores into z Scores

A desire to make meaningful comparisons forces us to convert raw scores into standardized scores. For example, let's say you know that after taking the midterm examination, you are 1 standard deviation above the mean in your statistics class. Is this good news? What if you are 0.5 standard deviation below the mean? Understanding a score's relation to the mean of its distribution gives us important information. For a statistics test, we know that being above the mean is good; for anxiety levels, we know that being above the mean is usually bad. z scores create an opportunity to make meaningful comparisons.

The only information we need to convert any raw score to a z score is the mean and standard deviation of the population of interest. In the midterm example, we are probably interested in comparing our grade with the grades of others in this course. In this case, the statistics class is the population of interest. Let's say that your score on the midterm is 2 standard deviations above the mean; your z score is 2.0. Imagine that a friend's score is 1.6 standard deviations below the mean; your friend's z score is −1.6. What would your z score be if you fell exactly at the mean in your statistics class? If you guessed 0, you're correct.

Figure 6-4 illustrates two important features of the z distribution. First, the z distribution always has a mean of 0. So, if you are exactly at the mean, then you are 0 standard deviations from the mean. Second, the z distribution always has a standard deviation of 1. If your raw score is 1 standard deviation above the mean, then you have a z score of 1.0.

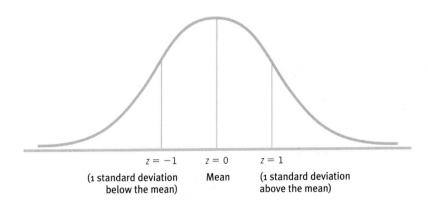

z = −1   z = 0   z = 1
(1 standard deviation   Mean   (1 standard deviation
below the mean)   above the mean)

FIGURE 6-4

The z Distribution

The z distribution always has a mean of 0 and a standard deviation of 1.

EXAMPLE 6.3

Let's calculate z scores without a calculator or formula. We'll use the distribution of scores on a statistics exam. (This example is illustrated in Figure 6-5.) If the mean on a statistics exam is 70, the standard deviation is 10, and your score is 80, what is your z score? In this case, you are exactly 10 points, or 1 standard deviation, above the mean, so your z score is 1.0. Now let's say your score is 50, which is 20 points, or 2 standard deviations, below the mean, so your z score is −2.0. What if your score is 85? Now you're 15 points, or 1.5 standard deviations, above the mean, so your z score is 1.5.

FIGURE 6-5

z Scores Intuitively

With a mean of 70 and a standard deviation of 10, we can calculate many z scores without a formula. A raw score of 50 has a z score of −2.0. A raw score of 60 has a z score of −1.0. A raw score of 70 has a z score of 0. A raw score of 80 has a z score of 1.0. A raw score of 85 has a z score of 1.5.

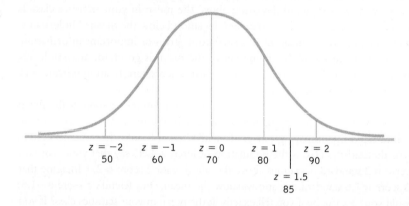

As you can see, we don't need a formula to calculate a z score when we're working with easy numbers. It is important, however, to learn the notation and language of statistics. So let's also convert z scores using a formula for when the numbers are not easy to work with. To calculate a particular z score, there are just two steps.

MASTERING THE FORMULA

6-1: The formula for a z score is:

$$z = \frac{(X - \mu)}{\sigma}$$

We calculate the difference between an individual score and the population mean, then divide by the population standard deviation.

STEP 1: Determine the distance of a particular person's score (X) from the population mean (μ): $X - \mu$.

STEP 2: Express this distance in terms of standard deviations by dividing by the population standard deviation, σ.

The formula, therefore, is:

$$z = \frac{(X - \mu)}{\sigma}$$

EXAMPLE 6.4

Let's take an example that is not so easy to calculate in our heads. The mean happiness score for the population of 157 countries we discussed earlier is 5.382, with a standard deviation of 1.138. Australia's score is 7.313. How can we convert this to a *z* score?

> **STEP 1: Subtract the population mean from your score.**

In this case, subtract the population mean, 5.382, from Australia's score, 7.313.

> **STEP 2: Divide by the population standard deviation.**

The population standard deviation is 1.138. Here are those steps in the context of the formula:

$$z = \frac{(X - \mu)}{\sigma} = \frac{(7.313 - 5.382)}{1.138} = 1.70$$

Australia's happiness score is 1.70 standard deviations above the mean.

We must be careful not to use a formula mindlessly. Always consider whether the answer makes sense. In this case, 1.70 is positive, indicating that the score is approaching 2 standard deviations above the mean. This makes sense because the raw score of 7.313 is also approaching 2 standard deviations above the mean of 5.382. If you do this quick check regularly, then you can correct mistakes before they cost you. ●

EXAMPLE 6.5

Let's take another example: The happiness score for Egypt is 4.362.

> **STEP 1: Subtract the population mean from your score.**

Here, subtract the population mean, 5.382, from Egypt's score, 4.362.

> **STEP 2: Divide by the population standard deviation.**

The population standard deviation is 1.138. Here are those steps in the context of the formula:

$$z = \frac{(X - \mu)}{\sigma} = \frac{(4.362 - 5.382)}{1.138} = -0.90$$

Egypt's happiness score is 0.90 standard deviation *below* the mean.

Don't forget the sign of the *z* score. Changing a *z* score from negative 0.90 to positive 0.90 makes a big difference! ●

Estimating z Scores Would you guess that the dog on the left has a positive or negative *z* score for size as compared to all dogs? What about the dog on the right? A dog that is very small is below average in size and would have a negative *z* score. A dog that is very large is above average in size and would have a positive *z* score.

EXAMPLE 6.6

With the global happiness example we've been using, let's now demonstrate that the mean of the *z* distribution is always 0 and the standard deviation is always 1. The mean is 5.382 and the standard deviation is 1.138. Let's calculate what the *z* score would be at the mean.

> **STEP 1:** Subtract the population mean from a score right at the mean.

We subtract the population mean, 5.382, from a score right at the mean, 5.382.

> **STEP 2:** Divide by the population standard deviation.

We divide the difference by 1.138. Here are those steps in the context of the formula:

$$z = \frac{(X - \mu)}{\sigma} = \frac{(5.382 - 5.382)}{1.138} = 0$$

If a country is exactly 1 standard deviation above the mean, its score would be $5.382 + 1.138 = 6.520$. (The country with the happiness score closest to this is Uruguay.) Let's calculate what the *z* score would be for this country.

> **STEP 1:** Subtract the population mean from a score exactly 1 standard deviation above the mean.

We subtract the population mean, 5.382, from a score exactly 1 standard deviation (1.138) above the mean, 6.520.

> **STEP 2:** Divide by the population standard deviation.

We divide the difference by 1.138. Here are those steps in the context of the formula:

$$z = \frac{(X - \mu)}{\sigma} = \frac{(6.520 - 5.382)}{1.138} = 1 \bullet$$

Transforming z Scores into Raw Scores

If we already know a *z* score, then we can reverse the calculations to determine the raw score. The formula is the same; we just plug in all the numbers instead of the *X*, then solve algebraically. Let's try it with the global happiness example.

EXAMPLE 6.7

The population mean is 5.382, with a standard deviation of 1.138. France has a z score of 0.963. What is its actual happiness score?

$$z = \frac{(X - \mu)}{\sigma} = 0.963 = \frac{(X - 5.382)}{1.138}$$

If we solve for X, we get 6.478. For those who prefer to minimize the use of algebra, we can do the algebra on the equation itself to derive a formula that gets the raw score directly. The formula is derived by multiplying both sides of the equation by σ, then adding μ to both sides of the equation. This isolates the X, as follows:

$$X = z(\sigma) + \mu$$

So, there are two steps to converting a z score to a raw score:

> **STEP 1:** Multiply the z score by the population standard deviation.

Multiply the z score, 0.963, by the population standard deviation, 1.138.

> **STEP 2:** Add the population mean to this product.

Add the population mean, 5.382, to this product.
Here are those steps in the context of the formula:

$$X = 0.963(1.138) + 5.382 = 6.478$$

Regardless of whether we use the original formula or the direct formula, the happiness score for France is 6.478. As always, think about whether the answer seems accurate. In this case, the answer does make sense because the score is above the mean and the z score is positive. ●

EXAMPLE 6.8

Let's try a country with a negative z score. Kenya's z score is −0.902.

> **STEP 1:** Multiply the z score by the population standard deviation.

Multiply the z score, −0.902, by the population standard deviation, 1.138.

> **STEP 2:** Add the population mean to this product.

Add the population mean, 5.382, to this product.

<aside>
MASTERING THE FORMULA

6-2: The formula to calculate the raw score from a z score is:

$$X = z(\sigma) + \mu$$

We multiply the z score by the population standard deviation, then add the population mean.
</aside>

Apples and Oranges Standardization allows us to compare apples with oranges. If we can standardize the raw scores on two different scales, converting both scores to z scores, we can then compare the scores directly.

Hafiz Ismail/EyeEm/Getty Images

Here are those steps in the context of the formula:

$$X = -0.902(1.138) + 5.382 = 4.356$$

Kenya's happiness score is 4.356. Don't forget the negative sign when doing this calculation.

As long as we know the mean and standard deviation of the population, we can do two things: (1) calculate the raw score from its z score, and (2) calculate the z score from its raw score.

Now that you understand z scores, let's question the saying that "you can't compare apples and oranges." We can take any apple from a normal distribution of apples, find its z score using the mean and standard deviation for the distribution of apples, convert the z score to a percentile, and discover that a particular apple is, say, larger than 85% of all apples. Similarly, we can take any orange from a normal distribution of oranges, find its z score using the mean and standard deviation for the distribution of oranges, convert the z score to a percentile, and discover that this particular orange is, say, larger than 97% of all oranges. The orange (with respect to other oranges) is bigger than the apple (with respect to other apples), and yes, that is an honest comparison. With standardization, we can compare anything, each relative to its own group.

The normal curve also allows us to convert scores to percentiles because 100% of the population is represented under the bell-shaped curve. This means that the midpoint is the 50th percentile. If an individual score on some test is located to the right of the mean, we know that the score lies above the 50th percentile. A score to the left of the mean is below the 50th percentile. To make more specific comparisons, we convert raw scores to z scores and z scores to percentiles using the z distribution. *The z distribution is a normal distribution of standardized scores—a distribution of z scores. And the standard normal distribution is a normal distribution of z scores.*

Most people are not content merely with knowing whether their own score is above or below the average score. After all, there is likely a big difference between scoring at the 51st percentile and scoring at the 99th percentile in national happiness, as shown in Figure 6-6. The standardized z distribution allows us to do the following:

1. Transform raw scores into standardized scores called z scores
2. Transform z scores back into raw scores

● The **z distribution** is a normal distribution of standardized scores.

● The **standard normal distribution** is a normal distribution of z scores.

The All-Encompassing z Distribution

The z distribution theoretically includes all possible scores, so when it's based on a normal distribution, we know that 50% of the scores are above the mean and 50% are below the mean. But the 51st percentile and the 99th percentile are still far from each other, so two people making a comparison usually want more precise information than whether or not they are above average.

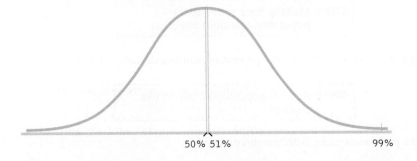

50% 51%   99%

3. Compare z scores to each other—even when the underlying raw scores are measured on different scales

4. Transform z scores into percentiles that are more easily understood ●

Using z Scores to Make Comparisons

In Figure 6-7, you'll find an example of how researchers use z scores as a standardization tool. Using the Google Ngram tool, researchers recorded the numbers of times that different emotion-related words were used in literature since 1900. To make direct comparisons, they converted all of the counts into z scores. By doing so, even if "fear" words were used more often than "disgust" words, the researchers could directly compare the patterns in the usage of emotion-related words.

Now let's look at an example you may have encountered in your own life. Imagine that a friend is taking a course in statistics at the same time that you are, but with a different professor. Each professor has a different grading scheme, so each class produces a different distribution of scores. Thanks to standardization, we can convert each raw score to a z score and compare raw scores from *different* distributions.

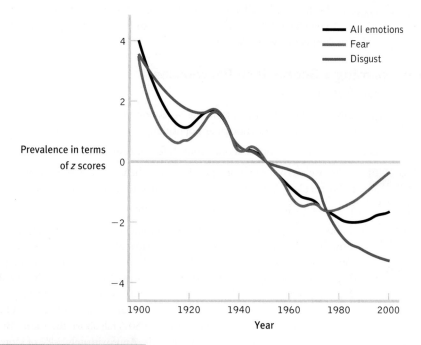

FIGURE 6-7

Using z Scores as a Standardization Tool in Research

Acerbi, Lampos, Garnett, and Bentley (2013) used Google Ngram to look at patterns in the use of emotion-related words in literature over time. They found that, in general, the prevalence of emotion-related words used in the 30 million books catalogued in Google books has decreased over the past century. The one exception was words related to "fear." This graph plots z scores to allow for the comparison of different emotion words. For example, if fear-related words were more common overall than disgust-related words, the lines would be far apart, making comparisons of trend lines difficult.

EXAMPLE 6.9

For example, let's say that you and your friend both took a quiz. You earned 92 out of 100; the distribution of your class had a mean of 78.1 and a standard deviation of 12.2. Your friend earned 8.1 out of 10; the distribution of his class had a mean of 6.8 with a standard deviation of 0.74. Again, we're only interested in the classes that took the test, so these are populations. Who did better?

We standardize the scores in terms of their respective distributions.

$$\text{Your score: } z = \frac{(X - \mu)}{\sigma} = \frac{(92 - 78.1)}{12.2} = 1.14$$

$$\text{Your friend's score: } z = \frac{(X - \mu)}{\sigma} = \frac{(8.1 - 6.8)}{0.74} = 1.76$$

First, let's check our work. Do these answers make sense? Yes—both you and your friend scored above the mean and have positive z scores. Second, we compare the z scores. Although you both scored well above the mean in terms of standard deviations, your friend did better with respect to his class than you did with respect to your class. ●

Making Comparisons z scores create a way to compare students taking different exams from different courses. If each exam score can be converted to a z score with respect to the mean and standard deviation for its particular exam, the two scores can then be compared directly.

Transforming z Scores into Percentiles

So z scores are useful because:

1. z scores give us a sense of where a score falls in relation to the mean of its population (in terms of the standard deviation of its population).

2. z scores allow us to compare scores from different distributions.

Yet we can be even more specific about where a score falls. An additional and particularly helpful use of z scores is that they also have this property:

3. z scores can be transformed into percentiles.

Because the shape of a normal curve is standard, we automatically know something about the percentage of any particular area under the curve. Think of the normal curve and the horizontal line below it as forming a shape. Like any shape, the area below the normal curve can be measured. We can quantify the space below a normal curve in terms of percentages.

Remember that the normal curve is, by definition, symmetric. This means that exactly 50% of scores fall below the mean and 50% fall above the mean. But Figure 6-8 demonstrates that we can be even more specific. Approximately 34% of scores fall between the mean and a z score of 1.0; and because of symmetry, 34% of scores also fall between the mean and a z score of −1.0. We also know that approximately 14% of scores fall between the z scores of 1.0 and 2.0, and 14% of scores fall between the z scores of −1.0 and −2.0. Finally, we know that approximately 2% of scores fall between the z scores of 2.0 and 3.0, and 2% of scores fall between the z scores of −2.0 and −3.0.

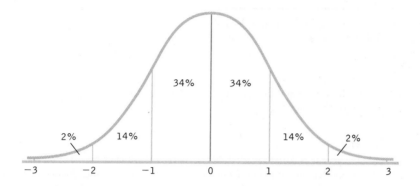

FIGURE 6-8

The Normal Curve and Percentages

The standard shape of the normal curve allows us to know the approximate percentages under different parts of the curve. For example, about 34% of scores fall between the mean and a *z* score of 1.0.

By simple addition, we can determine that approximately 68% (34 + 34 = 68) of scores fall within 1 standard deviation—or 1 *z* score—of the mean; that approximately 96% (14 + 34 + 34 + 14 = 96) of scores fall within 2 standard deviations of the mean; and that all or nearly all (2 + 14 + 34 + 34 + 14 + 2 = 100) scores fall within 3 standard deviations of the mean. So, if you know you are about 1 standard deviation above the mean on your statistics quiz, then you can add the 50% below the mean to the 34% between the mean and the *z* score of 1.0 that you earned on your quiz, and know that your score corresponds to approximately the 84th percentile.

If you know that you are about 1 standard deviation below the mean, you know that you are in the lower 50% of scores and that 34% of scores fall between your score and the mean. By subtracting, you can calculate that 50 − 34 = 16% of scores fall below yours. Your score corresponds to approximately the 16th percentile. Scores on standardized tests are often expressed as percentiles.

For now, it's important to understand that the *z* distribution forms a normal curve with a unimodal, symmetric shape. Because the shape is known and 100% of the population falls beneath the normal curve, we can determine the percentage of any area under the normal curve.

CHECK YOUR LEARNING

Reviewing the Concepts

> Standardization is a way to create meaningful comparisons between observations from different distributions. It can be done by transforming raw scores from different distributions into *z* scores, also known as standardized scores.

> A *z* score is the distance that a score is from the mean of its distribution in terms of standard deviations.

> We also can transform *z* scores to raw scores by reversing the formula for a *z* score.

> *z* scores correspond to known percentiles that communicate how an individual score compares with the larger distribution.

Clarifying the Concepts

6-4 Describe the process of standardization.

6-5 What do the numeric value and the sign (negative or positive) of a *z* score indicate?

continued on next page

Calculating the Statistics

6-6 The mean of a population is 14 and the standard deviation is 2.5. Using the formula, calculate z scores for the following raw scores:

a. 11.5

b. 18

6-7 Using the same population parameters as in Check Your Learning 6-6, calculate raw scores for the following z scores:

a. 2

b. −1.4

Applying the Concepts

6-8 The Consideration of Future Consequences (CFC) scale assesses the degree to which students are future-oriented. Researchers believe that a high CFC score is a positive indicator of a student's career potential. One study found a mean CFC score of 3.20, with a standard deviation of 0.70, for the 800 students in the sample (Adams, 2012).

a. If a student has a CFC score of 2.5, what is her z score? To what percentile does this z score roughly correspond?

b. If a student has a CFC score of 4.6, what is his z score? To what percentile does this z score roughly correspond?

c. If a student has a CFC score at the 84th percentile, what is her z score?

d. What is the raw score of the student at the 84th percentile? Use symbolic notation and the formula. Explain why this answer makes sense.

6-9 Samantha has high blood pressure but exercises; she has a wellness score of 84 on a scale with a mean of 93 and a standard deviation of 4.5 (a higher score indicates better health). Nicole is of normal weight but has high cholesterol; she has a wellness score of 332 on a scale with a mean of 312 and a standard deviation of 20.

a. Without using a formula, who would you say is in better health?

b. Using standardization, determine who is in better health. Provide details using symbolic notation.

Solutions to these Check Your Learning questions can be found in Appendix D.

c. Based on their z scores, what percentage of people are in better health than Samantha and Nicole, respectively?

● The **central limit theorem** refers to how a distribution of sample means is a more normal distribution than a distribution of scores, even when the population distribution is not normal.

MASTERING THE CONCEPT

6-4: The central limit theorem demonstrates that a distribution made up of the means of many samples (rather than individual scores) approximates a normal curve, even if the underlying population is not normally distributed.

The Central Limit Theorem

In the early 1900s, W. S. Gossett discovered how the predictability of the normal curve could improve quality control in the Guinness ale factory. One of the practical problems that Gossett faced was related to sampling yeast cultures: Too little yeast led to incomplete fermentation, whereas too much yeast led to a bitter-tasting beer. To test whether he could sample both accurately and economically, Gossett averaged samples of four observations to see how well they represented a known population of 3000 (Gossett, 1908, 1942; Stigler, 1999).

This small adjustment (taking the *average* of four samples rather than using just one sample) is possible because of the central limit theorem. *The **central limit theorem** refers to how a distribution of sample means is a more normal distribution than a distribution of scores, even when the population* *distribution is not normal.* Indeed, as sample size increases, a distribution of sample means more closely approximates a normal curve. More specifically, the central limit theorem demonstrates two important principles:

1. Repeated sampling approximates a normal curve, *even when the original population is not normally distributed.*
2. A distribution of means is less variable than a distribution of individual scores.

Instead of randomly sampling a single data point, Gossett randomly sampled four data points from the population of 3000 and computed the average. He did this repeatedly and used those many averages to create a distribution of means. *A **distribution of means** is a distribution composed of many means that are calculated from all possible samples of a given size, all taken from the same population.* Put another way, the numbers that make up the distribution of means are not individual scores; they are *means* of samples of individual scores. Distributions of means are frequently used to understand data across a range of contexts; for example, when a university reports the mean standardized test score of incoming first-year students, that mean would be understood in relation to a distribution of means instead of a distribution of scores.

● A **distribution of means** is a distribution composed of many means that are calculated from all possible samples of a given size, all taken from the same population.

Gossett experimented with using the average of four data points as his sample, but there is nothing magical about the number four. A mean test score for incoming students would have a far larger sample size. The important outcome is that a distribution of means more consistently produces a normal distribution (although with less variance) *even when the population distribution is not normal.* It might help your understanding to know that the central limit theorem works because a sample of four, for example, will minimize the effect of outliers. When an outlier is just one of four scores being sampled and averaged, the average won't be as extreme as the outlier.

A Distribution of Means A distribution of means reduces the influence of individual outliers such as the size of the giant Buddha on the left. When that extreme size is part of a sample that includes smaller, more typically sized Buddhas, such as the one on the right, the mean of that sample will be smaller than the size of the single large Buddha. That is why a distribution based on means is less variable than a distribution based on individual scores.

Rene Mattes/mauritius images/AGE Fotostock

klublu/Westend61/AGE Fotostock

In this section, we learn how to create a distribution of means, as well as how to calculate a *z* score for a mean (more accurately called a *z statistic* when calculated for means rather than scores). We also learn why the central limit theorem indicates that, when conducting hypothesis testing, a distribution of means is more useful than a distribution of scores.

Creating a Distribution of Means

The central limit theorem underlies many statistical processes that are based on a distribution of means. A distribution of means is more tightly clustered (has a smaller standard deviation) than a distribution of scores.

EXAMPLE 6.10

In class, we conduct a low-tech exercise with our students that demonstrates the central limit theorem in action. We start by writing the happiness scores in Table 6-1 on 157 individual index cards that can be mixed together in a hat.

1. First, we randomly pull one card at a time and record its score by marking it on a histogram. (In class, we create the histograms in this exercise on a whiteboard or smartboard.) After recording the score, we return the card to the container representing the population of scores and mix all the cards before pulling the next card. (Not surprisingly, this is known as *sampling with replacement*.) We continue

TABLE 6-1   The Population of Happiness Scores

These are the happiness scores, on a scale of 0 to 10, for all 157 countries in the World Happiness Report (Helliwell, Layard, & Sachs, 2017).

7.526	6.952	6.474	5.987	5.658	5.291	5.057	4.574	4.217	3.739
7.509	6.929	6.379	5.977	5.648	5.279	5.045	4.513	4.201	3.739
7.501	6.907	6.379	5.976	5.615	5.245	5.033	4.508	4.193	3.724
7.498	6.871	6.375	5.956	5.56	5.196	4.996	4.459	4.156	3.695
7.413	6.778	6.361	5.921	5.546	5.185	4.907	4.415	4.139	3.666
7.404	6.739	6.355	5.919	5.538	5.177	4.876	4.404	4.121	3.622
7.339	6.725	6.324	5.897	5.528	5.163	4.875	4.395	4.073	3.607
7.334	6.705	6.269	5.856	5.517	5.161	4.871	4.362	4.028	3.515
7.313	6.701	6.239	5.835	5.510	5.155	4.813	4.360	3.974	3.484
7.291	6.650	6.218	5.835	5.488	5.151	4.795	4.356	3.956	3.360
7.267	6.596	6.168	5.822	5.458	5.145	4.793	4.324	3.916	3.303
7.119	6.573	6.084	5.813	5.440	5.132	4.754	4.276	3.907	3.069
7.104	6.545	6.078	5.802	5.401	5.129	4.655	4.272	3.866	2.905
7.087	6.488	6.068	5.771	5.389	5.123	4.643	4.252	3.856	
7.039	6.481	6.005	5.768	5.314	5.121	4.635	4.236	3.832	
6.994	6.478	5.992	5.743	5.303	5.061	4.575	4.219	3.763	

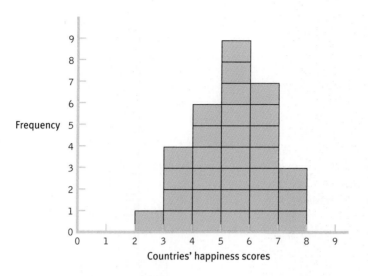

FIGURE 6-9

Creating a Distribution of Scores

This distribution is one of many that could be created by pulling 30 happiness scores, one at a time, and replacing the numbers between pulls, from the population of 157 countries. If you create a distribution of scores yourself from these data, it should look roughly bell-shaped like this one—that is, unimodal and symmetric. Source: Helliwell, Layard, & Sachs, 2017

until we have plotted at least 30 scores, drawing a square for each one so that bars emerge above each value. This creates the beginning of a *distribution of scores.* Using this method, we created the histogram in Figure 6-9.

2. Now, we randomly pull three cards at a time, compute the mean of these three scores, and record this mean on a different histogram. As before, we draw a square for each mean, with each stack of squares resembling a bar. Again, we return each set of cards to the population and mix before pulling the next set of three. We continue until we have plotted at least 30 values. This is the beginning of a *distribution of means.* Using this method, we created the histogram in Figure 6-10.

The distribution of scores in Figure 6-9, similar to those we create when we do this exercise in class, ranges from 2 to 8, with a peak in the middle. If we had a larger population, and if we pulled many more numbers, the distribution would become more and more normal. Notice that the distribution is centered roughly around the actual population mean, 5.382. Also notice that all, or nearly all, scores fall within 3 standard deviations of the mean. The population standard deviation of these scores is 1.138. So nearly all scores should fall within this range:

$$5.382 - 3(1.138) = 1.968 \text{ and } 5.382 + 3(1.138) = 8.796$$

In fact, the range of scores—1.968 through 8.796—in this population of 157 happiness scores is very close to this range.

Is there anything different about the distribution of means in Figure 6-10? Yes, there are not as many means at the far tails of the distribution as in the distribution of scores—we no longer have any values between 2 and 3 or between 7 and 8. However, there are no changes in the center of the distribution. The distribution of means is still centered on the actual mean of 5.382. This makes sense. The means of three scores each come from the same set of scores, so the mean of the individual sample means should be the same as the mean of the whole population of scores.

FIGURE 6-10

FIGURE 6-10

Creating a Distribution of Means

Compare this distribution of means to the distribution of scores in Figure 6-9. The mean is the same and it is still roughly bell-shaped. The spread is narrower, however, so there is a smaller standard deviation. This particular distribution is one of many similar distributions that could be created by pulling 30 means (the average of three numbers at a time) from the population of happiness scores for 157 countries. Source: Helliwell, Layard, & Sachs, 2017

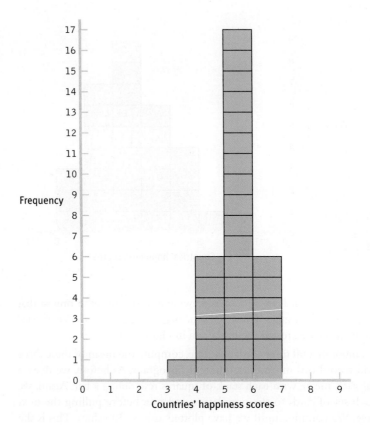

Why does the spread decrease when we create a distribution of means rather than a distribution of scores? When we plotted individual *scores*, each extreme score was plotted on the distribution. But when we plotted *means*, we averaged each extreme score with two other scores. So each time we pulled a score in the 70s, we tended to pull two lower scores as well; when we pulled a low score, such as 2.905, we tended to pull two higher scores as well.

What do you think would happen if we created a distribution of means of 10 scores rather than 3? As you might guess, the distribution would be even narrower because there would be more scores to balance the occasional extreme score. The mean of each set of 10 scores is likely to be even closer to the actual mean of 5.382. What if we created a distribution of means of 100 scores, or of 10,000 scores? The larger the sample size, the smaller the spread of the distribution of means. ●

Characteristics of the Distribution of Means

Because the distribution of means is less variable than the distribution of scores, the distribution of means needs its own standard deviation—a smaller standard deviation than we used for the distribution of individual scores.

The data presented in Figure 6-11 allow us to visually verify that the distribution of means needs a smaller standard deviation. Using the population mean of 5.382 and

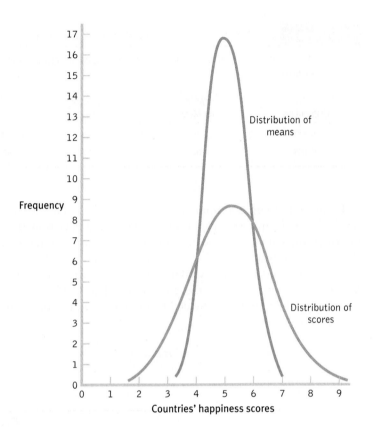

Frequency

Countries' happiness scores

Distribution of means

Distribution of scores

FIGURE 6-11

Using the Appropriate Measure of Spread

Because the distribution of means is narrower than the distribution of scores, it has a smaller standard deviation. This standard deviation has its own name: standard error. Source: Helliwell, Layard, & Sachs, 2017

standard deviation of 1.138, the z scores for the end scores of 3.894 and 6.560 are −1.31 and 1.04, respectively—not even close to 3 standard deviations. These z scores are wrong for this distribution. We need to use a standard deviation of sample *means* rather than a standard deviation of individual *scores*.

Language Alert! We use slightly modified language and symbols when we describe distributions of means instead of distributions of scores. The mean of a distribution of means is the same as the mean of a population of scores, but it uses the symbol μ_M (pronounced "mew sub em"). The μ indicates that it is the mean of a *population*, and the subscript M indicates that the population is composed of *sample means*—the means of all possible samples of a given size from a particular population of individual scores.

We also need a new symbol and a new name for the standard deviation of the distribution of means—the typical amount that a sample mean varies from the population mean. The symbol is σ_M (pronounced "sigma sub em"). The subscript M again stands for mean; this is the standard deviation of the population of means calculated for *all possible samples* of a given size. The symbol has its own name: *Standard error is the name for the standard deviation of a distribution of means.* Table 6-2 summarizes the alternative names that describe these related ideas.

MASTERING THE CONCEPT

6-5: A distribution of means has the same mean as a distribution of scores from the same population, but a smaller standard deviation.

● **Standard error** is the name for the standard deviation of a distribution of means.

TABLE 6-2	Parameters for Distributions of Scores Versus Means

When we determine the parameters of a distribution, we must consider whether the distribution is composed of scores or means.

Distribution	Symbol for Mean	Symbol for Spread	Name for Spread
Scores	μ	σ	Standard deviation
Means	μ_M	σ_M	Standard error

MASTERING THE FORMULA

6-3: The formula for standard error is:

$$\sigma_M = \frac{\sigma}{\sqrt{N}}$$

We divide the standard deviation for the population by the square root of the sample size.

Fortunately, there is a simple calculation that lets us know exactly how much smaller the standard error, σ_M, is than the standard deviation, σ. As we've noted, the larger the sample size, the narrower the distribution of means and the smaller the standard deviation of the distribution of means—the standard error. We calculate the standard error by taking into account the sample size used to calculate the means that make up the distribution. The standard error is the standard deviation of the population divided by the square root of the sample size, N. The formula is:

$$\sigma_M = \frac{\sigma}{\sqrt{N}}$$

EXAMPLE 6.11

Imagine that the standard deviation of the distribution of individual scores is 5 and we have a sample of 10 people. The standard error would be:

$$\sigma_M = \frac{\sigma}{\sqrt{N}} = \frac{5}{\sqrt{10}} = 1.58$$

The spread is smaller when we calculate means for samples of 10 people because any extreme scores are balanced by less extreme scores. With a larger sample size of 200, the spread is even smaller because there are many more scores close to the mean to balance out any extreme scores. The standard error would then be:

$$\sigma_M = \frac{\sigma}{\sqrt{N}} = \frac{5}{\sqrt{200}} = 0.35$$

A distribution of means faithfully obeys the central limit theorem. Even if the population of individual scores is *not* normally distributed, the distribution of means will approximate the normal curve if the samples are composed of at least 30 scores. The three graphs in Figure 6-12 depict (a) a distribution of individual scores that is extremely skewed in the positive direction, (b) the less skewed distribution that results when we create a distribution of means using samples of 2, and (c) the approximately normal curve that results when we create a distribution of means

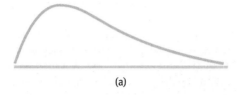

A severely skewed
distribution of scores
in a population

(a)

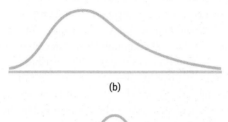

A less severely skewed
distribution of means using
samples of 2 from
the same population

(b)

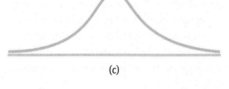

A normal distribution of
means using samples of 25
from the same population

(c)

FIGURE 6-12

**The Mathematical Magic of
Large Samples**

Even with a population of individual
scores that are not normally distributed,
the distribution of means approximates a
normal curve as the sample gets larger.

using samples of 25. We have learned three important characteristics of the distribution of means:

1. As sample size increases, the mean of a distribution of means remains the same.
2. The standard deviation of a distribution of means (called the *standard error*) is smaller than the standard deviation of a distribution of scores. As sample size increases, the standard error becomes ever smaller.
3. The shape of the distribution of means approximates the normal curve if the distribution of the population of individual scores has a normal shape or if the size of each sample that makes up the distribution is at least 30 (the central limit theorem). ●

Using the Central Limit Theorem to Make Comparisons with z Scores

z scores are a standardized version of raw scores based on the population. But we seldom have the entire population to work with, so we typically calculate the mean of a sample and calculate a *z* score based on a distribution of means. When we calculate the *z* score, we simply use a distribution of means instead of a distribution of scores. The *z* formula changes only in the symbols it uses:

$$z = \frac{(M - \mu_M)}{\sigma_M}$$

Note that we now use M instead of X because we are calculating a *z* score for a sample mean rather than for an individual score. Because the *z* score now represents a mean, not an actual score, it is often referred to as a z *statistic*. Specifically, the *z* statistic tells us how many standard errors a sample mean is from the population mean.

MASTERING THE FORMULA

6-4: The formula for *z* based on the mean of a sample is:

$$z = \frac{(M - \mu_M)}{\sigma_M}$$

We subtract the mean of the distribution of means from the mean of the sample, then we divide by the standard error, the standard deviation of the distribution of means.

EXAMPLE 6.12

Let's consider a distribution for which we know the population mean and standard deviation. Several hundred U.S. universities reported data from their counseling centers (Gallagher, 2009). (For this example, we'll treat this sample as the entire population of interest.) The study found that an average of 8.5 students per institution were hospitalized for mental illness for more than 1 year. For the purposes of this example, we'll assume a standard deviation of 3.8. Let's say we develop a prevention program to reduce the numbers of hospitalizations and we recruit 30 universities to participate. After 1 year, we calculate a mean of 7.1 hospitalizations at these 30 institutions. Is this an extreme sample mean, given the population?

To find out, let's imagine the distribution of means for samples of 30 hospitalization scores. We would collect the means the same way we collected the means of three heights in the earlier example—just with far more means. The average of all those means would have the same mean as the population but the spread would be narrower. The spread of the distribution is skinnier because any extreme hospitalization scores would now be part of a sample that likely included less extreme scores. So, the mean for each sample is less likely to be extreme than is an individual score. The distribution of all of these means, then, would be less variable than the distribution of scores. Here are the mean and standard error of the sample of universities, using proper symbolic notation:

$$\mu_M = \mu = 8.5$$

$$\sigma_M = \frac{\sigma}{\sqrt{N}} = \frac{3.8}{\sqrt{30}} = 0.694$$

At this point, we have all the information we need to calculate the z statistic:

$$z = \frac{(M - \mu_M)}{\sigma_M} = \frac{(7.1 - 8.5)}{0.694} = -2.02$$

From this z statistic, we could determine how extreme the mean number of hospitalizations is in terms of a percentage. Then we could draw a conclusion about whether we would be likely to find a mean number of hospitalizations of 7.1 in a sample of 30 universities if the prevention program did *not* work. The useful combination of a distribution of means and a z statistic has led us to a point where we're prepared for inferential statistics and hypothesis testing. ●

Data Ethics   Using z Scores to Keep Researchers Honest

In the chapter opener, we shared stories about identifying possible cheaters in tennis and sumo wrestling by looking for unusual cases, which are often identified as extreme z scores. This tactic also can be used to identify cheating researchers. How? The normal curve can help us identify extreme statistical results, and perhaps cheating researchers! Alan Gerber and Neil Malhotra (2006) looked at all studies published over a decade in two political science journals, and recorded the z statistics reported in these studies. Gerber and Malhotra combined positive and negative z statistics and depicted them in the histogram in Figure 6-13. These are the positive and negative scores combined, so think of this graph as one half of a distribution curve. In this case,

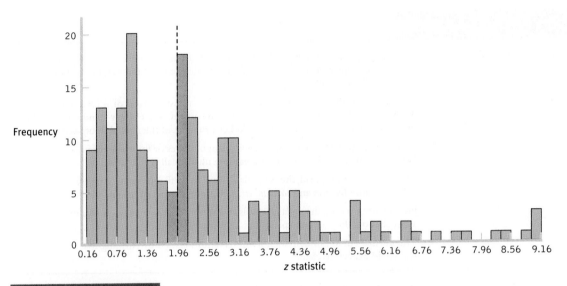

FIGURE 6-13

Identifying Cheaters

An understanding of distributions can help us identify cheaters. This histogram of *z* statistics for the journals studied by Gerber and Malhotra (2006) shows an unexpectedly short bar for findings with *z* statistics slightly smaller than 1.96 and an unexpectedly tall bar for findings with *z* statistics slightly larger than 1.96. This pattern is an indication that researchers might be manipulating their analyses to push their *z* statistics beyond the cutoffs and into the tails so that they can reject the null hypothesis.

any *z* statistic above 1.96 indicates that it was among the most extreme 5%. (In later chapters, we'll learn more about this 5% cutoff, but for now, it's only important to know that the 5% cutoff is arbitrary yet well established in statistical analyses; findings in the most extreme 5% are most likely to be published.) With this histogram, Gerber and Malhotra documented an apparent publication bias among researchers!

There is nothing magical about the 0.05 (5%) cutoff; it is simply a reasonable standard that gives us a reasonable chance of detecting a real finding while minimizing the likelihood of committing a Type I error. But guess what? The data don't know about the 0.05 standard, so we would not expect any clustering of reported findings. Let's look at the data.

If we think of this histogram as one-half of a normal curve, we notice a much lower frequency than would be expected for *z* statistics just below 1.96 (the 5% standard), as seen in the red bar just to the left of the dotted vertical line. And there was a much higher frequency than would be expected for *z* statistics just above 1.96, as seen in the red bar just to the right of the dotted vertical line. Gerber and Malhotra (2006) cite a "1 in 100 million" probability that the patterns they observed occurred just by chance (p. 3). What might account for this?

The authors suggest that the strict 5% cutoff is encouraging researchers to "play" with their data until they beat the cutoff. Some researchers may cheat in this way unwittingly, not realizing that they are biased. However, other researchers might cheat consciously, massaging the data with various analyses until it performs as they hope. (We'll explore this tactic more in the data ethics feature in Chapter 7.) The normal curve thus helped to identify a pattern of apparent cheating in social science publishing. Paying attention to the shape of distributions is not a sophisticated form of analysis. Yet such analysis can flag cheating in many contexts—from sports to behavioral science research.

CHECK YOUR LEARNING

Reviewing the Concepts

> According to the central limit theorem, a distribution of sample means based on 30 or more scores approximates the normal distribution, even if the original population is not normally distributed.

> A distribution of scores has the same mean as a distribution of means. However, a distribution of scores contains more extreme scores and a larger standard deviation than a distribution of means; this is another principle of the central limit theorem.

> *z* scores may be calculated from a distribution of scores or from a distribution of means. When we calculate a *z* score for a mean, we usually call it a *z* statistic.

> For the measure of spread, the two calculations use different terms: *standard deviation* for a distribution of scores and *standard error* for a distribution of means.

> Just as with *z* scores, the *z* statistic tells us about the relative position of a mean within a distribution; this can be expressed as a percentile.

> The normal curve can help identify observations caused by cheating that violate what we would expect by chance.

Clarifying the Concepts

6-10 What are the main ideas behind the central limit theorem?

6-11 Explain what a distribution of means is.

Calculating the Statistics

6-12 The mean of a distribution of scores is 57, with a standard deviation of 11. Calculate the standard error for a distribution of means based on samples of 35 people.

Applying the Concepts

6-13 Let's return to the selection of 30 CFC scores that we considered in Check Your Learning 6-2(b):

3.5	3.5	3.0	4.0	2.0	4.0	2.0	4.0	3.5	4.5
4.5	4.0	3.5	2.5	3.5	3.5	4.0	3.0	3.0	2.5
3.0	3.5	4.0	3.5	3.5	2.0	3.5	3.0	3.0	2.5

a. What is the range of these scores?

b. Take three means of 10 scores each from this sample of scores, one for each row. What is the range of these means?

c. Why is the range smaller for the *means* of samples of 10 scores than for the *individual* scores themselves?

Solutions to these Check Your Learning questions can be found in Appendix D.

d. The mean of these 30 scores is 3.32. The standard deviation is 0.69. Using symbolic notation and formulas (where appropriate), determine the mean and standard error of the distribution of means computed from samples of 10.

REVIEW OF CONCEPTS

LaunchPad
macmillan learning
Visit LaunchPad to access the e-book and to test your knowledge with LearningCurve.

The Normal Curve

Three ideas about the normal curve help us to understand inferential statistics. First, the *normal curve* describes the variability of many physical and psychological characteristics. Second, the normal curve may be translated into percentages, allowing us to standardize variables and make direct comparisons of scores on different measures. Third, a distribution of means, rather than a distribution of scores, produces a more normal curve. The last idea is based on the central limit theorem, by which we know that a distribution of means will be normally distributed and less variable as long as the samples from which the means are computed are of a sufficiently large size, usually at least 30.

Standardization, z Scores, and the Normal Curve

The process of *standardization* converts raw scores into z scores. Raw scores from any normal distribution can be converted to the z *distribution*. A normal distribution of z scores is called the *standard normal distribution*. z *scores* tell us how far a raw score falls from its mean in terms of standard deviation. We can also reverse the formula to convert z scores to raw scores. Standardization using z scores has two important applications. First, standardized scores—that is, z scores—can be converted to percentile ranks (and percentile ranks can be converted to z scores and then raw scores). Second, we can directly compare z scores from different raw-score distributions. z scores work the other way around as well.

The Central Limit Theorem

The z distribution can be used with a *distribution of means* in addition to a distribution of scores. Distributions of means have the same mean as the population of individual scores from which they are calculated, but a smaller spread, which means we must adjust for sample size. The standard deviation of a distribution of means is called the *standard error*. The decreased variability is due to the fact that extreme scores are balanced by less extreme scores when means are calculated. Distributions of means are normally distributed if the underlying population of scores is normal, or if the means are computed from sufficiently large samples, usually at least 30 individual scores. This second situation is described by the *central limit theorem*, the principle that a distribution of sample means will be normally distributed even if the underlying distribution of scores is not normally distributed, as long as there are enough scores—usually at least 30—in each sample. The characteristics of the normal curve allow us to make inferences from small samples using standardized distributions, such as the z distribution. We can use the z distribution for means, as well as for individual scores, if we determine the appropriate mean and standard deviation. The bell-shaped curve can also be used to catch cheaters when a pattern of scores violates what we would expect by chance.

SPSS

SPSS lets us understand each variable, identify its skewness, and explore how well it fits with a normal distribution. Enter the 157 happiness scores from Table 6-1.

We can identify outliers that might skew the normal curve by selecting Analyze → Descriptive Statistics → Explore. In the dialogue box, select Statistics → Outliers. Click "Continue." Choose the variable of interest, "Happiness," by

clicking it on the left and then using the arrow to move it to the right. Click "OK." The screenshot shown here depicts part of the output.

The output provides basic descriptive information for the variable of interest (i.e., mean, standard deviation, median, minimum, maximum, range, and so on), and then provides a description of extreme scores: the top five extreme scores and the bottom five extreme scores. By scrolling farther down in the output, SPSS (by default) will provide two types of graphs, both of which identify extreme scores using a statistical definition—values more than 1.5 interquartile ranges beyond the 25th or 75th percentiles. (See Chapter 4 for more information on interquartile ranges.) In addition to a frequency distribution, the box plot is a useful tool to visualize the shape (and skewness) in a distribution.

We encourage you to explore your data and the many features in SPSS, especially when you are analyzing your own data. SPSS is much easier to learn when you know why every number was included in the study in the first place. It's also much more interesting to test your own ideas!

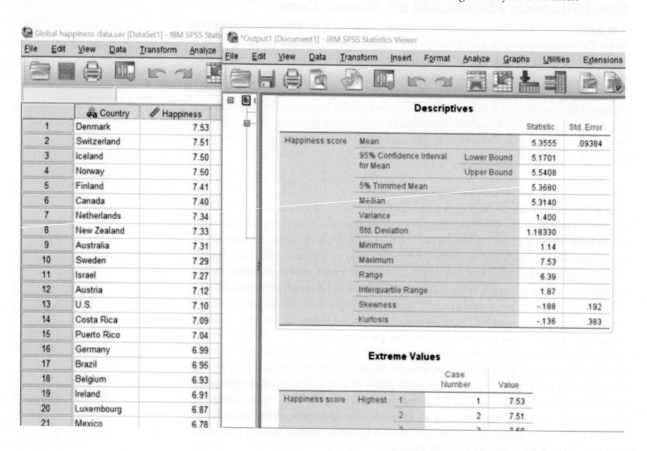

HOW IT WORKS

6.1 CONVERTING RAW SCORES TO z SCORES

Researchers reported that college students had healthier eating habits, on average, than did individuals who were neither college students nor college graduates (Georgiou et al., 1997). The researchers found that the 412 college students in the study ate breakfast a mean of 4.1 times per week, with a standard deviation of 2.4. Imagine that this is the entire population of interest.

Using symbolic notation and the formula, how can we calculate the *z* score for a student who eats breakfast six times per week? We can calculate the *z* score as follows:

$$z = \frac{(X - \mu)}{\sigma} = \frac{(6 - 4.1)}{2.4} = 0.79$$

Now, how can we calculate the *z* score for a student who eats breakfast twice a week? We can calculate this *z* score as follows:

$$z = \frac{(X - \mu)}{\sigma} = \frac{(2 - 4.1)}{2.4} = -0.88$$

6.2 STANDARDIZATION WITH *z* SCORES AND PERCENTILES

Who is doing better financially—Katy Perry, with respect to the 10 most powerful celebrities, or Tiger Woods, with respect to the 10 golfers with the highest incomes? www.Forbes.com publishes an annual list of the 10 most powerful celebrities in terms of earnings and media exposure, regardless of gender. In one year, Katy Perry ranked eighth on this list and earned $45 million that year. That same year www.Golfdigest .com listed the top 10 earners in golf. Woods topped the list, with $86.1 million. In comparison to his top 10 peers, did Woods really do better financially than Perry did in comparison to her top 10 peers?

For celebrities, the mean for the top 10 was $70.3 million, with a standard deviation of $41.4 million. Based on this, Kate Perry's *z* score is:

$$z = \frac{(X - \mu)}{\sigma} = \frac{(45 - 70.3)}{41.4} = -0.61$$

We can also calculate a range for her percentile rank. Fifty percent of scores fall below the mean. About 34% fall between the mean and a *z* score of −1.0, so: 50 − 34 = 16% of scores fall below a *z* score of −1. Therefore, Katy Perry is somewhere between the 16th and 50th percentiles among the top 10 most powerful celebrities.

For golf, the mean for the top 10 was $30.0 million, with a standard deviation of $21.1 million. Based on this, Tiger Woods's *z* score is:

$$z = \frac{(X - \mu)}{\sigma} = \frac{(86.1 - 30)}{21.1} = 2.66$$

We can also estimate his percentile rank. Fifty percent of scores fall below the mean; about 34% fall between the mean and 1 standard deviation above the mean; and about 14% fall between 1 and 2 standard deviations above the mean: 50 + 34 + 14 = 98. Woods is above the 98th percentile among the top 10 golfers with the highest incomes.

Tiger Woods outearned Katy Perry when each was compared to the top 10 earners in their respective fields.

EXERCISES

The solutions to the odd-numbered exercises can be found in Appendix C.

Clarifying the Concepts

6.1 Explain how the word *normal* is used in everyday conversation, then explain how statisticians use it.

6.2 What point on the normal curve represents the most commonly occurring observation?

6.3 How does the size of a sample of scores affect the shape of the distribution of data?

6.4 Explain how the word *standardize* is used in everyday conversation, then explain how statisticians use it.

6.5 What is a z score?

6.6 Give three reasons why z scores are useful.

6.7 What are the mean and the standard deviation of the z distribution?

6.8 Why is the central limit theorem such an important idea for dealing with a population that is not normally distributed?

6.9 What does the symbol μ_M stand for?

6.10 What does the symbol σ_M stand for?

6.11 What is the difference between standard deviation and standard error?

6.12 Why does the standard error become smaller simply by increasing the sample size?

6.13 What does a z statistic—a z score based on a distribution of means—tell us about a sample mean?

6.14 Each of the following equations has an error. Identify, fix, and explain the error in each of the following equations.

a. $\sigma_M = \dfrac{\mu}{\sqrt{N}}$

b. $z = \dfrac{(\mu - \mu_M)}{\sigma_M}$ (for a distribution of means)

c. $z = \dfrac{(M - \mu_M)}{\sigma}$ (for a distribution of means)

d. $z = \dfrac{(X - \mu)}{\sigma_M}$ (for a distribution of scores)

Calculating the Statistics

6.15 Create a histogram for these three sets of scores. Each set of scores represents a sample taken from the same population.

a. 6 4 11 7 7

b. 6 4 11 7 7 2 10 7 8 6 6 7 5 8

c. 6 4 11 7 7 2 10 7 8 6 6 7 5 8
7 8 9 7 6 9 3 9 5 6 8 11 8 3
8 4 10 8 5 5 8 9 9 7 8 7 10 7

d. What do you observe happening across these three distributions?

6.16 A population has a mean of 250 and a standard deviation of 47. Calculate z scores for each of the following raw scores:

a. 391

b. 273

c. 199

d. 160

6.17 A population has a mean of 1179 and a standard deviation of 164. Calculate z scores for each of the following raw scores:

a. 1000

b. 721

c. 1531

d. 1184

6.18 For a population with a mean of 250 and a standard deviation of 47, calculate the z score for 250. Explain the meaning of the value you obtain.

6.19 For a population with a mean of 250 and a standard deviation of 47, calculate the z scores for 203 and 297. Explain the meaning of these values.

6.20 For a population with a mean of 250 and a standard deviation of 47, convert each of the following z scores to raw scores.

a. 0.54

b. −2.66

c. −1.00

d. 1.79

6.21 For a population with a mean of 1179 and a standard deviation of 164, convert each of the following z scores to raw scores.

a. −0.23

b. 1.41

c. 2.06

d. 0.03

6.22 By design, the verbal subtest of the Graduate Record Examination (GRE) has a population mean of 500 and a population standard deviation of 100. Convert the following *z* scores to raw scores *without* using a formula.

  a. 1.5

  b. −0.5

  c. −2.0

6.23 By design, the verbal subtest of the Graduate Record Examination (GRE) has a population mean of 500 and a population standard deviation of 100. Convert the following *z* scores to raw scores using symbolic notation and the formula.

  a. 1.5

  b. −0.5

  c. −2.0

6.24 A study of the Consideration of Future Consequences (CFC) scale found a mean score of 3.20, with a standard deviation of 0.70, for the 800 students in the sample (Adams, 2012). (Treat this sample as the entire population of interest.)

  a. If the CFC score is 4.2, what is the *z* score? Use symbolic notation and the formula. Explain why this answer makes sense.

  b. If the CFC score is 3.0, what is the *z* score? Use symbolic notation and the formula. Explain why this answer makes sense.

  c. If the *z* score is 0, what is the CFC score? Explain.

6.25 Using the instructions in Example 6.9 on page 162, compare the following "apples and oranges": a score of 45 when the population mean is 51 and the standard deviation is 4, and a score of 732 when the population mean is 765 and the standard deviation is 23.

  a. Convert these scores to standardized scores.

  b. Using the standardized scores, what can you say about how these two scores compare to each other?

6.26 Compare the following scores:

  a. A score of 811 when $\mu = 800$ and $\sigma = 29$ against a score of 4524 when $\mu = 3127$ and $\sigma = 951$

  b. A score of 17 when $\mu = 30$ and $\sigma = 12$ against a score of 67 when $\mu = 88$ and $\sigma = 16$

6.27 Assume a normal distribution when answering the following questions.

  a. What percentage of scores falls below the mean?

  b. What percentage of scores falls between 1 standard deviation below the mean and 2 standard deviations above the mean?

  c. What percentage of scores lies beyond 2 standard deviations away from the mean (on both sides)?

  d. What percentage of scores is between the mean and 2 standard deviations above the mean?

  e. What percentage of scores falls under the normal curve?

6.28 Compute the standard error (σ_M) for each of the following sample sizes, assuming a population mean of 100 and a standard deviation of 20:

  a. 45

  b. 100

  c. 4500

6.29 A population has a mean of 55 and a standard deviation of 8. Compute μ_M and σ_M for each of the following sample sizes:

  a. 30

  b. 300

  c. 3000

6.30 Compute a *z* statistic for each of the following, assuming the population has a mean of 100 and a standard deviation of 20:

  a. A sample of 43 scores has a mean of 101.

  b. A sample of 60 scores has a mean of 96.

  c. A sample of 29 scores has a mean of 100.

6.31 A sample of 100 people had a mean depression score of 85; the population mean for this depression measure is 80, with a standard deviation of 20. A different sample of 100 people had a mean score of 17 on a different depression measure; the population mean for this measure is 15, with a standard deviation of 5.

  a. Convert these means to *z* statistics.

  b. Using the *z* statistics, what can you say about how these two means compare to each other?

Applying the Concepts

6.32 Normal distributions in real life: Many variables are normally distributed, but not all are. (Fortunately, the central limit theorem saves us when we conduct research on samples from nonnormal populations if the samples are larger than 30!) Which of the following are likely to be normally distributed, and which are likely to be non-normal? Explain your answers.

  a. In the population of students admitted to the highly selective University of Toronto, scores on the federal or provincial literacy test (required for university admissions)

b. In the population of secondary school students in New Zealand, the number of daily calories consumed

c. In the population of employed adults in San Antonio, Texas, the amount of time spent commuting to work

d. In the population of North American university students, the number of frequent flyer miles earned in a year

6.33 Distributions and getting ready for a date: We asked 150 students in our statistics classes how long, in minutes, they typically spend getting ready for a date. The scores ranged from 1 minute to 120 minutes, and the mean was 51.52 minutes. Here are the data for 40 of these students:

30 90 60 60   5 90   30 40 45 60

60 30 90 60 25 10   90 20 15 60

60 75 45 60 30 75   15 30 45   1

20 25 45 60 90 10 105 90 30 60

a. Construct a histogram for the 10 scores in the first row.

b. Construct a histogram for all 40 of these scores.

c. What happened to the shape of the distribution as you increased the number of scores from 10 to 40? What do you think would happen if the data for all 150 students were included? What if we included 10,000 scores? Explain this phenomenon.

d. Are these distributions of scores or distributions of means? Explain.

e. The data here are self-reported. That is, our students wrote down how many minutes they believe that they typically take to get ready for a date. This accounts for the fact that the data include many "pretty" numbers, such as 30, 60, or 90 minutes. What might have been a better way to operationalize this variable?

f. Do these data suggest any hypotheses that you might like to study? List at least one.

6.34 z scores and the GRE: By design, the verbal subtest of the GRE has a population mean of 500 and a population standard deviation of 100 (the quantitative subtest has the same mean and standard deviation).

a. Use symbolic notation to state the mean and the standard deviation of the GRE verbal test.

b. Convert a GRE score of 700 to a z score *without* using a formula.

c. Convert a GRE score of 550 to a z score *without* using a formula.

d. Convert a GRE score of 400 to a z score *without* using a formula.

6.35 The z distribution and hours slept: A sample of 150 statistics students reported the typical number of hours that they sleep on a weeknight. The mean number of hours was 6.65, and the standard deviation was 1.24. (For this exercise, treat this sample as the entire population of interest.)

a. What is *always* the mean of the z distribution?

b. Using the sleep data, demonstrate that your answer to part (a) is the mean of the z distribution. (*Hint:* Calculate the z score for a student who is exactly at the mean.)

c. What is *always* the standard deviation of the z distribution?

d. Using the sleep data, demonstrate that your answer to part (c) is the standard deviation of the z distribution. (*Hint:* Calculate the z score for a student who is exactly 1 standard deviation above or below the mean.)

e. How many hours of sleep do you typically get on a weeknight? What would your z score be, based on this population?

6.36 The z distribution applied to admiration ratings: A sample of 148 of our statistics students rated their level of admiration for Hillary Clinton on a scale of 1 to 7. The mean rating was 4.06, and the standard deviation was 1.70. (For this exercise, treat this sample as the entire population of interest.)

a. Use these data to demonstrate that the mean of the z distribution is always 0.

b. Use these data to demonstrate that the standard deviation of the z distribution is always 1.

c. Calculate the z score for a student who rated his admiration of Hillary Clinton as 6.1.

d. A student had a z score of −0.55. What rating did she give for her admiration of Hillary Clinton?

6.37 z statistics and CFC scores: We have already discussed summary parameters for CFC scores for the population of participants in a study by Adams (2012). The mean CFC score was 3.20, with a standard deviation of 0.70. (Remember that we treated the sample of 800 participants as the entire population.) Imagine that you randomly selected 40 people from this population and had them watch a series of videos on financial planning after graduation. The mean CFC score after watching the video was 3.62.

a. Why would it not make sense to compare the mean of this sample with the distribution of scores? Be sure to discuss the spread of distributions in your answer.

b. In your own words, what would the null hypothesis predict? What would the research hypothesis predict?

c. Using symbolic notation and formulas, what are the appropriate measures of central tendency and variability for the distribution from which this sample comes?

d. Using symbolic notation and the formula, what is the z statistic for this sample mean?

6.38 Converting z scores to raw CFC scores: A study using the Consideration of Future Consequences scale found a mean CFC score of 3.20, with a standard deviation of 0.70, for the 800 students in the sample (Adams, 2012).

a. Imagine that your z score on the CFC score is −1.2. What is your raw score? Use symbolic notation and the formula. Explain why this answer makes sense.

b. Imagine that your z score on the CFC score is 0.66. What is your raw score? Use symbolic notation and the formula. Explain why this answer makes sense.

6.39 The normal curve and real-life variables, part I: For each of the following variables, state whether the distribution of scores would likely approximate a normal curve. Explain your answer.

a. Number of movies that a college student watches in a year

b. Number of full-page advertisements in a magazine

c. Human birth weights in Canada

6.40 The normal curve and real-life variables, part II: For each of the following variables, state whether the distribution of scores would likely approximate a normal curve. Explain your answer.

a. Number of minutes that students check social media sites each week

b. Volume of water that people drink each day

c. The length, in minutes, of YouTube videos

6.41 The normal curve in the media: Statistics geeks rejoiced when the *New York Times* published an article on the normal curve (Dunn, 2013)! Biologist Casey Dunn wrote that "Many real-world observations can be approximated by, and tested against, the same expected pattern: the normal distribution." He described the normal curve as symmetric and bell-shaped with more observations gathered near the mean. He offered several examples: "The size of flowers, the physiological response to a drug, the breaking force in a batch of steel cables," but also noted that there are important exceptions, including household income. In your own words, explain to someone who has never taken statistics why household income, unlike Dunn's other examples, is not normally distributed.

6.42 Percentiles and eating habits: As noted in How It Works 6.1, Georgiou and colleagues (1997) reported that college students had healthier eating habits, on average, than did those individuals who were neither college students nor college graduates. The 412 students in the study ate breakfast a mean of 4.1 times per week, with a standard deviation of 2.4. (For this exercise, again imagine that this is the entire population of interest.)

a. What is the approximate percentile for a student who eats breakfast four times per week?

b. What is the approximate percentile for a student who eats breakfast six times per week?

c. What is the approximate percentile for a student who eats breakfast twice a week?

6.43 z scores and comparisons of sports teams: A common quandary faces sports fans who live in the same city but avidly follow different sports. How does one determine whose team did better with respect to its league division? In 2012, the Atlanta Braves baseball team and the Atlanta Falcons football team both did well. The Braves won 94 games and the Falcons won 13. Which team was better in 2012? The question, then, is: Were the Braves better, as compared to the other teams in Major League Baseball (MLB), than the Falcons, as compared to the other teams in the National Football League (NFL)? Some of us could debate this for hours, but it's better to examine some statistics. Let's operationalize performance over the season as the number of wins during regular season play.

a. In 2012, the mean number of wins for MLB teams was 81.00, with a standard deviation of 11.733. Because all teams were included, these are population parameters. What is the Braves' z score?

b. In 2012, the mean number of wins for all NFL teams was 7.969, with a standard deviation of 3.036. What is the Falcons' z score?

c. Which team did better, according to these data?

d. How many games would the team with the lower *z* score have had to win to beat the team with the higher *z* score?

e. List at least one other way we could have operationalized the outcome variable (i.e., team performance).

6.44 **The *z* distribution and comparing scores on two tests of English language learning:** The Test of English as a Foreign Language (TOEFL), with scores ranging from 0 to 120, has traditionally been the most commonly used exam of reading comprehension, vocabulary, writing, and grammar for English-language learners in the United States. The International English Language Testing System (IELTS), with scores ranging from 0 to 9, has traditionally been the most commonly used exam in most other English-speaking countries (Ben, 2018). Does it matter which one is used? If a researcher wanted to compare English-language learners' TOEFL and IELTS scores to see if they were equivalent, how could the researcher use *z* scores to test this?

6.45 **Raw scores, *z* scores, percentiles, and sports teams:** Let's look at baseball and football again. We'll look at data for all of the teams in Major League Baseball (MLB) and the National Football League (NFL), respectively.

a. In 2012, the mean number of wins for MLB teams was 81.00, with a standard deviation of 11.733. The perennial underdogs at the time, the Chicago Cubs, had a *z* score of −1.705. How many games did they win?

b. In 2012, the mean number of wins for all NFL teams was 7.969, with a standard deviation of 3.036. The New Orleans Saints had a *z* score of −0.319. How many games did they win?

c. The Indianapolis Colts were just below the 84th percentile in terms of NFL wins. How many games did they win? Explain how you obtained your answer.

d. Explain how you can examine your answers in parts (a), (b), and (c) to determine whether the numbers make sense.

6.46 **Distributions and life expectancy:** Researchers have reported that the projected life expectancy for South African men diagnosed with human immunodeficiency virus (HIV) at age 20 who receive antiretroviral therapy (ART) is 27.6 years (Johnson et al., 2013). Imagine that the researchers determined this by following 250 people

with HIV who were receiving ART and calculating the mean.

a. What is the dependent variable of interest?

b. What is the population?

c. What is the sample?

d. For the population, describe what the distribution of *scores* would be.

e. For the population, describe what the distribution of *means* would be.

f. If the distribution of the population were skewed, would the distribution of scores likely be skewed or approximately normal? Explain your answer.

g. Would the distribution of means be skewed or approximately normal? Explain your answer.

6.47 **Distributions, personality testing, and depression:** The revised version of the Minnesota Multiphasic Personality Inventory (MMPI-2) is the most frequently administered self-report personality measure. Test-takers respond to more than 500 true/false statements, and their responses are scored, typically by a computer, on a number of scales (e.g., hypochondriasis, depression, psychopathic deviation). Respondents receive a *T* score on each scale that can be compared to norms. (You're likely to encounter *T* scores if you take psychology classes, but it's good to be aware that they are different from the *t* statistic that you will learn about in a few chapters.) *T* scores are another way to standardize scores so that percentiles and cutoffs can be determined. The mean *T* score is always 50, and the standard deviation is always 10. Imagine that you administer the MMPI-2 to 95 respondents who have recently lost a parent; you wonder whether their scores on the depression scale will be, on average, higher than the norms. You find a mean score on the depression scale of 55 in your sample.

a. Using symbolic notation, report the mean and standard deviation of the population.

b. Using symbolic notation and formulas (where appropriate), report the mean and standard error for the distribution of means to which your sample will be compared.

c. In your own words, explain why it makes sense that the standard error is smaller than the standard deviation.

6.48 **Distributions, personality testing, and social introversion:** See the description of the MMPI-2 in the previous exercise. The mean *T* score is always 50, and the standard deviation is always 10. Imagine that you administer the MMPI-2 to 50 respondents who do not use Instagram or any other social media; you wonder whether their scores on the social introversion scale will be, on average, higher than the norms. You find a mean score on the social introversion scale of 60 in your sample.

a. Using symbolic notation, report the mean and standard deviation of the population.

b. Using symbolic notation and formulas (where appropriate), report the mean and standard error for the distribution of means to which your sample will be compared.

c. In your own words, explain why it makes sense that the standard error is smaller than the standard deviation.

6.49 Distributions and the General Social Survey: The General Social Survey (GSS) is a survey of approximately 2000 U.S. adults conducted each year since 1972, for a total of more than 38,000 participants. During several years of the GSS, participants were asked how many close friends they have. The mean for this variable is 7.44 friends, with a standard deviation of 10.98. The median is 5.00 and the mode is 4.00.

a. Are these data for a distribution of scores or a distribution of means? Explain.

b. What do the mean and standard deviation suggest about the shape of the distribution? (*Hint:* Compare the sizes of the mean and the standard deviation.)

c. What do the three measures of central tendency suggest about the shape of the distribution?

d. Let's say that these data represent the entire population. Pretend that you randomly selected a person from this population and asked how many close friends she or he had. Would you compare this person to a distribution of scores or to a distribution of means? Explain your answer.

e. Now pretend that you randomly selected a sample of 80 people from this population. Would you compare this sample to a distribution of scores or to a distribution of means? Explain your answer.

f. Using symbolic notation, calculate the mean and standard error of the distribution of means.

g. What is the likely shape of the distribution of means? Explain your answer.

6.50 A distribution of scores and the General Social Survey: Refer to the previous exercise. Again, pretend that the GSS sample is the entire population of interest.

a. Imagine that you randomly selected one person from this population who reported that he had 18 close friends. Would you compare his score to a distribution of scores or to a distribution of means? Explain your answer.

b. What is his *z* score? Based on this *z* score, what is his approximate percentile?

c. Does it make sense to calculate a percentile for this person? Explain your answer. (*Hint:* Consider the shape of the distribution.)

6.51 A distribution of means and the General Social Survey: Refer to Exercise 6.49. Again, pretend that the GSS sample is the entire population of interest.

a. Imagine that you randomly selected 80 people from this population, and that they had a mean of 8.7. Would you compare this sample mean to a distribution of scores or to a distribution of means? Explain your answer.

b. What is the *z* statistic for this mean? Based on this *z* statistic, what is the approximate percentile for this sample?

c. Does it make sense to calculate a percentile for this sample? Explain your answer. (*Hint:* Consider the shape of the distribution.)

6.52 Percentiles, raw scores, and credit card theft: Credit card companies will often call cardholders if the pattern of use indicates that the card might have been stolen. Let's say that you charge an average of $280 a month on your credit card, with a standard deviation of $75. The credit card company will call you anytime your purchases for the month exceed the 98th percentile. What is the dollar amount beyond which you'll get a call from your credit card company?

6.53 The *z* distribution and a rogue cardiologist: A cardiologist in Munster, Indiana, has been accused of conducting unnecessary heart surgeries (Cresswell, 2015). Investigators found that the rates for one heart procedure were in the top 10% in the country for the city where this doctor worked. Lawyers countered that there were older and sicker people in this part of the country; yet other afflictions of the elderly—for example, treatment for hip fractures—were no higher in this region. In your own words, explain how the *z* distribution might play a role in determining whether this cardiologist was conducting unnecessary surgeries.

6.54 **The z distribution and a "super recognizer":** According to a news article, "Friends call Constable [Gary] Collins Rain Man or Yoda or simply The Oracle. But to Scotland Yard, London's metropolitan police force, he is known as a 'super recognizer'" (Bennhold, 2015). Prosopagnosia, also known as face blindness, is a disorder in which the sufferer cannot recall faces, even of people they know well. About 2% of us experience face blindness. Collins is the opposite; he's among the 1% to 2% of us who recall almost every face they've ever seen. As you can imagine, this gives him an almost superhero ability to help solve crimes—a "Facebook of the mind." A snippet from a security camera, and Collins has a name for the suspect. Most of us, however, fall in between prosopagnosics and super recognizers.

a. Imagine a z distribution for face recognition ability. Give an estimate of the z score that Collins and other super recognizers are likely to fall above. Explain your answer.

b. Now give an estimate of the z score that people with face blindness are likely to fall below. Explain your answer.

c. Between approximately what z scores do most of us fall? Explain your answer.

Putting It All Together

6.55 **Probability and medical treatments:** The three most common treatments for blocked coronary arteries are medication, bypass surgery, and angioplasty, which is a medical procedure that involves clearing out arteries and that leads to higher profits for doctors than do the other two procedures. The highest rate of angioplasty in the United States is in Elyria, a small city in Ohio. A 2006 article in *The New York Times* stated that "the statistics are so far off the charts—Medicare patients in Elyria receive angioplasties at a rate nearly four times the national average—that Medicare and at least one commercial insurer are starting to ask questions" (Abelson, 2006). The rate, in fact, is three times as high as that of Cleveland, Ohio, which is located just 30 miles from Elyria.

a. What is the population in this example? What is the sample?

b. How did probability play a role in the decision of Medicare and the commercial insurer to begin investigations?

c. How might the z distribution help the investigators to detect possible fraud in this case?

d. If the insurers determine that physicians in Elyria are committing fraud, but the insurers are wrong, what kind of error would they have made? Explain.

e. Does Elyria's extremely high percentile mean that the doctors in town are committing fraud? Cite two other possible reasons for Elyria's status as an outlier.

6.56 **Rural friendships and the General Social Survey:** Earlier, we considered data from the GSS on numbers of close friends people reported having. The mean for this variable is 7.44, with a standard deviation of 10.98. Let's say that you decide to use the GSS data to test whether people who live in rural areas have a different mean number of friends than does the overall GSS sample. Again, treat the overall GSS sample as the entire population of interest. Let's say that you select 40 people living in rural areas and find that they have an average of 3.9 friends.

a. What is the independent variable in this study? Is this variable nominal, ordinal, or scale?

b. What is the dependent variable in this study? Is this variable nominal, ordinal, or scale?

c. What is the null hypothesis for this study?

d. What is the research hypothesis for this study?

e. Would we compare the sample data to a distribution of scores or to a distribution of means? Explain.

f. Using symbolic notation and formulas, calculate the mean and the standard error for the distribution of means.

g. Using symbolic notation and the formula, calculate the z statistic for this sample.

h. What is the approximate percentile for this sample?

i. Let's say that the researchers concluded that people in rural areas have fewer friends than does the general population (thus rejecting the null hypothesis). If they are incorrect, have they made a Type I or a Type II error? Explain.

6.57 **Cheating on standardized tests:** In their book *Freakonomics*, Levitt and Dubner (2009) describe alleged cheating among teachers in the Chicago public school system. Certain classrooms had suspiciously strong performances on standardized tests that often mysteriously declined the following year when a new teacher taught the same students. In about 5% of classrooms studied, Levitt and other researchers found blocks of correct answers, among most students, for the last few questions, an indication that the teacher had changed responses to difficult questions for most students. Let's assume cheating in a given classroom if the overall standardized test score for the class showed a surprising change from one year to the next.

a. How are the researchers operationalizing the variable of cheating in this study? Is this a nominal, ordinal, or scale variable?

b. Explain how researchers can use the *z* distribution to catch cheating teachers.

c. How might a histogram be useful to researchers who are trying to catch cheating teachers?

d. If researchers falsely conclude that teachers are cheating, what kind of error would they be committing? Explain.

6.58 Which was better, the book or the movie: FiveThirtyEight is a popular blog that uses statistics in creative ways to better understand politics, sports, science and health, economics, and culture. In one article (Hickey, 2015), the author uses *z* scores to standardize book reviews from www.goodreads.com (which uses a 1 to 5 scale) and movie reviews from www.imdb.com (which uses a scale of 0 to 100) for the top 500 movies that were based on novels.

a. Explain why converting to *z* scores would be necessary to find out which story had a better book compared to a movie, or which story had a better movie compared to the book.

b. What might be some sampling biases (think back to Chapter 5) found in using these online ratings?

6.59 Cheating in online gaming: Researchers used the normal curve to investigate cheating among online gamers playing a car racing game (Christensen et al., 2013). The graph shows the winning times for one version of the game.

a. Referring to Chapter 3, what kind of graph is this and why? (*Hint:* Imagine that the curve represents the outline of many bars stacked close together.)

b. In what ways does this graph resemble a normal curve? In what ways does it deviate from a normal curve? If there is skew, what kind of skew is represented here?

c. The researchers used outliers to identify cheaters. What are outliers?

d. The researchers reported that they used interquartile range (IQR) to identify outliers. What is the interquartile range and how did they likely use it to determine outliers?

e. The researchers analyzed data from almost 140,000 players who together generated approximately 2.2 million scores. If the researchers had recruited these players as participants in the study, what kind of a sample would this have been? Explain your answer.

f. One way that the researchers determined who was cheating was by calculating differences between the winning times logged by players' computers and the winning times logged by the servers to which their computers connected. Bigger differences were labeled "suspicious" because they indicated that the players may have artificially sped up or slowed down the game on their own computers. How could the normal curve be used to identify cheaters based on this difference measure?

g. The researchers reported other interesting results for race times based on type of game. They found that race times were faster when players competed against each other than when players competed against the computer. What types of variables are race times and type of game? Explain your answer.

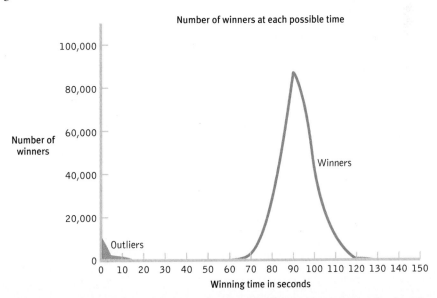

Number of winners at each possible time

Number of winners

Winners

Outliers

Winning time in seconds

Visit LaunchPad to access the e-book and to
test your knowledge with LearningCurve.

TERMS

normal curve (p. 150)

standardization (p. 154)

z score (p. 154)

z distribution (p. 160)

standard normal distribution (p. 160)

central limit theorem (p. 164)

distribution of means (p. 165)

standard error (p. 169)

FORMULAS

$$z = \frac{(X - \mu)}{\sigma}$$ (p. 156)

$$X = z(\sigma) + \mu$$ (p. 159)

$$\sigma_M = \frac{\sigma}{\sqrt{N}}$$ (p. 170)

$$z = \frac{(M - \mu_M)}{\sigma_M}$$ (p. 171)

SYMBOLS

z (p. 150)

μ_M (p. 169)

σ_M (p. 169)

Hypothesis Testing with z Tests

The z Table

Raw Scores, z Scores, and Percentages

The z Table and Distributions of Means

The Assumptions and Steps of Hypothesis Testing

The Three Assumptions for Conducting Analyses

The Six Steps of Hypothesis Testing

An Example of the z Test

Data Ethics: HARKing and *p*-Hacking

BEFORE YOU GO ON

- **You should understand how to calculate a z statistic for a distribution of scores and for a distribution of means (Chapter 6).**

- **You should understand that the z distribution allows us to determine the percentage of scores (or means) that fall below a particular z statistic (Chapter 6).**

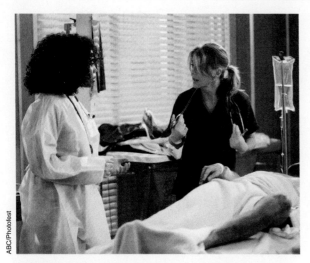

Misleadingly Dramatic? TV hospital dramas like *Grey's Anatomy* have a tendency to exaggerate the severity of injuries and the likelihood of death for trauma victims (Serrone et al., 2018). They also tend to embellish the road to recovery for TV survivors who are more likely to go straight home, as opposed to a rehabilitation hospital, than real-world trauma survivors. TV may create misleading perceptions of outcomes for trauma victims that doctors should address in their communication with patients. Helpful findings like this rely on hypothesis testing, including the *z* test that we introduce in this chapter.

Trauma patients and their relatives do not have time to learn about their medical conditions. After all, they've just been shot, hit by a car, or have experienced some other terrible bodily injury. Trauma patients must rely on what they already know about medical care, which, for many of us, is based on what we've seen on TV.

Researcher Rosemarie Serrone and her colleagues (2018) worried that TV depictions of trauma might be overly dramatic. Could such presentations mislead those who suffer actual trauma? To answer this question, Serrone's team engaged in some binge-watching (research is fun!). They recorded data for a sample of 290 fictional patients portrayed over 12 seasons of the popular hospital drama *Grey's Anatomy*. They then compared their sample to a population of actual trauma patients from the U.S. National Trauma Databank (NTDB).

Serrone and her colleagues reported a number of statistically significant differences between the means of their TV sample and the means for the population from the NTDB—all situations that could be analyzed with the *z* test we'll introduce in this chapter. For example, the TV patients were 10 years younger, on average, than the real-life patients (and, perhaps, more glamorous). And the TV patients received higher means on the injury severity scale (makes for more gripping television). Other differences were also apparent. On the one hand, TV patients were three times as likely to have needed surgery and three times as likely to have died as their real-world counterparts. On the other hand, TV survivors of trauma were more likely than real-world survivors to go straight home as opposed to a rehab hospital. After all, a quick recovery makes for a happy ending.

The researchers expressed concern that TV shows' need for drama misrepresents reality. These findings might help real-life doctors better communicate with actual trauma patients—and hypothesis testing helped to make this possible.

In this chapter, we start our exploration of hypothesis testing with the *z* test. We learn how the *z* distribution and the *z* test make fair comparisons possible through standardization. Specifically, we learn:

1. How to use a *z* table.
2. How to implement the basic steps of hypothesis testing.
3. How to conduct a *z* test to compare a single sample to a known population.

The z Table

In Chapter 6, we learned that (1) about 68% of scores fall within one *z* score of the mean, (2) about 96% of scores fall within two *z* scores of the mean, and (3) nearly all scores fall within three *z* scores of the mean. These guidelines are useful, but the table of *z* statistics and percentages is more specific. The *z* table is printed in its entirety in Appendix B.1, but for your convenience, we have provided an excerpt in Table 7-1. In this section, we learn how to use the *z* table to calculate percentages when the *z* score is not a whole number.

TABLE 7-1	Excerpt from the z Table

The z table provides the percentage of scores between the mean and a given z value. The full table includes positive z statistics from 0.00 to 4.50. The negative z statistics are not included because all we have to do is change the sign from positive to negative. Remember, the normal curve is symmetric: One side always mirrors the other. So, the percentages are the same for negative and positive z scores. See Appendix B.1 for the full table.

z	% Between Mean and z
⋮	⋮
0.97	33.40
0.98	33.65
0.99	33.89
1.00	34.13
1.01	34.38
1.02	34.61
⋮	⋮

Raw Scores, z Scores, and Percentages

Just as the same person might be called variations of a single name—"Christina," "Christy," or "Tina," for instance—z scores are just one of three different ways to identify the same point beneath the normal curve: raw score, z score, and percentile ranking. The z table is how we transition from one way of naming a score to another. More importantly, the z table gives us a way to state and test hypotheses by standardizing different kinds of observations onto the same scale.

For example, we can determine the percentage associated with a given z statistic by following two steps.

Step 1: Convert a raw score into a z score.
Step 2: Look up a given z score on the z table to find the percentage of scores *between the mean and that z score*.

Note that the z scores displayed in the z table are all positive, but that is just to save space. The normal curve is symmetric, so negative z scores (any scores below the mean) are the mirror image of positive z scores (any scores above the mean) (Figure 7-1).

MASTERING THE CONCEPT

7-1: We can use the z table to look up the percentage of scores between the mean of the distribution and a given z statistic.

FIGURE 7-1

The Standardized z Distribution

We can use a z table to determine the percentages below and above a particular z score. For example, 34% of scores fall between the mean and a z score of 1.

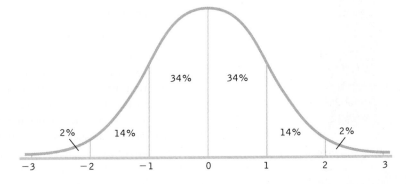

EXAMPLE 7.1

Here is an interesting way to learn how to use the z table: A research team (Sandberg, Bukowski, Fung, & Noll, 2004) wanted to know whether very short children tended to have poorer psychological adjustment than taller children and, therefore, should be treated with growth hormone. They categorized 15-year-old boys and girls into one of three groups—short (bottom 5%), average (middle 90%), or tall (top 5%)—based on published norms for a given age and gender (Centers for Disease Control and Prevention, National Center for Health Statistics, 2000; Sandberg et al., 2004). The mean height for 15-year-old boys was approximately 67.00 inches (170.18 centimeters), with a standard deviation of 3.19 inches (8.10 centimeters). For 15-year-old girls, the mean height was approximately 63.80 inches (162.05 centimeters), with a standard deviation of 2.66 inches (6.76 centimeters). We'll consider two 15-year-olds, one taller than average and the other shorter than average.

Jessica is 66.41 inches tall (just over 5 feet, 6 inches, or 167.64 centimeters).

> **STEP 1:** Convert her raw score to a z score, as we learned how to do in Chapter 6.

We use the mean ($\mu = 63.80$) and standard deviation ($\sigma = 2.66$) for the heights of girls:

$$z = \frac{(X - \mu)}{\sigma} = \frac{(66.41 - 63.80)}{2.66} = 0.98$$

> **STEP 2:** Look up 0.98 on the z table to find the associated percentage between the mean and Jessica's z score.

Once we know that the associated percentage is 33.65%, we can determine a number of percentages related to her z score. Here are three.

1. *Jessica's percentile rank—the percentage of scores below her score:* We add the percentage between the mean and the positive z score to 50%, which is the percentage of scores below the mean (50% of scores are on each side of the mean).

Jessica's percentile is 50% + 33.65% = 83.65%

Figure 7-2 shows this visually. As we can do when we are evaluating the calculations of z scores, we can run a quick mental check of the likely accuracy of the answer. We're interested in calculating the percentile of a *positive z score*. Because it is above the mean, we know that the answer must be higher than 50%. And it is.

FIGURE 7-2

Calculating the Percentile for a Positive z Score

Drawing curves helps us find someone's percentile rank. For Jessica's positive z score of 0.98, add the 50% below the mean to the 33.65% between the mean and her z score of 0.98; Jessica's percentile rank is 83.65%. Try drawing and labeling this curve for yourself. Research has demonstrated a "surprisingly powerful" effect of drawing on memory when learning new information (Fernandes, Wammes, & Meade, 2018).

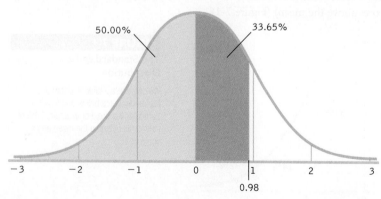

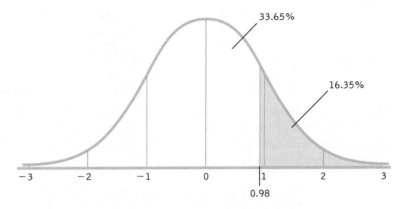

33.65%

16.35%

−3   −2   −1   0   1   2   3
0.98

FIGURE 7-3

Calculating the Percentage Above a Positive z Score

For a positive *z* score, we subtract the percentage between the mean and that *z* score from 50% (the total percentage above the mean) to get the percentage above that *z* score. Here, we subtract the 33.65% between the mean and the *z* score of 0.98 from 50%, which yields 16.35%. Drawing this curve on your own will help you remember what positive *z* scores look like.

2. *The percentage of scores above Jessica's score:* We subtract the percentage between the mean and the positive z score from 50%, which is the full percentage of scores above the mean:

$$50\% - 33.65\% = 16.35\%$$

So 16.35% of 15-year-old girls' heights are above Jessica's height. Figure 7-3 shows this visually. Here, it makes sense that the percentage would be smaller than 50%; because the z score is positive, we could not have more than 50% above it. As an alternative, a simpler method is to subtract Jessica's percentile rank of 83.65% from 100%. This gives us the same 16.35%. We could also look under the "In the tail" column in the z table in Appendix B.1.

3. *The scores at least as extreme as Jessica's z score, in both directions:* When we begin hypothesis testing, it will be useful to know the percentage of scores that are at least as extreme as a given z score. In this case, 16.35% of heights are extreme enough to have z scores above Jessica's z score of 0.98. But remember that the curve is symmetric. This means that another 16.35% of the heights are extreme enough to be below a z score of −0.98. So we can double 16.35% to find the total percentage of heights that are as far as or farther from the mean than is Jessica's height:

$$16.35\% + 16.35\% = 32.70\%$$

Thus 32.7% of heights are at least as extreme as Jessica's height in either direction. Figure 7-4 shows this visually.

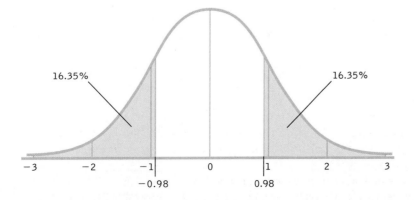

16.35%   16.35%

−3   −2   −1   0   1   2   3
−0.98   0.98

FIGURE 7-4

Calculating the Percentage at Least as Extreme as the z Score

For a positive *z* score, we double the percentage above that *z* score to get the percentage of scores that are at least as extreme—that is, at least as far from the mean—as the *z* score is. Here, we double 16.35% to calculate the percentage at least this extreme: 32.70%. Drawing this curve on your own will help you understand positive and negative *z* scores.

What group would Jessica fall in? Because 16.35% of 15-year-old girls are taller than Jessica, she is not in the top 5%. So she would be classified as being of average height, according to the researchers' definition of average. ●

EXAMPLE 7.2

Now let's repeat this process for a score below the mean. Manuel is 61.20 inches tall (about 5 feet, 1 inch or 154.94 centimeters), so we want to know if Manuel can be classified as short. Remember, for boys the mean height is 67.00 inches, and the standard deviation for height is 3.19 inches.

> **STEP 1: Convert his raw score to a *z* score.**

We use the mean ($\mu = 67.00$) and standard deviation ($\sigma = 3.19$) for the heights of boys:

$$z = \frac{(X - \mu)}{\sigma} = \frac{(61.20 - 67.00)}{3.19} = -1.82$$

> **STEP 2: Calculate the percentile, the percentage above, and the percentage at least as extreme for the negative *z* score for Manuel's height.**

We can again determine a number of percentages related to the *z* score; however, this time, we need to use the full table in Appendix B. The *z* table includes only positive *z* scores, so we look up 1.82 and find that the percentage between the mean and the *z* score is 46.56%. Of course, percentages are always positive, so don't add a negative sign here!

1. *Manuel's percentile score—the percentage of scores below his score:* For a negative *z* score, we subtract the percentage between the mean and the *z* score from 50% (which is the total percentage below the mean):

Manuel's percentile is 50% − 46.5% = 3.44% (Figure 7-5)

FIGURE 7-5

Calculating the Percentile for a Negative z Score

As with positive *z* scores, drawing curves helps us to determine the appropriate percentage for negative *z* scores. For a negative *z* score, we subtract the percentage between the mean and that *z* score from 50% (the percentage below the mean) to get the percentage below that negative *z* score, the percentile. Here we subtract the 46.56% between the mean and the *z* score of −1.82 from 50%, which yields 3.44%. Try drawing this one yourself.

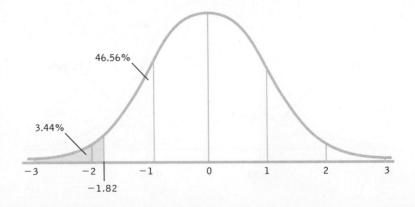

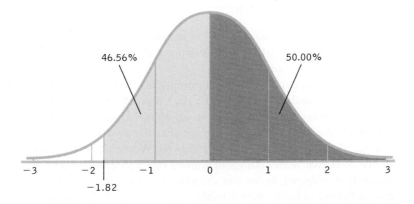

FIGURE 7-6

Calculating the Percentage Above a Negative z Score

For a negative z score, we add the percentage between the mean and that z score to 50% (the percentage above the mean) to get the percentage above that z score. Here we add the 46.56% between the mean and the z score of −1.82 to the 50% above the mean, which yields 96.56%.

2. *The percentage of scores above Manuel's score:* We add the percentage between the mean and the negative z score to 50%, the percentage above the mean:

$$50\% + 46.56\% = 96.56\%$$

So 96.56% of 15-year-old boys' heights fall above Manuel's height (Figure 7-6).

3. *The scores at least as extreme as Manuel's z score, in both directions:* In this case, 3.44% of 15-year-old boys have heights that are extreme enough to have z scores below −1.82. And because the curve is symmetric, another 3.44% of heights are extreme enough to be above a z score of 1.82. So we can double 3.44% to find the total percentage of heights that are as far as or farther from the mean than is Manuel's height:

$$3.44\% + 3.44\% = 6.88\%$$

So 6.88% of heights are at least as extreme as Manuel's in either direction (Figure 7-7). In what group would the researchers classify Manuel? Manuel has a percentile rank of 3.44%. He is in the lowest 5% of heights for boys of his age, so he would be classified as short. Now we can get to the question that drives this research. Does Manuel's short stature doom him to a life of few friends and poor social adjustment? Researchers compared the means of the three groups—short, average, and tall—on several measures of peer relations and social adjustment, but they did not find evidence of mean differences among the groups (Sandberg et al., 2004).

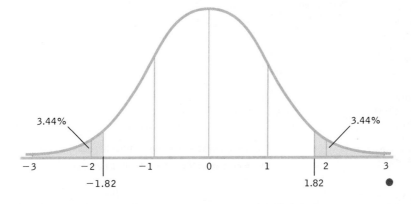

FIGURE 7-7

Calculating the Percentage at Least as Extreme as the z Score

With a negative z score, we double the percentage below that z score to get the percentage of scores that are at least as extreme—that is, at least as far from the mean—as the z score is. Here, we double 3.44% to calculate the percentage at least this extreme: 6.88%.

EXAMPLE 7.3

This example demonstrates (1) how to seamlessly shift among raw scores, *z* scores, and percentile ranks; and (2) why drawing a normal curve makes the calculations much easier to understand.

Christian Rudder, one of the founders of the online dating site OkCupid, writes a blog based on data from the site's users. The graph in Figure 7-8 shows the attractiveness ratings of heterosexual women and men who have profiles on OkCupid (Rudder, 2009). You can see that the distribution of women's ratings of men (the blue line) is positively skewed. Women tend to think men are not all that attractive. Men's ratings of women (the orange line), however, are roughly normally distributed, so we can calculate *z* scores for this distribution. (Women may judge men's looks more harshly, but according to Rudder they're also more likely than men to contact someone they view as less attractive, so it sort of evens out.) Rudder didn't provide the mean and standard deviation, but based on what we know about a normal distribution, we can estimate the mean to be 2.5 and the standard deviation to be 0.833. Let's imagine that Veena's rating is at the 63rd percentile. What was her raw score? Begin by drawing a curve, as in Figure 7-9. Then add a line at the point below which approximately 63% of scores fall. We know that this score is above the mean because 50% of scores fall below the mean, and 63% is larger than 50%.

Using the drawing as a guideline, we see that we have to calculate the percentage between the mean and the *z* score of interest. So, we subtract the 50% below the mean from Veena's rating, 63%:

$$63\% - 50\% = 13\%$$

We look up the closest percentage to 13% in the *z* table (which is 12.93%) and find an associated *z* score of 0.33. This is above the mean, so we do not label it with a

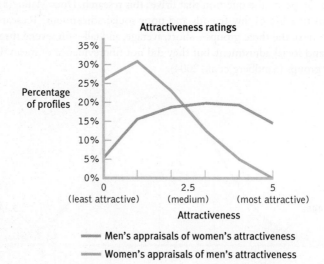

FIGURE 7-8

Calculating a Score from a Percentile

This graph combines two sets of data presented in an OkCupid article on heterosexual people's ratings of the opposite gender (Rudder, 2009). The *x*-axis represents a five-point scale of attractiveness, from least to most. The *y*-axis represents the percentage of profiles that receive that rating. The orange line represents men's appraisals of women's attractiveness, and the blue line represents women's appraisals of men's attractiveness. Most women rate men as fairly unattractive (note that no male profiles received a perfect score of five), whereas men's ratings of women's attractiveness follow the pattern of a normal distribution. Source: Rudder, C. (2009, November 17). Your looks and your inbox. *Oktrends*. Retrieved from theblog.okcupid .com/your-looks-and-your-inbox-8715c0f1561e

Attractiveness ratings

Percentage of profiles

Attractiveness

⎯⎯ Men's appraisals of women's attractiveness

⎯⎯ Women's appraisals of men's attractiveness

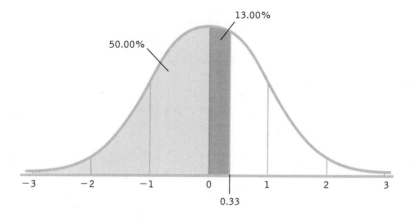

FIGURE 7-9

Calculating a Score from a Percentile

We convert a percentile to a raw score by calculating the percentage between the mean and the *z* score, and looking up that percentage on the *z* table to find the associated *z* score. We then convert the *z* score to a raw score using the formula. Here, we look up 13.00% on the *z* table (12.93% is the closest percentage) and find a *z* score of 0.33, which we can convert to a raw score.

negative sign. We then convert the z score to a raw score using the formula we learned in Chapter 6:

$$X = z(\sigma) + \mu = 0.33(0.833) + 2.5 = 2.7749$$

Veena, whose profile rating is at the 63rd percentile, has a raw score of 2.77. Double check! This score is above the mean of 2.5, and the percentage is above 50%. ●

The z Table and Distributions of Means

Let's shift our focus from the z score of an individual within a group to the z statistic for a group. There are a couple changes to the calculations. First, we will use means rather than individual scores because we are now studying a sample of many scores rather than studying one individual score. Fortunately, the z table can also be used to determine percentages and z statistics for distributions of means calculated from many people. The other change is that we need to calculate the mean and the standard error for the distribution of means before calculating the z statistic.

EXAMPLE 7.4

Let's now imagine that instead of looking at the rating of one person—Veena—we're interested in the average rating of a group. Maybe you wonder how the women at your university who are on OkCupid stack up with the whole population of women on OkCupid. You manage to convince OkCupid to give you the profile ratings for 30 women on your campus. Imagine that the mean rating for these 30 women is 2.84. Before we calculate the z statistic, let's use proper symbolic notation to indicate the mean and the standard error of this distribution of means:

$$\mu_M = \mu = 2.5$$

$$\sigma_M = \frac{\sigma}{\sqrt{N}} = \frac{0.833}{\sqrt{30}} = 0.152$$

Percentile for the Mean of a Sample

We can use the z table with sample means in addition to sample scores. The only difference is that we use the mean and standard error of the distribution of means rather than the distribution of scores. Here, the z score of 2.24 is associated with a percentage of 48.75% between the mean and z score. Added to the 50% below the mean, the percentile is 50% + 48.75% = 98.75%.

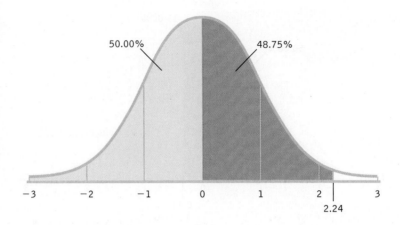

At this point, we have all the information we need to calculate the percentage using the two steps we learned earlier.

> **STEP 1:** We convert to a z statistic using the mean and standard error that we just calculated.

$$z = \frac{(M - \mu_M)}{\sigma_M} = \frac{(2.84 - 2.50)}{0.152} = 2.237$$

> **STEP 2:** We determine the percentage below this z statistic.

Draw it! Draw a curve that includes the mean of the z distribution, 0, and this z statistic, 2.237, rounded to 2.24 (Figure 7-10). Then shade the area in which we are interested: everything below 2.24. Now we look up the percentage between the mean and the z statistic of 2.24. The z table indicates that this percentage is 48.75, which we write in the section of the curve between the mean and 2.24. We write 50% in the half of the curve below the mean. We add 48.75% to the 50% below the mean to get the percentile rank, 98.75%. (Subtracting from 100%, only 1.25% of mean scores would be higher than the mean if they come from this population.) Based on this percentage, the average rating of a sample of women at your university is quite high. But we still can't arrive at a conclusion about whether these women are rated as significantly more attractive compared to the population average of 2.5 until we conduct a hypothesis test. ●

In the next section, we learn (1) the assumptions for conducting hypothesis testing; (2) the six steps of hypothesis testing using the z distribution; and (3) whether to reject or fail to reject the null hypothesis. In the last section, we demonstrate a z test.

CHECK YOUR LEARNING

Reviewing the Concepts	>	Raw scores, z scores, and percentile rankings are three ways to describe the same score within a normal distribution.
	>	If we know the mean and the standard deviation of a population, we can convert a raw score to a z score and then use the z table to determine percentages below, above, or at least as extreme as this z score.
	>	We can use the z table in reverse as well, taking a percentage and converting it into a z score and then a raw score.
	>	These same conversions can be conducted on a sample mean instead of on a score. The procedures are identical, but we use the mean and the standard error of the distribution of means, instead of the distribution of scores.

Clarifying the Concepts	7-1	What information do we need to know about a population of interest to use the z table?
	7-2	How do z scores relate to raw scores and percentile ranks?

Calculating the Statistics	7-3	If the percentage of scores between a z score of 1.37 and the mean is 41.47%, what percentage of scores lies between −1.37 and the mean?
	7-4	If 12.93% of scores fall between the mean and a z score of 0.33, what percentage of scores falls below this z score?

Applying the Concepts	7-5	Every year, the Educational Testing Service (ETS) administers the Major Field Test in Psychology (MFTP) to graduating psychology majors in the United States. Baylor University wondered how its students compared to the national average. On its Web site, Baylor reported that the mean and the standard deviation of the 18,073 U.S. students who took this exam were 156.8 and 14.6, respectively. Thirty-six students in Baylor's psychology and neuroscience department took the exam; these students had a mean score of 164.6.

a. What is the percentile rank for the sample of students at Baylor? Use symbolic notation and write out your calculations.

b. What percentage of samples of this size scored higher, on average, than the students at Baylor?

Solutions to these Check Your Learning questions can be found in Appendix D.

c. What can you say about how Baylor students compared to students across the nation?

The Assumptions and Steps of Hypothesis Testing

Whenever we analyze data, such as with the comparison of TV trauma patients with real-life trauma patients, the formal process of hypothesis testing is based on particular assumptions about the data. At times it might be safe to violate those assumptions and proceed through the six steps of formal hypothesis testing, but it is essential to understand the assumptions before making such a decision.

The Three Assumptions for Conducting Analyses

Think of "statistical assumptions" as the ideal conditions for hypothesis testing. More formally, *assumptions are the characteristics that we ideally require the population from which we are sampling to have so that we can make accurate inferences.* Why go

● An **assumption** is a characteristic that we ideally require the population from which we are sampling to have so that we can make accurate inferences.

through all the effort to understand and calculate statistics if you can't believe the story they tell?

The assumptions for the *z* test apply to several other hypothesis tests, especially ***parametric tests***, *which are inferential statistical analyses based on a set of assumptions about the population.* By contrast, ***nonparametric tests*** *are inferential statistical analyses that are not based on a set of assumptions about the population.* Learning the three main assumptions for parametric tests will help you to select the appropriate statistical test for your particular data set.

> ● A **parametric test** is an inferential statistical analysis based on a set of assumptions about the population.
>
> ● A **nonparametric test** is an inferential statistical analysis that is not based on a set of assumptions about the population.

Assumption 1: *The dependent variable is assessed using a scale measure.* If it's clear that the dependent variable is nominal or ordinal, we could not make this first assumption and thus should not use a parametric hypothesis test.

Assumption 2: *The participants are randomly selected.* Every member of the population of interest must have had an equal chance of being selected for the study. This assumption is often violated; it is more likely that participants are a convenience sample. If we violate this second assumption, we must be cautious when generalizing from a sample to the population.

> ● A **robust** hypothesis test is one that produces fairly accurate results even when the data suggest that the population might not meet some of the assumptions.

Assumption 3: *The distribution of the population of interest must be approximately normal.* Many distributions are approximately normal, but it is important to remember that there are exceptions to this guideline (Micceri, 1989). Because hypothesis tests deal with sample means rather than individual scores, as long as the sample size is at least 30 (recall the discussion about the central limit theorem), it is likely that this third assumption is met.

Many parametric hypothesis tests can be conducted even if some of the assumptions are not met (Table 7-2), and are robust against violations of some of these assumptions. ***Robust*** *hypothesis tests are those that produce fairly accurate results even when the data suggest that the population might not meet some of the assumptions.*

TABLE 7-2 The Three Assumptions for Hypothesis Testing

We must be aware of the assumptions for the hypothesis test that we choose, and we must be cautious in choosing to proceed with a hypothesis test when the data may not meet all of the assumptions. Note that in addition to these three assumptions, for many hypothesis tests, including the *z* test, the independent variable must be nominal.

The Three Assumptions	Breaking the Assumptions
1. Dependent variable is on a scale measure	Usually OK if the data are not clearly nominal or ordinal
2. Participants are randomly selected	OK if we are cautious about generalizing
3. Population distribution is approximately normal	OK if the sample includes at least 30 scores

These three statistical assumptions represent the ideal conditions and are more likely to produce valid research. *Meeting the assumptions improves the quality of research, but not meeting the assumptions doesn't necessarily invalidate research.*

The Six Steps of Hypothesis Testing

Hypothesis testing can be broken down into six standard steps.

Step 1: Identify the populations, comparison distribution, and assumptions.

When we first approach hypothesis testing, we consider the characteristics of the data to determine the distribution to which we will compare the sample. First, we state the populations represented by the groups to be compared. Then we identify the comparison distribution (e.g., a distribution of means). Finally, we review the assumptions of hypothesis testing. The information we gather in this step helps us to choose the appropriate hypothesis test (Chapter 18 provides a comprehensive guide for choosing the appropriate test).

Step 2: State the null and research hypotheses.

Hypotheses are about populations, *not* about samples. The null hypothesis is usually the "boring" one that posits no change or no difference between groups. The research hypothesis is usually the "exciting" one that posits that a given intervention will lead to a change or a difference—for instance, that a particular kind of psychotherapeutic intervention will reduce general anxiety. State the null and research hypotheses in both words and symbolic notation.

Step 3: Determine the characteristics of the comparison distribution.

State the relevant characteristics of the comparison distribution (the distribution based on the null hypothesis). In a later step, we will compare data from the sample (or samples) to the comparison distribution to determine how extreme the sample data are. For *z* tests, we will determine the mean and standard error of the comparison distribution. These numbers describe the distribution represented by the null hypothesis and will be used when we calculate the test statistic.

Step 4: Determine the critical values, or cutoffs.

The critical values, or cutoffs, of the comparison distribution indicate how extreme the data must be, in terms of the *z* statistic, to reject the null hypothesis. Often called simply *cutoffs*, these numbers are more formally called **critical values,** *the test statistic values beyond which we reject the null hypothesis.* In most cases, we determine two cutoffs: one for extreme samples below the mean and one for extreme samples above the mean.

The critical values, or cutoffs, are based on a somewhat arbitrary standard—the most extreme 5% of the comparison distribution curve: 2.5% on either end. At times, cutoffs are based on a less conservative percentage, such as 10%, or a more conservative percentage, such as 1%. Regardless of the chosen cutoff, the area beyond the cutoff, or critical value, is often referred to as the critical region. Specifically, *the **critical region** is the area in the tails of the comparison distribution in which the null hypothesis can be rejected.* These percentages are typically written as probabilities; that is, 5% would be written as 0.05. *The probabilities used to determine the critical values, or cutoffs, in hypothesis testing are **alpha levels*** (sometimes called p *levels*).

Step 5: Calculate the test statistic.

We use the information from step 3 to calculate the test statistic, in this case the *z* statistic. We can then directly compare the test statistic to the critical values to determine whether the sample is extreme enough to warrant rejecting the null hypothesis. If we use software to calculate the test statistic, we can also determine something called the *p* value. *The **p value** is the probability of finding this particular test statistic, or one even larger, if the null hypothesis is true—that is, if there is no difference between means.* The *p* value is something we'll come back to again and again throughout this book.

- A **critical value** is a test statistic value beyond which we reject the null hypothesis; often called a cutoff.

- The **critical region** is the area in the tails of the comparison distribution in which the null hypothesis can be rejected.

- The probability used to determine the critical values, or cutoffs, in hypothesis testing is an **alpha level** (sometimes called p *level*).

- The *p* **value** is the probability of finding this particular test statistic, or one even larger, if the null hypothesis is true—that is, if there is no difference between means.

Step 6: Make a decision.

Using the statistical evidence, we can now decide whether to reject or fail to reject the null hypothesis. Based on the available evidence, we either reject the null hypothesis if the test statistic is beyond the cutoffs, or we fail to reject the null hypothesis if the test statistic is not beyond the cutoffs. When we reject the null hypothesis, we know that the *p* value associated with the test statistic is smaller than the alpha level of 0.05.

These six steps of hypothesis testing are summarized in Table 7-3.

TABLE 7-3 The Six Steps of Hypothesis Testing
We use the same six basic steps with each type of hypothesis test.
1. Identify the populations, distribution, and assumptions, and then choose the appropriate hypothesis test.
2. State the null and research hypotheses, in both words and symbolic notation.
3. Determine the characteristics of the comparison distribution.
4. Determine the critical values, or cutoffs, that indicate the points beyond which we will reject the null hypothesis.
5. Calculate the test statistic.
6. Decide whether to reject or fail to reject the null hypothesis.

- A finding is **statistically significant** if the data differ from what we would expect by chance if there were, in fact, no actual difference.

Language Alert! When we reject the null hypothesis, we often refer to the results as "statistically significant." A finding is ***statistically significant*** *if the data differ from what we would expect by chance if there were, in fact, no actual difference.* The word *significant* is another one of those statistical terms with a very particular meaning. The phrase *statistically significant* does not necessarily mean that the finding is important or meaningful. A small difference between means could be statistically significant but not practically significant or important.

CHECK YOUR LEARNING

Reviewing the Concepts

> When we conduct hypothesis testing, we have to consider the assumptions for that particular test.

> Parametric statistics are those that are based on assumptions about the population distribution; nonparametric statistics have no such assumptions. Parametric statistics are often robust to violations of the assumptions.

> The three assumptions for a *z* test are that the dependent variable is on a scale measure, the sample is randomly selected, and the underlying population distribution is approximately normal.

> There are six standard steps for hypothesis testing. First, we identify the population, comparison distribution, and assumptions, all of which help us to choose the appropriate hypothesis test. Second, we state the null and research hypotheses. Third, we determine the characteristics of the comparison distribution. Fourth, we determine the critical values, or cutoffs, of the comparison distribution. Fifth, we calculate the test statistic. Sixth, we decide whether to reject or fail to reject the null hypothesis.

> The standard practice of statisticians is to consider scores to be statistically significant and to warrant rejection of the null hypothesis if they would occur less than 5% of the time based on the null hypothesis; observations that would occur more often than 5% of the time do not support this decision, and thus we would fail to reject the null hypothesis in these cases.

| Clarifying the Concepts | **7-6** | Explain the three assumptions made for most parametric hypothesis tests. |
| | **7-7** | How do critical values help us to make a decision about the hypothesis? |

| Calculating the Statistics | **7-8** | If a researcher always sets the critical region as 8% of the distribution, and the null hypothesis is true, how often will he reject the null hypothesis if the null hypothesis is true? |
| | **7-9** | Rewrite each of these percentages as a probability, or alpha level: |

    a. 15%

    b. 3%

    c. 5.5%

| Applying the Concepts | **7-10** | For each of the following scenarios, state whether each of the three basic assumptions for parametric hypothesis tests is met. Explain your answers and label the three assumptions (1) through (3). |

    a. Researchers compared the ability of experienced clinical psychologists versus clinical psychology graduate students to diagnose a patient, based on a 1-hour interview. For 2 months, either a psychologist or a student interviewed every outpatient at the local community mental health center who had already received diagnoses based on a number of criteria. For each diagnosis, the psychologists and graduate students were given a score of correct or incorrect.

    b. Behavioral scientists wondered whether animals raised in captivity would be healthier with diminished human contact. Twenty large cats (e.g., lions, tigers) were randomly selected from all the wild cats living in zoos in North America. Half were assigned to the control group—no change in human interaction. Half were assigned to the experimental group—no humans entered their cages except when the animals were not in them, one-way mirrors were used so that the animals could not see zoo visitors, and so on. The animals received a score for health over 1 year; points were given for various illnesses; a very few sickly animals had extremely high scores.

Solutions to these Check Your Learning questions can be found in Appendix D.

An Example of the z Test

In this section, we apply what we've learned about hypothesis testing—including the six steps—to a specific example of a z test. Just as the researchers in the chapter-opening story were able to compare the mean of a sample of TV trauma patients to the mean of the population of real-life trauma patients, this example pits a sample of Starbucks customers against a population. (The logic of the z test is a gateway to understanding all statistical tests; however, in practice, z tests are rarely used because researchers seldom have only one sample *and* know both the mean and the standard deviation of the population.)

EXAMPLE 7.5

New York City was the first U.S. city to require that chain restaurants post calorie counts for all menu items. Shortly after the new law was implemented, the research team of Bollinger, Leslie, and Sorensen (2010) decided to test the law's effectiveness. For more than a year, they gathered data on every transaction at Starbucks coffee shops in several cities. They determined a population mean of 247 calories in products purchased by customers at stores without calorie postings. Based on the range

The z Test and Calories on Menus We only use *z* tests when we have one sample and know the population mean and standard deviation, a rare situation. For example, on average, do people consume fewer calories when they know how many calories are in their favorite latte and doughnut? We can use the *z* test to compare the average numbers of calories that customers consume when calorie counts are either posted or not posted on their menu boards.

of 0 to 1208 calories in customer transactions, we estimate a standard deviation of approximately 201 calories, which we'll use as the population standard deviation for this example.

The researchers also recorded calories for a sample in New York City after calories were posted on Starbucks menus. They reported a mean of 232 calories per purchase, a decrease of 6%. For the purposes of this example, we'll assume a sample size of 1000. Here's how to apply hypothesis testing when comparing a sample of customers at Starbucks with calories posted on their menus to the general population of customers at Starbucks without calories posted on their menus.

We'll use the six steps of hypothesis testing to analyze the calorie data. These six steps will tell us if customers visiting a Starbucks with calories listed on the menu consume fewer calories, on average, than customers visiting a Starbucks without calories listed on the menu. In fact, we use the six-step approach so often in this book that it won't be long before it becomes an automatic way of thinking for you. Each step in the example below is followed by a summary that models how to report hypothesis tests.

> **STEP 1:** Identify the populations, distribution, and assumptions.

First, we identify the populations, comparison distribution, and assumptions, which help us to determine the appropriate hypothesis test. The *populations* are (1) all customers at those Starbucks with calories posted on the menu (whether or not the customers are in the sample) and (2) all customers at those Starbucks without calories posted on the menu. Because we are studying a sample rather than an individual, the *comparison distribution* is a distribution of means. We compare the mean of the sample of 1000 people visiting those Starbucks that have calories posted on the menu (selected from the population of all people visiting those Starbucks with calories posted) to a distribution of all possible means of samples of 1000 people (selected from the population of all people visiting those Starbucks that don't have calories posted on the menu). The *hypothesis test* will be a *z* test because we have only one sample and we know the mean and the standard deviation of the population from the published norms.

Now let's examine the *assumptions* for a *z* test. (1) The data are on a scale measure, calories. (2) We do not know whether sample participants were selected randomly from among all people visiting those Starbucks with calories posted on the menu. If they were not, the ability to generalize beyond this sample to other Starbucks customers would be limited. (3) The comparison distribution should be normal. The individual data points are likely to be positively skewed because the minimum score of 0 is much closer to the mean of 247 than it is to the maximum score of 1208. However, the sample size is 1000, which is greater than 30; so based on the central limit theorem, we know that the comparison distribution—the distribution of means—will be approximately normal.

Summary: Population 1: All customers at those Starbucks that have calories posted on the menu. Population 2: All customers at those Starbucks that don't have calories posted on the menu.

The comparison distribution will be a distribution of means. The hypothesis test will be a *z* test because there is only one sample and we know the population mean and standard deviation. This study meets two of the three assumptions and may meet the third. The dependent variable is scale. In addition, there are more than 30 participants in the sample, indicating that the comparison distribution will be normal. We do not know whether the sample was randomly selected, however, so we must be cautious when generalizing.

STEP 2: State the null and research hypotheses.

Next we state the null and research hypotheses in words and in symbols. Remember, hypotheses are always about populations, not samples. In most forms of hypothesis testing, there are two possible sets of hypotheses: directional (predicting either an increase or a decrease, but not both) or nondirectional (predicting a difference in either direction).

The first possible set of hypotheses is directional. The null hypothesis is that customers at those Starbucks that have calories posted on the menu do *not* consume fewer mean calories than customers at those Starbucks that don't have calories posted on the menu; in other words, they could consume the same or more mean calories, but not fewer. The research hypothesis is that customers at those Starbucks that have calories posted on the menu consume fewer mean calories than do customers at Starbucks that don't have calories posted on the menu. (Note that the direction of the hypotheses could be reversed.)

The symbol for the null hypothesis is H_0. The symbol for the research hypothesis is H_1. Throughout this text, we use μ for the mean because hypotheses are about populations and their parameters, not about samples and their statistics. So, in symbolic notation, the hypotheses are:

$$H_0: \mu_1 \geq \mu_2$$

$$H_1: \mu_1 < \mu_2$$

For the null hypothesis, the symbolic notation says that the mean calories consumed by those in population 1, customers at those Starbucks with calories posted on the menu, is not lower than the mean calories consumed by those in population 2, customers at those Starbucks without calories posted on the menu. For the research hypothesis, the symbolic notation says that the mean calories consumed by those in population 1 is lower than the mean calories consumed by those in population 2.

This hypothesis test is considered a one-tailed test. *A **one-tailed test** is a hypothesis test in which the research hypothesis is directional, positing either a mean decrease or a mean increase in the dependent variable, but not both, as a result of the independent variable.* One-tailed tests are rarely seen in the research literature; they are used only when the researcher is absolutely certain that the effect cannot go in the other direction or the researcher would not be interested in the result if it did.

● A **one-tailed test** is a hypothesis test in which the research hypothesis is directional, positing either a mean decrease or a mean increase in the dependent variable, but not both, as a result of the independent variable.

The second set of hypotheses is nondirectional. The null hypothesis states that customers at Starbucks with posted calories (whether in the sample or not) consume the same number of calories, on average, as customers at Starbucks without posted calories. The research hypothesis is that customers at Starbucks with posted calories (whether in the sample or not) consume a different average number of calories than do customers at Starbucks without posted calories. The means of the two populations are posited to be different, but neither mean is predicted to be lower or higher.

The hypotheses in symbols would be:

$$H_0: \mu_1 = \mu_2$$

$$H_1: \mu_1 \neq \mu_2$$

For the null hypothesis, the symbolic notation says that the mean number of calories consumed by those in population 1 is the same as the mean number of calories consumed by those in population 2. For the research hypothesis, the symbolic notation says that the mean number of calories consumed by those in population 1 is different from the mean number of calories consumed by those in population 2.

This hypothesis test is considered a two-tailed test. *A **two-tailed test** is a hypothesis test in which the research hypothesis does not indicate a direction of the mean difference or change in the dependent variable, but merely indicates that there will be a mean difference.* Two-tailed tests are much more common than are one-tailed tests. We will use two-tailed tests throughout this book unless we tell you otherwise. If a researcher expects a difference in a certain direction, he or she might have a one-tailed hypothesis; however, if the results are in the opposite direction, the researcher cannot then switch the direction of the hypothesis.

• A **two-tailed test** is a hypothesis test in which the research hypothesis does not indicate a direction of the mean difference or change in the dependent variable, but merely indicates that there will be a mean difference.

Summary: Null hypothesis: Customers at those Starbucks that have calories posted on the menu consume the same number of calories, on average, as do customers at Starbucks that don't have calories posted on the menu—$H_0: \mu_1 = \mu_2$. Research hypothesis: Customers at those Starbucks that have calories posted on the menu consume a different number of calories, on average, than do customers at those Starbucks that don't have calories posted on the menu—$H_1: \mu_1 \neq \mu_2$.

MASTERING THE CONCEPT

7-3: We conduct a one-tailed test if we have a directional hypothesis, such as that the sample will have a higher (or lower) mean than the population. We use a two-tailed test if we have a nondirectional hypothesis, such as that the sample will have a different mean than the population does.

> **STEP 3: Determine the characteristics of the comparison distribution.**

Now we determine the characteristics that describe the distribution with which we will compare the sample. For *z* tests, we must know the mean and the standard error of the population of scores; the standard error for samples of this size is calculated from the standard deviation of the population of scores. Here, the population mean for the number of calories consumed by the general population of Starbucks customers is 247, and the standard deviation is 201. The sample size is 1000. Because we use a sample mean in hypothesis testing, rather than a single score, we must use the standard error of the mean instead of the population standard deviation (of the scores). The characteristics of the comparison distribution are determined as follows:

$$\mu_M = \mu = 247$$

$$\sigma_M = \frac{\sigma}{\sqrt{N}} = \frac{201}{\sqrt{1000}} = 6.356$$

Summary: $\mu_M = 247; \sigma_M = 6.356$

STEP 4: Determine the critical values, or cutoffs.

Next we determine the critical values, or cutoffs, to which we can compare the test statistic. As stated previously, the research convention is to set the cutoffs to an alpha level of 0.05. For a two-tailed test, this indicates the most extreme 5%—that is, the 2.5% at the bottom of the comparison distribution and the 2.5% at the top. Because we calculate a test statistic for the sample—specifically a *z* statistic—we report cutoffs in terms of *z* statistics. We use the *z* table to determine the scores for the top and bottom 2.5%.

We know that 50% of the curve falls above the mean, and we know that 2.5% falls above the relevant *z* statistic. By subtracting (50% − 2.5% = 47.5%), we determine that 47.5% of the curve falls between the mean and the relevant *z* statistic. When we look up this percentage on the *z* table, we find a *z* statistic of 1.96. So the critical values are −1.96 and 1.96 (Figure 7-11).

Summary: The cutoff *z* statistics are −1.96 and 1.96.

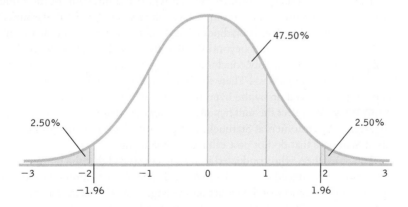

FIGURE 7-11

Determining Critical Values for a z Distribution

We typically determine critical values in terms of *z* statistics so we can easily compare a test statistic to determine whether it is beyond the critical values. Here, *z* scores of −1.96 and 1.96 indicate the most extreme 5% of the distribution, 2.5% in each tail.

STEP 5: Calculate the test statistic.

In step 5, we calculate the test statistic, in this case a *z* statistic, to find out what the data really say. We use the mean and standard error calculated in step 3:

$$z = \frac{(M - \mu_M)}{\sigma_M} = \frac{(232 - 247)}{6.356} = -2.36$$

Summary: $z = \frac{(232 - 247)}{6.356} = -2.36$

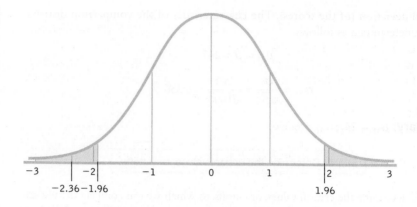

STEP 6: Make a decision.

Finally, we compare the test statistic to the critical values. We add the test statistic to the drawing of the curve that includes the critical *z* statistics (Figure 7-12). If the test statistic is in the critical region, we can reject the null hypothesis. In this example, the test statistic, −2.36, is in the critical region, so we reject the null hypothesis. An examination of the means tells us that the mean number of calories consumed by customers at those Starbucks with calories posted on the menu is lower than the mean number of calories consumed by customers at those Starbucks with no calories posted. So, even though we had nondirectional hypotheses, we can report the direction of the finding—that is, it appears that customers consume fewer calories, on average, at Starbucks that post calories on the menu than at Starbucks that do not post calories on the menu.

If the test statistic is not beyond the cutoffs, we fail to reject the null hypothesis. This means that we can only conclude that there is no evidence from this study to support the research hypothesis. There might be a real mean difference that is not extreme enough to be picked up by the hypothesis test. We just can't know.

Summary: We reject the null hypothesis. It appears that fewer calories are consumed, on average, by customers at Starbucks that post calories on the menus than by customers at Starbucks that do not post calories on the menu.

The researchers who conducted this study concluded that the posting of calories by restaurants does indeed seem to be beneficial. The 6% reduction may seem small, they admit, but they report that the reduction was larger—a 26% decrease in calories—among those consuming 250 or more calories per visit and among those making food purchases. Also, the researchers theorized that given data such as these, chains might respond by adding lower-calorie choices, leading to further reductions in average calories consumed. Research since then, though, suggests that the impact of the visible calorie counts has decreased over time or may not even exist (Cantor, Torres, Abrams, & Elbel, 2015; Long Tobias, Cradock, Batchelder, & Gortmaker, 2015). There is an intriguing caveat, though. If menus both include calorie counts and offer half-size options at half the price, people order healthier options (Haws & Liu, 2016). This effect goes away if the half-size options cost more than half-price. In those cases, most consumers will order the more economical full-sized version. And so research continues with ever-updated hypotheses. ●

Now that we've walked through the first hypothesis test of this text, we want to put hypothesis testing in context. Statistical analysis is just one step in the larger scientific process. In the scientific process, researchers first develop a hypothesis about the way the world works (e.g., menus that list calories lead to the consumption of fewer calories than menus that don't list calories). They then carefully design a study, after which they collect data (e.g., number of calories consumed). Researchers then run statistical hypothesis tests on the data (e.g., a z test). Finally, they use the results to update their original hypotheses (e.g., stores that are required to list calories have more low-calorie choices than stores that do not have this requirement).

After researchers complete these steps, they write a report that provides a precise description of the study, including their original hypotheses, what they did in the study, and what they found, including the actual statistics. (We'll talk more about reporting statistics in Chapter 18.) This report both communicates the researchers' findings to other scientists and to the public, and offers a template for those who want to do similar research. In the Data Ethics feature, we'll discuss some of the problems that can crop up in this system.

HARKing and *p*-Hacking   Data Ethics

xkcd (xkcd.com), a comic strip by physicist Randall Munroe, highlights the absurdity of science, including unethical research. In one strip, titled *Significant* (xkcd .com/882/), stick-figure scientists decide to investigate their hypothesis: "Jelly beans cause acne!" They fail to reject the null hypothesis, finding a $p > 0.05$. Maybe, they muse, it's only jelly beans of a certain color. So, they test 20 different colors, from magenta to turquoise to beige. Out of all 20 hypothesis tests, they have just one significant finding. For green jelly beans only, the *p* value associated with the test statistic is less than the alpha level of 0.05, and the researchers write their report using only this result. The cartoon punchline: A drawing of a newspaper headline blaring "GREEN JELLY BEANS LINKED TO ACNE!"

At the end of the last section, we outlined the steps of research, including the all-important step of writing a report. In a report, ethical researchers report their original hypotheses regardless of the results. That way, other scientists and the public know which hypothesis they set out to test and whether the data supported that hypothesis. If the stick-figure scientists had followed this practice, there would have been no dramatic headline.

For both good and bad reasons, actual scientific practice sometimes deviates from this norm. Academic journals—the primary place where scientists publish their reports—are more likely to publish "exciting" studies that reject the null hypothesis than "boring" studies that fail to reject the null hypothesis (Andrews & Kasy, 2017). Academic journals are particularly likely to publish studies when results confirm the specific hypotheses that researchers claim they set out to test. So, it can be tempting to change the hypotheses *after* seeing the results, a practice called HARKing (Hypothesizing After the Results are Known) that we introduced in the Chapter 1 Data Ethics feature (Kerr, 1998). HARKing is dangerous because it makes it seem as if

An Unscientific Headline Did these fictional researchers start out with the hypothesis that black cats reduce symptoms of depression, or were they engaging in HARKing? And how many hypothesis tests did they run? Did they also test the effects of calico cats, tabbies, and gingers and fail to find a decrease in depression? Then fancy cats like Siamese, Persian, and Norwegian Forest cats, and again fail? Ethical researchers report their original hypothesis and all of the statistical tests they conduct along the way.

● ***p*-Hacking** is the use of questionable research practices to increase the chances of achieving a statistically significant result.

the researcher predicted these particular results. HARKing also blurs the distinction between research meant to confirm a particular hypothesis (e.g., jelly beans cause acne) and research simply meant to explore data (e.g., do jelly beans of a specific color cause acne?). In the comic, the stick-figure scientists did not originally anticipate a specific green-jelly-bean result. In hindsight, though, they might devise a reason for this finding, perhaps the presence of a particular ingredient in the green jelly beans, and claim this as their original hypothesis. That would be HARKing.

There is debate on the extent to which different forms of HARKing are harmful (Kerr, 1998; Rubin, 2017). Clearly, updating one's original hypothesis in light of new data is part of science, and surprising results can be fruitful for suggesting future research. So, there are two main recommendations for reporting results: (1) Distinguish clearly between the original hypotheses and those developed after seeing the results, and (2) report all variables, experimental conditions, and analyses (Hollenbeck & Wright, 2017; Simmons, Nelson, & Simonsohn, 2011). This ethical practice allows researchers to explore data without misleading others about the strength of a surprising finding.

Another unethical research tactic related to HARKing is *p*-hacking, a term that combines the symbol *p* (which refers to the standard alpha level, or *p* level, of 0.05) with the term "hacking" (which is borrowed from the computer world and refers to underhanded methods). More specifically, ***p-hacking** is the use of questionable research practices to increase the chances of achieving a statistically significant result.* There are several ways to *p*-hack (Head, Holman, Lanfear, Kahn, & Jennions, 2015). Researchers might, for example, create criteria for removing certain scores—outliers, for example—*after* initial analyses have been performed, rather than before. They may analyze the data repeatedly throughout the data collection process—after collecting data from 30 participants, then 60, and so on—and stop data collection once they reject the null hypothesis. In addition, researchers may collect multiple dependent variables—assessing not only acne, but also indigestion, anxiety, and body image—but report only those dependent variables that reach statistical significance. Or, as our stick-figure scientists did, they may use multiple independent variables—different colors of jelly beans—but report only the one that reached statistical significance. (You can try *p*-hacking a simulated study yourself at the statistically focused Web site, FiveThirtyEight: fivethirtyeight.com/features/science-isnt-broken/#part1.) The problems of *p*-hacking and HARKing partly explain the push to preregister studies, discussed in the Chapter 1 Data Ethics feature, as behavioral scientists recognize the need for increased transparency in reporting of research. Maybe some of them were shamed by a comic strip.

CHECK YOUR LEARNING

Reviewing the Concepts	**>**	We conduct a z test when we have one sample and we know both the mean and the standard deviation of the population.
	>	We must decide whether to use a *one-tailed test*, in which the hypothesis is directional, or a *two-tailed test*, in which the hypothesis is nondirectional.
	>	One-tailed tests are rare in the research literature.
	>	Unethical researchers sometimes use HARKing, hypothesizing after the results are known, and p-hacking, playing with their data until they find statistically significant results, when analyzing their data.

Clarifying the Concepts	**7-11**	What does it mean to say a test is directional or nondirectional?

Calculating the Statistics	**7-12**	Calculate the characteristics (μ_M and σ_M) of a comparison distribution for a sample mean based on 53 participants when the population has a mean of 1090 and a standard deviation of 87.
	7-13	Calculate the z statistic for a sample mean of 1094 based on the sample of 53 people when $\mu = 1090$ and $\sigma = 87$.

Applying the Concepts	**7-14**	According to the Web site for the Coffee Research Institute (www.coffeeresearch .org/market/usa.htm), the average coffee drinker in the United States consumes 3.1 cups of coffee daily. Let's assume the population standard deviation is 0.9 cup. Jillian decides to study coffee consumption at her local coffee shop. She wants to know if people sitting and working in a coffee shop drink a different amount of coffee from what might be expected in the general U.S. population. Throughout the course of 2 weeks, she collects data on 34 people who spend most of the day at the coffee shop. The average number of cups consumed by this sample is 3.17 cups. Use the six steps of hypothesis testing to determine whether Jillian's sample is statistically significantly different from the population mean.

Solutions to these Check Your Learning questions can be found in Appendix D.

REVIEW OF CONCEPTS

The z Table

The z table has several uses when data are distributed normally. If we know an individual raw score, we can convert it to a z statistic and then determine percentages above, below, or at least as extreme as this score. Alternatively, if we know a percentage, we can look up a z statistic on the table and then convert it to a raw score. The table can be used in the same way with means instead of scores.

The Assumptions and Steps of Hypothesis Testing

Assumptions are the criteria that are met, ideally, before a hypothesis test is conducted. *Parametric tests* are those that require assumptions about the population, whereas *nonparametric tests* are those that do not. Three basic assumptions apply

LaunchPad
macmillan learning
Visit LaunchPad to access
the e-book and to test your
knowledge with LearningCurve.

to many parametric hypothesis tests—the dependent variable should be on a scale measure, the data should be from a randomly selected sample, and the population distribution should be normal (or there should be at least 30 scores in the sample). A *robust* hypothesis test is one that produces valid results even when all assumptions are not met.

There are six steps that apply to every hypothesis test. First, determine the populations, comparison distribution, and assumptions. This step helps us to choose the appropriate hypothesis test from the diagram in Chapter 18, Figure 18-1. Second, state the null and research hypotheses. Third, determine the characteristics of the comparison distribution to be used to calculate the test statistic. Fourth, determine the *critical values*, or *cutoffs*, usually based on an *alpha level*, or *p level*, of 0.05, that demarcate the most extreme 5% of the comparison distribution, the *critical region*. Fifth, calculate the test statistic. Sixth, use that test statistic to decide to reject or fail to reject the null hypothesis. We deem a finding *statistically significant* when we reject the null hypothesis. If we use software to calculate the test statistic, then we can also determine the p *value*, the probability of finding this particular test statistic, or one even larger, if the null hypothesis is true.

An Example of the z Test

z tests are conducted in the rare cases in which we have one sample and we know the mean and the standard deviation of the population. We must decide whether to use a *one-tailed test*, in which the hypotheses are directional, or a *two-tailed test*, in which the hypotheses are nondirectional.

Unethical researchers may play with their data after they analyze it based on their original hypotheses. Sometimes, they HARK (hypothesize after the results are known), pretending their original hypotheses matched their eventual findings. They may also engage in p-*hacking*, trying different hypotheses until one yields a statistically significant finding. More transparent reporting of research can prevent researchers from using these tactics.

SPSS

SPSS can be used to transform raw data from different scales into standardized data on one scale based on the *z* distribution. This allows us to look at standardized scores instead of raw scores. We can try this using the volcano data (numbers of volcanoes per country) from Chapter 2. To standardize the variable "seconds," select: Analyze → Descriptive Statistics → Descriptives. Select the relevant variable (i.e., "Volcanoes") by clicking it on the left side, then clicking the arrow to move it to the right. Check the "Save standardized values as variables" box and click "OK." Part of the new column of standardized variables under the heading "ZVolcanoes" is in the accompanying screenshot.

We can now see which countries fall below or above the sample mean by looking at the *z* score. For example, Chile, highlighted in yellow in the screenshot, has a *z* score of 0.155, indicating that it falls above the mean. The following country, China, has a *z* score of −0.464, indicating that it falls below the mean. Now that the number of volcanoes in each country has been standardized, we can use the *z* table to find percentages above or below a certain *z* score.

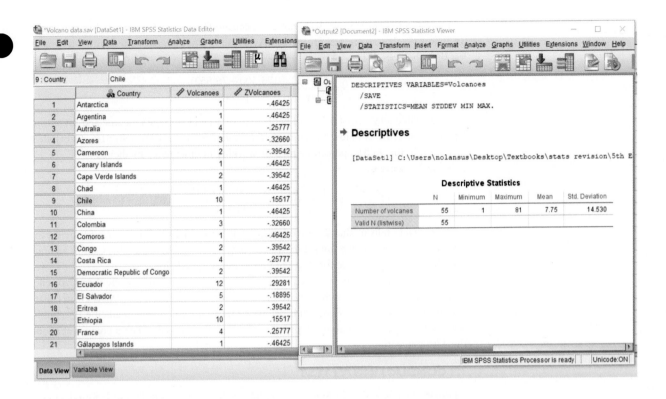

HOW IT WORKS

7.1 TRANSITIONING FROM RAW SCORES TO *z* SCORES AND PERCENTILES

Physician assistants (PAs) are increasingly central to the health care system in many countries. Students who graduated from U.S. PA programs reported their income (American Academy of Physician Assistants, 2005). The incomes of those working in emergency medicine had a mean of $76,553, a standard deviation of $14,001, and a median of $74,044. The incomes of those working in family/general medicine had a mean of $63,521, a standard deviation of $11,554, and a median of $62,935. How can we compare the income of Gabrielle, who earns $75,500 a year in emergency medicine, with that of Colin, who earns $64,300 a year in family/general medicine?

The *z* distribution should be used with individual scores only if the distribution is approximately normal, as seems to be the case here. For both distributions of incomes, the medians are relatively close to the means of their own distributions, suggesting that the distributions are not skewed. Additionally, the standard deviations are not large compared to the size of the respective means, which suggests that outliers are not inflating the standard deviation, which would also indicate skew.

From the information we have, we can calculate Gabrielle's z score and her percentile on income—that is, the percentage of PAs working in emergency medicine who make less than she does. Her z score is:

$$z = \frac{(X - \mu)}{\sigma} = \frac{(75,500 - 76,553)}{14,001} = -0.08$$

The z table tells us that 3.19% of people fall between Gabrielle's income and the mean. Because her score is below the mean, we calculate 50% − 3.19% = 46.81%. Gabrielle's income is in the 46.81st percentile for PAs working in emergency medicine.

Colin's z score is:

$$z = \frac{(X - \mu)}{\sigma} = \frac{(64,300 - 63,521)}{11,554} = 0.07$$

The z table tells us that 2.79% of people fall between Colin's income and the mean. Because his score is above the mean, we calculate 50% + 2.79% = 52.79%. Colin's income is in the 52.79th percentile for PAs working in general medicine.

Relative to those in their chosen fields, Colin is doing better financially than Gabrielle. Colin's z score of 0.07, which is above the mean for general medicine PAs, is greater than Gabrielle's z score of 20.08, which is below the mean for emergency medicine PAs. Similarly, Colin's income is at about the 53rd percentile, whereas Gabrielle's income is at about the 47th percentile.

7.2 CONDUCTING A z TEST

Summary data from the Consideration of Future Consequences (CFC) scale found a mean CFC score of 3.20 with a standard deviation of 0.70 for a large sample (Adams, 2012). (For the sake of this example, let's assume that this sample comprises the entire population of interest.) You wonder whether students who joined a career discussion group might have different CFC scores compared with those of the population. Forty-five students in your psychology department attended these discussion groups and then completed the CFC scale. The mean for this group is 3.45. From this information, how can we conduct all six steps of a two-tailed z test with an alpha level of 0.05?

Step 1: Population 1: All students who participated in career discussion groups. Population 2: All students who did not participate in career discussion groups.

The comparison distribution will be a distribution of means. The hypothesis test will be a z test because we have only one sample and we know the population mean and standard deviation. This study meets two of the three assumptions but does not seem to meet the third. The dependent variable is on a scale measure. In addition, there are more than 30 participants in the sample, indicating that the comparison distribution will be normal. The data were not randomly selected, however, so we must be cautious when generalizing.

Step 2: Null hypothesis: Students who participated in career discussion groups had the same mean CFC scores as students who did not participate: H_0: $\mu_1 = \mu_2$. Research hypothesis: Students who participated in career discussion groups had mean CFC scores that differed from those of students who did not participate: H_1: $\mu_1 \neq \mu_2$.

Step 3: $\mu_M = \mu = 3.20$; $\sigma_M = \frac{\sigma}{\sqrt{N}} = \frac{0.70}{\sqrt{45}} = 0.104$

Step 4: The critical z statistics are -1.96 and 1.96.

Step 5: $z = \dfrac{(M - \mu_M)}{\sigma_M} = \dfrac{(3.45 - 3.20)}{0.104} = 2.40$

Step 6: Reject the null hypothesis. It appears that students who participate in career discussions have higher mean CFC scores than do students who do not participate.

EXERCISES

The solutions to the odd-numbered exercises can be found in Appendix C.

Clarifying the Concepts

7.1 What is a percentile?

7.2 When we look up a z score on the z table, what information can we report?

7.3 How do we calculate the percentage of scores below a particular positive z score?

7.4 How is calculating a percentile for a mean from a distribution of means different from doing so for a score from a distribution of scores?

7.5 In statistics, what do we mean by *assumptions*?

7.6 What sample size is recommended to meet the assumption of a normal distribution of means, even when the underlying population of scores is not normal?

7.7 What is the difference between parametric tests and nonparametric tests?

7.8 What are the six steps of hypothesis testing?

7.9 What are critical values and the critical region?

7.10 What is the standard size of the critical region used by most statisticians?

7.11 What does *statistically significant* mean to statisticians?

7.12 What do these symbolic expressions mean: $H_0: \mu_1 = \mu_2$ and $H_1: \mu_1 \neq \mu_2$?

7.13 Using everyday language rather than statistical language, explain why the words *critical region* might have been chosen to define the area in which a z statistic must fall for a researcher to reject the null hypothesis.

7.14 Using everyday language rather than statistical language, explain why the word *cutoff* might have been chosen to define the point beyond which we reject the null hypothesis.

7.15 What is the difference between a one-tailed hypothesis test and a two-tailed hypothesis test in terms of critical regions?

7.16 Why do researchers typically use a two-tailed test rather than a one-tailed test?

7.17 Write the symbols for the null hypothesis and research hypothesis for a one-tailed test.

7.18 What is HARKing and why can it be harmful?

7.19 What is p-hacking and what are some examples of research behaviors that would constitute p-hacking?

Calculating the Statistics

7.20 Calculate the following percentages for a z score of -1.61, with a tail of 5.37%:

a. What percentage of scores falls above this z score?

b. What percentage of scores falls between the mean and this z score?

c. What proportion of scores falls above a z score of 1.61?

7.21 Calculate the following percentages for a z score of 0.74, with a tail of 22.96%:

a. What percentage of scores falls below this z score?

b. What percentage of scores falls between the mean and this z score?

c. What proportion of scores falls below a z score of -0.74?

7.22 Using the z table in Appendix B, calculate the following percentages for a z score of -0.08:

a. Above this z score

b. Below this z score

c. At least as extreme as this z score

7.23 Using the z table in Appendix B, calculate the following percentages for a z score of 1.71:

a. Above this z score

b. Below this z score

c. At least as extreme as this z score

7.24 Rewrite each of the following percentages as probabilities, or alpha levels:

a. 5%

b. 83%

c. 51%

7.25 Rewrite each of the following probabilities, or alpha levels, as percentages:

a. 0.19

b. 0.04

c. 0.92

7.26 If the critical values for a hypothesis test occur where 2.5% of the distribution is in each tail, what are the cutoffs for z?

7.27 For each of the following alpha levels, what percentage of the data will be in each critical region for a two-tailed test?

a. 0.05

b. 0.10

c. 0.01

7.28 State the percentage of scores in a one-tailed critical region for each of the following alpha levels:

a. 0.05

b. 0.10

c. 0.01

7.29 You are conducting a z test on a sample of 50 people with an average verbal score on the SAT, a university admissions test used in the U.S. and several other countries, of 542 (assume we know the population mean to be 500 and the standard deviation to be 100). Calculate the mean and the spread of the comparison distribution (μ_M and σ_M).

7.30 You are conducting a z test on a sample of 132 people for whom you observed a mean verbal score on the SAT, a university admissions test used in the U.S. and several other countries, of 490. The population mean is 500, and the standard deviation is 100. Calculate the mean and the spread of the comparison distribution (μ_M and σ_M).

7.31 If the cutoffs for a z test are −1.96 and 1.96, determine whether you would reject or fail to reject the null hypothesis in each of the following cases:

a. $z = 1.06$

b. $z = -2.06$

c. A z score beyond which 7% of the data fall in each tail

7.32 If the cutoffs for a z test are −2.58 and 2.58, determine whether you would reject or fail to reject the null hypothesis in each of the following cases:

a. $z = -0.94$

b. $z = 2.12$

c. A z score for which 49.6% of the data fall between z and the mean

7.33 Use the cutoffs of −1.65 and 1.65 and an alpha level of approximately 0.10, or 10%. For each of the following

values, determine whether you would reject or fail to reject the null hypothesis:

a. $z = 0.95$

b. $z = -1.77$

c. A z statistic that 2% of the scores fall above

7.34 You are conducting a z test on a sample for which you observe a mean weight of 150 pounds. The population mean is 160, and the standard deviation is 100.

a. Calculate a z statistic for a sample of 30 people.

b. Repeat part (a) for a sample of 300 people.

c. Repeat part (a) for a sample of 3000 people.

Applying the Concepts

7.35 **Percentiles and unemployment rates:** The U.S. Bureau of Labor Statistics' annual report published in 2011 provided adjusted unemployment rates for 10 countries. The mean was 7%, and the standard deviation was 1.85. For the following calculations, treat 7% as the population mean and 1.85 as the population standard deviation.

a. Australia's unemployment rate was 5.4. Calculate the percentile for Australia—that is, what percentage is less than that of Australia?

b. The United Kingdom's unemployment rate was 8.5. Calculate its percentile—that is, what percentage is less than that of the United Kingdom?

c. The unemployment rate in the United States was 8.9. Calculate its percentile—that is, what percentage is less than that of the United States?

d. The unemployment rate in Canada was 6.5. Calculate its percentile—that is, what percentage is less than that of Canada?

7.36 **Height and the z distribution, question 1:** Elena, a 15-year-old girl, is 58 inches (147.32 centimeters) tall. The Centers for Disease Control and Prevention (CDC) indicates that the average height for girls at this age is 63.80 inches, with a standard deviation of 2.66 inches.

a. Calculate Elena's z score.

b. What percentage of girls are taller than Elena?

c. What percentage of girls are shorter?

d. How much would Elena have to grow to be perfectly average?

e. If Sarah is in the 75th percentile for height at age 15, how tall is she?

f. How much would Elena have to grow to be at the 75th percentile with Sarah?

7.37 **Height and the z distribution, question 2:** Kona, a 15-year-old boy, is 72 inches (182.88 centimeters) tall.

According to the CDC, the average height for boys at this age is 67.00 inches, with a standard deviation of 3.19 inches.

a. Calculate Kona's *z* score.

b. What is Kona's percentile score for height?

c. What percentage of boys this age are shorter than Kona?

d. What percentage of heights are at least as extreme as Kona's, in either direction?

e. If Ian is in the 30th percentile for height as a 15-year-old boy, how tall is he? How does he compare to Kona?

7.38 Heights of girls and the *z* statistic: Imagine a class of thirty-three 15-year-old girls with an average height of 62.60 inches (159.00 centimeters). Remember, $\mu = 63.80$ inches and $\sigma = 2.66$ inches.

a. Calculate the *z* statistic.

b. How does this sample of girls compare to the distribution of sample means?

c. What is the percentile rank for this sample?

7.39 Heights of boys and the *z* statistic: Imagine a basketball team that comprises thirteen 15-year-old boys. The average height of the team is 69.50 inches (176.63 centimeters). Remember, $\mu = 67.00$ inches and $\sigma = 3.19$ inches.

a. Calculate the *z* statistic.

b. How does this sample of boys compare to the distribution of sample means?

c. What is the percentile rank for this sample?

7.40 The *z* distribution and statistics test scores: Imagine that your statistics professor lost all records of students' raw scores on a recent test. However, she did record students' *z* scores for the test, as well as the class average of 41 out of 50 points and the standard deviation of 3 points (treat these as population parameters). She informs you that your *z* score was 1.10.

a. What was your percentile score on this test?

b. Using what you know about *z* scores and percentiles, how did you do on this test?

c. What was your original test score?

7.41 The *z* statistic, distributions of means, and heights of girls: Using what we know about the height of 15-year-old girls (again, $\mu = 63.80$ inches (162.05 centimeters) and $\sigma = 2.66$ inches), imagine that a teacher finds the average height of 14 female students in one of her classes to be 62.40 inches.

a. Calculate the mean and the standard error of the distribution of mean heights.

b. Calculate the *z* statistic for this group.

c. What percentage of mean heights, based on a sample size of 14 students, would we expect to be shorter than this group?

d. How often do mean heights equal to or more extreme than this size occur in this population?

e. If statisticians define sample means that occur less than 5% of the time as "special" or rare, what would you say about this result?

7.42 The *z* statistic, distributions of means, and heights of boys: Another teacher decides to average the heights of all 15-year-old male students in his classes throughout the day. By the end of the day, he has measured the heights of 57 boys and calculated an average of 68.1 inches (172.97 centimeters; remember, for this population $\mu = 67$ inches and $\sigma = 3.19$ inches).

a. Calculate the mean and the standard error of the distribution of mean heights.

b. Calculate the *z* statistic for this group.

c. What percentage of groups of boys would we expect to have mean heights taller than this group, based on samples of this size (57)?

d. How often do mean heights equal to or more extreme than 68.1 inches occur in this population?

e. How does this result compare to the statistical significance cutoff of 5%?

7.43 Directional versus nondirectional hypotheses: For each of the following examples, identify whether the research has expressed a directional or a nondirectional hypothesis:

a. Musician David Teie worked with animal researchers to develop music specifically for cats—music that a typical cat might find relaxing (Stanford, 2015). Imagine that you decided to study whether cat-specific music led to decreased heart rate in feline listeners.

b. The National Sleep Foundation (2015) encourages U.S. high schools to start later in the morning to improve teenagers' sleep and school performance. Imagine you decide to conduct a study to see if teens who get to sleep an hour later have different grades than those who don't.

c. Smartphones are everywhere, and we are now available almost all of the time. Does this translate into a change in the closeness of our long-distance relationships?

7.44 Null hypotheses and research hypotheses: For each of the following examples, state the null hypothesis and the research hypothesis, in both words and symbolic notation:

a. Musician David Teie worked with animal researchers to develop music specifically for cats—music that a typical cat might find relaxing (Stanford, 2015). Imagine that you decided to study whether cat-specific music led to decreased heart rate in feline listeners. Use a one-tailed hypothesis.

b. The National Sleep Foundation (2015) encourages U.S. high schools to start later in the morning to improve teenagers' sleep and school performance. Imagine you decide to conduct a study to see if teens who get to sleep an hour later have different grades than those who don't.

c. Smartphones are everywhere, and we are now available to our friends and families almost all of the time. Does this translate into a change in the closeness of our long-distance relationships?

7.45 The *z* distribution and Hurricane Katrina: Hurricane Katrina hit New Orleans on August 29, 2005. The National Weather Service Forecast Office maintains online archives of climate data for all U.S. cities and areas. These archives allow us to find out, for example, how the rainfall in New Orleans that August compared to that in the other months of 2005. The table below shows the National Weather Service data (rainfall in inches) for New Orleans in 2005.

January	4.41
February	8.24
March	4.69
April	3.31
May	4.07
June	2.52
July	10.65
August	3.77
September	4.07
October	0.04
November	0.75
December	3.32

a. Calculate the *z* score for August, the month in which Hurricane Katrina hit. (*Note:* These are raw data for the population, rather than summaries, so you have to calculate the mean and the standard deviation first.)

b. What is the percentile for the rainfall in August? Does this surprise you? Explain.

c. When results surprise us, it is worthwhile to examine individual data points more closely or even to go beyond the data. The daily climate data as listed by this source for August 2005 shows the code "M" next to August 29, 30, and 31 for all climate statistics. The code says: "[REMARKS] ALL DATA MISSING AUGUST 29, 30, AND 31 DUE TO HURRICANE KATRINA." Pretend you were hired as a consultant to determine the percentile for that August. Write a brief paragraph for your report, explaining why the data you generated are likely to be inaccurate.

d. What raw scores mark the cutoff for the top and bottom 10% for these data? Based on these scores, which months had extreme data for 2005? Why should we not trust these data?

7.46 Steps 1 and 2 of hypothesis testing for a study of the Wechsler Adult Intelligence Scale–Revised: Boone (1992) examined scores on the Wechsler Adult Intelligence Scale-Revised (WAIS-R) for 150 adult psychiatric inpatients. He determined the "intrasubtest scatter" score for each inpatient. Intrasubtest scatter refers to patterns of responses in which respondents are almost as likely to get easy questions wrong as hard ones. In the WAIS-R, we expect more wrong answers near the end, as the questions become more difficult, so high levels of intrasubtest scatter would be an unusual pattern of responses. Boone wondered if psychiatric patients have different response patterns than nonpatients have. He compared the intrasubtest scatter for 150 patients to population data from the WAIS-R standardization group. Assume that he had access both to means and standard deviations for this population. Boone reported that "the standardization group's intrasubtest scatter was significantly greater than those reported for the psychiatric inpatients" and concluded that such scatter is normal.

a. What are the two populations?

b. What would the comparison distribution be? Explain.

c. What hypothesis test would you use? Explain.

d. Check the assumptions for this hypothesis test. Label your answers (1) through (3).

e. What does Boone mean when he says *significantly*?

f. State the null and research hypotheses for a two-tailed test in both words and symbols.

g. Imagine that you wanted to replicate this study. Based on the findings described here, state the null and research hypotheses for a one-tailed test in both words and symbols.

7.47 Passwords, redheads, and a *z* test: The BBC reported that red-haired women were more likely than others to choose strong passwords (Ward, 2013). How might a researcher study this? Computer scientist Cynthia Kuo and her colleagues (2006) conducted a study in which they gave passwords a score, with higher scores going to passwords that are not in "password crack dictionaries" that are used by hackers, that are longer, and that use a mix of letters, numbers, and symbols. They found a mean score of 15.7 with a standard deviation of 7.3. For the purposes of this exercise, treat these numbers as the population parameters. Based on your knowledge of the *z* test, explain how you might design a study to test the hypothesis that red-haired women create stronger passwords than others.

7.48 HARKing and medical research: Imagine that an international team of medical researchers hypothesized that a new drug might cure a life-threatening disease. They test their hypothesis by recruiting 50 participants; half receive the drug, while the other half serve as a control group. At the end of the multi-year study, the researchers fail to reject the null hypothesis, meaning they did not find evidence that the group receiving the drug fared any better than the control group. The researchers, however, are puzzled. Several of the researchers noticed that their older patients improved, whereas their younger patients did not. In hindsight, they can now devise a clear physiological difference between younger and older patients that would explain why the drug works for one group but not the other. When they reanalyze their data based on age, they find that older patients receiving the drug did, indeed, get better, whereas younger patients did not. The researchers write their report, presenting the hypothesis that they would see an age difference as if it were their hypothesis when the study began. Explain how this is an example of HARKing and why it might be dangerous in this particular case.

7.49 Same data set, different answers, and *p*-hacking: Brian Nosek and other researchers at the Center for Open Science gave the exact same set of data on football players (soccer players in the United States and Canada) to 29 different teams of researchers (Silberzahn et al., 2018). The researchers were all asked whether referees are more likely to give red cards—the harshest penalty for a rule violation—to dark-skinned players. The data set included many variables related to the players, including height, weight, number of games played, position, country of the league, and an ordinal measure of skin color. Of the 29 research teams, 25 came to the conclusion that dark-skinned players were statistically significantly more likely to receive red cards than lighter-skinned players. However, their assessment results varied widely, from "slightly more likely" to "three times as likely." Four of the research teams concluded that dark-skinned players were not statistically significantly more likely to receive red cards. Use the concept of *p*-hacking to describe potential reasons that different teams of researchers may have reached different conclusions using this exact same football data set.

7.50 Power posing, *p*-hacking, and mixed results: In 2010, a group of researchers published the finding that power posing—adopting a wide stance with one's hands on one's hips—improved self-reported feelings of power and increased testosterone levels in a sample of 42 participants (Carney, Cuddy, & Yap, 2010). Subsequent attempts to replicate the original study have yielded mixed results (Simmons & Simonsohn, 2017). Although some studies found the same effect, others found no effects of power posing, including one study that tested 200 participants (Ranehill et al., 2015). Sometimes there are good reasons that studies are not able to replicate previously published results, but sometimes this failure occurs because the original researchers engaged in unethical research practices. Use the concept of *p*-hacking to describe some potential reasons that there may be mixed results for the effects of power posing.

Putting It All Together

7.51 Patient adherence and orthodontics: A research report (Behenam & Pooya, 2006) begins, "There is probably no other area of health care that requires . . . cooperation to the extent that orthodontics does," and explores factors that affected the number of hours per day that Iranian patients wore their orthodontic appliances. The patients in the study reported that they used their appliances, on average, 14.78 hours per day, with a standard deviation of 5.31. We'll treat this group as the population for the purposes of this exercise. Let's say a researcher wanted to study whether a video with information about orthodontics led to an increase in the amount of time patients wore their appliances, but decided to use a two-tailed test to be conservative. Let's say he studied the next 15 patients at his clinic, asked them to watch the video, and then found that they wore their appliances, on average, 17 hours per day.

a. What is the independent variable? What is the dependent variable?

b. Did the researcher use random selection to choose his sample? Explain your answer.

c. Conduct all six steps of hypothesis testing. Be sure to label all six steps.

d. If the researcher's decision in step 6 were wrong, what type of error would he have made? Explain your answer.

e. If the researcher analyzed his data after every 10 patients and stopped once he had a statistically significantly result, which unethical practice would he have used? Why is this a potentially harmful practice?

7.52 The Graded Naming Test and sociocultural differences: Researchers often use *z* tests to compare their samples to known population norms. The Graded Naming Test (GNT) asks respondents to name objects in a set of 30 black-and-white drawings. The test, often used to detect brain damage, starts with easy words like *kangaroo* and gets progressively more difficult, ending with words like *sextant*. The GNT population norm for adults in England is 20.4. Roberts (2003) wondered whether a sample of Canadian adults had different scores than adults in England. If they were different, the English norms would not be valid for use in Canada. The mean for 30 Canadian adults was 17.5. For the purposes of this exercise, assume that the standard deviation of the adults in England is 3.2.

a. Conduct all six steps of a *z* test. Be sure to label all six steps.

b. Some words on the GNT are more commonly used in England. For example, a *mitre*, the headpiece worn by bishops, is worn by the archbishop of Canterbury in public ceremonies in England. No Canadian participant correctly responded to this item, whereas 55% of English adults correctly responded. Explain why we should be cautious about applying norms to people different from those on whom the test was normed.

c. When we conduct a one-tailed test instead of a two-tailed test, there are small changes in steps 2 and 4 of hypothesis testing. (*Note:* For this example, assume that those from populations other than the one on which it was normed will score lower, on average. That is, hypothesize that the Canadians will have a lower mean.) Conduct steps 2, 4, and 6 of hypothesis testing for a one-tailed test.

d. Under which circumstance—a one-tailed or a two-tailed test—is it easier to reject the null hypothesis? Explain.

e. If it becomes easier to reject the null hypothesis under one type of test (one-tailed versus two-tailed), does this mean that there is a bigger difference between the groups with a one-tailed test than with a two-tailed test? Explain.

f. When we change the alpha level that we use as a cutoff, there is a small change in step 4 of hypothesis testing. Although 0.05 is the most commonly used alpha level, other values, such as 0.01, are often used. For this example, conduct steps 4 and 6 of hypothesis testing for a two-tailed test and alpha level of 0.01, determining the cutoff and drawing the curve.

g. With which alpha level—0.05 or 0.01—is it easiest to reject the null hypothesis? Explain.

h. If it is easier to reject the null hypothesis with certain alpha levels, does this mean that there is a bigger difference between the samples with one alpha level versus the other alpha level? Explain.

7.53 Radiation levels on Japanese farms: Fackler (2012) reported in *The New York Times* that Japanese farmers have become skeptical of the Japanese government's assurances that radiation levels were within legal limits in the wake of the 2011 tsunami and radiation disaster at Fukushima. After reports of safe levels in Onami, more than 12 concerned farmers tested their crops and found dangerously high levels of cesium.

a. If the farmers wanted to conduct a *z* test comparing their results to the cesium levels found in areas that had not been exposed to the radiation, what would their sample be? Be specific.

b. Conduct step 1 of hypothesis testing.

c. Conduct step 2 of hypothesis testing.

d. Conduct step 4 of hypothesis testing for a two-tailed test and an alpha level of 0.05.

e. Imagine that the farmers calculated a *z* statistic of 3.2 for their sample. Conduct step 6 of hypothesis testing.

f. If the farmers' conclusions were incorrect, what type of error would they have made? Explain your answer.

g. Let's say that the farmers had originally predicted dangerously high levels of another type of radiation than cesium. Imagine that, when they found high levels of cesium, they reported this result as if it were what they originally predicted. Which unethical data practice would they have used? Why is this a potentially harmful practice?

 **LaunchPad**
macmillan learning

Visit LaunchPad to access the e-book and to test your knowledge with LearningCurve.

TERMS

assumption (p. 197)	critical value (p. 199)	statistically significant (p. 200)
parametric test (p. 198)	critical region (p. 199)	one-tailed test (p. 203)
nonparametric test (p. 198)	alpha level (p. 199)	two-tailed test (p. 204)
robust (p. 198)	*p* value (p. 199)	*p*-hacking (p. 208)

SYMBOLS

p	(p. 199)	H_0	(p. 203)	H_1	(p. 203)

Confidence Intervals, Effect Size, and Statistical Power

BEFORE YOU GO ON

- You should know how to conduct a *z* test (Chapter 7).

- You should understand the concept of statistical significance (Chapter 7).

STR/AFP/Getty Images

"Math Class Is Tough"   Teen Talk Barbie, with her negative proclamation about math class, was a lightning rod for discussions about gender stereotypes. Some of Barbie's negative press related to the fact that Barbie's message might doom girls to even poorer performance in mathematics. The media tend to play up gender differences instead of the less interesting (and more frequent) realities of gender similarities.

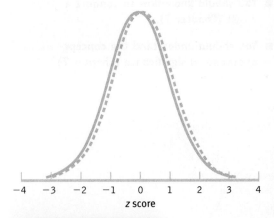

z score

FIGURE 8-1

A Gender Difference in Mathematics Performance

This graph represents the overlap in mathematical performance that would be expected if distributions for males and females differed, on average, by the amount that Hyde and colleagues (1990) reported in their meta-analysis. The solid line represents the distribution for females, and the dotted line represents the distribution for males.

"Want to go shopping? OK, meet me at the mall."

"Math class is tough."

With these and 268 other phrases, Teen Talk Barbie was introduced to the market in July, 1992. By September, it was being publicly criticized for its negative message about girls and math. At first the Mattel toy company refused to pull it from store shelves, citing more positive phrases in Barbie's repertoire, such as "I'm studying to be a doctor." But the bad press escalated, and by October Mattel had backed down. The controversy endured, however, and even showed up in a 1994 *Simpsons* episode when Lisa Simpson boycotted the fictional Malibu Stacy doll that had been programmed to say, "Thinking too much gives you wrinkles."

The controversy over gender differences in mathematical reasoning ability began after a study on the topic was published in the prestigious journal *Science*. Participants included about 10,000 male and female students in grades 7 through 10 who were already among the top 2% to 3% on standardized tests of mathematics (Benbow & Stanley, 1980). In this pre-selected sample, the boys' average score on the mathematics portion of the SAT test was 32 points higher than the girls' average score, a statistically significant difference that gained vast media attention (Jacob & Eccles, 1982). But the danger of reporting such a mean difference is the implication that all or most of the members of one group are different from all or most of the members of the other group. As we see from the overlapping distributions in Figure 8-1, such an assertion is far from the truth.

Language Alert! Part of this misunderstanding is caused by the language of statistics: "Statistically significant" does *not* mean "very important." The misunderstanding about Benbow and Stanley's study (1980) spread from researchers to the media to the general public. The issue gained even more attention when the release of Teen Talk Barbie inspired members of a guerrilla art group. The Barbie Liberation Organization switched the computer chips in talking Barbies and GI Joes and returned them to store shelves. Suddenly, GI Joe was chirping, in a voice uncannily like Barbie's, "Let's plan a great big wedding," as well as complaining that "Math class is tough."

It took a meta-analysis—a study of all the studies about a particular topic—to clarify the story these data were telling. Janet Hyde and colleagues conducted the meta-analysis by compiling the results from 259 mean differences in mathematical reasoning ability (Hyde, Fennema, & Lamon, 1990). These data represented 1,968,846 male participants and 2,016,836 female participants. Here's what the researchers discovered:

- The two distributions (one for males; another for females) overlapped almost completely (see Figure 8-1). The dotted-line curve represents male mathematical reasoning ability, and the solid-line curve represents female math reasoning ability.
- Mean gender differences in overall mathematical reasoning ability were small.

- The difference was smaller and *reversed* (favoring women and girls rather than men and boys) when the extreme tails of the distribution were eliminated (such as scores from participants in remedial or gifted programs).

Are you surprised that a small (but statistically significant) gender difference is almost completely overlapping? This is a case in which hypothesis testing alone inadvertently encouraged a profound misunderstanding (Jacob & Eccles, 1986). Stories like this one have led to an increasing emphasis on what Geoff Cumming (2012) calls "the new statistics." In this chapter, we'll talk about the push to use newer statistics, and we'll talk about three ways that statisticians do so. First, we compute confidence intervals, which provide a range of plausible mean differences. Second, we calculate effect sizes, which indicate the size of differences. Finally, we estimate the statistical power of the study to be sure that we have a sufficient sample size to detect a real difference. If we discover that we don't have enough statistical power, then we need to increase statistical power so that we can believe the results of our own study.

The New Statistics

In 2012, Geoff Cumming published *Understanding the New Statistics,* a book that shifted an academic discussion about how statistics is changing into the mainstream. Many researchers have criticized hypothesis testing and the black-and-white thinking it leads to (Gelman, 2018; Nuzzo, 2014). Indeed, the American Statistical Association recently released a statement that carefully defined p values in relation to traditional hypothesis testing, and offered guidelines for reducing their misuse (Wasserstein, 2016; Wasserstein & Lazar, 2016). What is the problem? In hypothesis testing, a finding is either significant or not significant, which actually tells us very little, as you'll learn in this chapter. Hypothesis testing can also lead researchers to "play" with their data until it edges under the arbitrary criterion of $p < 0.05$, a practice known as *p*-hacking that we introduced in Chapter 7. The "new statistics" help us to address these problems, though they are not actually new (Cumming, 2012). Rather, it is the use of these statistics in place of hypothesis testing that would be new for the social sciences.

What are the new statistics? They include effect sizes, confidence intervals, and meta-analysis, all of which are covered in this chapter. Statistical power, which is also covered here, is closely linked to these concepts. All of these new statistics help us to come up with an estimate for the thing that we are observing—the behavior, attitude, emotion, or cognition. Cumming observes that other sciences, like physics, report estimates: "the melting point of the plastic was $85.5 \pm 0.2°C$," for example (p. ix). The behavioral sciences, in contrast, tend to report that there is or is not a significant effect, which gives us less information than an estimate would.

It is important to note that the estimates that Cumming calls for are intervals rather than a single number. Interval estimates not only give us a range of plausible variables, but also give us a sense of the uncertainty behind statistics. When we report a single number, it seems as if that must be the real number. The interval estimate makes it clearer that we're not all that sure. In fact, in one study, researchers who interpreted data based only on the interval estimate tended to be more accurate than researchers who also took hypothesis testing into account (Coulson, Healey, Fidler, & Cumming, 2010).

Beyond the fact that estimates are more useful, journal editors increasingly expect researchers to include the new statistics in their research reports (Cumming, 2012; Funder et al., 2014; Lindsay, 2017). For example, both the American Psychological Association (APA) and the Association for Psychological Science (APS) have developed new guidelines for the ethical and transparent reporting of data analyses that includes an emphasis on the new statistics (Appelbaum et al., 2018; Association for Psychological Science, 2017). The journal *Basic and Applied Social Psychology* has even gone so far as to ban traditional hypothesis testing in articles that it publishes (Trafimow & Marks, 2015).

Researchers increasingly comply with these expectations. For example, in one major journal, 94% of studies published over several years reported effect sizes and 40% reported confidence intervals (Odgaard & Fowler, 2010). The behavioral sciences do continue to use hypothesis testing, which is why it is still helpful to learn it. But the field is shifting, which is why it is also essential to learn the new statistics. If you continue to study and work in the behavioral sciences, one day you may not use hypothesis testing at all. As Cumming (2012) puts it, "there's life beyond .05."

- A **point estimate** is a summary statistic from a sample that is just one number used as an estimate of the population parameter.

- An **interval estimate** is based on a sample statistic and provides a range of plausible values for the population parameter.

Confidence Intervals

In studies on gender differences in mathematics performance, researchers calculate a mean difference by subtracting a mean score for girls from a mean score for boys. All three summary statistics—the mean for boys, the mean for girls, and the difference between them—are point estimates. *A **point estimate** is a summary statistic from a sample that is just one number used as an estimate of the population parameter.* So, a mean taken from a sample is a point estimate, a single number used as an estimate for a population parameter. A point estimate, however, is rarely exactly accurate. We can increase accuracy by using an interval estimate when possible.

MASTERING THE CONCEPT

8-1: We can use a sample to calculate a point estimate—one plausible number, such as a mean—for the population. More realistically, we also can use a sample to calculate an interval estimate—a range of plausible numbers, such as a range of means—for the population.

Interval Estimates

*An **interval estimate** is based on a sample statistic and provides a range of plausible values for the population parameter.* Interval estimates are frequently used by the media, often when reporting political polls, and are usually constructed by adding and subtracting a margin of error from a point estimate.

EXAMPLE 8.1

For example, a Marist poll asked 938 adult respondents in the United States to select from five choices the word or phrase that they found "most annoying in conversation" (maristpoll.marist.edu/~107-whatever-takes-top-honors-as-most-annoying). "Whatever" was chosen by 47% of respondents, ahead of "you know" (25%), "it is what it is" (11%), "anyway" (7%), and "at the end of the day" (2%). The margin of error was reported to be ±3.2% (plus or minus 3.2%).

Because $47 - 3.2 = 43.8$ and $47 + 3.2 = 50.2$, the interval estimate for "whatever" is 43.8% to 50.2% (Figure 8-2). Interval estimates provide a range of plausible values, not just one statistic.

Pay attention to whether the interval estimates overlap. "You know" came in second, with 25%, giving an interval estimate of 21.8% to 28.2%. There's no

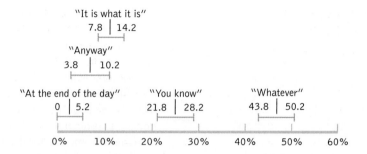

FIGURE 8-2

Intervals and Overlap

When two intervals, like those for "whatever" and "you know," do not overlap, we conclude that the population means are likely different. In the population, it seems that "whatever" really is more annoying than "you know." However, when two intervals do overlap, like those for "it is what it is" and "anyway," then it is plausible that the two phrases are perceived as equal—in this case, equally annoying—in the population.

overlap with the first-place word, a strong indication that "whatever" really was most annoying in the population as well as in the sample. However, if "you know" had received 42% of the vote, it would have placed only 5% behind "whatever," and it would have had an interval estimate of 38.8% to 45.2%. This range would have overlapped with the one for "whatever" (43.8% to 50.2%), an indication that both expressions could plausibly have been equally annoying in the population.

Language Alert! The terms "margin of error," "interval estimate," and "confidence interval" all represent the same idea. Specifically, *a confidence interval is an interval estimate based on a sample statistic; it includes the population mean a certain percentage of the time if the same population is sampled from repeatedly.* (*Note:* We are not saying that we are confident that the population mean falls in the interval; we are merely saying that we expect to find the population mean within a certain interval a certain percentage of the time—usually 95%—when we conduct this same study with the same sample size.)

The confidence interval is centered on the mean of the sample. A 95% confidence level is most commonly used, indicating the 95% that falls *between* the two tails (i.e., 100% − 5% = 95%). Note the terms used here: The confidence *level* is 95%, but the confidence *interval* is the range between the two values that surround the sample mean. ●

● A **confidence interval** is an interval estimate based on a sample statistic; it includes the population mean a certain percentage of the time if the same population is sampled from repeatedly.

Calculating Confidence Intervals with z Distributions

The symmetry of the z distribution makes it easy to calculate confidence intervals. We already conducted hypothesis testing in Chapter 7. Here is how confidence intervals can help us listen more closely to the story data tell.

EXAMPLE 8.2

What's your screen time? Nielsen, a company that tracks media usage, recently released its 2018 report. In the United States, adults spend an average of 11 hours each day consuming media, which includes television, radio, and any time spent in front of a computer, phone, or tablet (Nielsen Company, 2018). Let's assume that the average of 11 hours each day represents the population mean for adults and that the population standard deviation is 2 hours. And let's say we want to find out how the media consumption of U.S. teens stacks up against that of adults. Assume we collected data on a sample of 20 teenagers and determined that, on average, the teens in that sample spend 9 hours a day consuming media. This average is consistent with a 2015 survey on teen media consumption (Common Sense Media, 2015).

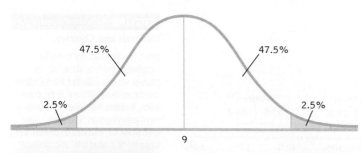

FIGURE 8-3

A 95% Confidence Interval, Part I

To begin calculating a confidence interval for a z distribution, we draw a normal curve, place the sample mean at its center, and indicate the percentages within and beyond the confidence interval.

In Chapter 7, we learned how to conduct a *z* test to determine whether a sample mean is statistically significantly different from a population mean. If we perform a hypothesis test to determine whether the amount of time U.S. teens spend consuming media differs from that spent by the population of U.S. adults, we would find a *z* statistic of −4.47. This *z* statistic is more extreme than the *z* critical value of 1.96 for an alpha level of .05, so we can reject the null hypothesis. We conclude that, on average, U.S. teens spend less time consuming media each day than do U.S. adults.

Of course, there is a lot more that we can say about teen media consumption. The sample average of 9 is just a point estimate. We can also calculate a more useful interval estimate—a confidence interval—around this average.

There are several steps to calculating a confidence interval.

> **STEP 1: Draw a picture of a distribution that will include the confidence interval.**

We draw a normal curve (Figure 8-3) that has the *sample* mean, 9, at its center. (This is different from the curve we drew for a *z* test when we had the population mean at the center.)

> **STEP 2: Indicate the bounds of the confidence interval on the drawing.**

We draw a vertical line from the mean to the top of the curve. For a 95% confidence interval, we also draw two small vertical lines to indicate the middle 95% of the normal curve (2.5% in each tail, for a total of 5%).

The curve is symmetric, so half of the 95% falls above and half falls below the mean. Half of 95 is 47.5, so we write 47.5% in the segments on either side of the mean. In the tails beyond the two lines that indicate the end of the middle 95%, we also write the appropriate percentages. You can see these percentages in Figure 8-3.

> **STEP 3: Determine the z statistics that fall at each line marking the middle 95%.**

FIGURE 8-4

A 95% Confidence Interval, Part II

The next step in calculating a confidence interval is identifying the z statistics that indicate each end of the interval. Because the curve is symmetric, the z statistics will have the same magnitude—one will be negative and one will be positive (−1.96 and 1.96).

To do this, we turn back to the versatile *z* table in Appendix B. The percentage between the mean and each of the *z* scores is 47.5%. When we look up this percentage in the *z* table, we find a *z* statistic of 1.96. (Note that this is identical to the cutoffs for the *z* test; this will always be the case because the alpha level of 0.05 corresponds to a confidence level of 95%.) We can now add the *z* statistics of −1.96 and 1.96 to the curve, as seen in Figure 8-4.

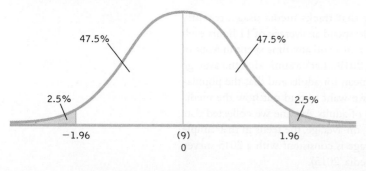

> **STEP 4:** Turn the *z* statistics back into raw means.

We use the formula for this conversion, but first we identify the appropriate mean and standard deviation. There are two important points to remember. First, we center the interval around the *sample* mean (not the *population* mean). So we use the sample mean of 9 in the calculations. Second, because we have a sample *mean* (rather than an individual *score*), we use a distribution of means. So we calculate standard error as the measure of spread:

$$\sigma_M = \frac{\sigma}{\sqrt{N}} = \frac{2}{\sqrt{20}} = 0.447$$

Using this mean and standard error, we calculate the raw mean at each end of the confidence interval, and add them to the curve, as in Figure 8-5:

$$M_{lower} = -z(\sigma_M) + M_{sample} = -1.96(0.447) + 9 = 8.12$$
$$M_{upper} = z(\sigma_M) + M_{sample} = 1.96(0.447) + 9 = 9.88$$

The 95% confidence interval, reported in brackets as is typical, is [8.12, 9.88].

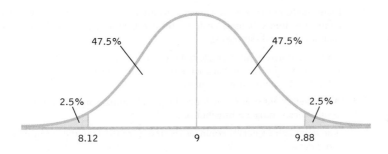

47.5%　　　47.5%

2.5%　　　2.5%

8.12　　　9　　　9.88

FIGURE 8-5

A 95% Confidence Interval, Part III

The final step in calculating a confidence interval is converting the *z* statistics that indicate each end of the interval into raw means.

> **STEP 5:** Check that the confidence interval makes sense.

The sample mean should fall exactly in the middle of the two ends of the interval.

$$8.12 - 9 = -0.88 \text{ and } 9.88 - 9 = 0.88$$

We have a match. The confidence interval ranges from 0.88 below the sample mean to 0.88 above the sample mean. We can think of this number, 0.88, as the margin of error.

To recap the steps for the creation of a confidence interval for a *z* statistic:

1. *Draw* a normal curve with the *sample* mean in the center.
2. *Indicate* the bounds of the confidence interval on either end, and write the percentages under each segment of the curve.

MASTERING THE FORMULA

8-1: The formula for the lower bound of a confidence interval using a *z* distribution is $M_{lower} = -z(\sigma_M) + M_{sample}$, and the formula for the upper bound is $M_{upper} = z(\sigma_M) + M_{sample}$. The first symbol in each formula refers to the mean at that end of the confidence interval. To calculate each bound, we multiply the *z* statistic by the standard error, then add the sample mean. The *z* statistic for the lower bound is negative, and the *z* statistic for the upper bound is positive.

3. *Look up* the z statistics for the lower and upper ends of the confidence interval in the z table. These are always -1.96 and 1.96 for a 95% confidence interval around a z statistic.

4. *Convert* the z statistics to raw means for each end of the confidence interval.

5. *Check* your answer; each end of the confidence interval should be exactly the same distance from the sample mean.

If we were to sample 20 U.S. teens from the same population over and over, the 95% confidence interval would include the population mean 95% of the time. Note that the population mean for U.S. adults, 11, falls outside of this interval. So, it is not plausible that the sample of U.S. teens comes from the null hypothesis population of U.S. adults.

The conclusions from both the z test and the confidence interval are the same, but the confidence interval gives us more information—an interval estimate, not just a point estimate. Moreover, as we noted earlier, there is evidence that reporting confidence intervals instead of the results of hypothesis testing can lead to more accurate interpretations of the findings (Coulson et al., 2010). ●

CHECK YOUR LEARNING

Reviewing the Concepts   >   Increasingly, researchers are expected to use the "new statistics"—effect sizes, confidence intervals, meta-analysis, and statistical power—in addition to or instead of traditional hypothesis testing.

> A point estimate is just a single number, such as a mean, that provides a plausible value for the population parameter. An interval estimate provides a range of plausible values for the population parameter.

> A confidence interval is one kind of interval estimate and can be created around a sample mean using a z distribution.

> The confidence interval confirms the results of the hypothesis test while adding more detail.

Clarifying the Concepts   8-1   Why are interval estimates better than point estimates?

Calculating the Statistics   8-2   If a poll determines that 21% of voters want to raise taxes, with a margin of error of 4%, what is the interval estimate? What is the point estimate?

Applying the Concepts   8-3   In How It Works 7.2, we conducted a z test based on the following information adapted from a study by Adams (2012) that used the Consideration of Future Consequences (CFC) scale as the dependent variable. The population mean CFC score was 3.20, with a standard deviation of 0.70. The sample was 45 students who joined a career discussion group, and the study examined whether this might have changed CFC scores. The mean for this group was 3.45.

a. Calculate the 95% confidence interval.

b. Explain what this confidence interval tells us.

Solutions to these Check Your Learning questions can be found in Appendix D.

c. Why is this confidence interval superior to the hypothesis test that we conducted in Chapter 7?

Effect Size

As we learned when we looked at the research on gender differences in mathematical reasoning ability, "statistically significant" does *not* mean that the findings from a study represent a meaningful difference. "Statistically significant" only means that those findings are unlikely to occur if, in fact, the null hypothesis is true. Geoff Cumming (2012) points out that hypothesis testing "relies on strange backward logic and can't give us direct information about what we want to know—the effect itself." Calculating an effect size moves us a little closer to the question we are most interested in: Is the pattern in a data set meaningful or important?

The Effect of Sample Size on Statistical Significance

The almost completely overlapping curves for mathematics performance in Figure 8-1 were "statistically significant" because the sample size was so big. Increasing sample size always increases the test statistic if all else stays the same. In Example 7.3, we used OkCupid data for men's ratings of women's online dating profiles (Rudder, 2009). Based on the reported distribution, we estimated the mean to be 2.5 and the standard deviation to be 0.833. We used the example of a fictional study in which you compare the mean rating of 2.84 for a sample of 30 women at your university to the overall OkCupid mean rating. Based on the sample size of 30, we reported the mean and standard error for the distribution of means as:

$$\mu_M = \mu = 2.50; \sigma_M = \frac{\sigma}{\sqrt{N}} = \frac{0.833}{\sqrt{30}} = 0.152$$

The test statistic calculated from these numbers was:

$$z = \frac{(M - \mu_M)}{\sigma_M} = \frac{(2.84 - 2.50)}{0.152} = 2.236$$

What would happen if we increased the sample size to 200? We'd have to recalculate the standard error to reflect the larger sample, and then recalculate the test statistic to reflect the smaller standard error.

$$\mu_M = \mu = 2.50; \sigma_M = \frac{\sigma}{\sqrt{N}} = \frac{0.833}{\sqrt{200}} = 0.059$$

$$z = \frac{(M - \mu_M)}{\sigma_M} = \frac{(2.84 - 2.50)}{0.059} = 5.763$$

What if we increased the sample size to 1000?

$$\mu_M = \mu = 2.50; \sigma_M = \frac{\sigma}{\sqrt{N}} = \frac{0.833}{\sqrt{1000}} = 0.026$$

$$z = \frac{(M - \mu_M)}{\sigma_M} = \frac{(2.84 - 2.50)}{0.026} = 13.077$$

What if we increased it to 100,000?

$$\mu_M = \mu = 2.50; \sigma_M = \frac{\sigma}{\sqrt{N}} = \frac{0.833}{\sqrt{100,000}} = 0.003$$

$$z = \frac{(M - \mu_M)}{\sigma_M} = \frac{(2.84 - 2.50)}{0.003} = 113.333$$

Misinterpreting Statistical Significance Statistical significance that is achieved by merely collecting a large sample can make a research finding appear to be far more important than it really is, just as a curved mirror can exaggerate a person's size.

Mary Hockenberry/Moment/Getty Images

Notice that each time we increased the sample size, the standard error decreased and the test statistic increased. The original test statistic, 2.24, was beyond the critical values of 1.96 and −1.96. And as the sample size increased, the test statistics (5.76, 13.08, and 113.33) were increasingly more extreme than the positive critical value. In their study of gender differences in mathematics performance, researchers studied 10,000 participants, a very large sample (Benbow & Stanley, 1980). It is not surprising, then, that a small difference would be a statistically significant difference.

Let's consider, logically, why it makes sense that a large sample should allow us to reject the null hypothesis more readily than a small sample. If we randomly selected five women at your university and they had a mean score well above the OkCupid average, we might say, "It could be chance." But if we randomly selected 1000 women with a mean rating well above the OkCupid average, it is very unlikely that we just happened to choose 1000 people with high scores.

But just because a real difference exists, that does not mean it is a large or meaningful difference. The difference we found with five people might be the same as the difference we found with 1000 people. As we demonstrated with multiple *z* tests with different sample sizes, we might fail to reject the null hypothesis with a small sample but then reject the null hypothesis for the same-size difference between means with a large sample.

Cohen (1990) used the small but statistically significant correlation between height and IQ to explain the difference between statistical significance and practical importance. The sample size was big: 14,000 children. Imagining that height and IQ were causally related, Cohen calculated that a person would have to grow by 3.5 feet to increase her IQ by 30 points (2 standard deviations). Or, to increase her height by 4 inches, she would have to increase her IQ by 233 points! Height may have been statistically significantly related to IQ, but there was no practical real-world application. A larger sample size should influence the level of confidence that the story is true, but it should not increase our confidence that the story is important.

Language Alert! When you come across the term *statistical significance*, do not interpret this as an indication of practical importance.

What Effect Size Is

Effect size can tell us whether a statistically significant difference might also be an important difference. **Effect size** *indicates the size of a difference and is unaffected by sample size.* Effect size tells us how much two populations *do not* overlap. Simply put, the less overlap, the bigger the effect size.

The amount of overlap between two distributions can be decreased in two ways. First, as shown in Figure 8-6, overlap decreases and effect size increases when means are farther apart. Second, as shown in Figure 8-7, overlap decreases and effect size increases when variability within each distribution of scores is smaller.

When we discussed gender differences in mathematical reasoning ability, you may have noticed that we described the size of the finding as "small," even though there was a statistically significant gender difference (Hyde, 2005). To determine that the size of the finding was "small," we calculated an effect size. Unlike statistical hypothesis testing, effect size is a standardized measure based on distributions of scores rather

---

MASTERING THE CONCEPT

8-2: As sample size increases, so does the test statistic (if all else stays the same). Because of this, a small difference might not be statistically significant with a small sample but might be statistically significant with a large sample.

● **Effect size** indicates the size of a difference and is unaffected by sample size.

timnewman/iStock/Getty Images

Larger Samples Give Us More Confidence in Our Conclusions Imagine your friend Carlos developed a procedure for house-training puppies based on what he learned in his behavior modification class, successfully training his new puppy in just one week. Meanwhile, Danica also developed a procedure for house-training puppies. She worked with a veterinary clinic to identify 10 households willing to try her procedure with their new puppies and then house-trained all 10 puppies in a week. We should have greater confidence in Danica's house-training procedure, because she demonstrated that it is effective in a larger sample.

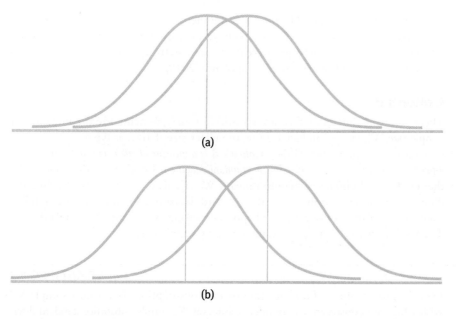

(a)

(b)

FIGURE 8-6

Effect Size and Mean Differences

When two population means are farther apart, as in (b), the overlap of the distributions is less and the effect size is bigger, even though the variability is the same in (a) and (b).

than distributions of means. Recall that we quantify the variability of a distribution of means with the standard error of the mean. To calculate the standard error of the mean, we divide the standard deviation by the sample size. This means that the standard error of the mean gets smaller as the sample size gets larger, and the distribution of means gets skinnier as the sample size gets larger.

In contrast, effect sizes are based only on the variability in the distribution of scores and do not depend on the sample size. This means that we can compare the effect sizes of different studies with each other, even when the studies

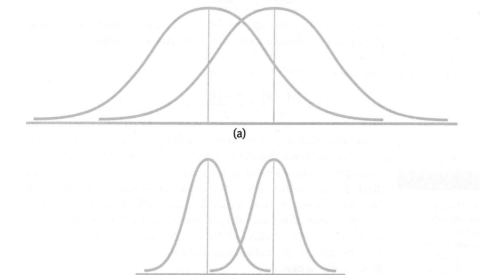

(a)

(b)

FIGURE 8-7

Effect Size and Standard Deviation

When two population distributions decrease their variability, or spread, as in (b), the overlap of the distributions is less and the effect size is bigger, even though the means are the same in (a) and (b).

have different sample sizes. Having a good understanding of effect sizes is important. Researchers who do are more likely to employ statistical practices that are closely aligned with the best practices of the new statistics (Badenes-Ribera, Frias-Navarro, Iotti, Bonilla-Campos, & Longobardi, 2018).

Cohen's d

There are many different effect-size statistics, but they all neutralize the influence of sample size. When we conduct a z test, the effect-size statistic is typically Cohen's d, developed by Jacob Cohen (1988). **Cohen's d** *is a measure of effect size that expresses the difference between two means in terms of standard deviation.* In other words, Cohen's d is the standardized difference between means. We calculate Cohen's d by dividing the difference between two means by the standard deviation. So, this calculation differs from the calculation of statistics for hypothesis testing, which uses the standard error. The result is that Cohen's d is not influenced by sample size.

● **Cohen's d** is a measure of effect size that expresses the difference between two means in terms of standard deviation.

EXAMPLE 8.3

Let's calculate Cohen's d for the same media consumption data from Example 8.2 with which we constructed a confidence interval. We simply substitute standard deviation for standard error. When we calculated the test statistic for the 20 U.S. teens, we first calculated standard error:

$$\sigma_M = \frac{\sigma}{\sqrt{N}} = \frac{2}{\sqrt{20}} = 0.447$$

We calculated the z statistic using the population mean of 11 and the sample mean of 9:

$$z = \frac{(M - \mu_M)}{\sigma_M} = \frac{(9 - 11)}{0.447} = -4.47$$

To calculate Cohen's d, we simply use the formula for the z statistic, substituting σ for σ_M (and μ for μ_M, even though these means are always the same). So we use 2 instead of 0.447 in the denominator. Cohen's d is based on the spread of the distribution of scores, rather than the distribution of means.

$$d = \frac{(M - \mu)}{\sigma} = \frac{(9 - 11)}{2} = -1.00$$

Now that we have the effect size, often written in shorthand as $d = -1.00$, we ask: What does it mean? First, we know that the two sample means are 1.00 standard deviation apart. Cohen developed guidelines for what constitutes a small effect (0.2), a medium effect (0.5), and a large effect (0.8). Based on these guidelines, $d = -1.00$ would be a large effect. Table 8-1 displays these guidelines, along with the amount of overlap between two curves that is indicated by an effect of that size. No sign is provided because it is the magnitude of an effect size that matters; an effect size of −0.5 is the same size as one of 0.5.

MASTERING THE FORMULA

8-2: The formula for Cohen's d for a z statistic is:

$$d = \frac{(M - \mu)}{\sigma}$$

It is the same formula as for the z statistic, except we divide by the population standard deviation rather than by standard error.

MASTERING THE CONCEPT

8-3: Because a statistically significant effect might not be an important one, we should calculate effect size in addition to conducting a hypothesis test. We can then report whether a statistically significant effect is small, medium, or large.

TABLE 8-1	Cohen's Conventions for Effect Sizes: *d*

Jacob Cohen published guidelines (or conventions) based on the overlap between two distributions to help researchers determine whether an effect is small, medium, or large. These numbers are not cutoffs; they are merely rough guidelines to help researchers interpret results.

Effect Size	Convention	Overlap
Small	0.2	85%
Medium	0.5	67%
Large	0.8	53%

Does an effect need to be large to be meaningful? Just because a statistically significant difference is small, that does not necessarily suggest it is not a meaningful difference. Sometimes a small effect can be meaningful (Matz, Gladstone, & Stillwell, 2017). Interpreting the meaningfulness of effect sizes depends on the context. For example, small effects may be sufficient to disprove a theory that predicted the opposite effect. However, small effects may not be sufficient for investing lots of money in government intervention programs. ●

Meta-Analysis

Many researchers consider meta-analysis to be the most important recent advancement in social science research (e.g., Rosenthal & DiMatteo, 2001). *A **meta-analysis** is a study that involves the calculation of a mean effect size from the individual effect sizes of more than one study.* Meta-analysis provides added statistical power by considering multiple studies simultaneously and helps to resolve debates fueled by contradictory research findings (Lam & Kennedy, 2005). Although the goal of meta-analysis, traditionally, has been to combine many studies, researchers are increasingly encouraging the use of meta-analysis with fewer studies—even as few as two (Cumming, 2012). Cumming argues that small meta-analyses can even replace hypothesis testing.

● A **meta-analysis** is a study that involves the calculation of a mean effect size from the individual effect sizes of more than one study.

The logic of the meta-analysis process is surprisingly simple. There are just four steps:

1. Select the topic of interest and decide exactly how to proceed *before* beginning to track down studies.
2. Locate every study that has been conducted and meets the criteria.
3. Calculate an effect size, often Cohen's *d*, for every study.
4. Calculate statistics—ideally, summary statistics, a hypothesis test, a confidence interval, and a visual display of the effect sizes (Rosenthal, 1995).

> **STEP 1:** Select the topic of interest and decide exactly how to proceed *before* beginning to track down studies.

Here are some of the considerations to keep in mind:

1. Make sure the necessary statistical information, either effect sizes or the summary statistics necessary to calculate effect sizes, is available.
2. Consider selecting only studies in which participants meet certain criteria, such as age, gender, or geographic location.
3. Consider eliminating studies based on the research design—for example, because they were not experimental in nature.

For example, British researcher Fidelma Hanrahan and her colleagues conducted a meta-analysis to examine the effectiveness of cognitive therapy in reducing levels of worrying in people with generalized anxiety disorder (Hanrahan, Field, Jones, & Davey, 2013). Before they began their meta-analysis, they developed criteria for the studies they would include; for example, they decided to include only studies that were true experiments and only studies in which the participants were between the ages of 18 and 65.

> **STEP 2: Locate every study that has been conducted and meets the criteria.**

Obvious places to start are PsycINFO, Google Scholar, and other electronic databases. For example, these researchers searched several databases using terms such as "generalized anxiety disorder," "cognitive," "therapy," and "anxiety" (Hanrahan et al., 2013). A key part of meta-analysis, however, is finding any studies that have been conducted but have not been published (Conn, Valentine, Cooper, & Rantz, 2003). Much of this "fugitive literature" (Rosenthal, 1995, p. 184) or "gray literature" (Lam & Kennedy, 2005) is unpublished simply because the studies did not find a significant difference. The overall effect size seems larger without these studies. We find these studies by using other sources—for example, by reading the proceedings of relevant conferences or contacting the primary researchers in the field to obtain any relevant unpublished findings. Hanrahan and her colleagues emailed the authors of the studies they located by using databases and asked whether they had any unpublished data.

> **STEP 3: Calculate an effect size, often Cohen's *d*, for every study.**

When the effect size has not been reported, the researcher must calculate it from summary statistics that were reported. These researchers were able to calculate 19 effect sizes from the 15 studies that met their criteria (some studies reported more than one effect) (Hanrahan et al., 2013).

> **STEP 4: Calculate statistics—ideally, summary statistics, a hypothesis test, a confidence interval, and a visual display of the effect sizes (Rosenthal, 1995).**

Most importantly, researchers calculate a mean effect size for all studies. In fact, we can apply all of the statistical insights we've learned: means, medians, standard deviations, confidence intervals and hypothesis testing, and visual displays of data.

In their meta-analysis of cognitive therapy for worry, Hanrahan and colleagues (2013) calculated several mean effect sizes. For example, the mean Cohen's *d* for the comparison of cognitive therapy with no therapy was 1.81. The confidence interval did not include 0, and the researchers were able to reject the null hypothesis that the effect size was 0. The mean Cohen's *d* for the comparison of cognitive therapy with other types of therapy was 0.63. The researchers were again able to reject the null hypothesis; however, they found an outlier that had a large effect size. The researchers found that when they omitted outliers, the mean dropped from 0.63 to 0.45, a smaller but still statistically significant effect. The researchers also included a graph—a *forest plot, which shows the confidence interval for the effect size of every study.* For example, Figure 8-8 shows a forest plot for the studies that compared cognitive therapy with no therapy. Based on this meta-analysis, the researchers concluded that cognitive therapy seems to be an effective treatment for worry.

Unpublished studies are key to a strong meta-analysis. Much of the fugitive literature of unpublished studies exists because studies with null results are less likely to appear in press (e.g., Begg, 1994). Twenty percent of the studies included in the meta-analysis conducted by Hanrahan and colleagues (2013) were unpublished at the time the meta-analysis was conducted, but there may have been other studies that these researchers were unable to locate. This has been called "the file drawer problem," and we will discuss two solutions to it.

The first solution involves additional analyses. The most common follow-up analysis was proposed by Robert Rosenthal (1991), and became aptly known as a *file drawer analysis, a statistical calculation, following a meta-analysis, of the number of studies with null results that would have to exist so that a mean effect size would no longer be statistically significant.* If just a few studies could render a mean effect size nonsignificant—that is, no longer statistically significantly different from zero—then the mean effect size should be viewed as likely to be an inflated estimate. If it would take several hundred studies in researchers' "file drawers" to render the effect nonsignificant, then it is safe to conclude that there really is a significant effect. For most research topics, it is not likely that there are hundreds of unpublished studies.

● A **forest plot** shows the confidence interval for the effect size of every study.

● A **file drawer analysis** is a statistical calculation, following a meta-analysis, of the number of studies with null results that would have to exist so that a mean effect size would no longer be statistically significant.

FIGURE 8-8

Forest Plot

This forest plot shows the effect sizes for the seven studies that compared cognitive therapy with no therapy in the treatment of worry among people with generalized anxiety disorder (Hanrahan et al., 2013). It also represents the overall effect size for the seven studies with the diamond at the bottom. Next to each effect size is the confidence interval for that effect size. The confidence interval for the overall effect size, 1.81, does not include 0. This is not surprising because the confidence intervals for the effect sizes of all seven studies do not include 0. The researchers were able to reject the null hypothesis that the overall effect size is 0.

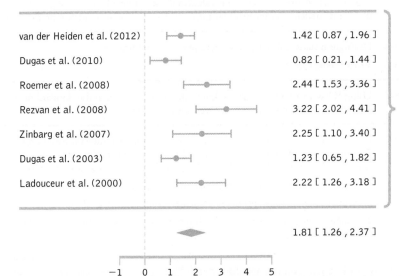

van der Heiden et al. (2012)	1.42 [0.87 , 1.96]
Dugas et al. (2010)	0.82 [0.21 , 1.44]
Roemer et al. (2008)	2.44 [1.53 , 3.36]
Rezvan et al. (2008)	3.22 [2.02 , 4.41]
Zinbarg et al. (2007)	2.25 [1.10 , 3.40]
Dugas et al. (2003)	1.23 [0.65 , 1.82]
Ladouceur et al. (2000)	2.22 [1.26 , 3.18]
	1.81 [1.26 , 2.37]

There are other variants of file drawer analysis, including analyses that allow researchers to examine their findings as if there were publication bias—that is, as if there were many studies out there with null results. The meta-analysis described here used a sensitivity analysis developed by Vevea and Woods (2005). Hanrahan and her colleagues (2013) concluded that the sensitivity analysis gave them "confidence that the estimated population effect sizes have not been severely inflated by unpublished studies not in the meta-analysis" (p. 126).

A second solution, replication or reproducibility, was introduced in Chapter 5 and will be discussed more fully in Chapter 9. Meta-analysis, despite concerns about the file drawer effect, can work together with replication to help us draw more reliable conclusions. As Geoff Cumming (2012) points out, meta-analysis, "even on messy social questions, can give conclusions that are well supported by evidence and have important practical implications" (p. 197). Given the drawbacks of hypothesis testing on its own, meta-analyses are increasingly a gold standard for research.

CHECK YOUR LEARNING

Reviewing the Concepts

> As sample size increases, the test statistic becomes more extreme and it becomes easier to reject the null hypothesis.

> A statistically significant result is not necessarily one with practical importance.

> Effect sizes are calculated with respect to distributions of scores, rather than distributions of means, so they are not inflated with increases in sample size.

> The size of an effect is based on the difference between two group means and the amount of variability within each group.

> Effect size for a z test is measured with Cohen's d, which is calculated much like a z statistic, but using standard deviation instead of standard error in the denominator.

> A meta-analysis is a study of studies that provides an average effect size across the many studies that asked the same research question.

> A researcher conducting a meta-analysis chooses a topic, decides on guidelines for a study's inclusion, tracks down every study on a given topic, and calculates an effect size for each. A mean effect size is calculated and reported, often along with a standard deviation, median, significance testing, confidence interval, and appropriate graphs.

Clarifying the Concepts

8-4 Distinguish statistical significance and practical importance.

8-5 What is effect size?

Calculating the Statistics

8-6 Using IQ as a variable, where we know the mean is 100 and the standard deviation is 15, calculate Cohen's d for an observed mean of 105.

Applying the Concepts

8-7 In Check Your Learning 8-3, you calculated a confidence interval based on CFC data. The population mean CFC score was 3.20, with a standard deviation of 0.70. The mean for the sample of 45 students who joined a career discussion group is 3.45.

a. Calculate the appropriate effect size for this study.

b. Citing Cohen's conventions, explain what this effect size tells us.

c. Based on the effect size, does this finding have any consequences or implications for anyone's life?

Solutions to these Check Your Learning questions can be found in Appendix D.

Statistical Power

The effect size statistic tells us that the public controversy over gender differences in mathematical ability was justified: The observed gender differences had no practical importance. Calculating statistical power is another way to limit such controversies from developing in the first place.

MASTERING THE CONCEPT

8-4: Statistical power is the likelihood of rejecting the null hypothesis when we should reject the null hypothesis. Researchers consider a probability of 0.80—an 80% chance of rejecting the null hypothesis if we should reject it—to be the minimum for conducting a study.

Making Correct Decisions

As described in Chapter 7, when we conduct a statistical null hypothesis test, we make a decision to either reject or fail to reject the null hypothesis. One problem with this analytical approach is that we don't have direct access to the truth about what we are studying. Instead, we make inferences based on the data we collected. Our decision could be right or wrong. But, a researcher's goal is to be correct as often as possible. There are two ways to be correct and two ways to be wrong. These four possibilities are shown in Table 8-2.

One way we can be wrong is to reject the null hypothesis when we should not have rejected it—a Type I error, or a false positive. With a Type I error, we claim an effect exists, when one really does not. A second way we can be wrong is failing to reject the null hypothesis when we should have rejected it—a Type II error, or a false negative. In this case, the null hypothesis is false: An effect does exist out in the world, but we don't detect it. These two types of errors were introduced in Chapter 5.

We can also make two types of correct decisions when conducting hypothesis testing. If the null hypothesis is true (left column of Table 8-2) and we fail to reject the null hypothesis, we have made a correct decision. In this case, we have said there is no effect, when in fact there is none. If the null hypothesis is false (right column of Table 8-2) and we reject the null hypothesis, that is also a correct decision. This type of correct decision is called *power*. A goal of research is to maximize statistical power.

Statistical Power Statistical power, like the progressive powers of a microscope used to show the fine details of a butterfly's wing, refers to the likelihood that we will detect differences that really exist.

TABLE 8-2	Our Decision Versus Truth About the Effect We Are Studying	
	In truth, no effect exists (Null hypothesis is true)	In truth, effect exists (Null hypothesis is false)
We reject the null hypothesis	Type I error ("false positive")	Correct decision (power)
We fail to reject the null hypothesis	Correct decision	Type II error ("false negative")

● **Statistical power** is a measure of the likelihood that we will reject the null hypothesis, given that the null hypothesis is false.

Power is a word that statisticians use in a very specific way. **Statistical power** *is a measure of the likelihood that we will reject the null hypothesis, given that the null hypothesis is false.* In other words, statistical power is the probability that we will reject the null hypothesis when we *should* reject the null hypothesis—the probability that we will not make a Type II error.

The calculation of statistical power ranges from a probability of 0.00 to a probability of 1.00 (or from 0% to 100%). Statisticians have historically used a probability of 0.80 as the minimum for conducting a study. Researchers want to maximize the power in their studies so that they can reject the null hypothesis if an effect truly exists. To that end, researchers will perform a power analysis prior to conducting a study. If they have an 80% chance of correctly rejecting the null hypothesis, then it is appropriate to conduct the study.

Conceptually, power is equal to the effect size times the sample size:

$$\text{Power} = \text{Effect Size} \times \text{Sample Size}$$

This means that we could achieve high power because the size of the effect is large—or, we could achieve high power because the size of the effect is small, but it is a large sample. To illustrate, in Example 8-3, we determined that the difference in media consumption between U.S. adults and teens was a large effect. So, we should statistically detect this difference even if we asked small samples of teens and adults about their media use. In contrast, the gender difference in math performance introduced at the beginning of this chapter (Benbow & Stanley, 1980) was a small effect. To detect this small effect, we would need a large sample.

As it turns out, the most practical way to increase statistical power for many behavioral studies is to add more participants. Fortunately, researchers can quantify the statistical power of their studies. One way to estimate a study's power is to refer to a published table like that in Jacob Cohen's (1992) article, "A Power Primer." However, we can estimate power even more precisely with new computing tools, such as the free software G*Power, which is available for both the Mac and the PC (Faul, Erdfelder, Lang, & Buchner, 2007; search online for G*Power).

Statistical power calculators like G*Power are versatile tools that are typically used in one of two ways. First, we can calculate power *after* conducting a study from several pieces of information. For most electronic power calculators, including G*Power, we determine power by inputting the effect size and sample size along with some additional information. Because we are calculating power after conducting the study, G*Power refers to these calculations as *post hoc*, which means "after the fact." Second, we can use electronic power calculators in reverse, *before* conducting a study, so as to identify the sample size necessary to achieve a given level of power. In this case, we use the power calculator to determine the sample size necessary to achieve the statistical power that we want before we conduct the study. G*Power refers to such calculations as *a priori*, which means "prior to."

Some statistical software, such as SPSS, will simultaneously provide post hoc power calculations with just the click of one button when conducting a hypothesis test. But, for a number of reasons, post hoc power calculation is not as meaningful as a priori power calculations for sample size planning (Dziak, Dierker, & Abar, 2018). Such an a priori power calculation is exactly the type of analysis performed by Eni Becker and her colleagues (2019) in their study of whether a computerized positivity-approach training would improve the depression symptoms of individuals at an inpatient clinic. Prior to conducting their study, these researchers used G*Power to determine that they would need a sample of 256 participants to achieve 89% power with an alpha level of .05.

To calculate this planned sample size, Becker's research team had to indicate the size of the effect they anticipated. They planned their sample size based on the assumption that any effect observed would be small. Of course, prior to running a study, we never know what the actual size of the effect will be. Researchers will sometimes examine the existing research literature or decide how large an effect size is needed to conduct a worthwhile study (Murphy & Myors, 2004). Some statisticians recommend erring on the side of using smaller, more conservative effect sizes in power calculations, which is what Becker and her colleagues did. Others recommend calculating power for a range of effect sizes (Anderson, Kelley, & Maxwell, 2017; Gelman & Carlin, 2014; McShane & Böckenholt, 2014).

On a practical level, statistical power calculations tell researchers how many participants are needed to conduct a study whose findings we can trust. Remember, however, that statistical power is based to some degree on hypothetical information, and it is just an estimate. We turn next to several factors that affect statistical power. ●

Five Factors That Affect Statistical Power

Here are five ways to increase the power of a statistical test, from the easiest to the most difficult:

1. **Increase alpha.** Increasing alpha is like changing the rules by widening the goal posts in football or the goal in soccer. In Figure 8-9, we see how statistical power increases when we increase an alpha level of 0.05 (see Figure 8-9a) to 0.10 (see Figure 8-9b). This has the side effect of increasing the probability

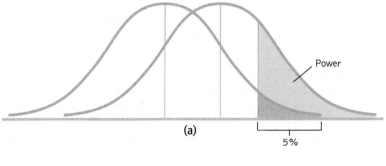

(a)
5%

(b)
10%

FIGURE 8-9

Increasing Alpha

As we increase alpha from the standard of 0.05 to a larger level, such as 0.10, statistical power increases. Because this also increases the probability of a Type I error, this is not usually a good method for increasing statistical power.

of a Type I error from 5% to 10%, however, so researchers rarely choose to increase statistical power in this manner.

2. **Turn a two-tailed hypothesis into a one-tailed hypothesis.** We have been using a simpler one-tailed test, which provides more statistical power. However, researchers usually begin with the more conservative two-tailed test. In Figure 8-10, we see the difference between the less powerful two-tailed test [part (a)] and the more powerful one-tailed test [part (b)]. The curves in part (a), with a two-tailed test, show less statistical power than do the curves in part (b). However, it is usually best to be conservative and use a two-tailed test.

FIGURE 8-10

Two-Tailed Versus One-Tailed Tests

A two-tailed test divides alpha into two tails. When we use a one-tailed test, putting the entire alpha into just one tail, we increase the chances of rejecting the null hypothesis, which translates into an increase in statistical power.

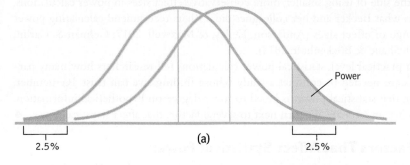
(a)
2.5%   2.5%
Power

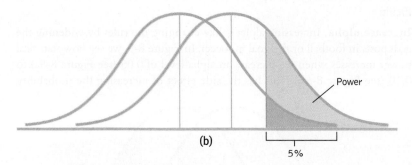
(b)
5%
Power

3. **Increase N.** As we demonstrated earlier in this chapter, increasing sample size leads to an increase in the test statistic, making it easier to reject the null hypothesis. The curves in Figure 8-11a represent a small sample size; those in Figure 8-11b represent a larger sample size. The curves are narrower in part (b) than in part (a) because a larger sample size means smaller standard error. We have direct control over sample size, so simply increasing N is often an easy way to increase statistical power.

4. **Exaggerate the mean difference between levels of the independent variable.** As seen in Figure 8-12, the mean of population 2 is farther from the mean of population 1 in part (b) than it is in part (a). The difference between means is not easily changed, but it can be done. For instance, if we were studying the effectiveness of group therapy for social phobia, we could increase the length of therapy from 3 months to 6 months. It is possible that a longer program would lead to a larger change in means than would the shorter program.

5. **Decrease standard deviation.** We see the same effect on statistical power if we find a way to decrease the standard deviation as when we increase sample size.

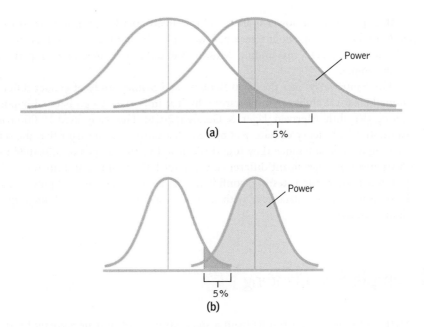

FIGURE 8-11

Increasing Sample Size or Decreasing Standard Deviation

As sample size increases, from part (a) to part (b), the distributions of means become more narrow and there is less overlap. Less overlap means more statistical power. The same effect occurs when we decrease standard deviation. As standard deviation decreases, also reflected from part (a) to part (b), the curves are narrower and there is less overlap—and more statistical power.

Look again at Figure 8-11, which reflects an increase in sample size. The curves can become narrower not just because the denominator of the standard error calculation is larger, but also because the numerator is smaller. When standard deviation is smaller, standard error is smaller and the curves are narrower. We can reduce standard deviation in two ways: (1) by using reliable measures from the beginning of the study, thus reducing error, or (2) by sampling from a more homogeneous group in which participants' responses are more likely to be similar to begin with.

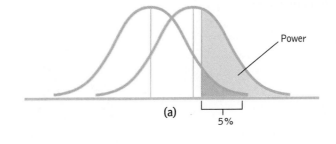
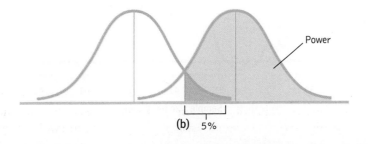

FIGURE 8-12

Increasing the Difference Between the Means

As the difference between means becomes larger, there is less overlap between curves. Here, the lower pair of curves has less overlap than the upper pair. Less overlap means more statistical power.

Because statistical power is affected by so many variables, it is important to consider it when reading about research. Always ask whether there was sufficient statistical power to detect a real finding. Most importantly, were there enough participants in the sample?

The controversy over the 1980 Benbow and Stanley study of gender differences in mathematical ability demonstrates why it is important to go beyond hypothesis testing (Vasishth, Mertzen, Jager, & Gelmen, 2018). The study used 10,000 participants, so it had plenty of statistical power. That means we can trust that the statistically significant difference they found was real. But the effect size informed us that this statistically significant difference was trivial. Combining all four ways of analyzing data (hypothesis testing, confidence intervals, effect size, and power analysis) helps us listen to the data story with all of its wonderful nuances and suggestions for future research.

Data Ethics | Sample Size Planning

Statistically significant results from a small sample will not necessarily be statistically significant when a larger sample is used. Of course, ethical researchers know that sampling variability plays a role in the results obtained (Simmons, Nelson, & Simonsohn, 2011). With a small sample, we are more likely to have sample data that do not represent the overall population. Fortunately, new advances in programming allow us to run computer simulations to see what happens with samples of different sizes. Figure 8-13 represents the results of a computer simulation performed by Joseph Simmons and his colleagues (2011), in which the researchers started with 10 participants in each of two groups and added one participant to each group at a time, performing a statistical hypothesis test after each addition. On the *y*-axis is the *p* value from that test.

FIGURE 8-13

Increasing Sample Size and *p* Values

The *p* values from a computer simulation in which one participant at a time was added to each of two groups (Simmons et al., 2011). In the simulated data, there was no difference between the two groups, but the *p* values from hypothesis testing suggest we would have rejected the null hypothesis in error for sample sizes between 21 and 28. We would have made a Type I error. Data from Simmons et al. (2011).

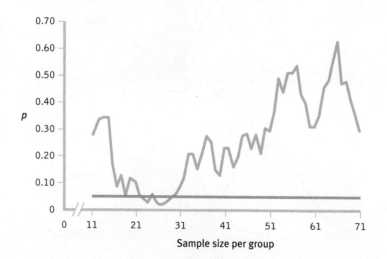

These are simulated ("made up") data, so we know that there is truly no difference between the two groups; that is, the effect size is zero. Thus, the null hypothesis is true, and we should not reject it. If we reject the null hypothesis because the *p* value is less than .05, we would have made a Type I error. The horizontal line in the graph represents the alpha level of .05. With sample sizes of 21 to 28 participants per group, we clearly would reject the null hypothesis in error. However, as we add more participants, we correctly fail to reject the null hypothesis. So, underpowered studies with small sample sizes increase the likelihood that statistically significant effects are false positives—that is, Type I errors (Button et al., 2013; Simmons et al., 2011).

Is actual scientific practice consistent with this computer simulation? The answer is yes. In fact, a meta-analysis inspecting the statistical power, effect sizes, and sample sizes of published neuroscience experiments points to a pervasive problem with underpowered studies (Button et al., 2013). The median statistical power was 21%, far below the recommended 80%. Even so, these studies rejected the null hypothesis at an alpha level of .05. How can this be? It turns out that studies rejecting the null hypothesis are more likely to get published than studies that do not reject the null hypothesis. In turn, it is likely that some portion of these published studies reflect Type I errors.

As further evidence of the sample-size problem, Katherine Button and her colleagues (2013) examined a set of studies looking for gender differences in animal models of spatial memory. They found the typical sample size per study to be 22 to 24. To achieve 80% power with that sample size, the effect size would need to be a large Cohen's *d*, in the range of 1.20 to 1.26. Unfortunately, the average range of effect sizes for these studies was only 0.49 to 0.69—effect sizes that are unlikely to be detectable with samples of only 22 to 24!

What does this mean for the behavioral sciences? Scott Maxwell and Ken Kelley (2011) suggest that the large number of underpowered studies in some disciplines can explain why published studies appear to contradict one another and why some researchers find statistically significant results whereas others do not. To illustrate, imagine that a number of different researchers all use small samples to study the same phenomenon. A small sample is less likely to represent the population, just by chance, so some researchers will reject the null hypothesis, but others will fail to reject the null hypothesis. The unfortunate result is an appearance of contradictory results.

To sum up, we are more likely to incorrectly reject the null hypothesis (Type I error) and to incorrectly fail to reject the null hypothesis (Type II error) with smaller samples. These are just some of the problems associated with underpowered studies (Ioannidis, 2008).

What is the remedy? Use a power calculator, such as G*Power, to plan your sample size based on the expected effect size before the study begins. Even then, it is not always easy to know which effect size to expect. Some researchers recommend correcting the expected effect size downward because of the bias toward publishing only significant effects (Anderson et al., 2017). Regardless of the method you use, the most important ethical guideline is to plan your sample size in advance, before you start collecting data.

CHECK YOUR LEARNING

Reviewing the Concepts

> Statistical power is the probability that we will reject the null hypothesis if we should reject it.

> Ideally, a researcher only conducts a study when there is 80% statistical power; that is, at least 80% of the time, the researcher will correctly reject the null hypothesis.

> Statistical power is affected by several factors, but most directly by sample size.

> Before conducting a study, researchers often determine the number of participants they need to ensure statistical power of 0.80.

> To get the most complete story about the data, it is best to combine the results of hypothesis testing with information gained from confidence intervals, effect size, and power.

> Smaller sample sizes can lead to both a lower likelihood of incorrectly rejecting the null hypothesis *and* a lower likelihood of incorrectly failing to reject the null hypothesis. These are additional reasons that, ethically, it's important to determine the appropriate sample size before collecting data.

Clarifying the Concepts   **8-8**   What are three ways to increase statistical power?

Calculating the Statistics   **8-9**   Check Your Learning 8-3 and 8-7 discussed a study aimed at changing CFC scores through a career discussion group. Imagine that those in the discussion group of 45 students have a mean CFC score of 3.45. Let's say that you know that the population mean CFC score is 3.20, with a standard deviation of 0.70. Calculate statistical power for this as a one-tailed test.

Applying the Concepts   **8-10**   Refer to Check Your Learning 8-9.

Solutions to these Check Your Learning questions can be found in Appendix D.

a. Explain what the number obtained in your statistical power calculation means.

b. Describe how the researchers might increase statistical power.

REVIEW OF CONCEPTS

 **LaunchPad**
macmillan learning

Visit LaunchPad to access the e-book and to test your knowledge with LearningCurve.

Confidence Intervals

A summary statistic, such as a mean, is a *point estimate* of the population mean. A more useful estimate is an *interval estimate*, a range of plausible numbers for the population mean. The most commonly used interval estimate is the *confidence interval*, which can be created around a mean using a z distribution. The confidence interval provides the same information as a hypothesis test and also gives us a range of values.

Effect Size

Knowing that a difference is statistically significant does not provide information about the size of the effect. A study with a large sample might find a small effect to be statistically significant, whereas a study with a small sample might fail to detect a large effect. To understand the importance of a finding, we must calculate an *effect size*. Effect sizes are independent of sample size because they are based on distributions of scores rather than distributions of means. One common effect-size measure is *Cohen's* d, which can be used when a z test has been conducted.

A *meta-analysis* is a study of studies in which the researcher chooses a topic, decides on guidelines for a study's inclusion, tracks down every study on a given topic, and calculates an effect size for each. A mean effect size is calculated and reported, often along with a standard deviation, median, hypothesis testing, confidence interval, and appropriate graphs. For example, researchers might create a *forest plot*, a graph that shows the confidence intervals for the effect sizes of all studies in the meta-analysis. A *file drawer analysis* can be performed to determine how many unpublished studies that failed to reject the null hypothesis must exist for the effect size to be rendered nonsignificantly different from zero.

Statistical Power

Statistical power is a measure of the likelihood that we will correctly reject the null hypothesis—that is, the chance that we will not commit a Type II error when the research hypothesis is true. Statistical power is affected most directly by sample size, but it is also affected by other factors. Researchers often use a computerized statistical power calculator to determine the appropriate sample size to achieve 0.80 statistical power. Smaller sample sizes can lead to both a lower likelihood of incorrectly rejecting the null hypothesis *and* a lower likelihood of incorrectly failing to reject the null hypothesis. These are additional reasons that, ethically, it's important to determine the appropriate sample size before collecting data.

HOW IT WORKS

8.1 CALCULATING CONFIDENCE INTERVALS

The Graded Naming Test (GNT) asks respondents to name objects in a set of 30 black-and-white drawings in an effort to detect brain damage. The GNT population norm for adults in England is 20.4. Researchers wondered whether a sample of Canadian adults had different scores from adults in England (Roberts, 2003). If the scores were different, the English norms would not be valid for use in Canada, perhaps because of differences in vocabulary between the two countries. The mean for 30 Canadian adults was 17.5. Assume that the standard deviation of the adults in England is 3.2. How can we calculate a 95% confidence interval for these data?

Given $\mu = 20.4$ and $\sigma = 3.2$, we can start by calculating standard error:

$$\sigma_M = \frac{\sigma}{\sqrt{N}} = \frac{3.2}{\sqrt{30}} = 0.584$$

We then find the z values that mark off the most extreme 0.025 in each tail, which are -1.96 and 1.96. We calculate the lower end of the interval as:

$$M_{lower} = -z(\sigma_M) + M_{sample} = -1.96(0.584) + 17.5 = 16.36$$

We calculate the upper end of the interval as:

$$M_{upper} = z(\sigma_M) + M_{sample} = 1.96(0.584) + 17.5 = 18.64$$

The 95% confidence interval around the mean of 17.5 is [16.36, 18.64].

How can we calculate the 90% confidence interval for the same data? In this case, we find the z values that mark off the most extreme 0.05 in each tail, which are -1.65 and 1.65. We calculate the lower end of the interval as:

$$M_{lower} = -z(\sigma_M) + M_{sample} = -1.65(0.584) + 17.5 = 16.54$$

We calculate the upper end of the interval as:

$$M_{upper} = z(\sigma_M) + M_{sample} = 1.65(0.584) + 17.5 = 18.46$$

The 90% confidence interval around the mean of 17.5 is [16.54, 18.46].

What can we say about these two confidence intervals in comparison to each other? The range of the 95% confidence interval is larger than that of the 90% confidence interval. When calculating the 95% confidence interval, we are describing where we think a larger portion of our sample means will fall if we repeatedly select samples of this size from the same population (95% as opposed to 90%) so that we have a larger range within which those means are likely to fall.

8.2 CALCULATING EFFECT SIZE

The Graded Naming Test (GNT) study has a population norm for adults in England of 20.4. Researchers found a mean for 30 Canadian adults of 17.5, and we assumed a standard deviation of adults in England of 3.2 (Roberts, 2003). How can we calculate the effect size for these data?

The appropriate measure of effect size for a z statistic is Cohen's d, which is calculated as:

$$d = \frac{(M - \mu)}{\sigma} = \frac{(17.5 - 20.4)}{3.2} = -0.91$$

Based on Cohen's conventions, this is a large effect size.

EXERCISES

The solutions to the odd-numbered exercises can be found in Appendix C.

Clarifying the Concepts

8.1 What specific danger exists when reporting a statistically significant difference between two means?

8.2 In your own words, define the word *confidence*—first as you would use it in everyday conversation and then as a statistician would use it in the context of a confidence interval.

8.3 Why do we calculate confidence intervals?

8.4 What are the five steps to create a confidence interval for the mean of a z distribution?

8.5 In your own words, define the word *effect*—first as you would use it in everyday conversation and then as a statistician would use it.

8.6 What effect does increasing the sample size have on standard error and the test statistic?

8.7 Relate effect size to the concept of overlap between distributions.

8.8 What does it mean to say an effect-size statistic neutralizes the influence of sample size?

8.9 What are Cohen's guidelines for small, medium, and large effects?

8.10 How does statistical power relate to Type II errors?

8.11 In your own words, define the word *power*—first as you would use it in everyday conversation and then as a statistician would use it.

8.12 How are statistical power and effect size different but related?

8.13 Traditionally, what minimum percentage chance of correctly rejecting the null hypothesis is suggested in order to proceed with an experiment?

8.14 Explain how increasing alpha increases statistical power.

8.15 List five factors that affect statistical power. For each, indicate how a researcher can leverage that factor to increase power.

8.16 What are the four basic steps of a meta-analysis?

8.17 What is the goal of a meta-analysis?

8.18 Why is it important for a researcher who is conducting a meta-analysis to find not only published studies but also unpublished studies?

8.19 How does a file drawer analysis make the findings from a meta-analysis more persuasive?

8.20 In statistics, concepts are often expressed in symbols and equations. For $M_{lower} = -z(\sigma) + M_{sample}$, (i) identify the incorrect symbol, (ii) state what the correct symbol is, and (iii) explain why the initial symbol was incorrect.

8.21 In statistics, concepts are often expressed in symbols and equations. For $d = \dfrac{(M - \mu)}{\sigma_M}$, (i) identify the incorrect symbol, (ii) state what the correct symbol is, and (iii) explain why the initial symbol was incorrect.

Calculating the Statistics

8.22 What are the potential negative consequences of an underpowered study?

8.23 What is the best way to avoid the negative consequences of an underpowered study?

8.24 In 2008, a Gallup poll asked people whether they were suspicious of steroid use among Olympic athletes. Thirty-five percent of respondents indicated that they were suspicious when they saw an athlete break a track-and-field record, with a 4% margin of error. Calculate an interval estimate.

8.25 In 2008, 22% of Gallup respondents indicated that they were suspicious of steroid use by athletes who broke world records in swimming. Calculate an interval estimate using a margin of error at 3.5%.

8.26 In 2013, the Gallup polling organization and the online publication *Inside Higher Ed* reported the results of a survey of 831 university presidents and chancellors. The report stated: "For results based on the sample size of 831 total respondents, one can say with 95 percent confidence that the margin of error attributable to sampling error is ±3.4 percentage points" (p. 6). Fourteen percent of respondents indicated that they strongly agreed that massive open online courses (MOOCs) could have a positive impact on higher education. Construct an interval estimate for the point estimate of 14%.

8.27 For each of the following confidence levels, indicate how much of the distribution would be placed in the cutoff region for a one-tailed z test.
a. 80%
b. 85%
c. 99%

8.28 For each of the following confidence levels, indicate how much of the distribution would be placed in the cutoff region for a two-tailed z test.
a. 80%
b. 85%
c. 99%

8.29 For each of the following confidence levels, look up the critical z value for a one-tailed z test.
a. 80%
b. 85%
c. 99%

8.30 For each of the following confidence levels, look up the critical z values for a two-tailed z test.
a. 80%
b. 85%
c. 99%

8.31 Calculate the 95% confidence interval for the following fictional data regarding daily TV viewing habits: $\mu = 4.7$ hours; $\sigma = 1.3$ hours; sample of 78 people, with a mean of 4.1 hours.

8.32 Calculate the 80% confidence interval for the same fictional data regarding daily TV viewing habits: $\mu = 4.7$ hours; $\sigma = 1.3$ hours; sample of 78 people, with a mean of 4.1 hours.

8.33 Calculate the 99% confidence interval for the same fictional data regarding daily TV viewing habits: $\mu = 4.7$ hours; $\sigma = 1.3$ hours; sample of 78 people, with a mean of 4.1 hours.

8.34 Calculate the standard error for each of the following sample sizes when $\mu = 1014$ and $\sigma = 136$:
a. 12
b. 39
c. 188

8.35 For a given variable, imagine we know that the population mean is 1014 and the standard deviation is 136. A sample mean of 1057 is obtained. Calculate the z statistic for this mean, using each of the following sample sizes:

   a. 12

   b. 39

   c. 188

8.36 Calculate the effect size for the mean of 1057 observed in Exercise 8.35 where $\mu = 1014$ and $\sigma = 136$.

8.37 Calculate the effect size for each of the following average SAT math scores. Remember, the SAT math exam is standardized such that $\mu = 500$ and $\sigma = 100$.

   a. Sixty-one people sampled have a mean of 480.

   b. Eighty-two people sampled have a mean of 520.

   c. Six people sampled have a mean of 610.

8.38 For each of the effect-size calculations in Exercise 8.37, identify the size of the effect using Cohen's guidelines. Remember, for the SAT math exam, $\mu = 500$ and $\sigma = 100$.

   a. Sixty-one people sampled have a mean of 480.

   b. Eighty-two people sampled have a mean of 520.

   c. Six people sampled have a mean of 610.

8.39 For each of the following d values, identify the size of the effect using Cohen's guidelines.

   a. $d = 0.79$

   b. $d = -0.43$

   c. $d = 0.22$

   d. $d = -0.04$

8.40 For each of the following d values, identify the size of the effect using Cohen's guidelines.

   a. $d = 1.22$

   b. $d = -1.22$

   c. $d = 0.13$

   d. $d = -0.13$

8.41 For each of the following z statistics, calculate the p value for a two-tailed test.

   a. 2.23

   b. −1.82

   c. 0.33

8.42 A meta-analysis reports an average effect size of $d = 0.11$, with a confidence interval of $d = 0.08$ to $d = 0.14$.

   a. Would a hypothesis test (assessing the null hypothesis that the average effect size is 0) lead us to reject the null hypothesis? Explain.

   b. Use Cohen's conventions to describe the average effect size of $d = 0.11$.

8.43 A meta-analysis reports an average effect size of $d = 0.11$, with a confidence interval of $d = -0.06$ to $d = 0.28$. Would a hypothesis test (assessing the null hypothesis that the average effect size is 0) lead us to reject the null hypothesis? Explain.

8.44 Assume you are conducting a meta-analysis over a set of five studies. The effect sizes for each study follow: $d = 0.67; d = 0.03; d = 0.32; d = 0.59; d = 0.22$.

   a. Calculate the mean effect size for these studies.

   b. Use Cohen's conventions to describe the mean effect size you calculated in part (a).

8.45 Assume you are conducting a meta-analysis over a set of five studies. The effect sizes for each study follow: $d = 1.23; d = 1.08; d = -0.35; d = 0.88; d = 1.69$.

   a. Calculate the mean effect size for these studies.

   b. Use Cohen's conventions to describe the mean effect size you calculated in part (a).

Applying the Concepts

8.46 **Margin of error and adult education:** According to a 2013 report by Public Agenda and the Kresge Foundation, online education is popular among adults planning to return to university. "The majority (73 percent) of adult prospective students want to take at least some classes online, and nearly 4 in 10 (37 percent) say it is absolutely essential for them that their future school offer online classes" (p. 25). The margin of error was reported to be 4.27. Calculate an interval estimate for each of these findings.

8.47 **Distributions and the Burakumin:** A friend reads in her *Introduction to Psychology* textbook about a minority group in Japan, the Burakumin, who are racially the same as other Japanese people but are viewed as outcasts because their ancestors were employed in positions that involved the handling of dead animals (e.g., butchers). In Japan, the text reported, mean IQ scores of Burakumin were 10 to 15 points below mean IQ scores of other Japanese people. In the United States, where Burakumin experienced no discrimination, there was no mean difference (from Ogbu, 1986, as reported in Hockenbury & Hockenbury, 2013). Your friend says to you: "Wow—when I taught English in Japan last summer, I had a

Burakumin student. He seemed smart; perhaps I was fooled." What should your friend consider about the two distributions, the one for Burakumin people and the one for other Japanese people?

8.48 Sample size, *z* statistics, and the Consideration of Future Consequences scale: Here are summary data from a *z* test regarding scores on the Consideration of Future Consequences scale (Petrocelli, 2003): The population mean (μ) is 3.20 and the population standard deviation (σ) is 0.70. Imagine that a sample of students had a mean of 3.45.

a. Calculate the test statistic for a sample of 5 students.

b. Calculate the test statistic for a sample of 1000 students.

c. Calculate the test statistic for a sample of 1,000,000 students.

d. Explain why the test statistic varies so much even though the population mean, population standard deviation, and sample mean do not change.

e. Why might sample size pose a problem for hypothesis testing and the conclusions we are able to draw?

8.49 Sample size, *z* statistics, and the Graded Naming Test: In an exercise in Chapter 7, we asked you to conduct a *z* test to ascertain whether the Graded Naming Test (GNT) scores for Canadian participants differed from the GNT norms based on adults in England. We also used these data in the How It Works section of this chapter. The mean for a sample of 30 adults in Canada was 17.5. The normative mean for adults in England is 20.4, and we assumed a population standard deviation of 3.2. With 30 participants, the *z* statistic was −4.97, and we were able to reject the null hypothesis.

a. Calculate the test statistic for 3 participants. How does the test statistic change compared to when *N* of 30 was used? Conduct step 6 of hypothesis testing. Does the conclusion change? If so, does this mean that the actual difference between groups changed? Explain.

b. Conduct steps 3, 5, and 6 for 100 participants. How does the test statistic change?

c. Conduct steps 3, 5, and 6 for 20,000 participants. How does the test statistic change?

d. What is the effect of sample size on the test statistic?

e. As the test statistic changes, has the underlying difference between groups changed? Why might this present a problem for hypothesis testing?

8.50 Cheating with hypothesis testing: Unsavory researchers know that one can cheat with hypothesis testing. That is, they know that a researcher can stack the deck in her or his favor, making it easier to reject the null hypothesis.

a. If you wanted to make it easier to reject the null hypothesis, what are three specific things you could do?

b. Would it change the actual difference between the samples? Why is this a potential problem with hypothesis testing?

8.51 Overlapping distributions and English-language tests for international students: International students who wish to study at English-speaking universities in Canada or the United States are required to take a test, such as the Test of English as a Foreign Language (TOEFL) or the International English Language Testing System (IELTS), if English is not their first language. In a report of mean TOEFL scores by country, people whose first language was Serbian scored a mean of 86 (2015). People whose first language was Portuguese scored a mean of 82. Tijana, from Serbia, and Tomas, from Portugal, both just took the TOEFL.

a. Can we tell which student will do better on the TOEFL? Explain your answer.

b. Draw a picture that represents what the two distributions, that for people whose first language is Serbian and that for people whose first language is Portuguese, might look like with respect to one another. (Note that scores on the TOEFL range from 0 to 120.)

8.52 Confidence intervals, effect sizes, and tennis serves: Let's assume the average speed of a serve in men's tennis is around 135 mph, with a standard deviation of 6.5 mph. Because these statistics are calculated over many years and many players, we will treat them as population parameters. We develop a new training method that will increase arm strength, the force of the tennis swing, and the speed of the serve (we hope). We recruit 9 professional tennis players to use our method. After 6 months, we test the speed of their serves and compute an average of 138 mph.

a. Using a 95% confidence interval, test the hypothesis that our method makes a difference.

b. Compute the effect size and describe its strength.

8.53 Confidence intervals and English-language tests for international students: The International English Language Testing System (IELTS) has six modules, one of which assesses listening skills. IELTS researchers reported that a recent mean for everyone who completed this module in one year was 6.00 and the standard deviation was 1.30 (2013). A sample of 63 international students who were accepted to study at the University of Melbourne in Australia had mean IELTS listening scores of 7.087 with a standard deviation of 0.754 (O'Loughlin & Arkoudis, 2009).

a. Calculate the 95% confidence interval for this sample.

b. State in your own words what we learn from this confidence interval.

c. What information does the confidence interval give us that we also get from a hypothesis test?

d. What additional information does the confidence interval give us that we do not get from a hypothesis test?

8.54 Confidence intervals and English-language tests for international students (continued): Using the IELTS listening data presented in the previous exercise, practice evaluating data using confidence intervals.

a. Compute the 80% confidence interval.

b. How do the conclusion and the confidence interval change as we move from 95% confidence to 80% confidence?

c. Why don't we talk about having 100% confidence?

8.55 Effect size and English-language tests for international students: In the two previous exercises, we considered the IELTS listening module, during which the population of all IELTS takers in a year had a mean score of 6.00 with a standard deviation of 1.30 (2013). A sample of 63 international students at the University of Melbourne had mean IELTS listening scores of 7.087 with a standard deviation of 0.754 (O'Loughlin & Arkoudis, 2009).

a. Calculate the appropriate measure of effect size for this sample.

b. Based on Cohen's conventions, is this a small, medium, or large effect?

c. Why is it useful to have this information in addition to the results of a hypothesis test?

8.56 Effect size and English-language tests for international students (continued): In the previous exercise, you calculated an effect size for data for 63 international students at the University of Melbourne. Imagine that you had a sample of 300 students. How would the effect size change? Explain why it would or would not change.

8.57 Confidence intervals, effect sizes, and Valentine's Day spending: According to the Nielsen Company, Americans spend $345 million on chocolate during the

week of Valentine's Day. Let's assume that we know the average married person spends $45, with a population standard deviation of $16. In February 2009, the U.S. economy was in the throes of a recession. Comparing data for Valentine's Day spending in 2009 with what is generally expected might give us some indication of the attitudes during the recession.

a. Compute the 95% confidence interval for a sample of 18 married people who spent an average of $38.

b. How does the 95% confidence interval change if the sample mean is based on 180 people?

c. If you were testing a hypothesis that things had changed under the financial circumstances of 2009 as compared to previous years, what conclusion would you draw in part (a) versus part (b)?

d. Compute the effect size based on these data and describe the size of the effect.

8.58 More about confidence intervals, effect sizes, and tennis serves: Let's assume the average speed of a serve in women's tennis is around 118 mph, with a standard deviation of 12 mph. We recruit 100 amateur tennis players to use our new training method this time, and after 6 months we calculate a group mean of 123 mph.

a. Using a 95% confidence interval, test the hypothesis that our method makes a difference.

b. Compute the effect size and describe its strength.

8.59 Confidence intervals, effect sizes, and tennis serves (continued): As in the previous exercise, assume the average speed of a serve in women's tennis is around 118 mph, with a standard deviation of 12 mph. But now we recruit only 26 amateur tennis players to use our method. Again, after 6 months we calculate a group mean of 123 mph.

a. Using a 95% confidence interval, test the hypothesis that our method makes a difference.

b. Compute the effect size and describe its strength.

c. How did changing the sample size from 100 (in Exercise 8.56) to 26 affect the confidence interval and effect size? Explain your answer.

8.60 Power analysis and enhancing memory: In a study of the effects of testing on enhancing memory, Akan and colleagues (2018) performed an a priori power analysis to determine the sample size they would need to detect a small to medium-sized effect ($d = 0.40$) with 80% power and an alpha level of .05. Their analysis indicated that they would need 52 participants.

a. Why did Akan and colleagues power their study to find an effect of size $d = 0.40$?

b. What would happen to the power of the study if the real effect size that Akan and colleagues were studying was smaller than $d = 0.40$?

c. What would be the easiest way for Akan and colleagues to increase their power without increasing their chances of making a Type I error?

8.61 Type I errors, Type II errors, and ego depletion: Ego depletion refers to the idea that we have a limited amount of self-control, which can be depleted. Exerting self-control in one situation will make it harder to exert self-control on later tasks. For example, maybe you're eating a healthy diet and successfully avoided the holiday cookies at work, but then couldn't resist the holiday cookies your grandparents sent you. Singh and Göritz (2018) investigated whether ego depletion interferes with working memory performance and found no statistically significant difference in working memory between an ego-depleted group and a control group at an alpha level of .05. The total sample size for their study was $N = 1385$. The researchers ran a power analysis to determine whether their study, with this large sample, would have had enough power to detect even a small effect. That is, they were trying to determine whether they rejected the null in error. The power analysis determined that their study had a power of 0.98 to detect a small effect.

a. Is it likely that Singh and Göritz made a Type II error? Why or why not?

b. What is the probability that Singh and Göritz made a Type I error?

8.62 Effect size and homeless families: A *New York Times* article reported on the growing problem of homelessness among families (Bellafante, 2013). The reporter wrote that families in a city-run program called Homebase had shorter stays than families not in the program—a difference of about 22.6 fewer nights in a shelter. However, the reporter observed, "Though this is a statistically significant result, it is hardly an impressive one, especially in light of the fact that the average stay for a family in the shelter system is now 13 months, up from 9 months in 2011, and the city is experiencing record levels of homelessness with 50,000 people, including 21,000 children, in shelters every night."

a. How is the reporter's observation about the size of the result—"hardly an impressive one"—related to the concept of effect size?

b. Imagine that a friend who has not taken statistics asks you to explain the difference between a statistically significant result and a large or "impressive"

effect. In your own words, how would you explain this difference to your friend?

8.63 Meta-analysis, mental health treatments, and cultural contexts: A meta-analysis examined studies that compared two types of mental health treatments for ethnic and racial minorities—the standard available treatments and treatments that were adapted to the clients' cultures (Griner & Smith, 2006). An excerpt from the abstract follows:

Many previous authors have advocated traditional mental health treatments be modified to better match clients' cultural contexts. Numerous studies evaluating culturally adapted interventions have appeared, and the present study used meta-analytic methodology to summarize these data. Across 76 studies the resulting random effects weighted average effect size was d = .45, *indicating a... benefit of culturally adapted interventions.* (p. 531)

a. What is the topic chosen by the researchers conducting the meta-analysis?

b. What type of effect size statistic did the researchers calculate for each study in the meta-analysis?

c. What was the mean effect size? According to Cohen's conventions, how large is this effect?

d. If a study chosen for the meta-analysis did not include an effect size, what summary statistics could the researchers use to calculate an effect size?

8.64 Meta-analysis, mental health treatments, and cultural contexts (continued): The research paper on culturally targeted therapy described in the previous exercise reported the following:

Across all 76 studies, the random effects weighted average effect size was d = .45 *(SE = .04,* p < .0001), *with a 95% confidence interval of* d = .36 *to* d = .53. *The data consisted of 72 nonzero effect sizes, of which 68 (94%) were positive and 4 (6%) were negative. Effect sizes ranged from* d = −48 *to* d = 2.7. (Griner & Smith, 2006, p. 535)

a. What is the confidence interval for the effect size?

b. Based on the confidence interval, would a hypothesis test lead us to reject the null hypothesis that the effect size is zero? Explain.

c. Why would a graph, such as a histogram, be useful when conducting a meta-analysis like this one? (*Hint:* Consider the problems when using a mean as the measure of central tendency.)

8.65 Meta-analysis and math performance: Below is an excerpt of an abstract from a published meta-analysis by Lindberg, Hyde, Petersen, and Linn (2010). Use this excerpt to describe what is done in each of the four steps of meta-analysis.

In this article, we use meta-analysis to analyze gender differences in recent studies of mathematics performance. First, we meta-analyzed data from 242 studies published between 1990 and 2007, representing the testing of 1,286,350 people. Overall, d = 0.05, indicating no gender difference, and variance ratio = 1.08, indicating nearly equal male and female variances. . . . These findings support the view that males and females perform similarly in mathematics.

8.66 **Meta-analysis and an examination of whether sex and violence sell:** Ohio State University researchers conducted a meta-analysis of 53 studies totaling almost 8500 participants (Lull & Bushman, 2015). Their goal was to determine whether advertising that included sex or violence helped to sell products. The researchers reported that "memory for brands and ads was significantly impaired in programs containing sex, violence, or both sex and violence, $d = -0.39$; 95% Cl $= -0.55$, -0.22" (p. 1029). (They found similar results for participants' reported intention to buy products associated with sex or violence.)

  a. What is the confidence interval for the effect size?

  b. Based on the confidence interval, would a hypothesis test lead us to reject the null hypothesis that the effect size is zero? Explain.

  c. Why would a graph, such as a forest plot, be useful when conducting a meta-analysis like this one? (*Hint:* Consider the problem when using a mean as the measure of central tendency.)

Putting It All Together

8.67 **Fantasy baseball:** Your roommate is reading *Fantasyland: A Season on Baseball's Lunatic Fringe* (Walker, 2006) and is intrigued by the statistical methods used by competitors in fantasy baseball leagues (in which competitors select a team of baseball players from across all major league teams, winning in the fantasy league if their eclectic roster of players outperforms the chosen mixes of other fantasy competitors). Among the many statistics reported in the book is a finding that Major League Baseball (MLB) players who have a third child show more of a decline in performance than players who have a first child or a second child. Your friend remembers that Kyle Seager of the Seattle Mariners recently had his third child and drops him from consideration for his fantasy team.

  a. Explain to your friend why a difference between means doesn't provide information about any specific player. Include a drawing of overlapping curves

as part of your answer. On the drawing, mark places on the *x*-axis that might represent a player from the distribution of those who recently had a third child (mark with an *X*) scoring *above* a player from the distribution of those who recently had a first or second child (mark with a *Y*).

  b. Explain to your friend that a statistically significant difference doesn't necessarily indicate a large effect size. How might a measure of effect size, such as Cohen's *d*, help us understand the importance of these findings and compare them to other predictors of performance that might have larger effects?

  c. Given that the reported association is true, can we conclude that having a third child *causes* a decline in performance? Explain your answer. What confounding variables might lead to the difference observed in this study?

  d. Given the relatively limited numbers of MLB players (and the relatively limited numbers of those who recently had a child—whether first, second, or third), what general guess would you make about the likely statistical power of this analysis?

8.68 **What does failing to reject the null mean?:** If a researcher fails to reject the null hypothesis, how would knowing information about the sample size and the expected effect size help to interpret the researcher's failure to reject the null hypothesis?

8.69 **Effect size and an intervention to increase college applications:** Caroline Hoxby and Sarah Turner (2013) conducted an experiment to determine whether a simple intervention could increase the number of college applications among low-income students. The intervention consisted of information about the college application process and about college costs that were specific to the student, along with an easy-to-implement waiver of college application fees. The following is an excerpt from a table. The intervention seemed to work with a statistically significant effect on this variable at an alpha level of 0.01.

Dependent variable	Effect in percentage change	Effect in effect size
Number of applications submitted	19.0%	0.247

  a. Describe the sample and population of this study.

  b. What is the independent variable and what are its levels?

c. What is the dependent variable?

d. The finding was statistically significant. Why is this not sufficient to determine that this intervention, which costs about $6 per student, is worthwhile?

e. What is the effect size for the dependent variable? How large is it, according to Cohen's conventions?

f. What does this effect size mean in terms of standard deviations in the context of this study?

g. The researchers also included the effect in percentage change. Explain what this means in the context of this study.

8.70 Sample size, effect size, and ESP: Bem (2011) reports nine experiments in which he presents evidence for extrasensory perception (ESP). For example, in Experiment 1, participants were shown two "curtains" side by side on a computer screen and told that there was a picture behind one curtain and nothing behind the second curtain. Participants were better than chance at guessing which curtain was hiding the picture, but only for erotic pictures. Below is a table of the sample size and effect size (Cohen's *d*) for each of the nine studies in Bem's 2011 report.

Experiment	Sample size	Cohen's *d*
1	100	0.25
2	150	0.20
3	100	0.25
4	100	0.25
5	100	0.22
6	150	0.15
7	200	0.09
8	100	0.19
9	50	0.42

a. What do you notice about the relation between sample size and effect size?

b. What problem or problems are suggested given the relation between sample size and effect size?

 **LaunchPad**
macmillan learning

Visit LaunchPad to access the e-book and to test your knowledge with LearningCurve.

TERMS

point estimate (p. 222)
interval estimate (p. 222)
confidence interval (p. 223)

effect size (p. 228)
Cohen's *d* (p. 230)
meta-analysis (p. 231)

forest plot (p. 233)
file drawer analysis (p. 233)
statistical power (p. 236)

FORMULAS

$M_{lower} = -z(\sigma_M) + M_{sample}$ (p. 225)

$M_{upper} = z(\sigma_M) + M_{sample}$ (p. 225)

Cohen's $d = \dfrac{(M - \mu)}{\sigma}$ for a *z* distribution   (p. 230)

SYMBOLS

Cohen's *d* (or just *d*)   (p. 230)

The Single-Sample *t* Test

The *t* Distributions

Estimating Population Standard Deviation from a Sample

Calculating Standard Error for the *t* Statistic

Using Standard Error to Calculate the *t* Statistic

The Single-Sample *t* Test

The *t* Table and Degrees of Freedom

The Six Steps of the Single-Sample *t* Test

Calculating a Confidence Interval for a Single-Sample *t* Test

Calculating Effect Size for a Single-Sample *t* Test

Data Ethics: Replication and Reproducibility

BEFORE YOU GO ON

■ You should know the six steps of hypothesis testing (Chapter 7).

■ You should know how to determine a confidence interval for a *z* statistic (Chapter 8).

■ You should understand the concept of effect size and know how to calculate Cohen's *d* for a *z* test (Chapter 8).

The Voice of a Stranger Have you ever dated someone you met online? If you did, you probably talked on the phone before meeting in person. Did you form an impression of what your date looked like from the sound of his or her voice? That may not be a bad tactic. Researchers used a single-sample *t* test to determine how much better than chance—50%—people matched voices with attractive or unattractive photos. And they found that people did statistically significantly better than chance, matching 72.6% correctly, on average.

So you've swiped right on Tinder, and after some back-and-forth messaging you've decided to actually talk to your potential date on the phone. How much of an impression do you form from someone's voice? If you decide to meet in person, would your date's physical appearance match the impression you had formed from her or his voice? Researchers Susan Hughes and Noelle Miller (2015) found that women tended to perceive high-pitched male voices as unattractive, but men tended to perceive high-pitched female voices as more attractive. Both men and women tended to perceive mid-pitched voices as "sexy." Hughes and Miller (2015) wanted to test whether people could match an attractive voice with an attractive face, so they presented 55 participants with two faces on a screen (one rated as attractive, the other as unattractive). Each participant heard 40 voices counting from 1 to 10 and each voice was paired with two photos. Then participants were asked which photo matched the voice.

The participants had a 50% chance of correctly matching the voice with the photo. But how much above 50% would convince you that participants were really making an association between voice and appearance? In this study, participants matched the voices and photos an average of 72.6% of the time. Is that a big enough difference that it's unlikely to have occurred by chance? Based on a single-sample *t* test, which we'll learn about in this chapter, Hughes and Miller concluded that people did indeed hold a stereotype that "what sounds beautiful looks beautiful." The researchers also found that people were confused when an attractive voice didn't match an attractive face, or vice versa. The researchers had just one sample (the participants in the experiment) and a comparison mean—the baseline expectation of 50% in the population if there were no significant difference. But that's all they needed to use the single-sample *t* test to answer their question. So let's say your potential Tinder date has an attractive voice. Based on this study's results, there's a pretty good chance that she or he will be physically attractive as well.

With a *t* distribution, we can compare one sample to a population when we don't know all the details about the parameters, and we can compare two samples to each other. There are two ways to compare two samples: by using a within-groups design or by using a between-groups design. For a within-groups design, we use a paired-samples *t* test, which we'll learn about in Chapter 10. For a between-groups design, we use an independent-samples *t* test, which we will learn about in Chapter 11.

MASTERING THE CONCEPT

9-1: There are three types of *t* tests: (1) We use a single-sample *t* test when comparing a sample mean to a population mean but do not know the population standard deviation. (2) We use a paired-samples *t* test, discussed in Chapter 10, when comparing two samples and every participant is in both samples—a within-groups design. (3) We use an independent-samples *t* test, discussed in Chapter 11, when comparing two samples and every participant is in only one sample—a between-groups design.

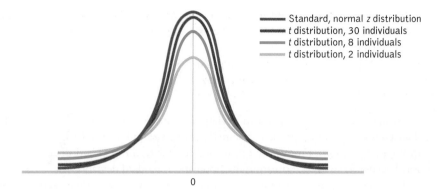

Standard, normal *z* distribution
t distribution, 30 individuals
t distribution, 8 individuals
t distribution, 2 individuals

0

FIGURE 9-1

The Wider and Flatter *t* Distributions

For smaller samples (such as of 2 or 8 individuals), the *t* distributions are wider and flatter than the *z* distribution. However, as the sample size increases (such as to 30 individuals), the *t* distributions look more like the *z* distribution. This makes sense because a larger sample size would be more similar to the entire population than a smaller sample size would.

The *t* Distributions

The *t* distributions (note the plural) help us specify how confident we can be about research findings. We want to know whether we can generalize what we have learned about one sample to a larger population. The *t* tests, based on the *t* distributions, tell us how confident we can be that a sample differs from the larger population.

The *t* distributions are more versatile than the *z* distribution because we can use them when (a) we don't know the population standard deviation, and (b) we compare two samples. Figure 9-1 demonstrates that there are many *t* distributions—one for each possible sample size. Just as we are less likely to believe gossip from only one or two people, we are less certain about what the population distribution really looks like when we have a small sample size. The uncertainty of a small sample size means that the *t* distributions become flatter and more spread out. However, as the sample size gets larger, the *t* distributions begin to merge with the *z* distribution because we gain confidence as more participants are added to a study, just as we become increasingly confident in gossip that is repeated by many independent sources.

Estimating Population Standard Deviation from a Sample

Before we conduct a single-sample *t* test, we must estimate the population standard deviation by using the sample standard deviation. Estimating the standard deviation is the only practical difference between conducting a *z* test with the *z* distribution and conducting a *t* test with the *t* distribution. Here is the sample standard deviation formula that we have used up until now:

$$SD = \sqrt{\frac{\Sigma(X - M)^2}{N}}$$

We need to make a correction to this formula to account for the fact that there is likely to be some level of error when we estimate the population standard deviation from a sample. Specifically, any given sample is likely to have somewhat less spread than does the entire population. One tiny alteration of this formula leads to a slightly larger and more accurate standard deviation. Instead of dividing by *N*, we divide by (*N* − 1) to get the mean of the squared deviations. Subtraction is the key. For example,

MASTERING THE FORMULA

9-1: The formula for standard deviation when estimating from a sample is:

$$s = \sqrt{\frac{\Sigma(X - M)^2}{(N - 1)}}$$

We subtract 1 from the sample size in the denominator to correct for the probability that the sample standard deviation slightly underestimates the actual standard deviation in the population.

if the numerator were 90 and the denominator (N) were 10, the answer would be 9; if we divide by $(N-1) = (10-1) = 9$, the answer would be 10, a slightly larger value. So the formula is:

$$s = \sqrt{\frac{\Sigma(X-M)^2}{(N-1)}}$$

Notice that we call this standard deviation s instead of SD. We still use Latin rather than Greek letters because it is a statistic (from a sample) rather than a parameter (from a population). From now on, we will calculate the standard deviation in this way because we will be estimating the population standard deviation.

Let's apply the new formula for standard deviation to a familiar activity: multitasking. Employees were observed at one of two high-tech companies for more than 1000 hours (Mark, Gonzalez, & Harris, 2005). The employees spent just 11 minutes, on average, on one project before being interrupted. Moreover, after each interruption, they needed an average of 25 minutes to get back to the original project! So maybe the reality is that multitasking actually reduces overall productivity.

Suppose you were a manager at one of these firms and decided to reserve a period from 1:00 to 3:00 each afternoon during which employees could not interrupt one another, but might still be interrupted by people outside the company. To test the intervention, you observe five employees and develop a score for each—time spent on a selected task before being interrupted. Here are the fictional data: 8, 12, 16, 12, and 14 minutes. In this case, we treat 11 minutes as the population mean, but we do not know the population standard deviation.

EXAMPLE 9.1

To calculate the estimated standard deviation for the population, there are two steps.

> **STEP 1: Calculate the sample mean.**

Even though we know the population mean (11 minutes), we use the sample mean to calculate the corrected sample standard deviation. The mean for these scores is:

$$M = \frac{(8+12+16+12+14)}{5} = 12.4$$

> **STEP 2: Use the sample mean in the corrected formula for the standard deviation.**

$$s = \sqrt{\frac{\Sigma(X-M)^2}{(N-1)}}$$

A Simple Correction: N − 1 When estimating variability, subtracting one person from a sample of three makes a big difference. Subtracting one person from a sample of thousands makes only a small difference. In this example, you would notice if one of the women disappeared from the photo on the left, but it would be almost impossible to notice if one of the crowd disappeared from the photo on the right.

Remember, the easiest way to calculate the numerator under the square root sign is by first organizing the data into columns, as shown here:

X	$X - M$	$(X - M)^2$
8	−4.4	19.36
12	−0.4	0.16
16	3.6	12.96
12	−0.4	0.16
14	1.6	2.56

The numerator is:

$$\Sigma(X - M)^2 = \Sigma(19.36 + 0.16 + 12.96 + 0.16 + 2.56) = 35.2$$

And given a sample size of 5, the corrected standard deviation is:

$$s = \sqrt{\frac{\Sigma(X - M)^2}{(N - 1)}} = \sqrt{\frac{35.2}{(5 - 1)}} = \sqrt{8.8} = 2.97 \; \bullet$$

Calculating Standard Error for the t Statistic

We now have an estimate of the standard deviation of the distribution of scores, but not an estimate of the spread of a distribution of means, the standard error. As we did with the z distribution, we make the spread smaller to reflect the fact that a distribution of means is less variable than a distribution of scores. We do this in exactly the same way that we adjusted for the *z* distribution. We divide *s* by $\sqrt{N}$. The formula for the standard error as estimated from a sample, therefore, is:

$$s_M = \frac{s}{\sqrt{N}}$$

Notice that we have replaced σ with *s* because we are using the corrected sample standard deviation rather than the population standard deviation.

EXAMPLE 9.2

Here's how we convert the corrected standard deviation of 2.97 to a standard error. The sample size was 5, so we divide by the square root of 5:

$$s_M = \frac{s}{\sqrt{N}} = \frac{2.97}{\sqrt{5}} = 1.33$$

So the standard error is 1.33. Just as the central limit theorem predicts, the standard error for the distribution of sample means is smaller than the standard deviation of sample scores. (*Note:* This step can lead to a common mistake. Because we implemented a correction when calculating *s*, students often want to implement an extra correction here by dividing by $\sqrt{N-1}$. Do not do this! We still divide by $\sqrt{N}$ in this step. There is no need for a further correction to the standard error.) ●

Using Standard Error to Calculate the *t* Statistic

- The *t* statistic indicates the distance of a sample mean from a population mean in terms of the estimated standard error.

We now have the tools necessary to conduct the single-sample *t* test. When conducting a single-sample *t* test, we calculate the **t** *statistic*, *the distance of a sample mean from a population mean in terms of the estimated standard error.* We introduce the formula for that *t* statistic here, and in the next section we go through all six steps for a single-sample *t* test. The formula is identical to that for the *z* statistic, except that it uses estimated standard error. Here is the formula for the *t* statistic for a distribution of means:

$$t = \frac{(M - \mu_M)}{s_M}$$

Note that the denominator is the only difference between this formula for the *t* statistic and the formula used to compute the *z* statistic for a sample mean. The corrected denominator makes the *t* statistic smaller and thereby reduces the probability of having an extreme *t* statistic. That is, a *t* statistic is not as extreme as a *z* statistic; in scientific terms, it's more conservative.

EXAMPLE 9.3

The t statistic for the sample of five scores representing minutes until interruptions is:

$$t = \frac{(M - \mu_M)}{s_M} = \frac{(12.4 - 11)}{1.33} = 1.05$$

As part of the six steps of hypothesis testing, the t statistic can help us make an inference about whether the ban on internal interruptions affected the average number of minutes until an interruption. ●

CHECK YOUR LEARNING

Reviewing the Concepts

> We use t distributions when we do not know the population standard deviation and are comparing only two groups.

> The two groups may be a sample and a population, or two samples as part of a within-groups design or a between-groups design.

> The formula for the t statistic for a single-sample t test is the same as the formula for the z statistic for a distribution of means, except that we use estimated standard error in the denominator rather than the actual standard error for the population.

> We calculate estimated standard error by dividing by $N - 1$, rather than dividing by N, when calculating standard error.

Clarifying the Concepts

9-1 What is the t statistic?

Calculating the Statistics

9-2 Calculate the standard deviation for a sample (SD) and as an estimate of the population (s) using the following data: 6, 3, 7, 6, 4, 5.

9-3 Calculate standard error for t for the data given in Check Your Learning 9-2.

Applying the Statistics

9-4 In the discussion of a study on multitasking (Mark et al., 2005), we imagined a follow-up study in which we measured time until a task was interrupted. For each of the five employees, let's now examine time until work on the initial task was resumed at 20, 19, 27, 24, and 18 minutes. Remember that the original research showed it took 25 minutes, on average, for an employee to return to a task after being interrupted.

a. What distribution would be used in this situation? Explain your answer.

b. Determine the appropriate mean and standard deviation (or standard error) for this distribution. Show all your work; use symbolic notation and formulas where appropriate.

Solutions to these Check Your Learning questions can be found in Appendix D.

c. Calculate the t statistic.

The Single-Sample *t* Test

- A **single-sample *t* test** is a hypothesis test in which we compare a sample from which we collect data to a population for which we know the mean but not the standard deviation.

To explore whether we can accurately guess how attractive a stranger is just by hearing a voice, researchers compared their sample mean to the population mean that would occur just by chance—50%. To do so, they used a ***single-sample t test**, a hypothesis test in which we compare a sample from which we collect data to a population for which we know the mean but not the standard deviation.* The logic of the single-sample *t* test is a model for other *t* tests that allow us to compare two samples—and all of the other more sophisticated statistical tests that will follow. You will soon be able to study just about anything you want.

The *t* Table and Degrees of Freedom

- **Degrees of freedom** is the number of scores that are free to vary when we estimate a population parameter from a sample.

When we use the *t* distributions, we use the *t* table. There are different *t* distributions for every sample size, and the *t* table takes sample size into account. However, we do not look up the actual sample size on the table. Rather, we look up ***degrees of freedom***, *the number of scores that are free to vary when we estimate a population parameter from a sample.*

Language Alert! The phrase "free to vary" refers to the number of scores that can take on different values when a given parameter is known.

EXAMPLE 9.4

MASTERING THE CONCEPT

9-2: *Degrees of freedom* refers to the number of scores that can take on different values when a given parameter is known. For example, if we know that the mean of three scores is 10, only two scores are free to vary. Once we know the values of two scores, we know the value of the third. If we know that two of the scores are 9 and 10, then we know that the third must be 11.

For example, the manager of a baseball team needs to assign nine players to particular spots in the batting order but only has to make eight decisions $(N - 1)$. Why? Because only one option remains after making the first eight decisions. So before the manager makes any decisions, there are $N - 1$, or $9 - 1 = 8$, degrees of freedom. After the second decision, there are $N - 1$, or $8 - 1 = 7$, degrees of freedom, and so on. But after the first 8 players have been assigned, there is no "freedom" when assigning the ninth player. There's only one spot left. ●

As in the baseball example, there is always one score that cannot vary once all of the others have been determined. For example, if we know that the mean of four scores is 6 and we know that three of the scores are 2, 4, and 8, then the last score must be 10. So the degrees of freedom is the number of scores in the sample minus 1. Degrees of freedom is written in symbolic notation as *df*, which is always italicized. The formula for degrees of freedom for a single-sample *t* test, therefore, is:

$$df = N - 1$$

MASTERING THE FORMULA

9-4: The formula for degrees of freedom for a single-sample *t* test is $df = N - 1$. To calculate degrees of freedom, we subtract 1 from the sample size.

Table 9-1 is an excerpt from a *t* table; the full table is in Appendix B. Notice the relation between degrees of freedom and the critical value needed to declare statistical significance. As degrees of freedom go up, the critical values go down. In the column corresponding to a one-tailed test at an alpha level of 0.05 with only 1 degree of freedom (two observations), the critical *t* value is 6.314. With only 1 degree of freedom, the two means have to be extremely far apart and/or the standard deviation has to be very small to declare a statistically significant difference. But with 2 degrees of freedom (three observations), the critical *t* value drops to 2.920. It is easier to reach the critical *t* value because we're more confident in making a reliable observation with three observations than with just two, just as we are more confident that a rumor is true

TABLE 9-1	Excerpt from the *t* Table

When conducting hypothesis testing, we use the *t* table to determine critical values for a given alpha level (0.10, 0.05, or 0.01), based on the degrees of freedom and whether the test is one- or two-tailed. The full table is in Appendix B.

	One-Tailed Tests			Two-Tailed Tests		
df	0.10	0.05	0.01	0.10	0.05	0.01
1	3.078	6.314	31.821	6.314	12.706	63.657
2	1.886	2.920	6.965	2.920	4.303	9.925
3	1.638	2.353	4.541	2.353	3.182	5.841
4	1.533	2.132	3.747	2.132	2.776	4.604
5	1.476	2.015	3.365	2.015	2.571	4.032

when we hear the same story from three independent observers rather than from just two people.

The pattern continues when we have four observations (with *df* of 3). The critical *t* value needed to declare statistical significance decreases from 2.920 to 2.353. The level of confidence in the observations increases and the critical value decreases.

The *t* distributions become closer to the *z* distribution as sample size increases. After all, if we kept increasing the sample size, we would eventually study the entire population and wouldn't need a pesky *t* test in the first place. But in the real world of research, the corrected standard deviation of a large enough sample is so similar to the actual standard deviation of the population that the *t* distribution is the same as the *z* distribution.

Check it out for yourself by comparing the *z* and *t* tables in Appendix B. For example, the *z* statistic for the 95th percentile—a percentage between the mean and the *z* statistic of 45%—is between 1.64 and 1.65. At a sample size of infinity, the *t* statistic for the 95th percentile is 1.645. Infinity (∞) indicates a very large sample size; a sample size of infinity itself is, of course, impossible.

Let's remind ourselves why the *t* statistic merges with the *z* statistic as sample size increases. More participants in a study—if they are a representative sample—correspond to increased confidence that we are making an accurate observation. So don't think of the *t* distributions as completely separate from the *z* distribution. Rather, think of the *z* statistic as a single-blade Swiss Army knife and the *t* statistic as a multiblade Swiss Army knife that still includes the single blade that is the *z* statistic.

Let's determine the cutoffs, or critical *t* values, for a research study using the full *t* table in Appendix B.

> **MASTERING THE CONCEPT**
>
> **9-3:** As sample size increases, the *t* distributions more and more closely approximate the *z* distribution. You can think of the *z* statistic as a single-blade Swiss Army knife and the *t* statistic as a multiblade Swiss Army knife that includes the single blade that is the *z* statistic.

EXAMPLE 9.5

The study: A researcher knows the mean number of calories lab rats will consume in half an hour if unlimited food is available. She wonders whether a new food will lead rats to consume a different number of calories—either more or fewer. She studies 38 rats and uses an alpha level of 0.05.

The cutoff(s): This is a two-tailed test because the research hypothesis allows for change in either direction. There are 38 rats, so the calculation for the degrees of freedom is:

$$df = N - 1 = 38 - 1 = 37$$

We want to look in the *t* table under two-tailed tests, in the column for 0.05 and in the row for a *df* of 37; however, there is no *df* of 37. In this case, we err on the side of being more conservative and choose the more extreme (i.e., larger) of the two possible critical *t* values, which is always the smaller *df*. Here, we look next to 35, where we see a value of 2.030. Because this is a two-tailed test, we will have critical values of −2.030 and 2.030. ●

The Six Steps of the Single-Sample *t* Test

Now we have all the tools necessary to conduct a single-sample *t* test. So let's consider a hypothetical study and conduct all six steps of hypothesis testing.

EXAMPLE 9.6

Nonparticipation in Therapy
Clients missing appointments can be a problem for both clients and therapists. A *t* test can compare the consequences between those who do and do not sign a contract to attend a set number of sessions.

Chapter 4 presented data that included the mean number of sessions attended by clients at a university counseling center. We noted that one study reported a mean of 4.6 sessions (Hatchett, 2003). Let's imagine that the counseling center hoped to increase participation rates by having students sign a contract to attend at least 10 sessions. Five students sign the contract and attend 6, 6, 12, 7, and 8 sessions, respectively. The researchers are interested only in their university, so they treat the mean of 4.6 sessions as a population mean.

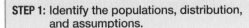

STEP 1: Identify the populations, distribution, and assumptions.

Population 1: All clients at this counseling center who sign a contract to attend at least 10 sessions. Population 2: All clients at this counseling center who do not sign a contract to attend at least 10 sessions.

The comparison distribution will be a distribution of means. The hypothesis test will be a single-sample *t* test because there is only one sample and we know the population mean but not the population standard deviation.

This study meets one of the three assumptions and may meet the other two: (1) The dependent variable is scale. (2) We do not know whether the data were randomly selected, however, so we must be cautious with respect to generalizing to other clients at this university who might sign the contract. (3) We do not know whether the population is normally distributed, and there are not at least 30 participants. However, the data from the sample do not suggest a skewed distribution.

STEP 2: State the null and research hypotheses.

Null hypothesis: Clients at this university who sign a contract to attend at least 10 sessions attend the same number of sessions, on average, as clients who do not sign such a contract—$H_0: \mu_1 = \mu_2$.

Research hypothesis: Clients at this university who sign a contract to attend at least 10 sessions attend a different number of sessions, on average, than do clients who do not sign such a contract—$H_1: \mu_1 \neq \mu_2$.

> **STEP 3: Determine the characteristics of the comparison distribution.**

$$\mu_M = 4.6; \; s_M = 1.114$$

Calculations:

$$\mu_M = \mu = 4.6$$

$$M = \frac{\Sigma X}{N} = \frac{(6+6+12+7+8)}{5} = 7.8$$

X	X − M	(X − M)²
6	−1.8	3.24
6	−1.8	3.24
12	4.2	17.64
7	−0.8	0.64
8	0.2	0.04

The numerator of the standard deviation formula is the sum of squares:

$$\Sigma(X - M)^2 = \Sigma(3.24 + 3.24 + 17.64 + 0.64 + 0.04) = 24.8$$

$$s = \sqrt{\frac{\Sigma(X - M)^2}{(N - 1)}} = \sqrt{\frac{24.8}{(5 - 1)}} = \sqrt{6.2} = 2.490$$

$$s_M = \frac{s}{\sqrt{N}} = \frac{2.490}{\sqrt{5}} = 1.114$$

> **STEP 4: Determine the critical values, or cutoffs.**

$$df = N - 1 = 5 - 1 = 4$$

For a two-tailed test with an alpha level of 0.05 and *df* of 4, the critical values are −2.776 and 2.776 (as seen in the curve in Figure 9-2).

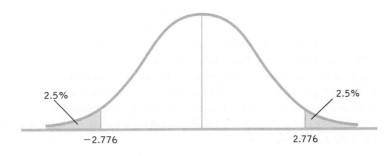

2.5%   2.5%

−2.776   2.776

FIGURE 9-2

Determining Cutoffs for a *t* Distribution

As with the *z* distribution, we typically determine critical values in terms of *t* statistics rather than means of raw scores so that we can easily determine whether the test statistic is beyond one of the cutoffs. Here, the cutoffs are −2.776 and 2.776, and they mark off the most extreme 5%, with 2.5% in each tail.

STEP 5: Calculate the test statistic.

$$t = \frac{(M - \mu_M)}{s_M} = \frac{(7.8 - 4.6)}{1.114} = 2.873$$

STEP 6: Make a decision.

Reject the null hypothesis. It appears that counseling center clients who sign a contract to attend at least 10 sessions do attend more sessions, on average, than do clients who do not sign such a contract (Figure 9-3).

FIGURE 9-3

Making a Decision

To decide whether to reject the null hypothesis, we compare the test statistic to the critical *t* values. In this case, the test statistic, 2.873, is beyond the cutoff of 2.776, so we can reject the null hypothesis.

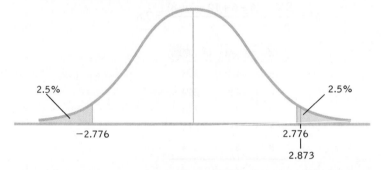

After completing the hypothesis test, we want to present the primary statistical information in a report. There is a standard American Psychological Association (APA) format for the presentation of statistics across the behavioral sciences so that the results are easily understood by the reader.

1. Write the symbol for the test statistic (e.g., *t*).
2. Write the degrees of freedom in parentheses.
3. Write an equal sign and then the value of the test statistic, typically to two decimal places.
4. Write a comma and then indicate the *p* value by writing "*p* =" and then the actual value. (Unless we use software to conduct the hypothesis test, we will not know the actual *p* value associated with the test statistic. In this case, we simply state whether the *p* value is beyond the critical value by saying $p < 0.05$ when we reject the null hypothesis or $p > 0.05$ when we fail to reject the null hypothesis.)

In the counseling center example, the statistics would read:

$$t(4) = 2.87, \, p < 0.05$$

The statistics typically follow a statement about the finding. For example, "It appears that counseling center clients who sign a contract to attend at least 10 sessions do attend more sessions, on average, than do clients who do not sign such a contract, $t(4) = 2.87$, $p < 0.05$." The report would also include the sample mean and standard deviation (not standard error) to two decimal points. Here, the descriptive statistics would read ($M = 7.80$, $SD = 2.49$). By convention, we use *SD* instead of *s* to symbolize the standard deviation. ●

Calculating a Confidence Interval for a Single-Sample *t* Test

We learned in the previous chapter that hypothesis testing is limited in what it tells us and is often misinterpreted. For these reasons, researchers should report confidence intervals and effect sizes whenever possible. These are reported in addition to hypothesis testing, and increasingly are used in place of hypothesis testing.

EXAMPLE 9.7

We can calculate a confidence interval with the single-sample *t* test data. The population mean was 4.6. We used the sample to estimate the population standard deviation to be 2.490 and the population standard error to be 1.114. The five students in the sample attended a mean of 7.8 sessions.

When we conducted hypothesis testing, we centered the curve on the mean according to the null hypothesis—the population mean of 4.6. Now we can use the same information to calculate the 95% confidence interval around the sample mean of 7.8.

> **STEP 1: Draw a picture of a *t* distribution that includes the confidence interval.**

We draw a normal curve (Figure 9-4) that has the sample mean, 7.8, at its center (instead of the population mean, 4.6).

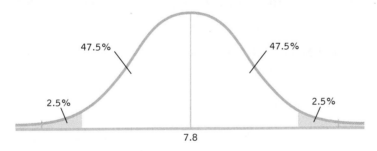

47.5%   47.5%

2.5%   2.5%

7.8

FIGURE 9-4

A 95% Confidence Interval for a Single-Sample *t* Test, Part I

To begin calculating a confidence interval for a single-sample *t* test, we place the sample mean, 7.8, at the center of a curve and indicate the percentages within and beyond the confidence interval.

> **STEP 2: Indicate the bounds of the confidence interval on the drawing.**

For a 95% confidence interval, we also draw two much smaller vertical lines that indicate the middle 95% of the *t* distribution (2.5% in each tail, for a total of 5%). We then write the appropriate percentages next to the segments of the curve.

> **STEP 3: Look up the *t* statistics that fall at each line marking the middle 95%.**

For a two-tailed test with an alpha level of 0.05 and a *df* of 4, the critical values are −2.776 and 2.776. We can now add these *t* statistics below the curve, as seen in Figure 9-5.

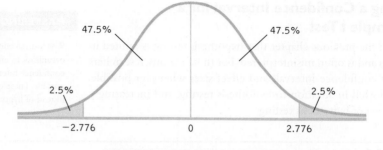

STEP 4: Convert the *t* statistics back into raw means.

As we did with the *z* test, we can use formulas for this conversion, but first we identify the appropriate mean and measure of spread. There are two important points to remember. First, we center the interval on the sample mean, so we use the sample mean of 7.8 in the calculations. Second, because we have a sample mean (rather than an individual score), we use a distribution of means. So we use the standard error of 1.114 as the measure of spread.

Using this mean and standard error, we calculate the raw mean at each end of the confidence interval, and add these means below the curve, as in Figure 9-6. The formulas are exactly the same as for the *z* test except that *z* is replaced by *t*, and σ_M is replaced by s_M.

$$M_{lower} = -t(s_M) + M_{sample} = -2.776(1.114) + 7.8 = 4.71$$
$$M_{upper} = t(s_M) + M_{sample} = 2.776(1.114) + 7.8 = 10.89$$

The 95% confidence interval—reported in brackets, as is typical—is [4.71, 10.89].

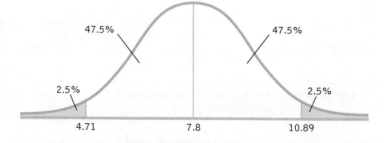

STEP 5: Verify that the confidence interval makes sense.

The sample mean should fall exactly in the middle of the two ends of the interval.

$$4.71 - 7.8 = -3.09; \text{ and } 10.89 - 7.8 = 3.09$$

We have a match. The confidence interval ranges from 3.09 below the sample mean to 3.09 above the sample mean. If we were to sample five students from the same population over and over, the 95% confidence interval would include the population mean 95% of the time. Note that the population mean, 4.6, does not fall within this interval. This means it is not plausible that this sample of students who signed contracts came from the population identified by the null hypothesis—students seeking treatment at the counseling center who did not sign a contract. We conclude that the sample comes from a different population, one in which students attend more mean sessions than does the general population. As with the *z* test, the conclusions from the hypothesis test and the confidence interval are the same, but the confidence interval gives us more information—an interval estimate, not just a point estimate. Because the conclusions are the same and the confidence interval gives more information, many researchers are now encouraging others to report *only* confidence intervals and not hypothesis tests. ●

Calculating Effect Size for a Single-Sample t Test

As with a *z* test, we can calculate the effect size (Cohen's *d*) for a single-sample *t* test.

EXAMPLE 9.8

Let's calculate the effect size for the counseling center study. Similar to what we did with the *z* test, we simply use the formula for the *t* statistic, substituting *s* for s_M (and μ for μ_M, even though these means are always the same). In this case, we use 2.490 instead of 1.114 in the denominator. Cohen's *d* is based on the spread of the distribution of individual scores, rather than the distribution of means.

$$\text{Cohen's } d = \frac{(M - \mu)}{s} = \frac{(7.8 - 4.6)}{2.490} = 1.29$$

The effect size, *d* = 1.29, tells us that the sample mean and the population mean are 1.29 standard deviations apart. According to the conventions we learned in Chapter 8 (that 0.2 is a small effect, 0.5 is a medium effect, and 0.8 is a large effect), this is a large effect. We can add the effect size when we report the statistics as follows: $t(4) = 2.87$, $p < 0.05$, $d = 1.29$. ●

> **MASTERING THE FORMULA**
>
> **9-6:** The formula for Cohen's *d* for a *t* statistic is:
>
> $$\text{Cohen's } d = \frac{(M - \mu)}{s}$$
>
> It is the same formula as for the *t* statistic, except that we divide by the population standard deviation (*s*) rather than by the population standard error (s_M).

Replication and Reproducibility   Data Ethics

In Chapter 5, we introduced the concept of replication on p. 122. Now that you've been introduced to hypothesis testing, we'll explore the benefits and challenges of replication for psychological science in more detail.

Psychologists Ed Diener and Robert Diener-Biswas (2019) conjure an interesting thought experiment. They ask you to imagine that you're driving to campus and you spot a pirate by the side of the road. Yes, a pirate. You might wonder whether that was *really* a pirate or just someone wearing "an unusual hat and a billowy shirt." But the researchers then ask you to imagine that you keep driving and see another

Power Posing and the Politics of Replication One of the most famous studies that failed to replicate was psychologist Amy Cuddy's work on power posing. Cuddy and her colleagues found that striking a pose like Cuddy's in this photo—she called these "open, expansive postures"—led to empowering changes in emotions and attitudes, but also to empowering changes in levels of testosterone and cortisol (Carney, Cuddy, & Yap, 2010). Want to ask for a raise? Power pose first. Cuddy soon found mainstream fame, including a viral Ted Talk (Cuddy, 2012). But the study failed to replicate, and there was a contentious public feud between Cuddy and her detractors (Simmons & Simonsohn, 2017). Some suggested that the attacks, more aggressive than those faced by many other researchers, were due to Cuddy's gender or to the fact that her public attention was somehow unseemly (Dominus, 2017). At this point, Cuddy has had the last word; although some of the physiological effects did not replicate, she found solid evidence for the effects of power posing on emotions and attitudes (Cuddy, Schultz, & Fosse, 2018). In the end, the science seems to have won out, although this situation has led many to call for more civility in the open-science movement (Sabeti, 2018).

● **Replication** is the repetition of a study that gives us confidence that a particular observation is true.

pirate. And then a few blocks later, another pirate. At some point, the researchers guess, you start believing your eyes and wonder why there are so many pirates near your university. Maybe it's "a pirate-themed conference" (p. 1)?

Diener and Diener-Biswas admit that it is a silly thought experiment, but nonetheless it's an example of *replication, the repetition of a study that gives us confidence that a particular observation is true.* Why is replication an important ethical data practice? If we conduct the same study with different samples and get the same results each time, it is more likely that the results are accurate. These later studies are then replications of the first study. So, if you think you see a pirate multiple times, then it is more likely that you are actually seeing pirates (or at least people dressed as pirates).

The problem is that, historically, social scientists rarely attempt to replicate (or reproduce) other scientists' findings. Academic scientists need to publish research to keep their jobs. But because journals tend to publish only new research, there isn't much incentive to repeat someone else's study. This emphasis on new findings is paralleled among the media, where a surprising or unusual finding, often based on a single study, is more likely to show up in the news than a replication of a study—what one researcher calls "sizzle over substance" (Levenson, 2017, p. 675).

This is starting to change, however. Increasingly, there's a push to "crowdsource" science (Baranski, 2015). This crowdsourcing of science can involve multiple researchers recruiting participants from their various universities or countries. Perhaps more important, though, crowdsourcing can involve researchers sharing their methodology and data online, which allows for more voices and more statistical analyses to contribute to a study's conclusions (Silberzahn & Uhlmann, 2015; Gilmore, Kennedy, & Adolph, 2018). It can also lead to other scientists jumping into the research fray via social media, questioning findings and sharing their questions. One journalist observed that "surprisingly high-level critiques of big [scientific] papers happen on Twitter each week," sometimes leading the authors of these papers to issue corrections (White, 2014).

The name for this crowdsourcing movement in research is "open science." If you put that term into a search engine, you'll find lots of examples of projects across different scientific disciplines and around the world, many of which involve students as researchers (Hawkins et al., 2018). For example, one crowdsourcing example is particularly exciting because it creates new opportunities for undergraduates. Psi Chi (2015), the International Honor Society in Psychology, has partnered with the Open Science Collaboration (Nosek et al., 2015) to test the reproducibility of well-known experiments.

As open science initiatives play out, we're discovering that many psychology studies have not been replicated by other researchers, which highlights the need for more replication. It's worth noting that the situation may be even worse in medical science, so it is not just psychological science that is facing this challenge (Begley & Ellis, 2012; Prinz, Schlange, & Asadullah, 2011). Regardless, in one highly publicized study published in the top journal *Science*, more than 100 researchers from more than 100 institutions around the world found that only 36% of a sample of important studies from top academic journals replicated; the remaining 64% of studies did *not* replicate (Open Science Collaboration, 2015). Some believe that failures to replicate may indicate that the original findings were Type I errors—incorrectly rejecting the null hypotheses. For example, one much-discussed study found a link between cleanliness and morality (Schnall, Benton, & Harvey, 2008). Specifically, participants who washed their hands after experiencing the emotion of disgust were less morally judgmental, on average, than were participants who did not wash their hands. Other researchers tried and failed to replicate this study (Johnson, Cheung, & Donnellan, 2014a).

The jury is still out, however, on whether the *Science* study really is evidence of a large-scale failure to replicate. In the case of the cleanliness and morality study, the lead author, psychologist Simone Schnall, published a critique of the failure to replicate her work, and the researchers who conducted the replication, in turn, responded to her critique (Bartlett, 2014; Johnson, Cheung, & Donnellan, 2014b; Schnall, 2014).

On a broader scale, Daniel Gilbert and his colleagues reanalyzed the full data set from the *Science* study (Gilbert, King, Pettigrew, & Wilson, 2016). Using different statistical techniques, these researchers came to the "opposite conclusion"—a fairly high level of replication of psychological research. Yet, that conclusion hasn't ended the debate. Some of the original researchers wrote a rebuttal saying that Gilbert and colleagues' conclusions are a "very optimistic assessment" and outline the ways in which they disagree with Gilbert and colleagues' statistical methodology (Anderson et al., 2016). These public debates about these findings in particular and replication efforts in general are helpful to making science more transparent.

But let's say that some of the studies really did fail to replicate. Some might think that such outcomes mean that psychological science is a failure itself, but many psychologists do not take this view, including some of the Open Science Collaboration researchers (Fanelli, 2018; Samarrai, 2015). One journalist called the push for reproducibility "an intensive background check" (Carey, 2018). Psychologist Lisa Feldman Barrett endorsed this viewpoint when she wrote in *The New York Times* about psychological science: The "failure to replicate is not a bug; it is a feature. It is what leads us along the path—the wonderfully twisty path—of scientific discovery" (2015). She pointed out that in some cases, a replication may be different in some ways, and the ways these differences affect the outcome can help scientists understand the exact context under which a finding occurs.

In her article, Barrett uses the example of a study in which rats froze at the sound of a tone that had been paired with an electric shock, but only under certain circumstances. In one study, they did not freeze; rather, they ran away. It turned out that the environment—in this case, the layout of the cage—affected whether the rat froze or not. What originally looked like a failure to replicate was, in fact, the progression toward a better understanding of fear in rats.

Related to Barrett's embrace of replication efforts, some scientists call for more nonexact replications of studies—both to test competing hypotheses and to expand the contexts in which a finding has been tested (Bless & Burger, 2016; Larzelere, Cox, & Swindle, 2015). Other scientists emphasize the need for replication efforts to include new samples of experimental stimuli as well as new samples of participants (Westfall, Judd, & Kenny, 2015). Most social scientists support the movement toward more replication, but a few think it has gone too far (Hamlin, 2017). Scientists against the replication movement call it "repligate" and describe replicators as scientific "bullies" (Bartlett, 2014). Most behavioral scientists, however, agree that replication is a good thing, whether it reproduces a finding, uncovers a Type I error, or helps us to tease apart the circumstances in which a finding seems to hold true and those in which it does not (Carey, 2015; Levenson, 2017). Some go even further, speculating that the openness and collaboration that the replication crisis has promoted leads to an exciting creativity in the behavioral sciences (Frankenhuis & Nettle, 2018; Vazire, 2018; Wagenmakers, Dutilh, & Sarafoglou, 2018).

We'll give Diener and Diener-Biswas the last word. "We are willing to consider unusual ideas if there is evidence to support them: We are open-minded. At the same time, we are critical and believe in replication. Scientists should be willing to consider unusual or risky hypotheses but ultimately allow good evidence to have the final say, not people's opinions" (p. 5, n.d.). We agree.

CHECK YOUR LEARNING

Reviewing the Concepts

> A single-sample *t* test is used to compare data from one sample to a population for which we know the mean but not the standard deviation.

> We consider degrees of freedom, or the number of scores that are free to vary, instead of *N* when we assess estimated *t* statistics against *t* distributions.

> As the sample size increases, confidence in the estimates improves, degrees of freedom increase, and the critical values for *t* decrease, making it easier to reach statistical significance. In fact, as sample size grows, the *t* distributions approach the *z* distribution.

> To conduct a single-sample *t* test, we follow the same six steps of hypothesis testing as we do for the *z* test, except that we estimate the standard deviation from the sample before we calculate standard error.

> We can calculate a confidence interval and an effect size, Cohen's *d*, for a single-sample *t* test.

> In the field of psychology, there's a growing push to replicate important research— that is, to repeat the study to see if the findings hold up.

Clarifying the Concepts

9-5   Explain the term *degrees of freedom*.

9-6   Why is a single-sample *t* test more useful than a *z* test?

Calculating the Statistics

9-7   Compute degrees of freedom for each of the following:

    a. An experimenter times how long it takes 35 rats to run through a maze with 8 pathways.

    b. Test scores for 14 students are collected and averaged over 4 semesters.

9-8   Identify the critical *t* value(s) for each of the following tests:

    a. A two-tailed test with alpha of 0.05 and 11 degrees of freedom

    b. A one-tailed test with alpha of 0.01 and *N* of 17

Applying the Concepts

Solutions to these Check Your Learning questions can be found in Appendix D.

9-9 Let's assume that according to university summary statistics, the average student misses 3.7 classes during a semester. Imagine that these are the data you have been working with (6, 3, 7, 6, 4, 5) for the number of classes missed by statistics students in your class. Conduct all six steps of hypothesis testing, using a two-tailed test with an alpha level of 0.05. (*Note:* You completed the work for step 3 in Check Your Learning 9-2 and 9-3.)

REVIEW OF CONCEPTS

The *t* Distributions

The *t* distributions are similar to the *z* distribution, except that in the former, we must estimate the standard deviation from the sample. When estimating the standard deviation, we make a mathematical correction to adjust for the increased likelihood of error. After estimating the standard deviation, the *t* statistic is calculated like the *z* statistic for a distribution of means. The *t* distributions can be used in three ways: (1) to compare the mean of a sample to a population mean when we don't know the population standard deviation (single-sample *t* test), (2) to compare two samples with a within-groups design (paired-samples *t* test—introduced in Chapter 10), and (3) to compare two samples with a between-groups design (independent-samples *t* test—introduced in Chapter 11).

LaunchPad
macmillan learning
Visit LaunchPad to access the e-book and to test your knowledge with LearningCurve.

The Single-Sample *t* Test

Like *z* tests, *single-sample* t *tests* are conducted in the rare cases in which there is one sample that we're comparing to a known population. The difference is that we only have to know the mean of the population to conduct a single-sample *t* test. There are many *t* distributions, one for every possible sample size. We look up the appropriate critical values on the *t* table based on *degrees of freedom*, a number calculated from the sample size. We can calculate a confidence interval and an effect size (Cohen's *d*) for a single-sample *t* test.

When we conduct hypothesis testing and reject the null hypothesis, we can never be sure whether the finding was a Type I error. For this reason, it is important to replicate important findings. The growing "open science" movement is helping to make it easier for scientists to attempt to replicate one another's work.

SPSS

Let's conduct a single-sample *t* test using the data on number of counseling sessions attended that we tested earlier in this chapter. The five scores were 6, 6, 12, 7, and 8.

Language Alert: The SPSS program uses an uppercase T rather than the lowercase, italicized *t* that you will use to report your results.

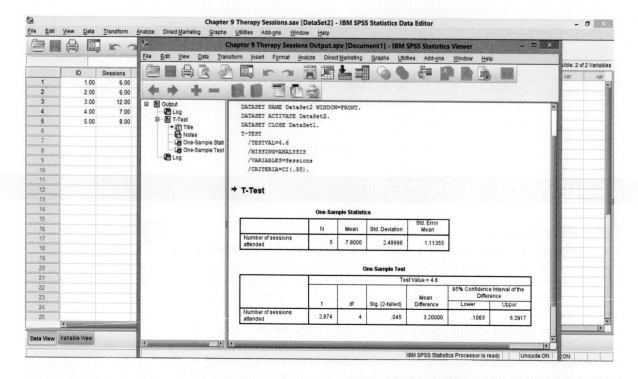

Select Analyze → Compare Means → One-Sample T Test. Highlight the dependent variable (Number of sessions attended) and click the arrow in the center to choose it. We have now told SPSS that we're interested in looking at the sample mean for this variable, number of sessions attended. We also need to tell SPSS the population to which we are comparing the sample mean. To do that, type the population mean to which we're comparing the sample, 4.6, next to "Test Value," and click "OK."

If we conduct this test using SPSS, we'll notice that the output presented includes two tables: a table with descriptive statistics for the dependent variable and a table that includes information used to calculate *t*. Both tables are in the screenshot here. In the second table, we should pay attention to three things: the *t* statistic in the first column, the *p* value in the significance column (in the third column), and the confidence interval (in the fifth and sixth columns). Notice that the *t* statistic, 2.874, is almost identical to the one we calculated earlier, 2.873. The difference is due solely to rounding decisions.

We can also see that the confidence interval is different from the one we calculated previously. This is an interval around the difference between the two means, rather than around the mean of the sample. The *p* value is under "Sig (2-tailed)." The *p* value of .045 is less than the chosen alpha level of .05, an indication that this is a statistically significant finding. All the information we used to hand calculate the *t* statistic should be the same as the information presented in these two SPSS output tables.

HOW IT WORKS

9.1 CONDUCTING A SINGLE-SAMPLE *t* TEST

The Web site Numbeo.com compiles statistics on quality of life issues from countries around the world based on data contributed by visitors to the site (2015). The Numbeo traffic index is calculated by taking into account the typical length of the commute to work, people's unhappiness with the length of their commute, the overall inefficiency of a country's transportation system, and an estimate of commute-related carbon dioxide emissions. The index ranges from 71 for Austria to 284.51 for Egypt, with higher numbers indicating more traffic and related problems. (For comparison, Canada has an index of 161.91

and the U.S. index is 154.2.) The mean for all countries listed in Numbeo is 138.69. For the purposes of this example, we'll treat these numbers as population parameters.

Imagine that 20 countries make a special effort to improve their traffic situations over a 5-year period. At the end of this time, the traffic indices are recalculated and these countries now have a mean index of 117.33 with a standard deviation of 45.04. Based on these data, how can we conduct all six steps of hypothesis testing for a two-tailed single-sample *t* test using an alpha level of 0.05? Let's walk through the steps.

Step 1: Population 1: Countries that did not make a special effort to improve the traffic situation over a 5-year period.

Population 2: Countries that made a special effort to improve the traffic situation over a 5-year period.

The comparison distribution will be a distribution of means. The hypothesis test will be a single-sample *t* test because there is only one sample and we know the population mean, but we do not know the population standard deviation. This study meets one of the three assumptions: The dependent variable is scale. We cannot assume that the countries in this sample were randomly selected from among all countries. In fact, it's likely those countries were self-selected; that is, they may have been motivated by other demands to make improvements. We must be cautious when generalizing. Last, there are fewer than 30 participants (i.e., countries), so we should be concerned about whether the comparison distribution is normal.

Step 2: Null hypothesis: Countries that made an effort to improve traffic conditions over a five-year time frame had the same traffic index score, on average, as countries that did not make explicit improvements—H_0: $\mu_1 = \mu_2$. Research hypothesis: Countries that made an effort to improve traffic conditions over a 5-year time frame had different traffic index scores, on average, than countries that did not make explicit improvements—H_1: $\mu_1 \neq \mu_2$.

Step 3: $\mu_M = \mu = 138.69$; $s_M = \dfrac{s}{\sqrt{N}} = \dfrac{45.04}{\sqrt{20}} = 10.072$

Step 4: $df = N - 1 = 20 - 1 = 19$

The critical values, based on 19 degrees of freedom, an alpha level of 0.05, and a two-tailed test, are −2.093 and 2.093.

Step 5: $t = \dfrac{(M - \mu_M)}{s_M} = \dfrac{(117.33 - 138.69)}{10.072} = -2.121$

Step 6: Reject the null hypothesis. It appears that the countries that made an effort to improve traffic conditions over a 5-year time frame had a lower traffic index score, on average, than did countries that did not make explicit improvements.

The statistics, as presented in a journal article, would read:

$$t(19) = -2.12, \ p < 0.05$$

(*Note:* If we had used software, we would report the actual *p* value instead of just whether the *p* value is larger or smaller than the critical *p* value.)

9.2 CALCULATING THE CONFIDENCE INTERVAL FOR A SINGLE-SAMPLE *t* TEST

How can we calculate a 95% confidence interval for these data?

Given $M = 117.13$ and $s = 45.05$, we can start by calculating standard error:

$$s_M = \frac{s}{\sqrt{N}} = \frac{45.04}{\sqrt{20}} = 10.072$$

We then find the *t* values that mark off the most extreme 0.025 in each tail and a *df* of 19, which are −2.093 and 2.093. We calculate the lower end of the interval as:

$$M_{lower} = -t(s_M) + M_{sample} = -2.093(10.072) + 117.13 = 96.049$$

We calculate the upper end of the interval as:

$$M_{upper} = t(s_M) + M_{sample} = 2.093(10.072) + 117.13 = 138.211$$

The 95% confidence interval is [96.05, 138.21].

9.3 CALCULATING EFFECT SIZE FOR A SINGLE-SAMPLE *t* TEST

How can we calculate effect size for these data? The appropriate measure of effect size for a single-sample *t* test is Cohen's *d*, which is calculated as:

$$\text{Cohen's } d = t = \frac{(M - \mu)}{s} = \frac{117.13 - 138.69}{45.04} = -0.48$$

Based on Cohen's conventions, this is a medium effect size.

EXERCISES

The solutions to the odd-numbered exercises can be found in Appendix C.

Clarifying the Concepts

9.1 When should we use a *t* distribution?

9.2 Why do we modify the formula for calculating standard deviation when using *t* tests (and divide by $N - 1$)?

9.3 How is the calculation of standard error different for a *t* test than for a *z* test?

9.4 Explain why the standard error for the distribution of sample means is smaller than the standard deviation of sample scores.

9.5 Define the symbols in the formula for the *t* statistic:

$$t = \frac{(M - \mu_M)}{s_M}$$

9.6 When is it appropriate to use a single-sample *t* test?

9.7 What does the phrase "free to vary," referring to a number of scores in a given sample, mean for statisticians?

9.8 How are the critical *t* values affected by sample size and degrees of freedom?

9.9 Why do the *t* distributions merge with the *z* distribution as sample size increases?

9.10 Explain what each part of the following statistical phrase means, as it would be reported in APA format: $t(4) = 2.87$, $p = 0.032$.

9.11 Why is a confidence interval more useful than a single-sample *t* test?

9.12 What is the appropriate effect size for a single-sample *t* test?

9.13 For a single-sample *t* test, how is a Cohen's *d* of 0.5 interpreted, according to Cohen's conventions?

9.14 What is replication and why is it important for behavioral science research?

9.15 If an effort to replicate a study fails, what are two things that the failure could indicate about the original study?

Calculating the Statistics

9.16 We use formulas to describe calculations. Find the error in each of the following formulas. Explain why each is incorrect and provide a correction.

   a. $s_M = \dfrac{s}{\sqrt{N-1}}$

   b. $t = \dfrac{(M - \mu_M)}{\sigma_M}$

9.17 For the data 93, 97, 91, 88, 103, 94, 97, calculate the standard deviation under the conditions in parts (a) and (b). Then, complete parts (c) and (d).

   a. For this sample

   b. As an estimate of the population

   c. Calculate the standard error for *t* using symbolic notation.

   d. Calculate the *t* statistic, assuming $\mu = 96$.

9.18 For the data 1.01, 0.99, 1.12, 1.27, 0.82, 1.04, calculate the standard deviation under the conditions in parts (a) and (b). Then, complete parts (c) and (d). (*Note:* You will have to carry some calculations out to the third decimal place to see the difference in calculations.)

   a. For the sample

   b. As an estimate of the population

   c. Calculate the standard error for *t* using symbolic notation.

   d. Calculate the *t* statistic, assuming $\mu = 0.96$.

9.19 Identify the critical *t* value in each of the following circumstances:

   a. One-tailed test, $df = 73$, alpha level of 0.10

   b. Two-tailed test, $df = 108$, alpha level of 0.05

   c. One-tailed test, $df = 38$, alpha level of 0.01

9.20 Calculate degrees of freedom and identify the critical *t* value for a single-sample *t* test in each of the following circumstances:

   a. Two-tailed test, $N = 8$, alpha level of 0.10

   b. One-tailed test, $N = 42$, alpha level of 0.05

   c. Two-tailed test, $N = 89$, alpha level of 0.01

9.21 Identify the critical *t* values for each of the following tests:

   a. A single-sample *t* test examining scores for 26 participants to see if there is any difference compared to the population, using an alpha level of 0.05

   b. A one-tailed, single-sample *t* test performed on scores on the Marital Satisfaction Inventory for 18 people who went through marriage counseling, as compared to the population of people who had not been through marital counseling, using an alpha level of 0.01

   c. A two-tailed, single-sample *t* test, using an alpha level of 0.05, with 34 degrees of freedom

9.22 Assume we know the following for a two-tailed, single-sample *t* test, at an alpha level of 0.05: $\mu = 44.3$, $N = 114$, $M = 43$, $s = 5.9$.

   a. Calculate the *t* statistic.

   b. Calculate a 95% confidence interval.

   c. Calculate the effect size using Cohen's *d*.

9.23 Assume we know the following for a two-tailed, single-sample *t* test: $\mu = 7$, $N = 41$, $M = 8.5$, $s = 2.1$.

   a. Calculate the *t* statistic.

   b. Calculate a 99% confidence interval.

   c. Calculate the effect size using Cohen's *d*.

9.24 Using Cohen's conventions, interpret the effect sizes that you calculated in:

   a. Exercise 9.22c

   b. Exercise 9.23c

9.25 Identify the critical *t* values for each of the following tests:

   a. Researchers wanted to know if marriage counseling improved participants' marital satisfaction. Scores were collected on the Marital Satisfaction Inventory for 15 people after a 12-week marriage counseling program. Using an alpha level of 0.01, identify the critical *t* value(s) for this one-tailed single-sample *t* test.

   b. A sample of fourth graders ($N = 44$) participated in a new curriculum for multiplication. A single-sample *t* test (using an alpha level of 0.05) was conducted to see if there was a significant difference between the scores of the students who participated in the new curriculum compared to the scores of all the students attending the same school. Identify the critical *t* value(s) for this two-tailed single-sample *t* test.

9.26 Market researchers collected information on smartphone data usage for Uber drivers. They wondered if Uber drivers use a higher amount of smartphone data compared to all other taxi drivers. A total of 31 Uber drivers reported their monthly data usage. Using an alpha level of 0.10, identify the critical *t* value(s) for this one-tailed single-sample *t* test.

Applying the Concepts

9.27 **The relation between the *z* distribution and the *t* distributions:** For the hypothesis tests described in parts (a) through (c), identify what the critical *z* value would have been if there had been just one sample and we knew the mean and standard deviation of the population:

a. A single-sample *t* test examining scores for 26 participants to see if there is any difference compared to the population, using an alpha level of 0.05

b. A one-tailed, single-sample *t* test performed on scores on the Marital Satisfaction Inventory for 18 people who went through marriage counseling, using an alpha level of 0.01

c. A two-tailed, single-sample *t* test, using an alpha level of 0.05, with 34 degrees of freedom

9.28 ***t* statistics and standardized tests:** On its Web site, the Princeton Review claims that students who have taken its course improve their Graduate Record Examination (GRE) scores, on average, by 210 points (based on the old scoring system). (No other information is provided about this statistic.) Treating this average gain as a population mean, a researcher wonders whether the far cheaper technique of practicing for the GRE on one's own would lead to a different average gain. She randomly selects five students from the pool of students at her university who plan to take the GRE. The students take a practice test before and after 2 months of self-study. They reported (fictional) gains of 160, 240, 340, 70, and 250 points. (Note that many experts suggest that the results from self-study are similar to those from a structured course for students who have the self-discipline to study on their own. Regardless of the format, preparation has been convincingly demonstrated to lead to increased scores, on average.)

a. Using symbolic notation and formulas (where appropriate), determine the appropriate mean and standard error for the distribution to which we will compare this sample. Show all steps of your calculations.

b. Using symbolic notation and the formula, calculate the *t* statistic for this sample.

c. As an interested consumer, what critical questions would you want to ask about the statistic reported by the Princeton Review? List at least three questions.

9.29 **Single-sample *t* test, military training, and anger:** Bardwell, Ensign, and Mills (2005) assessed the moods of 60 male U.S. Marines following a month-long training exercise conducted in cold temperatures and at high altitudes. Negative moods, including fatigue and anger, increased substantially during the training and lasted up to 3 months after the training ended. Mean mood scores were compared to population norms for three groups: college men, adult men, and male psychiatric outpatients. Let's examine the anger scores for six Marines at the end of training; these scores are fictional, but their mean and standard deviation are very close to the actual descriptive statistics for the sample: 14, 12, 13, 12, 14, 15.

a. The population mean anger score for college men is 8.90. Conduct all six steps of a single-sample *t* test. Report the statistics as you would in a journal article.

b. Now calculate the test statistic to compare this sample mean to the population mean anger score for adult men ($M = 9.20$). You do not have to repeat all the steps from part (a), but conduct step 6 of hypothesis testing and report the statistics as you would in a journal article.

c. Now calculate the test statistic to compare this sample mean to the population mean anger score for male psychiatric outpatients ($M = 13.5$). Do not repeat all the steps from part (a), but conduct step 6 of hypothesis testing and report the statistics as you would in a journal article.

d. What can we conclude overall about Marines' moods following high-altitude, cold-weather training?

e. For any findings for which you rejected the null hypothesis, explain how replication with another set of Marines might help to determine whether these findings might be a Type I error.

9.30 ***t* tests and the cost of Levi's jeans and H&M dresses in Halifax:** Numbeo is a crowdsourced Web site that gathers data on cities and countries around the world (numbeo.com/cost-of-living). The data are searchable by city or country. For example, when we looked up Halifax, Canada, we discovered that a pair of jeans ("Levis 501 or similar") goes for an average of $55.23 (Numbeo, 2017). The range was $40 to $70. And a summer dress from somewhere like Zara or H&M goes for an average of $42.37, with a range of $30 to $50. Numbeo also tells us that its Halifax data are based on contributions from 147 different people.

a. Let's say that Levi Strauss & Co. agreed to tell you the mean price (in Canadian dollars) of Levi's 501 jeans around the world. If you wanted to test whether Levi's 501 jeans in Halifax cost a different amount from the world price, what hypothesis test would you use? Explain your answer.

b. What additional information would you need to conduct the hypothesis test that you identified in part (a)?

c. Thinking back to Chapter 5, what kind of sample is this? What concerns might you have about this kind of a sample?

d. Numbeo doesn't tell us how many of the 147 contributors answered each of these questions. Why might the sample be even smaller than 147 for the average cost of summer dresses?

9.31 Cheating and a single-sample *t* test: Participants in a study (Chou, 2015) aimed at understanding cheating behaviors were asked to flip a coin 20 times and report—on the honor system—how many heads they received. The more heads, the more entries they would receive for a raffle for money. The catch? Some of them were randomly assigned to sign their name in ink on paper—old-school. Others were randomly assigned to check a box or type their name. Does signing your name make you more honest? If participants did not cheat, the probability of getting heads would be 50%, the population mean. The researchers reported that "a one-sample *t*-test . . . revealed that those who signed electronically reported getting significantly more heads than the statistical average ($M = 56.17\%$, $SD = 16.12$), $t(207) = 5.52$, $p < 0.001$)" but that participants who signed on paper in ink did not exhibit a significant effect "($M = 51.61\%$, $SD = 22.77$; $t(61) = 0.55$, $p = 0.57$)."

a. What does the number 207 indicate about the number of people in this particular sample?

b. What does the number 16.12 tell us about this particular distribution?

c. These findings do not give us any information about the effect size. Why would we want to know the value of Cohen's *d*?

d. Explain this finding in your own words.

9.32 Cultural change and replication: Psychologist Patricia Greenfield (2017) points out that failures to replicate do not necessarily indicate that the initial findings were wrong. She explains: "Data on the connection between social change and behavioral change point to a new role for 'replication': not to show that results can be duplicated, but to reveal behavioral effects of sociodemographic and cultural change in the intervening years between original and replicated procedure." Explain what she means in your own words.

9.33 A single-sample *t* test and Victoria's Secret perfume as an insect repellent: Biology researchers examined the mosquito-repelling effects of a control (no scent), insect repellents that contain DEET, natural insect repellents, and several beauty products (Rodriguez, Drake, Price, Hammond, & Hansen, 2015). In the control condition, on average, 61% of a swarm of mosquitoes chose to enter a chamber with a hand in it. For the purposes of this exercise, we'll treat this as the population mean. When the hand was sprayed with a high concentration of Victoria's Secret Bombshell perfume, only 17% of mosquitoes entered the chamber on average. The standard deviation for the sample of five perfumed hands was 12.052. (Interestingly, the perfume was almost as effective as bug spray with DEET; for example, Cutter Skinsations had a mean of 11%. The perfume worked better than Cutter's natural bug spray, which had a mean of 57% and better than the bug spray based on Avon's Skin So Soft lotion, a long-heralded home remedy, which had a mean of 48%.)

a. Explain why a single-sample *t* test is the appropriate hypothesis test to examine the effect of the perfume against the control.

b. Conduct all six steps of hypothesis testing for the effect of the perfume against the control.

c. Calculate the effect size for this hypothesis test. According to Cohen's conventions, how large is this effect?

d. Calculate the confidence interval for the sample mean for the perfume.

e. Explain how the confidence interval gives us the same information as the hypothesis test.

f. If you rejected the null hypothesis, how might replication help to determine whether these findings might be a Type I error?

g. If researchers attempted to replicate this study in a different laboratory in a different part of the world and failed to replicate it, explain why, other than a Type I error, this failure might have occurred.

Putting It All Together

9.34 Paid days off and the single-sample *t* test: The number of paid days off (e.g., vacation, sick leave) taken by eight employees at a small local business is compared to the national average. You are hired as a consultant by the new business owner to help her determine how many paid days off she should provide. In general, she wants to set some standard for her employees and for herself. Let's assume your search on the Internet for data on paid days off leaves you with the impression that the national average is 15 days. The data for the eight local employees during the last fiscal year are 10, 11, 8, 14, 13, 12, 12, and 27 days.

a. Write hypotheses for your research.

b. Which type of test would be appropriate to analyze these data so as to answer your question?

c. Before doing any computations, do you have any concerns about this research? Are there any questions you might like to ask about the data you have been given?

d. Calculate the appropriate *t* statistic. Show all of your work in detail.

e. Draw a statistical conclusion for this business owner.

f. Calculate the confidence interval.

g. Calculate and interpret the effect size.

h. Consider all the results you have calculated. How would you summarize the situation for this business owner? Identify the limitations of your analyses and discuss the difficulties of making comparisons between populations and samples. Make reference to the assumptions of the statistical test in your answer.

i. After further investigation, you discover that one of the data points, 27 days, was actually the owner's number of paid days off. Calculate the *t* statistic and draw a statistical conclusion, adapting for this new information by deleting that value. What changed in the re-analysis of the data?

j. Calculate and interpret the effect size, adapting for this new information by deleting the outlier of 27 days. What changed in the reanalysis of the data?

9.35 Death row and the single-sample *t* test: The Florida Department of Corrections publishes an online death row fact sheet. It reports the average time on death row prior to execution as 11.72 years but provides no standard deviation. This mean is a parameter because

it is calculated from the entire population of executed prisoners in Florida. Did the time spent on death row change over time? According to the execution list linked to the same Web site, the six prisoners executed in Florida during the years 2003, 2004, and 2005 spent 25.62, 13.09, 8.74, 17.63, 2.80, and 4.42 years on death row, respectively. (All were men, although Aileen Wuornos, the serial killer portrayed by Charlize Theron in the 2003 film *Monster*, was among the three prisoners executed by the state of Florida in 2002; Wuornos spent 10.69 years on death row.)

a. Using symbolic notation and formulas (where appropriate), determine the appropriate mean and standard error for the distribution of means. Show all steps of your calculations.

b. Using symbolic notation and the formula, calculate the *t* statistic for time spent on death row for the sample of executed prisoners.

c. The execution list provides data on all prisoners executed since the death penalty was reinstated in Florida in 1976. Included for each prisoner are the name, race, gender, date of birth, date of offense, date sentenced, date arrived on death row, date of execution, number of warrants, and years on death row. State at least one hypothesis, other than year of execution, that could be examined using a *t* distribution and the comparison mean of 11.72 years on death row. Be specific about your hypothesis (and if you are interested, you can search for the data online).

d. What additional information would you need to calculate a *z* score for the length of time Aileen Wuornos spent on death row?

e. Write hypotheses to address the question "Did the time spent on death row change over time?"

f. Using these data as "over time" and the mean of 11.72 years as the comparison, answer the question in part (e) based on the *t* statistic calculated in part (b), using alpha of 0.05.

g. Calculate the confidence interval for this statistic based on the data presented.

h. What conclusion would you make about the hypotheses based on this confidence interval? What can you say about the size of this confidence interval?

i. Calculate the effect size using Cohen's *d*.

j. Evaluate the size of this effect.

LaunchPad
macmillan learning

Visit LaunchPad to access the e-book and to
test your knowledge with LearningCurve.

TERMS

t statistic (p. 258)   degrees of freedom (p. 260)

single–sample *t* test (p. 260)   replication (p. 268)

FORMULAS

$$s = \sqrt{\frac{\Sigma(X - M)^2}{(N - 1)}} \quad \text{(p. 256)}$$

$$df = N - 1 \quad \text{(p. 260)}$$

$$M_{lower} = -t(s_M) + M_{sample} \quad \text{(p. 266)}$$

$$s_M = \frac{s}{\sqrt{N}} \quad \text{(p. 258)}$$

$$M_{upper} = t(s_M) + M_{sample} \quad \text{(p. 266)}$$

$$t = \frac{(M - \mu_M)}{s_M} \quad \text{(p. 258)}$$

$$\text{Cohen's } d = \frac{(M - \mu)}{s} \quad \text{(p. 267)}$$

SYMBOLS

t (p. 254) s_M (p. 258) df (p. 260)

The Paired-Samples *t* Test

BEFORE YOU GO ON

- **You should know how to conduct a
  single-sample *t* test (Chapter 9).**

- **You should know how to determine
  a confidence interval for a single-
  sample *t* test (Chapter 9).**

- **You should understand the concept
  of effect size and know how to
  calculate Cohen's *d* for a single-
  sample *t* test (Chapter 9).**

Holiday Weight Gain and Two-Group Studies Two-group studies (using before-and-after designs) indicate that the average holiday weight gain by university students is less than many people believe—only about 0.5 kilogram or 1 pound.

In many parts of the world, the winter holiday season is a time when family food traditions take center stage. Popular wisdom suggests that during this season, many people put on about 2 to 3 kilograms, or 5 to 7 pounds. But before-and-after studies suggest a weight gain of just over 0.5 kilogram or 1 pound (Díaz-Zavala et al., 2017; Hull, Radley, Dinger, & Fields, 2006; Roberts & Mayer, 2000). A small weight gain over the holidays might not seem so bad, but weight gained over the holidays tends to stay (Yanovski et al., 2000).

The fact that researchers used two groups in their study—students before the holidays and students after the holidays—is important for this chapter. With a *t* distribution, we can compare one sample to a population when we don't know all the details about the parameters, as we did in Chapter 9, and we can compare two samples to each other.

There are two ways to compare two samples: by using a within-groups design (as when the same people are weighed before and after the holidays) or by using a between-groups design (as when different people are in the preholiday sample than those in the postholiday sample). For a within-groups design, we use a paired-samples *t* test. The steps for a paired-samples *t* test are similar to those for a single-sample *t* test, which we learned about in Chapter 9. (For a between-groups design, we use an independent-samples *t* test, which we will learn about in Chapter 11.)

The Paired-Samples *t* Test

As we learned in the chapter opening, researchers found that weight gain over the holidays is far less than what folk wisdom had suggested. Guess what? The dreaded "freshman 15," which refers to a supposed gain of 15 pounds or about 7 kilograms in the first year living away at university, also appears to be a myth. One study found that male university students gained an average of 3.5 pounds (about 1.5 kilograms) between the beginning of the fall semester and November, and female students gained an average of 4.0 pounds (close to 2 kilograms) (Holm-Denoma, Joiner, Vohs, & Heatherton, 2008). We can use the paired-samples *t* test to make before-and-after comparisons.

● The **paired-samples *t* test** is used to compare two means for a within-groups design, a situation in which every participant is in both samples; also called a *dependent-samples* t *test*.

*The **paired-samples t test** (also called the *dependent-samples* t *test*) is used to compare two means for a within-groups design, a situation in which every participant is in both samples.* The paired-samples *t* test can be used to analyze the data from many studies. For example, if a participant is in both conditions (such as a memory task after ingesting a caffeinated beverage and again after ingesting a non-caffeinated beverage), then her score in one depends on her score in the other.

The steps for the paired-samples *t* test are almost the same as those for the single-sample *t* test. The major difference in the paired-samples *t* test is that we must first create difference scores for every participant. Because we'll be working with difference scores, we need to learn about a new distribution—a distribution of the means of these difference scores, or a distribution of *mean differences.*

Distributions of Mean Differences

We already learned about a distribution of scores and a distribution of means. Now we need to develop a distribution of *mean differences* for the preholiday and postholiday weight data. The goal is to establish a distribution that specifies the null hypothesis for a within-groups design.

Imagine that many university students' weights were measured before and after the winter holidays and written on individual cards. We begin by gathering data from a sample of three people from among this population of many university students. There are two cards for each person in the population, on which two weights are listed—one before the holidays and one after the holidays. We have one pair of cards for each student in the population (which is why one name for this test is the *paired-samples* t *test*). Let's walk through the steps to create a distribution of mean differences.

Step 1: Randomly choose three pairs of cards, replacing each pair of cards before randomly selecting the next.

Step 2: For each pair, calculate a difference score by subtracting the first weight from the second weight.

Step 3: Calculate the mean of the differences in weights for these three people. Then complete these three steps again. Randomly choose another three people from the population of many university students, calculate their difference scores, and calculate the mean of the three difference scores. And then complete these three steps again, and again, and again.

Let's walk through these steps once again, using an example.

Step 1: We randomly select one pair of cards and find that the first student weighed 140 pounds before the holidays and 144 pounds after the holidays. We replace those cards and randomly select another pair; the second student had before and after scores of 126 and 124, respectively. We replace those cards and randomly select another pair; the third student had before and after scores of 168 and 168, respectively.

Step 2: For the first student, the difference between weights, subtracting the before score from the after score, is $144 - 140 = 4$. She gained 4 pounds. For the second student, the difference between weights is $124 - 126 = -2$. He lost 2 pounds. For the third student, the difference between weights is $168 - 168 = 0$. Her weight did not change.

Step 3: The mean of these three difference scores $(4, -2, 0)$ is 0.667. The mean change in weight is a gain of 0.667 pound.

We would then choose three more students and calculate the mean of their difference scores. Eventually, we would have many mean differences to plot on a curve of mean differences—some positive, some negative, and some right at 0.

But this would just be the beginning of what this distribution of mean differences would look like. If we were to calculate the whole distribution of mean differences, then we would do this an uncountable number of times. When the authors of this book calculated 30 mean differences for pairs of weights, we got the distribution in Figure 10-1. If no mean difference is found when comparing weights from before

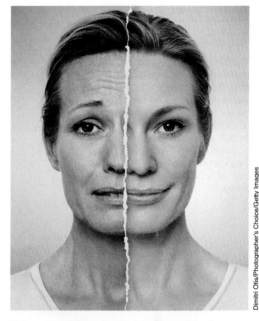

Before and After Don't be fooled by one dramatic before-and-after photo or testimonial. Before you start a potentially dangerous diet or have an expensive cosmetic procedure, ask for the results of an independently conducted paired-samples *t* test.

Dimitri Otis/Photographer's Choice/Getty Images

Creating a Distribution of Mean Differences

This distribution is one of many that could be created by pulling 30 mean differences—the average of three differences between pairs of weights, pulled one at a time from a population of pairs of weights—one preholiday and one postholiday. The population used here is one based on the null hypothesis—that there is no average difference in weight from before the holidays to after the holidays.

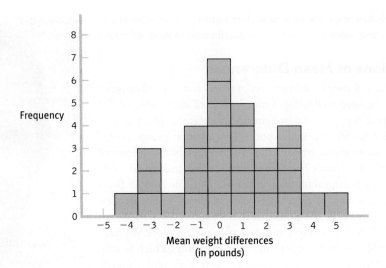

Mean weight differences (in pounds)

and after the holidays, as with the data we used to create Figure 10-1, the distribution would center on 0. According to the null hypothesis, we would expect no mean difference in weight—or a mean difference of 0—from before the holidays to after the holidays.

The Six Steps of the Paired-Samples *t* Test

In a paired-samples *t* test, each participant has two scores—one in each condition. When we conduct a paired-samples *t* test, we write the pairs of scores in two columns, side by side next to the same participant. We then subtract each score in one column from its paired score in the other column to create difference scores. Ideally, a positive difference score indicates an increase, and a negative difference score indicates a decrease. Typically, we subtract the first score from the second so that the difference scores match this logic. We will now walk through the six steps of hypothesis testing for the paired-samples *t* test.

EXAMPLE 10.1

News reports about the mental health of people who commit violent acts can contribute to widespread beliefs that people suffering from a severe mental illness such as schizophrenia tend to be violent (Pescosolido et al., 2010). Psychology researchers Ginny Chan and Philip Yanos (2018) hypothesized that when mental illness is suggested as the cause of a violent act, people pay particular attention to that suggestion and its importance even inflates over time. When no cause is indicated in a news report, we draw on our existing beliefs, which often include the stereotype that people with mental illnesses are violent.

In Chan and Yanos's study, participants read a news report about a deadly assault that either did or did not mention that the perpetrator suffered from schizophrenia. They asked participants right after reading the article to write down what they recalled about the story, and gave participants a score between 0 and 1, with 1 suggesting a higher probability that mental illness was a *cause* of the violence. (Remember, there was no stated link between schizophrenia and violence, even for those who read the version of the article that mentioned schizophrenia.) A week later, participants again wrote their recollections and received scores between 0 and 1.

Here are five participants' fictional data, which reflect similar means to those reported by the researchers, as well as a similar eventual outcome for the hypothesis test. The first person had a score of 0.3 right after reading the article and 0.5 a week later. For the second person, those scores were 0.2 and 0.4; for the third person, 0.1 and 0.5; for the fourth person, 0.1 and 0.3; and for the fifth person, 0.3 and 0.3.

> **STEP 1: Identify the populations, distribution, and assumptions.**

The paired-samples *t* test is like the single-sample *t* test in that we analyze a single sample of scores. For the paired-samples *t* test, however, we analyze difference scores. For the paired-samples *t* test, one population is reflected by each condition, but the comparison distribution is a *distribution of mean difference scores* (rather than a distribution of means). The comparison distribution is based on the null hypothesis that posits no mean difference. So the mean of the comparison distribution is 0. For the paired-samples *t* test, the three assumptions are the same as for the single-sample *t* test.

Summary: Population 1: People recalling details of the news article just after reading it. Population 2: People recalling details of the news article one week after reading it.

Mental illness and mass murder Researchers Ginny Chan and Philip Yanos found that when news reports of violence mentioned the perpetrator's mental illness, readers viewed the mental illness as a main cause of the crime, discounting the many other possible factors (2018). One alleged mass shooter was arrested in 2018 for the murder of four people in a Nashville, Tennessee, Waffle House restaurant. Did readers pay particular attention to reports of a diagnosis of schizophrenia in news reports about his horrific crime?

Allen Creative/Steve Allen/Alamy Stock Photo

The comparison distribution is a distribution of mean difference scores based on the null hypothesis. The hypothesis test is a paired-samples *t* test because there are two samples of scores and a within-groups design.

This study meets one of the three assumptions and may meet the other two: (1) The dependent variable is time, which is scale. (2) The participants were not randomly selected, however, so we must be cautious with respect to generalizing the findings. (In this case, some of the participants were university students and some were recruited via the crowdsourcing tool MTurk. In both cases, these were volunteer samples.) (3) We do not know whether the population is normally distributed, and there are not at least 30 participants; however, the data from this sample do not suggest a skewed distribution.

> **STEP 2: State the null and research hypotheses.**

This step is identical to that for the single-sample *t* test.

Summary: Null hypothesis: People who recall the details of a news article just after reading it will have the same mean level of belief that mental illness caused the violence as people who recall the details one week later—$H_0 : \mu_1 = \mu_2$. Research hypothesis: People who recall the details of a news article just after reading it will have a different mean level of belief that mental illness caused the violence as people who recall the details one week later—$H_1 : \mu_1 \neq \mu_2$.

> **STEP 3: Determine the characteristics of the comparison distribution.**

This step is similar to that for the single-sample *t* test. We determine the appropriate mean and standard error of the comparison distribution—the distribution based on the null hypothesis. With the paired-samples *t* test, however, there is a sample of difference scores and a comparison distribution of mean differences (instead of a sample of individual scores and a comparison distribution of means). According to the null hypothesis, there is no difference. So the mean of the comparison distribution is always 0, as long as the null hypothesis posits no difference.

For the paired-samples *t* test, standard error is calculated exactly as it is calculated for the single-sample *t* test, except we use the difference scores rather than the scores in each condition. To get the difference scores in the current example, we want to know what happens when we go from the initial condition (immediately after reading the article) to the second condition (one week after reading the article), so we subtract the first score from the second score. This means that a positive difference indicates an increase in belief that mental illness was a cause of the crime. (The test statistic will be the same if we reverse the order in which we subtract, but the sign will change.)

Summary: $\mu_M = 0$; $s_M = 0.063$

Calculations: (Notice that we crossed out the original scores once we created the column of difference scores. We did this to remind ourselves that all remaining calculations involve the differences scores, not the original scores.)

X	Y	Difference	Difference − Mean Difference	Squared Deviation
0.3	0.5	0.2	0	0
0.2	0.4	0.2	0	0
0.1	0.5	0.4	0.2	0.04
0.1	0.3	0.2	0	0
0.3	0.3	0.0	−0.2	0.04

The mean of the difference scores is calculated by adding up the differences for each participant and dividing by the sample size:

$$M_{difference} = 0.2$$

The numerator is the sum of squares, SS (which we learned about in Chapter 4):

$$SS = 0 + 0 + 0.04 + 0 + 0.04 = 0.08$$

The standard deviation, s, is:

$$s = \sqrt{\frac{0.08}{(5-1)}} = \sqrt{0.02} = 0.141$$

The standard error, s_M, is:

$$s_M = \frac{0.141}{\sqrt{5}} = 0.063$$

STEP 4: Determine the critical values, or cutoffs.

This step is the same as that for the single-sample t test, except that the degrees of freedom is the number of *participants* (not the number of scores) minus 1.
Summary: $df = N - 1 = 5 - 1 = 4$

The critical values, based on a two-tailed test and an alpha level of 0.05, are −2.776 and 2.776, as seen in the curve in Figure 10-2.

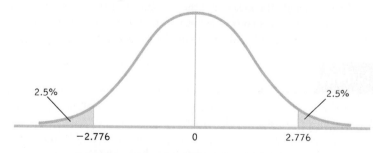

2.5%   2.5%

−2.776   0   2.776

FIGURE 10-2

Determining Cutoffs for a Paired-Samples *t* Test

We typically determine critical values in terms of *t* statistics rather than means of raw scores so that we can easily determine whether the test statistic is beyond one of the cutoffs.

STEP 5: Calculate the test statistic.

This step is identical to that for the single-sample t test, except that we use means of difference scores instead of means of individual scores. We subtract the mean difference score according to the null hypothesis, 0, from the mean difference score calculated for the sample. We then divide by standard error.

Summary: $t = \dfrac{(0.2 - 0)}{0.063} = 3.17$

STEP 6: Make a decision.

This step is identical to that for the single-sample *t* test.

Summary: Reject the null hypothesis. When we examine the means ($M_X = 0.2$; $M_Y = 0.4$), it appears that, on average, people's belief that mental illness caused the violence is higher, on average, a week after reading a news article about a deadly attack than just after reading the article, as shown by the curve in Figure 10-3. As the researchers concluded, "After a week of delay, participants reported more responses consistent with negative stereotypes" about people with mental illnesses (Chan & Yanos, 2018, p. 261).

FIGURE 10-3

Making a Decision

To decide whether to reject the null hypothesis, we compare the test statistic to the critical values. In this figure, the test statistic, 3.17, is beyond the cutoff of −2.776, so we can reject the null hypothesis.

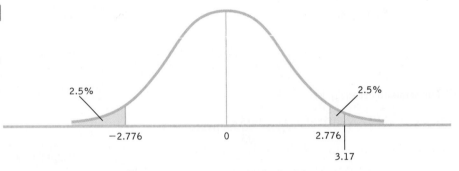

The statistics, as reported in a journal article, follow the same APA format as for a single-sample *t* test. (*Note:* Unless we use software, we can only indicate whether the *p* value is less than or greater than the cutoff alpha level of 0.05.) In the current example, the statistics would read:

$$t(4) = 3.17, \ p < 0.05$$

We also include the means and the standard deviations for the two samples. We calculated the means in step 6 of hypothesis testing, but we would also have to calculate the standard deviations for the two samples to report them. ●

CHECK YOUR LEARNING

Reviewing the Concepts > The paired-samples *t* test is used when we have data for all participants under two conditions—a within-groups design.

> In the paired-samples *t* test, we calculate a difference score for every individual in the study. The statistic is calculated using those difference scores.

> We use the same six steps of hypothesis testing that we used with the *z* test and with the single-sample *t* test.

| Clarifying the Concepts | **10-1** | How do we conduct a paired-samples *t* test? |
| | **10-2** | Explain what an individual difference score is, as it is used in a paired-samples *t* test. |

| Calculating the Statistics | **10-3** | Below are energy-level data (on a scale of 1 to 7, where 1 = feeling of no energy and 7 = feeling of high energy) for five students before and after lunch. Calculate the mean difference for these people so that loss of energy is a negative value. Assume you are testing the hypothesis that students go into what we call "food comas" after eating, versus lunch giving them added energy. |

Before lunch	After lunch
6	3
5	2
4	6
5	4
7	5

| Applying the Concepts | **10-4** | Using the energy-level data presented in Check Your Learning 10-3, test the hypothesis that students have different energy levels before and after lunch. Perform the six steps of hypothesis testing for a two-tailed paired-samples *t* test. |
| Solutions to these Check Your Learning questions can be found in Appendix D. | | |

Beyond Hypothesis Testing

Behavioral science organizations such as the APA encourage the inclusion of confidence intervals and effect sizes (as with the *z* test and the single-sample *t* test) for paired-samples *t* tests. We'll calculate both the confidence interval and the effect size for the example of stereotyping, mental illness, and violence.

Calculating a Confidence Interval for a Paired-Samples *t* Test

Let's start by determining the confidence interval for the mental health stereotyping example.

EXAMPLE 10.2

First, let's recap the information we need. The population mean difference according to the null hypothesis was 0, and we used the sample to estimate the population standard deviation to be 0.141 and the standard error to be 0.063. The five participants in the study sample had a mean difference of 0.2. We will calculate the 95% confidence interval around the sample mean difference of 0.2.

> **STEP 1: Draw a picture of a *t* distribution that includes the confidence interval.**

FIGURE 10-4

A 95% Confidence Interval for a Paired-Samples *t* Test, Part I

We start the confidence interval for a distribution of mean differences by drawing a curve with the sample mean difference, 0.2, in the center.

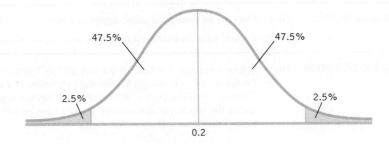

FIGURE 10-4

A 95% Confidence Interval for a Paired-Samples *t* Test, Part I

We start the confidence interval for a distribution of mean differences by drawing a curve with the sample mean difference, 0.2, in the center.

We draw a normal curve (Figure 10-4) that has the *sample* mean difference, 0.2, at its center instead of the *population* mean difference, 0.

> **STEP 2: Indicate the bounds of the confidence interval on the drawing.**

As before, 47.5% of the values fall on each side of the mean between the mean and the cutoff, and 2.5% fall in each tail.

> **STEP 3: Add the critical *t* statistics to the curve.**

For a two-tailed test with an alpha level of 0.05 and 4 *df*, the critical values are −2.776 and 2.776, as seen in Figure 10-5.

FIGURE 10-5

A 95% Confidence Interval for a Paired-Samples *t* Test, Part II

The next step in calculating a confidence interval for mean differences is identifying the *t* statistics that indicate each end of the interval. Because the curve is symmetric, the *t* statistics have the same magnitude—one is negative, −2.776, and one is positive, 2.776.

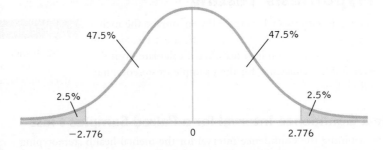

MASTERING THE FORMULA

10-1: The formula for the lower bound of a confidence interval for a paired-samples *t* test is: $M_{lower} = -t(s_M) + M_{sample}$. The formula for the upper bound of a confidence interval for a paired-samples *t* test is: $M_{upper} = t(s_M) + M_{sample}$. These are the same as for a single-sample *t* test, but remember that the means and standard errors are calculated from differences between pairs of scores, not individual scores.

> **STEP 4: Convert the critical *t* statistics back into raw mean differences.**

As we do with other confidence intervals, we use the sample mean difference (0.2) in the calculations and the standard error (0.063) as the measure of spread. We use the same formulas as for the single-sample *t* test, recalling that these means and standard errors are calculated from differences between two scores for each participant. We add these raw mean differences to the curve in Figure 10-6.

$$M_{lower} = -t(s_M) + M_{sample} = -2.776(0.063) + (0.2) = 0.03$$

$$M_{upper} = t(s_M) + M_{sample} = 2.776(0.063) + (0.2) = 0.37$$

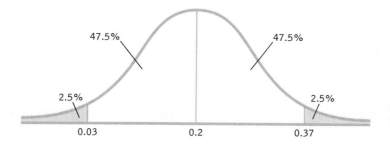

FIGURE 10-6

A 95% Confidence Interval for a Paired-Samples *t* Test, Part III

The final step in calculating a confidence interval for mean differences is converting the *t* statistics that indicate each end of the interval to raw mean differences, 0.03 and 0.37.

The 95% confidence interval, reported in brackets as is typical, is [0.03, 0.37].

> **STEP 5:** Verify that the confidence interval makes sense.

The sample mean difference should fall exactly in the middle of the two ends of the interval.

$$0.2 - 0.03 = 0.17 \text{ and } 0.2 - 0.37 = -0.17$$

We have a match. The confidence interval ranges from 0.17 below the sample mean difference to 0.17 above the sample mean difference. If we were to sample five people from the same population over and over, the 95% confidence interval would include the population mean 95% of the time. Note that the population mean difference according to the null hypothesis, 0, does not fall within this interval. This means it is not plausible that the difference between people's beliefs about the cause of the violence just after reading the article and people's beliefs one week later is 0.

As with other hypothesis tests, the conclusions from both the paired-samples *t* test and the confidence interval are the same, but the confidence interval gives us more information—an interval estimate, not just a point estimate. ●

Calculating Effect Size for a Paired-Samples *t* Test

As with a *z* test, we can calculate the effect size (Cohen's *d*) for a paired-samples *t* test.

EXAMPLE 10.3

Let's calculate the effect size for the mental health stereotyping study. Again, we simply use the formula for the *t* statistic, substituting s for s_M (and μ for μ_M, even though these means are always the same). In this case, we use 0.141 instead of 0.063 in the denominator. Cohen's *d* is now based on the spread of the distribution of individual differences between scores, rather than the distribution of mean differences.

$$\text{Cohen's } d = \frac{(M - \mu)}{s} = \frac{(0.2 - 0)}{0.141} = 1.42$$

The effect size, $d = 1.42$, tells us that the sample mean difference and the population mean difference are 1.42 standard deviations apart. This is a large effect. (In the original study with a much larger sample size, the effect size was 0.62, a medium effect.) Recall

MASTERING THE FORMULA

10-2: The formula for Cohen's *d* for a paired-samples *t* statistic is:

$$\text{Cohen's } d = \frac{(M - \mu)}{s}$$

It is the same formula as for the single-sample *t* statistic, except that the mean and standard deviation are for difference scores rather than individual scores.

that the sign is not relevant when interpreting the size of an effect: −1.42 and 1.42 are equivalent effect sizes. We can add the effect size when we report the statistics as follows: $t(4) = 3.17$, $p < 0.05$, $d = 1.42$. ●

| Data Ethics | Avoiding Order Effects Through Counterbalancing |

● **Order effects** refer to how a participant's behavior changes when the dependent variable is presented for a second time, sometimes called *practice effects*.

● **Counterbalancing** minimizes order effects by varying the order of presentation of different levels of the independent variable from one participant to the next.

Ethical researchers are attuned to the particular problems that can occur with a within-groups design (such as the paired-samples *t* test). Specifically, a within-groups design invites a particular kind of confounding variable into a study: order effects. *Order effects refer to how a participant's behavior changes when the dependent variable is presented for a second time.* (They're sometimes called *practice effects.*) Let's consider a study that could use a paired-samples *t* test. Behavioral scientists at Microsoft studied how 15 volunteers performed on a set of tasks under two conditions—while using a 15-inch computer monitor and while using a 42-inch monitor, the latter of which allows the user to have multiple programs in view at the same time (Czerwinski et al., 2003). Researchers recorded the time it took participants to complete the series of tasks under each condition. Can you spot the confound? Participants were likely to get faster the second time they completed the tasks. Their responses the second time around would be influenced by the practice of already having completed the tasks once.

Fortunately, there are fair ways to limit the confounding influence of order effects. *Counterbalancing minimizes order effects by varying the order of presentation of different levels of the independent variable from one participant to the next.* For example, half of the participants could be randomly assigned to complete the tasks on the 15-inch monitor

Order Effects You observe that your friends felt exhilarated after riding a roller coaster without loops (which turn riders upside-down), then felt nauseated after riding a roller coaster with loops. You conclude that loops lead to nausea. The problem is that there could be an order effect. Perhaps your friends would have felt nauseated after the second roller coaster ride whether or not it had loops. Counterbalancing would avoid this confound. Half of your friends would be randomly assigned to ride the one without loops first, then the one with loops; half of them would be randomly assigned to ride the one with loops first, then the one without loops. (Your second author gets queasy just thinking about roller coasters and would not participate in this experiment no matter what experimental controls were in place! But your first author would volunteer!)

first, then again on the 42-inch monitor. The other half could be randomly assigned to complete the tasks on the 42-inch monitor first, then again on the 15-inch monitor. In this case, any practice effect would be washed out by varying the order of the monitors.

There are other ways to reduce order effects. In the computer monitor example, we might decide to use a different set of tasks in each testing condition. The order in which the two different sets of tasks are given could be counterbalanced along with the order in which participants are assigned to the two different-sized monitors. Measures such as this can reduce order effects in within-groups research designs.

CHECK YOUR LEARNING

Reviewing the Concepts > We can calculate a confidence interval for a paired-samples *t* test. This provides us with an interval estimate rather than simply a point estimate. If 0 is *not* in the confidence interval, then it is not plausible that there is no difference between the sample and population mean differences.

> We also can calculate an effect size (Cohen's *d*) for a paired-samples *t* test.

> Order effects occur when participants' behavior is affected when a dependent variable is presented a second time.

> Order effects can be reduced through counterbalancing, a procedure in which the different levels of the independent variable are presented in different orders from one participant to the next.

Clarifying the Concepts **10-5** How does creating a confidence interval for a paired-samples *t* test give us the same information as hypothesis testing with a paired-samples *t* test?

10-6 How do we calculate Cohen's *d* for a paired-samples *t* test?

Calculating the Statistics **10-7** Assume that researchers asked five participants to rate their mood on a scale from 1 to 7 (1 being lowest, 7 being highest) before and after watching a funny video clip. The researchers reported that the average difference between the "before" mood score and the "after" mood score was $M = 1.0$, $s = 1.225$. They calculated a paired-samples *t* test, $t(4) = 1.13$, $p = 0.32$ and, using a two-tailed test with an alpha level of 0.05, failed to reject the null hypothesis.

a. Calculate the 95% confidence interval for this *t* test and describe how it results in the same conclusion as the hypothesis test.

b. Calculate and interpret Cohen's *d*.

Applying the Concepts **10-8** Using the energy-level data presented in Check Your Learning 10-3 and 10-4, let's go beyond hypothesis testing.

a. Calculate the 95% confidence interval and describe how it results in the same conclusion as the hypothesis test.

Solutions to these Check Your Learning questions can be found in Appendix D.

b. Calculate and interpret Cohen's *d*.

REVIEW OF CONCEPTS

LaunchPad
macmillan learning

Visit LaunchPad to access
the e-book and to test your
knowledge with LearningCurve.

The Paired-Samples *t* Test

We use a *paired-samples* t *test* when we have two samples and the same participants are in both samples; to conduct the test, we calculate a difference score for every individual in the study. The comparison distribution is a distribution of mean difference scores instead of the distribution of means that we used with a single-sample *t* test. Aside from the comparison distribution, the steps of hypothesis testing are similar to those for a single-sample *t* test.

Beyond Hypothesis Testing

As we can with a *z* test and a single-sample *t* test, we can calculate a confidence interval for a paired-samples *t* test. The confidence interval gives us an interval estimate rather than a point estimate. Its results match that of the hypothesis test. When we reject the null hypothesis, we know that the confidence interval will not include 0. We also can calculate an effect size (Cohen's *d*) for a paired-samples *t* test. This provides information about the size of the observed effect and can let us know if a statistically significant finding is likely to be practically important.

Paired-samples *t* tests are used when we compare two groups using a within-groups design, a situation in which we must be aware of order effects, also called practice effects. Order effects occur when participants' behavior changes when a dependent variable, such as a test or measure, is presented a second time. Researchers use counterbalancing to reduce order effects: They vary the order in which the different levels of the independent variable are presented from one participant to the next.

SPSS

For the paired-samples *t* test, let's use the data from Example 10.1 on news articles and stereotypes about violence and mental illness. Enter the data in two columns, with each participant having one score in the first column for his or her response immediately after reading and one score in the second column for his or her response one week later.

Select Analyze → Compare Means → Paired-Samples T Test. Choose the dependent variable under the first condition (immediate) by clicking it, then clicking the center arrow. Choose the dependent variable under the second condition (one_week) by clicking it, then clicking the center arrow.

"immediate" will now appear under the label "Variable 1," and "one_week" will now appear under the label "Variable 2." Then click "OK." The data and output are shown in the screenshot. Notice that the *t* statistic and confidence interval are very close to ours (3.17 and [0.03, 0.37]) except that the signs are different and there are slight differences due to rounding decisions. The difference in signs occurs because of the order in which one score was subtracted from the other score—that is, whether the score on the immediate response was subtracted from the score on the response one week later, or vice versa. The outcome is the same in either case. The *p* value is under "Sig. (2-tailed)" and is .034.

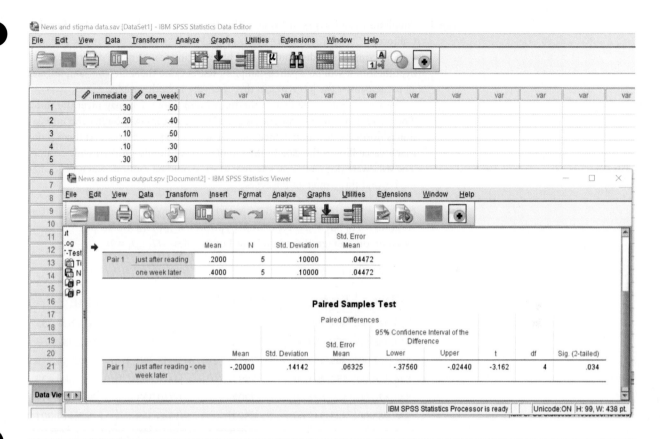

HOW IT WORKS

10.1 CONDUCTING A PAIRED-SAMPLES *t* TEST

Salary Wizard is an online tool that allows you to look up incomes for specific jobs for cities in the United States. We looked up the 25th percentile for income in U.S. dollars for six jobs in two cities: Boise, Idaho, and Los Angeles, California. The data are below.

	Boise	Los Angeles
Executive chef	$53,047.00	$62,490.00
Genetics counselor	$49,958.00	$58,850.00
Grants/proposal writer	$41,974.00	$49,445.00
Librarian	$44,366.00	$52,263.00
Public schoolteacher	$40,470.00	$47,674.00
Social worker (with bachelor's degree)	$36,963.00	$43,542.00

How can we conduct a paired-samples *t* test to determine whether income in one of these cities differs, on average, from income in the other? We'll use a two-tailed test and an alpha level of 0.05.

Step 1: Population 1: Job types in Boise, Idaho. Population 2: Job types in Los Angeles, California.

    The comparison distribution will be a distribution of mean differences. The hypothesis test will be a paired-samples t test because there are two samples, and all participants—the job types, in this case—are in both samples.

    This study meets the first of the three assumptions and may meet the third. The dependent variable, income, is scale. We do not know whether the population is normally distributed, there are not at least 30 participants, and there is not much variability in the data in the samples, so we should proceed with caution. The data were not randomly selected, so we should be cautious when generalizing beyond this sample of job types.

Step 2: Null hypothesis: Jobs in Boise pay the same, on average, as jobs in Los Angeles—$H_0 : \mu_1 = \mu_2$. Research hypothesis: Jobs in Boise pay different incomes, on average, than do jobs in Los Angeles—$H_1 : \mu_1 \neq \mu_2$.

Step 3: $\mu_M = \mu = 0; s_M = 438.919$

Boise	Los Angeles	Difference (D)	$(D - M_{difference})$	$(D - M_{difference})^2$
\$53,047.00	\$62,490.00	9443	1528.667	2,336,822.797
\$49,958.00	\$58,850.00	8892	977.667	955,832.763
\$41,974.00	\$49,445.00	7471	−443.333	196,544.149
\$44,366.00	\$52,263.00	7897	−17.333	300.433
\$40,470.00	\$47,674.00	7204	−710.333	504,572.971
\$36,963.00	\$43,542.00	6579	−1335.333	1,783,114.221

$M_{difference} = 7914.333$

$$SS = \Sigma(D - M_{difference})^2 = 5,777,187.334$$

$$s = \sqrt{\frac{\Sigma(D - M_{difference})^2}{(N-1)}} = \sqrt{\frac{5,777,187.334}{(6-1)}} = 1074.913$$

$$s_M = \frac{s}{\sqrt{N}} = \frac{1074.913}{\sqrt{6}} = \frac{1074.913}{2.449} = 438.919$$

Step 4: $df = N - 1 = 6 - 1 = 5$

    The critical values, based on 5 degrees of freedom, an alpha level of 0.05, and a two-tailed test, are −2.571 and 2.571.

Step 5: $t = \dfrac{(M_{difference} - \mu_{difference})}{s_M} = \dfrac{(7914.333 - 0)}{438.919} = 18.03$

Step 6: Reject the null hypothesis. It appears that jobs in Los Angeles pay more, on average, than do jobs in Boise.

    The statistics, as they would be presented in a journal article, are:

$$t(5) = 18.03, \; p < 0.05$$

10.2 CALCUATING THE CONFIDENCE INTERVAL FOR A PAIRED-SAMPLES *t* TEST

For the Salary Wizard example, given the sample mean difference, $M_{difference} = 7914.333$, and sample variance, $s = 1074.913$, we can start by calculating standard error:

$$s_M = \frac{s}{\sqrt{N}} = \frac{1074.913}{\sqrt{6}} = 438.919$$

We then find the *t* values that mark off the most extreme 0.025 in each tail and a *df* of 5, which are −2.571 and 2.571. We calculate the lower end of the interval as:

$$M_{lower} = -t(s_M) + M_{sample} = -2.571(438.919) + 7914.333 = 6785.872$$

We calculate the upper end of the interval as:

$$M_{upper} = t(s_M) + M_{sample} = 2.571(438.919) + 7914.333 = 9042.794$$

The 95% confidence interval is [6785.87, 9042.79].

10.3 CALCULATING EFFECT SIZE FOR A PAIRED-SAMPLES *t* TEST

How can we calculate effect size for the Salary Wizard data? The appropriate measure of effect size for a paired-samples *t* test is Cohen's *d*, which is calculated as:

$$\text{Cohen's } d = \frac{(M_{difference} - \mu_{difference})}{s} = \frac{7914.333 - 0}{1074.913} = 7.363$$

Based on Cohen's conventions, this is a very large effect size.

EXERCISES

The solutions to the odd-numbered exercises can be found in Appendix C.

Clarifying the Concepts

10.1 What do we mean when we say we have a distribution of mean differences?

10.2 When do we use a paired-samples *t* test?

10.3 Explain the distinction between the terms *independent samples* and *paired samples* as they relate to *t* tests.

10.4 How is a paired-samples *t* test similar to a single-sample *t* test?

10.5 How is a paired-samples *t* test different from a single-sample *t* test?

10.6 Why is the population mean almost always equal to 0 for the null hypothesis in the two-tailed, paired-samples *t* test?

10.7 If we calculate the confidence interval around the sample mean difference used for a paired-samples *t* test, and it includes the value of 0, what can we conclude?

10.8 If we calculate the confidence interval around the sample mean difference used for a paired-samples *t* test, and it does not include the value of 0, what can we conclude?

10.9 Why is a confidence interval more useful than a single-sample *t* test or a paired-samples *t* test?

10.10 What is the appropriate effect size for a paired-samples *t* test? How is the calculation different from the effect size for a single-sample *t* test?

10.11 What are order effects?

10.12 Identify and explain the technique for countering order effects using a within-groups research design.

10.13 Why might order effects lead a researcher to use a between-groups design rather than a within-groups design?

10.14 We introduced confounding variables (or confounds) in Chapter 1. Explain why order effects might be an example of a confound.

Calculating the Statistics

10.15 Identify critical *t* values for each of the following tests:

a. A one-tailed, paired-samples *t* test performed on before-and-after scores on the Marital Satisfaction Inventory for 18 people who went through marriage counseling, using an alpha level of 0.01.

b. A two-tailed, paired-samples *t* test performed on before-and-after scores on the Marital Satisfaction Inventory for 64 people who went through marriage counseling, using an alpha level of 0.05.

10.16 Assume 8 participants completed a mood scale before and after watching a funny video clip.

a. Identify the critical *t* value for a one-tailed, paired-samples *t* test with an alpha level of 0.01.

b. Identify the critical *t* values for a two-tailed, paired-samples *t* test with an alpha level of 0.01.

10.17 The following are scores for 8 students on two different exams.

Exam 1	Exam 2
92	84
67	75
95	97
82	87
73	68
59	63
90	88
72	78

a. Calculate the paired-samples *t* statistic for these exam scores.

b. Using a two-tailed test and an alpha level of 0.05, identify the critical *t* values and make a decision regarding the null hypothesis.

c. Assume you instead collected exam scores from 1000 students whose mean difference score and standard deviation were exactly the same as for these 8 students. Using a two-tailed test and an alpha level of 0.05, identify the critical *t* values and make a decision regarding the null hypothesis.

d. How did changing the sample size affect the decision regarding the null hypothesis?

10.18 The following are mood scores for 12 participants before and after watching a funny video clip (lower values indicate better mood).

Before	After	Before	After
7	2	4	2
5	4	7	3
5	3	4	1
7	5	4	1
6	5	5	3
7	4	4	3

a. Calculate the paired-samples *t* statistic for these mood scores.

b. Using a one-tailed hypothesis test that the video clip improves mood, and an alpha level of 0.05, identify the critical *t* values and make a decision regarding the null hypothesis.

c. Using a two-tailed hypothesis test with an alpha level of 0.05, identify the critical *t* values and make a decision regarding the null hypothesis.

10.19 Consider the following data:

Score 1	Score 2	Score 1	Score 2
45	62	15	26
34	56	51	56
22	40	28	33
45	48		

a. Calculate the paired-samples *t* statistic.

b. Calculate the 95% confidence interval.

c. Calculate the effect size for the mean difference.

10.20 Consider the following data.

Score 1	Score 2
23	16
30	12
28	25
30	27
14	6

a. Calculate the paired-samples *t* statistic.

b. Calculate the 95% confidence interval.

c. Calculate the effect size.

10.21 Assume we know the following for a paired-samples *t* test: $N = 13$, $M_{difference} = -0.77$, $s = 1.42$.

   a. Calculate the *t* statistic.

   b. Calculate a 95% confidence interval.

   c. Calculate the effect size using Cohen's *d*.

10.22 Assume we know the following for a paired-samples *t* test: $N = 32$, $M_{difference} = 1.75$, $s = 4.0$.

   a. Calculate the *t* statistic.

   b. Calculate a 95% confidence interval for a two-tailed test.

   c. Calculate the effect size using Cohen's *d*.

Applying the Concepts

10.23 **Brain exercises and a paired-samples *t* test:** Power-BrainRx, a Hong Kong–based for-profit company, promises to improve cognition. Its Web site lists testimonials, including one from a parent whose children "seemed to have better working memories, improved problem-solving ability like mathematics, more logical thinking, and better academic performance" following mental exercise training. There are numerous ads for companies like PowerBrainRx on the Internet and on late-night television, but there does not seem to be a lot of research examining the specific programs these companies are selling. How could you design a study for PowerBrainRx that would use a paired-samples *t* test to analyze the data?

10.24 ***t* tests and retail:** Many communities worldwide are lamenting the effects of so-called big box retailers (e.g., Walmart, Jysk) on their local economies, particularly on small, independently owned shops. Do these large stores affect the bottom lines of locally owned retailers? Imagine that you decide to test this premise. You assess earnings at 20 local stores for the month of October, a few months before a big box store opens. You then assess earnings the following October, correcting for inflation.

   a. What are the two populations?

   b. What is the comparison distribution? Explain.

   c. Which hypothesis test would you use? Explain.

   d. Check the assumptions for this hypothesis test.

   e. What is one flaw in drawing conclusions from this comparison over time?

   f. State the null and research hypotheses in both words and symbols.

10.25 **Paired-samples *t* tests, confidence intervals, and hockey goals:** Below are the numbers of goals scored by the leading scorers on the New Jersey Devils ice hockey team in the 2007–2008 and 2008–2009 seasons. On average, did the Devils play any differently in 2008–2009 than they did in 2007–2008?

Player	2007–2008	2008–2009
Elias	20	31
Zajac	14	20
Pandolfo	12	5
Langenbrunner	13	29
Gionta	22	20
Parise	32	45

   a. Conduct the six steps of hypothesis testing using a two-tailed test and an alpha level of 0.05.

   b. Report the test statistic in APA format.

   c. Calculate the confidence interval for the paired-samples *t* test you conducted in part (a). Compare the confidence interval to the results of the hypothesis test.

   d. Calculate the effect size for the mean difference between the 2007–2008 and 2008–2009 seasons.

10.26 **Paired-samples *t* test and graduate admissions:** Is it harder to get into graduate programs in psychology or in history? We randomly selected five institutions from among all U.S. institutions with graduate programs. The first number for each is the minimum grade-point average (GPA) for applicants to the psychology doctoral program, and the second is for applicants to the history doctoral program. These GPAs were posted on the Web site of the well-known university guide company Peterson's.

Wayne State University:	3.0, 2.75
University of Iowa:	3.0, 3.0
University of Nevada, Reno:	3.0, 2.75
George Washington University:	3.0, 3.0
University of Wyoming:	3.0, 3.0

   a. The participants are not people; explain why it is appropriate to use a paired-samples *t* test for this situation.

   b. Conduct all six steps of a paired-samples *t* test. Be sure to label all six steps.

c. Calculate the effect size and explain what this adds to your analysis.

d. Report the statistics as you would in a journal article.

10.27 Attitudes toward statistics and the paired-samples *t* test: A professor wanted to know if her students' attitudes toward statistics changed by the end of the course, so she asked them to fill out an "Attitudes Toward Statistics" scale at the beginning of the term and at the end of the term.

a. What kind of *t* test should she use to analyze the data?

b. If the average (mean) at the end of the class was higher than it was at the beginning, is that necessarily a statistically significant improvement?

c. Which situation makes it easier to declare that a certain mean difference is statistically significant: a class with 7 students or a class with 700 students? Explain your answer.

10.28 Paired-samples *t* tests, confidence intervals, and wedding-day weight loss: It seems that 14% of engaged women buy a wedding dress at least one size smaller than their current size. Why? Cornell researchers reported an alarming tendency for women who are engaged to sometimes attempt to lose an unhealthy amount of weight prior to their wedding (Neighbors & Sobal, 2008). The researchers found that engaged women weighed, on average, 152.1 pounds. The average ideal wedding weight reported by 227 women was 136.0 pounds. The data below represent the fictional weights of 8 women on the day they bought their wedding dress and on the day they got married. Did women lose weight for their wedding day?

Dress Purchase	Wedding Day
163	158
144	139
151	150
120	118
136	132
158	152
155	150
145	146

a. Conduct the six steps of hypothesis testing using a one-tailed test and an alpha level of 0.05.

b. Report the test statistic in APA format.

c. Calculate the confidence interval for the paired-samples *t* test that you conducted in part (a).

Compare the confidence interval to the results of the hypothesis test.

d. Calculate the effect size for this example. According to Cohen's conventions, how large is this effect?

10.29 Paired-samples *t* test, decorations in kindergarten classrooms, and science learning: Psychology researcher Anna Fisher and her colleagues studied whether kindergarten students learned better in decorated classrooms or undecorated classrooms, referred to as "sparse classrooms" (Fisher, Godwin, & Seltman, 2014). They wondered whether students would be less distracted and learn better without decorations such as posters, maps, and children's artwork. The same group of children had science lessons in a classroom without decorations and in a classroom with decorations. The students took a test on the material after each condition. Each child received a percentage-correct score, out of 100%, for each condition. In the journal article in which they reported their findings, the researchers wrote that the children's "learning scores were higher in the sparse-classroom condition ($M = 55\%$) than in the decorated-classroom condition ($M = 42\%$), paired-samples $t(22) = 2.95$, $p = .007$; this effect was of medium size, Cohen's $d = 0.65$."

a. What is the independent variable in this study and what are its levels?

b. What is the dependent variable in this study?

c. Why did the researchers analyze their data with a paired-samples *t* test?

d. How many children participated in this study? Explain how you determined your answer.

e. How do you know this result is statistically significant?

f. Using the means, explain the results to someone who has not taken statistics.

g. Why did the researchers report an effect size?

10.30 A paired-samples *t* test and English-language tests for international students: The International English Language Testing System (IELTS) is a test that assesses the English-language skills of international students who wish to study in an English-speaking country. It has six modules, one of which assesses listening skills. Researchers assessed IELTS listening skills for a sample of 63 international students at the University of Melbourne in Australia (O'Loughlin & Arkoudis, 2009). These students were assessed in order to be admitted to the university and then were reassessed during their final semester at the university. Below is a subset of the Australian sample. (The overall pattern of data, including the means and standard errors, is similar to that for the whole sample of 63 students.)

Time 1	Time 2
5.5	6.5
6.0	7.5
6.5	6.5
6.5	7.5
6.5	7.5
7.0	6.5
7.0	7.5
7.5	8.0
8.0	9.0
8.5	8.5

a. Conduct the six steps of hypothesis testing using a two-tailed test and an alpha level of 0.05.

b. Report the test statistic in APA format.

c. Calculate the confidence interval for the paired-samples *t* test that you conducted in part (a). Compare the confidence interval to the results of the hypothesis test.

d. Calculate the effect size for this example. According to Cohen's conventions, how large is this effect?

10.31 Email, stress, and a paired-samples *t* test: Researchers wondered if frequent checking of email increases stress (Kushlev & Dunn, 2015). They randomly assigned half of their participants to check email just three times a day for a week, and then in the second week, to check email as often as they wanted. The other half of participants checked their email as much as they wanted in the first week, and just three times a day in the second week. The researchers did find that participants were less stressed, on average, during the limited email week than during the unlimited email week. But they wanted to be sure that it really was limited email that led to this effect, so they conducted a paired-samples *t* test to be sure that participants were doing as they were told. The researchers reported that "confirming the success of our manipulation, people checked their email significantly fewer times per day in the *limited email* condition ($M = 4.70$, $SD = 4.10$) than in the *unlimited email* condition ($M = 12.54$, $SD = 8.02$; $t[115] = -10.23$, $p < .001$)." Was this because those who checked less frequently ended up getting less email or just ignored a lot of potentially stressful email? It doesn't seem like it. The researchers also reported

that "there were no significant differences between conditions in how many emails people received ($M_{limited} = 16.64$ vs. $M_{unlimited} = 16.04$, $t(114) = 1.31$, $p = .19$) or responded to ($M_{limited} = 5.30$ vs. $M_{unlimited} = 5.95$, $t(115) = -1.58$, $p = .12$), suggesting that our manipulation primarily affected how often people checked email rather than the volume of email they managed."

a. Why did the researchers use paired-samples *t* tests to explore their concerns about exactly what might be affecting stress levels in their study?

b. Explain why it would have been useful for the researchers to report confidence intervals in addition to the results of hypothesis testing.

c. Explain why it would have been useful for the researchers to report effect sizes in addition to the results of hypothesis testing.

d. Explain why the researchers assigned half of the participants to start with limited email and the other half to start with unlimited email. In your answer, use the terms *counterbalancing* and *order effects*, showing that you understand both of these terms in the context of this study.

e. Explain how the researchers' additional hypothesis tests, as described here, help them rule out some potential confounds.

Putting It All Together

10.32 Political bias in academia and a paired-samples *t* test: The following is an excerpt from the abstract (brief opening summary) from a published research study that examined a reported bias against conservatives in American academia (Fosse, Gross, & Ma, 2011).

> *The American professoriate contains a disproportionate number of people with liberal political views. Is this because of political bias or discrimination?...We sent two emails to directors of graduate study in the leading American departments of sociology, political science, economics, history, and English. The emails came from fictitious students who expressed interest in doing graduate work in the department....We analyze responses received in terms of frequency, timing, amount of information provided about the department, emotional warmth, and enthusiasm toward the student.* (p. 1)

One of the fictional emails was from a fictional student who mentioned working on the presidential campaign of John McCain, a well-known conservative, and one was from a fictional student who mentioned working on the presidential campaign of

Barack Obama, a well-known liberal. The researchers conducted a series of paired-samples *t* tests but did not find statistically significant differences on the various measures between ratings of the conservative and liberal students.

a. Why is this a within-groups design?

b. What is the independent variable and what are its levels?

c. What are the dependent variables, as listed in the study description, and what kind of variables are they?

d. Explain why it would have been possible to conduct a paired-samples *t* test.

e. Explain why there may have been order effects in this study.

f. How might the researchers have used counterbalancing?

g. Were the *p* values likely to be lower than or higher than 0.05? Explain your answer.

h. Given that the results were not statistically significant, what additional information would you want to know to determine whether there was sufficient statistical power?

10.33 **Hypnosis and the Stroop effect:** In Chapter 1, you were given an opportunity to complete the Stroop test, in which color words are printed in the wrong color; for example, the word *red* might be printed in the color blue. The conflict that arises when we try to name the color of ink the words are printed in but are distracted when the color word does not match the ink color increases reaction time and decreases accuracy. Several researchers have suggested that the Stroop effect can be decreased by hypnosis. Raz, Fan, and Posner (2005) used brain-imaging techniques to demonstrate that posthypnotic suggestion led highly hypnotizable people to see Stroop words as nonsense words. Imagine that you are working with Raz and colleagues and your assignment is to determine whether reaction times decrease (remember, a decrease is a good thing; it indicates that participants are faster) when highly hypnotizable people receive a posthypnotic suggestion to view the words as nonsensical. You conduct the experiment on six participants, once in each condition, and receive the following data; the first number is reaction time in seconds without the posthypnotic suggestion, and the second number is reaction time with the posthypnotic suggestion:

Participant 1:	12.6, 8.5
Participant 2:	13.8, 9.6
Participant 3:	11.6, 10.0
Participant 4:	12.2, 9.2
Participant 5:	12.1, 8.9
Participant 6:	13.0, 10.8

a. What is the independent variable and what are its levels? What is the dependent variable?

b. Conduct all six steps of a paired-samples *t* test as a two-tailed test. Be sure to label all six steps.

c. Report the statistics as you would in a journal article.

d. Now let's look at the effect of switching to a one-tailed test. Conduct steps 2, 4, and 6 of hypothesis testing for a one-tailed paired-samples *t* test. Under which circumstance—a one-tailed test or a two-tailed test—is it easier to reject the null hypothesis? If it becomes easier to reject the null hypothesis under one type of test (one-tailed versus two-tailed), does this mean that there is a bigger mean difference between the samples? Explain.

e. Now let's look at the effect of alpha level. Conduct steps 4 and 6 of hypothesis testing for an alpha level of 0.01 and a two-tailed test. With which alpha level—0.05 or 0.01—is it easiest to reject the null hypothesis with a two-tailed test? If it is easier to reject the null hypothesis with certain alpha levels, does this mean that there is a bigger mean difference between the samples? Explain.

f. Now let's look at the effect of sample size. Calculate the test statistic using only participants 1–3 and determine the new critical values. Is this test statistic closer to or farther from the cutoff? Does reducing the sample size make it easier or more difficult to reject the null hypothesis? Explain.

g. How might order effects influence the results of this study?

h. Could the researchers use a counterbalanced design? Why or why not? What might they do instead if they think order effects are a problem?

 **LaunchPad**
macmillan learning

Visit LaunchPad to access the e-book and to test your knowledge with LearningCurve.

TERMS

The Independent-Samples *t* Test

Conducting an Independent-Samples *t* Test

Beyond Hypothesis Testing

BEFORE YOU GO ON

- You should know the six steps of hypothesis testing (Chapter 7).

- You should understand the differences between a distribution of scores (Chapter 2), a distribution of means (Chapter 6), and a distribution of mean differences (Chapter 10).

- You should know how to conduct a single-sample *t* test and a paired-samples *t* test, including the calculations for the corrected versions of standard deviation and variance (Chapter 10).

- You should understand the basics of determining confidence intervals (Chapter 8).

- You should understand the concept of effect size and know the basics of calculating Cohen's *d* (Chapter 8).

Stella Cunliffe Stella Cunliffe created a remarkable career through her statistical reasoning and became the first female president of the Royal Statistical Society. As a statistician, she used hypothesis testing to improve quality control at the Guinness Brewing Company and to shape public policy in the criminology division at the British Home Office.

Stella Cunliffe, the first woman elected president of the Royal Statistical Society, built a path to success through two male-dominated industries: beer making and statistics. After living what she described as "a free and in many ways exciting life," she accepted a job at the Guinness Brewing Company. Cunliffe was a practical statistician whose insights helped her bypass long-standing social norms for gender. In her Royal Statistical Society presidential speech, she reminded her audience that applied "statistics are concerned much more with people than with vague ideas" (1976, p. 4).

For example, maintaining the quality of handmade beer barrels came down to a simple decision by the quality control worker: accept or reject. But that decision was biased because accepting meant kicking a barrel downhill and rejecting required pushing a barrel uphill, clearly the more arduous task. Cunliffe "de-biased" these judgments by moving the quality-control workstation so that it required equal effort either to accept or to reject a barrel—and saved Guinness a great deal of money by reducing the number of false positives (accepting barrels that should have been rejected). We can "de-bias" many experiments in the same way: by equalizing initial conditions through random assignment to independent groups.

In Chapter 9, we learned how to conduct a single-sample *t* test (comparing one sample to a population for which we know the mean but not the standard deviation). In Chapter 10, we learned how to conduct a paired-samples *t* test (such as a before/after design in which the same participants are in both groups). Here is a third situation calling for a *t* test: a two-group study in which each participant is in only one group. The scores for each group are independent of what happens in the other group. We also demonstrate how to determine a confidence interval and calculate an effect size for situations in which we have two independent groups.

Language Alert! The independent-samples *t* test is also called a *between-groups t test*.

Conducting an Independent-Samples *t* Test

- An **independent-samples *t* test** is used to compare two means for a between-groups design, a situation in which each participant is assigned to only one condition.

The **independent-samples t test** *is used to compare two means for a between-groups design, a situation in which each participant is assigned to only one condition.* This test uses a distribution of differences between means. This affects the *t* test in a few minor ways, most notably that it takes a bit more work when calculating a *t* test by hand (especially compared to using a computer!). The added calculation is that you have to estimate the appropriate standard error. It's not difficult—just a bit time consuming.

A Distribution of Differences Between Means

Because we have different people in each condition of the study, we cannot create a difference score for each person. We're looking at overall differences between two independent groups, so we need to develop a new type of distribution, a distribution of *differences between means*.

Let's use the Chapter 6 global happiness data to demonstrate how to create a distribution of differences between means (Helliwell, Layard, & Sachs, 2016).

Let's say that we were planning to collect data on two groups of three countries each and wanted to determine the comparison distribution for this research scenario. Remember that in Chapter 6, we used the example of a population of 157 countries. We described writing each country's happiness score on a card and putting the 157 cards in a bowl.

Let's use that example to create a distribution of differences between means. We'll walk through the steps for this process.

> **STEP 1:** We randomly select three cards, replacing each after selecting it, and calculate the mean of the happiness scores listed on them. This is the first group.

> **STEP 2:** We randomly select three other cards, replacing each after selecting it, and calculate their mean. This is the second group.

> **STEP 3:** We subtract the second mean from the first.

That's really all there is to it—except we repeat these three steps many more times. There are two samples, so there are two sample means, but we're building just *one* distribution of differences between those means.

EXAMPLE 11.1

Here's an example using the three steps.

> **STEP 1:** We randomly select three cards, replacing each after selecting it, and find that the happiness scores are 5.123, 6.269, and 5.155. We calculate a mean score of 5.516. This is the first group.

> **STEP 2:** We randomly select three other cards, replacing each after selecting it, and find that the happiness scores are 5.291, 6.725, and 6.361. We calculate a mean score of 6.126. This is the second group.

> **STEP 3:** We subtract the second mean from the first: $5.516 - 6.126 = -0.610$. (Note that it's fine to subtract the first from the second, as long as we're consistent in the arithmetic.)

We repeat the three-step process. Let's say that, this time, we calculate means of 6.228 and 4.576 for the two samples. Now the difference between means would be 6.228 − 4.576 = 1.652. We might repeat the three steps a third time and find means of 5.082 and 5.082, for a difference of 0. Eventually, we would have many differences between means—some positive, some negative, and some right at 0—and could plot them on a curve. But this would only be the beginning of what this distribution would look like. If we were to calculate the whole distribution, then we would do this many, many more times. When creating the beginning of a distribution of differences between means for the global happiness data, the authors calculated 30 differences between means, as shown in Figure 11-1. ●

FIGURE 11-1

Distribution of Differences Between Means

This graph represents the beginning of a distribution of differences between means. It includes only 30 differences, whereas the actual distribution would include all possible differences.

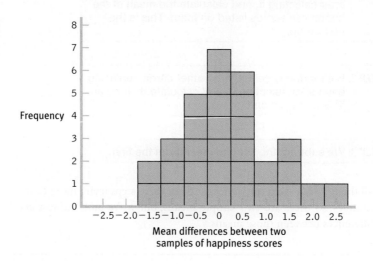

Mean differences between two samples of happiness scores

The Six Steps of the Independent-Samples *t* Test

We can use the same six steps of hypothesis testing to conduct an independent-samples *t* test. Let's look at an example.

EXAMPLE 11.2

Does the price of a product influence how much you like it? Payless, the discount shoe store, tricked fashion "influencers" into buying its shoes at up to an 1800% mark-up (Rhue, 2018). Payless invited 60 influencers to its fake luxury store, Palessi, and stocked it with outrageously overpriced Payless shoes. One influencer dropped $645 on a $30 pair! "Just stunning. Elegant, sophisticated," one shopper described the merchandise. Another said of a pair of fake leather sneakers, "I can tell it was made with high-quality material."

The success of Payless's prank could have been predicted by research. Economics researchers from Northern California, not far from prime wine country, wondered whether enjoyment of wine is influenced by price (Plassmann, O'Doherty, Shiv, & Rangel, 2008). In part of their study, they randomly assigned some wine drinkers to taste wine that was said to cost $10 per bottle and others to taste *the same wine* at a supposed price of $90 per bottle. (Note that we're altering some aspects of the design and statistical analysis of this study for teaching purposes, but the results are similar.) The researchers asked participants to rate, on a scale from 1 to 5, how much they liked the wine; they also used functional magnetic resonance imaging (fMRI), a brain-scanning technique, to determine whether differences were evident in areas of the brain that are typically activated when people experience a stimulus as pleasant (e.g., the medial orbitofrontal cortex). Which do you think participants preferred, the wine priced at $10 or the same wine priced at $90?

We will conduct an independent-samples *t* test using the ratings of how much nine people like the wine they were randomly assigned to taste (four tasting wine from the "$10" bottle and five tasting wine from the "$90" bottle). Remember, everyone is actually tasting wine from the *same* bottle! Notice that we do not need to have the same number of participants in each sample, although it is best if the sample sizes are fairly similar.

Price and Perception: Payless Versus Palessi Does the perceived price of a product influence how much you like it? The now-closed discount shoe store, Payless, launched a fake luxury store, Palessi, that displayed the same inexpensive shoes but with exorbitant prices (Rhue, 2018). Many of the "influencers" invited to shop at Palessi fell for the trick, sometimes paying multiple times the actual cost of the shoes. One excited influencer said she'd pay as much as $500 for a pair of sneakers, breathlessly predicting that she'd be asked, "where did you get those? Those are amazing!" If researchers asked some people to estimate the cost of the Payless sneakers and other people to estimate the cost of the same sneakers marketed as the Palessi luxury brand, we could conduct an independent-samples *t* test to determine if there is a statistically significant difference in the cost estimates.

Mean "liking ratings" of the wine

"$10" wine: 1.5   2.3   2.8   3.4

"$90" wine: 2.9   3.5   3.5   4.9   5.2

> **STEP 1: Identify the populations, distribution, and assumptions.**

In terms of determining the populations, this step is similar to that for the paired-samples *t* test: There are two populations—those told they are drinking wine from a $10 bottle and those told they are drinking wine from a $90 bottle. The comparison distribution for an independent-samples *t* test, however, will be a distribution of differences between means (rather than a distribution of mean difference scores). Table 11-1 summarizes the distributions we have encountered with the hypothesis tests we have learned so far.

TABLE 11-1	Hypothesis Tests and Their Distributions

We must consider the appropriate comparison distribution when we choose which hypothesis test to use.

Hypothesis Test	Number of Samples	Comparison Distribution
z test	One	Distribution of means
Single-sample *t* test	One	Distribution of means
Paired-samples *t* test	Two (same participants)	Distribution of mean difference scores
Independent-samples *t* test	Two (different participants)	Distribution of differences between means

As usual, the comparison distribution is based on the null hypothesis. As with the paired-samples *t* test, the null hypothesis for the independent-samples *t* test posits no mean difference. So the mean of the comparison distribution would be 0; this reflects a mean difference between means of 0. We compare the difference between the sample means to a difference of 0, which is what there would be if there were no difference between groups. The assumptions for an independent-samples *t* test are the same as those for the single-sample *t* test and the paired-samples *t* test.

Summary: Population 1: People told they are drinking wine from a $10 bottle. Population 2: People told they are drinking wine from a $90 bottle.

The comparison distribution will be a distribution of differences between means based on the null hypothesis. The hypothesis test will be an independent-samples *t* test because there are two samples composed of different groups of participants. This study meets one of the three assumptions. (1) The dependent variable is a rating on a liking measure, which can be considered a scale variable. (2) We do not know whether the population is normally distributed, and there are not at least 30 participants. However, the sample data do not suggest that the underlying population distribution is skewed. (3) The wine drinkers in this study were not randomly selected from among all wine drinkers, so we must be cautious with respect to generalizing these findings.

> **STEP 2: State the null and research hypotheses.**

This step for an independent-samples *t* test is identical to that for the previous *t* tests.

Summary: Null hypothesis: On average, people drinking wine they were told was from a $10 bottle give it the same rating as do people drinking wine they were told was from a $90 bottle—$H_0$: $\mu_1 = \mu_2$. Research hypothesis: On average, people drinking wine they were told was from a $10 bottle give it a different rating than do people drinking wine they were told was from a $90 bottle—$H_1$: $\mu_1 \neq \mu_2$.

> **STEP 3: Determine the characteristics of the comparison distribution.**

This step for an independent-samples *t* test is similar to that for previous *t* tests: We determine the appropriate mean and the appropriate standard error of the comparison distribution—the distribution based on the null hypothesis. According to the null hypothesis, no mean difference exists between the populations; that is, the difference between means is 0. So the mean of the comparison distribution is always 0, as long as the null hypothesis posits no mean difference.

Because there are two samples when we conduct an independent-samples *t* test, however, it is more complicated to calculate the appropriate measure of spread. There are five stages to this process. First, let's consider them in words; then we'll learn the calculations. These instructions are basic, and you'll understand them better when you do the calculations, but they'll help you to keep the overall framework in mind. (These verbal descriptions are keyed by letter to the calculation stages that follow them.)

a. Calculate the corrected variance for each sample. (Notice that we're working with variance, not standard deviation.)

b. Pool the variances. Pooling the variances involves taking an average of the two sample variances while accounting for any differences in the sizes of the two samples. Pooled variance is an estimate of the common population variance.

c. Convert the pooled variance from squared standard deviation (that is, variance) to squared standard error (another version of variance) by dividing the pooled variance by the sample size, first for one sample and then again for the second sample. These are the estimated variances for each sample's distribution of means.

d. Add the two variances (*squared* standard errors), one for each distribution of sample means, to calculate the estimated variance of the distribution of differences between means.

e. Calculate the square root of this form of variance (*squared* standard error) to get the estimated standard error of the distribution of differences between means.

Notice that stages (a) and (b) are an expanded version of the usual first calculation for a t test. Instead of calculating one corrected estimate of standard deviation, we're calculating two for an independent-samples t test—one for each sample. Also, for an independent-samples t test, we use variances instead of standard deviations. Because there are two calculations of variance, we combine them (i.e., the pooled variance). Stages (c) and (d) are an expanded version of the usual second calculation for a t test. Once again, we convert to standard error for each sample (only this time it is squared because we are working with variances) and combine the variances from each sample. In stage (e), we take the square root so that we have standard error. Let's examine the calculations.

a. We calculate corrected variance for each sample (corrected variance is the one we learned in Chapter 9 that uses $N - 1$ in the denominator). First, we calculate variance for X, the sample of people told they are drinking wine from a \$10 bottle. Be sure to use the mean of the ratings of the \$10 wine drinkers only, which we calculate to be 2.5. Notice that the symbol for this variance uses s^2, instead of SD^2 (just as the standard deviation used s instead of SD in the previous t tests). Also, we included the subscript X to indicate that this is variance for the first sample, whose scores are arbitrarily called X. (Remember: Don't take the square root. We want variance, not standard deviation.)

X	$X - M$	$(X - M)^2$
1.5	−1.0	1.00
2.3	−0.2	0.04
2.8	0.3	0.09
3.4	0.9	0.81

$$s_X^2 = \frac{\Sigma(X - M)^2}{N - 1} = \frac{(1.00 + 0.04 + 0.09 + 0.81)}{4 - 1} = \frac{1.94}{3} = 0.647$$

Now we do the same for Y, the people told they are drinking wine from a \$90 bottle. Remember to use the mean for Y; it's easy to forget and use the mean we calculated earlier for X. We calculate the mean for Y to be 4.0. The subscript Y indicates that this is the variance for the second sample, whose scores are arbitrarily called Y. (We could call these scores by any letter, but statisticians tend to call the scores in the first two samples X and Y.)

Y	$Y - M$	$(Y - M)^2$
2.9	−1.1	1.21
3.5	−0.5	0.25
3.5	−0.5	0.25
4.9	0.9	0.81
5.2	1.2	1.44

$$s_Y^2 = \frac{\Sigma(Y - M)^2}{N - 1} = \frac{(1.21 + 0.25 + 0.25 + 0.81 + 1.44)}{5 - 1} = \frac{3.96}{4} = 0.990$$

b. We pool the two estimates of variance. Because there are often different numbers of people in each sample, we cannot simply take their mean. We mentioned earlier in this book that estimates of spread taken from smaller samples tend to be less accurate. So we weight the estimate from the smaller sample a bit less and weight the estimate from the larger sample a bit more. We do this by calculating the proportion of degrees of freedom represented by each sample. Each sample has degrees of freedom of $N - 1$. We also calculate a total degrees of freedom that sums the degrees of freedom for the two samples. Here are the calculations:

$$df_X = N - 1 = 4 - 1 = 3$$
$$df_Y = N - 1 = 5 - 1 = 4$$
$$df_{total} = df_X + df_Y = 3 + 4 = 7$$

Using these degrees of freedom, we calculate a sort of average variance. **Pooled variance** *is a weighted average of the two estimates of variance—one from each sample—that are calculated when conducting an independent-samples* t *test.* The estimate of variance from the larger sample counts for more in the pooled variance than does the estimate from the smaller sample because larger samples tend to lead to somewhat more accurate estimates than do smaller samples. Here's the formula for pooled variance, and the calculations for this example:

$$s_{pooled}^2 = \left(\frac{df_X}{df_{total}}\right)s_X^2 + \left(\frac{df_Y}{df_{total}}\right)s_Y^2 = \left(\frac{3}{7}\right)0.647 + \left(\frac{4}{7}\right)0.990 = 0.277 + 0.566 = 0.843$$

(*Note:* If we had exactly the same number of participants in each sample, this would be an unweighted average—that is, we could compute the average in the usual way by summing the two sample variances and dividing by 2.)

c. Now that we have pooled the variances, we have an estimate of spread. This is similar to the estimate of the standard deviation in the previous t tests, but now it's based on two samples (and is an estimate of variance rather than standard deviation). The next calculation in the previous *t* tests was dividing standard deviation by $\sqrt{N}$ to get standard error. In this case, we divide by N instead of $\sqrt{N}$. Why? Because we are dealing with variances, not standard deviations. Variance is the square of standard deviation, so we divide by the square of $\sqrt{N}$, which is simply N. We do this once for each sample, using pooled variance as the estimate of spread. We use pooled variance because an estimate based on two samples is better than an estimate based on one sample. The key here is to divide by the appropriate N: in this case, 4 for the first sample and 5 for the second sample.

$$s_{M_X}^2 = \frac{s_{pooled}^2}{N_X} = \frac{0.843}{4} = 0.211$$

$$s_{M_Y}^2 = \frac{s_{pooled}^2}{N_Y} = \frac{0.843}{5} = 0.169$$

d. In stage (c), we calculated the variance versions of standard error for each sample, but we want only one such measure of spread when we calculate the test statistic. So, we combine the two variances, similar to the way in which we combined the two estimates of variance in stage (b). This stage is even simpler, however. We merely add the two variances together. When we sum them, we get the variance of the distribution of differences between means, symbolized as $s_{difference}^2$. Here are the formula and the calculations for this example:

$$s_{difference}^2 = s_{M_X}^2 + s_{M_Y}^2 = 0.211 + 0.169 = 0.380$$

e. We now have paralleled the two calculations of the previous *t* tests by doing two things: (1) We calculated an estimate of spread (we made two calculations, one for each sample, then combined them), and (2) we then adjusted the estimate for the sample size (again, we made two calculations, one for each sample, then combined them). The main difference is that we have kept all calculations as variances rather than standard deviations. At this final stage, we convert from variance form to standard deviation form. Because standard deviation is the square root of variance, we do this by simply taking the square root:

$$s_{difference} = \sqrt{s_{difference}^2} = \sqrt{0.380} = 0.616$$

Summary: The mean of the distribution of differences between means is $\mu_X - \mu_Y = 0$. The standard deviation of the distribution of differences between means is: $s_{difference} = 0.616$.

> **STEP 4: Determine critical values, or cutoffs.**

This step for the independent-samples *t* test is similar to those for previous *t* tests, but we use the total degrees of freedom, df_{total}.

Summary: The critical values, based on a two-tailed test, an alpha level of 0.05, and a df_{total} of 7, are −2.365 and 2.365 (as seen in the curve in Figure 11-2).

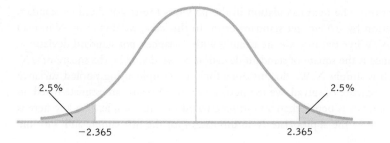

2.5%   2.5%

−2.365   2.365

STEP 5: Calculate the test statistic.

This step for the independent-samples *t* test is similar to the fifth step in previous *t*
tests. Here we subtract the population difference between means based on the null
hypothesis from the difference between means for the samples. The formula is:

$$t = \frac{(M_X - M_Y) - (\mu_X - \mu_Y)}{S_{difference}}$$

As in previous *t* tests, the test statistic is calculated by subtracting a number based
on the populations from a number based on the samples, then dividing by a version
of standard error. Because the population difference between means (according to the
null hypothesis) is almost always 0, many statisticians choose to eliminate the latter part
of the formula. So the formula for the test statistic for an independent-samples *t* test is
often abbreviated as:

$$t = \frac{(M_X - M_Y)}{S_{difference}}$$

You might find it easier to use the first formula, however, as it reminds us that we
are subtracting the population difference between means according to the null hypothesis (0) from the actual difference between the sample means. This format more closely
parallels the formulas of the test statistics we calculated in Chapter 9.

Summary: $t = \dfrac{(2.5 - 4.0) - 0}{0.616} = -2.44$

STEP 6: Make a decision.

This step for the independent-samples *t* test is identical to that for the previous *t* tests.
If we reject the null hypothesis, we need to examine the means of the two conditions
so that we know the direction of the effect.

Summary: Reject the null hypothesis. It appears that those persons told they are
drinking wine from a $10 bottle give it lower ratings, on average, than those told they
are drinking from a $90 bottle (as shown by the curve in Figure 11-3).

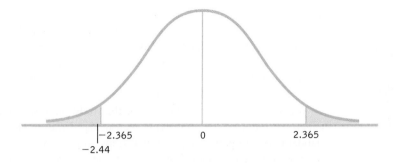

FIGURE 11-3

Making a Decision

As in previous *t* tests, to decide whether to reject the null hypothesis, we compare the test statistic to the critical values. In this figure, the test statistic, –2.44, is beyond the lower cutoff, –2.365. We reject the null hypothesis. It appears that those persons told they are drinking wine from a $10 bottle give it lower ratings, on average, than those told they are drinking wine from a $90 bottle.

This finding documents the fact that people report liking a more expensive wine better than a less expensive one—even when it's the same wine! The researchers documented a similar finding with a narrower gap between prices—$5 and $45. Naysayers might point out, however, that participants drinking an expensive wine may report liking it better than participants drinking an inexpensive wine simply because they are expected to say they like it better because of its price. However, the fMRI that was conducted, which is a more objective measure, yielded a similar finding. Those drinking the supposedly more expensive wines showed increased activation in brain areas such as the medial orbitofrontal cortex, essentially an indication in the brain that people are enjoying an experience. Expectations really do seem to influence us—even if we're "influencers." ●

Reporting the Statistics

To report the statistics as they would appear in a journal article, follow standard APA format. Be sure to include the degrees of freedom, the value of the test statistic, and the *p* value associated with the test statistic. (Note that because the *t* table in Appendix B only includes the *p* values of 0.10, 0.05, and 0.01, we cannot use it to determine the actual *p* value for the test statistic. Unless we use software, we can only report whether the *p* value is less than the critical alpha level.) In the current example, the statistics would read:

$$t(7) = -2.44, p < 0.05$$

In addition to the results of hypothesis testing, we would include the means and standard deviations for the two samples. We calculated the means in step 3 of hypothesis testing, and we also calculated the variances (0.647 for those persons told they were drinking from a $10 bottle and 0.990 for those told they were drinking from a $90 bottle). We can calculate the standard deviations by taking the square roots of the variances. The descriptive statistics can be reported in parentheses as:

($10 bottle: $M = 2.5, SD = 0.80$; $90 bottle: $M = 4.0, SD = 0.99$)

We might also want to include a graph. In Chapter 3, you learned how to make a bar graph. You also learned about ways to demonstrate the variability within the data, including by creating a violin plot. Now, we'll introduce a way to show variability directly on your bar graph, by adding error bars. **_Error bars_** *are vertical lines added to*

● **Error bars** are vertical lines added to bars or dots on a graph that represent the variability of those data and give us a sense of how precise an estimate summary statistic is.

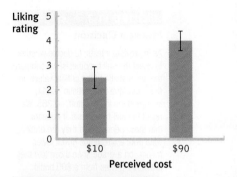

bars or dots on a graph that represent the variability of those data and give us a sense of how precise an estimate summary statistic is. Often, standard error is the specific measure of variability used to create error bars; remember, standard error is used to create confidence intervals, so essentially error bars are showing the confidence interval around a mean. Sometimes, however, researchers use standard deviation or another measure.

When calculating the *t* statistic for the study on how perceived price affects how much people like wine, we calculated the variance versions of standard error in part (c) of the calculations on pages 310 and 311—0.211 for the participants who thought the wine cost $10 and 0.169 for the participants who thought the wine cost $90. We can take the square roots of each variance to determine the standard errors for each group; these are 0.459 for the $10 group and 0.411 for the $90 group. If we create a bar graph for the two means, 2.5 and 4.0, we can add error bars. For each bar, add a line that represents the value of the standard error both above and below the top of the bar. For example, for the $10 group, the line runs 0.459 below the mean of 2.5 to 0.459 above the mean of 2.5. Figure 11-4 shows the bar graph with error bars.

CHECK YOUR LEARNING

Reviewing the Concepts > When we conduct an independent-samples *t* test, we cannot calculate individual difference scores. That is why we compare the mean of one sample with the mean of the other sample.

> The comparison distribution is a distribution of differences between means.

> We use the same six steps of hypothesis testing that we used with the *z* test and with the single-sample and paired-samples *t* tests.

> Conceptually, the *t* test for independent samples makes the same comparisons as the other *t* tests. However, the calculations are different, and the critical values are based on degrees of freedom from two samples.

> The appropriate graph for an independent-samples *t* test is a bar graph. We should add error bars, vertical lines at the top of each bar that indicate variability around each estimated mean, to the bar graph.

Clarifying the Concepts **11-1** In what situation do we conduct a paired-samples *t* test? In what situation do we conduct an independent-samples *t* test?

11-2 What is pooled variance?

Calculating the Statistics **11-3** Imagine you have the following data from two independent groups:

Group 1: 3, 2, 4, 6, 1, 2
Group 2: 5, 4, 6, 2, 6

Compute each of the following calculations needed to complete the final calculation of the independent-samples *t* test.

a. Calculate the corrected variance for each group.

b. Calculate the degrees of freedom and pooled variance.

c. Calculate the variance version of standard error for each group.

d. Calculate the variance of the distribution of differences between means, then convert this number to standard deviation.

e. Calculate the test statistic.

| Applying the Concepts | 11-4 | In the previous Check Your Learning exercise, you calculated several statistics; now let's consider a context for those numbers. Steele and Pinto (2006) examined whether people's level of trust in their direct supervisor affected their level of agreement with a policy supported by that leader. They found that the extent to which subordinates agreed with their supervisor was statistically significantly related to trust and showed no relation to gender, age, time on the job, or length of time working with the supervisor. We have presented fictional data to re-create these findings, where group 1 represents employees with low trust in their supervisor and group 2 represents the high-trust employees. The scores presented are the level of agreement with a decision made by a leader, from 1 (strongly disagree) to 7 (strongly agree). |

Group 1 (low trust in leader): 3, 2, 4, 6, 1, 2

Group 2 (high trust in leader): 5, 4, 6, 2, 6

a. State the null and research hypotheses.

b. Identify the critical values and make a decision.

c. Write your conclusion in a formal sentence that includes presentation of the statistic in APA format.

Solutions to these Check Your Learning questions can be found in Appendix D.

d. Explain why your results are different from those in the original research, despite having a similar mean difference.

Beyond Hypothesis Testing

After working at Guinness, the statistician Stella Cunliffe was hired by the British government's criminology department. She noticed that adult male prisoners who had short prison sentences returned to prison at a very high rate—an apparent justification for longer prison sentences. The genius of Stella Cunliffe was that she always looked carefully at the source of the original numbers. This time she discovered that the returning prisoners behind these numbers were almost all older people with mental health problems. They were trapped in the prison system because the mental hospitals would not take them; so, these data did not justify long, harsh prison sentences. Good researchers insist on knowing what the numbers *really* mean.

Two ways that researchers can understand more deeply the findings of a hypothesis test are by calculating a confidence interval and an effect size.

> **MASTERING THE CONCEPT**
>
> **11-2:** As we can with the *z* test, the single-sample *t* test, and the paired-samples *t* test, we can determine a confidence interval and calculate a measure of effect size—Cohen's *d*—when we conduct an independent-samples *t* test.

Calculating a Confidence Interval for an Independent-Samples *t* Test

Confidence intervals for an independent-samples *t* test are centered on the *difference between means* (rather than the means themselves). So we use the difference between means for the samples and the standard error for the difference between means, $s_{difference}$, which we calculate in an identical manner to the one used in hypothesis testing.

We use the formula for the independent-samples *t* statistic when calculating the raw differences between means. To do this, we use algebra on the original formula for an independent-samples *t* test to isolate the upper and lower mean differences. Here is the original *t* statistic formula:

$$t = \frac{(M_X - M_Y) - (\mu_X - \mu_Y)}{s_{difference}}$$

We replace the population mean difference, $(\mu_X - \mu_Y)$, with the sample mean difference $(M_X - M_Y)_{sample}$, because this is what the confidence interval is centered on. We also indicate that the first mean difference in the numerator refers to the bounds of the confidence intervals, the upper bound in this case:

$$t_{upper} = \frac{(M_X - M_Y)_{upper} - (M_X - M_Y)_{sample}}{s_{difference}}$$

With algebra, we isolate the upper bound of the confidence interval to create the following formula:

$$(M_X - M_Y)_{upper} = t(s_{difference}) + (M_X - M_Y)_{sample}$$

We create the formula for the lower bound of the confidence interval in exactly the same way, using the negative version of the *t* statistic:

$$(M_X - M_Y)_{lower} = -t(s_{difference}) + (M_X - M_Y)_{sample}$$

EXAMPLE 11.3

Let's calculate the confidence interval that parallels the hypothesis test we conducted earlier, comparing ratings of those who are told they are drinking wine from a $10 bottle and ratings of those told they are drinking wine from a $90 bottle (Plassmann et al., 2008). The difference between the means of these samples was calculated in the numerator of the *t* statistic. It is $2.5 - 4.0 = -1.5$. (Note that the order of subtraction in calculating the difference between means is irrelevant; we could just as easily have subtracted 2.5 from 4.0 and gotten a positive result, 1.5.) The standard error for the differences between means, $s_{difference}$, was calculated to be 0.616. The degrees of freedom were determined to be 7. Here are the five steps for determining a confidence interval for a difference between means:

> **STEP 1: Draw a normal curve with the sample difference between means in the center (as shown in Figure 11-5).**

FIGURE 11-5

A 95% Confidence Interval for Differences Between Means, Part I

As with a confidence interval for a single-sample *t* test, we start the confidence interval for a difference between means by drawing a curve with the sample difference between means in the center.

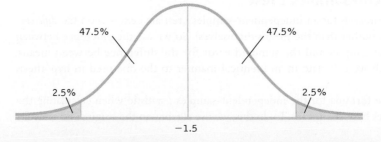

47.5%   47.5%

2.5%   2.5%

−1.5

STEP 2: Indicate the bounds of the confidence
interval on either end, and write the
percentages under each segment of the
curve (see Figure 11-5).

STEP 3: Look up the *t* statistics for the lower and
upper ends of the confidence interval in
the *t* table.

Use a two-tailed test and an alpha level of 0.05 (which corresponds to a 95% confidence interval). Use the degrees of freedom—7—that we calculated earlier. The table indicates a *t* statistic of 2.365. Because the normal curve is symmetric, the bounds of the confidence interval fall at *t* statistics of −2.365 and 2.365. (Note that these cutoffs are identical to those used for the independent-samples *t* test because the alpha level of 0.05 corresponds to a confidence level of 95%.) We add those *t* statistics to the normal curve, as in Figure 11-6.

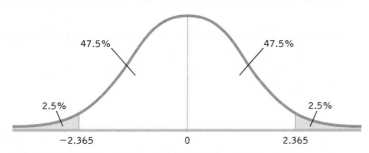

FIGURE 11-6

A 95% Confidence Interval for Differences Between Means, Part II

The next step in calculating a confidence interval is identifying the *t* statistics that indicate each end of the interval. Because the curve is symmetric, the *t* statistics have the same magnitude—one is negative and one is positive.

STEP 4: Convert the *t* statistics to raw differences
between means for the lower and upper
ends of the confidence interval.

For the lower end, the formula is:

$$(M_X - M_Y)_{lower} = -t(s_{difference}) + (M_X - M_Y)_{sample}$$
$$= -2.365(0.616) + (-1.5) = -2.96$$

For the upper end, the formula is:

$$(M_X - M_Y)_{upper} = t(s_{difference}) + (M_X - M_Y)_{sample}$$
$$= 2.365(0.616) + (-1.5) = -0.04$$

The confidence interval is [−2.96, −0.04], as shown in Figure 11-7.

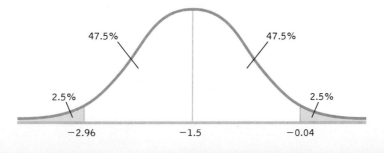

FIGURE 11-7

A 95% Confidence Interval for Differences Between Means, Part III

The final step in calculating a confidence interval is converting the *t* statistics that indicate each end of the interval into raw differences between means.

STEP 5: Check your answer.

Each end of the confidence interval should be exactly the same distance from the sample mean.

$$-2.96 - (-1.5) = -2.96 + 1.5 = -1.46$$
$$-0.04 - (-1.5) = -0.04 + 1.5 = 1.46$$

The interval checks out. The bounds of the confidence interval are calculated as the difference between sample means, plus or minus 1.46. Also, the confidence interval does not include 0; thus, it is not plausible that there is no difference between means. We can conclude that people told they are drinking wine from a $10 bottle give different ratings, on average, than those told they are drinking wine from a $90 bottle. When we conducted the independent-samples *t* test earlier, we rejected the null hypothesis and drew the same conclusion as we did with the confidence interval. But the confidence interval provides more information because it is an interval estimate rather than a point estimate. ●

Calculating Effect Size for an Independent-Samples *t* Test

As with all hypothesis tests, it is recommended that the results be supplemented with an effect size. For an independent-samples *t* test, as with other *t* tests, we can use Cohen's *d* as the measure of effect size.

EXAMPLE 11.4

The fictional data on which we conducted an independent-samples *t* test provided means of 2.5 for those persons told they were drinking wine from a $10 bottle and 4.0 for those told they were drinking wine from a $90 bottle (Plassmann et al., 2008). Previously, we calculated a standard error for the difference between means, $s_{difference}$, of 0.616. Here are the calculations we performed:

Stage (a) (variance for each sample):

$$s_X^2 = \frac{\Sigma(X - M)^2}{N - 1} = 0.647$$

$$s_Y^2 = \frac{\Sigma(Y - M)^2}{N - 1} = 0.990$$

Stage (b) (combining variances):

$$s_{pooled}^2 = \left(\frac{df_X}{df_{total}}\right)s_X^2 + \left(\frac{df_Y}{df_{total}}\right)s_Y^2 = 0.843$$

Stage (c) (variance form of standard error for each sample):

$$s_{M_X}^2 = \frac{s_{pooled}^2}{N_X} = 0.211; \; s_{M_Y}^2 = \frac{s_{pooled}^2}{N_Y} = 0.169$$

Stage (d) (combining variance forms of standard error):

$$s_{difference}^2 = s_{M_X}^2 + s_{M_Y}^2 = 0.380$$

Stage (e) (converting the variance form of standard error to the standard deviation form of standard error):

$$s_{difference} = \sqrt{s_{difference}^2} = 0.616$$

Because the goal is to disregard the influence of sample size in order to calculate Cohen's *d*, we want to use the standard deviation, rather than the standard error, in the denominator. So we can ignore the last three stages, all of which contribute to the calculation of standard error. That leaves stages (a) and (b). It makes more sense to use the one that includes information from both samples, so we focus our attention on stage (b). Here is where many students make a mistake. What we have calculated in stage (b) is pooled *variance*, not pooled *standard deviation*. We must take the square root of the pooled variance to get the pooled standard deviation, the appropriate value for the denominator of Cohen's *d*.

$$s_{pooled} = \sqrt{s_{pooled}^2} = \sqrt{0.843} = 0.918$$

The test statistic that we calculated for this study was:

$$t = \frac{(M_X - M_Y) - (\mu_X - \mu_Y)}{s_{difference}} = \frac{(2.5 - 4.0) - (0)}{0.616} = -2.44$$

For Cohen's *d*, we simply replace the denominator with standard deviation, s_{pooled}, instead of standard error, $s_{difference}$.

$$\text{Cohen's } d = \frac{(M_X - M_Y) - (\mu_X - \mu_Y)}{s_{pooled}} = \frac{(2.5 - 4.0) - (0)}{0.918} = -1.63$$

For this study, the effect size is reported as: *d* = 1.63. The two sample means are 1.63 standard deviations apart. According to the conventions that we learned in Chapter 8 and are shown again in Table 11-2, this is a large effect. ●

MASTERING THE FORMULA

11-8: For a two-sample, between-groups design, we calculate Cohen's *d* using the following formula:

$$\text{Cohen's } d = \frac{(M_X - M_Y) - (\mu_X - \mu_Y)}{s_{pooled}}$$

The formula is similar to that for the test statistic in an independent-samples *t* test, except that we divide by pooled standard deviation, rather than standard error, because we want a measure of variability not altered by sample size.

TABLE 11-2 Cohen's Conventions for Effect Sizes: *d*

Jacob Cohen has published guidelines (or conventions), based on the overlap between two distributions, to help researchers determine whether an effect is small, medium, or large. These numbers are not cutoffs; they are merely rough guidelines to help researchers interpret results.

Effect Size	Convention	Overlap
Small	0.2	85%
Medium	0.5	67%
Large	0.8	53%

Data Ethics: The Bayesian Approach to Statistics

Prior Beliefs about Pizza When we encounter new information in everyday life, we evaluate it in terms of what we already know. If your friend tells you your favorite pizza place is closing, and you were just there, you're not as likely to believe it as if you had not been by in months.

To combat troubling research practices in the behavioral sciences, some researchers point to Bayesian statistics as a solution (Wagenmakers et al., 2018). The Bayesian approach is an alternative way of thinking about probability that better aligns with people's intuitions about data. Because Bayesian statistics are less likely to be misinterpreted and misused, their use may lead to more ethical research practices (Dienes & Mclatchie, 2018).

The approach discussed so far in this book is the traditional approach, in which probability is based on what would happen in the long run if we repeat the same events over and over again. With the traditional approach, we calculate the probability of observing our data, assuming that the null hypothesis is true and assuming that we have repeatedly drawn samples from the population. One problem with this traditional approach is that it allows us only to reject or fail to reject the null hypothesis; we can never simply reject or accept the research hypothesis. *As a consequence, we do not learn the probability of our data occurring if the research hypothesis is true.* Ultimately, this is what we would like to know.

The Bayesian approach gives us this information. We can determine how likely our observed data are to occur under *any* hypothesis. Specifically, in the Bayesian approach, probability is defined as our degree of belief in a hypothesis—such as the research hypothesis—taking into account both the data that we have collected and the beliefs we had about that hypothesis prior to collecting the data. The mathematician Thomas Bayes (hence the name "Bayesian" statistics; 1793) proposed that we should not just rely on the data at hand but should also consider what we already know (Kruschke, 2010a). Bayesian analysis is built on the logic that each new piece of data is evaluated in terms of a growing set of prior beliefs (rather than in a vacuum). Furthermore, Bayesian statistics help us to take both prior beliefs—"priors" for short—and probabilities into account. We might respond, "Isn't that what statistics already do?" For the most part, the answer is "no." The traditional approach to statistical inference assumes that we never learn from prior experience—the comparison distribution is always some version of chance.

Researcher John Kruschke (2011) points out that the Bayesian approach is what we do in our daily lives: We examine new data and determine "how much we should change our beliefs relative to our prior beliefs" (p. 277; see also Gallistel, 2015b). Kruschke and Torrin Liddell (2018a) provide an example of belief updating that applies a Bayesian approach. Imagine you are a detective investigating a crime and have identified four suspects. Prior to the investigation, your belief about who is guilty is equally divided among all four suspects, as depicted in Figure 11-8a. The *prior* distribution *reflects the credibility or likelihood of the various values along the x-axis before we collect data.* But then you investigate and collect information (i.e., data). During your investigation, you learn that suspects W, X, and Y have strong alibis for the time of the crime. These new data—the alibis—prompt you to redistribute your beliefs about who likely committed the crime. *This redistribution of belief after collecting the data is the posterior.* As Figure 11-8b shows, after learning that suspects W, X, and Y have strong alibis, you

- The **prior** distribution reflects the credibility or likelihood of the various values along the *x*-axis before we collect data.

- The **posterior** is the redistribution of belief that occurs after collecting the data.

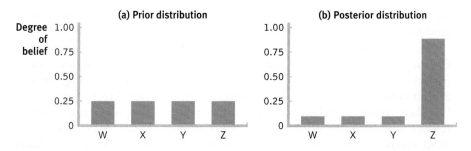

FIGURE 11-8

Prior and Posterior Distributions

(a) The prior distribution for the degree of belief that each of four suspects is guilty of the crime. (b) The posterior distribution for the degree of belief that each of four suspects is guilty of the crime, after learning that suspects W, X, and Y have strong alibis.
[Research from Kruschke & Liddell (2018a, Figure 1).]

would now think it very unlikely that they committed the crime; instead, you would now think it more likely that suspect Z committed the crime.

Here's an example of how you may already update your beliefs (the Bayesian approach) in your own life. Assume that you haven't been to your favorite childhood pizza restaurant in years, but a friend from back home mentions that she just walked by the restaurant today and it was closed for business. Because you haven't been there in years, your prior belief that the pizza place is open might look like the prior distribution depicted in Figure 11-9a: You have equal levels of confidence in the idea that it is open as well as in the idea that it is closed. Once your friend tells you that it is closed for business, you update your beliefs to the posterior distribution in Figure 11-9a. Now you have a strong belief that the pizza place is unlikely to be open for business.

Now imagine a different scenario: In this case, you just visited your favorite pizza place last night and then your friend tells you that she saw today that it was closed for business. Now your prior beliefs are like those in Figure 11-9b. You had a strong belief that the pizza place is open, because you just ate there. After hearing from your friend, you update your beliefs about the restaurant. Of course, you take into account your strong prior belief that the pizza place is open, so you do not update your beliefs as much as you did in Figure 11-9a. This little bit of data—one friend mentioning that the pizza restaurant is closed—is not enough to move you very far from your strong prior beliefs. But imagine you collect more data. You ask around and hear from several more friends that they, too, walked by the location today and saw the "Closed for Business" sign. Then you check the restaurant's Web site and find that it's down. These additional pieces of evidence may lead to a greater redistribution of your belief, as depicted in Figure 11-9c. At this point, you are fairly confident that the pizza place has closed.

Bayesian statistics offers several benefits (Kruschke & Liddell, 2018b; Wagenmakers et al., 2018). Unlike in traditional hypothesis testing, where all we can do is reject the null hypothesis, in Bayesian statistics, we can get evidence to support the null hypothesis, which may move publishers away from their strong bias of publishing only studies that reject the null hypothesis. Bayesian statistics also offers more intuitively interpretable interval estimates of population parameters than do traditional statistics: In Bayesian statistics, the posterior distribution tells us the likelihood of different possible values of the population parameter, taking into account both the data and

(a)

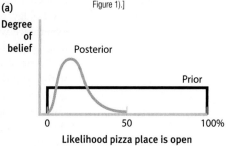

(b)

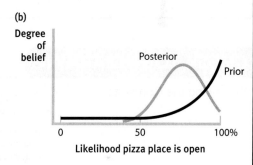

(c)

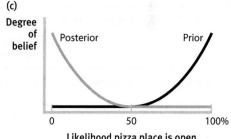

FIGURE 11-9

Redistributing Beliefs

The area under each curve represents where your belief is distributed along the *x*-axis. The narrower pink peaks, in (a) and (b), represent more confident beliefs in the corresponding value on the *x*-axis. The sloping pink line, in (c), represents less confidence in a precise point and beliefs that are distributed over a wider range of values.

the prior beliefs. Although traditional confidence intervals are often misinterpreted as providing this information, they actually do not (Wagenmakers et al., 2018).

Some researchers have pointed out that adopting Bayesian statistics does not necessarily save us from the various ethical problems currently facing the behavioral sciences (Kruschke & Liddell, 2018b; Simonsohn, 2014). But others, such as E. J. Wagenmakers and his colleagues (2018), argue that Bayesian analysis should replace traditional hypothesis testing (Kruschke, 2011). To facilitate this transition, Wagenmakers and his research team have developed software for performing Bayesian data analyses called JASP, which is available for free online. The students in one of the authors' classes created a manual for the JASP software, which is also available for free (shu.edu/psychology/resources.cfm). Additionally, if you are interested in getting more hands-on experience with the logic behind Bayesian data analyses, check out the free tutorial at tellmi.psy.lmu.de/felix/BayesLessons/BayesianLesson1.Rmd.

Eventually, Bayesian statistics may replace the traditional approach. For now, most statistics students still learn how to conduct traditional hypothesis testing. But if you go on to graduate school and have the opportunity to take a course in Bayesian analysis, we strongly encourage you to do so. The use of Bayesian analyses is definitely on the rise in the behavioral sciences, given some of its benefits over traditional hypothesis testing (e.g., Andrews & Baguley, 2013).

CHECK YOUR LEARNING

Reviewing the Concepts

> A confidence interval can be created with a *t* distribution around a difference between means.

> We can calculate an effect size, Cohen's *d*, for an independent-samples *t* test.

> Bayesian statistics is an alternative to traditional null hypothesis significance testing. The main difference is that it takes both prior beliefs—"priors" for short—and probabilities into account, whereas traditional hypothesis testing does not take into account prior beliefs.

Clarifying the Concepts

11-5   Why do we calculate confidence intervals?

11-6   How does considering the conclusions in terms of effect size help to prevent incorrect interpretations of the findings?

Calculating the Statistics

11-7   Use the hypothetical data on level of agreement with a supervisor, as listed here, to calculate the following. We already made some of these calculations for Check Your Learning 11-3.

> Group 1 (low trust in leader): 3, 2, 4, 6, 1, 2
> Group 2 (high trust in leader): 5, 4, 6, 2, 6

a.   Calculate the 95% confidence interval.

b.   Calculate effect size using Cohen's *d*.

Applying the Concepts

Solutions to these Check Your Learning questions can be found in Appendix D.

11-8   Explain what the confidence interval calculated in Check Your Learning 11-7 tells us. Why is this confidence interval superior to the hypothesis test that we conducted?

11-9   Interpret the meaning of the effect size calculated in Check Your Learning 11-7. What does this add to the confidence interval and hypothesis test?

REVIEW OF CONCEPTS

Conducting an Independent-Samples *t* Test

We use *independent-samples* t *tests* when we have two samples and different participants are in each sample. Because the samples comprise different people, we cannot calculate difference scores, so the comparison distribution is a distribution of differences between means. Because we are working with two separate samples of scores (rather than one set of difference scores) when we conduct an independent-samples *t* test, we need additional steps to calculate an estimate of spread. As part of these steps, we calculate estimates of variance from each sample and then combine them to create a *pooled variance*. We can present the statistics in APA style as we did with other hypothesis tests. We can also create a bar graph with a bar for each group's mean. Ideally, we include *error bars*, vertical lines at the top of each bar that indicate variability around each estimated mean.

Beyond Hypothesis Testing

As with other forms of hypothesis testing, it is useful to replace or supplement the independent-samples *t* test with a confidence interval. A confidence interval can be created around a difference between means using a *t* distribution. To understand the importance of a finding, we must also calculate an effect size. With an independent-samples *t* test, as with other *t* tests, a common effect-size measure is Cohen's *d*.

Bayesian statistics is an alternative to traditional null hypothesis significance testing. The main difference is that it takes both prior beliefs—"priors" for short—and probabilities into account, whereas traditional hypothesis testing does not take into account prior beliefs.

SPSS

We can conduct an independent-samples *t* test using SPSS for the wine-tasting data we presented earlier in this chapter. To begin, let's identify the variables included in the problem. First, there is the dependent variable: rating of the bottle of wine. Second, there is the independent variable: whether the participant was told it was a $10 bottle of wine or a $90 bottle of wine. This is a categorical variable that has two levels. We need to tell SPSS that this variable is categorical as well as the different levels for each category. To do so, participants are given a "1" if they were told that the wine was from a $10 bottle and a "2" if they were told that the wine was from a $90 bottle. We can then use the "Values" function in the Variable View to tell SPSS that 1 = $10 and 2 = $90. We also want to be sure to change the "Measures" function in the Variable View to "nominal" for this variable. For an independent-samples *t* test, the independent variable can either be a nominal variable or an ordinal variable. The dependent variable should always be a scale variable.

We place each participant's data in one row—an arbitrarily assigned ID number in the first column, a score for the stated cost of the wine in the second column, and a liking rating in the third column. Remember: As a rule of thumb, it is a good idea to give each participant an ID number. That way, we can always double-check any data that appear to be incorrect. We can now conduct the hypothesis test.

Note: When we are in Data View, we can switch between showing the actual value labels (i.e., $10 or $90 in this study) or the numbers assigned to each group (i.e., 1 or 2). Under the "view" menu at the top, we either check or uncheck the option "value labels" to turn the labels on or off. This does not change the data, but simply changes the way we see the data.

Select Analyze → Compare Means → Independent-Samples T Test. First, we choose the dependent variable, "Rating," by clicking it, then clicking the arrow in the upper center. We'll now see "Rating" in the box titled "Test Variable." Second, we choose the independent variable, "Cost," by clicking it, then clicking the arrow in the lower center. We'll now see "Cost" in the box titled "Grouping

Variable." Again, we need to tell SPSS what two groups we are comparing. To do so, we click the "Define Groups" button, then provide the values for each level of the independent variable. For example, we enter "1" for group 1 (the $10 group) and "2" for group 2 (the $90 group), and click "Continue." Then we click "OK."

The output is shown in the screenshot. In the first table, "Group Statistics," we see means and standard deviations for each group: participants told they were drinking wine from a $10 bottle and participants told they were drinking wine from a $90 bottle. For example, the output tells us that the mean for those told they were drinking

wine from a $10 bottle is 2.50, with a standard deviation of 0.80416.

In the second output table, "Independent-Samples Test," we focus our attention on the top line. We can see that the *t* statistic is −2.436, with a *p* value (under "Sig. (2-tailed)") of 0.045. The *t* statistic is the same as the one we calculated earlier, −2.44. We can also see the mean difference (the numerator used to calculate the *t* statistic), the standard error difference (the denominator used to calculate the *t* statistic), and the 95% confidence interval for the *t* statistic. These values should also match the previously calculated values presented in the example earlier.

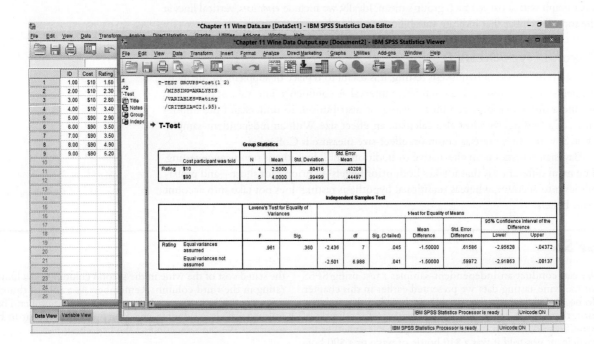

HOW IT WORKS

11.1 INDEPENDENT-SAMPLES *t* TEST

Does using social media stress us out? Australian researchers randomly assigned 138 Facebook users either to continue with their usual use of Facebook or to quit the social media platform entirely for 5 days (Vanman, Baker, & Tobin, 2018). Following this period, the researchers assessed a variety of dependent variables, including a change in cortisol levels in participants' saliva. (Cortisol is often referred to as the "stress hormone" because its level increases when people experience stress.) Following are fictional data for 9 people (4 in the group who continued using Facebook as usual and 5 in the group who abstained from using Facebook for 5 days); these fictional data have approximately the same means as in the original study.

Change in cortisol levels
Continued Facebook: 0.15, 0.05, 0.06, −0.10
No Facebook: 0.02, −0.13, − 0.29, − 0.11, − 0.34

How can we conduct all 6 steps of hypothesis testing for an independent-samples *t* test for this scenario, using a two-tailed test with critical values based on an alpha level of 0.05? Here are the steps:

Step 1: Population 1: People using Facebook. Population 2: People abstaining from Facebook.

The comparison distribution will be a distribution of differences between means based on the null hypothesis. The hypothesis test will be an independent-samples *t* test because there are two samples composed of different groups of participants. This study meets only the first of the three assumptions. (1) The dependent variable is change in cortisol level, which is a scale variable. (2) However, we do not know whether the population is normally distributed, and there are not at least 30 participants. Therefore, we must be cautious. (3) The people in this study were not randomly selected from among all people, so we must be cautious with respect to generalizing these findings.

Step 2: Null hypothesis: On average, people who continue to use Facebook have the same change in cortisol levels as people who abstain from Facebook for 5 days—H_0: $\mu_1 = \mu_2$. Research hypothesis: On average, people who continue to use Facebook have a different change in cortisol levels as compared with those who abstain from Facebook for 5 days—H_1: $\mu_1 \neq \mu_2$.

Step 3: $(\mu_1 - \mu_2) = 0$; $s_{difference} = 0.084$

Calculations:

a. $M_X = 0.040$

X	$X - M$	$(X - M)^2$
0.15	0.11	0.012
0.05	0.01	0.000
0.06	0.02	0.000
−0.10	−0.14	0.020

$$s_X^2 = \frac{\Sigma(X - M)^2}{N - 1} = \frac{(0.012 + 0.000 + 0.000 + 0.020)}{4 - 1} = 0.011$$

$$M_Y = -0.17$$

Y	$Y - M$	$(Y - M)^2$
0.02	0.19	0.036
−0.13	0.04	0.002
−0.29	−0.12	0.014
−0.11	0.06	0.004
−0.34	−0.17	0.029

$$s_Y^2 = \frac{\Sigma(Y - M)^2}{N - 1} = \frac{(0.036 + 0.002 + 0.014 + 0.004 + 0.029)}{5 - 1} = 0.021$$

b. $df_X = N - 1 = 4 - 1 = 3$

$df_Y = N - 1 = 5 - 1 = 4$

$df_{total} = df_X + df_Y = 3 + 4 = 7$

$$s_{pooled}^2 = \left(\frac{df_X}{df_{total}}\right)s_X^2 + \left(\frac{df_Y}{df_{total}}\right)s_Y^2 = \left(\frac{3}{7}\right)0.011 + \left(\frac{4}{7}\right)0.021 = 0.005 + 0.012 = 0.017$$

c. $s_{M_X}^2 = \frac{s_{pooled}^2}{N_X} = \frac{0.017}{4} = 0.004$

$s_{M_Y}^2 = \frac{s_{pooled}^2}{N_Y} = \frac{0.017}{5} = 0.003$

d. $s_{difference}^2 = s_{M_X}^2 + s_{M_Y}^2 = 0.004 + 0.003 = 0.007$

e. $s_{difference} = \sqrt{s_{difference}^2} = \sqrt{0.007} = 0.084$

Step 4: The critical values, based on a two-tailed test, an alpha level of 0.05, and a df_{total} of 7, are −2.365 and 2.365 (as seen in the curve in Figure 11-2 on page 312).

Step 5: $t = \dfrac{(0.040 - (-0.170)) - (0)}{0.084} = 2.50$

Step 6: Reject the null hypothesis. It seems that people who abstain from using Facebook show a greater average decrease in cortisol levels as compared with people who continue to use Facebook.

11.2 CONFIDENCE INTERVALS FOR AN INDEPENDENT-SAMPLES *t* TEST

How would we calculate a 95% confidence interval for the difference between means for the independent-samples *t* test we conducted in How It Works 11.1? Previously, we calculated the difference between the means of these samples to be $0.040 - (-0.170) = 0.210$; the standard error for the differences between means, $s_{difference}$, to be 0.084; and the degrees of freedom to be 7. (Note that the order of subtraction in calculating the difference between means is irrelevant; we could just as easily have subtracted 0.040 from −0.017 and gotten a negative result, −0.21.)

1. We draw a normal curve with the sample difference between means in the center.
2. We indicate the bounds of the 95% confidence interval on either end and write the percentages under each segment of the curve: 2.5% in each tail.
3. We look up the *t* statistics for the lower and upper ends of the confidence interval in the *t* table, based on a two-tailed test, an alpha of 0.05 (which corresponds to a 95% confidence interval), and the degrees of freedom—7—that we calculated earlier. Because the normal curve is symmetric, the bounds of the confidence interval fall at *t* statistics of −2.365 and 2.365. We add those *t* statistics to the normal curve.
4. We convert the *t* statistics to raw differences between means for the lower and upper ends of the confidence interval.

$$(M_X - M_Y)_{lower} = -t(s_{difference}) + (M_X - M_Y)_{sample} = -2.365(0.084) + (0.210) = 0.01$$

$$(M_X - M_Y)_{upper} = t(s_{difference}) + (M_X - M_Y)_{sample} = 2.365(0.084) + (0.210) = 0.41$$

The confidence interval around the difference between means is $[0.01, 0.41]$.
5. We check the answer; each end of the confidence interval should be exactly the same distance from the sample mean.

$$0.01 - (0.21) = -0.20$$
$$0.41 - (0.21) = 0.20$$

The interval checks out, and we know that the margin of error is 0.20.

11.3 EFFECT SIZE FOR AN INDEPENDENT-SAMPLES *t* TEST

How can we calculate an effect size for the independent-samples *t* test we conducted in How It Works 11.1? In How It Works 11.1, we calculated means of 0.04 for participants who continued to use Facebook and −0.17 for participants who abstained from using Facebook. Previously, we calculated a standard error for the difference between means, $s_{difference}$, of 0.084. This time, we'll take the square root of the pooled variance to get the pooled standard deviation, the appropriate value for the denominator of Cohen's *d*.

$$s_{pooled} = \sqrt{s^2_{pooled}} = \sqrt{0.017} = 0.130$$

For Cohen's *d*, we simply replace the denominator of the formula for the test statistic with the standard deviation, s_{pooled}, instead of the standard error, $s_{difference}$.

$$\text{Cohen's } d = \frac{(M_X - M_Y) - (\mu_X - \mu_Y)}{s_{pooled}} = \frac{(0.040 - (-0.170)) - (0)}{0.130} = 1.615$$

According to Cohen's conventions, this is a large effect. That's not surprising because with such a small sample size, we had to have a large effect to attain the same outcome—statistically significant—that the researchers did. In the actual study, there was a medium effect size.

11.4 REPORTING THE RESULTS OF HYPOTHESIS TESTING AND THE EFFECT SIZE IN A JOURNAL

How would we report the results of the hypothesis test and the effect size described in How It Works 11.1 and 11.3? The statistics would appear in a journal article as $t(7) = 2.50, p < 0.05, d = 1.62$, a large effect. In addition to the results of hypothesis testing, we would include the means and standard deviations for the two samples. We calculated the means in step 3 of hypothesis testing, and we also calculated the variances. We can calculate the standard deviations by taking the square roots of the variances. The descriptive statistics can be reported in parentheses as:

(Facebook: $M = 0.04, SD = 0.105$; No Facebook: $M = -0.17, SD = 0.145$)

EXERCISES

The solutions to the odd-numbered exercises can be found in Appendix C.

Clarifying the Concepts

11.1 When is it appropriate to use an independent-samples *t* test?

11.2 Explain random assignment and what it controls.

11.3 What are independent events?

11.4 Explain how the paired-samples *t* test helps us evaluate individual differences and the independent-samples *t* test helps us evaluate group differences.

11.5 As they relate to comparison distributions, what is the difference between *mean differences* and *differences between means*?

11.6 As measures of variability, what is the difference between standard deviation and variance?

11.7 What is the difference between s_X^2 and s_Y^2?

11.8 What is pooled variance?

11.9 Why would we want the variability estimate based on a larger sample to count more (to be more heavily weighted) than one based on a smaller sample?

11.10 Define the symbols in the following formula: $s_{difference}^2 = s_{M_X}^2 + s_{M_Y}^2$

11.11 How do confidence intervals relate to margin of error?

11.12 What is the difference between pooled variance and pooled standard deviation?

11.13 How does the size of the confidence interval relate to the precision of the prediction?

11.14 Why does the effect-size calculation use standard deviation rather than standard error?

11.15 Explain how we determine standard deviation (needed to calculate Cohen's *d*) from the several steps of calculations we made to determine standard error.

11.16 For an independent-samples *t* test, what is the difference between the formula for the *t* statistic and the formula for Cohen's *d*?

11.17 How do we interpret effect size using Cohen's *d*?

11.18 How does the Bayesian approach to statistics differ from the traditional approach?

11.19 Compare and contrast the characteristics of the prior and posterior distributions of the Bayesian statistical approach.

Calculating the Statistic

11.20 In the next column are several sample means. For each class, calculate the differences between the means for students who sit in the front versus the back of a classroom.

Mean Test Grades	Students in the Front	Students in the Back
Class 1	82.0	78.00
Class 2	79.5	77.41
Class 3	71.5	76.00
Class 4	72.0	71.30

11.21 Consider the following data from two independent groups:

Group 1: 97, 83, 105, 102, 92
Group 2: 111, 103, 96, 106

a. Calculate s^2 for group 1 and for group 2.

b. Calculate df_X, df_Y, and df_{total}.

c. Determine the critical values for *t*, assuming a two-tailed test with an alpha level of 0.05.

d. Calculate pooled variance, s^2_{pooled}.

e. Calculate the variance version of standard error for each group.

f. Calculate the variance and the standard deviation of the distribution of differences between means.

g. Calculate the *t* statistic.

h. Calculate the 95% confidence interval.

i. Calculate Cohen's *d*.

11.22 Consider the following data from two independent groups:

Liberals: 2, 1, 3, 2
Conservatives: 4, 3, 3, 5, 2, 4

a. Calculate s^2 for each group.

b. Calculate df_X, df_Y, and df_{total}.

c. Determine the critical values for *t*, assuming a two-tailed test with an alpha level of 0.05.

d. Calculate pooled variance, s^2_{pooled}.

e. Calculate the variance version of standard error for each group.

f. Calculate the variance and the standard deviation of the distribution of differences between means.

g. Calculate the *t* statistic.

h. Calculate the 95% confidence interval.

i. Calculate Cohen's *d*.

11.23 Find the critical *t* values for the following data sets:

a. Group 1 has 21 participants and group 2 has 16 participants. You are performing a two-tailed test with an alpha of 0.05.

b. You studied 3-year-old children and 6-year-old children, with samples of 12 and 16, respectively. You are performing a two-tailed test with an alpha of 0.01.

c. You have a total of 17 degrees of freedom for a two-tailed test and an alpha of 0.10.

Applying the Concepts

11.24 **Making a decision:** Numeric results for several independent-samples *t* tests are presented here. Decide whether each test is statistically significant, and report each result in the standard APA format.

a. A total of 73 people were studied, 40 in one group and 33 in the other group. The test statistic was calculated as 2.13 for a two-tailed test with an alpha level of 0.05.

b. One group of 23 people was compared to another group of 18 people. The *t* statistic obtained for their data was 1.77. Assume you were performing a two-tailed test with an alpha of 0.05.

c. One group of 9 mice was compared to another group of 6 mice, using a two-tailed test at an alpha of 0.01. The test statistic was calculated as 3.02.

11.25 **The independent-samples *t* test, hypnosis, and the Stroop effect:** Using data from Exercise 10.33 on the effects of posthypnotic suggestion on the Stroop effect (Raz, Fan, & Posner, 2005), let's conduct an independent-samples *t* test. For this test, we will pretend that two sets of people participated in the study, a between-groups design, whereas previously we considered data from a within-groups design. The first score for each original participant will be in the first sample—those not receiving a posthypnotic suggestion. The second score for each original participant will be in the second sample—those receiving a posthypnotic suggestion.

Sample 1: 12.6, 13.8, 11.6, 12.2, 12.1, 13.0
Sample 2: 8.5, 9.6, 10.0, 9.2, 8.9, 10.8

a. Conduct all six steps of an independent-samples *t* test. Be sure to label all six steps.

b. Report the statistics as you would in a journal article.

c. What happens to the test statistic when you switch from having all participants be in both samples to having two separate samples? Given the same numbers, is it easier to reject the null hypothesis with a within-groups design or with a between-groups design?

d. In your own words, why do you think it is easier to reject the null hypothesis in one of these situations than in the other?

e. Calculate the 95% confidence interval.

f. State in your own words what we learn from this confidence interval.

g. What information does the confidence interval give us that we also get from the hypothesis test?

h. What additional information does the confidence interval give us that we do not get from the hypothesis test?

i. Calculate the appropriate measure of effect size.

j. Based on Cohen's conventions, is this a small, medium, or large effect size?

k. Why is it useful to have this information in addition to the results of a hypothesis test?

11.26 **An independent-samples *t* test and getting ready for a date:** In an example we sometimes use in our statistics classes, several semesters' worth of male and female students were asked how long, in minutes, they spend getting ready for a date. The data reported below reflect the actual means and the approximate standard deviations for the actual data from 142 students.

Men: 28, 35, 52, 14

Women: 30, 82, 53, 61

a. Conduct all six steps of an independent-samples *t* test. Be sure to label all six steps.

b. Report the statistics as you would in a journal article.

c. Calculate the 95% confidence interval.

d. Calculate the 90% confidence interval.

e. How are the confidence intervals different from each other? Explain why they are different.

f. Calculate the appropriate measure of effect size.

g. Based on Cohen's conventions, is this a small, medium, or large effect size?

h. Why is it useful to have this information in addition to the results of a hypothesis test?

11.27 An independent-samples *t* test, gender, and talkativeness: "Are Women Really More Talkative Than Men?" is the title of an article that appeared in the journal *Science*. In the article, Mehl, Vazire, Ramirez-Esparza, Slatcher, and Pennebaker (2007) report the results of a study of 396 men and women. Each participant wore a microphone that recorded every word he or she uttered. The researchers counted the number of words uttered by men and women and compared them. The data below are fictional but they re-create the pattern that Mehl and colleagues observed:

Men: 16,345 17,222 15,646 14,889 16,701

Women: 17,345 15,593 16,624 16,696 14,200

a. Conduct all six steps of an independent-samples *t* test. Be sure to label all six steps.

b. Report the statistics as you would in a journal article.

c. Calculate the 95% confidence interval.

d. Express the confidence interval in writing, according to the format discussed in the chapter.

e. State in your own words what we learn from this confidence interval.

f. Calculate the appropriate measure of effect size.

g. Based on Cohen's conventions, is this a small, medium, or large effect size?

h. Why is it useful to have this information in addition to the results of a hypothesis test?

11.28 An independent-samples *t* test and getting people to turn off the light: Do you turn off the light when you leave the room? South Korean researchers wondered how they could increase the number of people who do (Ahn, Kim, & Aggarwal, 2013). They compared two poster campaigns. In one, an image of a light bulb was anthropomorphized by giving it eyes, nose, and a mouth, as well as adding the words, "I'm burning hot, turn me off when you leave!" (p. 225). In a second, there were no human features on the light bulb and the text simply said, "Our bulbs are burning hot, turn the lights off when you leave!" (p. 226). Participants were randomly assigned to view one of these posters and then were asked to rate a series of items about how likely they would be to behave in an environmentally friendly manner. The scale went from 1 (very unlikely) to 9 (very likely). The summary statistics for the data below approximate the actual means and standard errors in the study.

Anthropomorphism	Nonanthropomorphism
7.2	5.3
8.1	6.2
7.5	6.5
6.9	7.0
6.6	5.6
7.4	6.8
6.5	6.2

a. Conduct all six steps of an independent-samples *t* test. Be sure to label all six steps.

b. Report the statistics as you would in a journal article.

c. Is there a shortcut you could or did use to compute your hypothesis test? (*Hint:* There are equal numbers of participants in the two groups.)

d. Calculate the 95% confidence interval.

e. State in your own words what we learn from this confidence interval.

f. Explain why interval estimates are better than point estimates.

g. Calculate the appropriate measure of effect size.

h. Based on Cohen's conventions, is this a small, medium, or large effect size?

i. Why is it useful to have this information in addition to the results of a hypothesis test?

11.29 An independent-samples *t* test, award-winning television, and the theory of mind: Does watching award-winning fiction on television help us to understand other people? Psychologists Jessica Black and Jennifer Barnes (2015) tested whether people who watched award-winning fictional television shows like *Mad Men* and *The West Wing* performed better on a test of theory of mind than people who watch documentaries like episodes from the series *Shark Week* and *How the Universe Works*. After randomly watching either a high-quality fictional show or a documentary for about a half-hour, participants were asked to look at a series of 36 photos of people's eyes and decide if each person was jealous, panicked, arrogant, or hateful. Scores ranged from 0 (guessed no emotions correctly) to 36 (guessed every emotion correctly). The data below approximate the actual means and standard errors in the study.

TV Fiction	Documentary
28	27
30	26
31	28
27	29
29	29
29	28
31	27
27	26
29	

a. Conduct all six steps of an independent-samples *t* test. Be sure to label all six steps.

b. Report the statistics as you would in a journal article.

c. Calculate the 95% confidence interval.

d. State in your own words what we learn from this confidence interval.

e. Express the confidence interval, in a sentence, as a margin of error.

f. Calculate the appropriate measure of effect size.

g. Based on Cohen's conventions, is this a small, medium, or large effect size?

h. Why is it useful to have this information in addition to the results of a hypothesis test?

11.30 Choosing a hypothesis test: For each of the following three scenarios, state which hypothesis test you would use from among the four introduced so far: the *z* test, the single-sample *t* test, the paired-samples *t* test, and the independent-samples *t* test. (*Note:* In the actual studies described, the researchers did not always use one of these tests, often because the actual experiment had additional variables.) Explain your answer.

a. A study of 40 children who had survived a brain tumor revealed that the children were more likely to have behavioral and emotional difficulties than were children who had not experienced such a trauma (Upton & Eiser, 2006). Parents rated children's difficulties, and the ratings data were compared with known means from published population norms.

b. Talarico and Rubin (2003) recorded the memories of 54 students just after the terrorist attacks in the United States on September 11, 2001—some memories related to the terrorist attacks on that day (called *flashbulb memories* for their vividness and emotional content) and some everyday memories. They found that flashbulb memories were no more consistent over time than everyday memories, even though they were perceived to be more accurate.

c. The HOPE VI Panel Study (Popkin & Woodley, 2002) was initiated to test a U.S. program aimed at improving troubled public housing developments. Residents of five HOPE VI developments were examined at the beginning of the study so researchers could later ascertain whether their quality of life had improved. Means at the beginning of the study were compared to known national data sources (e.g., the U.S. Census, the American Housing Survey) that had summary statistics, including means and standard deviations.

11.31 Choosing a hypothesis test: For each of the following three scenarios, state which hypothesis test you would use from among the four introduced so far: the *z* test, the single-sample *t* test, the paired-samples *t* test, and the independent-samples *t* test. (*Note:* In the actual studies described, the researchers did not always use one of these tests, often because the actual experiment had additional variables.) Explain your answer.

a. Taylor and Ste-Marie (2001) studied eating disorders in 41 Canadian female figure skaters. They compared the figure skaters' data on the Eating Disorder Inventory to the means of known populations, including women with eating disorders. On average, the figure skaters were more similar to the population of women with eating disorders than to those without eating disorders.

b. In an article titled "A Fair and Balanced Look at the News: What Affects Memory for Controversial Arguments," Wiley (2005) found that people with a high level of previous knowledge about a given controversial topic (e.g., abortion, military intervention) had better average recall for arguments on both sides of that issue than did those with lower levels of knowledge.

c. Engle-Friedman and colleagues (2003) studied the effects of sleep deprivation. Fifty students were assigned to one night of sleep loss (students were required to call the laboratory every half-hour all night) and then one night of no sleep loss (normal sleep). The next day, students were offered a choice of math problems with differing levels of difficulty. Following sleep loss, students tended to choose less challenging problems.

11.32 Null and research hypotheses: Using the research studies described in the previous exercise, create null hypotheses and research hypotheses appropriate for the chosen statistical test:

a. Taylor and Ste-Marie (2001) studied eating disorders in 41 Canadian female figure skaters. They compared the figure skaters' data on the Eating Disorder Inventory to the means of known populations, including women with eating disorders. On average, the figure skaters were more similar to the population of women with eating disorders than to those without eating disorders.

b. In an article titled "A Fair and Balanced Look at the News: What Affects Memory for Controversial Arguments," Wiley (2005) found that people with a high level of previous knowledge about a given controversial topic (e.g., abortion, military intervention) had better average recall for arguments on both sides of that issue than did those with lower levels of knowledge.

c. Engle-Friedman and colleagues (2003) studied the effects of sleep deprivation. Fifty students were assigned to one night of sleep loss (students were required to call the laboratory every half-hour all night) and then one night of no sleep loss (normal sleep). The next day, students were offered a choice of math problems with differing levels of difficulty. Following sleep loss, students tended to choose less challenging problems.

11.33 Independent-samples *t* test and walking speed: The New York City Department of City Planning (2006) studied pedestrian walking speeds. The report stated that pedestrians who were en route to work walked a median of 4.41 feet per second, whereas tourist pedestrians walked a median of 3.79 feet per second. They did not report results of any hypothesis tests.

a. Why would an independent-samples *t* test be appropriate in this situation?

b. What would the null hypothesis and research hypothesis be in this situation?

11.34 Independent-sample *t* tests and the "fun theory": Volkswagen has created a series of videos based on its "fun theory," the idea that you can change behavior if you take an activity that is good for society and make it fun. (You can watch the videos at goodvertising.site/the-fun-theory.) For each of the following examples, state the independent variable (and its levels) as well as the dependent variable (and the types of variables that both of these are). Then, state whether you could use an independent-samples *t* test to analyze the data, and explain your answer.

a. A "Speed Camera Lottery"—in which an electronic sign told people how fast they were going so they could adjust their speed—was introduced. As people passed the electronic sign, a camera took a photo of their license plate. If they were speeding, they were mailed a ticket and had to pay a fine. If they were obeying the speed limit, they were entered into a lottery to win some of the money from those who paid speeding tickets. The average speed using the Speed Camera Lottery sign was 25 kilometers per hour, and the average speed with no lottery sign was 32 kilometers per hour.

b. At the exit of a subway station, stairs and an escalator were side by side. The stairs were turned into a piano, so that when you climbed them, you heard musical notes. While the Piano Staircase was in place, 66% more people took the stairs—rather than the escalator—than when the Piano Staircase was not in place.

c. A trash bin was designed so that when someone threw trash into it, there was a long whistling sound, followed by a thud, as if the trash were falling into an extremely deep bin. When the bin was used, an average of 72 kg of trash was disposed of in a day; when it was not used, an average of 31 kg of trash was disposed of in a day.

11.35 Cafeteria trays, food consumption, and an independent-samples *t* test: Kiho Kim and Stevia Morawski (2012) reported the following in the abstract (brief summary) of their published research study: "Here, we report on the results of an experiment to evaluate the effects of tray availability on food waste production and dish use in a university dining facility. We sampled 360 individual diners over a 6-day period and documented a 32% reduction in food waste and a 27% reduction in dish use when trays were unavailable."

a. What was the independent variable and what were its levels?

b. What were the dependent variables? How did the researchers likely operationalize their variables?

c. The researchers describe their study as an experiment. Explain what they mean by this.

d. Why would it be possible to use independent-samples *t* tests to analyze the data from their study?

11.36 Independent-sample *t* tests and "Blinded with Science": Researchers studied the effects of learning about the effectiveness of a new medication (Tal & Wansink, 2016). Some participants heard information about the medication; others heard the same information and saw a graph that depicted the data they had heard about. Thus, the two groups had identical information. Participants rated the effectiveness of the medication on a scale of 1–9, with 9 indicating a higher level of effectiveness. The researchers reported: "Participants given graphs expressed greater belief in the claims, rating the medication as more effective (6.83 of 9) than did participants given verbal description only (6.12 of 9): *t*(59) = −2.1, *p* = .04" (p. 4). The researchers titled their paper "Blinded with Science" because the mere presence of a scientific cue—a graph—altered perceptions of the medication.

a. What kind of *t* test did the researchers use? Explain your answer.

b. How do we know this finding is statistically significant?

c. How many participants were in this experiment?

d. Identify the means of the two groups.

e. What additional statistics would it have been helpful for the researchers to include?

11.37 Independent-sample *t* tests and note-taking—laptop or longhand: Researchers explored whether there were mean differences between students who were randomly assigned to take notes longhand and students who were randomly assigned to take notes on their laptops (Mueller & Oppenheimer, 2014). They had observed that students who took notes by hand performed better, on average, on conceptual questions—those that involved thinking beyond just recalling facts—than students who

took notes on their laptops. To explore reasons for this difference, they examined the students' notes. The researchers "found that laptop notes contained an average of 14.6% verbatim overlap with the lecture (*SD* = 7.3%), whereas longhand notes averaged only 8.8% (*SD* = 4.8%), *t*(63) = −3.77, *p* < .001, *d* = 0.94" (p. 3). They concluded that when people took notes longhand, they were more likely to put ideas in their own words, which likely led to deeper processing and better learning of information.

a. What kind of *t* test did the researchers use? Explain your answer.

b. How do we know this finding is statistically significant?

c. How many participants were in this experiment?

d. Identify the means of the two groups.

e. What is the effect size for this finding? Interpret what that means in terms of Cohen's conventions.

11.38 Gender, humor, and an independent-samples *t* test: Researchers at Stanford University examined brain activity in women and men during exposure to humorous cartoons (Azim, Mobbs, Jo, Menon, & Reiss, 2005). Using functional magnetic resonance imaging (fMRI), researchers observed more activity in the reward centers of women's brains than men's brains—the same reward centers that respond when you receive money or feel happy. The researchers suggested that this result might have occurred because women have lower expectations of humor than do men, so they find it more rewarding when something is actually funny. However, it's also possible that women and men tend to find different things funny. So, the researchers asked women and men to indicate the percentage of 30 cartoons that they perceived to be either "funny" or "unfunny." Below are fictional data for 9 people (4 women and 5 men); these fictional data have approximately the same means as in the original study.

Percentage of cartoons labeled as "funny"

Women: 84, 97, 58, 90

Men: 88, 90, 52, 97, 86

Conduct all six steps of hypothesis testing for an independent-samples *t* test for this scenario, using a two-tailed test with critical values based on an alpha level of 0.05.

11.39 Gender, humor, and a confidence interval for an independent-samples *t* test: Calculate a 95%

confidence interval for the independent-samples *t* test you conducted on the gender and humor data in the previous exercise.

11.40 Gender, humor, and effect size for an independent-samples *t* test: How can we calculate an effect size for the independent-samples *t* test we conducted in Exercise 11.38?

11.41 Gender, humor, and reporting statistical results in APA style: How would we report the results of the hypothesis test and the effect size calculation for the gender and humor data that you conducted in Exercises 11.38 and 11.40?

11.42 ESP and Bayesian belief updating: In Chapter 8, Exercise 8.71, we described a journal article in which Daryl Bem (2011) reported nine experiments, all providing evidence for extrasensory perception (ESP) using traditional statistical approaches. How might a Bayesian statistical approach come to a different conclusion? To illustrate for yourself, draw a prior distribution representing scientific consensus on the existence of ESP, with degree of belief on the *y*-axis and percent likelihood that ESP is real along the *x*-axis.

11.43 Sample size and Bayesian belief updating: The pizza place example that was introduced in the chapter, and in Figure 11-9, suggests an interaction between the strength of our prior beliefs and the amount of data that we have in determining how much we change our beliefs—that is, how different the posterior distribution is from the prior. What is this relation and what does it suggest about how sample size plays a role in Bayesian belief updating?

Putting It All Together

11.44 Gender and number words: Chang, Sandhofer, and Brown (2011) wondered whether mothers used number words more, on average, with their preschool sons than with their preschool daughters. Each participating family included one mother and one child—either female or male. The researchers speculated that early exposure to more number words might predispose children to like mathematics. They reported the following: "An independent-samples *t* test revealed statistically significant differences in the percentages of overall numeric speech used when interacting with boys compared with girls, $t(30) = 2.40$, $p < .05$, $d = .88$. That is, mothers used number terms with boys an average of 9.49% of utterances ($SD = 6.78$%) compared

with 4.64% of utterances with girls ($SD = 4.43$%)" (pp. 444–445).

a. Is this a between-groups or within-groups design? Explain your answer.

b. What is the independent variable? What is the dependent variable?

c. How many children were in the total sample? Explain how you determined this.

d. Is the sample likely randomly selected? Is it likely that the researchers used random assignment?

e. Were the researchers able to reject the null hypothesis? Explain.

f. What can you say about the size of the effect?

g. Describe how you could design an experiment to test whether exposure to more number words in preschool leads children to like mathematics more when they enter school.

11.45 School lunches: Alice Waters, owner of the Berkeley, California, restaurant Chez Panisse, has long been an advocate for the use of simple, fresh, organic ingredients in home and restaurant cooking. She has also turned her considerable expertise to school cafeterias. Waters (2006) praised changes in school lunch menus that have expanded nutritious offerings, but she hypothesizes that students are likely to circumvent healthy lunches by avoiding vegetables and smuggling in banned junk food unless they receive accompanying nutrition education and hands-on involvement in their meals. She has spearheaded an Edible Schoolyard program in Berkeley, which involves public school students in the cultivation and preparation of fresh foods, and states that such interactive education is necessary to combat growing levels of childhood obesity. "Nothing less," Waters writes, "will change their behavior."

a. In your own words, what is Waters predicting? Citing the confirmation bias, explain why Waters's program, although intuitively appealing, should not be instituted nationwide without further study.

b. Describe a simple between-groups experiment with a nominal independent variable with two levels and a scale dependent variable to test Waters's hypothesis. Specifically identify the independent variable, its levels, and the dependent variable. State how you will operationalize the dependent variable.

c. Which hypothesis test would be used to analyze this experiment? Explain your answer.

d. Conduct step 1 of hypothesis testing.

e. Conduct step 2 of hypothesis testing.

f. State at least one other way you could operationalize the dependent variable.

g. Let's say, hypothetically, that Waters discounted the need for the research you propose by citing her own data that the Berkeley school in which she instituted the program has lower rates of obesity than other California schools. Describe the flaw in this argument by discussing the importance of random selection and random assignment.

11.46 Graphic warnings, sugary beverages, and hypothesis testing: Researchers asked soda drinkers to view either the logo for their favorite soda or a graphic warning demonstrating the harmful effects of sugary beverages (e.g., tooth decay, obesity; Donnelly, Zatz, Svirsky, & John, 2018). They found that those participants who saw the warnings reported significantly greater negative moods than those who saw the logos, "(graphic warning: $M = -2.13, SD = 1.63$; no warning: $M = 2.29, SD = 1.47$), $t(200) = 20.18$, $p < .001$, $d = 2.84$," and reported a higher level of "intention to purchase water (graphic warning: $M = 4.24, SD = 2.04$; no warning: $M = 2.72, SD = 1.72$), $t(200) = 5.71$, $p < .001$, $d = 0.80$."

a. Is it likely that the researchers used random selection? Explain.

b. Is it likely that the researchers used random assignment? Explain.

c. What is the independent variable, and what are its levels?

d. What is (are) the dependent variable(s)?

e. Which hypothesis test would the researchers use? Explain.

f. What did the researchers conclude with respect to each dependent variable (e.g., reject the null hypothesis or fail to reject the null hypothesis)? How can we know this just from the reported statistics?

g. How large were these effects? Explain your answer.

h. How could the researchers redesign this study so that they could use a paired-samples *t* test? Why would counterbalancing be necessary?

i. The researchers reported: "The study was preregistered at ClinicalTrials.gov (https://clinicaltrials.gov/ct2/show/NCT02744859). Stimuli and data for this and both subsequent studies are available at the Open Science Framework (OSF; https://osf.io/rh8pv/)" (p. 1323). Why are preregistration

and the sharing of materials at the Open Science Framework both ethical data practices?

11.47 Independent-samples *t* test and the perils of informal email addresses: Is your email address something like hotstuff@fake-mail.com? You may not want to use it when you apply for a job or email your professors. Dutch psychologists studied the effect of using informal email addresses on the likelihood of being hired (van Toorenburg, Oostrom, & Pollet, 2015). The researchers asked employment recruiters to look at résumés that either had a formal email address based on the user's name, like sannejong@hotmail.com, or an informal email address, like luv_u_sanne@hotmail.com. Recruiters then rated the likelihood that they would hire the person whose résumés they looked at. The researchers reported that "hirability ratings regarding the résumés with informal email addresses were significantly lower, … $t(362) = 7.72, p < 0.001$, than the hirability ratings regarding résumés that featured a formal email address (Cohen's $d = 0.81$). The effect of the email address was as strong as the effect of spelling errors, … $t(362) = 7.66, p < 0.001$, Cohen's $d = 0.80$" (p. 137).

a. Explain why the researchers were able to test their hypotheses using independent-samples *t* tests.

b. For the first result described here, what is the independent variable and what are its levels? What is the dependent variable?

c. There is less information about the second result described here. For the information presented, what do you think the independent variable is and what are the likely levels? What is the dependent variable?

d. Is the sample likely randomly selected? Is it likely that the researchers used random assignment? Explain your answers.

e. The researchers assessed hirability by having recruiters rate four items on a scale of 1–6. For example, recruiters were asked to rate how likely they would be to interview the applicant. Describe one different way that the researchers might have operationalized hirability.

f. Explain why it would have been more helpful for the researchers to report confidence intervals instead of hypothesis tests.

g. Based on what information can the researchers say that "the effect of the e-mail address was as strong as the effect of spelling errors"? Explain your answer.

LaunchPad
macmillan learning

Visit LaunchPad to access the e-book and to
test your knowledge with LearningCurve.

TERMS

independent-samples *t* test (p. 304) error bars (p. 313) posterior (p. 320)

pooled variance (p. 310) prior (p. 320)

FORMULAS

$$df_{total} = df_X + df_Y \quad \text{(p. 310)}$$

$$s_{difference} = \sqrt{s^2_{difference}} \quad \text{(p. 311)}$$

$$(M_X - M_Y)_{lower} = -t(s_{difference}) + (M_X - M_Y)_{sample} \quad \text{(p. 316)}$$

$$s^2_{pooled} = \left(\frac{df_X}{df_{total}}\right)s^2_X + \left(\frac{df_Y}{df_{total}}\right)s^2_Y \quad \text{(p. 310)}$$

$$t = \frac{(M_X - M_Y) - (\mu_X - \mu_Y)}{s_{difference}}, \text{ often}$$

$$s_{pooled} = \sqrt{s^2_{pooled}} \quad \text{(p. 319)}$$

$$s^2_{M_X} = \frac{s^2_{pooled}}{N_X} \quad \text{(p. 311)}$$

$$\text{abbreviated as: } t = \frac{(M_X - M_Y)}{s_{difference}} \quad \text{(p. 312)}$$

$$\text{Cohen's } d = \frac{(M_X - M_Y) - (\mu_X - \mu_Y)}{s_{pooled}}$$

$$s^2_{M_Y} = \frac{s^2_{pooled}}{N_Y} \quad \text{(p. 311)}$$

$$(M_X - M_Y)_{upper} = t(s_{difference}) + (M_X - M_Y)_{sample} \quad \text{(p. 316)}$$

for a difference between means (p. 319)

$$s^2_{difference} = s^2_{M_X} + s^2_{M_Y} \quad \text{(p. 311)}$$

SYMBOLS

s^2_{pooled} (p. 310)

$s^2_{difference}$ (p. 311)

$s_{difference}$ (p. 311)

One-Way Between-Groups ANOVA

Using the *F* Distributions with Three or More Samples

Type I Errors When Making Three or More Comparisons

The *F* Statistic as an Expansion of the *z* and *t* Statistics

The *F* Distributions for Analyzing Variability to Compare Means

The *F* Table

The Language and Assumptions for ANOVA

One-Way Between-Groups ANOVA

Everything About ANOVA But the Calculations

The Logic and Calculations of the *F* Statistic

Making a Decision

Beyond Hypothesis Testing for the One-Way Between-Groups ANOVA

R^2 and Omega Squared, Effect Sizes for ANOVA

Post Hoc Tests

The Tukey *HSD* Test

Data Ethics: The Bonferroni Test

Here's the bad news: You are not very good at multitasking. Here's some additional bad news: You probably think you're pretty good at multitasking—especially when it comes to using your mobile phone while driving.

Usually, nothing bad happens when you drive and talk on your mobile phone, so many people probably conclude that they are pretty good at multitasking while driving. But here's a simple research question: Are we worse drivers when we talk on a hands-free device or when we have a conversation with the person in the passenger seat? A simple, two-group design analyzed with a *t* test will answer that question. But reality is often more complicated than a simple two-group design, and people drive while holding a conversation in a variety of ways.

To address the variety of conversations, researchers used a driving simulator with eight surrounding projection screens to create a series of dangerous driving situations, such as merging into traffic (Gaspar et al., 2014). There were four different experimental conditions: (1) driving alone, (2) driving and talking with a passenger seated next to them, (3) driving and talking on a videophone with a "remote passenger" in a separate room, and (4) driving and talking on a hands-free mobile phone. The third condition—with the videophone—used two projection screens that allowed the "remote passenger" to see both what the driver saw (the road ahead) and the driver's face—just like a real passenger. How dangerous do you think each of these situations is (Figure 12-1)?

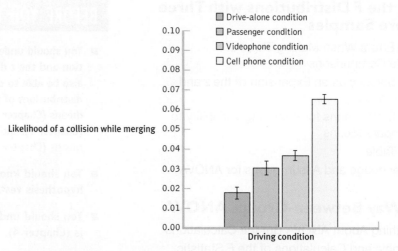

FIGURE 12-1

Comparing Three or More Groups

Researchers compared four groups in one study, which allowed them to discover that a conversation on a hands-free mobile phone was statistically significantly more dangerous than a conversation with a real passenger seated next to us, a conversation with a remote passenger using a videophone, or when driving alone (Gaspar et al., 2014).

For researchers, a four-group ANOVA is a bargain: multiple experiments for the price of one! In this chapter, we will learn about (a) the distributions used with ANOVA (the *F* distributions); (b) how to conduct an ANOVA when we have a between-groups design; (c) the effect-size statistic used with between-groups ANOVA; and (d) how to conduct a post hoc (or follow-up) test to determine exactly which groups are different from one another.

Using the *F* Distributions with Three or More Samples

The talking-while-driving study demonstrated that talking on a hands-free mobile phone was the most dangerous out of the four conditions. Comparing three or more groups is slightly more complicated than comparing two groups, so it requires comparison distributions that can accommodate that complexity: the *F* distributions.

Type I Errors When Making Three or More Comparisons

When comparing three or more groups, it is tempting to conduct an easy-to-understand *t* test on each of the possible comparisons. Unfortunately, there's a big downside to this approach: You may not be able to believe your own results. Why? Conducting numerous *t* tests greatly increases the probability of a Type I error (a false positive: rejecting the null hypothesis when the null hypothesis is true). Statisticians use a curious expression to describe the problem of too many possible comparisons: *inflating alpha*. For example, a study with three groups compares:

> Group 1 with group 2
> Group 1 with group 3
> Group 2 with group 3

That's three comparisons. If there were four groups, there would be six comparisons. With five groups, there would be 10 comparisons, and so on. With only one comparison, there is a 0.05 chance of having a Type I error in any given analysis if the null hypothesis is true, and a 0.95 chance of not having a Type I error when the null hypothesis is true. Those are pretty good odds, and we would tend to believe the conclusions in that study. However, Table 12-1 shows what happens when we conduct more studies on the same sample. The chances of not having a Type I error on the first analysis *and* not having a Type I error on the second analysis are $(0.95)(0.95) = (0.95)^2 = 0.903$, or about 90%. This means that the chance of having a Type I error is almost 10%. With three analyses, the chance of not having a Type I error is $(0.95)(0.95)(0.95) = (0.95)^3 = 0.857$, or about 86%. This means that there is about a 14% chance of having at least one Type I error. And so on, as we see in Table 12-1. ANOVA is a more powerful approach because it lets us test differences among three or more groups in just one test.

| TABLE 12-1 | The Probability of a Type I Error Increases as the Number of Statistical Comparisons Increases |

As the number of samples increases, the number of *t* tests necessary to compare every possible pair of means increases at an even greater rate. And with that, the probability of a Type I error quickly becomes far larger than 0.05.

Number of Means	Number of Comparisons	Probability of a Type I Error
2	1	0.050
3	3	0.143
4	6	0.265
5	10	0.401
6	15	0.537
7	21	0.659

The *F* Statistic as an Expansion of the *z* and *t* Statistics

We use *F* distributions because they allow us to conduct a single hypothesis test with multiple groups. *F* distributions are more conservative versions of the *z* distribution and the *t* distributions. Just as the *z* distribution is still part of the *t* distributions, the *t* distributions are also part of the *F* distributions—and they all rely on the characteristics of the normal bell-shaped curve. These distributions are like progressively more

z, t, and F Distributions
Statistical distributions are similar to the increasing complexity of ever-more sophisticated Swiss Army knives. Specifically, the *z*, *t*, and *F* distributions are three increasingly complex variations on one great idea: the normal curve.

complex versions of the Swiss Army knife: The z distribution has just one blade; the t distributions add some more tools; and the versatile F distributions can do everything the z and the t can do—as well as many more complex statistical tasks.

The hypothesis tests that we have learned so far—the z test and the three types of t tests—are calculated in similar ways. The numerator describes how far apart comparison groups are from each other (between-groups variability); the denominator describes other sources of variability, such as individual differences and chance (within-groups variability). For example, the average height of men is greater than the average height of women: between-groups variability. Yet not all men are the same height and not all women are the same height: within-groups variability. Many women are taller than many men, so there is considerable overlap between the two distributions. The F statistic calculates between-group variance and within-group variance to conduct the hypothesis test called *analysis of variance* (*ANOVA*; pronounced "ah-NO-vah"), *a hypothesis test typically used with one or more nominal (and sometimes ordinal) independent variables (with at least three groups overall) and a scale dependent variable.*

The *F* Distributions for Analyzing Variability to Compare Means

Comparing heights of men and women demonstrates that the **F** *statistic is a ratio of two measures of variance: (1) between-groups variance, which indicates differences among sample means, and (2) within-groups variance, the average of the sample variances.*

$$F = \frac{\text{between-groups variance}}{\text{within-groups variance}}$$

Let's begin with the numerator, called **between-groups variance** because it *is an estimate of the population variance, based on the differences among the means.* A big number in the numerator indicates a great deal of distance (or spread) between the means, suggesting that they come from different populations. A small number in the numerator indicates very little distance (or spread) between the means, suggesting that they come from the same population. With more than two means, we can't use simple subtraction to find a number that indicates how spread apart they are, so we calculate the variance among the sample means. For example, if we wanted to compare how fast people talk in Vancouver, Memphis, Chicago, and Toronto, then the number representing between-groups variance (in this case, the between-cities variance) is an estimate of the variability among the average number of words per minute spoken by the people representing each of those four cities.

The denominator of the F statistic is called the **within-groups variance**, *an estimate of the population variance, based on the differences within each of the three (or more) sample distributions.* For example, not everyone living in Vancouver, Memphis, Chicago, or Toronto speaks at the same pace. There are within-city differences in talking speeds, so within-groups variance refers to the average of the four variances.

To calculate the F statistic, we simply divide the between-groups variance by the within-groups variance. If the F statistic is a large number (when the between-groups variance is much larger than the within-groups variance), then we can infer that the sample means are different from one another. But we cannot make that inference

- **Analysis of variance (ANOVA)** is a hypothesis test typically used with one or more nominal (and sometimes ordinal) independent variables (with at least three groups overall) and a scale dependent variable.

- The **F statistic** is a ratio of two measures of variance: (1) between-groups variance, which indicates differences among sample means, and (2) within-groups variance, which is essentially an average of the sample variances.

- **Between-groups variance** is an estimate of the population variance, based on the differences among the means.

- **Within-groups variance** is an estimate of the population variance, based on the differences within each of the three (or more) sample distributions.

when the F statistic is close to the number 1 (the between-groups variance is about the same as the within-groups variance).

To summarize, we can think of within-groups variance as reflecting the difference between means that we'd expect just by chance. There is variability within any population, of course, so we would expect some difference among means just by chance. Between-groups variance reflects the difference between means that we found in the data. If this difference is much larger than the within-groups variance—what we'd expect by chance—then we can reject the null hypothesis and conclude that there is some difference between means.

The *F* Table

The F table is an expansion of the t table. Just as there are many t distributions represented in the t table—one for each possible sample size—there are many F distributions. Both tables include a wide range of sample sizes (represented by degrees of freedom) but the F table adds a third factor: the number of samples. (The t statistic is limited to two samples.) There is an F distribution for every possible combination of sample size (represented by one type of degrees of freedom) and number of samples (represented by another type of degrees of freedom).

The F table for two samples can even be used as a t test; the numbers are the same except that the F is based on variance and the t on the square root of the variance, the standard deviation. For example, if we look in the F table under two samples (that is, 1 degree of freedom) for a sample size of infinity for an alpha level of 0.05, we see 3.84. If we take the square root of this, we get 1.96. We can find 1.96 on the z table for an alpha of 0.05 (that is, 2.5% or 0.025 in each tail for a two-tailed test) and on the t table for an alpha level of 0.05 for a two-tailed test with a sample size of infinity. The connections between the z, t, and F distributions are summarized in Table 12-2.

TABLE 12-2 Connections Among Distributions

The z distribution is subsumed under the t distributions in certain specific circumstances, and both the z and t distributions are subsumed under the F distributions in certain specific circumstances.

	When Used	Links Among the Distributions
z	One sample; μ and σ are known	Subsumed under the t and F distributions
t	(1) One sample; only μ is known (2) Two samples	Same as z distribution if there is a sample size of infinity (∞), or a very large sample size
F	Three or more samples (but can be used with two samples)	Square of z distribution if there are only two samples and a sample size of infinity (∞), or a very large sample size; square of t distribution if there are only two samples

The Language and Assumptions for ANOVA

Here is a simple guide to the language that statisticians use to describe different kinds of ANOVAs (Landrum, 2005). The word *ANOVA* is almost always preceded by two adjectives that indicate (1) the number of independent variables and (2) the research design (between-groups or within-groups).

Study 1. What would you call an ANOVA with year in school (e.g., first year, sophomore) as the only independent variable and ratings of students' attachment to their

- A **one-way ANOVA** is a hypothesis test that includes both one nominal independent variable with more than two levels and a scale dependent variable.

- A **between-groups ANOVA** is a hypothesis test in which there are more than two samples, and each sample is composed of different participants.

- A **within-groups ANOVA** is a hypothesis test in which there are more than two samples, and each sample is composed of the same participants; also called a *repeated-measures ANOVA.*

- **Homoscedastic** populations are those that have the same variance; homoscedasticity is also called *homogeneity of variance.*

- **Heteroscedastic** populations are those that have different variances.

university as the dependent variable? Answer: A one-way between-groups ANOVA. *A one-way ANOVA is a hypothesis test that includes both one nominal independent variable with more than two levels and a scale dependent variable.* *A between-groups ANOVA is a hypothesis test in which there are more than two samples, and each sample is composed of different participants.*

Study 2. What if you wanted to test the same group of students every year? Answer: You would use a one-way within-groups ANOVA. *A within-groups ANOVA is a hypothesis test in which there are more than two samples, and each sample is composed of the same participants.* (This test is also called a *repeated-measures ANOVA.*)

Study 3. And what if you wanted to add gender to the first study, a research design we explore in Chapter 14? Now you have two independent variables: year in school *and* gender. Answer: You would use a two-way between-groups ANOVA.

All ANOVAs, regardless of type, share the same three assumptions that represent the optimal conditions for valid data analysis. (We'll learn about within-groups ANOVAs in Chapter 13 and two-way ANOVAs in Chapter 14.)

Assumption 1. *Random selection* is necessary if we want to generalize beyond a sample. Because of the difficulty of random sampling, researchers often substitute convenience sampling and then replicate their experiment with a new sample.

Assumption 2. A *normally distributed population* allows us to examine the distributions of the samples to get a sense of what the underlying population distribution might look like. This assumption becomes less important as the sample size increases.

Assumption 3. *Homoscedasticity* (also called *homogeneity of variance*) assumes that the samples all come from populations with the same variances. (*Heteroscedasticity* means that the populations do not all have the same variance.) **Homoscedastic** *populations are those that have the same variance.* **Heteroscedastic** *populations are those that have different variances.*

What if your study doesn't match these ideal conditions? You may have to throw away your data—but that is usually not necessary. You also can (a) report and justify your decision to violate those assumptions or (b) conduct a more conservative nonparametric test (see Chapter 17).

CHECK YOUR LEARNING

Reviewing the Concepts

> The *F* statistic, used in analysis of variance (ANOVA), is essentially an expansion of the *z* statistic and the *t* statistic that can be used to compare more than two samples.

> Like the *z* statistic and the *t* statistic, the *F* statistic is a ratio of a difference between group means (in this case, using a measure of variability) to a measure of variability within samples.

> One-way between-groups ANOVA is an analysis in which there is one independent variable with at least three levels and in which different participants are in each level of the independent variable. A within-groups ANOVA differs in that all participants experience all levels of the independent variable.

> The assumptions for ANOVA are that participants are randomly selected, the populations from which the samples are drawn are normally distributed, and those populations have the same variance (an assumption known as homoscedasticity).

Clarifying the Concepts   **12-1**   The *F* statistic is a ratio of what two kinds of variance?

12-2   What are the two types of research designs for a one-way ANOVA?

Calculating the Statistics	12-3	Calculate the F statistic, writing the ratio accurately, for each of the following cases:

a. Between-groups variance is 8.6 and within-groups variance is 3.7.

b. Within-groups variance is 123.77 and between-groups variance is 102.4.

c. Between-groups variance is 45.2 and within-groups variance is 32.1.

Applying the Concepts	12-4	Consider the research on multitasking that we explored in Chapter 9 (Mark, Gonzalez, & Harris, 2005). Let's say we compared three conditions to see which one would lead to the quickest resumption of a task following an interruption. In one condition, the control group, no changes were made to the working environment. In the second condition, a communication ban was instituted from 1:00 to 3:00 P.M. In the third condition, a communication ban was instituted from 11:00 A.M. to 3:00 P.M. We recorded the time, in minutes, until work on an interrupted task was resumed.

a. What type of distribution would be used in this situation? Explain your answer.

b. In your own words, explain how we would calculate between-groups variance. Focus on the logic rather than on the calculations.

Solutions to these Check Your Learning questions can be found in Appendix D.

c. In your own words, explain how we would calculate within-groups variance. Focus on the logic rather than on the calculations.

One-Way Between-Groups ANOVA

The talking-while-driving study showed us that it's dangerous when the person on the other end of the conversation doesn't know when difficult driving conditions are developing. But we needed to analyze the data from four groups with an ANOVA to reach that conclusion. In this section, we use another four-group study to apply the principles of ANOVA to hypothesis testing with a between-groups research design.

Everything About ANOVA But the Calculations

To introduce the steps of hypothesis testing for a one-way between-groups ANOVA, we use an international study about whether the economic makeup of a society affects the degree to which people behave in a fair manner toward others (Henrich et al., 2010).

EXAMPLE 12.1

The researchers studied people in 15 societies from around the world. For teaching purposes, we'll look at data from four types of societies—foraging, farming, natural resources, and industrial.

1. *Foraging.* Several societies, including ones in Bolivia and Papua New Guinea, were categorized as foraging societies. They acquired most of their food through hunting and gathering.

2. *Farming.* Some societies, including ones in Kenya and Tanzania, primarily practiced farming and tended to grow their own food.

3. *Natural resources.* Other societies, such as in Colombia, built their economies by extracting natural resources, such as trees and fish. Most food was purchased.

4. *Industrial.* In industrial societies, which include the major city of Accra in Ghana as well as rural Missouri in the United States, most food was purchased.

The Dictator Game Here a researcher introduces a fairness game to a woman from Papua New Guinea, one of the foraging societies. Using games, researchers were able to compare fairness behaviors among different types of societies—those that depend on foraging, farming, natural resources, or industry (Henrich et al., 2010). Because there are four groups and each participant is in only one group, the results can be analyzed with a one-way between-groups ANOVA.

Courtesy of Dr. David Tracer

The researchers wondered which groups would behave more fairly toward others—the first and second groups, which grew their own food, or the third and fourth groups, which depended on others for food. The researchers measured fairness through several games. In the Dictator Game, for example, two players were given a sum of money equal to approximately the daily minimum wage for that society. The first player (the dictator) could keep all of the money or give any portion of it to the other person. The proportion of money given to the second player constituted the measure of fairness. For example, it would be considered fairer to give the second player 40% of the money than to give him or her only 10% of the money.

This research design would be analyzed with a one-way between-groups ANOVA that uses the fairness measure, the proportion of money given to the second player, as the dependent variable. There is one independent variable (type of society) and it has four levels (foraging, farming, natural resources, and industrial). It is a between-groups design because each player lived in one and only one of those societies. It is an ANOVA because it analyzes variance by estimating the variability among the different types of societies and dividing it by the variability within the types of societies. The fairness scores below are from 13 fictional people, but the groups have almost the same mean fairness scores that the researchers observed in their actual (much larger) data set.

Foraging: 28, 36, 38, 31
Farming: 32, 33, 40
Natural resources: 47, 43, 52
Industrial: 40, 47, 45

Let's begin by applying a familiar framework: the six steps of hypothesis testing. We will learn the calculations in the next section.

> **STEP 1: Identify the populations, distribution, and assumptions.**

The first step of hypothesis testing is to identify the populations to be compared, the comparison distribution, the appropriate test, and the assumptions of the test. Let's summarize the fairness study with respect to this first step of hypothesis testing.

Summary: *The populations to be compared:* Population 1: All people living in foraging societies. Population 2: All people living in farming societies. Population 3: All people living in societies that extract natural resources. Population 4: All people living in industrial societies.

The comparison distribution and hypothesis test: The comparison distribution will be an *F* distribution. The hypothesis test will be a one-way between-groups ANOVA.

Assumptions: (1) The data are not selected randomly, so we must generalize only with caution. (2) We do not know if the underlying population distributions are normal, but the sample data do not indicate severe skew. (3) We will test homoscedasticity when we calculate the test statistics by checking whether the largest variance is not more than twice the smallest. (*Note:* Don't forget this step just because it comes later in the analysis.)

> **STEP 2: State the null and research hypotheses.**

The second step is to state the null and research hypotheses. As usual, the null hypothesis posits no difference among the population means. The symbols are the same as before, but with more populations: H_0: $\mu_1 = \mu_2 = \mu_3 = \mu_4$. However, the research hypothesis is more complicated because we can reject the null hypothesis even if only one group is different, on average, from the others. The research hypothesis that $\mu_1 \neq \mu_2 \neq \mu_3 \neq \mu_4$ does not include all possible outcomes, such as the hypothesis that the mean fairness scores for groups 1 *and* 2 are greater than the mean fairness scores for groups 3 *and* 4. The research hypothesis is that at least one population mean is different from at least one other population mean, so H_1 is that at least one μ is different from another μ.

Summary: Null hypothesis: People living in societies based on foraging, farming, the extraction of natural resources, and industry all exhibit, on average, the same fairness behaviors—H_0: $\mu_1 = \mu_2 = \mu_3 = \mu_4$. Research hypothesis: People living in societies based on foraging, farming, the extraction of natural resources, and industry do not all exhibit the same fairness behaviors, on average.

> **STEP 3: Determine the characteristics of the comparison distribution.**

The third step is to explicitly state the relevant characteristics of the comparison distribution. This step is an easy one in ANOVA because most calculations are in step 5. Here we merely state that the comparison distribution is an *F* distribution and provide the appropriate degrees of freedom. As we discussed, the *F* statistic is a ratio of two independent estimates of the population variance, between-groups variance and within-groups variance (both of which we calculate in step 5). Each variance estimate has its own degrees of freedom. The sample between-groups variance estimates the population variance through the difference among the means of the samples—four, in this case. The degrees of freedom for the between-groups variance estimate is the number of samples minus 1:

$$df_{between} = N_{groups} - 1 = 4 - 1 = 3$$

Because there are four groups (foraging, farming, the extraction of natural resources, and industry), the between-groups degrees of freedom is 3.

The sample within-groups variance estimates the variance of the population by averaging the variances of the samples, without regard to differences among the sample means. We first must calculate the degrees of freedom for each sample. Because there are four participants in the first sample (farming), we would calculate:

$$df_1 = n_1 - 1 = 4 - 1 = 3$$

where n represents the number of participants in the particular sample. We would then do this for the remaining samples. For this example, there are four samples, so the formula would be:

$$df_{within} = df_1 + df_2 + df_3 + df_4$$

For this example, the calculations would be:

$$df_1 = 4 - 1 = 3$$
$$df_2 = 3 - 1 = 2$$
$$df_3 = 3 - 1 = 2$$
$$df_4 = 3 - 1 = 2$$
$$df_{within} = 3 + 2 + 2 + 2 = 9$$

Summary: We would use the F distribution with 3 and 9 degrees of freedom.

STEP 4: Determine the critical value, or cutoff.

The fourth step is to determine a critical value, or cutoff, indicating how extreme the data must be to reject the null hypothesis. For ANOVA, we use an F statistic, for which the critical value on an F distribution will always be positive (because the F is based on estimates of variance and variances are always positive). We determine the critical value by examining the F table in Appendix B (excerpted in Table 12-3). The between-groups degrees of freedom are found in a row across the top of the table. Notice that, in the full table, this row only goes up to 6, as it is rare to have more than seven conditions, or groups, in a study. The within-groups degrees of freedom are in a column along the left-hand side of the table. Because the number of participants in a study can range from a few to many, the column continues for several pages, with the same range of values of between-groups degrees of freedom on the top of each page.

MASTERING THE FORMULA

12-1: The formula for the between-groups degrees of freedom is: $df_{between} = N_{groups} - 1$. We subtract 1 from the number of groups in the study.

MASTERING THE FORMULA

12-2: The formula for the within-groups degrees of freedom for a one-way between-groups ANOVA conducted with four samples is: $df_{within} = df_1 + df_2 + df_3 + df_4$. We sum the degrees of freedom for each of the four groups. We calculate the degrees of freedom for each group by subtracting 1 from the number of people in that sample. For example, for the first group, the formula is: $df_1 = n_1 - 1$.

TABLE 12-3	Excerpt from the *F* Table

We use the *F* table to determine a critical value for a given an alpha level, based on the degrees of freedom in the numerator (between-groups degrees of freedom) and the degrees of freedom in the denominator (within-groups degrees of freedom). Note that critical values are in boldface for **0.01**, regular type for 0.05, and italics for *0.10*.

Within-Groups Degrees of Freedom: Denominator	alpha level	Between-Groups Degrees of Freedom: Numerator			
		1	2	3	4 ...
9	**0.01**	**10.56**	**8.02**	**6.99**	**6.42**
	0.05	5.12	4.26	3.86	3.63
	0.10	*3.36*	*3.01*	*2.81*	*2.69*
10	**0.01**	**10.05**	**7.56**	**6.55**	**6.00**
	0.05	4.97	4.10	3.71	3.48
	0.10	*3.29*	*2.93*	*2.73*	*2.61*
11	**0.01**	**9.65**	**7.21**	**6.22**	**5.67**
	0.05	4.85	3.98	3.59	3.36
	0.10	*3.23*	*2.86*	*2.66*	*2.54*
12	**0.01**	**9.33**	**6.93**	**5.95**	**5.41**
	0.05	4.75	3.88	3.49	3.26
	0.10	*3.18*	*2.81*	*2.61*	*2.48*
13	**0.01**	**9.07**	**6.70**	**5.74**	**5.20**
	0.05	4.67	3.80	3.41	3.18
	0.10	*3.14*	*2.76*	*2.56*	*2.43*
14	**0.01**	**8.86**	**6.51**	**5.56**	**5.03**
	0.05	4.60	3.74	3.34	3.11
	0.10	*3.10*	*2.73*	*2.52*	*2.39*

Use the *F* table by first finding the appropriate within-groups degrees of freedom along the left-hand side of the page: 9. Then find the appropriate between-groups degrees of freedom along the top: 3. The place in the table where this row and this column intersect contains three numbers: alpha levels for 0.01, 0.05, and 0.10. Researchers usually use the middle one, 0.05, which for this study is 3.86 (Figure 12-2).
Summary: The cutoff, or critical value, for the *F* statistic for an alpha of 0.05 is 3.86, as displayed in the curve in Figure 12-2.

STEP 5: Calculate the test statistic.

In the fifth step, we calculate the test statistic. We use the two estimates of the between-groups variance and the within-groups variance to

FIGURE 12-2

Determining Cutoffs for an *F* Distribution

We determine a single critical value on an *F* distribution. Because *F* is a squared version of *t* (or *z* in some circumstances), we have only one cutoff for a two-tailed test.

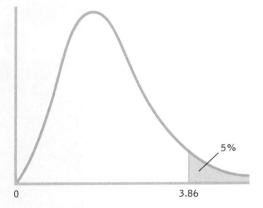

calculate the *F* statistic. We compare the *F* statistic to the cutoff to determine whether to reject the null hypothesis. We will learn to do these calculations in the next section. **Summary:** To be calculated in the next section.

> **STEP 6: Make a decision.**

In the final step, we decide whether to reject or fail to reject the null hypothesis. If the *F* statistic is beyond the critical value, then we know that it is in the most extreme 5% of possible test statistics *if* the null hypothesis is true. We can then reject the null hypothesis and conclude, "It seems that people exhibit different fairness behaviors, on average, depending on the type of society in which they live." ANOVA only tells us that at least one mean is significantly different from another; it does not tell us *which* societies are different from each other.

If the test statistic is not beyond the critical value, then we must fail to reject the null hypothesis. The test statistic would not be very rare if the null hypothesis were true. In this circumstance, we report only that there is no evidence from the present study to support the research hypothesis.

Summary: Because the decision we will make must be evidence-based, we cannot make it until we complete step 5, in which we calculate the probabilities associated with that evidence. We will complete step 6 in the Making a Decision section on p. 356. ●

MASTERING THE CONCEPT

12-2: When conducting an ANOVA, we use the same six steps of hypothesis testing that we've already learned. One of the differences from what we've learned is that we calculate an *F* statistic, the ratio of between-groups variance to within-groups variance.

The Logic and Calculations of the *F* Statistic

In this section, we first review the logic behind ANOVA's use of between-groups variance and within-groups variance. Then we apply the same six steps of hypothesis testing we have used in previous statistical tests to make a data-driven decision about what story the data are trying to tell us. Our goal in performing the calculations of ANOVA is to understand the *sources* of all the variability in a study.

Gender Differences in Height
Men, on average, are slightly taller than women (between-groups variance). However, neither men nor women are all the same height within their groups (within-groups variance). *F* is between-groups variability divided by within-groups variability.

As we noted earlier, grown men, on average, are slightly taller than grown women, on average. We call that "between-groups variability." We also noted that not all women are the same height and not all men are the same height. We call that "within-groups variability." The F statistic is simply an estimate of between-groups variability (in the numerator) divided by an estimate of within-groups variability (in the denominator).

$$F = \frac{\text{between-groups variability}}{\text{within-groups variability}}$$

Quantifying Overlap with ANOVA On average, men are taller than women; however, many women are taller than many men, so their distributions overlap. The amount of overlap is influenced by the distance between the means (between-groups variability) and the amount of spread (within-groups variability). In Figure 12-3, there is a great deal of overlap between the foraging and farming groups; the means are close together

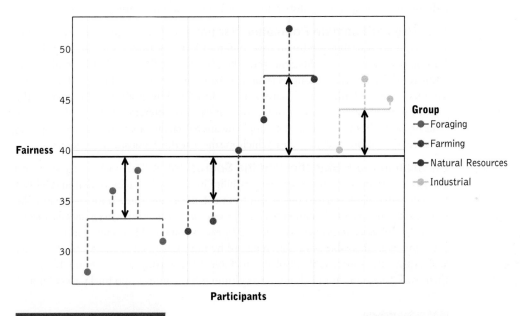

Participants

FIGURE 12-3

The Logic of ANOVA

This graph shows all 13 data points in the fairness study, with each group represented by a different color. The colored horizontal lines represent the means for the four groups. The colored, dashed vertical lines connect each dot to the mean for its group, and represent the variability *within* that group. For example, the four green lines between the dots and the green horizontal line represent the variability within the foraging group. The within-groups variance used as the denominator in the calculation of the *F* statistic in ANOVA is based on the variability represented by the colored vertical lines for all four groups. Because this is the denominator, as this variability gets smaller, the overall *F* gets larger. The overall black horizontal line across the middle represents the grand mean of all 13 data points. The four black vertical arrows represent the distance of each group mean from the grand mean. The between-groups variance used as the numerator in the calculation of the *F* statistic is based on this variability. Because this is the numerator, as this variability gets larger, the overall *F* gets larger. So, we can increase the *F* statistic if we either increase the variability between the group means—represented by the black arrows—or decrease the variability within each group—represented by the colored dashed lines.

and the distributions of the individual dots are spread out. There also is overlap between the natural resources and industrial groups; again, the means are relatively similar and the individual dots are spread out. Distributions with a lot of overlap suggest that any differences among them are probably due to chance. The groups in Figure 12-3 that have similar means would not contribute to a larger overall F statistic.

There is less overlap, however, between the foraging and farming groups on the one hand, and the natural resources and industrial groups on the other hand, mostly because the means are farther apart; the within-groups variability, reflected by the individual dots, is roughly similar. Larger differences between means contribute to a larger overall F statistic, in this case because the numerator would be larger. Distributions with little overlap are less likely to be drawn from the same population. It is also less likely that any differences among them are due to chance. There would be even less overlap among the distributions if the individual dots were less spread out—if they were all closer to their means. If this were the case, then there would be a larger F statistic because the within-groups variability—represented in the denominator of the F statistic—would be smaller. Both a larger numerator and a smaller denominator indicate less overlap among distributions and contribute to a larger F statistic.

Two Ways to Estimate Population Variance Between-groups variability and within-groups variability estimate two different kinds of variance in the population. If those two estimates are the same, then the F statistic will be 1.0. For example, if the estimate of the between-groups variance is 32 and the estimate of the within-groups variance is also 32, then the F statistic is $32/32 = 1.0$. This is a bit different from the z and t tests, in which a z or t of 0 would mean no difference at all. Here, an F of 1 means no difference at all. As the sample means get farther apart, the between-groups variance (the numerator) increases, which means that the F statistic also increases.

Calculating the F Statistic with the Source Table The goal of any statistical analysis is to understand the *sources* of variability in a study. We achieve that in ANOVA by calculating many squared deviations from the mean and three sums of squares. We organize the results into *a **source table** that presents the important calculations and final results of an ANOVA in a consistent and easy-to-read format*. A source table is shown in Table 12-4; the symbols in this table would be replaced by numbers in an actual source table. We will explain the source table displayed in Table 12-4 starting with column 1; we will then work backward from column 5 to column 4 to column 3 and finally to column 2.

● A **source table** presents the important calculations and final results of an ANOVA in a consistent and easy-to-read format.

TABLE 12-4   The Source Table Organizes the ANOVA Calculations

A source table helps researchers organize the most important calculations necessary to conduct an ANOVA, as well as the final results of the ANOVA. The numbers 1–5 in the first row are used in this particular table only to help you understand the format of source tables; they would not be included in an actual source table.

1 Source	2 SS	3 df	4 MS	5 F
Between	$SS_{between}$	$df_{between}$	$MS_{between}$	F
Within	SS_{within}	df_{within}	MS_{within}	
Total	SS_{total}	df_{total}		

Column 1: Source. One possible source of population variance comes from the spread *between* means; a second source comes from the spread *within* each sample. In this chapter, the row labeled "Total" allows us to check the calculations of the sum of squares (*SS*) and degrees of freedom (*df*). Now let's work backward through the source table to learn how it describes these two familiar sources of variability.

Column 5: F. We calculate *F* using simple division: between-groups variance divided by within-groups variance.

Column 4: MS. *MS* is the conventional symbol for variance in ANOVA. It stands for "mean square" because variance is the arithmetic mean of the squared deviations for between-groups variance ($MS_{between}$) and within-groups variance (MS_{within}). We divide $MS_{between}$ by MS_{within} to calculate *F*.

Column 3: df. We calculate the between-groups degrees of freedom ($df_{between}$) and the within-groups degrees of freedom (df_{within}), and then add the two together to calculate the total degrees of freedom:

$$df_{total} = df_{between} + df_{within}$$

In our version of the fairness study, $df_{total} = 3 + 9 = 12$. A second way to calculate df_{total} is:

$$df_{total} = N_{total} - 1$$

where N_{total} refers to the total number of people in the entire study. In our abbreviated version of the fairness study, there were four groups, with 4, 3, 3, and 3 participants in the groups, and $4 + 3 + 3 + 3 = 13$. We calculate total degrees of freedom for this study as $df_{total} = 13 - 1 = 12$. If we calculate degrees of freedom both ways and the answers don't match up, then we know we have to go back and check the calculations.

Column 2: SS. We calculate three *sums of squares*. One *SS* represents between-groups variability ($SS_{between}$), a second represents within-groups variability (SS_{within}), and a third represents total variability (SS_{total}). The first two sums of squares add up to the third; calculate all three to be sure they match.

The source table is a convenient summary because it describes everything we have learned about the sources of numerical variability. Once we calculate the sums of squares for between-groups variance and within-groups variance, there are just two steps.

Step 1: Divide each sum of squares by the appropriate degrees of freedom—the appropriate version of $(N - 1)$. We divide the $SS_{between}$ by the $df_{between}$ and the SS_{within} by the df_{within}. We then have the two variance estimates ($MS_{between}$ and MS_{within}).

Step 2: Calculate the ratio of $MS_{between}$ and MS_{within} to get the *F* statistic. Once we have the sums of squared deviations, the rest of the calculation is simple division.

Sums of Squared Deviations Language Alert! The term "deviations" is another word used to describe variability. ANOVA analyzes three different types of statistical deviations: (1) deviations between groups, (2) deviations within groups, and (3) total deviations. We begin by calculating the sum of squares for each type of deviation, or source of variability: between, within, and total.

It is easiest to start with the total sum of squares, SS_{total}. Organize all the scores and place them in a single column with a horizontal line dividing each sample from the next. Use the data (from our version of the fairness study) in the column labeled "*X*"

MASTERING THE FORMULA

12-3: One formula for the total degrees of freedom for a one-way between-groups ANOVA is: $df_{total} = df_{between} + df_{within}$. We sum the between-groups degrees of freedom and the within-groups degrees of freedom. An alternative formula is: $df_{total} = N_{total} - 1$. We subtract 1 from the total number of people in the study—that is, from the number of people in all groups.

● The **grand mean** is the mean of every score in a study, regardless of which sample the score came from.

12-4: The grand mean is the mean score of all people in a study, regardless of which sample the score came from. The formula is:

$$GM = \frac{\Sigma(X)}{N_{total}}$$

We add up everyone's score, then divide by the total number of people in the study.

of Table 12-5 as a model; X stands for each of the 13 individual scores listed below. Each set of scores is displayed next to its sample; the means are underneath the names of each respective sample. (We have included subscripts on each mean in the first column—*for* for foraging, *nr* for natural resources, and so on—to indicate its sample.)

To calculate the total sum of squares, subtract the overall mean from each score, including everyone in the study, regardless of sample. The mean of all the scores is called the *grand mean*, and its symbol is GM. *The **grand mean** is the mean of every score in a study, regardless of which sample the score came from:*

$$GM = \frac{\Sigma(X)}{N_{total}}$$

The grand mean of these scores is 39.385. (As usual, we write each number to three decimal places until we get to the final answer, F. We report the final answer to two decimal places.)

The third column in Table 12-5 shows the deviation of each score from the grand mean. The fourth column shows the squares of these deviations. For example, for the first score, 28, we subtract the grand mean:

$$28 - 39.385 = -11.385$$

Then we square the deviation:

$$(-11.385)^2 = 129.618$$

TABLE 12-5 Calculating the Total Sum of Squares

The total sum of squares is calculated by subtracting the overall mean, called the *grand mean*, from every score to create deviations, then squaring the deviations and summing the squared deviations.

Sample	X	$(X - GM)$	$(X - GM)^2$
Foraging	28	−11.385	129.618
	36	−3.385	11.458
$M_{for} = 33.250$	38	−1.385	1.918
	31	−8.385	70.308
Farming	32	−7.385	54.538
	33	−6.385	40.768
$M_{farm} = 35.000$	40	0.615	0.378
Natural resources	47	7.615	57.988
	43	3.615	13.068
$M_{nr} = 47.333$	52	12.615	159.138
Industrial	40	0.615	0.378
	47	7.615	57.988
$M_{ind} = 44.000$	45	5.615	31.528
	$GM = 39.385$		$SS_{total} = \textbf{629.074}$

Below the fourth column in Table 12-5, we have summed the squared deviations: 629.074. This is the total sum of squares, SS_{total}. The formula for the total sum of squares is:

$$SS_{total} = \Sigma(X - GM)^2$$

The model for calculating the within-groups sum of squares is shown in Table 12-6. This time the deviations are around the mean of each particular group (separated by horizontal lines) instead of around the grand mean. For the four scores in the first sample, we subtract their sample mean, 33.25. For example, the calculation for the first score is:

$$(28 - 33.25)^2 = 27.563$$

For the three scores in the second sample, we subtract their sample mean, 35.0. We do the same for all four samples. (*Note:* Don't forget to switch means when you get to each new sample!)

Once we have all the deviations, we square them and sum them to calculate the within-groups sum of squares, 167.419, the number below the fourth column. Because we subtract the sample mean, rather than the grand mean, from each score, the formula is:

$$SS_{within} = \Sigma(X - M)^2$$

Notice how the weighting for sample size is built into the calculation: The first sample has four scores and contributes four squared deviations to the total. The other samples have only three scores, so they contribute only three squared deviations.

MASTERING THE FORMULA

12-5: The total sum of squares in an ANOVA is calculated using the following formula: $SS_{total} = \Sigma(X - GM)^2$. We subtract the grand mean from every score, then square these deviations. We then sum all the squared deviations.

MASTERING THE FORMULA

12-6: The within-groups sum of squares in a one-way between-groups ANOVA is calculated using the following formula: $SS_{within} = \Sigma(X - M)^2$. From each score, we subtract its group mean. We then square these deviations. We sum all the squared deviations for everyone in all groups.

TABLE 12-6 Calculating the Within-Groups Sum of Squares

The within-groups sum of squares is calculated by taking each score and subtracting the mean of the sample from which it comes—not the grand mean—to create deviations, then squaring the deviations and summing the squared deviations.

Sample	X	$(X - M)$	$(X - M)^2$
Foraging	28	−5.25	27.563
	36	2.75	7.563
$M_{for} = 33.250$	38	4.75	22.563
	31	−2.25	5.063
Farming	32	−3.000	9.000
	33	−2.000	4.000
$M_{farm} = 35.000$	40	5.000	25.000
Natural resources	47	−0.333	0.111
	43	−4.333	18.775
$M_{nr} = 47.333$	52	4.667	21.781
Industrial	40	−4.000	16.000
	47	3.000	9.000
$M_{ind} = 44.000$	45	1.000	1.000
	GM = 39.385		$SS_{within} = $ **167.419**

Finally, we calculate the between-groups sum of squares. Remember, the goal for this step is to estimate how much each *group*—not each *individual participant*—deviates from the overall grand mean, so we use means rather than individual scores in the calculations. For each of the 13 people in this study, we subtract the grand mean from the mean of the group to which that individual belongs.★

For example, the first person has a score of 28 and belongs to the group labeled "foraging," which has a mean score of 33.25. The grand mean is 39.385. We ignore this person's individual score and subtract 39.385 (the grand mean) from 33.25 (the group mean) to get the deviation score, −6.135. The next person, also in the group labeled "foraging," has a score of 36. The group mean of that sample is 33.25. Once again, we ignore that person's individual score and subtract 39.385 (the grand mean) from 33.25 (the group mean) to get the deviation score, also −6.135.

In fact, we subtract 39.385 from 33.25 for all four scores, as you can see in Table 12-7. When we get to the horizontal line between samples, we look for the next sample mean. For all three scores in the next sample, we subtract the grand mean, 39.385, from the sample mean, 35.0, and so on.

Notice that individual scores are *never* involved in the calculations, just the sample means and the grand mean. Also notice that the first group (foraging), with four participants,

---

TABLE 12-7 Calculating the Between-Groups Sum of Squares

The between-groups sum of squares is calculated by subtracting the grand mean from the sample mean for every score to create deviations, then squaring the deviations and summing the squared deviations. The individual scores themselves are not involved in any calculations.

Sample	X	$(M - GM)$	$(M - GM)^2$
Foraging	28	−6.135	37.638
	36	−6.135	37.638
$M_{for} = 33.250$	38	−6.135	37.638
	31	−6.135	37.638
Farming	32	−4.385	19.228
	33	−4.385	19.228
$M_{farm} = 35.000$	40	−4.385	19.228
Natural resources	47	7.948	63.171
	43	7.948	63.171
$M_{nr} = 47.333$	52	7.948	63.171
Industrial	40	4.615	21.298
	47	4.615	21.298
$M_{ind} = 44.000$	45	4.615	21.298
	$GM = 39.385$		$SS_{between} = \mathbf{461.643}$

★There is a shortcut to the formula for the between–groups sum of squares, but it can be used only when there are equal numbers of participants in each group. In that case, we need to subtract the grand mean from each mean just once—not for every individual. After squaring and summing the deviations for each mean, we then multiply that sum of squares by the number of participants in each sample. The formula is:

$$SS_{between} = n\left[\Sigma(M - GM)^2\right]$$

where n is the number of participants in each sample.

has more weight in the calculation than the other three groups, which each have only three participants. The third column of Table 12-7 includes the deviations and the fourth includes the squared deviations. The between-groups sum of squares, in bold under the fourth column, is 461.643. The formula for the between-groups sum of squares is:

$$SS_{between} = \Sigma(M - GM)^2$$

Now is the moment of arithmetic truth. Were the calculations correct? To find out, we add the within-groups sum of squares (167.419) to the between-groups sum of squares (461.643) to see if they equal the total sum of squares (629.074). Here's the formula:

$$SS_{total} = SS_{within} + SS_{between} = 629.062 = 167.419 + 461.643$$

Indeed, the total sum of squares, 629.074, is almost equal to the sum of the other two sums of squares, 167.419 and 461.643, which is 629.062. The calculations were correct (the slight difference is due to rounding decisions).

To recap (Table 12-8), for the total sum of squares, we subtract the *grand mean* from each individual *score* to get the deviations. For the within-groups sum of squares, we subtract the appropriate *sample mean* from every *score* to get the deviations. And for the between-groups sum of squares, we subtract the *grand mean* from the appropriate *sample mean*, once for each score, to get the deviations; for the between-groups sum of squares, the actual scores are never involved in any calculations.

TABLE 12-8	The Three Sums of Squares of ANOVA

The calculations in ANOVA are built on the foundation we learned in Chapter 4, sums of squared deviations. We calculate three types of sums of squares, one for between-groups variance, one for within-groups variance, and one for total variance. Once we have the three sums of squares, most of the remaining calculations involve simple division.

Sum of Squares	To Calculate the Deviations, Subtract the . . .	Formula
Between-groups	Grand mean from the sample mean (for each score)	$SS_{between} = \Sigma(M - GM)^2$
Within-groups	Sample mean from each score	$SS_{within} = \Sigma(X - M)^2$
Total	Grand mean from each score	$SS_{total} = \Sigma(X - GM)^2$

Now we insert these numbers into the source table to calculate the *F* statistic. See Table 12-9 for the source table that lists all the formulas and Table 12-10 for the completed source table. We divide the between-groups sum of squares and the

TABLE 12-9	A Source Table with Formulas

This table summarizes the formulas for calculating an *F* statistic.

Source	SS	df	MS	F
Between	$\Sigma(M - GM)^2$	$N_{groups} - 1$	$\dfrac{SS_{between}}{df_{between}}$	$\dfrac{MS_{between}}{MS_{within}}$
Within	$\Sigma(X - M)^2$	$df_1 + df_2 + \cdots + df_{last}$	$\dfrac{SS_{within}}{df_{within}}$	
Total	$\Sigma(X - GM)^2$	$N_{total} - 1$		

[Expanded formula: $df_{within} = (N_1 - 1) + (N_2 - 1) + \cdots + (N_{last} - 1)$]

MASTERING THE FORMULA

12-9: We calculate the mean squares from their associated sums of squares and degrees of freedom. For the between-groups mean square, we divide the between-groups sum of squares by the between-groups degrees of freedom:

$$MS_{between} = \frac{SS_{between}}{df_{between}}$$

For the within-groups mean square, we divide the within-groups sum of squares by the within-groups degrees of freedom:

$$MS_{within} = \frac{SS_{within}}{df_{within}}$$

MASTERING THE FORMULA

12-10: The formula for the F statistic is:

$$F = \frac{MS_{between}}{MS_{within}}$$

We divide the between-groups mean square by the within-groups mean square.

within-groups sum of squares by their associated degrees of freedom to get the between-groups variance and the within-groups variance. The formulas are:

$$MS_{between} = \frac{SS_{between}}{df_{between}} = \frac{461.643}{3} = 153.881$$

$$MS_{within} = \frac{SS_{within}}{df_{within}} = \frac{167.419}{9} = 18.602$$

We then divide the between-groups variance by the within-groups variance to calculate the F statistic. The formula, in bold in Table 12-9, is:

$$F = \frac{MS_{between}}{MS_{within}} = \frac{153.881}{18.602} = 8.27$$

TABLE 12-10	A Completed Source Table

Once we calculate the sums of squares and the degrees of freedom, the rest is just simple division. We use the first two columns of numbers to calculate the variances and the F statistic. We divide the between-groups sum of squares and within-groups sum of squares by their associated degrees of freedom to get the between-groups variance and within-groups variance. Then we divide the between-groups variance by the within-groups variance to get the F statistic, 8.27.

Source	SS	df	MS	F
Between-groups	461.643	3	153.881	**8.27**
Within-groups	167.419	9	18.602	
Total	629.074	12		

Making a Decision

Now we have to come back to the six steps of hypothesis testing for ANOVA to fill in the gaps in steps 1 and 6. We finished steps 2 through 5 in the previous section.

Step 1: ANOVA assumes that participants were selected from populations with equal variances. Statistical software, such as SPSS, tests this assumption while analyzing the overall data. For now, we can use the last column from the within-groups sum of squares calculations in Table 12-6. Variance is computed by dividing the sum of squares by the sample size minus 1. We can add the squared deviations for each sample, then divide by the sample size minus 1. Table 12-11 shows the calculations for variance within each of the four samples. Because the largest variance, 20.917, is not more than twice the smallest variance, 13.0, we have met the assumption of equal variances.

Step 6: Now that we have the test statistic, we compare it with 3.86, the critical F value that we identified in step 4. The F statistic we calculated was 8.27, and Figure 12-4 demonstrates that the F statistic is beyond the critical value: We can reject the null hypothesis. It appears that people living in some types of societies are fairer, on average, than are people living in other types of societies. And congratulations on making your way through your first ANOVA! Statistical software will do all of these calculations for you, but understanding how the computer produces those numbers adds to your overall understanding.

The ANOVA, however, only allows us to conclude that at least one mean is different from at least one other mean. The next section describes how to determine which groups are different.

TABLE 12-11	Calculating Sample Variances

We calculate the variances of the samples by dividing each sum of squares by the sample size minus 1 to check one of the assumptions of ANOVA. For unequal sample sizes, as we have here, we want the largest variance (20.917 in this case) to be no more than twice the smallest (13.0 in this case). Two times 13.0 is 26.0, which is more than 20.917, so we meet this assumption.

Sample	Foraging	Farming	Natural Resources	Industrial
Squared deviations	27.563	9.000	0.111	16.000
	7.563	4.000	18.775	9.000
	22.563	25.000	21.781	1.000
	5.063			
Sum of squares:	62.752	38.000	40.667	26.000
$N-1$:	3	2	2	2
Variance	**20.917**	**19.000**	**20.334**	**13.000**

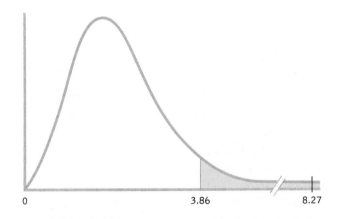

FIGURE 12-4

Making a Decision with an F Distribution

We compare the F statistic that we calculated for the samples to a single cutoff, or critical value, on the appropriate F distribution. We can reject the null hypothesis if the test statistic is beyond—more to the right than—the cutoff. Here, the F statistic of 8.27 is beyond the cutoff of 3.86, so we can reject the null hypothesis.

0   3.86   8.27

Summary: We reject the null hypothesis. It appears that mean fairness levels differ based on the type of society in which a person lives. In a scientific journal, these statistics are presented in a similar way to the z and t statistics but with separate degrees of freedom in parentheses for between-groups and within-groups: $F(3, 9) = 8.27, p < 0.05$. (*Note:* Report the actual p value when analyzing ANOVA with statistical software.)

CHECK YOUR LEARNING

Reviewing the Concepts > One-way between-groups ANOVA uses the same six steps of hypothesis testing that we learned in Chapter 7, but with a few minor changes in steps 3 and 5.

> In step 3, we merely state the comparison distribution and provide two different types of degrees of freedom, *df* for the between-groups variance and *df* for the within-groups variance.

continued on next page

> In step 5, we complete the calculations, using a source table to organize the results. First, we estimate population variance by considering the differences among means (between-groups variance). Second, we estimate population variance by calculating a weighted average of the variances within each sample (within-groups variance).

> The calculation of variability requires several means, including sample means and the grand mean, which is the mean of all scores, regardless of which sample the scores came from.

> We divide between-groups variance by within-groups variance to calculate the F statistic.

> Before making a decision based on the F statistic, we check whether the assumption of equal sample variances is met. This assumption is met when the largest sample variance is not more than twice the amount of the smallest variance.

Clarifying the Concepts

12-5   If the F statistic is beyond the cutoff, what does that tell us? What doesn't that tell us?

12-6   What is the primary subtraction that enters into the calculation of $SS_{between}$?

Calculating the Statistics

12-7   Calculate each type of degrees of freedom for the following data, assuming a between-groups design:

Group 1: 37, 30, 22, 29
Group 2: 49, 52, 41, 39
Group 3: 36, 49, 42

a. $df_{between} = N_{groups} - 1$

b. $df_{within} = df_1 + df_2 + \cdots + df_{last}$

c. $df_{total} = df_{between} + df_{within}$, or $df_{total} = N_{total} - 1$

12-8   Using the data in Check Your Learning 12-7, compute the grand mean.

12-9   Using the data in Check Your Learning 12-7, compute each type of sum of squares.

a.   Total sum of squares

b.   Within-groups sum of squares

c.   Between-groups sum of squares

12-10   Using all of your calculations in Check Your Learning 12-7 to 12-9, perform the simple division to complete an entire between-groups ANOVA source table for these data.

Applying the Concepts

12-11   Let's create a context for the data provided in the preceding Calculating the Statistics exercises. Hollon, Thase, and Markowitz (2002) reviewed the efficacy of different treatments for depression, including medications, electroconvulsive therapy, psychotherapy, and placebo treatments. These data recreate some of the basic findings the researchers present regarding psychotherapy. Each group is meant to represent people who received a different psychotherapy-based treatment, including psychodynamic therapy in group 1, interpersonal therapy in group 2, and cognitive-behavioral therapy in group 3. The scores presented here represent the extent to which someone responded to the treatment, with higher numbers indicating greater efficacy of treatment.

Group 1 (psychodynamic therapy): 37, 30, 22, 29
Group 2 (interpersonal therapy): 49, 52, 41, 39
Group 3 (cognitive-behavioral therapy): 36, 49, 42

a.   Write hypotheses, in words, for this research.

b.   Check the assumptions of ANOVA.

Solutions to these Check Your Learning questions can be found in Appendix D.

c.   Determine the critical value for F. Using your calculations from the previous Check Your Learning exercise, make a decision about the null hypothesis for these treatment options.

Beyond Hypothesis Testing for the One-Way Between-Groups ANOVA

Is driving while talking on a hands-free mobile phone really more dangerous than talking with a passenger sitting next to us? Do expectations for fairness differ across types of societies? Hypothesis testing is a good way to start answering such questions. We can obtain more specific answers by (1) calculating effect size (as we did with z tests and t tests) and (2) conducting post hoc tests to determine exactly which groups are significantly different from each other.

R^2 and Omega Squared, Effect Sizes for ANOVA

In Chapter 8, we learned how to use Cohen's d to calculate an estimate of effect size. However, Cohen's d applies only when we are subtracting one mean from another (as for a z test or a t test). With ANOVA, most often we calculate R^2 (pronounced "r squared"), *an estimate of the proportion of variance in the dependent variable that is accounted for by the independent variable.* [We could also calculate a similar statistic called η^2 (pronounced "eta squared"). We can interpret η^2 exactly as we interpret R^2.] After we introduce R^2, we'll discuss omega squared, a more conservative measure of effect size that is increasingly being used.

Like the F statistic, R^2 is a ratio; however, it calculates the proportion of variance accounted for by the independent variable out of all of the variance. Its numerator uses only the between-groups sum of squares, $SS_{between}$, to indicate variability among the means (ignoring the variability within each sample). The denominator uses total variability (both between-groups variance and within-groups variance), which is the total sum of squares: SS_{total}. The formula is:

$$R^2 = \frac{SS_{between}}{SS_{total}}$$

EXAMPLE 12.2

Let's apply this to the ANOVA we conducted on fairness across different types of societies. We can use the statistics in the source table we created earlier to calculate R^2:

$$R^2 = \frac{SS_{between}}{SS_{total}} = \frac{461.643}{629.074} = 0.73$$

Table 12-12 displays Jacob Cohen's conventions for R^2 that, like Cohen's d, indicate whether the effect size is small, medium, or large. This R^2 of 0.73 is large. This is not surprising; if we can reject the null hypothesis when the sample size is small, then the effect size must be large.

We can also turn the proportion into the more familiar language of percentages by multiplying by 100. We can then say that a specific percentage of the variance in the dependent variable is accounted for by the independent variable. In this case, we

- **R^2** is an estimate of the proportion of variance in the dependent variable that is accounted for by the independent variable.

TABLE 12-12	Cohen's Conventions for Effect Sizes: R^2

The following guidelines, called *conventions* by statisticians, are meant to help researchers decide how important an effect is. These numbers are not cutoffs; they are merely rough guidelines to help researchers interpret results.

Effect Size	Convention
Small	0.01
Medium	0.06
Large	0.14

● **Omega squared** (ω^2) is an estimate of the proportion of variance in the dependent variable that is accounted for by the independent variable; it is less biased than other estimates.

MASTERING THE FORMULA

12-12: The formula for the less-biased effect size we can use with one-way between-groups ANOVA is:

$$\omega^2 = \frac{SS_{between} - ((df_{between})(MS_{within}))}{SS_{total} + MS_{within}}$$

This calculation is a ratio, similar to the calculation for the F statistic. For the numerator of ω^2, we subtract the product of the between-groups degrees of freedom and the within-groups mean square from the between-groups sum of squares. For the denominator, we add the total sum of squares and the within-groups mean square. The resulting ω^2 will always be smaller than R^2 for the same data.

could say that an estimated 73% of the variability in sharing is due to the type of society. (Note that the overall pattern of results match those of the original study; however, the actual effect size was smaller than this.) ●

As we explained previously, R^2 is the most commonly used measure of effect size. It's important to remember, however, that this is just an estimate (as are all statistics), based on the data from the sample of the actual effect size in the population. Some statisticians have noted that R^2 is a biased estimate, which tends to be larger than the true effect size in the population (Albers & Lakens, 2018). Because of this bias, these statisticians recommend a less-used, but also less-biased, estimate of effect size, called omega squared (ω^2). **Omega squared** (ω^2) *is an estimate of the proportion of variance in the dependent variable that is accounted for by the independent variable; it is less biased than other estimates.* You can think of omega squared as an attempt at correcting the bias of R^2.

Like R^2, omega squared can be calculated from the information in the source table. The formula is $\omega^2 = \frac{SS_{between} - ((df_{between})(MS_{within}))}{SS_{total} + MS_{within}}$. Notice that, compared to R^2, omega squared has a smaller numerator because we are subtracting from the between-groups sum of squares. It also has a larger denominator because we are adding to the total sum of squares. This leads to an overall lower effect-size estimate.

Let's calculate omega squared for the fairness study, using the information from the source table we calculated earlier:

$$\omega^2 = \frac{SS_{between} - ((df_{between})(MS_{within}))}{SS_{total} + MS_{within}} = \frac{461.643 - ((3)(18.602))}{629.074 + 18.602} = \frac{405.837}{647.676} = 0.627$$

We can use the same conventions in Table 12-12 to interpret omega squared. The omega squared of 0.63 (or 63%) is still quite large; however, it is smaller than the R^2 of 0.73 (or 73%). (We should note that because omega squared is, by design, smaller than R^2, sometimes the correction is too large. In fact, the correction occasionally results in a negative value, even though it is technically impossible to have a negative effect size. When omega squared is negative, researchers are split between whether it is best to report the calculated negative effect or simply round it up to 0 (Albers & Lakin, 2018).)

MASTERING THE CONCEPT

12-4: ANOVA tells us only that there is a difference between at least two of the means in the study. We need a post hoc test to determine which pairs of means are statistically significantly different from each other.

Post Hoc Tests

The statistically significant F statistic means that some difference exists somewhere in the study. The R^2 and ω^2 tell us that the difference is large, but we still don't know which pairs of means are responsible for these effects. Here's an easy way to figure it out: Graph the data.

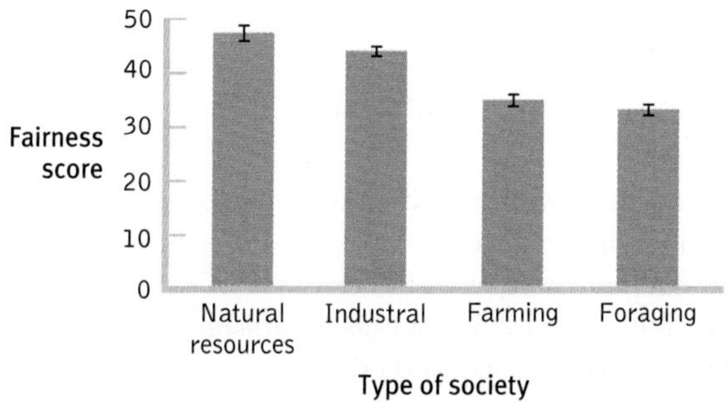

FIGURE 12-5

Which Types of Societies Are Different in Terms of Fairness?

This graph depicts the mean fairness scores of people living in each of four different types of societies. The error bars represent standard error for each sample. When we conduct an ANOVA and reject the null hypothesis, we know only that there is a difference somewhere; we do not know where the difference lies. We can see several possible combinations of differences by examining the means on this graph. A post hoc test will let us know which specific pairs of means are significantly different from one another.

The picture will suggest which means are different, but those differences still need to be confirmed with a post hoc test. *A **post hoc test** is a statistical procedure frequently carried out after the null hypothesis has been rejected in an analysis of variance; it allows us to make multiple comparisons among several means.* The name of the test, post hoc, means "after this" in Latin; these tests are often referred to as *follow-up tests.* (Post hoc tests are not conducted if we fail to reject the null hypothesis, because we already know that there are no statistically significant differences among means.)

For example, the fairness study produced the following mean scores: foraging, 33.25; farming, 35.0; industrial, 44.0; and natural resources, 47.333. The ANOVA told us to reject the null hypothesis, so something is going on in this data set. The Pareto chart (organized by highest to lowest) and a post hoc test will tell us "where the action is" in this statistically significant ANOVA.

The Pareto chart in Figure 12-5 helps us think through the possibilities. For example, people in industrial societies and in societies that extract natural resources might exhibit higher levels of fairness, on average, than people in foraging or farming societies (groups 1 and 2 versus groups 3 and 4). Or people in societies that extract natural resources might be higher, on average, only compared with those in foraging societies (group 1 versus group 4). Maybe all four groups are different from one another, on average. There are so many possibilities that we need a post hoc test to reach a statistically valid conclusion. There are many post hoc tests and most are named for their founders, almost exclusively people with fabulous names—for example, Bonferroni, Scheffé (pronounced "sheff-ay"), and Tukey (pronounced "two-key"). We will focus on the Tukey *HSD* test here.

The Tukey *HSD* Test

*The **Tukey HSD test** is a widely used post hoc test that determines the differences between means in terms of standard error; the HSD is compared to a critical value.* The Tukey *HSD* test (also called the *q test*) stands for "*h*onestly *s*ignificant *d*ifference" because it allows us to make multiple comparisons to identify differences that are "honestly" there.

In the Tukey *HSD* test, we (1) calculate differences between each pair of means, (2) divide each difference by the standard error, and (3) compare the *HSD* for each pair of means to a critical value (a *q* value, found in Appendix B) to determine whether the means are different enough to reject the null hypothesis. The formula for the Tukey *HSD* test is a variant of the *z* test and *t* tests for any two sample means:

$$HSD = \frac{(M_1 - M_2)}{s_M}$$

● A **post hoc test** is a statistical procedure frequently carried out after the null hypothesis has been rejected in an analysis of variance; it allows us to make multiple comparisons among several means; often referred to as a *follow-up test*.

● The **Tukey *HSD* test** is a widely used post hoc test that determines the differences between means in terms of standard error; the *HSD* is compared to a critical value; sometimes called the *q test*.

MASTERING THE FORMULA

12-13: To conduct a Tukey *HSD* test, we first calculate standard error:

$$s_M = \sqrt{\frac{MS_{within}}{N}}$$

We divide the MS_{within} by the sample size and take the square root. We can then calculate the *HSD* for each pair of means:

$$HSD = \frac{(M_1 - M_2)}{s_M}$$

For each pair of means, we subtract one from the other and divide by the standard error we calculated earlier.

MASTERING THE FORMULA

12-14: When we conduct an ANOVA with different-size samples, we have to calculate a harmonic mean, N':

$$N' = \frac{N_{groups}}{\Sigma(1/N)}$$

To do that, we divide the number of groups in the study by the sum of 1 divided by the sample size for every group.

The formula for the standard error is:

$$s_M = \sqrt{\frac{MS_{within}}{N}}$$

In this case, N is the sample size within each group, with the assumption that all samples have the same number of participants.

When samples are different sizes, as in the example of societies, we have to calculate a weighted sample size, also known as a *harmonic mean*, N' (pronounced "N prime") before we can calculate standard error:

$$N' = \frac{N_{groups}}{\Sigma(1/N)}$$

EXAMPLE 12.3

We calculate N' by dividing the number of groups (the numerator) by the sum of 1 divided by the sample size for every group (the denominator). For the example in which there were four participants in foraging societies and three in each of the other three types of societies, the formula is:

$$N' = \frac{4}{\left(\frac{1}{4} + \frac{1}{3} + \frac{1}{3} + \frac{1}{3}\right)} = \frac{4}{1.25} = 3.20$$

MASTERING THE FORMULA

12-15: When we conduct an ANOVA with different-size samples, we have to calculate standard error using N':

$$s_M = \sqrt{\frac{MS_{within}}{N'}}$$

To do that, we divide MS_{within} by N' and take the square root.

When sample sizes are not equal, we use a formula for s_M based on N' instead of N:

$$s_M = \sqrt{\frac{MS_{within}}{N'}} = \sqrt{\frac{18.602}{3.20}} = 2.411$$

Now we use simple subtraction to calculate *HSD* for each pair of means. Which comes first doesn't matter; for example, we could subtract the mean for foraging societies from the mean for farming societies, or vice versa. We can ignore the sign of the answer because it is contingent on the arbitrary decision of which mean to subtract from the other.

Foraging (33.250) versus farming (35.000):

$$HSD = \frac{(33.250 - 35.000)}{2.411} = -0.73$$

Foraging (33.250) versus natural resources (47.333):

$$HSD = \frac{(33.250 - 47.333)}{2.411} = -5.84$$

Foraging (33.250) versus industrial (44.000):

$$HSD = \frac{(33.250 - 44.000)}{2.411} = -4.46$$

Farming (35.000) versus natural resources (47.333):

$$HSD = \frac{(35.000 - 47.333)}{2.411} = -5.12$$

Farming (35.000) versus industrial (44.000):

$$HSD = \frac{(35.000 - 44.000)}{2.411} = -3.73$$

Natural resources (47.333) versus industrial (44.000):

$$HSD = \frac{(47.333 - 44.000)}{2.411} = -1.38$$

Now all we need is a critical value from the q table in Appendix B (excerpted in Table 12-13) to which we can compare the HSDs. The numbers of means being compared (levels of the independent variable) are in a row along the top of the q table, and the within-groups degrees of freedom are in a column along the left-hand side. We first look up the within-groups degrees of freedom for the test, 9, along the left column. We then go across from 9 to the numbers below the number of means being compared, 4. For an alpha level of 0.05, the cutoff q is 4.41. Again, the sign of the HSD does not matter. This is a two-tailed test, and any HSD above 4.41 or below −4.41 would be considered statistically significant.

TABLE 12-13	Excerpt from the q Table

Like the F table, we use the q table to determine critical values for a given alpha level, based on the number of means being compared and the within-groups degrees of freedom. Note that critical values are in regular type for 0.05 and boldface for 0.01.

Within-Groups Degrees of Freedom	alpha level	k = Number of Treatments (levels)		
		. . . 3	4	5 . . .
8	.05	4.04	4.53	4.89
	.01	**5.64**	**6.20**	**6.62**
9	.05	3.95	4.41	4.76
	.01	**5.43**	**5.96**	**6.35**
10	.05	3.88	4.33	4.65
	.01	**5.27**	**5.77**	**6.14**

The q table indicates three statistically significant differences whose HSDs are beyond the critical value of −4.41: −5.84, −4.46, and −5.12. It appears that people in foraging societies are less fair, on average, than people in societies that depend on natural resources and people in industrial societies. In addition, people in farming societies are less fair, on average, than are people in societies that depend on natural resources. We have not rejected the null hypothesis for any other pairs, so we can only conclude that there is not enough evidence to determine whether their means are different.

What might explain these differences? The researchers observed that people who purchase food routinely interact with other people in an economic market. They concluded that higher levels of market integration are associated with higher levels of fairness (Henrich et al., 2010). Social norms of fairness may develop in market societies that require cooperative interactions between people who do not know each other.

How much faith can we have in these findings? Cautious confidence and replication are recommended; researchers could not randomly assign people to live in particular societies, so some third variable may explain the relation between market integration and fairness. ●

Data Ethics | The Bonferroni Test

For many researchers, the Tukey *HSD* test is the default post hoc test, and in many cases, it really is the best choice. But the ethical researcher thinks about which post hoc test to choose before automatically conducting a Tukey *HSD* test. One other post hoc test that is often used is the Bonferroni test. It is more conservative than the Tukey *HSD* test, meaning that the test makes it more difficult to reject the null hypothesis. Also, the Bonferroni test is easy to implement.

The ***Bonferroni test*** *is a post hoc test that provides a stricter critical value for every comparison of means.* Normally, social scientists use a cutoff level of 0.05. With a Bonferroni test, sometimes called the *Bonferroni correction, Bonferroni adjustment*, or *Dunn Multiple Comparison test*, we use a smaller critical region to make it more difficult to reject the null hypothesis. To use a Bonferroni test, we determine the number of comparisons we plan to make. Table 12-14 states the number of comparisons for two through seven means.

● The **Bonferroni test** (also sometimes called the *Bonferroni correction, Bonferroni adjustment,* or *Dunn Multiple Comparison test*) is a post hoc test that provides a stricter critical value for every comparison of means.

TABLE 12-14 | The Bonferroni Test: Few Groups, Many Comparisons

Even with a few means, we must make many comparisons to account for every possible difference. Because we run the risk of incorrectly rejecting the null hypothesis just by chance if we run so many tests, it is a wise idea to use a more conservative procedure, such as the Bonferroni test, when comparing means. The Bonferroni test requires that we divide an overall alpha level, such as 0.05, by the number of comparisons we will make.

Number of Means	Number of Comparisons	Bonferroni Alpha Level (overall alpha $= 0.05$)
2	1	0.05
3	3	0.017
4	6	0.008
5	10	0.005
6	15	0.003
7	21	0.002

The Bonferroni test is straightforward. We merely divide the alpha level by the number of comparisons. For an alpha level of 0.05 and four means, as in the fairness study, we make six comparisons using a 0.008 alpha level (0.05/6) for each comparison. We then conduct a series of independent-samples t tests using the more extreme alpha level to determine the cutoffs. That is, the difference between means would have to be in the extremely narrow tails of a t distribution, at 0.008 (0.8%), before we would be willing to reject the null hypothesis.

In each case, the alpha levels for every comparison add up to 0.05, so we are still using a 0.05 alpha level overall. For example, when we make six comparisons at the 0.008 level, we have a $(0.008 + 0.008 + 0.008 + 0.008 + 0.008 + 0.008) = 6(0.008) = 0.05$ alpha level overall. Even though the overall alpha level remains at 0.05, the alpha levels for the individual comparisons rapidly become very extreme (see Table 12-14). The difference between two means must be quite extreme before we can reject the null hypothesis. We may fail to detect real differences that are not quite extreme enough, which is a Type II error.

Despite this limitation, the Bonferroni test is a versatile one. Some researchers use it to create a more "severe test" (Mayo, 2018) even in cases where they're not doing a post hoc test after an ANOVA. For example, when conducting a series of separate statistical analyses, researchers might choose to use the stricter alpha level of a Bonferroni test. This stricter alpha level will decrease the chances of a Type I error.

Readers of research also sometimes apply a Bonferroni correction. If you're concerned that a researcher may have engaged in p-hacking, for example, you might decide to count the number of analyses the researcher conducted, divide the alpha level by that number, and compare the actual p values for each analysis to the more severe test of the smaller alpha level. Because it is easy to divide an alpha level of 0.05 by the number of tests, this tactic can be quickly implemented while reading published results. In fact, in line with the growing practice of applying a Bonferroni correction after the fact, some researchers have called for a lower standard alpha level, such as 0.005 (Ioannidis, 2018).

CHECK YOUR LEARNING

Reviewing the Concepts

> As with other hypothesis tests, it is recommended that we calculate a measure of effect size when we have conducted an ANOVA. The most commonly reported effect size for ANOVA is R^2. Another estimate of effect size, omega squared (ω^2) is increasingly used because it is a less-biased estimate than R^2.

> If we are able to reject the null hypothesis with ANOVA, we're not finished. We must conduct a post hoc test, such as a Tukey HSD test, to determine exactly which pairs of means are significantly different from one another.

> When computing a post hoc Tukey HSD test on samples with unequal N's, we need to calculate a weighted sample size, called N'.

> The Bonferroni test is a more conservative post hoc test than the Tukey HSD test. It makes it more difficult to reject the null hypothesis.

Clarifying the Concepts

12-12 When do we conduct a post hoc test, such as a Tukey HSD test, and what does it tell us?

12-13 How is R^2 interpreted?

continued on next page

Calculating the Statistics	**12-14** Assume that a researcher is interested in whether reaction time varies as a function of grade level. After measuring the reaction times of 10 children in fourth grade, 12 children in fifth grade, and 13 children in sixth grade, the researcher conducts an ANOVA and finds an $SS_{between}$ of 336.360 and an SS_{total} of 522.782.

          a. Calculate R^2.

          b. Write a sentence interpreting this R^2. Be sure to do so in terms of the independent and dependent variables described for this study.

12-15 If the researcher in the previous Check Your Learning exercise rejected the null hypothesis after performing the ANOVA and intended to perform Tukey *HSD* post hoc comparisons, what would the critical value of the *q* statistic be for the comparisons?

12-16 If the researcher in the previous Check Your Learning exercise were to conduct post hoc tests using the Bonferroni test, what would the adjusted alpha level be?

Applying the Concepts	**12-17** Perform Tukey *HSD* post hoc comparisons on the data you analyzed in Check Your Learning 12-10. For which comparisons do you reject the null hypothesis?
Solutions to these Check Your Learning questions can be found in Appendix D.	**12-18** Calculate the effect size for the data you analyzed in Check Your Learning 12-10 and interpret its meaning.

REVIEW OF CONCEPTS

LaunchPad
macmillan learning
Visit LaunchPad to access the e-book and to test your knowledge with LearningCurve.

Using the *F* Distribution with Three or More Samples

We use the *F statistic* when we want to compare three or more samples. As with the *z* and *t* statistics, the *F* statistic is calculated by dividing a measure of the differences among sample means (*between-groups variance*) by a measure of variability within the samples (*within-groups variance*). The hypothesis test based on the *F* statistic is called *analysis of variance (ANOVA)*.

ANOVA offers a solution to the problem of having to run multiple *t* tests, because it allows for multiple comparisons in just one statistical analysis. There are several different types of ANOVA, and each has two descriptors. One indicates the number of independent variables, such as *one-way ANOVA* for one independent variable. The other indicates whether participants are in only one condition (*between-groups ANOVA*) or in every condition (*within-groups ANOVA*). The major assumptions for ANOVA are random selection of participants, normally distributed underlying populations, and *homoscedasticity*, which means that all populations have the same variance (versus *heteroscedasticity*, which means that the populations do not all have the same variance). As with previous statistical tests, most real-life analyses do not meet all of these assumptions.

One-Way Between-Groups ANOVA

The one-way between-groups ANOVA uses the six steps of hypothesis testing that we have already learned, but with some modifications, particularly to steps 3 and 5. Step 3 is simpler than with *t* tests; we only have to state that the comparison distribution is an *F* distribution and provide the degrees of freedom. In step 5, we calculate the

F statistic; a *source table* helps us to keep track of the calculations. The F statistic is a ratio of two different estimates of population variance, both of distributions of scores rather than distributions of means. The denominator, within-groups variance, is similar to the pooled variance of the independent-samples t test; it's basically a weighted average of the variance within each sample. The numerator, between-groups variance, is an estimate based on the difference between the sample means, but it is then inflated to represent a distribution of scores rather than a distribution of means. As part of the calculations of between-groups variance and within-groups variance, we need to calculate a *grand mean*, the mean score of every participant in the study.

A large between-groups variance and a small within-groups variance indicate a small degree of overlap among samples and likely a small degree of overlap among populations. A large between-groups variance divided by a small within-groups variance produces a large F statistic. If the F statistic is beyond a prescribed cutoff, or critical value, then we can reject the null hypothesis.

Beyond Hypothesis Testing for the One-Way Between-Groups ANOVA

It is also recommended, as with other hypothesis tests, that we calculate an effect size—usually R^2—when we conduct an ANOVA. Omega squared (ω^2) is an another estimate of effect size that is being used more often. It is similar to, but less biased than, R^2. In addition, when we reject the null hypothesis in an ANOVA, we know only that at least one of the means is different from at least one other mean. But we do not know exactly where the differences lie until we conduct a *post hoc test* such as the *Tukey HSD test*. The Bonferroni test is a more conservative post hoc test and is helpful to researchers who want to explore a data set while minimizing the probability of making a Type I error.

SPSS

In this chapter, we conducted a one-way between-groups ANOVA to compare people in four different types of societies regarding how fairly they behaved in a game, as assessed by the proportion of money that participants gave to a second player in that game. The type of society is a nominal independent variable, and the proportion of money is a scale dependent variable. To conduct a one-way between-groups ANOVA using SPSS, we enter the data so that all of the data for each participant is in a single row. For example, a person would have a score in the first column indicating the type of society in which he or she lives, perhaps a 1 for foraging or a 3 for natural resources. That person would also have a score in the second column indicating fairness level—the proportion of money he or she gave to a second player. The data as they should be entered are visible behind the output on the screenshot shown here. Remember: We can change how we view categorical data by selecting "View" and either checking or unchecking the box "value labels." In the screenshot, "value labels" is turned on.

Once the data have been entered, we can instruct SPSS to conduct the ANOVA by selecting Analyze → Compare Means → One-Way ANOVA. Now select the variables from the list. The independent variable named "Society" goes in the box marked "Factor," and the dependent variable named "Fairness" goes in the box labeled "Dependent List." Now, select "Post Hoc," then "Tukey," and then click "Continue." To request descriptive statistics—like the means and standard deviations for each group—select "Options," then "Descriptive," and then click "Continue." Click "OK" to run the ANOVA.

The SPSS output will provide four different tables. The first table (not included in the screenshot) includes the descriptive statistics for each level of the independent variable. The second table is the source table. Notice that the sums of squares, degrees of freedom, mean squares, and F statistic match the ones we calculated earlier. Any slight differences are due to differences in rounding decisions. The last column, titled "Sig.," says .006. This number indicates that the actual p value of this test statistic

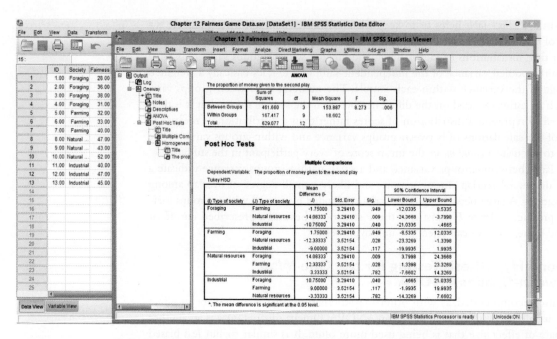

is just 0.006, which is less than the 0.05 alpha level typically used in hypothesis testing and an indication that we can reject the null hypothesis.

Below the source table, we can see the output for the post hoc test (the table labeled "Multiple Comparisons"). Mean differences with an asterisk are statistically significant at an alpha level of 0.05. The output here matches the post hoc test we conducted earlier. Each line in the table indicates a comparison between two groups. For example, the first line compares the foraging and farming groups and includes the mean difference and standard error for that comparison, as well as the p value: .949. This p value is above the 0.05 standard, so there is not a statistically significant difference between these two means. Note that SPSS includes asterisks to indicate significant mean differences. Also, this table provides several redundant comparisons. For example, the first line compares foraging to farming, and the fourth line compares farming to foraging. These two comparisons are the same, just with a different order. Regardless of the order, the conclusion about the comparison is the same.

The Tukey post hoc test in SPSS provides an additional table after the Multiple Comparisons table (labeled "Homogeneous Subsets" and shown in the right column). The conclusions made using this table will be the same as the conclusions we make using the "Multiple Comparisons" table and with the hand calculations we made earlier. This table provides the means for each level of the independent variable and provides us with two pieces of information. First, means found in the same column are not statistically significantly different from each other. Second, means found in different columns are statistically significantly different from each other. For example, the first column includes the means for the foraging and farming

groups, so we can conclude that there is not a statistically significant difference between these groups. For the second column, we can see the means for the farming and industrial groups, so these two means also are not statistically significantly different from each other. The patterns in the column, therefore, allow us to determine visually which means are in the same column and are not statistically significantly different. Additionally, we can see which means are not in the same column and are statistically significantly different. For example, the mean for the foraging group and the mean for the industrial group are never in the same column. We can conclude, then, that the foraging and industrial groups are statistically significantly different from each other. Regardless of which table we use to interpret the results of the post hoc tests, the conclusions will be the same.

Homogeneous Subsets

The proportion of money given to the second player

Tukey HSD[a,b]

Type of society	N	Subset for alpha = 0.05		
		1	2	3
Foraging	4	33.2500		
Farming	3	35.0000	35.0000	
Industrial	3		44.0000	44.0000
Natural resources	3			47.3333
Sig.		.954	.103	.765

Means for groups in homogeneous subsets are displayed.

a. Uses Harmonic Mean Sample Size = 3.200.

b. The group sizes are unequal. The harmonic mean of the group sizes is used. Type I error levels are not guaranteed.

HOW IT WORKS

12.1 CONDUCTING A ONE-WAY BETWEEN-GROUPS ANOVA

Who do you think is more outgoing, first-born or later-born siblings? Rohrer, Egloff, and Schmukle (2015) used three nationally based data sets from the United States, Great Britain, and Germany to understand the relations between a person's birth-order position and his or her personality. Each national data set used a different measure of personality, but all measures were theoretically based on the Big Five personality traits: extroversion, emotional stability, agreeableness, conscientiousness, and openness. The researchers standardized scores from each personality measure so comparisons could be made among all participants. They used a method similar to z scores, but with a mean of 50 rather than 0. The researchers also adjusted the personality scores for age, as "changes in personality over time … are inherently confounded with birth order" (p. 5).

Here is an abbreviated version of this study with fictional data for the personality trait extroversion. The means of these data points, however, are the actual means of the study. The findings from this smaller, fictional data set match the findings from the large, multinational study. The data represent participants with two siblings (i.e., families with three children).

Oldest Sibling: 47.15, 51.25, 49.75, 52.45

Middle Sibling: 47.55, 49.7, 50.8, 53.75

Youngest Sibling: 47.97, 49.49, 50.21, 53.89

In this study, the independent variable was birth-order position, with three levels: oldest, middle, and youngest. The dependent variable was the standardized personality score for extroversion. So there is one ordinal independent variable with three between-groups levels and one scale dependent variable. How can we conduct a one-way between-groups ANOVA?

Summary of Step 1

Population 1: People who are the oldest child in a family of three siblings. Population 2: People who are the middle child in a family of three siblings. Population 3: People who are the youngest child in a family of three siblings.

The comparison distribution will be an F distribution. The hypothesis test will be a one-way between-groups ANOVA. The participants were unlikely to have been randomly selected from among all children in families in which there are three siblings, so we should be cautious when generalizing conclusions from this study. We do not know if the underlying population distributions are normal, and this fictional example does not have a sufficient sample size that we can assume normal distributions based on the central limit theorem. (The actual study, however, did have a large sample size, so this assumption would have been met.) To see if we meet the homoscedasticity assumption, we will check whether the largest variance is no greater than twice the smallest variance. From the calculations that follow, we see that the largest variance, 6.66 for middle children, is not more than twice the smallest, 5.22 for the oldest children, so we have met the homoscedasticity assumption. (The following information is taken from the calculation of SS_{within}.)

Sample	Oldest	Middle	Youngest
Squared deviations	9.000	8.410	5.856
	1.210	0.563	0.810
	0.160	0.123	0.032
	5.290	10.890	12.250
Sum of Squares	15.660	19.986	18.948
$N-1$	3	3	3
Variance	**5.220**	**6.662**	**6.316**

Summary of Step 2

Null hypothesis: Extroversion as a personality trait is the same, on average, regardless of a person's birth-order position—$H_0 : \mu_1 = \mu_2 = \mu_3$. Research hypothesis: Extroversion as a personality trait is not the same, on average, for oldest children, middle children, and younger children—H_1 is that at least one μ is different from at least one other μ.

Summary of Step 3

$$df_{between} = N_{groups} - 1 = 3 - 1 = 2$$
$$df_1 = 4 - 1 = 3; df_2 = 4 - 1 = 3; df_3 = 4 - 1 = 3$$
$$df_{within} = 3 + 3 + 3 = 9$$

The comparison distribution will be an F distribution with 2 and 9 degrees of freedom.

Summary of Step 4

The critical F statistic based on an alpha level of 0.05 is 4.26.

Summary of Step 5

$$df_{total} = 2 + 9 = 11 \text{ or } df_{total} = 12 - 1 = 11$$
$$SS_{total} = \Sigma(X - GM)^2 = 54.794$$

Sample	X	$(X - GM)$	$(X - GM)^2$
Oldest	47.15	−3.180	10.112
$M_{oldest} = 50.15$	51.25	0.920	0.846
	49.75	−0.580	0.336
	52.45	2.120	4.494
Middle	47.55	−2.780	7.728
$M_{middle} = 50.45$	49.70	−0.630	0.397
	50.80	0.470	0.221
	53.75	3.420	11.696
Youngest	47.97	−2.360	5.570
$M_{youngest} = 50.39$	49.49	−0.840	0.706
	50.21	−0.120	0.014
	53.89	3.560	12.674
$GM = 50.33$			$SS_{total} = \textbf{54.794}$

$$SS_{within} = \Sigma(X - M)^2 = 54.594$$

Sample	X	$(X - M)$	$(X - M)^2$
Oldest	47.15	−3.000	9.000
$M_{oldest} = 50.15$	51.25	1.100	1.210
	49.75	−0.400	0.160
	52.45	2.300	5.290
Middle	47.55	−2.900	8.410
$M_{middle} = 50.45$	49.70	−0.750	0.563
	50.80	0.350	0.123
	53.75	3.300	10.890
Youngest	47.97	−2.420	5.856
$M_{youngest} = 50.39$	49.49	−0.900	0.810
	50.21	−0.180	0.032
	53.89	3.500	12.250
$GM = 50.33$			$SS_{within} = \textbf{54.594}$

$$SS_{between} = \Sigma(M - GM)^2 = 0.200$$

Sample	X	$(M - GM)$	$(M - GM)^2$
Oldest	47.15	−0.18	0.032
$M_{oldest} = 50.15$	51.25	−0.18	0.032
	49.75	−0.18	0.032
	52.45	−0.18	0.032
Middle	47.55	0.12	0.014
$M_{middle} = 50.45$	49.70	0.12	0.014
	50.80	0.12	0.014
	53.75	0.12	0.014
Youngest	47.97	0.06	0.004
$M_{youngest} = 50.39$	49.49	0.06	0.004
	50.21	0.06	0.004
	53.89	0.06	0.004
$GM = 50.33$			$SS_{between} = \textbf{0.200}$

$$MS_{between} = \frac{SS_{between}}{df_{between}} = \frac{0.200}{2} = 0.100$$

$$MS_{within} = \frac{SS_{within}}{df_{within}} = \frac{54.594}{9} = 6.066$$

$$F = \frac{MS_{within}}{MS_{between}} = \frac{0.100}{6.066} = 0.016$$

Source	SS	df	MS	F
Between	0.20	2	0.10	0.02
Within	54.59	9	6.07	
Total	54.79	11		

Summary of Step 6

The F statistic, 0.02, is not beyond the cutoff of 4.26. We cannot reject the null hypothesis. We do not have evidence that there is a mean difference in extroversion among oldest children, middle children, or youngest children. Post hoc tests are not completed because we cannot reject the null hypothesis. How It Works 12.2 demonstrates how to calculate the effect size for this example.

12.2 EFFECT SIZE FOR A ONE-WAY BETWEEN-GROUPS ANOVA

How would we calculate an effect size for the one-way between-groups ANOVA we conducted in How It Works 12.1?

$$R^2 = \frac{SS_{between}}{SS_{total}} = \frac{0.200}{54.594} = 0.004$$

According to Cohen's conventions for effect sizes (R^2), this is a very small effect.

EXERCISES

The solutions to the odd-numbered exercises can be found in Appendix C.

Clarifying the Concepts

12.1 What is an ANOVA?

12.2 What do the F distributions allow us to do that the t distributions do not?

12.3 The F statistic is a ratio of between-groups variance and within-groups variance. What are these two types of variance?

12.4 What is the difference between a within-groups (repeated-measures) ANOVA and a between-groups ANOVA?

12.5 What are the three assumptions for a between-groups ANOVA?

12.6 The null hypothesis for ANOVA posits no difference among population means, as in other hypothesis tests, but the research hypothesis in this case is a bit different. Why?

12.7 Why is the F statistic always positive?

12.8 Define the word *source* as you would use it in everyday conversation. Provide at least two different meanings that might be used. Then define the word as a statistician would use it.

12.9 Explain the concept of *sum of squares.*

12.10 The total sum of squares for a one-way between-groups ANOVA is found by adding which two statistics together?

12.11 What is the grand mean?

12.12 How do we calculate the between-groups sum of squares?

12.13 What do we typically use to measure effect size for a z test or a t test? What do we use to measure effect size for an ANOVA?

12.14 What are Cohen's conventions for interpreting effect size using R^2?

12.15 What is omega squared?

12.16 Why are researchers increasingly calculating omega squared rather than R^2?

12.17 What does *post hoc* mean, and when are these tests needed with ANOVA?

12.18 Define the symbols in the following formula:

$$N' = \frac{N_{groups}}{\Sigma(1/N)}$$

12.19 Find the error in the statistics language in each of the following statements about z, t, or F distributions or their related tests. Explain why it is incorrect and provide the correct word.

a. The professor reported the mean and standard error for the final exam in the statistics class.

b. Before we can calculate a t statistic, we must know the population mean and the population standard deviation.

c. The researcher calculated the parameters for her three samples so that she could calculate an F statistic and conduct an ANOVA.

d. For her honors project, Evelyn calculated a z statistic so that she could compare the mean video game scores of a sample of students who had ingested caffeine with a sample of students who had not ingested caffeine.

12.20 Find the incorrectly used symbol or symbols in each of the following statements or formulas. For each statement or formula, (i) state which symbol(s) is/are used incorrectly, (ii) explain why the symbol(s) in the original statement is/are incorrect, and (iii) state which symbol(s) *should* be used.

a. When calculating an F statistic, the numerator includes the estimate for the between-groups variance, s.

b. $SS_{between} = (X - GM)^2$

12.21 Find the incorrectly used symbol or symbols in each of the following statements or formulas. For each statement or formula, (i) state which symbol(s) is/are used incorrectly, (ii) explain why the symbol(s) in the original statement is/are incorrect, and (iii) state which symbol(s) should be used.

a. $SS_{within} = (X - M)$

b. $F = \sqrt{t}$

12.22 What are the necessary steps for performing a Bonferroni post hoc comparison?

12.23 Explain what statisticians mean when they say that a Bonferroni post hoc comparison is more conservative than a Tukey HSD test.

12.24 Why would a researcher use a Bonferroni test when conducting several separate statistical analyses?

12.25 Why would the reader of a research study use a Bonferroni test?

Calculating the Statistics

12.26 For the following data, assuming a between-groups design, determine:

Group 1: 11, 17, 22, 15
Group 2: 21, 15, 16

Group 3: 7, 8, 3, 10, 6, 4
Group 4: 13, 6, 17, 27, 20

a. $df_{between}$
b. df_{within}
c. df_{total}
d. The critical value, assuming a p value of 0.05
e. The mean for each group and the grand mean
f. The total sum of squares
g. The within-groups sum of squares
h. The between-groups sum of squares
i. The rest of the ANOVA source table for these data
j. Tukey HSD values

12.27 For the following data, assuming a between-groups design, determine:

1990: 45, 211, 158, 74
2000: 92, 128, 382
2010: 273, 396, 178, 248, 374

a. $df_{between}$
b. df_{within}
c. df_{total}
d. The critical value, assuming a p value of 0.05
e. The mean for each group and the grand mean
f. The total sum of squares
g. The within-groups sum of squares
h. The between-groups sum of squares
i. The rest of the ANOVA source table for these data
j. The effect size and an indication of its size

12.28 Calculate the F statistic, writing the ratio accurately, for each of the following cases:

a. Between-groups variance is 29.4 and within-groups variance is 19.1

b. Within-groups variance is 0.27 and between-groups variance is 1.56

c. Between-groups variance is 4595 and within-groups variance is 3972

12.29 Calculate the F statistic, writing the ratio accurately, for each of the following cases:

a. Between-groups variance is 321.83 and within-groups variance is 177.24

b. Between-groups variance is 2.79 and within-groups variance is 2.20

c. Within-groups variance is 41.60 and between-groups variance is 34.45

12.30 An incomplete one-way between-groups ANOVA source table is shown below. Compute the missing values.

Source	SS	df	MS	F
Between	191.450	—	47.863	—
Within	104.720	32	—	
Total	—	36		

12.31 An incomplete one-way between-groups ANOVA source table is shown below. Compute the missing values.

Source	SS	df	MS	F
Between	—	2	—	—
Within	89	11	—	
Total	132	—		

12.32 Use the source table in 12.30 to answer the following questions.

a. What is R^2 for these data?

b. What is ω^2 for these data?

12.33 Use the source table in 12.31 to answer the following questions.

a. What is R^2 se data?

b. What is ω^2 for these data?

12.34 Each of the following is a calculated F statistic with its degrees of freedom. Using the F table, estimate the level of significance for each. You can do this by indicating whether its likelihood of occurring is greater than or less than an alpha level shown in the table.

a. $F = 4.11$, with 3 $df_{between}$ and 30 df_{within}

b. $F = 1.12$, with 5 $df_{between}$ and 83 df_{within}

c. $F = 2.28$, with 4 $df_{between}$ and 42 df_{within}

12.35 A researcher designs an experiment in which the single independent variable has four levels. If the researcher performed an ANOVA and rejected the null hypothesis, how many post hoc comparisons would she make (assuming she was making all possible comparisons)?

12.36 A researcher designs an experiment in which the single independent variable has five levels. If the researcher performed an ANOVA and rejected the null hypothesis, how many post hoc comparisons would he make (assuming he was making all possible comparisons)?

12.37 A researcher designs an experiment in which the single independent variable has seven levels. If the researcher performed an ANOVA and rejected the null

hypothesis, how many post hoc comparisons would she make (assuming she was making all possible comparisons)?

12.38 Irwin and colleagues (2004) conducted a study on adherence to an exercise program. Participants were asked to attend a monthly group education program to help them change their exercise behavior. Attendance was taken and participants were divided into three categories: those who attended fewer than 5 sessions, those who attended between 5 and 8 sessions, and those who attended between 9 and 12 sessions. The researchers assessed the number of minutes of exercise per week for all participants. Assume that you plan to do Bonferroni post hoc comparisons if the ANOVA is statistically significant.

a. With a desired alpha level of 0.05 overall, what would the cutoff p value be for each comparison using a Bonferroni test?

b. With a desired alpha level of 0.01 overall, what would the cutoff p value be for each comparison using a Bonferroni test?

c. Using statistical software, we performed all of the possible pairwise independent-samples t tests on a subset of data that matches the sample means in the study (see Exercise 12.45); the actual p values (listed in the Sig. column in SPSS) associated with each of those tests appear below. Assuming an overall alpha level of 0.05, decide whether to reject or fail to reject the null hypothesis for each comparison.

<5 versus 5–8: $p = 0.041$

<5 versus 9–12: $p = 0.001$

5–8 versus 9–12: $p = 0.060$

Applying the Concepts

12.39 **Comedy versus news and hypothesis testing:** Focusing on coverage of the U.S. presidential election, Julia R. Fox, a telecommunications professor at Indiana University, wondered whether *The Daily Show*, despite its comedy format, was a valid source of news. She coded a number of half-hour episodes of *The Daily Show* as well as a number of half-hour episodes of the network news (Indiana University Media Relations, 2006). Fox reported that the average amounts of "video and audio substance" were not statistically significantly different between the two types of shows. Her analyses are described as "second by second," so, for this exercise, assume that all outcome variables are measures of time.

a. As the study is described, what are the independent and dependent variables? For nominal variables, state the levels.

b. As the study is described, what type of hypothesis test would Fox use?

c. Now imagine that Fox added a third category, a cable news channel such as CNN. Based on this new information, state the independent variable or variables and the levels of any nominal independent variables. What hypothesis test would she use?

12.40 **The comparison distribution:** For each of the following situations, state whether the distribution of interest is the z distribution, a t distribution, or an F distribution. Explain your answer.

a. A city employee locates a U.S. Census report that includes the mean and standard deviation for income in the state of Wyoming and then takes a random sample of 100 residents of the city of Cheyenne. He wonders whether residents of Cheyenne earn more, on average, than Wyoming residents as a whole.

b. A researcher studies the effect of different contexts on work interruptions. Using discreet video cameras, she observes employees working in enclosed offices in the workplace, in open cubicles in the workplace, and in home offices.

c. An honors student wondered whether an education in statistics reduces the tendency to believe advertising that cites data. He compares social science majors who had taken statistics and social science majors who had not taken statistics with respect to their responses to an interactive advertising assessment.

12.41 **The comparison distribution:** For each of the following situations, state whether the distribution of interest is the z distribution, a t distribution, or an F distribution. Explain your answer.

a. A student reads in her *Introduction to Psychology* textbook that the mean IQ is 100. She asks 10 friends what their IQ scores are (they attend a university that assesses everyone's IQ score) to determine whether her friends are smarter than average.

b. Is the presence of books in the home a marker of a stable family? A social worker counted the number of books on view in the living rooms of all the families he visited over the course of one year. He categorized families into four groups: no books visible, only children's books visible, only adult books visible, and both children's and adult books visible. The department for which he worked had stability ratings for each family based on a number of measures.

c. Which television show leads to more learning? A researcher assessed the vocabularies of a sample of children randomly assigned to watch *Sesame Street* as much as they wanted for a year but to not watch *The Wiggles*. She also assessed the vocabularies of a sample of children randomly assigned to watch *The Wiggles* as much as they wanted for a year but not to watch *Sesame Street*. She compared the average vocabulary scores for the two groups.

12.42 **Links among distributions:** The z, t, and F distributions are closely linked. In fact, it is possible to use an F distribution in all cases in which a t or a z could be used.

a. If you calculated an F statistic of 4.22 but you could have used a t statistic (i.e., the situation met all criteria for using a t statistic), what would the t statistic have been? Explain your answer.

b. If you calculated an F statistic of 4.22 but you could have used a z statistic, what would the z statistic have been? Explain your answer.

c. If you calculated a t statistic of 0.67 but you could have used a z statistic, what would the z statistic have been? Explain your answer.

d. Cite at least one possible reason that all three types of distributions (i.e., z, t, and F) are still in use when we really only need an F distribution.

12.43 **International students and type of ANOVA:** Catherine Ruby (2006), a doctoral student at New York University, conducted an online survey to ascertain the reasons that international students chose to attend graduate school in the United States. One of several dependent variables that she considered was reputation; students were asked to rate the importance in their decision of factors such as the reputation of the institution, the institution's and program's academic accreditations, and the reputation of the faculty. Students rated factors on a 1–5 scale, and then all reputation ratings were averaged to form a summary score for each respondent. For each of the following scenarios, state the independent variable with its levels (the dependent variable is reputation in all cases). Then state what kind of an ANOVA she would use.

a. Ruby compared the importance of reputation among graduate students in different types of programs: arts and sciences, education, law, and business.

b. Imagine that Ruby followed these graduate students for 3 years and assessed their rating of reputation once a year.

c. Ruby compared international students working toward a master's, a doctoral, or a professional degree (e.g., MBA) on reputation.

d. Imagine that Ruby followed international students from their master's program to their doctoral program to their postdoctoral fellowship, assessing their ratings of reputation once at each level of their training.

12.44 Type of ANOVA in study of remembering names: Do people remember names better under different circumstances? In a fictional study, a cognitive psychologist studied memory for names after a group activity that lasted 20 minutes. Participants were not told that this was a study of memory. After the group activity, participants were asked to name the other group members. The researcher randomly assigned 120 participants to one of three conditions: (1) group members introduced themselves once (one introduction only), (2) group members were introduced by the experimenter and by themselves (two introductions), and (3) group members were introduced by the experimenter and themselves and also wore name tags throughout the group activity (two introductions and name tags).

a. Identify the type of ANOVA that should be used to analyze the data from this study.

b. State what the researcher could do to redesign this study so it would be analyzed with a one-way within-groups ANOVA. Be specific.

12.45 Exercise and education programs: Irwin and colleagues (2004) conducted research on adherence to an exercise regimen. We give an overview of the study in exercise 12.38. Here are the data:

<5 sessions: 155, 120, 130
5–8 sessions: 199, 160, 184
9–12 sessions: 230, 214, 195, 209

a. What is the independent variable in this study? What are its levels?

b. What is the dependent variable in this study?

c. Use the six steps of hypothesis testing to conduct a one-way between-groups ANOVA.

d. What is R^2 for these data? How large is this effect according to Cohen's conventions?

e. What is ω^2 for these data? How large is this effect according to Cohen's conventions?

12.46 Exercise and post hoc tests: Use the same data from the previous exercise in this exercise.

a. Explain why it is necessary to conduct a post hoc test such as a Tukey *HSD* test when an ANOVA is statistically significant.

b. Conduct a Tukey *HSD* test. Show all calculations.

c. Explain why we cannot assume that two groups have the same means when we fail to reject the null hypothesis using a Tukey *HSD* test. Refer to the current example in your answer.

12.47 Grade-point average and comparing the *t* and *F* distributions: Based on your knowledge of the relation of the *t* and *F* distributions, complete the software output tables below. The table for the independent-samples *t* test and the table for the one-way between-groups ANOVA were calculated using the identical fictional data comparing grade-point averages (GPAs).

a. What is the *F* statistic? Show your calculations. (*Hint:* The "Mean Square" column includes the two estimates of variance used to calculate the *F* statistic.)

b. What is the *t* statistic? Show your calculations. [*Hint:* Use the *F* statistic that you calculated in part (a).]

Independent Samples Test

				t-test for Equality of Means				
						Standard Error Difference	95% Confidence Interval of the Difference	
	t	*df*	Sig. (2-tailed)	Mean Difference			Lower	Upper
GPA		82		−.28251		.12194	−.52508	−.03993

ANOVA

GPA	Sum of Squares	*df*	Mean Square	*F*	Sig.
Between groups	4.623	1	4.623		.005
Within groups	42.804	82	.522		
Total	47.427	83			

c. In statistical software output, "Sig." refers to the actual alpha level of the statistic. We can compare the actual alpha level to a cutoff alpha level such as 0.05 to decide whether to reject the null hypothesis. For the t test, what is the "Sig."? Explain how you determined this. (*Hint:* Would we expect the "Sig." for the independent-samples t test to be the same as or different from that for the one-way between-groups ANOVA?)

12.48 Consideration of Future Consequences and two kinds of hypothesis testing: Two samples of students, one composed of social science majors and one composed of students with other majors, completed the Consideration of Future Consequences scale (CFC). The accompanying tables include the output from software for an independent-samples t test and a one-way between-groups ANOVA on these data.

a. Demonstrate that the results of the independent-samples t test and the one-way between-groups ANOVA are the same. (*Hint:* Find the t statistic for the t test and the F statistic for the ANOVA.)

b. In statistical software output, "Sig." refers to the actual alpha level of the statistic. We can compare the actual alpha level to a cutoff alpha level such as 0.05 to decide whether to reject the null hypothesis. What are the "Sig." levels for the two tests here—the independent-samples t test and the one-way between-groups ANOVA? Are they the same or different? Explain why this is the case.

c. In the CFC ANOVA, the column titled "Mean Square" includes the estimates of variance. Show how the F statistic was calculated from two types of variance. (*Hint:* Look at the far-left column to determine which estimate of variance is which.)

d. Looking at the table titled "Group Statistics," how many participants were in each sample?

e. Looking at the table titled "Group Statistics," what is the mean CFC score for the social science majors?

Independent Samples Test

	t	df	Sig. (2-tailed)	Mean Difference	Standard Error Difference	95% Confidence Interval of the Difference	
						Lower	Upper
CFC scores	−.650	28	.521	−.17500	.26930	−.72664	.37664

ANOVA

CFC Scores

	Sum of Squares	df	Mean Square	F	Sig.
Between Groups	.204	1	.204	.422	.521
Within Groups	13.538	28	.483		
Total	13.742	29			

Group Statistics

Major		N	Mean	Standard Deviation	Standard Error Mean
CFC Scores	Other	10	3.2000	.88819	.28087
	Social Science	20	3.3750	.58208	.13016

12.49 **Instructors on Facebook and one-way ANOVA:** Researchers investigated whether the amount of self-disclosure on Facebook affected student perceptions of the instructor, the class, and the classroom environment (Mazer, Murphy, & Simonds, 2007). Students were randomly assigned to view one of three Facebook pages of an instructor. The pages were identical except that one instructor had high self-disclosure, one had medium self-disclosure, and one had low self-disclosure. Self-disclosure was "manipulated in photographs, biological information, and posts" (p. 6). The researchers reported that "Participants who accessed the Facebook Web site of a teacher high in self-disclosure anticipated higher levels of motivation and affective learning and a more positive classroom climate" (p. 1).

  a. What is the independent variable, what kind of variable is it, and what are its levels?

  b. What is the first dependent variable mentioned, and what kind of variable is this?

  c. Is this a between-groups design or a within-groups design? Explain your answer.

  d. Based on your answers to parts (a) through (c), what kind of ANOVA would the researchers use to analyze the data? Explain your answer.

  e. Is this a true experiment? Explain your answer, and explain what this means for the researchers' conclusion.

12.50 **Post hoc tests and *p* values:** The most recent version of the *Publication Manual of the American Psychological Association* (American Psychological Association, 2010) recommends reporting the exact *p* values for all statistical tests to two decimal places (previously, it recommended reporting $p < 0.05$ or $p > 0.05$). Explain how this reporting format allows a reader to more critically interpret the results of post hoc comparisons reported by an author.

12.51 **Post hoc tests, bilingualism, and language skills:** Researchers Raluca Barac and Ellen Bialystok (2012) conducted a study in which they compared the language skills of 104 six-year-old children who were in one of four groups. Some children spoke only English. Others were bilingual, speaking English along with Chinese, French, or Spanish. The children completed the Peabody Picture Vocabulary Test (PPVT) as a measure of their vocabulary. An excerpt from the results section of the published journal article follows: "A one-way ANOVA on PPVT scores showed a main effect of language group, $F(3, 100) = 8.27$, $p < .0001$. Post hoc Bonferroni contrasts indicated that the monolingual children and the Spanish-English bilingual children

outperformed the other two bilingual groups who did not differ from each other."

  a. What is the independent variable, what kind of variable is it, and what are its levels? What is the dependent variable and what kind of variable is it?

  b. How do we know that this finding is statistically significant?

  c. Why was the one-way ANOVA not sufficient to draw a conclusion from these data?

  d. Explain what is meant here by the Bonferroni test.

  e. Summarize this finding in your own words.

12.52 **Romantic love and post hoc tests:** Researchers who conducted a study of brain activation and romantic love divided their analyses into two groups (Aron et al., 2005). Some analyses—those for which they had developed specific hypotheses prior to data collection—used an alpha level of 0.05. The rest of the analyses used an alpha level of 0.001.

  a. Explain why the researchers' plan to have different alpha levels for the two groups was a wise one.

  b. Suggest one method by which the researchers could have come up with an alpha level of 0.001 as their cutoff.

Putting It All Together

12.53 **Trust in leadership and one-way between-groups ANOVA:** In Chapter 11, we introduced a study by Steele and Pinto (2006) that examined whether people's level of trust in their direct supervisor was related to their level of agreement with a policy supported by that leader. Steele and Pinto found that the extent to which subordinates agreed with their supervisor was related to trust and showed no relation to gender, age, time on the job, or length of time working with the supervisor. Let's assume we used a scale that sorted employees into three groups: low trust, moderate trust, and high trust in supervisors. Following are fictional data regarding level of agreement with a leader's decision for these three groups. The scores presented are the level of agreement with a decision made by a leader, ranging from 1, the least agreement, to 40, the highest level of agreement. *Note:* These fictional data are different from those presented in Chapter 11.

  Employees with low trust in their leader: 9, 14, 11, 18

  Employees with moderate trust in their leader: 14, 35, 23

  Employees with high trust in their leader: 27, 33, 21, 34

a. What is the independent variable? What are its levels?

b. What is the dependent variable?

c. Conduct all six steps of hypothesis testing for a one-way between-groups ANOVA.

d. How would you report the statistics in a journal article?

e. Conduct a Tukey *HSD* test. What did you learn?

f. Why is it not possible to conduct a *t* test in this situation?

g. What is R^2 for these data? How large is this effect according to Cohen's conventions?

h. What is ω^2 for these data? How large is this effect according to Cohen's conventions?

12.54 Orthodontics and one-way between-groups ANOVA: Iranian researchers studied factors affecting patients' likelihood of wearing orthodontic appliances, noting that orthodontics is perhaps the area of health care with the highest need for patient cooperation (Behenam & Pooya, 2007). Among their analyses, they compared students in primary school, junior high school, and high school. The data that follow have almost exactly the same means as the researchers found in their study, but with far smaller samples. The score for each student is his or her daily hours of wearing the orthodontic appliance.

> Primary school: 16, 13, 18
> Junior high school: 8, 13, 14, 12
> High school: 20, 15, 16, 18

a. What is the independent variable? What are its levels?

b. What is the dependent variable?

c. Conduct all six steps of hypothesis testing for a one-way between-groups ANOVA.

d. How would you report the statistics in a journal article?

e. Conduct a Tukey *HSD* test. What did you learn?

f. Calculate the traditional effect size for this sample.

g. Calculate the more conservative estimate of effect size for this sample. How does this estimate differ from the one you calculated in part (f)?

h. Based on Cohen's conventions, are these small, medium, or large effect sizes?

i. Why is it useful to know the effect size in addition to the results of a hypothesis test?

j. How could this study be conducted using a within-groups design?

12.55 ANOVA, award-winning television, and the theory of mind: Can watching high-quality television dramas improve our theory of mind—our ability to understand others? Psychologists Jessica Black and Jennifer Barnes (2015) explored this question in a study in which participants were randomly assigned to watch 42 minutes of an award-winning television drama like *The Good Wife,* 42 minutes of an award-winning television documentary such as an episode of *Through the Wormhole,* or no television at all. (*Note:* Exercise 11.29 is about a different study reported in this same journal article.) Next, all participants were asked to look at a series of 36 photos of people's eyes and decide if each person was jealous, panicked, arrogant, or hateful. Scores ranged from 0 (guessed no emotions correctly) to 36 (guessed every emotion correctly). The researchers analyzed the data and found that the "mean ... differed across the three groups, $F(2, 173) = 6.04$, $p = .003$, partial $\eta^2 = .065$." (Partial η^2 can be interpreted in the same way as R^2.) The means were 28.02 for the drama group, 26.55 for the documentary group, and 25.30 for the control group. The researchers reported a significant difference only between the means for the drama group and control group.

a. What is the independent variable in this study? What are its levels?

b. What is the dependent variable in this study?

c. Is this an experiment or a correlational study? Explain your answer.

d. What statistical analysis did the researchers use? Explain your answer.

e. Explain the statistics reported in the research excerpt. What does each of these mean?

f. Explain what the researchers likely did to determine which means were significantly different from each other.

g. Explain the overall pattern of results in your own words.

h. The effect size is given in terms of partial η^2. What does this tell us about the effect size?

i. Let's say you prefer documentaries to dramas. You notice that the mean for documentaries is also higher than the mean for controls, and decide that documentaries are helpful, too. Why is this statement problematic from a statistical point of view?

j. If the one significant mean difference observed in this study is an incorrect conclusion, what kind of error is this? Explain your answer.

k. The researchers represented these research findings in a graph similar to the one shown here. Cite at least two ways you would revise the graph to fit with what you learned in Chapter 3.

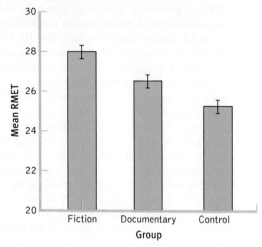

12.56 ANOVA and taking notes: Researchers studied the type of note taking that would lead to the best performance on conceptual questions on a test (Mueller & Oppenheimer, 2014). Conceptual questions are those in which students have to apply the material, rather than just answer fact-based questions. Students were randomly assigned to one of the following groups:

1. Take notes by hand (the longhand group)

2. Take notes on their laptops as usual (the laptop-nonintervention group)

3. Take notes on their laptops with instructions to try to put the notes in their own words (the laptop-intervention group)

Because people tend to take notes verbatim on their laptops, the researchers speculated that those in the laptop-nonintervention group would learn less, on average, than those in the other two groups. The researchers reported that "results showed that on conceptual-application questions, longhand participants performed better (z-score $M = 0.28, SD = 1.04$) than laptop-nonintervention participants (z-score $M = -0.15, SD = 0.85$), $F(1, 89) = 11.98, p = .017, \eta_p^2 = .12$. Scores for laptop-intervention participants (z-score $M = -0.11, SD = 1.02$) did not significantly differ from those for either laptop-nonintervention ($p = .91$) or longhand ($p = .29$) participants" (p. 1162).

a. What is the independent variable in this study? What are its levels?

b. What is the dependent variable in this study?

c. Is this an experiment or a correlational study? Explain your answer.

d. The report of the statistics provides us with z-score M rather than M. Explain what these researchers are reporting here.

e. Which groups are significantly different from each other? Describe two ways that we know this.

f. The effect size is given in terms of η_p^2. What does this tell us about the effect size? (Note: The subscript p means "partial," and indicates that this effect size is just for this particular finding. You may ignore the p in your answer. Remember that η^2 is roughly equivalent to R^2.)

g. A friend hears this finding and says, "I don't want to take notes longhand, but I'll think about typing the notes in my own words. The mean z-score of $-.11$ is higher than the mean z-score of $-.15$." Why is this statement problematic from a statistical point of view?

h. If the finding of no significant difference between the longhand group and the laptop-intervention group is wrong, what kind of error is this? Explain your answer.

LaunchPad
macmillan learning

Visit LaunchPad to access the e-book and to test your knowledge with LearningCurve.

TERMS

analysis of variance (ANOVA) (p. 340)

F statistic (p. 340)

between-groups variance (p. 340)

within-groups variance (p. 340)

one-way ANOVA (p. 342)

between-groups ANOVA (p. 342)

within-groups ANOVA (p. 342)

homoscedastic (p. 342)

heteroscedastic (p. 342)

source table (p. 350)

grand mean (p. 352)

R^2 (p. 359)

omega squared $\left(\omega^2\right)$ (p. 360)

post hoc test (p. 361)

Tukey HSD test (p. 361)

Bonferroni test (p. 364)

FORMULAS

$df_{between} = N_{groups} - 1$ (p. 346)

$df_{within} = df_1 + df_2 + \cdots 1\, df_{last}$ (in which df_1, df_2, etc., are the degrees of freedom, $N - 1$, for each sample) [formula for a one-way between-groups ANOVA]   (p. 346)

$df_{total} = df_{between} + df_{within}$ [formula for a one-way between-groups ANOVA]   (p. 351)

$df_{total} = N_{total} - 1$ (p. 351)

$GM = \dfrac{\Sigma(X)}{N_{total}}$ (p. 352)

$SS_{total} = \Sigma(X - GM)^2$ (p. 353)

$SS_{within} = \Sigma(X - M)^2$ [formula for a one-way between-groups ANOVA]   (p. 353)

$SS_{between} = \Sigma(M - GM)^2$ (p. 355)

$SS_{total} = SS_{within} + SS_{between}$ [alternative formula for a one-way between-groups ANOVA]   (p. 355)

$MS_{between} = \dfrac{SS_{between}}{df_{between}}$ (p. 356)

$MS_{within} = \dfrac{SS_{within}}{df_{within}}$ (p. 356)

$F = \dfrac{MS_{between}}{MS_{within}}$ (p. 356)

$R^2 = \dfrac{SS_{between}}{SS_{total}}$ [formula for a one-way between-groups ANOVA]   (p. 359)

$\omega^2 = \dfrac{SS_{between} - ((df_{between})(MS_{within}))}{SS_{total} + MS_{within}}$ (p. 360)

$s_M = \sqrt{\dfrac{MS_{within}}{N}}$, if equal sample sizes   (p. 361)

$HSD = \dfrac{(M_1 - M_2)}{s_M}$, for any two sample means   (p. 361)

$N' = \dfrac{N_{groups}}{\Sigma(1/N)}$ (p. 362)

$s_M = \sqrt{\dfrac{MS_{within}}{N'}}$, if unequal sample sizes   (p. 362)

SYMBOLS

F (p. 338)

$df_{between}$ (p. 346)

df_{within} (p. 346)

$MS_{between}$ (p. 350)

MS_{within} (p. 350)

df_{total} (p. 350)

$SS_{between}$ (p. 350)

SS_{within} (p. 350)

SS_{total} (p. 350)

GM (p. 352)

R^2 (p. 359)

ω^2 (p. 360)

HSD (p. 361)

N' (p. 362)

One-Way Within-Groups ANOVA

One-Way Within-Groups **ANOVA**

The Benefits of Within-Groups ANOVA

The Six Steps of Hypothesis Testing

Beyond Hypothesis Testing for the One-Way Within-Groups **ANOVA**

R^2, the Effect Size for ANOVA

The Tukey *HSD* Test

Data Ethics: "WEIRD" Samples and Good Reporting Practices

Within-Groups Design
Whenever researchers have people provide ratings of several items—such as here, with different types of coffee—they are using a within-groups design. If the order of the flavors is varied for each person, the researcher is using counterbalancing.

"What's in a name?" Juliet asks Romeo. "That which we call a rose/By any other name would smell as sweet." A group of Canadian researchers decided to test Juliet's assertion (Djordjevic et al., 2007). They assigned names associated with positive, negative, or neutral odors to 15 different odors and then presented them to participants, who were asked to rate the pleasantness and the intensity of the aroma. Positive names for aromas included "cinnamon stick" and "jasmine tea." Negative names for odors included "rotten fish" and "dry vomit." Neutral names were 2-digit numbers such as "36."

The researchers used a within-groups design, which means that each participant smelled the same odor with a positive name, a negative name, and a neutral name. Having each participant experience each level of the independent variable is one of the advantages of using a within-groups design: Researchers require fewer participants. The research team found that participants generally rated aromas with positive names as more pleasant and odors with negative names as more intense.

This odor study also demonstrates why this chapter is divided into two parts. The first part discusses the one-way within-groups ANOVA, which shows how to determine the probability that any differences are real (such as the differences between odor ratings based on a positive, negative, or neutral name). The second part takes us beyond hypothesis testing and discusses how to calculate the size of those differences.

One-Way Within-Groups ANOVA

There is not much difference between Chapters 12 and 13. Chapter 12 taught you how to conduct the multiple-group equivalent of an independent-samples *t* test, the one-way between-groups ANOVA. You have also learned how to calculate effect size and conduct a post hoc test for a one-way between-groups ANOVA. Chapter 13 draws on the same ideas, but this time you will be learning how to conduct the multiple-group equivalent of a paired-samples *t* test, called a *one-way within-groups ANOVA* (also known as a *one-way repeated-measures ANOVA*). Just as you did for the one-way between-groups ANOVA, you will learn how to calculate effect size and conduct a post hoc test for the one-way within-groups ANOVA. If you understand how a between-groups design differs from a within-groups design, then you already understand the key concept involved.

EXAMPLE 13.1

Have you ever participated in a taste test? If you have, then you were probably a participant in a within-groups experiment. A couple of decades ago, when pricier microbrew beers were becoming popular in North America, the journalist James Fallows, who loves beer, found himself spending increasingly more on a bottle of beer. He began to wonder whether he was getting his money's worth for these more expensive beers. So, he recruited 12 colleagues, all self-professed beer snobs, to participate in a taste test to see whether they really could tell whether a beer was expensive or cheap (Fallows, 1999).

Fallows wanted to know whether his recruits could distinguish among widely available American beers that were categorized into three groups based on price—"high-end" beers like Sam Adams, "mid-range" beers like Budweiser, and "cheap" beers like Busch. All of these beers are lagers, a type of beer chosen because it can be found at every price point. Here are data—mean scores on a scale of 0–100 for each category of beer—for five of the participants. (*Note:* For teaching purposes, the means are slightly different and have been rounded to the nearest whole number; the take-home data story, however, remains the same.)

Participant	Cheap Beer	Mid-Range Beer	High-End Beer
1	40	30	53
2	42	45	65
3	30	38	64
4	37	32	43
5	23	28	38

The Benefits of Within-Groups ANOVA

Fallows only reported his overall findings. If he had conducted hypothesis testing, then he would have used a one-way within-groups ANOVA, the appropriate statistic when there is one nominal or ordinal independent variable (type of beer) that has more than two levels (cheap, mid-range, and high-end), a scale dependent variable (ratings of beers), and participants who experience every level of the independent variable (each participant tasted the beers in every category).

The beauty of the within-groups design is that it reduces errors that are due to differences between the groups, because each group includes exactly the same participants. The beer study could not be influenced by individual taste preferences, amount of alcohol typically consumed, tendency to be critical or lenient when rating, and so on. This enables us to reduce the within-groups variability associated with differences among the people in the study across groups. The lower within-groups variability means a smaller denominator for the F statistic and a larger F statistic that makes it easier to reject the null hypothesis.

> **MASTERING THE CONCEPT**
>
> **13-1:** We use a one-way within-groups ANOVA when there is one independent variable with at least three levels, a scale dependent variable, and participants who are in every group.

The Six Steps of Hypothesis Testing

We'll use the data from the beer taste test to walk through the same six steps of hypothesis testing that we have used for every other statistical test.

EXAMPLE 13.2

> **STEP 1:** Identify the populations, distribution, and assumptions.

The one-way within-groups ANOVA requires an additional assumption compared to the one-way between-groups ANOVA: We must be careful to avoid order effects. In the beer study, order may have influenced participants' judgments because all participants tasted the beers in the same order: a mid-range beer, followed by a high-end beer, followed by a cheap beer, followed by another cheap beer, and so on. Perhaps the first sip of beer tastes the best, no matter what kind of beer is being tasted. Ideally, Fallows would have used counterbalancing, so that participants tasted the beers in different orders.

Summary: Population 1: People who drink cheap beer. Population 2: People who drink mid-range beer. Population 3: People who drink high-end beer.

The comparison distribution and hypothesis test: The comparison distribution is an *F* distribution. The hypothesis test is a one-way within-groups ANOVA.

Assumptions: (1) The participants were not selected randomly, so we must generalize with caution. (2) We do not know if the underlying population distributions are normal, but the sample data do not indicate severe skew. (3) After we calculate the test statistic, we will test the homoscedasticity assumption by checking whether the largest variance is more than twice the smallest. (4) The experimenter did not counterbalance, so there may be order effects.

> **STEP 2: State the null and research hypotheses.**

This step is identical to that for a one-way between-groups ANOVA.

Summary: Null hypothesis: People who drink cheap, mid-range, and high-end beer rate their beverages the same, on average—H_0: $\mu_1 = \mu_2 = \mu_3$. Research hypothesis: People who drink cheap, mid-range, and high-end beer do not rate their beverages the same, on average—H_1 is that at least one μ is different from another μ.

> **STEP 3: Determine the characteristics of the comparison distribution.**

We state that the comparison distribution is an *F* distribution and determine the degrees of freedom. Instead of three, we now calculate four kinds of degrees of freedom—between-groups, subjects, within-groups, and total. The subjects degrees of freedom corresponds to a sum of squares for differences across participants: the *subjects sum of squares,* or $SS_{subjects}$. In a one-way within-groups ANOVA, we calculate between-groups degrees of freedom and subjects degrees of freedom first because we multiply these two together to calculate the within-groups degrees of freedom.

We calculate the between-groups degrees of freedom exactly as before:

$$df_{between} = N_{groups} - 1 = 3 - 1 = 2$$

We next calculate the degrees of freedom that pairs with $SS_{subjects}$. Called $df_{subjects}$, it is calculated by subtracting 1 from the actual number of subjects, not from the number of data points. We use a lowercase *n* to indicate that this is the number of participants in a single sample (even though they're all in every sample). The formula is:

$$df_{subjects} = n - 1 = 5 - 1 = 4$$

Once we know the between-groups degrees of freedom and the subjects degrees of freedom, we calculate the within-groups degrees of freedom by multiplying the first two:

$$df_{within} = (df_{between})(df_{subjects}) = (2)(4) = 8$$

Note that the within-groups degrees of freedom is smaller than we would have calculated for a one-way between-groups ANOVA. For a one-way between-groups ANOVA, we would have subtracted 1 from each sample ($5 - 1 = 4$) and summed them to get 12. The within-groups degrees of freedom is smaller because we exclude variability related to differences among the participants from the within-groups sum of squares, and the degrees of freedom must reflect that.

Finally, we calculate total degrees of freedom using either method we learned earlier. We can sum the other degrees of freedom:

$$df_{total} = df_{between} + df_{subjects} + df_{within} = 2 + 4 + 8 = 14$$

Alternatively, we can use the second formula we learned before, treating the total number of participants as every data point, rather than every person. We know, of course, that there are just five participants and that they participate in all three levels of the independent variable, but for this step, we count the 15 total data points:

$$df_{total} = N_{total} - 1 = 15 - 1 = 14$$

We have calculated the 4 degrees of freedom that we will include in the source table. However, we only report the between-groups and within-groups degrees of freedom at this step.

Summary: We use the F distribution with 2 and 8 degrees of freedom.

> **STEP 4: Determine the critical values, or cutoffs.**

The fourth step is identical to that for a one-way between-groups ANOVA. We use the between-groups degrees of freedom and within-groups degrees of freedom to look up a critical value on the F table in Appendix B.

Summary: The critical value for the F statistic for an alpha level of 0.05 and 2 and 8 degrees of freedom is 4.46.

> **STEP 5: Calculate the test statistic.**

As before, we calculate the test statistic in the fifth step. To start, we calculate four sums of squares—one each for between-groups, subjects, within-groups, and total. For each sum of squares, we calculate deviations between two different types of means or scores, square the deviations, and then sum the squared differences. We calculate a squared deviation for *every* score; so for each sum of squares in this example, we sum 15 squared deviations.

As we did with the one-way between-groups ANOVA, let's start with the total sum of squares, SS_{total}. We calculate this exactly as we calculated it previously:

$$SS_{total} = \Sigma(X - GM)^2 = 2117.732$$

Type of Beer	Rating (X)	($X - GM$)	($X - GM$)^2
Cheap	40	−0.533	0.284
Cheap	42	1.467	2.152
Cheap	30	−10.533	110.944
Cheap	37	−3.533	12.482
Cheap	23	−17.533	307.406
Mid-range	30	−10.533	110.944
Mid-range	45	4.467	19.954
Mid-range	38	−2.533	6.416
Mid-range	32	−8.533	72.812
Mid-range	28	−12.533	157.076
High-end	53	12.467	155.426
High-end	65	24.467	598.634
High-end	64	23.467	550.700
High-end	43	2.467	6.086
High-end	38	−2.533	6.416
$GM = 40.533$			$\Sigma(X - GM)^2 = 2117.732$

Next, we calculate the between-groups sum of squares. It, too, is the same as for a one-way between-groups ANOVA:

$$SS_{between} = \Sigma(M - GM)^2 = 1092.130$$

Type of Beer	Rating (X)	Group Mean (M)	($M - GM$)	($M - GM$)^2
Cheap	40	34.4	−6.133	37.614
Cheap	42	34.4	−6.133	37.614
Cheap	30	34.4	−6.133	37.614
Cheap	37	34.4	−6.133	37.614
Cheap	23	34.4	−6.133	37.614
Mid-range	30	34.6	−5.933	35.200
Mid-range	45	34.6	−5.933	35.200
Mid-range	38	34.6	−5.933	35.200
Mid-range	32	34.6	−5.933	35.200
Mid-range	28	34.6	−5.933	35.200
High-end	53	52.6	12.067	145.612
High-end	65	52.6	12.067	145.612
High-end	64	52.6	12.067	145.612
High-end	43	52.6	12.067	145.612
High-end	38	52.6	12.067	145.612
$GM = 40.533$				$\Sigma(M - GM)^2 = 1092.130$

So far, the calculations of the sums of squares for a one-way within-groups ANOVA have been the same as they were for a one-way between-groups ANOVA. We left the subjects sum of squares and within-groups sum of squares for last. Here is where we see some changes. We want to remove the variability caused by participant differences from the estimate of variability across conditions. So we calculate the subjects sum of squares separately from the within-groups sum of squares. To do that, we subtract the grand mean from each participant's mean *for all of his or her scores.* We first have to calculate a mean for each participant across the three conditions. For example, the first participant had ratings of 40 for cheap beers, 30 for mid-range beers, and 53 for high-end beers. This participant's mean is 41.

So the formula for the subjects sum of squares is:

$$SS_{subjects} = \Sigma(M_{participant} - GM)^2 = 729.738$$

MASTERING THE FORMULA

13-4: The subjects sum of squares in a one-way within-groups ANOVA is calculated using the following formula: $SS_{subjects} = \Sigma(M_{participant} - GM)^2$. For each score, we subtract the grand mean from that participant's mean for all of his or her scores and square this deviation. Note that we do not use the scores in any of these calculations. We sum all the squared deviations.

Participant	Type of Beer	Rating (X)	Participant Mean ($M_{participant}$)	($M_{participant} - GM$)	($M_{participant} - GM$)^2
1	Cheap	40	41	0.467	0.218
2	Cheap	42	50.667	10.134	102.698
3	Cheap	30	44	3.467	12.02
4	Cheap	37	37.333	−3.2	10.24
5	Cheap	23	29.667	−10.866	118.07
1	Mid-range	30	41	0.467	0.218
2	Mid-range	45	50.667	10.134	102.698
3	Mid-range	38	44	3.467	12.02
4	Mid-range	32	37.333	−3.2	10.24
5	Mid-range	28	29.667	−10.866	118.07
1	High-end	53	41	0.467	0.218
2	High-end	65	50.667	10.134	102.698
3	High-end	64	44	3.467	12.02
4	High-end	43	37.333	−3.2	10.24
5	High-end	38	29.667	−10.866	118.07
		$GM = 40.533$			$\Sigma(M_{participant} - GM)^2 = 729.738$

We have just one sum of squares left to go. To calculate the within-groups sum of squares from which we've removed the subjects sum of squares, we take the total sum of squares and subtract the two others that we've calculated so far—the between-groups sum of squares and the subjects sum of squares. The formula is:

$$SS_{within} = SS_{total} - SS_{between} - SS_{subjects}$$

$$= 2117.732 - 1092.130 - 729.738 = 295.864$$

We now have enough information to fill in the first three columns of the source table—the source, SS, and df columns. We calculate the rest of the source table as we did for a one-way between-groups ANOVA. For each of the three sources—between-groups,

MASTERING THE FORMULA

13-5: The within-groups sum of squares for a one-way within-groups ANOVA is calculated using the following formula: $SS_{within} = SS_{total} - SS_{between} - SS_{subjects}$. We subtract the between-groups sum of squares and the subjects sum of squares from the total sum of squares.

subjects, and within-groups—we divide the sum of squares by the degrees of freedom to get its variance, MS.

$$MS_{between} = \frac{SS_{between}}{df_{between}} = \frac{1092.130}{2} = 546.065$$

$$MS_{subjects} = \frac{SS_{subjects}}{df_{subjects}} = \frac{729.738}{4} = 182.435$$

$$MS_{within} = \frac{SS_{within}}{df_{within}} = \frac{295.864}{8} = 36.981$$

We then calculate two F statistics—one for between-groups and one for subjects. For the between-groups F statistic, we divide its MS by the within-groups MS. For the subjects F statistic, we divide its MS by the within-groups MS.

$$F_{between} = \frac{MS_{between}}{MS_{within}} = \frac{546.065}{36.981} = 14.766$$

$$F_{subjects} = \frac{MS_{subjects}}{MS_{within}} = \frac{182.435}{36.981} = 4.933$$

The completed source table is shown here:

Source	SS	df	MS	F
Between-groups	1092.130	2	546.065	14.766
Subjects	729.738	4	182.435	4.933
Within-groups	295.864	8	36.981	
Total	2117.732	14		

Here is a recap of the formulas used to calculate a one-way within-groups ANOVA:

Source	SS	df	MS	F
Between-groups	$\Sigma(M - GM)^2$	$N_{groups} - 1$	$\frac{SS_{between}}{df_{between}}$	$\frac{MS_{between}}{MS_{within}}$
Subjects	$\Sigma(M_{participant} - GM)^2$	$n - 1$	$\frac{SS_{subjects}}{df_{subjects}}$	$\frac{MS_{subjects}}{MS_{within}}$
Within-groups	$SS_{total} - SS_{between} - SS_{subjects}$	$(df_{between})(df_{subjects})$	$\frac{SS_{within}}{df_{within}}$	
Total	$\Sigma(X - GM)^2$	$N_{total} - 1$		

We calculated two F statistics, but we're really only interested in the between-groups F statistic, 14.766, that tells us whether there is a statistically significant difference between groups.

Summary: The F statistic associated with the between-groups difference is 14.77.

STEP 6: Make a decision.

This step is identical to that for the one-way between-groups ANOVA.

Summary: The F statistic, 14.77, is beyond the critical value, 4.46. We reject the null hypothesis. It appears that mean ratings of beers differ based on the type of beer in terms of price category, although we cannot yet know exactly which means differ. We report the statistics in a journal article as $F(2, 8) = 14.77, p < 0.05$. (*Note:* If we used software, we would report the exact p value.) ●

CHECK YOUR LEARNING

Reviewing the Concepts > We use one-way within-groups ANOVA when the problem involves a nominal or ordinal independent variable with at least three levels, a scale dependent variable, and participants who experience all levels of the independent variable.

> Because all participants experience all levels of the independent variable, we reduce the within-groups variability by reducing individual differences; each person serves as a control for himself or herself. A possible concern with this design is order effects.

> One-way within-groups ANOVA uses the same six steps of hypothesis testing that are used for one-way between-groups ANOVA—with one major exception. We calculate statistics for four sources rather than three. The fourth source, which is in addition to between-groups, within-groups, and total, is typically called "subjects."

Clarifying the Concepts **13-1** Why is the within-groups variability, or sum of squares, smaller for the within-groups ANOVA compared to the between-groups ANOVA?

Calculating the Statistics **13-2** Calculate the four degrees of freedom for the following groups, assuming a within-groups design:

	Participant 1	Participant 2	Participant 3
Group 1	7	9	8
Group 2	5	8	9
Group 3	6	4	6

a. $df_{between} = N_{groups} - 1$

b. $df_{subjects} = n - 1$

c. $df_{within} = (df_{between})(df_{subjects})$

d. $df_{total} = df_{between} + df_{subjects} + df_{within}$; or $df_{total} = N_{total} - 1$

13-3 Calculate the four sums of squares for the data in the previous Check Your Learning exercise:

a. $SS_{total} = \Sigma(X - GM)^2$

b. $SS_{between} = \Sigma(M - GM)^2$

c. $SS_{subjects} = \Sigma(M_{participant} - GM)^2$

d. $SS_{within} = SS_{total} - SS_{between} - SS_{subjects}$

13-4 Using all of your calculations in the two previous Check Your Learning exercises, perform the simple division to complete an ANOVA source table for these data.

continued on next page

Applying the Concepts

13-5 Let's create a context for the data presented in Check Your Learning 13-2. Suppose a car dealer wants to sell a car by having people test drive it and two other cars in the same class (e.g., midsize sedans). The data from these three groups might represent the ratings, ranging from 1 (low quality) to 10 (high quality), that drivers gave the driving experience after test-driving the cars. Using the F values you calculated in the previous exercise, complete the following:

a. Write hypotheses, in words, for this study.

b. How might you conduct this research such that you would satisfy the fourth assumption of the within-groups ANOVA?

c. Determine the critical value for F and make a decision about the outcome of this research.

Solutions to these Check Your Learning questions can be found in Appendix D.

Beyond Hypothesis Testing for the One-Way Within-Groups ANOVA

Hypothesis testing with a one-way within-groups ANOVA can tell us whether people can, on average, distinguish between types of beer based on price category—that is, whether people give beers different mean ratings based on price. Effect sizes help us figure out whether these differences are large enough to matter. The Tukey HSD test can tell us exactly which means are statistically significantly different from each other.

R^2, the Effect Size for ANOVA

The calculations for R^2 for a one-way within-groups ANOVA and a one-way between-groups ANOVA are similar. As before, the numerator is a measure of the variability that takes into account just the differences among means, $SS_{between}$. The denominator, however, takes into account the total variability, SS_{total}, but removes the variability caused by differences among participants, $SS_{subjects}$. This enables us to determine the variability explained only by between-groups differences. The formula is:

$$R^2 = \frac{SS_{between}}{(SS_{total} - SS_{subjects})}$$

EXAMPLE 13.3

Let's apply this to the ANOVA we just conducted. We can use the statistics in the source table shown on p. 349 to calculate R^2:

$$R^2 = \frac{SS_{between}}{(SS_{total} - SS_{subjects})} = \frac{1092.130}{(2117.732 - 729.738)} = 0.787$$

The conventions for R^2 are the same as those shown in Table 12-12 (see p. 322). This effect size of 0.79 is a very large effect: 79% of the variability in ratings of beer is explained by price. ●

The Tukey HSD Test

We use the same procedure that we used for a one-way between-groups ANOVA, the Tukey HSD test. Let's look at the calculations for the beer-tasting example.

EXAMPLE 13.4

We calculate an *HSD* for each pair of means by first calculating the standard error:

$$s_M = \sqrt{\frac{MS_{within}}{N}} = \sqrt{\frac{36.981}{5}} = 2.720$$

The standard error allows us to calculate *HSD* for each pair of means.
Cheap beer (34.4) versus mid-range beer (34.6):

$$HSD = \frac{(34.4 - 34.6)}{2.720} = -0.074$$

Cheap beer (34.4) versus high-end beer (52.6):

$$HSD = \frac{(34.4 - 52.6)}{2.720} = -6.691$$

Mid-range beer (34.6) versus high-end beer (52.6):

$$HSD = \frac{(34.6 - 52.6)}{2.720} = -6.618$$

Now we look up the critical value in the *q* table in Appendix B. For a comparison of three means with within-groups degrees of freedom of 8 and an alpha level of 0.05, the cutoff *q* is 4.04. As before, the sign of each *HSD* does not matter.

The *q* table indicates two statistically significant differences for which the *HSDs* are beyond the critical values: −6.691 and −6.618. It appears that high-end beers elicit

Anna Furman/Shutterstock

Within-Groups Designs in Everyday Life We often use a within-groups design without even knowing it. A bride might use a within-groups design when she has all of her bridesmaids (the participants) try on several different possible dresses (the levels of the study). They would then choose the dress that is most flattering, on average, on the bridesmaids. We even have an intuitive understanding of order effects. A bride, for example, might ask her bridesmaids to try on the dress that she prefers either first or last (but not in the middle) so they'll remember it better and be more likely to prefer it!

higher average ratings compared to cheap beers; high-end beers also elicit higher average ratings compared to mid-range beers. No statistically significant difference is found between cheap beers and mid-range beers.

What might explain these differences? It's not surprising that expensive beers came out ahead of cheap and mid-range beers, but Fallows was surprised that no observable average difference was found between cheap and mid-range beers, which led to this advice that he gave to his beer-drinking colleagues: Buy high-end beer "when [you] want an individual glass of lager to be as good as it can be," but buy cheap beer "at all other times, since it gives the maximum taste and social influence per dollar invested." The mid-range beers? Not worth the money.

How much faith can we have in these findings? As behavioral scientists, we critically examine the design and procedures. Did the darker color of Sam Adams (the beer that received the highest average ratings) give it away as a high-end beer? The beers were labeled with letters (Budweiser was labeled with F). Yet, in line with many academic grading systems, the letter A has a positive connotation and F has a negative one. Were there order effects? Did the testers get more lenient (or critical) with every swallow? The panel of tasters was mostly Microsoft employees and was all men. Would we get different results for non-tech employees or with female participants? Science is a slow but sure way of knowing that depends on replication of experiments. ●

Data Ethics — "WEIRD" Samples and Good Reporting Practices

President-elect Harry Truman holds up a *Chicago Tribune* newspaper with the erroneous headline "Dewey Defeats Truman." The error highlights the importance of sampling issues.

On the morning after the 1948 presidential election in the United States, the *Chicago Tribune* printed 150,000 papers with the headline "DEWEY BEATS TRUMAN." The problem? It was Harry Truman, not Thomas Dewey, who won that election. This famous and embarrassing gaffe was not fake news. Instead, it resulted from a sampling problem (Cooper, 2018; Curran & Takata, 2002). Recall that with inferential statistics, we make inferences about a population based on a smaller set of cases we have studied—the sample. The same is true with pollsters: They predict what all voters will do by sampling a subset of voters before the election. The accuracy of these predictions based on samples depends on several factors, with perhaps the most important being how well the polled sample represents the entire population of voters.

Unfortunately for the *Chicago Tribune*, a printing strike meant that the paper had to print the first edition of its election coverage before the election was finalized, relying on pre-election polls that gave Dewey a comfortable lead over Truman. A major problem with those polls is that they were conducted by phone, which not all households had in 1948. Those households with phones were wealthier, so the real population used for predicting the 1948 U.S. presidential election was "voters who had telephones" (and not "all voters"). As it turns out, wealthier voters favored Dewey, but the whole U.S. voting population favored Truman.

Sampling problems and over-generalizations are not confined to distant elections. Joseph Henrich and colleagues (2010) argue that it is far too common for researchers in the behavioral sciences to make sweeping generalizations to all of humanity after conducting research using a sample of participants who are highly unrepresentative of the human population (Rad, Martingano, & Ginges, 2018). For example, in a review of psychological studies published in the six top journals of the American Psychological Association, Jeffrey Arnett (2008) found that 96% of studies used samples from Europe, North American, Australia, or Israel. These studies made claims about how the "human" mind works and how "human" behavior works. But they sampled from only 12% of the human population! This sampling bias led Henrich and his fellow researchers to conclude that most behavioral science research is conducted with **WEIRD samples**, *which are samples of participants from countries that are Western, Educated, Industrialized, Rich, and Democratic.* These countries represent a small portion of the world's population, yet most behavioral science research is conducted on samples from these countries.

● **WEIRD samples** are samples of participants from countries that are Western, Educated, Industrialized, Rich, and Democratic.

How do we prevent sweeping over-generalizations like those sometimes reported in articles using WEIRD samples? Daniel Simons, Yuichi Shoda, and Stephen Lindsey (2017) have suggested that all papers reporting the results of studies should include a **constraints on generality (COG) statement**, *a statement of the target population to which the study results should generalize*, when discussing what can be concluded from the study. Having to explicitly state the target population may prevent researchers from over-generalizing about what happens in *all of humanity*. Such overstated claims may embarrass researchers when another researcher fails to replicate a study with a sample from a different population.

● A **constraints on generality (COG) statement** is a statement of the target population to which the study results should generalize.

Making explicit statements about the target population also makes it easier for other researchers to replicate the findings of studies. According to some researchers, replication failures result from sampling from different target populations (Simons et al., 2017). It's not difficult to see how university students in the United Kingdom might be different from those in the United States. To illustrate with a ridiculous example, assume a veterinarian advertises the ultimate training procedure for house pets. The claim suggests that the target population is all house pets. However, if the training procedure was developed and tested only with dogs, it may not be suitable for other types of house pets. Pet owners with cats, ferrets, and snakes who attempt to use the training procedure—only to find that it fails (a replication failure)—would be in an uproar. However, if the pet owners had been told that it was the ultimate training procedure for dogs (a less broad and more strict definition of the target population), then finding out that the procedure does not work for cats would not be a replication failure. It is possible that being explicit about the reasonable target population for studies will also help with the WEIRD problem in the behavioral sciences. At the very least, it should make the problem much more explicit.

CHECK YOUR LEARNING

Reviewing the Concepts

> It is recommended, as it is for other hypothesis tests, that we calculate a measure of effect size, R^2, for a one-way within-groups ANOVA.

> As with one-way between-groups ANOVA, if we are able to reject the null hypothesis with a one-way within-groups ANOVA, we're not finished. We must conduct a post hoc test, such as a Tukey *HSD* test, to determine exactly which pairs of means are significantly different from one another.

> Too often, behavioral science research is based on samples from WEIRD populations—Western, Educated, Industrialized, Rich, and Democratic. Because of this, ethical researchers are careful to outline, sometimes in a constraints on generality (COG) statement, exactly what their sample is and to which populations it will generalize.

Clarifying the Concepts

13-6 How does the calculation of the effect size R^2 differ between the one-way within-groups ANOVA and the one-way between-groups ANOVA?

13-7 How does the calculation of the Tukey *HSD* differ between the one-way within-groups ANOVA and the one-way between-groups ANOVA?

Calculating the Statistics

13-8 A researcher measured the reaction time of six participants at three different times and found the mean reaction time at time 1 ($M_1 = 155.833$), time 2 ($M_2 = 206.833$), and time 3 ($M_3 = 251.667$). The researcher rejected the null hypothesis after performing a one-way within-groups ANOVA. For the ANOVA, $df_{between} = 2$, $df_{within} = 10$, and $MS_{within} = 771.256$.

  a. Calculate the *HSD* for each of the three mean comparisons.

  b. What is the critical value of q for this Tukey *HSD* test?

  c. For which comparisons do we reject the null hypothesis?

13-9 Use the following source table to calculate the effect size R^2 for the one-way within-groups ANOVA.

Source	SS	df	MS	F
Between	27,590.486	2	13,795.243	17.887
Subjects	16,812.189	5	3362.438	4.360
Within	7712.436	10	771.244	
Total	52,115.111	17		

Applying the Concepts

Solutions to these Check Your Learning questions can be found in Appendix D.

13-10 In Check Your Learning 13-4 and 13-5, we conducted an analysis of driver-experience ratings following test drives.

  a. Calculate R^2 for this ANOVA, and state what size effect this is.

  b. Which follow-up tests are needed for this ANOVA, if any?

REVIEW OF CONCEPTS

LaunchPad
macmillan learning

Visit LaunchPad to access the e-book and to test your knowledge with LearningCurve.

One-Way Within-Groups ANOVA

We use a one-way within-groups ANOVA (also called a *repeated-measures ANOVA*) when there is one nominal or ordinal variable with at least three levels and a scale dependent variable, and every participant experiences every level of the independent variable. We use the same six steps of hypothesis testing for one-way within-groups ANOVA as we do for one-way between-groups ANOVA, except that for the former, we calculate statistics for four sources instead of three. We still calculate statistics for the between-groups, within-groups, and total sources, but we also calculate statistics for a fourth source, "subjects." Although we calculate two F statistics, one for the between-groups variability and one for the subjects variability, we compare the between-groups F statistic to a critical value and either reject or fail to reject the null hypothesis.

Beyond Hypothesis Testing for the One-Way Within-Groups ANOVA

As we do with the one-way between-groups ANOVA, we calculate a measure of effect size, usually R^2, and we conduct a post hoc test, such as the Tukey HSD test, if we reject the null hypothesis.

Behavioral science research has been criticized for its over-reliance on samples from *WEIRD populations*—Western, Educated, Industrialized, Rich, and Democratic. Ethical researchers are encouraged to be specific about the populations to which their findings might apply, sometimes using a *constraints on generality (COG) statement*.

SPSS

To conduct a one-way within-groups ANOVA in SPSS using the beer-rating data from the chapter, we enter the data so that each participant has one row with all of his data. This results in a different format from that of the data entered for a one-way between-groups ANOVA. In that case, we had a score for each participant's level of the independent variable and a score for the dependent variable. For a within-groups

ANOVA, each participant has multiple scores on the dependent variable. The levels of the independent variable are indicated in the titles for each of the three columns in SPSS. For example, as seen on the left of the SPSS screenshot, the first participant has scores of 40 for the cheap beer, 30 for the mid-range beer, and 53 for the high-end beer. Instruct SPSS to conduct the ANOVA by selecting Analyze → General

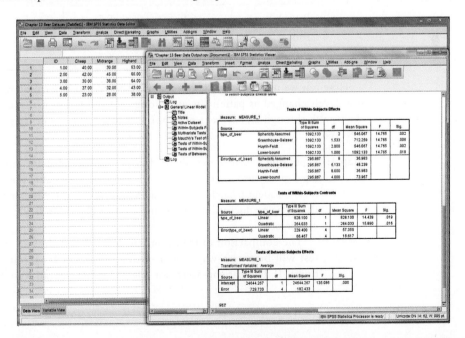

Linear Model → Repeated Measures. (Remember that *repeated measures* is another way to say "within groups" when describing ANOVA.) Next, under "Within-Subject Factor Name," change the generic "factor1" to the actual name of the independent variable, such as "type_of_beer" (using underscores between words because SPSS doesn't recognize spaces in a variable name). Next to "Number of Levels," type "3" to represent the number of levels of the independent variable in this study. Now click "Add," followed by "Define." Define the levels by clicking each of the three levels, then clicking the arrow button, in turn. To see the results of the ANOVA, click "OK." You can see the entered data, and the output, in the screenshot.

The output includes more tables than in the between-groups ANOVA SPSS output. The one we want to pay attention to is titled "Tests of Within-Subjects Effects." This table provides four *F* values and four "Sig." values (the actual *p* values). There are several more advanced considerations that play into deciding which one to use; for the purposes of this introduction to SPSS, we simply note that the *F* values are all the same, and all match the *F* of 14.77 that we calculated previously. Moreover, all of the *p* values are less than the cutoff of 0.05. As we could when we conducted this one-way within-groups ANOVA by hand, we can reject the null hypothesis.

HOW IT WORKS

13.1 CONDUCTING A ONE-WAY WITHIN-GROUPS ANOVA

Researchers followed the progress of 42 people undergoing inpatient rehabilitation following a spinal cord injury (White, Driver, & Warren, 2010). They assessed the patients on a variety of measures on three separate occasions—when they were admitted to the rehabilitation facility, 3 weeks later, and at discharge. Following are data that reflect the patients' symptoms of depression on the Patient Health Questionnaire-9 (PHQ-9). (The data for these three fictional patients have the same means as the actual larger data set, as well as the same outcome in terms of the decision in step 6 of the ANOVA performed here.)

	Admission	Three Weeks	Discharge
Patient 1	6.1	5.5	5.3
Patient 2	6.9	5.7	4.2
Patient 3	7.4	6.5	4.9

How can we use one-way within-groups ANOVA to determine whether depression levels changed as patients went through rehabilitation for spinal cord injury? We'll walk through all six steps of hypothesis testing for a one-way within-groups ANOVA.

Step 1: Population 1: People just admitted to an inpatient rehabilitation facility following a spinal cord injury. Population 2: People 3 weeks after they were admitted to an inpatient rehabilitation facility following a spinal cord injury. Population 3: People being discharged from an inpatient rehabilitation facility following spinal cord injury.

The comparison distribution will be an *F* distribution. The hypothesis test will be a one-way within-groups ANOVA. Regarding the assumptions: (1) The patients were not selected randomly (all were from the same hospital), so we must generalize with caution. (2) We do not know if the underlying population distributions are normal, but the sample data do not indicate severe skew. (3) To see if we meet the homoscedasticity assumption, we will check whether the variances are similar (typically, when the largest variance is not more than twice the smallest) when we calculate the test statistic. (4) The experimenter could not counterbalance, so order effects might be present. With different levels of a time-related variable, it is not possible to assign someone to be measured at, for example, the final time point before the first time point.

Step 2: Null hypothesis: People in an inpatient rehabilitation hospital for a spinal cord injury have the same levels of depression, on average, at admission, 3 weeks later, and at discharge—H_0: $\mu_1 = \mu_2 = \mu_3$. Research hypothesis: People in an inpatient rehabilitation hospital for a spinal cord injury do not have the same levels of depression, on average, at admission, 3 weeks later, and at discharge—H_1 is that at least one μ is different from another μ.

Step 3: We use an F distribution with 2 and 4 degrees of freedom.

$$df_{between} = N_{groups} - 1 = 3 - 1 = 2$$
$$df_{subjects} = n - 1 = 3 - 1 = 2$$
$$df_{within} = (df_{between})(df_{subjects}) = (2)(2) = 4$$
$$df_{total} = df_{between} + df_{subjects} + df_{within} = 2 + 2 + 4 = 8$$
$$(or\ df_{total} = N_{total} - 1 = 9 - 1 = 8)$$

Step 4: The critical value for the F statistic for an alpha level of 0.05 and 2 and 4 degrees of freedom is 6.95.

Step 5: $SS_{total} = \Sigma(X - GM)^2 = 8.059$

Time	X	X − GM	(X − GM)²
Admission	6.1	0.267	0.071
Admission	6.9	1.067	1.138
Admission	7.4	1.567	2.455
Three weeks	5.5	−0.333	0.111
Three weeks	5.7	−0.133	0.018
Three weeks	6.5	0.667	0.445
Discharge	5.3	−0.533	0.284
Discharge	4.2	−1.633	2.667
Discharge	4.9	−0.933	0.87
	GM = 5.833		$\Sigma(X - GM)^2 = 8.059$

$$SS_{between} = \Sigma(M - GM)^2 = 6.018$$

Time	X	Group Mean (M)	M − GM	(M − GM)²
Admission	6.1	6.8	0.967	0.935
Admission	6.9	6.8	0.967	0.935
Admission	7.4	6.8	0.967	0.935
Three weeks	5.5	5.9	0.067	0.004
Three weeks	5.7	5.9	0.067	0.004
Three weeks	6.5	5.9	0.067	0.004
Discharge	5.3	4.8	−1.033	1.067
Discharge	4.2	4.8	−1.033	1.067
Discharge	4.9	4.8	−1.033	1.067
GM = 5.833				$\Sigma(M - GM)^2 = 6.018$

$$SS_{subjects} = \Sigma(M_{participant} - GM)^2 = 0.846$$

Participant	Time	X	Participant Mean ($M_{participant}$)	$M_{participant} - GM$	$(M_{participant} - GM)^2$
1	Admission	6.1	5.633	−0.2	0.040
2	Admission	6.9	5.6	−0.233	0.054
3	Admission	7.4	6.267	0.434	0.188
1	Three weeks	5.5	5.633	−0.2	0.040
2	Three weeks	5.7	5.6	−0.233	0.054
3	Three weeks	6.5	6.267	0.434	0.188
1	Discharge	5.3	5.633	−0.2	0.040
2	Discharge	4.2	5.6	−0.233	0.054
3	Discharge	4.9	6.267	0.434	0.188
GM = 5.833					$\Sigma(M_{participant} - GM)^2 = 0.846$

$$SS_{within} = SS_{total} - SS_{between} - SS_{subjects} = 8.059 - 6.018 - 0.846 = 1.195$$

We now have enough information to fill in the first three columns of the source table—the source, SS, and df columns—and to divide each sum of squares by the degrees of freedom to get the variance, MS.

$$MS_{between} = \frac{SS_{between}}{df_{between}} = \frac{6.018}{2} = 3.009$$

$$MS_{subjects} = \frac{SS_{subjects}}{df_{subjects}} = \frac{0.846}{2} = 0.423$$

$$MS_{within} = \frac{SS_{within}}{df_{within}} = \frac{1.195}{4} = 0.299$$

We then calculate two F statistics—one for between-groups and one for subjects—by dividing each MS by the within-groups MS.

$$F_{between} = \frac{MS_{between}}{MS_{within}} = \frac{3.009}{0.299} = 10.06$$

$$F_{subjects} = \frac{MS_{subjects}}{MS_{within}} = \frac{0.423}{0.299} = 1.41$$

The completed source table is:

Source	SS	df	MS	F
Between	6.018	2	3.009	10.06
Subjects	0.846	2	0.423	1.41
Within	1.195	4	0.299	
Total	8.059	8		

We want to know if there's a statistically significant difference between groups, so we'll look at the between-groups F statistic, 10.06.

Step 6: The F statistic, 10.06, is beyond the critical value, 6.95. We can reject the null hypothesis. It appears that depression scores differ based on the time point during rehabilitation. A post hoc test is necessary to know exactly which pairs of means are significantly different.

13.2 CALCULATING THE EFFECT SIZE FOR A ONE-WAY WITHIN-GROUPS ANOVA

How can we calculate the effect size for these data?

The appropriate measure of effect size for a one-way within-groups ANOVA is R^2, which is calculated as:

$$R^2 = \frac{SS_{between}}{\left(SS_{total} - SS_{subjects}\right)} = \frac{6.018}{(8.059 - 0.846)} = 0.834$$

Based on the conventions for R^2, this is a very large effect: 83% of the variability in depression scores is explained by the time during rehabilitation.

13.3 CALCULATING THE TUKEY *HSD* POST HOC TEST FOR A ONE-WAY WITHIN-GROUPS ANOVA

The F test calculated in How It Works 13.1 tells us only that there is a statistically significant difference; we cannot determine any significant differences without conducting a post hoc test. How can we calculate the Tukey *HSD* test for a one-way within-groups ANOVA?

First, we must calculate the standard error:

$$s_M = \sqrt{\frac{MS_{within}}{N}} = \sqrt{\frac{0.299}{9}} = 0.182$$

Then, we calculate an *HSD* for each mean pair comparison:

To compare the mean depression rate at time of admission ($M = 6.8$) to the mean depression rate 3 weeks into rehabilitation ($M = 5.9$), we calculate:

$$HSD = \frac{6.8 - 5.9}{0.182} = 4.945$$

To compare the mean depression rate at time of admission ($M = 6.8$) to the mean depression rate at discharge ($M = 4.8$), we calculate:

$$HSD = \frac{6.8 - 4.8}{0.182} = 10.989$$

To compare the mean depression rate at 3 weeks into rehabilitation ($M = 5.9$) to the mean depression rate at discharge ($M = 4.8$), we calculate:

$$HSD = \frac{5.9 - 4.8}{0.182} = 6.044$$

The critical value in the q table for a comparison of three means with within-groups degrees of freedom of 4 and an alpha level of 0.05 is 5.04. Only two of the comparisons are statistically significant (comparisons where the *HSD* is beyond the critical value): the comparison of the mean depression rate at time of admission and time of discharge, and the comparison of the mean depression rate at 3 weeks into rehabilitation and time of discharge.

EXERCISES

The solutions to the odd-numbered exercises can be found in Appendix C.

Clarifying the Concepts

13.1 What are the four assumptions for a within-groups ANOVA?

13.2 What are order effects?

13.3 Explain the source of variability called "subjects."

13.4 What is the advantage of the design of the within-groups ANOVA over that of the between-groups ANOVA?

13.5 What is counterbalancing?

13.6 Why is it appropriate to counterbalance when using a within-groups design?

13.7 How do we calculate the sum of squares for subjects?

13.8 How does the calculation of df_{within} in a between-groups ANOVA differ from the calculation in a within-groups ANOVA?

13.9 How could we turn a between-groups study into a within-groups study?

13.10 What are some situations in which it might be impossible—or not make sense—to turn a between-groups study into a within-groups study?

13.11 How is the calculation of effect size different for a one-way between-groups ANOVA versus a one-way within-groups ANOVA?

13.12 What does WEIRD stand for, and what is the problem that led to the coining of this term?

13.13 What is a constraints on generality (COG) statement?

13.14 How might a constraints on generality statement help research progress?

Calculating the Statistics

13.15 For the following data, assuming a within-groups design, determine:

	Person			
	1	2	3	4
Level 1 of the independent variable	7	16	3	9
Level 2 of the independent variable	15	18	18	13
Level 3 of the independent variable	22	28	26	29

a. $df_{between} = N_{groups} - 1$

b. $df_{subjects} = n - 1$

c. $df_{within} = (df_{between})(df_{subjects})$

d. $df_{total} = df_{between} + df_{subjects} + df_{within}$, or $df_{total} = N_{total} - 1$

e. $SS_{total} = \Sigma(X - GM)^2$

f. $SS_{between} = \Sigma(M - GM)^2$

g. $SS_{subjects} = \Sigma(M_{participant} - GM)^2$

h. $SS_{within} = SS_{total} - SS_{between} - SS_{subjects}$

i. The rest of the ANOVA source table for these data

j. The effect size

k. The Tukey HSD statistic for the comparisons between level 1 and level 3

13.16 For the following data, assuming a within-groups design, determine:

	Person					
	1	2	3	4	5	6
Level 1	5	6	3	4	2	5
Level 2	6	8	4	7	3	7
Level 3	4	5	2	4	0	4

a. $df_{between} = N_{groups} - 1$

b. $df_{subjects} = n - 1$

c. $df_{within} = (df_{between})(df_{subjects})$

d. $df_{total} = df_{between} + df_{subjects} + df_{within}$, or $df_{total} = N_{total} - 1$

e. $SS_{total} = \Sigma(X - GM)^2$

f. $SS_{between} = \Sigma(M - GM)^2$

g. $SS_{subjects} = \Sigma(M_{participant} - GM)^2$

h. $SS_{within} = SS_{total} - SS_{between} - SS_{subjects}$

i. The rest of the ANOVA source table for these data

j. The critical F value and your decision about the null hypothesis

k. If appropriate, the Tukey HSD statistic for all possible mean comparisons

l. The critical q value; then, make a decision for each comparison in part (k)

m. The effect size

13.17 For the following incomplete source table for a one-way within-groups ANOVA:

Source	SS	df	MS	F
Between	941.102	2	—	—
Subjects	3807.322	—	—	—
Within	—	20	—	
Total	5674.502	—		

a. Complete the missing information.

b. Calculate R^2.

13.18 Assume that a researcher had 14 individuals participate in all three conditions of her experiment. Use this information to complete the source table below.

Source	SS	df	MS	F
Between	60	—	—	—
Subjects	—	—	—	—
Within	50	—	—	
Total	136	—		

13.19 An incomplete one-way between-groups ANOVA source table is shown below. Compute the missing values.

Source	SS	df	MS	F
Between	56.570	—	28.285	2.435
Subjects	83.865	—	10.483	—
Within	—	16		
Total	326.265	26		

13.20 An incomplete one-way between-groups ANOVA source table is shown below. There were 3 conditions and 6 participants. Compute the missing values.

Source	SS	df	MS	F
Between	0.588	—	—	—
Subjects	0.236	—	—	—
Within	0.126	—	—	
Total	—	—		

Applying the Concepts

13.21 **Fear of dogs and one-way within-groups ANOVA:** Imagine a researcher wanted to assess people's fear of dogs as a function of the size of the dog. He assessed fear among people who indicated they were afraid of dogs, using a 30-point scale from 0 (no fear) to 30 (extreme fear). The researcher exposed each participant to three different dogs, a small dog weighing 20 pounds, a medium-sized dog weighing 55 pounds, and a large dog weighing 110 pounds, and assessed the fear level after each exposure. Here are some hypothetical data; note that these are the data from Exercise 13.15, on which you have already calculated numerous statistics:

	Person			
	1	2	3	4
Small dog	7	16	3	9
Medium dog	15	18	18	13
Large dog	22	28	26	29

a. State the null and research hypotheses.

b. Determine whether the assumptions of random selection and order effects were met.

c. In Exercise 13.15, you calculated the effect size for these data. What does this statistic tell us about the effect of size of dog on fear levels?

d. In Exercise 13.15, you calculated a Tukey HSD test for the difference between levels 1 (small dog) and 3 (big dog). What can you conclude about the effect of size of dog on fear levels based on this statistic?

13.22 Chewing-gum commercials and one-way within-groups ANOVA: Commercials for chewing gum make claims about how long the flavor will last. In fact, some commercials claim that the flavor lasts too long, affecting sales and profit. Let's put these claims to a test. Imagine a student decides to compare four different gums using five participants. Each randomly selected participant was asked to chew a different piece of gum each day for 4 days, such that at the end of the 4 days, each participant had chewed all four types of gum. The order of the gums was randomly determined for each participant. After 2 hours of chewing, participants recorded the intensity of flavor from 1 (not intense) to 9 (very intense). Here are some hypothetical data:

	Person				
	1	2	3	4	5
Gum 1	4	6	3	4	4
Gum 2	8	6	9	9	8
Gum 3	5	6	7	4	5
Gum 4	2	2	3	2	1

a. Conduct all six steps of the hypothesis test.

b. Are any additional tests warranted? Explain your answer.

13.23 Pessimism and one-way within-groups ANOVA: Researchers Busseri, Choma, and Sadava (2009) asked a sample of individuals who scored as pessimists on a measure of life orientation about past, present, and projected future satisfaction with their lives. Higher scores on the life-satisfaction measure indicate higher satisfaction. The data below reproduce the pattern of means that the researchers observed in self-reported life satisfaction of the sample of pessimists for the three time points. Do pessimists predict a gloomy future for themselves?

	Person				
	1	2	3	4	5
Past	18	17.5	19	16	20
Present	18.5	19.5	20	17	18
Future	22	24	20	23.5	21

a. Perform steps 5 and 6 of hypothesis testing. Be sure to complete the source table when calculating the F ratio for step 5.

b. If appropriate, calculate the Tukey HSD for all possible mean comparisons. Find the critical value of q and make a decision regarding the null hypothesis for each of the mean comparisons.

c. Calculate the R^2 measure of effect size for this ANOVA.

13.24 Optimism and one-way within-groups ANOVA: The previous exercise describes a study conducted by Busseri and colleagues (2009) using a group of pessimists. These researchers asked the same question of a group of optimists: Optimists rated their past, present, and projected future satisfaction with their lives. Higher scores on the life-satisfaction measure indicate higher satisfaction. The data below reproduce the pattern of means that the researchers observed in self-reported life satisfaction of the sample of optimists for the three time points. Do optimists see a rosy future ahead?

	Person				
	1	2	3	4	5
Past	22	23	25	24	26
Present	25	26	27	28	29
Future	24	27	26	28	29

a. Perform steps 5 and 6 of hypothesis testing. Be sure to complete the source table when calculating the F ratio for step 5.

b. If appropriate, calculate the Tukey HSD for all possible mean comparisons. Find the critical value of q and make a decision regarding the null hypothesis for each of the mean comparisons.

c. Calculate the R^2 measure of effect size for this ANOVA.

13.25 Wagging tails and one-way within-groups ANOVA: How does a dog's tail wag in response to seeing different people and other pets? Quaranta, Siniscalchi, and Vallortigara (2007) investigated the amplitude and direction of a dog's tail wagging in response to seeing its owner, an unfamiliar cat, and an unfamiliar dog. The fictional data below are measures of amplitude. These data reproduce the pattern of results in the study, averaging leftward tail wags and rightward tail wags. Use these data to construct the source table for a one-way within-groups ANOVA.

Dog Participant	Owner	Cat	Other Dog
1	69	28	45
2	72	32	43
3	65	30	47
4	75	29	45
5	70	31	44

13.26 Memory, post hoc tests, and effect size: Luo, Hendriks, and Craik (2007) were interested in whether people might better remember lists of words if the lists were paired with either pictures or sound effects. They asked participants to memorize lists of words under three different learning conditions. In the first condition, participants just saw a list of nouns that they were to remember (word-alone condition). In the second condition, the words were also accompanied by a picture of the object (picture condition). In the third condition, the words were accompanied by a sound effect matching the object (sound effect condition). The researchers measured the proportion of words participants got correct in a later recognition test. Fictional data from four participants produce results similar to those of the original study. The average proportion of words recognized was $M = 0.54$ in the word-alone condition, $M = 0.69$ in the picture condition, and $M = 0.838$ in the sound effect condition. The source table below depicts the results of the ANOVA on the data from the four fictional participants.

Source	SS	df	MS	F
Between	0.177	2	0.089	8.900
Subjects	0.002	3	0.001	0.100
Within	0.059	6	0.010	
Total	0.238	11		

a. Is it appropriate to perform post hoc comparisons on the data? Why or why not?

b. Use the information provided in the ANOVA table to calculate R^2. Interpret the effect size using Cohen's conventions. State what this R^2 means in terms of the independent and dependent variables used in this study.

13.27 Wagging tails, hypothesis-test decision making, and post hoc tests: Assume that we recruited a different sample of five dogs and attempted to replicate the Quaranta and colleagues (2007) study described in Exercise 13.25. The source table for our fictional replication appears below. Find the critical F value and make a decision regarding the null hypothesis. Based on this decision, is it appropriate to conduct post hoc comparisons? Why or why not?

Source	SS	df	MS	F
Between	58.133	2	29.067	0.066
Subjects	642.267	4	160.567	0.364
Within	532.533	8	441.567	
Total	4232.933	14		

13.28 Pilots' mental efforts and a one-way within-groups ANOVA: Researchers examined the amount of mental effort that participants felt they were expending on a cognitively complex task, piloting an unmanned air vehicle (UAV) (Ayaz, Shewokis, Bunce, Izzetoglu, Willems, & Onaral, 2012). The researchers used the Task Load Index (TLX), a measure that assesses participants' perception of their mental effort following a series of approach and landing tasks in simulated UAV tasks. They wondered whether expertise would have an effect on perceptions of mental effort. In the results section, the researchers reported the results of their analyses, a series of one-way repeated-measures ANOVA. "The results indicated a significant main effect of practice level (beginner/intermediate/advanced conditions) for mental demand $(F(2, 8) = 17.87, p < 0.01, \eta^2 = 0.817)$, effort $(F(2, 8) = 16.32, p < 0.01, \eta^2 = 0.803)$, and frustration $(F(2, 8) = 8.60, p < 0.01, \eta^2 = 0.682)$." The researchers went on to explain that mental demand, effort, and frustration all tended to decrease with expertise.

a. What is the independent variable in this study?

b. What are the dependent variables in this study?

c. Explain why the researchers were able to use a one-way within-groups ANOVA in this situation.

d. η^2 is roughly equivalent to R^2. How large is each of these effects, based on Cohen's conventions?

e. The researchers drew a specific conclusion beyond that there was some difference, on average, in the dependent variables, depending on the particular levels of the independent variable. What additional test were they likely to have conducted? Explain your answer.

13.29 Negativity bias and constraints on generality: In a recent article, Amber Boydstun and her colleagues (2019) described a study on the effects of negativity bias in a political context. Negativity bias is the finding that people's decisions are more influenced by negatively framed information (e.g., number of jobs lost) than they are by positively framed information (e.g., number of jobs saved). When interpreting their results, Boydstun and colleagues devoted a whole section of their paper to constraints on generalization, in which they discussed various conditions under which they would expect their results to generalize (or not). For example, they said, "We expect that our results would generalize to any sample of U.S. participants below age 50 who identify as Democrat, Republican, or Independent leaning Democrat or Republican." How does this COG statement help future researchers who are also interested in negativity bias in a political context?

13.30 Negativity bias and WEIRD: Refer to the description of the study by Amber Boydstun and her colleagues (2019) in the previous exercise. How is the COG statement provided by the authors related to the WEIRD problem?

Putting It All Together

13.31 An app to track alcohol use and interpreting the results of a one-way within-groups ANOVA: Australian researcher Antoinette Poulton and her colleagues (2018) investigated the use of a smartphone app to monitor alcohol consumption. The same individuals participated in the study for 21 days; the researchers analyzed the average alcohol weekly intake for each person across the 3 weeks of the study. The researchers reported: "A one-way repeated measures ANOVA showed significant differences between weekly totals of app data, $F(2, 1321) = 38.67, p < 0.001, \eta_p^2 = 0.06$" (p. 38). (Note: Poulton et al. reported corrected degrees of freedom, so we changed them here to match what you learned in this chapter.) The researchers then compared each of the three pairs and reported that the average alcohol intake, as recorded on the app "during the first week ($M = 9.14, SD = 10.90$) was significantly higher than that recorded in either of

the subsequent weeks ($p < 0.001$); there was no difference between average total intake recorded in the second ($M = 8.02, SD = 9.70$) and third weeks ($M = 7.11, SD = 9.48, p = 0.449$)" (p. 38). The researchers speculated that the average number of weekly drinks reported on the app may have declined from week 1 to weeks 2 and 3 for two possible reasons: Participants may have tired of logging their drinking, or the act of actually tracking their drinking may have led participants to drink less.

a. Why is this an example of a within-groups ANOVA (often called a repeated-measures ANOVA)?

b. How do we know that the ANOVA resulted in a statistically significant finding?

c. What do the means and standard deviations suggest about the shape of the distribution?

d. Partial η^2 can be interpreted like R^2. What can we learn from the η_p^2 reported in these statistics?

e. Why did the researchers conduct additional analyses beyond the ANOVA?

f. The researchers reported "no difference" between the average alcohol intakes in the second and third weeks. Why can we not make a decision that there is no difference between groups? How could the researchers have clarified this?

g. The researchers compared pairs of scores—week 1 versus week 2, for example. They reported that "Paired comparisons were Bonferroni-corrected" (p. 37). What do they mean by this? Why did they use a Bonferroni correction?

h. Why might the use of a Bonferroni correction fall under Deborah Mayo's (2018) concept of severe testing?

13.32 ANOVA, athletes, and social support: Researchers examined differences among student-athletes' perceptions of different kinds of support related to their sports (Adams, Coffee, & Lavallee, 2015). Male athletes at a Scottish University who played one of seven sports—including cricket, basketball, and badminton—were surveyed about the level of support they received in four areas. Students provided ratings for each of these four areas, with higher scores indicating more support. The means for the four areas in this study were 8.47 for emotional support (mood-related), 8.42 for esteem support (encouragement), 7.63 for informational support (technical advice), and 6.66 for tangible support (help in planning, for example). Here is the description of the analyses from the researchers: "A one-way repeated measures analysis of variance (ANOVA) was conducted to determine the differences…. [Effect size] values were interpreted by following the guidelines proposed by Cohen" (p. 41). The researchers included the following statistics: $F(3, 68) = 29.88, p < .001$. They also reported that: "Pairwise comparisons between all four types of social support indicated a significant difference between all support types except that between emotional support and esteem support (95% CI = $-0.342 - 0.428, p = 1.000$)" (p. 42). Finally, the researchers reported an effect size of 0.57 for the statistically significant comparisons. (Note that they reported partial η^2 for effect size, which you may recall is interpreted like R^2.)

a. What is the independent variable in this study? What are its levels?

b. What is the dependent variable in this study? Which type of variable is it?

c. Is this an experiment or a correlational study? Explain your answer.

d. The researchers explain that they used a one-way repeated-measures ANOVA, another way to say one-way within-groups ANOVA. Explain why they used this statistical analysis.

e. The researchers reported that they interpreted the effect size using Cohen's guidelines. Explain how they would have interpreted the effect size that they found.

f. Explain the statistics that the researchers reported. What does each of these mean? (*Hint:* For the pairwise comparisons, the researchers likely conducted paired-samples t tests. Also, "CI" refers to confidence interval.)

g. Explain the overall pattern of results in your own words.

h. If the one mean difference in this study that was *not* statistically significant is an incorrect conclusion, what kind of error is this? Explain your answer.

i. The researchers also reported that "a Bonferroni adjustment was used to adjust the p value from the initial .05 to .017 for the pairwise comparison of the results." Based on what you learned in the Data Ethics feature of Chapter 12, what does this mean? Why did the researchers make this adjustment?

j. Create a graph that depicts the differences among these means. Follow the graphing guidelines you learned in Chapter 3.

 **LaunchPad**
macmillan learning

Visit LaunchPad to access the e-book and to test your knowledge with LearningCurve.

TERMS

WEIRD sample (p. 395)

constraints of generality (COG) statement (p. 395)

FORMULAS

$df_{subjects} = n - 1$ (p. 386)

$df_{within} = (df_{between})(df_{subjects})$ [formula for a one-way within-groups ANOVA] (p. 387)

$df_{total} = df_{between} + df_{subjects} + df_{within}$ [formula for a one-way within-groups ANOVA] (p. 387)

$SS_{subjects} = \Sigma(M_{participant} - GM)^2$ (p. 389)

$SS_{within} = SS_{total} - SS_{between} - SS_{subjects}$ [formula for a one-way within-groups ANOVA] (p. 389)

$MS_{subjects} = \dfrac{SS_{subjects}}{df_{subjects}}$ (p. 390)

$F_{subjects} = \dfrac{MS_{subjects}}{MS_{within}}$ (p. 390)

$R^2 = \dfrac{SS_{between}}{(SS_{total} - SS_{subjects})}$ [formula for a one-way within-groups ANOVA] (p. 392)

SYMBOLS

$df_{subjects}$ (p. 386)
$SS_{subjects}$ (p. 386)

$MS_{subjects}$ (p. 390)
$F_{subjects}$ (p. 390)

Two-Way Between-Groups ANOVA

Two-Way ANOVA

Understanding Interactions in ANOVA

Conducting a Two-Way Between-Groups ANOVA

BEFORE YOU GO ON

- **You should understand the six steps of hypothesis testing (Chapter 7).**

- **You should be able to conduct and interpret a one-way between-groups ANOVA (Chapter 12).**

- **You should understand the concept of effect size (Chapter 8) and the measure of effect size for ANOVA, R^2 (Chapter 12).**

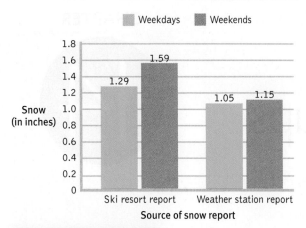

FIGURE 14-1

Ski Bums, Beware!

This bar graph tells a useful story for consumers about a statistically significant interaction. Ski resorts tend to exaggerate the amount of snowfall, especially snowfall on weekends.

Jonathan Zinman and Eric Zitzewitz are social science researchers and ski bums who live in New Hampshire. They had become annoyed when they hit the slopes, only to find that snowfall reports had clearly been exaggerated. So they collected snowfall data both from ski resorts and the weather station for weekdays (when fewer people go skiing or snowboarding) and for the more profitable weekends. Figure 14-1 summarizes what they found: The ski resorts reported greater snowfall than weather stations did, an effect that was even more pronounced on weekends, when such an exaggeration was likely to draw more paying customers.

In the study by Zinman and Zitzewitz (2009), the dependent variable is the amount of snow reported, in inches. But there are two independent variables (source of the snow report and time of the week), and each seems to have its own effect on the amount of snow reported. Ski resorts reported more snowfall, on average, when we disregard whether it fell on weekdays or weekends, than weather stations did. This is called a *main effect* of the source of the snow report. Figure 14-1 also shows that snow reports are higher on weekends than on weekdays when we disregard the source of the snow report. This is called a *main effect* of time of the week.

But there is a third finding, and it's the most interesting one: Only ski resorts, and not weather stations, bumped up their estimates even more on the weekend than they did during the week! So the variable for the source of the report interacted with the variable for the time of week, making its own unique impact on the reported amount of snowfall. This is called an *interaction* between the variables for the source of the snow report and the time of week.

Armed with empirical evidence of biased reporting, these researchers concluded that skiers and snowboarders could fight back. Zinman and Zitzewitz (2009) wrote: "Near the end of our sample period, a new iPhone application feature makes it easier for skiers to share information on ski conditions in real time. Exaggeration falls sharply, especially at resorts with better iPhone reception." It's a great reminder that we can question reported data, create new data, and take advantage of social media to share information in meaningful ways.

With two independent variables and one dependent variable, this experiment contains three comparisons that might influence a skier's decision about whether to hit the slopes: (1) the source of the snowfall report (ski resort versus weather station), (2) the time of week (weekday versus weekend), and (3) the combined effects of the source of snowfall report *and* the time of week. In this study, researchers discovered that the combined effects were the most important of the influences on the amount of snowfall reported. The effect of the source of the snowfall report on the amount of snow reported depended on whether it was a weekday or a weekend.

Crowdsourcing Snowfall Data Internet-savvy skiers and snowboarders can share information about conditions on the slopes in real time, foiling attempts by ski resorts to exaggerate snowfall amounts. This exaggeration had been exposed through a statistical interaction.

In this chapter, we examine a hypothesis test that checks for the presence of combined effects, also called *interactions*. *A statistical **interaction** occurs in a factorial design when two or more independent variables have an effect on the dependent variable in combination that neither independent variable has on its own.* We learn about interactions in relation to a research design that has *two* nominal (or sometimes ordinal) independent variables, one scale dependent variable, and a between-groups design. We learn how the six steps of hypothesis testing apply to this statistical test, and how to calculate effect sizes for this test.

Two-Way ANOVA

Skiing-related decisions (and many other behaviors) are routinely influenced by multiple variables, so we need a way to measure the interactive effects of multiple variables.

A two-way ANOVA (analysis of variance) allows us to compare levels from two independent variables plus the joint effects of those two variables. *A **two-way ANOVA** is a hypothesis test that includes two nominal independent variables, regardless of their numbers of levels, and a scale dependent variable.* We can also have ANOVAs with more than two independent variables. As the number of independent variables increases, the number increases in the name of the ANOVA—three-way, four-way, five-way, and so on. Table 14-1 shows a range of possibilities for naming ANOVAs.

Regardless of the number of independent variables, we can use the research designs that we have already discussed. As with other hypothesis tests, a between-groups design is one in which every participant is in only one condition, and a within-groups design is one in which every participant is in all conditions. A mixed design is one in which one of the independent variables is between-groups and one is within-groups. In this chapter, we focus on the ANOVA that uses the second modifier from column 1 and the first modifier from column 2: the two-way between-groups ANOVA.

Language Alert! There is a catch-all phrase for two-way, three-way, and higher-order ANOVAs: Any ANOVA with at least two independent variables can be called a *factorial ANOVA*, *a statistical analysis used with one scale dependent variable and at least two nominal independent variables (also called factors).* This is also called a *multifactorial ANOVA*. **Factor** *is another word used to describe an independent variable in a study with more than one independent variable.*

- A statistical **interaction** occurs in a factorial design when two or more independent variables have an effect on the dependent variable in combination that neither independent variable has on its own.

- A **two-way ANOVA** is a hypothesis test that includes two nominal independent variables, regardless of their numbers of levels, and a scale dependent variable.

- A **factorial ANOVA** is a statistical analysis used with one scale dependent variable and at least two nominal independent variables (also called *factors*); also called a *multifactorial ANOVA*.

- **Factor** is a term used to describe an independent variable in a study with more than one independent variable.

TABLE 14-1	How to Name an ANOVA

ANOVAs are typically described by two adjectives, one from the first column and one from the second. So, we could have a one-way between-groups ANOVA or a one-way within-groups ANOVA, a two-way between-groups ANOVA or a two-way within-groups ANOVA, and so on. If at least one independent variable is between-groups and at least one is within-groups, it is a mixed-design ANOVA.

Number of Independent Variables: Pick One	Participants in One or All Samples: Pick One	Always Follows Descriptors
One-way	Between-groups	ANOVA
Two-way	Within-groups	
Three-way	Mixed-design	

In this section, we learn more about the situations in which we use a two-way ANOVA, as well as the language that is used in reference to this type of hypothesis test. Then we learn about the three outcomes we can examine with a two-way ANOVA.

Why We Use Two-Way ANOVA

Behavioral science researchers understand the benefits of the two-way ANOVA. Let's look at a study where the interaction tells a more interesting and more complete story than the main effects. In recent years, a great deal of research has demonstrated gender discrimination in science, technology, engineering, and mathematics fields—the so-called STEM fields. In one experiment, for example, faculty members viewed an application for a laboratory manager position (Moss-Racusin, Dovidio, Brescoll, Graham, & Handelsman, 2012). The applications were identical, except half had a male name (John) and half had a female name (Jennifer). The faculty members rated John as more competent and more "hireable," on average, than Jennifer, and were more likely to offer John a higher salary and career mentoring. Remember, their applications were *identical*. Imagine that you read this summary. How much credibility would you give it?

EXAMPLE 14.1

Ian Handley and his research team (2015) based their own study on the lab manager experiment you just read about. They wondered about the effect of gender on perceptions of research on gender disparities in STEM: Would male faculty members be less open, on average, to the findings described above, than female faculty members? They also wondered about the effect of academic discipline: Would faculty members in STEM fields be less open to these findings, on average, than faculty members in other fields?

To examine these hypotheses, the researchers could have conducted two studies—one comparing male and female faculty members and another comparing faculty members in STEM and non-STEM fields. But conducting separate studies is limiting. The researchers were actually even more interested in whether the pattern of gender differences would be different within STEM fields than it is outside of STEM fields.

Jennifer or John? Are you surprised that faculty members preferred an applicant named John over one named Jennifer for a lab manager position—even though they had identical applications (Moss-Racusin et al., 2012)? Your answer may be depend on your background. One study found that the likelihood that professors would find this research credible depends on the interaction of two factors—their gender and their academic discipline (Handley et al., 2015). Two-way ANOVAs can help us to understand the interactions between multiple factors.

A single study simultaneously examining gender and academic discipline is more efficient than two studies examining each independent variable separately. Two-way ANOVAs allow researchers to examine both hypotheses while using the resources, time, and energy that they would devote to a single study. And a two-way ANOVA yields even more information than two separate experiments.

Specifically, a two-way ANOVA allows researchers to explore exactly what Handley and his colleagues wanted to explore: interactions. Does the effect of gender depend on the particular levels of another independent variable, academic discipline? A two-way ANOVA can examine (1) the effect of gender, (2) the effect of academic discipline, *and* (3) the ways in which gender and academic discipline might combine to create some entirely new, and often unexpected, effect. ●

The More Specific Vocabulary of Two-Way ANOVA

Every ANOVA, we learned, has two descriptors, one indicating the number of independent variables and one indicating the research design. Many researchers expand the first descriptor to provide even more information about the independent variables. Let's consider these expanded descriptors in the context of the study on people's perceptions of research on gender discrimination in STEM fields. Were Handley and his colleagues to conduct just one study that examined both gender and academic discipline, they would recruit both female and male faculty members in STEM fields and female and male faculty members in non–STEM fields. This research design is shown in Table 14-2.

| **TABLE 14-2** | Interactions in Perceptions of Gender Discrimination Research |

A two-way ANOVA allows researchers to examine two independent variables (gender and academic discipline), as well as the ways in which they might interact, simultaneously.

	STEM fields (S)	Non-STEM fields (NS)
Women (W)	W & S	W & NS
Men (M)	M & S	M & NS

When we draw the design of a study, such as in Table 14-2, we call each box of the design a *cell, a box that depicts one unique combination of levels of the independent variables in a factorial design*. When cells contain numbers, they are usually means of the scores of all participants who were assigned to that combination of levels. Many social science researchers hope to have about 30 participants in each cell—that's why experiments can quickly become very expensive. In the study we're considering here, participants are included in one of four cells depending on their gender and academic discipline. Each participant is included in one of the two levels of the variable "gender" (women or men) listed in the rows of the table of cells.

Each participant is *also* included in one of the two levels of the variable "academic discipline" (STEM or non-STEM field) listed in the rows of the table of cells. A participant might be included in the women and STEM groups (upper-left cell), men and non-STEM groups (lower-right cell), or either of the other two combinations.

Language Alert! This leads us to the new ANOVA vocabulary. Instead of the descriptor *two-way*, many researchers refer to an ANOVA with this arrangement of cells as a *2 × 2 ANOVA* (pronounced "two by two," not "two times two"). As with the two-way descriptor, the ANOVA is described with a second modifier—usually *between-groups* or *within-groups*. Because participants would be categorized in only one gender and only one type of academic discipline, the hypothesis test could be called either a *two-way between-groups ANOVA* or a *2 × 2 between-groups ANOVA*. (An added benefit to the method of naming ANOVAs by the numbers of levels in each independent variable is the ease of calculating the total number of cells. Simply multiply the levels of the independent variables. In this case, the 2 × 2 ANOVA would have (2 × 2) = 4 cells.)

● A **cell** is a box that depicts one unique combination of levels of the independent variables in a factorial design.

Two Main Effects and an Interaction

Two-way ANOVAs produce *three* F statistics: one for the first independent variable, one for the second independent variable, and one for the interaction between the

● A **main effect** occurs in a factorial design when one of the independent variables has an influence on the dependent variable.

two independent variables. The F statistics for each of the two independent variables describe *main effects. A **main effect** occurs in a factorial design when one of the independent variables has an influence on the dependent variable.* We evaluate whether there is a main effect by disregarding the influence of any other independent variables in the study—we temporarily pretend that the other variable doesn't exist.

So, with two independent variables, Handley and his colleagues would have two possibilities for a main effect. For example, after testing their participants in a two-way ANOVA, they might find a main effect of "gender," temporarily pretending that the variable "academic discipline" hadn't even been included in the study. For example, male faculty members might be less receptive, on average, to the conclusions of the gender discrimination research than female faculty members. That's the first F statistic. They also might find a main effect of "academic discipline," temporarily pretending that the variable "gender" hadn't even been included in the study. For example, faculty members in STEM fields might be less receptive, on average, to the gender discrimination research than faculty members in non-STEM fields. That's the second F statistic.

The third F statistic in a two-way ANOVA has the potential to be the most interesting because it is complicated by multiple, interacting variables. For example, the researchers might find a larger gender difference among faculty members in STEM fields than among faculty members in non-STEM fields. In other words, the effect of gender on the perception of this research might be different among STEM faculty members than among non-STEM faculty members. Alternatively, the researchers might find a larger difference between STEM and non-STEM faculty members among men than among women. In other words, the effect of academic discipline on the perception of this research might be different depending on the gender of the faculty member.

Each of the three F statistics has its own between-groups sum of squares (SS), degrees of freedom (df), mean square (MS), and critical value, but they all share a within-groups mean square (MS_{within}). The source table is shown in Table 14-3. The symbols in the body of the table are replaced by the specific values of these statistics in an actual source table.

TABLE 14-3 An Expanded Source Table

This source table is the framework into which we place the calculations for the two-way between-groups ANOVA with independent variables of gender and academic discipline—here listed as "discipline" for short. It tells three stories: one each for the two main effects, which are listed first, and one for the interaction.

Source	SS	df	MS	F
Gender	SS_{gender}	df_{gender}	MS_{gender}	F_{gender}
Discipline	$SS_{discipline}$	$df_{discipline}$	$MS_{discipline}$	$F_{discipline}$
Gender × Discipline	$SS_{gender \times discipline}$	$df_{gender \times discipline}$	$MS_{gender \times discipline}$	$F_{gender \times discipline}$
Within	SS_{within}	df_{within}	MS_{within}	
Total	SS_{total}	df_{total}		

CHECK YOUR LEARNING

Reviewing the Concepts

> Factorial ANOVAs are used with multiple independent variables because they allow us to examine several hypotheses in a single study and explore interactions.

> Factorial ANOVAs are often referred to by the levels of their independent variables (e.g., 2×3) rather than the number of independent variables (e.g., two-way). Sometimes the independent variables are called *factors*.

> A two-way ANOVA can have two main effects (one for each independent variable) and one interaction (the combined influence of both variables). Each effect and interaction has its own set of statistics, including its own *F* statistic, which are displayed in an expanded source table.

Clarifying the Concepts 14-1 What is a factorial ANOVA?

14-2 What is an interaction?

Calculating the Statistics 14-3 Determine how many factors are in each of the following designs:

a. The effect of three diet programs and two exercise programs on weight loss.

b. The effect of three diet programs, two exercise programs, and three different personal metabolism types on weight loss.

c. The effect of gift certificate value ($15, $25, $50, and $100) on the amount people spend over that value.

d. The effect of gift certificate value ($15, $25, $50, and $100) and store quality (low end versus high end) on consumer overspending.

Applying the Concepts 14-4 Adam Alter, then a graduate student at Princeton University, and his advisor, Daniel Oppenheimer, studied whether names of stocks affected selling prices (Alter & Oppenheimer, 2006). They found that stocks with pronounceable ticker-code names, like "BAL," tended to sell at higher prices than did stocks with unpronounceable names, like "BDL." They examined this effect 1 day, 1 week, 6 months, and 1 year after the stock was offered for sale. The effect was strongest 1 day after the stocks were initially offered.

a. What are the "participants" in this study?

b. What are the independent variables and what are their levels?

c. What is the dependent variable?

d. Using the descriptors from Chapter 12, what would you call the hypothesis test that would be used?

e. Using the new descriptors from *this* chapter, what would you call the hypothesis test that would be used?

Solutions to these Check Your Learning questions can be found in Appendix D.

f. How many cells are there? Explain how you calculated this answer.

Understanding Interactions in ANOVA

A two-way ANOVA is like a "buy 1, get 3" clearance sale. We get three distinct findings by conducting just one study. The first finding by New Hampshire ski bums Jonathan Zinman and Eric Zitzewitz concerned the effect of the source of the snowfall reports. Their second finding concerned the effect of when the snowfall report was issued (time of week). The third finding related to the combined effects (the interaction) of the source of the snowfall reports *and* the time of week the snowfall reports were issued. The interaction informed us that the effect of the source of a snowfall report depended on when the report was issued (time of week). A statistical interaction occurs when any subgroup represents a significant exception in any direction to the general trend in the data.

In this section, we explore the concept of an interaction in a two-way ANOVA in more depth. We look at a real-life example of an interaction, then introduce two different types of interactions—quantitative and qualitative.

Interactions and Public Policy

Hurricane Katrina, which ravaged New Orleans in 2005, demonstrates the importance of understanding interactions. First, the hurricane itself was an interaction among several weather variables. The devastating effects of the hurricane depended on particular levels of other variables, such as where it made landfall and the speed of its movement across the Gulf of Mexico.

Interactions were relevant for the people affected by Hurricane Katrina as well. For example, one would think that Hurricane Katrina would have been universally bad for the health of all those displaced people—a main effect of a hurricane on health care. However, there were exceptions to that rule, and three researchers from the Tulane University School of Public Health and Tropical Diseases in New Orleans proposed a startling interaction regarding the effects of the hurricane on health care for pregnant women (Buekens, Xiong, & Harville, 2006).

Some women gave birth in the squalor of the public shelter in New Orleans's Superdome sports stadium or in alleys while waiting for rescuers. When it comes to pregnant women, the first priority of disaster relief agencies is to provide obstetric and neonatal care. Massive relief efforts sometimes mean that access to care for pregnant women is actually improved in the aftermath of a disaster. Of course, the quality of health care certainly doesn't improve for everybody, which means that an interaction is involved. So the quality of health care improved for pregnant women in the aftermath of the disaster, whereas it became worse for almost everyone else. In the language of two-way ANOVA, the effect of a disaster (one independent variable with two levels: disaster versus no disaster) on the quality of health care (the dependent variable) depends on the type of health care needed (the second independent variable, also with two levels: obstetric/neonatal versus all other types of health care).

HARAZ N. GHANBARI/AP Images

Disaster Relief and Pregnant Women
This refugee from Hurricane Katrina and her newborn baby received care at a shelter in Louisiana. There was a surprising interaction after Hurricane Katrina: For some pregnant women, massive relief efforts actually *improved* their access to health care.

Interpreting Interactions

The two-way between-groups ANOVA allows us to separate between-groups variance into three finer categories: the two main effects and an interaction effect. The interaction effect is a blended effect resulting from the interaction between the two independent variables; it is not a separate individual variable. The interaction effect is like mixing chocolate syrup into a glass of milk; the two liquids blend into something familiar yet new.

Two terms often used to describe interactions are *quantitative* and *qualitative* (e.g., Newton & Rudestam, 1999). *A **quantitative interaction** is an interaction in which the effect of one independent variable is strengthened or weakened at one or more levels of the other independent variable, but the direction of the initial effect does not change.* The researcher ski bums, Jonathan Zinman and Eric Zitzewitz, found a quantitative interaction when they discovered that resort snowfall reports were always exaggerated compared to weather reports, and especially on the weekends. More specifically, the effect of one independent variable is modified in the presence of another independent variable. Some social scientists refer to interactions like this one as a significant difference in differences. The weekday–weekend difference is significantly larger among ski resort reports than among weather reports.

*A **qualitative interaction** is an interaction of two (or more) independent variables in which one independent variable reverses its effect depending on the level of the other independent variable.* In a qualitative interaction, the effect of one variable doesn't just become stronger or weaker; it actually reverses direction in the presence of another variable. Let's examine a quantitative interaction.

● A **quantitative interaction** is an interaction in which the effect of one independent variable is strengthened or weakened at one or more levels of the other independent variable, but the direction of the initial effect does not change.

● A **qualitative interaction** is an interaction of two (or more) independent variables in which one independent variable reverses its effect depending on the level of the other independent variable.

EXAMPLE 14.2

The gender discrimination in STEM fields example is a helpful illustration of a quantitative interaction. Let's examine what the researchers found. Male faculty members in STEM fields "evaluated the research less favorably" than did female faculty members in STEM fields. There was not a similar statistically significant difference between male and female faculty members in non-STEM fields (Handley et al., 2015). So, there was a gender difference among STEM professors, but not among non-STEM professors. Let's look at the actual means from the study in Table 14-4. Higher scores indicate a more favorable view, on average, of the research. (For the purposes of this research, we will assume equal sample sizes across cells.)

TABLE 14-4   A Table of Means

We use a table to display the cell and marginal means so that we can interpret any main effects. Higher numbers indicate a more favorable view of the gender discrimination research.

	STEM	Non-STEM	
Women	4.80	4.54	4.67
Men	4.02	4.55	4.285
	4.41	4.545	

First, we consider the main effects; then we consider the overall pattern that constitutes the interaction. If there is a significant interaction, we ignore any significant main effects. The significant interaction supersedes any significant main effects.

Table 14-4 includes mean perception scores for the four cells of the study. It also includes numbers in the margins of the table, to the right of and below the cells; these numbers are also means, but are for every participant in a given row or in a given column. Each of these is called a **marginal mean**, *the mean of a row or a column in a table that shows the cells of a study with a two-way ANOVA design.* In Table 14-4, for example, the mean across from the row for female, 4.67, is the mean perception score of every female faculty member in the study, regardless of her academic discipline. The mean below the column for STEM fields, 4.41, is the mean perception score of every faculty member in a STEM field in the study, regardless of his or her gender.

The easiest way to understand the main effects is to make a smaller table for each, with only the appropriate marginal means. Separate tables let us focus on one main

● A **marginal mean** is the mean of a row or a column in a table that shows the cells of a study with a two-way ANOVA design.

TABLE 14-5 The Main Effect of Gender

This table shows only the marginal means that demonstrate the main effect of gender. Because we have isolated these marginal means, we cannot get distracted or confused by the other means in the table.

Women	4.67
Men	4.285

TABLE 14-6 The Main Effect of Academic Discipline

This table shows only the marginal means that demonstrate the main effect of academic discipline. Because we have isolated these marginal means, we cannot get distracted or confused by the other means in the table.

STEM	Non-STEM
4.41	4.545

TABLE 14-7 Examining the Overall Pattern of Means

A first step in understanding an interaction is examining the overall pattern of means in the cells.

	STEM	Non-STEM
Women	4.80	4.54
Men	4.02	4.55

effect at a time without being distracted by the means in the cells. For the main effect of gender, we construct a table with two cells, as shown in Table 14-5. The table makes it easy to see that women had more favorable views of the gender disparity research, on average, than did men.

Let's now consider the second main effect, that for academic discipline. As before, we construct a table (such as Table 14-6) that shows only the means for academic discipline, as if gender were not included in the study. We kept the means for gender in rows and the means for academic discipline in columns, just as they were in the original table. You may, however, arrange them either way, using whichever order makes sense to you. Table 14-6 shows that views of gender disparity research for non-STEM fields were higher, on average, than for STEM fields. Both results would need to be verified with a hypothesis test, but we seem to have two main effects: (1) a main effect of gender (women, on average, had a more favorable view of the gender disparity research than men did) and (2) a main effect of academic discipline (faculty members in non-STEM fields had a more favorable view of the gender disparity research compared to faculty members in STEM fields).

But that's not the whole story. Here's where the interaction comes in. Now we ignore the marginal means and get back to the means in the cells themselves, seen again in Table 14-7. Here we can see the overall pattern by framing it in two different ways. We can start by considering gender. Was there a gender difference in perceptions of the gender disparity research? It depends. Specifically, it depends on whether the faculty member was in a STEM field or a non-STEM field. The researchers report that the tiny gender difference among faculty members in non-STEM fields is *not* statistically significant (Handley et al., 2015). But the gender difference among faculty members in STEM fields *is* significantly different with a substantial effect size. The Cohen's d of 0.74 is close to Cohen's guideline of 0.8 for a large effect. So, men seemed to have a less favorable view of the gender disparity research than women did, but only if they were in STEM fields.

We can also frame the question by starting with academic discipline. Did academic discipline lead to different perceptions of the gender disparity research? It depends. Specifically, it depends on whether the faculty members were male or female. It seemed to make a difference for men; the difference between the means for men in STEM fields and men in non-STEM fields was statistically significant. The difference between the means for women in STEM fields and women in non-STEM fields, however, was not statistically significant. This is a quantitative interaction because the *strength* of the effect varies under certain conditions, but the *direction* does not (considering only the statistically significant findings as different).

People sometimes perceive an interaction where there is none. On the one hand, if men always had less favorable impressions of the gender disparity research than women did, regardless of their academic discipline, there would be no interaction. On the other hand, there is an interaction in the example we have been considering because gender has a significant effect only among STEM faculty members. The tendency to see an interaction when there is none can be diminished by constructing a bar graph, as in Figure 14-2.

The bar graph helps us to see the overall pattern, but one more step is necessary: to connect each set of bars with a line. If the lines intersect (or would eventually intersect if they were extended), that is an indication that there may be an interaction. We have two choices that match the two ways we framed the interaction in words above: (1) As in Figure 14-3, we could connect the bars for one of the independent variables, academic discipline. We would connect the two bars for STEM fields and the two bars for non-STEM fields. (2) Alternatively, as in Figure 14-4, we could connect the bars for the two genders. We would connect the two bars for female faculty members and the two bars for male faculty members.

In Figure 14-3, notice that the lines do not intersect, but they're not parallel to each other either. If the lines were extended far enough, eventually those connecting the two bars for each type of academic discipline would intersect. Perfectly parallel lines indicate the likely absence of an interaction, but we almost never see perfectly parallel lines emerging from real-life data sets; real-life data are usually messy. Nonparallel lines may indicate a statistically significant interaction, but we have to conduct an ANOVA to be sure. Only if the lines are significantly different from parallel, we can reject the null hypothesis that there is no interaction—and we want to interpret an interaction only if we reject the null hypothesis. In the case of this study, the researchers reported a statistically significant

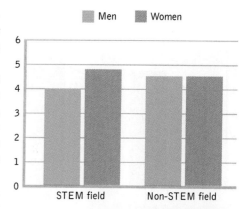

FIGURE 14-2

Bar Graphs and Interactions

Bar graphs help us determine if there really is an interaction. The bars in this graph help us to see that there seems to be a gender difference among faculty members in STEM fields but not among faculty members in non-STEM fields.

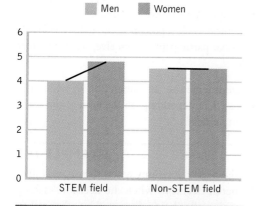

FIGURE 14-3

Are the Lines Parallel? Part I

We add lines to bar graphs to help us determine whether there really is an interaction. We draw a line connecting the bars for the male and female faculty members in STEM fields. We then draw a line connecting the bars for the male and female faculty members in non-STEM fields. Were the two lines to continue, they would eventually intersect, an indication of an interaction. The presence of a significant interaction was confirmed by the researchers who reported it in their publication (Handley et al., 2015).

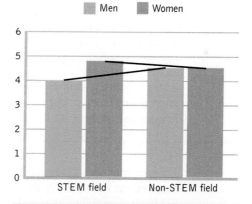

FIGURE 14-4

Are the Lines Parallel? Part II

There are always two ways to examine the pattern of the bar graphs. Here, we draw two lines, one connecting the two bars for the female faculty members and one connecting the two bars for the male faculty members. You can see that the lines are about to intersect, an indication of interaction. The presence of a significant interaction was confirmed by the researchers in their publication (Handley et al., 2015).

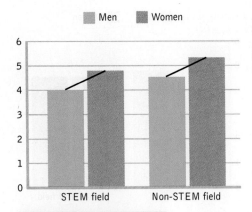

FIGURE 14-5

Parallel Lines

The two lines are exactly parallel. Were they to continue indefinitely, they would never intersect. Were this true among the population (not just this sample), there would be no interaction.

interaction with an effect size of 0.03 (using a measure similar to R^2). According to Cohen's conventions, this is a small-to-medium effect.

Some social scientists refer to an interaction as a significant difference in differences. In the context of the gender disparity study, there is a significant gender difference among faculty members in STEM fields but not among faculty members in non-STEM fields. This is an example of a significant difference between differences. This interaction is represented graphically whenever the lines connecting the bars are significantly different from parallel.

However, if women had similarly higher perceptions of the gender disparity research, as compared to men, in non-STEM fields as in STEM fields, the graph would look like the one in Figure 14-5. In this case, there is still a gender difference, on average, in STEM fields, but there is also a gender difference, on average, in non-STEM fields, and there is likely no interaction. If these were the real data, then gender would have the same effect on perceptions of the gender disparity research, regardless of academic discipline. When in doubt about whether there is an interaction or just two main effects that add up to a greater effect, draw a graph and connect the bars with lines.

However, you shouldn't just draw lines and skip the step of creating the bar graph. Ali and Peebles (2013) found that line graphs were more frequently misinterpreted than bar graphs. In one of their experiments, students randomly assigned to interpret line graphs were significantly more likely than students randomly assigned to interpret bar graphs to ignore the variable on the *x*-axis. Those interpreting line graphs were more often also unable to explain the finding at all than were those interpreting bar graphs. In addition, Zacks and Tversky (1997) reported that some people view lines as indicating a continuous variable in a line graph. A participant in one of their experiments viewed a line graph and stated: "The more male a person is, the taller he/she is" (p. 148). A bar graph would likely have led that participant to perceive, accurately, that men are, on average, taller than women. ●

Let's recall the definition of a qualitative interaction: an interaction in which the effect of one independent variable *reverses* its effect depending on the level of the other independent variable. We'll explore an example next.

EXAMPLE 14.3

Do you think that, on average, people make better decisions when they consciously focus on the decision? Or do they make better decisions when the decision-making process is unconscious (i.e., making the decision after being distracted by other tasks)? Researchers in the Netherlands conducted a series of studies in which participants were asked to decide between two options following either conscious or unconscious thinking about the choice. The studies were analyzed with two-way ANOVAs (Dijksterhuis, Bos, Nordgren, & van Baaren, 2006).

In one study, participants were asked to choose one of four cars. One car was objectively the best of the four, and one was objectively the worst. Some participants made a less complex decision; they were told 4 characteristics of each car. Some participants made a more complex decision; they were told 14 characteristics of each car. After learning about the cars, half the participants in each group were randomly assigned to think consciously about the cars for 4 minutes before making a decision. Half were randomly assigned to distract themselves for 4 minutes by solving anagrams before making a decision. The research design, with two independent variables, is shown in Table 14–8. The first independent variable is complexity, with two levels: less complex (4 attributes) and more complex (14 attributes). The second independent variable is type of decision making, with two levels: conscious thought and unconscious thought (distraction).

TABLE 14-8 A Two-Way Between-Groups ANOVA

Dutch researchers designed a study to examine what style of decision making led to the best choices in less complex and more complex situations. Would you predict an interaction? In other words, would the lines connecting bars on a graph be different from parallel? And if they are different from parallel, how are they different? If they are different just in strength, we are predicting a quantitative interaction. If the direction of effect actually reverses, we are predicting a qualitative interaction.

	Conscious thought	Unconscious thought (distraction)
Less complex (4 attributes of each car)	Less complex; conscious	Less complex; unconscious
More complex (14 attributes of each car)	More complex; conscious	More complex; unconscious

The researchers calculated a score for each participant that reflected his or her ability to differentiate between the objectively best and objectively worst cars in the group. This score represents the dependent variable, and higher numbers indicate a better ability to differentiate between the best and worst cars. Table 14-9 presents the cell means and marginal means for this experiment. For the teaching purposes of this example, note that (1) the cell means are approximate, (2) the marginal means assume the same number of participants in each cell, and (3) all the observed differences are statistically significant. (In a real research situation, we would conduct an ANOVA to determine statistical significance.)

TABLE 14-9 Decision-Making Tactics

To understand the main effects and overall pattern of a two-way ANOVA, we start by examining the cell means and marginal means.

	Conscious thought	Unconscious thought (distraction)	
Less complex	5.5	2.3	3.9
More complex	0.6	5.0	2.8
	3.05	3.65	

Because there was an overall pattern—an interaction—the researchers did not pay attention to the main effects in this study; an interaction trumps any main effects. However, let's examine the main effects to get some practice. We'll create tables for each of the two main effects so that we can examine them independently (Tables 14–10 and 14–11). The marginal means indicate that when the type of decision making is ignored entirely, people make better decisions, on average, in less complex situations than in more complex situations. The marginal means also suggest that when complexity of decision is ignored, people make better

TABLE 14-10 Main Effect of Complexity of Decision

These marginal means suggest that, overall, participants are better at making less complex decisions.

Less complex	3.9
More complex	2.8

TABLE 14-11	Main Effect of Type of Decision Making

These marginal means suggest that, overall, participants are better at making decisions when the decision making is unconscious—that is, when the participants are distracted.

Conscious	Unconscious
3.05	3.65

decisions, on average, when the decision-making process is unconscious than when it is conscious.

However, if there is also a significant interaction, then these main effects don't tell the whole story. The interaction demonstrates that the effect of the decision-making method *depends* on the complexity of the decision. Conscious decision making tends to be better than unconscious decision making in less complex situations, but unconscious decision making tends to be better than conscious decision making in more complex situations. This reversal of direction is what makes this a qualitative interaction. It's not just the strength of the effect that changes, but the actual direction!

A bar graph, shown in Figure 14-6, makes the pattern of the data far clearer. We can actually see the qualitative interaction.

FIGURE 14-6

Graphing Decision-Making Methods

This bar graph displays the interaction far better than a table or words can. We can see that it is a qualitative interaction; there is an actual reversal of direction of the effect of decision-making method in less complex situations versus more complex situations.

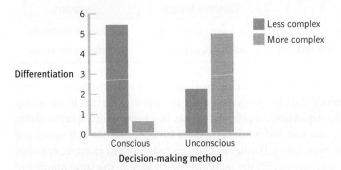

As we do with a quantitative interaction, we add lines to determine whether they are parallel (no matter how long the lines are) or intersect (or would do so if extended far enough), as in Figure 14-7. Here we see that the lines intersect without even having to extend them beyond the graph. This is likely an interaction. Type of decision making has an effect on differentiation between best cars and worst cars, but it depends on the complexity of the decision. Those individuals making a less complex decision tend to make better choices if they use conscious thought. Those making a more complex decision tend to make better choices if they use unconscious thought. We would, as these researchers did, verify this finding by conducting a hypothesis test before rejecting the null hypothesis that there is no interaction.

The qualitative interaction of the decision-making method and the complexity of the situation was not likely to have been predicted by common sense. In such instances, we

FIGURE 14-7

The Intersecting Lines of a Qualitative Interaction

When we draw two lines, one for the two bars that represent less complex situations and one for the two bars that represent more complex situations, we can easily see that they intersect. Lines that intersect, or would intersect if we extended them, indicate a possible interaction.

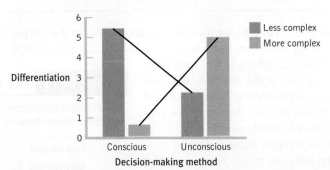

should be cautious before generalizing the findings. In this case, the research was carefully conducted and the researchers replicated their findings across several situations. For example, the researchers found similar effects in a real-life context when the less complex situation was shopping at a department store that sold clothing and kitchen products, and the more complex situation was purchasing furniture at IKEA. Such an intriguing finding would not have been possible without the inclusion of two independent variables in one study, which required that researchers use a two-way ANOVA capable of testing for an interaction.

So what do these findings mean for us as we approach the decisions we face every day? Which sunblock should we buy to best protect against UV rays? Should we go to graduate school or get a job following graduation? Should we consciously consider characteristics of sunblocks but "sleep on" graduate school–related factors? Research would suggest that the answer to the last question is yes (Dijksterhuis et al., 2006). Yet if the history of social science research is any indication, other factors (not included in these studies) likely could affect the quality of our decisions. And so the research process continues. ●

Choosing IKEA Furniture When making decisions, such as which chairs to buy, do we make better choices after conscious or unconscious deliberation? Research by Dijksterhuis and colleagues (2006) suggests that less complex decisions, like buying clothing or kitchen products, are typically better after conscious deliberation, whereas more complex decisions, like buying furniture at IKEA, are typically better after unconscious deliberation.

CHECK YOUR LEARNING

Reviewing the Concepts > A two-way ANOVA is represented by a grid in which cells represent each unique combination of independent variables. Means are calculated for cells, and are called cell means. Means are also computed for each level of an independent variable, by itself, regardless of the levels of the other independent variable. These means, found in the margins of the grid, are called marginal means.

> When there is a statistically significant interaction, the main effects are considered to be modified by an interaction. As a result, we focus only on the overall pattern of cell means that reveals the interaction.

> Two categories of interactions describe the overall pattern of cell means: quantitative and qualitative interactions.

> The most common interaction is a quantitative interaction, in which the effect of the first independent variable depends on the levels of the second independent variable, but the differences at each level vary only in the strength of the effect.

> Qualitative interactions are those in which the effect of the first independent variable depends on the levels of the second independent variable, but the direction of the effect actually reverses.

> There are three ways to identify a statistically significant interaction: (1) visually, whenever the lines connecting the means of each group are significantly different from parallel; (2) conceptually, when we need to use the idea of "it depends" to tell the data's story; and (3) statistically, when the *p* value associated with an interaction in a source table is less than 0.05, as with other hypothesis tests. This last method, the statistical analysis, is the only objective way to assess the interaction.

Clarifying the Concepts   **14-5**   What is the difference between a quantitative interaction and a qualitative interaction?

14-6   Why do we ignore any main effects when there is an interaction? (We often say the main effects are *trumped* by an interaction.)

continued on next page

Calculating the Statistics   **14-7**   Data are presented here for two hypothetical independent variables (IVs) and their combinations.

IV 1, level A; IV 2, level A: 2, 1, 1, 3

IV 1, level B; IV 2, level A: 5, 4, 3, 4

IV 1, level A; IV 2, level B: 2, 3, 3, 3

IV 1, level B; IV 2, level B: 3, 2, 2, 3

a. Figure out how many cells are in this study's table, and draw a grid to represent them.

b. Calculate cell means and write them in the cells of the grid.

c. Calculate marginal means and write them in the margins of the grid.

d. Draw a bar graph of these data.

Applying the Concepts   **14-8**   Researchers wondered whether students' genders and attractiveness influence their grades (Hernández-Julián & Peters, 2015). The researchers had a group of unbiased people rate the attractiveness of more than 5000 male and female students based on their university photos. These students were divided into three categories of attractiveness: below average, average, and above average. The researchers also had access to students' grades on a grade-point average (GPA) scale of 0 to 4. The results, as summarized in a news story about this research, indicated that "among similarly qualified female students—those who are physically attractive earn better grades than others. For male students, there is no significant relationship between attractiveness and grades" (Jaschik, 2016).

a. What are the independent variables in this study, and what are the levels of the independent variables?

b. What is the dependent variable in this study? What type of variable is it?

c. Based on your answers to (a) and (b), explain why it would be possible to conduct an ANOVA on these data. Using the language introduced in this chapter, what kind of ANOVA would it be?

d. Explain why the summary of the research indicates that there is an interaction.

e. Construct a table showing the cells. Include numbers in the cells that demonstrate the pattern of the interaction. (There are many possible specific numbers that would work.)

f. Is the interaction qualitative or quantitative? Explain your answer.

g. The researchers noted two possible explanations for these findings—that the more attractive women were simply smarter and that the professors were biased toward more attractive women. Explain why this presents a confound in this study. (The researchers conducted the same study in online courses where appearance is not a factor, and the attractiveness effect for women was not statistically significant, pointing to professor bias.)

Solutions to these Check Your Learning questions can be found in Appendix D.

Conducting a Two-Way Between-Groups ANOVA

Understanding interactions makes it easier to explain patterns in the data. For example, it is easy to understand why a ski resort would be tempted to exaggerate snowfall reports—especially right before a big, money-making weekend. Conducting a two-way ANOVA (with two independent variables) is the only way to test whether the effect of one independent variable *depends* on the levels of another independent variable.

Behavioral scientists explore interactions by using two-way ANOVAs. Fortunately, hypothesis testing for a two-way between-groups ANOVA uses the same logic as for a one-way between-groups ANOVA. For example, the null hypothesis is exactly the same: There are no mean differences between groups. Type I and Type II errors still pose the same threats to decision making. We compare an F statistic to a critical F value to make a decision. The main way that a two-way ANOVA differs from a one-way ANOVA is that three ideas are being tested and each idea is a separate source of variability.

The three ideas being tested in a two-way between-groups ANOVA are the main effect of the first independent variable, the main effect of the second independent variable, and the interaction effect of the two independent variables. A fourth source of variability in a two-way ANOVA is within-groups variance. Let's learn how to separate and measure these four sources of variance by evaluating a commonly used educational method to improve public health: myth busting.

The Six Steps of Two-Way ANOVA

Two-way ANOVAs use the same six hypothesis-testing steps that you already know. The main difference is that you essentially perform most of the steps three times—once for each main effect and once for the interaction. Let's look at an example.

EXAMPLE 14.4

Does myth busting really improve public health? Here are some myths and facts. From the Web site of the Canadian Mental Health Association (2018):

Myth: "People who experience mental illnesses can't work."
Fact: "Whether you realize it or not, workplaces are filled with people who have experienced mental illnesses. Mental illnesses don't mean that someone is no longer capable of working."

From the Web site for the World Health Organization (2018):

Myth: "Disasters bring out the worst in human behavior."
Fact: "Although isolated cases of antisocial behavior exist, the majority of people respond spontaneously and generously."

A group of Canadian researchers examined the effectiveness of myth busting (Skurnik, Yoon, Park, & Schwarz, 2005). They wondered whether the effectiveness of debunking false medical claims depends on the age of the person targeted by the message. In one study, they compared two groups of adults: younger adults, ages 18–25, and older adults, ages 71–86. Participants were presented with a series of claims and were told that each claim was either true or false. (In reality, all claims were true, partly because researchers did not want to run the risk that participants would misremember false claims as being true.) In some cases, the claim was presented once, and in other cases, it was repeated three times. In either case, the accurate information was presented after each "false" statement. (Note that for our teaching purposes, we have slightly altered the study's design.)

The two independent variables in this study were age, with two levels (younger, older), and number of repetitions, with two levels (once, three times). The dependent variable, proportion of responses that were wrong after a 3-day delay, was calculated for

Do We Remember the Medical Myth or the Fact? Skurnik and colleagues (2005) studied the factors that influence the misremembering of false medical claims as facts. They asked: When a physician tells a patient a false claim, then debunks it with the facts, does the patient remember the false claim or the facts? A source table examines each factor in the study and tells us how much of the variability in the dependent variable is explained by that factor.

each participant. This was a two-way between-groups ANOVA—more specifically, a 2×2 between-groups ANOVA. From this name, we know that the table has four cells: $(2 \times 2) = 4$. There were 64 participants—16 in each cell. But here we use an example with 12 participants—3 in each cell. Here are the data that we'll use; they have similar means to those in the actual study, and the F statistics are similar as well.

Experimental Conditions	Proportion of Responses That Were Wrong	Mean
Younger, one repetition	0.25, 0.21, 0.14	0.20
Younger, three repetitions	0.07, 0.13, 0.16	0.12
Older, one repetition	0.27, 0.22, 0.17	0.22
Older, three repetitions	0.33, 0.31, 0.26	0.30

Let's consider the steps of hypothesis testing for a two-way between-groups ANOVA in the context of this example.

> **STEP 1: Identify the populations, distribution, and assumptions.**

The first step of hypothesis testing for a two-way between-groups ANOVA is very similar to that for a one-way between-groups ANOVA. First, we state the populations, but we specify that they are broken down into more than one category. In the current example, there are four populations, so there are four cells (as shown in Table 14-12). As we do the calculations, the first independent variable, age, appears in the rows of the table, and the second independent variable, number of repetitions, appears in the columns of the table.

TABLE 14-12 Studying the Memory of False Claims Using a Two-Way ANOVA

The study of memory for false claims has two independent variables: age (younger, older) and number of repetitions (one, three).

	One repetition (1)	Three repetitions (3)
Younger (Y)	Y; 1	Y; 3
Older (0)	0; 1	0; 3

There are four populations, each with labels representing the levels of the two independent variables to which they belong.

Population 1 (Y; 1): Younger adults who hear one repetition of a false claim
Population 2 (Y; 3): Younger adults who hear three repetitions of a false claim
Population 3 (O; 1): Older adults who hear one repetition of a false claim
Population 4 (O; 3): Older adults who hear three repetitions of a false claim

We next consider the characteristics of the data to determine the distributions to which we compare the sample. There are more than two groups, so we need to consider variances to analyze differences among means. Therefore, we use F distributions. Finally, we list the hypothesis test that we use for those distributions and check the assumptions for that test. For F distributions, we use ANOVA—in this case, two-way between-groups ANOVA.

The assumptions are the same for all types of ANOVA: The sample should be selected randomly; the populations should be distributed normally; and the population variances should be equal. Let's explore those assumptions a bit further.

(1) These data were not randomly selected. Younger adults were recruited from a university, and older adults were recruited from the local community. Because random sampling was not used, we must be cautious when generalizing from these samples. (2) The researchers did not report whether they investigated the shapes of the distributions of their samples to assess the shapes of the underlying populations. (3) The researchers did not provide standard deviations of the samples as an indication of whether the population spreads might be approximately equal—the condition known as homoscedasticity, which we explored in Chapter 12. We typically explore these assumptions using the sample data.

Summary: Population 1 (Y; 1): Younger adults who hear one repetition of a false claim. Population 2 (Y; 3): Younger adults who hear three repetitions of a false claim. Population 3 (O; 1): Older adults who hear one repetition of a false claim. Population 4 (O; 3): Older adults who hear three repetitions of a false claim.

The comparison distributions will be F distributions. The hypothesis test will be a two-way between-groups ANOVA. Assumptions: (1) The data are not from random samples, so we must generalize only with caution. (2) From the published research report, we do not know if the underlying population distributions are normal. (3) We do not know if the population variances are approximately equal (homoscedasticity).

> **STEP 2:** State the null and research hypotheses.

The second step, to state the null and research hypotheses, is similar to that for a one-way between-groups ANOVA, except that we now have three sets of hypotheses, one for each main effect and one for the interaction. Those for the two main effects are the same as those for the one effect of a one-way between-groups ANOVA (see the summary below). If there are only two levels, then we can simply say that the two levels are not equal; if there are only two levels and there is a statistically significant difference, the difference must be between those two levels. Note that because there are two independent variables, we clarify which variable we are referring to by using initial letters or abbreviations for the levels of each (e.g., Y for younger and O for older). If an independent variable has more than two levels, the research hypothesis would be that any two levels of the independent variable are not equal.

The hypotheses for the interaction are typically stated in words but not in symbols. The null hypothesis is that the effect of one independent variable is not dependent on the levels of the other independent variable. The research hypothesis is that the effect of one independent variable depends on the levels of the other independent variable. It does not matter which independent variable we list first (e.g., "The effect of age is not dependent…" or "The effect of number of repetitions is not dependent…"). Write the hypotheses in the way that makes the most sense to you.

Summary: The hypotheses for the main effect of the first independent variable, age, are as follows. Null hypothesis: On average, compared with older adults, younger adults have the same proportion of responses that are wrong when remembering which claims are myths—$H_0: \mu_Y = \mu_O$. Research hypothesis: On average, compared with older adults, younger adults have a different proportion of responses that are wrong when remembering which claims are myths—H_1: $\mu_Y \neq \mu_O$.

The hypotheses for the main effect of the second independent variable, number of repetitions, are as follows. Null hypothesis: On average, those who hear one repetition have the same proportion of responses that are wrong when remembering which claims are myths compared with those who hear three repetitions—H_0: $\mu_1 = \mu_3$. Research hypothesis: On average, those who hear one repetition have a different proportion of responses that are wrong when remembering which claims are myths compared with those who hear three repetitions—H_1: $\mu_1 \neq \mu_3$.

The hypotheses for the interaction of age and number of repetitions are as follows. Null hypothesis: The effect of number of repetitions is not dependent on the levels of age. Research hypothesis: The effect of number of repetitions depends on the levels of age.

> **STEP 3: Determine the characteristics of the comparison distribution.**

The third step is similar to that of a one-way between-groups ANOVA, except that there are three comparison distributions, all of them F distributions. We need to provide the appropriate degrees of freedom for each of these: two main effects and one interaction. As before, each F statistic is a ratio of between-groups variance and within-groups variance. Because there are three effects, there are three between-groups variance estimates, each with its own degrees of freedom. There is only one within-groups variance estimate, with its degrees of freedom for all three.

For each main effect, the between-groups degrees of freedom is calculated as for a one-way ANOVA: the number of groups minus 1. The first independent variable, age, is in the rows of the table of cells, so the between-groups degrees of freedom is:

$$df_{rows(age)} = N_{rows} - 1 = 2 - 1 = 1$$

The second independent variable, number of repetitions, is in the columns of the table of cells, so the between-groups degrees of freedom is:

$$df_{columns(reps)} = N_{columns} - 1 = 2 - 1 = 1$$

We now need a between-groups degrees of freedom for the interaction, which we calculate by multiplying the degrees of freedom for the two main effects:

$$df_{interaction} = (df_{rows(age)})(df_{columns(reps)}) = (1)(1) = 1$$

The within-groups degrees of freedom is calculated like that for a one-way between-groups ANOVA, as the sum of the degrees of freedom in each of the cells. In the current example, there are three participants in each cell, so the within-groups degrees of freedom is calculated as follows, with N representing the number in each cell:

$$df_{Y,1} = N - 1 = 3 - 1 = 2$$
$$df_{Y,3} = N - 1 = 3 - 1 = 2$$
$$df_{O,1} = N - 1 = 3 - 1 = 2$$
$$df_{O,3} = N - 1 = 3 - 1 = 2$$
$$df_{within} = df_{Y,1} + df_{Y,3} + df_{O,1} + df_{O,3} = 2 + 2 + 2 + 2 = 8$$

For a check on our work, we calculate the total degrees of freedom just as we did for the one-way between-groups ANOVA. We subtract 1 from the total number of participants:

$$df_{total} = N_{total} - 1 = 12 - 1 = 11$$

We now add up the three between-groups degrees of freedom and the within-groups degrees of freedom to see if they equal 11. We have a match:

$$11 = 1 + 1 + 1 + 8$$

Finally, for this step, we list the distributions with their degrees of freedom for the three effects. Note that, although the between-groups degrees of freedom for the three effects are the same in this case, they are often different. For example, if one independent variable had three levels and the other had four, the between-groups degrees of freedom for the main effects would be 2 and 3, respectively, and the between-groups degrees of freedom for the interaction would be 6.
Summary: Main effect of age: *F* distribution with 1 and 8 degrees of freedom. Main effect of number of repetitions: *F* distribution with 1 and 8 degrees of freedom. Interaction of age and number of repetitions: *F* distribution with 1 and 8 degrees of freedom. (*Note:* It is helpful to include all degrees of freedom calculations in this step.)

> **MASTERING THE FORMULA**
>
> **14-5:** There are two ways to calculate the total degrees of freedom. We can subtract 1 from the total number of participants in the entire study:
>
> $$df_{total} = N_{total} - 1$$
>
> Alternatively, we can add the three between-groups degrees of freedom and the within-groups degrees of freedom. It's a good idea to calculate it both ways as a check on our work.

STEP 4: Determine the critical values, or cutoffs.

Again, this step for the two-way between-groups ANOVA is just an expansion of that for the one-way version. We now need three critical values, but we determine them just as we determined them before. We use the *F* table in Appendix B.

For each main effect and for the interaction, we look up the within-groups degrees of freedom, which is always the same for each effect, along the left-hand side and the appropriate between-groups degrees of freedom across the top of the table. The place on the grid where this row and this column intersect contains three numbers. From top to bottom, the table provides cutoffs for alpha levels of 0.01, 0.05, and 0.10. As usual, we typically use 0.05. In this instance, it happens that the critical value is the same for all three effects because the between-groups degrees of freedom is the same for all three. But when the between-groups degrees of freedom are different, there are different critical values. Here, we look up the between-groups degrees of freedom of 1, within-groups degrees of freedom of 8, and an alpha level of 0.05. The cutoff for all three is 5.32, as seen in Figure 14-8.
Summary: There are three critical values (which in this case are all the same), as seen in the curve in Figure 14-8. The critical *F* value for the main effect of age is 5.32. The critical *F* value for the main effect of number of repetitions is 5.32. The critical *F* value for the interaction of age and number of repetitions is 5.32.

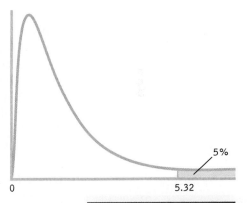

FIGURE 14-8

Determining Cutoffs for an *F* Distribution

We determine the critical values for an *F* distribution for a two-way between-groups ANOVA just as we did for a one-way between-groups ANOVA, except that we calculate three cutoffs, one for each main effect and one for the interaction. In this case, the between-groups degrees of freedom are the same for all three, so the cutoffs are the same.

> **STEP 5: Calculate the test statistic.**

As with the one-way between-groups ANOVA, the fifth step for the two-way between-groups ANOVA is the most time consuming. As you might guess, it's similar to what we already learned, but we have to calculate three F statistics instead of one. We learn the logic and the specific calculations for this step in the next section.

> **STEP 6: Make a decision.**

This step is the same as for a one-way between-groups ANOVA, except that we compare each of the three F statistics to its appropriate cutoff F statistic. If the F statistic is beyond the critical value, then we know that it is in the most extreme 5% of possible test statistics *if* the null hypothesis is true. After making a decision for each F statistic, we present the results in one of three ways.

First, if we are able to reject the null hypothesis for the interaction, then we draw a specific conclusion with the help of a table and graph. Because we have more than two groups, we use a post hoc test, such as the ones that we learned in Chapter 12. When there are three effects, post hoc tests are typically implemented separately for each main effect and for the interaction (Hays, 1994). If the interaction is statistically significant, then it might not matter whether the main effects are also significant; if they are also significant, then those findings are usually qualified by the interaction, and are not described separately. The overall pattern of cell means tells the whole story.

Second, if we are not able to reject the null hypothesis for the interaction, then we focus on any significant main effects, drawing a specific directional conclusion for each. In this study, each independent variable has only two levels, so there is no need for a post hoc test. If there were three or more levels, however, then each significant main effect would require a post hoc test to determine exactly where the differences lie.

Third, if we do not reject the null hypothesis for either main effect or the interaction, then we can conclude only that there is insufficient evidence from this study to support the research hypotheses. We will complete step 6 of hypothesis testing for this study in the next section, after we consider the calculations of the source table for a two-way between-groups ANOVA. ●

Identifying Four Sources of Variability in a Two-Way ANOVA

In this section, we complete step 5 for a two-way between-groups ANOVA. The calculations are similar to those for a one-way between-groups ANOVA, except that we calculate three F statistics. We use a source table with elements like those shown in Table 14-18 on page 434.

First, we calculate the total sum of squares (Table 14-13). We calculate this number in exactly the same way as we do for a one-way ANOVA. We subtract the grand mean, in this case 0.21, from every score to create deviations, then square the deviations, and finally sum the squared deviations:

$$SS_{total} = \Sigma(X - GM)^2 = 0.0672$$

MASTERING THE FORMULA

14-6: We calculate the total sum of squares using the following formula:

$$SS_{total} = \Sigma(X - GM)^2$$

We subtract the grand mean from every score to create deviations, then square the deviations, and finally sum the squared deviations.

TABLE 14-13   Calculating the Total Sum of Squares

The total sum of squares is calculated by subtracting the overall mean, called the *grand mean,* from every score to create deviations, then squaring the deviations and summing them: $\Sigma(X-GM)^2 = 0.0672$.

	X	$(X-GM)$	$(X-GM)^2$
Y, 1	0.25	$(0.25-0.21) = 0.04$	0.0016
	0.21	$(0.21-0.21) = 0.00$	0.0000
	0.14	$(0.14-0.21) = -0.07$	0.0049
Y, 3	0.07	$(0.07-0.21) = -0.14$	0.0196
	0.13	$(0.13-0.21) = -0.08$	0.0064
	0.16	$(0.16-0.21) = -0.05$	0.0025
0, 1	0.27	$(0.27-0.21) = 0.06$	0.0036
	0.22	$(0.22-0.21) = 0.01$	0.0001
	0.17	$(0.17-0.21) = -0.04$	0.0016
0, 3	0.33	$(0.33-0.21) = 0.12$	0.0144
	0.31	$(0.31-0.21) = 0.10$	0.0100
	0.26	$(0.26-0.21) = 0.05$	0.0025

We now calculate the between-groups sums of squares for the two main effects. Both are calculated similarly to the between-groups sum of squares for a one-way between-groups ANOVA. Table 14-14 shows the cell means, marginal means, and grand mean. The between-groups sum of squares for the main effect of the independent variable age would be the sum, for every score, of the marginal mean minus the grand mean, squared. We list all 12 scores in Table 14-15, marking the divisions among the cells. For each of the six younger participants, those in the top six rows of Table 14-15, we subtract the grand mean, 0.21, from the marginal mean, 0.16. For the six older participants, those in the bottom six rows, we subtract 0.21 from the marginal mean, 0.26. We square all of these deviations and then add them to calculate the sum of squares for the rows, the independent variable of age:

$$SS_{between(rows)} = \Sigma(M_{row(age)} - GM)^2 = 0.03$$

MASTERING THE FORMULA

14-7: We calculate the between-groups sum of squares for the first independent variable, that in the rows of the table of cells, using the following formula:

$$SS_{between(rows)} = \Sigma(M_{row} - GM)^2$$

For every participant, we subtract the grand mean from the marginal mean for the appropriate row for that participant. We square these deviations and sum the squared deviations.

TABLE 14-14   Means for False Medical Claims Study

The study of the misremembering of false medical claims as true had two independent variables, age and number of repetitions. The cell means and marginal means for error rates are shown in the table. The grand mean is 0.21.

	One repetition (1)	Three repetitions (3)	
Younger (Y)	0.20	0.12	0.16
Older (0)	0.22	0.30	0.26
	0.21	0.21	0.21

TABLE 14-15   Calculating the Sum of Squares for the First Independent Variable

The sum of squares for the first independent variable is calculated by subtracting the overall mean (the grand mean) from the mean for each level of that variable—in this case, age—to create deviations, then squaring the deviations and summing them: $\Sigma(M_{row(age)} - GM)^2 = 0.03$.

	X	$(M_{row(age)} - GM)$	$(M_{row(age)} - GM)^2$
Y, 1	0.25	$(0.16 - 0.21) = -0.05$	0.0025
	0.21	$(0.16 - 0.21) = -0.05$	0.0025
	0.14	$(0.16 - 0.21) = -0.05$	0.0025
Y, 3	0.07	$(0.16 - 0.21) = -0.05$	0.0025
	0.13	$(0.16 - 0.21) = -0.05$	0.0025
	0.16	$(0.16 - 0.21) = -0.05$	0.0025
O, 1	0.27	$(0.26 - 0.21) = 0.05$	0.0025
	0.22	$(0.26 - 0.21) = 0.05$	0.0025
	0.17	$(0.26 - 0.21) = 0.05$	0.0025
O, 3	0.33	$(0.26 - 0.21) = 0.05$	0.0025
	0.31	$(0.26 - 0.21) = 0.05$	0.0025
	0.26	$(0.26 - 0.21) = 0.05$	0.0025

We repeat this process for the second possible main effect, that of the independent variable in the columns (Table 14-16). The between-groups sum of squares for number of repetitions, then, would be the sum, for every score, of the marginal mean minus the grand mean, squared. We again list all 12 scores, marking the divisions among the cells. For each of the six participants who had one repetition, those in the left-hand column of Table 14-14 and in rows 1–3 and 7–9 of Table 14-16, we subtract the grand mean, 0.21, from the marginal mean, 0.21. For each of the six participants who had three repetitions, those in the right-hand column of Table 14-14 and in rows 4–6 and 10–12 of Table 14-16, we subtract 0.21 from the marginal mean, 0.21. (*Note:* It is a coincidence that in this case the marginal means are exactly the same.) We square all of these deviations and add them to calculate the between-groups sum of squares for the columns, the independent variable of number of repetitions. Again, the calculations for the between-groups sum of squares for each main effect are just like the calculations for a one-way between-groups ANOVA:

$$SS_{between(columns)} = \Sigma(M_{columns(reps)} - GM)^2 = 0$$

The within-groups sum of squares is calculated in exactly the same way as for the one-way between-groups ANOVA (Table 14-17). The cell mean is subtracted from each of the 12 scores. The deviations are squared and summed:

$$SS_{within} = \Sigma(X - M_{cell})^2 = 0.018$$

TABLE 14-16	Calculating the Sum of Squares for the Second Independent Variable

The sum of squares for the second independent variable is calculated by subtracting the overall mean (the grand mean) from the mean for each level of that variable—in this case, number of repetitions—to create deviations, then squaring the deviations and summing them: $\Sigma(M_{column(reps)} - GM)^2 = 0$.

	X	$(M_{column(reps)} - GM)$	$(M_{column(reps)} - GM)^2$
Y, 1	0.25	$(0.21 - 0.21) = 0$	0
	0.21	$(0.21 - 0.21) = 0$	0
	0.14	$(0.21 - 0.21) = 0$	0
Y, 3	0.07	$(0.21 - 0.21) = 0$	0
	0.13	$(0.21 - 0.21) = 0$	0
	0.16	$(0.21 - 0.21) = 0$	0
0, 1	0.27	$(0.21 - 0.21) = 0$	0
	0.22	$(0.21 - 0.21) = 0$	0
	0.17	$(0.21 - 0.21) = 0$	0
0, 3	0.33	$(0.21 - 0.21) = 0$	0
	0.31	$(0.21 - 0.21) = 0$	0
	0.26	$(0.21 - 0.21) = 0$	0

TABLE 14-17	Calculating the Within-Groups Sum of Squares

The within-groups sum of squares is calculated the same way for a two-way ANOVA as for a one-way ANOVA. We take each score and subtract the mean of the cell from which it comes—not the grand mean—to create deviations; then we square the deviations and sum them: $\Sigma(X - M_{cell})^2 = 0.018$.

	X	$\Sigma(X - M_{cell})$	$\Sigma(X - M_{cell})^2$
Y, 1	0.25	$(0.25 - 0.20) = 0.05$	0.0025
	0.21	$(0.21 - 0.20) = 0.01$	0.0001
	0.14	$(0.14 - 0.20) = -0.06$	0.0036
Y, 3	0.07	$(0.07 - 0.12) = -0.05$	0.0025
	0.13	$(0.13 - 0.12) = 0.01$	0.0001
	0.16	$(0.16 - 0.12) = 0.04$	0.0016
0, 1	0.27	$(0.27 - 0.22) = 0.05$	0.0025
	0.22	$(0.22 - 0.22) = 0.00$	0.0000
	0.17	$(0.17 - 0.22) = -0.05$	0.0025
0, 3	0.33	$(0.33 - 0.30) = 0.03$	0.0009
	0.31	$(0.31 - 0.30) = 0.01$	0.0001
	0.26	$(0.26 - 0.30) = -0.04$	0.0016

TABLE 14-18 The Expanded Source Table and the Formulas

This source table includes all of the formulas for the calculations necessary to conduct a two-way between-groups ANOVA.

Source	SS	df	MS	F
Age (between/rows)	$\Sigma(M_{between(rows)} - GM)^2$	$N_{rows} - 1$	$\dfrac{SS_{between(rows)}}{df_{between(rows)}}$	$\dfrac{MS_{between(rows)}}{MS_{within}}$
Repetitions (between/columns)	$\Sigma(M_{between(columns)} - GM)^2$	$N_{columns} - 1$	$\dfrac{SS_{between(columns)}}{df_{between(columns)}}$	$\dfrac{MS_{between(columns)}}{MS_{within}}$
Age × repetitions (between/interaction)	$SS_{total} - (SS_{between(rows)} + SS_{between(columns)} + SS_{within})$	$(df_{rows})(df_{columns})$	$\dfrac{SS_{interaction}}{df_{interaction}}$	$\dfrac{MS_{interaction}}{MS_{within}}$
Within	$\Sigma(X - M_{cell})^2$	$df_{cell\,1} + df_{cell\,2} + df_{cell\,3} + df_{cell\,4}$ (and so on for any additional cells)	$\dfrac{SS_{within}}{df_{within}}$	
Total	$\Sigma(X - GM)^2$	$N_{total} - 1$		

MASTERING THE FORMULA

14-10: To calculate the between-groups sum of squares for the interaction, we subtract the two between-groups sums of squares for the independent variables and the within-groups sum of squares from the total sum of squares. The formula is:
$SS_{between(interaction)} = SS_{total} - (SS_{between(rows)} + SS_{between(columns)} + SS_{within})$.

All we need now is the between-groups sum of squares for the interaction. We calculate this by subtracting the other between-groups sums of squares (those for the two main effects) and the within-groups sum of squares from the total sum of squares. The between-groups sum of squares for the interaction is essentially what is left over when the main effects are accounted for. Mathematically, any variability that is predicted by these variables, but is not directly predicted by either independent variable on its own, is attributed to the interaction. The formula is:

$$SS_{between(interaction)} = SS_{total} - (SS_{between(rows)} + SS_{between(columns)} + SS_{within})$$

The calculations are:

$$SS_{between(interaction)} = 0.0672 - (0.03 + 0 + 0.018) = 0.0192$$

Now we complete step 6 of hypothesis testing by calculating the F statistics using the formulas in Table 14-18. The results are shown in the source table (Table 14-19). The main effect of age is statistically significant because the F statistic, 13.04, is larger than the critical value of 5.32. The means tell us that older participants tend to make more mistakes, remembering more medical myths as true, than do younger

MASTERING THE FORMULA

14-11: The formulas to calculate the four mean squares are shown in Table 14-18. There are three between-groups mean squares—one for each main effect and one for the interaction—and one within-groups mean square. For each mean square, we divide the appropriate sum of squares by its related degrees of freedom. The formulas for the three F statistics, one for each main effect and one for the interaction, are also shown in Table 14-18. For each of the three effects, we divide the appropriate between-groups mean square by the within-group mean square. The denominator is the same in all three cases.

TABLE 14-19 The Expanded Source Table and False Medical Claims

This expanded source table shows the actual sums of squares, degrees of freedom, mean squares, and F statistics for the study on false medical claims.

Source	SS	df	MS	F
Age (A)	0.0300	1	0.0300	13.04
Repetitions (R)	0.0000	1	0.0000	0.00
A × R	0.0192	1	0.0192	8.35
Within	0.0180	8	0.0023	
Total	0.0672	11		

participants. The main effect of number of repetitions is not statistically significant, however, because the F statistic of 0.00 is not larger than the cutoff of 5.32. It is unusual to have an F statistic of 0.00. Even when there is no statistically significant effect, there is usually some difference among means due to random sampling. The interaction is also statistically significant because the F statistic of 8.35 is larger than the cutoff of 5.32. Therefore, we construct a bar graph of the cell means, as seen in Figure 14-9, to interpret the interaction.

FIGURE 14-9

Interpreting the Interaction

The nonparallel lines demonstrate the interaction. The bars tell us that, on average, repetition decreases errors for younger people but increases them for older people. Because the direction reverses, this is a qualitative interaction.

In Figure 14-9, the lines connecting the bars are not parallel; in fact, they intersect without even having to extend them beyond the graph. We see that among younger participants, the proportion of responses that were incorrect was *lower*, on average, with three repetitions than with one repetition. Among older participants, the proportion of responses that were incorrect was *higher*, on average, with three repetitions than with one repetition. Does repetition help? It depends. It helps for younger people but is detrimental for older people. Specifically, repetition tends to help younger people distinguish between myth and fact. But the mere repetition of a medical myth tends to lead older people to be more likely to view it as fact. The researchers speculate that older people remember that they are familiar with a statement but forget the context in which they heard it. This is a qualitative interaction because the direction of the effect of repetition *reverses* from one age group to another.

Effect Size for Two-Way ANOVA

With a two-way ANOVA, as with a one-way ANOVA, we calculate R^2 as the measure of effect size. As before, we use sums of squares as indicators of variability. For each of the three effects—the two main effects and the interaction—we divide the appropriate between-groups sum of squares by the total sum of squares minus the sums of squares for both of the other effects. We subtract the sums of squares for the other two effects from the total so that we isolate the effect size for a single effect at a time. For example, if we want to determine effect size for the main effect in the rows, we divide the sum of squares for the rows by the total sum of squares minus the sum of squares for the column and the sum of squares for the interaction.

For the first main effect, the one in the rows of the table of cells, the formula is:

$$R^2_{rows} = \frac{SS_{rows}}{(SS_{total} - SS_{columns} - SS_{interaction})}$$

MASTERING THE FORMULA

14-12: To calculate effect size for two-way ANOVA, we perform three R^2 calculations, one for each main effect and one for the interaction. In each case, we divide the appropriate between-groups sum of squares by the total sum of squares minus the sums of squares for the other two effects. For example, the effect size for the interaction is calculated using this formula:

$$R^2_{interaction} = \frac{SS_{interaction}}{(SS_{total} - SS_{rows} - SS_{columns})}.$$

For the second main effect, the one in the columns of the table of cells, the formula is:

$$R^2_{columns} = \frac{SS_{columns}}{(SS_{total} - SS_{rows} - SS_{interaction})}$$

For the interaction, the formula is:

$$R^2_{interaction} = \frac{SS_{interaction}}{(SS_{total} - SS_{rows} - SS_{columns})}$$

EXAMPLE 14.5

Let's apply this to the ANOVA we just conducted. We use the statistics in the source table shown in Table 14-19 to calculate R^2 for each main effect and the interaction. Here are the calculations for the main effect of age:

$$R^2_{rows(age)} = \frac{SS_{rows(age)}}{(SS_{total} - SS_{columns(repetition)} - SS_{interaction})}$$

$$= \frac{0.0300}{(0.0672 - 0.000 - 0.0192)} = 0.625$$

Here are the calculations for the main effect of repetitions:

$$R^2_{columns(repetitions)} = \frac{SS_{columns(repetitions)}}{(SS_{total} - SS_{rows(age)} - SS_{interaction})}$$

$$= \frac{0.000}{(0.0672 - 0.0300 - 0.0192)} = 0.000$$

Here are the calculations for the interaction:

$$R^2_{interaction} = \frac{SS_{interaction}}{(SS_{total} - SS_{rows(age)} - SS_{columns(repetitions)})}$$

$$= \frac{0.0192}{0.0672 - 0.0300 - 0.0000} = 0.516$$

TABLE 14-20 Cohen's Conventions for Effect Sizes: R^2

The following guidelines, called *conventions* by statisticians, are meant to help researchers decide how important an effect is. These numbers are not cutoffs; they are merely rough guidelines to help researchers interpret results.

Effect Size	Convention
Small	0.01
Medium	0.06
Large	0.14

The conventions are the same as those presented in Chapter 12, shown again here in Table 14-20. From this table, we can see that the R^2 values of 0.63 for the main effect of age and 0.52 for the interaction are very large. The R^2 value of 0.00 for the main effect of repetitions indicates that there is no observable effect in this study. ●

Variations on ANOVA

We've already seen the flexibility that ANOVA offers in terms of both independent variables and research design. Yet ANOVA is even more flexible than we've seen so far in this and the previous two chapters. In Chapter 13, we described within-groups ANOVAs in which the participants experience all of the research conditions. Researchers also use four slightly more complicated designs.

1. *A **mixed-design ANOVA** is used to analyze the data from a study with at least two independent variables; at least one variable must be within-groups and at least one variable must be between-groups.* In other words, a mixed design includes both a between-groups variable and a within-groups variable.

2. *A **multivariate analysis of variance (MANOVA)** is a form of ANOVA in which there is more than one dependent variable.* The word *multivariate* refers to the number of dependent variables, not the number of independent variables. (Remember, a plain old ANOVA already can handle multiple independent variables.)

3. ***Analysis of covariance (ANCOVA)** is a type of ANOVA in which a covariate is included so that statistical findings reflect effects after a scale variable has been statistically removed.* Specifically, a ***covariate** is a scale variable that we suspect associates, or covaries, with the independent variable of interest.* So ANCOVA statistically subtracts the effect of a possible confounding variable.

4. We can also combine the features of a MANOVA and an ANCOVA. A ***multivariate analysis of covariance (MANCOVA)** is an ANOVA with multiple dependent variables and a covariate.* MANOVAs, ANCOVAs, and MANCOVAs can all have a between-groups design, a within-groups design, or even a mixed design. Table 14-21 shows variations on ANOVA.

- A **mixed-design ANOVA** is used to analyze the data from a study with at least two independent variables; at least one variable must be within-groups and at least one variable must be between-groups.

- A **multivariate analysis of variance (MANOVA)** is a form of ANOVA in which there is more than one dependent variable.

- **Analysis of covariance (ANCOVA)** is a type of ANOVA in which a covariate is included so that statistical findings reflect effects after a scale variable has been statistically removed.

- A **covariate** is a scale variable that we suspect associates, or covaries, with the independent variable of interest.

- A **multivariate analysis of covariance (MANCOVA)** is an ANOVA with multiple dependent variables and a covariate.

TABLE 14-21 Variations on ANOVA

There are many variations on ANOVA that allow us to analyze a variety of research designs. A MANOVA allows us to include more than one dependent variable. An ANCOVA allows us to include covariates to correct for third variables that might influence our study. A MANCOVA allows us to include both more than one dependent variable and a covariate.

	Independent Variables	Dependent Variables	Covariate
ANOVA	Any number	Only one	None
MANOVA	Any number	More than one	None
ANCOVA	Any number	Only one	At least one
MANCOVA	Any number	More than one	At least one

EXAMPLE 14.6

Let's consider an example of a mixed-design ANOVA. Researchers explored the effects of different types of emails on exam grades later in the course (Forsyth, Lawrence, Burnette, & Baumeister, 2007). There were three independent variables. The first independent variable was previous grade. There were two levels of this independent variable—students who had a grade of C on the first exam and those with a grade of D or F on the first exam. The second independent variable was type of email. Students could receive three types of emails over the semester: emails intended to bolster their self-esteem, emails intended to help students take responsibility for their grades, and emails that just included review questions (control group).

The third independent variable was type of exam grade. The researchers assessed two types of exam grades: the second midterm exam grades and the final exam grades. Because every student took both exams, this third independent variable was within-groups. Thus, the research design had two between-groups independent variables and one within-groups independent variable. This is an example of a three-way, mixed-design ANOVA. Specifically, this ANOVA would be referred to as a 2 (grade: C, D/F) × 3 (type of email: control, self-esteem, take responsibility) × 2 (exam: midterm, final) mixed-design ANOVA. ●

Let's consider an example of a MANCOVA, an analysis that includes both (a) multiple dependent variables and (b) at least one covariate.

(a) We sometimes use a multivariate analysis when we have several similar dependent variables. Aside from the use of multiple dependent variables, multivariate analyses are not all that different from those with one dependent variable. Essentially, the calculations treat the group of dependent variables as one dependent variable. Although we can follow up a MANOVA by considering the different univariate (single dependent variable) ANOVAs embedded in the MANOVA, we often are most interested in the effect of the independent variables on the composite of dependent variables.

(b) In some situations, we might suspect that a third variable is affecting the dependent variable. In these cases, we might conduct an ANCOVA or MANCOVA. We might, for example, have level of education as one of the independent variables and worry that age, which is likely related to level of education, is actually what is influencing the dependent variable, not education. In this case, we could include age as a covariate.

The inclusion of a covariate means that the analysis will look at the effects of the independent variables on the dependent variables after statistically removing the effect of one or more third variables. At its most basic, conducting an ANCOVA is almost like conducting an ANOVA at each level of the covariate. If age were the covariate, with level of education as the independent variable and income as the dependent variable, then we'd essentially be looking at a regular ANOVA for each age. We want to answer the question: Given a certain age, does education predict income? Of course, this is a simplified explanation, but that's the basic logic behind the procedure. If the calculations show that education has an effect on income among 33-year-olds, 58-year-olds, and every other age group, then we know that there is a main effect of education on income, over and above the effect of age.

EXAMPLE 14.7

Let's see how it works. Researchers conducted a MANCOVA to analyze the results of a study examining military service and marital status within the context of men's satisfaction within their romantic relationships (McLeland & Sutton, 2005). The independent variables were military service (military, nonmilitary) and marital status (married, unmarried). There were two dependent variables, both measures of relationship satisfaction: the Kansas Marital Satisfaction Scale (KMSS) and the ENRICH Marital Satisfaction Scale (EMS). The researchers also included the covariate of age.

Initial analyses also found that age was significantly associated with relationship satisfaction: Older men tended to be more satisfied than younger men. The researchers wanted to be certain that it was military status and marital status, not age, that affected relationship satisfaction, so they controlled for age as a covariate. The MANCOVA led to only one statistically significant finding: Military men were less satisfied than nonmilitary men with respect to their relationships, when controlling for the age of the men. That is, given a certain age, military men of that age are likely to be less satisfied with their relationships than are nonmilitary men of that age. ●

How Data Detectives Fact-Check Statistics   Data Ethics

You may have noticed that we greatly prefer to use real-life examples in this text, but that we sometimes include fictional examples or real examples with fewer data points than the original study. In these instances, we have to come up with reasonable numbers with which to work. Sounds easy, right? We can just invent, say, sample sizes, F values, degrees of freedom, p values, means, standard deviations, and effect sizes, and be done with it—roll the dice or use a random numbers generator. We could, but we don't. We want the degrees of freedom to make sense in relation to the sample size, the p values to make sense given the test statistics and degrees of freedom, and the effect sizes to be consistent with the means and standard deviations. After all, once you learn statistics, you can call us out on anything that doesn't match up in this text (and we hope you will)!

This kind of internal consistency for statistics might not matter much for a fictional example in a textbook, but it matters a great deal in the real world. If researchers' numbers don't make sense as a whole, it means that something has gone wrong. Maybe they cheated, and engaged in a particularly egregious form of p-hacking: "Um, I'll just mistype this 0.143 p value as 0.049. Oops!" More likely, they were sloppy in their reporting. Perhaps they cut and pasted one statistical result, but forgot to update the test statistic. Either way, such errors can lead to a false impression that is compounded when others cite it in their own research (the "retweet" of the publication world) or report on it in news articles. And it can stymie meta-analysts who use data from previous research. Like a game of telephone—in which one participant after another whispers a phrase to the next person, often ending up with hilariously inaccurate results—mistakes made when reporting data can become exaggerated over time.

Traditionally, it has been a time-consuming task to find these statistical errors. When reading this text, for example, you probably didn't try to find places where our numbers don't add up, so to speak. You're not alone. We don't, as a rule, do this extra work when we read journal articles. Fortunately, as in much of life these days, there's an app for that!

Statistical Reference	Computed p Value	Consistency
t(41) = 2.88, p < .05	0.00630	Consistent
F(2, 86) = 3.75, p = .027	0.02745	Consistent
t(41) = 15.3, p < .001	0.00000	Consistent
t(41) = 1.28, p = .104	0.20774	Inconsistency

FIGURE 14.10

Statcheck on the Web

Here's a snapshot of the results after submitting a research article to statcheck. We see four of the article's statistical tests, each of which appears in the leftmost column as the APA-style reported statistic. In the middle column are the p values that should be associated with those statistics (based on the degrees of freedom and the value of the test statistic), as calculated by statcheck. In the rightmost column, statcheck indicates whether results do or do not match the correct p value. Of the four tests for this paper, one had an incorrect p value reported and is marked as an "inconsistency." In this particular instance, the incorrect p value did not qualitatively change our interpretation of the results. The authors failed to reject the null hypothesis, and that would be true with the corrected p value as well.

Okay, it's not exactly an app. It's a free software package developed by Dutch psychology researchers Sacha Epskamp and Michèle Nuijten (2016) that you can install on your computer as a sort of data detective that can analyze statistical results in a Word or PDF file; called "statcheck," this package was created using the free statistical software R that we've mentioned previously in this textbook (Epskamp & Nuijten, 2016). If you want to try it, you can download it here: mbnuijten.com/statcheck/quick-install. If you want things to be even easier, just upload your paper here: statcheck.io. As an example, Figure 14-10 shows a statcheck screenshot of four statistical tests from a paper written by one of your authors. As long as your paper is in APA style, statcheck automatically compares all of the statistics within a particular result to make sure they're consistent, saving you—and your readers—a lot of time and calculations.

Of course, even before you or any other researcher use statcheck on data in a journal article, statcheck has already made its own contributions to the field (Nuijten, Hartgerink, van Assen, Epskamp, & Wicherts, 2016). Using statcheck on more than 250,000 p values in eight top-notch psychology journals, Nuijten and her colleagues found that more than half of the articles they examined had at least one p value that didn't match up with the test statistic and degrees of freedom. More worrisome, approximately 12% of papers had a p value that was so far off that it could have altered the researchers' conclusion. Even more worrisome, the mistakes tended to occur with p values that were statistically significant. Were researchers engaging in p-hacking to push their p values just below the magic alpha level of 0.05?

The program statcheck sounds like a positive for science, but some have criticized its use on previously published papers, many of which were not written in the current era of open science and ethical data practices. Prominent psychologist Susan Fiske called for civility in criticism of others' research, calling statcheck a "'gotcha' algorithm" because the results were made public (Letzter, 2016). Others are grateful to the statcheck creators for the easy-to-use tool. Researcher Michael Kane had one paper called out after errors were caught by statcheck, and he even tweeted about it (Resnick, 2016). He told a reporter, "I don't mind my work being checked up on. I think it's generally a good thing for the field."

There's a bright side to the statcheck controversy and the alarming results this software has uncovered. The subsequent discussion has provided additional encouragement for researchers to engage in the ethical, open science practices that we've been describing in the Data Ethics features throughout this book. Among the solutions, Nuijten and her colleagues (2016) suggest that researchers use statcheck on their own and others' results, and that everyone share their data so that other researchers can keep sneaky researchers honest and help honest researchers find their errors. When in doubt, statcheck it.

CHECK YOUR LEARNING

Reviewing the Concepts

> The six steps of hypothesis testing for a two-way between-groups ANOVA are similar to those for a one-way between-groups ANOVA.

> Because we have the possibility of two main effects and an interaction, each step is broken down into three parts, with three sets of hypotheses, comparison distributions, critical F values, F statistics, and conclusions.

> An expanded source table helps us to keep track of the calculations.

> Statistically significant F statistics require post hoc tests to determine where differences lie when there are more than two groups.

> We calculate a measure of effect size, R^2, for each main effect and for the interaction.

> Factorial ANOVAs can have a mixed design in addition to a between-groups design or within-groups design. In a mixed design, at least one of the independent variables is between-groups and at least one of the independent variables is within-groups.

> Researchers can also include multiple dependent variables, not just multiple independent variables, in a single study, which are then analyzed with a MANOVA.

> Researchers can add a covariate to an ANOVA and conduct an ANCOVA, which allows us to control for the effect of a variable that is related to the independent variable.

> Researchers can include multiple dependent variables and one or more covariates in an analysis called a MANCOVA.

> Tools like statcheck can help ethical researchers make sure their own statistics are consistent. They can also help readers to check the statistics in published reports of research.

Clarifying the Concepts

14-9 What is the basic difference between the six steps of hypothesis testing for a two-way between-groups ANOVA and a one-way between-groups ANOVA?

14-10 What are the four sources of variability in a two-way ANOVA?

Calculating the Statistics

14-11 Compute the three between-groups degrees of freedom (both main effects and the interaction), the within-groups degrees of freedom, and the total degrees of freedom for the following data: (Note: IV 1 refers to the first independent variable and IV 2 refers to the second independent variable.)

IV 1, level A; IV 2, level A: 2, 1, 1, 3

IV 1, level B; IV 2, level A: 5, 4, 3, 4

IV 1, level A; IV 2, level B: 2, 3, 3, 3

IV 1, level B; IV 2, level B: 3, 2, 2, 3

14-12 Using the degrees of freedom you calculated in the previous Check Your Learning exercise, determine critical values, or cutoffs, using an alpha level of 0.05, for the F statistics of the two main effects and the interaction.

continued on next page

Applying the Concepts   **14-13**   Researchers explored the effects of different types of emails on students' exam grades later in a course (Forsyth et al., 2007). Let's look at two of their independent variables. The first independent variable was previous grade: students who had a grade of C on the first exam versus those with a grade of D or F on the first exam. The second independent variable was type of email that students received: emails intended to bolster their self-esteem, emails intended to help students take responsibility for their grades, and emails that just included review questions (control group). The accompanying table shows the cell means for the final exam grades (note that some of these are approximate, but all represent actual findings). For simplicity, assume there were 84 participants in the study evenly divided among cells.

	Self-esteem (SE)	Take responsibility (TR)	Control group (CG)
C	67.31	69.83	71.12
D/F	47.83	60.98	62.13

a. From step 1 of hypothesis testing, list the populations for this study.

b. Conduct step 2 of hypothesis testing.

c. Conduct step 3 of hypothesis testing.

d. Conduct step 4 of hypothesis testing.

Solutions to these Check Your Learning questions can be found in Appendix D.

e. The *F* statistics are 20.84 for the main effect of the independent variable of initial grade, 1.69 for the main effect of the independent variable of type of email, and 3.02 for the interaction. Conduct step 6 of hypothesis testing.

REVIEW OF CONCEPTS

LaunchPad
macmillan learning
Visit LaunchPad to access the e-book and to test your knowledge with LearningCurve.

Two-Way ANOVA

Factorial ANOVAs (also called *multifactorial ANOVAs*), those with more than one independent variable (or *factor*), permit us to test more than one hypothesis in a single study. They also allow us to examine *interactions* between independent variables. Factorial ANOVAs are often named by referring to the levels of their independent variables (e.g., 2 × 2) rather than the number of independent variables (e.g., two-way). With a *two-way ANOVA*, we can examine two *main effects* (one for each independent variable) and one interaction (the way in which the two variables might work together to influence the dependent variable). Because we are examining three hypotheses, we calculate three sets of statistics for a two-way ANOVA.

Understanding Interactions in ANOVA

Researchers typically interpret interactions by examining the overall pattern of cell means. A *cell* is one condition in a study. We typically write the mean of a group in its cell. We write the *marginal means* for each row to the right of the cells and the marginal means for each column below the cells. If the main effect of one independent variable is stronger under certain conditions of the second independent variable, there is a *quantitative interaction*. If the direction of the main effect actually reverses under certain conditions of the second independent variable, there is a *qualitative interaction*.

Conducting a Two-Way Between-Groups ANOVA

A two-way between-groups ANOVA uses the same six steps of hypothesis testing that we used previously, with minor changes. Because we test for two main effects and one interaction, each step is broken down into three parts. Specifically, we have three sets of hypotheses, three comparison distributions, three critical F values, three F statistics, and three conclusions. We use an expanded source table to aid in the calculations of the F statistics. We also calculate a measure of effect size, R^2, for each of the main effects and for the interaction.

There are several ways to expand on ANOVA. A mixed-design ANOVA has at least one between-groups independent variable and at least one within-groups independent variable. We also can include multiple dependent variables, not just multiple independent variables, in a single study, analyzed with a multivariate analysis of variance (MANOVA). Alternatively, we can add a covariate to the ANOVA and conduct an analysis of covariance (ANCOVA), which allows us to control for the effect of a variable that we believe might be related to our independent variable. Finally, we can include multiple dependent variables and a covariate in an analysis called a multivariate analysis of covariance (MANCOVA).

New statistical tools (e.g., statcheck) allow researchers to check the statistics in their write-ups of their results to ensure they are consistent. They also provide a way to check the statistics in published studies.

SPSS

Let's use SPSS to conduct a two-way ANOVA for the data on myth busting that we used in this chapter. We enter the data in three columns—one for each participant's scores on each independent variable (age and number of repetitions) and one for each participant's score on the dependent variable (false memory).

We instruct SPSS to conduct the ANOVA by selecting Analyze → General Linear Model → Univariate and selecting the variables. (Even though there are two independent variables, we still choose univariate, which means one variable, instead of multivariate, which means many variables. That's because this choice refers to the dependent variable

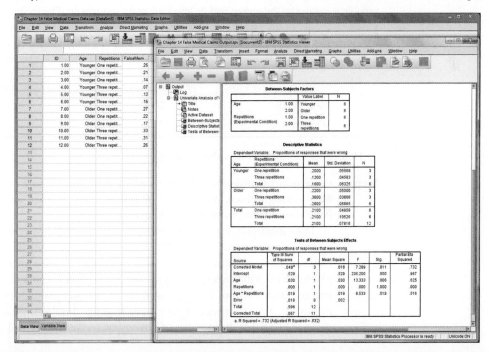

rather than the independent variable, and there's just one dependent variable, false memory.)

Select the dependent variable, false memory, by highlighting it and clicking the arrow next to "Dependent Variable." Select the independent variables (called "fixed factors" here), age and repetitions, by clicking each of them, then clicking the arrow next to "Fixed Factor(s)." To include specific descriptive statistics, as well as a measure of effect size, select "Options," then select "Descriptive statistics" and "Estimates of effect size." Then, select "Continue." Finally, click "OK" to run the analysis.

The output in the screenshot shown here includes the same statistics that we calculated earlier. The small differences are due only to rounding decisions. For example, we see that the F statistic for the main effect of age is 13.333. Its p value is found in the column headed "Sig." and is .006. This is well below the typical alpha level of 0.05, which tells us that this is a statistically significant effect. The effect size is found in the final column, "Partial Eta Squared," which can be interpreted as we learned to interpret R^2. The effect size of .625 indicates that this is a very large effect.

HOW IT WORKS

14.1 CONDUCTING A TWO-WAY BETWEEN-GROUPS ANOVA

The online dating Web site Match.com allows users to post personal ads in an effort to meet potential romantic partners. Each person is asked to specify a range from the youngest age that would be acceptable for a dating partner to the oldest acceptable age. The following data were randomly selected from the ads of 25-year-old people living in the New York City area. The scores represent the youngest acceptable ages listed by those in the sample. So, in the first line, the first of the five 25-year-old women who are seeking men states that she will not date a man younger than 26 years old.

25-year-old women seeking men: 26, 24, 25, 24, 25

25-year-old men seeking women: 18, 21, 22, 22, 18

25-year-old women seeking women: 22, 25, 22, 25, 25

25-year-old men seeking men: 23, 25, 24, 22, 20

There are two independent variables and one dependent variable. The first independent variable is gender of the seeker, and its levels are male and female. The second independent variable is gender of the person being sought, and its levels are men and women. The dependent variable is the youngest acceptable age of the person being sought. Based on these variables, how can we conduct a two-way between-groups ANOVA on these data? The cell means are:

	Female seekers	Male seekers
Men sought	24.8	22.8
Women sought	23.8	20.2

Here are the six steps of hypothesis testing for this example.

Step 1: Population 1 (female, men): Women seeking men. Population 2 (male, women): Men seeking women. Population 3 (female, women): Women seeking women. Population 4 (male, men): Men seeking men.

The comparison distributions will be F distributions. The hypothesis test will be a two-way between-groups ANOVA. Assumptions: The data are not from random samples, so we must generalize with caution. From these small sample sizes, it's hard to tell if the underlying population distributions are normal, so we should proceed with caution. The homogeneity of variance assumption is violated because the largest variance (3.70) is more than five times as large as the smallest variance (0.70). For the purposes of demonstration, we will proceed anyway.

Step 2:   The hypotheses for the main effect of the first independent variable, gender of seeker, are as follows: Null hypothesis: On average, male and female seekers report the same youngest acceptable ages for their partners—H_0: $\mu_M = \mu_F$. Research hypothesis: On average, male and female seekers report different youngest acceptable ages for their partners—H_0: $\mu_M \neq \mu_F$.

The hypotheses for the main effect of the second independent variable, gender of person sought, are as follows: Null hypothesis: On average, those seeking men and those seeking women report the same youngest acceptable ages for their partners—H_0: $\mu_M = \mu_W$. Research hypothesis: On average, those seeking men and those seeking women report different youngest acceptable ages for their partners—H_0: $\mu_M \neq \mu_W$.

The hypotheses for the interaction of gender of seeker and gender of person sought are as follows: Null hypothesis: The effect of the gender of the seeker on the youngest acceptable ages for partners does not depend on the gender of the person sought. Research hypothesis: The effect of the gender of the seeker on the youngest acceptable ages for partners does depend on the gender of the person sought.

Step 3: $df_{columns(seeker)} = 2 - 1 = 1$

$df_{rows(sought)} = 2 - 1 = 1$

$df_{interaction} = (1)(1) = 1$

$df_{within} = df_{F,M} + df_{M,W} + df_{F,M} + df_{M,M} = 4 + 4 + 4 + 4 = 16$

Main effect of gender of seeker: F distribution with 1 and 16 degrees of freedom
Main effect of gender of sought: F distribution with 1 and 16 degrees of freedom
Interaction of seeker and sought: F distribution with 1 and 16 degrees of freedom

Step 4:   Critical F for main effect of seeker: 4.49
Critical F for main effect of sought: 4.49
Critical F for interaction of seeker and sought: 4.49

Step 5: $SS_{total} = \Sigma(X - GM)^2 = 103.800$

$SS_{column(seeker)} = \Sigma(M_{column(seeker)} - GM)^2 = 39.200$

$SS_{row(sought)} = \Sigma(M_{row(sought)} - GM)^2 = 16.200$

$SS_{within} = \Sigma(X - M_{cell})^2 = 45.200$

$SS_{interaction} = SS_{total} - (SS_{row} + SS_{column} + SS_{within}) = 3.200$

Source	SS	df	MS	F
Seeker gender	39.200	1	39.200	13.876
Sought gender	16.200	1	16.200	5.735
Seeker 3 sought	3.200	1	3.200	1.133
Within	45.200	16	2.825	
Total	103.800	19		

Step 6:   There is a significant main effect of gender of the seeker and a significant main effect of gender of the person being sought. We can reject the null hypotheses for both of these main effects. Male seekers are willing to accept younger

partners, on average, than are female seekers. Those seeking women are willing to accept younger partners, on average, than are those seeking men. We cannot reject the null hypothesis for the interaction; we can conclude only that there is not sufficient evidence that the effect of the gender of the seeker on the youngest acceptable age depends on the gender of the person sought.

14.2 CALCULATING EFFECT SIZE FOR A TWO-WAY BETWEEN-GROUPS ANOVA

How can we compute and interpret the effect sizes, R^2, for each main effect and the interaction for the ANOVA we conducted in How It Works 14.1? Here are the effect size calculations and interpretations, according to Cohen's conventions, for each of the three effects.

For the main effect of seeker gender:

$$R^2_{rows} = \frac{SS_{rows}}{(SS_{total} - SS_{columns} - SS_{interaction})} = \frac{39.2}{(103.8 - 16.2 - 3.2)} = 0.46$$

This is a large effect size.

For the main effect of sought gender:

$$R^2_{columns} = \frac{SS_{columns}}{(SS_{total} - SS_{rows} - SS_{interaction})} = \frac{16.2}{(103.8 - 39.2 - 3.2)} = 0.26$$

This is a large effect size.

For the interaction:

$$R^2_{interaction} = \frac{SS_{interaction}}{(SS_{total} - SS_{rows} - SS_{columns})} = \frac{3.2}{(103.8 - 39.2 - 16.2)} = 0.07$$

This is a medium effect size.

EXERCISES

The solutions to the odd-numbered exercises can be found in Appendix C.

Clarifying the Concepts

14.1 What is a two-way ANOVA?

14.2 What is a factor?

14.3 In your own words, define the word *cell*, first as you would use it in everyday conversation and then as a statistician would use it.

14.4 What is a four-way within-groups ANOVA?

14.5 What is the difference in information provided when we say *two-way ANOVA* versus *2 × 3 ANOVA*?

14.6 What are the three different F statistics in a two-way ANOVA?

14.7 What is a marginal mean?

14.8 What are the three ways to identify a statistically significant interaction?

14.9 How do bar graphs help us identify and interpret interactions? Explain how adding lines to the bar graph can help.

14.10 Why is a bar graph a better choice than a line graph for depicting the means of a two-way ANOVA?

14.11 In step 6 of hypothesis testing for a two-way between-groups ANOVA, we make a decision for each F statistic. What are the three possible outcomes with respect to the overall pattern of results?

14.12 When are post hoc tests needed for a two-way between-groups ANOVA?

14.13 Explain the following formula in your own words: $SS_{interaction} = SS_{total} - (SS_{rows} + SS_{columns} + SS_{within})$.

14.14 In your own words, define the word *interaction*, first as you would use it in everyday conversation and then as a statistician would use it.

14.15 What effect-size measure is used with two-way ANOVA?

14.16 What is a two-way mixed-design ANOVA?

14.17 How is an ANCOVA different from an ANOVA?

14.18 How is a MANOVA different from an ANOVA?

14.19 When might a researcher decide to use a MANOVA rather than an ANOVA?

14.20 When might a researcher decide to use an ANCOVA rather than an ANOVA?

14.21 What is a two-way mixed-design MANOVA?

14.22 What is statcheck?

14.23 How is statistical tools' ability to check the consistency of statistics helpful both to individual researchers and to the field as a whole?

Calculating the Statistics

14.24 For each of the following scenarios, what are two names for the ANOVA that would be conducted to analyze the data?

a. A researcher examined the effect of gender and pet ownership (no pets, one pet, more than one pet) on a measure of loneliness.

b. In a study on memory, participants completed a memory task once each week for 4 weeks—twice after sleeping 8 hours and twice after sleeping 4 hours. In each sleep condition, the participants completed the task after ingesting a caffeinated beverage and again, on another day, after ingesting a "placebo" beverage that they were told contained caffeine.

c. A study examined the impact of students' Instagram profiles on numbers of Instagram friends. The researchers were interested in the effect of (1) the profile photo—either an identifiable photo of the student or a photo of someone or something else (e.g., a dog)—and (2) bio length—either short (fewer than 75 characters) or long (75 characters or more).

14.25 Identify the factors and their levels in the following research designs.

a. Men's and women's enjoyment of two different sporting events, Sport 1 and Sport 2, are compared using a 20-point enjoyment scale.

b. The amount of underage drinking, as documented in formal incident reports, is compared at "dry" university campuses (no alcohol at all) and "wet" campuses (those that enforce the legal age for possession of alcohol). Three different types of universities are considered: state institutions, private schools, and schools with a religious affiliation.

c. The extent of contact with juvenile authorities is compared for youth across three age groups (12–13, 14–15, 16–17), considering both gender and family composition (two parents, single parent, or no identified authority figure).

14.26 State how many cells there should be for each of these studies. Then, create an empty grid to represent those cells.

a. Men's and women's enjoyment of two different sporting events, Sport 1 and Sport 2, are compared using a 20-point enjoyment scale.

b. The amount of underage drinking, as documented in formal incident reports, is compared at "dry" university campuses (no alcohol at all) and "wet" campuses (those that enforce the legal age for possession of alcohol). Three different types of universities are considered: state institutions, private schools, and schools with a religious affiliation.

c. The extent of contact with juvenile authorities is compared for youth across three age groups (12–13, 14–15, 16–17), considering both gender and family composition (two parents, single parent, or no identified authority figure).

14.27 Use these "enjoyment" ratings to perform the following tasks:

	Ice hockey	Figure skating
Men	19, 17, 18, 17	6, 4, 8, 3
Women	13, 14, 18, 8	11, 7, 4, 14

a. Calculate the cell and marginal means.

b. Draw a bar graph.

c. Calculate the five different degrees of freedom, and indicate the critical F value based on each set of degrees of freedom, assuming the alpha level is 0.01.

d. Calculate the total sum of squares.

e. Calculate the between-groups sum of squares for the independent variable gender.

f. Calculate the between-groups sum of squares for the independent variable sporting event.

g. Calculate the within-groups sum of squares.

h. Calculate the sum of squares for the interaction.

i. Create a source table.

14.28 Use these data—incidents of reports of underage drinking at universities—to perform the following tasks:

"Dry" campus, state school: 47, 52, 27, 50

"Dry" campus, private school: 25, 33, 31

"Wet" campus, state school: 77, 61, 55, 48

"Wet" campus, private school: 52, 68, 60

a. Calculate the cell and marginal means. Notice the unequal Ns.

b. Draw a bar graph.

c. Calculate the five different degrees of freedom, and indicate the critical F value based on each set of degrees of freedom, assuming the alpha level is 0.05.

d. Calculate the total sum of squares.

e. Calculate the between-groups sum of squares for the independent variable campus.

f. Calculate the between-groups sum of squares for the independent variable school.

g. Calculate the within-groups sum of squares.

h. Calculate the sum of squares for the interaction.

i. Create a source table.

14.29 Using what you know about the expanded source table, fill in the missing values in the table shown here:

Source	SS	df	MS	F
Gender	248.25	1		
Parenting style	84.34	3		
Gender × style	33.60			
Within	1107.20	36		
Total				

14.30 Using the information in the source table provided here, compute R^2 values for each effect. Using Cohen's conventions, explain what these values mean.

Source	SS	df	MS	F
A (rows)	0.267	1	0.267	0.004
B (columns)	3534.008	2	1767.004	24.432
A × B	5.371	2	2.686	0.037
Within	1157.167	16	72.323	
Total	4696.813	21		

14.31 Using the information in the source table provided here, compute R^2 values for each effect. Using Cohen's conventions, explain what these values mean.

Source	SS	df	MS	F
A (rows)	30.006	1	30.006	0.511
B (columns)	33.482	1	33.482	0.570
A × B	1.720	1	1.720	0.029
Within	587.083	10	58.708	
Total	652.291	13		

Applying the Concepts

14.32 **An app for tracking alcohol use, and ANOVA:** In Exercise 13.31 (page 406), we described a study investigating the use of an app for tracking alcohol consumption on the number of drinks a person consumed over a 3-week period. Participants logged each time they had a drink, and the researchers summed the number of drinks that each participant had each week. The researchers analyzed whether there was a significant difference in the number of drinks consumed across the 3 weeks of the study (Poulton, Pana, Bruns, Sinott, & Hestera, 2018). Let's imagine that we've redesigned their study.

a. What are the independent variables and their levels?

b. What kind of ANOVA would we use?

14.33 **Health-related myths and the type of ANOVA:** Consider the study we used as an example for a two-way between-groups ANOVA in this chapter. Older and younger people were randomly assigned to hear either one repetition or three repetitions of a health-related myth, accompanied by the accurate information that "busted" the myth.

a. Explain why this study would be analyzed with a between-groups ANOVA.

b. How could this study be redesigned to use a within-groups ANOVA? (*Hint:* Think long term.)

14.34 **Memory and choosing the type of ANOVA:** In a fictional study, a cognitive psychologist studied memory for names after a group activity. The researcher randomly assigned 120 participants to one of three conditions: (1) group members introduced themselves once, (2) group members were introduced by the experimenter and by themselves, and (3) group members were introduced by the experimenter and themselves, and they wore name tags throughout the group activity.

a. How could the researcher redesign this study so it would be analyzed with a two-way between-groups ANOVA? Be specific. (*Note:* There are several possible ways that the researcher could do this.)

b. How could the researcher redesign this study so it would be analyzed with a two-way mixed-design ANOVA? Be specific. (*Note:* There are several possible ways the researcher could do this.)

14.35 **Anger, culture, and choosing the type of ANOVA:** Researchers explored the effect of the expression of anger on physical health in two cultures—the United States and Japan (Kitayama et al., 2015). They noted that previous research linked the expression of anger with health problems, but this research had been conducted in Western cultures. In their cross-cultural study, the researchers found that high levels of anger (compared with low levels of anger) led to worse health, including higher blood pressure, among American participants, but better health among Japanese participants. The researchers speculate that in the United States, anger tends to indicate that people have experienced negative events. The researchers believe that, in Japan, anger tends to indicate that people feel "empowered and entitled"—positive feelings that tend to occur only among people in Japan who have more control over their lives.

a. List any independent variables, along with the levels.

b. What is the dependent variable?

c. What kind of ANOVA would the researchers use?

d. Name this ANOVA using the more specific language that enumerates the numbers of levels.

e. Use your answer to part (d) to calculate the number of cells. Explain how you made this calculation.

f. Draw a table that depicts the cells of this ANOVA.

g. Is this a quantitative or qualitative interaction? Explain your answer.

14.36 Racism, juries, and interactions: In a study of racism, Nail, Harton, and Decker (2003) had U.S. participants read a scenario in which a police officer assaulted a motorist. Half the participants read about a black officer who assaulted a white motorist, and half read about a white officer who assaulted a black motorist. Participants were categorized based on political orientation: liberal, moderate, or conservative. Participants were told that the officer was acquitted of assault charges in state court but was found guilty of violating the motorist's rights in federal court. Double jeopardy occurs when an individual is tried twice for the same crime. Participants were asked to rate, on a scale of 1–7, the degree to which the officer had been placed in double jeopardy by the second trial.

The researchers reported the interaction as $F(2, 58) = 10.93, p < 0.0001$. The means for the *liberal* participants were 3.18 for those who read about the black officer and 1.91 for those who read about the white officer. The means for the *moderate* participants were 3.50 for those who read about the black officer and 3.33 for those who read about the white officer. The means for the *conservative* participants were 1.25 for those who read about the black officer and 4.62 for those who read about the white officer.

a. Draw a table of cell means that includes the actual means for this study.

b. Do the reported statistics indicate that there is a significant interaction? If yes, describe the interaction in your own words.

c. Draw a bar graph that depicts the interaction. Include lines that connect the tops of the bars and show the pattern of the interaction.

d. Is this a quantitative or qualitative interaction? Explain.

e. Change the cell mean for the conservative participants who read about a black officer so that this is now a quantitative interaction.

f. Draw a bar graph that depicts the pattern that includes the new cell means.

g. Change the cell means for the moderate and conservative participants who read about a black officer so that there is now no interaction.

h. Draw a bar graph that depicts the pattern that includes the new cell means.

14.37 Self-interest, ANOVA, and interactions: Ratner and Miller (2001) wondered whether people are uncomfortable when they act in a way that's not obviously in their own self-interest. They randomly assigned 33 women and 32 men to read a fictional passage saying that government funding would soon be cut for research into a gastrointestinal illness that mostly affected either (1) women or (2) men. They were then asked to rate, on a 1–7 scale, how comfortable they would be "attending a meeting of concerned citizens who share your position" on this cause (p. 11). A higher rating indicates a greater degree of comfort. The journal article reported the statistics for the interaction as $F(1, 58) = 9.83, p < 0.01$. Women who read about women had a mean of 4.88, whereas those who read about men had a mean of 3.56. Men who read about women had a mean of 3.29, whereas those who read about men had a mean of 4.67.

a. What are the independent variables and their levels? What is the dependent variable?

b. What kind of ANOVA did the researchers conduct?

c. Do the reported statistics indicate that there is a significant interaction? Explain your answer.

d. Draw a table that includes the cells of the study. Include the cell means.

e. Draw a bar graph that depicts these findings.

f. Describe the pattern of the interaction in words. Is this a qualitative or a quantitative interaction? Explain your answer.

g. Draw a new table of cells, but change the means for male participants reading about women so that there is now a quantitative, rather than a qualitative, interaction.

h. Draw a bar graph of the means in part (g).

i. Draw a new table of cells, but change the means for male participants reading about women so that there is no interaction.

14.38 Gender, negotiating a salary, and an interaction: Eleanor Barkhorn (2012) reported in *The Atlantic* about differences in women's and men's negotiating styles. She first explained that researchers did not find a significant difference in how likely women and men are to negotiate salaries. But this did not tell the whole story. Barkhorn wrote: "Women are more likely to negotiate when an employer explicitly says that wages are negotiable. Men, on the other hand, are more likely to negotiate when the employer does not directly state that they can negotiate."

For each of the following, state whether the finding is a result of examining a main effect or examining an interaction. Explain your answer.

a. The finding that women and men do not significantly differ, on average, in their likelihood of negotiating.

b. The finding of a gender difference in the circumstances under which one will negotiate.

14.39 The cross-race effect, main effects, and interactions: Hugenberg, Miller, and Claypool (2007) conducted a study to better understand the cross-race effect, in which people have a difficult time recognizing members of different racial groups—colloquially known as the "they all look the same to me" effect. In a variation on this study, white participants in the United States viewed either 20 black faces or 20 white faces for 3 seconds each. Half the participants were told to pay particular attention to distinguishing features of the faces. Later, participants were shown 40 black faces or 40 white faces (the same race that they were shown in the prior stage of the experiment), 20 of which were new. Each participant received a score that measured his or her recognition accuracy.

The researchers reported two effects, one for the race of the people in the pictures, $F(1, 136) = 23.06$, $p < 0.001$, such that white faces were more easily recognized, on average, than black faces. There also was a significant interaction of the race of the people in the pictures and the instructions, $F(1, 136) = 5.27$, $p < 0.05$. When given no instructions, the mean recognition scores were 1.46 for white faces and 1.04 for black faces. When given instructions to pay attention to distinguishing features, the mean recognition scores were 1.38 for white faces and 1.23 for black faces.

a. What are the independent variables and their levels? What is the dependent variable?

b. What kind of ANOVA did the researchers conduct?

c. Do the reported statistics indicate that there is a significant main effect? If yes, describe it.

d. Why is the main effect not sufficient in this situation to understand the findings? Be specific about why the main effect is misleading by itself.

e. Do the reported statistics indicate that there is a significant interaction? Explain your answer.

f. Draw a table that includes the cells of the study and the cell means.

g. Draw a bar graph that depicts these findings.

h. Describe the pattern of the interaction in words. Is this a qualitative or a quantitative interaction? Explain your answer.

14.40 Grade-point average, fraternities, sororities, and two-way between-groups ANOVA: A sample of students from our statistics classes reported their grade-point averages (GPAs), indicated their genders, and stated whether they were in the university's Greek system (i.e., in a fraternity or sorority). Following are the GPAs for the different groups of students:

Men in a fraternity: 2.6, 2.4, 2.9, 3.0
Men not in a fraternity: 3.0, 2.9, 3.4, 3.7, 3.0
Women in a sorority: 3.1, 3.0, 3.2, 2.9
Women not in a sorority: 3.4, 3.0, 3.1, 3.1

a. What are the independent variables and their levels? What is the dependent variable?

b. Draw a table that lists the cells of the study design. Include the cell means.

c. Conduct all six steps of hypothesis testing.

d. Draw a bar graph for all statistically significant effects.

e. Is there a significant interaction? If yes, describe it in words and indicate whether it is a qualitative or a quantitative interaction. Explain.

f. Compute the effect sizes, R^2, for the main effects and interaction. Using Cohen's conventions, interpret the effect-size values.

14.41 Age, online dating, and two-way between-groups ANOVA: The data below were from the same 25-year-old participants described in How It Works 14.1, but now the scores represent the oldest age that would be acceptable in a dating partner.

25-year-old women seeking men: 40, 35, 29, 35, 35
25-year-old men seeking women: 26, 26, 28, 28, 28
25-year-old women seeking women: 35, 35, 30, 35, 45
25-year-old men seeking men: 33, 35, 35, 36, 38

a. What are the independent variables and their levels? What is the dependent variable?

b. Draw a table that lists the cells of the study design. Include the cell means.

c. Conduct all six steps of hypothesis testing.

d. Is there a significant interaction? If yes, describe it in words, indicate whether it is a quantitative or a qualitative interaction, and draw a bar graph.

e. Compute the effect sizes, R^2, for the main effects and interaction. Using Cohen's conventions, interpret the effect-size values.

14.42 Helping, payment, and two-way between-groups ANOVA: Heyman and Ariely (2004) were interested in whether effort and willingness to help were affected by the form and amount of payment offered in return for effort. They predicted that when money was used as payment, in what is called a *money market*, effort would increase as a function of payment level. By comparison, if effort were performed out of altruism, in what is called a *social market,* the level of effort would be consistently high and unaffected by level of payment. In one of their studies, university students were asked to estimate another student's willingness to help load a sofa into a van in return for a cash payment or candy of equivalent value. Willingness to help was assessed using an 11-point scale ranging from "Not at all likely to help" to "Will help for sure." Data are presented here to re-create some of their findings.

Cash payment, low amount of $0.50: 4, 5, 6, 4

Cash payment, moderate amount of $5.00: 7, 8, 8, 7

Candy payment, low amount valued at $0.50: 6, 5, 7, 7

Candy payment, moderate amount valued at $5.00: 8, 6, 5, 5

a. What are the independent variables and their levels?

b. What is the dependent variable?

c. Draw a table that lists the cells of the study design. Include the cell and marginal means.

d. Create a bar graph.

e. Using this graph and the table of cell means, describe what effects you see in the pattern of the data.

f. Write the null and research hypotheses.

g. Complete all of the calculations and construct a full source table for these data.

h. Determine the critical value for each effect at an alpha level of 0.05.

i. Make your decisions. Is there a significant interaction? If yes, describe it in words and indicate whether it is a qualitative or a quantitative interaction. Explain.

j. Compute the effect sizes, R^2, for the main effects and interaction. Using Cohen's conventions, interpret the effect-size values.

k. Why might the researchers want to use a tool like statcheck once they write up their results?

14.43 Helping, payment, and interactions: Expanding on the work of Heyman and Ariely (2004) as described in the previous exercise, let's assume a higher level of payment was included and the following data were collected. (Notice that all data are the same as earlier, with the addition of new data under a high payment amount.)

Cash payment, low amount of $0.50: 4, 5, 6, 4

Cash payment, moderate amount of $5.00: 7, 8, 8, 7

Cash payment, high amount of $50.00: 9, 8, 7, 8

Candy payment, low amount, valued at $0.50: 6, 5, 7, 7

Candy payment, moderate amount, valued at $5.00: 8, 6, 5, 5

Candy payment, high amount, valued at $50.00: 6, 7, 7, 6

a. What are the independent variables and their levels? What is the dependent variable?

b. Draw a table that lists the cells of the study design. Include the cell and marginal means.

c. Create a new bar graph of these data.

d. Do you think there is a significant interaction? If yes, describe it in words.

e. Now that one independent variable has three levels, which additional analyses are needed? Explain what you would do and why. Based on the graph you created, where do you think there would be significant differences?

14.44 Exercise, well-being, and type of ANOVA: Cox, Thomas, Hinton, and Donahue (2006) studied the effects of exercise on well-being. There were three independent variables: age (18–20 years old, 35–45 years old), intensity of exercise (low, moderate, high), and time point (15, 20, 25, and 30 minutes). The dependent variable was positive well-being. Every participant was assessed at all intensity levels and all time points. (Generally, moderate-intensity exercise and high-intensity exercise led to higher levels of positive well-being than did low-intensity exercise.)

a. What type of ANOVA would the researchers conduct?

b. The researchers included two covariates related to the physical effects of exercise, measures of hemoglobin and serum ferritin. Which statistical test would they use? Explain.

c. The researchers conducted separate analyses for three dependent variables: perceived fatigue, psychological distress, and positive well-being. If they wanted to include all three dependent variables in the analysis described in part (a), which statistical test would they use? Explain.

d. If the researchers wanted to use all three dependent variables in the analysis described in part (b), the analysis that included covariates, which statistical test would they use? Explain.

14.45 Body weight, salary, and the need for covariates: A nutritional software program called DietPower offers encouragement to its users when they sign in each day. In one instance, the program states that people at their ideal body weight tend to have higher salaries than do people who are overweight and then explicitly states that losing weight might lead to an increase in pay!

a. Why is this a problematic statement? List at least two confounding variables that might affect this finding.

b. Imagine that you were going to conduct a study that compared the salaries of two groups: people who were overweight and people who were at their ideal body weight. Why would it be useful to include one or more covariates? What scale variables might you include as covariates?

14.46 Math performance and type of ANOVA: Imagine that a university professor is interested in the effects of a new instructional method on the math performance of first-year university students. All students take a math pretest and then are randomly assigned to a class in which the new instructional method is used or a class in which the old method is used. At the end of the semester, the professor gives all students the same final exam and has all students complete a national standardized test that assesses math ability.

a. What is the independent variable and what are its levels?

b. Which scale variable could the professor use as a covariate in the statistical analysis of this study?

c. What are the dependent variables assessed by the professor?

d. Which type of ANOVA could be used to analyze the results of this study?

14.47 College students, anxiety, depression, and a MANOVA: Jason Nelson and Noel Gregg (2012)

conducted a study of colege students with disabilities. They reported that: "A $3 \times 3 \times 2$ MANOVA was conducted to determine the effect of level of educational attainment (transitioning adolescents and college underclassmen—that is, freshmen and sophomores—and college upperclassmen—that is, juniors and seniors), disability status (dyslexia, ADHD, and ADHD/dyslexia), and gender on BDI-II and BAI scores" (p. 249). (The BDI is the Beck Depression Inventory, which assesses symptoms of depression; the BAI is the Beck Anxiety Inventory, which assesses symptoms of anxiety.)

a. What are the independent variables in this study and what are their levels?

b. What are the dependent variables in this study?

c. Based on these variables, explain why the researchers conducted a MANOVA.

d. The researchers report that there was only one significant effect in this MANOVA. Specifically, "Tukey's *HSD* post hoc tests indicated college underclassmen with disabilities had higher BAI ($M = 9.10$, $SD = 8.37$) and BDI-II scores ($M = 9.30$, $SD = 8.92$) than did transitioning adolescents with disabilities (BAI: $M = 5.18$, $SD = 6.18$; BDI-II: $M = 4.50$, $SD = 5.40$). The effect sizes for these group differences on the BAI ($d = .50$) and BDI-II ($d = .59$) were medium in magnitude."

i. Put these findings into plain English and in your own words.

ii. Explain why the researchers conducted Tukey *HSD* tests.

iii. Why did the researchers report Cohen's *d* when they conducted a form of ANOVA (i.e., MANOVA)? (*Hint:* Think about the number of means in their comparisons.)

14.48 Gender, pizza, and an interaction: Researchers examined whether men and women eat different amounts of food in the company of same-sex dining partners versus opposite-sex dining partners (Kniffin, Sigirci, & Wansink, 2016). From an evolutionary perspective, the researchers wondered which of the following two hypotheses would receive support: (1) Men—most of them presumably heterosexual—would show off by eating more in the presence of women to attract a mate; or (2) men would show off by eating more in the presence of other men in an effort to demonstrate status or dominance. Restaurant diners were observed eating lunch. Research assistants counted the number of pizza slices eaten by each diner in the study, along with the genders of their dining companions. The graph here depicts the results.

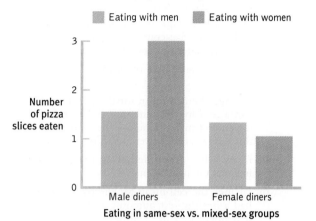

Eating in same-sex vs. mixed-sex groups

a. Based on this graph, what type of ANOVA did the researchers conduct?

b. Does it seem as if there is a main effect of the gender of the diner? If yes, explain the effect in your own words. If not, explain your answer.

c. Does it seem as if there is a main effect of type of the gender of the diner's lunch companion? If yes, explain the effect in your own words. If not, explain your answer.

d. Describe the interaction in your own words. Is this a quantitative interaction or a qualitative interaction? Explain your answer.

e. Which of the competing hypotheses received support from this study?

f. A link from the online version of the published article leads readers to additional information, including that the researchers conducted "a robustness check that affirms the main findings" of the study. The researchers also provide their data and details on the specific ways in which they conducted their statistical analyses. Explain, based on the concepts of severe testing and the open science movement, why the researchers might have provided this information.

14.49 **Negotiation, an interaction, and a graph:** German psychologist David Loschelder and his colleagues (2014) conducted an experiment on negotiations. They cited tennis player Andy Roddick's agent, who thought it was always detrimental to make an initial offer: "The first offer gives you an insight into [the other party's] thought process." The researchers wondered if this was always true. So, they conducted an experiment with two independent variables. One independent variable was the person's role in the negotiations—either the person starting the negotiation (the sender) or the person being targeted (the receiver). The second independent variable was the type of information in the initial offer—different or the same. That is, the sender was either asking for something that is different from what the other partner wanted or asking for something that the other person also wanted. For example, if you are negotiating with a new employer, you might ask for five weeks of vacation and a higher salary than you think you can get. And maybe the employer was already prepared to give you five weeks vacation. So, the researchers thought the type of information that matches what the other person wants (like the information about vacation time) might give the receiver a bargaining chip. Knowing what the sender really wants might let you lowball on other aspects of the negotiation. So, the employer can then grant the vacation time, and perhaps not have to offer the higher salary. The graph here depicts the results of this experiment, in which success in the negotiation was measured in the percentage of a pool of money that could be earned.

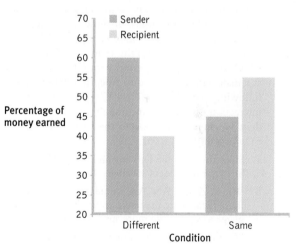

a. Based on this graph, which type of ANOVA did the researchers conduct?

b. Does it seem as if there's a main effect of role in the negotiations (sender or receiver)? If yes, explain the effect in your own words. If not, explain your answer.

c. Does it seem as if there's a main effect of type of information provided? If yes, explain the effect in your own words? If not, explain your answer.

d. Describe the interaction in your own words. Is this a quantitative interaction or a qualitative interaction? Explain your answer.

e. Based on what you learned about graphing in Chapter 3, explain an important problem with the *y*-axis.

Putting It All Together

14.50 **Skepticism, self-interest, and two-way ANOVA:** A study on motivated skepticism examined whether participants were more likely to be skeptical when it served their self-interest (Ditto & Lopez, 1992). Ninety-three participants completed a fictitious medical test that told them they had high levels of a certain enzyme, TAA. Participants were randomly assigned to be told either that high levels of TAA had potentially unhealthy consequences or potentially healthy consequences. They were also randomly assigned to complete a dependent measure before or after the TAA test. The dependent measure assessed their perception of the accuracy of the TAA test on a scale of 1 (very inaccurate) to 9 (very accurate). Ditto and Lopez found the following means for those who completed the dependent measure before taking the TAA test: unhealthy result, 6.6; healthy result, 6.9. They found the following means for those who completed the dependent measure after taking the TAA test: unhealthy result, 5.6; healthy result, 7.3. From their ANOVA, they reported statistics for two findings. For the main effect of test outcome, they reported the following statistic: $F(1, 73) = 7.74, p < 0.01$. For the interaction of test outcome and timing of the dependent measure, they reported the following statistic: $F(1, 73) = 4.01, p < 0.05$.

a. State the independent variables and their levels. State the dependent variable.

b. Which kind of ANOVA would be used to analyze these data? State the name using the original language as well as the more specific language.

c. Use the more specific language of ANOVA to calculate the number of cells in this research design.

d. Draw a table of cell means, marginal means, and the grand mean. Assume that equal numbers of participants were assigned to each cell (even though this was not the case in the actual study).

e. Describe the significant main effect in your own words.

f. Draw a bar graph that depicts the main effect.

g. Why is the main effect misleading by itself?

h. Is the main effect qualified by a statistically significant interaction? Explain. Describe the interaction in your own words.

i. Draw a bar graph that depicts the interaction. Include lines that connect the tops of the bars and show the pattern of the interaction.

j. Is this a quantitative or qualitative interaction? Explain.

k. Change the cell mean for the participants who had a healthy test outcome and completed the dependent measure before the TAA test so that this is now a qualitative interaction.

l. Draw a bar graph depicting the pattern that includes the new cell mean.

m. Change the cell mean for the participants who had a healthy test outcome and completed the dependent measure before the TAA test so that there is now no interaction.

n. Draw a bar graph that depicts the pattern that includes the new cell mean.

14.51 **Feedback and ANOVA:** Stacey Finkelstein and Ayelet Fishbach (2012) examined the impact of feedback in the learning process. The following is an excerpt from their abstract: "This article explores what feedback people seek and respond to. We predict and find a shift from positive to negative feedback as people gain expertise. We document this shift in a variety of domains, including feedback on language acquisition, pursuit of environmental causes, and use of consumer products. Across these domains, novices sought and responded to positive feedback, and experts sought and responded to negative feedback" (p. 22).

a. Based on the abstract, what are the independent variables and what are their levels?

b. What are possible dependent variables, based on the description in the abstract?

c. The researchers conducted several experiments, one of which examined students in beginning and advanced French classes. Here is the result of one analysis: "The analysis also yielded the predicted expertise × feedback interaction $(F(1, 79) = 7.31, p < .01)$." Is this interaction statistically significant? Explain your answer.

d. Which important statistic is missing from their report? Why would it be helpful to include this statistic?

e. The results in part (c) are represented by the accompanying graph. We would, of course, have to conduct additional analyses to know exactly which bars are significantly different from each other. That said, what does the overall pattern seem to indicate for this analysis?

f. How would you redesign this graph in line with what you learned in Chapter 3? Give at least two specific suggestions.

g. This study was conducted in the United States. Is this likely to be a sample from a WEIRD population? Explain your answer.

h. Why would it be helpful for the researchers to include a COG (constraints on generality) statement? In your answer, explain what a COG statement is.

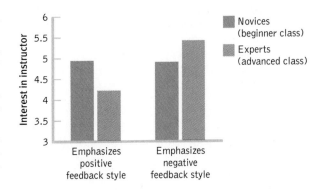

LaunchPad
macmillan learning

Visit LaunchPad to access the e-book and to test your knowledge with LearningCurve.

TERMS

interaction (p. 411)

two-way ANOVA (p. 411)

factorial ANOVA (p. 411)

factor (p. 411)

cell (p. 413)

main effect (p. 414)

quantitative interaction (p. 417)

qualitative interaction (p. 417)

marginal mean (p. 417)

mixed-design ANOVA (p. 437)

multivariate analysis of variance (MANOVA) (p. 437)

analysis of covariance (ANCOVA) (p. 437)

covariate (p. 437)

multivariate analysis of covariance (MANCOVA) (p. 437)

FORMULAS

$df_{rows} = N_{rows} - 1$ (p. 428)

$df_{columns} = N_{columns} - 1$ (p. 428)

$df_{interaction} = (df_{rows})(df_{columns})$ (p. 428)

$df_{within} = df_{cell\,1} + df_{cell\,2} + df_{cell\,3} \cdots + df_{cell\,last}$
(p. 428)

$df_{total} = N_{total} - 1$ (p. 429)

$SS_{total} = \Sigma(X - GM)^2$ for each score   (p. 430)

$SS_{between(rows)} = \Sigma(M_{row} - GM)^2$ for each score   (p. 431)

$SS_{between(columns)} = \Sigma(M_{column} - GM)^2$ for each score   (p. 432)

$SS_{within} = \Sigma(X - M_{cell})^2$ for each score   (p. 432)

$SS_{between(interaction)} = SS_{total} - (SS_{between(rows)} + SS_{between(columns)} + SS_{within})$ (p. 434)

$R^2_{rows} = \dfrac{SS_{rows}}{(SS_{total} - SS_{columns} - SS_{interaction})}$
(p. 435)

$R^2_{columns} = \dfrac{SS_{columns}}{(SS_{total} - SS_{rows} - SS_{interaction})}$
(p. 436)

$R^2_{interaction} = \dfrac{SS_{interaction}}{(SS_{total} - SS_{rows} - SS_{columns})}$
(p. 436)

Correlation

BEFORE YOU GO ON

- You should know the difference between correlational research and experimental research (Chapter 1).

- You should understand how to calculate the deviations of scores from a mean (Chapter 4).

- You should understand the concept of sum of squares (Chapter 4).

- You should understand the six steps of hypothesis testing (Chapter 7).

- You should understand the concept of effect size (Chapter 8).

Eric Audras/PhotoAlto/Alamy

A Correlation Between Cheating and Grades Does cheating lead to poorer grades? Researchers can't say whether cheating causes lower grades, but there is a negative correlation between cheating and final exam grade.

John Snow's map of the London cholera epidemic (Chapter 1) revealed a *correlation*, a systematic association (or relation) between two variables. Researchers from the Massachusetts Institute of Technology (MIT) also used a correlation to reveal the dangers of academic cheating (Palazzo, Lee, Warnakulasooriya, & Pritchard, 2010). They compared the final exam scores of 428 physics students with how frequently they had copied computerized homework assignments from classmates. They assumed that the minority of students who finished their homework within a ridiculously short time—less than 10% of them—had cheated. You might expect cheating to boost grades—after all, that is the point of cheating, isn't it? But you'd be wrong. The more a student cheated during the semester (variable 1), the lower his or her final exam grade (variable 2) was.

What might be going on here? Students' preexisting abilities in math and physics were not correlated with cheating, so these were not weak students who were also incompetent at cheating. Their computerized homework revealed a correlation that suggested another possible answer: Cheaters procrastinated by starting their homework too late to complete it without cheating. Did they have outside jobs, suffer from anxiety, or have other commitments that cut into homework time? *Correlations can't tell us which explanation is right*, but they can force us to think about the possible explanations.

This chapter demonstrates how to (1) assess the direction and size of a correlation, (2) identify limitations of correlation, and (3) calculate the most common form of correlation: *r*, the Pearson correlation coefficient. We then use the six steps of hypothesis testing to determine whether a correlation is statistically significant.

The Meaning of Correlation

A correlation is exactly what its name suggests: a co-relation between two variables. Lots of everyday observations are co-related: junk food eaten and body fat, distance driven and the wear on tires, air conditioner usage and the electric bill. If you can measure any two variables, you can calculate the degree to which they are co-related.

- A **correlation coefficient** is a statistic that quantifies a relation between two variables.

- A **positive correlation** is an association between two variables such that participants with high scores on one variable tend to have high scores on the other variable as well, and those with low scores on one variable tend to have low scores on the other variable.

The Characteristics of Correlation

A **correlation coefficient** *is a statistic that quantifies a relation between two variables.* In this chapter, we learn how to quantify a relation—that is, we learn to calculate a correlation coefficient—when the data are linearly related. A linear relation means that the data form an overall pattern through which it would make sense to draw a straight line—that is, the dots on a scatterplot are roughly clustered around a line, rather than, say, a curve. You can actually see—and understand—the data story with just a glance. There are three main characteristics of the correlation coefficient.

1. The correlation coefficient can be either positive or negative.
2. The correlation coefficient always falls between −1.00 and 1.00.
3. It is the strength (also called the *magnitude*) of the coefficient, not its sign, that indicates how large it is.

The first important characteristic of the correlation coefficient is that it can be either positive or negative. A positive correlation has a positive sign (e.g., +0.32, or more typically, just 0.32), and a negative correlation has a negative sign (e.g., −0.32). *A **positive correlation** is an association between two variables such that participants with high scores on one variable tend to have high scores on the other variable as well, and those with low scores on one variable tend to have low scores on the other variable.*

Contrary to what some people think, when participants with low scores on one variable tend to have low scores on the other, it is *not* a negative correlation. A positive correlation describes a situation in which participants tend to have *similar* scores, with respect to the mean and spread, on both variables—whether both scores are low, medium, or high. The line that summarizes a scatterplot with a positive correlation slopes upward and to the right.

MASTERING THE CONCEPT

15-1: The sign indicates the direction of the correlation, positive or negative. A positive correlation occurs when people who are high on one variable tend to be high on the other as well, and people who are low on one variable tend to be low on the other. A negative correlation occurs when people who are high on one variable tend to be low on the other.

EXAMPLE 15.1

The scatterplot in Figure 15.1 shows a positive correlation between the numbers of words infants hear and their vocabulary 2 years later. These data are based on actual findings by researcher Rochelle Newman and her colleagues (2016). (The means and standard deviations are similar, although the overall correlation is somewhat higher than in the original research.) The *x*-axis reflects the number of different words infants' mothers used during a 15-minute play session when their children were younger than 7 months. The *y*-axis reflects the child's vocabulary size at age 2.

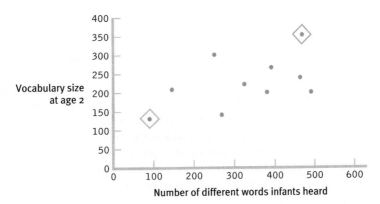

FIGURE 15-1

A Positive Correlation

These data points depict a positive correlation between the diversity of vocabulary infants hear from their mothers and their vocabulary at age 2. Those who hear more different words at a very young age tend to have bigger vocabularies at age 2, and those who hear fewer different words tend to have smaller vocabularies later on.

For example, the dot in the green diamond indicates a child whose mother used only 91 different words when she or he was an infant and had a vocabulary of 132 words at age 2; this child was lower than average on both scores. The dot in the red diamond is for a child who heard 469 different words as an infant during the same 15-minute play session, and then had a vocabulary of 353 different words at age 2; this child is higher than average on both scores. This makes sense because a good deal of research indicates that children who hear more words from their parents develop better language skills, on average. ●

EXAMPLE 15.2

● A **negative correlation** is an association between two variables in which participants with high scores on one variable tend to have low scores on the other variable.

The scatterplot in Figure 15-2 shows the negative correlation of −0.43 between cheating and final exam grade for the MIT study. *A **negative correlation** is an association between two variables in which participants with high scores on one variable tend to have low scores on the other variable.* The line that summarizes a scatterplot with a negative correlation slopes downward and to the right. Each dot represents one person's values on both variables. The proportion of homework copied during the semester is on the horizontal *x*-axis, and the final exam grade (converted to standardized *z* scores) is on the vertical *y*-axis. For example, the dot in the green diamond indicates a student who copied less than 0.2, or 20%, of the homework, and scored almost 2 standard deviations above the mean on the final exam. The dot in the red diamond indicates a student who copied almost 80% of the homework and scored more than 3 standard deviations below the mean on the final exam. Even though most dots are not as extreme as the pattern of the two students we just described, the overall trend is for students who copied more to perform more poorly on the final—a linear relation.

FIGURE 15-2

A Negative Correlation

In this negative correlation from the MIT study, those students who cheat more tend to have a lower final grade; those who cheat less tend to have a higher final grade.

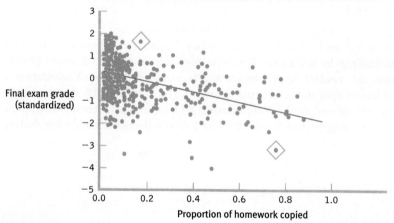

A second important characteristic of the correlation coefficient is that it always falls between −1.00 and 1.00. Both −1.00 and 1.00 are perfect correlations. If we calculate a coefficient that is outside this range, we have made a mistake in the calculations. A correlation coefficient of 1.00 indicates a perfect positive correlation; every point on the scatterplot falls on one line, as seen in the imaginary relation between absences and exam grades depicted in Figure 15-3. Higher scores on one variable are associated with higher

MASTERING THE CONCEPT

15-2: A correlation coefficient always falls between −1.00 and 1.00. The size of the coefficient, not its sign, indicates how large it is.

FIGURE 15-3

A Perfect Positive Correlation

Every dot falls exactly on a straight line that moves up and to the right. This perfect, positive correlation is not real. More absences almost certainly don't lead to higher grades—and certainly they don't for every student.

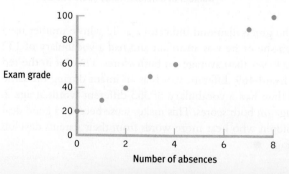

scores on the other variable, and lower scores on one variable are associated with lower scores on the other variable. When a correlation coefficient is either −1.00 or 1.00, knowing someone's score on one variable tells you exactly what that person's score is on the other variable: The scores are perfectly related.

A correlation coefficient of −1.00 indicates a perfect negative correlation. Every point on the scatterplot falls on one line, as seen in the imaginary relation between absences and exam grades depicted in Figure 15-4, but now higher scores on one variable go with lower scores on the other variable. As with a perfect positive correlation, knowing someone's score on one variable tells you that person's exact score on the other variable. A correlation of 0.00 falls right in the middle of the two extremes and indicates no correlation—no association between the two variables.

The third useful characteristic of the correlation coefficient is that its sign—positive or negative—indicates only the direction of the association, not the strength or size of the association. So a correlation coefficient of −0.35 is the same size as one of 0.35. A correlation coefficient of −0.67 is larger than one of 0.55. Don't be fooled by a negative sign; the sign indicates the *direction* of the relation, not the *strength*.

The strength of the correlation is determined by how close to "perfect" the data points are. The closer the data points are to the imaginary line that one could draw through them, the closer the correlation is to being perfect (either −1.00 or 1.00), and the stronger the relation between the two variables is. The farther the points are from this imaginary line, the farther the correlation is from being perfect (and so, closer to 0.00), and the weaker the relation between the two variables is.

How big does a correlation coefficient have to be to be considered important? As he did for effect sizes, Jacob Cohen (1988) published standards, shown in Table 15-1, to help us interpret the correlation coefficient. Very few findings in the behavioral sciences have correlation coefficients of 0.50 or larger because any particular outcome—a student's exam grade, for example—is likely influenced by

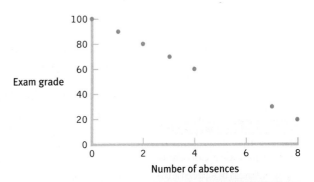

Exam grade / **Number of absences**

FIGURE 15-4

A Perfect Negative Correlation

When every pair of scores falls on the same line on a scatterplot and higher scores on one variable are associated with lower scores on the other variable, there is a perfect negative correlation of −1.00, a situation that almost never happens in real life.

The Seesawing Negative Correlation When two variables are negatively correlated, a high score on one variable indicates a likely low score on the other variable—just like children on a seesaw.

TABLE 15-1 How Strong Is an Association?

Cohen (1988) published guidelines to help researchers determine the strength of a correlation from the correlation coefficient. In behavioral science research, however, it is extremely unusual to have a correlation as high as 0.50, and some researchers have disputed the utility of Cohen's conventions for many behavioral science contexts.

Size of the Correlation	Correlation Coefficient
Small	0.10
Medium	0.30
Large	0.50

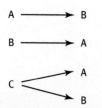

FIGURE 15-5

Three Possible Causal Explanations for a Correlation

Any correlation can be explained in one of several ways. The first variable, A, might cause the second variable, B. Or the reverse could be true—the second variable, B, could cause the first variable, A. Finally, a third variable, C, could cause both A and B. In fact, there could be many "third" variables.

MASTERING THE CONCEPT

15-3: Just because two variables are related, it doesn't mean one causes the other. It could be that the first causes the second, the second causes the first, or a third variable causes both. Correlation does not indicate causation.

many variables. For example, a student's exam grade is likely influenced by absences from class, attention level, hours of studying, interest in the subject matter, and IQ, among other things. So, the correlation of −0.43 between cheating and exam grades found among MIT students is a large correlation for the behavioral sciences.

Correlation Is Not Causation

In addition to appreciating what correlations indicate about the relation between variables, you also need to understand what correlations do *not* reveal about that relation. Correlations *only* provide clues to causality; they do *not* demonstrate or test for causality; they *only* quantify the strength and direction of the relation between variables. Your appreciation for what correlations do *not* reveal suggests that you are thinking scientifically. For example, we know that there was a strong negative correlation in the MIT study between cheating and final exam grade; it is not unreasonable to think that cheating causes bad grades. However, there are three possible reasons for this observed correlation.

First, variable A (cheating) could cause variable B (poor grades). Second, variable B (poor grades) could cause variable A (cheating). Third, variable C (some other influence) could cause the correlation between variable A (cheating) and variable B (poor grades). You can think of these three possibilities as the A-B-C model (Figure 15-5).

Knowing that correlation does *not* imply causation coaxes our brains into thinking of alternative explanations. The MIT researchers found that physics and math ability did not correlate with cheating, so that's an unlikely answer. But we also mentioned working, anxiety, and other time commitments. You can probably think of even more possibilities.

Here's another real-life example. Researchers studied the exercise habits of almost 9000 older adults in Denmark (Schnohr et al., 2018). They found positive correlations between longevity (how long people lived) and the number of hours per week that participants typically engaged in the solitary pursuits of running or cycling. The more people cycled or ran, the longer they lived. But the researchers found much stronger positive correlations between longevity and weekly hours of engagement in group exercise activities such as tennis and soccer, suggesting that the social aspects of group sports may lead to longer lives. That could be true, but we can't draw any causal conclusions from a correlational study. It may not be the social aspects of the sport that increase lifespan; perhaps the real cause is something about the people who choose these particular sports. Were the tennis and soccer players generally outgoing, which is why they chose social sports? Were they already in better shape, and so less concerned with others observing their fitness? Were the cognitive aspects of tennis and soccer—having to make strategic decisions—related to longevity? Even the researchers addressed their study's limitations stemming from the lack of random assignment, noting "we cannot be sure that the associations observed in our study represent a causal relationship" (p. 1783). Never confuse correlation with causation.

One final caveat: Correlation may not even always be correlation. Perhaps two things are statistically associated just by chance and have no actual underlying relation. Type I errors can occur with correlation, too, and if you look hard enough, you're bound to find some strange things that relate to each other. Tyler Vigen hosts a fun Web site called Spurious Correlations. A ***spurious correlation*** *is one in which two variables vary together, but there is no connection between the variables. Instead, their quantitative association is due purely to chance.* Among the crazy, probably-not-true correlations he's highlighted are a link between the number of letters in the winning word in the U.S. national spelling bee and the number of fatalities from poisonous spider bites. Should the spelling bee organizers choose shorter words to save the lives of potential spider-bite victims? Of course not. This correlation is almost certainly spurious. (We'll explore spurious correlations in more depth in this chapter's data ethics feature.)

● A **spurious correlation** is one in which two variables vary together, but there is no connection between the variables. Instead, their quantitative association is due purely to chance.

CHECK YOUR LEARNING

Reviewing the Concepts
> A correlation coefficient is a statistic that quantifies a relation between two variables.

> The correlation coefficient always falls between −1.00 and 1.00.

> When two variables are related such that people with high scores on one variable tend to have high scores on the other, and people with low scores on one variable tend to have low scores on the other, we describe the variables as positively correlated.

> When two variables are related such that people with high scores on one variable tend to have low scores on the other, we describe the variables as negatively correlated.

> When two variables are not related, there is no correlation and they have a correlation coefficient close to 0.

> The strength of a correlation, captured by the number value of the coefficient, is independent of its sign. Cohen established standards for evaluating the strength of association.

> Correlation is not equivalent to causation. In fact, a correlation does not help us evaluate the merits of different causal explanations.

> When two variables are correlated, this association might occur because the first variable, A, causes the second, B; or because the second variable, B, causes the first, A. Alternatively, a third variable, C, could cause both of the correlated variables, A and B.

> Spurious correlations are associations that look real—and are statistically significantly correlated—but are probably not true links.

Clarifying the Concepts   **15-1**   There are three main characteristics of the correlation coefficient. What are they?

15-2   Why doesn't correlation indicate causation?

Calculating the Statistics   **15-3**   Use Cohen's guidelines to describe the strength of the following coefficients:

a. −0.60

b. 0.35

c. 0.04

15-4   Draw a hypothetical scatterplot to depict the following correlation coefficients:

a. −0.60

b. 0.35

c. 0.04

continued on next page

Applying the Concepts

15-5 A writer for *Runner's World* magazine debated the merits of running while listening to music (Seymour, 2006). The writer interviewed a clinical psychologist, whose response to the debate about whether to listen to music while running was: "I like to do what the great ones do and try to emulate that. What are the Kenyans doing?"

Let's say a researcher conducted a study in which he determined the correlation between the percentage of a country's marathon runners who train while listening to music and the average marathon finishing time for that country's runners. (Note that in this case the participants are countries, not people.) Let's say the researcher finds a strong positive correlation. That is, the greater the proportion of a country's runners who train with music, the longer the average marathon finishing time. Remember, in a marathon, a longer time is bad. So this fictional finding is that training with music is associated with slower marathon finishing times; the United States, for example, would have a higher percentage of music use and higher (slower) finishing times than Kenya.

Using the A–B–C model, provide three possible explanations for this finding.

Solutions to these Check Your Learning questions can be found in Appendix D.

The Pearson Correlation Coefficient

• The **Pearson correlation coefficient** is a statistic that quantifies a linear relation between two scale variables.

The most widely used correlation coefficient is the ***Pearson correlation coefficient****, a statistic that quantifies a linear relation between two scale variables.* In other words, a single number is used to describe the direction and strength of the relation between two variables when their overall pattern indicates a straight-line relation. The Pearson correlation coefficient is symbolized by the italic letter r when it is a statistic based on sample data and by the Greek letter ρ (written as "rho" and pronounced "row," even though it looks a bit like the Latin letter p). We use ρ when we're referring to the population parameter for the correlation coefficient, such as when we're writing the hypotheses for significance testing.

Calculating the Pearson Correlation Coefficient

The correlation coefficient can be used as a descriptive statistic that describes the direction and strength of an association between two variables. However, it can also be used as an inferential statistic that relies on a hypothesis test to determine whether the correlation coefficient is significantly different from 0 (no correlation). In this section, we construct a scatterplot from the data and learn how to calculate the correlation coefficient. Then we walk through the steps of hypothesis testing.

EXAMPLE 15.3

Every couple of semesters, we have a student who avows that she does not have to attend statistics classes regularly to do well because she can learn it all from the book. What do you think? Table 15-2 displays the data for 10 students in one of our statistics classes. The second column shows the number of absences over the semester (out of 29 classes total) for each student, and the third column shows each student's final exam grade.

TABLE 15-2	Is Skipping Class Related to Statistics Exam Grades?

Here are the scores for 10 students on two scale variables: number of absences from class in one semester and exam grade.

Student	Absences	Exam Grade
1	4	82
2	2	98
3	2	76
4	3	68
5	1	84
6	0	99
7	4	67
8	8	58
9	7	50
10	3	78

Let's begin with a visual exploration of the scatterplot in Figure 15-6. The data, overall, have a pattern through which we could imagine drawing a straight line, so it makes sense to use the Pearson correlation coefficient. Look more closely at the scatterplot. Are the dots clustered closely around the imaginary line? If they are, then the correlation is probably close to 1.00 or −1.00; if they are not, then the correlation is probably closer to 0.00.

A positive correlation results when a high score (above the mean) on one variable tends to indicate a high score (also above the mean) on the other variable. A negative correlation results when a high score (above the mean) on one variable tends to indicate a low score (below the mean) on the other variable. We can determine whether an individual falls above or below the mean by calculating deviations from the mean for each score. If participants tend to have two positive deviations (both scores above the mean) or two negative deviations (both scores below the mean), then the two

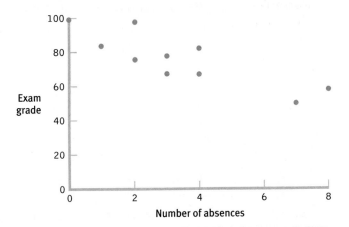

FIGURE 15-6

Always Start with a Scatterplot

Let your eyes do the work! Look at the scatterplot *before* calculating a correlation coefficient. Do the dots appear to form a straight line? Do they flow up and to the right (positive) or down and to the right (negative)? The dots in this scatterplot cluster tightly around an imaginary straight line that goes down and to the right so the correlation will probably be fairly close to −1.00.

variables are likely to be positively correlated. If participants tend to have one positive deviation (above the mean) and one negative deviation (below the mean), then the two variables are likely to be negatively correlated. That's a big part of how the formula for the correlation coefficient does its work.

Think about why calculating deviations from the mean makes sense. With a positive correlation, high scores are above the mean and so would have positive deviations. The product of a pair of high scores would be positive. Low scores are below the mean and would have negative deviations. The product of a pair of low scores would also be positive. When we calculate a correlation coefficient, part of the process involves adding up the products of the deviations. If most of these are positive, we get a positive correlation coefficient.

Let's consider a negative correlation. High scores, which are above the mean, would have positive deviations. Low scores, which are below the mean, would have negative deviations. The product of one positive deviation and one negative deviation would be negative. If most of the products of the deviations are negative, we would get a negative correlation coefficient.

The process we just described is the calculation of the numerator of the correlation coefficient. Table 15-3 shows us the calculations. The first column has the number of absences for each student. The second column shows the deviations from the mean, 3.40. The third column has the exam grade for each student. The fourth column shows the deviations from the mean for that variable, 76.00. The fifth column shows the products of the deviations. Below the fifth column, we see the sum of the products of the deviations, −304.0.

As we see in Table 15-3, the pairs of scores tend to fall on either side of the mean—that is, for each student, a negative deviation on one score tends to indicate a positive deviation on the other score. For example, student 6 was never absent, so she has a score of 0, which is well below the mean, and she got a 99 on the exam, well above the mean. By comparison, student 9 was absent 7 times, well above the mean, and she got a 50 on the exam, well below the mean. So most of the products of the deviations

TABLE 15-3 Calculating the Numerator of the Correlation Coefficient

Absences (X)	($X - M_X$)	Exam Grade (Y)	($Y - M_Y$)	($X - M_X$)($Y - M_Y$)
4	0.6	82	6	3.6
2	−1.4	98	22	−30.8
2	−1.4	76	0	0.0
3	−0.4	68	−8	3.2
1	−2.4	84	8	−19.2
0	−3.4	99	23	−78.2
4	0.6	67	−9	−5.4
8	4.6	58	−18	−82.8
7	3.6	50	−26	−93.6
3	−0.4	78	2	−0.8
$M_X = 3.400$		$M_Y = 76.000$		$\Sigma[(X - M_X)(Y - M_Y)] = -304.0$

are negative, and when we sum the products, we get a negative total. This indicates a negative correlation.

You might have noticed that this number, −304.0, is not between −1.00 and 1.00. The problem is that this number is influenced by two factors—sample size and variability. First, the more people in the sample, the more deviations there are to contribute to the sum. Second, if the scores in the study were more variable, the deviations would be larger and so would the sum of the products. So we have to correct for these two factors in the denominator.

It makes sense that we would have to correct for variability. In Chapter 6, we learned that z scores provide an important function in statistics by allowing us to standardize. You may remember that the formula for the z score that we first learned was $z = \dfrac{(X - M)}{SD}$. In the calculations in the numerator for correlation, we already subtracted the mean from the scores when we created deviations, but we didn't divide by the standard deviation. If we correct for variability in the denominator, that takes care of one of the two factors for which we have to correct.

But we also have to correct for sample size. Recall that when we calculate standard deviation, the last two steps are (1) dividing the sum of squared deviations by the sample size, N, to remove the influence of the sample size and to calculate variance; and (2) taking the square root of the variance to get the standard deviation. So, to factor in sample size along with standard deviation (which we just mentioned allows us to factor in variability), we can go backward in the calculations. If we multiply variance by sample size, we get the sum of squared deviations, or sum of squares. Because of this, the denominator of the correlation coefficient is based on the sums of squares for both variables. To make the denominator match the numerator, we multiply the two sums of squares together, and then we take their square root, as we would with standard deviation. Table 15-4 shows the calculations for the sum of squares for the two variables, absences and exam grades.

TABLE 15-4 Calculating the Denominator of the Correlation Coefficient

Absences (X)	$(X - M_X)$	$(X - M_X)^2$	Exam Grade (Y)	$(Y - M_Y)$	$(Y - M_Y)^2$
4	0.6	0.36	82	6	36
2	−1.4	1.96	98	22	484
2	−1.4	1.96	76	0	0
3	−0.4	0.16	68	−8	64
1	−2.4	5.76	84	8	64
0	−3.4	11.56	99	23	529
4	0.6	0.36	67	−9	81
8	4.6	21.16	58	−18	324
7	3.6	12.96	50	−26	676
3	−0.4	0.16	78	2	4
		$\Sigma(X - M_X)^2 = 56.4$			$\Sigma(Y - M_Y)^2 = 2262$

15-1: The formula for the correlation coefficient is:

$$r = \frac{\Sigma[(X - M_X)(Y - M_Y)]}{\sqrt{(SS_X)(SS_Y)}}$$

We divide the sum of the products of the deviations for each variable by the square root of the products of the sums of squares for each variable. This calculation has a built-in standardization procedure: It subtracts a mean from each score and divides by some kind of variability. By using sums of squares in the denominator, it also takes sample size into account.

We now have all of the ingredients necessary to calculate the correlation coefficient. Here's the formula:

$$r = \frac{\Sigma[(X - M_X)(Y - M_Y)]}{\sqrt{(SS_X)(SS_Y)}}$$

The numerator is the sum of the products of the deviations for each variable (see Table 15-3).

> **STEP 1:** For each score, calculate the deviation from its mean.

> **STEP 2:** For each participant, multiply the deviations for his or her two scores.

> **STEP 3:** Sum the products of the deviations.

The denominator is the square root of the product of the two sums of squares. The sums of squares calculations are in Table 15-4.

> **STEP 1:** Calculate a sum of squares for each variable.

> **STEP 2:** Multiply the two sums of squares.

> **STEP 3:** Take the square root of the product of the sums of squares.

Let's apply the formula for the correlation coefficient to the example data:

$$r = \frac{\Sigma[(X - M_X)(Y - M_Y)]}{\sqrt{(SS_X)(SS_Y)}} = \frac{-304.0}{\sqrt{(56.4)(2262.0)}} = \frac{-304.0}{357.179} = -0.85$$

Here, the Pearson correlation coefficient, r, is -0.85. This is a very strong negative correlation. When we examine the scatterplot in Figure 15-6 carefully, we notice that there aren't any glaring individual exceptions to this rule. The data tell a consistent story. So what should students learn from this result? Go to class! ●

Hypothesis Testing with the Pearson Correlation Coefficient

We said earlier that correlation could be used in two ways: (1) as a descriptive statistic to simply describe a relation between two variables *and* (2) as an inferential statistic.

EXAMPLE 15.4

Here we outline the six steps for hypothesis testing with a correlation coefficient. Usually when we conduct hypothesis testing with correlation, we want to test whether a correlation is statistically significantly different from no correlation—an r of 0.

> **STEP 1:** Identify the populations, distribution, and assumptions.

Population 1: Students like those whom we studied in Example 15.3. Population 2: Students for whom there is no correlation between number of absences and exam grade.

The comparison distribution is a distribution of correlations taken from the population, but with the characteristics of our study, such as a sample size of 10. In this case, it is a distribution of all possible correlations between the numbers of absences and exam grades when 10 students are considered.

The first two assumptions are like those for other parametric tests. (1) The data must be randomly selected, or external validity will be limited. In this case, we do not know how the data were selected, so we should generalize with caution. (2) The underlying population distributions for the two variables must be approximately normal. In our study, it's difficult to tell if the distribution is normal because there are so few data points.

The third assumption is specific to correlation: Each variable should vary equally, no matter the magnitude of the other variable. That is, number of absences should show the same amount of variability at each level of exam grade; conversely, exam grade should show the same amount of variability at each number of absences. You can get a sense of this by looking at the scatterplot in Figure 15-7. In our study, it's hard to determine whether the amount of variability is the same for each variable across all levels of the other variable because there are so few data points. But it seems as if there's variability of between 10 and 20 points on exam grade at each number of absences. The center of that variability decreases as we increase in number of absences, but the range stays roughly the same. It also seems that there's variability of between two and three absences at each exam grade. Again, the center of that variability decreases as exam grade increases, but the range stays roughly the same.

MASTERING THE CONCEPT

15-5: As with other statistics, we can conduct hypothesis testing with the correlation coefficient. We compare the correlation coefficient to critical values on the *r* distribution.

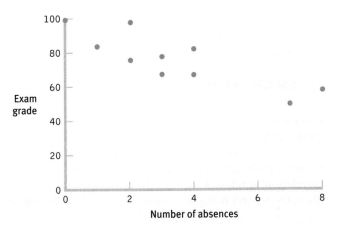

FIGURE 15-7

Using a Scatterplot to Examine the Assumptions

We can use a scatterplot to see whether one variable varies equally at each level of the other variable. With only 10 data points, we can't be certain. But this scatterplot suggests a variability of between 10 and 20 points on exam grade at each number of absences and a variability of between two and three absences at each exam grade.

> **STEP 2:** State the null and research hypotheses.

Null hypothesis: There is no correlation between number of absences and exam grade—H_0: $\rho = 0$. Research hypothesis: There is a correlation between number of absences and exam grade—H_1: $\rho \neq 0$. (*Note:* We use the Greek letter rho because hypotheses are about population parameters.)

> **STEP 3:** Determine the characteristics of the comparison distribution.

The comparison distribution is an r distribution with degrees of freedom calculated by subtracting 2 from the sample size, which for Pearson correlation is the number of participants rather than the number of scores:

$$df_r = N - 2$$

In our study, degrees of freedom is calculated as follows:

$$df_r = N - 2 = 10 - 2 = 8$$

So the comparison distribution is an r distribution with 8 degrees of freedom.

> **STEP 4:** Determine the critical values, or cutoffs.

MASTERING THE FORMULA

15-2: When conducting hypothesis testing for the Pearson correlation coefficient, r, we calculate degrees of freedom by subtracting 2 from the sample size. For Pearson correlation, the sample size is the number of participants, not the number of scores. The formula is:

$$df_r = N - 2$$

Now we can look up the critical values in the r table in Appendix B. Like the z table and the t table, the r table includes only positive values. For a two-tailed test, we take the negative and positive versions of the critical test statistic indicated in the table. The critical values for an r distribution with 8 degrees of freedom for a two-tailed test with an alpha level of 0.05 are -0.632 and 0.632.

> **STEP 5:** Calculate the test statistic.

We already calculated the test statistic, r, in the preceding section. It is -0.85.

> **STEP 6:** Make a decision.

The test statistic, $r = -0.85$, is larger in magnitude than the critical value of -0.632. We can reject the null hypothesis and conclude that number of absences and exam grade seem to be negatively correlated. ●

Partial Correlation

● **Partial correlation** is a technique that quantifies the degree of association between two variables that remains when the correlations of these two variables with a third variable are mathematically eliminated.

In the group sports and longevity example we considered earlier, we wondered about other variables that might be related both to a propensity to play group sports such as tennis or soccer and to a long life. What are the effects of personality, fitness, education, and other factors? In behavioral science research, we are often interested in the relations among more than one variable. Fortunately, correlation provides a helpful way—through using *partial correlation*—to think about the relative influence of multiple variables. ***Partial correlation is a technique***

Applying Correlation in Psychometrics

Here's an in-demand career available to students of the behavioral sciences: *psychometrics, which is the branch of statistics used in the development of tests and measures.* Not surprisingly, *the statisticians and psychologists who develop tests and measures are called psychometricians.* Psychometricians use the statistical procedures referred to in this textbook, particularly those for which correlation forms the mathematical backbone. Psychometricians make sure that elections are fair, they test for cultural biases in standardized tests, they identify high-achieving employees, and they make a wide range of social contributions—and we don't have nearly enough of them. *The New York Times* reported (Herszenhorn, 2006) a "critical shortage" of such experts and intense competition for the few who are available—who are being offered U.S. salaries as high as $200,000 per year! Psychometricians use correlation to examine two important aspects of the development of measures—reliability and validity.

- **Psychometrics** is the branch of statistics used in the development of tests and measures.

- **Psychometricians** are the statisticians and psychologists who develop tests and measures.

Reliability

In Chapter 1, we defined a reliable measure as one that is consistent. For example, if we measure shyness, then a reliable measure leads to nearly the same score every time a person takes the shyness test. One particular type of reliability is test–retest reliability. *Test–retest reliability refers to whether the scale being used provides consistent information every time the test is taken.* To calculate a measure's test–retest reliability, the measure is given twice to the *same sample,* typically with a delay between tests. The participants' scores for the first time they complete the measure are correlated with their scores for the second time they complete the measure. A large correlation indicates that the measure yields the same results consistently over time—that is, good test–retest reliability (Cortina, 1993).

Another way to measure the reliability of a test is by assessing its internal consistency so as to verify that all the items were measuring the same idea (DeVellis, 1991). Initially, researchers measured internal consistency via *split-half* reliability, correlating the odd-numbered items (1, 3, 5, ...) with the even-numbered items (2, 4, 6, ...). If this correlation coefficient is large, then the test has high internal consistency. The odd–even approach is easy to understand, but computers now allow researchers to take a more sophisticated approach. A computer can calculate the average of *every possible* split-half reliability.

Consider a 10-item measure. A computer can calculate correlations between the odd-numbered items and the even-numbered items, between the first 5 items and the last 5 items, between items 1, 2, 4, 8, 10 and items 3, 5, 6, 7, 9, and so on for every combination of two groups of 5 items. The computer can then calculate what is essentially (although not always exactly) the average of all possible split-half correlations (Cortina, 1993). The average of these is called *coefficient alpha* (or *Cronbach's alpha,* in honor of the statistician who developed it). *Coefficient alpha (symbolized as α) is a commonly used estimate of a test's or measure's reliability, or internal consistency,*

- **Test–retest reliability** refers to whether the scale being used provides consistent information every time the test is taken.

- **Coefficient alpha**, symbolized as α, is a commonly used estimate of a test's or measure's reliability, or internal consistency, and is calculated by taking the average of all possible split-half correlations; sometimes called *Cronbach's alpha.*

Correlation and Reliability Correlation is used by psychometricians to help professional sports teams assess the reliability of athletic performance, such as how fast a pitcher can reliably throw a baseball.

MICHAEL MANNING/AP Images

15-7: Correlation is used to calculate reliability either through test–retest reliability or through a measure of internal consistency such as coefficient alpha.

and is calculated by taking the average of all possible split-half correlations. Coefficient alpha is used frequently across a wide range of fields, including psychology, education, sociology, political science, medicine, economics, criminology, and anthropology (Cortina, 1993). (Note that this alpha is different from the alpha level.) In this era of data ethics, however, you will start to see some newer measures of reliability that some consider to be more accurate. Researcher Daniel McNeish (2018), for example, encourages the use of other statistics such as omega total and coefficient H. He even provides detailed instructions for calculating these and other statistics in the statistical software R and Excel.

Validity

In Chapter 1, we defined a valid measure as one that assesses what it was designed or intended to assess. Many researchers consider validity to be the most important concept in the field of psychometrics (e.g., Nunnally & Bernstein, 1994). It can be a great deal more work to measure validity than reliability, however, so that work is not always done. In fact, it is quite possible to have a reliable test, one that measures a variable, such as shyness, consistently over time and is internally consistent but is still not valid. Just because the items on a test all measure the same thing doesn't mean that they're measuring what we want them to measure or what we think they are measuring.

For example, one of the best-known personality tests is the Myers–Briggs Type Inventory (MBTI), which assigns people to one of 16 personality categories. Some swear by it, and the MBTI is widely used in settings ranging from hiring to career guidance. Writer Lauren Apfel (2019) wrote: "My belief in the power of this system stems from the fact that my own type—which presents itself to me consistently, no matter how many times I take the test or which version I take—is eerily spot on." The consistency that Apfel describes is an indicator of the MBTI's reliability, although it turns out that her experience may not be universal. Researchers have found that one-third to one-half of those who take the MBTI end up with a different personality type when taking it again just a few weeks later (Pittenger, 2005). But even for those who have consistent results on the MBTI, is Apfel's claim of its validity accurate?

Validity and Personality Quizzes Correlation can help establish the validity of a personality test—a more difficult task than establishing reliability. Magazine publishers and Web sites probably never check the reliability or validity of the quizzes they develop. Think of them as mere entertainment.

Unfortunately, research does not find that MBTI results are predictive in areas its proponents say it should be, such as relationships, education, or careers (e.g., Pittenger, 2005). Beyond that, research hasn't even distinguished among the 16 different personality types (Hunsley, Lee, Wood, & Taylor, 2015). It seems that the MBTI is not a valid measure, and most researchers suggest using caution when using this instrument, especially in real-world contexts such as hiring. Why is it still so popular? For one thing, the company that makes the test earns a lot of money by marketing it (Stromberg & Caswell, 2015). For another thing, the MBTI focuses on the positive aspects of personality, so it "flatters those who take it" (Kindley, 2016, p. 44). The bottom line? We agree with the reporters who, after reviewing the research on the MBTI's lack of validity, suggested that it be used only as "a fun interesting activity, like a BuzzFeed quiz" (Stromberg & Caswell, 2015).

It takes a psychometrician who understands correlation to test the validity of measures like the MBTI. Typically, a psychometrician finds other measures with which to correlate a new measure. For instance, a new scale to measure anxiety might be correlated with an existing measure known to be valid, or with physiological measures of anxiety such as heart rate. If the new anxiety measure correlates with other measures, this is evidence of its validity.

CHECK YOUR LEARNING

Reviewing the Concepts

> Correlation is a central part of psychometrics, the statistics of the construction of tests and measures.

> Psychometricians, the statisticians who practice psychometrics, use correlation to establish the reliability and the validity of a test.

> Test–retest reliability can be estimated by correlating the same participants' scores on the same test at two different time points.

> Coefficient alpha, now widely used to establish reliability, is essentially calculated by taking the average of all possible split-half correlations (i.e., not just the odds versus the evens).

> A measure is valid when it assesses what it was designed or intended to assess.

Clarifying the Concepts

15-11 How does the field of psychometrics make use of correlation?

15-12 What does coefficient alpha measure and how is it calculated?

Calculating the Statistics

15-13 A researcher develops a new measure of extraversion and correlates it with an existing measure of extraversion. She calculates a Pearson correlation coefficient of −0.032.

a. Is she assessing reliability or validity? Explain your answer.

b. What does this correlation coefficient suggest?

Applying the Concepts

15-14 *Cosmopolitan* magazine often has quizzes that claim to assess readers' relationships. One quiz, titled "Is He Devoted to You?," asks readers, "Be honest: Do you ever worry that he might cheat on you?" Does this item assess a man's devotion to his partner or his partner's jealousy? It also asks, "When you introduced him to your closest friends, he said:" and then offers three options—(1) "I've heard so much about all of you! So, how'd you become friends?" (2) "'Hi,' then silence—he looked a bit bored." and (3) "'Nice to meet you' with a big smile." Does this measure the man's devotion or his social skills? Such a quiz might be reliable, but is it a valid measure of devotion?

Imagine that *Cosmopolitan* hired a psychometrician to assess the reliability and validity of its quizzes, and she administered this 10-item quiz to 100 readers of that magazine who had boyfriends.

a. How could the psychometrician establish the reliability of the quiz? That is, which of the methods introduced in this chapter could she use in this case? Be specific, and cite at least two ways.

b. How could the psychometrician establish the validity of the quiz? Be specific, and cite at least two ways.

Solutions to these Check Your Learning questions can be found in Appendix D.

c. Choose one of your criteria from part (b) and explain why it might not actually measure the underlying variable of interest. That is, explain how your criterion itself might not be valid.

REVIEW OF CONCEPTS

Visit LaunchPad to access
the e-book and to test your
knowledge with LearningCurve.

The Meaning of Correlation

Correlation is an association between two variables and is quantified by a *correlation coefficient*. A *positive correlation* indicates that a participant who has a high score on one variable is likely to have a high score on the other variable, and someone with a low score on one variable is likely to have a low score on the other variable. A *negative correlation* indicates that someone with a high score on one variable is likely to have a low score on the other variable. All correlation coefficients must fall between −1.00 and 1.00. The strength of the correlation is independent of its sign.

Correlation coefficients are useful, but they can be misleading. When interpreting a correlation coefficient, we must be certain not to confuse correlation with causation. We cannot know the causal direction in which two variables are related from a correlation coefficient, nor can we know if there is a hidden third variable that causes the apparent relation.

The Pearson Correlation Coefficient

The *Pearson correlation coefficient* is used when two scale variables are linearly related, as determined from a scatterplot. Calculating a correlation coefficient involves three steps. (1) We calculate the deviation of each score from its mean, multiply the deviations for each variable for each participant, and sum the products of the deviations. (2) We multiply the sums of squares for each variable, then take the square root of the product. (3) We divide the sum of the products of the deviations (from step 1) by the square root of the product of the sums of squares (from step 2). We can use the six steps of hypothesis testing to determine whether the correlation coefficient is statistically significantly different from 0 on the *r* distribution.

With partial correlation, researchers quantify the degree of association between two variables that remains when the correlations of these two variables with a third variable are mathematically eliminated. Researchers use partial correlation when a third variable may be influencing the correlation of the first two variables.

Ethical researchers will be aware of the limitations inherent in research that uses big data—extremely large data sets that are often available online. Researchers should be careful not to confuse correlation with causation in their conclusions and should be aware that some findings might be spurious—that is, Type I errors.

Applying Correlation in Psychometrics

Psychometrics is the statistics of the development of tests and measures. *Psychometricians* assess the reliability and validity of a test. Reliability is sometimes measured by *test–retest reliability*, whereby participants' scores on the same measure at two different points in time are correlated. With *coefficient alpha*, a computer essentially calculates the average of all possible split-half correlations (e.g., odd and even items, first and second halves of items). Validity is sometimes assessed by correlating a new measure with existing measures that have been shown to be valid.

SPSS

Enter the data for the example used to calculate the correlation coefficient in this chapter: numbers of absences and exam grades (Table 15-2 on p. 465). Be sure to put each student's two scores on the same row. Check that both are listed as scale variables.

To view a scatterplot, select: Graphs → Chart Builder → Gallery → Scatter/Dot. (*Note:* The first time you click "Chart Builder," you may have to then click "OK" to indicate that you have correctly listed the variables as scale, ordinal, or nominal.) Choose "Scatter/Dot" from the list of charts at the bottom. Select and drag the first scatterplot option to the large box on top. Then select the variables to be included in the scatterplot by dragging the independent variable, absences, to the *x*-axis and the dependent variable, grade, to the *y*-axis. Click "OK."

If the scatterplot indicates that we have met the assumptions for a Pearson correlation coefficient, we can analyze the data. Select: Analyze → Correlate → Bivariate. (*Note:* Bivariate means that you are analyzing two variables.) Then select the two variables to be analyzed, absences and grade, and move them into the Variables list. "Pearson" will already be checked as the type of correlation coefficient to be calculated. (*Note:* If more than two variables are selected, SPSS will build a correlation matrix of all possible pairs of variables.) Click "OK" to see the Output screen. The screenshot here shows the output for the Pearson correlation coefficient. Notice that the correlation coefficient is −0.851, the same as the coefficient that we calculated by hand earlier. The two asterisks indicate that it is statistically significant at an alpha level of less than 0.01. You can see under the correlation coefficient that the actual *p* value is 0.002.

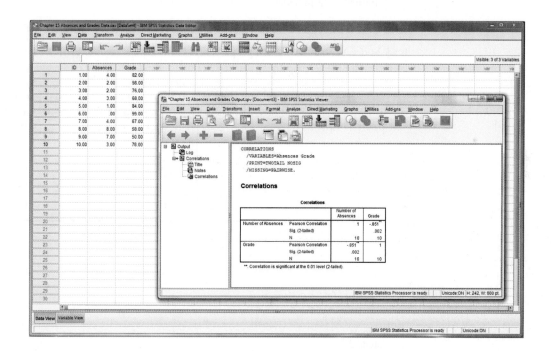

HOW IT WORKS

15.1 UNDERSTANDING CORRELATION COEFFICIENTS

A newspaper report summarized a relation between temperature and numbers of homicides in the United States (Asher, 2018). (The actual relation was positive; the reporter wrote: "In Philadelphia, for example, there were 2.6 shooting victims per day on average when it was cold, 3.4 on pleasant days, and 4.4 on hot ones.") From each fictional correlation coefficient below, what do we know about the relation between the two variables?

1. 1.00: This correlation coefficient reflects a perfect positive relation between temperature and number of homicides. This correlation is the strongest correlation of the six options, and, if true, would allow us to perfectly predict the number of homicides from the temperature.

2. −0.001: This correlation coefficient reflects a lack of relation between temperature and number of homicides. This is the weakest correlation of the six options.

3. 0.56: This correlation coefficient reflects a large positive relation between temperature and number of homicides.

4. −0.27: This coefficient reflects a medium negative relation between temperature and number of homicides.

5. −0.98: This coefficient reflects a large (close to perfect) negative relation between temperature and number of homicides.

6. 0.09: This coefficient reflects a small positive relation between temperature and number of homicides.

15.2 CALCULATING THE PEARSON CORRELATION COEFFICIENT

Is age associated with how much people study? How can we calculate the Pearson correlation coefficient for the accompanying data (taken from students in some of our statistics classes)?

Student	Age	Number of Hours Studied per Week	Student	Age	Number of Hours Studied per Week
1	19	5	6	23	25
2	20	20	7	22	15
3	20	8	8	20	10
4	21	12	9	19	14
5	21	18	10	25	15

Step 1: First, construct a scatterplot:

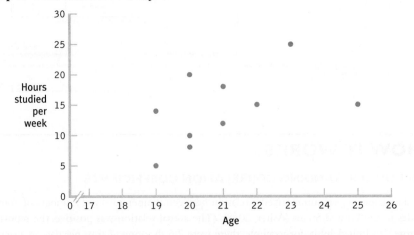

We see from the scatterplot that the data, overall, have a pattern through which we could imagine drawing a straight line. So, it is safe to calculate the Pearson correlation coefficient.

Step 2: Next, calculate the numerator of the Pearson correlation coefficient. The numerator is the sum of the product of the deviations for each variable. The mean for age is 21, and the mean for hours studied is 14.2. We use these means to calculate each score's deviation from its mean. We then multiply the deviations for each student's two scores and sum the products of the deviations. Here are the calculations:

Age (X)	$(X - M_X)$	Hours studied (Y)	$(Y - M_Y)$	$(X - M_X)(Y - M_Y)$
19	−2	5	−9.2	18.4
20	−1	20	5.8	−5.8
20	−1	8	−6.2	6.2
21	0	12	−2.2	0
21	0	18	3.8	0
23	2	25	10.8	21.6
22	1	15	0.8	0.8
20	−1	10	−4.2	4.2
19	−2	14	−0.2	0.4
25	4	15	0.8	3.2
$M_X = 21$		$M_Y = 14.2$		$\Sigma[(X - M_X)(Y - M_Y)] = 49.0$

The numerator is 49.0.

Step 3: Calculate the denominator of the Pearson correlation coefficient. The denominator is the square root of the product of the two sums of squares. We first calculate a sum of squares for each variable. The calculations are here:

Age (X)	$(X - M_X)$	$(X - M_X)^2$	Hours studied (Y)	$(Y - M_Y)$	$(Y - M_Y)^2$
19	−2	4	5	−9.2	84.64
20	−1	1	20	5.8	33.64
20	−1	1	8	−6.2	38.44
21	0	0	12	−2.2	4.84
21	0	0	18	3.8	14.44
23	2	4	25	10.8	116.64
22	1	1	15	0.8	0.64
20	−1	1	10	−4.2	17.64
19	−2	4	14	−0.2	0.04
25	4	16	15	0.8	0.64
$M_X = 21$	$\Sigma(X - M_X)^2 = 32$		$M_Y = 14.2$		$\Sigma(Y - M_Y)^2 = 311.6$

We now multiply the two sums of squares, then take the square root of the product of the sums of squares.

$$\sqrt{(SS_X)(SS_Y)} = \sqrt{(32)(311.6)} = 99.856$$

Step 4: Finally, we can put the numerator and denominator together to calculate the Pearson correlation coefficient:

$$r = \frac{\Sigma[(X - M_X)(Y - M_Y)]}{\sqrt{(SS_X)(SS_Y)}} = \frac{49.0}{99.856} = 0.49$$

Now that we have calculated the Pearson correlation coefficient (0.49), we determine what the statistic tells us about the direction and the strength of the association between the two variables (age and number of hours studied). This is a positive correlation. Higher ages tend to be associated with longer hours spent studying, and lower ages tend to be associated with fewer hours spent studying.

EXERCISES

The solutions to the odd-numbered exercises can be found in Appendix C.

Clarifying the Concepts

15.1 What is a correlation coefficient?

15.2 What is a linear relation?

15.3 Describe a perfect correlation, including its possible coefficients.

15.4 What is the difference between a *positive correlation* and a *negative correlation*?

15.5 What *magnitude* of a correlation coefficient is large enough to be considered important, or worth talking about?

15.6 When we have a straight-line relation between two variables, we use a Pearson correlation coefficient. What does this coefficient describe?

15.7 Explain how the correlation coefficient can be used as a descriptive statistic or an inferential statistic.

15.8 How are deviation scores used in assessing the relation between variables?

15.9 Explain how the sum of the product of deviations determines the sign of the correlation.

15.10 Why can we not infer causation from correlation?

15.11 What is meant by a spurious correlation, and why might it be a Type I error?

15.12 What are the null and research hypotheses for correlations?

15.13 What are the three basic steps to calculate the Pearson correlation coefficient?

15.14 Describe the third assumption of hypothesis testing with correlation.

15.15 What is the difference between test–retest reliability and coefficient alpha?

15.16 Why is a correlation coefficient never greater than 1 (or less than −1)?

15.17 In your own words, briefly explain the difference between a Pearson correlation coefficient and a partial correlation coefficient.

15.18 How does partial correlation begin to address the third variable problem?

15.19 What is the big data approach?

15.20 What is the relation between big data and spurious correlations?

Calculating the Statistics

15.21 Determine whether the data in each of the graphs provided would result in a negative or positive correlation coefficient.

a.

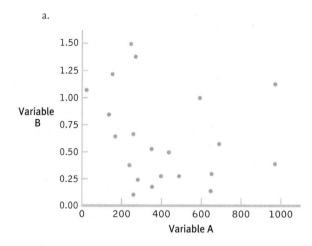

b.

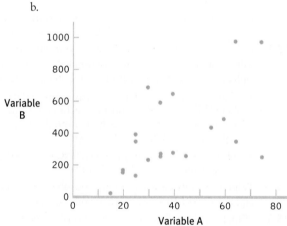

c.

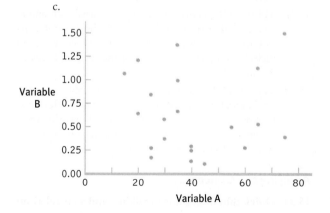

15.22 Decide which of the three correlation coefficient values below goes with each of the scatterplots presented in Exercise 15.21.

a. 0.545

b. 0.018

c. −0.20

15.23 Use Cohen's guidelines to describe the strength of the following correlation coefficients:

a. −0.28

b. 0.79

c. 1.0

d. −0.015

15.24 For each of the pairs of correlation coefficients provided, determine which one indicates a stronger relation between variables:

a. −0.28 and −0.31

b. 0.79 and 0.61

c. 1.0 and −1.0

d. −0.15 and 0.13

15.25 Using the following data:

X	Y
0.13	645
0.27	486
0.49	435
0.57	689
0.84	137
0.64	167

a. Create a scatterplot.

b. Calculate deviation scores and products of the deviations for each individual, and then sum all products. This is the numerator of the correlation coefficient equation.

c. Calculate the sum of squares for each variable. Then compute the square root of the product of the sums of squares. This is the denominator of the correlation coefficient equation.

d. Divide the numerator by the denominator to compute the coefficient, r.

e. Calculate degrees of freedom.

f. Determine the critical values, or cutoffs, assuming a two-tailed test with an alpha level of 0.05.

15.26 Using the following data:

X	Y
394	25
972	75
349	25
349	65
593	35
276	40
254	45
156	20
248	75

a. Create a scatterplot.

b. Calculate deviation scores and products of the deviations for each individual, and then sum all products. This is the numerator of the correlation coefficient equation.

c. Calculate the sum of squares for each variable. Then compute the square root of the product of the sums of squares. This is the denominator of the correlation coefficient equation.

d. Divide the numerator by the denominator to compute the coefficient, r.

e. Calculate degrees of freedom.

f. Determine the critical values, or cutoffs, assuming a two-tailed test with an alpha level of 0.05.

15.27 Using the following data:

X	Y
40	60
45	55
20	30
75	25
15	20
35	40
65	30

a. Create a scatterplot.

b. Calculate deviation scores and products of the deviations for each individual, and then sum all products. This is the numerator of the correlation coefficient equation.

c. Calculate the sum of squares for each variable. Then compute the square root of the product of

the sums of squares. This is the denominator of the correlation coefficient equation.

d. Divide the numerator by the denominator to compute the coefficient, r.

e. Calculate degrees of freedom.

f. Determine the critical values, or cutoffs, assuming a two-tailed test with an alpha level of 0.05.

15.28 Calculate the degrees of freedom and the critical values, or cutoffs, assuming a two-tailed test with an alpha level of 0.05, for each of the following designs:

a. Forty students were recruited for a study about the relation between knowledge regarding academic integrity and values held by students, with the idea that students with less knowledge would care less about the issue than students with more knowledge.

b. Twenty-seven couples are surveyed regarding their years together and their relationship satisfaction.

15.29 Calculate the degrees of freedom and the critical values, or cutoffs, assuming a two-tailed test with an alpha level of 0.05, for each of the following designs:

a. Data are collected to examine the relation between size of dog and rate of bone and joint health issues. Veterinarians from around the country contributed data on 3113 dogs.

b. Hours spent studying per week was correlated with credit-hour load for 72 students.

15.30 Which of the following is not a possible coefficient alpha: 1.67, 0.12, −0.88? Explain your answer.

15.31 Which of the following is not a possible coefficient alpha: 0.0, 1.0, or 2.0? Explain your answer.

15.32 There is a 0.86 correlation between variables A and B. The partial correlation between A and B, after controlling for a third variable, is 0.67. Does this third variable completely account for the relation between A and B? Explain your answer.

15.33 There is a 0.86 correlation between variables A and B. The partial correlation between A and B, after controlling for a third variable, is 0.86. Does this third variable completely account for the relation between A and B? Explain your answer.

Applying the Concepts

15.34 **Quick thinking, smooth talking, and a correlation:** Australian psychologist William von Hippel and his colleagues examined the premise that the ability to think quickly would be related to social skills in a paper titled "Quick Thinkers Are Smooth Talkers" (von Hippel, Ronay, Baker, Kjelsaas, & Murphy, 2016). They summarized their findings by saying: "Participants who were able to answer common-knowledge questions more rapidly and to respond more rapidly in general were evaluated by their peers as being more charismatic than participants who responded more slowly. These findings are consistent with the notion that mental speed facilitates social functioning" (p. 121). Are the researchers describing a positive correlation or a negative correlation? Explain your answer.

15.35 **Grip strength, mortality, and correlation:** An international team of researchers studied the association between grip strength (using a tool that measures the strength of participants' hands) and mortality among adults in 17 countries (Leong et al., 2015). They reported that "Low grip strength is associated with higher ... fatality rates" (p. 271). Are the researchers describing a positive correlation or a negative correlation? Explain your answer.

15.36 **Awe and correlation in the news:** *The New York Times* reported on a study that examined the link between positive emotions and health. First citing previous research connecting negative moods with poor health, the reporter said: "Far less is known, however, about the health benefits of specific upbeat moods—whether contentment, say, might promote good health more robustly than joy or pride does. A new study singles out one surprising emotion as a potent medicine: awe" (Reynolds, 2015). What is awe? The reporter interviewed one of the researchers, Dacher Keltner, who said that awe is something that "will pass the goose-bumps test." Keltner explained that "Some people feel awe listening to music, others watching a sunset or attending a political rally or seeing kids play."

a. If this study were an experiment, how might the researchers have studied the emotion of awe as a medicine?

b. Why is it unlikely that the researchers conducted a true experiment?

c. The researchers actually conducted a correlational study (Stellar, John-Henderson, Anderson, Gordon, McNeil, & Keltner, 2015). They used elevated levels of interleukin-6 (IL-6), a measure of inflammation, as a marker of poorer health in their participants. They examined a number of positive emotions, and reported that "awe had the strongest relationship with IL-6 of any positive

emotion." Is this relation likely to be positive or negative? Explain your answer.

d. Why can the researchers not conclude that awe causes a change in levels of inflammation?

e. Why should the reporter avoid the word "medicine" in her article?

15.37 **Debunking astrology with correlation:** *The New York Times* reported that an officer of the International Society for Astrological Research, Anne Massey, stated that a certain phase of the planet Mercury, the retrograde phase, leads to breakdowns in areas as wide-ranging as communication and travel (Newman, 2006). The *Times* reporter, Andy Newman, documented the likelihood of breakdown on a number of variables, and discovered that, contrary to Massey's hypothesis, New Jersey Transit commuter trains were less likely to be late, although by just 0.4%, during the retrograde phase. In contrast, and consistent with Massey's hypothesis, the rate of baggage complaints at LaGuardia airport increased a tiny amount during retrograde periods. Newman's findings were contradictory across all examined variables—rates of theft, computer crashes, traffic disruptions, delayed plane arrivals—with some variables backing Massey and others not. Transportation statistics expert Bruce Schaller said, "If all of this is due to randomness, that's the result you'd expect." Astrologer Massey counters that the pattern she predicts would only emerge across thousands of years of data.

a. Do reporter Newman's data suggest a correlation between Mercury's phase and breakdowns?

b. Why might astrologer Massey believe there is a correlation? Discuss the confirmation bias and illusory correlations (Chapter 5) in your answer.

c. How do transportation expert Schaller's statement and Newman's contradictory results relate to what you learned about probability in Chapter 5? Discuss expected relative-frequency probability in your answer.

d. If there were indeed a small correlation that one could observe only across thousands of years of data, how useful would that knowledge be in terms of predicting events in your own life?

e. Write a brief response to Massey's contention of a correlation between Mercury's phases and breakdowns in aspects of day-to-day living.

f. If the rate of baggage complaints at La Guardia is correlated with retrograde periods, why might this be a spurious correlation?

15.38 Obesity, age at death, and correlation: In a newspaper column, Paul Krugman (2006) mentioned obesity (as measured by body mass index) as a possible correlate of age at death.

a. Describe the implied correlation between these two variables. Is it likely to be positive or negative? Explain.

b. Draw a scatterplot that depicts the correlation you described in part (a).

15.39 Exercise, number of friends, and correlation: Does the amount that people exercise correlate with the number of friends they have? The accompanying table contains data collected in some of our statistics classes. The first and third columns show hours exercised per week and the second and fourth columns show the number of close friends reported by each participant.

Hours of Exercise	Number of Friends	Hours of Exercise	Number of Friends
1	4	8	4
0	3	2	4
1	2	10	4
6	6	5	7
1	3	4	5
6	5	2	6
2	4	7	5
3	5	1	5
5	6		

a. Create a scatterplot of these data. Be sure to label both axes.

b. What does the scatterplot suggest about the relation between these two variables?

c. Would it be appropriate to calculate a Pearson correlation coefficient? Explain your answer.

15.40 Externalizing behavior, anxiety, and correlation: As part of their study on the relation between rejection and depression in adolescents (Nolan, Flynn, & Garber, 2003), researchers collected data on externalizing behaviors (e.g., acting out in negative ways, such as causing fights) and anxiety. They wondered whether externalizing behaviors were related to feelings of anxiety. Some of the data are presented in the accompanying table.

Externalizing Behaviors	Anxiety	Externalizing Behaviors	Anxiety
9	37	6	33
7	23	2	26
7	26	6	35
3	21	6	23
11	42	9	28

a. Create a scatterplot of these data. Be sure to label both axes.

b. What does the scatterplot suggest about the relation between these two variables?

c. Would it be appropriate to calculate a Pearson correlation coefficient? Explain your answer.

d. Construct a second scatterplot, but this time add a participant who scored 1 on externalizing behaviors and 45 on anxiety. Would you expect the correlation coefficient to be positive or negative now? Small in magnitude or large in magnitude?

e. The Pearson correlation coefficient for the first set of data is 0.65; for the second set of data it is 0.12. Explain why the correlation changed so much with the addition of just one participant.

15.41 Externalizing behavior, anxiety, and hypothesis testing for correlation: Using the data in the previous exercise, perform all six steps of hypothesis testing to explore the relation between externalizing and anxiety.

15.42 Direction of a correlation: For each of the following pairs of variables, would you expect a positive correlation or a negative correlation between the two variables? Explain your answer.

a. How hard the rain is falling and your commuting time

b. How often you say no to dessert and your body fat

c. The amount of wine you consume with dinner and your alertness after dinner

15.43 Cats, mental health problems, and the direction of a correlation: You may be aware of the stereotype about the "crazy" person who owns a lot of cats. Have you wondered whether the stereotype is true? As a researcher, you decide to assess 100 people on two variables: (1) the number of cats they own and (2) their level of mental health problems (a higher score indicates more problems).

a. Imagine that you found a positive relation between these two variables. What might you expect for someone who owns a lot of cats? Explain.

b. Imagine that you found a positive relation between these two variables. What might you expect for someone who owns no cats or just one cat? Explain.

c. Imagine that you found a negative relation between these two variables. What might you expect for someone who owns a lot of cats? Explain.

d. Imagine that you found a negative relation between these two variables. What might you expect for someone who owns no cats or just one cat? Explain.

15.44 Cats, mental health problems, and scatterplots: Consider the scenario in the previous exercise again. The two variables under consideration were (1) number of cats owned and (2) level of mental health problems (with a higher score indicating more problems). Each possible relation between these variables would be represented by a different scatterplot. Using data for approximately 10 participants, draw a scatterplot that depicts a correlation between these variables for each of the following:

a. A weak positive correlation

b. A strong positive correlation

c. A perfect positive correlation

d. A weak negative correlation

e. A strong negative correlation

f. A perfect negative correlation

g. No (or almost no) correlation

15.45 Trauma, femininity, and correlation: Graduate student Angela Holiday (2007) conducted a study examining perceptions of combat veterans suffering from mental illness. Participants read a description of either a male or female soldier who had recently returned from combat in Iraq and who was suffering from depression. Participants rated the situation (combat in Iraq) with respect to how traumatic they believed it was; they also rated the combat veterans on a range of variables, including scales that assessed how masculine and how feminine they perceived the person to be. Among other analyses, Holiday examined the relation between the perception of the situation as traumatic and the perception of the veteran as being masculine or feminine. When the person was male, the perception of the situation as traumatic was strongly positively correlated with the perception of the man as feminine but was only weakly positively correlated with the perception of the man as masculine. What would you expect when the person was female? The accompanying table presents some of the data for the perception of the situation as traumatic (on a scale of 1 – 10, with 10 being the most traumatic) and the perception of the woman as feminine (on a scale of 1 – 10, with 10 being the most feminine).

Perceived Trauma	Perceived Femininity
5	6
6	5
4	6
5	6
7	4
8	5

a. Draw a scatterplot for these data. Does the scatterplot suggest that it is appropriate to calculate a Pearson correlation coefficient? Explain.

b. Calculate the Pearson correlation coefficient.

c. State what the Pearson correlation coefficient tells us about the relation between these two variables.

d. Explain why the pattern of pairs of deviation scores enables us to understand the relation between the two variables. (That is, consider whether pairs of deviations tend to have the same sign or opposite signs.)

15.46 Trauma, femininity, and hypothesis testing for correlation: Using the data and your work in the previous exercise, perform the remaining five steps of hypothesis testing to explore the relation between trauma and femininity. In step 6, be sure to evaluate the size of the correlation using Cohen's guidelines. [You completed step 5, the calculation of the correlation coefficient, in 15.45(b).]

15.47 Trauma, masculinity, and correlation: See the description of Holiday's experiment in Exercise 15.45. We calculated the correlation coefficient for the relation between the perception of a situation as traumatic and the perception of a woman's femininity. Now let's look at data to examine the relation between the perception of a situation as traumatic and the perception of a woman's masculinity (on a scale of 1 – 10, with 10 being the most masculine).

Perceived Trauma	Perceived Masculinity
5	3
6	3
4	2
5	2
7	4
8	3

a. Draw a scatterplot for these data. Does the scatterplot suggest that it is appropriate to calculate a Pearson correlation coefficient? Explain.

b. Calculate the Pearson correlation coefficient.

c. State what the Pearson correlation coefficient tells us about the relation between these two variables.

d. Explain why the pattern of pairs of deviation scores enables us to understand the relation between the two variables. (That is, consider whether pairs of deviation scores tend to share the same sign or to have opposite signs.)

e. Explain how the relations between the perception of a situation as traumatic and the perception of a woman as either masculine or feminine differ from those same relations with respect to men.

15.48 **Trauma, masculinity, and hypothesis testing for correlation:** Using the data and your work in the previous exercise, perform the remaining five steps of hypothesis testing to explore the relation between trauma and masculinity. In step 6, be sure to evaluate the size of the correlation using Cohen's guidelines. [You completed step 5, the calculation of the correlation coefficient, in 15.47(b).]

15.49 **Traffic, running late, and bias:** A friend tells you that there is a correlation between how late she's running and the amount of traffic. Whenever she's going somewhere and she's behind schedule, there's a lot of traffic. And when she has plenty of time, the traffic is sparser. She tells you that this happens no matter what time of day she's traveling or where she's going. She concludes that she's cursed with respect to traffic.

a. Explain to your friend how other phenomena, such as coincidence, superstition, and the confirmation bias (Chapter 5), might explain her conclusion.

b. How could she quantify the relation between these two variables: the degree to which she is late

and the amount of traffic? In your answer, be sure to explain how you might operationalize these variables. Of course, they could be operationalized in many different ways.

c. Let's say your friend tries to quantify her bad luck and examines a range of associations between pairs of variables. She finds a correlation between the amount of time she has to spend outside on a given day and the amount of precipitation on that day. Why might this be a spurious correlation?

15.50 **IQ-boosting water and illusory correlation:** The trashy tabloid *Weekly World News* published an article—"Water from Mountain Falls Can Make You a Genius"—stating that drinking water from a special waterfall in a secret location in Switzerland "boosts IQ by 14 points—in the blink of an eye!" Hans and Inger Thurlemann, two hikers lost in the woods, drank some of the water, noticed an improvement in their thinking, and instantly found their way out of the woods. The more water they drank, the smarter they seemed to get. They credited the "miracle water" with enhancing their IQs. They brought some of the water home to their friends, who also claimed to notice an improvement in their thinking. Explain how a reliance on anecdotes may have led the Thurlemanns to perceive an illusory correlation (Chapter 5).

15.51 **Driving a convertible, correlation, and causality:** How safe are convertibles? *USA Today* (Healey, 2006) examined the pros and cons of convertible automobiles. The Insurance Institute for Highway Safety determined that, depending on the model, 52 to 99 drivers of 1 million registered convertibles died in a car crash. The average rate of deaths for all passenger cars was 87. "Counter to conventional wisdom," the reporter wrote, "convertibles generally aren't unsafe."

a. What does the reporter suggest about the safety of convertibles?

b. Can you think of another explanation for the fairly low fatality rates? (*Hint:* The same article reported that convertibles "are often second or third cars.")

c. Given your explanation in part (b), suggest data that might make for a more appropriate comparison.

15.52 **Standardized tests, correlation, and causality:** A *New York Times* editorial ("Public vs. Private Schools," 2006) cited a finding by the U.S. Department of Education that standardized test scores were significantly higher among students in private schools than among students in public schools.

a. What are the researchers suggesting with respect to causality?

b. How could this correlation be explained by reversing the direction of hypothesized causality? Be specific.

c. How might a third variable account for this correlation? Be specific. Note that there are many possible "third" variables. (*Note:* In the actual study, the difference between types of school disappeared when the researchers statistically controlled for related third variables including race, gender, parents' education, and family income.)

15.53 Arts education, correlation, and causality: The Broadway musical *Annie* and the Entertainment Industry Foundation teamed up to promote arts education programs for underserved children. In an ad in *The New York Times*, they said, "Students in arts education programs perform better and stay in school longer."

a. What are the musical (*Annie*) and the foundation suggesting with respect to causality?

b. How could this correlation be explained by reversing the direction of hypothesized causality? Be specific.

c. How might a third variable account for this correlation? Be specific. Note that there are many possible "third" variables.

15.54 Correlation versus causation and hate crimes: Using municipalities (i.e., towns, cities) in Germany as participants, researchers found an association between the numbers of anti-refugee posts on social media and the numbers of violent acts against refugees (Müller & Schwarz, 2018). (Note that this was true only among municipalities where social media use was high.) They concluded that the results indicated a link "between online hate speech and real-life violent crime." Describe this correlation in your own words. Does this correlation indicate that online hate speech *causes* violent crime in a community?

15.55 Correlation versus causation, iPhones, and millennials: One newspaper headline, noting that 18- to 34-year-olds were increasingly likely to move back home following the 2007 release of the iPhone, asked: "Did the Release of the iPhone Cause Millennials to Move Back in with Their Parents?" (Novak, 2018). The reporter noted that "the implication, of course, is that people are spending all their money on technology instead of buying homes or renting."

a. If this is indeed a real correlation, can we draw a causal conclusion that technology expenditures

cause millennials to move home? Explain your answer.

b. Is it likely that technology expenditures led young people to move back home? What are some alternative explanations? Might this correlation simply be a coincidence and not a true association?

15.56 Facebook likes and correlation: Be careful what you "like." Researchers examined the relations between the number of Facebook "likes" a person has posted and the researchers' ability to correctly identify various characteristics of the person, including gender, age, sexual orientation, ethnicity, religion, political beliefs, personality traits, and intelligence (Kosinski, Stillwell, & Graepel, 2013). The accompanying graph shows the relations between number of likes and accuracy of identifying gender, age, and the personality characteristic of openness, respectively.

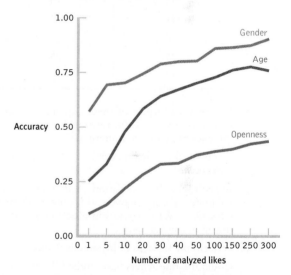

a. In your own words, what story is this graph telling?

b. Based on what you learned in Chapter 3 about graphs, explain why the *x*-axis is misleading, and describe how you would redesign the graph.

15.57 Swearing, vocabulary, and correlation: Psychology researchers set out to test the folk assumption that people swear a lot because their overall vocabulary is limited (Jay & Jay, 2015). They asked participants to name as many taboo words, described as "curse words or swear words" (p. 253), as they could in one minute. They then asked participants to repeat the task but with other categories of words, such as naming as many animals as they could in one minute. The accompanying table provides fictional data that have the same overall pattern—similar means, standard deviations, and statistical significance of the correlation coefficient—as the data in the actual study.

Number of Taboo Words (X)	Number of Animals (Y)
9	23
5	20
4	17
12	28
14	26
10	16
9	17
11	18
14	23
6	21
7	25
13	19

a. Create a scatterplot of these data and describe your impression of the relation between these variables based on the scatterplot.

b. Compute the Pearson correlation coefficient for these data.

c. Explain why the correlation coefficient you just computed is a descriptive statistic, not an inferential statistic. What would you need to do to make this an inferential statistic?

d. Perform the six steps of hypothesis testing.

e. Could the researchers have studied this phenomenon with an experiment rather than a correlational study? Explain your answer.

15.58 **Romantic love, brain activation, and reliability:** Aron and colleagues (2005) found a correlation between intense romantic love (as assessed by the Passionate Love Scale [PLS]) and activation in a specific region of the brain [as assessed by functional magnetic resonance imaging [fMRI]). The PLS (Hatfield & Sprecher, 1986) assessed the intensity of romantic love by asking people in romantic relationships to rate their agreement with a series of statements, such as "I want _____ physically, emotionally, and mentally" and "Sometimes I can't control my thoughts; they are obsessively on _____," replacing the blanks with the name of their partner.

a. How might we examine the reliability of this measure using test–retest reliability techniques? Be specific and explain the role of correlation.

b. Would test–retest reliability be appropriate for this measure? That is, is there likely to be a practice effect? Explain.

c. How could we examine the reliability of this measure using coefficient alpha? Be specific and explain the role of correlation.

d. What is the idea that this measure is trying to assess?

e. What would it mean for this measure to be valid? Be specific.

15.59 **A biased exam question, validity, and correlation:** New York State's fourth-grade English exam led to an outcry from parents because of a question that was perceived to be an unfair measure of fourth graders' performance. Students read a story, "Why the Rooster Crows at Dawn," that described an arrogant rooster who claims to be king, and Brownie, "the kindest of all the cows," who eventually acts in a mean way toward the rooster. In the beginning the rooster does whatever he wants, but by the end, the cows, led by Brownie, have convinced him that as self-proclaimed king, he must be the first to wake up in the morning and the last to go to sleep. To the cows' delight, the arrogant rooster complies. Students were then asked to respond to several questions about the story, including one that asked: "What causes Brownie's behavior to change?" Several parents started a Web site to point out problems with the test, particularly with this question. Students, they argued, were confused because it seemed that it was the rooster's behavior, not the cow's behavior, that changed. The correct answer, according to a quote on the Web site from an unnamed state official, was that the cow started out kind and ended up mean.

a. This test item was supposed to evaluate writing skills. According to the Web site, test items should lead to good student writing; be unambiguous; test for writing, not another skill; and allow for objective, reliable scoring. If students were marked down for talking about the rooster rather than the cow, as alleged by the Web site, would it meet these criteria? Explain. Does this seem to be a valid question? Explain.

b. The Web site states that New York City schools use the tests to, among other things, evaluate teachers and principals. The logic behind this, ostensibly, is that good teachers and administrators cause higher test performance. List at least two possible third variables that might lead to better performance in some schools than in other schools, other than the presence of good teachers and administrators.

15.60 **Reliability and personality tests:** A meta-analysis compared the reliability of personality tests that are free with those that cost money (Hamby, Taylor, Snowden, & Peterson, 2016). All of the personality tests were based on the Big Five model of personality. The researchers reported that "free scales possessed significantly higher alpha coefficients than for-pay scales for each of the Big Five traits" (p. 422).

a. What is meant by a meta-analysis here?

b. What is meant by alpha coefficients here?

c. The researchers reported that the alpha coefficients were "significantly higher" for free personality tests than for tests that cost money. What does the phrase "significantly higher" indicate?

d. These findings indicate that free personality tests are likely to be reliable, or at least more so than for-pay personality tests. Does that mean that these tests are worth taking?

15.61 **Flu epidemics and correlation:** In 2009, researchers at Google demonstrated that they could detect the spread of flu epidemics in the United States based on the correlation between a set of Google search terms that users were entering and the number of doctor's visits for the flu (Ginsberg et al., 2009). These data allowed them to detect the spread of the epidemic about one week faster than the Centers for Disease Control and Prevention. Is this a big data success or a big data failure? Why?

15.62 **Divorce rate, margarine consumption, and big data:** Using data from the National Vital Statistics Reports and the U.S. Department of Agriculture, Tyler Vigen (2015) demonstrated a strong correlation of $r = 0.99$ between the divorce rate in Maine and the per capita consumption of margarine in the United States. Is this a big data success or a big data failure? Why?

Putting It All Together

15.63 **Health care spending, longevity, and correlation:** *The New York Times* columnist Paul Krugman (2006) used the idea of correlation in a newspaper column when he asked, "Is being an American bad for your health?" Krugman explained that the United States has higher per capita spending on health care than any country in the world and yet is surpassed by many countries in life expectancy [Krugman cited a study by Banks, Marmot, Oldfield, and Smith (2006), published in the *Journal of the American Medical Association*].

a. Name the "participants" in this study.

b. What are the two scale variables being studied, and how was each of them operationalized? Suggest at least one alternative way, other than life expectancy, to operationalize health.

c. What was the study finding, and why might this finding be surprising? If the finding described here holds true across countries, would this be a negative correlation or a positive correlation? Explain.

d. Some people thought race or income might be a third variable related to higher spending and lower life expectancy. But Krugman further reported that a comparison of non-Hispanic white people from America and from England (thus taking race out of the equation) yielded a surprising finding: The wealthiest third of Americans have poorer health than do even the *least* wealthy third of the English. What are some other possible third variables that might affect both of the variables in this study?

e. Why is this research considered a correlational study rather than a true experiment?

f. Why would it not be possible to conduct a true experiment to determine whether the amount of health care spending causes changes in health?

15.64 **Availability of food, amount eaten, and correlation:** Did you know that sometimes you eat more just because the food is in front of you? Geier, Rozin, and Doros (2006) studied how portion size affected the amount people consumed. They discovered interesting things such as that people eat more M&M's when the candies are dispensed using a big spoon as compared with when a small spoon is used. They investigated whether people eat more when more food is available. Hypothetical data are presented in the table for the amount of candy presented in a bowl for customers to take and the amount of candy taken by the end of each day of the study.

Number of Pieces Presented	Number of Pieces Taken
10	3
25	14
50	26
75	44
100	36
125	57
150	41

a. What are the two variables in this study? What type of variable is each?

b. Create a scatterplot of these data.

c. Describe your impression of the relation between these variables based on the scatterplot.

d. Compute the Pearson correlation coefficient for these data.

e. Summarize your findings using Cohen's guidelines.

f. Perform the remaining steps of hypothesis testing.

g. What limitations are there to the conclusions you can draw based on this correlation?

h. Use the A-B-C model to explain possible causes for the relation between these variables.

15.65 **High school athletic participation and correlation:** Researchers examined longitudinal data to explore the long-term effects of high school athletic participation in the United States (Lutz, Cornish, Gonnerman, Ralston, & Baker, 2009). They reported three findings. First, they found that high school athletic participation was related to a number of positive outcomes. These included increases in high school grade point average, university completion, earnings as an adult, and various positive health behaviors. Second, they found that a number of other variables affected the relation between high school athletic participation and these positive outcomes; these other variables included race, gender, and type of school (e.g., public, private). Third, they found that high school athletic participation was related to several negative outcomes among male athletes; these included increases in alcohol consumption, sexist and homophobic attitudes, and violence.

a. How might high school athletic participation be operationalized as a nominal variable? Be specific.

b. How might high school athletic participation be operationalized as a scale variable? Be specific.

c. Why might correlation be a useful tool with data like those used in this study? (Assume the use of scale variables.)

d. Did the researchers report positive correlations? If yes, list at least two. Explain why these are positive correlations.

e. Did the researchers report negative correlations? If yes, list at least two. Explain why these are negative correlations.

f. Use the A-B-C model to offer three different causal explanations for the correlation between high school athletic participation and positive health behaviors.

g. Why might partial correlation be useful in this study? Give at least one specific example of how it might be useful.

15.66 **Mental health and partial correlation:** A study by Nolan and colleagues (2003) examined the relation between externalizing behaviors (acting out) and anxiety in adolescents. Depression has been shown to relate to both of these variables. What role might depression play in the observed positive relation between these variables? The accompanying correlation matrix displays the Pearson correlation coefficients, as calculated by computer software, for each pair of the variables of interest: depression, externalizing, and anxiety. The Pearson correlation coefficients for each pair of variables are at the intersection in the chart of the two variables. For example, the correlation coefficient for the association between depression (top row) and externalizing (second column of correlations) is 0.635, a very strong positive correlation.

a. Given that the authors calculated correlation coefficients, what kind of variables are depression, anxiety, and externalizing? Explain your answer.

	Correlations		
	Depression	Externalizing	Anxiety
Depression Pearson Correlation	1	0.635(★★)	0.368(★★)
Sig. (2-tailed)		.000	.000
N	220	219	207
Externalizing Pearson Correlation	0.635(★★)	1	0.356(★★)
Sig. (2-tailed)	.000		.000
N	219	220	207
Anxiety Pearson Correlation	0.368(★★)	0.356(★★)	1
Sig. (2-tailed)	.000	.000	
N	207	207	207

★★Correlation is significant at the 0.01 level (2-tailed).

b. What is the correlation coefficient for the association between depression and anxiety? Explain what this correlation coefficient tells us about the relation between these variables.

c. What is the correlation coefficient for the association between anxiety and externalizing? Explain what this correlation coefficient tells us about the relation between these variables.

d. The partial correlation of anxiety and externalizing is 0.17, controlling for the variable of depression. How is this different from the original Pearson correlation coefficient between these two variables?

e. Why is the partial correlation coefficient different from the original Pearson correlation coefficient between these two variables? What did we learn by calculating a partial correlation?

f. Why can we not draw causal conclusions with respect to these findings?

LaunchPad
macmillan learning

Visit LaunchPad to access the e-book and to test your knowledge with LearningCurve.

TERMS

correlation coefficient (p. 458)
positive correlation (p. 459)
negative correlation (p. 460)
spurious correlation (p. 463)

Pearson correlation coefficient (p. 464)
partial correlation (p. 470)
big data (p. 472)
psychometrics (p. 475)

psychometricians (p. 475)
test–retest reliability (p. 475)
coefficient alpha (p. 475)

FORMULAS

$$r = \frac{\Sigma[(X - M_X)(Y - M_Y)]}{\sqrt{(SS_X)(SS_Y)}}$$ (p. 468)

$df_r = N - 2$ (p. 470)

SYMBOLS

r (p. 464)

ρ (p. 464)

α (p. 475)

Regression

Simple Linear Regression

Prediction Versus Relation

Regression with *z* Scores

Determining the Regression Equation

The Standardized Regression Coefficient and
  Hypothesis Testing with Regression

Interpretation and Prediction

Regression and Error

Applying the Lessons of Correlation to Regression

Regression to the Mean

Multiple Regression

Understanding the Equation

Multiple Regression in Everyday Life

Data Ethics: Ethical Landmines in Predicting
Individual Behavior

BEFORE YOU GO ON

- You should understand the six steps
  of hypothesis testing (Chapter 7).

- You should understand the concept
  of effect size (Chapter 8).

- You should understand the concept
  of correlation (Chapter 15).

- You should be able to explain
  the limitations of correlation
  (Chapter 15).

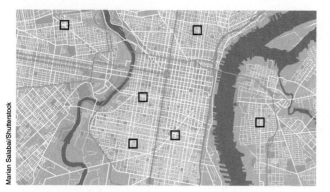

Predictive Policing Predictive policing technologies, such as PredPol (predpol.com), can be used to highlight potential areas where crimes are likely to be committed. The red boxes in this figure indicate high-risk areas.

What if we could predict crimes and stop them before they ever happened? This sounds like science fiction, perhaps because it is the idea behind the 1956 Philip K. Dick short story "Pre-Crime," which was the basis for the 2002 movie *Minority Report*. Both versions depict a future in which people are arrested and placed in detention camps before they commit a crime. But predicting crimes is more than the stuff of fiction. Predictive policing—using statistical methods to predict future crime—made headlines in 2011 when *Time* magazine named the city of Santa Cruz's predictive policing as one of the most important inventions of the year (City of Santa Cruz, 2012; Gerstner, 2018).

Since then, many cities in the United States and in Europe have invested in predictive policing technologies, and police agencies can purchase commercially available software packages for this purpose (Hardyns & Rummens, 2018). Santa Cruz's predictive policing focused on identifying the location and timing of future burglaries and vehicle thefts. Technologies like those used by the city of Santa Cruz collect a lot of data regarding crimes, such as the date and time of crimes, Global Positioning System (GPS)–identified locations from police vehicles, the types of houses that are burglarized, the addresses and placements of the houses (e.g., near road or set back from road), and the burglar's method of entry. The city of Santa Cruz then uses statistical methods to predict the likelihood of future crimes in an area.

For example, one software package performs statistical analyses to predict the likelihood and location of a future crime three times daily, based on up-to-the minute crime data (Gerstner, 2018). This program sends live alerts to on-duty police officers about locations in which a crime is likely to occur soon, so they can then increase patrols in that area.

Are these technologies effective? After using the technology to guide its policing efforts, Santa Cruz saw an 11% drop in the number of home burglaries committed in the city. Other cities have observed noticeable drops in crime after employing these techniques as well, although some cities have observed no discernable drop in crime (Hardyns & Rummens, 2018).

One statistical method used by predictive policing software packages is regression—the topic of this chapter. In this chapter, we will build on our knowledge of correlation to create prediction tools. We begin by learning how to use data from a single variable to make predictions about another variable. Then, after discussing the limitations of regression, we examine how it can be extended to use multiple variables simultaneously to predict an outcome, similar to using lots of different pieces of information to predict the likelihood of a crime.

Simple Linear Regression

Correlation is a marvelous tool because it allows us to know the direction and strength of a relation between two variables. We can also use a correlation coefficient to develop a *prediction tool*—an equation to predict a person's score on one variable from his or her score on a different variable. Language Alert! When we were dealing with experimental research designs that we analyzed with ANOVA or *t*-tests, we used the terms *independent variable* and *dependent variable*. Those terms imply causation: We manipulate an independent variable, which causes a change in the dependent variable. Because regression builds on correlation, we cannot make any causal claims. That is why we use new terms to refer to the variables. In regression, we have a *predictor variable* and an *outcome variable*. The predictor variable is the variable that we use to make a best guess about what an individual's score will be on the outcome variable. Although the predictor variable is similar to the independent variable and the outcome variable is similar to the dependent variable, we modify our language to say predictor variables and outcome variables because we cannot assume causation.

Being able to predict the future is powerful stuff, but it's not magic—it's statistics. Of course, statistical prediction requires building in some margin of error. For example, many universities use variables such as high school grades and standardized test scores to predict the success of prospective students. They aren't perfect predictions, but they are much better than gazing into a crystal ball. Similarly, insurance companies input demographic data into an equation to predict the likelihood of a class of people (such as young male drivers) to submit a claim. Mark Zuckerberg, the founder of Facebook, is even alleged to have used data from Facebook users to predict breakups of romantic relationships. He used predictor variables, such as the amount of time looking at others' Facebook profiles, changes in postings to others' Facebook walls, and photo-tagging patterns, to predict the outcome variable: the end of a relationship as evidenced by the user's Facebook relationship status. He was right about one-third of the time ("Can Facebook Predict Your Breakup?," 2010).

Ridesharing Services Predict Decline in Public Transportation Use. Ridesharing services such as Uber and Lyft provide commuters with a convenient transportation alternative. But, what is their effect on the use of public transportation? Using data from five major cities in the U.S. spanning 2002–2018, researcher Michael Graehler and his colleagues (Graehler, Mucci, & Erhardt, 2019) used regression to predict public transportation ridership. They found that train ridership decreased by 1.3% and bus ridership decreased by 1.7% for every year that ridesharing services had been in a city. City governments could use the information gained from this regression analysis to predict future public transportation needs.

Roman Tiraspolsky/Alamy

Prediction Versus Relation

The name for the prediction tool that we've been discussing is *regression*, a statistical technique that can provide specific quantitative information that predicts relations between variables. More specifically, ***simple linear regression*** *is a statistical tool that lets us predict a person's score on an outcome variable from his or her score on one predictor variable.*

Simple linear regression allows us to calculate the equation for a straight line that describes the data. Once we can graph that line, we can look at any point on the *x*-axis and find its corresponding point on the *y*-axis. That corresponding point is what we predict for *y*. (*Note:* As with the Pearson correlation coefficient, we are not able to use simple linear regression if the data do not form the pattern of a straight line.) Let's consider an example of research that uses regression techniques, and then walk through the steps to develop a regression equation.

Christopher Ruhm, an economist, often uses regression in his research. In one study, he wanted to explore the reasons for his finding that the death rate *decreases* when unemployment goes up—a surprising negative relation between the death rate and an economic indicator (Ruhm, 2000). He took this relation a step further, into the realm of prediction: He found that an increase of 1% in unemployment predicted a decrease in the death rate of 0.5%, on average. In other words, a *poorer* economy predicted *better* health!

● **Simple linear regression** is a statistical tool that lets us predict a person's score on an outcome variable from his or her score on one predictor variable.

To explore the reasons for this surprising finding, Ruhm (2006) conducted regression analyses for variables related to health (smoking, obesity, and physical activity) and variables related to the economy (income, unemployment, and the length of the workweek). He analyzed data from a sample of nearly 1.5 million participants collected from telephone surveys over more than a decade. Among other things, Ruhm found that a decrease in working hours predicted decreases in smoking, obesity, and physical inactivity.

Regression can take us a step beyond correlation. Regression can provide specific quantitative predictions that more precisely explain relations among variables.

For example, Ruhm reported that a decrease in the workweek of just 1 hour predicted a 1% decrease in physical inactivity. Ruhm suggested that shorter working hours free up time for physical activity—something he might not have thought of without the more specific quantitative information provided by regression. Let's now conduct a simple linear regression analysis using information that we're already familiar with: z scores.

Regression with z Scores

To illustrate the case of regression, we will imagine a therapist who wants to understand the level of depression his clients are likely to experience. This research-savvy therapist knows that stressful life events are associated with higher levels of depression (Legget, Burgard, & Zivin, 2016). So, knowing how many stressful life events a client has had in the past 2 years may help the therapist better understand how depressed each of his clients may be.

Let's assume the therapist is working with a client named Raphael, who has experienced three stressful life events in the past 2 years. We can refer to the size and direction of the correlation ($r = 0.58$) to predict his current depression score. Doing so may help the therapist determine how best to help Raphael. To make this prediction, we start with a statistic we are more familiar with: z scores. If we know Raphael's z score on one variable (the predictor), we can multiply by the correlation coefficient to calculate his predicted z score on a second variable (the outcome). Remember that z scores indicate how far a score falls from the mean in terms of standard deviations. The formula, called the *standardized regression equation* because it uses z scores, is:

$$z_{\hat{Y}} = (r_{XY})(z_X)$$

The subscripts in the formula indicate that the first z score is for the outcome variable, Y, and that the second z score is for the predictor variable, X. The ^ symbol over the subscript Y, called a "hat" by statisticians, refers to the fact that this variable is predicted. This is the z score for "Y hat"—the z score for the *predicted* score on the outcome variable, not the actual score. We cannot, of course, predict the actual score, and the "hat" reminds us of this. When we refer to this score, we can either say "the predicted score for Y" (with no hat, because we have specified with words that it is predicted) or we can use the hat, $\hat{Y}$, to indicate that it is predicted. (We would not use both expressions because that would be redundant.) The subscripts X and Y for the Pearson correlation coefficient, r, indicate that this is the correlation between variables X and Y.

EXAMPLE 16.1

To get a better understanding of the standardized regression equation, let's examine what would happen with different values of the predictor variable, the number of stressful life events. If Raphael's number of stressful life events were identical to the mean number of stressful life events, then he'd have a z score of 0. If we multiply that by the correlation coefficient, then he'd have a predicted z score of 0 on the Beck Depression Inventory:

$$z_{\hat{Y}} = (0.58)(0) = 0$$

So if Raphael's score is right at the mean on the predictor variable, then we'd predict that he'd be right at the mean on the outcome variable.

If Raphael had more stressful life events than average and had a z score of 1.0 on the predictor variable (1 standard deviation above the mean), then his predicted score on the outcome variable would be 0.58 (that is, 0.58 standard deviation above the mean):

$$z_{\hat{Y}} = (0.58)(1) = 0.58$$

If his z score were −2 (that is, if it were 2 standard deviations below the mean), his predicted z score on the outcome variable would be −1.16 (that is, 1.16 standard deviations below the mean):

$$z_{\hat{Y}} = (0.58)(-2) = -1.16$$

Notice two things: First, because this is a positive correlation, a score above the mean on stressful life events predicts a score above the mean on the Beck Depression Inventory and vice versa. Second, the predicted z score on the outcome variable is closer to its mean than is the z score for the predictor variable. Table 16-1 illustrates this for several z scores.

This regressing of the outcome variable—the fact that it is closer to its mean—is called ***regression to the mean***, *the tendency of scores that are particularly high or low to drift toward the mean over time.*

● **Regression to the mean** is the tendency of scores that are particularly high or low to drift toward the mean over time.

TABLE 16-1   Regression to the Mean

One reason that regression equations are so named is because they predict a z score on the outcome variable that is closer to the mean than is the z score on the predictor variable. Scores regress, or go backward, toward the mean. In fact, this phenomenon is often called *regression to the mean*. The following predicted z scores for the outcome variable, Y, were calculated by multiplying the z score for the predictor variable, X, by the Pearson correlation coefficient of 0.58.

z Score for the Predictor Variable, X	Predicted z Score for the Outcome Variable, Y
−2.0	−1.16
−1.0	−0.58
0.0	0.00
1.0	0.58
2.0	1.16

In the social sciences, many phenomena demonstrate regression to the mean. For example, parents who are very tall tend to have children who are somewhat shorter than they are, although probably still above average. And parents who are very short tend to have children who are somewhat taller than they are, although probably still below average. We explore this concept in more detail later in this chapter.

When we don't have a person's z score on the predictor variable, we have to perform the additional step of converting his or her raw score to a z score. In addition, when we calculate a predicted z score on the outcome variable, we can use the formula that determines a raw score from a z score. Let's try it. ●

EXAMPLE 16.2

We already know that Raphael has had three stressful life events. What would we predict for his depression score?

> **STEP 1: Calculate the z score.**

We first have to calculate Raphael's z score on number of stressful life events. Using the mean (1.900) and the standard deviation (1.663), we calculate:

$$z_X = \frac{(X - M_X)}{SD_X} = \frac{(3 - 1.900)}{1.663} = 0.661$$

> **STEP 2: Multiply the z score by the correlation coefficient.**

We multiply this z score by the correlation coefficient to get his predicted z score on the outcome variable, the depression score:

$$z_{\hat{Y}} = (r_{XY})(z_X) = (0.58)(0.661) = 0.383$$

> **STEP 3: Convert the z score to a raw score.**

We convert from the predicted z score on Y, 0.383, to a predicted raw score for Y, using the mean and standard deviation of the depression scores in Table 16-2:

$$\hat{Y} = z_Y(SD_Y) + M_Y = 0.383(9.358) + 15.700 = 19.284$$

If Raphael had three stressful life events, this number would reflect more than the average, so we would expect him to have a higher than average depression score. And the formula makes this very prediction—that Raphael's depression score would be 19.28, which is higher than the mean (15.70).

The admissions counselor, the insurance salesperson, and Mark Zuckerberg of Facebook, however, are unlikely to have the time or interest to do conversions

TABLE 16-2	Is Experiencing Stressful Life Events Related to Depression?

Here are the scores for 10 individuals on two scale variables: participants' number of stressful life events experienced in the past 2 years and their Beck Depression Inventory score. The correlation between these variables is 0.58, but regression can take us a step further. We can develop a regression equation to assist with prediction.

Individual	Number of stressful life events	Beck Depression Inventory score
1	1	24
2	2	20
3	2	18
4	1	10
5	3	18
6	0	0
7	4	30
8	0	2
9	5	15
10	1	20
Mean	1.900	15.700
Standard deviation	1.663	9.358

from raw scores to z scores and back, so the z score regression equation is not useful in a practical sense for situations in which we must make ongoing predictions using the same variables. It is very useful, however, as a tool to help us develop a regression equation we can use with raw scores, a procedure we look at in the next section. ●

Determining the Regression Equation

You may remember the equation for a line that you learned in geometry class. The version you likely learned was: $y = m(x) + b$. (In this equation, b is the intercept and m is the slope.) In statistics, we use a slightly different version of this formula:

$$\hat{Y} = a + b(X)$$

In the regression formula, a is the ***intercept***, *the predicted value for* Y *when* X *is equal to 0, which is the point at which the line crosses, or intercepts, the y-axis.* In Figure 16-1, the intercept is 5. b is the ***slope***, *the amount that* Y *is predicted to increase for an increase of one unit in* X. In Figure 16-1, the slope is 2. As X increases from 3 to 4, for example, we see an increase in what we predict for a Y of 2: from 11 to 13. The equation, therefore, is: $\hat{Y} = 5 + 2(X)$. If the score on X is 6, for example, the predicted score for Y is: $\hat{Y} = 5 + 2(6) = 5 + 12 = 17$. We can verify this on the line in Figure 16-1. Here, we were given the regression equation and regression line, but usually we have to determine them from the data. In this section, we learn the process of calculating a regression equation from data.

MASTERING THE FORMULA

16-2: The simple linear regression equation uses the formula:

$$\hat{Y} = a + b(X)$$

In this formula, X is the raw score on the predictor variable and $\hat{Y}$ is the predicted raw score on the outcome variable. a is the intercept of the line, and b is its slope.

● The **intercept** is the predicted value for Y when X is equal to 0, which is the point at which the line crosses, or intercepts, the y-axis.

● The **slope** is the amount that Y is predicted to increase for an increase of one unit in X.

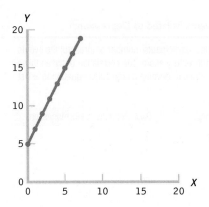

FIGURE 16-1

The Equation for a Line

The equation for a line includes the intercept, the point at which the line crosses the y-axis; here the intercept is 5. It also includes the slope, the amount that Y increases for an increase of one unit in X. Here, the slope is 2. The equation, therefore, is: $\hat{Y} = 5 + 2(X)$.

EXAMPLE 16.3

Once we have the equation for a line, it's easy to input any value for X to determine the predicted value for Y. Let's imagine that our therapist encounters another client, Tia, who had two stressful life events in the past 2 years. If we had a regression equation, then we could input Tia's score of 2 on X and find her predicted score on Y. But first we have to develop the regression equation. Using the z score regression equation to find the intercept and slope enables us to "see" where these numbers come from in a way that makes sense (Aron & Aron, 2002). For this, we use the z score regression equation: $z_{\hat{Y}} = (r_{XY})(z_X)$.

We start by calculating a, the intercept, a process that takes three steps.

> **STEP 1: Find the z score for an X of 0.**

We know that the intercept is the point at which the line crosses the y-axis when X is equal to 0. So we start by finding the z score for an X of 0 using the mean and standard deviation from our predictor in Table 16-2, number of stressful life events, in the formula:

$$z_X = \frac{(X - M_X)}{SD_X} = \frac{(0 - 1.900)}{1.663} = -1.143$$

> **STEP 2: Use the z score regression equation to calculate the predicted z score on Y.**

We use the z score regression equation $z_{\hat{Y}} = (r_{XY})(z_X)$, to calculate the predicted z score on Y for an X of 0.

$$z_{\hat{Y}} = (r_{XY})(z_X) = (0.58)\,(-1.143) = -0.663$$

> **STEP 3: Convert the z score to its raw score.**

We convert the z score for $\hat{Y}$ to its raw score using mean and standard deviation of the outcome variable from Table 16-2 in the formula:

$$\hat{Y} = z_{\hat{Y}}(SD_Y) + M_Y = -1.143(9.358) + 15.700 = 9.496$$

We have the intercept! When X is 0, $\hat{Y}$ is 9.496. That is, we would predict that someone with no stressful life events in the past 2 years would have a depression score of 9.496.

Next, we calculate b, the slope, a process that is similar to the one for calculating the intercept, but calculating the slope takes four steps rather than three. We know that the slope is the amount that $\hat{Y}$ increases when X increases by 1. So all we need to do is calculate what we would predict for an X of 1. We can then compare the $\hat{Y}$ increases for an X of 0 to the $\hat{Y}$ for an X of 1. The difference between the two is the slope.

> **STEP 1: Find the z score for an X of 1.**

We find the z score for an X of 1, using the mean and standard deviation for our predictor in the formula:

$$z_X = \frac{(X - M_X)}{SD_X} = \frac{(1 - 1.900)}{1.663} = -0.541$$

> **STEP 2: Use the z score regression equation to calculate the predicted z score on Y.**

We use the z score regression equation, $z_{\hat{Y}} = (r_{XY})(z_X)$, to calculate the predicted z score on Y for an X of 1:

$$z_{\hat{Y}} = (r_{XY})(z_X) = (0.58)(-0.541) = -0.314.$$

> **STEP 3: Convert the z score to its raw score.**

We convert the z score for $\hat{Y}$ to its raw score, using the mean and standard deviation for the outcome variable in the formula:

$$\hat{Y} = z_{\hat{Y}}(SD_Y) + M_Y = -0.314(9.358) + 15.700 = 12.762$$

> **STEP 4: Determine the slope.**

The prediction is that a person with one stressful life event would have a depression score of 12.762. As X, number of stressful life events, increased from 0 to 1, what happened to Y? First, ask yourself if it increased or decreased. An increase would mean a positive slope, and a decrease would mean a negative slope. Here, we see an increase in depression scores as the number of stressful life events increased. Next, determine how much it increased or decreased. In this case, the increase is 3.266 (calculated as $12.762 - 9.496 = 3.266$). So, the slope here is 3.27.

We now have the intercept and the slope and can put them into the equation: $\hat{Y} = a + b(X)$, which becomes $\hat{Y} = 9.50 + 3.27(X)$. We can use this equation to predict Tia's depression score based on her number of stressful life events, two.

$$\hat{Y} = 9.50 + 3.27(X) = 9.50 + 3.27(2) = 16.04$$

Based on the sample of data in Table 16-2, we predict that Tia would have a depression score of 16.04, given that she has had two stressful life events. We could have predicted this same score for Tia using the z score regression equation. The difference is that now we can input any score into the raw-score regression equation, and it does all the work of converting for us. The admissions counselor, the insurance salesperson, and the Facebook founder have an easy formula and don't have to know z scores to use it.

We can also use the regression equation to draw the regression line and get a visual sense of what it looks like. We do this by calculating at least two points on the regression line, usually for one low score on X and one high score on X. We would always have $\hat{Y}$ for two scores, 0 and 1 (although in some cases these numbers won't make sense, such as for the variable of human body temperature; you'd never have a temperature that low!). Because these scores are low on the scale for number of stressful life events, we would choose a high score as well; 5 is the highest score in the original data set, so we can use that:

$$\hat{Y} = 9.50 + 3.27(X) = 9.50 + 3.27(5) = 25.85$$

For someone with five stressful life events, we predict a depression score of 25.85. We now have three points, as shown in Table 16-3. It's useful to have three points because the third point serves as a check on the other two. If the three points do not fall in a straight line, we have made an error.

We then draw a line through the dots—but it's not just any line. This line, which you can see in Figure 16-2, is the regression line,

TABLE 16-3 Drawing a Regression Line

We calculate at least two, and preferably three, pairs of scores for X and $\hat{Y}$. Ideally, at least one is low on the scale for X and at least one is high.

X	$\hat{Y}$
0	9.50
1	12.76
5	25.85

FIGURE 16-2

The Regression Line

To draw a regression line, we plot at least two, and preferably three, pairs of scores for X and $\hat{Y}$. We then draw a line through the dots.

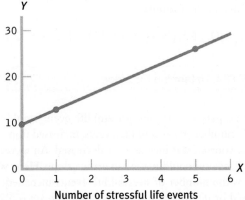

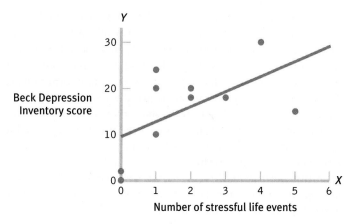

FIGURE 16-3

The Line of Best Fit

The regression line is the line that best fits the points on the scatterplot. Statistically, the regression line is the line that leads to the least amount of error in prediction.

which has another name that is wonderfully intuitive: the line of best fit. If you have ever had some clothes tailored to fit your body, perhaps for a wedding or other special occasion, then you know that there really is such a thing as a "best fit."

In regression, the meaning of "the line of best fit" is the same as that characteristic in a tailored set of clothes. We couldn't make the line a little steeper, or raise or lower it, or manipulate it in any way that would make it represent those dots any better than it already does. When we look at the scatterplot around the line in Figure 16-3, we see that the line goes precisely through the middle of the data. Statistically, this is the line that leads to the least amount of error in prediction.

Language Alert! Notice that the line we just drew starts in the lower left of the graph and ends in the upper right, meaning that it has a positive slope. The word *slope* is often used when discussing, say, ski slopes. A positive slope means that the line looks like it's going uphill as we move from left to right. This makes sense because the calculations for the regression equation are based on the correlation coefficient, and the scatterplot associated with a positive correlation coefficient has dots that also go "uphill." If the slope were negative the line would start in the upper left of the graph and end in the lower right. A negative slope means that the line looks like it's going downhill as we move from left to right. Again, this makes sense, because we base the calculations on a negative correlation coefficient, and the scatterplot associated with a negative correlation coefficient has dots that also go "downhill." ●

The Line of Best Fit The line of best fit in regression has the same characteristics as tailored clothes; there is nothing we could do to that line that would make it fit the data any better.

The Standardized Regression Coefficient and Hypothesis Testing with Regression

The steepness of the slope tells us the amount that the outcome variable changes as the predictor variable increases by 1. So, for the stressful life events and depression example, the slope of 3.27 tells us that for each additional stressful life event, we can

16-3: The standardized regression coefficient, β, is calculated by multiplying the slope of the regression equation by the square root of the sum of squares for the predictor variable divided by the square root of the sum of squares for the outcome variable:

$$\beta = (b)\frac{\sqrt{SS_X}}{\sqrt{SS_Y}}$$

• The **standardized regression coefficient**, a standardized version of the slope in a regression equation, is the predicted change in the outcome variable in terms of standard deviations for an increase of 1 standard deviation in the predictor variable; symbolized by β and often called *beta weight*.

predict that the depression score will be 3.27 points higher. Let's say that another therapist was interested in using the number of stressful life events to predict depression scores, but instead of using the full 21-item Beck Depression Inventory, used the short form of this inventory, which has only 13 items. How could the therapist use the regression equation developed with the 21-item form to make predictions on the 13-item form? The problem here is that the slope of 3.27 for the 21-item form will not be an accurate predictor for the shorter form, whose scores have a narrower range.

This problem might remind you of the problems we faced in comparing scores on different scales. To appropriately compare scores, we standardized them using the z statistic. We can standardize slopes in a similar way by calculating the standardized regression coefficient. *The **standardized regression coefficient**, a standardized version of the slope in a regression equation, is the predicted change in the outcome variable in terms of standard deviations for an increase of 1 standard deviation in the predictor variable.* It is symbolized by β and is often called a *beta weight* because of its symbol (pronounced "beta"). It is calculated using the formula:

$$\beta = (b)\frac{\sqrt{SS_X}}{\sqrt{SS_Y}}$$

We calculated the slope, 3.27, earlier in this chapter. To complete the equation, we need to calculate the sum of squares for both of the variables. Table 16-4 illustrates these calculations. At the bottom of the table, we can see that the sum of squares for the predictor variable of stressful life events is 24.90 and the sum of squares for the outcome variable of depression score is 788.10. By inputting these numbers into the formula, we calculate:

$$\beta = (b)\frac{\sqrt{SS_X}}{\sqrt{SS_Y}} = (3.27)\frac{\sqrt{24.90}}{\sqrt{788.10}} = (3.27)\frac{4.990}{28.073} = 0.58$$

TABLE 16-4 Calculating the Sum of Squares for the Standardized Regression Equation

We calculate the sum of squares for the predictor variable (X) and the outcome variable (Y) to use in the equation for the standardized regression coefficient (β).

Stressful life events (X)	($X - M_X$)	($X - M_X$)^2	Depression score (Y)	($Y - M_Y$)	($Y - M_Y$)^2
1	−0.900	0.810	24	8.300	68.890
2	0.100	0.010	20	4.300	18.490
2	0.100	0.010	18	2.300	5.290
1	−0.900	0.810	10	−5.700	32.490
3	1.100	1.210	18	2.300	5.290
0	−1.900	3.610	0	−15.700	246.490
4	2.100	4.410	30	14.300	204.490
0	−1.900	3.610	2	−13.700	187.690
5	3.100	9.610	15	−0.700	0.490
1	−0.900	0.810	20	4.300	18.490
		$\Sigma(X - M_X)^2 = 24.900$			$\Sigma(Y - M_Y)^2 = 788.100$

Notice that this result is the same as the Pearson correlation coefficient of 0.58. In fact, for simple linear regression, the standardized regression coefficient is always exactly the same as the correlation. Any difference would be due to rounding decisions for both calculations. Both the standardized regression coefficient and the correlation coefficient indicate the change in standard deviation that we expect when the predictor variable increases by 1 standard deviation. Note that the correlation coefficient is *not* the same as the standardized regression coefficient when an equation includes more than one predictor variable, a situation we'll encounter later in the section "Multiple Regression."

Because the standardized regression coefficient is the same as the correlation coefficient with simple linear regression, the outcome of hypothesis testing is also identical. The hypothesis-testing process that we used to test whether the correlation coefficient is statistically significantly different from 0 can also be used to test whether the standardized regression coefficient is statistically significantly different from 0. Recall that for the correlation coefficient, the degrees of freedom is $N - 2$. Thus, in this case, the two-tailed critical value of r, based on 8 degrees of freedom and an alpha level of 0.05, is 0.632. The calculated r of 0.58 is not larger than this critical value. So, in this case, despite the value of the correlation being large (as determined by the conventions given in Table 15-1 from Chapter 15), it is not statistically significant.

> **MASTERING THE CONCEPT**
>
> **16-2:** A standardized regression coefficient is the standardized version of a slope, much like a z statistic is a standardized version of a raw score. For simple linear regression, the standardized regression coefficient is identical to the correlation coefficient. This means that when we conduct hypothesis testing and conclude that a correlation coefficient is statistically significantly different from 0, we can draw the same conclusion about the standardized regression coefficient.

CHECK YOUR LEARNING

Reviewing the Concepts

> Regression builds on correlation, enabling us not only to quantify the relation between two variables but also to predict a score on an outcome variable from a score on a predictor variable.

> With the standardized regression equation, we simply multiply a person's z score on the predictor variable by the Pearson correlation coefficient to predict that person's z score on an outcome variable.

> We use the standardized regression equation to build the raw score regression equation that can predict a raw score on an outcome variable from a raw score on the predictor variable.

> The raw-score regression equation is easier to use because the equation itself does the transformations from raw score to z score and back.

> We can graph the regression line, $\hat{Y} = a + b(X)$, based on values for the y intercept, a, the predicted value on Y when X is 0; and the slope, b, which is the change in Y expected for a one-unit increase in X.

> The slope, which captures the nature of the relation between the variables, can be standardized by calculating the standardized regression coefficient. The standardized regression coefficient tells us the predicted change in the outcome variable in terms of standard deviations for every increase of 1 standard deviation in the predictor variable.

> With simple linear regression, the standardized regression coefficient is identical to the Pearson correlation coefficient.

continued on next page

| Clarifying the Concepts | **16-1** | What is simple linear regression? |
| | **16-2** | What purpose does the regression line serve? |

| Calculating the Statistics | **16-3** | Let's assume we know that women's heights and weights are correlated and the Pearson coefficient is 0.28. Let's also assume that we know the following descriptive statistics: For women's height, the mean is 5 feet 4 inches (64 inches), with a standard deviation of 2 inches; for women's weight, the mean is 155 pounds, with a standard deviation of 15 pounds. Sarah is 5 feet 7 inches tall. How much would you predict she weighs? To answer this question, complete the following steps: |

a. Transform the raw score for the predictor variable into a z score.

b. Calculate the predicted z score for the outcome variable.

c. Transform the z score for the outcome variable back into a predicted raw score.

16-4 Given the regression line $\hat{Y} = 12 + 0.67(X)$, make predictions for each of the following:

a. $X = 78$

b. $X = -14$

c. $X = 52$

| Applying the Concepts | **16-5** | In Exercise 15.57, we explored the relation between number of taboo words said in 1 minute and the number of animal words said in 1 minute. We computed a correlation of 0.353 between these variables. The fictional data are presented below. |

Number of taboo words (X)	Number of animals (Y)
9	23
5	20
4	17
12	28
14	26
10	16
9	17
11	18
14	23
6	21
7	25
13	19

a. What is the intercept?

b. What is the slope?

c. What is the regression equation?

d. Interpret both the y intercept and the slope in this regression equation.

e. Compute the standardized regression coefficient.

f. Explain what a strong correlation means for the predictive ability of the regression line.

g. What conclusion would you make if you performed a hypothesis test for this regression?

Solutions to these Check Your Learning questions can be found in Appendix D.

Interpretation and Prediction

In this section, we learn how to calculate effect sizes and measures of prediction error so that we can interpret how well a regression equation predicts behavior. Then we discuss why regression doesn't allow us to designate causation as we interpret data; for instance, Christopher Ruhm (2000) could not say that higher unemployment caused better health. This discussion of causation then leads us to a familiar warning about interpreting the meaning of regression, this time due to the process called *regression to the mean*.

Regression and Error

For many different reasons, predictions are full of errors. For example, we might predict an individual's depression score based on the number of stressful life events she has experienced, but we could be wrong in our prediction. Other factors, such as her sleep, diet, and exercise habits, as well as her coping skills, are all likely to influence her likelihood of becoming depressed. The number of stressful life events is highly unlikely to be a perfect predictor.

Errors in prediction lead to variability—and that is something we can measure. For *t* tests and ANOVAs, for example, we use standard deviation and standard error to calculate the variability around the mean. For regression, we calculate the variability around the line of best fit. Figure 16-4 illustrates that there is less variability—or error—when the data points are clustered tightly around the line of best fit. There is more variability—or error—when the data points are far away from the line of best fit.

(a)

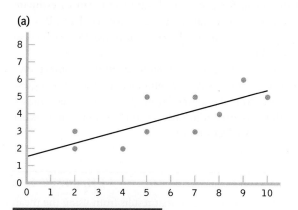

(b)

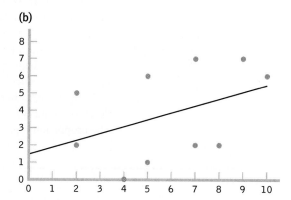

FIGURE 16-4

The Standard Error of the Estimate

Data points clustered closely around the line of best fit, as in graph (a), are described by a small standard error of the estimate. Data points clustered far away from the line of best fit, as in graph (b), are described by a large standard error of the estimate. We have a higher level of confidence in the predictive ability of the predictor variable when the data points are tightly clustered around the line of best fit, as in (a) (that is, there is much less error), and we have a lower level of confidence in the predictive ability of the predictor variable when the data points vary widely around the line of best fit, as in (b) (that is, there is much more error).

● The **standard error of the estimate** is a statistic that indicates the average vertical distance between a regression line and the actual data points.

With linear regression, there are two common ways of quantifying how well the regression line captures the variability in the data. One of these is called *the **standard error of the estimate**, a statistic that indicates the average vertical distance between a regression* *line and the actual data points*. The standard error of the estimate is essentially the standard deviation of the actual data points around the regression line. A smaller standard error of the estimate means that there is less error and that we're doing much better in our predictions than if there had been a larger standard error. Visually, this means that the actual scores are closer to the regression line, as in Figure 16-4a. Conversely, with a larger standard error of the estimate, we're doing much worse in our predictions than if there had been a smaller standard error. Visually, the actual scores are farther away from the regression line, as in Figure 16-4b. A second way to quantify how well the regression line captures the data is to calculate the proportionate reduction in error.

● The **proportionate reduction in error** is a statistic that quantifies how much more accurate predictions are when we use the regression line instead of the mean as a prediction tool; also called the *coefficient of determination*.

The ***proportionate reduction in error*** *is a statistic that quantifies how much more accurate predictions are when we use the regression line instead of the mean as a prediction tool.* (Note that the proportionate reduction in error is sometimes called the *coefficient of determination*.) More specifically, the proportionate reduction in error is a statistic that quantifies how much more accurate predictions are when scores are predicted using a specific regression equation rather than predicting the mean score for everyone. We turn first to the calculation of the proportionate reduction in error; we then revisit the standard error of the estimate, which is easily calculated once we have calculated the proportionate reduction in error.

Earlier in this chapter, we noted that if we did not have a regression equation, the best we could do is predict the mean for everyone. So, after seeing 10 clients with the Beck Depression Inventory scores shown in Table 16-2, a therapist would predict the next client to have an inventory score of 15.7. There would obviously be a great deal of error if we predicted the mean for everyone. Using the mean to estimate scores is a reasonable way to proceed if that's all the information we have. But the regression line provides a more precise picture of the relation between variables, so using a regression equation reduces error.

We can actually quantify how much better the regression equation is compared to the mean: We calculate the proportion of error that we eliminate by using the regression equation, rather than the mean, to make a prediction. (In this next section, we learn the long way to calculate this proportion in order to understand exactly what the proportion represents. Then we learn a shortcut.)

EXAMPLE 16.4

Using a sample, we can calculate the amount of error that results from using the mean as a predictive tool. We quantify that error by determining how far off a person's score on the outcome variable (depression score) is from the mean, as seen in the column labeled "Error $(Y - M_Y)$" in Table 16-5.

For example, for individual 1, the error is $24 - 15.7 = 8.3$. We then square these errors for all 10 individuals and sum them. This is the sum of squared errors. Here, the sum of squared errors is 788.10 (the sum of the values in the "Squared Error" column). Note that this is the same sum of squares that we calculated in the right side of Table 16-4 for depression scores. It is the total variability around the mean of Y, which is the same as saying it is the total error for predicting Y. So, it is a measure of the error that would result if we predicted the mean for every person in the sample. We call this particular type of sum of squared errors the *sum of squares total, SS_{total}*. It represents the

TABLE 16-5	Calculating Error When We Predict the Mean for Everyone

If we do not have a regression equation, the best we can do is predict the mean for Y for every individual. When we do that, we will of course have some error, because not everyone will have exactly the mean value for Y. This table presents the squared errors for each individual when we predict the mean for each of them. The sum is 788.10.

Individual	Depression score (Y)	Mean (Y)	Error ($Y - M_Y$)	Squared error ($Y - M_Y)^2$
1	24	15.7	8.3	68.89
2	20	15.7	4.3	18.49
3	18	15.7	2.3	5.29
4	10	15.7	−5.7	32.49
5	18	15.7	2.3	5.29
6	0	15.7	−15.7	246.49
7	30	15.7	14.3	204.49
8	2	15.7	−13.7	187.69
9	15	15.7	−0.7	0.49
10	20	15.7	4.3	18.49

worst-case scenario, the total error we would have if there were no regression equation. We can visualize this error on a graph that depicts a horizontal line for the mean, as seen in Figure 16-5. We can add the actual points, as we would in a scatterplot, and draw vertical lines from each point to the mean. These vertical lines give us a visual sense of the error that results from predicting the mean for everyone.

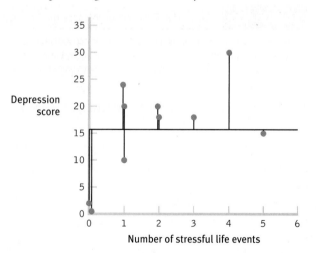

FIGURE 16-5

Visualizing Error

A graph with a horizontal line for the mean, 15.7, allows us to visualize the error that would result if we predicted the mean for everyone. We draw lines for each person's point on a scatterplot to the mean. Those lines are a visual representation of error.

The regression equation can't make the predictions any worse than they would be if we just predicted the mean for everyone. But it's not worth the time and effort to use a regression equation if it doesn't lead to a substantial improvement over just predicting the mean. As we can with the mean, we can calculate the amount of error from using the regression equation with the sample. We can then see how much better we do with the regression equation than with the mean.

First, we calculate what we would predict for each student if we used the regression equation. We do this by plugging each X into the regression equation. Here are the calculations using the equation $\hat{Y} = 9.50 - 3.27(X)$:

$$\hat{Y} = 9.50 - 3.27(1); \hat{Y} = 12.77$$
$$\hat{Y} = 9.50 - 3.27(2); \hat{Y} = 16.04$$
$$\hat{Y} = 9.50 - 3.27(2); \hat{Y} = 16.04$$
$$\hat{Y} = 9.50 - 3.27(1); \hat{Y} = 12.77$$
$$\hat{Y} = 9.50 - 3.27(3); \hat{Y} = 19.31$$
$$\hat{Y} = 9.50 - 3.27(0); \hat{Y} = 9.50$$
$$\hat{Y} = 9.50 - 3.27(4); \hat{Y} = 22.58$$
$$\hat{Y} = 9.50 - 3.27(0); \hat{Y} = 9.50$$
$$\hat{Y} = 9.50 - 3.27(5); \hat{Y} = 25.85$$
$$\hat{Y} = 9.50 - 3.27(1); \hat{Y} = 12.77$$

The $\hat{Y}$'s, or predicted scores for Y, that we just calculated are presented in Table 16-6, where the errors are calculated based on the predicted scores rather than the mean. For example, for student 1, the error is the actual score minus the predicted score: $24 - 12.77 = 11.23$. As before, we square the errors and sum them. The sum of squared errors based on the regression equation is 526.577. We call this the *sum of squared errors,* SS_{error}, because it represents the error that we'd have if we predicted Y using the regression equation.

TABLE 16-6 Calculating Error When We Use the Regression Equation to Predict

When we use a regression equation for prediction, as opposed to using the mean, we have less error. However, we still have some error because not every participant falls exactly on the regression line. This table presents the squared errors for each participant when we predict each one's score on Y using the regression equation. The sum is 526.577.

Individual	Depression score (Y)	Predicted ($\hat{Y}$)	Error ($Y - \hat{Y}$)	Squared error ($Y - \hat{Y}$)^2
1	24	12.77	11.23	126.113
2	20	16.04	3.96	15.682
3	18	16.04	1.96	3.842
4	10	12.77	−2.77	7.673
5	18	19.31	−1.31	1.716
6	0	9.50	−9.50	90.250
7	30	22.58	7.42	55.056
8	2	9.50	−7.50	56.250
9	15	25.85	−10.85	117.723
10	20	12.77	7.23	52.273

As before, we can visualize this error on a graph that includes the regression line, as seen in Figure 16-6. We again add the actual points, as in a scatterplot, and we draw vertical lines from each point to the regression line. These vertical lines give us a visual sense of the error that results from predicting Y for everyone using the regression equation. Notice that these vertical lines in Figure 16-6 tend to be shorter than those connecting each person's point with the mean in Figure 16-5.

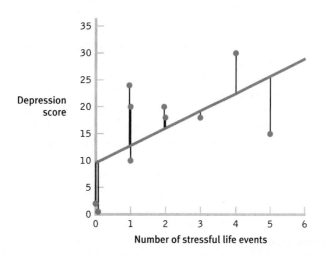

FIGURE 16-6

Visualizing Error

A graph that depicts the regression line allows us to visualize the error that would result if we predicted Y for everyone using the regression equation. We draw lines for each person's point on a scatterplot to the regression line. Those lines are a visual representation of error.

So how much better did we do? The error we predict by using the mean for everyone in this sample is 788.10. The error we predict by using the regression equation for everyone in this sample is 526.577. Remember that the measure of how well the regression equation predicts is called the proportionate *reduction* in error. What we want to know is how much error we have gotten rid of—reduced—by using the regression equation instead of the mean. The amount of error we've reduced is $788.10 - 526.577 = 261.523$. But the word *proportionate* indicates that we want a proportion of the total error that we have reduced, so we set up a ratio to determine this. We have reduced 261.523 of the original 788.10, or $\dfrac{261.523}{788.10} = 0.332$.

We have reduced 0.332, or 33.2%, of the original error by using the regression equation versus using the mean to predict Y. This ratio can be calculated using an equation that represents what we just calculated—the proportionate reduction in error, symbolized as:

$$r^2 = \frac{(SS_{total} - SS_{error})}{SS_{total}} = \frac{(788.10 - 526.577)}{788.10} = 0.332$$

To recap, we simply have to do the following:

1. Determine the error associated with using the mean as the predictor.
2. Determine the error associated with using the regression equation as the predictor.
3. Subtract the error associated with the regression equation from the error associated with the mean.
4. Divide the difference (calculated in step 3) by the error associated with using the mean. ●

MASTERING THE FORMULA

16-4: The proportionate reduction in error is calculated by subtracting the error generated using the regression equation as a prediction tool from the total error that would occur if we used the mean as everyone's predicted score. We then divide this difference by the total error:

$$r^2 = \frac{(SS_{total} - SS_{error})}{SS_{total}}$$

We can interpret the proportionate reduction in error as we did the effect-size estimate for ANOVA. It represents the same statistic.

The proportionate reduction in error tells us how good the regression equation is. Here is another way to state it: The proportionate reduction in error is a measure of the amount of variance in the outcome variable that is explained by the predictor variable. Did you notice the symbol for the proportionate reduction in error? The symbol is r^2. Perhaps you see the connection with another number we have calculated. Yes, we could simply square the correlation coefficient!

The longer calculations are important however, to see the difference between the error in prediction from using the regression equation and the error in prediction from simply predicting the mean for everyone. Once you have calculated the proportionate reduction in error the long way a few times, you'll have a good sense of exactly what you're calculating. In addition to the relation of the proportionate reduction in error to the correlation coefficient, it is the same as another number we've calculated—the effect size for ANOVA, R^2. In both cases, this number represents the proportion of variance in the one variable that is explained by a second variable. For the case of regression, that is the proportion of variance in the outcome variable that is explained by the predictor. For the case of ANOVA, it was the proportion of variance in the dependent variable that is explained by the independent variable.

Because the proportionate reduction in error can be calculated by squaring the correlation coefficient, we can have a sense of the amount of error that would be reduced simply by looking at the correlation coefficient. A correlation coefficient that is high in magnitude, whether negative or positive, indicates a strong relation between two variables. If two variables are highly related, it makes sense that one of them would be a good predictor of the other. And it makes sense that when we use one variable to predict the other, we will reduce error.

Recall that when we calculated the effect size for ANOVA in Chapter 12 we calculated omega squared, ω^2, which we said was a less-biased effect size estimate than r^2. As in the ANOVA case, the proportionate reduction in error, or r^2, is thought to be a biased estimate of the effect size of our regression equation, overestimating the size of the effect. For the case of regression, a common correction is to calculate the **adjusted r^2**, *a less biased and more conservative estimate of effect size for the regression equation than is r:*

$$r_{adjusted}^2 = 1 - \frac{(1 - r^2)(N - 1)}{N - p - 1}$$

In this equation, r^2 is the proportionate reduction in error that we calculated earlier, N is the total sample size, and p is the number of predictor variables that we used in the regression equation. In the case of simple linear regression, p will always be 1, because there is just one predictor variable. We can calculate this unbiased estimate of effect size for predicting depression scores from number of stressful life events:

$$r_{adjusted}^2 = 1 - \frac{(1 - 0.332)(10 - 1)}{10 - 1 - 1} = 1 - \frac{6.012}{8} = 1 - 0.752 = 0.248$$

We can see that the effect size estimate of 0.248 is smaller than the original estimate of 0.332. This more conservative estimate is thought to more accurately estimate the effect size we would likely observe if we used the number of stressful life events to predict depression scores in the future in a different sample.

Finally, let's return to the standard error of the estimate. Figure 16-4 provided a visual sense of what a smaller or larger standard error of the estimate would look like in terms of our prediction ability. We can also precisely quantify the standard error of the estimate using some of the same information that we used to calculate the proportionate reduction in error. We can precisely quantify the standard error of the estimate with the following equation:

$$\sigma_{estimate} = \sqrt{\frac{\Sigma(Y - \hat{Y})^2}{N}}$$

MASTERING THE FORMULA

16-6: The standard error of the estimate tells us the average error around the regression line. It is calculated by dividing the sum of squared error by the sample size and taking the square root:

$$\sigma_{estimate} = \sqrt{\frac{\Sigma(Y - \hat{Y})^2}{N}}$$

The standard error of the estimate is for the regression line, what the measure of standard deviation is for the mean.

The numerator of this equation is the sum of squared errors when using the regression equation. Earlier, we calculated the squared errors for each individual when using the regression equation to predict their depression score; these results appear in the rightmost column of Table 16-6. Summing these squared errors gave us 526.577. We can use this value in our equation for the standard error of the estimate:

$$\sigma_{estimate} = \sqrt{\frac{\Sigma(Y - \hat{Y})^2}{N}} = \sqrt{\frac{526.577}{10}} = \sqrt{52.658} = 7.26$$

This tells us that the average deviation of each individual score from the regression line is 7.26. Thus, the average error, in this sample, for predicting depression scores from the number of stressful life events is 7.26. On average, we will be 7.26 units off from the actual depression score.

Applying the Lessons of Correlation to Regression

In addition to understanding the ways in which regression can help us, it is important to understand the limitations associated with using regression. It is extremely rare that the data analyzed in a regression equation are from a true experiment (one that used randomization to assign participants to conditions). Typically, we cannot randomly assign participants to conditions when the predictor variable is a scale variable (rather than a nominal variable), as is usually the case with regression. So, the results are subject to the same limitations in interpretation that we discussed with respect to correlation.

In Chapter 15, we introduced the A-B-C model of understanding correlation. We noted that the correlation between number of absences and exam grade could be explained if skipping class (A) harmed one's grade (B); if a bad grade (B) led one to skip class more often (A) because of frustration; or if a third variable (C)—such as intelligence—led both to the awareness that going to class is a good thing (A) and to good grades (B). When drawing conclusions from regression, we must consider the same set of possible confounding variables that limited our confidence in the findings following a correlation.

In fact, regression, like correlation, can be wildly inaccurate in its predictions. As with the Pearson correlation coefficient, a good statistician questions causality *after* the statistical analysis (to identify potential confounding variables). But one more source of error can affect fair-minded interpretations of regression analyses: regression to the mean.

Regression to the Mean

In the study that we considered earlier in this chapter (Ruhm, 2006), economic factors predicted several indicators of health. The study also reported that "the drop in tobacco use disproportionately occurs among heavy smokers, the fall in body weight among the severely obese, and the increase in exercise among those who were completely inactive" (p. 2). What Ruhm describes captures the meaning of the word *regression*, as defined by its early proponents. Those who were most extreme on a given variable regressed (toward the mean). In other words, they became somewhat less extreme on that variable.

Francis Galton (Charles Darwin's cousin) was the first to describe the phenomenon of regression to the mean, and he did so in a number of contexts (Bernstein, 1996). For example, Galton asked nine people—including Darwin—to plant sweet pea seeds in the widely scattered locations in Britain where these people lived. Galton found that the variability among the seeds he sent out to be planted was larger than among the seeds that were produced by these plants. The largest seeds produced seeds smaller than they were. The smallest seeds produced seeds larger than they were.

Similarly, among people, Galton documented that, although tall parents tend to have taller-than-average children, their children tend to be a little shorter than they are. And although short parents tend to have shorter-than-average children, their children tend to be a little taller than they are. Galton noted that if regression to the mean did *not* occur, with tall people and large sweet peas producing offspring even taller or larger, and short people and small sweet peas producing offspring even shorter or smaller, "the world would consist of nothing but midgets and giants" (quoted in Bernstein, 1996, p. 167).

You can probably think of lots of additional examples of regression to the mean. Kevin Pemoulie, chef and co-owner of the now-closed Thirty Acres restaurant in Jersey City, New Jersey, talked about regression to the mean in sports and upscale, foodie restaurants (Tishgart, 2015). Pemoulie (2015) asked his readers, "Are you aware of the curse of John Madden? Each year, EA Sports puts out a John Madden football game, and the guy who's on the cover of the game almost inevitably gets hurt or costs his team a championship.... [Los Angeles restaurant] Alma is literally the John Madden problem: It was the No. 1 restaurant" on a highly respected list of the best newcomers to the restaurant scene in 2012, a list that Pemoulie's Thirty Acres was also on. Thirty Acres and Alma both closed in 2015.

An understanding of regression to the mean can help us make better choices in our daily lives. For example, regression to the mean is a particularly important concept to remember when we begin to save for retirement and have to choose the specific allocations of our savings. Table 16-7 shows data from *Morningstar*, an investment publication. The percentages represent the increase in that investment vehicle over two 5-year periods: 1984–1989 and 1989–1994 (Bernstein, 1996). As most descriptions

Regression to the Mean Tall parents tend to have children who are taller than average, but not as tall as they are. Similarly, short parents (like the older parents in this photograph) tend to have children who are shorter than average, but not as short as they are. Francis Galton was the first to document this phenomenon, which came to be called *regression to the mean*.

Jack Hollingsworth/Getty Images

TABLE 16-7   Regression to the Mean: Investing

Bernstein (1996) presented these data from *Morningstar*, an investment publication, demonstrating regression to the mean in action. Notice that the category that showed the highest performances during the first time period (international stocks) had declined by the second time period, whereas the category with the poorest performances in the first time period (aggressive growth) had improved by the second time period.

Five Years to Objective	1984–1989 (percent increase)	1989–1994 (percent increase)
International stocks	20.6	9.4
Income	14.3	11.2
Growth and income	14.2	11.9
Growth	13.3	13.9
Small company	10.3	15.9
Aggressive growth	8.9	16.1
Average	13.6	13.1

of mutual funds remind potential investors, previous performance is not necessarily indicative of future performance. Consider regression to the mean in your own investment decisions. It might help you ride out a decrease in a mutual fund rather than panic and sell before the likely drift back toward the mean. And it might help you avoid buying into the fund that's been on top for several years, knowing that it stands a chance of sliding back toward the mean.

CHECK YOUR LEARNING

Reviewing the Concepts

> Error based on the mean is referred to as the sum of squares total (SS_{total}), whereas error based on the regression equation is referred to as the sum of squared errors (SS_{error}).

> Proportionate reduction in error, r^2, is the amount of error we have eliminated by using a particular regression equation to predict a person's score on the outcome variable versus simply predicting the mean on the outcome variable for that person.

> The standard error of the estimate tells us the average error in predicting each of our data points using the regression equation.

> The adjusted r^2 is a less-biased and more conservative estimate of effect size than is r^2.

> Findings from regression analyses are subject to the same types of limitations as correlation. Regression, like correlation, does not tell us about causation.

> People with extreme scores at one point in time tend to have less extreme scores (scores closer to the mean) at a later point in time, a phenomenon called *regression to the mean*.

Clarifying the Concepts

16-6   Distinguish the standard error of the estimate around the line of best fit from the error of prediction around the mean.

16-7   Explain how, for regression, the strength of the correlation is related to the proportionate reduction in error.

continued on next page

Calculating the Statistics 16-8 Data are provided here with means, standard deviations, a correlation coefficient, and a regression equation: $r = -0.77$, $\hat{Y} = 7.846 - 0.431(X)$.

X	Y
5	6
6	5
4	6
5	6
7	4
8	5
$M_X = 5.833$	$M_Y = 5.333$
$SD_X = 1.344$	$SD_Y = 0.745$

a. Using this information, calculate the sum of squared errors for the mean, SS_{total}.

b. Now, using the regression equation provided, calculate the sum of squared errors for the regression equation, SS_{error}.

c. Using your work from parts (a) and (b), calculate the proportionate reduction in error for these data.

d. Check that this calculation of r^2 equals the square of the correlation coefficient.

Applying the Concepts 16-9 Earlier you read about regression to the mean in a football video game and in the world of high-end restaurants. Many athletes and sports fans believe that an appearance on the cover of *Sports Illustrated (SI)* is a curse. Shortly after appearing on the cover of *SI*, players or teams often have a particularly poor performance. This tendency is documented in the pages of (what else?) *Sports Illustrated* and even has a name, the "*SI* jinx" (Wolff, 2002). In fact, of 2456 covers, *SI* counted 913 "victims." And their potential victims have noticed: After the New England Patriots football team won their league championship, their coach at the time, Bill Parcells, called his daughter, then an *SI* staffer, and ordered: "No cover." Using your knowledge about the limitations of regression, what would you say to Coach Parcells?

Solutions to these Check Your Learning questions can be found in Appendix D.

Multiple Regression

In regression analysis, we explain more of the variability in the outcome variable if we can discover genuine predictors that are separate and distinct. This involves **orthogonal variables,** *predictor variables that make separate and distinct contributions in the prediction of a outcome variable, as compared with the contributions of the other predictor variables.* Orthogonal variables do not overlap each other. For example, when exploring which variables are associated with better health outcomes such as low blood pressure and an absence of heart disease, both the amount of physical activity and diet would likely make separate contributions to the prediction of health outcomes. Their contributions would likely be orthogonal because one can be physically active but eat an unhealthy diet, and eating well does not require that one also exercises.

● An **orthogonal variable** is a predictor variable that makes a separate and distinct contribution in the prediction of an outcome variable, as compared with the contributions of another variable.

The statistical technique we consider next is a way of quantifying (1) whether multiple pieces of evidence really are better than one, and (2) precisely how much better each additional piece of evidence actually is.

Understanding the Equation

Just as a regression equation using one predictor variable is a better predictor than the mean, a regression equation using more than one predictor variable is likely to be an even better predictor. This makes sense in the same way that knowing a baseball player's historical batting average *plus* knowing that the player continues to suffer from a serious injury is likely to improve our ability to predict the player's future performance. So it is not surprising that multiple regression is far more common than simple linear regression. ***Multiple regression*** *is a statistical technique that includes two or more predictor variables in a prediction equation.*

Let's return to our example of predicting depression scores from number of stressful life events. We may be able to improve the accuracy of our prediction by adding another predictor, sleep disturbance or insomnia, which is known to be associated with higher rates of depression (Legget et al., 2016). Table 16-8 repeats the data from Table 16-2, with the added variable of a sleep disturbance score from a hypothetical measure of sleep problems, with scores ranging from 0 to 12 and for which higher scores indicate greater sleep problems.

● **Multiple regression** is a statistical technique that includes two or more predictor variables in a prediction equation.

MASTERING THE CONCEPT

16-5: Multiple regression predicts scores on a single outcome variable from scores on more than one predictor variable. Because behavior tends to be influenced by many factors, multiple regression allows us to better predict a given outcome.

TABLE 16-8	Predicting Depression Scores from Two Variables

Multiple regression allows us to develop a regression equation that predicts an outcome variable from two or more predictor variables. Here we will use these data to develop a regression equation that predicts depression scores from number of stressful life events and sleep disturbances.

Individual	Number of stressful life events	Sleep disturbance score	Beck Depression Inventory score
1	1	12	24
2	2	10	20
3	2	9	18
4	1	7	10
5	3	9	18
6	0	0	0
7	4	12	30
8	0	5	2
9	5	8	15
10	1	12	20
Mean	1.900	8.400	15.700
Standard Deviation	1.663	3.747	9.358

The computer software for regression gives us the printout seen in Figure 16-7. The column in which we're interested is the one labeled "B," under "Unstandardized Coefficients." The first number, across from "(Constant)," is the intercept. The intercept is called *constant* because it does not change; it is not multiplied by any value of a predictor variable. The intercept here is −4.117. The second number is the slope for the predictor variable, number of stressful life events. Number of stressful life events is

Coefficients^a

Model		Unstandardized Coefficients		Standardized Cofficients		
		B	Std. Error	Beta	t	Sig.
1	(Constant)	−4.117	2.737		−1.504	0.176
	Life Events	1.194	0.749	0.212	1.594	0.155
	Sleep Problems	2.089	0.332	0.837	6.287	0.000

a. Outcome Variable: Depression Score

> **FIGURE 16-7**
>
> **SPSS Output for Regression**
>
> Computer software provides the information necessary for the multiple regression equation. All necessary coefficients are in column B under "Unstandardized Coefficients." The constant −4.117 is the intercept; the number next to "Life Events," 1.194, is the slope for that predictor; and the number next to "Sleep Problems," 2.089, is the slope for that predictor variable.

positively correlated with depression scores, so the slope, 1.194, is positive. The third number in this column is the slope for the predictor variable of sleep disturbance score. Having sleep disturbances is also positively correlated with depression scores. So, the slope for this predictor variable, 2.089, is also positive. We can put these numbers into a regression equation, with X_1 representing the first variable, stressful life events, and X_2 representing the second variable, sleep disturbances:

$$\hat{Y} = -4.117 + 1.194(X_1) + 2.089(X_2)$$

Once we develop the multiple regression equation, we can input raw scores for number of stressful life events and sleep disturbance score to determine an individual's predicted score on Y. Imagine that an individual had two stressful life events, but was sleeping pretty well, with a low sleep disturbance score of 2. What would we predict her depression score to be?

$$\hat{Y} = -4.117 + 1.194(X_1) + 2.089(X_2)$$
$$= -4.117 + 1.194(2) + 2.089(2)$$
$$= -4.117 + 2.388 + 4.178 = 2.449$$

Based on these two variables, we predict a depression score of 2.449. How good is this multiple regression equation? From software, we calculated that the proportionate reduction in error for this equation is a whopping 0.899. By using a multiple regression equation with the predictor variables of number of stressful life events and sleep disturbance score, we have reduced 90% of the error that would result from predicting the mean of 15.70 for everyone.

When we calculate proportionate reduction in error for a multiple regression, the symbol changes

Multiple Predictor Variables Researchers use multiple regression when they have measured at least two predictor variables that they believe predict the outcome variable. For example, researchers might explore whether hours spent playing violent video games, scores on a personality measure, and numbers of close friends predict aggression levels in children.

slightly. The symbol is now R^2 instead of r^2. The capitalization of this statistic is an indication that the proportionate reduction in error is based on more than one predictor variable.

The software also gives us the adjusted R^2 for this multiple regression, 0.871. So, even when penalizing the regression for the additional predictors, the regression equation improves our ability to predict to depression scores by 87.1% compared to using the mean alone.

Multiple Regression in Everyday Life

With the development of increasingly more powerful computers and the availability of ever-larger amounts of electronic data, tools based on multiple regression have proliferated. Now the general public can access many of them online (Darlin, 2006; Rosenbloom, 2015). Many apps and Web sites, including Flyr, Hopper, Kayak, and Google Flights, predict the price of an airline ticket for specific routes, travel dates, and, most important, purchase dates. Often using the same data available to travel agents, along with additional predictor variables such as the weather and even which sports teams' fans might be traveling to a championship game, forecasting tools mimic the regression equations used by the airlines. Airlines predict how much money potential travelers are willing to pay on a given date for a given flight and use these predictions to adjust their fares so they can earn the most money.

Online forecasting tools are attempting an end run, using mathematical prediction tools, to help savvy airline consumers either beat or wait out the airlines' price hikes. In 2007, one early forecasting site claimed a 74.5% accuracy rate for its predictions. Zillow.com does for real estate what the forecasting sites do for airline tickets. Using archival land records, Zillow predicts U.S. housing prices and claims to be accurate to within 10% of the actual selling price of a given home.

Amazon.com is trying to take the prediction game to a new level. In 2014 the company filed a patent for "anticipatory shipping" (Bensinger, 2014). Amazon could take advantage of its immense database of customer information to ship products to distribution centers closer to customers, or even load products onto trucks—all *before* customers make a purchase! Amazon indicated that it might base its shipping behavior on customers' searches, wish lists, and previous orders, as well as their online behavior, down to noticing the amount of time a customer spends with her cursor over a particular product.

What's interesting about prediction tools is that they all depend on the predictor variables that the researchers choose. Different inputs lead to different predictions. Let's take just one example—the predictive tools that Amazon and Netflix use to determine what books, movies, or other media you might like. In describing the difference, a reporter asked readers to imagine they were in a brick-and-mortar store (Domingos, 2015). Based on their individual regression equations, "Amazon would be more likely to walk you over to shelves you've frequented previously; Netflix would take you to unfamiliar and seemingly odd sections of the store but lead you to stuff you'd end up loving." Is one better than the other? Perhaps not. You have to pay for each item you order from Amazon, so you may not be as likely to take risks. With Netflix, everything is included in your monthly subscription, so an offbeat recommendation is much less of a gamble. Prediction is not an exact science, but it is certainly an exciting one—and one that provides exciting opportunities for the statistically inclined. Like the future of visual displays of data, the future of the regression equation is limited only by the creativity of the rising generation of behavioral scientists and statisticians.

Data Ethics Ethical Landmines in Predicting Individual Behavior

Regression techniques have long been used to make predictions about human behavior. Recently, however, the amount of data available has exploded. In particular, with the increase in the amount of data that are automatically collected about individual people, efforts to predict what individual people will do have increased dramatically. For example, Gmail users may notice advertisements appearing on their Gmail page that are related to their recent Web searches. Advertisers use past search behavior to predict future purchasing behavior. But perhaps more insidious than predicting future purchases is predicting an individual's likelihood of committing a crime—a prediction that raises a number of ethical conundrums.

At the beginning of this chapter, we discussed policing techniques focused on predicting locations where future crimes are likely to occur. There is also person-based predictive policing, which involves using past data to determine *who* is likely to commit a crime in the future. Police in Chicago have used these methods to create a Strategic Subject List (SSL; City of Chicago Data Portal, 2017). The SSL provides a risk score for all individuals with arrest records, indicating each person's risk of being involved in a future shooting, either as the shooter or as the victim. Police then concentrate their investigative efforts on high-risk individuals.

Department of Pre-Crime Regression techniques have been used to make predictions about human behavior for many years. Today, the enormous amount of data available has led to the development of policing techniques focused on predicting who is likely to commit crimes in the future. Unfortunately, using these predictive tools can also create ethical dilemmas.

Similar to Chicago's SSL is a predictive tool called COMPAS, which has been used since 2000 and employs 137 variables, such as history of substance abuse and number of criminal associates, to determine the likelihood that a criminal defendant will commit a crime in the next 2 years (Dressel & Farid, 2018). It has been used by judges when making sentencing decisions and by parole boards when making parole determinations. In other words, individuals deemed high risk by COMPAS may receive longer sentences and may be less likely to be paroled. But how accurate are these predictive tools? One study of COMPAS's performance for 7000 individuals found it was approximately 65% accurate for both black and white defendants (Angwin, Larson, Mattu, & Kirchner, 2016). However, the errors that it made for each of these types of defendants were in opposite directions: It was more likely to incorrectly predict that a white defendant *would not* reoffend and, conversely, to incorrectly predict that a black defendant *would* reoffend. As a consequence, white individuals were more likely to erroneously receive shorter sentences as a result of the COMPAS predictions, whereas black individuals were more likely to erroneously receive longer sentences as a result of the predictions.

In addition to this obvious problem, the use of these predictive tools creates other ethical dilemmas. Even when race is not used as an explicit predictor in the statistical analysis, the use of other variables that may be correlated with race (for example, whether someone's parents were ever arrested, how many of a person's friends use illegal drugs) can lead to racial profiling by these predictive tools (Angwin et al., 2016). Furthermore, these predictive tools are only as good as the data on which they are built. Because those data come from the justice system, any biases, racial or otherwise, that are inherent in the judicial system will be perpetuated by the statistical predictions (Fitzpatrick, Gorr, & Neill, 2019). For example, black individuals are 3.7 times more likely than white individuals to be arrested for marijuana possession, even given the same circumstances of possession (American Civil Liberties Union, 2013). Based on these data, the statistical programs making criminal predictions would predict that black individuals would commit more marijuana-related crimes. The programs would also make this prediction about future crimes, perpetuating the bias of the police officers. Finally, these criminal predictive tools violate a long-standing principle in the U.S. justice system—that a person is innocent until proven guilty. Should someone receive a longer sentence now for a hypothetical future crime not yet committed? These types of questions do not have straightforward answers.

If you are interested in learning more, you might check out *Pre-Crime,* a 2017 documentary film covering the ethical dilemmas associated with predictive policing.

CHECK YOUR LEARNING

Reviewing the Concepts

> Multiple regression is used to predict an outcome variable from more than one predictor variable. Ideally, these variables are distinct from one another in such a way that they contribute uniquely to the predictions.

> We can develop a multiple regression equation and input specific scores for each predictor variable to determine the predicted score on the outcome variable.

> Multiple regression is the backbone of many online tools that we can use for predicting everyday variables such as home prices or traffic.

> Using regression to predict an individuals' future behavior can lead to a number of ethical problems, particularly when we intervene (e.g., extend a prison sentence) based on these predictions.

> All regressions have some amount of error, and the regressions are only as good as the variables we use for our predictions.

Clarifying the Concepts 16-10 What is multiple regression, and what are its benefits over simple linear regression?

Calculating the Statistics 16-11 Write the equation for the line of prediction using the following output from a multiple regression analysis:

Coefficients[a]

Model		Unstandardized Coefficients B	Unstandardized Coefficients Std. Error	Standardized Coefficients Beta	t	Sig.
1	(Constant)	5.251	4.084		1.286	.225
	Variable A	.060	.107	.168	.562	.585
	Variable B	1.105	.437	.758	2.531	.028

a. Dependent Variable: Outcome variable

continued on next page

16-12 Use the equation for the line you created in the previous Check Your Learning exercise to make predictions for each of the following:

    a. $X_1 = 40$, $X_2 = 14$

    b. $X_1 = 101$, $X_2 = 39$

    c. $X_1 = 76$, $X_2 = 20$

Applying the Concepts

16-13 As regression analyses become more common in situations that we encounter every day, there are bound to be problems (Kirchner, 2015). Below are two examples of problematic regression equations. For each, state the likely predictor variable or variables and the likely outcome variable or variables. Be as specific as you can. Based just on the information provided, is this an example of a simple linear regression or a multiple regression? Explain your answer.

    a. *The Wall Street Journal* (Valentino-Devries, Singer-Vine, & Soltani, 2012) reported that the office supply store Staples used a regression to determine prices for customers in different locations. Customers who lived farther away from office supply stores that are competitors to Staples were charged higher prices than those who lived closer to competitors. The problem? Customers living farther from competitors' stores were more likely to be living in poor or rural regions. The reporter pointed out that "it diminishes the Internet's role as an equalizer."

    b. A 2015 report examined the predictive equations used in sentencing those convicted of crimes in an attempt to predict the likelihood that an individual would become a repeat offender (Barry-Jester, Casselman, & Goldstein, 2015). Beyond the person's criminal record, the equations used information like age, job history, and patterns of crime within the person's family. The reporter asked, "Is it fair to score people based on not only their own past criminal behavior, but on statistics about other people who fit the same profile?"

Solutions to these Check Your Learning questions can be found in Appendix D.

REVIEW OF CONCEPTS

LaunchPad
macmillan learning
Visit LaunchPad to access the e-book and to test your knowledge with LearningCurve.

Simple Linear Regression

Regression is an expansion of correlation in that it allows us not only to quantify a relation between two variables but also to quantify one variable's ability to predict another variable. We can predict an outcome variable's z score from a predictor variable's z score, or we can do a bit more initial work and predict an outcome variable's raw score from a predictor variable's raw score. The latter method uses the equation for a line with an *intercept* and a *slope*.

We use *simple linear regression* when we predict one outcome variable from one predictor variable when the two variables are linearly related. We can graph this line using the regression equation, plugging in low and high values of X and plotting those values with their associated predicted values on Y, then connecting the dots to form the regression line.

Just as we can standardize a raw score by converting it to a z score, we can standardize a slope by converting it to a *standardized regression coefficient*. This number indicates the predicted change on the outcome variable in terms of standard deviation for every increase of 1 standard deviation in the predictor variable. For simple linear regression, the standardized regression coefficient is the same as the Pearson correlation coefficient. Hypothesis testing that determines whether the correlation coefficient is statistically significantly different from 0 also indicates whether the standardized regression coefficient is statistically significantly different from 0.

Interpretation and Prediction

A regression equation is rarely a perfect predictor of scores on the outcome variable. There is always some prediction error, which can be quantified by the *standard error of the estimate*, the number that describes the typical amount that an observation falls from the regression line. We can also quantify how much better the regression equation is at predicting the outcome compared to using the mean alone. To do this, we can calculate the proportionate reduction in error, symbolized as r^2, which is a measure of the size of the effect. We can also calculate a less-biased estimate of effect size, adjusted r^2. In addition, regression suffers from the same drawbacks as correlation. For example, we cannot know if the predictive relation is causal; the posited direction could be the reverse (with Y causally predicting X), or there could be a third variable at work.

When we use regression, we must also be aware of the phenomenon called regression to the mean, in which extreme values tend to become less extreme over time.

Multiple Regression

We use *multiple regression* when we have more than one predictor variable, as is usual in most research in the behavioral sciences. Multiple regression is particularly useful when we have *orthogonal variables*, predictor variables that make separate contributions to the prediction of an outcome variable. Multiple regression has led to the development of many Web-based prediction tools that allow us to make educated guesses about such outcomes as airplane ticket prices.

Using regression to predict an individual's future behavior raises a number of ethical problems, particularly when we intervene (e.g., extend a prison sentence) based on these predictions. All regressions have some amount of error, and the regressions are only as good as the variables we use for our predictions.

SPSS

The most common form of regression analysis in SPSS uses at least two scale variables: the predictor variable and the outcome variable. Note that SPSS uses the terms "independent variable" for the predictor and "dependent variable" for the outcome. Let's use the depression and stressful life events data as an example. Once again, begin by visualizing the data.

Request the scatterplot of the data by selecting: Graphs → Chart Builder → Gallery → Scatter/Dot. Drag the upper-left sample graph to the large box on top. Then select the variables to be included in the scatterplot by dragging the predictor variable, "stressful life events," to the *x*-axis, and the outcome

variable, "depression," to the *y*-axis. Click "OK." Double-click on the graph to make changes using the Chart Editor. To add the regression line, click "Elements," then "Fit Line at Total." Close the Chart Editor by clicking the x in the upper right-hand corner.

To analyze the linear regression, select: Analyze → Regression → Linear. Select "stressful life events" as the independent (predictor) variable and "grade" as the dependent (outcome) variable.

As usual, click on "OK" to see the Output screen. Part of the output is shown in the screenshot here. In the box

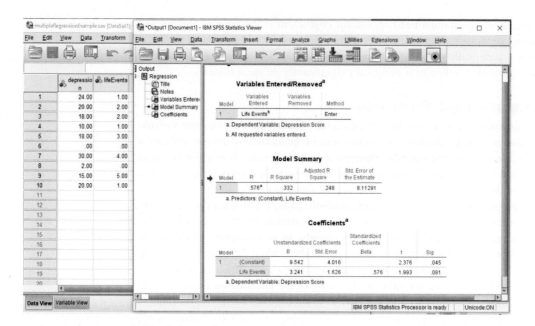

titled "Model Summary," we can see the correlation coefficient of .576 under "R" and the proportionate reduction of error, .332, under "R Square." In the box titled "Coefficients," we can look in the first column under "B" to determine the regression equation. The intercept, 9.542, is across from "(Constant)," and the slope, 3.241, is across from "Life Events." (Any slight differences from the numbers we calculated earlier are due to rounding decisions.)

HOW IT WORKS

16.1 REGRESSION WITH z SCORES

Shannon Callahan, a former student in the experimental psychology master's program at Seton Hall University, conducted a study that examined evaluations of faculty members on Ratemyprofessor.com. She wondered if professors who were rated high on "clarity" were more likely to be viewed as "easy." Callahan found a significant correlation of 0.267 between the average easiness rating a professor garnered and the average rating he or she received with respect to clarity of teaching.

If we know that a professor's z score on clarity is 2.2 (an indication that she is very clear), how could we predict her z score on easiness?

$$z_{\hat{Y}} = (r_{XY})(z_X) = (0.267)(2.2) = 0.59$$

When there's a positive correlation, we predict a z score above the mean when the professor's original z score is above the mean.

And if a professor's z score on clarity is -1.8 (an indication that she's not very clear), how could we predict her z score on easiness?

$$z_{\hat{Y}} = (r_{XY})(z_X) = (0.267)(-1.8) = -0.48$$

When there's a positive correlation, we predict a z score below the mean when the professor's original z score is below the mean.

16.2 REGRESSION WITH RAW SCORES

Using Shannon Callahan's data, how can we develop the regression equation so that we can work directly with raw scores? To do this, we need a little more information. For this data set, the mean clarity score is 3.673, with a standard deviation of 0.890; the mean easiness score is 2.843, with a standard deviation of 0.701. As noted before, the correlation between these variables is 0.267.

To calculate the regression equation, we need to find the intercept and the slope. We determine the *intercept* by calculating what we predict for Y (easiness) when X (clarity) equals 0. Given the means, the standard deviations, and the correlation calculated above, we first find z_X:

$$z_X = \frac{(X - M_X)}{SD_X} = \frac{(0 - 3.673)}{0.890} = -4.127$$

We then calculate the predicted z score for easiness:

$$z_{\hat{Y}} = (r_{XY})(z_X) = (0.267)(-4.127) = -1.102$$

Finally, we transform the predicted easiness z score into the predicted easiness raw score:

$$\hat{Y} = z_{\hat{Y}}\,(SD_Y) + M_Y = -1.102(0.701) + 2.843 = 2.070$$

The intercept, therefore, is 2.070.

To determine the *slope*, we calculate what we would predict for Y (easiness) when X (clarity) equals 1, and determine how much that differs from what we would predict when X equals 0. The z score for X corresponding to the raw score of 1 is:

$$z_X = \frac{(X - M_X)}{SD_X} = \frac{(1 - 3.673)}{0.890} = -3.003$$

We then calculate the predicted z score for easiness:

$$z_{\hat{Y}} = (r_{XY})(z_X) = (0.267)(-3.003) = -0.802$$

Finally, we transform the predicted easiness z score into the predicted easiness raw score:

$$\hat{Y} = z_{\hat{Y}}\,(SD_Y) + M_Y = -0.802(0.701) + 2.843 = 2.281$$

The difference between the predicted Y when X equals 1 (2.281) and that when X equals 0 (2.070) yields the slope, which is $2.281 - 2.070 = 0.211$. So the regression equation is:

$$\hat{Y} = 2.07 + 0.21(X)$$

We can then use this regression equation to calculate a professor's predicted easiness score from his or her clarity score. Let's say a professor has a clarity score of 3.2. We would use the regression equation to predict his easiness score as follows:

$$\hat{Y} = 2.07 + 0.21(X) = 2.07 + 0.21(3.2) = 2.74$$

This result makes sense because she is below the mean on clarity, so, given that there is a positive correlation, we predict his score to fall below the mean on easiness.

EXERCISES

The solutions to the odd-numbered exercises can be found in Appendix C.

Clarifying the Concepts

16.1 What does regression add above and beyond what we learn from correlation?

16.2 How does the regression line relate to the correlation of two variables?

16.3 Is there any difference between $\hat{Y}$ and a predicted score for Y? Explain your answer.

16.4 What does each of the symbols stand for in the formula for the regression equation: $z_{\hat{Y}} = (r_{XY})(z_X)$?

16.5 The equation for a line is $\hat{Y} = a + b(X)$. Define the symbols a and b.

16.6 What are the three steps to calculate the intercept?

16.7 When is the intercept not meaningful or useful?

16.8 What does the slope tell us?

16.9 Why do we also call the regression line the line of best fit?

16.10 How are the sign of the correlation coefficient and the sign of the slope related?

16.11 What is the difference between a small standard error of the estimate and a large one?

16.12 Why are explanations of the causes behind relations explored with regression limited in the same way they are with correlation?

16.13 What is the connection between regression to the mean and the bell-shaped normal curve?

16.14 Explain why the regression equation is a better source of predictions than the mean.

16.15 What is SS_{total}?

16.16 When drawing error lines between data points and the regression line, why is it important that these lines be perfectly vertical?

16.17 What are the basic steps to calculate the proportionate reduction in error?

16.18 What information does the proportionate reduction in error give us?

16.19 What is an orthogonal variable?

16.20 If you know the correlation coefficient, how can you determine the proportionate reduction in error?

16.21 Why is multiple regression often more useful than simple linear regression?

16.22 What is the difference between the symbol for the effect size for simple linear regression and the symbol for the effect size for multiple regression?

16.23 Imagine that you calculate the standard error of the estimate of a regression equation and find it to be 6.2. What does this tell you about the amount of error in predictions based on this particular regression equation?

16.24 What is adjusted r^2, and how does it differ from r^2?

16.25 In what ways have regression tools been used to predict individuals' future behavior?

16.26 What are some of the ethical issues associated with using regression to predict individuals' future behavior?

Calculating the Statistics

16.27 Using the following information, make a prediction for Y, given an X score of 2.9:

Variable X: $M = 1.9$, $SD = 0.6$

Variable Y: $M = 10$, $SD = 3.2$

Pearson correlation of variables X and $Y = 0.31$

a. Transform the raw score for the predictor variable into a z score.

b. Calculate the predicted z score for the outcome variable.

c. Transform the z score for the outcome variable back into a raw score.

16.28 Using the following information, make a prediction for Y, given an X score of 8:

Variable X: $M = 12$, $SD = 3$

Variable Y: $M = 74$, $SD = 18$

Pearson correlation of variables X and $Y = 0.46$

a. Transform the raw score for the predictor variable into a z score.

b. Calculate the predicted z score for the outcome variable.

c. Transform the z score for the outcome variable back into a raw score.

d. Calculate the intercept, a.

e. Calculate the slope, b.

f. Write the equation for the line.

g. Draw the line on an empty scatterplot, basing the line on predicted Y values for X values of 0, 1, and 48.

16.29 Let's assume we know that age is related to bone density, with a Pearson correlation coefficient of −0.19. (Notice that the correlation is negative, indicating that bone density tends to be lower at older ages than at younger ages.) Assume we also know the following descriptive statistics:

Age of people studied: 55 years on average, with a standard deviation of 12 years

Bone density of people studied: 1000 mg/cm^2 on average, with a standard deviation of 95 mg/cm^2

Virginia is 76 years old. What would you predict her bone density to be? To answer this question, complete the following steps:

a. Transform the raw score for the predictor variable into a z score.

b. Calculate the predicted z score for the outcome variable.

c. Transform the z score for the outcome variable back into a raw score.

d. Calculate the intercept, a.

e. Calculate the slope, b.

f. Write the equation for the line.

g. Draw the line on an empty scatterplot, basing the line on predicted Y values for X values of 0, 1, and 18.

16.30 Given the regression line $\hat{Y} = -6 + 0.41(X)$, make predictions for each of the following:

a. $X = 25$

b. $X = 50$

c. $X = 75$

16.31 Given the regression line $\hat{Y} = 49 - 0.18(X)$, make predictions for each of the following:

a. $X = -31$

b. $X = 65$

c. $X = 14$

16.32 Data are provided here with descriptive statistics, a correlation coefficient, and a regression equation: $r = 0.426$, $\hat{Y} = 219.974 + 186.595(X)$.

X	Y
0.13	200.00
0.27	98.00
0.49	543.00
0.57	385.00
0.84	420.00
1.12	312.00
$M_X = 0.57$	$M_Y = 326.333$
$SD_X = 0.333$	$SD_Y = 145.752$

Using this information, compute the following estimates of prediction error:

a. Calculate the sum of squared errors for the mean, SS_{total}.

b. Now, using the regression equation provided, calculate the sum of squared errors for the regression equation, SS_{error}

c. Using your work, calculate the proportionate reduction in error for these data.

d. Check that this calculation of r^2 equals the square of the correlation coefficient.

e. Compute the standard error of the estimate.

f. Compute the standardized regression coefficient.

16.33 Data are provided here with descriptive statistics, a correlation coefficient, and a regression equation: $r = 0.52$, $\hat{Y} = 2.643 + 0.469(X)$.

X	Y
4.00	6.00
6.00	3.00
7.00	7.00
8.00	5.00
9.00	4.00
10.00	12.00
12.00	9.00
14.00	8.00
$M_X = 8.75$	$M_Y = 6.75$
$SD_X = 3.031$	$SD_Y = 2.727$

Using this information, compute the following estimates of prediction error:

a. Calculate the sum of squared errors for the mean, SS_{total}.

b. Now, using the regression equation provided, calculate the sum of squared errors for the regression equation, SS_{error}

c. Using your work, calculate the proportionate reduction in error for these data.

d. Check that this calculation of r^2 equals the square of the correlation coefficient.

e. Compute the standard error of the estimate.

f. Compute the standardized regression coefficient.

16.34 Use this output from a multiple regression analysis to answer the following questions:

Coefficients[a]

Model		Unstandardized Coefficients		Standardized Coefficients	t	Sig.
		B	Std. Error	Beta		
1	(Constant)	3.977	1.193		3.333	.001
	Variable 1	.414	.096	.458	4.313	.000
	Variable 2	-.019	.011	-.181	-1.704	.093

a. Dependent Variable: Outcome (Y)

a. Write the equation for the line of prediction.

b. Use the equation for part (a) to make predictions for: Variable 1 = 6, variable 2 = 60.

c. Use the equation for part (a) to make predictions for: Variable 1 = 9, variable 2 = 54.3.

d. Use the equation for part (a) to make predictions for: Variable 1 = 13, variable 2 = 44.8.

16.35 Use this output from a multiple regression analysis to answer the following questions:

Coefficients[a]

Model		Unstandardized Coefficients		Standardized Coefficients	t	Sig.
		B	Std. Error	Beta		
1	(Constant)	1.675	.563		2.972	.004
	SAT	.001	.000	.321	2.953	.004
	Rank	-.008	.003	-.279	-2.566	.012

a. Dependent Variable: GPA

a. Write the equation for the line of prediction.

b. Use the equation for part (a) to make predictions for: SAT = 1030, rank = 41.

c. Use the equation for part (a) to make predictions for: SAT = 860, rank = 22.

d. Use the equation for part (a) to make predictions for: SAT = 1060, rank = 8.

Applying the Concepts

16.36 Birth weight, blood pressure, and regression: A meta-analysis found a negative correlation between birth weight and blood pressure later in life (Mu et al., 2012).

a. Explain what is meant by a negative correlation between these two variables.

b. If you were to examine these two variables with simple linear regression instead of correlation, how would you frame the question?

(*Hint:* The research question for correlation would be: Is birth weight related to blood pressure?)

c. What is the difference between simple linear regression and multiple regression?

d. If you were to conduct a multiple regression instead of a simple linear regression, what other predictor variables might you include?

16.37 Predictive policing: *The New York Times* reported on predictive policing, a strategy based on formulas that "forecast" whether a particular person is likely to commit a crime (Elgion & Williams, 2015). What are the predictive data that the police consider? They look at personal connections—whether in real life or on social media—with victims of homicides, members of gangs, or people in prison. They also look at whether people are unemployed or have a history of drug or alcohol problems.

a. What are the predictor variables in this example?

b. What is the outcome variable?

c. What other variables might predict this outcome variable? Name at least three.

d. The same article that described predictive policing also discussed critiques of this method. The reporters noted that these tactics "legitimize the profiling of racial minorities who live in poor, high-crime neighborhoods, and prompted officers to enforce laws selectively." Based on this example, explain why regression is not a perfect science—why can regression lead to problems with prediction?

16.38 Age, hours studied, and prediction: In How It Works 15.2, we calculated the correlation coefficient between students' age and number of hours they study per week. The correlation between these two variables is 0.49.

a. Elif's z score for age is −0.82. What would we predict for the z score for the number of hours she studies per week?

b. John's z score for age is 1.2. What would we predict for the z score for the number of hours he studies per week?

c. Eugene's z score for age is 0. What would we predict for the z score for the number of hours he studies per week?

d. For part (c), explain why the concept of regression to the mean is not relevant (and why you didn't really need the formula).

16.39 Consideration of Future Consequences scale, z scores, and raw scores: A study of Consideration of Future Consequences (CFC) found a mean score of 3.51, with a standard deviation of 0.61, for the 664 students in the sample (Petrocelli, 2003).

a. Imagine that your z score on the CFC score was −1.2. What would your raw score be? Use symbolic notation and the formula. Explain why this answer makes sense.

b. Imagine that your z score on the CFC score was 0.66. What would your raw score be? Use symbolic notation and the formula. Explain why this answer makes sense.

16.40 IMDB, z scores, and raw scores: The 23,396 films on the Internet Movie Database (IMBD) have a mean of 6.2 and a standard deviation of 1.4 (Moertel, 2006). They are roughly normally distributed. (Note that this population includes all films that were reviewed by at least 100 people.)

a. Convert the following z scores to raw scores without using a formula: (i) −1.0, (ii) 1.0, (iii) 0.0

b. Now convert the same z scores to raw scores using symbolic notation and the formula: (i) −1.0, (ii) 1.0, (iii) 0.0

16.41 Hours studied, grade, and regression: A regression analysis of data from some of our statistics classes yielded the following regression equation for the predictor variable (hours studied) and the outcome variable (grade-point average [GPA]): $\hat{Y} = 2.96 + 0.02(X)$.

a. If you plan to study 8 hours per week, what would you predict your GPA will be?

b. If you plan to study 10 hours per week, what would you predict your GPA will be?

c. If you plan to study 11 hours per week, what would you predict your GPA will be?

d. Create a graph and draw the regression line based on these three pairs of scores.

e. Determine the number of hours you'd have to study to have a predicted GPA that is the maximum possible, 4.0. Why is it misleading to make predictions for anyone who plans to study this many hours (or more)?

16.42 Precipitation, violence, and limitations of regression: Does the level of precipitation predict violence? Dubner and Levitt (2006b) reported on various studies that found links between rain and violence. They mentioned one study by Miguel, Satyanath, and Sergenti that found that decreased rain was linked with an increased likelihood of civil war across a number of African countries they examined. Referring to the study's authors, Dubner and Levitt state, "The causal effect of a drought, they argue, was frighteningly strong."

a. What is the predictor variable in this study?

b. What is the outcome variable?

c. What possible third variables might play a role in this connection? Is it just the lack of rain that's causing violence, or is it something else? (*Hint:* Consider the likely economic base of many African countries.)

16.43 Cola consumption, bone mineral density, and limitations of regression: Does one's cola consumption predict one's bone mineral density? Using regression analyses, nutrition researchers found that older women who drank more cola (but not more of other carbonated drinks) tended to have lower bone mineral density, a risk factor for osteoporosis (Tucker, Morita, Qiao, Hannan, Cupples, & Kiel, 2006). Cola intake, therefore, does seem to predict bone mineral density.

a. Explain why we cannot conclude that cola intake causes a decrease in bone mineral density.

b. The researchers included a number of possible third variables in their regression analyses. Among the included variables were physical activity score, smoking, alcohol use, and calcium intake. They included the possible third variables first, and then added the bone density measure. Why would they have used multiple regression in this case? Explain.

c. How might physical activity play a role as a third variable? Discuss its possible relation to both bone density and cola consumption.

d. How might calcium intake play a role as a third variable? Discuss its possible relation to both bone density and cola consumption.

16.44 Tutoring, mathematics performance, and problems with regression: A researcher conducted a study in which children with problems learning mathematics were offered the opportunity to purchase time with special tutors. The number of weeks that children met with their tutors varied from 1 to 20. The researcher found that the number of weeks of tutoring predicted these children's mathematics performance and recommended that parents of such children send them for tutoring.

a. List one problem with that interpretation. Explain your answer.

b. If you were to develop a study that uses a multiple regression equation instead of a simple linear regression equation, what additional variables might be good predictor variables? List at least one variable that can be manipulated (e.g., weeks of tutoring) and at least one variable that cannot be manipulated (e.g., parents' years of education).

16.45 Anxiety, depression, and simple linear regression: We analyzed data from a larger data set that one of the authors used for previous research (Nolan, Flynn, & Garber, 2003). In the current analyses, we used regression to look at factors that predict anxiety over a 3-year period. Shown below is the output for the regression analysis examining whether depression at year 1 predicted anxiety at year 3.

Coefficients(a)

	Unstandardized Coefficients		Standardized Coefficients	t	Sig.
	B	Std. Error	Beta		
(Constant)	24.698	.566		43.665	.000
Depression Year 1	.161	.048	.235	3.333	.001

a. Dependent Variable: Anxiety Year 3

a. From this software output, write the regression equation.

b. As depression at year 1 increases by 1 point, what happens to the predicted anxiety level for year 3? Be specific.

c. If someone has a depression score of 10 at year 1, what would we predict for her anxiety score at year 3?

d. If someone has a depression score of 2 at year 1, what would we predict for his anxiety score at year 3?

16.46 Anxiety, depression, and multiple regression: We conducted a second regression analysis on the data from the previous exercise. In addition to depression at year 1, we included a second predictor variable to predict anxiety at year 3. We also included anxiety at year 1. (We might expect that the best predictor of anxiety at a later point in time is one's anxiety at an earlier point in time.) Here is the output for that analysis.

Coefficients(a)

	Unstandardized Coefficients		Standardized Coefficients	t	Sig.
	B	Std. Error	Beta		
(Constant)	17.038	1.484		11.482	.000
Depression Year 1	-.013	.055	-.019	-.237	.813
Anxiety Year 1	.307	.056	.442	5.521	.000

a. Dependent Variable: Anxiety Year 3

a. From this software output, write the regression equation.

b. As the first predictor variable, depression at year 1, increases by 1 point, what happens to the predicted score on anxiety at year 3?

c. As the second predictor variable, anxiety at year 1, increases by 1 point, what happens to the predicted score on anxiety at year 3?

d. Compare the predictive utility of depression at year 1 using the regression equation in the previous exercise and using the regression equation you just wrote in part (a) of this exercise. In which regression equation is depression at year 1 a better predictor? Given that we're using the same sample, is depression at year 1 actually better at predicting anxiety at year 3 in one regression equation versus the other? Why do you think there's a difference?

e. The table at the top of the next page is the correlation matrix for the three variables. As you can see, all three are highly correlated with one another. If we look at the intersection of each pair of variables, the number next to "Pearson correlation" is the correlation coefficient. For example, the correlation between "Anxiety year 1" and "Depression year 1" is .549. Which two variables show the strongest correlation? How might this explain the fact that depression at year 1 seems to be a better predictor when it's the only predictor variable than when anxiety at year 1 also is included? What does this tell us about the importance of including third variables in the regression analyses when possible?

f. Let's say you want to add a fourth predictor variable. You have to choose among three possible predictor variables: (1) a variable highly correlated with both predictor variables and the outcome variable, (2) a variable highly correlated with the outcome variable but not correlated with either predictor variable, and (3) a variable not correlated with either of the predictor variables or with the outcome variable. Which of the three variables is likely to make the multiple regression equation better? That is, which is likely to

Correlations

		Depression Year 1	Anxiety Year 1	Anxiety Year 3
Depression Year 1	Pearson Correlation	1	.549(**)	.235(**)
	Sig. (2-tailed)		.000	.001
	N	240	240	192
Anxiety Year 1	Pearson Correlation	.549(**)	1	.432(**)
	Sig. (2-tailed)	.000		.000
	N	240	240	192
Anxiety Year 3	Pearson Correlation	.235(**)	.432(**)	1
	Sig. (2-tailed)	.001	.000	
	N	192	192	192

** Correlation is significant at the 0.01 level (2-tailed).

increase the proportionate reduction in error? Explain.

16.47 Cohabitation, divorce, and prediction: A study by the Institute for Fiscal Studies (Goodman & Greaves, 2010) found that parents' marital status when a child was born predicted the likelihood of the relationship's demise. Parents who were cohabitating when their child was born had a 27% chance of breaking up by the time the child was 5, whereas those who were married when their child was born had a 9% chance of breaking up by the time the child was 5—a difference of 18%. The researchers, however, reported that cohabiting parents tended to be younger, less affluent, less likely to own a home, less educated, and more likely to have an unplanned pregnancy. When the researchers statistically controlled for these variables, they found that there was just a 2% difference between cohabitating and married parents.

a. What are the predictor and outcome variables used in this study?

b. Were the researchers likely to have used simple linear regression or multiple regression for their analyses? Explain your answer.

c. In your own words, explain why the ability of marital status at the time of a child's birth to predict divorce within 5 years almost disappeared when other variables were considered.

d. Name at least one additional "third variable" that might have been at play in this situation. Explain your answer.

16.48 Google, the flu, and third variables: *The New York Times* reported: "Several years ago, Google, aware of how many of us were sneezing and coughing, created a fancy equation on its Web site to figure out just how many people had influenza. The math works like this: people's location + flu-related search queries on Google + some really smart algorithms = the number of people with the flu in the United States" (Bilton, 2013; http://bits.blogs.nytimes.com/2013/02/24/disruptions-google-flu-trends-shows-problems-of-big-data-without-context/).

a. A friend who knows you're taking statistics asks you to explain what this means in statistical terms. In your own words, what is it likely that the Google statisticians did?

b. The problem was that Google's "fancy equation" didn't work. It estimated that 11% of the U.S. population had the flu, but the real number was only 6%. *The New York Times* article warned against taking data out of context. What do you think may have gone wrong in this case? (*Hint:* Think about your own Google searches and the varied reasons you have for conducting those searches.)

16.49 Sugar, diabetes, and multiple regression: A *New York Times* reporter wrote: "A study published in the journal *PLOS ONE* links increased consumption of sugar with increased rates of diabetes by examining the data on sugar availability and the rate of diabetes in 175 countries over the past decade. And after accounting for many other factors, the researchers found that increased sugar in a population's food supply was linked to higher diabetes rates independent of rates of obesity" (Bittman, 2013).

a. Explain how the researchers may have used multiple regression to analyze these data.

b. Why did the reporter emphasize that the researchers accounted for many other factors?

c. List at least three other factors that the researchers may have included.

d. The reporter also wrote: "In other words, according to this study, obesity doesn't cause diabetes: sugar does. The study demonstrates this with the same level of confidence that linked cigarettes and lung cancer in the 1960s." Explain in your own words why Bittman likely feels justified in drawing a causal conclusion from correlational research.

16.50   The age of a country, the level of concern for the environment, and multiple regression: Researchers analyzed the impact of the age of a country on the overall level of concern for the environment (Hershfield, Bang, & Weber, 2014). They noted that some countries—Sweden, for example—are more likely to enact environmentally friendly legislation, whereas others, like India, are less likely to do so. They predicted that older countries—those with more of a history—would be more likely to be future-oriented and therefore develop environmentally friendly policies. So, they conducted a regression to examine whether a country's age predicted a country's score on a measure called the Environmental Performance Index (EPI). They controlled for wealth, as measured by a country's gross domestic product (GDP) and a scale that assessed a government's overall stability. They reported that, "even after controlling for these factors, however, we found that country age accounted for approximately 6% of the variation in country-level environmental performance." They reported a p value of 0.001.

a. Explain how you know researchers used multiple regression in this case.

b. What is the most likely reason that researchers controlled for wealth and stability in their multiple regression?

c. List at least one additional variable that the researchers might have considered controlling for.

Putting It All Together

16.51   Age, hours studied, and regression: In How It Works 15.2, we calculated the correlation coefficient between students' age and the number of hours they study per week. The mean for age is 21, and the standard deviation is 1.789. The mean for hours studied is 14.2, and the standard deviation is 5.582. The correlation between these two variables is 0.49. Use the z score formula.

a. João is 24 years old. How many hours would we predict he studies per week?

b. Kimberly is 19 years old. How many hours would we predict she studies per week?

c. Seung is 45 years old. Why might it not be a good idea to predict how many hours per week he studies?

d. From a mathematical perspective, why is the word *regression* used? [*Hint:* Look at parts (a) and (b), and discuss the scores on the first variable with respect to their mean versus the predicted scores on the second variable with respect to their mean.]

e. Calculate the regression equation.

f. Use the regression equation to predict the number of hours studied for a 17-year-old student and for a 22-year-old student.

g. Using the four pairs of scores that you have [age and predicted hours studied from part (b), and the predicted scores for a score of 0 and 1 from calculating the regression equation], create a graph that includes the regression line.

h. Why is it misleading to include young ages such as 0 and 5 on the graph?

i. Construct a graph that includes both the scatterplot for these data and the regression line. Draw vertical lines to connect each dot on the scatterplot with the regression line.

j. Construct a second graph that includes both the scatterplot and a line for the mean for hours studied, 14.2. The line will be horizontal and will begin at 14.2 on the y-axis. Draw vertical lines to connect each dot on the scatterplot with the line representing the mean.

k. Part (i) is a depiction of the error we make if we use the regression equation to predict hours studied. Part (j) is a depiction of the error we make if we use the mean to predict hours studied (i.e., if we predict that everyone has the mean of 14.2 on hours studied per week). Which one appears to have less error? Briefly explain why the error is less in one situation.

l. Calculate the proportionate reduction in error the long way.

m. Explain what the proportionate reduction in error that you calculated in part (l) tells us. Be specific about what it tells us about making predictions using the regression equation versus making predictions using the mean.

n. Demonstrate how the proportionate reduction in error could be calculated using the shortcut. Why does this make sense? That is, why does the correlation coefficient give us a sense of how useful the regression equation will be?

o. Compute the standardized regression coefficient.

p. How does this coefficient relate to other information you know?

q. Draw a conclusion about your analysis based on what you know about hypothesis testing with regression.

16.52 **Corporate political contributions, profits, and regression:** Researchers studied whether corporate political contributions predicted profits (Cooper, Gulen, & Ovtchinnikov, 2007). From archival data, they determined how many political candidates each company supported with financial contributions, as well as each company's profit in terms of a percentage. The accompanying table shows data for five companies. (*Note:* The data points are hypothetical but are based on averages for companies falling in the 2nd, 4th, 6th, and 8th deciles in terms of candidates supported. A decile is a range of 10%, so the 2nd decile includes those with percentiles between 10 and 19.9.)

Number of candidates supported	Profit (%)
6	12.37
17	12.91
39	12.59
62	13.43
98	13.42

a. Create the scatterplot for these scores.

b. Calculate the mean and standard deviation for the variable "number of candidates supported."

c. Calculate the mean and standard deviation for the variable "profit."

d. Calculate the correlation between number of candidates supported and profit.

e. Calculate the regression equation for the prediction of profit from number of candidates supported.

f. Create a graph and draw the regression line.

g. What do these data suggest about the political process?

h. What third variables might be at play here?

i. Compute the standardized regression coefficient.

j. How does this coefficient relate to other information you know?

k. Draw a conclusion about your analysis based on what you know about hypothesis testing with simple linear regression.

LaunchPad
macmillan learning

Visit LaunchPad to access the e-book and to test your knowledge with LearningCurve.

TERMS

simple linear regression (p. 497)
regression to the mean (p. 499)
intercept (p. 501)
slope (p. 501)

standardized regression coefficient (p. 506)
standard error of the estimate (p. 509)

proportionate reduction in error (p. 510)
adjusted r^2 (p. 514)
orthogonal variable (p. 518)
multiple regression (p. 519)

FORMULAS

$z_{\hat{Y}} = (r_{XY})(z_X)$ (p. 498)

$\hat{Y} = a + b(X)$ (p. 501)

$\beta = (b)\dfrac{\sqrt{SS_X}}{\sqrt{SS_Y}}$ (p. 506)

$r^2 = \dfrac{(SS_{total} - SS_{error})}{SS_{total}}$ (p. 513)

$r^2_{adjusted} = 1 - \dfrac{(1 - r^2)(N - 1)}{N - p - 1}$ (p. 514)

$\sigma_{estimate} = \sqrt{\dfrac{\Sigma(Y - \hat{Y})^2}{N}}$ (p. 515)

SYMBOLS

$\hat{Y}$ (p. 498)

a (p. 501)

b (p. 501)

β (p. 506)

SS_{total} (p. 510)

SS_{error} (p. 512)

r^2 (p. 513)

$r^2_{adjusted}$ (p. 514)

$\sigma_{estimate}$ (p. 515)

R^2 (p. 521)

Chi-Square Tests

Nonparametric Statistics

An Example of a Nonparametric Test

When to Use Nonparametric Tests

Chi-Square Tests

Chi-Square Test for Goodness of Fit

Chi-Square Test for Independence

Adjusted Standardized Residuals

Beyond Hypothesis Testing

Cramér's *V*, the Effect Size for Chi Square

Graphing Chi-Square Percentages

Data Ethics: Relative Risk

BEFORE YOU GO ON

- You should be able to differentiate between a parametric and a nonparametric hypothesis test (Chapter 7).

- You should know the six steps of hypothesis testing (Chapter 7).

- You should understand the concept of effect size (Chapter 8).

Check out the last selfie you posted. What does it say about you? German researchers Nicola Döring, Anne Reif, and Sandra Poeschl (2016) conducted a study that suggested that, for many of us, our selfies reflect our gender. They looked at 500 selfies—half of men and half of women—and counted how many times the photos met various gender stereotypes. They counted how often the people in the selfies exhibited stereotypically feminine behaviors or postures like lying down, looking away, or appearing seductive—

Selfies and Gender Stereotypes Do we fall back on gender stereotypes when we pose for our selfies? Research suggests that we do (Döring, Reif, & Poeschl, 2016). Women are more likely than men to pose in a seductive manner, such as with "duckface," whereas men are more likely than women to pose showing off muscles.

such as what is sometimes called "duckface." They also counted stereotypically masculine behaviors such as showing off muscles.

How would you analyze data like these? There is no scale variable. The researchers are just counting behaviors in selfies; they're not giving the selfies some kind of a score. So, these are nominal data—you either exhibit a behavior—such as duckface—or you don't. As you may realize, we don't yet have the tools to handle a study with only nominal data. We've learned about only parametric tests so far, the ones summarized in Table 17-1. In this chapter, we'll learn about nonparametric tests, which allow us to analyze data when there is no scale dependent variable.

So what did Döring and her colleagues find? Using the nonparametric chi-square tests, they found that women and men did indeed tend to fall back on gender stereotypes in their selfie poses. In fact, the gender stereotyping was even more pronounced than what we see in advertisements.

This chapter helps us to explore hypotheses about nonparametric data by explaining when to use a nonparametric test and by demonstrating how to use two nonparametric tests based on nominal data.

Nonparametric hypothesis tests allow us to distinguish between pattern and chance when observational data do not have a scale dependent variable. We use the chi-square statistic when all of the data are nominal variables—as in the selfie study. If we can count the frequency of any event and assign each frequency to one (and only one) category, then the chi-square statistic lets us test for the independence of those categories and estimate effect sizes.

TABLE 17-1	**A Summary of Research Designs**

We have encountered several research designs so far, most of which fall in one of two categories. Some designs—those listed in category I—include at least one scale independent variable and a scale dependent variable. Other designs—those listed in category II—include a nominal (or sometimes ordinal) independent variable and a scale dependent variable. Until now, we have not encountered a research design with a nominal independent variable and a nominal dependent variable, or a research design with an ordinal dependent variable.

I. Scale Independent Variable and Scale Dependent Variable	II. Nominal Independent Variable and Scale Dependent Variable
Correlation	z test
Regression	All kinds of t tests
	All kinds of ANOVAs

Nonparametric Statistics

Selfies are not just a place where gender stereotypes run wild. They can even be dangerous. The headline of a British newspaper warned us that "Selfies Are Killing More People Than Shark Attacks," with 12 people dying while taking selfies—from falls, for example—in the first half of the year but only 8 being killed by sharks (Sandhu, 2015). This is another example of a study based on nominal data—counts of people in categories—rather than scale data. Many studies, like the study on the dangers of selfies, violate parametric assumptions for hypothesis testing (especially the assumption that the data be drawn from a normally distributed population). The chi-square statistic provides a solution because it is a more conservative nonparametric statistic that is *not* based on critical assumptions about the population.

An Example of a Nonparametric Test

Nonparametric statistics are exciting because they expand the universe of things that we can study. For example, what do you think would make you more likely to recycle? What if you identified with an object? Would that lead you to be more likely to recycle it than to toss it in the trash? Behavioral scientist Remi Trudel and his colleagues (2016) explored this question. Participants were handed a paper cup and asked whether they could tell whether it contained tap water or bottled water (although the researchers didn't care about that at all). One-third of participants were handed a paper cup with their name written on it and spelled correctly (e.g., Ashley), one-third with their name spelled incorrectly (e.g., Ashli), and one-third with no name. After sampling water and completing questionnaires, participants were told to "dispose of your cup on the way out." Just outside of the lab were two bins, one for trash and one for recycling.

The hypothesis is that people will be more likely to recycle if they identify with an object. So, in Trudel and colleagues' study, participants would be more likely to recycle the paper cup with their name spelled correctly than either the cup with their name spelled incorrectly or the cup with no name. The independent variable is type of name on the paper cup (spelled correctly, spelled incorrectly, or no name). The dependent variable is method of disposal, with two levels (recycling or trash). This is a new statistical situation because method of disposal, of course, is not a scale variable. Both the independent variable and the dependent variable are nominal. (We'll explore their results in more detail later.)

This new situation (two nominal variables) calls for a new statistic and a new hypothesis test: The chi-square statistic is symbolized as χ^2 (pronounced "kai square"—rhymes with *sky*) and relies on the chi-square distribution.

When to Use Nonparametric Tests

We use a nonparametric test when (1) the dependent variable is nominal, (2) the dependent variable is ordinal, or (3) the sample size is small and the population of interest may be skewed.

Situation 1 (a nominal dependent variable) occurs whenever we categorize the observations: trash or recycling, dog lover or cat lover, driver's license or no driver's license. We often think of our world in terms of categories.

Situation 2 (an ordinal dependent variable) describes rank, such as in athletic competitions, class position, or preferred flavor of ice cream. Top 10 lists and favorite nephews are also ordinal observations.

MASTERING THE CONCEPT

17-1: We use nonparametric tests when (1) the dependent variable is nominal, (2) the dependent variable is ordinal, or (3) the sample size is small and we suspect that the underlying population distribution is not normal.

Situation 3 (a small sample size, usually of less than 30, and a potentially skewed population) occurs less frequently. It would be difficult to recruit enough participants to study the brain patterns among people who have won the Nobel Prize in literature, no matter how hard we tried or how much we paid people to participate.

Although nonparametric tests expand the range of variables available for research, they have two big problems: (1) Confidence intervals and effect-size measures are not typically available for nominal or ordinal data and (2) nonparametric tests tend to have less statistical power than parametric tests. This increases the risk of a Type II error: We are less likely to reject the null hypothesis when we should reject it (that is, when there is a real difference between groups). Nonparametric tests are often the backup plan, not the go-to statistical tests.

CHECK YOUR LEARNING

Reviewing the Concepts

> We use a nonparametric test when we cannot meet the assumptions of a parametric test, primarily the assumptions of having a scale dependent variable and a normally distributed population.

> The most common situations in which we use a nonparametric test are when we have a nominal or ordinal dependent variable or a small sample in which the data for the dependent variable suggest that the underlying population distribution might be skewed.

Clarifying the Concepts

17-1 Distinguish a parametric test from a nonparametric test.

17-2 When do we use nonparametric tests?

Calculating the Statistics

17-3 For each of the following situations, identify the independent and dependent variables and how they are measured (nominal, ordinal, or scale).

a. *The New York Times* publishes an annual list of recommended travel destinations. The "52 Places to Go in 2019" ranked list included Puerto Rico; Hampi, India; and Eilat, Israel, among the top 10 recommendations (nytimes.com/interactive/2019/travel/places-to-visit.html). Imagine if the newspaper also ranked the typical costs of traveling to each destination to see if these were related to each destination's overall ranking.

b. Imagine that *The New York Times* gave every destination a score on how interesting it is (on a scale of 1–10), and then compared the destinations in Asia and South America.

c. You might be interested in whether the 1–10 scores for how interesting destinations are is related to (or predicted by) how expensive those locales are in terms of the typical amount a traveler would spend each day.

d. *The New York Times* added posts on its Facebook page for each of the 52 destinations. Readers could add recommendations in the comments on each post. For example, Aalborg, Denmark, garnered 28 recommendations, whereas 5 people had recommendations for Gambia. Does the number of recommendations differ among destinations in Europe, Africa, and North America?

Applying the Concepts

Solutions to these Check Your Learning questions can be found in Appendix D.

17-4 For each of the situations listed in the previous Check Your Learning exercise, state the category (I or II) from Table 17-1 from which you would choose the appropriate hypothesis test. If you would not choose a test from either category I or II, simply list category III—other. Explain why you chose I, II, or III.

Chi-Square Tests

Selfie research is beginning to be a legitimate area of scholarship. Australian researchers recently presented their ideas on the rise of controversial selfies, such as selfies at funerals (Gibbs, Nansen, Carter, & Kohn, 2014). It might be interesting to explore the circumstances under which people take selfies at funerals. For example, are they more common at funerals of young people? Of those who died tragically in accidents? These are testable ideas, and this chapter describes what is being tested in two common kinds of chi-square statistical tests: (1) the *chi-square test for goodness of fit*, *a nonparametric hypothesis test that is used when there is one nominal variable,* and (2) the *chi-square test for independence*, *a nonparametric hypothesis test that is used when there are two nominal variables*. Both chi-square tests involve the by-now familiar six steps of hypothesis testing.

Both chi-square tests use the chi-square statistic: χ^2. The chi-square statistic is based on the chi-square distribution. As with t and F distributions, there are several chi-square distributions, depending on the degrees of freedom. After we introduce chi-square tests, we'll introduce several ways of determining the size of a finding, including by calculating an effect and graphing the finding. In addition, in the Data Ethics feature, we'll explore the easy-to-understand, but also easy-to-misinterpret, relative risk.

- The **chi-square test for goodness of fit** is a nonparametric hypothesis test that is used when there is one nominal variable.

- The **chi-square test for independence** is a nonparametric hypothesis test that is used when there are two nominal variables.

Chi-Square Test for Goodness of Fit

The chi-square test for goodness of fit calculates a statistic based on just one variable. There is no independent variable or dependent variable—just one categorical variable with two or more categories into which participants are placed. In fact, the chi-square test for goodness of fit received its name because it measures how good the fit is between the observed data in the various categories of a single nominal variable and the data we would expect according to the null hypothesis. If there's a really good fit with the null hypothesis, then we cannot reject the null hypothesis. If we hope to receive empirical support for the research hypothesis, then we're actually hoping for a *bad fit* between the observed data and what we expect according to the null hypothesis.

> **MASTERING THE CONCEPT**
>
> **17-2:** When we only have nominal variables, we use the chi-square statistic. Specifically, we use a chi-square test for goodness of fit when there is one nominal variable, and we use a chi-square test for independence when there are two nominal variables.

EXAMPLE 17.1

For example, researchers reported that the best youth soccer players in the world were more likely to have been born early in the year than later (Dubner & Levitt, 2006a). As one example, they reported that 52 elite youth players in Germany were born in January, February, or March, whereas only 4 players were born in October, November, or December. (Those born in other months were not included in this study.)

The null hypothesis predicts that when a person was born will not make any difference; the research hypothesis predicts that the month a person was born will matter when it comes to being an elite soccer player. Assuming that births in the general population are evenly distributed across months of the year, the null hypothesis posits that equal numbers of elite soccer players were born in the first 3 months and

Are Elite Soccer Players Born in the Early Months of the Year?
Based on data for elite German youth soccer players, a chi-square test for goodness of fit showed a statistically significant effect: Players were more likely to be born in the first 3 months than in the last 3 months of the year (Dubner & Levitt, 2006a).

the last 3 months of the year. With 56 participants in the study (52 born in the first 3 months and 4 in the last 3 months), equal frequencies lead us to expect 28 players to have been born in the first 3 months and 28 in the last 3 months just by chance. The birth months don't appear to be evenly distributed, but is this a real pattern, or just chance?

Like previous hypothesis tests, the chi-square goodness of fit test uses the six steps of hypothesis testing.

> **STEP 1:** Identify the populations, distribution, and assumptions.

There are always two populations involved in a chi-square test: one population that matches the frequencies of participants like those we observed and another population that matches the frequencies of participants like those we would expect according to the null hypothesis. In this case, there is a population of elite German youth soccer players with birth dates like those we observed and a population of elite German youth soccer players with birth dates like those in the general population. The comparison distribution is a chi-square distribution. There's just one nominal variable, birth month, so we'll conduct a chi-square test for goodness of fit.

The first assumption is that the variable (birth month) is nominal. The second assumption is that each observation is independent; no single participant can be in more than one category. The third assumption is that participants were randomly selected. If not, it may be unwise to confidently generalize beyond the sample. A fourth assumption is that there is a minimum number of expected participants in every category (also called a *cell*)—at least 5 and preferably more. An alternative guideline (Delucchi, 1983) is for there to be at least five times as many participants as cells. In any case, the chi-square tests seem robust to violations of this last assumption.

Summary: Population 1: Elite German youth soccer players with birth dates like those we observed. Population 2: Elite German youth soccer players with birth dates like those in the general population.

The comparison distribution is a chi-square distribution. The hypothesis test will be a chi-square test for goodness of fit because there is one nominal variable only, birth months. This study meets three of the four assumptions: (1) The one variable is nominal. (2) Every participant is in only one cell (you can't be born in both January and November). (3) This is not a randomly selected sample of all elite soccer players. The sample includes only German youth soccer players in the elite leagues. We must be cautious in generalizing beyond young German elite players.

(4) There are more than five times as many participants as cells (the table has two cells, and $2 \times 5 = 10$). We have 56 participants, far more than the 10 necessary to meet this guideline.

> **STEP 2:** State the null and research hypotheses.

For chi-square tests, it's easiest to state the hypotheses in words only, rather than in both words and symbols.

Summary: Null hypothesis: Elite German youth soccer players have the same pattern of birth months as those in the general population. Research hypothesis: Elite German youth soccer players have a different pattern of birth months than those in the general population.

> **STEP 3:** Determine the characteristics of the comparison distribution.

The only task at this step is to determine the degrees of freedom. In most previous hypothesis tests, the degrees of freedom have been based on sample size. For the chi-square hypothesis tests, however, the degrees of freedom are based on the numbers of categories, or cells, in which participants can be counted. The degrees of freedom for a chi-square test for goodness of fit is the number of categories minus 1:

$$df_{\chi^2} = k - 1$$

Here, k is the symbol for the number of categories. The current example has only two categories: Each soccer player in this study was born in either the first 3 months of the year or the last 3 months of the year:

$$df_{\chi^2} = 2 - 1 = 1$$

Summary: The comparison distribution is a chi-square distribution, which has 1 degree of freedom: $df_{\chi^2} = 2 - 1 = 1$.

> **STEP 4:** Determine the critical value, or cutoff.

To determine the cutoff, or critical value, for the chi-square statistic, we use the chi-square table in Appendix B-4. χ^2 is based on squares and can never be negative, so there is just one critical value. An excerpt from Appendix B-4 that applies to the soccer study is given in Table 17-2. We look under the alpha level, usually 0.05, and across from the appropriate degrees of freedom, in this case, 1. For this situation, the critical chi-square statistic is 3.841.

MASTERING THE FORMULA

17-1: We calculate the degrees of freedom for the chi-square test for goodness of fit by subtracting 1 from the number of categories, represented in the formula by k. The formula is:

$$df_{\chi^2} = k - 1$$

As an example, here are the calculations for the category "first 3 months":

$$O - E = (52 - 28) = 24$$

$$(O - E)^2 = (24)^2 = 576$$

$$\frac{(O - E)^2}{E} = \frac{576}{28} = 20.571$$

Once we complete the table, the last step is easy. We just add up the numbers in the sixth column. In this case, the chi-square statistic is $20.571 + 20.571 = 41.14$. We can finish the formula by adding a summation sign to the formula in the sixth column. Note that we don't have to divide this sum by anything, as we've done with other statistics. We already did the dividing before we summed. This sum is the chi-square statistic. Here is the formula:

$$\chi^2 = \Sigma \left[\frac{(O - E)^2}{E} \right]$$

Summary: $\chi^2 = \Sigma \left[\dfrac{(O - E)^2}{E} \right] = 20.571 + 20.571 = 41.14$

STEP 6: Make a decision.

This last step is identical to that of previous hypothesis tests. We reject the null hypothesis if the test statistic is beyond the critical value, and we fail to reject the null hypothesis if the test statistic is not beyond the critical value. In this case, the test statistic, 41.14, is far beyond the cutoff, 3.841, as seen in Figure 17-2. We reject the null hypothesis. Because there are only two categories, it's clear where the difference lies. It appears that elite German youth soccer players are more likely to have been born in the first 3 months of the year, and less likely to have been born in the last 3 months of the year, than members of the general population. (If we had failed to reject the null hypothesis, we could only have concluded that these data did not provide sufficient evidence to show that elite German youth soccer players have a different likelihood

FIGURE 17-2

Making a Decision

As with other hypothesis tests, we make a decision with a chi-square test by comparing the test statistic to the cutoff, or critical value. We see here that 41.14 would be *far* to the right of 3.841.

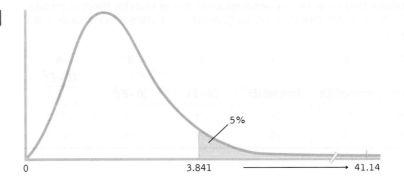

of being born in the first, versus the last, 3 months of the year than those in the general population.)

Summary: Reject the null hypothesis; it appears that elite German youth soccer players are more likely to have been born in the first 3 months of the year, and less likely to have been born in the last 3 months of the year, than people in the general population.

We report these statistics in a journal article in almost the same format that we've seen previously. We report the degrees of freedom, the value of the test statistic, and whether the p value associated with the test statistic is less than or greater than the cutoff based on the alpha level of 0.05. (As usual, we would report the actual p value if we conducted this hypothesis test using software.) In addition, we report the sample size in parentheses with the degrees of freedom. In the current example, the statistics read:

$$\chi^2(1, N = 56) = 41.14, \ p < 0.05$$

The researchers who conducted this study imagined four possible explanations: "a) certain astrological signs confer superior soccer skills; b) winter-born babies tend to have higher oxygen capacity, which increases soccer stamina; c) soccer-mad parents are more likely to conceive children in springtime, at the annual peak of soccer mania; d) none of the above" (Dubner & Levitt, 2006a). What's your guess?

Dubner and Levitt (2006a) picked (d) and suggested another alternative. Participation in German youth soccer leagues has a strict cutoff date: December 31. Compared to those born in December, children born the previous January are likely to be more physically and emotionally mature, perceived as more talented, chosen for the best leagues, and given better coaching—a self-fulfilling prophecy. All this from a simple chi-square test for goodness of fit! ●

Chi-Square Test for Independence

The chi-square test for goodness of fit analyzes just one nominal variable. The chi-square test for independence analyzes *two* nominal variables.

Like the correlation coefficient, the chi-square test for independence does not require that we identify independent and dependent variables. However, specifying an independent variable and a dependent variable can help us articulate hypotheses. The chi-square test for independence is so named because it is used to determine whether the two variables—no matter which one is considered to be the independent variable—are independent of each other. Let's take a closer look at whether the choice to recycle something or toss it in the trash is independent of (that is, depends on) whether you identify with it, as operationalized by whether a paper cup has your name correctly written on it, incorrectly written on it, or not written on it at all.

MBI/Stockbroker/Alamy

A Choice Which factors affect how likely you are to recycle? If you identify more closely with an object, are you more likely to extend its "life" by recycling it as opposed to throwing it in the trash?

EXAMPLE 17.2

In the recycling study, 159 people were randomly assigned to one of three groups (Trudel et al., 2016). (Note that the researchers did not provide the exact numbers of people in each cell, but we roughly determined them from the percentages they provided.) Of those participants, 53 were given a paper cup on which their name was spelled correctly, 53 were given a cup with their name spelled incorrectly, and 53 were given a cup with no name on it. The participants then had to choose whether to recycle the paper cup or throw it in the trash. Of the 53 people whose name was spelled correctly, 25 chose to recycle. But only 13 of the 53 people with cups with incorrectly spelled names and 14 of the 53 people with cups with no names chose to recycle. The cells for these observed frequencies can be seen in Table 17-5. The table of cells for a chi-square test for independence is called a *contingency table* because it helps us see if the outcome of one variable (e.g., recycling the cup versus throwing it in the trash) is contingent on the other variable (correctly spelled name on the cup versus incorrectly spelled or no name). Let's implement the six steps of hypothesis testing for a chi-square test for independence.

TABLE 17-5 Observed Recycling Rates

This table depicts the cells and their frequencies for the study on whether the likelihood of recycling an object depended on the degree to which the person identified with it.

	Observed	
	Recycling	Trash
Correctly spelled name	25	28
Incorrectly spelled name	13	40
No name	14	39

> **STEP 1: Identify the populations, distribution, and assumptions.**

Summary: Population 1: People like those whom we observed who received cups on which their names were correctly spelled. Population 2: People like those whom we observed who received cups on which their names were incorrectly spelled. Population 3: People like those whom we observed who received cups with no name on them.

The comparison distribution is a chi-square distribution. The hypothesis test will be a chi-square test for independence because there are two nominal variables. This study meets three of the four assumptions: (1) The two variables are nominal. (2) Every participant is in only one cell. (3) The participants were not, however, randomly selected from the population. We must be cautious in generalizing beyond this sample of university students. (4) There are more than five times as many participants as cells (159 participants and 6 cells; $6 \times 5 = 30$). We have far more participants, 159, than the 30 necessary to meet this guideline.

> **STEP 2: State the null and research hypotheses.**

Summary: Null hypothesis: Likelihood of recycling depends on identification with an object, operationalized by the type of cup received (correctly spelled name, incorrectly spelled name, or no name). Research hypothesis: Likelihood of recycling does not depend on identification with an object, operationalized by the type of cup received.

STEP 3: Determine the characteristics of the comparison distribution.

For a chi-square test for independence, we calculate degrees of freedom for each variable and then multiply the two to get the overall degrees of freedom. The degrees of freedom for the variable in the rows of the contingency table are:

$$df_{row} = k_{row} - 1$$

The degrees of freedom for the variable in the columns of the contingency table are:

$$df_{column} = k_{column} - 1$$

The overall degrees of freedom are:

$$df_{\chi^2} = (df_{row})(df_{column})$$

To expand this last formula, we write:

$$df_{\chi^2} = (k_{row} - 1)(k_{column} - 1)$$

So, the degrees of freedom for this chi-square test is:

$$df_{\chi^2} = (k_{row} - 1)(k_{column} - 1) = (3-1)(2-1) = 2$$

Summary: The comparison distribution is a chi-square distribution, which has 2 degrees of freedom: $df_{\chi^2} = (k_{row} - 1)(k_{column} - 1) = (3-1)(2-1) = 2$.

STEP 4: Determine the critical values, or cutoffs.

Summary: The critical value, or cutoff, for the chi-square statistic, based on an alpha level of 0.05 and 2 degrees of freedom, is 5.991 (Figure 17-3).

0   5.991

5%

FIGURE 17-3

The Cutoff for a Chi-Square Test for Independence

The shaded region is beyond the critical value for a chi-square test for independence with an alpha level of 0.05 and 2 degrees of freedom. If the test statistic falls within this shaded area, we will reject the null hypothesis.

> **STEP 5:** Calculate the test statistic.

The next step, determining the appropriate expected frequencies, is the most important in the calculation of the chi-square test for independence. Errors are often made in this step, and if the wrong expected frequencies are used, the chi-square statistic derived from them will also be wrong. Many students want to divide the total number of participants (here, 159) by the number of cells (here, 6) and place equivalent frequencies in all cells for the expected data. Here, that would mean that the expected frequencies would be 26.5.

But this would not make sense. Of the 159 university students, only 52 chose to recycle; $52/159 = 0.327$, or 32.7%, chose to recycle. If recycling rates do not depend on identification with an object, then we would expect the same percentage of cups to get recycled, 32.7%, regardless of the type of cup received. If we have expected frequencies of 26.5 in all 6 cells, then we have a 50%, not a 32.7%, recycling rate. We must always consider the specifics of the situation.

In the current study, we already calculated that 32.7% of all participants recycled. If recycling is independent of identification with an object, then we would expect 32.7% of all participants who received a cup with their name correctly spelled to recycle the cup, 32.7% of participants who received a cup with their name incorrectly spelled to recycle it, and 32.7% of participants who received a cup with no name on it to recycle it. Based on this percentage, $100 - 32.7 = 67.3\%$ of participants in each of these conditions would throw their cup in the trash. Again, we expect the same recycling rates and trash rates in all three groups if recycling does not depend on identification with an object (the cup).

Table 17-6 shows the observed data, and it also shows totals for each row, each column, and the whole table. From Table 17-6, we see that 53 participants received a cup on which their name was correctly spelled. From our earlier calculations, we would expect 32.7% of them to recycle the cup.

$$(0.327)(53) = 17.331$$

The same would be true for the other two groups.

We now repeat the same procedure for throwing the cup in the trash. We would expect 67.3% of participants in all three groups to choose not to recycle. For the participants who received a cup with their correctly spelled name, we would expect 67.3% of them to throw their cup in the trash:

$$(0.673)(53) = 35.669$$

TABLE 17-6 Observed Frequencies

This table depicts the cells and their frequencies for the recycling study. It also includes row totals (53, 53, 53), column totals (52, 107), and the grand total for the whole table (159).

	Observed		
	Recycling	Trash	
Correctly spelled name	25	28	53
Incorrectly spelled name	13	40	53
No name	14	39	53
	52	107	159

The same would be true for the other two groups. (Note that the two expected frequencies for the first row are the same as the two expected frequencies for the second and third rows, but only because the same number of people were in each cup condition, 53. If these three numbers were different, we would not see the same expected frequencies in the three rows.)

The method of calculating the expected frequencies that we described here is ideal because it is directly based on our own thinking about the frequencies in the rows and in the columns. Sometimes, however, our thinking can get muddled, particularly when the two (or more) row totals do not match and the two (or more) column totals do not match. For these situations, a simple set of rules leads to accurate expected frequencies. For each cell, we divide its column total ($Total_{column}$) by the grand total (N) and multiply that by the row total ($Total_{row}$):

$$\frac{Total_{column}}{N}(Total_{row})$$

MASTERING THE FORMULA

17-4: When conducting a chi-square test for independence, we can calculate the expected frequencies in each cell by taking the total for the column that the cell is in, dividing it by the total in the study, and then multiplying by the total for the row that the cell is in:

$$\frac{Total_{column}}{N}(Total_{row})$$

As an example, the observed frequency of those who received a cup with their name correctly spelled on it and then recycled it is 25. The row total for this cell is 53. The column total is 52. The grand total, N, is 159. The expected frequency, therefore, is:

$$\frac{Total_{column}}{N}(Total_{row}) = \frac{52}{159}(53) = (0.327)(53) = 17.331$$

Notice that this result is identical to what we calculated without a formula. The middle step above shows that, even with the formula, we actually did calculate the recycling rate overall, by dividing the column total (52) by the grand total (159). We then calculated how many in that row of 53 participants we would expect to recycle using this overall rate:

$$(0.327)(53) = 17.331$$

The formula follows the logic of the test and keeps us on track when there are multiple calculations.

As a final check on the calculations, shown in Table 17-7, we can add up the frequencies to be sure that they still match the row, column, and grand totals. For example, if we add the three numbers in the first column, 17.331, 17.331, and 17.331, we

TABLE 17-7   Expected Frequencies with Totals

This table includes the expected frequencies for each of the six cells. The expected frequencies should still add up to the row totals (53, 53, 53), column totals (52, 107), and the grand total for the whole table (159).

	Expected		
	Recycling	Trash	
Correctly spelled name	17.331	35.669	53
Incorrectly spelled name	17.331	35.669	53
No name	17.331	35.669	53
	52	107	159

get 51.933 (different from 52 only because of rounding decisions). If we had made the mistake of dividing the 159 participants into cells by dividing by 6, we would have had 26.5 in each cell; then the total for the first column would have been $26.5 + 26.5 + 26.5 = 79.5$, which is not a match with 52. This final check ensures that we have the appropriate expected frequencies in the cells.

The remainder of the fifth step is identical to that for a chi-square test for goodness of fit, as seen in Table 17-8. As before, we calculate the difference between each observed frequency and its matching expected frequency, square these differences, and divide each squared difference by the appropriate expected frequency. We add up the numbers in the final column of the table to calculate the chi-square statistic.

Summary: $\chi^2 = \Sigma\left[\dfrac{(O-E)^2}{E}\right] = 3.394 + 1.649 + 1.082 + 0.526 + 0.640 + 0.311 = 7.602$

TABLE 17-8 The Chi-Square Calculations

For the chi-square test for independence calculations, we use the same format as we did for the chi-square test for goodness of fit. We calculate the difference between each observed frequency and expected frequency, square the difference, then divide each square by its appropriate expected frequency. Finally, we add up the numbers in the last column, which gives us the chi-square statistic.

Category	Observed (O)	Expected (E)	($O-E$)	($O-E$)^2	$\dfrac{(O-E)^2}{E}$
Correctly spelled name; chose recycling	25	17.331	7.669	58.814	3.394
Correctly spelled name; chose trash	28	35.669	−7.669	58.814	1.649
Incorrectly spelled name; chose recycling	13	17.331	−4.331	18.758	1.082
Incorrectly spelled name; chose trash	40	35.669	4.331	18.758	0.526
No name; chose recycling	14	17.331	−3.331	11.096	0.640
No name; chose trash	39	35.669	3.331	11.096	0.311

STEP 6: Make a decision.

We can now compare the test statistic, 7.602, to the critical value, 5.991. Because the test statistic is beyond the critical value, we can reject the null hypothesis.

Summary: Reject the null hypothesis; it appears that the likelihood of recycling depends on identification with an object, as operationalized by the type of cup received (correctly spelled name, incorrectly spelled name, or no name) (Figure 17-4).

The statistics, as reported in a journal article, would follow the format we learned for a chi-square test for goodness of fit as well as for other hypothesis tests in earlier chapters. We report the degrees of freedom and sample size, the value of the test statistic, and whether the p value associated with the test statistic is less than or greater than the critical value based on the alpha level of 0.05. (We would report the actual p value if we conducted this hypothesis test using software.) In the current example, the statistics would read:

$$\chi^2(2, N = 159) = 7.60, p < 0.05$$

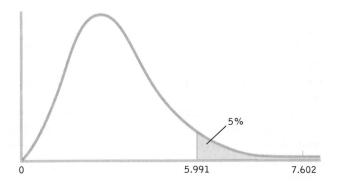

FIGURE 17-4

The Decision

Because the chi-square statistic, 7.602, is beyond the critical value, 5.991, we can reject the null hypothesis. It is unlikely that the likelihood of recycling depends on identification with an object.

A chi-square test tells us that there is a statistically significant effect, but it does not tell us exactly where differences lie. If there are just four cells, we know that all four observed counts are different from the expected counts, but if one variable has more than two levels, we must take an additional step and conduct a type of post hoc test that can be used to determine exactly where any differences lie among the cells of a chi-square design. We'll introduce that procedure, the calculation of adjusted standardized residuals, in the next section.

Adjusted Standardized Residuals

Chi-square tests present a problem when there are more than two levels of one of the variables. A significant chi-square hypothesis test means only that at least some of the cells' observed frequencies are statistically significantly different from their corresponding expected frequencies. We cannot know how many cells or exactly which ones are significantly different without an additional step. That next step is the calculation of a statistic for each cell based on its residual.

A cell's residual is the difference between the expected frequency and the observed frequency for that cell, but we take it a step further. We calculate *an **adjusted standardized residual***, *the difference between the observed frequency and the expected frequency for a cell in a chi-square research design, divided by the standard error.* In other words, an adjusted standardized residual (often called just *adjusted residual* by software) is a measure of the number of standard errors that an observed frequency falls from its associated expected frequency.

Does this sound familiar? The adjusted standardized frequency is kind of like a *z* statistic for each cell (Agresti & Franklin, 2006). A larger adjusted standardized residual indicates that an observed frequency is further from its expected frequency than a smaller adjusted standardized residual indicates. And as with a *z* statistic, we're not concerned with the sign. A large positive adjusted standardized residual and a large negative adjusted standardized residual tell us the same thing. If it's large enough, then we're willing to conclude that the observed frequency really is different from what we would expect if the null hypothesis were true.

Also like a *z* statistic, any time a cell has an adjusted standardized residual that is at least 2 (whether the sign is positive or negative), we are willing to conclude that the

● **Adjusted standardized residual** is the difference between the observed frequency and the expected frequency for a cell in a chi-square research design, divided by the standard error; also called *adjusted residual*.

cell's observed frequency is different from its expected frequency. Some statisticians prefer a more stringent criterion, drawing this conclusion only if an adjusted standardized residual is larger than 3 (again, whether the sign is positive or negative). Regardless of the criterion used, the method and logic for determining the probabilities of z statistics and determining adjusted standardized residuals are the same.

Adjusted standardized residuals are too complicated to calculate without the aid of a computer, but we'll show you a software printout of the adjusted standardized residuals for the recycling study. Figure 17-5 shows the printout from the SPSS software package. The rows labeled "Count" include the observed frequencies. The "Expected Count" rows include the expected frequencies. The "Adjusted Residual" rows include the adjusted standardized residuals. So, for example, the upper-left-hand cell has data for participants who received a cup on which their name was spelled correctly and chose to recycle it; the observed frequency for this cell was 25, the expected frequency was 17.3, and the adjusted standardized residual was 2.7. Any adjusted standardized residual greater than 2 or less than −2 indicates that the observed frequency is further from the expected frequency than we would expect if the two variables were independent of each other. In this case, only the adjusted standardized residuals for the two groups with correctly spelled names were greater than 2 or less than −2. We can conclude only that these two observed frequencies are further from their corresponding expected frequencies than would likely occur if the null hypothesis were true.

Condition * Decision Cross Tabulation

			Decision		Total
			Recycling	Trash	
Condition	Name spelled correctly	Count	25	28	53
		Expected Count	17.3	35.7	53.0
		Adjusted Residual	2.7	−2.7	
	Name misspelled	Count	13	40	53
		Expected Count	17.3	35.7	53.0
		Adjusted Residual	−1.6	1.6	
	No name	Count	14	39	53
		Expected Count	17.3	35.7	53.0
		Adjusted Residual	−1.2	1.2	
Total		Count	52	107	159
		Expected Count	52.0	107.0	159.0

FIGURE 17-5

Adjusted Standardized Residuals

Software calculates an adjusted standardized residual, called *adjusted residual* by most software packages, for each cell. It is calculated by taking the residual for each cell, calculating the difference between the observed frequency and expected frequency, and dividing by standard error. When an adjusted standardized residual is greater than 2 or less than −2, we typically conclude that the observed frequency is different from the expected frequency.

CHECK YOUR LEARNING

Reviewing the Concepts

> The chi-square tests are used when all variables are nominal.

> The chi-square test for goodness of fit is used with one nominal variable.

> The chi-square test for independence is used with two nominal variables; usually one can be thought of as the independent variable and one as the dependent variable.

> Both chi-square hypothesis tests use the same six steps of hypothesis testing with which we are familiar.

> A statistically significant chi-square hypothesis test does not tell us exactly which cells are further from their expected frequencies than would occur if the two variables were independent. We must calculate adjusted standardized residuals to identify these cells.

Clarifying the Concepts

17-5 When do we use chi-square tests?

17-6 What are observed frequencies and expected frequencies?

Calculating the Statistics

17-7 Imagine a town that boasts clear blue skies 80% of the time. You get to work in that town one summer for 78 days and record the following data. (*Note:* For each day, you picked just one label.)

Clear blue skies: 59 days

Cloudy/hazy/gray skies: 19 days

a. Calculate degrees of freedom for this chi-square test for goodness of fit.

b. Determine the observed and expected frequencies.

c. Calculate the differences and squared differences between frequencies, and calculate the chi-square statistic. Use the six-column format provided here.

Category	Observed (O)	Expected (E)	$O - E$	$(O - E)^2$	$\dfrac{(O - E)^2}{E}$
Clear blue skies					
Unclear skies					

Applying the Concepts

17-8 The Chicago Police Department conducted a study comparing two types of lineups for suspect identification: simultaneous lineups and sequential lineups (Mecklenburg, Malpass, & Ebbesen, 2006). In simultaneous lineups, witnesses saw the suspects all at once, either live or in photographs, and then made their selection. In sequential lineups, witnesses saw the people in the lineup one at a time, either live or in photographs, and said yes or no to suspects one at a time. After numerous high-profile cases in which DNA evidence exonerated people who had been convicted, including many on death row, many police departments shifted to sequential lineups in the hope of reducing incorrect identifications. Several previous studies had indicated the superiority of sequential lineups with respect to accuracy. Over one year, three jurisdictions in Illinois compared the two types of lineups. Of 319 simultaneous lineups, 191 led to identification of the suspect, 8 led to identification of another person in the lineup, and 120 led to no identification. Of 229 sequential lineups, 102 led to identification of the suspect, 20 led to identification of another person in the lineup, and 107 led to no identification.

continued on next page

a. Who or what are the participants in this study? Identify the independent variable and its levels as well as the dependent variable and its levels.

b. Conduct all six steps of hypothesis testing.

c. Report the statistics as you would in a journal article.

d. Why is this study an example of the importance of using two-tailed rather than one-tailed hypothesis tests?

Solutions to these Check Your Learning questions can be found in Appendix D.

MASTERING THE FORMULA

17-5: The formula for Cramér's V, the effect size typically used with the chi-square statistic, is:

$$\text{Cramér's } V = \sqrt{\frac{\chi^2}{(N)(df_{row/column})}}$$

The numerator is the chi-square statistic, χ^2. The denominator is the product of the sample size, N, and either the degrees of freedom for the rows or the degrees of freedom for the columns, whichever is smaller. We take the square root of this quotient to get Cramér's V.

● **Cramér's V** is the standard effect size used with the chi-square test for independence; also called *Cramér's phi*, symbolized as ϕ.

Beyond Hypothesis Testing

In the selfie study that introduced this chapter, Döring and her colleagues (2016) conducted a chi-square analysis that supported their hypothesis that women and men fall back on gender stereotypes in their selfie poses. For a statistically significant finding like this, we would want to know more. For example, we might ask how large the gender difference was and we might want to see the difference in a graph.

Most nonparametric hypothesis tests do not have associated effect-size measures, but chi square does. Using the recycling example, we'll introduce Cramér's V, the effect size for chi square, as one method to determine how large a finding is. We'll then show how to depict chi-square findings visually in a graph so that we can see how large the effect is. In the Data Ethics feature, we'll also demonstrate how to calculate and interpret relative risk, another way to understand the size of an effect by quantifying the chances of a given outcome.

Cramér's V, the Effect Size for Chi Square

Many nonparametric hypothesis tests do not have associated effect-size measures, but chi square does. As with other hypothesis tests, the effect size helps us to make claims about the importance of a study's finding. **Cramér's V** *is the standard effect size used with the chi-square test for independence*. It is also called *Cramér's phi* (pronounced "fie"— rhymes with *fly*) and symbolized by ϕ. Once we have calculated the test statistic, it is easy to calculate Cramér's V by hand. The formula is:

$$\text{Cramér's } V = \sqrt{\frac{\chi^2}{(N)(df_{row/column})}}$$

where χ^2 is the test statistic we just calculated, N is the total number of participants in the study (the lower-right number in the contingency table), and $df_{row/column}$ is the degrees of freedom for either the category in the rows or the category in the columns, whichever is smaller.

EXAMPLE 17.3

For the recycling example, we calculated a chi-square statistic of 7.602, there were 159 participants, and the degrees of freedom for the categories were 1 and 2, respectively. So, the smaller degrees of freedom is 1. (When neither degrees of freedom

TABLE 17-9	Conventions for Determining Effect Size Based on Cramér's V

Jacob Cohen (1992) developed guidelines to determine whether particular effect sizes should be considered small, medium, or large. The effect-size guidelines vary depending on the size of the contingency table. There are different guidelines based on whether the smaller of the two degrees of freedom (row or column) is 1, 2, or 3.

Effect Size	When $df_{row/column} = 1$	When $df_{row/column} = 2$	When $df_{row/column} = 3$
Small	0.10	0.07	0.06
Medium	0.30	0.21	0.17
Large	0.50	0.35	0.29

value is smaller than the other, of course, it doesn't matter which one we choose.) The effect size for the recycling study, therefore, is:

$$\text{Cramér's } V = \sqrt{\frac{\chi^2}{(N)(df_{row/column})}} = \sqrt{\frac{7.602}{(159)(1)}} = \sqrt{.048} = 0.219$$

Now that we have the effect size, we must ask what it means. As with other effect sizes, Jacob Cohen (1992) has developed guidelines, shown in Table 17-9, for determining whether a particular effect is small, medium, or large. The guidelines vary based on the size of the contingency table. When the smaller of the two degrees of freedom for the row and column is 1, we use the guidelines in the second column. When the smaller of the two degrees of freedom is 2, we use the guidelines in the third column. Finally, when it is 3, we use the guidelines in the fourth column. As with the other guidelines for judging effect sizes, such as those for Cohen's d, the guidelines are not cutoffs, but rather rough indicators to help researchers gauge a finding's importance.

The effect size for the recycling study was 0.22. The smaller of the two degrees of freedom values, that for the row and that for the column, was 1. So we use the second column in Table 17-9. This Cramér's V falls about halfway between the effect-size guidelines for a small effect (0.10) and a medium effect (0.30). We would call this a small-to-medium effect. We can build on the report of the statistics by adding the Cramér's V to the end:

$$\chi^2(2, N = 159) = 7.60, p < 0.05, \text{Cramér's } V = 0.22 \ \bullet$$

Graphing Chi-Square Percentages

In addition to calculating Cramér's V, we can graph the data. A visual depiction of the pattern of results is an effective way to understand the size of the relation between two variables assessed using the chi-square statistic. We don't graph the frequencies, however. Instead, we graph proportions or percentages.

EXAMPLE 17.4

For participants who received a cup with their name spelled correctly, we calculate the proportion who recycled the cup and the proportion who threw it in the trash. For the participants who received a cup with their name spelled incorrectly or with no name on it, we again calculate the proportion who recycled it and who threw it in the trash. The calculations for the proportions are below.

In each case, we're dividing the number of a given outcome by the total number of participants in that group. The proportions are called *conditional proportions* because we're not calculating the proportions out of all participants in the study; we're calculating proportions for participants in a certain condition. We calculate the proportion of participants who recycled their cups, for example, conditional on their having received a cup on which their names were spelled correctly.

Correctly spelled name
    Recycling: 25/53 = 0.472
    Trash: 28/53 = 0.528
Incorrectly spelled name
    Recycling: 13/53 = 0.245
    Trash: 40/53 = 0.755
No name
    Recycling: 14/53 = 0.264
    Trash: 39/53 = 0.736

We can put those proportions into a table (such as Table 17-10). For each category of cup (correctly spelled name, incorrectly spelled name, no name), the proportions should add up to 1.00; or if we used percentages, they should add up to 100%.

TABLE 17-10   Conditional Proportions

To construct a graph depicting the results of a chi-square test for independence, we first calculate conditional proportions. For example, we calculate the proportions of participants who recycled, conditional on having received a cup with their name spelled correctly: 25/53 = 0.472.

	Conditional Proportions		
	Recycling	Trash	
Correctly spelled name	0.472	0.528	1.00
Incorrectly spelled name	0.245	0.755	1.00
No name	0.264	0.736	1.00

We can now graph the conditional proportions, as in Figure 17-6. Alternatively we could have simply graphed the three rates at which participants recycled—0.472, 0.245, and 0.264—given that the rates at which they tossed their cups in the trash are based on these rates. This graph is depicted in Figure 17-7. In both cases, we include the scale of proportions on the y-axis from 0 to 1.0 so that the graph does not mislead the viewer into thinking that rates are higher than they are. ●

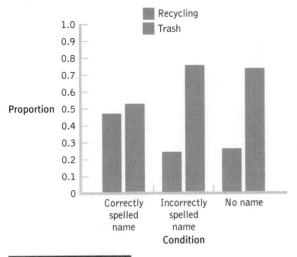

FIGURE 17-6

Graphing and Chi Square

When we graph the data for a chi-square test for independence, we graph conditional proportions rather than frequencies. The proportions allow us to compare the rates at which people recycle in the three conditions.

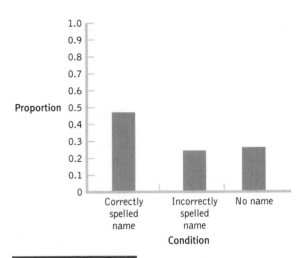

FIGURE 17-7

A Simpler Graph of Conditional Proportions

Because the rates at which people throw their cups in the trash are based on the rates at which they recycled their cups, we can simply graph one set of rates. Here we see the rates at which people recycled in each of the three conditions.

Relative Risk

Public health statisticians like John Snow (Chapter 1) are called epidemiologists. They often think about the size of an effect with chi square in terms of ***relative risk***, *a measure created by making a ratio of two conditional proportions.* It is also called *relative likelihood* or *relative chance.* As we'll see, these statistics can be used by ethical researchers to clarify their findings, but they can also be misused to unnecessarily scare the public. First, let's calculate the relative likelihood for two conditions of the recycling experiment—recycling rates for those with a cup on which their name was spelled correctly as compared with rates for those with a cup on which their name was misspelled.

As with Figure 17-6, we calculate the likelihood that people will recycle their cup given that they were given a cup with their named spelled correctly by dividing the number of people in this group who recycled (25) by the total number of people in this group (53):

$$25/53 = 0.472$$

We then calculate the likelihood that people will recycle their cup given that they were given a cup with their name spelled incorrectly by dividing the number of people in this group who recycled (13) by the total number of people in this group (53)

$$13/53 = 0.245$$

● **Relative risk** is a measure created by making a ratio of two conditional proportions; also called *relative likelihood* or *relative chance.*

MASTERING THE CONCEPT

17-3: We can quantify the size of an effect with chi square through relative risk, also called *relative likelihood.* By making a ratio of two conditional proportions, we can say, for example, that one group is twice as likely to show some outcome or, conversely, that the other group is one-half as likely to show that outcome.

If we divide the likelihood that people will recycle their cup given that they were given a cup with their name spelled correctly by the likelihood that people will recycle their cup given that they were given a cup with their name spelled incorrectly on it, then we get the relative likelihood:

$$0.472/0.245 = 1.927$$

Based on the relative risk calculation, the likelihood of recycling when your cup has your name correctly spelled on it is 1.93 times (or about twice) the likelihood of recycling when your cup has your name incorrectly spelled on it. This matches the impression that we get from the graph.

Alternatively we can reverse the ratio, dividing the chance that people will recycle their cup given that they were given a cup on which their name was spelled incorrectly by the chance that people will recycle their cup given that they were given a cup on which their name was spelled correctly. This is the relative likelihood for the reversed ratio:

$$0.245/0.472 = 0.519$$

This number gives us the same information in a different way. The likelihood of recycling when your cup has your name incorrectly spelled on it is 0.52 times (or about half) the likelihood of recycling when your cup has your name correctly spelled on it. Again, this matches the graph; one bar is about half that of the other. As you may have guessed, we could also calculate the relative likelihood of recycling a cup with a correctly spelled name rather than a cup with no name, and of recycling a cup with an incorrectly spelled name than a cup with no name. *Note:* When this calculation is made with respect to diseases or other bad things, it is referred to as *relative risk* (rather than relative likelihood).

How do ethics play into this? Relative likelihood and relative risk are easily understood by the general public. Because they are more "approachable" statistics, they're a helpful addition to the arsenal of an ethical researcher who is trying to be honest and clear when reporting statistics. The unethical researcher, however, can exploit relative likelihood and relative risk to exaggerate or minimize findings by leaving out base rates.

● The **base rate** is the underlying probability of a particular occurrence.

In statistics, *the **base rate** is the underlying probability of a particular occurrence.* If, for example, a certain disease occurs in just 0.01% of the population (that is, 1 in 10,000) and is twice as likely to occur among people who eat ice cream, then the rate is 0.02% (2 in 10,000) among those who eat ice cream. Psychologist Gerd Gigerenzer (2009) described one well-known example. In 1995, the British Committee on Safety of Medicines warned of a relative risk of about 2 for the development of thrombosis, a dangerous blood clot, among women who took a new type of birth control pill as compared with women who took an older type of birth control pill. Media coverage of this finding led to widespread terror among women who had taken the new pill. Yet, only 1 in 7,000 of those who took the older pill had experienced a thrombosis. A relative risk of 2 meant that twice as many women would develop one—so, now 2 out of 7,000 were likely to experience a thrombosis. Gigerenzer concluded that "had the committee and the media reported the absolute risk increase [from 1 in 7,000 to 2 in 7,000], it would not have caused such panic" (p. 567). Relative risks and relative likelihoods can be used to scare the general public unnecessarily—which is one more reason that ethical researchers should be thoughtful and clear when reporting their findings.

CHECK YOUR LEARNING

Reviewing the Concepts

> The appropriate effect-size measure for the chi-square test for independence is Cramér's *V.*

> We can depict the effect size visually by calculating and graphing conditional proportions so that we can compare the rates of a certain outcome in each of two or more groups.

> Another way to consider the size of an effect is through relative risk, a ratio of conditional proportions for each of two groups.

Clarifying the Concepts **17-9** What is the effect-size measure for chi-square tests and how is it calculated?

Calculating the Statistics **17-10** In the selfie research we discussed at the beginning of this chapter, we talked about gender stereotypes in people's poses and behaviors (Döring et al., 2016). Out of 250 women's selfies, 29 showed a "kissing pout," better known as duckface. Out of 250 men's selfies, 6 did. Calculate the relative likelihood of taking a duckface selfie if you're a woman as opposed to a man.

Applying the Concepts **17-11** In Check Your Learning 17-8, you were asked to conduct a chi-square test on a Chicago Police Department study comparing two types of lineups for suspect identification: simultaneous lineups and sequential lineups (Mecklenburg et al., 2006).

a. Calculate the appropriate measure of effect size for this study.

b. Create a graph of the conditional proportions for these data.

Solutions to these Check Your Learning questions can be found in Appendix D.

c. Calculate the relative likelihood of a suspect being accurately identified in the simultaneous lineups versus the sequential lineups.

REVIEW OF CONCEPTS

Nonparametric Statistics

Nonparametric hypothesis tests are used when a study's design does not meet the assumptions of a parametric test. This often occurs when there is a nominal or ordinal dependent variable or a small sample in which the data suggest a skewed population distribution. Given the choice, we should use a parametric test because these tests tend to have more statistical power and because we can more frequently calculate confidence intervals and effect sizes for parametric hypothesis tests.

LaunchPad
macmillan learning

Visit LaunchPad to access the e-book and to test your knowledge with LearningCurve.

Chi-Square Tests

We use the *chi-square test for goodness of fit* when there is only one variable and it is nominal. We use the *chi-square test for independence* when there are two nominal variables; typically, for the purposes of articulating hypotheses, one variable is thought of as the independent variable and the other is thought of as the dependent variable. With both chi-square tests, we analyze whether the data that we observe match what we would expect according to the null hypothesis. Both tests use the same basic six steps of hypothesis testing that we learned previously. For statistically significant chi-square tests with more than four cells, we must conduct an additional analysis to know exactly which observed counts are different from the expected counts. We can determine this by calculating adjusted standardized residuals, the distances of the observed frequencies from their corresponding expected frequencies in terms of standard errors.

Beyond Hypothesis Testing

We usually calculate an effect size as well; the most commonly calculated effect size with chi square is *Cramér's* V, also called *Cramér's phi*. We can also create a graph that depicts the conditional proportions of an outcome for each group. Alternatively we can calculate *relative risk* (*relative likelihood* or *relative chance*) to more easily compare the rates of certain outcomes in each of two groups. Ethical researchers can report relative risks to help their audience better understand a finding, but they must be cautious and communicate the base rates as well.

SPSS

In SPSS, we can conduct both a chi-square test for goodness of fit and a chi-square test for independence. Using data from the soccer player example, we enter the data for the one variable: whether or not a soccer player was born in the first 3 months. We enter the data as a nominal variable. Remember, with nominal and ordinal variables we have to tell SPSS the names for each category (see Chapter 11 for a refresher on

how to enter nominal data in SPSS). In this example, we can use 1 to represent soccer players who were born in the first 3 months and 2 to represent soccer players who were born in the last 3 months.

To conduct a chi-square test for goodness of fit, select: Analyze → Nonparametric Tests → Legacy Dialogue → Chi-square.

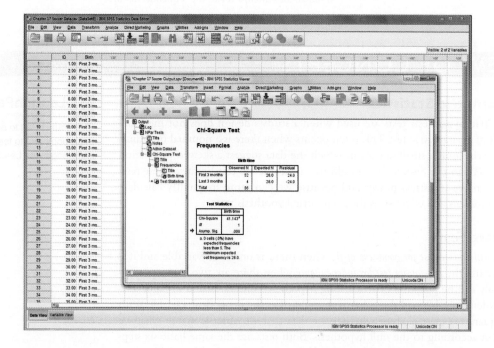

Select the variable of interest, in this example "birth," and move it into the Test Variable List. In this example, we hypothesize that soccer players have the sample patterns of birth months as those in the general population, meaning that we expect that all categories will be equal. If, however, we expect a different proportion (as in the How It Works 17.1 example), we would need to enter those proportions into the Expected Values. For now, we can keep the default selected, all categories equal. Click "OK" to run the analysis.

The output on the previous page displays two tables. The first table provides the observed values for each level in the variable, the expected values, and the residual. The second table, "Test Statistics," provides the chi-square value, the degrees of freedom, and the *p* value (next to "Asymp, Sig."). The chi-square value of 41.193 and the degrees of freedom of 1 match what we calculated earlier in the chapter. The *p* value here is less than 0.05; therefore, we reject the null hypothesis. (Any slight differences we see in this table versus what we calculated earlier are due to rounding decisions.)

We can also conduct a chi-square test for independence using SPSS. To demonstrate how, we will use data from the recycling study. Each participant gets a score on each variable: one for the cup condition (name spelled correctly, name spelled incorrectly, no name) and one for the participant's decision (recycling, trash). As you can see on the screenshot on this page, we gave the levels of each variable numbers—1, 2, and 3 for the three levels of the cup condition, and 1 and 2 for the two decision levels. Select: Analyze → Descriptive Statistics → Crosstabs. (Select a nominal variable for the row and a nominal variable for the column; we selected cup condition for the rows and decision for the columns, but it doesn't matter which we choose.) Click "Statistics" and select two boxes "Chi-Square" and "Phi & Cramér's *V*" (for effect sizes). Click "Continue," and then click "OK" to run the analysis.

Most of the output, along with a view of some of the data, can be seen in the screenshot on this page. In the top box of the output, we can see that the chi-square statistic (in the box titled "Chi-Square Tests" in the row labeled "Pearson Chi-Square") is 7.601, almost the same as the one we calculated by hand earlier. In the box titled "Symmetric Measures," we can see the Cramér's *V* statistic of .219, exactly the same as we calculated earlier. (Again, any slight differences we see in this table versus what we calculated earlier are due to rounding decisions.)

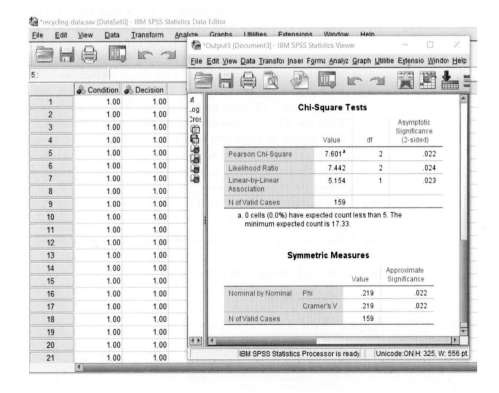

HOW IT WORKS

17.1 CONDUCTING A CHI-SQUARE TEST FOR GOODNESS OF FIT

Have you heard of the Bechdel Test? Allison Bechdel developed a simple rubric to determine if a movie (or other fictional work) was at least trying for gender equality. The test: You have to be able to answer "yes" to three questions: (1) Are there at least two women in the film? (2) Who talk to each other? (3) About something other than a man? It's surprisingly hard to find films that meet these criteria. Researchers examined the effect of the screenwriters' genders on films' gender equality (Friedman, Daniels, & Blinderman, 2016). Of high-earning films written entirely by men, 53% failed the Bechdel Test. What about similarly successful films with at least one female writer? In a sample of 61 top films that had at least one woman on the writing team, 23 failed the Bechdel Test and 38 passed. (For fun, check out the researchers' Bechdel Test simulator on poly-graph.co/bechdel. You can see the likelihood that a film will pass the Bechdel Test given a particular director, producer, and writer. For example, a film directed by Tina Fey, produced by Judd Apatow, and written by Shonda Rimes would only have an 11% chance of failing.) How can we use the Bechdel Test to conduct the six steps of hypothesis testing for a chi-square test for goodness of fit for the films with at least one female writer?

Step 1: Population 1: High-earning films with at least one woman on the writing team. Population 2: High-earning films written entirely by men.

    The comparison distribution is a chi-square distribution. The hypothesis test will be a chi-square test for goodness of fit because we have one nominal variable only. This study meets three of the four assumptions: (1) The one variable is nominal. (2) Every participant is in only one cell (either passing the Bechdel Test or not passing the test). (3) There are far more than five times as many participants as cells (there are 61 films included in the sample and only two cells). (4) We do not know how the 61 films (top films with at least one woman on the writing team) were selected and therefore do not know if they were randomly selected. This limits our ability to generalize beyond the films in this sample.

Step 2: Null hypothesis: Films with at least one female writer will be just as likely to pass the Bechdel Test as films written entirely by men. Research hypothesis: Films with at least one woman writer will pass the Bechdel Test at a different rate than films written entirely by men.

Step 3: The comparison distribution is a chi-square distribution that has 1 degree of freedom: $df_{\chi^2} = 2 - 1 = 1$.

Step 4: The critical chi-square value, based on an alpha level of 0.05 and 1 degree of freedom, is 3.841, as seen in the curve in Figure 17-1 earlier in this chapter.

Step 5: Observed (among films with at least 1 woman writer)

Pass	Fail
38	23

Expected (based on 53%—or 0.53—of films written entirely by men failing the test)

Pass	Fail
(0.47)(61) = 28.67	(0.53)(61) = 32.33

	Observed (O)	Expected (E)	$O - E$	$(O - E)^2$	$\dfrac{(O - E)^2}{E}$
Pass	38	28.67	9.33	87.049	3.036
Fail	23	32.33	−9.33	87.049	2.693

$$\chi^2 = \Sigma \left[\frac{(O - E)^2}{E} \right] = 3.036 + 2.693 = 5.729$$

Step 6: Reject the null hypothesis; it appears that films with at least one woman writer pass the Bechdel Test more often than do films written entirely by men.

The statistics, as reported in a journal article, would read:

$$\chi^2 (1, N = 61) = 5.73, p < 0.05$$

17.2 CONDUCTING A CHI-SQUARE TEST FOR INDEPENDENCE

Do people who move far from their hometown have a more exciting life? Since 1972, the General Social Survey (GSS) has asked approximately 40,000 adults in the United States numerous questions about their lives. During several years of the GSS, participants were asked, "In general, do you find life exciting, pretty routine, or dull?" (a variable called LIFE) and "When you were 16 years old, were you living in the same (city/town/country)?" (a variable called MOBILE16). How can we use these data to conduct the six steps of hypothesis testing for a chi-square test for independence?

In this case, there are two nominal variables. The independent variable is where a person lives relative to when he or she was 16 years old (same city, or same state but different city, or different state). The dependent variable is how the person finds life (exciting, routine, dull). Here are the data:

	Exciting	**Routine**	**Dull**
Same city	4890	6010	637
Same state/different city	3368	3488	337
Different state	4604	4139	434

Step 1: Population 1: People like those in this sample. Population 2: People from a population in which a person's characterization of life as exciting, routine, or dull does not depend on where that person is living relative to when he or she was 16 years old.

　　The comparison distribution is a chi-square distribution. The hypothesis test will be a chi-square test for independence because there are two nominal variables. This study meets all four assumptions: (1) The two variables are nominal. (2) Every participant is in only one cell. (3) There are more than five times as many participants as there are cells (there are 27,907 participants and 9 cells). (4) The GSS sample uses a form of random selection.

Step 2: Null hypothesis: The proportion of people who find life to be exciting, routine, or dull does not depend on where they live relative to where they lived when they were 16 years old. Research hypothesis: The proportion of people who find life exciting, routine, or dull differs depending on where they live relative to where they lived when they were 16 years old.

Step 3: The comparison distribution is a chi-square distribution with 4 degrees of freedom:

$$df_{\chi^2} = (k_{row} - 1)(k_{column} - 1) = (3 - 1)(3 - 1) = (2)(2) = 4$$

Step 4: The critical chi-square statistic, based on an alpha level of 0.05 and 4 degrees of freedom, is 9.488.

Step 5:

	Observed (Expected in parentheses)			
	Exciting	**Routine**	**Dull**	
Same city	4890 (5317.264)	6010 (5637.656)	637 (582.080)	11,537
Same state/different city	3368 (3315.167)	3488 (3514.922)	337 (362.911)	7193
Different state	4604 (4229.569)	4139 (4484.421)	434 (463.010)	9177
	12,862	13,637	1408	27,907

$$\frac{Total_{column}}{N}(Total_{row}) = \frac{12,862}{27,907}(11,537) = 5317.264$$

$$\frac{Total_{column}}{N}(Total_{row}) = \frac{12,862}{27,907}(7193) = 3315.167$$

$$\frac{Total_{column}}{N}(Total_{row}) = \frac{12,862}{27,907}(9177) = 4229.569$$

$$\frac{Total_{column}}{N}(Total_{row}) = \frac{13,637}{27,907}(11,537) = 5637.656$$

$$\frac{Total_{column}}{N}(Total_{row}) = \frac{13,637}{27,907}(7193) = 3514.922$$

$$\frac{Total_{column}}{N}(Total_{row}) = \frac{13,637}{27,907}(9177) = 4484.421$$

$$\frac{Total_{column}}{N}(Total_{row}) = \frac{1408}{27,907}(11,537) = 582.080$$

$$\frac{Total_{column}}{N}(Total_{row}) = \frac{1408}{27,907}(7193) = 362.911$$

$$\frac{Total_{column}}{N}(Total_{row}) = \frac{1408}{27,907}(9177) = 463.010$$

Category	$(O - E)^2$	$\dfrac{(O - E)^2}{E}$
Same city; exciting	182,554.526	34.332
Same city; routine	138,640.054	24.592
Same city; dull	3016.206	5.182
Same state/different city; exciting	2791.326	0.842
Same state/different city; routine	724.794	0.206
Same state/different city; dull	671.38	1.850
Different state; exciting	140,198.574	33.147
Different state; routine	119,315.667	26.607
Different state; dull	841.580	1.818

$$\chi^2 = \Sigma\left[\frac{(O - E)^2}{E}\right] = 128.576$$

Step 6: Reject the null hypothesis. The calculated chi-square statistic exceeds the critical value. How exciting a person finds life does appear to vary with where the person lives relative to where he or she lived when he or she was 16 years old.

We would present these statistics in a journal article as:

$$\chi^2(4, \ N = 27,907) = 128.58, \ p < 0.05.$$

17.3 CALCULATING CRAMÉR'S V

What is the effect size, Cramér's V, for the chi-square test for independence we conducted in How It Works 17.2?

$$V = \sqrt{\frac{\chi^2}{(N)(df_{row/column})}} = \sqrt{\frac{128.576}{(27,907)(2)}} = \sqrt{\frac{128.576}{55,814}} = 0.048$$

According to Cohen's conventions, this is a small effect size. With this piece of information, we'd present the statistics in a journal article as:

$$\chi^2(4, \ N = 27,907) = 128.58 < 0.05, \ \text{Cramér's } V = 0.05$$

EXERCISES

Clarifying the Concepts

17.1 Distinguish among nominal, ordinal, and scale data.

17.2 What are the three main situations in which we use a nonparametric test?

17.3 What is the difference between the chi-square test for goodness of fit and the chi-square test for independence?

17.4 What are the four assumptions for the chi-square tests?

17.5 List two ways in which statisticians use the word *independence* or *independent* with respect to concepts introduced earlier in this book. Then describe how *independence* is used by statisticians with respect to chi square.

17.6 What are the hypotheses when conducting the chi-square test for goodness of fit?

17.7 How are the degrees of freedom for the chi-square hypothesis tests different from those of most other hypothesis tests?

17.8 Why is there just one critical value for a chi-square test, even when the hypothesis is a two-tailed test?

17.9 What information is presented in a contingency table in the chi-square test for independence?

17.10 How are adjusted standardized residuals calculated?

17.11 How are adjusted standardized residuals used as a post hoc test for chi-square tests?

17.12 What measure of effect size is used with chi square?

17.13 Define the symbols in the following formula:

$$\chi^2 = \Sigma\left[\frac{(O-E)^2}{E}\right]$$

17.14 What is the formula $\frac{Total_{column}}{N}(Total_{row})$ used for?

17.15 What information does the measure of relative likelihood provide?

17.16 To calculate relative likelihood, what must we first calculate?

17.17 What is the difference between relative likelihood and relative risk?

17.18 Why might relative likelihood be easier to understand as an effect size than Cramér's V?

17.19 Which graph is most useful for displaying the results of a chi-square test for independence?

Calculating the statistics

17.20 For each of the following, (i) identify the incorrect symbol, (ii) state what the correct symbol should be, and (iii) explain why the initial symbol was incorrect.
  a. For the chi-square test for goodness of fit:
     $df_{\chi^2} = N - 1$
  b. For the chi-square test for independence:
     $df_{\chi^2} = (k_{row} - 1) + (k_{column} - 1)$
  c. $\chi^2 = \Sigma\left[\frac{(M-E)^2}{E}\right]$
  d. Cramér's $V = \sqrt{\frac{\chi^2}{(N)(k_{row/column})}}$
  e. Expected frequency for each cell $= \frac{k_{column}}{(N)(k_{row})}$

17.21 For each of the following, identify the independent variable(s), the dependent variable(s), and the level of measurement (nominal, ordinal, scale).

a. The number of loads of laundry washed per month was tracked for first-year students and seniors living in university dorms.

b. A researcher interested in people's need to maintain their social image collected data on the number of kilometers on someone's car and his or her rank for "need for approval" out of the 183 people studied.

c. A professor of social science was interested in whether involvement in campus life is significantly impacted by whether a student lives on or off campus. Thirty-seven students living on campus and 37 students living off campus were asked whether they were an active member of a club.

17.22 Use this calculation table for the chi-square test for goodness of fit to complete this exercise.

Category	Observed (O)	Expected (E)	O − E	(O − E)²	$\frac{(O-E)^2}{E}$
1	48	60			
2	46	30			
3	6	10			

a. Calculate degrees of freedom for this chi-square test for goodness of fit.

b. Perform all of the calculations to complete this table.

c. Compute the chi-square statistic.

17.23 Use this calculation table for the chi-square test for goodness of fit to complete this exercise.

Category	Observed (O)	Expected (E)	O − E	(O − E)²	$\frac{(O-E)^2}{E}$
1	750	625			
2	650	625			
3	600	625			
4	500	625			

a. Calculate degrees of freedom for this chi-square test for goodness of fit.

b. Perform all of the calculations to complete this table.

c. Compute the chi-square statistic.

17.24 Following are some data to use in a chi-square test for independence.

	Observed		
	Accidents	No Accidents	
Rain	19	26	45
No rain	20	71	91
	39	97	136

a. Calculate the degrees of freedom for this test.

b. Complete this table of expected frequencies.

	Expected	
	Accidents	No Accidents
Rain		
No rain		

c. Calculate the test statistic.

d. Calculate the appropriate measure of effect size.

e. Calculate the relative likelihood of accidents, given that it is raining.

17.25 The following data are from a study of lung cancer patients in Turkey (Yilmaz et al., 2000). Use these data to calculate the relative likelihood of the patient being a smoker, given that a person is female rather than male.

	Nonsmoker	Smoker
Female	186	13
Male	182	723

17.26 The following table (output from SPSS) represents the observed frequencies for the data presented in Exercise 17.24 and the adjusted standardized residuals for each of the cells. Using this information and the criterion of 2, indicate for which of these cells there is a significant difference between the observed and the expected frequencies.

		Observed		
		Accident	No Accident	
Rain	Observed	19	26	45
	Adjusted Residual	2.5	−2.5	
No rain	Observed	20	71	91
	Adjusted Residual	−2.5	2.5	
		39	97	136

17.27 The following table represents the observed frequencies for hypothetical data on housing status and having a car. The table also includes the adjusted standardized residuals for each of the cells. Using this information and the criterion of 2, indicate for which of these cells there is a significant difference between the observed and the expected frequencies.

		Observed		
		No car	Car	
On campus	Observed	33	11	44
	Adjusted residual	4.7	−4.7	
Off campus	Observed	8	28	36
	Adjusted residual	−4.7	4.7	
		41	39	80

Applying the Concepts

17.28 **A nonparametric test and gender differences in obeying bicycling laws:** Students at Hunter College studied bicycle safety in New York City (Tuckel & Milczarski, 2014). They reported data on cyclists who were riding their own bikes and were not cycling as part of their job (they were not, for example, riding as delivery workers). They reported that 28.4% of male cyclists stopped completely at a red light, whereas 38.3% of female cyclists did so. Of the sample, 30.9% of male cyclists and 35.4% of female cyclists paused but then rolled through the red light. And 40.7% of male cyclists and 26.3% of female cyclists just ran the light. What hypothesis test would the researchers conduct? Explain your answer.

17.29 **Gender, salary negotiation, and chi square:** Researchers investigated whether language in job postings affected the likelihood that women and men would negotiate regarding salary (Leibbrandt & List, 2012). Some job postings clearly indicated that the salary was negotiable, and others contained no such statement. The postings were otherwise identical. The researchers examined the behavior of almost 2500 applicants for one of the jobs in these advertisements. The graph shows the proportions of women and men who negotiated in response to either type of listing.

a. What are the variables in this study, what are their levels, and what types of variables are they?

b. Explain why the researchers would have been able to use chi square in this study. Which type of chi-square test would have been appropriate?

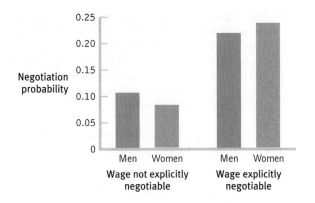

c. Based on the graph, explain in your own words what the researchers found.

17.30 Gender, the Oscars, and nonparametric tests: In 2010, Sandra Bullock won an Academy Award for best actress. Shortly thereafter, she discovered that her husband was cheating on her. Headlines erupted about a supposed Oscar curse that befalls women, and many in the media wondered whether ambitious women—whether actors or corporate leaders—are more likely than ambitious men to run the risk of ruining their family lives. Reporters breathlessly listed female actors who were divorced within a couple of years of winning an Oscar—Julia Roberts, Helen Hunt, Kate Winslet, Halle Berry, and Reese Witherspoon among them.

a. A good researcher always asks, "Compared to what?" In this case, what would be an appropriate comparison group to use to determine whether there really is a gender difference in likelihood of relationship breakups among Oscar winners? Explain your answer.

b. Kate Harding (2010) reported that many men—including Russell Crowe, William Hurt, Dustin Hoffman, Robert Duvall, and Clark Gable—experienced the same outcome. Indeed, Harding counted 15 best actor winners, compared with just 8 best actress winners, who divorced not long after winning an Oscar. If she wanted to conduct statistical analyses, what test would Harding use? Explain your answer.

c. Explain how an illusory correlation, bolstered by a confirmation bias, might have led to the headlines despite evidence to the contrary.

17.31 Parametric or nonparametric test? For each of the following research questions, state whether a parametric or nonparametric hypothesis test is more appropriate. Explain your answers.

a. Are women more or less likely than men to be economics majors?

b. At a small company with 15 staff and one top boss, do those with a university education tend to make a different amount of money than those without one?

c. At your high school, did athletes or nonathletes tend to have higher grade-point averages?

d. At your high school, did athletes or nonathletes tend to have higher class ranks?

e. Compare car accidents in which the occupants were wearing seat belts with accidents in which the occupants were not wearing seat belts. Do seat belts seem to make a difference in the numbers of accidents that lead to no injuries, nonfatal injuries, and fatal injuries?

f. Compare car accidents in which the occupants were wearing seat belts with accidents in which the occupants were not wearing seat belts. Were those wearing seat belts driving at slower speeds, on average, than those not wearing seat belts?

17.32 Types of variables and student evaluations of professors: Weinberg, Fleisher, and Hashimoto (2007) studied almost 50,000 students' evaluations of their professors in nearly 400 economics courses at The Ohio State University over a 10-year period. For each of their findings, outlined here state (i) the independent variable or variables, and, where appropriate, their levels; (ii) the dependent variable(s); and (iii) which category of research design is being used:

    I—Scale independent variable(s) and scale dependent variable

    II—Nominal independent variable(s) and scale dependent variable

    III—Only nominal variables

Explain your answer to part (iii).

a. The researchers found that students' ratings of their professors were predictive of grades in the class for which the professor was evaluated.

b. The researchers also found that students' ratings of their professors were not predictive of grades for other, related future classes. (The researchers stated that these first two findings suggest that student ratings of professors are tied to their current grades but not to learning—which would affect future grades.)

c. The researchers found that male professors received statistically significantly higher student ratings, on average, than did female professors.

d. The researchers reported, however, that average levels of students' learning (as assessed by grades in related future classes) were not statistically significantly different between those who had male professors and those who had female professors.

e. The researchers might have been interested in whether there were proportionally more female professors teaching upper-level than lower-level courses and proportionally more male professors teaching lower-level than upper-level courses (perhaps a reason for the lower average ratings of female professors).

f. The researchers found no statistically significant differences in average student evaluations among non-tenure-track lecturers, graduate student teaching associates, and tenure-track faculty members.

17.33 Sexual orientation, activism, and types of variables: Researcher Eric Swank (2018) analyzed survey data to determine whether people who are gay or lesbian are more likely than those who are heterosexual to become activists for various causes. Spoiler alert: Gays and lesbians are more likely than heterosexual people to be activists for a range of causes, including movements for peace and for the environment. For each of the findings outlined here, state (i) the independent variable or variables, and, where appropriate, their levels; (ii) the dependent variable(s); and (iii) which category of research design is being used:

  I—Scale independent variable(s) and scale dependent variable

  II—Nominal independent variable(s) and scale dependent variable

  III—Only nominal variables

Explain your answer to part (iii).

a. Swank reported that "gays and lesbians were about twenty times more likely to join LGB justice campaigns than heterosexuals" (p. 176).

b. Swank cited previous research that found "sexual minorities seem to know more gays and lesbians than heterosexuals [do]" (p. 180).

c. Survey respondents were asked to "rate their emotional warmth or coldness towards gays and lesbians . . . with scores ranging from 0 to 100" (p. 180). What if you wondered whether this variable were related to the number of gays/lesbians whom each survey respondent knows?

17.34 Researching selfies and types of variables: Here are three ways to assess data related to selfies: (1) numbers of selfies taken in a month, (2) whether you took

any selfies this past month, and (3) where you rank in terms of the number of selfies you took in the past month. For example, Abdul might have taken 11 selfies last month, which would mean he had taken selfies. He also may have been the 23rd most frequent selfie-taker over the last month.

a. Which of these variables could be considered a nominal variable? Explain.

b. Which of these variables is most clearly an ordinal variable? Explain.

c. Which of these variables is a scale variable? Explain.

d. Which of these variables gives us the most information about Abdul's selfie-taking?

e. If we were to use one of these variables in an analysis, which variable (as the dependent variable) would lead to the lowest chance of a Type II error? Explain why.

17.35 Immigration, crime, and research design: "Do Immigrants Make Us Safer?" asked the title of a *New York Times Magazine* article (Press, 2006). The article reported findings from several U.S.-based studies, including several conducted by Harvard sociologist Robert Sampson in Chicago. For each of the following findings, draw the table of cells that would comprise the research design. Include the labels for each row and column.

a. Mexican immigrants were more likely to be married (versus single) than either blacks or whites.

b. People living in immigrant neighborhoods were 15% less likely than were people living in non-immigrant neighborhoods to commit crimes. This finding was true among both those living in households headed by a married couple and those living in households not headed by a married couple.

c. The crime rate was higher among second-generation than among first-generation immigrants; moreover, the crime rate was higher among third-generation than among second-generation immigrants.

17.36 Sex selection and hypothesis testing: Across all of India, there are only 933 girls for every 1000 boys (Lloyd, 2006), evidence of a bias that leads many parents to illegally select for boys or to kill their infant girls. (Note that this translates into a proportion of girls of 0.483.) In Punjab, a region of India in which residents tend to be more educated than in other regions, there are only 798 girls for every 1000 boys. Assume that you are a researcher interested in whether sex selection is more or less prevalent in educated regions of India, and that 1798 children from Punjab constitute the entire sample. (*Hint:* You will use the proportions from the national database for comparison.)

a. How many variables are there in this study? What are the levels of any variable you identified?

b. Which hypothesis test would be used to analyze these data? Justify your answer.

c. Conduct the six steps of hypothesis testing for this example. (*Note:* Be sure to use the correct proportions for the expected values, not the actual numbers for the population.)

d. Report the statistics as you would in a journal article.

17.37 Gender, op-ed writers, and hypothesis testing: Richards (2006) reported data from a study by *The American Prospect* on the genders of op-ed writers who addressed the topic of abortion in *The New York Times.* Over a 2-year period, *The American Prospect* counted 124 articles that discussed abortion (from a wide range of political and ideological perspectives). Of these, just 21 were written by women.

a. How many variables are there in this study? What are the levels of any variable you identified?

b. Which hypothesis test would be used to analyze these data? Justify your answer.

c. Conduct the six steps of hypothesis testing for this example.

d. Report the statistics as you would in a journal article.

17.38 Romantic music, behavior, chi square, and effect size: Guéguen, Jacob, and Lamy (2010) investigated whether exposure to romantic music affects dating behavior. The participants, young, single, heterosexual French women, waited for the experiment to start in a room in which songs with either romantic lyrics or neutral lyrics were playing. After a few minutes, each woman who participated completed a marketing survey administered by a young male confederate. During a break, the confederate asked the participant for her phone number. Of the women who listened to romantic music, 52.2% (23 out of 44) gave him her phone number, whereas 27.9% (12 out of 43) of the women who listened to neutral music did so. The researchers conducted a chi-square test for independence, and found the following results: $(\chi^2(1, N = 83) = 5.37, p < .02)$.

a. Calculate Cramér's V. What size effect is this?

b. Calculate the relative likelihood of providing her phone number for women listening to romantic music versus neutral music. Explain what we learn from this relative likelihood.

17.39 The General Social Survey, an exciting life, and relative risk: In How It Works 17.2, we walked through a chi-square test for independence using two items from the General Social Survey (GSS)—LIFE and MOBILE16. Use these data to answer the following questions.

a. Construct a table that shows only the appropriate conditional proportions for this example. For example, the percentage of people who find life exciting, given that they live in the same city, is 42.4. The proportion, therefore, is 0.424.

b. Construct a graph that displays these conditional proportions.

c. Calculate the relative risk (or relative likelihood) of finding life exciting if one lives in a different state compared to if one lives in the same city as one did at 16.

17.40 Gender, ESPN, and chi square: Many of the numbers we see in the news could be analyzed with chi square. The feminist blog *Culturally Disoriented* examined the photos in the 2012 "body issue" of *ESPN The Magazine*—the publication's annual spread of photographs of nude athletes. The blogger reported: "Female athlete after female athlete was photographed not as a talented, powerful sportswoman, but as . . . eye candy" (culturallydisoriented.wordpress.com/2012/07/12/the-bodies-we-want-female-athletes-in-espn-magazines-body-issue). The blogger reported that there were 19 photos of male athletes and 17 of female athletes. Of these, 15 of the men were in active poses and 9 of the women were in active poses. Active poses were typically those in which they were engaged in their sport, whereas the passive photos looked more like a modeling shoot—"where they're just looking hot for the camera," in the words of *Culturally Disoriented.*

a. Why is a chi-square statistical analysis a good choice for these data? Which kind of chi-square test should you use? Explain your answer.

b. Conduct the six steps of hypothesis testing for this example.

c. Calculate an effect size. Explain why there might be a fairly substantial effect size even though we were not able to reject the null hypothesis.

d. Report the statistics as you would in a journal article.

e. Construct a table that shows only the appropriate conditional proportions for this example—that is, the proportion of people in active poses given that they are men or women.

f. Construct a graph that displays these conditional proportions.

g. Calculate the relative likelihood of being photographed in an active pose if you are a male athlete compared to if you are a female athlete.

17.41 Premarital doubts, divorce, and chi square: In an article titled "Do Cold Feet Warn of Trouble Ahead?," researchers studied 464 married heterosexual spouses to determine whether doubts before marriage were predictive of marital troubles, and divorce, later on (Lavner, Karney, & Bradbury, 2012). The following is an excerpt from the results section of their paper: "For husbands, 9% of those who reported not having premarital doubts divorced by four years ($n = 10$ of 117) compared with 14% of those who did report premarital doubts ($n = 15$ of 106); these groups did not differ significantly, $\chi^2(1, n = 223) = 1.76, p > .10$. Among wives, 8% of those who reported not having premarital doubts divorced by four years ($n = 11$ of 141) compared with 19% of those who did report premarital doubts ($n = 16$ of 84). Chi-square analyses indicated that these rates differed significantly, $\chi^2(1, n = 225) = 6.31, p < .05$."

a. What are the variables in this study, and what are their levels?

b. Explain why the researchers were able to use chi-square tests. Which kind of chi-square tests did they use?

c. What changes would the APA want to see in the reporting of these results?

d. Explain in your own words what the researchers found.

17.42 Police lineups, SPSS, and adjusted standardized residual: In Check Your Learning 17-8, we introduced the example of the Chicago Police Department's study of lineups. The printout from SPSS software at the bottom of this page depicts the data for the six cells.

a. For simultaneous lineups, what is the observed frequency for the identification of suspects?

b. For sequential lineups, what is the expected frequency for the identification of a person other than the suspect?

c. For simultaneous lineups, what is the adjusted standardized residual for cases in which there was no identification? What does this number indicate?

d. If you were to use an adjusted standardized residual criterion of 2 (regardless of the sign), for which cells would you conclude that the difference between observed frequency and expected frequency is greater than you would expect if the two variables were independent?

e. Repeat part (d) for an adjusted standardized residual criterion of 3 (regardless of the sign).

17.43 Reporter Aaron Carroll (2018) reported described a new study that warned of the risks of drinking, even a little. Carroll wrote, "The news warns that even one drink per day carries a risk. But how great is that risk? For each set of 100,000 people who have one drink a day per year, 918 can expect to experience one of 23 alcohol-related problems in any year. Of those who drink nothing, 914 can expect to experience a problem." That means that, out of 100,000 people, only four additional people will be harmed by consuming one drink a day, as opposed to none. (Carroll adds the caveat that, of course, no one is suggesting that drinking is healthy, and emphasizes that heavy drinking has been definitively shown to be related to health problems.)

a. Why is it important to understand the actual risk, as opposed to relative risk, in cases like this?

b. Why might a graph be helpful in this case?

c. Why would it be helpful to calculate Cramér's V in a case like this?

Identification			Type of Lineup		Total
---	---	---	Simultaneous	Sequential	
Identification	Suspect	Count	191	102	293
		Expected Count	170.6	122.4	293.0
		Adjusted Residual	3.5	-3.5	
	Another Person	Count	8	20	28
		Expected Count	16.3	11.7	28.0
		Adjusted Residual	-3.3	3.3	
	No Identification	Count	120	107	227
		Expected Count	132.1	94.9	227.0
		Adjusted Residual	-2.1	2.1	
Total		Count	319	229	548

d. Carroll also reported that data like these "can be very confounded, meaning that unmeasured factors might be the actual cause of the harm. Perhaps people who drink also smoke tobacco. Perhaps people who drink are also poorer." Explain what he means by confounded—that is, that there might be a confound. From a research design perspective, why might these other variables be implicated in the increase in health problems?

17.44 Utah was the first U.S. state to implement a particularly strict drunk-driving law. As reporter Christopher Ingraham (2017) wrote, "At a [blood alcohol content (BAC)] of .08, a driver's odds of getting into a crash are about four times greater than a sober driver's. At .05, however, the crash risk is halved relative to the risk at .08—although it's worth pointing out that even at .05, your odds of a crash are still double what they'd be if you were completely sober." (Based on these data, some countries, such as Hungary, allow no alcohol for drivers—absolutely none.)

a. What is the relative risk of crashing with a BAC of .08 as compared to a BAC of zero—that is, if you were entirely sober?

b. What is the relative risk of crashing with a BAC of .05 as compared to a BAC of zero—that is, if you were entirely sober?

c. What is the relative risk of crashing with a BAC of .08 as compared to a BAC of .05?

Putting It All Together

17.45 Gender bias, poor growth, and hypothesis testing: Grimberg, Kutikov, and Cucchiara (2005) wondered whether gender biases were evident in referrals of children for poor growth. They believed that boys were more likely to be referred even when there was no problem—which is bad for boys because families of short boys might falsely view their height as a medical problem. They also believed that girls were less likely to be referred even when there was a problem—which is bad for girls because real problems might not be diagnosed and treated. They studied all new patients at the Children's Hospital of Philadelphia

Diagnostic and Research Growth Center who were referred for potential problems related to short stature. Of the 182 boys who were referred, 27 had an underlying medical problem, 86 did not but were below norms for their age, and 69 were of normal height according to growth charts. Of the 96 girls who were referred, 39 had an underlying medical problem, 38 did not but were below norms for their age, and 19 were of normal height according to growth charts.

a. How many variables are there in this study? What are the levels of any variable you identified?

b. Which hypothesis test would be used to analyze these data? Justify your answer.

c. Conduct the six steps of hypothesis testing for this example.

d. Calculate the appropriate measure of effect size. According to Cohen's conventions, what size effect is this?

e. Report the statistics as you would in a journal article.

f. Draw a table that includes the conditional proportions for boys and for girls.

g. Create a graph with bars showing the proportions for all six conditions.

h. Among only children who are below height norms, calculate the relative risk of having an underlying medical condition if one is a boy as opposed to a girl. Show your calculations.

i. Explain what we learn from this relative risk.

j. Now calculate the relative risk of having an underlying medical condition if one is a girl. Show your calculations.

k. Explain what we learn from this relative risk.

Gender * Problem Crosstabulation

			Problem			
			Underlying medical condition	Below norms	Normal height	Total
Gender	Boy	Count	27	86	69	182
		Expected Count	43.2	81.2	57.6	182.0
		Adjusted Residual	-4.8	1.2	3.1	
	Girl	Count	39	38	19	96
		Expected Count	22.8	42.8	30.4	96.0
		Adjusted Residual	4.8	-1.2	-3.1	
Total		Count	66	124	88	278
		Expected Count	66.0	124.0	88.0	278.0

l. Explain how the calculations in parts (h) and (j) provide us with the same information in two different ways.

m. The printout from SPSS software at the bottom of the previous page depicts the data for the six cells. For each cell, there is an observed frequency (count), expected frequency (expected count), and adjusted standardized residual (adjusted residual). For boys, what are the observed and expected frequencies for having an underlying medical condition?

n. For boys, what is the adjusted standardized residual for those with an underlying medical condition? What does this number indicate? If you used an adjusted standardized residual criterion of 2 (regardless of the sign), for which cells would you conclude that the difference between observed frequency and expected frequency is greater than you would expect if the two variables were independent? What if you used an adjusted standardized residual criterion of 3 (regardless of the sign)? Are the results different from those using a criterion of 2? If yes, explain how.

17.46 **The prisoner's dilemma, cross-cultural research, and hypothesis testing:** In a classic prisoner's dilemma game with money for prizes, players who cooperate with each other both earn good prizes. If, however, your opposing player cooperates but you do not (the term used is *defect*), you receive an even bigger payout and your opponent receives nothing. If you cooperate but your opposing player defects, he or she receives that bigger payout and you receive nothing. If you both defect, you each get a small prize. Because of this, most players of such games choose to defect, knowing that if they cooperate but their partners don't, they won't win anything. The strategies of U.S. and Chinese students were compared. The researchers hypothesized that those from the market economy (United States) would cooperate less (i.e., would defect

more often) than would those from the nonmarket economy (China). Here are the observed values.

	Defect	Cooperate
China	31	36
United States	41	14

a. How many variables are there in this study? What are the levels of any variables you identified?

b. Which hypothesis test would be used to analyze these data? Justify your answer.

c. Conduct the six steps of hypothesis testing for this example, using the above data.

d. Calculate the appropriate measure of effect size. According to Cohen's conventions, what size effect is this?

e. Report the statistics as you would in a journal article.

f. Draw a table that includes the conditional proportions for participants from China and from the United States.

g. Create a graph with bars showing the proportions for all four conditions.

h. Create a graph with two bars showing just the proportions for the defections for each country.

i. Calculate the relative risk (or relative likelihood) of defecting, given that one is from China versus the United States. Show your calculations.

j. Explain what we learn from this relative risk.

k. Now calculate the relative risk of defecting, given that one is from the United States versus China. Show your calculations.

l. Explain what we learn from this relative risk.

m. Explain how the calculations in parts (i) and (k) provide us with the same information in two different ways.

 **LaunchPad**
macmillan learning

Visit LaunchPad to access the e-book and to test your knowledge with LearningCurve.

TERMS

chi-square test for goodness of fit (p. 541)
chi-square test for independence (p. 541)

adjusted standardized residual (p. 553)
Cramér's *V* (p. 556)

relative risk (p. 559)
base rate (p. 560)

FORMULAS

$df_{\chi^2} = k - 1$ (degrees of freedom for chi-square test for goodness of fit)   (p. 543)

$\chi^2 = \Sigma\left[\dfrac{(O-E)^2}{E}\right]$ (p. 546)

$df_{\chi^2} = (k_{row} - 1)(k_{column} - 1)$ (degrees of freedom for chi-square test for independence)   (p. 549)

Expected frequency for each cell $= \dfrac{Total_{column}}{N}(Total_{row})$,

where we use the overall number of participants, N, along with the totals for the rows and columns for each particular cell   (p. 551)

Cramér's $V = \sqrt{\dfrac{\chi^2}{(N)df_{row/column}}}$

(p. 556)

SYMBOLS

χ^2 (p. 539)

k (p. 543)

Cramér's V (p. 556)

Cramér's ϕ (p. 556)

Choosing and Reporting Statistics

Choosing the Right Statistical Test

Category 1: Two Scale Variables

Category 2: Nominal Independent Variable(s) and a Scale Dependent Variable

Category 3: Only Nominal Variables

Reporting Statistics

Overview of Reporting Statistics

Justifying the Study

Reporting the Traditional *and* the New Statistics

Data Ethics: Open Data Practices

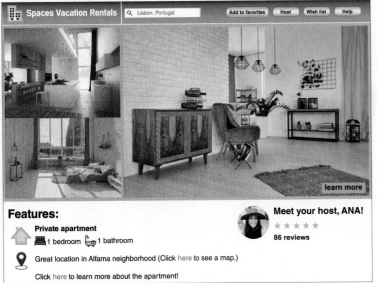

What Do You Look for in a Vacation Rental? When you look at listings on Airbnb, VRBO, or HomeAway, which factors do you consider? You're probably aware of the importance of location, great photos, a clever description, and amenities such as parking and pools, but are you aware of the importance of the host's photo? Research shows that factors related to hosts and their photos, such as attractiveness, are enticing to guests; attractive hosts can even charge more (Ert, Fleischer, & Magen, 2016; Jaeger, Sleegers, Evans, Stel, & van Beest, 2018).

From Australia to Zimbabwe, vacation rentals are booming because of what some call "the Airbnb effect," named after the best known of the short-term rental online platforms. These disruptive rental platforms have had mixed effects. They reduce lodging costs for travelers but also decrease hotel profits and can lead to rent hikes for people living in the local area (Gerdeman, 2018; van der Zee, 2016). In a boon for behavioral scientists, all of this activity plays out online, offering ready-made opportunities to explore data from around the world. Researchers have been using these data to try to understand what drives consumer spending and the role that stereotypes—such as those about attractive people—may play in travelers' choices.

Of course, behavioral scientists have lots of decisions to make before they begin to conduct research. Listings for vacation rentals are complex and include a great deal of information. A range of variables can potentially be selected, many of which could be either independent variables (predictor variables, in the case of regression), predicting how well a listing will do, or dependent variables (outcome variables, in the case of regression), indicating how well a listing did. Price, for example, can predict whether people will book a place but can also suggest that a rental site has high demand. Some of these variables are nominal, such as top host classifications and badges (e.g., "Superhost" status) or the availability of parking. Other variables are scale, such as cost per night, guests' ratings, and attractiveness ratings of host photos.

In the first section of this chapter, we'll explore how researchers have analyzed data from vacation rental sites using multiple combinations of nominal and scale variables, and then we'll use these examples to demonstrate how to choose the right statistical test. After that, we'll explore a different study—one on whether giving advice or receiving advice motivates us more—as we demonstrate how to most clearly (and most ethically) report results. By learning how to report statistical findings, you'll also become more skilled in reading the findings in journal articles, particularly important if you continue to study the behavioral sciences.

Choosing the Right Statistical Test

Let's begin at the beginning. Good researchers choose the appropriate statistical test before they even start their study. This step is important both to ensure that the researchers collect useful data and to reduce the likelihood that researchers will engage in unethical behavior, such as changing their analysis plan after they see the data—the sketchy maneuver known as *p*-hacking. To choose the appropriate statistical test, researchers first identify any independent and dependent variables, then figure out exactly how each will be operationalized. Attractiveness of hosts, for example, could be operationalized as a nominal variable in a "hot or not" style, or it could be utilized as a scale variable by rating the photos. In either case, the score could be a combination of the verdicts of multiple raters—the mode in the case of the nominal variable versus the mean or the median in the case of the scale variable. Ideally, before starting data collection, the researcher would document these details in a preregistration report, along with the planned statistical analyses.

Let's look at how some researchers approached their chosen variables and statistical analyses for vacation rentals. As we do this, we'll use Figure 18-1 as a decision tree.

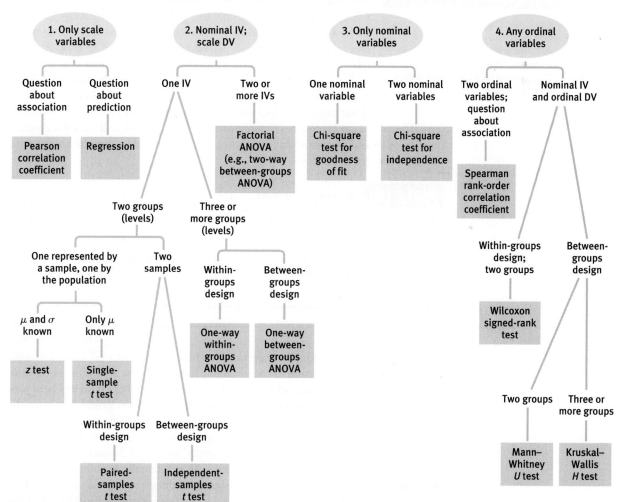

Four Categories of Hypothesis Tests (IV = independent variable; DV = dependent variable)

FIGURE 18-1

Choosing the Appropriate Hypothesis Test

By asking the right questions about our variables and research design, we can choose the appropriate hypothesis test for our research.

Start at the top and choose one of four categories based on the types of variables: (1) All variables are scale; (2) there is a nominal independent variable or variables and a scale dependent variable; (3) all variables are nominal; or (4) any variable is ordinal. (*Note:* We didn't address the fourth category, studies that have at least one ordinal variable, in this text, so we won't discuss it further. We included that category in the decision tree because if you go on to conduct or read research beyond this course, you're likely to encounter some of these tests.) Let's start by looking at a situation that involves two scale variables. (For additional practice using this decision tree to choose the right statistical test, go to the Which Test Is Best? interactive activity in LaunchPad.)

Category 1: Two Scale Variables

For a research design with only two scale variables, we have two choices for how to analyze the data. The only question we have to answer is this: Does the research question pertain to the strength of an association (or relation) between two variables, or does it pertain to predicting the value of one variable from another variable? If the research question is about association, then we choose the Pearson correlation coefficient. If it is about prediction, then we choose regression. The choices for this category (labeled as 1 on Figure 18-1) are presented in Table 18-1. Recall from the chapters on correlation and regression that the relations between variables must be linear to use the tests presented in this text.

TABLE 18-1 Category 1 Statistics

When both the independent variable and the dependent variable are scale, we calculate either a Pearson correlation coefficient or a regression equation.

Research Question: Association (Relation)	Research Question: Prediction
Pearson correlation coefficient	Regression equation

EXAMPLE 18.1

Let's look at an example for two scale variables. Israeli researcher Eyal Ert and his colleagues (2016) asked participants to choose among lodging options in Stockholm, Sweden, including several Airbnb apartments. For each apartment, the host's photo had been previously scored by multiple raters as to how trustworthy the person looked. The researchers found that the apartments of the trustworthy-looking Airbnb host were more likely to be chosen than the other apartments. They wondered, though, if that choice occurred because participants had relied on previous guests' reviews or because the hosts who looked trustworthy really *were* more trustworthy. To examine this hypothesis, Ert and his colleagues examined whether perception of trustworthiness and actual trustworthiness were related. They measured perceived trustworthiness on a scale of 1–10 based on the host's photo and actual trustworthiness based on the host's reputation, indicated by the average number of stars—from 1 to 5—awarded by previous guests. Which test did they use to determine whether these two variables are related? Given that this study involves two scale variables, we know that the researchers should choose a test from category 1.

The next decision deals with the research question. Are the researchers asking about an association between two variables, perceived trustworthiness and actual trustworthiness (host's reputation), or about whether one variable predicts the other? In this case, the researchers are asking if there is a relation, or association, between the two variables, so they would choose the Pearson correlation coefficient.

And that's exactly what they did. The researchers reported a Pearson correlation coefficient of −0.03. This finding was not statistically significant, and it's not even close to a small effect, according to Cohen's (1988) conventions. In this case, the researchers cannot conclude that there is a relation between these two variables. This outcome suggests that the perception of a host's trustworthiness based on a photo drives consumer choices, regardless of the host's actual reputation as determined by previous reviews. Because the researchers were careful not to accept the null hypothesis, however, they urged caution in concluding that there is no relation. ●

Category 2: Nominal Independent Variable(s) and a Scale Dependent Variable

If the research design includes one or more nominal independent variables and a scale dependent variable, then the researcher has several choices to make.

EXAMPLE 18.2

Let's walk through those choices using a research example. A team of researchers from Norway, Iceland, and the United Kingdom investigated whether the facial expressions of Airbnb hosts in their photos would influence people's ratings of how likely they were to rent a particular apartment (Fagerstrøm, Pawar, Sigurdsson, Foxall, & Yani-de-Soriano, 2017). They paired each listing with one of several facial expressions, including negative (i.e., angry) and positive (i.e., joyful). Next, they asked 139 Norwegian undergraduate students to rate 20 Airbnb apartments in New York City in terms of how likely they would be to rent them for a hypothetical winter vacation. A host's negative facial expression tended to decrease participants' likelihood that they would rent, whereas a host's positive facial expression tended to increase participants' likelihood that they would rent. For all analyses, researchers asked participants to rate the likelihood that they would rent on a scale from 0, "Not at all likely to rent," to 7, "Certainly would like to rent" (p. 126). The researchers then wondered whether these outcomes varied by the gender of the participant: For example, did women and men who viewed a negative facial expression give different ratings with respect to the likelihood that they would rent? What test would they use to answer this question?

We know that this is a category 2 test because there is one nominal independent variable, gender, and one scale dependent variable, likelihood rating on a scale of 0 to 7. The next question pertains to the number of independent variables. If there is just *one independent variable*, then we must determine how many levels it has. There are three possibilities:

1. If there are *two levels, but just one sample*—that is, one level is represented by the sample and one level by the population—then we use either a *z* test or a single-sample *t* test. We will rarely know enough about a population

that we need to collect data from only a single sample, so these statistical tests aren't conducted very often. If this is the case, however, and we know both the population mean and the population standard deviation, then we can use a *z* test. If this is the case and we know only the population mean (but not the population standard deviation), then we use the single sample *t* test.

2. If there are *two levels, each represented by a sample*—either a single sample in which everyone participates in both levels or two different samples, one for each level—then we use either a paired-samples *t* test (if all participants are in both levels of the independent variable) or an independent-samples *t* test (if participants are in only one level of the independent variable).

3. If there are *three or more levels*, then we use a form of a one-way ANOVA. We examine the research design to determine whether it is a between-groups ANOVA (participants are in just one level of the independent variable) or a within-groups ANOVA (participants are in all levels of the independent variable).

If there are *at least two independent variables*, we must use a form of factorial ANOVA. Recall that we name ANOVAs according to the number of independent variables (one-way, two-way, three-way) and the research design (between-groups, within-groups). Table 18-2 summarizes the decisions about data that fall into category 2 and have one independent variable. For studies with two or more independent variables, use a factorial ANOVA. Table 18-3 provides guidelines to help you determine the specific type of factorial ANOVA needed.

> **MASTERING THE CONCEPT**
>
> 18-2: When a research design has at least one nominal independent variable and a scale dependent variable, we use some kind of *t* test or some kind of ANOVA.

TABLE 18-2   Category 2 Statistics

When there are one or more nominal independent variables and a scale dependent variable, examine the data to see which test is appropriate to use. Begin by determining the number of independent variables. If there is just one independent variable, use the accompanying chart. (When there are two or more independent variables, we use a form of ANOVA; see Table 18-3.) The first two columns in this chart identify the number of levels of the independent variable and the number of samples. For two levels but one sample, choose either the *z* test and single-sample *t* test, depending on whether you know the population standard deviation; for two levels and two samples, choose either the paired-samples *t* test or the independent-samples *t* test, depending on the research design. For three or more levels (and the matching number of samples), choose either a one-way between-groups ANOVA or a one-way within-groups ANOVA, again basing your decision on the research design.

Number of Levels of Independent Variable	Number of Samples	Information About Population	Research Design	Hypothesis Test
Two	One (compared with the population)	Mean and standard deviation	—	*z* test
Two	One (compared with the population)	Mean only	—	Single-sample *t* test
Two	Two	—	Within-groups	Paired-samples *t* test
Two	Two	—	Between-groups	Independent-samples *t* test
Three (or more)	Three (or more)	—	Between-groups	One-way between-groups ANOVA
Three (or more)	Three (or more)	—	Within-groups	One-way within-groups ANOVA

TABLE 18-3	How to Name an ANOVA

ANOVAs are typically described by two adjectives, one from the first column and one from the second. So, we could have a one-way between-groups ANOVA or a one-way within-groups ANOVA, a two-way between-groups ANOVA or a two-way within-groups ANOVA, and so on. If at least one independent variable is between-groups and at least one is within-groups, it is a mixed-design ANOVA.

Number of Independent Variables: Pick One	Participants in One or All Samples: Pick One	Always Follows Descriptors
One-way	Between-groups	ANOVA
Two-way	Within-groups	
Three-way	Mixed-design	

In the study of whether participant's gender affected the likelihood to rent from a host with a negative expression in their photo, there is just one independent variable, gender. Next, we determine how many groups, or levels, the independent variable has. In this case, gender has two levels—female and male. Now we determine whether the two groups are both represented by two samples or by one sample and one population. In this case, there are two samples—one of male participants and one of female participants. We've narrowed our choices down to two possibilities: one for within-groups designs and one for between-groups designs. For this study, participants fall into only one group, either female or male, so it is a between-groups design. Therefore, we will analyze the data with an independent-samples t test.

And that's just what the researchers did. For those participants who viewed hosts with negative facial expressions, the researchers found a statistically significant gender difference. Women gave lower ratings, on average, than did men for their likelihood of renting apartments in which the hosts had a negative expression (although neither group gave high ratings). The lesson: Smile in your host photos. ●

Category 3: Only Nominal Variables

Now we'll explore a study that includes only nominal variables.

EXAMPLE 18.3

At this point, you might be wondering whether the host photo is the main determinant of where people will stay. Fortunately, it's not. Surprisingly, reviews don't seem to affect consumer choices, although other factors such as location and price do have an impact (Ert et al., 2016; Fagerstrøm et al., 2017). But other host characteristics might factor into decisions. For example, an analysis of Airbnb listings in dozens of German cities showed that the Airbnb designation for stellar hosts, "Superhost" status, translates into higher prices (Teubner, Saade, Hawlitschek, & Weinhardt, 2016). A team of researchers from Australia, Canada, and the United States wondered: Is it actually the Superhost badge or something about the Superhosts themselves that leads to their success (Gibbs, Guttentag, Gretzel, Yao, & Morton, 2018)? Are Superhosts just savvier hosts to start with?

Airbnb encourages hosts to vary their prices depending on factors such as the time of year, length of stay, and special events (e.g., the World Cup is in town). Airbnb uses an algorithm to recommend prices to its hosts, and hosts are free to implement Airbnb's suggested "dynamic pricing," as it's called in the travel industry, or just keep a stable price. The researchers analyzed Airbnb listings from five Canadian cities and recorded how many Superhosts and non-Superhosts varied the price of their listing on 0–5% of days, 5–10% of days, 10–25% of days, and 25% or more days. Airbnb has determined that hosts who vary their prices more tend to earn more money. Here is the breakdown in terms of percentages for Superhosts and non-Superhosts who varied their prices at the four different rates:

	Percentage of days with price variations				
	0–5% of days	5–10% of days	10–25% of days	25% or more days	Total
Non-Superhost	53.9%	11.9%	16.4%	17.8%	100.0%
Superhost	23.9%	16.3%	31.7%	28.2%	100.1%

Note: The row for Superhosts adds up to 100.1% only because of rounding decisions.

For example, 53.9% of non-Superhosts and 23.9% of Superhosts varied their daily price less than 5% of the time. Based on the table of data, it seems as if Superhosts are over-represented among those who varied their prices a lot, and under-represented among those who varied their prices a little. Is this a statistically significant effect? How would the researchers analyze these data?

This research design has only nominal variables—that is, the cells contain counts, not means. The table shows the counts after they've been converted to percentages, but they were generated by counting how many of the two types of hosts fell into each category. In this situation, we have two options, both of which are nonparametric tests. The only question we have to answer is whether we have one or two nominal variables. If we have one nominal variable, we choose the chi-square test for goodness of fit. If we have two nominal variables, we choose the chi-square test for independence. The decision for category 3 is represented in Table 18-4.

MASTERING THE CONCEPT

18-3: When a research design has only nominal variables, there are two choices for how to analyze the data: (1) If there is just one nominal variable, we choose the chi-square test for goodness of fit. (2) If there are two nominal variables, we choose the chi-square tests for independence.

TABLE 18-4   Category 3 Statistics

When we have only nominal variables, then we choose one of the two chi-square tests.

One Nominal Variable	Two Nominal Variables
Chi-square test for goodness of fit	Chi-square test for independence

In the case of the Superhost study, there are two nominal variables—type of host (Superhost, non-Superhost) and frequency of price variation (0–5%, 5–10%, 10–25%, and 25% or more). In consequence, we would choose a chi-square test for independence. And that's exactly what this research team did. They were able to reject the null hypothesis and conclude that Superhosts were indeed more likely to vary their pricing than non-Superhosts—just as the table of data suggested. So, it might not be the Superhost badge itself that attracts renters, but rather the specific behaviors that differentiate the Superhosts from the rest of the pack. ●

CHECK YOUR LEARNING

Reviewing the Concepts > Researchers should identify their variables and choose the appropriate statistical test before beginning a study. Ideally, researchers should preregister these details so they can't change their plan later on.

> If a study includes only scale variables, then the appropriate statistical test is the Pearson correlation coefficient or regression.

> If a study includes at least one nominal independent variable and a scale dependent variable, then the appropriate statistical test is either some kind of a *t* test or some kind of an ANOVA.

> If a study includes only nominal variables, then the appropriate statistical test is either a chi-square test for goodness of fit or a chi-square test for independence.

Clarifying the Concepts **18-1** Why is it important to identify the appropriate statistical test before beginning a study?

Calculating the Statistics **18-2** For each of the following types of variables, which test would you choose?

a. One nominal variable.

b. Two scale variables with a question about prediction.

c. One nominal independent variable with four levels and one scale dependent variable; all participants experience all four levels of the independent variable.

d. One nominal independent variable with two levels, one of which is represented by a sample and one of which is represented by the population, and a scale dependent variable; the population mean and standard deviation are known.

Applying the Concepts **18-3** For each of the following real-life studies, state the variables, identify which type of variable each is, indicate which is the independent variable and which is the dependent variable, and note the appropriate statistical test. Explain why you suggested that test.

a. Researchers compared travelers who had used Airbnb with those who had never used Airbnb. They found that the two groups gave different mean ratings on a 1–5 scale for a range of variables. Those travelers who had never used Airbnb gave a higher rating to the importance of security when making their lodging choices than did previous Airbnb users (Varma, Jukic, Pestek, Shultza, & Nestorov, 2016).

b. Researchers found that several host behaviors significantly predicted how much they could charge (Chen & Xie, 2017). For example, the amount of time a host typically takes to respond to a rental request predicts a higher price for that listing. (Quicker responses predict higher prices.)

c. One study found that people traveling with friends were more likely to choose a vacation rental like Airbnb, whereas people traveling with family were more likely to choose a hotel (Poon & Huang, 2017).

Reporting Statistics

You made a plan, preregistered your study, then collected and analyzed your data. Now what? At this point, it's time to share your findings with the world! The ultimate goal for most researchers is to write up their results, likely with the hope of publishing them—the mark of success for researchers. In this section, we'll walk through

Conference Presentations as a First Step Toward Publication
Many researchers present their findings at a conference before they submit them for publication. This allows researchers to share their findings earlier and to get earlier feedback from others in the field—both marks of open science. Here, your author Tom Heinzen presents research at the International Convention of Psychological Science on using games to teach!

the process of writing your results, point out data ethics pitfalls to avoid, and explore some of the reasons that the traditional benchmarks used for publication in a traditional print peer-reviewed journal may be detrimental to the health of the behavioral sciences.

Overview of Reporting Statistics

If you're writing up your results, you'll probably need more guidance than this chapter provides, but this overview will help you read and interpret results sections so that you can understand the journal articles you're likely to encounter in your behavioral science courses. If you are lucky enough to get to write up your own research one day, we recommend three resources, all of which expand on the guidance we offer in this section:

1. The *Publication Manual of the American Psychological Association* is the "bible" of research writing in the behavioral sciences (American Psychological Association [APA], 2010). The *APA Publication Manual* offers specific advice on everything from which symbols are italicized to how to format a table. It's not a gripping read, but it's essential to anyone who wants to write in APA style.

2. In 2018, an APA task force headed by psychologist Mark Appelbaum published a more detailed and comprehensive set of guidelines for writing results sections, *The Journal Article Reporting Standards for Quantitative Research in Psychology: The APA Publications and Communications Board Task Force Report* (Appelbaum et al., 2018). This article has been nicknamed JARS, short for *Journal Article Reporting Standards*. JARS outlines standards for reporting more traditional hypothesis tests, but also for reporting results from replication studies and from relatively newer techniques such as meta-analysis. The authors include extensive tables that are essential resources for reporting the results from various analytic approaches.

3. Here's the fun one: Psychologist Marianne Fallon's (2018) article, "Writing Quantitative Empirical Manuscripts with Rigor and Flair (Yes, It's Possible)," is itself written with rigor and flair. Perhaps most importantly, it's published in the *Psi Chi Journal of Psychological Research*, a journal aimed at a wide audience that includes undergraduates. Indeed, *Psi Chi Journal* encourages undergraduates to submit articles for consideration. (Psi Chi is the international honor society for psychology students.) Fallon offers concrete advice on reporting the results of your statistical analyses in a way that is clear and accurate, but also lively and approachable. True to her own advice, she manages this feat with warmth and wit.

We'll break our guidelines for reporting statistics into two sections (APA, 2010). Along the way, we'll frequently refer to advice from JARS and Fallon. But first, let's place our discussion of reporting statistics in the context of the entire manuscript that researchers will be writing. Since the 1970s, the IMRAD format has been the standard for most scientific writing (Wu, 2011). IMRAD stands for the four parts of a research report: Introduction, Methods, Results, and Discussion. Briefly, the Introduction summarizes previous research that informed the current study and outlines the current study and the researcher's hypotheses. The Methods section outlines exactly how the current research was conducted. The Results section provides a description of the analyses and the findings. Finally, the Discussion section places the findings in context. The statistics that you learned to calculate in this text are usually reported in the Results section or, in a few cases, in the Methods section:

- *In the Methods section,* we tell the reader how we collected our data. As part of this discussion, we justify the study by including information about how we planned our sample size, such as based on the result of a power analysis. We also outline our plan for data analysis. We include information about where the study has been preregistered, if we took that step. Finally, we provide any psychometric statistics related to the reliability and validity of the measures we used.
- *In the Results section,* where we describe our analyses and findings, we report the traditional statistics, which include any relevant descriptive statistics and the results of hypothesis testing. In addition, we report the newer statistics that are now required by the APA, including effect sizes and confidence intervals (APA, 2010).

Throughout the research process, you should focus on transparency, ideally both preregistering your plan before you conduct your study and sharing your results after you conduct it, often in online supplemental materials (Appelbaum et al., 2018; Chambers, 2017). It also pays to focus on writing clearly. When possible, avoid jargon and use straightforward language. In Fallon's (2018) words: "Sacrificing accessible prose to sound scientifically rigorous is a false choice; it alienates potential future scientists (who have to start somewhere!) as well as the public."

> **MASTERING THE CONCEPT**
>
> **18-4:** Most of the statistics you learned to calculate in this text are reported in either the Methods section or the Results section of a research manuscript.

> **MASTERING THE CONCEPT**
>
> **18-5:** In the Methods section, we indicate whether the study has been preregistered, how we planned the sample size, the data analysis plan, and any relevant psychometric statistics.

> **MASTERING THE CONCEPT**
>
> **18-6:** In the Results section, we describe our analyses and findings from both traditional hypothesis testing and the new statistics.

EXAMPLE 18.4

Let's walk through these sections of the research report using a real-life example. In an article titled "Dear Abby: Should I Give Advice or Receive It?," Lauren Eskreis-Winkler and her colleagues (2018) contrasted the motivational effects of giving and receiving advice in four experiments: one experiment with a sample of middle school students with respect to doing homework and three experiments with samples of adults recruited from MTurk with respect to goals like saving money or losing weight. (MTurk is the online participant recruitment network that we introduced in Chapter 5.) Although we'll focus more on the middle school experiment here, we'll also reference the MTurk experiments along the way because the researchers used more open-science practices with that research. So, which do you think would motivate you more: giving advice or receiving it from an expert? ●

Justifying the Study

Ethical researchers, such as Eskreis-Winkler and her colleagues, will justify their study, ideally by preregistering how they plan to collect and analyze the data. (See the Data Ethics feature in Chapter 1 for a discussion of preregistration.) Researchers who preregister their study are announcing their plan in advance so they can't change it later to retroactively fit the data collected. If a study was preregistered, then the researchers should report where they preregistered their study as well as the basics of what they preregistered.

A preregistration typically includes two main pieces of information, both of which should be reported in a Methods section even if a study was not preregistered. First, we report how we planned our sample size. This might include statistical power analyses that were conducted before the data were collected to guide the determination of the sample size. Determining sample size first, via a power analysis, is important for two reasons: (1) It gives us confidence that we'll have enough power to detect the effect that we hypothesize and (2) it helps us avoid unethical practices like *p*-hacking (for example, analyzing the data after 20 participants, 40 participants, and so on, and then stopping when the results reach statistical significance). Second, we outline the data analysis plan that we developed in advance, including any guidelines for discarding data. For example, if participants finish a survey or task too quickly (or take a ridiculously long time), that performance might indicate that they responded without thinking or got distracted. In such cases, researchers might decide a cutoff range of completion times before they collect data. Researchers should also specify the statistical analyses that they plan to use *before* beginning data collection.

Beyond the information that would be included in preregistration, we report any statistics related to the reliability and validity of the measured variables. All of this information usually goes in the Methods section of the paper. To summarize the statistics-related aspects of the study planning, we include these four items in the Methods section:

1. Whether the study was preregistered, and if so, where can readers see the preregistration
2. How we planned the sample size, often using a statistical power analysis
3. The data analysis plan, including any rules for discarding data
4. Psychometric data for each scale used (reliability and validity information)

Let's see how Eskreis-Winkler and her colleagues approached the Methods section. We'll start by giving you a bit more detail about one of the studies, the experiment with middle schoolers and motivation to do homework. The researchers randomly assigned the students to either give or receive advice. Those who gave advice read a letter from an actual fourth-grader asking for help, which concluded, "When the school day is over, I sort of check out but I need to be online to learn vocabulary. How do you motivate yourself to do stuff like this?" (Eskreis-Winkler et al., 2018, p. 1799). Participants were asked to write a response to the fourth-grader with their best advice. Those who received advice read a letter from an "expert teacher" that stated, in part, "Trying your hardest is always the way to go. You should always try and do BETTER. Don't settle" (p. 1799). Participants in this group were asked to write a reply to the teacher.

The neat part is how the researchers operationalized the dependent variable—without having to rely on self-reports. The middle school used an online vocabulary study program, and the researchers determined the actual numbers of minutes that students were logged in to the vocabulary program during the 4 weeks after they either gave or received advice. The experiments with the participants recruited on MTurk were similar, but with advice related to goals such as saving money.

Let's explore how these researchers presented the key four items about the study in their Methods section:

Advice and Motivation Universities recruit peer advisors to help other students, but does advising their peers actually motivate themselves more?

1. *Whether the study was preregistered, and if so, where can readers see the preregistration.* The researchers did not preregister Experiment 1 on the middle schoolers, although they did preregister Experiments 2 through 4 on the MTurkers. For Experiment 2, for example, they stated: "This study was preregistered on AsPredicted (aspredicted.org/9vk44.pdf)" (p. 1800). So, for Experiments 2 through 4, the researchers' outline of the data analysis plan was given in the preregistration materials, and anyone could click and read it.

2. *The sample size as determined by a statistical power analysis.* The researchers did not provide information about a power analysis to determine the sample size for Experiment 1 (middle schoolers), although they did for Experiments 2 through 4 (MTurkers). They used G*Power, which we introduced in Chapter 8. For Experiments 2 through 4, they reported: "A G*Power analysis revealed that we would have 80% power to detect a medium-sized effect ($d = 0.50$) with alpha set to .05 if we recruited 88 participants per condition, which is what we did in this and subsequent experiments" (p. 1800). They noted that they based the effect size of 0.50 used in the power analysis on effect sizes from their own earlier studies. (Eskreis-Winkler and colleagues may not have used a power analysis to determine sample size for Experiment 1 because they were constrained by their sample size in the first place, so a power analysis wouldn't have mattered. They apparently had access to one U.S. school district, and they simply invited *all* middle school students in this district to participate: 318 students did.)

3. *The data analysis plan, including any rules for discarding data.* The researchers clearly outlined their data analysis plan. For Experiment 1, for example, the researchers noted that some invited participants were not included because they were absent on the first day of the study or did not consent to participate. All other students were included in the analysis. In other words, no data were discarded in this study.

4. *Psychometric data for each scale used (reliability and validity information).* Not all studies require the reporting of psychometric data. For Experiment 1, for example, the researchers were interested in the number of minutes for which students engaged in online vocabulary practice. Because this measure does not consist of a series of individual questions or items, there would not be any psychometric data, such as reliability and validity statistics.

Reporting the Traditional *and* the New Statistics

Now let's outline what goes in the Results section before we tell you the results of this study. We'll find out if the participants found it more motivating to give advice or receive it. The Results section—in Fallon's words, "the big reveal!"—should parallel your research questions and match what you described in your Methods section. Before you present your findings, you'll want to provide the reader with all the background information needed. For starters, you'll want to describe how you followed your own rules for discarding data and let the reader know the outcome of these rules. How many data points did you drop and why?

Next, you'll include any relevant summary statistics. For analyses with a scale dependent variable, include traditional summary statistics such as means, standard deviations, and sample sizes for each cell in the research design (Appelbaum et al., 2018). Also, remember to follow the new-statistics recommendation of including confidence intervals (CIs) for your means or mean differences. These are typically labeled as "95% CI," with the actual interval following in brackets. For analyses with only nominal dependent variables (that is, chi-square analyses), the traditional summaries include the frequencies (counts), sample sizes, and adjusted standardized residuals for each cell. There won't be means or standard deviations because there are no scores on a scale measure.

These summary statistics are sometimes presented first in a Results section and appear after a description of each hypothesis test. The actual presentation depends on how complicated the data are. If there are only two or three cells, then the summary statistics are typically written out in the text; with four or more cells, these statistics are more cleanly displayed in a table or figure.

It's finally time to share your findings. Did you reject the null hypothesis or fail to reject it? Reports of hypothesis tests typically follow a format much like the one we describe here:

1. *Hypotheses and tests:* Reiterate the hypothesis to be tested and then describe the test that was conducted, including the independent and dependent variables.

2. *Assumptions:* Note whether you met the assumptions for the statistical test you used, and if you didn't, explain why you decided it was acceptable to proceed. Remember that many hypothesis tests are robust to violations of some of the assumptions, at least some of the time.

3. *Traditional findings:* Next, present the traditional results of the hypothesis test. Usually, these include the symbol for the statistic, the degrees of freedom, the actual value of the statistic, and, if using software, the actual p value associated with that statistic.

4. *New statistics:* In addition to the traditional results, you should follow the new-statistics recommendations of reporting the effect size, often just after the p value. The format for reporting the traditional statistics and effect sizes is described after each hypothesis test in this text and is summarized in Table 18-5.

TABLE 18-5	Summary of the Results Section

To summarize this aspect of Results sections:

- Describe exactly how many data points you discarded, and for what reasons, as you follow your predetermined rules for deleting data.

- Include traditional summary statistics: means, standard deviations, and either sample sizes for each cell (when the dependent variable is scale) or frequencies (counts) for each cell (when the dependent variable is nominal). These are often included after each hypothesis test.

- Include confidence intervals, the "new" summary statistic.

- For each hypothesis test conducted:

  - Discuss whether you met the assumptions for the hypothesis tests you planned to do, and if not, why you decided to proceed anyway.

  - Include a brief summary of the hypotheses and hypothesis testing.

  - Report the traditional results of hypothesis testing: the symbol for the statistic used, the degrees of freedom, the actual value of the statistic, and the p value associated with this statistic (if using software).

  - When reporting the hypothesis test, also include the "new" statistics of effect size and confidence intervals, as appropriate.

  - Provide a statement that summarizes the results of the hypothesis test.

  - Use tables and figures to clarify patterns in the findings.

- Include all results, even for findings that are not statistically significant. They can enlighten your reader and help a future meta-analyst.

Throughout the Results section, think again about the concept of severe testing: Are you giving your hypothesis a tough test or an easy one? (Mayo, 2018). If you're actively looking for flaws, let your reader know; when you're reading others' research, ask yourself whether they challenged their hypotheses sufficiently (Chambers, 2017). In addition, note whether any of your analyses were exploratory—that is, if you conducted an analysis spurred by something you learned *after* you collected your data, rather than an analysis that you planned to do *before* you collected data. It's perfectly ethical to explore sometimes; just be sure to report that you did so.

Finally, consider whether tables or graphs can help you elevate your story to an epic tale. Tables provide a straightforward, easily scannable resource and are the minimalist's way of showcasing data. Moreover, data visualizations often tell a story in a clearer and more engaging way than words can possibly do. Think about the power of the graphs that depicted mood, as expressed via Twitter, over the course of each

Severe Testing of Divers We can't know from these photos which of these two women is the better diver, but we might feel safer concluding that the diver on the right (high dive) is. After all, the woman on the left (low dive) may very well be able to dive off the higher platform, but we just don't know from her dive here. If you're choosing a new member for your diving team, you would likely choose the diver who engaged in the more severe test, the high dive.

FIGURE 18-2

The Compelling Simplicity of Graphs

This simple graph displays the qualities that Airbnb users seek when choosing a place to stay (on the left), the qualities sought by those who have never used Airbnb (right), and those that matter to both groups (middle). It's much easier to understand the story that this research tells from a clear graph than from lines of text providing the same information.

Data from Varma et al., 2016.

MASTERING THE CONCEPT

18-7: A clear, compelling graph can tell the story of your data far better than many words, with the added side effect of streamlining the write-up of the data.

day of the week (Figure 3-6 on p. 63) or the complexity of the bubble graph correlating health and positive emotions in countries around the world—color-coded by continent (Figure 3-14 on p. 71). These kinds of graphs entice the viewer into spending time with the data and the tales they tell. But even simpler data can still paint a compelling picture. Figure 18-2, for example, shows the factors that travelers take into account when choosing a place to stay (Varma et al., 2016). The factors on the left (in yellow) are those that matter to Airbnb guests, whereas the factors on the right (in blue) are those that matter to travelers who have never used Airbnb. The ones in the overlapping section in the middle (in green) matter to both groups of travelers. Obviously, it is much easier to understand this data story by looking at a minimalist graph than by reading a paragraph of text.

With graphs like these, Fallon (2018) points out, your readers may not even read your text. "Admit it," she calls out her readers, "you have at one point skimmed (skipped?) over some text in a Results section and focused on the tables and figures?" (p. 193). She doesn't judge, though. Like us, she acknowledges the ways in which a compelling graph or table can tell a story more powerfully and streamline the accompanying text at the same time. Do your readers a favor and make it easy for them to *see* your story. And when you're reading a Results section, don't be ashamed of turning to the visuals first.

After presenting the statistics, you have two options:

- If you *failed to reject the null hypothesis,* simply state that you do not have evidence for your hypothesis. Do not accept the null hypothesis—that is, do not say that there is no difference, because hypothesis testing does not tell you that.
- If you *rejected the null hypothesis,* write a brief statement summarizing the results, indicating the direction and size of any effects.

In the Results section, though, you should focus just on what your results mean with respect to your original hypotheses. At this point, you shouldn't go beyond your findings or, for example, discuss your conclusion in light of the general theories in the field or in terms of potential implications and applications. Appropriately, all of this discussion and speculation goes in the Discussion section. (Sometimes, however, the Results and Discussion sections are combined, particularly when a report includes more than one experiment. In this case, a more general discussion section typically appears at the end that grounds the various findings in the existing literature.)

But here's one "do" (as opposed to a "don't"): Always present the results of every hypothesis test that you conducted, even when you failed to reject the null hypothesis. If you have a lot of hypothesis tests, you might report them in a table or an appendix to avoid an overly long Results section, but you must report them. Why? Other researchers can learn a lot by seeing the actual numbers, particularly the effect sizes. Did you fail to reject the null hypothesis, yet find a medium-to-large effect? Maybe that outcome occurred because you didn't have enough statistical power. And some researchers may one day want to include your work in a meta-analysis—reporting all the statistics both gives them the tools they need and gives you credibility as a force to be reckoned with, a genuine severe tester!

For the study of middle schoolers who gave or received advice, the researchers started the Results section with flair. Readers might wonder what a seventh-grader would write in response to the fourth-grader's note. One seventh-grader wrote, in part, "As you become older, you start to realize what is really important. I realized that school and academics are the most important thing. It is still fun to do things outside of school, but you have to realize what is important to you" (Eskreis-Winkler et al., 2018, p. 1799). So mature! This is the kind of detail that helps you, as a reader, understand why giving advice might be powerful with respect to our own motivation. It also adds to the stylish writing endorsed by Fallon (2018). The researchers then launch into the expected statistical details:

1. *Hypotheses and tests:* The researchers clearly outlined their statistical analyses, tying them directly to their hypotheses.

2. *Assumptions:* The researchers did not address the assumptions for the analysis they conducted, an independent-samples *t* test. They did, however, indicate that all 318 students who participated were included in the analyses, which means they did not discard any data. In a footnote, they also reported higher variability among the scores in one group, the students who gave advice, because there was one outlier. As ethical researchers, they analyzed their data without the outlier, and it did not change their conclusions. Consequently, they reported the analysis with all of the data. This is a good example of severe testing, subjecting the data to additional tests to see if they still hold up (Mayo, 2018).

3/4. *Traditional findings and new statistics:* The researchers then gave us their bottom line, integrating the traditional and new statistics:

> Supporting our hypothesis, over the 4 weeks following the intervention, middle-school students who gave advice spent more time per week studying vocabulary ($M = 26.58$ min; $SD = 12.33$) than students who received advice ($M = 23.27$ min; $SD = 8.30$), $t(316) = 2.83$, $p = .005$, $d = 0.32$, 95% confidence interval (CI) = [0.10, 0.54]. (p. 1799)

In this one statement, the researchers provide a wealth of information. First, they give the summary statistics—means and standard deviations for both groups, although they did not include confidence intervals for these values. Then, they report the results of the traditional statistical analysis, along with the effect size, which is small-to-medium, and a confidence interval for the effect size. How did we know that the confidence interval was for the effect size? If in doubt as to what point estimate the confidence interval surrounds, see which score falls exactly in the middle of the confidence interval. In this case, Cohen's *d*, 0.32, falls exactly in the middle between 0.10 and 0.54. This confidence interval for the effect size is useful because 0 is not in the confidence interval; therefore, it is not plausible that there is no effect. The verdict from Experiment 1 is this: The next time you have a chance to give some motivating advice, know that it could motivate *you*, too!

Data Ethics Open Data Practices

Besides preregistering studies, researchers should report any ethical data practices that they used *after* they collected their data. Are the researchers willing to share their data with other scientists who want to reanalyze it? Do the researchers share enough details of the statistical analyses that others can re-create what they did? These kinds of details are often included in a note at the end of the manuscript. In some journals, that note is labeled "Open Practices" and can include badges like the ones depicted here that indicate the manuscript has met certain criteria.

Badges That Reward Transparency in Science The Open Science Framework developed badges that journals can use to provide an incentive for researchers to practice ethical and transparent science. The blue badge for "Open Data" indicates that the researchers have made their data available for others to analyze. The yellow badge for "Open Materials" indicates that the researchers have made their experimental materials available to help others replicate their work. The red badge indicates that the study was preregistered.

How did Lauren Eskreis-Winkler and her colleagues (2018) do in terms of open practices in their study contrasting giving versus receiving advice? They win all the stars! A quick glance at the last page of their manuscript reveals that they earned all three of the badges depicted here based on their practices for Experiments 2 through 4 (on the MTurkers). The journal included images of the three badges in an Open Practices note at the end of their paper, and the researchers explained that others could access their data and materials through the Open Science Framework at osf.

io/dp2aq. They reported that they had preregistered three of the experiments and provided specifics about how to view these notifications at a preregistration site called AsPredicted. For example, one of their experiments was preregistered here: aspredicted.org/9vk44.pdf. You can expect that ethical and transparent research practices like these will become more common over time—so watch for them.

Finally, remember the lessons imparted in the Data Ethics features throughout the book, especially the feature on replication and reproducibility in Chapter 9. A major problem of the psychological science "industrial complex" is that it's far more exciting when researchers reject the null hypothesis. The pressure to get the p value to less than 0.05 is so profound that it drives a lot of researchers to behave in unethical ways, usually unwittingly. For readers of behavioral science news, the emphasis on "exciting" results also means that a lot of exciting findings are Type I errors and a lot of truly good research never sees the light of, well, even a blog post.

Some of you will go on to careers in which you conduct your own research, calculate statistics, and write your results—ideally as an ethical researcher and, yes, as a severe tester. But most of you will go on to the many varied careers for which a behavioral sciences degree prepares you. For those of you in the latter camp, your skills in understanding and interpreting statistics are among your most marketable.

Our final word: Whenever you read about behavioral science in the news, ask yourself questions about ethics and severe testing. If you can't glean that information from the news article, dig deeper. You now know how to read the Results sections of the primary sources, peer-reviewed journal articles. Read them, think critically about them, ask good questions, and then share your knowledge. You're now a statistical thinker, and an ethical one at that!

CHECK YOUR LEARNING

Reviewing the Concepts

> Researchers report aspects of their statistical analyses in the Methods section and the Results section of their research report.

> In the Methods section, researchers justify their study by reporting how they determined their sample size, decided in advance how to discard any data, and detailed their statistical analysis plan. Ideally, this information will be preregistered online as evidence of the advance plan.

> In the Results section, researchers report summary statistics, the results of traditional statistical analyses, and any appropriate new statistics. They use tables or graphs to present large amounts of numbers or to clarify findings.

> In the interest of transparency and to help future meta-analysts, all results should be reported, even if they are not statistically significant.

> The open-science movement encourages researchers to report any transparent practices that they used in a note at the end of the manuscript. This information may include whether a study was preregistered and whether the researchers have made their materials or data publicly available. Some journals offer badges—colorful symbols that appear in an article—to reward transparent researchers.

continued on next page

| Clarifying the Concepts | **18-4** | Which statistical information is important to include in the Methods section of a manuscript? |
| | **18-5** | Which statistical information is important to include in the Results section of a manuscript? |

| Calculating the Statistics | **18-6** | Does each of the following belong in the Methods section or the Results section? |

    a. A statistical power analysis conducted to determine sample size

    b. Coefficient alpha as a measure of reliability

    c. Cohen's d

    d. The p value associated with the test statistic

    e. Whether the study was preregistered

    f. How many data points researchers ended up discarding in an actual study

| Applying the Concepts | **18-7** | Canadian and U.S. researchers randomly assigned research participants to either use their smartphones or not during a social interaction (Dwyer, Kushlev, & Dunn, 2018). Those who used their phones reported feeling statistically significantly more distracted, on average, than those who did not, and reported lower mean rates of enjoyment of the interactions. Answer these questions about the following statements from the researchers' Methods and Results sections of their manuscript. |

    a. The researchers stated that, "using G*Power3, we calculated that we would need a sample size of $N = 200$ for 80% power" (p. 234). They further stated that they "estimated an effect size of $d = 0.4$" to conduct the power analysis. Why might the researchers have chosen statistical power of 80% and a d of 0.4 for their power analysis? And why is it important to include the power analysis in their research report?

    b. The researchers reported that they preregistered their study "on the Open Science Framework (tinyurl.com/z7xe43d)" (p. 236). Which details did they likely preregister?

    c. During the study, participants completed surveys that assessed variables such as distraction and social connection. The researchers wrote that "for the full survey, see tinyurl.com/hau2wck" (p. 236). Which Open Science Framework badge could they earn through an action like this? Explain your answer.

    d. The researchers also reported: "We found that phone use had a small negative effect on well-being, $d = -0.31$, ... 95% CI [-0.43, -0.12]." Explain what the d and the CI mean in this context. In which section of the research report would information like this be included?

REVIEW OF CONCEPTS

LaunchPad
macmillan learning
Visit LaunchPad to access
the e-book and to test your
knowledge with LearningCurve.

Choosing the Right Statistical Test

Two of the most important statistical skills are being able to choose the appropriate statistical test and to write up your results for other researchers and the public. It's important to decide on the experimental variables and statistical test before beginning a study. Ideally, researchers will record these details in advance on one of the online preregistration sites now available.

Choosing the appropriate statistical test involves a deep understanding of the types of variables you're studying. For a study with only scale variables, the appropriate statistical test is the Pearson correlation coefficient or regression. For a study with at least one nominal independent variable and a scale dependent variable, the appropriate statistical test is either some kind of *t* test or some kind of ANOVA. For a study with only nominal variables, the appropriate statistical test is either a chi-square test for goodness of fit or a chi-square test for independence.

Reporting Statistics

All of the statistical procedures covered in this book will be reported in a manuscript that outlines a study's findings—in the Methods section and the Results section. In the Methods section, researchers outline how they determined their sample size, how they planned to delete any data, and how they planned to analyze their data. Ideally, researchers preregister these details online.

In the Results section, researchers report summary statistics, traditional statistics, the new statistics, and any appropriate tables or graphs. Ethically, researchers should report all results, even if those findings are not statistically significant, so as not to imply that every analysis they conducted was statistically significant. Beyond this, researchers should explicitly report any open-science practices that they used, including whether a study was preregistered and whether the researchers have made their materials or data publicly available. Some journals offer badges to acknowledge these practices.

HOW IT WORKS

18.1 CHOOSING THE RIGHT STATISTICAL TEST

Can public health policies change the amount of sugary beverages that people drink? In a series of studies, researcher Leslie John and her colleagues (2017) varied the conditions under which people consumed soda. In one study, participants chose from various sugary beverage options. First, they could choose whether to order a medium drink or a large drink. Second, they were placed in one of the following conditions: no refills, self-service refills, waiter-service refills. The researchers then determined how many beverage calories each participant consumed. How would you choose which statistical test to use?

Initially, the researchers would choose one of the four categories. To do this, they would identify the independent variable(s) and the dependent variable, and determine which type of variables they are.

- In this study, there are three variables.
- The two independent variables are both nominal; one is size of drink with two levels (small and large), and the second is type of refill, with three levels (no refill, self-service refill, and waiter-service refill).
- The dependent variable is calories consumed, which is a scale variable.
- Both independent variables are nominal and the dependent variable is scale, so we look under category 2 on Figure 18-1.

The next decision involves the number of independent variables. There are two independent variables, so we know we need to use a factorial ANOVA. We are then directed to Table 18-3 on p. 583. Because there are two independent variables, we use a two-way ANOVA. Both independent variables are between-groups. Participants receive only one size of beverage and they are in only one refill condition. So, this is a two-way between-groups ANOVA.

18.2 REPORTING STATISTICS

In the sugary-beverages study, the researchers reported main effects for each independent variable and the interaction. Here we'll look just at the reporting of the interaction for the 341 participants with data included in this analysis. The test statistic was 15.42 and the p value was less than 0.001. The researchers included a graph like the one shown here instead of listing all of the means and standard deviations. They did not report an effect size. How would you report the results of this analysis?

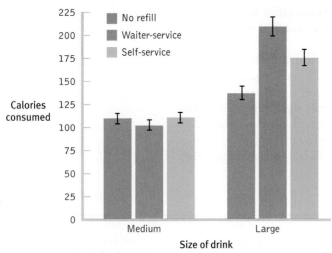

Data from John et al., 2017.

First, you calculate the between-groups and within-groups degrees of freedom for this analysis. The between-groups degrees of freedom for the first independent variable would be $2 - 1 = 1$, and that for the second would be $3 - 1 = 2$. We multiply those values to get the between-groups degrees of freedom for the interaction: $1 \times 2 = 2$. The within-groups degrees of freedom is the sum of the degrees of freedom for each of the six cells. Because we subtract 1 from the sample size in each cell, we know we can subtract 6 from the overall sample size to get the within-groups degrees of freedom: $341 - 6 = 335$.

Now we're ready to report the results. Here's what John and her colleagues (2017) reported:

> [To examine our hypotheses,] we ran a 3×2 ANOVA. . . . These [main effects] were qualified by a significant interaction between portion limit and drink size, $F(2, 335) = 15.42$, $p < .001$ (Fig. 3). (p. 625)

Note that these researchers called the refill condition "portion limit" and that Fig. 3 refers to the actual figure number in their manuscript for the graph depicting these results.

The researchers then conducted follow-up one-way ANOVAs to determine which groups of cells were significantly different from each other. They reported:

> Follow-up tests revealed that for the medium drink, consumption was similar across service styles, $F(2, 197) = 1.07$, $p = .34$. For the large drink, . . . consumption differed by service style, $F(2, 138) = 11.69$, $p < .001$. (p. 625)

So, the researchers didn't find evidence that refill condition mattered among those who ordered the medium drink, but type of refill did make a difference among those who ordered the large drink. We would need an additional post hoc test to determine which of the three bars differed from each other, but it appears that the availability of refills led to higher mean calorie consumption, and if it was even easier—served by a waiter—participants drank even more, on average.

EXERCISES

The solutions to the odd-numbered exercises can be found in Appendix C.

Clarifying the Concepts

18.1 How many and what types of variables are analyzed with a Pearson correlation coefficient? What is the research question that a Pearson correlation coefficient addresses?

18.2 How many and what types of variables are analyzed with a regression analysis? What is the research question that a regression analysis addresses?

18.3 How many and what types of variables are analyzed with a z test? What do we need to know about the levels of the independent variable? What do we need to know about the population?

18.4 How many and what types of variables are analyzed with a single-sample t test? What do we need to know about the levels of the independent variable? What do we need to know about the population?

18.5 How many and what types of variables are analyzed with a paired-samples t test? What research design would be used?

18.6 How many and what types of variables are analyzed with an independent-samples t test? What research design would be used?

18.7 How many and what types of variables are analyzed with a one-way within-groups ANOVA? What research design would be used?

18.8 How many and what types of variables are analyzed with a one-way between-groups ANOVA? What research design would be used?

18.9 What are the possibilities for the types of variables and research designs that would be analyzed with a factorial ANOVA?

18.10 How many and what types of variables are analyzed with a two-way between-groups ANOVA? What research design would be used?

18.11 How many and what types of variables are analyzed with a chi-square test for goodness of fit?

18.12 How many and what types of variables are analyzed with a chi-square test for independence?

18.13 Based on the decision tree presented in Figure 18-1, what are the possible appropriate statistical tests for when there is at least one ordinal variable? (You only have to list the tests for this exercise.)

18.14 What is the *Publication Manual of the American Psychological Association*, and why is it useful to researchers writing up the results of a study?

18.15 What is JARS, and why is it useful to researchers writing up the results of a study?

18.16 In which section of a paper should researchers report information about how they determined their sample size or their planned statistical analyses?

18.17 In which section of a paper should researchers report information about their test statistic, p value, and effect size?

18.18 When researchers preregister a study or provide data or materials at the time they publish their research, they either provide a permanent online link or upload a time-stamped document that cannot be altered. From the perspective of ethical, transparent science, why is this necessary?

18.19 Which Open Science badges exist and what does each mean?

Calculating the Statistics

18.20 Researchers conducted an independent-samples t test and calculated a test statistic of 13.48 with a sample of 392 people. The p value was less than 0.001. Means were 546 with a standard deviation of 122, and 411 with a standard deviation of 49. The 95% confidence interval for the difference between the two means ranged from 115 to 154. The effect size was 1.69. How would you report these statistics in APA style?

18.21 Researchers compared 630 women and 570 men on a scale variable and calculated a test statistic of 7.50 with a sample of 392 people. The p value was less than 0.001. The mean for women was 54.7 with a standard deviation of 31.36, and the mean for men was 47.2 with a standard deviation of 31.75. The effect size was 0.24. How would you report these statistics in APA style?

18.22 Researchers compared three groups on a scale variable and calculated a test statistic of 2.39 with a sample of 559 people. The p value was 0.09. The mean for the first group was 94.52 with a standard deviation of 95.93; the mean for the second group was 77.07 with a standard deviation of 66.28; and the mean for the third group was 79.17 with a standard deviation of 86.86. The effect size was 0.34. How would you report these statistics in APA style?

18.23 Researchers conducted a chi-square test for goodness of fit comparing two groups and calculated a test statistic of 10.030. This corresponded to a p value of 0.002. They calculated an effect size of 0.09. There were 298 people in the analysis. How would you report these statistics in APA style?

18.24 For a study in which they assessed scores on a scale dependent variable, researchers reported a coefficient alpha of 0.81 for that measure, as well as a correlation of 0.67 between that measure and a similar one. Would they report these statistics in the Methods section or the Results section of their research report? Explain your answer.

18.25 Researchers conducted a study that compared two groups on a scale variable, and reported a confidence interval around the difference between means of [–0.26, 1.74].

   a. Would the researchers report the confidence interval in the Methods section or the Results section of their research report? Explain your answer.

   b. Based on this confidence interval, would the researchers have rejected the null hypothesis or failed to reject the null hypothesis? Explain your answer.

18.26 For one of the main effects of a two-way ANOVA, researchers reported the following: $F(1, 124) = 5.50$, $p = 0.02$.

   a. Would the researchers report these statistics in the Methods section or the Results section of their research report? Explain your answer.

   b. We know from the p value, which is less than the typical alpha level of 0.05, that the researchers were able to reject the null hypothesis. Why is this not sufficient to determine that this is an important finding? What additional information should the researchers report?

18.27 Researchers reported that they planned to collect data for a sample size of $N = 128$ to attain 80% power to detect a finding with a medium effect size, an alpha level of 0.05, and a two-tailed test.

   a. Would the researchers report these statistics in the Methods section or the Results section of their research report? Explain your answer.

   b. What are the ethical implications of reporting the planned sample size based on a statistical power analysis?

Applying the Concepts

18.28 **Swearing and choosing the right statistical test:** British linguistics researcher Jack Grieve created maps of which swear words are most common across regions of the United States (Carey, 2015). Using data from billions of tweets worldwide, he had a computer count the frequency of a range of curse words, and documented the geographic patterns in which words were most popular. The "F word," for example, is most common on the east and west coasts and in the south. The much milder "darn," by contrast, is least common in those regions. For this example, state the variables, identify what type of variable each is, indicate which is the independent variable and which is the dependent variable, and note the appropriate statistical test. Explain why you suggested that test.

18.29 **Cats versus dogs and choosing the right statistical test:** The American Veterinary Association (AVA) published data on dog and cat ownership in the United States (Duff, 2017). For each example, state the variables, identify what type of variable each is, indicate which is the independent variable and which is the dependent variable, and note the appropriate statistical test. Explain why you suggested that test.

   a. The data set enabled researchers to determine which are "cat states" and which are "dog states." Specifically, for each state, the AVA provided numbers of U.S. cat-owning households and numbers of U.S. dog-owning households. Each state, therefore, had a score for number of cat households and a score for number of dog households. Some states, such as Maine and Massachusetts, have far more cat households than dog households. Other states, such as Arkansas and Alabama, show the opposite pattern. We might ask whether, overall, states tend to have more dog households or more cat households.

   b. One commenter, @ninja, responded to the data from part (a): "Great data set! I wonder if there is any [relation] between urbanization and cat ownership (versus dog ownership)." Imagine that you had data for every state for both population density and number of households with cats. How could you answer @ninja's question?

   c. Another commenter, @spagolish, also responded to the data from part (a): "You can't just ignore that the mean number of cats per household trends higher than the mean # of dogs per household. While there may be fewer cat lovers those with cats appear to have a greater need for more of them." How could you respond to @spagolish's comment?

18.30 **Ride-sharing data and choosing the right statistical test:** One of your authors lives in an urban area and sometimes relies on ride-sharing apps to get around. Her year-end report from Uber included two data points based on her own history with the app. The following questions quote from the report, but also suggest hypothetical studies that might use these data. For each question, state the variables, identify what type of variable each is, indicate which is the independent variable and which is the dependent variable, and note the appropriate statistical test. Explain why you suggested that test.

a. "You joined 1777 days ago." Do early adopters of Uber use the ride-sharing service more often than newer users do? More specifically, does the number of days since you've joined Uber predict how many times a month you use the service?

b. Based on a rider rating of 4.9, Uber wrote, "Thanks for being such a great passenger," which, admittedly, the company likely says to everyone. Do those who typically ride during the day have higher ratings than those who typically ride at night?

18.31 Ride-sharing data around the world and choosing the right statistical test: One of your authors lives in an urban area and sometimes relies on ride-sharing apps to get around. Her year-end report from Uber included a number of data points, many of which involved how Uber is used around the world. The following questions quote from the report, but also suggest hypothetical studies that might use these data. For each question, state the types of variables, indicate which is the independent variable and which is the dependent variable, and note the appropriate statistical test. Explain why you suggested that test.

a. New York is known as the city that never sleeps, but Uber thinks Chicago, known as the Windy City, may have stolen that title: "The Windy City is also the city that never sleeps. It had the most rides between 2 am and 6 am. Maybe the wind keeps them up?" Do cities with frequently changing weather have more Uber riders in the wee hours of the night? Imagine you could categorize cities as either having changeable weather or non-changeable weather.

b. Which countries use Uber the most? The top three in Uber's global rankings are the United States, Brazil, and India. Uber reports that "riders in these countries really went the distance this year, traveling more miles than anyone else." Is having a higher gross domestic product (in terms of U.S. dollars) related to more Uber rides in a country? (Trick question! See category 4 on the decision tree.)

c. Uber has an offshoot app called Uber Eats. Yes, you can order an Uber for your food! The company tracked the most popular orders, including "the world's most popular sugar fix," doughnuts. Uber apparently delivered so many of the circular treats that it can legitimately report that "people ordered enough to fill the Eiffel Tower 4 times." Suppose you wondered whether food-ordering behavior varied between those who live in North America versus Europe. More specifically, does the ratio of orders of burritos, pizza, and doughnuts vary between North America and Europe?

d. Which is the most forgetful city in the world? According to Uber, it's New York City. "The Big Apple has a short memory when it comes to their belongings. We would give them a medal, but they'd probably forget it in an Uber trip." New York City attracts a lot of tourists as well as a lot of day visitors from the surrounding areas in upstate New York and Long Island, New Jersey, and Connecticut. And, of course, there are locals. Do these three groups—tourists, day-trippers, and locals—differ in the number of belongings they have ever left behind in an Uber car in New York City? (We acknowledge that the mean number of belongings for each group will be a small number because most will leave nothing.)

18.32 Cows with names and choosing the right statistical test: "Ermintrude, Daisy and La vache qui rit may produce as much as 454 pints more [milk] each year than cows with no names" (Gammell, 2009). So began a news report about a study of 516 British dairy farmers, in which cows with names were found to produce more milk than cows without names. Why? Agriculture professor Catherine Douglas, one of the researchers behind this study, suggested that "Just as people respond better to the personal touch, cows also feel happier and more relaxed if they are given a bit more one-to-one attention." What statistical test might she have used?

18.33 Airport security, floppy-eared dogs, perceived friendliness, and choosing the right statistical test: A recent news headline asked, "Do Floppy-Eared Dogs Look Friendlier?" It then responded to its own question, also in the headline: "The T.S.A. Thinks So" (Mervosh, 2019). The Transportation Security Administration (TSA), which handles safety and security in U.S. airports, uses the keen noses of dogs to detect explosives. But the dogs work in public places, which can lead to fear among the traveling public. Are floppy-eared dogs less scary? Imagine that you wanted to conduct a study on this topic. Each participant sees either a photo of a floppy-eared dog or that same photo manipulated so that the dog has pointy ears. Participants must label the dog as friendly, neutral, or scary. What statistical test would you use?

18.34 **Food, negotiations, and choosing the right statistical test:** Whether it's a diplomatic engagement or just a family holiday, eating together can go a long way toward getting people on the same wavelength. One study looked at whether eating similar foods actually has an effect on how well we collaborate (Woolley & Fishbach, 2017). In a mock strike negotiation, participants were given roles as either managers or union leaders and told to negotiate an hourly wage for workers; the dependent variable was the number of strike days until a deal was reached. At the same time, participants were given a taste test. In a slight variation of the actual study, imagine that participants were given foods that ranged from very different to very similar on a rating scale. Might the similarity of foods affect how people negotiate? (The researchers found that increased similarity of foods predicted a lower number of strike days.) What statistical test would you use?

18.35 **Photoshop, body image, and choosing the right statistical test:** The lingerie company Aerie stopped modifying the photos of its models in an ad campaign that it called Aerie Real. Psychology researchers wondered whether this was just a publicity stunt or whether it could have a positive impact on the women who viewed the ads (Convertino, Rodgers, Franko, & Jodoin, 2016). They randomly assigned 200 women to two groups. One group saw photos of Aerie models that were digitally modified, and a second group saw photos from the new Aerie Real campaign. All participants then completed the Body Image State Scale, which includes six questions that participants rate on a scale of 1–9. Overall, the researchers did not find a statistically significant difference between the two groups (although they did find a positive effect of the Aerie Real campaign among women who were more focused on physical appearances). What statistical test might they have used?

Putting It All Together

18.36 **Giving versus receiving, choosing the right statistical test, interpreting data, and data ethics:** In what some people call the "hedonic treadmill," the pleasure we receive from something tends to go down

over time. A rare night out at a fancy restaurant brings much happiness, but if you go every night, that effect diminishes. U.S. researchers wondered if this effect would be true for the happiness we feel when giving to others (O'Brien & Kassirer, 2019). Participants came to the researchers' lab, where they received five envelopes, each containing $5. Some participants were randomly assigned to spend $5 on themselves every day for 5 days or to spend $5 on someone else every day for 5 days. At the end of each day, participants completed a survey that assessed their happiness on a scale of 1–7. The accompanying graph shows the results.

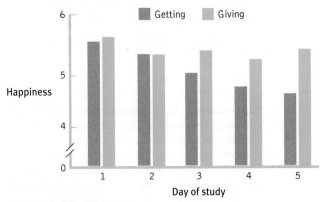

Data from O'Brien and Kassirer, 2019.

a. For this example, state the variables, identify what type of variable each is, indicate which is the independent variable and which is the dependent variable, and note the appropriate statistical test. Explain why you suggested that test.

b. This graph shows differences among means, but does not show variability for each group. Why is it more ethical to show variability for each group, and how could this graph be designed to show variability? (*Note:* The original graph did show variability.)

c. Toward the beginning of their Methods section, the researchers reported: "All data, materials, and preregistration files can be found at https://osf.io/njea2/" (p. 195). Explain what that means and what you might find at the link.

d. The researchers wondered whether the difficulty of the task—spending money on others (giving) versus yourself (getting)—could have affected happiness. They asked the two groups to rate difficulty and reported the following statistics for an independent-samples t test: "(getting: $M = 1.93$, $SD = 1.35$; giving: $M = 2.00$, $SD = 1.37$), $t(90) = -0.24$, $p = .811$, $d = 0.05$, 95% CI for the mean difference $= [-0.63, 0.50]$" (p. 198).

Explain what each of these statistics means in the context of this experiment and in your own words.

e. Toward the end of their manuscript, the researchers reported: "All data and materials have been made publicly available via the Open Science Framework (OSF) and can be accessed at osf.io/njea2" (p. 203). Explain what this means and explain why this is an example of good data ethics practices.

f. Were the researchers likely to have recruited their participants from a crowdsourcing site like MTurk? Explain your answer.

18.37 **Attractive hosts and the price of a vacation rental, choosing the right statistical test, interpreting data, and data ethics:** Researchers in the Netherlands examined whether a variety of characteristics of New York City vacation rental listings, including the attractiveness of the hosts, predicted the price of that listing (Jaeger, Sleegers, Evans, Stel, & van Beest, 2018). The researchers recruited participants from MTurk and asked them to rate the photos of 1020 people, without knowing that these individuals were Airbnb hosts, on a scale of 0–11. Photos were rated by an average of 26 participants, and the researchers took the median score for each photo and used that as the attractiveness score of the host. They used the prices for a given day for all Airbnb apartments.

a. For this example, state the variables, identify what type of variable each is, indicate which is the independent variable and which is the dependent variable, and note the appropriate statistical test. Explain why you suggested that test.

b. What are the pros and cons of using a sample of participants from a crowdsourcing platform like MTurk?

c. Toward the beginning of their Methods section, the researchers reported: "This study was pre-registered and all data and analysis scripts are available at the Open Science Framework (https://osf.io/3enh8/). We report how our sample size was determined, all data exclusions, and all measures in the study." Explain what that means, what you might find at the link, and why these are ethical data practices.

d. The researchers reported: "we did find a positive effect of host attractiveness, $\beta = 0.011$, $SE = 0.0048$, $t(1,010) = 2.34$, $p = .020$, 95% CI [0.0018, 0.021].... Specifically, a one standard deviation increase in perceived attractiveness was associated with a 2.78% price increase" (p. 4). In your own words, describe what the researchers found. Refer to the statistics in your answer.

e. The analysis in part (d) was actually part of a larger analysis, a multiple regression. Explain why the researchers likely used multiple regression as an analytical technique.

f. In their discussion, the researchers point out that their work is correlational in nature, rather than experimental, "which precludes us from making any causal claims" (p. 8, 2018). In your own words, what does this mean? What else may cause attractiveness to predict price?

 **LaunchPad**
macmillan learning

Visit LaunchPad to access the e-book and to test your knowledge with LearningCurve.

● Appendix A

REFERENCE FOR BASIC MATHEMATICS

This appendix serves as a reference for the basic mathematical operations that are used in the book. We provide quick reference tables to help you with symbols and notation; instruction on the order of operations; guidelines for converting fractions, decimals, and percentages; and examples of how to solve basic algebraic equations. Most of you will be familiar with much of this material. However, the inclusion of this reference can help you to solve problems throughout this book, particularly when you come across material that appears unfamiliar.

We include a diagnostic quiz for you to assess your current comfort level with the material. Following the diagnostic test, we provide

instruction and reference tables for each section so that you can review the concepts, apply the concepts through worked problems, and review your skills with a brief self-quiz.

Section A.1   Diagnostic Test: Skills Evaluation
Section A.2   Symbols and Notation: Arithmetic Operations
Section A.3   Order of Operations
Section A.4   Proportions: Fractions, Decimals, and Percentages
Section A.5   Solving Equations with a Single Unknown Variable
Section A.6   Answers to Diagnostic Test and Self-Quizzes

A.1 Diagnostic Test: Skills Evaluation

This diagnostic test is divided into four parts that correspond to the sections of the basic mathematics review that follows. The purpose of the diagnostic test is to help you understand which areas you need to review prior to completing work in this book. (Answers to each of the questions can be found at the end of the review on page A-7.)

SECTION 1 (Symbols and Notation: Arithmetic Operations)

1. $8 + 2 + 14 + 4 =$ _____
2. $4 \times (-6) =$ _____
3. $22 - (-4) + 3 =$ _____
4. $8 \times 6 =$ _____
5. $36 \div (-9) =$ _____
6. $13 + (-2) + 8 =$ _____
7. $44 \div 11 =$ _____
8. $-6 \, (-3) =$ _____
9. $-6 - 8 =$ _____
10. $-14 / -2 =$ _____

SECTION 2 (Order of Operations)

1. $3 \times (6 + 4) - 30 =$ _____
2. $4 + 6(2 + 1) + 6 =$ _____
3. $(3 - 6) \times 2 + 5 =$ _____
4. $4 + 6 \times 2 =$ _____
5. $16 / 2 + 6(3 - 1) =$ _____
6. $2^2(12 - 8) =$ _____
7. $5 - 3(4 - 1) =$ _____
8. $7 \times 2 - (9 - 3) \times 2 =$ _____
9. $15 \div 5 + (6 + 2) / 2 =$ _____
10. $15 - 3^2 + 5(2) =$ _____

SECTION 3 (Proportions: Fractions, Decimals, and Percentages)

1. Convert 0.42 into a fraction _____
2. Convert $\dfrac{6}{10}$ into a decimal _____
3. Convert $\dfrac{4}{5}$ into a percentage _____
4. $\dfrac{6}{13} + \dfrac{4}{13} =$ _____
5. $0.8 \times 0.42 =$ _____
6. 40% of 120 = _____
7. $\dfrac{2}{7} + \dfrac{2}{5} =$ _____
8. $\dfrac{2}{5} \times 80 =$ _____
9. $\dfrac{1}{4} \div \dfrac{1}{3} =$ _____
10. $\dfrac{4}{7} \times \dfrac{5}{9} =$ _____

SECTION 4 (Solving Equations with a Single Unknown Variable)

1. $5X - 13 = 7$ _____
2. $3(X - 2) = 9$ _____
3. $X/3 + 2 = 10$ _____
4. $X(-3) + 2 = -16$ _____
5. $X(6 - 4) + 3 = 15$ _____
6. $X/4 + 3 = 6$ _____
7. $3X + (-9)/(-3) = 24$ _____
8. $9 + X/4 = 12$ _____
9. $4X - 5 = 19$ _____
10. $5 + (-2) + 3X = 9$ _____

A.2 Symbols and Notation: Arithmetic Operations

SYMBOLS AND NOTATION

The basic mathematical symbols used throughout this book are listed in Table A.1. These include the most common arithmetic operations, and you will likely find that you are familiar with them. However, it is worth your time to review the reference table and material that outline the operations using positive and negative numbers. If you have spent little time solving math equations recently, familiarizing yourself with this material can help you avoid making common mistakes.

TABLE A-1	Symbols and Notations	
+	Addition	$8 + 3 = 11$
−	Subtraction	$14 - 6 = 8$
×, ( )	Multiplication	$4 \times 3 = 12,\ 4(3) = 12$
÷, /	Division	$12 \div 6 = 2, 12/6 = 2$
>	Greater than	$7 > 5$
<	Less than	$4 < 9$
≥	Greater than or equal to	$7 \geq 5, 4 \geq 4$
≤	Less than or equal to	$5 \leq 9, 6 \leq 6$
≠	Not equal to	$5 \neq 3$

ARITHMETIC OPERATIONS: Worked Examples

Adding, Subtracting, Multiplying, and Dividing with Positive and Negative Numbers

1. Adding with positive numbers: Add the two (or series of) numbers to produce a sum.
   a. $4 + 7 = 11$
   b. $7 + 4 + 9 = 20$
   c. $4 + 6 + 7 + 2 = 19$

2. Adding with negative numbers: Sum the absolute values of each number and place a negative sign in front of the sum. (*Hint:* When a positive sign directly precedes a negative sign, change both signs to a single negative sign.)
   a. $-6 + (-4) = -10$
      $-6 - 4 = -10$
   b. $-3 + (-2) = -5$
      $-3 - 2 = -5$

3. Adding two numbers with opposite signs: Find the difference between the two numbers and assign the sign (positive or negative) of the larger number to the answer.
   a. $17 + (-9) = 8$
   b. $-16 + 10 = -6$

4. Subtracting one number from another number. (*Hint:* When subtracting a negative number from another number, two negative signs come in sequence, as in part (a). To solve the equations, change the two sequential negative signs into a single positive sign.)
   a. $5 - (-4) = 9$
      $5 + 4 = 9$
   b. $5 - 8 = -3$
   c. $-6 - 3 = -9$

5. Multiplying two positive numbers produces a positive result.
   a. $6 \times 9 = 54$
   b. $6(9) = 54$
   c. $4 \times 3 = 12$
   d. $4(3) = 12$

6. Multiplying two negative numbers produces a positive result.
   a. $-3 \times -9 = 27$
   b. $-3(-9) = 27$
   c. $-4 \times (-3) = 12$
   d. $-4(-3) = 12$

7. Multiplying one positive number and one negative number produces a negative result.
   a. $-3 \times 9 = -27$
   b. $-3(9) = -27$
   c. $4 \times (-3) = -12$
   d. $4(-3) = -12$

8. Dividing two positive numbers produces a positive result.
   a. $12 \div 4 = 3$
   b. $12 / 4 = 3$
   c. $16 \div 8 = 2$
   d. $16 / 8 = 2$

9. Dividing two negative numbers produces a positive result.
   a. $-12 \div -4 = 3$
   b. $-12 / -4 = 3$
   c. $-16 \div (-8) = 2$
   d. $-16 / (-8) = 2$

10. Dividing a positive number by a negative number (or dividing a negative number by a positive number) produces a negative result.
    a. $-12 \div 4 = -3$
    b. $-12 / 4 = -3$
    c. $16 \div (-8) = -2$
    d. $16 / (-8) = -2$

SELF-QUIZ #1: Symbols and Notation: Arithmetic Operations

(Answers to this quiz can be found on page A-7.)

1. $4 \times 7 =$
2. $6 + 3 + 9 =$
3. $-6 - 3 =$
4. $-27 / 3 =$
5. $4(9) =$
6. $12 + (-5) =$
7. $16(-3) =$
8. $-24 / -3 =$
9. $75 \div 5 =$
10. $-7(-4) =$

A.3 Order of Operations

Equations and formulas often include a number of mathematical operations combining addition, subtraction, multiplication, and division. Some also include exponents and square roots. In complex equations with more than one operation, it is important to perform the operations in a specific sequence. Deviating from this sequence can produce a wrong answer. Table A.2 lists the order of operations for quick reference.

TABLE A-2   Order of Operations

Rule of Operation	Example
1. Complete any calculations within parentheses first.	1a. $(6+2) - 4 \times 3/2^2 + 6 =$ 1b. $8 - 4 \times 3/2^2 + 6 =$
2. Complete any squaring (or raising to another exponent) second.	2a. $8 - 4 \times 3/2^2 + 6 =$ 2b. $8 - 4 \times 3/4 + 6 =$
3. From left to right, complete all multiplication and division operations. This may require multiple steps.	3a. $8 - 4 \times 3/4 + 6 =$ 3b. $8 - 12/4 + 6 =$ 3c. $8 - 12/4 + 6 =$ 3d. $8 - 3 + 6 =$
4. Complete all the addition and subtraction operations.	4a. $8 - 3 + 6 =$ 4b. $5 + 6 =$ 4c. $11 = 11$

ORDER OF OPERATIONS: Worked Examples

1.
$$-3 + 6(4) - 7 =$$ Multiplication
$$-3 + 24 - 7 =$$ Addition
$$21 - 7 =$$ Subtraction
$$14 = 14$$ Answer

2.
$$2(8) + 6/3 \times 8 =$$ Multiplication
$$16 + 6/3 \times 8 =$$ Division
$$16 + 2 \times 8 =$$ Multiplication
$$16 + 16 =$$ Addition
$$32 = 32$$ Answer

3.
$$3^2 + 6/3 - 12(2) =$$ Square (raise exponent)
$$9 + 6/3 - 12(2) =$$ Division
$$9 + 2 - 12(2) =$$ Multiplication
$$9 + 2 - 24 =$$ Addition
$$11 - 24 =$$ Subtraction
$$-13 = -13$$ Answer

4.
$$(10 + 6) - 6^2/4 + 3(10) =$$ Within parentheses
$$16 - 6^2/4 + 3(10) =$$ Square (raise exponent)
$$16 - 36/4 + 3(10) =$$ Division
$$16 - 9 + 3(10) =$$ Multiplication
$$16 - 9 + 30 =$$ Subtraction
$$7 + 30 =$$ Addition
$$37 = 37$$ Answer

5.
$$8 + (-4) + 3(12 - 8) =$$ Within parentheses
$$8 + (-4) + 3(4) =$$ Multiplication
$$8 + (-4) + 12 =$$ Addition
$$4 + 12 =$$ Addition
$$16 = 16$$ Answer

SELF-QUIZ #2: Order of Operations

(Answers to this quiz can be found on page A-7.)

1. $3(7) - 12/3 + 2 =$
2. $4/2 + 6 - 2(3) =$
3. $-5(4) + 16 =$
4. $8 + (-16)/4 =$
5. $6 - 3 + 5 - 3(5) + 10 =$
6. $4^2/8 - 4(3) + (8 - 3) =$
7. $(14 - 6) + 72/9 + 4 =$
8. $(54 - 18)/4 + 7 \times 3 =$
9. $32 - 4(3 + 4) + 8 =$
10. $100 \times 3 - 87 =$

A.4 Proportions: Fractions, Decimals, and Percentages

A proportion is a part in relation to a whole. When we look at fractions, we understand the denominator (the bottom number) to be the number of equal parts that make up the whole. The numerator represents the proportion of parts of that whole that are present. Fractions can be converted into decimals by dividing the numerator by the denominator. Decimals can then be converted into percentages by multiplying by 100 (Table A.3). It is important to use the percent symbol (%) when differentiating decimals from percentages. Additionally, decimals are often rounded to the nearest hundredth before they are converted into a percentage.

TABLE A-3	Proportions: Converting Fractions to Decimals to Percentages

 $= 2/8$ $= 0.25$ $= 25\%$

 $= 5/8$ $= 0.625$ $= 62.5\%$ or 63%

 $= 10/20$ $= 0.50$ $= 50\%$

FRACTIONS

Equivalent Fractions

The same proportion can be expressed in a number of equivalent fractions. Equivalent fractions are found by multiplying both the numerator and the denominator by the same number.

$$\frac{1}{2} = \frac{2}{4} = \frac{6}{12} = \frac{30}{60}$$

In this case, we multiply each side of $\frac{1}{2}$ by 2 to reach the equivalent $\frac{2}{4}$, then by 3 to reach the equivalent $\frac{6}{12}$, then by 5 to reach the equivalent $\frac{30}{60}$. Or we could have multiplied the numerator and denominator of the original $\frac{1}{2}$ by 30 to reach our concluding $\frac{30}{60}$.

Fractions can also be reduced to a simpler form by dividing the numerator and denominator by the same number. Be sure to divide each by a number that will result in a whole number for both the numerator and the denominator.

$$\frac{25}{75} = \frac{5}{15} = \frac{1}{3}$$

By dividing each side by 5, the fraction was reduced from $\frac{25}{75}$ to $\frac{5}{15}$. By further dividing by 5, we reduce the fraction to its simplest form, $\frac{1}{3}$. Or we could have divided the numerator and denominator of the original $\frac{25}{75}$ by 25, resulting in the simplest expression of this fraction, $\frac{1}{3}$.

Adding and Subtracting Fractions with the Same Denominator

Finding equivalent fractions is essential to adding and subtracting two or more fractions. To add or subtract, each fraction must have the same denominator. If the two fractions already have the same denominator, add or subtract the numbers in the numerators only.

$$\frac{2}{7} + \frac{1}{7} = \frac{3}{7} \qquad \frac{4}{5} - \frac{3}{5} = \frac{1}{5}$$

In each of these instances, we are adding or subtracting from the same whole (or same pie, as in lines 1 and 2 of Table A.3). In the first equation, we are increasing our proportion of 2 by 1 to equal 3 pieces of the whole. In the second equation, we are reducing the number of proportions from 4 by 3 to equal just 1 piece of the whole.

Adding and Subtracting Fractions with Different Denominators

When adding or subtracting two proportions with different denominators, it is necessary to find a common denominator before performing the operation. It is often easiest to multiply each side (numerator and denominator) by the number equal to the denominator of the other fraction. This provides an easy route to finding a common denominator.

$$\frac{2}{5} + \frac{1}{6} =$$

Multiply the numerator and denominator of $\frac{2}{5}$ by 6, equaling $\frac{12}{30}$.
Multiply the numerator and denominator of $\frac{1}{6}$ by 5, equaling $\frac{5}{30}$.

$$\frac{12}{30} + \frac{5}{30} = \frac{17}{30}$$

Multiplying Fractions

When multiplying fractions, it is not necessary to find common denominators. Just multiply the two numerators in each fraction and the two denominators in each fraction.

$$\frac{4}{7} \times \frac{5}{8} = \frac{(4 \times 5)}{(7 \times 8)} = \frac{20}{56}$$

(*Note:* This fraction can be reduced to a simpler equivalent by dividing both the numerator and the denominator by 4. The result is $\frac{5}{14}$.)

Dividing Fractions

When dividing a fraction by another fraction, invert the second fraction and multiply as just described.

$$\frac{1}{3} \div \frac{2}{3} = \frac{1}{3} \times \frac{3}{2} = \frac{(1 \times 3)}{(3 \times 2)} = \frac{3}{6}$$

(*Note:* This can be reduced to a simpler equivalent by dividing both the numerator and the denominator by 3. The result is one-half, $\frac{1}{2}$.)

SELF-QUIZ #3: Fractions

(Answers to this quiz can be found on page A-7.)

1. $\frac{2}{5} + \frac{1}{5} =$

2. $\frac{2}{7} \times \frac{4}{5} =$

3. $\frac{11}{15} - \frac{2}{5} =$

4. $\frac{3}{5} \div \frac{6}{8} =$

5. $\frac{3}{8} + \frac{1}{4} =$

6. $\frac{1}{8} \div \frac{4}{5} =$

7. $\frac{8}{9} - \frac{5}{9} + \frac{2}{9} =$

8. $\frac{2}{7} + \frac{1}{3} =$

9. $\frac{4}{15} \times \frac{3}{5} =$

10. $\frac{6}{7} - \frac{3}{4} =$

DECIMALS

Converting Decimals to Fractions

Decimals represent proportions of a whole, similar to fractions. Each decimal place represents a factor of 10. So, the first decimal place represents that number over 10, the second decimal place represents that number over 100, the third decimal place represents that number over 1000, the fourth decimal place represents that number over 10,000, and so on.

To convert a decimal to a fraction, take the number as the numerator and place it over 10, 100, 1000, and so on based on how many numbers are to the right of the decimal point. For example:

$$0.6 = \frac{6}{10} \qquad 0.58 = \frac{58}{100}$$

$$0.926 = \frac{926}{1000} \qquad 0.7841 = \frac{7841}{10,000}$$

Adding and Subtracting Decimals

When adding or subtracting decimal points, it is necessary to keep the decimal points in a vertical line. Then add or subtract each vertical row as you normally would.

```
  3.83          4.4992
+1.358         -1.738
_____        _____
  5.188         2.7612
```

Multiplying Decimals

Multiplying decimals requires two basic steps. First, multiply the two decimals just as you would any numbers, paying no concern to where the decimal point is located. Once you have completed that operation, add the number of places to the right of the decimal in each number and count off that many decimal points in the solution line. That is your answer, which you may round up to three decimal places (two for the final answer).

```
    4.26 (two decimal places)              0.532 (three decimal places)
  ×0.398 (three decimal places)            ×0.8 (one decimal place)
  _____                                   _____
    3408                                   0.4256 (four decimal places)
    3834
   1278
  _____
1.69548 (five decimal places)
```

Dividing Decimals

When dividing decimals, it is easiest to multiply each decimal by the factor of 10 associated with the number of places to the right of the decimal point. So, if one of the numbers has two numbers to the right of the decimal point and the other number has one, each number should be multiplied by 100. For example:

$$0.7 \div 1.32 = \frac{0.7}{1.32}$$

Then multiply each side by the factor of 10 associated with the most spaces to the right of the decimal point in either number. In this case, that is 2, so we multiply each side by 100.

$$0.7 \times 100 = 70$$
$$1.32 \times 100 = 132$$

The new fraction is $\frac{70}{132}$, which we can solve: $70 \div 132 = 0.530$

SELF-QUIZ #4: Decimals

(Answers to this quiz can be found on page A-7.)

1. $1.83 \times 0.68 =$

2. $2.637 + 4.2 =$

3. $1.894 - 0.62 =$

4. $0.35 \div 0.7 =$

5. $3.419 \times 0.12 =$

6. $\frac{0.82}{1.74} =$

7. $0.125 \div 0.625 =$
8. $0.44 \times 0.163 =$
9. $0.8 + 1.239 =$
10. $13.288 - 4.46 =$

PERCENTAGES

Converting Percentages to Fractions or Decimals

Convert a percentage into a fraction by removing the percentage symbol and placing the number over a denominator of 100.

$$82\% = \frac{82}{100} \quad \text{or} \quad \frac{41}{50} \quad \text{or} \quad 0.82$$

$$20\% = \frac{20}{100} \quad \text{or} \quad \frac{1}{5} \quad \text{or} \quad 0.2$$

Multiplying with Percentages

In statistics, it is often necessary to determine the percentage of a whole number when analyzing data. To multiply with a percentage, convert the percentage to a decimal (see Table A.3) and solve the equation. To convert a percentage to a decimal, remove the percentage symbol and move the decimal point two places to the left.

$$80\% \text{ of } 45 = 80\% \times 45 = 0.80 \times 45 = 36$$
$$25\% \text{ of } 94 = 25\% \times 94 = 0.25 \times 94 = 23.5$$

SELF-QUIZ #5: Percentages

(Answers to this quiz can be found on page A-7.)

1. $45\% \times 100 =$
2. $22\% \text{ of } 80 =$
3. $35\% \text{ of } 90 =$
4. $80\% \times 23 =$
5. $58\% \times 60 =$
6. $32 \times 16\% =$
7. $125 \times 73\% =$
8. $24 \times 75\% =$
9. $69\% \text{ of } 224 =$
10. $51\% \times 37 =$

A.5 Solving Equations with a Single Unknown Variable

When solving equations with an unknown variable, isolate the unknown variable on one side of the equation. By isolating the variable, you free up the other side of the equation so you can solve it to a single number, which gives you the value of the variable.

To isolate the variable, add, subtract, multiply, or divide each side of the equation to solve the operations on the side of the equation that contains the variable (Table A.4).

TABLE A-4	Solving Equations with a Single Variable
Addition $X + 7 = 18$ $X + 7 - 7 = 18 - 7$ $X = 11$	Subtracting 7 from each side zeros the addition operation.
Subtraction $X - 13 = 27$ $X - 13 + 13 = 27 + 13$ $X = 40$	Adding 13 to each side zeros the subtraction operation.
Multiplication $X \times 5 = 20$ $X \times 5 / 5 = 20 / 5$ $X = 4$	Dividing each side by 5 zeros the multiplication operation.
Division $X / 5 = 40$ $X / 5 \times 5 = 40 \times 5$ $X = 200$	Multiplying each side by 5 zeros the division operation.
Multiple Operations $4X + 6 = 18$ $4X + 6 - 6 = 18 - 6$ $4X = 12$ $4X / 4 = 12 / 4$ $X = 3$	When isolating a variable, work *backward* through the order of operations (see Table A.2). Isolate addition and subtraction operations first. Then isolate operations for multiplication and division.

SOLVING EQUATIONS WITH A SINGLE UNKNOWN VARIABLE: Worked Examples

1. $X + 12 = 42$
   $X + 12 - 12 = 42 - 12$
   $X = 30$

2. $X - 13 = -5$
   $X - 13 + 13 = -5 + 13$
   $X = 8$

3. $(X - 3)/6 = 2$
   $(X - 3)/6 \times 6 = 2 \times 6$
   $X - 3 = 12$
   $X - 3 + 3 = 12 + 3$
   $X = 15$

4. $(3X + 4)/2 = 8$

$(3X + 4)/2 \times 2 = 8 \times 2$

$3X + 4 = 16$

$3X + 4 - 4 = 16 - 4$

$3X = 12$

$3X/3 = 12/3$

$X = 4$

5. $(X - 2)/3 = 7$

$(X - 2)/3 \times 3 = 7 \times 3$

$X - 2 = 21$

$X - 2 + 2 = 21 + 2$

$X = 23$

SELF-QUIZ #6: Solving Equations with a Single Unknown Variable

(Answers to this quiz can be found in the right column.)

1. $7X = 42$

$X =$

2. $87 - X + 16 = 57$

$X =$

3. $X - 17 = -6$

$X =$

4. $5X - 4 = 21$

$X =$

5. $X - 10 = -4$

$X =$

6. $X/8 = 20$

$X =$

7. $(X + 17)/3 = 10$

$X =$

8. $2(X + 4) = 24$

$X =$

9. $X(3 + 12) - 20 = 40$

$X =$

10. $34 - X/6 = 27$

$X =$

A.6 Answers to Diagnostic Test and Self-Quizzes

Answers to Diagnostic Test

Section 1

1. 28; **2.** −24; **3.** 29; **4.** 48; **5.** −4; **6.** 19; **7.** 4; **8.** 18; **9.** −14; **10.** 7

Section 2

1. 0; **2.** 28; **3.** −1; **4.** 16; **5.** 20; **6.** 16; **7.** −4; **8.** 2; **9.** 7; **10.** 16

Section 3

1. $\frac{42}{100}$ or $\frac{21}{50}$; **2.** 0.6; **3.** 80%; **4.** $\frac{10}{13}$; **5.** 0.336; **6.** 48; **7.** $\frac{24}{35}$; **8.** 32; **9.** $\frac{3}{4}$; **10.** $\frac{20}{63}$

Section 4

1. 4; **2.** 5; **3.** 24; **4.** 6; **5.** 6; **6.** 12; **7.** 7; **8.** 12; **9.** 6; **10.** 2

Answers for Self-Quiz #1: Symbols and Notation

1. 28; **2.** 18; **3.** −9; **4.** −9; **5.** 36; **6.** 7; **7.** −48; **8.** 8; **9.** 15; **10.** 28

Answers for Self-Quiz #2: Order of Operations

1. 19; **2.** 2; **3.** −4; **4.** 4; **5.** 3; **6.** −5; **7.** 20; **8.** 30; **9.** 12; **10.** 213

Answers for Self-Quiz #3: Fractions

1. $\frac{3}{5}$; **2.** $\frac{8}{35}$; **3.** $\frac{1}{3}$ or $\frac{5}{15}$ or $\frac{25}{75}$; **4.** $\frac{24}{30}$ or $\frac{4}{5}$; **5.** $\frac{5}{8}$; **6.** $\frac{5}{32}$; **7.** $\frac{5}{9}$; **8.** $\frac{13}{21}$; **9.** $\frac{12}{75}$ or $\frac{4}{25}$; **10.** $\frac{3}{28}$

Answers for Self-Quiz #4: Decimals

1. 1.244; **2.** 6.837; **3.** 1.274; **4.** $\frac{35}{70}$ or $\frac{1}{2}$ or 0.5; **5.** 0.41028; **6.** $\frac{82}{174}$ or $\frac{41}{87}$ or 0.47; **7.** $\frac{125}{625}$ or $\frac{1}{5}$ or 0.2; **8.** 0.07172; **9.** 2.039; **10.** 8.828

Answers for Self-Quiz #5: Percentages

1. 45; **2.** 17.6; **3.** 31.5; **4.** 18.4; **5.** 34.8; **6.** 5.12; **7.** 91.25; **8.** 18; **9.** 154.56; **10.** 18.87

Answers for Self-Quiz #6: Solving Equations with a Single Unknown Variable

1. 6; **2.** 46; **3.** 11; **4.** 5; **5.** 6; **6.** 160; **7.** 13; **8.** 8; **9.** 4; **10.** 42

Appendix B

STATISTICAL TABLES

TABLE B-1 The z Distribution

Normal curve columns represent percentages between the mean and the *z* scores and percentages beyond the *z* scores in the tail.

Mean z   Mean z   Mean z   Mean z

z	% Mean to z	% in Tail	z	% Mean to z	% in Tail
0.00	0.00	50.00	0.25	9.87	40.13
0.01	0.40	49.60	0.26	10.26	39.74
0.02	0.80	49.20	0.27	10.64	39.36
0.03	1.20	48.80	0.28	11.03	38.97
0.04	1.60	48.40	0.29	11.41	38.59
0.05	1.99	48.01	0.30	11.79	38.21
0.06	2.39	47.61	0.31	12.17	37.83
0.07	2.79	47.21	0.32	12.55	37.45
0.08	3.19	46.81	0.33	12.93	37.07
0.09	3.59	46.41	0.34	13.31	36.69
0.10	3.98	46.02	0.35	13.68	36.32
0.11	4.38	45.62	0.36	14.06	35.94
0.12	4.78	45.22	0.37	14.43	35.57
0.13	5.17	44.83	0.38	14.80	35.20
0.14	5.57	44.43	0.39	15.17	34.83
0.15	5.96	44.04	0.40	15.54	34.46
0.16	6.36	43.64	0.41	15.91	34.09
0.17	6.75	43.25	0.42	16.28	33.72
0.18	7.14	42.86	0.43	16.64	33.36
0.19	7.53	42.47	0.44	17.00	33.00
0.20	7.93	42.07	0.45	17.36	32.64
0.21	8.32	41.68	0.46	17.72	32.28
0.22	8.71	41.29	0.47	18.08	31.92

z	% Mean to z	% in Tail	z	% Mean to z	% in Tail
0.23	9.10	40.90	0.48	18.44	31.56
0.24	9.48	40.52	0.49	18.79	31.21
0.50	19.15	30.85	0.90	31.59	18.41
0.51	19.50	30.50	0.91	31.86	18.14
0.52	19.85	30.15	0.92	32.12	17.88
0.53	20.19	29.81	0.93	32.38	17.62
0.54	20.54	29.46	0.94	32.64	17.36
0.55	20.88	29.12	0.95	32.89	17.11
0.56	21.23	28.77	0.96	33.15	16.85
0.57	21.57	28.43	0.97	33.40	16.60
0.58	21.90	28.10	0.98	33.65	16.35
0.59	22.24	27.76	0.99	33.89	16.11
0.60	22.57	27.43	1.00	34.13	15.87
0.61	22.91	27.09	1.01	34.38	15.62
0.62	23.24	26.76	1.02	34.61	15.39
0.63	23.57	26.43	1.03	34.85	15.15
0.64	23.89	26.11	1.04	35.08	14.92
0.65	24.22	25.78	1.05	35.31	14.69
0.66	24.54	25.46	1.06	35.54	14.46
0.67	24.86	25.14	1.07	35.77	14.23
0.68	25.17	24.83	1.08	35.99	14.01
0.69	25.49	24.51	1.09	36.21	13.79
0.70	25.80	24.20	1.10	36.43	13.57
0.71	26.11	23.89	1.11	36.65	13.35
0.72	26.42	23.58	1.12	36.86	13.14
0.73	26.73	23.27	1.13	37.08	12.92
0.74	27.04	22.96	1.14	37.29	12.71
0.75	27.34	22.66	1.15	37.49	12.51
0.76	27.64	22.36	1.16	37.70	12.30
0.77	27.94	22.06	1.17	37.90	12.10
0.78	28.23	21.77	1.18	38.10	11.90
0.79	28.52	21.48	1.19	38.30	11.70
0.80	28.81	21.19	1.20	38.49	11.51
0.81	29.10	20.90	1.21	38.69	11.31
0.82	29.39	20.61	1.22	38.88	11.12
0.83	29.67	20.33	1.23	39.07	10.93
0.84	29.95	20.05	1.24	39.25	10.75

TABLE B-I   continued

z	% Mean to z	% in Tail	z	% Mean to z	% in Tail
0.85	30.23	19.77	1.25	39.44	10.56
0.86	30.51	19.49	1.26	39.62	10.38
0.87	30.78	19.22	1.27	39.80	10.20
0.88	31.06	18.94	1.28	39.97	10.03
0.89	31.33	18.67	1.29	40.15	9.85
1.30	40.32	9.68	1.70	45.54	4.46
1.31	40.49	9.51	1.71	45.64	4.36
1.32	40.66	9.34	1.72	45.73	4.27
1.33	40.82	9.18	1.73	45.82	4.18
1.34	40.99	9.01	1.74	45.91	4.09
1.35	41.15	8.85	1.75	45.99	4.01
1.36	41.31	8.69	1.76	46.08	3.92
1.37	41.47	8.53	1.77	46.16	3.84
1.38	41.62	8.38	1.78	46.25	3.75
1.39	41.77	8.23	1.79	46.33	3.67
1.40	41.92	8.08	1.80	46.41	3.59
1.41	42.07	7.93	1.81	46.49	3.51
1.42	42.22	7.78	1.82	46.56	3.44
1.43	42.36	7.64	1.83	46.64	3.36
1.44	42.51	7.49	1.84	46.71	3.29
1.45	42.65	7.35	1.85	46.78	3.22
1.46	42.79	7.21	1.86	46.86	3.14
1.47	42.92	7.08	1.87	46.93	3.07
1.48	43.06	6.94	1.88	46.99	3.01
1.49	43.19	6.81	1.89	47.06	2.94
1.50	43.32	6.68	1.90	47.13	2.87
1.51	43.45	6.55	1.91	47.19	2.81
1.52	43.57	6.43	1.92	47.26	2.74
1.53	43.70	6.30	1.93	47.32	2.68
1.54	43.82	6.18	1.94	47.38	2.62
1.55	43.94	6.06	1.95	47.44	2.56
1.56	44.06	5.94	1.96	47.50	2.50
1.57	44.18	5.82	1.97	47.56	2.44
1.58	44.29	5.71	1.98	47.61	2.39
1.59	44.41	5.59	1.99	47.67	2.33
1.60	44.52	5.48	2.00	47.72	2.28
1.61	44.63	5.37	2.01	47.78	2.22
1.62	44.74	5.26	2.02	47.83	2.17
1.63	44.84	5.16	2.03	47.88	2.12

z	% Mean to z	% in Tail	z	% Mean to z	% in Tail
1.64	44.95	5.05	2.04	47.93	2.07
1.65	45.05	4.95	2.05	47.98	2.02
1.66	45.15	4.85	2.06	48.03	1.97
1.67	45.25	4.75	2.07	48.08	1.92
1.68	45.35	4.65	2.08	48.12	1.88
1.69	45.45	4.55	2.09	48.17	1.83
2.10	48.21	1.79	2.50	49.38	0.62
2.11	48.26	1.74	2.51	49.40	0.60
2.12	48.30	1.70	2.52	49.41	0.59
2.13	48.34	1.66	2.53	49.43	0.57
2.14	48.38	1.62	2.54	49.45	0.55
2.15	48.42	1.58	2.55	49.46	0.54
2.16	48.46	1.54	2.56	49.48	0.52
2.17	48.50	1.50	2.57	49.49	0.51
2.18	48.54	1.46	2.58	49.51	0.49
2.19	48.57	1.43	2.59	49.52	0.48
2.20	48.61	1.39	2.60	49.53	0.47
2.21	48.64	1.36	2.61	49.55	0.45
2.22	48.68	1.32	2.62	49.56	0.44
2.23	48.71	1.29	2.63	49.57	0.43
2.24	48.75	1.25	2.64	49.59	0.41
2.25	48.78	1.22	2.65	49.60	0.40
2.26	48.81	1.19	2.66	49.61	0.39
2.27	48.84	1.16	2.67	49.62	0.38
2.28	48.87	1.13	2.68	49.63	0.37
2.29	48.90	1.10	2.69	49.64	0.36
2.30	48.93	1.07	2.70	49.65	0.35
2.31	48.96	1.04	2.71	49.66	0.34
2.32	48.98	1.02	2.72	49.67	0.33
2.33	49.01	0.99	2.73	49.68	0.32
2.34	49.04	0.96	2.74	49.69	0.31
2.35	49.06	0.94	2.75	49.70	0.30
2.36	49.09	0.91	2.76	49.71	0.29
2.37	49.11	0.89	2.77	49.72	0.28
2.38	49.13	0.87	2.78	49.73	0.27
2.39	49.16	0.84	2.79	49.74	0.26
2.40	49.18	0.82	2.80	49.74	0.26

TABLE B-I continued

z	% Mean to z	% in Tail	z	% Mean to z	% in Tail
2.41	49.20	0.80	2.81	49.75	0.25
2.42	49.22	0.78	2.82	49.76	0.24
2.43	49.25	0.75	2.83	49.77	0.23
2.44	49.27	0.73	2.84	49.77	0.23
2.45	49.29	0.71	2.85	49.78	0.22
2.46	49.31	0.69	2.86	49.79	0.21
2.47	49.32	0.68	2.87	49.79	0.21
2.48	49.34	0.66	2.88	49.80	0.20
2.49	49.36	0.64	2.89	49.81	0.19
2.90	49.81	0.19	2.97	49.85	0.15
2.91	49.82	0.18	2.98	49.86	0.14
2.92	49.82	0.18	2.99	49.86	0.14
2.93	49.83	0.17	3.00	49.87	0.13
2.94	49.84	0.16	3.50	49.98	0.02
2.95	49.84	0.16	4.00	50.00	0.00
2.96	49.85	0.15	4.50	50.00	0.00

TABLE B-2 The t Distributions

 or

df	One-Tailed Tests Alpha Level			Two-Tailed Tests Alpha Level		
	0.10	0.05	0.01	0.10	0.05	0.01
1	3.078	6.314	31.821	6.314	12.706	63.657
2	1.886	2.920	6.965	2.920	4.303	9.925
3	1.638	2.353	4.541	2.353	3.182	5.841
4	1.533	2.132	3.747	2.132	2.776	4.604
5	1.476	2.015	3.365	2.015	2.571	4.032
6	1.440	1.943	3.143	1.943	2.447	3.708
7	1.415	1.895	2.998	1.895	2.365	3.500
8	1.397	1.860	2.897	1.860	2.306	3.356
9	1.383	1.833	2.822	1.833	2.262	3.250
10	1.372	1.813	2.764	1.813	2.228	3.170
11	1.364	1.796	2.718	1.796	2.201	3.106
12	1.356	1.783	2.681	1.783	2.179	3.055

TABLE B-2 continued

	One-Tailed Tests Alpha Level			Two-Tailed Tests Alpha Level		
df	0.10	0.05	0.01	0.10	0.05	0.01
13	1.350	1.771	2.651	1.771	2.161	3.013
14	1.345	1.762	2.625	1.762	2.145	2.977
15	1.341	1.753	2.603	1.753	2.132	2.947
16	1.337	1.746	2.584	1.746	2.120	2.921
17	1.334	1.740	2.567	1.740	2.110	2.898
18	1.331	1.734	2.553	1.734	2.101	2.879
19	1.328	1.729	2.540	1.729	2.093	2.861
20	1.326	1.725	2.528	1.725	2.086	2.846
21	1.323	1.721	2.518	1.721	2.080	2.832
22	1.321	1.717	2.509	1.717	2.074	2.819
23	1.320	1.714	2.500	1.714	2.069	2.808
24	1.318	1.711	2.492	1.711	2.064	2.797
25	1.317	1.708	2.485	1.708	2.060	2.788
26	1.315	1.706	2.479	1.706	2.056	2.779
27	1.314	1.704`	2.473	1.704	2.052	2.771
28	1.313	1.701	2.467	1.701	2.049	2.764
29	1.312	1.699	2.462	1.699	2.045	2.757
30	1.311	1.698	2.458	1.698	2.043	2.750
35	1.306	1.690	2.438	1.690	2.030	2.724
40	1.303	1.684	2.424	1.684	2.021	2.705
60	1.296	1.671	2.390	1.671	2.001	2.661
80	1.292	1.664	2.374	1.664	1.990	2.639
100	1.290	1.660	2.364	1.660	1.984	2.626
120	1.289	1.658	2.358	1.658	1.980	2.617
∞	1.282	1.645	2.327	1.645	1.960	2.576

TABLE B-3 The F Distributions

Within-Groups df	Significance (Alpha) Level	Between-Groups Degrees of Freedom					
		1	2	3	4	5	6
1	**0.01**	**4052**	**5000**	**5404**	**5625**	**5764**	**5859**
	0.05	162	200	216	225	230	234
	0.10	39.9	49.5	53.6	55.8	57.2	58.2

TABLE B-3   continued

Within-Groups df	Significance (Alpha) Level	Between-Groups Degrees of Freedom					
		1	2	3	4	5	6
2	**0.01**	**98.50**	**99.00**	**99.17**	**99.25**	**99.30**	**99.33**
	0.05	18.51	19.00	19.17	19.25	19.30	19.33
	0.10	*8.53*	*9.00*	*9.16*	*9.24*	*9.29*	*9.33*
3	**0.01**	**34.12**	**30.82**	**29.46**	**28.71**	**28.24**	**27.91**
	0.05	10.13	9.55	9.28	9.12	9.01	8.94
	0.10	*5.54*	*5.46*	*5.39*	*5.34*	*5.31*	*5.28*
4	**0.01**	**21.20**	**18.00**	**16.70**	**15.98**	**15.52**	**15.21**
	0.05	7.71	6.95	6.59	6.39	6.26	6.16
	0.10	*4.55*	*4.33*	*4.19*	*4.11*	*4.05*	*4.01*
5	**0.01**	**16.26**	**13.27**	**12.06**	**11.39**	**10.97**	**10.67**
	0.05	6.61	5.79	5.41	5.19	5.05	4.95
	0.10	*4.06*	*3.78*	*3.62*	*3.52*	*3.45*	*3.41*
6	**0.01**	**13.75**	**10.93**	**9.78**	**9.15**	**8.75**	**8.47**
	0.05	5.99	5.14	4.76	4.53	4.39	4.28
	0.10	*3.78*	*3.46*	*3.29*	*3.18*	*3.11*	*3.06*
7	**0.01**	**12.25**	**9.55**	**8.45**	**7.85**	**7.46**	**7.19**
	0.05	5.59	4.74	4.35	4.12	3.97	3.87
	0.10	*3.59*	*3.26*	*3.08*	*2.96*	*2.88*	*2.83*
8	**0.01**	**11.26**	**8.65**	**7.59**	**7.01**	**6.63**	**6.37**
	0.05	5.32	4.46	4.07	3.84	3.69	3.58
	0.10	*3.46*	*3.11*	*2.92*	*2.81*	*2.73*	*2.67*
9	**0.01**	**10.56**	**8.02**	**6.99**	**6.42**	**6.06**	**5.80**
	0.05	5.12	4.26	3.86	3.63	3.48	3.37
	0.10	*3.36*	*3.01*	*2.81*	*2.69*	*2.61*	*2.55*
10	**0.01**	**10.05**	**7.56**	**6.55**	**6.00**	**5.64**	**5.39**
	0.05	4.97	4.10	3.71	3.48	3.33	3.22
	0.10	*3.29*	*2.93*	*2.73*	*2.61*	*2.52*	*2.46*
11	**0.01**	**9.65**	**7.21**	**6.22**	**5.67**	**5.32**	**5.07**
	0.05	4.85	3.98	3.59	3.36	3.20	3.10
	0.10	*3.23*	*2.86*	*2.66*	*2.54*	*2.45*	*2.39*
12	**0.01**	**9.33**	**6.93**	**5.95**	**5.41**	**5.07**	**4.82**
	0.05	4.75	3.89	3.49	3.26	3.11	3.00
	0.10	*3.18*	*2.81*	*2.61*	*2.48*	*2.40*	*2.33*
13	**0.01**	**9.07**	**6.70**	**5.74**	**5.21**	**4.86**	**4.62**
	0.05	4.67	3.81	3.41	3.18	3.03	2.92
	0.10	*3.14*	*2.76*	*2.56*	*2.43*	*2.35*	*2.28*

TABLE B-3 continued

Within-Groups df	Significance (Alpha) Level	Between-Groups Degrees of Freedom					
		1	2	3	4	5	6
14	**0.01**	**8.86**	**6.52**	**5.56**	**5.04**	**4.70**	**4.46**
	0.05	4.60	3.74	3.34	3.11	2.96	2.85
	0.10	*3.10*	*2.73*	*2.52*	*2.40*	*2.31*	*2.24*
15	**0.01**	**8.68**	**6.36**	**5.42**	**4.89**	**4.56**	**4.32**
	0.05	4.54	3.68	3.29	3.06	2.90	2.79
	0.10	*3.07*	*2.70*	*2.49*	*2.36*	*2.27*	*2.21*
16	**0.01**	**8.53**	**6.23**	**5.29**	**4.77**	**4.44**	**4.20**
	0.05	4.49	3.63	3.24	3.01	2.85	2.74
	0.10	*3.05*	*2.67*	*2.46*	*2.33*	*2.24*	*2.18*
17	**0.01**	**8.40**	**6.11**	**5.19**	**4.67**	**4.34**	**4.10**
	0.05	4.45	3.59	3.20	2.97	2.81	2.70
	0.10	*3.03*	*2.65*	*2.44*	*2.31*	*2.22*	*2.15*
18	**0.01**	**8.29**	**6.01**	**5.09**	**4.58**	**4.25**	**4.02**
	0.05	4.41	3.56	3.16	2.93	2.77	2.66
	0.10	*3.01*	*2.62*	*2.42*	*2.29*	*2.20*	*2.13*
19	**0.01**	**8.19**	**5.93**	**5.01**	**4.50**	**4.17**	**3.94**
	0.05	4.38	3.52	3.13	2.90	2.74	2.63
	0.10	*2.99*	*2.61*	*2.40*	*2.27*	*2.18*	*2.11*
20	**0.01**	**8.10**	**5.85**	**4.94**	**4.43**	**4.10**	**3.87**
	0.05	4.35	3.49	3.10	2.87	2.71	2.60
	0.10	*2.98*	*2.59*	*2.38*	*2.25*	*2.16*	*2.09*
21	**0.01**	**8.02**	**5.78**	**4.88**	**4.37**	**4.04**	**3.81**
	0.05	4.33	3.47	3.07	2.84	2.69	2.57
	0.10	*2.96*	*2.58*	*2.37*	*2.23*	*2.14*	*2.08*
22	**0.01**	**7.95**	**5.72**	**4.82**	**4.31**	**3.99**	**3.76**
	0.05	4.30	3.44	3.05	2.82	2.66	2.55
	0.10	*2.95*	*2.56*	*2.35*	*2.22*	*2.13*	*2.06*
23	**0.01**	**7.88**	**5.66**	**4.77**	**4.26**	**3.94**	**3.71**
	0.05	4.28	3.42	3.03	2.80	2.64	2.53
	0.10	*2.94*	*2.55*	*2.34*	*2.21*	*2.12*	*2.05*
24	**0.01**	**7.82**	**5.61**	**4.72**	**4.22**	**3.90**	**3.67**
	0.05	4.26	3.40	3.01	2.78	2.62	2.51
	0.10	*2.93*	*2.54*	*2.33*	*2.20*	*2.10*	*2.04*
25	**0.01**	**7.77**	**5.57**	**4.68**	**4.18**	**3.86**	**3.63**
	0.05	4.24	3.39	2.99	2.76	2.60	2.49
	0.10	*2.92*	*2.53*	*2.32*	*2.19*	*2.09*	*2.03*

TABLE B-3 continued

Within-Groups df	Significance (Alpha) Level	Between-Groups Degrees of Freedom					
		1	2	3	4	5	6
26	**0.01**	**7.72**	**5.53**	**4.64**	**4.14**	**3.82**	**3.59**
	0.05	4.23	3.37	2.98	2.74	2.59	2.48
	0.10	*2.91*	*2.52*	*2.31*	*2.18*	*2.08*	*2.01*
27	**0.01**	**7.68**	**5.49**	**4.60**	**4.11**	**3.79**	**3.56**
	0.05	4.21	3.36	2.96	2.73	2.57	2.46
	0.10	*2.90*	*2.51*	*2.30*	*2.17*	*2.07*	*2.01*
28	**0.01**	**7.64**	**5.45**	**4.57**	**4.08**	**3.75**	**3.53**
	0.05	4.20	3.34	2.95	2.72	2.56	2.45
	0.10	*2.89*	*2.50*	*2.29*	*2.16*	*2.07*	*2.00*
29	**0.01**	**7.60**	**5.42**	**4.54**	**4.05**	**3.73**	**3.50**
	0.05	4.18	3.33	2.94	2.70	2.55	2.43
	0.10	*2.89*	*2.50*	*2.28*	*2.15*	*2.06*	*1.99*
30	**0.01**	**7.56**	**5.39**	**4.51**	**4.02**	**3.70**	**3.47**
	0.05	4.17	3.32	2.92	2.69	2.53	2.42
	0.10	*2.88*	*2.49*	*2.28*	*2.14*	*2.05*	*1.98*
35	**0.01**	**7.42**	**5.27**	**4.40**	**3.91**	**3.59**	**3.37**
	0.05	4.12	3.27	2.88	2.64	2.49	2.37
	0.10	*2.86*	*2.46*	*2.25*	*2.11*	*2.02*	*1.95*
40	**0.01**	**7.32**	**5.18**	**4.31**	**3.83**	**3.51**	**3.29**
	0.05	4.09	3.23	2.84	2.61	2.45	2.34
	0.10	*2.84*	*2.44*	*2.23*	*2.09*	*2.00*	*1.93*
45	**0.01**	**7.23**	**5.11**	**4.25**	**3.77**	**3.46**	**3.23**
	0.05	4.06	3.21	2.81	2.58	2.42	2.31
	0.10	*2.82*	*2.43*	*2.21*	*2.08*	*1.98*	*1.91*
50	**0.01**	**7.17**	**5.06**	**4.20**	**3.72**	**3.41**	**3.19**
	0.05	4.04	3.18	2.79	2.56	2.40	2.29
	0.10	*2.81*	*2.41*	*2.20*	*2.06*	*1.97*	*1.90*
55	**0.01**	**7.12**	**5.01**	**4.16**	**3.68**	**3.37**	**3.15**
	0.05	4.02	3.17	2.77	2.54	2.38	2.27
	0.10	*2.80*	*2.40*	*2.19*	*2.05*	*1.96*	*1.89*
60	**0.01**	**7.08**	**4.98**	**4.13**	**3.65**	**3.34**	**3.12**
	0.05	4.00	3.15	2.76	2.53	2.37	2.26
	0.10	*2.79*	*2.39*	*2.18*	*2.04*	*1.95*	*1.88*

Within-Groups df	Significance (Alpha) Level	Between-Groups Degrees of Freedom					
		1	2	3	4	5	6
65	0.01	7.04	4.95	4.10	3.62	3.31	3.09
	0.05	3.99	3.14	2.75	2.51	2.36	2.24
	0.10	2.79	2.39	2.17	2.03	1.94	1.87
70	0.01	7.01	4.92	4.08	3.60	3.29	3.07
	0.05	3.98	3.13	2.74	2.50	2.35	2.23
	0.10	2.78	2.38	2.16	2.03	1.93	1.86
75	0.01	6.99	4.90	4.06	3.58	3.27	3.05
	0.05	3.97	3.12	2.73	2.49	2.34	2.22
	0.10	2.77	2.38	2.16	2.02	1.93	1.86
80	0.01	6.96	4.88	4.04	3.56	3.26	3.04
	0.05	3.96	3.11	2.72	2.49	2.33	2.22
	0.10	2.77	2.37	2.15	2.02	1.92	1.85
85	0.01	6.94	4.86	4.02	3.55	3.24	3.02
	0.05	3.95	3.10	2.71	2.48	2.32	2.21
	0.10	2.77	2.37	2.15	2.01	1.92	1.85
90	0.01	6.93	4.85	4.01	3.54	3.23	3.01
	0.05	3.95	3.10	2.71	2.47	2.32	2.20
	0.10	2.76	2.36	2.15	2.01	1.91	1.84
95	0.01	6.91	4.84	4.00	3.52	3.22	3.00
	0.05	3.94	3.09	2.70	2.47	2.31	2.20
	0.10	2.76	2.36	2.14	2.01	1.91	1.84
100	0.01	6.90	4.82	3.98	3.51	3.21	2.99
	0.05	3.94	3.09	2.70	2.46	2.31	2.19
	0.10	2.76	2.36	2.14	2.00	1.91	1.83
200	0.01	6.76	4.71	3.88	3.41	3.11	2.89
	0.05	3.89	3.04	2.65	2.42	2.26	2.14
	0.10	2.73	2.33	2.11	1.97	1.88	1.80
1000	0.01	6.66	4.63	3.80	3.34	3.04	2.82
	0.05	3.85	3.00	2.61	2.38	2.22	2.11
	0.10	2.71	2.31	2.09	1.95	1.85	1.78
∞	0.01	6.64	4.61	3.78	3.32	3.02	2.80
	0.05	3.84	3.00	2.61	2.37	2.22	2.10
	0.10	2.71	2.30	2.08	1.95	1.85	1.78

TABLE B-4	The Chi-Square Distributions

	Significance (Alpha) Level		
df	0.10	0.05	0.01
1	2.706	3.841	6.635
2	4.605	5.992	9.211
3	6.252	7.815	11.345
4	7.780	9.488	13.277
5	9.237	11.071	15.087
6	10.645	12.592	16.812
7	12.017	14.067	18.475
8	13.362	15.507	20.090
9	14.684	16.919	21.666
10	15.987	18.307	23.209

TABLE B-5	The q Statistic (Tukey HSD Test)

Within-Groups df	Significance (Alpha) Level	k = Number of Treatments (Levels)										
		2	3	4	5	6	7	8	9	10	11	12
4	0.05	3.93	5.04	5.76	6.29	6.71	7.05	7.35	7.60	7.83	8.03	8.21
	0.01	6.51	8.12	9.17	9.96	10.58	11.10	11.54	11.92	12.26	12.57	12.84
5	0.05	3.64	4.60	5.22	5.67	6.03	6.33	6.58	6.80	6.99	7.17	7.32
	0.01	5.70	6.98	7.80	8.42	8.91	9.32	9.67	9.97	10.24	10.48	10.70
6	0.05	3.46	4.34	4.90	5.30	5.63	5.90	6.12	6.32	6.49	6.65	6.79
	0.01	5.24	6.33	7.03	7.56	7.97	8.32	8.61	8.87	9.10	9.30	9.48
7	0.05	3.34	4.16	4.68	5.06	5.36	5.61	5.82	6.00	6.16	6.30	6.43
	0.01	4.95	5.92	6.54	7.01	7.37	7.68	7.94	8.17	8.37	8.55	8.71
8	0.05	3.26	4.04	4.53	4.89	5.17	5.40	5.60	5.77	5.92	6.05	6.18
	0.01	4.75	5.64	6.20	6.62	6.96	7.24	7.47	7.68	7.86	8.03	8.18
9	0.05	3.20	3.95	4.41	4.76	5.02	5.24	5.43	5.59	5.74	5.87	5.98
	0.01	4.60	5.43	5.96	6.35	6.66	6.91	7.13	7.33	7.49	7.65	7.78
10	0.05	3.15	3.88	4.33	4.65	4.91	5.12	5.30	5.46	5.60	5.72	5.83
	0.01	4.48	5.27	5.77	6.14	6.43	6.67	6.87	7.05	7.21	7.36	7.49
11	0.05	3.11	3.82	4.26	4.57	4.82	5.03	5.20	5.35	5.49	5.61	5.71
	0.01	4.39	5.15	5.62	5.97	6.25	6.48	6.67	6.84	6.99	7.13	7.25

Within-Groups df	Significance (Alpha) Level	\(k\) = Number of Treatments (Levels)										
		2	3	4	5	6	7	8	9	10	11	12
12	0.05	3.08	3.77	4.20	4.51	4.75	4.95	5.12	5.27	5.39	5.51	5.61
	0.01	**4.32**	**5.05**	**5.50**	**5.84**	**6.10**	**6.32**	**6.51**	**6.67**	**6.81**	**6.94**	**7.06**
13	0.05	3.06	3.73	4.15	4.45	4.69	4.88	5.05	5.19	5.32	5.43	5.53
	0.01	**4.26**	**4.96**	**5.40**	**5.73**	**5.98**	**6.19**	**6.37**	**6.53**	**6.67**	**6.79**	**6.90**
14	0.05	3.03	3.70	4.11	4.41	4.64	4.83	4.99	5.13	5.25	5.36	5.46
	0.01	**4.21**	**4.89**	**5.32**	**5.63**	**5.88**	**6.08**	**6.26**	**6.41**	**6.54**	**6.66**	**6.77**
15	0.05	3.01	3.67	4.08	4.37	4.59	4.78	4.94	5.08	5.20	5.31	5.40
	0.01	**4.17**	**4.84**	**5.25**	**5.56**	**5.80**	**5.99**	**6.16**	**6.31**	**6.44**	**6.55**	**6.66**
16	0.05	3.00	3.65	4.05	4.33	4.56	4.74	4.90	5.03	5.15	5.26	5.35
	0.01	**4.13**	**4.79**	**5.19**	**5.49**	**5.72**	**5.92**	**6.08**	**6.22**	**6.35**	**6.46**	**6.56**
17	0.05	2.98	3.63	4.02	4.30	4.52	4.70	4.86	4.99	5.11	5.21	5.31
	0.01	**4.10**	**4.74**	**5.14**	**5.43**	**5.66**	**5.85**	**6.01**	**6.15**	**6.27**	**6.38**	**6.48**
18	0.05	2.97	3.61	4.00	4.28	4.49	4.67	4.82	4.96	5.07	5.17	5.27
	0.01	**4.07**	**4.70**	**5.09**	**5.38**	**5.60**	**5.79**	**5.94**	**6.08**	**6.20**	**6.31**	**6.41**
19	0.05	2.96	3.59	3.98	4.25	4.47	4.65	4.79	4.92	5.04	5.14	5.23
	0.01	**4.05**	**4.67**	**5.05**	**5.33**	**5.55**	**5.73**	**5.89**	**6.02**	**6.14**	**6.25**	**6.34**
20	0.05	2.95	3.58	3.96	4.23	4.45	4.62	4.77	4.90	5.01	5.11	5.20
	0.01	**4.02**	**4.64**	**5.02**	**5.29**	**5.51**	**5.69**	**5.84**	**5.97**	**6.09**	**6.19**	**6.28**
24	0.05	2.92	3.53	3.90	4.17	4.37	4.54	4.68	4.81	4.92	5.01	5.10
	0.01	**3.96**	**4.55**	**4.91**	**5.17**	**5.37**	**5.54**	**5.69**	**5.81**	**5.92**	**6.02**	**6.11**
30	0.05	2.89	3.49	3.85	4.10	4.30	4.46	4.60	4.72	4.82	4.92	5.00
	0.01	**3.89**	**4.45**	**4.80**	**5.05**	**5.24**	**5.40**	**5.54**	**5.65**	**5.76**	**5.85**	**5.93**
40	0.05	2.86	3.44	3.79	4.04	4.23	4.39	4.52	4.63	4.73	4.82	4.90
	0.01	**3.82**	**4.37**	**4.70**	**4.93**	**5.11**	**5.26**	**5.39**	**5.50**	**5.60**	**5.69**	**5.76**
60	0.05	2.83	3.40	3.74	3.98	4.16	4.31	4.44	4.55	4.65	4.73	4.81
	0.01	**3.76**	**4.28**	**4.59**	**4.82**	**4.99**	**5.13**	**5.25**	**5.36**	**5.45**	**5.53**	**5.60**
120	0.05	2.80	3.36	3.68	3.92	4.10	4.24	4.36	4.47	4.56	4.64	4.71
	0.01	**3.70**	**4.20**	**4.50**	**4.71**	**4.87**	**5.01**	**5.12**	**5.21**	**5.30**	**5.37**	**5.44**
∞	0.05	2.77	3.31	3.63	3.86	4.03	4.17	4.28	4.39	4.47	4.55	4.62
	0.01	**3.64**	**4.12**	**4.40**	**4.60**	**4.76**	**4.88**	**4.99**	**5.08**	**5.16**	**5.23**	**5.29**

TABLE B-6 | The Pearson Correlation Coefficient

To be statistically significant, the sample correlation coefficient, r, must be greater than or equal to the critical value in the table.

$df = N - 2$	Critical Value for One-Tailed Test Alpha Level		$df = N - 2$	Critical Value for Two-Tailed Test Alpha Level	
	0.05	0.01		0.05	0.01
1	0.988	0.9995	1	0.997	0.9999
2	0.900	0.980	2	0.950	0.990
3	0.805	0.934	3	0.878	0.959
4	0.729	0.882	4	0.811	0.917
5	0.669	0.833	5	0.754	0.874
6	0.622	0.789	6	0.707	0.834
7	0.582	0.750	7	0.666	0.798
8	0.549	0.716	8	0.632	0.765
9	0.521	0.685	9	0.602	0.735
10	0.497	0.658	10	0.576	0.708
11	0.476	0.634	11	0.553	0.684
12	0.458	0.612	12	0.532	0.661
13	0.441	0.592	13	0.514	0.641
14	0.426	0.574	14	0.497	0.623
15	0.412	0.558	15	0.482	0.606
16	0.400	0.542	16	0.468	0.590
17	0.389	0.528	17	0.456	0.575
18	0.378	0.516	18	0.444	0.561
19	0.369	0.503	19	0.433	0.549
20	0.360	0.492	20	0.423	0.537
21	0.352	0.482	21	0.413	0.526
22	0.344	0.472	22	0.404	0.515
23	0.337	0.462	23	0.396	0.505
24	0.330	0.453	24	0.388	0.496
25	0.323	0.445	25	0.381	0.487
26	0.317	0.437	26	0.374	0.479
27	0.311	0.430	27	0.367	0.471
28	0.306	0.423	28	0.361	0.463
29	0.301	0.416	29	0.355	0.456
30	0.296	0.409	30	0.349	0.449
35	0.275	0.381	35	0.325	0.418
40	0.257	0.358	40	0.304	0.393
45	0.243	0.338	45	0.288	0.372

TABLE B-6 continued

	Critical Value for One-Tailed Test Alpha Level			Critical Value for Two-Tailed Test Alpha Level	
$df = N - 2$	0.05	0.01	$df = N - 2$	0.05	0.01
50	0.231	0.322	50	0.273	0.354
60	0.211	0.295	60	0.250	0.325
70	0.195	0.274	70	0.232	0.302
80	0.183	0.256	80	0.217	0.283
90	0.173	0.242	90	0.205	0.267
100	0.164	0.230	100	0.195	0.254

TABLE B-7 Random Digits

19223	95034	05756	28713	96409	12531	42544	82853
73676	47150	99400	01927	27754	42648	82425	36290
45467	71709	77558	00095	32863	29485	82226	90056
52711	38889	93074	60227	40011	85848	48767	52573
95592	94007	69971	91481	60779	53791	17297	59335
68417	35013	15529	72765	85089	57067	50211	47487
82739	57890	20807	47511	81676	55300	94383	14893
60940	72024	17868	24943	61790	90656	87964	18883
36009	19365	15412	39638	85453	46816	83485	41979
38448	48789	18338	24697	39364	42006	76688	08708
81486	69487	60513	09297	00412	71238	27649	39950
59636	88804	04634	71197	19352	73089	84898	45785
62568	70206	40325	03699	71080	22553	11486	11776
45149	32992	75730	66280	03819	56202	02938	70915
61041	77684	94322	24709	73698	14526	31893	32592
14459	26056	31424	80371	65103	62253	50490	61181
38167	98532	62183	70632	23417	26185	41448	75532
73190	32533	04470	29669	84407	90785	65956	86382
95857	07118	87664	92099	58806	66979	98624	84826
35476	55972	39421	65850	04266	35435	43742	11937
71487	09984	29077	14863	61683	47052	62224	51025
13873	81598	95052	90908	73592	75186	87136	95761
54580	81507	27102	56027	55892	33063	41842	81868
71035	09001	43367	49497	72719	96758	27611	91596
96746	12149	37823	71868	18442	35119	62103	39244

Appendix C

SOLUTIONS TO ODD-NUMBERED END-OF-CHAPTER PROBLEMS

Chapter 1

1-1 Descriptive statistics organize, summarize, and communicate a group of numerical observations. Inferential statistics use sample data to make general estimates about the larger population.

1-3 The four types of variables are nominal, ordinal, interval, and ratio. A nominal variable is used for observations that have categories, or names, as their values. An ordinal variable is used for observations that have rankings (i.e., 1st, 2nd, 3rd) as their values. An interval variable has numbers as its values; the distance (or interval) between pairs of consecutive numbers is assumed to be equal. A ratio variable meets the criteria for interval variables but also has a meaningful zero point. Interval and ratio variables are both often referred to as scale variables.

1-5 Discrete variables can only be represented by specific numbers, usually whole numbers; continuous variables can take on any values, including those with great decimal precision (e.g., 1.597).

1-7 A confounding variable (also called a *confound*) is any variable that systematically varies with the independent variable so that we cannot logically determine which variable affects the dependent variable. Researchers attempt to control confounding variables in experiments by randomly assigning participants to conditions. The hope with random assignment is that the confounding variable will be spread equally across the different conditions of the study, thus neutralizing its effects.

1-9 An operational definition specifies the operations or procedures used to measure or manipulate an independent or dependent variable.

1-11 When conducting experiments, the researcher randomly assigns participants to conditions or levels of the independent variable. When random assignment is not possible, such as when studying something like gender or marital status, correlational research is used. Correlational research allows us to examine how variables are related to each other; experimental research allows us to make assertions about how an independent variable causes an effect in a dependent variable.

1-13 **a.** "This was an experiment." (not "This was a correlational study.")

b. "the independent variable of caffeine" (not "the dependent variable of caffeine")

c. "A university assessed the validity" (not "A university assessed the reliability")

d. "In a between-groups experiment" (not "In a within-groups experiment")

1-15 Data ethics refer to best research practices that enable transparency in research design and statistical analysis, as well as the fair and clear interpretation and reporting of findings. The push toward ethical data practices is sometimes called "open science."

1-17 Preregistration is an ethical and transparent research practice in which researchers report their research design and analysis plan before they conduct a study. Researchers can preregister studies online by outlining their research design and statistical analyses. Preregistration is important because researchers have a time-stamped record of their plans. They cannot later claim that they intended to study and analyze different hypotheses in different ways.

1-19 The sample is the 2500 Canadians who work out every week. The population is all Canadians.

1-21 The sample is the 100 customers who completed the survey. The population is all of the customers at the grocery store.

1-23 **a.** 73 people

b. All people who shop in grocery stores similar to the one where data were collected

c. Inferential statistic

d. Answer may vary, but here is one way that the amount of fruit and vegetable items purchased could be operationalized as a nominal variable: People could be labeled as having a "healthy diet" or an "unhealthy diet."

e. Answers may vary, but one way is to rank people according to how many fruits and vegetables they purchased, so that the person who purchased the most is ranked 1, the person who purchased the second most is ranked 2, and so on.

f. Answers may vary, but the number of items could be counted or weighed.

1-25 **a.** The independent variables are pet ownership and social activity. The dependent variable is loneliness.

b. There are two levels of pet ownership, owning no pets or owning at least one pet, and two levels of social activity, went out with friends or family either not at all or at least once over the past week.

c. Answers may vary, but loneliness could be operationalized as responses to a questionnaire about each respondent's feelings.

1-27 a. 300 million is based on a sample. The researchers would not have been able to assess the entire population—every single person in the world.

b. The 300 million is an inferential statistic because it is being used to draw conclusions about the prevalence of depression in the population.

1-29 a. Ordinal

b. Scale

c. Nominal

1-31 a. Discrete

b. Continuous

c. Discrete

d. Discrete

1-33 a. The independent variables are temperature and rainfall. Both are continuous scale variables.

b. The dependent variable is experts' ratings. This is a discrete scale variable.

c. The researchers wanted to know if the wine experts are consistent in their ratings—that is, if they're reliable.

d. This observation would suggest that Robert Parker's judgments are valid. His ratings seem to be measuring what they intend to measure—wine quality.

1-35 a. *Forbes* is operationalizing earnings as all of a comedian's pre-tax gross income from all sources, provided that he earned the majority of his money from live performances.

b. Erin Gloria Ryan likely has a problem with this definition because not all comedians perform live as their primary source of income. In her article, she explains: "The *Forbes* list isn't a brofest because men 100% dominate the top echelons of comedy . . . [It] employs an outdated definition of what comedy is and who is earning money from it that is always going to skew male. The game is rigged."

c. *Forbes* could operationalize the earnings of comedians as pretax gross income, as they are already doing, *but* they could include all comedians, whether they earned most of their money from concerts, TV or Internet shows, movies, books, MP3 sales, or any other comedy-related source. This would remove the restriction that most income must come from concert sales. According to Ryan, this broader definition would have put Ellen DeGeneres in first place; she earned $53 million in 2013. Other female comedians who would have leaped onto this list include Sofía Vergara, Tina Fey, Amy Poehler, and Chelsea Handler.

1-37 a. An experiment requires random assignment to conditions. It would not be ethical to randomly assign some people to

vape and some people not to vape, so this research had to be correlational.

b. Other unhealthy behaviors may be associated with vaping, such as drinking alcohol or using illegal drugs. These other unhealthy behaviors might be confounded with vaping.

c. The e-cigarette industry could claim it was not the vaping that was harming people, but rather the other activities in which vapers tend to engage or fail to engage.

d. You could randomly assign people to either a vaping group or a nonvaping group and assess their health over time.

1-39 a. Answers may vary, but one hypothesis could be "Charging for plastic bags increases the likelihood that a customer will bring his or her own bags."

b. You could observe the number of customers who bring their own bags at stores that do not charge for plastic bags and at other stores that do charge for plastic bags. You could then determine the percentages of customers who bring their own bags in each situation.

c. You could randomly assign certain days of the week to charge for plastic bags, and other days to not charge for plastic bags. As in part (b), you could then determine the percentages of customers who bring their own bags in each situation.

1-41 a. This is a good analogy because it describes the process by which researchers "aim" at a hypothesis, find something else entirely, then pretend that the "something else entirely" was what they were shooting at all along. The scientific method can't work if the researchers change the target to match the finding.

b. If researchers preregistered their research, then everyone would know if they moved their "target" after they knew their findings. HARKing wouldn't be possible!

1-43 a. Researchers could have randomly assigned some people who are HIV-positive to take the oral vaccine and other people who are HIV-positive not to take the oral vaccine. The second group would likely take a placebo.

b. This would have been a between-groups experiment because the people who are HIV-positive would have been in only one group: either vaccine or no vaccine.

c. This limits the researchers' ability to draw causal conclusions because the participants who received the vaccine may have been different in some way from those who did not receive the vaccine. There may have been a confounding variable that led to these findings. For example, those who received the vaccine might have had better access to health care and better sanitary conditions to begin with, making them less likely to contract cholera regardless of the vaccine's effectiveness.

d. The researchers might not have used random assignment because it would have meant recruiting participants, likely immunizing half, then following up with all of them. The researchers likely did not want to deny the vaccine to people who were HIV-positive because they might have contracted cholera and died without it.

e. If the researchers preregistered their study, that would mean that they detailed, in advance, exactly how they would recruit their participants, how they would assign them to groups (if they were indeed using random assignment), and how they would analyze their results statistically.

1-45 **a.** A "good charity" is operationally defined as one that spends more of its money for the cause it is supporting and less for fundraising or administration.

b. The rating is a scale variable, as it has a meaningful zero point, has equal distance between intervals, and is continuous.

c. The tier is an ordinal variable, as it involves ranking the organizations into categories (1st, 2nd, 3rd, 4th, or 5th tier) and it is discrete.

d. The type of charity is a nominal variable, as it uses names or categories to classify the values (e.g., health and medical needs) and it is discrete.

e. Measuring finances is more objective and easier to measure than some of the criteria mentioned by Ord, such as importance of the problem and competency and honesty.

f. Charity Navigator's ratings are more likely to be reliable than GiveWell's ratings because they are based on an objective measure. It is more likely that different assessors would come up with the same rating for Charity Navigator than for GiveWell.

g. GiveWell's ratings are likely to be more valid than Charity Navigator's, provided that they can attain some level of reliability. GiveWell's more comprehensive rating system incorporates a better-rounded assessment of a charity.

h. This would be a correlational study because donation funds, the independent variable, would not be randomly assigned based on country but measured as they naturally occur.

i. This would be an experiment because the levels of donation funds, the independent variable, are randomly assigned to different regions to determine the effect on death rate.

Chapter 2

2-1 Raw scores are the original data, to which nothing has been done.

2-3 A frequency table is a visual depiction of data that shows how often each value occurred; that is, it shows how many scores are at each value. Values are listed in one column, and the numbers of individuals with scores at that value are listed in the second column. A grouped frequency table is a visual depiction of data that reports the frequency within each given interval, rather than the frequency for each specific value.

2-5 Bar graphs typically provide scores for nominal data, whereas histograms typically provide frequencies for scale data. Also, the categories in bar graphs do not need to be arranged in a particular order and the bars should not touch, whereas the intervals in histograms are arranged in a meaningful order (lowest to highest) and the bars should touch each other.

2-7 A histogram looks like a bar graph but is usually used to depict scale data, with the values (or midpoints of intervals) of the variable on the x-axis and the frequencies on the y-axis.

2-9 In everyday conversation, you might use the word *distribution* in a number of different contexts, from the distribution of food to a marketing distribution. A statistician would use *distribution* only to describe the way that a set of scores, such as a set of grades, is distributed. A statistician is looking at the overall pattern of the data—what the shape is, where the data tend to cluster, and how they trail off.

2-11 With positively skewed data, the distribution's tail extends to the right, in a positive direction, and with negatively skewed data, the distribution's tail extends to the left, in a negative direction.

2-13 A ceiling effect occurs when there are no scores above a certain value; a ceiling effect leads to a negatively skewed distribution because the upper part of the distribution is constrained.

2-15 Like a histogram, a dot plot shows the overall shape of the distribution.

2-17 17.95% and 40.67%

2-19 0.10% and 96.77%

2-21 0.04, 198.22, and 17.89

2-23 The full range of data is 68 minus 2, plus 1, or 67. The range (67) divided by the desired seven intervals gives us an interval size of 9.57, or 10 when rounded. The seven intervals are 0–9, 10–19, 20–29, 30–39, 40–49, 50–59, and 60–69.

2-25 Four countries had at least 30 volcanoes.

2-27 Serial killers would create positive skew, adding high numbers of murders to the data that are clustered around 1.

2-29 **a.** For the university population, the range of ages extends farther to the right (with a larger number of years) than to the left, creating positive skew.

b. The fact that youthful prodigies have limited access to university creates a sort of floor effect that makes low scores less possible.

2-31 **a.** First, we put the data in order from lowest to highest: 2, 2, 2.5, 2.5, 2.5, 3, 3, 3, 3, 3.5, 3.5, 3.5, 3.5, 3.5, 3.5, 3.5, 4, 4, 4, 4.5, 4.5

Then we set up the x-axis and draw the dots:

b. This distribution has a slight negative skew.

2-33 a.

Percentage	Frequency	Percentage
10	1	5.26
9	0	0.00
8	0	0.00
7	0	0.00
6	0	0.00
5	2	10.53
4	2	10.53
3	4	21.05
2	4	21.05
1	5	26.32
0	1	5.26

b. In 10.53% of these schools, exactly 4% of the students reported that they wrote between 5 and 10 twenty-page papers that year.

c. This is not a random sample. It includes schools that chose to participate in this survey and opted to have their results made public.

d.

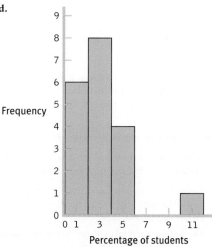

Percentage of students

e. One

f. The data are clustered around 1% to 4%, with a high outlier, 10%.

2-35 a.

Interval	Frequency
80–84	7
75–79	9
70–74	5
65–69	3
60–64	3
55–59	2
50–54	1

b. There are many possible answers. One research hypothesis might be that the economic status of different regions of the world predicts life expectancies.

c.

Life expectancies

d. The data presented here demonstrate a negatively skewed distribution. There are more countries that have a life expectancy on the higher end—longer than 70 years—than there are in the rest of the distribution.

2-37 a. Extroversion scores are most likely to have a normal distribution. Most people would fall toward the middle, with some people having higher levels and some having lower levels.

b. The distribution of finishing times for a marathon is likely to be positively skewed. The floor is the fastest possible time, a little over 2 hours; however, some runners take as long as 6 hours or more. Unfortunately for the very, very slow but unbelievably dedicated runners, many marathons shut down the finish line 6 hours after the start of the race.

c. The distribution of numbers of meals eaten in a dining hall in a semester on a three-meal-a-day plan is likely to be negatively skewed. The ceiling is three times per day, multiplied by the number of days; most people who choose to pay for the full plan would eat many of these meals. A few would hardly ever eat in the dining hall, pulling the tail in a negative direction.

2-39

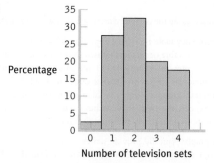

Number of television sets

2-41 a. A histogram based on these data is likely to be negatively skewed. The scale is 1–10 and most films are rated above the midpoint. Very few are as low as *Gunday*.

b. There is more likely to be a ceiling effect. With most films earning high ratings, it seems that the limiting factor is the top score of 10. No film earned the lowest possible score of 1, and few were as low as *Gunday's* 1.4. So, there doesn't seem to be a floor effect of 1.

c. IMDb ratings don't seem to be a good way to operationalize movie quality. Audience ratings may be based on something other than how good the film is. In this case, many of those who rated *Gunday* based their scores on politics rather than on the qualities of the film itself. Another way to operationalize movie quality is a rating based on critics' reviews, such as the system used by rottentomatoes.com. This site provides an average rating from critics, based on published reviews, in addition to one by movie audiences. Critics are unlikely to rate a movie simply based on politics.

2-43 a. First, we order the scores from lowest to highest:

6 6 6 6 6 6 6 6 6 6 7 7 7 7 7
7 7 7 7 7 7 8 8 8 8 8 8 8 8 8
9 9 9 9 10 10 11 12 13 14 15 15

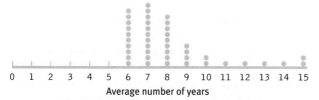

Average number of years

b. In most of the universities sampled, it takes between six and nine years, on average, to earn the doctorate degree. But the distribution is positively skewed, with a number of universities having a longer time to earn the degree.

2-45 a.

Percentages	Frequency	Percentage
35–39.9	1	5
30–34.9	2	10
25–29.9	2	10
20–24.9	4	20
15–19.9	5	25
10–14.9	4	20
5–9.9	1	5
0–4.9	1	5

b.

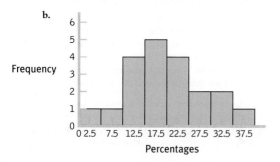

Percentages

c. These data are centered on 17.5% and are relatively normally distributed.

d. The bulk of the data would need to be shifted from the middle of the distribution toward the left. The resulting distribution would center on a lower percentage of obesity, such as 7.5%, with a tail in the positive direction. Fewer countries would have high rates of obesity. Knowing which countries were in the middle and top parts of the distribution would allow us to target anti-obesity efforts toward those geographic regions.

e. These data are from correlational research. The researchers observed the weights of people in the countries in which they already lived. They did not randomly assign people to live in certain countries.

2-47 a.

Former Students Now in Top Jobs	Frequency	Percentage
13	1	1.85
12	0	0.00
11	0	0.00
10	0	0.00
9	1	1.85
8	3	5.56
7	4	7.41
6	5	9.26
5	9	16.67
4	8	14.81
3	23	42.59

b.

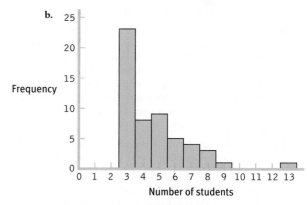

Number of students

c. This distribution is positively skewed.

d. The researchers operationalized the variable of mentoring success as numbers of students placed into top professorial positions. There are many other ways this variable could have been operationalized. For example, the researchers might have counted numbers of student publications while in graduate school or might have asked graduates to rate their satisfaction with their graduate mentoring experiences.

e. The students might have attained their positions as professors because of the prestige of their advisor, not because of his mentoring.

f. There are many possible answers to this question. For example, the attainment of a top professorial position might be predicted by the prestige of the institution, the number of publications while in graduate school, or the graduate student's academic ability.

Chapter 3

3-1 The five techniques for misleading with graphs are the biased scale lie, the sneaky sample lie, the interpolation lie, the extrapolation lie, and the inaccurate values lie.

3-3 Each dot on a scatterplot represents an individual's scores on two scale variables. It falls above the individual's score on the x-axis and across from the individual's score on the y-axis.

3-5 With scale data, a scatterplot allows for a helpful visual analysis of the relation between two variables. If the data points appear to fall approximately along a straight line, the variables may have a linear relation. If the data form a line that changes direction along its path, the variables may have a nonlinear relation. If the data points show no particular relation, it is possible that the two variables are not related.

3-7 A bar graph is a visual depiction of data in which the independent variable is nominal or ordinal and the dependent variable is scale. Each bar typically represents the mean value of the dependent variable for each category. A Pareto chart is a specific type of bar graph in which the categories along the x-axis are ordered from highest bar on the left to lowest bar on the right.

3-9 A pictorial graph is a visual depiction of data typically used for a nominal independent variable with very few levels (categories) and a scale dependent variable. Each level uses a picture or symbol to represent its value on the scale dependent variable. A pie chart is a graph in the shape of a circle, with a slice for every level. The size of each slice represents the proportion (or percentage) of each category. In most cases, a bar graph is preferable to a pictorial graph or a pie chart.

3-11 The independent variable typically goes on the horizontal x-axis and the dependent variable goes on the vertical y-axis.

3-13 Moiré vibrations are any visual patterns that create a distracting impression of vibration and movement. A grid is a background pattern, almost like graph paper, on which the data representations, such as bars, are superimposed. Ducks are features of the data that have been dressed up to be something other than merely data.

3-15 Like a traditional scatterplot, the locations of the points on the bubble graph simultaneously represent the values that a single case (or country) has on two scale variables. The graph as a whole depicts the relation between these two variables.

3-17 Bar graphs just tell us group means. Without including some depiction of variability, we can't know the shape of a distribution or whether there are extreme scores.

3-19 Total dollars donated per year is scale data. A time plot would nicely show how donations varied across years.

3-21 a. The independent variable is news source and the dependent variable is knowledge about current affairs.

b. Nominal

c. Scale

d. The best graph for these data would be a bar graph because there is a nominal independent variable and a scale dependent variable.

3-23 Linear, because the data could be fit with a line drawn from the upper-left to the lower-right corner of the graph.

3-25 a. Bar graph

b. Line graph; more specifically, a time plot

c. The y-axis should go down to 0.

d. The lines in the background are grids, and the three-dimensional effect is a type of duck.

e. 3.20%, 3.22%, 2.80%

f. If the y-axis started at 0, all of the bars would appear to be about the same height. The differences would be minimized.

3-27 The minimum value is 0.04 and the maximum is 0.36, so the axis could be labeled from 0.00 to 0.40. We might choose to mark every 0.05 value:

0.00   0.05   0.10   0.15   0.20   0.25   0.30   0.35   0.40

3-29 The relation between physical health and positive emotions seems to be positive, with the data fitting a line moving from the lower-left to the upper-right corner of the graph. As positive emotions increase, self-reported physical health also tends to increase.

3-31 a. For this study, the independent and dependent variables are scale because a numerical value represents each variable. For example, international representation is measured by how many countries are represented by the average number of different authors for each journal; impact score is measured using a scale that ranges from 0 to 30.

b. This graph is a scatterplot. A scatterplot is appropriate for these data because there are two scale variables of interest.

c. This graph demonstrates that there is a positive relation between impact score and the average number of countries represented by the authors for each journal in the study, such that the more countries represented the higher the impact score. This graph demonstrates that there seems to be a linear relation between the two variables.

3-33 a. The independent variable is country and the dependent variable is male suicide rate.

b. Country is a nominal variable and suicide rate is a scale variable.

c. The best graph for these data would be a bar graph or a Pareto chart. Because there are six categories or countries to list along the *x*-axis, it may be best to arrange them in order from highest to lowest using a Pareto chart.

d. A time series plot could show year on the *x*-axis and suicide rate on the *y*-axis. Each country would be represented by a different color line.

3-35 a.   **Relation between percentage with university degree and GDP (in trillions of USD)**

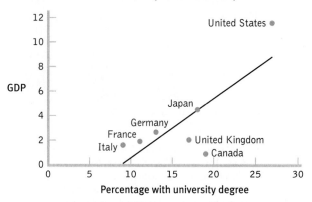

b. The percentage of residents with a university degree appears to be related to GDP. As the percentage with a university degree increases, so does GDP.

c. It is possible that an educated populace has the skills to make that country productive and profitable. Conversely, it is possible that a productive and profitable country has the money needed for the populace to be educated.

3-37 a. The independent variable is the subfield in psychology. The independent variable is a nominal variable because there are unique categories or levels. There are 10 different levels for the independent variable: clinical psychology, cognitive psychology, counseling psychology, developmental psychology, experimental psychology, industrial/organizational psychology, neuroscience, school psychology, social psychology, and other applied psychology.

b. The dependent variable is the overall acceptance rate. The dependent variable is a scale variable because there are numbers as the values. The units for the dependent variable are the percentages of number of people accepted into a specific doctoral program. The minimum value is 7% and the maximum value is 29%.

c. The default will differ, depending on which software is used. Here is one example.

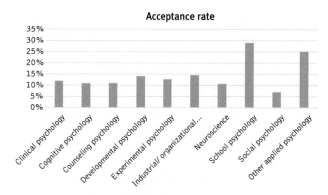

d. The redesign will differ, depending on which software is used. In this example, we updated the title, added the *x*-axis label, added the *y*-axis label, rotated the *y*-axis label to read horizontally, removed the unnecessary lines in the background, added tick marks to the *y*-axis, and enlarged the *x*-axis so that "Industrial/organizational psychology" was not cut off.

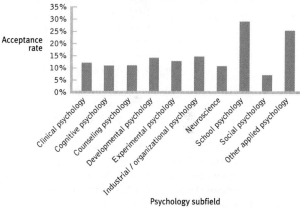

e. Answers may vary. Here are some examples of potential follow-up research questions. What are the graduation rates for each subfield? How likely are graduates to get a job within each subfield? On average, how many years does each program take to complete? Are there differences in the number of credits, internship hours, and other requirements for each subfield? Are there gender differences in the applicant pool for each subfield?

f. Pictures could be used instead of bars. For example, using the Greek letter ψ (Psi) would be appropriate considering the data are about psychology doctoral programs and ψ is often used as a symbol for psychology.

g. If ψ becomes wider as it gets taller (to represent a higher acceptance rate), the overall size would be proportionally larger than the increase in donation rate it is meant to represent. A bar graph is not subject to this problem because graphmakers are not likely to make bars wider as they get taller.

3-39 a. One independent variable is time frame; it has two levels: 1945–1950 and 1996–1998. The other independent variable is type of graduate program; it also has two levels: clinical psychology and experimental psychology.

b. The dependent variable is percentage of graduates who had a mentor while in graduate school.

c.

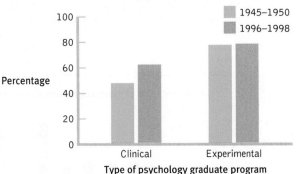

Percentage of mentoring by time frame and type of psychology graduate program

d. These data suggest that clinical psychology graduate students were more likely to have been mentored if they were in school in the 1996–1998 time frame than if they were in school during the 1945–1950 time frame. There does not appear to be such a difference among experimental psychology students.

e. This was not a true experiment. Students were not randomly assigned to time period or type of graduate program.

f. A time series plot would be inappropriate with so few data points. It would suggest that we could interpolate between these data points. It would suggest a continual increase in the likelihood of being mentored among clinical psychology students, as well as a stable trend, albeit at a high level, among experimental psychology students.

g. The story based on two time points might be falsely interpreted as a continual increase of mentoring rates for the clinical psychology students and a plateau for the experimental psychology students. The expanded data set suggests that the rates of mentoring have fluctuated over the years. Without the four time points, we might be seduced by interpolation into thinking that the two scores represent the end points of a linear trend. We cannot draw conclusions about time points for which we have no data—especially when we have only two points, but even when we have more points.

3-41 a. The details will differ, depending on the software used. Here is one example.

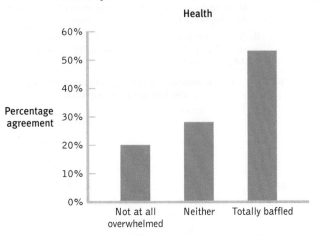

b. The default options that students choose to override will differ. For the bar graph shown here, we changed the default settings by (1) adding a title, (2) adding a y-axis label, (3) rotating the y-axis label to read horizontally, (4) eliminating lines in the background, and (5) adding tick marks for the y-axis.

3-43 a. The graph is a scatterplot: individual points are identified for two scale variables—academic standing and "hotness."

b. The variables are academic standing and "hotness."

c. The graph could be redesigned to get rid of moiré vibrations, such as the colored background; the grid (the background pattern of graph paper); and the duck (the woman in the background image). In addition, the scoring on the x-axis could be reversed so that 0 indicated the lowest academic score and 100 indicated the highest academic score. It's more intuitive for a low number to match a low score, and for a high number to match a high score.

3-45 Each student's advice will differ. The following is an example of advice:

Business and women: Eliminate all the pictures, including the woman, piggy banks, the dollar signs in the background, and the icons to the right (e.g., house). The two bars near the top could mislead us into thinking they indicated quantities, even though they are the same length for two different median wages. Either eliminate the bars or size them so that they are appropriate to the dollars they represent. Ideally, the two median wages would be presented in a bar graph. Eliminate unnecessary words (e.g., "The Mothers of Business Invention").

3-47 a. The graph proposes that Type I regrets of action are initially intense but decline over the years, while Type II regrets of inaction are initially mild but become more intense over the years.

b. There are two independent variables: type of regret (a nominal variable) and age (a scale variable). There is one dependent variable: intensity of regrets (also a scale variable).

c. This is a graph of a theory. No data have been collected, so there are no statistics of any kind.

d. The story that this theoretical relation suggests is that regrets over things a person has done are intense shortly after the actual behavior but decline over the years. In contrast, regrets over things a person has not done but wishes he or she had are initially low in intensity but become more intense as the years go by.

3-49 a. These data tell us that most domestic Canadian students—59%—strongly agreed or somewhat agreed that international students have improved their universities' reputations. Far fewer—15%—strongly disagreed or somewhat disagreed with this statement, and 27% reserved judgment for some reason.

b. To understand this pie chart, we have to look back and forth between the label and each "pie slice" that it describes. We then need to mentally compare the various percentages in the graph. A bar graph would allow for easier comparisons among the possible responses.

c.

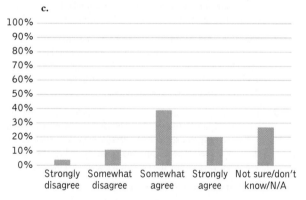

d. In this case, it makes sense to keep the possible responses in order from most negative to most positive (with the catch-all "other" category at the end). If we arranged the bars in order of height—somewhat disagree, not sure/don't know/N/A, strongly disagree, somewhat agree, and strongly agree—the story is not as easy to understand. This graph allows us to "see" that Canadian students tend to hold positive opinions toward the effect of international students on their universities' reputations.

3-51 a. The primary flaw in this graph is that it is very misleading. It looks like murders went down after "Stand Your Ground" but they actually went up. The *y*-axis is rotated 180 degrees, so that 0 is at the top of the graph, and 1000

is at the bottom of the graph where the *y*-axis intersects with the *x*-axis.

b. Answers to this question should include revising the graph so that the *y*-axis begins with 0 at the point of intersection with the *x*-axis, adding a *y*-axis label, and reducing clutter by including fewer years along the *x*-axis.

3-53 a. Using the word cloud, we can see that "social life," "activities," and "health" are three top areas perceived to be related to well-being for participants. "Social life" is the largest word, and can be interpreted as the most frequently used term. "Activities" and "health" follow as the second and third most frequently discussed areas of well-being. Older adults want to have fun in addition to being healthy.

b. Based on this word cloud, further research questions might focus on specific elements of social life, such as activities. Additionally, further research might consider the importance of health in the context of well-being for communities of older adults.

3-55 a. The independent variable is song type, with two levels: romantic song and nonromantic song.

b. The dependent variable is dating behavior.

c. This is a between-groups study because each participant is exposed to only one level or condition of the independent variable.

d. Dating behavior was operationalized by giving one's phone number to an attractive person of the opposite sex. This may not be a valid measure of dating behavior, as we do not know if the participant actually intended to go on a date with the researcher. Giving one's phone number might not necessarily indicate an intention to date.

e. We would use a bar graph because there is one nominal independent variable and one scale dependent variable.

f. The default graph will differ, depending on which software is used. Here is one example:

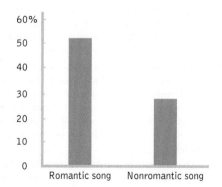

g. The default options that students choose to override will differ. Here is one example.

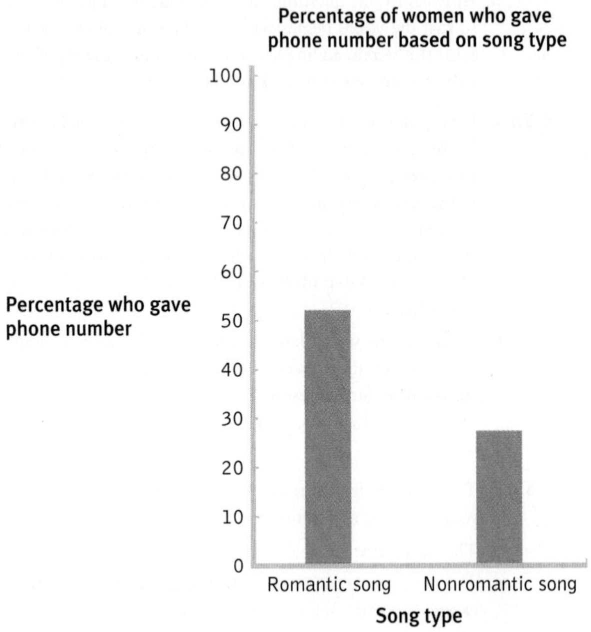

Percentage of women who gave phone number based on song type

Bar graph with y-axis labeled "Percentage who gave phone number" ranging from 0 to 100, and x-axis labeled "Song type" with categories "Romantic song" (~52%) and "Nonromantic song" (~27%).

3-57 a. (i) The independent variable was type of media with two levels, audio and film/TV show. It was operationalized based on the way in which the story was delivered. (ii) The dependent variables were all physiological measures of interest. They were operationalized as heart rate and body temperature. (iii) Because these measures were assessed over one minute for each excerpt, the best graph for these data is a time plot.

b. (i) The independent variable was country with six levels; it's clear how that would be operationalized. (ii) The dependent variable was amount of sleep, operationalized as average hours of sleep for people in each country. (iii) Because country is a nominal variable and hours of sleep is a scale variable, the best type of graph is a bar graph. Even better, a Pareto chart would allow viewers to easily determine the order among the countries in this sample.

c. (i) The independent variable was the countries' average income, operationalized by determining the GDP per person for each country. (ii) The dependent variable was happiness, operationalized as self-reported level of happiness by residents in a country. (iii) Because both GDP per person and happiness score are scale variables, the best type of graph is a scatterplot.

d. (i) The independent variable was frequency—specifically, how often the new partner sleeps over. It was operationalized as the number of nights per week or month that the partner stays the night. (ii) The dependent variable was whether the new partner should kick in for the costs of the place; it was

operationalized as yes or no, with percentages calculated for each frequency. (iii) Because participants responded across a range of time points, from once a month to six times a week, the best graph for these data is a time plot.

Chapter 4

4-1 The mean is the arithmetic average of a group of scores; it is calculated by summing all the scores and dividing by the total number of scores. The median is the middle score of all the scores when a group of scores is arranged in ascending order. If there is no single middle score, the median is the mean of the two middle scores. The mode is the most common score of all the scores in a group of scores.

4-3 The mean takes into account the actual numeric value of each score. The mean is the mathematic center of the data. It is the center balance point in the data, such that the sum of the deviations (rather than the number of deviations) below the mean equals the sum of deviations above the mean.

4-5 The mean might not be useful in a bimodal or multimodal distribution because in these distributions the mathematical center of the distribution is not the number that describes what is typical or most representative of that distribution.

4-7 The mean is affected by outliers because the numeric value of the outlier is used in the computation of the mean. The median typically is not affected by outliers because its computation is based on the data in the middle of the distribution, and outliers lie at the extremes of the distribution.

4-9 The range is the difference between the highest score and the lowest score in the data set. Thus, the range is completely driven by the most extreme scores in the data set and is susceptible to the effects of outliers. The interquartile range is based on the middle 50% of the data. Unlike the range, it is not affected by outliers.

4-11 The first quartile is the 25th percentile.

4-13 The standard deviation is the typical amount each score in a distribution varies from the mean of the distribution.

4-15 The standard deviation is a measure of variability in terms of the values of the measure used to assess the variable, whereas the variance is squared values. Squared values simply don't make intuitive sense to us, so we take the square root of the variance and report this value, the standard deviation.

4-17 a. The mean is calculated:

$$M = \frac{\Sigma X}{N} = \frac{(15 + 34 + 32 + 46 + 22 + 36 + 34 + 28 + 52 + 28)}{10}$$

$$= \frac{327}{10} = 32.70$$

The median is found by arranging the scores in numeric order—15, 22, 28, 28, 32, 34, 34, 36, 46, 52—then dividing the number of scores, 10, by 2 and adding 1/2 to get

5.5. The mean of the 5th and 6th scores in the ordered list of scores is the median—$(32 + 34)/2 = 33$—so 33 is the median.

The mode is the most common score. In these data, two scores appear twice, so we have two modes, 28 and 34.

b. Adding the value of 112 to the data changes the calculation of the mean in the following way:

$(15 + 34 + 32 + 46 + 22 + 36 + 34 + 28 + 52 + 28 + 112)/11 = 439/11 = 39.91$

The mean gets larger with this outlier.

There are now 11 data points, so the median is the 6th value in the ordered list, which is 34.

The modes are unchanged at 28 and 34.

This outlier increases the mean by approximately 7 values; it increases the median by 1; and it does not affect the mode at all.

c. The range is: $X_{highest} - X_{lowest} = 52 - 15 = 37$

The variance is: $SD^2 = \dfrac{\Sigma(X - M)^2}{N}$

We start by calculating the mean, which is 32.70. We then calculate the deviation of each score from the mean and the square of that deviation.

$$SD^2 = \frac{\Sigma(X - M)^2}{N} = \frac{1036.10}{10} = 103.61$$

X	$X - M$	$(X - M)^2$
15	−17.70	313.29
34	1.30	1.69
32	−0.70	0.49
46	13.30	176.89
22	−10.70	114.49
36	3.30	10.89
34	1.30	1.69
28	−4.70	22.09
52	19.30	372.49
28	−4.70	22.09

The standard deviation is: $SD = \sqrt{SD^2}$ or

$$SD = \sqrt{\frac{\Sigma(X - M)^2}{N}} = \sqrt{103.61} = 10.18$$

4-19 a. The mean is calculated as:

$$M = \frac{\Sigma X}{N} = \frac{[-3.7 + (-1.7) + 5.9 + 16.4 + 29.5 + \cdots + 1.7]}{12}$$

$$= \frac{244.2}{12} = 20.35°F$$

The median is found by arranging the temperatures in numeric order:

$-3.7, -1.7, 1.7, 5.9, 13.6, 16.4, 24, 29.5, 34.6, 38.5, 42.1, 43.3$

There are 12 data points, so the mean of the 6th and 7th data points gives us the median: $(16.4 + 24)/2 = 20.20°F$.

b. The mean is calculated as:

$$M = \frac{\Sigma X}{N} = \frac{[47 + (-46) + (-38) + (-20) + \cdots + 46]}{12}$$

$$= \frac{-163}{12} = -13.58°F$$

The median is found by arranging the temperatures in numeric order:

$-47, -46, -46, -38, -20, -20, -5, -2, 8, 9, 20, 24$

There are 12 data points, so the mean of the 6th and 7th data points gives us the median: $[-20 + (-5)]/2 = -25/2 = -12.50°F$.

There are two modes: both −46 and −20 were recorded twice.

c. The mean is calculated as:

$$M = \frac{\Sigma X}{N} = \frac{[173 + 166 + 180 + \cdots + 178]}{12} = \frac{2022}{12}$$

$$= 168.50 \text{ mph}$$

The median is found by arranging the wind gusts in numeric order:

136, 142, 154, 161, 163, 164, 166, 173, 174, 178, 180, 231

There are 12 data points, so the mean of the 6th and 7th data points gives us the median: $(164 + 166)/2 = 165$ mph.

There is no mode among these wind gusts.

d. For the wind-gust data, we could create 10 mph intervals and calculate the mode as the interval that occurs most often. There are four recorded gusts in the $160 - 169$ mph interval, three in the $170 - 179$ interval, and only one in the other intervals. So, the $160 - 169$ mph interval could be presented as the mode.

e. The range is: $X_{highest} - X_{lowest} = 43.3 - (-3.7) = 47°F$

The variance is: $SD^2 = \dfrac{\Sigma(X - M)^2}{N}$

X	$X - M$	$(X - M)^2$
−3.7	−24.05	578.403
−1.7	−22.05	486.203
5.9	−14.45	208.803
16.4	−3.95	15.603
29.5	9.15	83.723
38.5	18.15	329.423
43.3	22.95	526.703
42.1	21.75	473.063
34.6	14.25	203.063
24	3.65	13.323
13.6	−6.75	45.563
1.7	−18.65	347.823

We start by calculating the mean, which is 20.35°F. We then calculate the deviation of each score from the mean and the square of that deviation.

The variance is: $SD^2 = \dfrac{\Sigma(X - M)^2}{N} = \dfrac{3311.696}{12} = 275.975$

The standard deviation is: $SD = \sqrt{SD^2}$ or

$SD = \sqrt{\dfrac{\Sigma(X - M)^2}{N}} = \sqrt{275.975} = 16.61°F$

f. The range is $X_{highest} - X_{lowest} = 24 - (-47) = 71°F$

The variance is: $SD^2 = \dfrac{\Sigma(X - M)^2}{N}$

We already calculated the mean, −13.583°F. We now calculate the deviation of each score from the mean and the square of that deviation.

The variance is: $SD^2 = \dfrac{\Sigma(X - M)^2}{N} = \dfrac{7620.018}{12}$

$= 635.077$

X	X − M	(X − M)²
−47	−33.417	1116.696
−46	−32.417	1050.862
−38	−24.417	596.190
−20	−6.417	41.178
−2	11.583	134.166
8	21.583	465.826
24	37.583	1412.482
20	33.583	1127.818
9	22.583	509.992
−5	8.583	73.668
−20	−6.417	41.178
−46	−32.417	1050.862

The standard deviation is: $SD = \sqrt{SD^2}$ or

$SD = \sqrt{\dfrac{\Sigma(X - M)^2}{N}} = \sqrt{635.077} = 25.20°F$

g. For the peak wind-gust data, the range is $X_{highest} - X_{lowest} = 231 - 136 = 95$ mph

The variance is: $SD^2 = \dfrac{\Sigma(X - M)^2}{N}$

We start by calculating the mean, which is 168.50 mph. We then calculate the deviation of each score from the mean and the square of that deviation.

X	X − M	(X − M)²
173	4.50	20.25
166	−2.50	6.25
180	11.50	132.25
231	62.50	3906.25
164	−4.50	20.25
136	−32.50	1056.25
154	−14.50	210.25
142	−26.50	702.25
174	5.50	30.25
161	−7.50	56.25
163	−5.50	30.25
178	9.50	90.25

The variance is: $SD^2 = \dfrac{\Sigma(X - M)^2}{N} = \dfrac{6261}{12} = 521.75$

The standard deviation is: $SD = \sqrt{SD^2}$ or

$SD = \sqrt{\dfrac{\Sigma(X - M)^2}{N}} = \sqrt{520.75} = 22.82$ mph

4-21 Calculating the interquartile range requires that we order the observations from lowest to highest, find the first and third quartiles, and subtract the first from the third. Here are the data sorted from lowest to highest:

1 1 1 2 2 2 2 3 3 3 3 3 3 4 4 5 6 7 7 8 12

Q1 is the median of the first half of the observations, which is 2. Q3 is the median of the second half of the observations, which is 5.50. The $IQR = Q3 - Q1$, or $IQR = 5.50 - 2 = 3.50$.

4-23 The interquartile range of 18.50 is so much smaller than the range of 95 because there is an outlier of 231 mph in the wind-gust data. This outlier affects the range but not the interquartile range.

4-25 The mean for salary is often greater than the median for salary because the high salaries of top management inflate the mean but not the median. If we are trying to attract people to our company, we may want to present the typical salary as whichever value is higher—in most cases, the mean. However, if we are going to offer someone a low salary, presenting the median might make them feel better about that amount!

4-27 There are few participants in this study (only seven) so a single extreme score would influence the mean more than it would influence the median. The median is a more trustworthy indicator than the mean when there is only a handful of scores.

4-29 In April 1934, a wind gust of 231 mph was recorded. This data point is rather far from the next closest record of 180 mph. If this extreme score were excluded from analyses of central tendency, the mean would be lower, the median would change only slightly, and the mode would be unaffected.

4-31 There are many possible answers to this question. All answers will include a distribution that is skewed, perhaps one that has outliers. A skewed distribution would affect the mean but not the median. One example would be the variable of number of foreign countries visited; the few jet-setters who have been to many countries would pull the mean higher. The median is more representative of the typical score.

4-33 a. These ads are likely presenting outlier data.

 b. To capture the experience of the typical individual who uses the product, the ad could include the mean result and the standard deviation. If the distribution of outcomes is skewed, it would be best to present the median result.

4-35 a. $M = \dfrac{\Sigma X}{N} = \dfrac{(0 + 5 + 3 \cdots + 5)}{19} = \dfrac{53}{19} = 2.789$

 b. The formula for variance is $SD^2 = \dfrac{\Sigma(X - M)^2}{N}$

 We start by creating three columns: one for the scores, one for the deviations of the scores from the mean, and one for the squares of the deviations.

 We can now calculate variance:

$SD^2 = \dfrac{\Sigma(X - M)^2}{N}$

$= \dfrac{(7.779 + 4.889 + 0.045 + 0.045 + \cdots + 0.045 + 4.889)}{19}$

$= \dfrac{91.167}{19} = 4.798$

X	X − M	(X − M)²
0	−2.789	7.779
5	2.211	4.889
3	0.211	0.045
3	0.211	0.045
1	−1.789	3.201
10	7.211	51.999
2	−0.789	0.623
2	−0.789	0.623
3	0.211	0.045
1	−1.789	3.201
2	−0.789	0.623
4	1.211	1.467

(Table continued)

X	X − M	(X − M)²
2	−0.789	0.623
1	−0.789	3.201
1	−0.789	3.201
1	−0.789	3.201
4	1.211	1.467
3	0.211	0.045
5	2.211	4.889

 c. We calculate standard deviation the same way we calculate variance, but we then take the square root:

$SD = \sqrt{\dfrac{\Sigma(X - M)^2}{N}} = \sqrt{4.798} = 2.19$

 d. The typical score is around 2.79, and the typical deviation from 2.79 is around 2.19.

4-37 There are many possible answers to these questions. The following are only examples.

 a. 70, 70. There is no skew; the mean is not pulled away from the median.

 b. 80, 70. There is positive skew; the mean is pulled up, but the median is unaffected.

 c. 60, 70. There is negative skew; the mean is pulled down, but the median is unaffected.

4-39 a. Because the policy for which violations were issued changed during this time frame, we cannot make accurate comparisons before and after Hurricane Sandy. The conditions for issuing violations were not constant; thus, the policy change would be a likely explanation for a change in the data.

 b. The removal of violations in Zone A, which appears to have been most affected by infestations after the hurricane, would result in eliminating an otherwise extreme number, or outlier, of issued violations. This would lead to inaccurate data as it does not accurately portray the number of rat violations, only the number of rat violations issued under the current policy.

4-41 It would probably be appropriate to use the mean because the data are scale; we would assume we have a large number of data points available to us; and the mean is the most commonly used measure of central tendency. Because of the large amount of data available, the effect of outliers is minimized. All of these factors would support the use of the mean for presenting information about the heights or weights of large numbers of people.

4-43 We cannot directly compare the mean ages reported by Canada with the median ages reported by the United States because it is likely that there were some older outliers in both Canada and the United States, and these outliers would affect the means reported by Canada much more than they would affect the medians reported by the United States.

4-45 a. The researchers reported an increase in early literacy among students in the intervention group (those whose parents received the text messages) as compared with the students who were not in the intervention group (those whose parents did *not* receive texts). The intervention seemed to work. That is, those in the intervention group as a whole ended up higher in literacy skills as compared with the mean for the nonintervention group. The increase was between 0.21 and 0.34 deviations. We know that the standard deviation indicates the difference of a typical student from the mean. So, the shift for the group as a whole is *not* as big as the amount that the typical student differs from the mean. It's just part of a standard deviation.

b. The researchers used a between-groups design because each student could only be in one group—either the group in which parents received the text messages or the group in which the parents did not receive the text messages.

4-47 a.

Interval	Frequency
60–69	1
50–59	5
40–49	9
30–39	5
20–29	8
10–19	2

b.

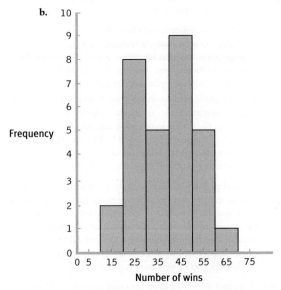

c. $M = \dfrac{\Sigma X}{N} = \dfrac{[60 + 44 + 39 + 29 + \cdots + 23]}{30}$

$= \dfrac{1144}{30} = 38.133$

With 30 scores, the median would be between the 15th and 16th scores: $(30/2) + 0.5 + 15.5$. The 15th and 16th scores are 39 and 40, respectively, so the median is 39.50. The mode is 29; there are three scores of 29.

d. Software reports that the range is 42 and the standard deviation is 11.59.

e. The summary will differ for each student but should include the following information: The data appear to be roughly symmetric and unimodal, maybe a bit negatively skewed. There are no glaring outliers.

f. Answers will vary. One example is whether number of wins is related to the average age of a team's players.

Chapter 5

5-1 It is rare to have access to an entire population. That is why we study samples and use inferential statistics to estimate what is happening in the population.

5-3 Generalizability refers to the ability of researchers to apply findings from one sample or in one context to other samples or contexts.

5-5 Crowdsourcing in research is the process of collecting data by recruiting a very large group of people, often online.

5-7 Random sampling means that every member of a population has an equal chance of being selected to participate in a study. Random assignment means that each selected participant has an equal chance of being in any of the experimental conditions.

5-9 Random assignment is a process in which all participants (regardless of how they were selected) have an equal chance of being in any of the experimental conditions. This avoids bias across experimental conditions.

5-11 An illusory correlation is a belief that two events are associated when in fact they are not.

5-13 Students' answers will vary. Personal probability is a person's belief about the probability of an event occurring: for example, someone's belief about the likelihood that she or he will complete a particular task.

5-15 In reference to probability, the term *trial* refers to each occasion that a given procedure is carried out. For example, each time we flip a coin, it is a trial. *Outcome* refers to the result of a trial. For coin-flip trials, the outcome is either heads or tails. *Success* refers to the outcome for which we're trying to determine the probability. If we are testing for the probability of heads, then success is heads.

5-17 The independent variable is the variable the researcher manipulates. Independent trials or events are those that do not affect each other; the flip of a coin is independent of another flip of a coin because the two events do not affect each other.

5-19 A null hypothesis is a statement that postulates that there is no mean difference between populations or that the mean difference is in a direction opposite of that anticipated by the researcher. A research hypothesis, also called an alternative hypothesis, is a statement that postulates that there is a mean difference between populations or sometimes, more specifically, that there is a mean difference in a certain direction, positive or negative.

5-21 We commit a Type I error when we reject the null hypothesis but the null hypothesis is true. We commit a Type II error when we fail to reject the null hypothesis but the null hypothesis is false.

5-23 The lists will be different for each student. Each student generates a list of six numbers by telling the site they want a list of 6 numbers that range from 1 to 10. They would instruct the program that the numbers should not remain unique and should not be sorted. One possible outcome is that in each of the six groups of 10 passengers that go through the checkpoint, we would check the ninth, ninth, tenth, first, tenth, and eighth passengers, respectively.

5-25 The lists will be different for each student. Each student generates a list of 7 numbers by telling the site they want a list of 7 numbers that range from 1 to 5. They would instruct the program that the numbers should not remain unique and should not be sorted. Here's one example of what the output could look like: 5, 3, 5, 5, 2, 2, and 2. So, the first person is assigned to the fifth condition, the second person to the third condition, and so on.

5-27 Illusory correlation is particularly dangerous because people might perceive there to be an association between two variables that does not in fact exist. Because we often make decisions based on associations, it is important that those associations be real and be based on objective evidence. For example, a parent might perceive an illusory correlation between body piercings and trustworthiness, believing that a person with a large number of body piercings is untrustworthy. This illusory correlation might lead the parent to unfairly eliminate anyone with a body piercing from consideration when choosing babysitters.

5-29 The probability of winning is estimated as the number of people who have already won out of the total number of contestants, or $8/266 = 0.03$.

5-31 **a.** 0.627

  b. 0.003

  c. 0.042

5-33 **a.** Expected relative-frequency probability

  b. Personal probability

  c. Personal probability

  d. Expected relative-frequency probability

5-35 Most of us believe we can think randomly. However, it is extremely difficult for us to come up with a string of four numbers in which we determined each of the numbers completely independently. We may choose numbers with some

meaning for us, perhaps without even realizing we are doing so. We also tend to consider the previous numbers when we come up with each new one. As the BBC article reported, people are lazy when it comes to choosing PINs and passwords. "They use birthdays, wedding days, the names of siblings or children or pets. They use their house number, street name or pick on a favourite pop star" (Ward, 2013). So, the best advice would be to let a random numbers table choose your PIN.

5-37 **a.** The independent variable is type of news information, with two levels: information about an improving job market and information about a declining job market.

  b. The dependent variable is psychologists' attitudes toward their careers.

  c. The null hypothesis would be that, on average, the psychologists who received the positive article about the job market have the same attitude toward their career as those who read a negative article about the job market. The research hypothesis would be that a difference, on average, exists between the two groups.

5-39 Although we all believe we can think randomly if we want to, we do not, in fact, generate numbers independently of the ones that came before. We tend to glance at the preceding numbers in an effort to make the next ones "random." Yet once we do this, the numbers are not independent and therefore are not random. Moreover, even if we can keep ourselves from looking at the previous numbers, the numbers we generate are not likely to be random. For example, if we were born on the sixth of the month, then we may be more likely to choose 6's than other digits. Humans just don't think randomly.

5-41 **a.** The researchers are using crowdsourcing, a technique in which many participants are recruited, usually online. This is a form of a volunteer sample.

  b. The main benefit here is the ability to collect data more quickly than usual.

  c. One ethical problem might be the compensation that participants receive. In this case, participants play Mozak for free, earning only points and levels.

5-43 **a.** It is unlikely the journalist's results would be representative of the U.S. population. Instead, participants who complete the survey are more likely to be representative of people who subscribe to or frequently read the Gizmodo blog *Throb*. This sample would likely include only people who use the Internet and read this specific blog. Not everyone in the U.S. population uses the Internet and reads the blog *Throb*.

  b. Those most likely to volunteer are those who have stumbled across, or searched for, this particular blog.

  c. The journalist's perspective seems to be that teens primarily either are misinformed or have incorrect information about sex. However, her interpretation of the forums she reviewed could be framed as a positive opportunity where misinformation about sex is discussed and corrected. Additionally, it is possible that teenagers who are well informed about sex do not frequent online forums about sex. Her perspective—that most teenagers are misinformed about sex—might attract readers who are actively seeking out clarifications about sex using the Internet and ultimately reading her contributions to the blog *Throb*. But inviting people to participate in this manner often leads to a confirmation bias in research. This method of sampling involves convenience and volunteer sampling (as opposed to random sampling), where the sample is likely to reflect a specific population of individuals who read the blog *Throb*, which endorses a specific perspective about teenagers' knowledge about sex.

d. It does not matter how large a sample is if it is not representative. With respect to external validity, it would be far preferable to have a smaller but representative sample than a very large but unrepresentative sample.

5-45 If a depressed person has negative thoughts about himself or herself and about the world, confirmation bias may make it difficult to change those thoughts because confirmation bias would lead this person to pay more attention to and better remember negative events than positive events. For example, he or she might remember the one friend who slighted him or her at a party but not the many friends who were excited to see him or her.

5-47 a. *Probability* refers to the proportion of Waldos that we expect to see in these two 1.5-inch bands in the long run. In the long run, given 53% of Waldos falling in these bands, we would expect the proportion of Waldos to be 0.53.

b. *Proportion* refers to the observed fraction of Waldos in these bands—the number of successes (Waldo in one of these bands) divided by the number of trials (total Waldo illustrations used). In this case, the proportion of Waldos in one of these bands is 0.53.

c. *Percentage* refers to the proportion multiplied by 100: $0.53(100) = 53\%$, as reported by Blatt in this case. The media often report percentage versions of probabilities.

d. Although it is improbable that this pattern would occur just by chance, Blatt did not analyze every *Where's Waldo?* illustration that exists. It does seem that this is more than coincidence, but we might expect a fluctuation in the short run. We can't know for certain that the *Where's Waldo?* game has a bias.

5-49 These polls could be considered independent trials if they were conducted for each state individually, and if the state currently being polled did not have any information about the polling results from other states. However, these are not truly independent trials, as state-by-state polls are often presented in the media as they take place, thus potentially influencing voters in states that have not yet been polled.

5-51 a. The null hypothesis is that the average tendency to develop false memories is either unchanged or is lowered by the repetition of false information. The research hypothesis is that false memories are higher, on average, when false information is repeated than when it is not.

b. The null hypothesis is that the average outcome is the same or worse whether or not structured assessments are used. The research hypothesis is that the average outcome is better when structured assessments are used than when they are not used.

c. The null hypothesis is that average employee morale is the same whether employees work in enclosed offices or in cubicles. The research hypothesis is that average employee morale is different when employees work in enclosed offices versus in cubicles.

d. The null hypothesis is that ability to speak one's native language is the same, on average, whether or not a second language is taught from birth. The research hypothesis is that the ability to speak one's native language is different, on average, when a second language is taught from birth than when no second language is taught.

5-53 a. If this conclusion is incorrect, the researcher has made a Type I error. The researcher rejected the null hypothesis when the null hypothesis is really true. (Of course, he or she never knows whether there has been an error! She or he just has to acknowledge the possibility.)

b. If this conclusion is incorrect, the researcher has made a Type I error. She has rejected the null hypothesis when the null hypothesis is really true.

c. If this conclusion is incorrect, the researcher has made a Type II error. He has failed to reject the null hypothesis when the null hypothesis is not true.

d. If this conclusion is incorrect, the researcher has made a Type II error. She has failed to reject the null hypothesis when the null hypothesis is not true.

5-55 a. Confirmation bias has guided his logic in that he looked for specific events that occurred during the day to fit the horoscope but ignored the events that did not fit the prediction.

b. If this conclusion is incorrect, they have made a Type I error. Dean and Kelly would have failed to reject the null hypothesis when the null hypothesis is not true.

c. If an event occurs regularly or a research finding is replicated many times and by other researchers and in a range of contexts, then it is likely the event or finding is not occurring in error or by chance alone.

5-57 a. The population in which you would be interested is all people who already had read *Harry Potter and the Half-Blood Prince*.

b. The sample would be just bel 78. It is dangerous to rely on just one review, bel 78's testimonial. She clearly felt strongly about the book if she spent the time to post her review. She is not likely to be representative of the typical reader of this book.

c. This is a large sample, but it is not likely representative of those who had read this book. Not only does this sample consist solely of Amazon users, but it consists of readers who chose to post a review. It is likely that those who took the time to write and post a review were those who felt more strongly about the book than did the typical reader.

d. In this case, the population of interest would be all Amazon users who had read this book. We would need Amazon to generate a list of everyone who bought the book (something that the company would not do because of ethical considerations), and we would have to randomly select a sample from this population. We would then have to identify the people who actually read the book (who may not be the buyers) and elicit the ratings from the randomly selected sample.

e. We could explain that testimonials are typically written by those who feel most strongly about a book. The sample of reviewers, therefore, is unlikely to be representative of the population of readers.

5-59 a. The population of interest is male students with alcohol problems. The sample is the 64 students who were ordered to meet with a school counselor.

b. Random selection was not used. The sample comprised 64 male students who had been ordered to meet with a school counselor; they were not chosen out of all male students with alcohol problems.

c. Random assignment was used. Each participant had an equal chance of being assigned to either of the two conditions.

d. The independent variable is type of counseling. It has two levels: BMI and AE. The dependent variable is number of alcohol-related problems at follow-up.

e. The null hypothesis is that the mean number of alcohol-related problems at follow-up is the same, regardless of type of counseling (BMI or AE). The research hypothesis is that students who undergo a BMI have different mean numbers of alcohol-related problems at follow-up than do students who participate in AE.

f. The researchers rejected the null hypothesis.

g. If the researchers were incorrect in their decision, then they made a Type I error, rejecting the null hypothesis when the null hypothesis is true. The consequences of this type of error are that a new treatment that is no better, on average, than the standard treatment would be implemented. This might lead to unnecessary costs to train counselors to implement the new treatment.

5-61 a. First, the researchers are making their data available online. This is an ethical practice because it allows other researchers to check their statistical analyses and make sure they didn't cut corners to get the statistical result they desired. Second, the researchers preregistered their hypothesis, statistical analyses, and sample size. This is an ethical practice because it means that they cannot vary these procedures after the fact to find the results they desired.

b. HARKing stands for "hypothesizing after the results are known." Researchers who HARK wait to see their results, and then work backward, developing hypotheses that fit what they found, rather than discussing their findings in light of what they actually hypothesized. Because the researchers preregistered their hypotheses, they cannot later change them, and therefore cannot HARK.

c. Mechanical Turk (MTurk for short) is a service provided by Amazon that allows researchers to quickly collect data from many, many participants. This form of data collection is called crowdsourcing and is a form of a volunteer sample.

d. The benefits of crowdsourcing include speedy data collection and the opportunity to have a more representative sample than the typical sample of undergraduate university students that many researchers use.

e. One of the drawbacks of crowdsourcing is the main flaw that accompanies any volunteer sample—that is, it might not be a representative sample. A second drawback is the possibility of fraud; bots (automatic software) may be responding instead of actual people. A third drawback is an ethical one: Are the participants earning a fair amount of money for the work that they're doing?

Chapter 6

6-1 In everyday conversation, the word *normal* is used to refer to events or objects that are common or that typically occur. Statisticians use the word to refer to distributions that conform to a specific bell-shaped curve, with a peak in the middle where most of the observations lie, and symmetric areas underneath the curve on either side of the midpoint. This normal curve represents the pattern of occurrence of many different kinds of events.

6-3 The distribution of sample scores approaches normal as the sample size increases, assuming the population is normally distributed.

6-5 A z score is a way to standardize data; it expresses how far a data point is from the mean of its distribution in terms of standard deviations.

6-7 The mean is 0 and the standard deviation is 1.0.

6-9 The symbol μ_M stands for the mean of the distribution of means. The μ indicates that it is the mean of a *population*, and the subscript M indicates that the population is composed of *sample means*—the means of all possible samples of a given size from a particular population of individual scores.

6-11 Standard deviation is the measure of spread for a distribution of scores in a single sample or in a population of scores. Standard error is the standard deviation (or measure of spread) in a distribution of means of all possible samples of a given size from a particular population of individual scores.

6-13 The z statistic tells us how many standard errors a sample mean is from the population mean.

6-15 a.

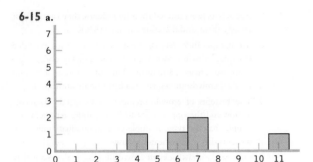

b.

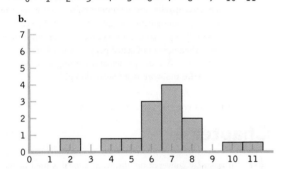

c.

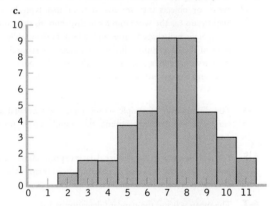

d. As the sample size increases, the distribution approaches the shape of the normal curve.

6-17 a. $z = \dfrac{(X - \mu)}{\sigma} = \dfrac{1000 - 1179}{164} = -1.09$

b. $z = \dfrac{721 - 1179}{164} = -2.79$

c. $z = \dfrac{1531 - 1179}{164} = 2.15$

d. $z = \dfrac{1184 - 1179}{164} = 0.03$

6-19 $z = \dfrac{203 - 250}{47} = -1.0$

$z = \dfrac{(297 - 250)}{47} = 1.0$

Each of these scores is 47 points away from the mean, which is the value of the standard deviation. The z scores of -1.0 and 1.0 express that the first score, 203, is 1 standard deviation below the mean, whereas the other score, 297, is 1 standard deviation above the mean.

6-21 a. $X = z(\sigma) + \mu = -0.23(164) + 1179 = 1141.28$

b. $X = 1.41(164) + 1179 = 1410.24$

c. $X = 2.06(164) + 1179 = 1516.84$

d. $X = 0.03(164) + 1179 = 1183.92$

6-23 a. $X = z(\sigma) + \mu = 1.5(100) + 500 = 650$

b. $X = z(\sigma) + \mu = -0.5(100) + 500 = 450$

c. $X = z(\sigma) + \mu = -2.0(100) + 500 = 300$

6-25 a. $z = \dfrac{45 - 51}{4} = -1.5$

$z = \dfrac{732 - 765}{23} = -1.43$

b. Both of these scores fall below the means of their distributions, resulting in negative z scores. One score (45) is a little farther below its mean than the other (732).

6-27 a. 50%

b. 82% (34 + 34 + 14)

c. 4% (2 + 2)

d. 48% (34 + 14)

e. 100% or nearly 100%

6-29 a. $\mu_M = \mu = 55$, and $\sigma_M = \dfrac{8}{\sqrt{30}} = 1.46$

b. $\mu_M = \mu = 55$, and $\sigma_M = \dfrac{8}{\sqrt{300}} = 0.46$

c. $\mu_M = \mu = 55$, and $\sigma_M = \dfrac{8}{\sqrt{3000}} = 0.15$

6-31 a. $z = \dfrac{(M - \mu_M)}{\frac{\sigma}{\sqrt{N}}} = \dfrac{85 - 80}{\frac{20}{\sqrt{100}}} = \dfrac{5}{\frac{20}{10}} = \dfrac{5}{2} = 2.50$

$z = \dfrac{(M - \mu_M)}{\frac{\sigma}{\sqrt{N}}} = \dfrac{17 - 15}{\frac{5}{\sqrt{100}}} = \dfrac{2}{\frac{5}{10}} = \dfrac{2}{0.50} = 4.00$

b. The first sample had a mean that was 2.50 standard deviations above the population mean, whereas the second sample had a mean that was 4 standard deviations above the mean. Compared to the population mean (as measured by this scale), both samples are extreme scores; however, a z score of 4.0 is even more extreme than a z score of 2.5.

6-33 a. Histogram for the 10 scores:

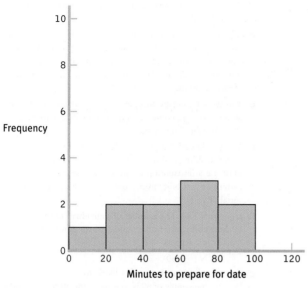

Minutes to prepare for date

b. Histogram for the 40 scores:

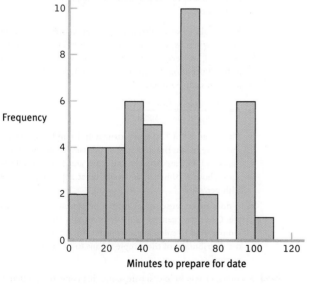

Minutes to prepare for date

c. The shape of the distribution became more normal as the number of scores increased. If we added more scores, the distribution would become more and more normal. This happens because many physical, psychological, and behavioral variables are normally distributed. With smaller samples, this might not be clear. But as the sample size approaches the size of the population, the shape of the sample distribution approaches that of the population.

d. These are distributions of scores, as each individual score is represented in the histograms on its own, not as part of a mean.

e. There are several possible answers to this question. For example, instead of using retrospective self-reports, we could have had students send a text message as they began to get ready; they would then have sent another text when they were ready. This would have led to scores that would be closer to the actual time it took the students to get ready.

f. There are several possible answers to this question. For example, we could examine whether there was a mean gender difference in time spent getting ready for a date.

6-35 a. The mean of the z distribution is always 0.

b. $z = \dfrac{(X - \mu)}{\sigma} = \dfrac{(6.65 - 6.65)}{1.24} = 0$

c. The standard deviation of the z distribution is always 1.

d. A student who is 1 standard deviation above the mean would have a score of $6.65 + 1.24 = 7.89$. This person's z score would be: $z = \dfrac{(X - \mu)}{\sigma} = \dfrac{(7.89 - 6.65)}{1.24} = 1$

e. The answer will differ for each student but will involve substituting one's own score for X in this equation:

$$z = \dfrac{(X - 6.65)}{1.24}$$

6-37 a. It would not make sense to compare the mean of this sample to the distribution of individual scores because, in a sample of means, the occasional extreme individual score is balanced by less extreme scores that are also part of the sample. Thus, there is less variability.

b. The null hypothesis would state that the population from which the sample was drawn has a mean of 3.20. The research hypothesis would state that the mean for the population from which our sample was drawn is not 3.20.

c. $\mu_M = \mu = 3.20$

$$\sigma_M = \dfrac{\sigma}{\sqrt{N}} = \dfrac{0.70}{\sqrt{40}} = 0.111$$

d. $z = \dfrac{(M - \mu_M)}{\sigma_M} = \dfrac{(3.62 - 3.20)}{0.111} = 3.78$

6-39 a. Yes, the distribution of the number of movies college students watch in a year would likely approximate a normal curve. You can imagine that a small number of students watch an enormous number of movies and that a small number watch very few but that most watch a moderate number of movies between these two extremes.

b. Yes, the number of full-page advertisements in magazines is likely to approximate a normal curve. We could find magazines that have no or just one or two full-page advertisements and some that are chock-full of them, but most magazines have some intermediate number of full-page advertisements.

c. Yes, human birth weights in Canada could be expected to approximate a normal curve. Few infants would weigh in at the extremes of very light or very heavy, and the weight of most infants would cluster around some intermediate value.

6-41 Household income is positively skewed. Most households cluster around a relatively low central tendency, but the 1-percenters—the Mark Zuckerbergs and Lady Gagas of the world—pull the tail of the distribution in a positive direction.

6-43 a. $z = \dfrac{(X - \mu)}{\sigma} = \dfrac{(94.00 - 81.00)}{11.733} = 1.11$

b. $z = \dfrac{(X - \mu)}{\sigma} = \dfrac{(13.00 - 7.969)}{3.036} = 1.66$

c. According to these data, the Falcons had a better regular season (they had a higher z score) than did the Braves.

d. The Braves would have had to have won 101 regular season games to have a slightly higher z score than the Falcons:

$z = \dfrac{(X - \mu)}{\sigma} = \dfrac{(101.00 - 81.00)}{11.733} = 1.70$

e. There are several possible answers to this question. For example, we could have summed the teams' scores for every game (as compared to other teams' scores within their leagues).

6-45 a. $X = z(\sigma) + \mu = -1.705(11.733) + 81.00 = 61$ games (rounded to a whole number)

b. $X = z(\sigma) + \mu = -0.319(3.036) + 7.969 = 7$ games (rounded to a whole number)

c. Fifty percent of scores fall below the mean, so 34% $(84 - 50 = 34)$ fall between the mean and the Colts' score. We know that 34% of scores fall between the mean and a z score of 1.0, so the Colts have a z score of 1.0. $X = z(\sigma) + \mu = 1(3.036) + 7.969 = 11$ games (rounded to a whole number).

d. We can examine our answers to be sure that negative z scores match up with answers that are below the mean and positive z scores match up with answers that are above the mean.

6-47 a. $\mu = 50$; $\sigma = 10$

b. $\mu_M = \mu = 50$; $\sigma_M = \dfrac{\sigma}{\sqrt{N}} = \dfrac{10}{\sqrt{95}} = 1.03$

c. When we calculate the mean of the scores for 95 individuals, the most extreme MMPI-2 depression scores will likely be balanced by scores toward the middle. It would be rare to have an extreme mean of the scores for 95 individuals. Thus, the spread is smaller than is the spread for all of the individual MMPI-2 depression scores.

6-49 a. These are the data for a distribution of scores rather than means because they have been obtained by entering each individual score into the analysis.

b. Comparing the sizes of the mean and the standard deviation suggests that there is positive skew. A person can't have

fewer than zero friends, so the distribution would have to extend in a positive direction to have a standard deviation larger than the mean.

c. Because the mean is larger than either the median or the mode, it suggests that the distribution is positively skewed. There are extreme scores in the positive end of the distribution that are causing the mean to be more extreme than the median or mode.

d. You would compare this person to a distribution of scores. When making a comparison of an individual score, we must use a distribution of scores.

e. You would compare this sample to a distribution of means. When making a comparison involving a sample mean, we must use a distribution of means because it has a different pattern of variability from a distribution of scores (it has less variability).

f. $\mu_M = \mu = 7.44$. The number of individuals in the sample is 80. Substituting 80 in the standard error equation yields

$\sigma_M = \dfrac{\sigma}{\sqrt{N}} = \dfrac{10.98}{\sqrt{80}} = 1.23$

g. The distribution of means is likely to be a normal curve. Because the sample of 80 is well above the 30 recommended to see the central limit theorem at work, we expect that the distribution of the sample means will approximate a normal distribution.

6-51 a. You would compare this sample mean to a distribution of means. When we are making a comparison involving a sample mean, we need to use a distribution of means because it is this distribution that indicates the variability we are likely to see in sample means.

b. $z = \dfrac{(M - \mu_M)}{\sigma_M} = \dfrac{(8.7 - 7.44)}{1.228} = 1.03$

This z statistic of 1.03 is approximately 1 standard deviation above the mean. Because 50% of the sample are below the mean and 34% are between the mean and 1 standard deviation above it, this sample would be at approximately the 84th percentile.

c. It does make sense to calculate a percentile for this sample. Given the central limit theorem and the size of the sample used to calculate the mean (80), we would expect the distribution of the sample means to be approximately normal.

6-53 z scores can help us to compare scores that come from different distributions. In this example, the number of heart surgeries conducted per doctor might have a different distribution compared to the number of hip surgeries conducted per doctor. By converting raw scores (i.e., number of surgeries for each doctor) in each distribution to a z score, we can see if this specific cardiologist is particularly high on the national distribution for numbers of heart surgeries and compare this to the level of hip surgeries in Munster with respect to the national distribution for numbers of hip surgeries.

6-55 a. The population is all patients treated for blocked coronary arteries in the United States. The sample is Medicare patients in Elyria, Ohio, who received angioplasty.

b. Medicare and the commercial insurer compared the angioplasty rate in Elyria to that in other towns. Given that the rate was so far above that of other towns, they decided that such a high angioplasty rate was unlikely to happen just by chance. Thus, they used probability to make a decision to investigate.

c. Medicare and the commercial insurer could look at the z distribution of angioplasty rates in cities from all over the country. Locating the rate of Elyria within that distribution would indicate exactly how extreme or unlikely its angioplasty rates are.

d. The error made would be a Type I error, as they would be rejecting the null hypothesis that there is no difference among the various towns in rates of angioplasty, and concluding that there is a difference, when there really is no difference.

e. Elyria's extremely high rates do not necessarily mean the doctors are committing fraud. One could imagine that an area with a population composed mostly of retirees (that is, more elderly people) would have a higher rate of angioplasty. Conversely, perhaps Elyria has a talented set of surgeons who are renowned for their angioplasty skills and people from all over the country come there to have angioplasty.

6-57 a. The researchers are operationally defining cheating as the change in standardized test score for a given classroom. This variable is a scale variable.

b. Researchers could establish a cutoff z statistic at which those who had a mean change larger than that z statistic would be considered "suspicious." For example, a classroom with a z statistic of 2 or more may have cheated on this year's test.

c. A histogram would provide an easy visual to see where a given classroom falls on the distribution. A researcher could even draw lines indicating the cutoffs and see which classrooms fall beyond them.

d. They would be committing a Type I error, because they would be rejecting the null hypothesis that there is no difference in a classroom's test scores from one year to the next when there really is no difference and they should have failed to reject the null hypothesis.

6-59 a. This graph is closest to a histogram because it gives frequencies for a range of scores.

b. The graph is like a normal curve in that it is symmetric, unimodal, and bell-shaped for the most part. There is skew, however, in that there is a tail to the left representing those players who win the game in extremely fast times. This skew represents negative skew because the tail is to the left of the curve.

c. Outliers are extreme scores that are either very high or very low in comparison with the rest of the scores in the sample.

d. The interquartile range is a measure of the distance between the first and third quartiles—that is, the data that fall between the 25th percentile and the 75th percentile. They may have identified outliers as those that fell below the 25th percentile or above the 75th percentile. In this case, cheaters would have particularly fast scores, so researchers would be interested in those below the 25th percentile.

e. This would have been a crowdsourced sample. A crowdsourced sample is one that is recruited from a very large group of people, usually online.

f. The researchers could create a curve of all difference scores. Noncheaters would be at or close to 0 because there should be no difference between the times on their computers and the times on the servers. Those who cheated would be those in the tails of the distribution, as their computer times would be much slower or much faster than the server time.

g. Race time in seconds is a ratio variable because it has numbers as its values, the distance between pairs of consecutive numbers is assumed to be equal, and zero is meaningful when it comes to time. Ratio variables, along with interval variables, are often referred to as scale variables. Type of game is a nominal variable because it has categories—play against others versus play against computer—as its values.

Chapter 7

7-1 A percentile is the percentage of scores that fall below a certain point on a distribution.

7-3 We add the percentage between the mean and the positive z score to 50%, which is the percentage of scores below the mean (50% of scores are on each side of the mean).

7-5 In statistics, *assumptions* are the characteristics we ideally require the population from which we are sampling to have so that we can make accurate inferences.

7-7 *Parametric tests* are statistical analyses based on a set of assumptions about the population. By contrast, *nonparametric tests* are statistical analyses that are not based on assumptions about the population.

7-9 *Critical values*, often simply called *cutoffs*, are the test statistic values beyond which we reject the null hypothesis. The *critical region* refers to the area in the tails of the distribution in which the null hypothesis will be rejected if the test statistic falls there.

7-11 A *statistically significant* finding is one in which we have rejected the null hypothesis because the pattern in the data differed from what we would expect by chance. The word *significant* has a particular meaning in statistics. "Statistical significance" does *not* mean that the finding is necessarily important or meaningful. Statistical significance only means that we are justified in believing that the pattern in the data is likely to reoccur; that is, the pattern is likely genuine.

7-13 *Critical region* may have been chosen because values of a test statistic describe the area beneath the normal curve that represents a statistically significant result.

7-15 For a one-tailed test, the critical region (usually 5%, or an alpha level of 0.05) is placed in only one tail of the distribution; for a two-tailed test, the critical region must be split in half and shared between both tails (usually 2.5%, or 0.025, in each tail).

7-17 The following are the two options for one-tailed test hypotheses.

1) Null hypothesis: H_0: $\mu_1 \geq \mu_2$

   Research hypothesis: H_1: $\mu_1 < \mu_2$

2) Null hypothesis: H_0: $\mu_1 \leq \mu_1$

   Research hypothesis: H_1: $\mu_1 > \mu_2$

7-19 *p*-hacking occurs when researchers use questionable statistical methods to increase their chances of finding a statistically significant result. Some of these practices include repeatedly analyzing data after collecting data from small numbers of participants and then stopping data collection as soon as they reach significance. Or, researchers might selectively exclude extreme data points, after looking at the data, so that their results will reach significance. Researchers might also study multiple dependent variables, but report only those that reach significance. Or, researchers might include additional experimental conditions, but report only those that reach significance.

7-21 a. If 22.96% are beyond this *z* score (in the tail), then 77.04% are below it (100% − 22.96%).

b. If 22.96% are beyond this *z* score, then 27.04% are between it and the mean (50% − 22.96%).

c. Because the curve is symmetric, the area beyond a *z* score of −0.74 is the same as that beyond 0.74. Expressed as a proportion, 22.96% appears as 0.2296.

7-23 a. The percentage above is the percentage in the tail, 4.36%.

b. The percentage below is calculated by adding the area below the mean, 50%, and the area between the mean and this *z* score, 45.64%, to get 95.64%.

c. The percentage at least as extreme is computed by doubling the amount beyond the *z* score, 4.36%, to get 8.72%.

7-25 a. 19%

b. 4%

c. 92%

7-27 a. 2.5% in each tail

b. 5% in each tail

c. 0.5% in each tail

7-29 $\mu_M = \mu = 500$

$$\sigma_M = \frac{\sigma}{\sqrt{N}} = \frac{100}{\sqrt{50}} = 14.14$$

7-31 a. Fail to reject the null hypothesis because 1.06 does not exceed the cutoff of 1.96.

b. Reject the null hypothesis because −2.06 is more extreme than −1.96.

c. Fail to reject the null hypothesis because a *z* statistic with 7% of the data in the tail occurs between ±1.48 and ±1.47, which are not more extreme than ±1.96.

7-33 a. Fail to reject the null hypothesis because 0.95 does not exceed 1.65.

b. Reject the null hypothesis because −1.77 is more extreme than −1.65.

c. Reject the null hypothesis because the critical value resulting in 2% in the tail falls within the 5% cutoff region in each tail.

7-35 a. $z = \frac{(X - \mu)}{\sigma} = \frac{5.4 - 7}{1.85} = \frac{-1.6}{1.85} = -0.86$

The percentage below is 19.49%.

b. $z = \frac{(X - \mu)}{\sigma} = \frac{8.5 - 7}{1.85} = \frac{1.5}{1.85} = 0.81$

The percentage below is 50% + 29.10% = 79.10%.

c. $z = \frac{(X - \mu)}{\sigma} = \frac{8.9 - 7}{1.85} = \frac{1.9}{1.85} = 1.03$

The percentage below is 50% + 34.85% = 84.85%.

d. $z = \frac{(X - \mu)}{\sigma} = \frac{6.5 - 7}{1.85} = \frac{-0.5}{1.85} = -0.27$

The percentage below is 39.36%.

7-37 a. $z = \frac{(X - \mu)}{\sigma} = \frac{72 - 67}{3.19} = 1.57$

b. 44.18% of scores are between this *z* score and the mean. We need to add this to the area below the mean, 50%, to get the percentile score of 94.18%.

c. 94.18% of boys are shorter than Kona at this age.

d. If 94.18% of boys are shorter than Kona, that leaves 5.82% in the tail. To compute how many scores are at least as extreme, we double this to get 11.64%.

e. We look at the *z* table to find a critical value that puts 30% of scores in the tail, or as close as we can get to 30%. A *z* score of −0.52 puts 30.15% in the tail. We can use that *z* score to compute the raw score for height:

$$X = -0.52(3.19) + 67 = 65.34 \text{ inches}$$

At 72 inches tall, Kona is 6.66 inches taller than Ian.

7-39 a. $z = \frac{(M - \mu_M)}{\sigma_M} = \frac{69.5 - 67}{\frac{3.19}{\sqrt{13}}} = 2.83$

b. The *z* statistic indicates that this sample mean is 2.83 standard deviations above the expected mean for samples of size 13. In other words, this sample of boys is, on average, exceptionally tall.

c. The percentile rank is 99.77%, meaning that 99.77% of sample means would be of lesser value than the one obtained for this sample.

7-41 a. $\mu_M = \mu = 63.8$

$$\sigma_M = \frac{\sigma}{\sqrt{N}} = \frac{2.66}{\sqrt{14}} = 0.711$$

b. $z = \frac{(M - \mu_M)}{\sigma_M} = \frac{62.4 - 63.8}{0.711} = -1.97$

c. 2.44% of sample means would be shorter than this mean.

d. We double 2.44% to account for both tails, so we get 4.88% of the time.

e. The average height of this group of 15-year-old females is rare, or statistically significant.

7-43 a. This is a directional hypothesis because a decrease in heart rate is predicted.

b. This is a nondirectional hypothesis because any change of grades is of interest, not just a decrease or an increase in grades.

c. This hypothesis is nondirectional because any change is of interest, not just a decrease or an increase in closeness of relationships.

7-45 a.

	X	$(X - \mu)$	$(X - \mu)^2$
January	4.41	0.257	0.066
February	8.24	4.087	16.704
March	4.69	0.537	0.288
April	3.31	−0.843	0.711
May	4.07	−0.083	0.007
June	2.52	−1.633	2.667
July	10.65	6.497	42.211
August	3.77	−0.383	0.147
September	4.07	−0.083	0.007
October	0.04	−4.113	16.917
November	0.75	−3.403	11.580
December	3.32	−0.833	0.694

$\mu = 4.153$; $SS = \Sigma(X - \mu)^2 = 91.999$;

$$\sigma^2 = \frac{\Sigma(X - \mu)^2}{N} = \frac{(91.999)}{12} = 7.667$$

$$\sigma = \sqrt{\sigma^2} = \sqrt{7.667} = 2.769$$

August: $X = 3.77$

$$z = \frac{(X - \mu)}{\sigma} = \frac{(3.77 - 4.153)}{2.769} = -0.14$$

b. The table tells us that 44.43% of scores fall in the tail beyond a z score of −0.14. So, the percentile for August is 44.43%. This is surprising because it is below the mean, and it was the month in which a devastating hurricane hit New Orleans. (*Note:* It is helpful to draw a picture of the curve when calculating this answer.)

c. Paragraphs will be different for each student but will include the fact that a monthly total based on missing data is inaccurate. The mean and the standard deviation based on this population, therefore, are inaccurate. Moreover, even if we had these data points, they would likely be large and would increase the total precipitation for August; August would likely be an outlier, skewing the overall mean. The median would be a more accurate measure of central tendency than the mean under these circumstances.

d. We would look up the z score that has 10% in the tail. The closest z score is 1.28, so the cutoffs are −1.28 and 1.28. (*Note:* It is helpful to draw a picture of the curve that includes these z scores.) We can then convert these z scores to raw scores. $X = z(\sigma) + \mu = -1.28(2.769) + 4.153 = 0.61$; $X = z(\sigma) + \mu = 1.28(2.769) + 4.153 = 7.70$. Only October (0.04) is below 0.61. Only February (8.24) and July (10.65) are above 7.70. These data are likely inaccurate, however, because the mean and the standard deviation of the population are based on an inaccurate mean from August. Moreover, it is quite likely that August would have been in the most extreme upper 10% if there were complete data for this month.

7-47 Because we have a population mean and a population standard deviation, we can use a z test. To conduct this study, we would need a sample of red-haired women. Ideally, we would recruit at least 30 women so that we could be assured that the underlying population distribution was normal (based on the central limit theorem). Each participant would create a password, and we would rate the strength of her password using Kuo's scoring system. We would take the mean of all of the password scores. We would then conduct all six steps of hypothesis testing to determine whether the sample mean for red-haired women was statistically significantly higher than the population mean of 15.7.

7-49 The researchers were given a data set with lots of different variables; so, even though the researchers were all given the same research question, they may have tested different combinations of the different variables and then reported only the statistical tests that reached statistical significance. Some of the researchers may have used different criteria for excluding extreme cases. Some may have found these differences in only one, but not all, of the leagues and reported the result for the one league for which they rejected the null hypothesis. Similarly, some researchers might have divided the data in different ways, such as looking separately at tall and short players.

7-51 a. The independent variable is whether a patient received the video with information about orthodontics. One group received the video; the other group did not. The dependent variable is the number of hours per day patients wore their appliances.

b. The researcher did not use random selection when choosing his sample. He selected the next 15 patients to come into his clinic.

c. *Step 1:* Population 1 is patients who did not receive the video. Population 2 is patients who received the video. The comparison distribution will be a distribution of means. The hypothesis test will be a *z* test because there is only one sample and we know the population mean and the standard deviation. This study meets the assumption that the dependent variable is a scale measure. We might expect the distribution of number of hours per day people wear their appliances to be normally distributed, but from the information provided it is not possible to tell for sure. Additionally, the sample includes fewer than 30 participants, so the central limit theorem may not apply here. The distribution of sample means may not approach normality. Finally, the participants were not randomly selected. Therefore, we may not want to generalize the results beyond this sample.

Step 2: Null hypothesis: Patients who received the video do not wear their appliances a different mean number of hours per day than patients who did not receive the video: $H_0: \mu_1 = \mu_2$.

Research hypothesis: Patients who received the video wear their appliances a different mean number of hours per day than patients who did not receive the video: $H_1: \mu_1 \neq \mu_2$.

Step 3: $\mu_M = \mu = 14.78$; $\sigma_M = \dfrac{\sigma}{\sqrt{N}} = \dfrac{5.31}{\sqrt{15}} = 1.371$

Step 4: The cutoff *z* statistics, based on an alpha level of 0.05 and a two-tailed test, are −1.96 and 1.96. (*Note:* It is helpful to draw a picture of the normal curve and include these *z* statistics on it.)

Step 5: $z = \dfrac{(X - \mu_M)}{\sigma_M} = \dfrac{(17 - 14.78)}{1.371} = 1.62$

(*Note:* It is helpful to add this *z* statistic to your drawing of the normal curve that includes the cutoff *z* statistics.)

Step 6: Fail to reject the null hypothesis. We cannot conclude that receiving the video improves average patient compliance.

d. The researcher would have made a Type II error. He would have failed to reject the null hypothesis when a mean difference actually existed between the two populations.

e. He would have engaged in *p*-hacking, an unethical data practice that increases the chance of a statistically significant result. This is a potentially harmful practice because it may lead to Type I errors. In this case, by stopping when he attained the result he wanted, the researcher doesn't know if that result would have held up with a larger sample size. It may just be a chance finding.

7-53 a. Their sample would be the 12 farmers' crops tested for cesium.

b. *Step 1:* Population 1 is the crops exposed to radiation. Population 2 is the normal, nonradiated crops. The comparison distribution will be a distribution of means. The hypothesis test will be a *z* test because there is only one sample and we can obtain the population mean and the standard deviation for nonradiated crops. This study meets the assumption that the dependent variable is a scale measure. We might expect the levels of cesium to be normally distributed, but from the information provided it is not possible to tell for sure. Additionally, the sample includes crops from fewer than 30 farms, so the central limit theorem may not apply here. The distribution of sample means may not approach normality. Finally, the crops were not randomly selected. Therefore, we may not want to generalize the results beyond this sample.

c. *Step 2:* Null hypothesis: The average cesium level in crops tested after the 2011 tsunami and radiation disaster at Fukushima does not differ from the average cesium level in areas that were not exposed to radiation: $H_0: \mu_1 = \mu_2$.

Research hypothesis: The average cesium level in crops tested after the 2011 tsunami and radiation disaster at Fukushima differs from the average cesium level in areas that were not exposed to radiation: $H_1: \mu_1 \neq \mu_2$.

d. *Step 4:* The cutoff *z* statistics, based on an alpha level of 0.05 and a two-tailed test, are −1.96 and 1.96. (*Note:* It is helpful to draw a picture of the normal curve and include these *z* statistics on it.)

e. *Step 6:* Reject the null hypothesis. It appears that the crops in the areas near Fukushima have higher average cesium levels than the average levels in areas that were not exposed to radiation.

f. They would have made a Type I error because they rejected the null hypothesis when there actually was no mean difference.

g. They would have engaged in HARKing, hypothesizing after the results are known. This is a potentially harmful practice because when researchers pretend they had predicted the actual outcome of a study, it makes that finding seem stronger.

Chapter 8

8-1 There may be a statistically significant difference between group means, but the difference might not be meaningful or have a real-life application.

8-3 Confidence intervals add details to the hypothesis test. Specifically, they tell us a range within which the population mean would fall 95% of the time if we were to conduct repeated hypothesis tests using samples of the same size from the same population.

8-5 In everyday language, we use the word *effect* to refer to the outcome of some event. Statisticians use the word in a similar way when they look at effect sizes. They want to assess a given outcome. For statisticians, the outcome is any change in a dependent variable, and the event creating the outcome is an independent variable. When statisticians calculate an effect size, they are calculating the size of an outcome.

8-7 If two distributions overlap a lot, then we would probably find a small effect size and not be willing to conclude that the distributions are necessarily different. If the distributions do not overlap much, this would be evidence for a larger effect or a meaningful difference between them.

8-9 According to Cohen's guidelines for interpreting the d statistic, a small effect is around 0.2, a medium effect is around 0.5, and a large effect is around 0.8.

8-11 In everyday language, we use the word *power* to mean either an ability to get something done or an ability to make others do things. Statisticians use the word *power* to refer to the ability to detect an effect, given that one exists.

8-13 80%

8-15 A researcher could increase statistical power by (1) increasing the alpha level; (2) performing a one-tailed test instead of a two-tailed test; (3) increasing the sample size; (4) maximizing the difference in the levels of the independent variable (e.g., giving a larger dose of a medication); and (5) decreasing variability in the distributions by using, for example, reliable measures and homogeneous samples. Researchers want statistical power in their studies. In many instances, the most practical way to increase statistical power is to increase the sample size.

8-17 The goal of a meta-analysis is to find the mean of the effect sizes from many different studies that all manipulated the same independent variable and measured the same dependent variable.

8-19 A file drawer analysis allows us to calculate the number of studies with null results that would have to exist so that a mean effect size would no longer be statistically significant. If it would take many studies (e.g., hundreds) to render the effect nonsignificant, then a statistically significant meta-analysis finding would be more persuasive. Specifically, we would be more convinced that a mean effect size really is statistically significantly different from zero.

8-21 (i) σ_M is incorrect. (ii) The correct symbol is σ. (iii) Because we are calculating Cohen's d, a measure of effect size, we divide by the standard deviation, σ, not the standard error of the mean. We use standard deviation rather than standard error because effect size is independent of sample size.

8-23 The best way to avoid the negative consequences of an underpowered study is to perform a power analysis in advance, before collecting data for the study, to determine the required sample size for a minimum of 80% statistical power.

8-25 In this study, 18.5% to 25.5% of respondents were suspicious of steroid use among swimmers.

8-27 **a.** 20%
　　b. 15%
　　c. 1%

8-29 **a.** A z of 0.84 leaves 19.77% in the tail.
　　b. A z of 1.04 leaves 14.92% in the tail.
　　c. A z of 2.33 leaves 0.99% in the tail.

8-31 We know that the cutoffs for the 95% confidence interval are $z = \pm 1.96$. The standard error is calculated as:

$$\sigma_M = \frac{\sigma}{\sqrt{N}} = \frac{1.3}{\sqrt{78}} = 0.147$$

Now we can calculate the lower and upper bounds of the confidence interval.

$$M_{lower} = -z(\sigma_M) + M_{sample} = -1.96(0.147) + 4.1 = 3.812 \text{ hours}$$
$$M_{upper} = z(\sigma_M) + M_{sample} = 1.96(0.147) + 4.1 = 4.388 \text{ hours}$$

The 95% confidence interval can be expressed as [3.81, 4.39].

8-33 z values of ± 2.58 put 0.49% in each tail, without going over, so we will use those as the critical values for the 99% confidence interval. The standard error is calculated as:

$$\sigma_M = \frac{\sigma}{\sqrt{N}} = \frac{1.3}{\sqrt{78}} = 0.147$$

Now we can calculate the lower and upper bounds of the confidence interval.

$$M_{lower} = -z(\sigma_M) + M_{sample} = -2.58(0.147) + 4.1 = 3.721 \text{ hours}$$
$$M_{upper} = z(\sigma_M) + M_{sample} = 2.58(0.147) + 4.1 = 4.479 \text{ hours}$$

The 99% confidence interval can be expressed as [3.72, 4.48].

8-35 **a.** $\sigma_M = \dfrac{\sigma}{\sqrt{N}} = \dfrac{136}{\sqrt{12}} = 39.261$

$z = \dfrac{(M - \mu_M)}{\sigma_M} = \dfrac{1057 - 1014}{39.261} = 1.10$

b. $\sigma_M = \dfrac{\sigma}{\sqrt{N}} = \dfrac{136}{\sqrt{39}} = 21.777$

$z = \dfrac{1057 - 1014}{21.777} = 1.97$

c. $\sigma_M = \dfrac{\sigma}{\sqrt{N}} = \dfrac{136}{\sqrt{188}} = 9.919$

$z = \dfrac{1057 - 1014}{9.919} = 4.34$

8-37 **a.** Cohen's $d = \dfrac{(M - \mu)}{\sigma} = \dfrac{(480 - 500)}{100} = -0.20$

b. Cohen's $d = \dfrac{(M - \mu)}{\sigma} = \dfrac{(520 - 500)}{100} = 0.20$

c. Cohen's $d = \dfrac{(M - \mu)}{\sigma} = \dfrac{(610 - 500)}{100} = 1.10$

8-39 **a.** Large
　　b. Medium
　　c. Small
　　d. No effect (very close to zero)

8-41 a. The percentage beyond the z statistic of 2.23 is 1.29%. Doubled to take into account both tails, this is 2.58%. Converted to a proportion by dividing by 100, we get a p value of 0.0258, or 0.03.

b. For −1.82, the percentage in the tail is 3.44%. Doubled, it is 6.88%. As a proportion, it is 0.0688, or 0.07.

c. For 0.33, the percentage in the tail is 37.07%. Doubled, it is 74.14%. As a proportion, it is 0.7414, or 0.74.

8-43 We would fail to reject the null hypothesis because the confidence interval around the mean effect size includes 0.

8-45 a. The mean effect size is $d = 0.91$.

b. This is a large effect size.

8-47 Your friend is not considering the fact that the two distributions, that of IQ scores of Burakumin and that of IQ scores of other Japanese, will have a great deal of overlap. The fact that one mean is higher than another does not imply that all members of one group have higher IQ scores than all members of another group. Any individual member of either group, such as your friend's former student, might fall well above the mean for his or her group (and the other group) or well below the mean for his or her group (and the other group). Research reports that do not give an indication of the overlap between two distributions risk misleading their audience.

8-49 a. *Step 3:*

$$\mu_M = \mu = 20.4; \; \sigma_M = \frac{\sigma}{\sqrt{N}} = \frac{3.2}{\sqrt{3}} = 1.848$$

Step 4: The cutoff z statistics are −1.96 and 1.96.
Step 5:

$$z = \frac{(M - \mu_M)}{\sigma_M} = \frac{(17.5 - 20.4)}{1.848} = -1.57$$

Step 6: Fail to reject the null hypothesis; we can conclude only that there is not sufficient evidence that Canadian adults have different average GNT scores from English adults. The conclusion has changed, but the actual difference between groups has not. The smaller sample size led to a larger standard error and a smaller test statistic. This makes sense because an extreme mean based on just a few participants is more likely to have occurred by chance than is an extreme mean based on many participants.

b. *Step 3:*

$$\mu_M = \mu = 20.4; \; \sigma_M = \frac{\sigma}{\sqrt{N}} = \frac{3.2}{\sqrt{100}} = 0.32$$

Step 5:

$$z = \frac{(M - \mu_M)}{\sigma_M} = \frac{(17.5 - 20.4)}{0.32} = -9.06$$

Step 6: Reject the null hypothesis. It appears that Canadian adults have lower average GNT scores than English adults. The test statistic has increased along with the increase in sample size.

c. *Step 3:*

$$\mu_M = \mu = 20.4; \; \sigma_M = \frac{\sigma}{\sqrt{N}} = \frac{3.2}{\sqrt{20,000}} = 0.023$$

Step 5:

$$z = \frac{(M - \mu_M)}{\sigma_M} = \frac{(17.5 - 20.4)}{0.023} = -126.09$$

The test statistic is now even larger, as the sample size has grown even larger. Step 6 is the same as in part (b).

d. As sample size increases, the test statistic increases. A mean difference based on a very small sample could have occurred just by chance. Based on a very large sample, that same mean difference is less likely to have occurred just by chance.

e. The underlying difference between groups has not changed. This might pose a problem for hypothesis testing because the same mean difference is statistically significant under some circumstances but not others. A very large test statistic might not indicate a very large difference between means; therefore, a statistically significant difference might not be an important difference.

8-51 a. No, we cannot tell which student will do better on the TOEFL. It is likely that the distributions of TOEFL scores for people from Serbia and people from Portugal have a great deal of overlap. Just because one group, on average, does better than another group does not mean that everyone in one group does better than everyone in another group.

b. Answers to this will vary, but the two distributions should overlap and the mean of the distribution for people whose first language is Serbian should be farther to the right (i.e., higher) than the mean for people whose first language is Portuguese. The figure here shows one example.

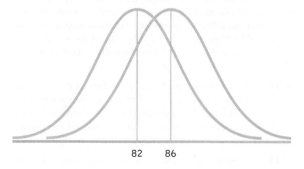

82   86

8-53 a. Given $\mu = 6.00, \sigma = 1.30$, and $N = 63$, we calculate $\sigma_M =$
$\frac{\sigma}{\sqrt{N}} = \frac{1.30}{\sqrt{63}} = 0.16$. To calculate the 95% confidence interval, we find the z values that mark off the most extreme 0.025 in each tail, which are −1.96 and 1.96. We calculate the lower end of the interval as $M_{lower} = -z(\sigma_M) + M_{sample} = -1.96(0.16) + 7.087 = 6.766$ and the upper end of the interval as $M_{upper} = z(\sigma_M) + M_{sample} = 1.96(0.16) + 7.087 =$

7.408. The confidence interval around the mean of 7.087 is [6.77, 7.41] when rounded to two decimal places for the final answer.

b. Because 6.00, the null-hypothesized value of the population mean, does not fall within this confidence interval, it is not plausible that the scores of the 63 international students at the University of Melbourne are the same, on average, as the scores for the population of students who completed this listening module of the IELTS. One explanation for the difference is that the sample may come from a different population.

c. Because the confidence interval does not include the hypothesized population mean of 6.00, we would reject the null hypothesis if we conducted a hypothesis test. It is plausible that the sample came from a different population.

d. In addition to letting us know that it is unlikely that the sample of University of Melbourne international students came from the same population as the IELTS test-takers, the confidence interval tells us a range of plausible values for the IELTS for international students at the University of Melbourne.

8-55 a. The appropriate measure of effect size for a z statistic is Cohen's d, which is calculated as:

$$d = \frac{(M - \mu)}{\sigma} = \frac{7.087 - 6.00}{1.30} = 0.836$$

b. Based on Cohen's conventions, this is a large effect size.

c. The hypothesis test tells us only whether a sample mean is likely to have been obtained by chance, whereas the effect size gives us the additional information of how much overlap there is between the distributions. Cohen's d, in particular, tells us how far apart two means are in terms of standard deviation. Because it's based on standard deviation, not standard error, Cohen's d is independent of sample size and therefore has the added benefit of allowing us to compare across studies. In summary, effect size tells us the magnitude of the effect, giving us a sense of how important or practical this finding is, and allows us to standardize the results of the study. Here, we know that there's a large effect.

8-57 a. We know that the cutoffs for the 95% confidence interval are $z = \pm 1.96$. Standard error is calculated as:

$$\sigma_M = \frac{\sigma}{\sqrt{N}} = \frac{16}{\sqrt{18}} = 3.771$$

Now we can calculate the lower and upper bounds of the confidence interval.

$$M_{lower} = -z(\sigma_M) + M_{sample} = -1.96(3.771) + 38 = \$30.61$$
$$M_{upper} = z(\sigma_M) + M_{sample} = 1.96(3.771) + 38 = \$45.39$$

The 95% confidence interval can be expressed as [\$30.61, \$45.39].

b. Standard error is now calculated as:

$$\sigma_M = \frac{\sigma}{\sqrt{N}} = \frac{16}{\sqrt{180}} = 1.193$$

Now we can calculate the lower and upper bounds of the confidence interval.

$$M_{lower} = -z(\sigma_M) + M_{sample} = -1.96(1.193) + 38 = \$35.66$$
$$M_{upper} = z(\sigma_M) + M_{sample} = 1.96(1.193) + 38 = \$40.34$$

The 95% confidence interval can be expressed as [\$35.66, \$40.34].

c. The null-hypothesized mean of \$45 falls in the 95% confidence interval when N is 18. Because of this, we cannot claim that spending was lower in 2009 than what we would normally expect. When N is increased to 180, the confidence interval becomes narrower because standard error is reduced. As a result, the mean of \$45 no longer falls within the interval, and we can now conclude that Valentine's Day spending was different in 2009 from what was expected based on previous population data.

d. Cohen's $d = \dfrac{(M - \mu)}{\sigma} = \dfrac{(38 - 45)}{16} = -0.44$, close to a medium effect size.

8-59 a. Standard error is calculated as:

$$\sigma_M = \frac{\sigma}{\sqrt{N}} = \frac{12}{\sqrt{26}} = 2.353$$

Now we can calculate the lower and upper bounds of the confidence interval.

$$M_{lower} = -z(\sigma_M) + M_{sample} = -1.96(2.353) + 123$$
$$= 118.39 \text{ mph}$$
$$M_{upper} = z(\sigma_M) + M_{sample} = 1.96(2.353) + 123$$
$$= 127.61 \text{ mph}$$

The 95% confidence interval can be expressed as [118.39, 127.61].

Because the population mean of 118 mph does not fall within the confidence interval around the new mean, we can conclude that the program had an impact. In fact, we can conclude that the program seemed to increase the average speed of women's serves.

b. Cohen's $d = \dfrac{(M - \mu)}{\sigma} = \dfrac{(123 - 118)}{12} = 0.42$, close to a medium effect.

c. Because standard error, which utilizes sample size in its calculation, is part of the calculations for confidence interval, the interval becomes narrower as the sample size increases; however, because sample size is eliminated from the calculation of effect size, the effect size does not change.

8-61 a. It is unlikely that the researchers made a Type II error. A Type II error occurs when the researcher fails to reject the null hypothesis, but that hypothesis is in fact true. The power of the study was .98, which means that the researchers would have a 98% chance of rejecting the null hypothesis if the null hypothesis were true. That is a very good chance. So, there is only a 2% chance that the researchers made a Type II error.

b. The researchers set their alpha to .05, so the probability that they would make a Type I error is .05, or 5%.

8-63 a. The topic is the effectiveness of culturally adapted therapies.

b. The researchers used Cohen's *d* as a measure of effect size for each study in the analysis.

c. The mean effect size they found was 0.45. According to Cohen's conventions, this is close to a medium effect.

d. The researchers could use the group means and standard deviations to calculate a measure of effect size.

8-65 *Step 1:* The authors of the article first selected a topic of interest: gender differences in mathematical performance. They identified the necessary statistical information: Cohen's *d*. The authors likely wanted to include journal articles that compared men and women on mathematical tasks. Any study that did not fit this criterion was likely to have not been included. Additionally, they probably only included studies that had similar research designs.

Step 2: After identifying the criteria, the authors attempted to locate every relevant study. Because the authors note that they included only published studies, it is likely that they did not include (or perhaps even search for) unpublished studies on gender differences and mathematical performance.

Step 3: The authors then either identified or calculated an effect size for every study that met the inclusion criteria.

Step 4: Last, the authors calculated summary statistics (*d* = 0.05, variance ratio = 1.08). It is likely the authors included a visual display of the effect sizes.

8-67 a. A statistically significant difference just indicates that the difference between the means is unlikely to be due to chance. It does not tell us that there is *no* overlap in the distributions of the two populations we are considering. It is likely that there is overlap between the distributions and that some players with three children actually perform better than some players with two or fewer children. The drawings of distributions will vary; the two curves will overlap, but the mean of the distribution representing two or fewer children should be farther to the right than the mean of the distribution representing three or more children. However, the *X* for the player who had a third child should be to the right of the *Y* for the player who had a first or second child.

b. A difference can be statistically significant even if it is very small. In fact, if there are enough observations in a sample, even a tiny difference will approach statistical significance. Statistical significance does not indicate the importance or size of an effect—we need measures of effect size, which are not influenced by sample size, to understand the importance of an effect. These measures of effect size allow us to compare different predictors of performance. For example, in this case, it is likely that

other aspects of a player's stats are more strongly associated with his performance and therefore would have a larger effect size. We could make the decision about whom to include in the fantasy team on the basis of the largest predictors of performance.

c. Even if the association is true, we cannot conclude that having a third child causes a decline in baseball performance. There are a number of possible causal explanations for this relation. It could be the reverse; perhaps those players who are not performing as well in their careers end up devoting more time to family, so not playing well could lead to having more children. Alternatively, a third variable could explain both (a) having three children and (b) poorer baseball performance. For example, perhaps less competitive or more laid-back players have more children and also perform more poorly.

d. The sample size for this analysis is likely small, so the statistical power to detect an effect is likely small as well.

8-69 a. The sample is the group of low-income students utilized for the study by Hoxby and Turner (2013). The population is low-income students applying to college.

b. The independent variable is the intervention, with two levels—no intervention and intervention.

c. The dependent variable is the number of applications submitted.

d. Just because a finding is statistically significant, it does not mean that it is practically significant. Justification for the impact of using the intervention based on a cost-benefit analysis may be needed.

e. The effect size for number of applications submitted was 0.247. This is a small effect size, according to Cohen's conventions.

f. Effect sizes demonstrate the difference between two means in terms of standard deviations. Thus, for the number of applications submitted, the means for the two groups were 0.247 standard deviations apart.

g. The intervention increased the average number of applications submitted by 19%.

Chapter 9

9-1 We should use a *t* distribution when we do not know the population standard deviation and are comparing two groups.

9-3 For both tests, standard error is calculated as the standard deviation divided by the square root of *N*. For the *z* test, the population standard deviation is calculated with *N* in the denominator. For the *t* test, the population standard deviation is estimated by dividing the sum of squared deviations by $N - 1$.

9-5 t stands for the t statistic, M is the sample mean, μ_M is the mean of the distribution of means, and s_M is the standard error as estimated from a sample.

9-7 *Free to vary* refers to the number of scores that can take on different values if a given parameter is known.

9-9 As the sample size increases, we can feel more confident in the estimate of the variability in the population. Remember, this estimate of variability (s) is calculated with $N-1$ in the denominator so as to inflate the estimate somewhat. As the sample increases from 10 to 100, for example, and then up to 1000, subtracting 1 from N has less of an impact on the overall calculation. As this happens, the t distributions approach the z distribution, where we in fact knew the population standard deviation and did not need to estimate it.

9-11 The confidence interval gives us more information—an interval estimate, not just a point estimate.

9-13 A Cohen's d of 0.5 always indicates a medium effect, whether it accompanies a single-sample t test or any other hypothesis test.

9-15 The failure to replicate a finding can potentially mean a few things. The conclusion from the original study may have been a Type I error (an incorrect rejection of the null hypothesis that led the researcher to state that there is a statistically significant finding). Or the failure to replicate may be a Type II error (an incorrect failure to reject the null hypothesis). Differences in findings might also reflect differences in the research context, perhaps because of differences between laboratories, samples, or researchers. Or perhaps the phenomenon itself has changed over the time that passed between replications. There are potentially other explanations, especially if there is even the smallest shift in methodology, but these are often the primary explanations.

9-17 **a.** First we need to calculate the mean:

$$M = \frac{\Sigma X}{N} = \frac{93 + 97 + 91 + 88 + 103 + 94 + 97}{7} = \frac{663}{7} = 94.714$$

We then calculate the deviation of each score from the mean and the square of that deviation.

X	$X - M$	$(X - M)^2$
93	−1.714	2.938
97	2.286	5.226
91	−3.714	13.794
88	−6.714	45.078
103	8.286	68.658
94	−0.714	0.510
97	2.286	5.226

Numerator: $\Sigma(X - M)^2 = 141.430$

The standard deviation is:

$$SD = \sqrt{\frac{\Sigma(X - M)^2}{N}} = \sqrt{\frac{141.430}{7}} = \sqrt{20.204} = 4.49$$

b. When estimating the population variability, we calculate s:

$$s = \sqrt{\frac{\Sigma(X - M)^2}{N - 1}} = \sqrt{\frac{141.430}{7 - 1}} = \sqrt{23.572} = 4.855$$

c. $s_M = \dfrac{s}{\sqrt{N}} = \dfrac{4.855}{\sqrt{7}} = 1.835$

d. $t = \dfrac{(M - \mu)}{s_M} = \dfrac{(94.714 - 96)}{1.835} = -0.70$

9-19 **a.** Because 73 df is not on the table, we go to 60 df (we do not go to the closest value, which would be 80, because we want to be conservative and go to the next-lowest value for df) to find the critical value of 1.296 in the upper tail. If we are looking in the lower tail, the critical value is −1.296.

b. ±1.984

c. Either −2.438 or 2.438

9-21 **a.** This is a two-tailed test with $df = 25$, so the critical t values are ±2.060.

b. $df = 17$, so the critical t value is 2.567, assuming you're anticipating an increase in marital satisfaction.

c. $df = 33$, so the critical t values are ±2.043.

9-23 **a.** $t = \dfrac{(M - \mu_M)}{s_M} = \dfrac{(8.5 - 7)}{\left(\dfrac{2.1}{\sqrt{41}}\right)} = 4.57$

b. $M_{lower} = -t(s_M) + M_{sample} = -2.705(0.328) + 8.5 = 7.61$

$M_{upper} = t(s_M) + M_{sample} = 2.705(0.328) + 8.5 = 9.39$

c. $d = \dfrac{(M - \mu)}{s} = \dfrac{(8.5 - 7)}{2.1} = 0.71$

9-25 **a.** The critical value for the test would be 2.624. The df is 14. It is a one-tailed test, with an alpha level of .01.

b. The critical values for the test would be −2.021 and 2.021. The df is 43, but the table only includes critical t values for $df = 40$ and $df = 50$. We use the more conservative critical t values, which would be for a df of 40. It is a two-tailed test, with an alpha level of .05.

9-27 **a.** ±1.96

b. Either −2.33 or +2.33, depending on the tail of interest

c. ±1.96

9-29 **a.** *Step 1:* Population 1 is male U.S. Marines following a month-long training exercise. Population 2 is college men. The comparison distribution will be a distribution of means. The hypothesis test will be a single-sample t test because there is only one sample and we know the population mean but not the standard deviation. This study meets one of the three assumptions and may meet another. The dependent variable, anger, appears to be scale. The data were not likely randomly selected, so we must be cautious with respect to generalizing to all Marines who complete this training. We do not know whether the population is normally distributed, and there are not at least 30 participants. However, the data from the sample do not suggest a skewed distribution.

Step 2: Null hypothesis: Male U.S. Marines after a month-long training exercise have the same average anger levels as college men: $H_0: \mu_1 = \mu_2$.

Research hypothesis: Male U.S. Marines after a month-long training exercise have different average anger levels than college men: $H_1: \mu_1 \neq \mu_2$.

Step 3: $\mu_M = \mu = 8.90$; $s_M = 0.494$

X	$X - M$	$(X - M)^2$
14	0.667	0.445
12	−1.333	1.777
13	−0.333	0.111
12	−1.333	1.777
14	0.667	0.445
15	1.667	2.779

$M = 13.333$

$SS = \Sigma(X - M)^2 = \Sigma(0.445 + 1.777 + 0.111 + 1.777 + 0.445 + 2.779) = 7.334$

$$s = \sqrt{\frac{\Sigma(X - M)^2}{N - 1}} = \sqrt{\frac{SS}{(N - 1)}} = \sqrt{\frac{7.334}{6 - 1}} = \sqrt{1.467} = 1.211$$

$$s_M = \frac{s}{\sqrt{N}} = \frac{1.211}{\sqrt{6}} = 0.494$$

Step 4: $df = N - 1 = 6 - 1 = 5$; the critical values, based on 5 degrees of freedom, an alpha level of 0.05, and a two-tailed test, are −2.571 and 2.571. (*Note:* It is helpful to draw a curve that includes these cutoffs.)

Step 5: $t = \dfrac{(M - \mu_M)}{s_M} = \dfrac{(13.333 - 8.90)}{0.494} = 8.97$

(*Note:* It is helpful to add this t statistic to the curve that you drew in step 4.)

Step 6: Reject the null hypothesis. It appears that male U.S. Marines just after a month-long training exercise have higher average anger levels than college men have; $t(5) = 8.97$, $p < 0.05$.

b. $t = \dfrac{(M - \mu_M)}{s_M} = \dfrac{(13.333 - 9.20)}{0.494} = 8.37$. Reject the null hypothesis; it appears that male U.S. Marines just after a month-long training exercise have higher average anger levels than adult men; $t(5) = 8.37$, $p < 0.05$.

c. $t = \dfrac{(M - \mu_M)}{s_M} = \dfrac{(13.333 - 13.5)}{0.494} = -0.34$. Fail to reject the null hypothesis; we conclude that there is no evidence from this study to support the research hypothesis; $t(5) = -0.34$, $p > 0.05$.

d. We can conclude that Marines' anger scores just after high-altitude, cold-weather training are, on average, higher than those of college men and adult men. We cannot conclude, however, that they are different, on average, from those of male psychiatric outpatients. With respect to the latter difference, we can only conclude that there is no evidence to support that there is a difference between Marines' mean anger scores and those of male psychiatric outpatients.

e. Replicating this finding with another set of Marines would support the initial finding about mood and high-altitude, cold-weather training. The finding for the original (fictional) sample of just six Marines may have been due to chance. If other samples show the same result, it becomes less and less likely that the finding was due just to chance.

9-31 a. 207 is the degrees of freedom, which is 1 less than the sample size. So, 208 people were in this sample.

b. 16.12 is the standard deviation. It tells us that the typical score deviates from the mean of 56.17 by about 16%.

c. This is a statistically significant finding, but we do not know how large or important it is. Cohen's d would let us know if this effect is worth making real-life changes.

d. When people sign their names electronically, they report higher than chance outcomes for getting heads when flipping a coin, an indication of cheating. There is no such finding when people sign their names with ink on paper.

9-33 a. A single-sample t test is the appropriate hypothesis test because we are comparing a sample to a population. There is only one sample and we know the population mean, but we do not know the population standard deviation.

b. *Step 1:* Population 1: The number of mosquitos that chose to enter a chamber with a hand in it with no perfume or insect repellent (control condition).

Population 2: The number of mosquitos that chose to enter a chamber with a hand in it sprayed with a high concentration of Victoria's Secret Bombshell perfume.

The comparison distribution will be a distribution of means. The hypothesis test will be a single-sample t test because we have only one sample and we know the population mean, but we do not know the population standard deviation. This study meets at least one of the three assumptions: The dependent variable is scale. It is not likely that the five hands were randomly selected from all hands in the population. Last, we do not know whether the population is normally distributed, and there are only 5 participants (i.e., hands with perfume).

Step 2: Null hypothesis: The percentage of mosquitos that approached a hand with perfume is the same as the percentage of mosquitos that approached the hand with no perfume (or insect repellent)—$H_0: \mu_1 = \mu_2$.

Research hypothesis: A different percentage of mosquitos approached a hand with perfume compared to mosquitos that approached the hand with no perfume (or insect repellent)—$H_0: \mu_1 = \mu_2$.

Step 3:

$$\mu_M = \mu = 61\%$$

$$s_M = \frac{s}{\sqrt{N}} = \frac{12.052}{\sqrt{5}} = 5.390$$

Step 4: $df = N - 1 = 5 - 1 = 4$

The critical values, based on 4 degrees of freedom with an alpha level of 0.05 and a two-tailed test, are −2.776 and 2.776.

Step 5:

$$t = \frac{(M - \mu_M)}{s_M} = \frac{17\% - 61\%}{5.390} = -8.163$$

Step 6: Reject the null hypothesis. It appears that significantly fewer mosquitos approached the hand with perfume compared to mosquitos that experienced the control condition, no perfume. The statistics, as presented in a journal article, would read: $t(4) = -8.163$, $p < 0.05$

c. Cohen's $d = t = \frac{(M - \mu)}{s} = \frac{17\% - 61\%}{12.052} = -3.65$
Based on Cohen's conventions, this is a huge effect size. (Cohen considered 0.8 to be a large effect.)

d. Calculate the confidence interval for the sample mean for the perfume.

Given $M = 17\%$ and $s = 12.052$, standard error is:

$$s_M = \frac{s}{\sqrt{N}} = \frac{12.052}{\sqrt{5}} = 5.390$$

$M_{lower} = -t(s_M) + M_{sample} = -2.776(5.390) + 17\% = 2.037\%$

We calculate the upper end of the interval as:

$M_{upper} = t(s_M) + M_{sample} = 2.776(5.390) + 17\% = 31.963\%$

The 95% confidence interval around the mean of 17% is [2.04%, 31.96%].

e. The population mean, 61%, does not fall within the 95% confidence interval for a sample mean of 17%. We can conclude that the sample of perfumed hands placed in the chamber with the mosquitoes came from a different population than the mosquitoes who experienced the control condition. The confidence interval allows us to make the same conclusion as the t test, but it gives us more information with an interval estimate as opposed to a point estimate.

f. Replication studies help to increase our confidence in a particular finding. If this finding is replicated, then we have more confidence that Victoria's Secret Bombshell perfume repels mosquitoes. Without a replication study,

this finding might be limited to this specific sample or this particular location.

g. Failure to replicate may be a reflection of the research context. For example, the perfume may not be as effective in a warmer climate, with a different breed of mosquitoes, or using a different type of chamber.

9-35 a. The appropriate mean: $\mu_M = \mu = 11.72$

The calculations for the appropriate standard deviation (in this case, standard error, s_M) are:

$$M = \frac{\Sigma X}{N} = \frac{(25.62 + 13.09 + 8.74 + 17.63 + 2.80 + 4.42)}{6} = 12.05$$

X	X − M	(X − M)²
25.62	13.57	184.145
13.09	1.04	1.082
8.74	−3.31	10.956
17.63	5.58	31.136
2.80	−9.25	85.563
4.42	−7.63	58.217

Numerator: $\Sigma(X - M)^2 = \Sigma(184.145 + 1.082 + 10.956 + 31.136 + 85.563 + 58.217) = 371.099$

$$s = \sqrt{\frac{\Sigma(X - M)^2}{(N - 1)}} = \sqrt{\frac{371.099}{(6 - 1)}} = \sqrt{74.220} = 8.615$$

$$s_M = \frac{s}{\sqrt{N}} = \frac{8.615}{\sqrt{6}} = 3.517$$

b. $t = \frac{(M - \mu_M)}{s_M} = \frac{(12.05 - 11.72)}{3.517} = 0.09$

c. There are several possible answers to this question. Among the hypotheses that could be examined are whether the length of stay on death row depends on gender, race, or age. Specifically, given prior evidence of a racial bias in the implementation of the death penalty, we might hypothesize that black and Hispanic prisoners have shorter times to execution than do prisoners overall.

d. We would need to know the population standard deviation. If we were really interested in this, we could calculate the standard deviation from the entire online execution list.

e. The null hypothesis states that the average time spent on death row in recent years is equal to what it has been historically (no change): $H_0: \mu_1 = \mu_2$. The research hypothesis is that there has been a change in the average time spent on death row: $H_1: \mu_1 \neq \mu_2$.

f. The t statistic we calculated was 0.09. The critical t values for a two-tailed test, alpha level of 0.05, and df of 5, are ±2.571. We fail to reject the null hypothesis and conclude that we do not have sufficient evidence to indicate a change in time spent on death row.

g. $M_{lower} = -t(s_M) + M_{sample} = -2.571(3.517) + 12.05$

$= 3.01$ years

$M_{upper} = t(s_M) + M_{sample} = 2.571(3.517) + 12.05 = 21.09$ years

The 95% confidence interval around the mean of 12.05 is [3.01, 21.09].

h. Because the population mean of 11.72 years is within the very large range of the confidence interval, we fail to reject the null hypothesis. This confidence interval is so large that it is not useful. The large size of the confidence interval is due to the large variability in the sample (s_M) and the small sample size (resulting in a large critical t value).

i. $d = \dfrac{(M - \mu)}{s} = \dfrac{(12.05 - 11.72)}{8.615} = 0.04$

j. This is a small effect.

Chapter 10

10-1 We can understand the meaning of a distribution of mean differences by reviewing how the distribution is created in the first place. A distribution of mean differences is constructed by measuring the difference scores for a sample of individuals and then averaging those differences. This process is performed repeatedly, using the same population and samples of the same size. Once a collection of mean differences is gathered, they can be displayed on a graph (in most cases, they form a bell-shaped curve).

10-3 The term *paired samples* is used to describe a test that compares an individual's scores in both conditions; it is also called a *paired-samples* t *test*. *Independent samples* refer to groups that do not overlap in any way, including membership; the observations made in one group in no way relate to or depend on the observations made in another group.

10-5 Unlike in a single-sample t test, in the paired-samples t test there are two scores for every participant; we take the difference between these scores before calculating the sample mean difference that will be used in the t test.

10-7 If the confidence interval around the mean difference score includes the value of 0, then 0 is a plausible mean difference. If we conduct a hypothesis test for these data, we would fail to reject the null hypothesis.

10-9 As with other hypothesis tests, the conclusions from both the single-sample t test or paired-samples t test and the confidence interval are the same, but the confidence interval gives us more information—an interval estimate, not just a point estimate.

10-11 Order effects occur when performance on a task changes because the dependent variable is being presented for a second time.

10-13 Because order effects result in a change in the dependent variable that is not directly the result of the independent variable of interest, the researcher may decide to use a between-groups design, particularly when counterbalancing is not possible. For example, a researcher may be interested in how the amount of practice affects the acquisition of a new language. It would not be possible for the same participants to be in both a group that has small amounts of practice and a group that has large amounts of practice.

10-15 a. $df = 17$, so the critical t value is 2.567, assuming you're anticipating an increase in marital satisfaction.

b. $df = 63$, so the critical t values are ± 2.001.

10-17 a.

Difference (D)	D – M	(D – M)²
−8	−9.25	85.563
8	6.75	45.563
2	0.75	0.563
5	3.75	14.063
−5	−6.25	39.063
4	2.75	7.563
−2	−3.25	10.563
6	4.75	22.563

$M_{difference} = 1.25$

$SS = \Sigma(D - M)^2 = 225.504$

$s = \sqrt{\dfrac{SS}{N-1}} = \sqrt{\dfrac{225.504}{7}} = 5.676$

$s_M = \dfrac{s}{\sqrt{N}} = \dfrac{5.676}{\sqrt{8}} = 2.007$

$t = \dfrac{(M - \mu_M)}{s_M} = \dfrac{(1.25 - 0)}{2.007} = 0.62$

b. With $df = 7$, the critical t values are ± 2.365. The calculated t statistic of 0.62 does not exceed the critical value. Therefore, we fail to reject the null hypothesis.

c. When increasing N to 1000, we need to recalculate s_M and the t test.

$s_M = \dfrac{s}{\sqrt{N}} = \dfrac{5.676}{\sqrt{1000}} = 0.179$

$t = \dfrac{(1.25 - 0)}{0.179} = 6.98$

The critical values with $df = 999$ are $t = \pm 1.98$. Because the calculated t exceeds one of the t critical values, we reject the null hypothesis.

d. Increasing the sample size increased the value of the t statistic and decreased the critical t values, making it easier for us to reject the null hypothesis.

10-19 a.

Difference (D)	D − M	(D − M)²
17	5.429	29.474
22	10.429	108.764
18	6.429	41.332
3	−8.571	73.462
11	−0.571	0.326
5	−6.571	43.178
5	−6.571	43.178

$M_{difference} = 11.571$

$SS = \Sigma(D - M)^2 = 339.714$

$s = \sqrt{\dfrac{SS}{N-1}} = \sqrt{\dfrac{339.714}{6}} = 7.525$

$s_M = \dfrac{s}{\sqrt{N}} = \dfrac{7.525}{\sqrt{7}} = 2.844$

$t = \dfrac{(M - \mu_M)}{s_M} = \dfrac{(11.571 - 0)}{2.844} = 4.07$

b. With $N = 7$, $df = 6$, $t = \pm 2.447$:

$M_{lower} = -t(s_M) + M_{sample} = -2.447(2.844) + 11.571 = 4.61$

$M_{upper} = t(s_M) + M_{sample} = 2.447(2.844) + 11.571 = 18.53$

c. $d = \dfrac{(M - \mu_M)}{s} = \dfrac{(11.571 - 0)}{7.525} = 1.54$

10-21 a. $s_M = \dfrac{s}{\sqrt{N}} = \dfrac{1.42}{\sqrt{13}} = 0.394$

$t = \dfrac{(-0.77 - 0)}{0.394} = -1.95$

b. $M_{lower} = -t(s_M) + M_{sample} = -2.179(0.394) + (-0.77)$
$= -1.63$

$M_{upper} = t(s_M) + M_{sample} = 2.179(0.394) + (-0.77) = 0.09$

c. $d = \dfrac{(M - \mu)}{s} = \dfrac{(-0.77 - 0)}{1.42} = -0.54$

10-23 A study using a paired-samples t test design would compare people before and after training using the program of mental exercises designed by PowerBrainRx. Population 1 would be people before the mental exercises training. Population 2 would be people after the mental exercises training.

The comparison distribution is a distribution of mean differences. The participants receiving mental exercises training are the same in both samples. So, we would calculate a difference score for each participant and a mean difference score for the study. The mean difference score would be compared to a distribution of all possible mean difference scores for a sample of this size and based on

the null hypothesis. In this case, the mean difference score would be compared to 0. Because there are two samples and all participants are in both samples, we would use a paired-samples t test.

10-25 a. *Step 1:* Population 1 is the Devils players in the 2007–2008 season. Population 2 is the Devils players in the 2008–2009 season. The comparison distribution is a distribution of mean differences. We meet one assumption: The dependent variable, goals, is scale. We do not, however, meet the assumption that the participants are randomly selected from the population. We may also not meet the assumption that the population distribution of scores is normally distributed (the scores do not appear normally distributed and the N is not at least 30).

Step 2: Null hypothesis: The team performed no differently, on average, between the 2007–2008 and 2008–2009 seasons: H_0: $\mu_1 = \mu_2$.

Research hypothesis: The team performed differently, on average, between the 2007–2008 and 2008–2009 seasons: H_1: $\mu_1 \neq \mu_2$.

Step 3: $\mu = 0$ and $s_M = 3.682$

Difference (D)	D − M	(D − M)²
11	4.833	23.358
6	−0.167	0.028
−7	−13.167	173.370
16	9.833	96.688
−2	−8.167	66.670
13	6.833	46.690

$M_{difference} = 6.167$

$SS = \Sigma(D - M)^2 = 406.834$

$s = \sqrt{\dfrac{SS}{N-1}} = \sqrt{\dfrac{406.834}{5}} = 9.020$

$s_M = \dfrac{s}{\sqrt{N}} = \dfrac{9.020}{\sqrt{6}} = 3.682$

Step 4: The critical t values with a two-tailed test, an alpha level of 0.05, and 5 degrees of freedom, are ± 2.571.

Step 5: $t = \dfrac{(M - \mu_M)}{s_M} = \dfrac{(6.167 - 0)}{3.682} = 1.67$

Step 6: Fail to reject the null hypothesis because the calculated t statistic of 1.67 does not exceed the critical t value.

b. $t(5) = 1.67$, $p > 0.05$ (*Note:* If we had used software, we would provide the actual p value.)

c. $M_{lower} = -t(s_M) + M_{sample} = -2.571(3.682) - 6.167$
$= -3.30$

g. Participants might get faster at completing the Stroop test as a result of practice with it. If so, their reaction times would be faster the second time they complete the task regardless of whether they had the posthypnotic suggestion.

h. The researchers could use counterbalancing by having some people complete the Stroop task in the posthypnotic suggestion condition first, and others complete the Stroop task in the no-suggestion condition first. So, if the researchers are concerned about order effects, they could use counterbalancing or switch to a between-groups design.

Chapter 11

11-1 An independent-samples *t* test is used when we do not know the population parameters and are comparing two groups that are composed of unrelated participants or observations.

11-3 Independent events are things that do not affect each other. For example, the lunch you buy today does not impact the hours of sleep the authors of this book will get tonight.

11-5 The comparison distribution for the paired-samples *t* test is made up of *mean differences*—the average of many difference scores. The comparison distribution for the independent-samples *t* test is made up of *differences between means*, or the differences we can expect to see between group means if the null hypothesis is true.

11-7 Both of these represent corrected variance within a group (s^2), but one is for the *X* variable and the other is for the *Y* variable. Because these are corrected measures of variance, $N-1$ is in the denominator of the equations.

11-9 We assume that larger samples do a better job of estimating the population than smaller samples do, so we would want the variability measure based on the larger sample to count more.

11-11 We can take the confidence interval's upper bound and lower bound, compare those to the point estimate in the numerator, and get the margin of error. So, if we predict a score of 7 with a confidence interval of [4.3, 9.7], we can also express this as a margin of error of 2.7 points (7±2.7). Confidence interval and margin of error are simply two ways to say the same thing.

11-13 Larger ranges mean less precision in making predictions, just as widening the goal posts in rugby or in American football mean that you can be less precise when trying to kick the ball between the posts. Smaller ranges indicate we are doing a better job of predicting the phenomenon within the population. For example, a 95% confidence interval that spans a range from 2 to 12 is larger than a 95% confidence interval from 6 to 8. Although the percentage range has stayed the same, the width of the distribution has changed.

11-15 We would take several steps back from the final calculation of standard error to the step in which we calculated pooled variance. Pooled variance is the variance version, or squared version, of standard deviation. To convert pooled variance to the pooled standard deviation, we take its square root.

11-17 Guidelines for interpreting the size of an effect based on Cohen's *d* were presented in Table 11-2. Those guidelines state that 0.2 is a small effect, 0.5 is a medium effect, and 0.8 is a large effect.

11-19 Both the prior and the posterior distributions are distributions of belief. On the *y*-axis, they represent the credibility or likelihood—that is, our degree of belief—of each of the possible values along the *x*-axis. The prior distribution represents our distribution of belief before we've begun data collection. After we collect data, the posterior distribution is our updated distribution of belief, taking into account both our prior beliefs about the likelihood of values along the *x*-axis and what the data tell us about the likelihood of values along the *x*-axis.

11-21 **a.** Group 1 is treated as the *X* variable; $M_X = 95.8$.

X	X − M	(X − M)²
97	1.2	1.44
83	−12.8	163.84
105	9.2	84.64
102	6.2	38.44
92	−3.8	14.44

$$s_X^2 = \frac{\Sigma(X-M)^2}{N-1} = \frac{(1.44+163.84+84.64+24.44+14.44)}{5-1}$$
$$= 75.7$$

Group 2 is treated as the *Y* variable; $M_Y = 104$.

Y	Y − M	(Y − M)²
111	7	49
103	−1	1
96	−8	64
106	2	4

$$s_Y^2 = \frac{\Sigma(Y-M)^2}{N-1} = \frac{(49+1+64+4)}{4-1} = 39.333$$

b. Treating group 1 as *X* and group 2 as *Y*, $df_X = N-1 = 5-1 = 4$, $df_Y = 4-1 = 3$, and $df_{total} = df_X + df_Y = 4+3 = 7$.

c. −2.365, 2.365

d. $s_{pooled}^2 = \left(\frac{df_X}{df_{total}}\right)s_X^2 + \left(\frac{df_Y}{df_{total}}\right)s_Y^2 = \left(\frac{4}{7}\right)75.7 + \left(\frac{3}{7}\right)39.333$
$$= 43.257 + 16.857 = 60.114$$

e. For group 1: $s^2_{M_X} = \dfrac{s^2_{pooled}}{N_X} = \dfrac{60.114}{5} = 12.023$

For group 2: $s^2_{M_Y} = \dfrac{s^2_{pooled}}{N_Y} = \dfrac{60.114}{4} = 15.029$

f. $s^2_{difference} = s^2_{M_X} + s^2_{M_Y} = 12.023 + 15.029 = 27.052$

The standard deviation of the distribution of differences between means is:

$s_{difference} = \sqrt{s^2_{difference}} = \sqrt{27.052} = 5.201$

g. $t = \dfrac{(M_X - M_Y)}{s_{difference}} = \dfrac{(95.8 - 104) - (0)}{5.201} = -1.58$

h. The critical t values for the 95% confidence interval for a df of 7 are -2.365 and 2.365.

$(M_X - M_Y)_{lower} = -t(s_{difference}) + (M_X - M_Y)_{sample}$
$= -2.365(5.201) + (-8.2) = -20.50$

$(M_X - M_Y)_{upper} = t(s_{difference}) + (M_X - M_Y)_{sample}$
$= 2.365(5.201) + (-8.2) = 4.10$

The confidence interval is $[-20.50, 4.10]$.

i. To calculate Cohen's d, we need to calculate the pooled standard deviation for the data:

$s_{pooled} = \sqrt{s^2_{pooled}} = \sqrt{60.114} = 7.753$

Cohen's $d =$

$\dfrac{(M_X - M_Y) - (\mu_X - \mu_Y)}{s_{pooled}} = \dfrac{(95.8 - 104) - (0)}{7.753} = -1.06$

11-23 a. df_{total} is 35, and the cutoffs are -2.030 and 2.030.

b. df_{total} is 26, and the cutoffs are -2.779 and 2.779.

c. -1.740 and 1.740

11-25 a. *Step 1:* Population 1 is highly hypnotizable people who receive a posthypnotic suggestion. Population 2 is highly hypnotizable people who do not receive a posthypnotic suggestion. The comparison distribution will be a distribution of differences between means. The hypothesis test will be an independent-samples t test because there are two samples and every participant is in only one sample. This study meets one of the three assumptions and may meet another. The dependent variable, reaction time in seconds, is scale. The data were not likely randomly selected, so we should be cautious when generalizing beyond the sample. We do not know whether the population is normally distributed, and there are fewer than 30 participants, but the sample data do not suggest skew.

Step 2: Null hypothesis: Highly hypnotizable individuals who receive a posthypnotic suggestion have the same average Stroop reaction times as highly hypnotizable individuals who receive no posthypnotic suggestion—$H_0: \mu_1 = \mu_2$.

Research hypothesis: Highly hypnotizable individuals who receive a posthypnotic suggestion have different average Stroop reaction times than highly hypnotizable individuals who receive no posthypnotic suggestion—$H_1: \mu_1 \neq \mu_2$.

Step 3: $(\mu_1 - \mu_2) = 0$; $s_{difference} = 0.463$

Calculations:

$M_X = 12.55$

X	$X - M$	$(X - M)^2$
12.6	0.05	0.003
13.8	1.25	1.563
11.6	−0.95	0.903
12.2	−0.35	0.123
12.1	−0.45	0.203
13.0	0.45	0.203

$s^2_X = \dfrac{\Sigma(X - M)^2}{N - 1}$

$= \dfrac{(0.003 + 1.563 + 0.903 + 0.123 + 0.203 + 0.203)}{6 - 1}$

$= 0.600$

$M_Y = 9.50$

Y	$Y - M$	$(Y - M)^2$
8.5	−1.0	1.000
9.6	0.1	0.010
10.0	0.5	0.250
9.2	−0.3	0.090
8.9	−0.6	0.360
10.8	1.3	1.690

$s^2_Y = \dfrac{\Sigma(Y - M)^2}{N - 1}$

$= \dfrac{(1.0 + 0.01 + 0.25 + 0.09 + 0.36 + 1.69)}{6 - 1}$

$= 0.680$

$df_X = N_X - 1 = 6 - 1 = 5$

$df_Y = N_Y - 1 = 6 - 1 = 5$

$df_{total} = df_X + df_Y = 5 + 5 = 10$

$s^2_{pooled} = \left(\dfrac{df_X}{df_{total}}\right)s^2_X + \left(\dfrac{df_Y}{df_{total}}\right)s^2_Y = \left(\dfrac{5}{10}\right)0.600 + \left(\dfrac{5}{10}\right)0.680$

$= 0.300 + 0.340 = 0.640$

$s^2_{M_X} \dfrac{s^2_{pooled}}{N_X} = \dfrac{0.640}{6} = 0.107$

$$s^2_{M_Y} = \frac{s^2_{pooled}}{N_Y} = \frac{0.640}{6} = 0.107$$

$$s^2_{difference} = s^2_{M_X} + s^2_{M_Y} = 0.107 + 0.107 = 0.214$$

$$s_{difference} = \sqrt{s^2_{difference}} = \sqrt{0.214} = 0.463$$

Step 4: The critical values, based on a two-tailed test, an alpha level of 0.05, and df_{total} of 10, are −2.228 and 2.228. (*Note:* It is helpful to draw a curve that includes these cutoffs.)

Step 5: $t = \dfrac{(12.55 - 9.50) - (0)}{0.463} = \dfrac{3.05}{0.463} = 6.59$

(*Note:* It is helpful to add this t statistic to the curve that you drew in step 4.)

Step 6: Reject the null hypothesis; it appears that highly hypnotizable people have faster Stroop reaction times when they receive a posthypnotic suggestion than when they do not.

b. $t(10) = 6.59$, $p < 0.05$. (*Note:* If we used software to conduct the t test, we would report the actual p value associated with this test statistic.)

c. When there are two separate samples, the t statistic becomes smaller. Thus, it becomes more difficult to reject the null hypothesis with a between-groups design than with a within-groups design.

d. In the within-groups design and the calculation of the paired-samples t test, we create a set of difference scores and conduct a t test on that set of difference scores. This means that any overall differences that participants have on the dependent variable are subtracted out and do not go into the measure of overall variability that is in the denominator of the t statistic.

e. To calculate the 95% confidence interval, first calculate:

$$s_{difference} = \sqrt{s^2_{difference}} = \sqrt{s^2_{M_X} + s^2_{M_Y}}$$

$$= \sqrt{\frac{s^2_{pooled}}{N_X} + \frac{s^2_{pooled}}{N_Y}}$$

$$= \sqrt{\frac{0.640}{6} + \frac{0.640}{6}} = \sqrt{0.214} = 0.463$$

The critical t statistics for a distribution with $df = 10$ that correspond to an alpha level of 0.05—that is, the values that mark off the most extreme 0.025 in each tail—are −2.228 and 2.228.

Then calculate:

$(M_X - M_Y)_{lower} = -t(s_{difference}) + (M_X - M_Y)_{sample} = -2.228$
$(0.463 + (12.55 - 9.5) = -1.032 + 3.05 = 2.02$
$(M_X - M_Y)_{upper} = t(s_{difference}) + (M_X - M_Y)_{sample} =$
$2.228(0.463) + (12.55 - 9.5) = 1.032 + 3.05 = 4.08$

The 95% confidence interval around the difference between means of 3.05 is [2.02, 4.08].

f. Were we to draw repeated samples (of the same sizes) from these two populations, 95% of the time the confidence interval would contain the true population parameter.

g. Because the confidence interval does not include 0, it is not plausible that there is no difference between means. Were we to conduct a hypothesis test, we would be able to reject the null hypothesis and could conclude that the means of the two samples are different.

h. In addition to determining statistical significance, the confidence interval allows us to determine a range of plausible differences between means. An interval estimate gives us a better sense than does a point estimate of how precisely we can estimate from this study.

i. The appropriate measure of effect size for a t statistic is Cohen's d, which is calculated as:

$$d = \frac{(M_X - M_Y) - (\mu_X - \mu_Y)}{s_{pooled}} = \frac{(12.55 - 9.5) - (0)}{\sqrt{0.640}} = 3.81$$

j. Based on Cohen's conventions, this is a large effect size.

k. It is useful to have effect-size information because the hypothesis test tells us only whether we were likely to have obtained our sample mean by chance. The effect size tells us the magnitude of the effect, giving us a sense of how important or practical this finding is, and allows us to standardize the results of the study so that we can compare across studies. Here, we know that there's a large effect.

11-27 a. *Step 1:* Population 1 consists of men. Population 2 consists of women. The comparison distribution is a distribution of differences between means. We will use an independent-samples t test because men and women cannot be in both conditions, and there are two groups. Of the three assumptions, we meet one because the dependent variable, number of words uttered, is a scale variable. We do not know whether the data were randomly selected or whether the population is normally distributed, and there is a small N, so we should be cautious in drawing conclusions.

Step 2: Null hypothesis: There is no mean difference in the number of words uttered by men and women—H_0: $\mu_1 = \mu_2$. Research hypothesis: Men and women utter a different number of words, on average—H_1: $\mu_1 \neq \mu_2$.

Step 3: $(\mu_1 - \mu_2) = 0$; $= s_{difference} = 612.565$
Calculations (treating women as X and men as Y):

$$M_X = 16,091.600$$

X	X − M	(X − M)²
17,345	1253.400	1,571,011.560
15,593	−498.600	248,601.960
16,624	532.400	283,499.760
16,696	604.400	365,299.360
14,200	−1891.600	3,578,150.560

$$s^2_X = \frac{\Sigma(X - M)^2}{N - 1} = \frac{(6,046,513.200)}{5 - 1} = 1,511,628.300$$

$$M_Y = 16,160.600$$

Y	$Y - M$	$(Y - M)^2$
16,345	184.400	34,003.360
17,222	1061.400	1,126,569.960
15,646	−514.600	264,813.160
14,889	−1271.600	1,616,966.560
16,701	540.400	292,032.160

$$s_Y^2 = \frac{\Sigma(Y - M)^2}{N-1} = \frac{(3,334,385.200)}{5-1} = 833,596.300$$

$df_X = N - 1 = 5 - 1 = 4$

$df_Y = N - 1 = 5 - 1 = 4$

$df_{total} = df_X + df_Y = 8$

$$s_{pooled}^2 = \left(\frac{df_X}{df_{total}}\right)s_X^2 + \left(\frac{df_Y}{df_{total}}\right)s_Y^2$$

$$= \left(\frac{4}{10}\right)1,511,628.300 + \left(\frac{4}{10}\right)833,596.300$$

$$= 938,089.84$$

$$s_{M_X}^2 = \frac{s_{pooled}^2}{N_X} = \frac{938,089.84}{5} = 187,617.968$$

$$s_{M_Y}^2 = \frac{s_{pooled}^2}{N_Y} = \frac{938,089.84}{5} = 187,617.968$$

$$s_{difference}^2 = s_{M_X}^2 + s_{M_Y}^2 = 187,617.968 + 187,617.968$$

$$= 375,235.936$$

$$s_{difference} = \sqrt{s_{difference}^2} = \sqrt{375,235.936} = 612.565$$

Step 4: The critical values, based on a two-tailed test, an alpha level of 0.05, and a df_{total} of 8, are −2.306 and 2.306.

Step 5: $t = \dfrac{(16,091.600 - 16,160.600) - (0)}{612.565} = -0.11$

Step 6: We fail to reject the null hypothesis. The calculated t statistic of −0.11 is not more extreme than the critical t values.

b. $t(8) = -0.11$, $p > 0.05$. (*Note:* If we used software to conduct the t test, we would report the actual p value associated with this test statistic.)

c. $(M_X - M_Y)_{lower} = -t(s_{difference}) + (M_X - M_Y)_{sample}$
$$= -2.306(612.565) + (-69.000)$$
$$= -1481.575$$
$(M_X - M_Y)_{upper} = t(s_{difference}) + (M_X - M_Y)_{sample}$
$$= 2.306(612.565) + (-69.000)$$
$$= 1343.575$$

d. The 95% confidence interval around the observed mean difference of −69.00 is [−1481.58, 1343.58].

e. The confidence interval does not include 0 (the hypothesized mean difference if the two samples had the same mean). The conclusion about the null hypothesis is the same for both the hypothesis test and the confidence interval.

f. First, we need the appropriate measure of variability. In this case, we calculate pooled standard deviation by taking the square root of the pooled variance:

$$s_{pooled} = \sqrt{s_{pooled}^2} = \sqrt{938,089.84} = 968.550$$

Now we can calculate Cohen's d:

$$d = \frac{(M_X - M_Y)}{s} = \frac{(16,091.600 - 16,160.600) - (0)}{968.550}$$
$$= -0.07$$

g. This is a small effect.

h. Effect size tells us how big the difference we observed between means was, uninfluenced by sample size. Often, this measure will help us understand whether we want to continue along our current research lines; that is, if a strong effect is indicated but we fail to reject the null hypothesis, we might want to replicate the study with more statistical power. In this case, however, the failure to reject the null hypothesis is accompanied by a small effect.

11–29 a. *Step 1:* Population 1 is people who watch fictional shows. Population 2 is people who watch documentaries. The hypothesis test will be an independent-samples t test because there are two samples and every participant is in only one sample. This study meets two of the three assumptions and may meet another. The dependent variable, number of pictures in which the participant correctly identified the emotion (a measure of theory of mind), is a scale variable. Participants were not likely to have been randomly selected, so we must generalize with caution. In addition, we do not know whether the population is normally distributed, and there are fewer than 30 participants. Thus, we should be cautious in drawing conclusions from these data.

Step 2: Null hypothesis: The mean number of correctly identified emotions will not differ between people who watch TV fiction compared to people who watch documentaries—$H_0: \mu_1 = \mu_2$.

Research hypothesis: People who watch TV fiction will correctly identify a different number of emotions, on average, than people who watch documentaries—$H_1: \mu_1 \neq \mu_2$.

Step 3: $(\mu_1 - \mu_2) = 0$; $s_{difference} = 0.664$

Calculations:

$$M_X = 29$$

TV Fiction		
28	−1	1
30	1	1
31	2	4
27	−2	4
29	0	0
29	0	0
31	2	4
27	−2	4
29	0	0

$$s_X^2 = \frac{\Sigma(X - M)^2}{N - 1} = \frac{18}{9 - 1} = 2.250$$

$$M_Y = 27.5$$

Documentary		
27	−0.5	0.25
26	−1.5	2.25
28	0.5	0.25
29	1.5	2.25
29	1.5	2.25
28	0.5	0.25
27	−0.5	0.25
26	−1.5	2.25

$$s_Y^2 = \frac{\Sigma(Y - M)^2}{N - 1} = \frac{10}{8 - 1} = 1.429$$

$$df_X = N_X - 1 = 9 - 1 = 8$$
$$df_Y = N_Y - 1 = 8 - 1 = 7$$
$$df_{total} = df_X + df_Y = 8 + 7 = 15$$

$$s_{pooled}^2 = \left(\frac{df_X}{df_{total}}\right)s_X^2 + \left(\frac{df_Y}{df_{total}}\right)s_Y^2 = \left(\frac{8}{15}\right)2.250$$

$$+ \left(\frac{7}{15}\right)1.429 = 1.200 + 0.667 = 1.867$$

$$s_{M_X}^2 = \frac{s_{pooled}^2}{N_X} = \frac{1.867}{9} = 0.207$$

$$s_{M_Y}^2 = \frac{s_{pooled}^2}{N_Y} = \frac{1.867}{8} = 0.233$$

$$s_{difference}^2 = s_{M_X}^2 + s_{M_Y}^2 = 0.207 + 0.233 = 0.440$$

$$s_{difference} = \sqrt{s_{difference}^2} = \sqrt{0.440} = 0.663$$

Step 4: The critical values, based on a two-tailed test, an alpha level of 0.05, and df_{total} of 15, are −2.132 and 2.132. (*Note:* It is helpful to draw a curve that includes these cutoffs.)

Step 5:

$$t = \frac{(M_X - M_Y)}{s_{difference}} = \frac{(29 - 27.5)}{0.663} = \frac{1.5}{0.663} = 2.262$$

(*Note:* It is helpful to add this *t* statistic to the curve that you drew in step 4.)

Step 6: Reject the null hypothesis; we conclude that there is evidence from this study to support the research hypothesis. It appears that people who view TV fiction are better, on average, at identifying others' emotions than are people who view documentaries.

b. $t(15) = 2.26$, $p < 0.05$ (*Note:* If we used software to conduct the *t* test, we would report the actual *p* value associated with this test statistic.)

c. To calculate the 95% confidence interval, we find the *t* statistics that correspond to an alpha level of 0.05 that we identified earlier, −2.132 and 2.132. We calculate the lower end of the interval as:

$$(M_X - M_Y)_{lower} = -t(s_{difference}) + (M_X - M_Y)_{sample}$$
$$= -2.132(0.663) + 1.5 = 0.086$$

We calculate the upper end of the interval as:

$$(M_X - M_Y)_{upper} = t(s_{difference}) + (M_X - M_Y)_{sample}$$
$$= 2.132(0.663) + 1.5 = 2.914$$

The 95% confidence interval around the difference between means of 1.5 is [0.09, 2.91].

d. The confidence interval does not include 0 (the hypothetical mean difference if the two samples had the same mean). The conclusion about the null hypothesis is the same for both the hypothesis test and the confidence interval. It appears that there is a mean difference between the two groups.

e. The margin of error is 1.415, and each end of the confidence interval should be exactly the same distance from the sample mean difference.

$$0.085 - (1.5) = -1.415$$
$$2.915 - (1.5) = 1.415$$

f. The appropriate measure of effect size is:

$$\text{Cohen's } d = \frac{(M_X - M_Y) - (\mu_X - \mu_Y)}{s_{pooled}} = \frac{1.5}{1.366} = 1.098$$

g. Based on Cohen's conventions, this is a large effect.

h. The effect size supplements the point estimate of the *t* test, and the confidence interval. A statistically significant finding may not be a large or important one. The effect size tells us how big of an effect watching fictional TV has on a test of theory of mind—a large effect, in fact.

11-31 a. We would use a single-sample *t* test because there is one sample of figure skaters and are comparing that sample to a population (women with eating disorders) for which we know the mean.

b. We would use an independent-samples *t* test because there are two samples, and no participant can be in both samples. One cannot have both a high level and a low level of knowledge about a topic.

c. We would use a paired-samples *t* test because there are two samples, but every student is assigned to both samples—one night of sleep loss and one night of no sleep loss.

11-33 a. We would use an independent-samples *t* test because there are two samples, and no participant can be in both samples. One cannot be a pedestrian en route to work and a tourist pedestrian at the same time. (Note that although the researchers reported medians, we could calculate means for this study as well.)

b. Null hypothesis: People en route to work tend to walk at the same pace, on average, as people who are tourists—H_0: $\mu_1 = \mu_2$. Research hypothesis: People en route to work tend to walk at a different pace, on average, than do those who are tourists—H_1: $\mu_1 \neq \mu_2$.

11-35 a. The independent variable is the tray availability, with levels of not available and available.

   b. The dependent variables are food waste and dish use. Food waste was likely operationalized by weight or volume of food disposed, whereas dish use was likely operationalized by number of dishes used or dirtied.

   c. This study is an experiment because the environment was manipulated or controlled by the researchers. It assumes that the individuals were randomly sampled from the population and randomly assigned to one of the two levels of the independent variable.

   d. We would use an independent-samples t test because there is a scale dependent variable, there are two samples, and no participant can be in both samples. One cannot have trays available and not available at the same time.

11-37 a. The researchers used an independent-samples t test. We know this because there were two separate groups, so this was a between-groups design. The researchers were comparing the difference between means.

   b. We know that the finding is statistically significant because we are told that the p value is less than 0.001. Researchers often report very small p values this way rather than saying, for example, $p = 0.0000054$.

   c. There were 65 participants. There were 63 total degrees of freedom. This would have been calculated by summing the degrees of freedom for each group. The degrees of freedom for each group was the sample size minus 1.

   d. There was a mean of 14.6% verbatim overlap with the lecture for students taking notes on laptops, and a mean of 8.8% verbatim overlap with the lecture for students taking notes longhand.

   e. The effect size is 0.94. This is a large effect, according to Cohen's conventions.

11-39 In Exercise 11.38, you calculated the difference between the means of these samples to be $82.25 - 82.6 = -0.35$; the standard error for the differences between means, $s_{difference}$, to be 11.641; and the degrees of freedom to be 7. (Note that the order of subtraction in calculating the difference between means is irrelevant; we could just as easily have subtracted 82.25 from 82.6 and gotten a positive result, 0.35.)

1. We draw a normal curve with the sample difference between means in the center.

2. We indicate the bounds of the 95% confidence interval on either end and write the percentages under each segment of the curve: 2.5% in each tail.

3. We look up the t statistics for the lower and upper ends of the confidence interval in the t table, based on a two-tailed

test, an alpha level of 0.05 (which corresponds to a 95% confidence interval), and the degrees of freedom (7) that we calculated earlier. Because the normal curve is symmetric, the bounds of the confidence interval fall at t statistics of -2.365 and 2.365. We add those t statistics to the normal curve.

4. We convert the t statistics to raw differences between means for the lower and upper ends of the confidence interval.
$$(M_X - M_Y)_{lower} = -t(s_{difference}) + (M_X - M_Y)_{sample}$$
$$= -2.365(11.641) + (-0.35) = -27.88$$
$$(M_X - M_Y)_{upper} = t(s_{difference}) + (M_X - M_Y)_{sample}$$
$$= 2.365(11.641) + (-0.35) = 27.18$$

The confidence interval is $[-27.88, \ 27.18]$.

5. We check the answer; each end of the confidence interval should be exactly the same distance from the sample mean.

$$-27.88 - (-0.35) = -27.53$$
$$27.18 - (-0.35) = 27.53$$

The interval checks out, and we know that the margin of error is 27.53.

11-41 The statistics would appear in a journal article as follows: $t(7) = -0.03$, $p > 0.05$, $d = -0.02$. In addition to the results of hypothesis testing and the effect size, we would include the means and standard deviations for the two samples. We calculated the means in step 3 of hypothesis testing, and we also calculated the variances. We can calculate the standard deviations by taking the square roots of the variances. The descriptive statistics can be reported in parentheses as follows: (Women: $M = 82.25$, $SD = 17.02$; Men: $M = 82.60$, $SD = 17.60$).

11-43 The general relation is that if there is a very strong prior, we will need a lot more evidence to move away from that prior. So, if the data are inconsistent with our prior belief, but those data are sparse, the posterior distribution will still look a lot like the prior distribution. That is, our beliefs will not change that much. However, if we have a strong prior belief, and then we observe a lot of data that are inconsistent with that belief, we will make large changes to our initial belief. In this case, the posterior distribution will look very different from the prior distribution—it will look more like the data.

11-45 a. Waters is predicting lower levels of obesity among children who are in the Edible Schoolyard program than among children who are not in the program. Waters and others who believe in her program are likely to notice successes and overlook failures. Solid research is necessary before instituting such a program nationally, even though it sounds extremely promising.

   b. Students could be randomly assigned to participate in the Edible Schoolyard program or to continue with their usual lunch plan. The independent variable is the program, with two levels (Edible Schoolyard, control), and the dependent variable could be weight. Weight is easily operationalized by weighing children, perhaps after one year in the program.

c. We would use an independent-samples t test because there are two samples and no student is in both samples.

d. *Step 1:* Population 1 is all students who participated in the Edible Schoolyard program. Population 2 is all students who did not participate in the Edible Schoolyard program. The comparison distribution will be a distribution of differences between means. The hypothesis test will be an independent-samples t test. This study meets all three assumptions. The dependent variable, weight, is scale. The data would be collected using a form of random selection. In addition, there would be more than 30 participants in the sample, indicating that the comparison distribution would likely be normal.

e. *Step 2:* Null hypothesis: Students who participate in the Edible Schoolyard program weigh the same, on average, as students who do not participate—H_0: $\mu_1 = \mu_2$.

Research hypothesis: Students who participate in the Edible Schoolyard program have different weights, on average, than students who do not participate—H_1: $\mu_1 \neq \mu_2$.

f. The dependent variable could be nutrition knowledge, as assessed by a test, or body mass index (BMI).

g. There are many possible confounds when we do not conduct a controlled experiment. For example, the Berkeley school might be different to begin with. After all, the school allowed Waters to begin the program, and perhaps it had already emphasized nutrition. Random selection allows us to have faith in the ability to generalize beyond our sample. Random assignment allows us to eliminate confounds, other variables that may explain any differences between groups.

11-47 a. This study used a between-groups design. Recruiters looked at one of two résumés: one with a formal email address or one with an informal email address. This makes two separate samples, whose means could easily be compared. In addition, the dependent variable, hirability ratings, was scale.

b. The independent variable is the type of résumé looked at. This variable has two levels: formal email address or informal email address. The dependent variable is a rating of hirability.

c. The independent variable is likely the same: type of résumé, with two levels. However, the two levels might have to do with spelling errors. One résumé may have had many spelling errors and another résumé may have had no spelling errors. The dependent variable is likely the same: a rating of hirability.

d. Yes, it is possible that the sample was a random selection of recruiters. They may have had access to a full list of recruiters from a professional organization, in which case they could have randomly selected their participants. And it is likely that the researchers used random assignment when sending emails to recruiters in their sample.

e. Answers will vary. One possible way to measure hirability is to ask a yes or no question: Based on this résumé, is this person hirable? A second possible way is for recruiters to review multiple résumés and have them rank the résumés, with 1 being the most hirable.

f. Confidence intervals provide a range of possible estimates, as opposed to the point estimate identified in the hypothesis test.

g. Cohen's d measures effect size. The reported Cohen's d for email address on hirability is 0.81, and the reported Cohen's d for spelling errors on hirability is 0.80. Both of these effects are equally large, suggesting that résumés with an informal email address and/or many spelling errors are more likely to be viewed negatively than those with formal email addresses or no spelling errors.

Chapter 12

12-1 An ANOVA is a hypothesis test with at least one nominal or ordinal independent variable (with at least three total groups) and a scale dependent variable.

12-3 Between-groups variance is an estimate of the population variance based on the differences among the means; within-groups variance is an estimate of the population variance based on the differences within each of the three (or more) sample distributions.

12-5 The three assumptions are that the participants were randomly selected, the underlying populations are normally distributed, and the underlying variances of the different conditions are similar, or *homoscedastic*.

12-7 The F statistic is calculated as the ratio of two variances. Variability, and the variance measure of it, is always positive—it always exists. Variance is calculated as the sum of squared deviations, and squaring both positive and negative values makes them positive.

12-9 With sums of squares, we add up all the squared values. Deviations from the mean always sum to 0. By squaring these deviations, we can sum them and they will not sum to 0. Sums of squares are measures of variability of scores from the mean.

12-11 The grand mean is the mean of every score in a study, regardless of which sample the score came from.

12-13 Cohen's d; R^2

12-15 Omega squared is an estimate of effect size that, similar to R^2, estimates the proportion of variance in the dependent variable that is accounted for by the independent variable.

12-17 *Post hoc* means "after this." These tests are needed when an ANOVA is significant and we want to discover where significant differences exist between the groups.

12-19 a. *Standard error* is wrong. The professor is reporting the spread for a distribution of scores, the *standard deviation*.

  b. *t statistic* is wrong. We do not use the population standard deviation to calculate a *t* statistic. The sentence should say *z statistic* instead.

  c. *Parameters* is wrong. Parameters are numbers that describe populations, not samples. The researcher calculated *statistics*.

  d. *z statistic* is wrong. Evelyn is comparing two means; thus, she would have calculated a *t* statistic.

12-21 a. (i) The formula is missing the summation symbol, Σ, and it is missing the squared term. (ii) When calculating SS_{within}, you must square the deviation of each score from its own group mean and then sum those deviation scores. (iii) The formula should read $SS_{within} = \Sigma(X - M)^2$.

  b. (i) The square root symbol is on the wrong side of the equation. (ii) *F* is a term based on variance, which means it is a squared term. *t* is the square root of *F*. (iii) The formula should read $t = \sqrt{F}$.

12-23 When statisticians state that one test is more conservative than another, they are saying that there is a lower risk of a Type I error but a higher risk of Type II error. That is, it sets the bar to reject the null hypothesis higher.

12-25 A reader might be suspicious that a researcher has engaged in *p*-hacking, and subject the findings to a Bonferroni test. It's easy to divide the alpha level of 0.05 by the number of tests, and then apply that new alpha level to published results.

12-27 a. $df_{between} = N_{groups} - 1 = 3 - 1 = 2$

  b. $df_{within} = df_1 + df_2 + \cdots + df_{last} = (4-1) + (3-1) + (5-1) = 3 + 2 + 4 = 9$

  c. $df_{total} = df_{between} + df_{within} = 2 + 9 = 11$

  d. The critical value for a between-groups degrees of freedom of 2 and a within-groups degrees of freedom of 9 at an alpha level of 0.05 is 4.26.

  e. $M_{1990} = \dfrac{\Sigma(X)}{N} = \dfrac{45 + 211 + 158 + 74}{4} = 122$

  $M_{2000} = \dfrac{\Sigma(X)}{N} = \dfrac{92 + 128 + 382}{3} = 200.667$

  $M_{2010} = \dfrac{\Sigma(X)}{N} = \dfrac{273 + 396 + 178 + 248 + 374}{5} = 293.80$

  $GM = \dfrac{\Sigma(X)}{N_{total}} = \dfrac{\left(\begin{array}{c} 45 + 211 + 158 + 74 + 92 + 128 + \\ 382 + 273 + 396 + 178 + 248 + 374 \end{array}\right)}{12}$
  $= 213.25$

f. (*Note:* The total sum of squares may not exactly equal the sum of the between-groups and within-groups sums of squares because of rounding decisions.)

The total sum of squares is calculated here as $SS_{total} = \Sigma(X - GM)^2$:

Sample	X	$(X - GM)$	$(X - GM)^2$
1990	45	−168.25	28,308.063
$M_{1990} = 122$	211	−2.25	5.063
	158	−55.25	3052.563
	74	−139.25	19,390.563
2000	92	−121.25	14,701.563
$M_{2000} = 200.667$	128	−85.25	7267.563
	382	168.75	28,476.563
2010	273	59.75	3570.063
$M_{2010} = 293.8$	396	182.75	33,397.563
	178	−35.25	1242.563
	248	34.75	1207.563
	374	160.75	25,840.563
$GM = 213.25$			$SS_{total} = \mathbf{166{,}460.256}$

g. The within-groups sum of squares is calculated here as $SS_{within} = \Sigma(X - M)^2$:

Sample	X	$(X - M)$	$(X - M)^2$
1990	45	−77	5929.00
$M_{1990} = 122$	211	89	7921.00
	158	36	1296.00
	74	−48	2304.00
2000	92	−108.667	11,808.517
$M_{2000} = 200.667$	128	−72.667	5280.493
	382	181.333	32,881.657
2010	273	−20.8	432.64
$M_{2010} = 293.8$	396	102.2	10,444.84
	178	−115.8	13,409.64
	248	−45.8	2097.64
	374	80.2	6432.04
$GM = 213.25$			$SS_{within} = \mathbf{100{,}237.467}$

h. The between-groups sum of squares is calculated here as $SS_{between} = \Sigma(M - GM)^2$:

Sample	X	$(M - GM)$	$(M - GM)^2$
1990	45	−91.25	8326.563
$M_{1990} = 122$	211	−91.25	8326.563
	158	−91.25	8326.563
	74	−91.25	8326.563
2000	92	−12.583	158.332
$M_{2000} = 200.667$	128	−12.583	158.332
	382	−12.583	158.332
2010	273	80.55	6488.303
$M_{2010} = 293.8$	396	80.55	6488.303
	178	80.55	6488.303
	248	80.55	6488.303
	374	80.55	6488.303
$GM = 213.25$			$SS_{between} = \mathbf{66,222.763}$

i. $MS_{between} = \dfrac{SS_{between}}{df_{between}} = \dfrac{66,222.763}{2} = 33,111.382$

$MS_{within} = \dfrac{SS_{within}}{df_{within}} = \dfrac{100,237.467}{9} = 11,137.496$

$F = \dfrac{MS_{between}}{MS_{within}} = \dfrac{33,111.382}{11,137.496} = 2.97$

Source	SS	df	MS	F
Between	66,222.763	2	33,111.382	2.97
Within	100,237.467	9	11,137.496	
Total	166,460.256	11		

j. Effect size is calculated as $R^2 = \dfrac{SS_{between}}{SS_{total}} = \dfrac{66,222.763}{166,460.256} =$ 0.40. According to Cohen's conventions for R^2, this is a very large effect.

12-29 a. $F = \dfrac{\text{between-groups variance}}{\text{within-groups variance}} = \dfrac{321.83}{177.24} = 1.82$

b. $F = \dfrac{2.79}{2.20} = 1.27$

c. $F = \dfrac{34.45}{41.60} = 0.83$

12-31

Source	SS	df	MS	F
Between	43	2	21.500	2.66
Within	89	11	8.091	
Total	132	13		

12-33 a. $R^2 = \dfrac{SS_{between}}{SS_{total}} = \dfrac{43}{132} = 0.326$

b. $\omega^2 = \dfrac{SS_{between} - ((df_{between})(MS_{within}))}{SS_{total} + MS_{within}}$

$= \dfrac{43 - ((2)(8.091))}{132 + 8.091} = \dfrac{26.818}{140.091} = 0.191$

12-35 With four groups, there would be a total of six different comparisons.

12-37 With seven groups, there would be a total of 21 different comparisons. The first group would be compared with groups 2, 3, 4, 5, 6, and 7. The second group would be compared with groups 3, 4, 5, 6, and 7. The third group would be compared with groups 4, 5, 6, and 7. The fourth group would be compared with groups 5, 6, and 7. The fifth group would be compared with groups 6 and 7. And the sixth group would be compared with group 7.

12-39 a. The independent variable is type of program. The levels are *The Daily Show* and network news. The dependent variable is the number of seconds of substantive video and audio reporting.

b. The hypothesis test that Fox would use is an independent-samples *t* test.

c. The independent variable is still type of program, but now the levels are *The Daily Show*, network news, and cable news. The hypothesis test would be a one-way between-groups ANOVA.

12-41 a. A *t* distribution; we are comparing the mean IQ of a sample of 10 to the population mean of 100; this student knows only the population mean—she doesn't know the population standard deviation.

b. An *F* distribution; we are comparing the mean ratings of four samples—families with no books visible, with only children's books visible, with only adult books visible, and with both types of books visible.

c. A *t* distribution; we are comparing the average vocabulary scores of two groups.

12-43 a. The independent variable in this case is the type of program in which students are enrolled; the levels are arts and sciences, education, law, and business. Because every student is enrolled in only one program, Ruby would use a one-way between-groups ANOVA.

b. Now the independent variable is year, with levels of first, second, or third. Because the same participants are repeatedly measured, Ruby would use a one-way within-groups ANOVA.

c. The independent variable in this case is type of degree, and its levels are master's, doctoral, and professional. Because every student is in only one type of degree program, Ruby would use a one-way between-groups ANOVA.

d. The independent variable in this case is stage of training, and its levels are master's, doctoral, and postdoctoral. Because the same students are repeatedly measured, Ruby would use a one-way within-groups ANOVA.

12-45 a. In this study, the independent variable was attendance, with three levels: < 5 sessions, 5–8 sessions, and 9–12 sessions.

b. The dependent variable was number of minutes of exercise per week.

c. Summary of Step 1

Population 1: People who attended fewer than 5 sessions of a group exercise-education program. Population 2: People who attended 5–8 sessions of a group exercise-education program. Population 3: People who attended 9–12 sessions of a group exercise-education program.

The comparison distribution will be an F distribution. The hypothesis test will be a one-way between-groups ANOVA. The data were not selected randomly, so we must generalize only with caution. We do not know if the underlying population distributions are normal, but the sample data do not indicate severe skew. To see if we meet the homoscedasticity assumption, we will check whether the largest variance is no greater than twice the smallest variance. From the calculations below, we see that the largest variance, 387, is not more than twice the smallest, 208.67, so we have met the homoscedasticity assumption. (The following information is taken from the calculation of SS_{within}.)

Sample	< 5	5–8	9–12
Squared deviations	400	324	324
	225	441	4
	25	9	289
			9
Sum of squares	650	774	626
$N - 1$	2	2	3
Variance	325	387	208.67

Summary of Step 2

Null hypothesis: People in different categories of attendance at a group exercise-education program exercise the same average number of minutes per week— $H_0: \mu_1 = \mu_2 = \mu_3$ Research hypothesis: People in different categories of attendance at a group exercise-education program do not exercise the same average number of minutes per week—H_1 is that at least one μ is different from another μ.

Summary of Step 3

$df_{between} = N_{groups} - 1 = 3 - 1 = 2$

$df_1 = 3 - 1 = 2;\ df_2 = 3 - 1 = 2;\ df_3 = 4 - 1 = 3$

$df_{within} = 2 + 2 + 3 = 7$

The comparison distribution will be the F distribution with 2 and 7 degrees of freedom.

Summary of Step 4

The critical F statistic based on an alpha level of 0.05 is 4.74.

Summary of Step 5

$df_{total} = 2 + 7 = 9$ or $df_{total} = 10 - 1 = 9$

$SS_{total} = \Sigma(X - GM)^2 = 12{,}222.40$

Sample	X	$(X - GM)$	$(X - GM)^2$
< 5	155	−24.6	605.16
$M_{<5} = 135$	120	−59.6	3552.16
	130	−49.6	2460.16
5–8	199	19.4	376.36
$M_{5-8} = 181$	160	−19.6	384.16
	184	4.4	19.36
9–12	230	50.4	2540.16
$M_{9-12} = 212$	214	34.4	1183.36
	195	15.4	237.16
	209	29.4	864.36
$GM = 179.60$			$SS_{total} = \mathbf{12{,}222.40}$

$SS_{within} = \Sigma(X - M)^2 = 2050.00$

Sample	X	$(X - M)$	$(X - M)^2$
< 5	155	20	400
$M_{<5} = 135$	120	−15	225
	130	−5	25
5–8	199	18	324
$M_{5-8} = 181$	160	−21	441
	184	3	9
9–12	230	18	324
$M_{9-12} = 212$	214	2	4
	195	−17	289
	209	−3	9
$GM = 179.60$			$SS_{within} = \mathbf{2050.00}$

$SS_{between} = \Sigma(M - GM)^2 = 10{,}172.40$

Sample	X	$(M - GM)$	$(M - GM)^2$
< 5	155	−44.6	1989.16
$M_{<5} = 135$	120	−44.6	1989.16
	130	−44.6	1989.16
5–8	199	1.4	1.96
$M_{5-8} = 181$	160	1.4	1.96
	184	1.4	1.96
9–12	230	32.4	1049.76
$M_{9-12} = 212$	214	32.4	1049.76
	195	32.4	1049.76
	209	32.4	1049.76
$GM = 179.60$			$SS_{between} = \mathbf{10{,}172.40}$

$$SS_{total} = SS_{within} + SS_{between} = 12,222.40 = 2050.00 + 10,172.40$$

$$MS_{between} = \frac{SS_{between}}{df_{between}} = \frac{10,172.40}{2} = 5086.20$$

$$MS_{within} = \frac{SS_{within}}{df_{within}} = \frac{2050.00}{7} = 292.857$$

$$F = \frac{MS_{between}}{MS_{within}} = \frac{5086.20}{292.857} = 17.37$$

Source	SS	df	MS	F
Between	10,172.40	2	5086.200	17.37
Within	2050.00	7	292.857	
Total	12,222.40	9		

Summary of Step 6

The F statistic, 17.37, is beyond the cutoff of 4.74. We can reject the null hypothesis. It appears that people in different categories of attendance at a group exercise-education program do exercise a different average number of minutes per week. However, the results from this ANOVA do not tell us where specific differences lie. The ANOVA tells us only that there is at least one difference between means. We must conduct a post hoc test to determine exactly which pairs of means are different.

d. $R^2 = \dfrac{SS_{between}}{SS_{total}} = \dfrac{10,172.40}{12,222.40} = 0.832$

This is a very large effect.

e. $\omega^2 = \dfrac{SS_{between} - ((df_{between})(MS_{within}))}{SS_{total} + MS_{within}}$

$$= \frac{10,172.40 - ((2)(292.857))}{12,222.40 + 292.857} = \frac{9586.686}{12,515.257} = 0.766$$

This is a very large effect.

12-47 a. $F = \dfrac{MS_{between}}{MS_{within}} = \dfrac{4.623}{0.522} = 8.856$

b. $t = \sqrt{F} = \sqrt{8.856} = 2.98$

c. The "Sig." for t is the same as that for the ANOVA, 0.005, because the F distribution reduces to the t distribution when we are dealing with two groups.

12-49 a. The independent variable is instructor self-disclosure, which is a nominal variable with three levels—high, medium, and low self-disclosure.

b. The first dependent variable mentioned is levels of motivation, which is a scale variable.

c. This is a between-groups design because students are exposed to only one of the three types of instructor self-disclosure via the Facebook pages.

d. A one-way between-subjects ANOVA would be used to analyze the data.

e. This is a true experiment as participants were randomly assigned to levels of a manipulated independent variable. This means that the researchers can draw a causal conclusion. That is, they can conclude that high self-disclosure causes "higher levels of motivation and affective learning and a more positive classroom climate," as compared with low and medium levels of self-disclosure.

12-51 a. The independent variable is languages spoken, which is a nominal variable with four levels—monolingual (English), bilingual (Spanish-English), bilingual (French-English), and bilingual (Chinese-English). The dependent variable is vocabulary skills as assessed by the PPVT, a scale variable.

b. We know that the finding is statistically significant because the p value of 0.0001 is less than the typical cutoff alpha level of 0.05.

c. The findings from the one-way ANOVA tell us only that there is at least one difference among the groups but not which specific groups are statistically significantly different from each other.

d. The Bonferroni test is a more conservative post hoc test. It is used to determine a critical value that is stricter than that based on an alpha level of 0.05. We can use this more conservative critical value to determine whether we can reject the null hypothesis when comparing the four levels of the independent variable.

e. Statistically significant mean differences between mean vocabulary scores exist between the monolingual children and the bilingual (Chinese-English) children and between the monolingual children and the bilingual (French-English) children. They also exist between the bilingual (Spanish-English) children and the bilingual (Chinese-English) children and between the bilingual (Spanish-English) children and the bilingual (French-English) children. However, the monolingual children and bilingual (Spanish-English) children did not statistically significantly differ from each other, on average, nor did the bilingual (Chinese-English) and bilingual (French-English) children statistically significantly differ from each other, on average.

12-53 a. Level of trust in the leader is the independent variable. It has three levels: low, moderate, and high.

b. The dependent variable is level of agreement with a policy supported by the leader or supervisor.

c. *Step 1:* Population 1 is employees with low trust in their leader. Population 2 is employees with moderate trust in their leader. Population 3 is employees with high trust in their leader. The comparison distribution will be an F distribution. The hypothesis test will be a one-way between-groups ANOVA. We do not know if employees were randomly selected. We also do not know if the underlying distributions are normal, and the sample sizes are small so we must proceed with caution. To check the final assumption, that we have homoscedastic variances, we will calculate variance for each group.

Sample	Low Trust	Moderate Trust	High Trust
Squared deviations	16	100	3.063
	1	121	18.063
	4	1	60.063
	25		27.563
Sum of squares	46	222	108.752
$N-1$	3	2	3
Variance	15.33	111	36.25

Because the largest variance, 111, is much more than twice as large as the smallest variance, we can conclude we have heteroscedastic variances. Violation of this third assumption of homoscedastic samples means we should proceed with caution. Because these data are intended to give you practice calculating statistics, proceed with your analyses. When conducting real research, we would want to have much larger sample sizes and to more carefully consider meeting the assumptions.

Step 2: Null hypothesis: There are no mean differences between these three groups: The mean level of agreement with a policy does not vary across the three trust levels—$H_0: \mu_1 = \mu_2 = \mu_3$.

Research hypothesis: There are mean differences between some or all of these groups: The mean level of agreement depends on trust.

Step 3: $df_{between} = N_{groups} - 1 = 3 - 1 = 2$

$df_{within} = df_1 + df_2 + \cdots + df_{last} = (4-1) + (3-1) +$
$\qquad (4-1) = 3 + 2 + 3 = 8$

$df_{total} = df_{between} + df_{within} = 2 + 8 = 10$

The comparison distribution will be an F distribution with 2 and 8 degrees of freedom.

Step 4: The critical value for the F statistic based on an alpha level of 0.05 is 4.46.

Step 5: $GM = 21.727$

Total sum of squares is calculated here as $SS_{total} = \Sigma(X - GM)^2$:

Sample	X	$(X - GM)$	$(X - GM)^2$
Low trust	9	−12.727	161.977
$M_{low} = 13$	14	−7.727	59.707
	11	−10.727	115.069
	18	−3.727	13.891
Moderate trust	14	−7.727	59.707
$M_{mod} = 24$	35	13.273	176.173
	23	1.273	1.621

(Table continued)

Sample	X	$(X - GM)$	$(X - GM)^2$
High trust	27	5.273	27.805
$M_{high} = 28.75$	33	11.273	127.081
	21	−0.727	0.529
	34	12.273	150.627

$$GM = 21.727 \qquad SS_{total} = \mathbf{894.187}$$

Within-groups sum of squares is calculated here as $SS_{within} = \Sigma(X - M)^2$:

Sample	X	$(X - M)$	$(X - M)^2$
Low trust	9	−4	16.00
$M_{low} = 13$	14	1	1.00
	11	−2	4.00
	18	5	25.00
Moderate trust	14	−10	100.00
$M_{mod} = 24$	35	11	121.00
	23	−1	1.00
High trust	27	−1.75	3.063
$M_{high} = 28.75$	33	4.25	18.063
	21	−7.75	60.063
	34	5.25	27.563

$$GM = 21.727 \qquad SS_{within} = 376.752$$

Between-groups sum of squares is calculated here as $SS_{between} = \Sigma(M - GM)^2$:

Sample	X	$(M - GM)$	$(M - GM)^2$
Low trust	9	−8.727	76.161
$M_{low} = 13$	14	−8.727	76.161
	11	−8.727	76.161
	18	−8.727	76.161
Moderate trust	14	2.273	5.167
$M_{mod} = 24$	35	2.273	5.167
	23	2.273	5.167
High trust	27	7.023	49.323
$M_{high} = 28.75$	33	7.023	49.323
	21	7.023	49.323
	34	7.023	49.323

$$GM = 21.727 \qquad SS_{between} = 517.437$$

$$MS_{between} = \frac{SS_{between}}{df_{between}} = \frac{517.437}{2} = 258.719$$

$$MS_{within} = \frac{SS_{within}}{df_{within}} = \frac{376.752}{8} = 47.094$$

$$F = \frac{MS_{between}}{MS_{within}} = \frac{258.719}{47.094} = 5.49$$

Source	SS	df	MS	F
Between	517.437	2	258.719	5.49
Within	376.752	8	47.094	
Total	894.187	10		

Step 6: The F statistic, 5.49, is beyond the cutoff of 4.46, so we can reject the null hypothesis. The mean level of agreement with a policy supported by a supervisor varies across level of trust in that supervisor. Remember: The research design and data did not meet the three assumptions of this statistical test, so we should be careful in interpreting this finding.

d. $F(2,8) = 5.49$, $p < 0.05$. (Note: We would include the actual p value if we used software to conduct this analysis).

e. Because there are unequal sample sizes, we must calculate a weighted sample size.

$$N' = \frac{N_{groups}}{\Sigma\left(\frac{1}{N}\right)} = \frac{3}{\left(\frac{1}{4}+\frac{1}{3}+\frac{1}{4}\right)} = \frac{3}{0.25+0.333+0.25}$$

$$= \frac{3}{0.833} = 3.601$$

$$s_M = \sqrt{\frac{MS_{within}}{N'}} = \sqrt{\frac{47.094}{3.601}} = 3.616$$

Now we can compare the three groups.

Low trust ($M = 13$) versus moderate trust ($M = 24$):

$$HSD = \frac{13-24}{3.616} = -3.04$$

Low trust ($M = 13$) versus high trust ($M = 28.75$):

$$HSD = \frac{13-28.75}{3.616} = -4.36$$

Moderate trust ($M = 24$) versus high trust ($M = 28.75$):

$$HSD = \frac{24-28.75}{3.616} = -1.31$$

According to the q table, the critical value is 4.04 for an alpha level of 0.05 when we are comparing three groups and have within-groups degrees of freedom of 8. We obtained one q value (-4.36) that exceeds this cutoff. Based on the calculations, there is a statistically significant difference between the mean level of agreement by employees with low trust in their supervisors compared to those with high trust. Because the sample sizes here were so small and we did not meet the three assumptions of ANOVA, we should be careful in making strong statements about this

finding. In fact, these preliminary findings would encourage additional research.

f. It is not possible to conduct a t test in this situation because there are more than two groups or levels of the independent variable.

g. $R^2 = \frac{SS_{between}}{SS_{total}} = \frac{517.437}{894.187} = 0.575$

This is a very large effect.

h. $\omega^2 = \frac{SS_{between} - ((df_{between})(MS_{within}))}{SS_{total} + MS_{within}}$

$$= \frac{517.437 - ((2)(47.094))}{894.187 + 47.094} = \frac{423.249}{941.281} = 0.450$$

This is a very large effect.

12-55 a. The independent variable in this study is the type of television show watched. There are three levels: watching a drama, watching a documentary, or watching no television.

b. The dependent variable in this study is the number of emotions guessed correctly. It is a scale variable.

c. This is an experiment. We know this because the researchers manipulated the independent variable—type of television show watched—and randomly assigned participants to levels of the independent variable.

d. The researchers conducted a one-way between-groups ANOVA. We know this because the analysis included a categorical independent variable that had more than two levels and a dependent variable that was scale. Additionally, an F statistic is reported in the findings.

e. The values in the parentheses tell us that there are two between-groups degrees of freedom and 173 within-groups degrees of freedom. If we add 1 to the first number, we know that the analysis included 3 different groups. If we then add the two numbers in the parentheses together ($2 + 173$), we get 175, which is the degrees of freedom for the total sample. If we add 1 to the total degrees of freedom, we then know the sample size: 176 participants. The third number presented (6.04) is the test statistic: the calculated or observed F value. The fourth number presented, .003, is the p value. The p value is less than the standard alpha level of 0.05, which means that there is a statistically significant difference. The last number presented, .065, is the effect size. According to Cohen's conventions for R^2 (which we can use to interpret partial η^2), this is a medium effect.

f. An F statistic demonstrates only there is a statistically significant mean difference among at least two different levels of the independent variable; it does not indicate where those specific differences lie. It is likely the researchers conducted a post hoc test, such as a Tukey HSD test, to determine which means were significantly different from each other.

g. Participants who watched a drama television show accurately identified significantly more emotions, on average, compared to the control group (people who did not watch any television prior to making judgments about emotions in pictures).

However, there were no statistically significant mean differences between the drama group and the documentary group. Similarly, there were no statistically significant mean differences between the documentary group and the control group. We can only conclude that watching a drama series seems to increase accuracy, on average, compared to not watching TV.

h. According to Cohen's conventions for R^2 (which we can use to interpret partial η^2), this is a medium effect.

i. Although the mean for documentaries is higher than the mean for the control group, this comparison is not statistically significantly different. Documentaries might be helpful, but we do not have supporting evidence from this study.

j. This would be considered a Type I error: when we incorrectly reject the null hypothesis.

k. The label for the y-axis should be horizontal. The y-axis should begin at 0, not 20. The y-axis and x-axis should be labeled appropriately (e.g., "Mean score correct emotion identification" for y-axis, and "Condition" for x-axis).

Chapter 13

13-1 The four assumptions are that (1) the data are randomly selected; (2) the underlying population distributions are normal; (3) the variability is similar across groups, known as homoscedasticity; and (4) there are no order effects.

13-3 The "subjects" variability is noise in the data caused by each participant's personal variability compared with the other participants. It is calculated by comparing each person's mean response across all levels of the independent variable with the grand mean, which is the overall mean response across all levels of the independent variable.

13-5 Counterbalancing involves exposing participants to the different levels of the independent variable in different orders.

13-7 To calculate the sum of squares for subjects, we first calculate an average of each participant's scores across the levels of the independent variable. Then we subtract the grand mean from each participant's mean. We repeat this subtraction for each score the participant has—that is, for as many times as there are levels of the independent variable. Once we have the deviation scores, we square each of them and then sum the squared deviations to get the sum of squares for participants.

13-9 If we have a between-groups study in which different people are participating in the different conditions, then we can turn it into a within-groups study by having all the people in the sample participate in all the conditions.

13-11 The calculations for R^2 for a one-way within-groups ANOVA and a one-way between-groups ANOVA are similar. In both one-way ANOVAs, the numerator is a measure of the variability that takes into account just the differences among means, $SS_{between}$. The denominator, however, is different for the within-groups ANOVA, as it takes into account the total variability, SS_{total}, similarly to the between-groups ANOVA, but removes the variability due to differences among participants, $SS_{subjects}$. This enables the researcher to determine the variability explained only by between-groups differences.

13-13 A constraints on generality statement is an explicit statement of the target population to which the results of a study are intended to generalize.

13-15 a. $df_{between} = N_{groups} - 1 = 3 - 1 = 2$

b. $df_{subjects} = n - 1 = 4 - 1 = 3$

c. $df_{within} = (df_{between})(df_{subjects}) = (2)(3) = 6$

d. $df_{total} = df_{between} + df_{subjects} + df_{within} = 2 + 3 + 6 = 11$, or we can calculate it as $df_{total} = N_{total} - 1 = 12 - 1 = 11$

e. $SS_{total} = \Sigma(X - GM)^2 = 754$

Level	(X)	X − GM	(X − GM)²
1	7	−10	100
1	16	−1	1
1	3	−14	196
1	9	−8	64
2	15	−2	4
2	18	1	1
2	18	1	1
2	13	−4	16
3	22	5	25
3	28	11	121
3	26	9	81
3	29	12	144
	$GM = 17$		$\Sigma(X - GM)^2 = 754$

f. $SS_{between} = \Sigma(M - GM)^2 = 618.504$

Level	Rating (X)	Group Mean (M)	M − GM	(M − GM)²
1	7	8.75	−8.25	68.063
1	16	8.75	−8.25	68.063
1	3	8.75	−8.25	68.063
1	9	8.75	−8.25	68.063
2	15	16	−1	1.000
2	18	16	−1	1.000
2	18	16	−1	1.000
2	13	16	−1	1.000
3	22	26.25	9.25	85.563
3	28	26.25	9.25	85.563
3	26	26.25	9.25	85.563
3	29	26.25	9.25	85.563
	$GM = 17$			$\Sigma(M - GM)^2 = 618.504$

Next, we calculate HSD for each pair of means.

For past versus present: $HSD = \dfrac{(18.1 - 18.6)}{0.753} = -0.66$

For past versus future: $HSD = \dfrac{(18.1 - 22.1)}{0.753} = -5.31$

For present versus future: $HSD = \dfrac{(18.6 - 22.1)}{0.753} = -4.65$

The critical value of q at an alpha level of 0.05 is 4.04. Thus, we reject the null hypothesis for the past versus future comparison and for the present versus future comparison, but not for the past versus present comparison. These results indicate that the mean self-reported life satisfaction of pessimists is not significantly different for their past and present, but they expect to have greater life satisfaction in the future, on average.

c. $R^2 = \dfrac{SS_{between}}{(SS_{total} - SS_{subjects})} = \dfrac{47.5}{(73.6 - 3.429)} = 0.68$

13-25 $df_{between} = N_{groups} - 1 = 2$

$df_{subjects} = n - 1 = 4$

$df_{within} = (df_{between})(df_{subjects}) = 8$

$df_{total} = N_{total} - 1 = 14$

For the total sum of squares: $SS_{total} = \Sigma(X - GM)^2 = 4207.335$

Stimulus	X	$(X - GM)$	$(X - GM)^2$
Owner	69	20.667	427.125
Owner	72	23.667	560.127
Owner	65	16.667	277.789
Owner	75	26.667	711.129
Owner	70	21.667	469.459
Cat	28	−20.333	413.431
Cat	32	−16.333	266.767
Cat	30	−18.333	336.099
Cat	29	−19.333	373.765
Cat	31	−17.333	300.433
Dog	45	−3.333	11.109
Dog	43	−5.333	28.441
Dog	47	−1.333	1.777
Dog	45	−3.333	11.109
Dog	44	−4.333	18.775

$GM = 48.333 \qquad SS_{total} = 4207.335$

For sum of squares between: $SS_{between} - \Sigma(M - GM)^2 = 4133.735$

Stimulus	X	Group Mean (M)	$(M - GM)$	$(M - GM)^2$
Owner	69	70.2	21.867	478.166
Owner	72	70.2	21.867	478.166
Owner	65	70.2	21.867	478.166
Owner	75	70.2	21.867	478.166
Owner	70	70.2	21.867	478.166
Cat	28	30	−18.333	336.099
Cat	32	30	−18.333	336.099
Cat	30	30	−18.333	336.099
Cat	29	30	−18.333	336.099
Cat	31	30	−18.333	336.099
Dog	45	44.8	−3.533	12.482
Dog	43	44.8	−3.533	12.482
Dog	47	44.8	−3.533	12.482
Dog	45	44.8	−3.533	12.482
Dog	44	44.8	−3.533	12.482

$GM = 48.333 \qquad SS_{between} = 4133.735$

For sum of squares subjects: $SS_{subjects} = \Sigma(M_{participant} - GM)^2 = 12.675$

Stimulus	X	Participant Mean $(M_{participant})$	$M_{participant} - GM$	$(M_{participant} - GM)^2$
Owner	69	47.333	−1.000	1.000
Owner	72	49.000	0.667	0.445
Owner	65	47.333	−1.000	1.000
Owner	75	49.667	1.334	1.780
Owner	70	48.333	0.000	0.000
Cat	28	47.333	−1.000	1.000
Cat	32	49.000	0.667	0.445
Cat	30	47.333	−1.000	1.000
Cat	29	49.667	1.334	1.780
Cat	31	48.333	0.000	0.000
Dog	45	47.333	−1.000	1.000
Dog	43	49.000	0.667	0.445
Dog	47	47.333	−1.000	1.000
Dog	45	49.667	1.334	1.780
Dog	44	48.333	0.000	0.000

$GM = 48.333 \qquad SS_{subjects} = 12.675$

$$SS_{within} = SS_{total} - SS_{between} - SS_{subjects} = 60.925$$

Source	SS	df	MS	F
Between	4133.735	2	2066.868	271.38
Subjects	12.675	4	3.169	0.42
Within	60.925	8	7.616	
Total	4207.335	14		

13.27 At an alpha level of 0.05, the critical F value is 4.46. Because the calculated F statistic does not exceed the critical F value, we would fail to reject the null hypothesis. Because we failed to reject the null hypothesis, it would not be appropriate to perform post hoc comparisons.

13-29 Because the constraints on generality statement explicitly designates the target population, future researchers who were interested in doing a direct replication could identify a sample from this exact same target population. Additionally, researchers may be interested in attempting to extend the results of the study by seeing if the effects are similar or different in a population of participants older than the age of 50, or if the effect is similar among members of political groups in different countries.

13-31 **a.** The researchers analyzed data for the same participants at three different time points.

b. The p value for the ANOVA was 0.001, well below the typical alpha level of 0.05.

c. The standard deviations are larger than the means, which suggests that outliers are pulling the mean higher. Indeed, the number of drinks cannot go below zero, so there is a floor effect. This suggests a positively skewed distribution.

d. We know there is an estimated effect size of 0.06, which is a medium effect.

e. A statistically significant ANOVA tells us only that there is a difference between at least two of the groups in the study. It does not tell us which groups are statistically significant. We must conduct post hoc analyses, such as a Tukey HSD test or a Bonferroni test, to determine where the actual differences lie.

f. We have only two possible decisions when we conduct hypothesis testing: We can reject the null hypothesis or fail to reject the null hypothesis. When we say there is no difference, we are, in effect, accepting the null hypothesis of no difference. The researchers could have clarified that point by stating that there is "no statistically significant difference" between groups.

g. The researchers are stating that they used a Bonferroni correction to be more conservative in their analyses. They divided the alpha level by the number of comparisons, 3, and used this new alpha level of 0.017. They did this to reduce the chances of a Type I error.

h. Severe testing refers to the practice of holding your data up to a more difficult standard when conducting hypothesis testing. Severe testing reduces the chances of a Type I error. Using a Bonferroni correction is an example of making it more difficult to reject the null hypothesis; thus, any statistically significant finding is more likely to be a true finding.

Chapter 14

14.1 A two-way ANOVA is a hypothesis test that includes two nominal (or sometimes ordinal) independent variables and a scale dependent variable.

14.3 In everyday conversation, the word *cell* conjures up images of a prison or a small room in which someone is forced to stay, or of one of the building blocks of a plant or animal. In statistics, the word *cell* refers to a single condition in a factorial ANOVA that is characterized by its values on each of the independent variables.

14.5 A two-way ANOVA has two independent variables. When we express that as a 2×3 ANOVA, we get added detail: The first number tells us that the first independent variable has two levels, and the second number tells us that the other independent variable has three levels.

14.7 A marginal mean is the mean of a row or a column in a table that shows the cells of a study with a two-way ANOVA design.

14.9 Bar graphs allow us to visually depict the relative changes across the different levels of each independent variable. By adding lines that connect the bars within each series, we can assess whether the lines appear parallel, significantly different from parallel, or intersecting. Intersecting and significantly nonparallel lines are indications of interactions.

14.11 First, we may be able to reject the null hypothesis for the interaction. (If the interaction is statistically significant, then it might not matter whether the main effects are significant; if they are also significant, then those findings are usually qualified by the interaction and they are not described separately. The overall pattern of cell means can tell the whole story.) Second, if we are not able to reject the null hypothesis for the interaction, then we focus on any significant main effects, drawing a specific directional conclusion for each. Third, if we do not reject the null hypothesis for either the main effect or the interaction, then we can conclude only that there is insufficient evidence from this study to support the research hypotheses.

14.13 This is the formula for the between-groups sum of squares for the interaction; we can calculate it by subtracting the other between-groups sums of squares (those for the two main effects) and the within-groups sum of squares from the total sum of squares. (The between-groups sum of squares for the interaction is essentially what is left over when the main effects are accounted for.)

14.15 We can use R^2 to calculate effect size similarly to how we did for a one-way ANOVA according to Cohen's conventions. An effect size can be calculated for each main effect and for the interaction.

14.17 An ANCOVA and an ANOVA both have one or more nominal (or sometimes ordinal) independent variables and a single scale dependent variable, but an ANCOVA uses another scale variable as a covariate. Any variability in the dependent variable that is associated with this covariate is removed so that the effects of the independent variables can be observed without being contaminated by differences on the covariate.

14.19 If a researcher used multiple scale dependent variables that all assessed similar constructs, the researcher should use a MANOVA.

14.21 A two-way mixed-design MANOVA is an analysis used for a study in which there are two independent variables, and each participant experiences all levels of one independent variable, but only one level of the other independent variable. That is, one variable is between-groups and one variable is within-groups. In addition, there are multiple (at least two) dependent variables that are being measured for each participant.

14.23 Statistical tools like statcheck can help individual researchers make sure their statistics are consistent and can help readers of research determine when a report has statistical inconsistencies. They are important to the field because they have already identified numerous errors in published papers, along with a potential bias—that is, errors tend to be in the direction of making nonsignificant findings fall in the statistically significant range.

14.25 a. There are two independent variables or factors: gender and sporting event. Gender has two levels, male and female, and sporting event has two levels, Sport 1 and Sport 2.

b. Type of campus is one factor that has two levels: dry and wet. The second factor is type of university, which has three levels: state, private, and religious.

c. Age group is the first factor, with three levels: 12–13, 14–15, and 16–17. Gender is a second factor, with two levels: female and male. Family composition is the last factor, with three levels: two parents, single parent, no identified authority figure.

14.27 a.

	Ice hockey	Figure skating	
Men	$M = (19+17+18+17)/4 = 17.75$	$M = (6+4+8+3)/4 = 5.25$	$(17.75+5.25)/2 = 11.50$
Women	$M = (13+14+18+8)/4 = 13.25$	$M = (11+7+4+14)/4 = 9$	$(13.25+9)/2+11.125$
	$(17.75+13.25)/2 = 15.5$	$(5.25+9)/2 = 7.125$	

b.

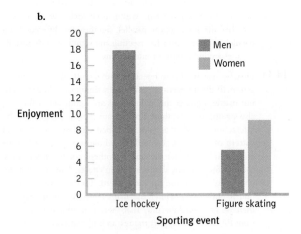

c. $df_{rows(gender)} = N_{rows} - 1 = 2 - 1 = 1$
$df_{columns(sport)} = N_{columns} - 1 = 2 - 1 = 1$
$df_{interaction} = (df_{rows})(df_{columns}) = (1)(1) = 1$
$df_{within} = df_{M,H} + df_{M,S} + df_{W,H} + df_{W,S} = 3 + 3 + 3 + 3 = 12$
$df_{total} = N_{total} - 1 = 16 - 1 = 15$

We can also check that this answer is correct by adding all of the other degrees of freedom together:

$$1 + 1 + 1 + 12 = 15$$

The critical value for an F distribution with 1 and 12 degrees of freedom, at an alpha level of 0.01, is 9.33. The main effects and the interaction will all have the same critical value.

d. $GM = 11.313$
$SS_{total} = \Sigma(X - GM)^2$ for each score $= 475.438$

	X	$X - GM$	$(X - GM)^2$
Men, hockey	19	7.687	59.090
	17	5.687	32.342
	18	6.687	44.716
	17	5.687	32.342
Men, skating	6	−5.313	28.228
	4	−7.313	53.480
	8	−3.313	10.976
	3	−8.313	69.106
Women, hockey	13	1.687	2.846
	14	2.687	7.220

(Table continued)

	X	X − GM	(X − GM)²
	18	6.687	44.716
	8	−3.313	10.976
Women, skating	11	−0.313	0.098
	7	−4.313	18.602
	4	−7.313	53.480
	14	2.687	7.220

$\Sigma = 475.438$

e. Sum of squares for gender: $SS_{between(rows)} = \Sigma(M_{row} - GM)^2$ for each score = 0.560

	X	(M_{row} − GM)	(M_{row} − GM)²
Men, hockey	19	0.187	0.035
	17	0.187	0.035
	18	0.187	0.035
	17	0.187	0.035
Men, skating	6	0.187	0.035
	4	0.187	0.035
	8	0.187	0.035
	3	0.187	0.035
Women, hockey	13	−0.188	0.035
	14	−0.188	0.035
	18	−0.188	0.035
	8	−0.188	0.035
Women, skating	11	−0.188	0.035
	7	−0.188	0.035
	4	−0.188	0.035
	14	−0.188	0.035

$\Sigma = 0.560$

f. Sum of squares for sporting event: $SS_{between(columns)} = \Sigma(M_{column} - GM)^2$ for each score = 280.560

	X	(M_{column} − GM)	(M_{column} − GM)²
Men, hockey	19	4.187	17.531
	17	4.187	17.531
	18	4.187	17.531
	17	4.187	17.531
Men, skating	6	−4.188	17.539
	4	−4.188	17.539

(Table continued)

	X	(M_{column} − GM)	(M_{column} − GM)²
	8	−4.188	17.539
	3	−4.188	17.539
Women, hockey	13	4.187	17.531
	14	4.187	17.531
	18	4.187	17.531
	8	4.187	17.531
Women, skating	11	−4.188	17.539
	7	−4.188	17.539
	4	−4.188	17.539
	14	−4.188	17.539

$\Sigma = 280.560$

g. $SS_{within} = \Sigma(X - M_{cell})^2$ for each score = 126.256

	X	(X − M_{cell})	(X − M_{cell})²
Men, hockey	19	1.25	1.563
	17	−0.75	0.563
	18	0.25	0.063
	17	−0.75	0.563
Men, skating	6	0.75	0.563
	4	−1.25	1.563
	8	2.75	7.563
	3	−2.25	5.063
Women, hockey	13	−0.25	0.063
	14	0.75	0.563
	18	4.75	22.563
	8	−5.25	27.563
Women, skating	11	2	4.000
	7	−2	4.000
	4	−5	25.000
	14	5	25.000

$\Sigma = 126.256$

h. We use subtraction to find the sum of squares for the interaction. We subtract all other sources from the total sum of squares, and the remaining amount is the sum of squares for the interaction.

$SS_{gender \times sport} = SS_{total} - (SS_{gender} + SS_{sport} + SS_{within})$
$= 475.438 - (0.560 + 280.560 + 126.256)$
$= 68.062$

i.

Source	SS	df	MS	F
Gender	0.560	1	0.560	0.05
Sporting event	280.560	1	280.560	26.67
Gender × sport	68.062	1	68.062	6.47
Within	126.256	12	10.521	
Total	475.438	15		

14.29

Source	SS	df	MS	F
Gender	248.25	1	248.25	8.07
Parenting style	84.34	3	28.113	0.91
Gender × style	33.60	3	11.20	0.36
Within	1107.20	36	30.756	
Total	1473.39	43		

14.31 For the main effect A:

$$R^2_{rows} = \frac{SS_{rows}}{\left(SS_{total} - SS_{columns} - SS_{interaction}\right)}$$

$$= \frac{30.006}{\left(652.291 - 33.482 - 1.720\right)} = 0.049$$

According to Cohen's conventions, this is approaching a medium effect size.

For the main effect B:

$$R^2_{columns} = \frac{SS_{columns}}{\left(SS_{total} - SS_{rows} - SS_{interaction}\right)}$$

$$= \frac{33.482}{\left(652.291 - 30.006 - 1.720\right)} = 0.054$$

According to Cohen's conventions, this is approaching a medium effect size.

For the interaction:

$$R^2_{interaction} = \frac{SS_{interaction}}{\left(SS_{total} - SS_{rows} - SS_{columns}\right)}$$

$$= \frac{1.720}{\left(652.291 - 30.006 - 33.482\right)} = 0.003$$

According to Cohen's conventions, this is smaller than a small effect size.

14.33 a. This study would be analyzed with a between-groups ANOVA because different groups of participants were assigned to the different treatment conditions.

b. This study could be redesigned to use a within-groups ANOVA by testing the same group of participants on some myths repeated once and some repeated three times both when the participants are young and then again when they are old.

14.35 a. There are two independent variables: country and anger. Country has two levels: Japan and the United States. Anger has two levels: low or high.

b. The dependent variable is health outcomes.

c. There are two independent variables and one dependent variable for these data. A two-way ANOVA would be the appropriate hypothesis test because it allows us to compare levels from two independent variables, as well as explore the combined effects of the two independent variables, on the dependent variable.

d. A 2×2 between-groups ANOVA would be the appropriate test to use.

e. There are two variables, each with two levels. By multiplying the number of levels for each variable (two multiplied by two), we know that we need four cells.

f.

	Low levels of anger	High levels of anger
Japan		
United States		

g. This is a quantitative interaction because the direction of the effect of one independent variable, level of anger, among people in Japan is opposite of the direction of the effect among people in the United States.

14.37 a. The first independent variable is the gender said to be most affected by the illness, and its levels are men and women. The second independent variable is the gender of the participant, and its levels are male and female. The dependent variable is level of comfort, on a scale of 1–7.

b. The researchers conducted a two-way between-groups ANOVA.

c. The reported statistics do indicate that there is a significant interaction because the probability associated with the F statistic for the interaction is less than 0.05.

d.

	Female participants	Male participants
Illness affects women	4.88	3.29
Illness affects men	3.56	4.67

e. Bar graph for the interaction:

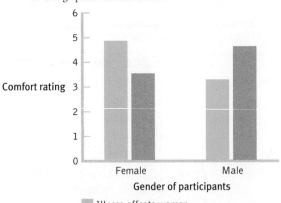

f. This is a qualitative interaction. Female participants indicated greater average comfort about attending a meeting regarding an illness that affects women than about attending a meeting regarding an illness that affects men. Male participants had the opposite pattern of results; male participants indicated greater average comfort about attending a meeting regarding an illness that affects men as opposed to one that affects women.

g.

	Female participants	Male participants
Illness affects women	4.88	**4.80**
Illness affects men	3.56	4.67

Note: There are several cell means that would work.

h. Bar graph for the new means:

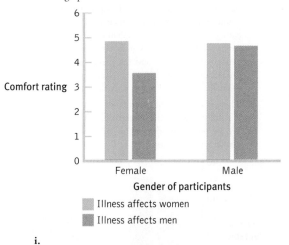

i.

	Female participants	Male participants
Illness affects women	4.88	**5.99**
Illness affects men	3.56	4.67

14.39 a. The first independent variable is the race of the face, and its levels are white and black. The second independent variable is the type of instruction given to the participants, and its levels are no instruction and instruction to attend to distinguishing features. The dependent variable is the measure of recognition accuracy.

b. The researchers conducted a two-way between-groups ANOVA.

c. The reported statistics indicate that there is a significant main effect of race. On average, the white participants who saw white faces had higher recognition scores than did white participants who saw black faces.

d. The main effect is misleading because those who received instructions to attend to distinguishing features actually had lower mean recognition scores for the white faces than did those who received no instruction, whereas those who received instructions to attend to distinguishing features had higher mean recognition scores for the black faces than did those who received no instruction.

e. The reported statistics do indicate that there is a significant interaction because the probability associated with the F statistic for the interaction is less than 0.05.

f.

	Black face	White face
No instruction	1.04	1.46
Distinguishing features instruction	1.23	1.38

g. Bar graph of findings:

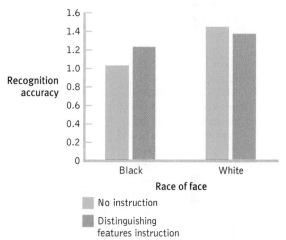

h. When given instructions to pay attention to distinguishing features of the faces, participants' average recognition of the black faces was higher than when given no instructions, whereas their average recognition of the white faces was worse than when given no instruction. This is a qualitative interaction because the direction of the effect changes between black and white.

14.41 a. The first independent variable is gender of the seeker, and its levels are men and women. The second independent variable is gender of the person being sought, and its levels are men and women. The dependent variable is the oldest acceptable age of the person being sought.

b.

	Women seekers	Men seekers
Men sought	34.80	35.40
Women sought	36.00	27.20

c. *Step 1:* Population 1 (women, men) is women seeking men. Population 2 (men, women) is men seeking women. Population 3 (women, women) is women seeking women. Population 4 (men, men) is men seeking men. The comparison distributions will be F distributions. The hypothesis test will be a two-way between-groups ANOVA.

Assumptions: The data are not from random samples, so we must generalize with caution. From the small sample sizes, it's difficult to know if the underlying population distributions are normally distributed, so we must proceed with caution. The assumption of homogeneity of variance is violated because the largest variance (29.998) is much larger than the smallest variance (1.188). For the purposes of this exercise, however, we will conduct this ANOVA.

Step 2: Main effect of first independent variable—gender of seeker:

Null hypothesis: On average, men and women report the same oldest acceptable ages for a partner—$\mu_M = \mu_W$.

Research hypothesis: On average, men and women report different oldest acceptable ages for a partner—$\mu_M \neq \mu_W$.

Main effect of second independent variable—gender of person sought:

Null hypothesis: On average, those seeking men and those seeking women report the same oldest acceptable ages for a partner—$\mu_M = \mu_W$.

Research hypothesis: On average, those seeking men and those seeking women report different oldest acceptable ages for a partner—$\mu_M \neq \mu_W$.

Interaction: Seeker × sought:

Null hypothesis: The effect of the gender of the seeker does not depend on the gender of the person sought.

Research hypothesis: The effect of the gender of the seeker does depend on the gender of the person sought.

Step 3: $df_{columns(seeker)} = 2 - 1 = 1$

$df_{rows(sought)} = 2 - 1 = 1$

$df_{interaction} = (1)(1) = 1$

$df_{within} = df_{W,M} + df_{M,W} + df_{W,W} + df_{M,M}$
$= 4 + 4 + 4 + 4 = 16$

Main effect of gender of seeker: F distribution with 1 and 16 degrees of freedom

Main effect of gender of sought: F distribution with 1 and 16 degrees of freedom

Interaction of seeker and sought: F distribution with 1 and 16 degrees of freedom

Step 4: Cutoff F for main effect of seeker: 4.49

Cutoff F for main effect of sought: 4.49

Cutoff F for interaction of seeker and sought: 4.49

Step 5: $SS_{total} = \Sigma(X - GM)^2 = 454.559$

$SS_{column(seeker)} = \Sigma(M_{column(seeker)} - GM)^2 = 84.050$

$SS_{row(sought)} = \Sigma(M_{row(sought)} - GM)^2 = 61.260$

$SS_{within} = \Sigma(X - M_{cell})^2 = 198.800$

$SS_{interaction} = SS_{total} - (SS_{row} + SS_{column} + SS_{within}) = 110.449$

Source	SS	df	MS	F
Seeker gender	84.050	1	84.050	6.76
Sought gender	61.260	1	61.260	4.93
Seeker × sought	110.449	1	110.449	8.89
Within	198.800	16	12.425	
Total	454.559	19		

Step 6: There is a significant main effect of gender of the seeker; it appears that women are willing to accept older dating partners, on average, than are men. There is also a significant main effect of gender of the person being sought; it appears that those seeking men are willing to accept older dating partners, on average, than are those seeking women. Additionally, there is a significant interaction between the gender of the seeker and the gender of the person being sought. Because there is a significant interaction, we ignore the main effects and report only the interaction.

d. There is a significant quantitative interaction because there is a difference for male seekers, but not for female seekers. We are not seeing the reversal of direction necessary for a qualitative interaction.

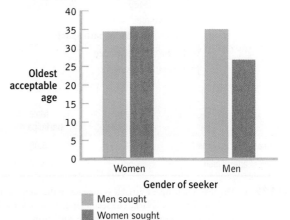

e. For the main effect of seeker gender:

$$R^2_{seeker} = \frac{SS_{seeker}}{(SS_{total} - SS_{sought} - SS_{interaction})}$$

$$= \frac{84.05}{454.559 - 61.26 - 110.449} = 0.30$$

According to Cohen's conventions, this is a large effect size.

For the main effect of sought gender:

$$R^2_{sought} = \frac{SS_{sought}}{(SS_{total} - SS_{seeker} - SS_{interaction})}$$

$$= \frac{61.26}{454.559 - 84.05 - 110.449} = 0.24$$

According to Cohen's conventions, this is a large effect size. For the interaction:

$$R^2_{seeker} = \frac{SS_{interaction}}{(SS_{total} - SS_{seeker} - SS_{sought})}$$

$$= \frac{110.449}{454.559 - 84.05 - 61.26} = 0.36$$

According to Cohen's conventions, this is a large effect size.

14.43 a. The independent variables are type of payment, still with two levels, and level of payment, now with three levels (low, moderate, and high). The dependent variable is still willingness to help, as assessed with the 11-point scale.

b.

	Low amount	Moderate amount	High amount	
Cash payment	4.75	7.50	8.00	6.75
Candy payment	6.25	6.00	6.50	6.25
	5.50	6.75	7.25	

c.

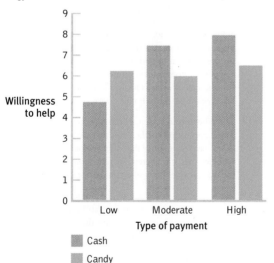

d. There does still seem to be the same qualitative interaction, such that the effect of the level of payment depends on the type of payment. When candy payments are used, the level seems to have no mean impact. However, when cash payments are used, willingness to help is higher, on average, at each successive level of payment.

e. Post hoc tests would be needed. Specifically, we would need to compare the three levels of payment to see where specific significant differences exist. Based on the graph we created, it appears as if willingness to help does not vary significantly across the three levels of payment for candy, whereas it does seem to vary across the three levels of payment for cash.

14.45 a. This is problematic because it suggests a causal relation for correlational data. There are many possible confounds. It could be that people with high energy are more likely both to exercise (and lose weight) and to work long hours (and make more money). It could be that education level is associated with both weight and income. The act of losing weight might not cause one's income to change at all.

b. If you can include covariates, you can eliminate alternative explanations. Several scale variables could potentially be included as covariates. For example, if you include education level as a covariate and there is still a link between weight and income, you can eliminate education level as a possible confound.

14.47 a. The independent variables are educational attainment (levels: transitioning adolescents, college underclassmen, college upperclassmen), disability status (levels: dyslexia, ADHD, ADHD/dyslexia), and gender (levels: male, female).

b. The dependent variables are depression as assessed by the BDI-II and anxiety as assessed by the BAI.

c. The researchers conducted a MANOVA because multiple dependent variables were being analyzed at the same time.

d. (i) Upperclassmen with disabilities have higher levels of depression and anxiety, on average, than do transitioning adolescents with disabilities.

(ii) Tukey *HSD* tests were likely conducted because statistically significant effects were found for the main effect of educational attainment. Because there were three levels, the researchers would not have known from a statistically significant effect which pairs of the three means were statistically significantly different from each other. The Tukey *HSD* tests allowed the researchers to test each pair of educational attainment levels for mean differences in anxiety and for mean differences in depression.

(iii) Usually the appropriate effect size with ANOVA and its various forms, including MANOVA, is R^2. However, in this case, the researchers reported Cohen's *d* because the Tukey *HSD* tests assess the difference between pairs of means, and Cohen's *d* reports the differences in terms of standard deviation between pairs of means.

14.49 a. The researchers conducted a two-way between-groups ANOVA.

b. By averaging the percentages for each pair of bars, we can estimate that the mean for sender is around 52 or 53, and the mean for receiver is around 47 or 48. So, there does appear to be a main effect of role in the negotiations. Senders—the people who kick off the negotiations—end up doing better, on average, than do receivers.

    c. It does not seem that there is a main effect of type of information provided. The mean of the two bars for each is around 50.

    d. There seems to be a qualitative interaction. It seems to be better to be the sender (the one initiating the negotiation) if the sender is *not* providing information about areas in which she or he is willing to acquiesce, whereas it seems better to be the receiver if the sender *is* providing information about what she or he will settle for.

    e. The *y*-axis should begin at 0. Otherwise, the graph would exaggerate the differences between groups.

14.51 a. The independent variables are type of feedback (levels: positive, negative), level of expertise (levels: novice, expert), and domain (level: feedback on language acquisition, pursuit of environmental causes, use of consumer products).

    b. The dependent variable appears to be levels of seeking behavior and response behavior.

    c. This interaction is statistically significant, as the *p* value is less than 0.05.

    d. The statistic missing from this report is a measure of effect size, such as R^2. The effect size helps us figure out whether something that is statistically significant is also practically important.

    e. The bar graph illustrates what appears to be a qualitative interaction. Experts sought and responded more to negative feedback than novices did; novices sought and responded more to positive feedback than experts did.

    f. Suggestions may vary. The graph needs a clear, specific title; the *y*-axis should go down to 0; and the label on the *y*-axis should be rotated so that it reads left to right.

    g. Yes, a U.S. sample is likely to be from a WEIRD (Western, Educated, Industrial, Rich, Democratic) population.

    h. A COG statement outlines the population to which a given study is likely to apply—that is, is likely to generalize to. It would be helpful to include a COG statement because then readers would be aware that this sample is likely from a WEIRD population.

Chapter 15

15-1 A correlation coefficient is a statistic that quantifies the relation between two variables.

15-3 A perfect relation occurs when the data points fall exactly on the line we fit through the data. A perfect relation results in a correlation coefficient of −1.0 or 1.0.

15-5 According to Cohen (1988), a correlation coefficient of 0.50 is a large correlation, and 0.30 is a medium one. However, it is unusual in social science research to have a correlation as high as 0.50. The decision of whether a correlation is worth talking about is sometimes based on whether it is statistically significant, as well as what practical effect a correlation of a certain size indicates.

15-7 When used to capture the relation between two variables, the correlation coefficient is a descriptive statistic. When used to draw conclusions about the greater population, such as with hypothesis testing, the coefficient serves as an inferential statistic.

15-9 Positive products of deviations, indicating a positive correlation, occur when both members of a pair of scores tend to result in a positive deviation or when both members tend to result in a negative deviation. Negative products of deviations, indicating a negative correlation, occur when members of a pair of scores tend to result in opposite-valued deviations (one negative and the other positive).

15-11 Spurious correlations are associations that look real, but are not. If you calculate correlation coefficients between enough pairs of variables, some of them are likely to be statistically significant. If there's no actual underlying correlation, this would be a Type I error.

15-13 (1) We calculate the deviation of each score from its mean, multiply the two deviations for each participant, and sum the products of the deviations. (2) We calculate a sum of squares for each variable, multiply the two sums of squares, and take the square root of the product of the sums of squares. (3) We divide the sum from step 1 by the square root in step 2.

15-15 Test–retest reliability involves giving the same group of people the exact same test with some amount of time (perhaps a week) between the two administrations of the test. Test–retest reliability is then calculated as the correlation between their scores on the two administrations of the test. Calculation of coefficient alpha does not require giving the same test two times. Rather, coefficient alpha is based on correlations between different halves of the test items from a single administration of the test.

15-17 The difference between a Pearson correlation coefficient and a partial correlation coefficient is that the partial correlation coefficient has factored out the influence of one or more additional variables; thus, it is a better representation of the relation between the two variables because it controls for other related variables.

15-19 Big data refers to the use of computing technology to search through very large data sets for statistical patterns and correlations, often in the absence of hypotheses.

15-21 a. These data appear to be negatively correlated.

    b. These data appear to be positively correlated.

    c. Neither; these data appear to have a very small correlation, if any.

15-23 a. −0.28 is a medium correlation.

    b. 0.79 is a large correlation.

    c. 1.0 is a perfect correlation.

    d. −0.015 is almost no correlation.

15-25 a.

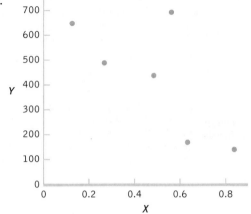

b.

X	$(X - M_X)$	Y	$(Y - M_Y)$	$(X - M_X)(Y - M_Y)$
0.13	−0.36	645	218.50	−78.660
0.27	−0.22	486	59.50	−13.090
0.49	0.00	435	8.50	0.000
0.57	0.08	689	262.50	21.000
0.84	0.35	137	−289.50	−101.325
0.64	0.13	167	−259.50	−38.925
$M_X = 0.49$		$M_Y = 426.5$		$\Sigma[(X - M_X)(Y - M_Y)] = -211.0$

c.

X	$(X - M_X)$	$(X - M_X)^2$	Y	$(Y - M_Y)$	$(Y - M_Y)^2$
0.13	−0.36	0.130	645	218.50	47,742.25
0.27	−0.22	0.048	486	59.50	3540.25
0.49	0.00	0.000	435	8.50	72.25
0.57	0.08	0.006	689	262.50	68,906.25
0.84	0.35	0.123	137	−289.50	83,810.25
0.64	0.13	0.023	167	−259.50	67,340.25

$$\Sigma(X - M_X)^2 = 0.330 \qquad \Sigma(Y - M_Y)^2 = 271,411.50$$

$$\sqrt{(SS_X)(SS_Y)} = \sqrt{(0.330)(271,411.50)} = \sqrt{89,565.795} = 299.275$$

d. $r = \dfrac{\Sigma[(X - M_X)(Y - M_Y)]}{\sqrt{(SS_X)(SS_Y)}} = \dfrac{-211.0}{299.275} = -0.71$

e. $df_r = N - 2 = 6 - 2 = 4$

f. −0.811 and 0.811; this is not a statistically significant correlation.

15-27 a.

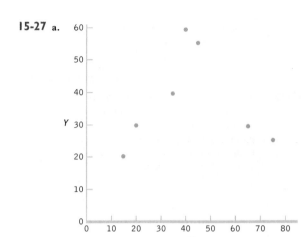

b.

X	$(X - M_X)$	Y	$(Y - M_Y)$	$(X - M_X)(Y - M_Y)$
40	−2.143	60	22.857	−48.983
45	2.857	55	17.857	51.017
20	−22.143	30	−7.143	158.167
75	32.857	25	−12.143	−398.983
15	−27.143	20	−17.143	465.312
35	−7.143	40	2.857	−20.408
65	22.857	30	−7.143	163.268
$M_X = 42.143$		$M_Y = 37.143$		$\Sigma[(X - M_X)(Y - M_Y)] = 42.854$

c.

X	$(X - M_X)$	$(X - M_X)^2$	Y	$(Y - M_Y)$	$(Y - M_Y)^2$
40	−2.143	4.592	60	22.857	522.442
45	2.857	8.162	55	17.857	318.872
20	−22.143	490.312	30	−7.143	51.022
75	32.857	1079.582	25	−12.143	147.452
15	−27.143	736.742	20	−17.143	293.882
35	−7.143	51.022	40	2.857	8.162
65	22.857	522.442	30	−7.143	51.022

$$\Sigma(X - M_X)^2 = 2892.854 \qquad \Sigma(Y - M_Y)^2 = 1392.854$$

$$\sqrt{(SS_X)(SS_Y)} = \sqrt{(2892.854)(1392.854)}$$
$$= \sqrt{4,029,323.265} = 2007.317$$

d. $r = \dfrac{\Sigma[(X - M_X)(Y - M_Y)]}{\sqrt{(SS_X)(SS_Y)}} = \dfrac{42.854}{2007.317} = 0.02$

e. $df_r = N - 2 = 7 - 2 = 5$

f. −0.754 and 0.754; this is not a statistically significant correlation.

15-29 a. $df_r = N - 2 = 3113 - 2 = 3111$. The highest degrees of freedom listed on the table is 100, with cutoffs of −0.195 and 0.195.

b. $df_r = N - 2 = 72 - 2 = 70$; −0.232 and 0.232

15-31 2.0 is not a possible coefficient alpha, as this score must be between −1.0 and +1.0.

15-33 The third variable does not account for any of the correlation between A and B. The partial correlation, taking into account the third variable, is exactly the same as the original correlation between A and B.

15-35 The researchers are describing a negative relation. As grip strength increases, fatality rates decrease; when grip strength decreases, there are higher fatality rates.

15-37 a. Newman's data do not suggest a correlation between Mercury's phases and breakdowns. There was no consistency in the report of breakdowns during one of the phases.

b. Massey may observe a correlation because she already believes that there is a relation between astrological events and human events. As you learned in Chapter 5, confirmation bias refers to the tendency to pay attention to those events that confirm our prior beliefs. Confirmation bias may lead Massey to observe an illusory correlation (i.e., she perceives a correlation that does not actually exist) because she attends only to those events that confirm her prior belief that the phase of Mercury is related to breakdowns.

c. Given that there are two phases of Mercury (and assuming they're equal in length), half of the breakdowns that occur would be expected to occur during the retrograde phase and the other half during the nonretrograde phase, just by chance. Expected relative-frequency probability refers to the expected frequency of events. So in this example we would expect 50% of breakdowns to occur during the retrograde phase and 50% during the nonretrograde phase. If we base our conclusions on only a small number of observations of breakdowns, the observed relative-frequency probability is more likely to differ from the expected relative-frequency probability because we are less likely to have a representative sample of breakdowns.

d. This correlation would not be useful in predicting events in your own life because no relation would be observed in this limited time span.

e. Available data do not support the idea that a correlation exists between Mercury's phases and breakdowns.

f. If you calculate correlation coefficients between enough pairs of variables, some of them are likely to be statistically significant. If there is no actual underlying correlation, this would be a Type I error. Some call these spurious correlations, meaning associations that look real, but are not.

15-39 a. The accompanying scatterplot depicts the relation between hours of exercise and number of friends. Note that you could have chosen to put hours of exercise along the y-axis and number of friends along the x-axis.

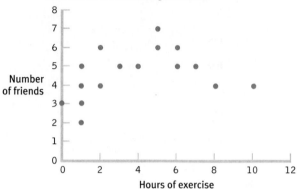

b. The scatterplot suggests that as the number of hours of exercise each week increases from 0 to 5, there is an increase in the number of friends, but as the hours of exercise continue to increase past 5, there is a decrease in the number of friends.

c. It would not be appropriate to calculate a Pearson correlation coefficient with this set of data. The scatterplot suggests a nonlinear relation between exercise and number of friends, and the Pearson correlation coefficient measures only the extent of linear relation between two variables.

15-41 *Step 1:* Population 1: Adolescents like those we studied. Population 2: Adolescents for whom there is no relation between externalizing behavior and anxiety. The comparison distribution is made up of correlation coefficients based on many, many samples of our size, 10 people, randomly selected from the population.

We do not know if the data were randomly selected (first assumption), so we must be cautious when generalizing the findings. We also do not know if the underlying population distribution for externalizing behaviors and anxiety in adolescents is normally distributed (second assumption). The sample size is too small to make any conclusions about this assumption, so we should proceed with caution. The third assumption, unique to correlation, is that the variability of one variable is equal across the levels of the other variable. Because we have such a small data set, it is difficult to evaluate this assumption. However, we can see from the scatterplot that the data are somewhat consistently variable.

Step 2: Null hypothesis: There is no correlation between externalizing behavior and anxiety among adolescents—$H_0 : \rho = 0$.

Research hypothesis: There is a correlation between externalizing behavior and anxiety among adolescents—$H_1 : \rho \neq 0$.

Step 3: The comparison distribution is a distribution of Pearson correlations, r, with the following degrees of freedom: $df_r = N - 2 = 10 - 2 = 8$.

Step 4: The critical values for an r distribution with 8 degrees of freedom for a two-tailed test with an alpha level of 0.05 are −0.632 and 0.632.

Step 5: The Pearson correlation coefficient is calculated in three steps. First, we calculate the numerator:

X	$(X - M_X)$	Y	$(Y - M_Y)$	$(X - M_X)(Y - M_Y)$
9	2.40	37	7.60	18.24
7	0.40	23	−6.40	−2.56
7	0.40	26	−3.40	−1.36
3	−3.60	21	−8.40	30.24
11	4.40	42	12.60	55.44
6	−0.60	33	3.60	−2.16
2	−4.60	26	−3.40	15.64
6	−0.60	35	5.60	−3.36
6	−0.60	23	−6.40	3.84
9	2.40	28	−1.40	−3.36

$M_X = 6.60$ $M_Y = 29.40$ $\Sigma[(X - M_X)(Y - M_Y)] = 110.60$

Second, we calculate the denominator:

X	$(X - M_X)$	$(X - M_X)^2$	Y	$(Y - M_Y)$	$(Y - M_Y)^2$
9	2.40	5.76	37	7.60	57.76
7	0.40	0.16	23	−6.40	40.96
7	0.40	0.16	26	−3.40	11.56
3	−3.60	12.96	21	−8.40	70.56
11	4.40	19.36	42	12.60	158.76
6	−0.60	0.36	33	3.60	12.96
2	−4.60	21.16	26	−3.40	11.56
6	−0.60	0.36	35	5.60	31.36
6	−0.60	0.36	23	−6.40	40.96
9	2.40	5.76	28	−1.40	1.96

$\Sigma(X - M_X)^2 = 66.40$ $\Sigma(Y - M_Y)^2 = 438.40$

$$\sqrt{(SS_X)(SS_Y)} = \sqrt{(66.40)(438.40)} = \sqrt{29,109.76} = 170.616$$

Finally, we compute r:

$$r = \frac{\Sigma[(X - M_X)(Y - M_Y)]}{\sqrt{(SS_X)(SS_Y)}} = \frac{110.60}{170.616} = 0.65$$

The test statistic, $r = 0.65$, is larger in magnitude than the critical value of 0.632. We can reject the null hypothesis and conclude that there is a strong positive correlation between the level of externalizing behaviors performed by adolescents and their level of anxiety.

15-43 a. You might expect a person who owns a lot of cats to tend to have many mental health problems. Because the two variables are positively correlated, as cat ownership increases, the number of mental health problems tends to increase.

b. You might expect a person who owns no cats or just one cat to tend to have few mental health problems. Because the variables are positively correlated, people who have a low score on one variable are also likely to have a low score on the other variable.

c. You might expect a person who owns a lot of cats to tend to have few mental health problems. Because the two variables are negatively related, as one variable increases, the other variable tends to decrease. This means a person who owns a lot of cats would likely have a low score on the mental health variable.

d. You might expect a person who owns no cats or just one cat to tend to have many mental health problems. Because the two variables are negatively related, as one variable decreases, the other variable tends to increase, which means that a person with fewer cats would likely have more mental health problems.

15-45 a. The accompanying scatterplot depicts a negative linear relation between perceived femininity and perceived trauma. Because the relation appears linear, it is appropriate to calculate the Pearson correlation coefficient for these data. (*Note:* The number (2) indicates that two participants share that pair of scores.)

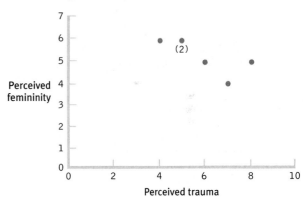

b. The Pearson correlation coefficient is calculated in three steps. Step 1 is calculating the numerator:

X	$(X - M_x)$	Y	$(Y - M_Y)$	$(X - M_x)(Y - M_Y)$
5	−0.833	6	0.667	−0.556
6	0.167	5	−0.333	−0.056
4	−1.833	6	0.667	−1.223
5	−0.833	6	0.667	−0.556
7	1.167	4	−1.333	−1.556
8	2.167	5	−0.333	−0.722

$M_X = 5.833$ $M_Y = 5.333$ $\Sigma[(X - M_X)(Y - M_Y)] = -4.669$

Step 2 is calculating the denominator:

X	$(X-M_X)$	$(X-M_X)^2$	Y	$(Y-M_Y)$	$(Y-M_Y)^2$
5	−0.833	0.694	6	0.667	0.445
6	0.167	0.028	5	−0.333	0.111
4	−1.833	3.360	6	0.667	0.445
5	−0.833	0.694	6	0.667	0.445
7	1.167	1.362	4	−1.333	1.777
8	2.167	4.696	5	−0.333	0.111

$$\Sigma[(X-M_X)^2 = 10.834 \qquad \Sigma(Y-M_Y)^2 = 3.334$$

$$\sqrt{(SS_X)(SS_Y)} = \sqrt{(10.834)(3.334)} = \sqrt{36.121} = 6.010$$

Step 3 is computing r:

$$r = \frac{\Sigma\left[(X-M_X)(Y-M_Y)\right]}{\sqrt{(SS_X)(SS_Y)}} = \frac{-4.669}{6.010} = -0.78$$

c. The correlation coefficient reveals a strong negative relation between perceived femininity and perceived trauma: As trauma increases, perceived femininity tends to decrease.

d. Those participants who had positive deviation scores on trauma tended to have negative deviation scores on femininity (and vice versa), meaning that when a person's score on one variable was above the mean for that variable (positive deviation), his or her score on the second variable was typically below the mean for that variable (negative deviation). So, having a high score on one variable was associated with having a low score on the other, which is a negative correlation.

15-47 a. The accompanying scatterplot depicts a positive linear relation between perceived trauma and perceived masculinity. The data appear to be linearly related; therefore, it is appropriate to calculate a Pearson correlation coefficient.

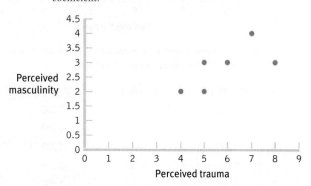

b. The Pearson correlation coefficient is calculated in three steps. Step 1 is calculating the numerator:

X	$(X-M_X)$	Y	$(Y-M_Y)$	$(X-M_X)(Y-M_Y)$
5	−0.833	3	0.167	−0.139
6	0.167	3	0.167	0.028
4	−1.833	2	−0.833	1.527
5	−0.833	2	−0.833	0.694
7	1.167	4	1.167	1.362
8	2.167	3	0.167	0.362

$$M_X = 5.833 \qquad M_Y = 2.833 \qquad \Sigma[(X-M_X)(Y-M_Y)] = 3.834$$

Step 2 is calculating the denominator:

X	$(X-M_X)$	$(X-M_X)^2$	Y	$(Y-M_Y)$	$(Y-M_Y)^2$
5	−0.833	0.694	3	0.167	0.028
6	0.167	0.028	3	0.167	0.028
4	−1.833	3.360	2	−0.833	0.694
5	−0.833	0.694	2	−0.833	0.694
7	1.167	1.362	4	1.167	1.362
8	2.167	4.696	3	0.167	0.028

$$\Sigma[(X-M_X)^2 = 10.834 \qquad \Sigma(Y-M_Y)^2 = 2.834$$

$$\sqrt{(SS_X)(SS_Y)} = \sqrt{(10.834)(2.834)} = \sqrt{30.704} = 5.541$$

Step 3 is computing r:

$$r = \frac{\Sigma[(X-M_X)(Y-M_Y)]}{\sqrt{(SS_X)(SS_Y)}} = \frac{3.834}{5.541} = 0.69$$

c. The correlation coefficient is large and positive. This means that as ratings of trauma increased, ratings of masculinity tended to increase as well.

d. For most of the participants, the sign of the deviation for the trauma variable is the same as that for the masculinity variable, which indicates that those participants scoring above the mean on one variable also tended to score above the mean on the second variable (and likewise for the lowest scores). Because the scores for each participant tend to fall on the same side of the mean, this is a positive relation.

e. When the soldier was a woman, the perception of the situation as traumatic was strongly negatively correlated with the perception of the woman as feminine. This relation is the opposite to that observed when the soldier was a man. When the soldier was a man, the perception of the situation as traumatic was strongly positively correlated with the perception of the man as feminine. Regardless of whether the soldier was a man or a woman, there was a positive correlation between the perception of the situation as traumatic and the perception of masculinity, but the observed correlation was stronger for the perceptions of women than for the perceptions of men.

15-49 a. Because your friend is running late, she is likely more concerned about traffic than she otherwise would be. Thus, she may take note of traffic only when she is running late, leading her to believe that the amount of traffic correlates with how late she is. Furthermore, having this belief, in the future she may think only of cases that confirm her belief that a relation exists between how late she is and traffic conditions, reflecting a confirmation bias. Alternatively, traffic conditions might be worse when your friend is running late, but that could be a coincidence. A more systematic study of the relation between your friend's behavior and traffic conditions would be required before she could conclude that a relation exists.

b. There are a number of possible answers to this question. For example, we could operationalize the degree to which she is late as the number of minutes past her intended departure time that she leaves for her destination. We could operationalize the amount of traffic as the number of minutes the car is being driven at less than the speed limit (given that your friend would normally drive right at the speed limit).

c. If you calculate correlation coefficients between enough pairs of variables, some of them are likely to be statistically significant just by chance. If there's no actual underlying correlation, this would be a Type I error. Some call these spurious correlations, meaning associations that look real, but are not.

15-51 a. The reporter suggests that convertibles are not generally less safe than other cars.

b. Convertibles may be driven less often than other cars, as they may be considered primarily a recreational vehicle. If they are driven less, owners have fewer chances to get into accidents while driving them.

c. A more appropriate comparison may be to determine the number of fatalities that occur per every 100 hours driven in various kinds of cars.

15-53 a. The researchers are suggesting that participation in arts education programs causes students to tend to perform better and stay in school longer.

b. It could be that those students who perform better and stay in school longer are more likely to be interested in, and therefore participate in, arts education programs.

c. There are many possible answers. For example, the socioeconomic status of the students' families may be associated with performance in school, years of schooling, and participation in arts education programs, with higher socioeconomic status tending to lead to improved performance, staying in school longer, and higher participation in arts education programs.

15-55 a. We cannot draw a causal correlation. Many other factors might potentially lead both to technology expenditures and to the trend of millennials moving home.

b. Many other factors may be at work here. In fact, the link may be coincidental. The reporter blamed student debt for the trend of millennials moving back home and said, "There's no evidence that this has anything to do with the iPhone."

15-57 a. The accompanying scatterplot depicts a positive linear relation between number of taboo words and number of animal words. The data appear to be linearly related; therefore, it is appropriate to calculate a Pearson correlation coefficient.

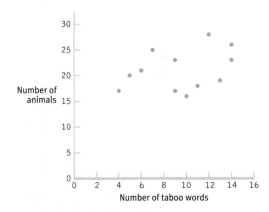

b. Step 1 is calculating the numerator:

Number of taboo words (X)	$(X - M_X)$	Number of animals (Y)	$(Y - M_Y)$	$(X - M_X)(Y - M_Y)$
9	−0.5	23	1.917	−0.959
5	−4.5	20	−1.083	4.874
4	−5.5	17	−4.083	22.457
12	2.5	28	6.917	17.293
14	4.5	26	4.917	22.127
10	0.5	16	−5.083	−2.542
9	−0.5	17	−4.083	2.042
11	1.5	18	−3.083	−4.625
14	4.5	23	1.917	8.627
6	−3.5	21	−0.083	0.291
7	−2.5	25	3.917	−9.793
13	3.5	19	−2.083	−7.291
$M_X = 9.5$		$M_Y = 21.083$		$\Sigma[(X - M_X)(Y - M_Y)] = 52.501$

Step 2 is calculating the denominator:

Number of taboo words (X)	$(X - M_X)$	$(X - M_X)^2$	Number of animals (Y)	$(Y - M_Y)$	$(Y - M_Y)^2$
9	−0.5	0.25	23	1.917	3.675
5	−4.5	20.25	20	−1.083	1.173
4	−5.5	30.25	17	−4.083	16.671
12	2.5	6.25	28	6.917	47.845
14	4.5	20.25	26	4.917	24.177
10	0.5	0.25	16	−5.083	25.837
9	−0.5	0.25	17	−4.083	16.671
11	1.5	2.25	18	−3.083	9.505
14	4.5	20.25	23	1.917	3.675
6	−3.5	12.25	21	−0.083	0.007
7	−2.5	6.25	25	3.917	15.343
13	3.5	12.25	19	−2.083	4.339

$$\Sigma(X - M_X)^2 = 131 \qquad \Sigma(Y - M_Y)^2 = 168.918$$

$$r = \frac{\Sigma[(X - M_X)(Y - M_Y)]}{\sqrt{(SS_X)(SS_Y)}} = \frac{52.501}{\sqrt{(131)(168.918)}} = \frac{52.501}{148.756} = 0.353$$

c. The correlation coefficient we just computed is a descriptive statistic because we can use it to describe only this particular sample. To turn this correlation coefficient into an inferential statistic, we would need to conduct a hypothesis test. The hypothesis test will determine if the correlation coefficient is significantly different from zero.

d. *Step 1:* Population 1: Participants like those whom Jay and Jay (2015) studied. Population 2: Participants for whom there is no relation between the number of taboo words and the number of animal words that they could list in a minute. The comparison distribution is made up of correlation coefficients based on samples of this size (12 people) selected from the population. We do not know if these data were randomly selected, so we must be cautious when generalizing the findings. We also do not know if the underlying population distributions are normally distributed. The sample size is too small to draw any conclusions about this assumption, so we should proceed with caution. Additionally, because we have such a small data set, it is difficult to evaluate whether the variability of the number of taboo words listed is equal across all levels of the second variable, the number of animal words listed. Similarly, we cannot easily evaluate whether the variability of the number of animal words listed is similar across all levels of the number of taboo words listed.

Step 2: Null hypothesis: There is no correlation between the number of taboo words said and the number of animal words said—$H_0: \rho = 0$.

Research hypothesis: There is a correlation between the number of taboo words said and the number of animal words said—$H_1: \rho \neq 0$.

Step 3: The comparison distribution is a distribution of Pearson correlation coefficients, r, with the following degrees of freedom: $df_r = N - 2 = 12 - 2 = 10$.

Step 4: The critical values for an r distribution with 10 degrees of freedom for a two-tailed test with an alpha level of 0.05 are −0.576 and 0.576.

Step 5: (same as the solution for 15.57b):

$$M_X = 9.5$$
$$M_Y = 21.083$$
$$\Sigma[(X - M_X)(Y - M_Y)] = 52.501$$
$$\Sigma(X - M_X)^2 = SS_X = 131$$
$$\Sigma(Y - M_Y)^2 = SS_Y = 168.918$$

$$r = \frac{\Sigma[(X - M_X)(Y - M_Y)]}{\sqrt{(SS_X)(SS_Y)}} = \frac{52.501}{\sqrt{(131)(168.918)}} = \frac{52.501}{148.756} = 0.353$$

Step 6: The test statistic, $r = 0.35$, is not larger in magnitude than the critical value of 0.576, so we fail to reject the null hypothesis. We cannot conclude that there is a relation between the number of taboo words said and the number of animal words said. Because the sample size is rather small and we calculated such a strong correlation with this small sample, we would be encouraged to replicate the study with a larger sample to increase the statistical power so that we may more fully explore this relation. In fact, the researchers who conducted this study did find that this correlation was statistically significant, but they had many more participants than in our fictional example.

e. It is unlikely you could study this phenomenon using an experimental design because it would be difficult to manipulate a person's vocabulary size.

15-59 a. If students were marked down for talking about the rooster rather than the cow, the reading test would not meet the established criteria. The question asked on the test is ambiguous because the information regarding what caused the cow's behavior to change is not explicitly stated in the story. Furthermore, the correct answer to the question provided on the Web site is not actually an answer to the question itself. The question states, "What caused Brownie's behavior to change?" The answer that the cow started out kind and ended up mean is a description of *how* her behavior changed, not what caused her behavior to change. This question does not appear to be a valid question because it does not appear to provide an accurate assessment of students' *writing* ability.

b. One possible third variable that could lead to better performance in some schools over others is the average socioeconomic status of the families whose children attend the school. Schools in wealthier areas or counties would have students of higher socioeconomic status, who might be expected to perform better on a test of writing skill. Another possible third variable that could lead to better performance in some schools over others is the type of reading and writing curriculum implemented in the school. Different ways of teaching the material may be more effective than others, regardless of the effectiveness of the teachers who are actually presenting the material.

15-61 This would be a big data success. Although the precise reason or causal mechanism for the correlation is unknown, using this correlation might help health care providers target resources for fighting the flu in a timely manner.

15-63 a. The participants in the study are the various countries for which rates were obtained.

  b. The two variables are health care spending and health, as assessed by life expectancy. Health care spending was operationalized as the amount spent per capita on health care, whereas life expectancy is the average age at death. Another way to operationalize health could be rates of various diseases, such as heart disease, or obesity via body mass index (BMI).

  c. The study finding was that there is a negative correlation between health care spending and life expectancy, in which countries, such as the United States, that have higher rates of spending on health care per capita have lower life expectancies. One would suspect the opposite to be true: that the more a country spends on health care, the healthier the population would be, thus resulting in higher life expectancy.

  d. Other possible third variables could be the typical body weight in a country, the typical exercise levels in a country, accident rates, access to health care, access to or knowledge of preventive health measures, stereotypes, or a country's typical diet.

  e. This study is a correlational study, not a true experiment, because countries were not assigned to certain levels of health care spending, and then assessed for life expectancy. The data were obtained from naturally occurring events.

  f. It would not be possible to conduct a true experiment on this topic, as doing so would require a manipulation in the health care spending for various countries for the entire population for a long period of time, which would not be realistic, practical, or ethical to implement.

15-65 a. High school athletic participation might be operationalized as a nominal variable by indicating whether a student participates in athletics (levels: yes or no), or by categorizing each student according to the type of athletics (levels: none, football, baseball, and so on.) in which they participate.

  b. High school athletic participation might be operationalized as a scale variable by counting the number of sports in which a student participates (e.g., 0, 1, 2), or by counting the number of days on which a student participates in sports annually.

  c. Correlation is a useful tool to quantify the relation between two scale variables, especially when manipulation of either variable does not or cannot occur, and measuring either variable on a nominal or ordinal level would result in information being lost.

  d. The researchers reported the following positive correlations: high school athletic participation and high school GPA; high school athletic participation and university completion; high school athletic participation and earnings as an adult; and high school athletic participation and various positive health behaviors. There are several other positive correlations among only male students, including the following: high school athletic performance and alcohol consumption; high school athletic performance and sexist attitudes; high school athletic performance and homophobic attitudes; and high school athletic performance and violence. These are all positive correlations because as high school athletic participation increases, so does each of these variables.

  e. There are no negative correlations reported; in all cases, an increase in one variable tended to accompany an increase in the other variable.

  f. One possible causal explanation is that high school athletic participation (A) tends to cause positive health behaviors (B). A second possible causal explanation is that positive health behaviors (B) tend to cause high school athletic participation (A). A third possible causal explanation is that some other variable, such as socioeconomic status (C), could tend to affect both high school athletic participation and positive health behaviors.

  g. Partial correlation might be useful in this study because it would allow us to factor out, or control for, the contribution of a third (or fourth) variable to a relation between two variables. For example, we could calculate the partial correlation between high school athletic participation and university completion, controlling for high school or university GPA.

Chapter 16

16-1 Regression allows us to make predictions based on the relation established in the correlation. Regression also allows us to consider the contributions of several variables.

16-3 There is no difference between these two terms. They are two ways to express the same thing.

16-5 a is the intercept, the predicted value for Y when X is equal to 0, which is the point at which the line crosses, or intercepts, the y-axis. b is the slope, the amount that Y is predicted to increase for an increase of 1 in X.

16-7 The intercept is not meaningful or useful when it is impossible to observe a value of 0 for X. If height is being used to predict weight, it would not make sense to talk about the weight of someone with no height.

16-9 The line of best fit in regression means that we couldn't make the line a little steeper, or raise or lower it, in any way that would allow it to represent those dots any better than it already does. This is why we can look at the scatterplot around this line and observe that the line goes precisely through the middle of the dots. Statistically, this is the line that leads to the least amount of error in prediction.

16-11 Data points clustered closely around the line of best fit are described by a small standard error of the estimate; this allows us to have a high level of confidence in the predictive ability of the predictor variable. Data points clustered far away from the line of best fit are described by a large standard error of the estimate, and result in our having a low level of confidence in the predictive ability of the predictor variable.

16-13 If regression to the mean did not occur, every distribution would look bimodal, like a valley. Instead, the end result of the phenomenon of regression to the mean is that things look unimodal, like a hill or what we call the normal, bell-shaped curve. Remember that the center of the bell-shaped curve is the mean, and this is where the bulk of data cluster, thanks to regression to the mean.

16-15 The sum of squares total, SS_{total}, represents the worst-case scenario, the total error we would have in the predictions if there were no regression equation and we had to predict the mean for everybody.

16-17 The basic steps to calculate the proportionate reduction in error are: (1) Determine the error associated with using the mean as the predictor. (2) Determine the error associated with using the regression equation as the predictor. (3) Subtract the error associated with the regression equation from the error associated with the mean. (4) Divide the difference (calculated in step 3) by the error associated with using the mean.

16-19 An orthogonal variable is a predictor variable that makes a separate and distinct contribution in the prediction of an outcome variable, as compared with the contributions of another predictor variable.

16-21 Multiple regression is often more useful than simple linear regression because it allows us to take into account the contribution of multiple predictor variables, and increase the accuracy of prediction of the outcome variable, thus reducing the prediction error. Because behaviors are complex and tend to be influenced by many factors, multiple regression allows us to better predict a given outcome.

16-23 When making predictions from the regression equation, we would expect that our predictions for the value of the outcome variable would be off by 6.2, on average.

16-25 Regression tools have been used to predict the likelihood that a person will commit a crime in the future. They have also been used by Facebook to predict whether users are at risk for suicide based on their Facebook activity.

16-27 a. $z_X = \dfrac{X - M_X}{SD_X} = \dfrac{2.9 - 1.9}{0.6} = 1.667$

b. $z_{\hat{Y}} = (r_{XY})(z_X) = (0.31)(1.667) = 0.517$

c. $\hat{Y} = z_{\hat{Y}}(SD_Y) + M_Y = (0.517)(3.2) + 10 = 11.65$

16-29 a. $z_X = \dfrac{X - M_X}{SD_X} = \dfrac{76 - 55}{12} = 1.75$

b. $z_{\hat{Y}} = (r_{XY})(z_X) = (-0.19)(1.75) = -0.333$

c. $\hat{Y} = z_{\hat{Y}}(SD_Y) + M_Y = (-0.333)(95) + 1000 = 968.37$

d. The y intercept occurs when X is equal to 0. We start by finding a z score:

$$z_X = \dfrac{X - M_X}{SD_X} = \dfrac{0 - 55}{12} = -4.583$$

This is the z score for an X of 0. Now we need to figure out the predicted z score on Y for this X value:

$$z_{\hat{Y}} = (r_{XY})(z_X) = (-0.19)(-4.583) = 0.871$$

The final step is to convert the predicted z score on this predicted Y to a raw score:

$$\hat{Y} = z_{\hat{Y}}(SD_Y) + M_Y = (0.871)(95) + 1000 = 1082.745$$

This is the y intercept.

e. The slope can be found by comparing the predicted Y value for an X value of 0 (the intercept) and an X value of 1. Using the same steps as in part (a), we can compute the predicted Y score for an X value of 1.

$$z_X = \dfrac{X - M_X}{SD_X} = \dfrac{1 - 55}{12} = -4.5$$

This is the z score for an X of 1. Now we need to figure out the predicted z score on Y for this X value:

$$z_{\hat{Y}} = (r_{XY})(z_X) = (-0.19)(-4.5) = 0.855$$

The final step is to convert the predicted z score on this predicted Y to a raw score:

$$\hat{Y} = z_{\hat{Y}}(SD_Y) + M_Y = (0.855)(95) + 1000 = 1081.225$$

We compute the slope by measuring the change in Y with this one-unit increase in X:

$$1081.225 - 1082.745 = -1.52$$

This is the slope.

f. $\hat{Y} = 1082.745 - 1.52(X)$

g. To draw the line, we must compute one more $\hat{Y}$ value. This time we can use the regression equation to make the prediction:

$$\hat{Y} = 1082.745 - 1.52(48) = 1009.785$$

Now we can draw the regression line.

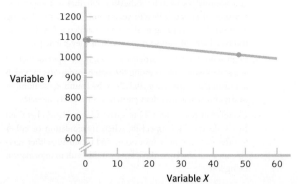

16-31 a. $\hat{Y} = 49 + (-0.18)(X) = 49 + (-0.18)(-31) = 54.58$
  b. $\hat{Y} = 49 + (-0.18)(65) = 37.3$
  c. $\hat{Y} = 49 + (-0.18)(14) = 46.48$

16-33 a. The sum of squared error for the mean, SS_{total}:

X	Y	M_Y	Error	Squared Error
4	6	6.75	−0.75	0.563
6	3	6.75	−3.75	14.063
7	7	6.75	0.25	0.063
8	5	6.75	−1.75	3.063
9	4	6.75	−2.75	7.563
10	12	6.75	5.25	27.563
12	9	6.75	2.25	5.063
14	8	6.75	1.25	1.563

$$SS_{total} = \Sigma(Y - M_Y)^2 = 59.504$$

b. The sum of squared error for the regression equation, SS_{error}:

X	Y	Regression Equation	$\hat{Y}$	Error $(Y - \hat{Y})$	Squared Error
4	6	$\hat{Y} = 2.643 + 0.469(4)$	$= 4.519$	1.481	2.193
6	3	$\hat{Y} = 2.643 + 0.469(6)$	$= 5.457$	−2.457	6.037
7	7	$\hat{Y} = 2.643 + 0.469(7)$	$= 5.926$	1.074	1.153
8	5	$\hat{Y} = 2.643 + 0.469(8)$	$= 6.395$	−1.395	1.946
9	4	$\hat{Y} = 2.643 + 0.469(9)$	$= 6.864$	−2.864	8.202
10	12	$\hat{Y} = 2.643 + 0.469(10)$	$= 7.333$	4.667	21.781
12	9	$\hat{Y} = 2.643 + 0.469(12)$	$= 8.271$	0.729	0.531
14	8	$\hat{Y} = 2.643 + 0.469(14)$	$= 9.209$	−1.209	1.462

$$SS_{total} = \Sigma(Y - \hat{Y})^2 = 43.305$$

c. The proportionate reduction in error for these data:
$$r^2 = \frac{(SS_{total} - SS_{error})}{SS_{total}} = \frac{(59.504 - 43.305)}{59.504} = 0.272$$

d. This calculation of r^2, 0.272, equals the square of the correlation coefficient, $r^2 = (0.52)(0.52) = 0.270$. These numbers are slightly different due to rounding decisions.

e. We can plug the sample size and the SS_{error} calculated for part (b) into the equations for the standard error of the estimate:
$$\sigma_{estimate} = \sqrt{\frac{\Sigma(Y - \hat{Y})^2}{N}} = \sqrt{\frac{43.305}{8}} = \sqrt{5.413} = 2.327$$

f. The standardized regression coefficient is equal to the correlation coefficient for simple linear regression, 0.52. We can also check that this is correct by computing β:

X	$(X - M_X)$	$(X - M_X)^2$	Y	$(Y - M_Y)$	$(Y - M_Y)^2$
4	−4.75	22.563	6	−0.75	0.563
6	−2.75	7.563	3	−3.75	14.063
7	−1.75	3.063	7	0.25	0.063
8	−0.75	0.563	5	−1.75	3.063
9	0.25	0.063	4	−2.75	7.563
10	1.25	1.563	12	5.25	27.563
12	3.25	10.563	9	2.25	5.063
14	5.25	27.563	8	1.25	1.563

$$\Sigma(X - M_X)^2 = 73.504 \qquad \Sigma(Y - M_Y)^2 = 59.504$$

$$\beta = (b)\frac{\sqrt{SS_X}}{\sqrt{SS_Y}} = (0.469)\frac{\sqrt{73.504}}{\sqrt{59.504}} = (0.469)\frac{8.573}{7.714} = 0.521$$

16-35 a. $\hat{Y} = 1.675 + (0.001)(X_{SAT}) + (-0.008)(X_{rank})$; or
  $\hat{Y} = 13675 + 0.001(X_{SAT}) - 0.008(X_{rank})$
  b. $\hat{Y} = 1.675 + (0.001)(1030) - 0.008(41)$
    $= 1.675 + 1.03 - 0.328 = 2.377$
  c. $\hat{Y} = 1.675 + (0.001)(860) - 0.008(22)$
    $= 1.675 + 0.86 - 0.176 = 2.359$
  d. $\hat{Y} = 1.675 + (0.001)(1060) - 0.008(8)$
    $= 1.675 + 1.06 - 0.064 = 2.671$

16-37 a. The predictor variables include personal connections with victims, personal connections with gang members, personal connections with people in prison, unemployment, and history of drug or alcohol problems.
  b. The outcome variable is the likelihood of committing a crime.
  c. Several other variables might predict a person's likelihood of committing a crime. Some examples might include the person's level of education, the person's current criminal record, the level of poverty in the community in which the person lives, and the person's positive connections to the community such as membership in a church or participation with a volunteer organization.
  d. Regressions can lead to problems with prediction because predictions can have unforeseen consequences. There may be hidden confounding variables that may mean that regression-based decisions are not fair or accurate ones. Therefore, it is important to consider confounding variables when developing a regression model. Additionally, regressions are unable to make statements about causality. Only experimental studies (i.e., methodologically controlled studies) can demonstrate causality. Finally, regression toward the mean, such that extreme scores tend to become less extreme, makes regression models problematic with respect to making accurate predictions.

In this example, there are many possible confounding variables that might predict crime. When including variables in a regression model, it is important to consider whether the predictor variables are related. For example, quality public education and access to public transportation might be related as they are both services provided by the government. It is important to consider whether variables are orthogonal when developing regression models.

Similarly, for this example, using a regression model to make predictions can lead to the confusion of correlation and causation. Having a personal connection with an imprisoned person might predict crime, but we have no evidence that this connection causes crime. Data that are not based on an experimental design should be interpreted cautiously.

16-39 a. $X = z(\sigma) + \mu = -1.2(0.61) + 3.51 = 2.778$. This answer makes sense because the raw score of 2.778 is a bit more than 1 standard deviation below the mean of 3.51.

b. $X = z(\sigma) + \mu = 0.66(0.61) + 3.51 = 3.913$. This answer makes sense because the raw score of 3.913 is slightly more than 0.5 standard deviation above the mean of 3.51.

16-41 a. 3.12

b. 3.16

c. 3.18

d. The accompanying graph depicts the regression line for GPA and hours studied.

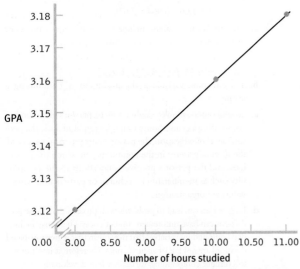

e. We can calculate the number of hours one would need to study to earn a 4.0 by substituting 4.0 for $\hat{Y}$ in the regression equation and solving for X: $4.0 = 2.96 + 0.02(X)$. To isolate the X, we subtract 2.96 from the left side of the equation and divide by 0.02: $X = (4.0 - 2.96)/0.02 = 52$. This regression equation predicts that we would have to study 52 hours per week to earn a 4.0. It is misleading to make predictions about what will happen when a person studies this many hours because the regression equation for prediction is almost certainly based on a sample that studied far fewer hours. Even though the relation between hours studied and GPA was linear within the range of studied scores, outside of that range it may have a different slope or no longer be linear, or the relation may not even exist.

16-43 a. We cannot conclude that cola consumption causes a decrease in bone mineral density because there are a number of different kinds of causal relations that could lead to the predictive relation observed by Tucker and colleagues. There may be some characteristic about these older women that both causes them to drink cola and leads to a decrease in bone mineral density. For example, perhaps overall poorer health habits lead to an increased consumption of cola and a decrease in bone mineral density.

b. Multiple regression allows us to assess the contributions of more than one predictor variable to the outcome variable. Performing this multiple regression allowed the researchers to explore the unique contributions of a third variable, such as physical activity, in addition to bone density.

c. Physical activity might produce an increase in bone mineral density, as exercise is known to increase bone density. Conversely, it is possible that physical activity might produce a decrease in cola consumption because people who exercise more might instead drink beverages that are more likely to keep them hydrated (such as water or sports drinks).

d. Calcium intake should produce an increase in bone mineral density, thereby producing a positive relation between calcium intake and bone density. It is possible that consumption of cola means less consumption of beverages with calcium in them, such as milk, producing a negative relation between cola consumption and bone density.

16-45 a. $\hat{Y} = 24.698 + 0.161(X)$, or predicted year 3 anxiety = $24.698 + 0.161$ (year 1 depression)

b. As depression at year 1 increases by 1 point, predicted anxiety at year 3 increases, on average, by the slope of the regression equation, which is 0.161.

c. We would predict that her year 3 anxiety score would be 26.31.

d. We would predict that his year 3 anxiety score would be 25.02.

16-47 a. The predictor variable in this study was marital status, and the outcome variable was chance of breaking up.

b. It appears that the researchers initially conducted a simple linear regression and then conducted a multiple regression analysis to account for the other variables (e.g., age, financial status) that may have been confounded with marital status in predicting the outcome variable.

c. Answers will differ, but the focus should be on the statistically significant contribution these other variables had in predicting the outcome variable, which appear to be more important than, and perhaps explain, the relation between marital status and the break-up of the relationship.

d. Another "third variable" in this study could have been length of relationship before the child was born. Married couples may have been together longer than cohabitating couples, and it may be that those who were together longer before the birth of the child, regardless of their marital status, are more likely to stay together than those who had been together for only a short period of time prior to the birth.

16-49 a. Multiple regression may have been used to predict countries' diabetes rates based on consumption of sugar while controlling for rates of obesity and other variables.

b. Accounting for other factors allowed the reporter to exclude the impact of potentially confounding variables. This is important because other variables, such as rates of obesity, could have contributed to the relation between sugar consumption and rates of diabetes across countries. Factoring out other variables allows us to eliminate these potential confounds as explanations for a relation.

c. Numerous other factors may have been included. For example, the researchers may have controlled for countries' gross domestic product, median educational attainment, health care spending, unemployment rates, and so on.

d. Let's consider the A-B-C model of understanding possible causal explanations within correlation to understand why it is most likely that A (sugar consumption) causes B (rates of diabetes). First, it doesn't make sense that B (rates of diabetes) causes A (increased sugar consumption). Second, although it's still possible that one or more additional variables (C) account for the relation between A (sugar consumption) and B (diabetes rates), this explanation is not likely because the researchers controlled for most of the obvious possible confounding variables.

16-51 a. To predict the number of hours João studies per week, we use the formula $z_{\hat{Y}} = (r_{XY})(z_X)$ to find the predicted z score for the number of hours he studies; then we can transform the predicted z score into his raw score. First, translate his predicted raw score for age into a z score for age: $z_X = \frac{(X - M_X)}{SD_X} = \frac{(24 - 21)}{1.789} = 1.677$. Then calculate his predicted z score for number of hours studied: $z_{\hat{Y}} = (r_{XY})(z_X) = (0.49)(1.677) = 0.82$. Finally, translate the z score for hours studied into the raw score for hours studied: $\hat{Y} = 0.82(5.582) + 14.2 = 18.777$.

b. First, translate Kimberly's age raw score into an age z score: $z_X = \frac{(X - M_X)}{SD_X} = \frac{(19 - 21)}{1.789} = -1.118$. Then calculate the predicted z score for hours studied: $z_{\hat{Y}} = (r_{XY})(z_X) = (0.49)(-1.118) = -0.548$. Finally, translate the z score for hours studied into the raw score for hours studied: $\hat{Y} = -0.548(5.582) + 14.2 = 11.141$.

c. Seung's age is well above the mean age of the students sampled. The relation that exists for traditional-age students may not exist for students who are much older. Extrapolating beyond the range of the observed data may lead to erroneous conclusions.

d. From a mathematical perspective, the word *regression* refers to a tendency for extreme scores to drift toward the mean. In the calculation of regression, the predicted score is closer to its mean (i.e., less extreme) than the score used for prediction. For example, in part (a) the z score used for predicting was 1.677 and the predicted z score was 0.82, a less extreme

score. Similarly, in part (b) the z score used for predicting was −1.118 and the predicted z score was −0.548, which is again a less extreme score.

e. First, we calculate what we would predict for Y when X equals 0; that number, −17.908, is the intercept.

$$z_X = \frac{(X - M_X)}{SD_X} = \frac{(0 - 21)}{1.789} = -11.738$$

$$z_{\hat{Y}} = (r_{XY})(z_X) = (0.49)(-11.738) = -5.752$$

$$\hat{Y} = z_{\hat{Y}}(SD_Y) + M_Y = -5.752(5.582) + 14.2 = -17.908$$

Note that this prediction is negative (it doesn't make sense to have a negative number of hours) because the number for age, 0, is not a number that would actually be used in this situation—it's another example of the dangers of extrapolation, but it still is necessary to determine the regression equation.

Then we calculate what we would predict for Y when X equals 1: The amount that this number, −16.378, differs from the prediction when X equals 0 is the slope.

$$z_X = \frac{(X - M_X)}{SD_X} = \frac{(1 - 21)}{1.789} = -11.179$$

$$z_{\hat{Y}} = (r_{XY})(z_X) = (0.49)(-11.179) = -5.478$$

$$\hat{Y} = z_{\hat{Y}}(SD_Y) + M_Y = -5.478(5.582) + 14.2 = -16.378$$

When X equals 0, −17.908 is the prediction for Y. When X equals 1, −16.378 is the prediction for Y. The latter number is 1.530 higher $[-16.378 - (-17.908) = 1.530]$—that is, more positive—than the former. when you're calculating the difference, remember to consider whether the prediction for Y was more positive or more negative when X increased from 0 to 1.

Thus, the regression equation is: $\hat{Y} = -17.91 + 1.53(X)$.

f. Substituting 17 for X in the regression equation for part (e) yields 8.1. Substituting 22 for X in the regression equation yields 15.75. We would predict that a 17-year-old would study 8.1 hours and a 22-year-old would study 15.75 hours.

g. The accompanying graph depicts the regression line for predicting hours studied per week from a person's age.

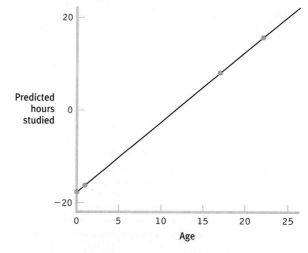

h. It is misleading to include young ages such as 0 and 5 on the graph because people of that age would never be college students.

i. The accompanying graph shows the scatterplot and regression line relating age and number of hours studied. Vertical lines from each observed data point are drawn to the regression line to represent the error prediction from the regression equation.

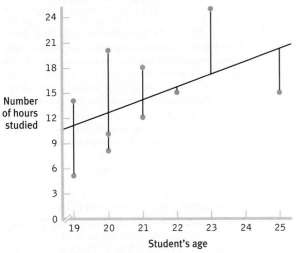

Student's age

j. The accompanying scatterplot relating age and number of hours studied includes a horizontal line at the mean number of hours studied. Vertical lines between the observed data points and the mean represent the amount of error in predicting from the mean.

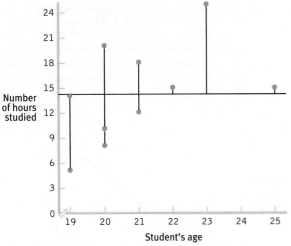

Student's age

k. There appears to be less error in part (i), where the regression line is used to predict hours studied. This occurs because the regression line is the line that minimizes the distance between the observed scores and the line drawn through them. That is, the regression line is the *one* line that can be drawn through the data that produces the minimum error.

l. To calculate the proportionate reduction in error the long way, we first calculate the predicted Y scores (column 3) for each of the observed X scores in the data set and determine how much those predicted Y scores differ from the observed Y scores (column 4), and then we square them (column 5).

Age	Observed Hours Studied	Predicted Hours Studied	Observed − Predicted	Square of Observed − Predicted	Observed − Mean	Square of Observed − Mean
19	5	11.16	−6.16	37.946	−9.2	84.64
20	20	12.69	7.31	53.436	5.8	33.64
20	8	12.69	−4.69	21.996	−6.2	38.44
21	12	14.22	−2.22	4.928	−2.2	4.84
21	18	14.22	3.78	14.288	3.8	14.44
23	25	17.28	7.72	59.598	10.8	116.64
22	15	15.75	−0.75	0.563	0.8	0.64
20	10	12.69	−2.69	7.236	−4.2	17.64
19	14	11.16	2.84	8.066	−0.2	0.04
25	15	20.34	−5.34	28.516	0.8	0.64

We then calculate SS_{error}, which is the sum of the squared error when using the regression equation as the basis of prediction. This sum, calculated by adding the numbers in column 5, is 236.573. We then subtract the mean from each score (column 6), and square these differences (column 7). Next, we calculate SS_{total} which is the sum of the squared error when using the mean as the basis of prediction. This sum is 311.6. Finally, we calculate the proportionate reduction in error as $r^2 = \frac{(SS_{total} - SS_{error})}{SS_{total}} = 0.24$.

m. The r^2 calculated in part (l) indicates that 24% of the variability in hours studied is accounted for by a student's age. By using the regression equation, we have reduced the error of the prediction by 24% as compared with using the mean.

n. To calculate the proportionate reduction in error the short way, we would square the correlation coefficient. The correlation between age and hours studied is 0.49. Squaring 0.49 yields 0.24. It makes sense that the correlation coefficient could be used to determine how useful the regression equation will be because the correlation coefficient is a measure of the strength of association between two variables. If two variables are strongly related, we are better able to use one of the variables to predict the values of the other.

o. Here are the computations needed to compute β:

X	$(X - M_X)$	$(X - M_X)^2$	Y	$(Y - M_Y)$	$(Y - M_Y)^2$
19	−2	4	5	−9.2	84.64
20	−1	1	20	5.8	33.64
20	−1	1	8	−6.2	38.44
21	0	0	12	−2.2	4.84
21	0	0	18	3.8	14.44
23	2	4	25	10.8	116.64
22	1	1	15	0.8	0.64
20	−1	1	10	−4.2	17.64
19	−2	4	14	−0.2	0.04
25	4	16	15	0.8	0.64

$$\Sigma(X - M_X)^2 = 32 \qquad \Sigma(Y - M_Y)^2 = 311.6$$

$$\beta = (b)\frac{\sqrt{SS_X}}{\sqrt{SS_Y}} = (1.53)\frac{\sqrt{32}}{\sqrt{311.6}} = 0.490$$

p. The standardized regression coefficient is equal to the correlation coefficient, 0.49, for simple linear regression.

q. The hypothesis test for regression is the same as that for correlation. The critical values for r with 8 degrees of freedom at an alpha level of 0.05 are −0.632 and 0.632. With a correlation of 0.49, we fail to exceed the cutoff and therefore fail to reject the null hypothesis. The same is true for the regression equation. We do not have a statistically significant regression and should be careful not to claim that the slope is different from 0.

Chapter 17

17-1 Nominal data are those that are categorical in nature; they cannot be ordered in any meaningful way, and they are often thought of as simply named. Ordinal data can be ordered, but we cannot assume even distances between points of equal separation. For example, the difference between the second and third scores may not be the same as the difference between the seventh and the eighth scores. Scale data are measured on either the interval or ratio level; we can assume equal intervals between points along these measures.

17-3 The chi-square test for goodness of fit is a nonparametric hypothesis test used with one nominal variable. The chi-square test for independence is a nonparametric test used with two nominal variables.

17-5 Throughout the book, we have referred to independent variables, those variables that we hypothesize to have an effect on the dependent variable. We also described how statisticians refer to observations that are independent of one another, such as a between-groups research design requiring that observations be taken from independent samples. Here, with regard to chi square, *independence* takes on a similar meaning. We are testing whether the effect of one variable is independent of the other—that the proportion of cases across the levels of one variable does not depend on the levels of the other variable.

17-7 In most previous hypothesis tests, the degrees of freedom have been based on sample size. For the chi-square hypothesis tests, however, the degrees of freedom are based on the numbers of categories, or cells, in which participants can be counted. For example, the degrees of freedom for the chi-square test for goodness of fit is the number of categories minus 1: $df_{\chi^2} = k - 1$. Here, k is the symbol for the number of categories.

17-9 The contingency table presents the observed frequencies for each cell in the study.

17-11 If a researcher obtains a significant chi-square value but one of the variables has more than two levels, the researcher can determine which cells of the table differ from expectations by comparing the value of the adjusted standardized residual for that cell to a criterion. The criterion adopted by many researchers is 2, such that if the adjusted standardized residual is greater than 2, the observed values for that cell differ significantly from the expected values.

17-13 This is the formula to calculate the chi-square statistic. The symbols represent the sum, for each cell, of the squared difference between each observed frequency and its matching expected frequency, divided by the expected value for its cell.

17-15 Relative likelihood indicates the relative chance of an outcome (i.e., how many times more likely the outcome is, given the group membership of an observation). For example, we might determine the relative likelihood that a person would be a victim of bullying, given that the person is a boy versus a girl.

17-17 Relative likelihood and relative risk are exactly the same measure, but relative likelihood is typically called *relative risk* when it comes to health and medical situations because it describes a person's risk for a disease or health outcome.

17-19 The most useful graph for displaying the results of a chi-square test of independence is a bar graph that uses the conditional proportions rather than the frequencies, thus allowing us to compare the rates across the various levels of each variable.

17-21 **a.** The independent variable is year in school, which is nominal (first-years or seniors). The dependent variable is number of loads of laundry, which is scale.

  b. The independent variable is need for approval, which is ordinal (rank). The dependent variable is kilometers on a car, which is scale.

  c. The independent variable is place of residence, which is nominal (on or off campus). The dependent variable is whether the student is an active member of a club, which is also nominal (active or not active).

17-23 a. $df_{\chi^2} = k - 1 = 4 - 1 = 3$

b.

Category	Observed (O)	Expected (E)	O − E	$(O-E)^2$	$\dfrac{(O-E)^2}{E}$
1	750	625	750 − 625 = 125	15,625	25
2	650	625	650 − 625 = 25	625	1
3	600	625	600 − 625 = −25	625	1
4	500	625	500 − 625 = −125	15,625	25

c. $\chi^2 = \left[\dfrac{(O-E)^2}{E}\right] = 25 + 1 + 1 + 25 = 52$

17-25 The conditional probability of being a smoker, given that a person is female, is $\dfrac{13}{199} = 0.065$, and the conditional probability of being a smoker, given that a person is male, is $\dfrac{723}{905} = 0.799$. The relative likelihood of being a smoker given that one is female rather than male is $\dfrac{0.065}{0.799} = 0.08$. These Turkish women with lung cancer were less than one-tenth as likely to be smokers as were the male lung cancer patients.

17-27 All four adjusted residuals are greater than 2 or less than −2. We can conclude that all four observed frequencies are further from their corresponding expected frequencies than would likely occur if the null hypothesis were true.

17-29 a. The first variable is gender, which is nominal (male or female). The second variable is salary negotiation, which also is nominal (wage not explicitly negotiable or wage explicitly negotiable).

b. A chi-square test for independence would be appropriate because both variables are nominal.

c. The researchers found that both genders seemed to be more likely to negotiate when the ad stated that the wage was negotiable than when that was not stated; however, when the job posting stated that the wage was negotiable, women seemed to be somewhat more likely than men to negotiate, whereas, when wage was not explicitly mentioned as negotiable in the job posting, men seemed to be more likely than women to negotiate.

17-31 a. A nonparametric test would be appropriate because both of the variables are nominal: gender and major.

b. A nonparametric test is more appropriate because the sample size is small and the data are unlikely to be normally distributed; the "top boss" is likely to have a much higher income than the other employees. This outlier would lead to a nonnormal distribution.

c. A parametric test would be appropriate because the independent variable (type of student: athlete versus nonathlete) is nominal and the dependent variable (grade point average) is scale.

d. A nonparametric test would be appropriate because the independent variable (athlete versus nonathlete) is nominal and the dependent variable (class rank) is ordinal.

e. A nonparametric test would be appropriate because the research question is about the relation between two nominal variables: seat-belt wearing and type of injuries.

f. A parametric test would be appropriate because the independent variable (seat-belt use: no seat belt versus seat belt) is nominal and the dependent variable (speed) is scale.

17-33 a. (i) Sexual orientation, with levels of gay/lesbian and heterosexual. (ii) Involvement in LGB justice campaigns, with levels of involved and not involved. (iii) This is a category III research design because the independent variable, sexual orientation, is nominal and the dependent variable, involvement in LGB justice campaigns, is also nominal.

b. (i) Sexual orientation, with levels of sexual minority and heterosexual. (ii) Number of gays/lesbians whom each person knows. (iii) This is a category II research design because the independent variable, sexual orientation, is nominal and the dependent variable, number of gays/lesbians whom each person knows, is scale.

c. (i) Emotional warmth or coldness scores on a scale of 1–100. (ii) Number of gays/lesbians whom each person knows. (iii) This is a category I research design because both the independent variable and the dependent variable are scale.

17-35 a.

	Mexican	White	Black
Married			
Single			

b.

	Married Head of Household	
	Immigrant Neighborhood	Nonimmigrant Neighborhood
Committed crime		
No crime		

	Unmarried Head of Household	
	Immigrant Neighborhood	Nonimmigrant Neighborhood
Committed crime		
No crime		

c.

	First Generation	Second Generation	Third Generation
Committed crime			
No crime			

17-37 a. There is one variable, the gender of the op-ed writers. Its levels are men and women.

b. A chi-square test for goodness of fit would be used because we have data on a single nominal variable from one sample.

c. *Step 1:* Population 1 is op-ed contributors, in proportions of men and women who are like those in our sample. Population 2 is op-ed contributors, in proportions of men and women who are like those in the general population. The comparison distribution is a chi-square distribution. The hypothesis test will be a chi-square test for goodness of fit because there is only one nominal variable. This study meets three of the four assumptions: (1) The variable under study is nominal. (2) Each observation is independent of all the others. (3) There are more than five times as many participants as there are cells (there are 124 op-ed articles and only two cells). (4) This is not, however, a randomly selected sample of op-eds, so we must generalize with caution; specifically, we should not generalize beyond *The New York Times*.

Step 2: Null hypothesis: The proportions of male and female op-ed contributors are the same as those in the population as a whole.

Research hypothesis: The proportions of male and female op-ed contributors are different from those in the population as a whole.

Step 3: The comparison distribution is a chi-square distribution with 1 degree of freedom: $df_{\chi^2} = 2 - 1 = 1$.

Step 4: The critical χ^2, based on an alpha level of 0.05 and 1 degree of freedom, is 3.841.

Step 5:

Observed (Proportions of Men and Women)	
Men	Women
103	21

Expected (Based on the General Population)	
Men	Women
62	62

Category	Observed (O)	Expected (E)	O − E	(O − E)²	$\frac{(O-E)^2}{E}$
Men	103	62	41	1681	27.113
Women	21	62	−41	1681	27.113

$$\chi^2 = \Sigma\left[\frac{(O-E)^2}{E}\right] = 27.113 + 27.113 = 54.226$$

Step 6: Reject the null hypothesis. The calculated chi-square statistic exceeds the critical value. It appears that the proportion of op-eds written by women versus men is not the same as the proportion of men and women in the population. Specifically, there are fewer women than in the general population.

d. $\chi^2(1, N = 124) = 54.23, p < 0.05$

17-39 a. The accompanying table shows the conditional proportions.

	Exciting	Routine	Dull	
Same city	0.424	0.521	0.055	1.00
Same state/different city	0.468	0.485	0.047	1.00
Different state	0.502	0.451	0.047	1.00

b. The accompanying graph shows these conditional proportions.

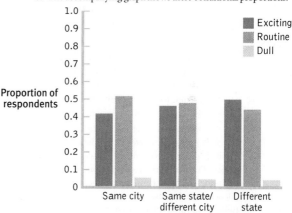

c. The relative likelihood of finding life exciting if one lives in a different state as opposed to the same city is $\frac{0.502}{0.424} = 1.18$.

17-41 a. There are two nominal variables—premarital doubts (yes or no) and divorced by 4 years (yes or no).

b. Chi-square tests for independence were used because there were two nominal variables. These tests were conducted for husbands and wives separately.

c. n should be reported as N. The specific p values for each hypothesis test should be provided. An effect size—Cramér's V in these cases—should be reported for each hypothesis test.

d. The researchers could not conclude that the likelihood of husbands being divorced by 4 years was dependent on premarital doubts. However, premarital doubts did seem to be related to being divorced by 4 years for wives.

17-43 a. An increase from 914 to 918 out of 100,000 people is an increase of just 4 people. That means that only 4 additional people will be affected by the single drink per day—that's not even close to 1%. In fact, it translates to a relative risk of 1.004. But even a much higher relative risk of 2, doubling the impact, would mean that only about an additional 1% of those who consumed one drink each day would be affected. The actual risk is just not that high.

b. A graph would highlight the tiny difference between the 914 out of 100,000 and the 918 out of 100,000. Both are less than 1%, and the difference between them is tiny.

c. Cramér's V quantifies the effect, which would emphasize how small this particular effect is.

d. A confound is any variable that systematically varies with the independent variable—drinking, in this case. When there is a confound, we cannot differentiate which variable is a causal factor in the levels of the dependent variable— health issues, in this case. It is possible that other factors might be confounding the relation between drinking and health issues because this is a correlational study. The researchers did not randomly assign people to amount of drinks; it would have been unethical to conduct an experiment in this situation.

17-45 a. There are two variables in this study. The independent variable is the referred child's gender (boy, girl) and the dependent variable is the diagnosis (problem, no problem but below norms, no problem and normal height).

b. A chi-square test for independence would be used because we have data on two nominal variables.

c. *Step 1:* Population 1 is referred children like those in this sample. Population 2 is referred children from a population in which growth problems do not depend on the child's gender. The comparison distribution is a chi-square distribution. The hypothesis test will be a chi-square test for independence because we have two nominal variables. This study meets three of the four assumptions. (1) The two variables are nominal. (2) Every participant is in only one cell. (3) There are more than five times as many participants as there are cells (there are 278 participants and six cells). (4) The sample, however, was not randomly selected, so we must use caution when generalizing.

Step 2: Null hypothesis: The proportion of boys in each diagnostic category is the same as the proportion of girls in each category.

Research hypothesis: The proportion of boys in each diagnostic category is different from the proportion of girls in each category.

Step 3: The comparison distribution is a chi-square distribution that has 2 degrees of freedom:

$df_{\chi^2} = (k_{row} - 1)\,(k_{column} - 1) = (2-1)(3-1) = 2.$

Step 4: The critical χ^2, based on an alpha level of 0.05 and 2 degrees of freedom, is 5.99.

Step 5:

	Observed			
	Medical Problem	No Problem/ Below Norm	No Problem/ Normal Height	
Boys	27	86	69	182
Girls	39	38	19	96
	66	124	88	278

$\dfrac{Total_{column}}{N}(Total_{row}) = \dfrac{66}{278}(182) = 43.134$

$\dfrac{Total_{column}}{N}(Total_{row}) = \dfrac{66}{278}(96) = 22.752$

$\dfrac{Total_{column}}{N}(Total_{row}) = \dfrac{124}{278}(182) = 81.172$

$\dfrac{Total_{column}}{N}(Total_{row}) = \dfrac{124}{278}(96) = 42.816$

$\dfrac{Total_{column}}{N}(Total_{row}) = \dfrac{88}{278}(182) = 57.694$

$\dfrac{Total_{column}}{N}(Total_{row}) = \dfrac{88}{278}(96) = 30.432$

	Expected			
	Medical Problem	No Problem/ Below Norm	No Problem/ Normal Height	
Boys	43.134	81.172	57.694	182
Girls	22.752	42.816	30.432	96
	65.886	123.988	88.126	278

Category	Observed (O)	Expected (E)	O − E	(O − E)²	$\dfrac{(O-E)^2}{E}$
Boy; med prob	27	43.134	−16.134	260.306	6.035
Boy; no prob/below	86	81.172	4.828	23.31	0.287
Boy; no prob/norm	69	57.694	11.306	127.826	2.216
Girl; med prob	39	22.752	16.248	263.998	11.603
Girl; no prob/below	38	42.816	−4.816	23.194	0.542
Girl; no prob/norm	19	30.432	−11.432	130.691	4.295

$$\chi^2 = \Sigma\left[\frac{(O-E)^2}{E}\right] = 6.035 + 0.287 + 2.216 + 11.603$$
$$+\, 0.542 + 4.295 = 24.978$$

Step 6: Reject the null hypothesis. The calculated chi-square value exceeds the critical value. It appears that the proportion of boys in each diagnostic category is not the same as the proportion of girls in each category.

d. Cramér's $V = \sqrt{\dfrac{\chi^2}{df_{row/column}}} = \sqrt{\dfrac{24.978}{(278)(1)}} = 0.300$

According to Cohen's conventions, this is a medium effect size.

e. $\chi^2(1, N = 278) = 24.98$, $p < 0.05$, Cramér's $V = 0.30$.

f. The accompanying table shows the conditional proportions.

	Medical Problem	No Problem/ Below Norm	No Problem/ Normal Height	
Boys	0.148	0.473	0.379	1.00
Girls	0.406	0.396	0.198	1.00

g. The accompanying graph shows all six conditions.

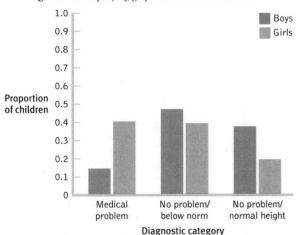

h. Here, we're interested only in the children who are below height norms, so we'll exclude the 69 boys and 19 girls who were of normal height. Of the 113 boys below normal height, 27 were diagnosed with a medical problem. Of the 77 girls below normal height, 39 were diagnosed with a medical problem. The conditional proportion for boys is 0.239 and for girls is 0.506. This makes the relative risk for having a medical condition, given that one is a boy as opposed to a girl, $\frac{0.239}{0.506} = 0.472$.

i. Referred boys below normal height are about half as likely to have a medical condition as are referred girls below normal height.

j. If referred for short stature, the relative risk for having a medical condition, given that one is a girl, is $\frac{0.506}{0.239} = 2.117$.

k. If referred for short stature, girls below normal height are about twice as likely to have a medical condition as are boys below normal height.

l. The two relative risks give us complementary information. Saying that boys are half as likely to have a medical condition implies that girls are twice as likely to have a medical condition.

m. The observed frequency is 27. The expected frequency is 43.2.

n. The adjusted standardized residual for boys is −4.8. This number indicates that the observed frequency for boys is 4.8 standard errors below the expected frequency for boys. The cells for boys and for girls with an underlying medical condition exceed the criterion of 2, as do the cells for both boys and girls who are of normal height. Using the new criterion of 3 does not change the conclusion regarding which cells have observed frequencies significantly different from expected.

Chapter 18

18-1 Pearson correlation coefficients are used when there are two scale variables and the research question addresses an association between them.

18-3 A z test is used when there is one nominal independent variable and one scale dependent variable in cases when the independent variable has two levels—one represented by a sample and one represented by a population. We must know the population mean and standard deviation.

18-5 A paired-samples t test is used when there is one nominal independent variable and one scale dependent variable in cases when the independent variable has two levels and there is a within-groups design.

18-7 A one-way within-groups ANOVA is used when there is one nominal independent variable and one scale dependent variable in cases when the independent variable has three or more levels and there is a within-groups design.

18-9 A factorial ANOVA is used when there are at least two nominal independent variables and a scale dependent variable. If all independent variables are between-groups, then it is a between-groups ANOVA; if all independent variables are within-groups, then it is a within-groups ANOVA. If one or more independent variables are between-groups and one or more are within-groups, then it is considered a mixed-design ANOVA.

18-11 A chi-square test for goodness of fit is used when there is one nominal variable.

18-13 For cases in which there is at least one ordinal variable, the decision tree in Figure 18-1 outlines four options: the Spearman rank-order correlation coefficient, the Wilcoxon signed-rank test, the Mann–Whitney U test, and the Kruskal–Wallis H test.

18-15 JARS is short for *The Journal Article Reporting Standards for Quantitative Research in Psychology: The APA Publications and Communications Board Task Force Report* (Appelbaum et al., 2018). It provides overviews of the standards for reporting statistics, including both more traditional hypothesis tests and newer techniques such as meta-analysis.

18-17 Results section

18-19 The three badges that journals can use are the blue badge for "Open Data," which indicates that the researchers have made their data available for others to analyze; the yellow badge for "Open Materials," which indicates that the researchers have made their experimental materials available to help others replicate their work; and the red badge for "Preregistered." These badges tell readers that the researchers have met the criteria for scientific transparency in each of these particular areas, and provide an incentive for researchers to use ethical data practices.

18-21 There was a statistically significant effect of gender on the dependent variable, $t(1198) = 7.50$, $p < 0.001$, $d = 0.24$; this was a small effect. The group of women ($M = 54.7$, $SD = 31.36$) had a higher mean than the group of men ($M = 47.2$, $SD = 31.75$).

18-23 There was a statistically significant effect, $\chi^2(298) = 10.030$, $p = .002$, Cramér's $V = .09$, a small effect. (*Note:* To draw a conclusion, we would need to know the numbers or percentages in each cell.)

18-25 a. The researchers would report these statistics in the Results section. Confidence intervals are among the new statistics that are included along with or instead of the results of traditional hypothesis testing.

b. The researchers would fail to reject the null hypothesis. The confidence interval includes 0, an indication that it is plausible that there is no difference between the means.

18-27 a. The researchers would report these statistics in the Methods section. They are reporting the results of a power analysis that they conducted before collecting data in order to determine the sample size for their study. Information about statistical power goes in the Methods section to justify the chosen sample size.

b. Ethical researchers plan their research before they begin collecting data (and ideally they preregister these details). Conducting a power analysis before collecting data decreases the chances that a researcher will engage in p-hacking, which consists of a range of unethical practices that includes stopping data collection when a traditional hypothesis test results in a test statistic associated with a p value less than 0.05.

18-29 a. There are two variables. The first is type of pet, which is the independent variable; it is nominal and has two levels—dog and cat. The second variable, numbers of households, is a scale variable and is the dependent variable. (The states are the "participants" in this study.) This study involves one nominal independent variable and one scale dependent variable; the nominal independent variable has two levels, both of which are represented by the same sample of states; and the research design is within-groups. The appropriate statistical test is a paired-samples t test.

b. Population density is a scale variable, as is the number of cats per household. Because both are scale variables, we know that this hypothesis will be analyzed with either a Pearson correlation coefficient or a regression analysis. Because the question focuses on association rather than prediction, the data would be analyzed with a Pearson correlation coefficient.

c. Type of household, the independent variable, is a nominal variable with two levels—cat household or dog household. Number of animals in that household, the dependent variable, is a scale variable. This study involves one nominal independent variable and one scale dependent variable; the nominal independent variable has two levels, each of which

is represented by a separate sample; and the research design is between-groups. So, the appropriate statistical test is an independent-samples t test.

18-31 a. Weather, the independent variable, is a nominal variable with two levels, changeable or nonchangeable. Numbers of riders between 2 A.M. and 6 A.M., the dependent variable, is a scale variable. This study involves one nominal independent variable and one scale dependent variable; the nominal independent variable has two levels, each of which is represented by a separate sample; and the research design is between-groups. So, the appropriate statistical test is an independent-samples t test.

b. The countries' rankings in terms of Uber rides are ordinal data, and gross domestic product in U.S. dollars is a scale variable. Because this study has one ordinal variable, this is a category 4 situation—and based on what this chapter says, you could stop there. (For those of you who went further, this study involves an ordinal variable and a scale variable that could be converted to an ordinal variable. The question focuses on association, so you would use a Spearman correlation coefficient.)

c. There are two variables. The first is part of the world, which is the more obvious independent variable and is nominal. It has two levels—North America and Europe. The second, type of food, has three levels—burritos, pizza, and doughnuts. It is the more obvious dependent variable and also is nominal. Because both variables are nominal, we know that the most appropriate statistical test is one of the two chi-square tests. Because there are two nominal variables, the most appropriate test is a chi-square test for independence.

d. Type of rider, the independent variable, is a nominal variable with three levels: tourists, day-trippers, and locals. The number of belongings ever left behind, the dependent variable, is a scale variable. This study involves one nominal independent variable and one scale dependent variable; the nominal independent variable has three levels; and the research design is between-groups. So, the appropriate statistical test is a one-way, between-groups ANOVA.

18-33 There are two variables. The first is dog ears, which is the more obvious independent variable and is nominal. It has two levels—floppy and pointy. The second, perception of the dog, has three levels—friendly, neutral, and scary. It is the more obvious dependent variable and also is nominal. Because both variables are nominal, we know that the most appropriate statistical test is one of the two chi-square tests. Because there are two nominal variables, the most appropriate test is a chi-square test for independence.

18-35 Type of photo, the independent variable, is a nominal variable with two levels: digitally modified or from the Aerie Real campaign. The dependent variable is scores on the Body Image State Scale, a scale variable. This study involves one nominal independent variable and one scale dependent variable; the nominal independent variable has two levels; and the research design is between-groups. So, the appropriate statistical test is an independent-samples *t* test.

18-37 a. There are two variables: the attractiveness of the host on a scale of 0–11 and price. Because both are scale variables, we know that this hypothesis will be analyzed with either a Pearson correlation coefficient or a regression. Because the question focuses on prediction rather than association, these data would be analyzed with a regression analysis.

b. On the one hand, crowdsourcing platforms such as MTurk allow researchers to recruit a more representative sample than they would typically recruit if they relied on university undergraduates. In addition, they can collect data relatively quickly. On the other hand, the samples are still volunteer samples, so they may not really be representative; there may be fraudulent activity on MTurk with responses coming from bots; and there are ethical issues related to the low pay that many MTurkers receive.

c. The researchers preregistered their study—that is, they outlined their research methods and planned their statistical analyses before they collected the data. This information was posted at the link noted here. At this link, as the researchers explain, you'll find information about how they determined their sample size, under which conditions they would discard data, and how they planned to conduct their statistical analyses. They also included their materials. These are ethical practices because preregistration means that the researchers can't later change their approach depending on the specific data they collected. By providing their data and their data analysis scripts—or how they actually analyzed the data—the researchers enable others to check whether they analyzed their data correctly. By providing their materials, they help others replicate their study if they wish.

d. The researchers found a standardized regression coefficient, β, of 0.011. This is the predicted change in price, in terms of standard deviation, for each standard deviation in attractiveness. The researchers used the *t* statistic to determine if this was statistically significant; we know it is because the *p* value is less than 0.05. The researchers also include a confidence interval for the standardized regression coefficient; we know that is what the confidence interval indicates because 0.011 falls roughly in the middle between the two bounds of the confidence interval. Because 0 is not in the interval, it is not plausible that there is no increase in price when attractiveness has a higher rating. The researchers also translated the 0.011 standard deviation into understandable numbers by telling us that as a host's attractiveness rises by one standard deviation, the price tends to increase by 2.78%. So, the attractiveness of a host does predict the price: The more attractive the host, the more that person can charge for the rental.

e. A multiple regression is used when two or more independent variables predict the dependent variable. In this case, the researchers likely used variables other than attractiveness to predict price. In fact, they used ratings of hosts' trustworthiness based on their photos, but they did not find that it statistically significantly predicted price.

f. In this kind of study, it's not possible to randomly assign attractive hosts to particular listings, so perhaps something else leads to the price increase. Many third variables that the researchers didn't consider or couldn't control for could potentially be at play. For example, maybe attractive hosts secure better apartments, so it's actually the apartments that are drawing the higher prices.

Appendix D

CHECK YOUR LEARNING SOLUTIONS

Chapter 1

1-1 Data from samples are used in inferential statistics to make an inference about the larger population.

1-2 **a.** The average grade for your statistics class would be a descriptive statistic because it's being used only to describe the tendency of people in your class with respect to a statistics grade.

b. In this case, the average grade would be an inferential statistic because it is being used to estimate the results of a population of students taking statistics.

1-3 **a.** 1500 Americans

b. All Americans

c. The 1500 Americans in the sample know 600 people, on average.

d. The entire population of Americans has many acquaintances, on average. The sample mean, 600, is an estimate of the unknown population mean.

1-4 Discrete observations can take on only specific values, usually whole numbers; continuous observations can take on a full range of values.

1-5 **a.** These data are continuous because they can take on a full range of values.

b. The variable is a ratio observation because there is a true zero point.

c. On an ordinal scale, Lorna's score would be 2 (or 2nd).

1-6 **a.** This variable is a scale variable because it meets the criteria for an interval variable (the distance between pairs of consecutive numbers is assumed to be equal).

b. This variable is a nominal variable because there are categories (received a warning or not) that have no specific order.

c. This variable is a scale variable because it meets the criteria for a ratio variable (there is a meaningful zero; there can be zero hours spent logged into the Uber app).

d. This variable is an ordinal variable because drivers are ranked.

e. This variable is a nominal variable because there are categories (taken the class or not) that have no specific order.

1-7 Independent; dependent

1-8 **a.** There are two independent variables: beverage and subject to be remembered. The dependent variable is memory.

b. Beverage has two levels: caffeine and no caffeine. The subject to be remembered has three levels: numbers, word lists, and aspects of a story.

1-9 **a.** Whether or not trays were available

b. Trays were available; trays were not available

c. Food waste; food waste could have been measured via volume or weight as it was thrown away.

d. The measure of food waste would be consistent over time.

e. The measure of food waste was actually measuring how much food was wasted.

1-10 Experimental research involves random assignment to conditions; correlational research examines associations where random assignment is not possible and variables are not manipulated.

1-11 Random assignment helps to distribute the levels of confounding variables evenly across all conditions so that the levels of the independent variable are what truly vary across groups or conditions.

1-12 **a.** Answers may vary; operational definitions explicitly define ways to measure a variable of interest. Uber is identifying ways to measure performance of their drivers. Two examples of operational definitions that Uber used are rankings of top drivers and whether drivers have received a warning.

b. Answers may vary; cancellation rate may not be a good operational definition to measure performance because there are potentially thoughtful reasons for why a driver may cancel a ride, such as traffic that would delay a pick-up longer than would be expected or receiving a rude message from a potential passenger.

1-13 **a.** Researchers could randomly assign a certain number of women to be told about a gender difference on the test and randomly assign a certain number of other women to be told that no gender difference existed on this test.

b. If researchers did not use random assignment, any gender differences might be due to confounding variables. The women in the two groups might be different in some way (e.g., in math ability or belief in stereotypes) to begin with.

c. There are many possible confounds. Women who already believed the stereotype might do so because they had always performed poorly in mathematics, whereas those who did not believe the stereotype might be those who always did particularly well in math. Women who believed the stereotype might be those who were discouraged from studying math because "girls can't do math," whereas those who did not believe the stereotype might be those who were encouraged to study math because "girls are just as good as boys in math."

d. Math performance is operationalized as scores on a math test.

e. Researchers could have two math tests that are similar in difficulty. All women would take the first test after being told that women tend not to do as well as men on this test. After taking that test, they would be given the second test after being told that women tend to do as well as men on this test.

Chapter 2

2-1 Frequency tables, grouped frequency tables, and histograms

2-2 A frequency is a count of how many times a score appears. A grouped frequency is a count for a defined interval, or group, of scores.

2-3 **a.**

Interval	Frequency
100–104	4
95–99	14
90–94	6
85–89	4
80–84	2
75–79	6
70–74	6
65–69	3
60–64	5

b.

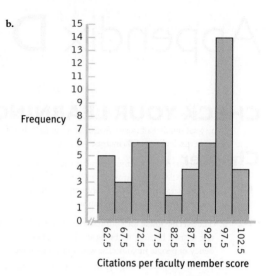

2-4 **a.** We can now get a sense of the overall pattern of the data.

b. Schools in different academic systems may place different emphases on faculty conducting independent research and getting published, as well as have varying ranges of funding or other resources to assist faculty research and publication.

2-5 A normal distribution is a specific distribution that is symmetric around a center high point: It looks like a bell. A skewed distribution is asymmetric or lopsided to the left or to the right, with a long tail of data to one side.

2-6 Negative; positive

2-7 This distribution is negatively skewed due to the data trailing off to the left and the bulk of the data clustering together on the right.

2-8 **a.** Early-onset Alzheimer's disease would create negative skew in the distribution for age of onset.

b. Because all humans eventually die, there is a sort of ceiling effect.

2-9 Being aware of these exceptional early-onset cases allows medical practitioners to be open to such surprising diagnoses. In addition, exceptional cases like these often give us great insight into the underlying mechanisms of disease.

Chapter 3

3-1 The purpose of a graph is to reveal and clarify relations between variables.

3-2 There were 43,405 nurses in 2010–2011 and 46,573 in 2011–2012. The difference is $46,573 - 43,405 = 3168$. This is a graphing lie because the graph appears to show a spike of many multiples of the total number of nurses that there were in 2010–2011. But in reality, this is about a 7% increase.

3-3 The graph on the left is misleading. It shows a sharp decline in annual traffic deaths in Connecticut from 1955 to 1956, but we cannot draw valid conclusions from just two data points. The graph on the right is a more accurate and complete depiction of the data. It includes nine, rather than two, data points and suggests that the sharp 1-year decline was the beginning of a clear downward trend in traffic fatalities that extended through 1959. It also shows that there had been previous 1-year declines of similar magnitude—from 1951 to 1952 and from 1953 to 1954. Also, the y-axis does not go down to 0, which exaggerates any differences.

3-4 Scatterplots and line graphs both depict the relation between two scale variables.

3-5 We should typically avoid using pictorial graphs and pie charts because the data can almost always be presented more clearly in a table or in a bar graph.

3-6 The line graph known as a time plot, or time series plot, allows us to calculate or evaluate how a variable changes over time.

3-7 **a.** A scatterplot is the best graph choice to depict the relation between two scale variables such as depression and stress.

   b. A time plot, or time series plot, is the best graph choice to depict the change in a scale variable, such as the rise or decline in the number of facilities, over time.

   c. For one scale variable, such as number of siblings, the best graph choice would be a histogram.

   d. In this case, there is a nominal variable (region of the United States) and a scale variable (years of education). The best choice would be a bar graph, with one bar depicting the mean years of education for each region. In a Pareto chart, the bars would be arranged from highest to lowest, allowing for easier comparisons.

   e. Calories and hours are both scale variables, and the question is about prediction rather than relation. In this case, we would calculate and graph a line of best fit.

3-8 Chartjunk is any unnecessary information or feature in a graph that detracts from the viewer's understanding.

3-9 **a.** Scatterplot or line graph

   b. Bar graph

   c. Scatterplot or line graph

3-10

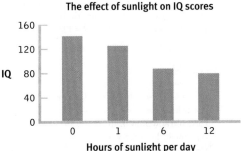

The effect of sunlight on IQ scores

The accompanying graph improves on the chartjunk graph in several ways. First, it has a clear, specific title. Second, all axes are labeled left to right. Third, there are no abbreviations. The units of measurement, IQ and hours of sunlight per day, are included. The y-axis has 0 as its minimum, the colors are simple and muted, and all chartjunk has been eliminated. This graph wasn't as much fun to create, but it offers a far clearer presentation of the data! (*Note:* We are treating hours as an ordinal variable.)

Chapter 4

4-1 Statistics are calculated for samples; they are usually symbolized by Latin letters (e.g., M). Parameters are calculated for populations; they are usually symbolized by Greek letters (e.g., μ).

4-2 An outlier has the greatest effect on the mean, because the calculation of the mean takes into account the numeric value of each data point, including that outlier.

4-3 **a.** $M = \dfrac{\Sigma X}{N}$

$$= (10 + 8 + 22 + 5 + 6 + 1 + 19 + 8 + 13 + 12 + 8)/11$$

$$= 112/11 = 10.18$$

The median is found by arranging the scores in numeric order—1, 5, 6, 8, 8, 8, 10, 12, 13, 19, 22—then dividing the total number of scores, 11, by 2 and adding 1/2 to get 6. The 6th score in our ordered list of scores is the median, and in this case the 6th score is the number 8.

The mode is the most common score. In these data, the score 8 occurs most often (three times), so 8 is our mode.

   b. $M = \dfrac{\Sigma X}{N}$

$$= (122.5 + 123.8 + 121.2 + 125.8 + 120.2 + 123.8 + 120.5 + 119.8 + 126.3 + 123.6)/10$$

$$= 122.7/10 = 122.75$$

The data ordered are: 119.8, 120.2, 120.5, 121.2, 122.5, 123.6, 123.8, 123.8, 125.8, 126.3. Again, we find the median by ordering the data and then dividing the number of scores (here there are 10 scores) by 2 and adding 1/2. In this case, we get 5.5, so the mean of the 5th and 6th data points is the median. The median is $(122.5 + 123.6)/2 = 123.05$.

The mode is 123.8, which occurs twice in these data.

c. $M = \dfrac{\Sigma X}{N}$

$= (0.100 + 0.866 + 0.781 + 0.555 + 0.222 + 0.245$
$+ 0.234)/7$

$= 3.003/7 = 0.429$

Note that three decimal places are included here (rather than the standard two places used throughout this book) because the data are carried out to three decimal places.

The median is found by first ordering the data: 0.100, 0.222, 0.234, 0.245, 0.555, 0.781, 0.866. Then the total number of scores, 7, is divided by 2 to get 3.5, to which 1/2 is added to get 4. So, the 4th score, 0.245, is the median. There is no mode in these data. All scores occur once.

4-4 a. $M = \dfrac{\Sigma X}{N}$

$= (1 + 0 + 1 + 2 + 5 + ... 4 + 6)/20 = 50/20 = 2.50$

b. In this case, the scores would comprise a sample taken from the whole population, and this mean would be a statistic. The symbol, therefore, would be either M or $\bar{X}$.

c. In this case, the scores would constitute the entire population of interest, and the mean would be a parameter. Thus, the symbol would be μ.

d. To find the median, we would arrange the scores in order: 0, 0, 1, 1, 1, 1, 2, 2, 2, 2, 2, 3, 3, 3, 3, 4, 5, 6, 7. We would then divide the total number of scores, 20, by 2 and add 1/2, which is 10.5. The median, therefore, is the mean of the 10th and 11th scores. Both of these scores are 2; therefore, the median is 2.

e. The mode is the most common score—in this case, there are six 2's, so the mode is 2.

f. The mean is a little higher than the median. This indicates that there are potential outliers pulling the mean higher; outliers would not affect the median.

4-5 By incorrectly labeling the debate as a regular edition of the newsmagazine program, the mean number of viewers for the show would be much higher as a result of the outlier from this special programming event, thus resulting in more advertising dollars for NBC.

4-6 Variability is the concept of variety in data, often measured as deviation around some center.

4-7 The range tells us the span of the data, from highest to lowest score. It is based on just two scores. The standard deviation tells us how far the typical score falls from the mean. The standard deviation takes every score into account.

4-8 a. The range is: $X_{highest} - X_{lowest} = 22 - 1 = 21$

The variance is:

$$SD^2 = \frac{\Sigma(X - M)^2}{N}$$

We start by calculating the mean, which is 10.182. We then calculate the deviation of each score from the mean and the square of that deviation.

X	$X - M$	$(X - M)^2$
10	−0.182	0.033
8	−2.182	4.761
22	11.818	139.665
5	−5.182	26.853
6	−4.182	17.489
1	−9.182	84.309
19	8.818	77.757
8	−2.182	4.761
13	2.818	7.941
12	1.818	3.305
8	−2.182	4.761

$$SD^2 = \frac{\Sigma(X - M)^2}{N} = \frac{371.635}{11} = 33.785$$

The standard deviation is: $SD = \sqrt{SD^2}$ or

$$SD = \sqrt{\frac{\Sigma(X - M)^2}{N}} = \sqrt{33.785} = 5.81$$

b. The range is: $X_{highest} - X_{lowest} = 126.3 - 119.8 = 6.5$

The variance is:

$$SD^2 = \frac{\Sigma(X - M)^2}{N}$$

We start by calculating the mean, which is 122.750. We then calculate the deviation of each score from the mean and the square of that deviation.

X	$X - M$	$(X - M)^2$
122.500	−0.250	0.063
123.800	1.050	1.103
121.200	−1.550	2.403
125.800	3.050	9.303
120.200	−2.550	6.503
123.800	1.050	1.103
120.500	−2.250	5.063
119.800	−2.950	8.703
126.300	3.550	12.603
123.600	0.850	0.723

$$SD^2 = \frac{\Sigma(X - M)^2}{N} = \frac{47.570}{10} = 4.757$$

The standard deviation is: $SD = \sqrt{SD^2}$

$$SD = \sqrt{\frac{\Sigma(X-M)^2}{N}} = \sqrt{4.757} = 2.18$$

c. The range is: $X_{highest} - X_{lowest} - 0.866 - 0.100 = 0.766$

The variance is:

$$SD^2 = \frac{\Sigma(X-M)^2}{N}$$

We start by calculating the mean, which is 0.429. We then calculate the deviation of each score from the mean and the square of that deviation.

X	X − M	(X − M)²
0.100	−0.329	0.108
0.866	0.437	0.191
0.781	0.352	0.124
0.555	0.126	0.016
0.222	−0.207	0.043
0.245	−0.184	0.034
0.234	−0.195	0.038

$$SD^2 = \frac{\Sigma(X-M)^2}{N} = \frac{0.554}{7} = 0.079$$

The standard deviation is: $SD = \sqrt{SD^2}$ or

$$SD = \sqrt{\frac{\Sigma(X-M)^2}{N}} = \sqrt{0.079} = 0.28$$

4-9 a. range $= X_{highest} - X_{lowest} = 1460 - 450 = 1010$

b. We do not know whether scores cluster at some point in the distribution—for example, near one end of the distribution—or whether the scores are more evenly spread out.

c. The formula for variance is:

$$SD^2 = \frac{\Sigma(X-M)^2}{N}$$

The first step is to calculate the mean, which is 927.500. We then create three columns: one for the scores, one for the deviations of the scores from the mean, and one for the squares of the deviations.

X	X − M	(X − M)²
450	−477.50	228,006.25
670	−257.50	66,306.25
1130	202.50	41,006.25
1460	532.50	283,556.25

We can now calculate variance:

$$SD^2 = \frac{\Sigma(X-M)^2}{N}$$

$$= (228,006.25 + 66,306.25 + 41,006.25 + 283,556.25) / 4$$

$$= 618,875 / 4 = 154,718.75.$$

d. We calculate standard deviation the same way we calculate variance, but we then take the square root.

$$SD = \sqrt{\frac{\Sigma(X-M)^2}{N}} = \sqrt{154,718.75} = 393.34$$

e. If the researcher were interested only in these four students, these scores would represent the entire population of interest, and the variance and standard deviation would be parameters. Therefore, the symbols would be σ^2 and σ, respectively.

f. If the researcher hoped to generalize from these four students to all students at the university, these scores would represent a sample, and the variance and standard deviation would be statistics. Therefore, the symbols would be SD^2, s^2, or MS for variance and SD or s for standard deviation.

Chapter 5

5-1 The risks of sampling are that we might not have a representative sample, and sometimes it is difficult to know whether the sample is representative. If we didn't realize that the sample was not representative, then we might draw conclusions about the population that are inaccurate.

5-2 The lists will be different for each student. Students would generate a list of six numbers by telling the site that they want one set of numbers, six numbers per set, numbers ranging from 1 to 80, each number in the set being unique, and numbers sorted from least to greatest. Here's an example of what the output might look like: 42, 45, 59, 68, 72, and 80.

5-3 The lists will be different for each student. Students would generate a list of six numbers by telling the site they want a list of six numbers that range from 0 to 1. They would instruct the program that the numbers should not remain unique and should not be sorted. Here's one example of what the output could look like: 001010.

5-4 a. The likely population is all patients who will undergo surgery; the researcher would not be able to access this population, and therefore random selection could not be used. Random assignment, however, could be used. The psychologist could randomly assign half of the patients to counseling and half to a control group.

b. The population is all children in this school system; the psychologist could identify all of these children and thus could use random selection. The psychologist could also use random assignment. She could randomly assign half the children to the interactive online textbook and half to the printed textbook.

c. The population is patients in therapy; because the whole population could not be identified, random selection could not be used. Moreover, random assignment could not be used. It is not possible to assign people to either have or not have a diagnosed personality disorder.

5-5 We regularly make personal assessments about how probable we think an event is, but we base these evaluations on our opinions about things rather than on systematically collected data. Statisticians are interested in objective probabilities that are based on unbiased research.

5-6 **a.** probability = successes/trials = 5/100 = 0.05

b. 8/50 = 0.16

c. 130/1044 = 0.12

5-7 A statistician would explain that in the universe of cat adoptions, it's not surprising that, every once in a while, two cat brothers would get adopted by different people who eventually would meet. A statistician would urge you to consider the underlying probabilities. How many pairs of cat siblings get adopted every year? Out of all of those pairs of adoptions, is it really that surprising that at least one of them would one day lead to a reunion, especially in a relatively small city like Petaluma?

5-8 When we reject the null hypothesis, we are saying we reject the idea that there is no mean difference in the dependent variable across the levels of our independent variable. Rejecting the null hypothesis means we can support the research hypothesis that there is a mean difference.

5-9 The null hypothesis assumes that no mean difference would be observed, so the mean difference in grades would be zero.

5-10 **a.** The null hypothesis is that a decrease in temperature does not affect mean academic performance (or does not decrease mean academic performance).

b. The research hypothesis is that a decrease in temperature does affect mean academic performance (or decreases mean academic performance).

c. The researchers would reject the null hypothesis.

d. The researchers would fail to reject the null hypothesis.

5-11 We make a Type I error when we reject the null hypothesis but the null hypothesis is correct. We make a Type II error when we fail to reject the null hypothesis but the null hypothesis is false.

5-12 In this scenario, a Type I error would be imprisoning a person who is really innocent, and 7 convictions out of 280 innocent people calculates to be 0.025, or 2.5%.

5-13 In this scenario, a Type II error would be failing to convict a guilty person, and 11 acquittals for every 35 guilty people calculates to be 0.314, or 31.4%.

5-14 **a.** If the virtual-reality glasses really don't have any effect, this is a Type I error, which is made when the null hypothesis is rejected but is really true.

b. If the virtual-reality glasses really do have an effect, this is a Type II error, which is made when the researchers fail to reject the null hypothesis but the null hypothesis is not true.

Chapter 6

6-1 Unimodal means there is one mode or high point to the curve. Symmetric means the left and right sides of the curve have the same shape and are mirror images of each other.

6-2 **a.**

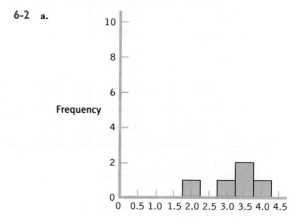

b.

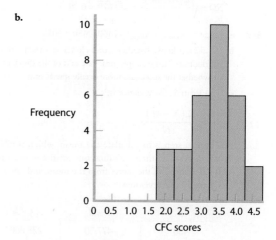

6-3 The shape of the distribution becomes more normal as the size of the sample increases (although the larger sample appears to be somewhat negatively skewed).

6-4 In standardization, we convert individual scores to standardized scores for which we know the percentiles.

6-5 The numeric value tells us how many standard deviations a score is from the mean of the distribution. The sign tells us whether the score is above or below the mean.

6-6 **a.** $z = \dfrac{(X - \mu)}{\sigma} = \dfrac{11.5 - 14}{2.5} = -1.0$

b. $z = \dfrac{(X - \mu)}{\sigma} = \dfrac{18 - 14}{2.5} = 1.6$

6-7 **a.** $X = z(\sigma) + \mu = 2(2.5) + 14 = 19$

b. $X = z(\sigma) + \mu = 1.4(2.5) + 14 = 10.5$

6-8 **a.** $z = \dfrac{(X - \mu)}{\sigma} = \dfrac{2.50 - 3.20}{0.70} = -1.00$;

approximately 16% of students have a CFC score of 2.5 or less.

b. $z = \dfrac{(X - \mu)}{\sigma} = \dfrac{4.60 - 3.20}{0.70} = 2.00$; this score is at approximately the 98th percentile.

c. This student has a z score of 1.

d. $X = z(\sigma) + \mu = 1(0.70) + 3.20 = 3.90$; this answer makes sense because 3.90 is above the mean of 3.20, as a z score of 1 would indicate.

6-9 **a.** Nicole is in better health because her score is above the mean for her measure, whereas Samantha's score is below the mean.

b. Samantha's z score is $z = \dfrac{(X - \mu)}{\sigma} = \dfrac{84 - 93}{4.5} = -2.0$

Nicole's z score is

$z = \dfrac{(X - \mu)}{\sigma} = \dfrac{332 - 312}{20} = 1.0$

Nicole is in better health, being 1 standard deviation above the mean, whereas Samantha is 2 standard deviations below the mean.

c. We can conclude that approximately 98% of the population is in better health than Samantha, who is 2 standard deviations below the mean. We can conclude that approximately 16% of the population is in better health than Nicole, who is 1 standard deviation above the mean.

6-10 The central limit theorem asserts that a distribution of sample means approaches the shape of the normal curve as sample size increases. It also asserts that the spread of the distribution of sample means gets smaller as the sample size gets larger.

6-11 A distribution of means is composed of many means that are calculated from all possible samples of a particular size from the same population.

6-12 $\sigma_M = \dfrac{\sigma}{\sqrt{N}} = \dfrac{11}{\sqrt{35}} = 1.86$

6-13 **a.** The scores range from 2.0 to 4.5, which gives us a range of $4.5 - 2.0 = 2.5$.

b. The means are 3.4 for the first row, 3.4 for the second row, and 3.15 for the third row [e.g., for the first row, $M = (3.5 +$

$3.5 + 3.0 + 4.0 + 2.0 + 4.0 + 2.0 + 4.0 + 3.5 + 4.5)/10 = 3.4$]. These three means range from 3.15 to 3.40, which gives us a range of $3.40 - 3.15 = 0.25$.

c. The range is smaller for the means of samples of 10 scores than for the individual scores because the more extreme scores are balanced by lower scores when samples of 10 are taken. Individual scores are not attenuated in that way.

d. The mean of the distribution of means will be the same as the mean of the individual scores: $\mu_M = \mu = 3.32$. The standard error will be smaller than the standard deviation; we must divide by the square root of the sample size of 10:

$\sigma_M = \dfrac{\sigma}{\sqrt{N}} = \dfrac{0.69}{\sqrt{10}} = 0.22$

Chapter 7

7-1 We need to know the mean, μ, and the standard deviation, σ, of the population.

7-2 Raw scores are used to compute z scores, and z scores are used to determine what percentage of scores fall below and above that particular position on the distribution. A z score can also be used to compute a raw score.

7-3 Because the curve is symmetric, the same percentage of scores (41.47%) lies between the mean and a z score of -1.37 as between the mean and a z score of 1.37.

7-4 Fifty percent of scores fall below the mean, and 12.93% fall between the mean and a z score of 0.33.

$50\% + 12.93\% = 62.93\%$

7-5 **a.** $\mu_M = \mu = 156.8$

$\sigma_M = \dfrac{\sigma}{\sqrt{N}} = \dfrac{14.6}{\sqrt{36}} = 2.433$

$z = \dfrac{(M - \mu_M)}{\sigma_M} = \dfrac{(164.6 - 156.8)}{2.433} = 3.21$

50% below the mean; 49.87% between the mean and this score; $50 + 49.87 = 99.87$th percentile.

b. $100 - 99.87 = 0.13\%$ of samples of this size scored higher than the students at Baylor.

c. At the 99.87th percentile, these 36 students from Baylor are truly outstanding. If these students are representative of their majors, clearly these results reflect positively on Baylor's psychology and neuroscience department.

7-6 For most parametric hypothesis tests, we assume that (1) the dependent variable is assessed on a scale measure—that is, equal changes are reflected by equal distances on the measure; (2) the participants are randomly selected, meaning everyone has the same chance of being selected; and (3) the distribution of the population of interest is approximately normal.

7-7 If a test statistic is more extreme than the critical value, then the null hypothesis is rejected. If a test statistic is less extreme than the critical value, then we fail to reject the null hypothesis.

7-8 If the null hypothesis is true, he will reject it 8% of the time.

7-9 **a.** 0.15

b. 0.03

c. 0.055

7-10 **a.** (1) The dependent variable—diagnosis (correct versus in-correct)—is nominal, not scale, so this assumption is not met. Based only on this, we should not proceed with a hypothesis test based on a z distribution. (2) The samples include only outpatients seen over two specific months and only those at one community mental health center. The sample is not randomly selected, so we must be cautious about generalizing from it. (3) The populations are not normally distributed because the dependent variable is nominal.

b. (1) The dependent variable, health score, is likely scale. (2) The participants were randomly selected; all wild cats in zoos in North America had an equal chance of being selected for this study. (3) The data are not normally distributed; we are told that a few animals had very high scores, so the data are likely positively skewed. Moreover, there are fewer than 30 participants in this study. It is probably not a good idea to proceed with a hypothesis test based on a z distribution.

7-11 A directional test indicates that either a mean increase or a mean decrease in the dependent variable is hypothesized, but not both. A nondirectional test does not indicate a direction of mean difference for the research hypothesis, just that there is a mean difference.

7-12 $\mu_M = \mu = 1090$

$$\sigma_M = \frac{\sigma}{\sqrt{N}} = \frac{87}{\sqrt{53}} = 11.95$$

7-13 $z = \frac{(M - \mu_M)}{\sigma_M} = \frac{(1094 - 1090)}{11.95} = 0.33$

7-14 *Step 1:* Population 1 is coffee drinkers who spend the day in coffee shops. Population 2 is all coffee drinkers in the United States. The comparison distribution will be a distribution of means. The hypothesis test will be a z test because there is only one sample and we know the population mean and standard deviation. This study meets two of the three assumptions and may meet the third. The dependent variable, the number of cups coffee drinkers drank, is scale. In addition, there are more than 30 participants in the sample, indicating that the comparison distribution is normal. The data were not randomly selected, however, so we must be cautious when generalizing.

Step 2: The null hypothesis is that people who spend the day working in the coffee shop drink the same amount of coffee, on average, as those in the general U.S. population: $H_0: \mu_1 = \mu_2$.

The research hypothesis is that people who spend the day in coffee shops drink a different amount of coffee, on average, than those in the general U.S. population: $H_1: \mu_1 \neq \mu_2$.

Step 3: $\mu_M = \mu = 3.10$

$$\sigma_M = \frac{\sigma}{\sqrt{N}} = \frac{0.9}{\sqrt{34}} = 0.154$$

Step 4: The cutoff z statistics are -1.96 and 1.96.

Step 5: $z = \frac{(M - \mu_M)}{\sigma_M} = \frac{(3.17 - 3.10)}{0.154} = 0.45$

Step 6: Because the z statistic does not exceed the cutoffs, we fail to reject the null hypothesis. We did not find any evidence that the sample was different from what was expected according to the null hypothesis.

Chapter 8

8-1 Interval estimates provide a range of scores in which we have some confidence the population statistic will fall, whereas point estimates use just a single value to describe the population.

8-2 The interval estimate is 17% to 25% ($21\% - 4\% = 17\%$ and $21\% + 4\% = 25\%$); the point estimate is 21%.

8-3 **a.** First, we draw a normal curve with the sample mean, 3.20, in the center. Then we put the bounds of the 95% confidence interval on either end, writing the appropriate percentages under the segments of the curve: 2.5% beyond the cutoffs on either end and 47.5% between the mean and each cutoff. Now we look up the z statistics for these cutoffs; the z statistic associated with 47.5%, the percentage between the mean and the z statistic, is 1.96. Thus, the cutoffs are -1.96 and 1.96. Next, we calculate standard error so that we can convert these z statistics to raw means:

$$\sigma_M = \frac{\sigma}{\sqrt{N}} = \frac{0.70}{\sqrt{45}} = 0.104$$

$M_{lower} = -z(\sigma_M) + M_{sample} = -1.96(0.104) + 3.45 = 3.25$

$M_{upper} = z(\sigma_M) + M_{sample} = 1.96(0.104) + 3.45 = 3.65$

Finally, we check whether the answer makes sense by demonstrating that each end of the confidence interval is the same distance from the mean: $3.25 - 3.45 = -0.20$ and $3.65 - 3.45 = 0.20$. The confidence interval is [3.25, 3.65].

b. If we were to conduct this study over and over, with the same sample size, we would expect the population mean to fall in that interval 95% of the time. Thus, it provides a range of plausible values for the population mean. Because the null-hypothesized population mean of 3.20 is not a plausible value, we can conclude that those who attended the discussion group seem to have higher mean CFC scores than those who did not. This conclusion matches that of the hypothesis test, in which we rejected the null hypothesis.

c. The confidence interval is superior to the hypothesis test because not only does it lead to the same conclusion, but it also gives us an interval estimate, rather than a point estimate, of the population mean.

8-4 Statistical significance means that the observation meets the standard for special events, typically something that occurs less than 5% of the time. Practical importance means that the outcome really matters.

8-5 Effect size is a standardized value that indicates the size of a difference with respect to a measure of spread, but is not affected by sample size.

8-6 Cohen's $d = \dfrac{(M - \mu)}{\sigma} = \dfrac{(105 - 100)}{15} = 0.33$

8-7 **a.** We calculate Cohen's d, the effect size appropriate for data analyzed with a z test. We use standard deviation in the denominator, rather than standard error, because effect sizes are for distributions of scores rather than distributions of means.

Cohen's $d = \dfrac{(M - \mu)}{\sigma} = \dfrac{(3.45 - 3.20)}{0.70} = 0.36$

b. Cohen's conventions indicate that 0.2 is a small effect and 0.5 is a medium effect. This effect size, therefore, would be considered a small-to-medium effect.

c. If the career discussion group is easily implemented in terms of time and money, the small-to-medium effect might be worth the effort. For university students, a higher mean level of Consideration of Future Consequences might translate into a higher mean level of readiness for life after graduation, a premise that we could study.

8-8 Three ways to increase power are to increase alpha, to conduct a one-tailed test rather than a two-tailed test, and to increase N. All three of these techniques serve to increase the chance of rejecting the null hypothesis. (We could also increase the difference between means, or decrease variability, but these are more difficult.)

8-9 *Step 1:* We know the following information about population 2: $\mu = 3.20$, $\sigma = 0.70$. We assume the following about population 1 based on the information from the sample: $N = 45$, $M = 3.45$. We need to calculate standard error based on the standard deviation for population 2 and the size of the sample:

$$\sigma_M = \dfrac{\sigma}{\sqrt{N}} = \dfrac{0.70}{\sqrt{45}} = 0.104$$

Step 2: Because the sample mean is higher than the population mean, we will conduct this one-tailed test by examining only the high end of the distribution. We need to find the cutoff that marks where 5% of the data fall in the tail. We know that the z cutoff for a one-tailed test is 1.64. Using that z statistic, we can calculate a raw score.

$$M = z(\sigma_M) + \mu_M + 1.64(0.104) + 3.20 = 3.371$$

This mean of 3.371 marks the point beyond which 5% of all means based on samples of 45 observations will fall.

Step 3: For the distribution based on population 1, centered on 3.45, we need to calculate how often means of 3.371 (the cutoff) and greater occur. We do this by calculating the z statistic for the raw mean of 3.371 with respect to the sample mean of 3.45.

$$z = \dfrac{3.371 - 3.45}{0.104} = -0.76$$

We now look up this z statistic on the table and find that 22.36% falls toward the tail and 27.64% falls between this z statistic and the mean. We calculate power as the proportion of observations between this z statistic and the tail of interest, which is at the high end. So we would add 27.64% and 50% to get statistical power of 77.64%.

8-10 **a.** The statistical power calculation means that, if population 1 really does exist, we have a 77.64% chance of observing a sample mean, based on 45 observations, that will allow us to reject the null hypothesis. We fall just short of the desired 80% statistical power.

b. We can increase statistical power by increasing the sample size, extending or enhancing the career discussion group such that we create a bigger effect, or by changing alpha.

Chapter 9

9-1 The t statistic indicates the distance of a sample mean from a population mean in terms of the estimated standard error.

9-2 First, we need to calculate the mean:

$$M = \dfrac{\Sigma X}{N} = (6 + 3 + 7 + 6 + 4 + 5)/6 = 31/6 = 5.167$$

We then calculate the deviation of each score from the mean and the square of that deviation.

X	$X - M$	$(X - M)^2$
6	0.833	0.694
3	−2.167	4.696
7	1.833	3.360
6	0.833	0.694
4	−1.167	1.362
5	−0.167	0.028

Numerator: $\Sigma(X - M)^2 = (0.694 + 4.696 + 3.360 + 0.694 + 1.362 + 0.028)^2 = 10.834$

The standard deviation is:

$$SD = \sqrt{\frac{\Sigma(X-M)^2}{N}} = \sqrt{\frac{10.834}{6}} = \sqrt{1.806} = 1.344$$

When estimating the population variability, we calculate s:

$$s = \sqrt{\frac{\Sigma(X-M)^2}{N-1}} = \sqrt{\frac{10.834}{6-1}} = \sqrt{2.167} = 1.472$$

9-3 $\quad s_M = \frac{s}{\sqrt{N}} = \frac{1.472}{\sqrt{6}} = 0.601$

9-4 **a.** We would use a distribution of means, specifically a t distribution. It is a distribution of means because there is a sample consisting of more than one individual. It is a t distribution because we are comparing one sample to a population, but we know only the population mean, not its standard deviation.

b. The appropriate mean: $\mu_M = \mu = 25$. The calculations for the appropriate standard deviation (in this case, standard error, s_M):

$$M = \frac{\Sigma X}{N} = (20+19+27+24+18)/5$$
$$= 108/5 = 21.6$$

X	$X-M$	$(X-M)^2$
20	−1.6	2.56
19	−2.6	6.76
27	5.4	29.16
24	2.4	5.76
18	−3.6	12.96

Numerator: $\Sigma(X-M)^2 = (2.56+6.76+29.16+5.76+12.96)^2$
$$= 57.2$$

$$s = \sqrt{\frac{\Sigma(X-M)^2}{(N-1)}} = \sqrt{\frac{57.2}{5-1}} = \sqrt{14.3} = 3.782$$

$$s_M = \frac{s}{\sqrt{N}} = \frac{3.782}{\sqrt{5}} = 1.691$$

c. $t = \frac{(M-\mu_M)}{s_M} = \frac{(21.6-25)}{1.691} = -2.01$

9-5 *Degrees of freedom* is the number of scores that are free to vary, or take on any value, when a population parameter is estimated from a sample.

9-6 A single-sample t test is more useful than a z test because it requires only that we know the population mean (not the population standard deviation).

9-7 **a.** $df = N-1 = 35-1 = 34$

b. $df = N-1 = 14-1 = 13$

9-8 **a.** ±2.201

b. Either −2.584 or +2.584, depending on the tail of interest

9-9 *Step 1:* Population 1 is statistics students. Population 2 is all university students.

The distribution will be a distribution of means, and we will use a single-sample t test. We meet the assumption that the dependent variable is scale. We do not know if the sample was randomly selected, and we do not know if the population variable is normally distributed. Some caution should be exercised when drawing conclusions from these data.

Step 2: The null hypothesis is H_0: $\mu_1 = \mu_2$; that is, statistics students miss the same number of classes, on average, as the general population.

The research hypothesis is H_1: $\mu_1 \neq \mu_2$; that is, statistics students miss a different number of classes, on average, than the general population.

Step 3: $\mu_M = \mu = 3.7$

$$M = \frac{\Sigma X}{N} = (6+3+7+6+4+5)/6 = 31/6 = 5.167$$

$$s = \sqrt{\frac{\Sigma(X-M)^2}{N-1}} = \sqrt{\frac{10.834}{6-1}} = \sqrt{2.167} = 1.472$$

$$s_M = \frac{s}{\sqrt{N}} = \frac{1.472}{\sqrt{6}} = 0.601$$

Step 4: $df = N-1 = 6-1 = 5$

For a two-tailed test with an alpha level of 0.05 and 5 degrees of freedom, the cutoffs are ±2.571.

Step 5: $t = \frac{(M-\mu_M)}{s_M} = \frac{(5.167-3.7)}{0.601} = 2.441$

Step 6: Because the calculated t value falls short of the critical values, we fail to reject the null hypothesis.

Chapter 10

10-1 For a paired-samples t test, we calculate a difference score for every individual. We then compare the average difference observed to the average difference we would expect based on the null hypothesis. If there is no difference, then all difference scores should average to 0.

10-2 An individual difference score is a calculation of change or difference for each participant. For example, we might subtract weight before the holiday break from weight after the break to evaluate how many pounds an individual lost or gained.

10-3 We want to subtract the before-lunch energy level from the after-lunch energy level to get values that reflect loss of energy as a negative value and an increase of energy with food as a positive value. The mean of these differences is −1.4.

Before Lunch	After Lunch	After − Before
6	3	$3-6=-3$
5	2	$2-5=-3$
4	6	$6-4=2$
5	4	$4-5=-1$
7	5	$5-7=-2$

10-4 *Step 1:* Population 1 is students for whom we're measuring energy levels before lunch. Population 2 is students for whom we're measuring energy levels after lunch.

The comparison distribution is a distribution of mean difference scores. We use the paired-samples t test because each participant contributes a score to each of the two samples we are comparing.

We meet the assumption that the dependent variable is a scale measurement. However, we do not know whether the participants were randomly selected or if the population is normally distributed, and the sample is less than 30.

Step 2: The null hypothesis is that there is no difference in mean energy levels before and after lunch—$H_0: \mu_1 = \mu_2$.

The research hypothesis is that there is a mean difference in energy levels—$H_1: \mu_1 \neq \mu_2$.

Step 3:

Difference (D)	($D-M$)	($D-M$)^2
−3	−1.6	2.56
−3	−1.6	2.56
2	3.4	11.56
−1	0.4	0.16
−2	−0.6	0.36

$M_{difference} = -1.4$

$$s = \sqrt{\frac{\Sigma(X-M)^2}{(N-1)}} = \sqrt{\frac{17.2}{(5-1)}} = \sqrt{4.3} = 2.074$$

$$s_M = \frac{s}{\sqrt{N}} = \frac{2.074}{\sqrt{5}} = 0.928$$

$\mu_M = 0$, $s_M = 0.928$

Step 4: The degrees of freedom is $5-1=4$, and the cutoffs, based on a two-tailed test and an alpha level of 0.05, are ±2.776.

Step 5: $t = \frac{(-1.4-0)}{0.928} = -1.51$

Step 6: Because the test statistic, −1.51, did not exceed the critical value of −2.776, we fail to reject the null hypothesis.

10-5 The null hypothesis for the paired-samples t test is that the mean difference score is 0—that is, $\mu_M = 0$. Therefore, if the confidence interval around the mean difference does not include 0, we know that the sample mean is unlikely to have come from a distribution with a mean of 0 and we can reject the null hypothesis.

10-6 We calculate Cohen's d by subtracting 0 (the population mean based on the null hypothesis) from the sample mean and dividing by the standard deviation of the difference scores.

10-7 a. We first find the t values associated with a two-tailed hypothesis test and an alpha level of 0.05. These are ±2.776. We then calculate s_M by dividing s by the square root of the sample size, which results in $s_M = 0.548$.

$M_{lower} = -t(s_M) + M_{sample} = -2.776(0.548) + 1.0 = -0.52$

$M_{upper} = t(s_M) + M_{sample} = 2.776(0.548) + 1.0 = 2.52$

The confidence interval can be written as [−0.52, 2.52]. Because this confidence interval includes 0, we would fail to reject the null hypothesis. Zero is one of the likely mean differences we would get when repeatedly sampling from a population with a mean difference score of 1.

b. We calculate Cohen's d as:

$$d = \frac{(M-\mu)}{s} = \frac{(1-0)}{1.225} = 0.82$$

This is a large effect size.

10-8 a. $M_{lower} = -t(s_M) + M_{sample} = -2.776(0.928) + (-1.4) = -3.98$

$M_{upper} = t(s_M) + M_{sample} = 2.776(0.928) + (-1.4) = 1.18$

The confidence interval can be written as [−3.98, 1.18]. Notice that the confidence interval spans 0, the null-hypothesized difference between mean energy levels before and after lunch. Because the null value is within the confidence interval, we fail to reject the null hypothesis.

b. $d = \frac{(M-\mu)}{s} = \frac{(-1.4-0)}{2.074} = -0.68$

This is a medium-to-large effect size, according to Cohen's guidelines.

Chapter 11

11-1 When the data we are comparing are collected using the same participants in both conditions, we use a paired-samples t test; each participant contributes two values to the analysis. When we are comparing two independent groups and no participant is in more than one condition, we use an independent-samples t test.

11-2 Pooled variance is a weighted combination of the variability in both groups in an independent-samples t test.

11-3 a. Group 1 is treated as the X variable; its mean is 3.0.

X	$X - M$	$(X - M)^2$
3	0	0
2	-1	1
4	1	1
6	3	9
1	-2	4
2	-1	1

$$s_X^2 = \frac{\Sigma(X - M)^2}{N - 1} = \frac{(0 + 1 + 1 + 9 + 4 + 1)}{6 - 1} = 3.2$$

Group 2 is treated as the Y variable; its mean is 4.6.

Y	$Y - M$	$(Y - M)^2$
5	0.4	0.16
4	-0.6	0.36
6	1.4	1.96
2	-2.6	6.76
6	1.4	1.96

$$s_Y^2 = \frac{\Sigma(Y - M)^2}{N - 1} = \frac{(0.16 + 0.36 + 1.96 + 6.76 + 1.96)}{5 - 1}$$
$$= 28$$

b. $df_X = N - 1 = 6 - 1 = 5$

$df_Y = N - 1 = 5 - 1 = 4$

$df_{total} = df_X + df_Y = 5 + 4 = 9$

$$s_{pooled}^2 = \left(\frac{df_X}{df_{total}}\right)s_X^2 + \left(\frac{df_Y}{df_{total}}\right)s_Y^2 = \left(\frac{5}{9}\right)3.2 + \left(\frac{4}{9}\right)2.8$$
$$= 1.778 + 1.244 = 3.022$$

c. The variance version of standard error is calculated for each sample as:

$$s_{M_X}^2 = \frac{s_{pooled}^2}{N_X} = \frac{3.022}{6} = 0.504$$

$$s_{M_Y}^2 = \frac{s_{pooled}^2}{N_Y} = \frac{3.022}{5} = 0.604$$

d. The variance of the distribution of differences between means is:

$$s_{difference}^2 = s_{M_X}^2 + s_{M_Y}^2 = 0.504 + 0.604 = 1.108$$

This can be converted to standard deviation units by taking the square root:

$$s_{difference} = \sqrt{s_{difference}^2} = \sqrt{1.108} = 1.053$$

e. $t = \dfrac{(M_X - M_Y) - (\mu_X - \mu_Y)}{s_{difference}} = \dfrac{(3 - 4.6) - (0)}{1.053} = -1.52$

11-4 a. The null hypothesis asserts that there is no average between-groups difference; employees with low trust in their leader show the same mean level of agreement with decisions as those with high trust in their leader. Symbolically, this would be written H_0: $\mu_1 = \mu_2$.

The research hypothesis asserts that mean level of agreement is different between the two groups—H_1: $\mu_1 \neq \mu_2$.

b. The critical values, based on a two-tailed test, an alpha level of 0.05, and df_{total} of 9, are -2.262 and 2.262.

The t value we calculated, -1.519, does not exceed the cutoff of -2.262, so we fail to reject the null hypothesis.

c. Based on these results, we did not find evidence that mean level of agreement with a decision is different across the two levels of trust, $t(9) = -1.519, p > 0.05$.

d. Despite having similar means for the two groups, we failed to reject the null hypothesis, whereas the original researchers rejected the null hypothesis. The failure to reject the null hypothesis is likely due to the low statistical power from the small samples we used.

11-5 We calculate confidence intervals to determine a range of plausible values for the population parameter, based on the data.

11-6 Effect size tells us how large or small the difference we observed is, regardless of sample size. Even when a result is statistically significant, it might not be important. Effect size helps us evaluate practical significance.

11-7 a. The upper and lower bounds of the confidence interval are calculated as:

$$(M_X - M_Y)_{lower} = -t(s_{difference}) + (M_X - M_Y)_{sample}$$
$$= -2.262(1.053) + (-1.6) = -3.98$$
$$(M_X - M_Y)_{upper} = t(s_{difference}) + (M_X - M_Y)_{sample}$$
$$= 2.262(1.053) + (-1.6) = 0.78$$

The confidence interval is $[-3.98, 0.78]$.

b. To calculate Cohen's d, we need to calculate the pooled standard deviation for the data:

$$s_{pooled} = \sqrt{s_{pooled}^2} = \sqrt{3.022} = 1.738$$

$$\text{Cohen's } d = \frac{(M_X - M_Y) - (\mu_X - \mu_Y)}{s_{pooled}} = \frac{(3 - 4.6) - (0)}{1.738}$$
$$= -0.92$$

11-8 The confidence interval provides us with a range of differences between means in which we could expect the population mean difference to fall 95% of the time, based on samples of this size.

Whereas the hypothesis test evaluates the point estimate of the difference between means—(3 − 4.6), or −1.6, in this case—the confidence interval gives us a range, or interval estimate, of [−3.98, 0.78].

11-9 The effect size we calculated, Cohen's d of −0.92, is a large effect according to Cohen's guidelines. Beyond the hypothesis test and confidence interval, which both lead us to fail to reject the null hypothesis, the size of the effect indicates that we might be on to a real effect here. We might want to replicate the study with more statistical power in an effort to better test this hypothesis.

Chapter 12

12-1 The F statistic is a ratio of between-groups variance and within-groups variance.

12-2 The two types of research design for a one-way ANOVA are a within-groups design and a between-groups design.

12-3 a. $F = \dfrac{\text{between-groups variance}}{\text{within-groups variance}} = \dfrac{8.6}{3.7} = 2.324$

b. $F = \dfrac{102.4}{123.77} = 0.827$

c. $F = \dfrac{45.2}{32.1} = 1.408$

12-4 a. We would use an F distribution because there are more than two groups.

b. We would determine the variance among the three sample means—the means for those in the control group, for those in the 2-hour communication ban, and for those in the 4-hour communication ban.

c. We would determine the variance within each of the three samples, and we would take a weighted average of the three variances.

12-5 If the F statistic is beyond the cutoff, then we can reject the null hypothesis—meaning that there is a significant mean difference (or differences) somewhere in the data, but we do not know where the difference lies.

12-6 When calculating $SS_{between}$, we subtract the grand mean (GM) from the mean of each group (M). We do this for every score.

12-7 a. $df_{between} = N_{groups} - 1 = 3 - 1 = 2$

b. $df_{within} = df_1 + df_2 + \ldots + df_{last} = (4-1) + (4-1) + (3-1)$
$= 3 + 3 + 2 = 8$

c. $df_{total} = df_{between} + df_{within} = 2 + 8 = 10$

12-8 $GM = \dfrac{\Sigma(X)}{N_{total}}$

$= \dfrac{(37 + 30 + 22 + 29 + 49 + 52 + 41 + 39 + 36 + 49 + 42)}{11}$

$= 38.727$

12-9 a. Total sum of squares is calculated here as $SS_{total} = \Sigma(X - GM)^2$:

Sample	X	$(X - GM)$	$(X - GM)^2$
Group 1	37	−1.727	2.983
$M_1 = 29.5$	30	−8.727	76.161
	22	−16.727	279.793
	29	−9.727	94.615
Group 2	49	10.273	105.535
$M_2 = 45.25$	52	13.273	176.173
	41	2.273	5.167
	39	0.273	0.075
Group 3	36	−2.727	7.437
$M_3 = 42.333$	49	10.273	105.535
	42	3.273	10.713
	$GM = 38.73$		$SS_{total} = 864.187$

b. Within-groups sum of squares is calculated here as $SS_{within} = \Sigma(X - M)^2$.

Sample	X	$(X - M)$	$(X - M)^2$
Group 1	37	7.500	56.250
$M_1 = 29.5$	30	0.500	0.250
	22	−7.500	56.250
	29	−0.500	0.250
Group 2	49	3.750	14.063
$M_2 = 45.25$	52	6.750	45.563
	41	−4.250	18.063
	39	−6.250	39.063
Group 3	36	−6.333	40.107
$M_3 = 42.333$	49	6.667	44.449
	42	−0.333	0.111
	$GM = 38.73$		$SS_{within} = 314.419$

c. Between-groups sum of squares is calculated here as $SS_{between} = \Sigma(M - GM)^2$:

Sample	X	$(M - GM)$	$(M - GM)^2$
Group 1	37	−9.227	85.138
$M_1 = 29.5$	30	−9.227	85.138
	22	−9.227	85.138
	29	−9.227	85.138
Group 2	49	6.523	42.550
$M_2 = 45.25$	52	6.523	42.550
	41	6.523	42.550
	39	6.523	42.550
Group 3	36	3.606	13.003
$M_3 = 42.333$	49	3.606	13.003
	42	3.606	13.003

$$GM = 38.73 \qquad SS_{between} = 549.761$$

12-10 $MS_{between} = \dfrac{SS_{between}}{df_{between}} = \dfrac{549.761}{2} = 274.881$

$MS_{within} = \dfrac{SS_{within}}{df_{within}} = \dfrac{314.419}{8} = 39.302$

$F = \dfrac{SS_{between}}{df_{within}} = \dfrac{274.881}{39.302} = 6.99$

Source	SS	df	MS	F
Between	549.761	2	274.881	6.99
Within	314.419	8	39.302	
Total	864.187	10		

12-11 a. According to the null hypothesis, there are no mean differences in efficacy among these three treatment conditions; they would all come from one underlying distribution. The research hypothesis states that there are mean differences in efficacy across some or all of these treatment conditions.

b. There are three assumptions: (1) the participants were selected randomly, (2) the underlying populations are normally distributed, and (3) the underlying populations have similar variances. Although we can't say much about the first two assumptions, we can assess the last one using the sample data.

Sample	Group 1	Group 2	Group 3
Squared deviations of scores from sample means	56.25	14.063	40.107
	0.25	45.563	44.449
	56.25	18.063	0.111
	0.25	39.063	
Sum of squares	113	116.752	84.667
$N - 1$	3	3	2
Variance	37.67	38.92	42.33

Because these variances are all close together, with the biggest being no more than twice as large as the smallest, we can conclude that we meet the third assumption of homoscedastic samples.

c. The critical value for F with a p value of 0.05, two between-groups degrees of freedom, and 8 within-groups degrees of freedom, is 4.46. The F statistic exceeds this cutoff, so we can reject the null hypothesis. There are mean differences between these three groups, but we do not know where.

12-12 If we are able to reject the null hypothesis when conducting an ANOVA, then we must also conduct a post hoc test, such as a Tukey HSD test, to determine which pairs of means are significantly different from one another.

12-13 R^2 tells us the proportion of variance in the dependent variable that is accounted for by the independent variable.

12-14 a. $R^2 = \dfrac{SS_{between}}{SS_{total}} = \dfrac{336.360}{522.782} = 0.64$

b. Children's grade level accounted for 64% of the variability in reaction time. This is a large effect.

12-15 The number of levels of the independent variable is 3 and df_{within} is 32. At an alpha level of 0.05, the critical values of the q statistic are −3.49 and 3.49.

12-16 The adjusted alpha level is the alpha level for the experiment divided by the number of comparisons being made, which in this case is $\dfrac{0.05}{3} = 0.017$.

12-17 Because there are unequal sample sizes, we must calculate a weighted sample size.

$$N' = \dfrac{N_{groups}}{\Sigma\left(\dfrac{1}{N}\right)} = \dfrac{3}{\left(\dfrac{1}{4} + \dfrac{1}{4} + \dfrac{1}{3}\right)}$$

$$= \dfrac{3}{0.25 + 0.25 + 0.333} = \dfrac{3}{0.833} = 3.601$$

$s_M = \sqrt{\dfrac{MS_{within}}{N'}}$, then equals $\sqrt{\dfrac{39.302}{3.601}} = 3.304$

Now we can compare the three treatment groups.

Psychodynamic therapy ($M = 29.50$) versus interpersonal therapy ($M = 45.25$):

$$HSD = \dfrac{29.50 - 45.25}{3.304} = -4.77$$

Psychodynamic therapy ($M = 29.5$) versus cognitive-behavioral therapy ($M = 42.333$):

$$HSD = \dfrac{29.50 - 42.333}{3.304} = -3.88$$

Interpersonal therapy ($M = 45.25$) versus cognitive-behavioral therapy ($M = 42.333$):

$$HSD = \dfrac{45.25 - 42.333}{3.304} = 0.88$$

We look up the critical value for this post hoc test on the q table. We look in the row for 8 within-groups degrees of freedom, and then in the column for 3 treatment groups. At an alpha level of 0.05, the value in the q table is 4.04, so the cutoffs are −4.04 and 4.04.

There is just one significant difference, which is between psychodynamic therapy and interpersonal therapy: Tukey $HSD = -4.77$. Specifically, clients responded at statistically significantly higher rates to interpersonal therapy than to psychodynamic therapy, with a difference between means of 15.75 points on this scale.

12-18 Effect size is calculated as follows:

$$R^2 = \frac{SS_{between}}{SS_{total}} = \frac{549.761}{864.187} = 0.64$$

According to Cohen's conventions for R^2, this is a very large effect.

Chapter 13

13-1 For the one-way between-groups ANOVA, we calculate one kind of variability that occurs within groups: within-groups variability. But for the one-way within-groups ANOVA, the variability that occurs within groups is divided into two types: subjects variability and within-groups variability. Subjects variability assesses how much each person's overall mean differs from the others', assessed by comparing each person's mean score to the grand mean. We can remove this from the within-groups variability because the same people are in each group, and they would be the same across levels of the independent variable on many variables that may affect the dependent variable. This makes the within-groups variability smaller.

13-2 a. $df_{between} = N_{groups} - 1 = 3 - 1 = 2$

   b. $df_{subject} = n - 1 = 3 - 1 = 2$

   c. $df_{within} = (df_{between})(df_{subjects}) = (2)(2) = 4$

   d. $df_{total} = df_{between} + df_{subjects} + df_{within} = 2 + 2 + 4 = 8$; or we can calculate it as $df_{total} = N_{total} - 1 = 9 - 1 = 8$

13-3 a. $SS_{total} = \Sigma(X - GM)^2 = 24.886$

Group	Rating (X)	X − GM	(X − GM)²
1	7	0.111	0.012
1	9	2.111	4.456
1	8	1.111	1.234
2	5	−1.889	3.568
2	8	1.111	1.234
2	9	2.111	4.456
3	6	−0.889	0.790
3	4	−2.889	8.346
3	6	−0.889	0.790

$GM = 6.889$ $\Sigma(X - GM)^2 = 24.886$

b. $SS_{between} = \Sigma(M - GM)^2 = 11.556$

Group	Rating (X)	Group Mean (M)	M − GM	(M − GM)²
1	7	8	1.111	1.234
1	9	8	1.111	1.234
1	8	8	1.111	1.234
2	5	7.333	0.444	0.197
2	8	7.333	0.444	0.197
2	9	7.333	0.444	0.197
3	6	5.333	−1.556	2.421
3	4	5.333	−1.556	2.421
3	6	5.333	−1.556	2.421

$GM = 6.889$ $\Sigma(M - GM)^2 = 11.556$

c. $SS_{subject} = \Sigma\left(M_{participant} - GM\right)^2 = 4.221$

Participant	Group	Rating (X)	Participant Mean ($M_{participant}$)	$M_{participant}$ − GM	($M_{participant}$ − GM)²
1	1	7	6	−0.889	0.790
2	1	9	7	0.111	0.012
3	1	8	7.667	0.778	0.605
1	2	5	6	−0.889	0.790
2	2	8	7	0.111	0.012
3	2	9	7.667	0.778	0.605
1	3	6	6	−0.889	0.790
2	3	4	7	0.111	0.012
3	3	6	7.667	0.778	0.605

$GM = 6.889$ $\Sigma(M_{participant} - GM)^2 = 4.221$

d. $SS_{within} = SS_{total} - SS_{between} - SS_{subjects}$
$$= 24.886 - 11.556 - 4.221 = 9.109$$

13-4 $MS_{between} = \dfrac{SS_{between}}{df_{between}} = \dfrac{11.556}{2} = 5.778$

$MS_{subjects} = \dfrac{SS_{subjects}}{df_{subjects}} = \dfrac{4.221}{2} = 2.111$

$MS_{within} = \dfrac{SS_{within}}{df_{within}} = \dfrac{9.109}{4} = 2.277$

$F_{between} = \dfrac{SS_{between}}{df_{within}} = \dfrac{5.778}{2.277} = 2.538$

$F_{subjects} = \dfrac{SS_{subjects}}{df_{within}} = \dfrac{2.111}{2.277} = 0.927$

Source	SS	df	MS	F
Between-groups	11.556	2	5.778	2.54
Subjects	4.221	2	2.111	0.93
Within-groups	9.109	4	2.277	
Total	24.886	8		

13-5 a. Null hypothesis: People rate the driving experience of these three cars the same, on average—H_0: $\mu_1 = \mu_2 = \mu_3$. Research hypothesis: People do not rate the driving experience of these three cars the same, on average.

b. Order effects are addressed by counterbalancing. We could create a list of random orders of the three cars to be driven. Then, as a new customer arrives, we would assign him or her to the next random order on the list. With a large enough sample size (much larger than the three participants we used in this example), we could feel confident that this assumption would be met using this approach.

c. The critical value for the F statistic for an alpha level of 0.05 and 2 and 4 degrees of freedom is 6.95. The between-groups F statistic of 2.54 does not exceed this critical value. We cannot reject the null hypothesis, so we cannot conclude that there are differences among mean ratings of cars.

13-6 In both cases, the numerator in the ratio is $SS_{between}$, but the denominators differ in the two cases. For the between-groups ANOVA, the denominator of the R^2 calculation is SS_{total}. For the within-groups ANOVA, the denominator of the R^2 calculation is $SS_{total} - SS_{subjects}$, which takes into account the fact that we are subtracting out the variability caused by differences among participants (subjects sum of square) from the measure of error.

13-7 There are no differences in the way that the Tukey HSD is calculated. The formula for the calculation of the Tukey HSD is exactly the same for both the between-groups ANOVA and the within-groups ANOVA.

13-8 a. First, we calculate s_M:

$$s_M = \sqrt{\frac{MS_{within}}{N}} = \sqrt{\frac{771.256}{6}} = 11.338$$

Next, we calculate HSD for each pair of means.

For time 1 versus time 2:

$$HSD = \frac{(155.833 - 206.833)}{11.338} = -4.498$$

For time 1 versus time 3:

$$HSD = \frac{(155.833 - 251.667)}{11.338} = -8.452$$

For time 2 versus time 3:

$$HSD = \frac{(206.833 - 251.667)}{11.338} = -3.954$$

b. There is an independent variable with three levels and $df_{within} = 10$, so the q cutoff value at an alpha level of 0.05 is 3.88. Because we are performing a two-tailed test, the cutoff values are 3.88 and −3.88.

c. We reject the null hypothesis for all three of the mean comparisons because all of the HSD calculations exceed the critical value of −3.88. This tells us that all three of the group means are statistically significantly different from one another.

13-9 $R^2 = \dfrac{SS_{between}}{SS_{total} - SS_{subjects}} = \dfrac{27,590.486}{(52,115.111 - 16,812.189)} = 0.78$

13-10 a. $R^2 = \dfrac{SS_{between}}{(SS_{total} - SS_{subjects})} = \dfrac{11.556}{(24.886 - 4.221)} = 0.56$

This is a large effect size.

b. Because the F statistic did not exceed the critical value, we failed to reject the null hypothesis. As a result, Tukey HSD tests are not necessary.

Chapter 14

14-1 A factorial ANOVA is a statistical analysis used with one scale dependent variable and at least two nominal (or sometimes ordinal) independent variables (also called factors).

14-2 A statistical interaction occurs in a factorial design when the two independent variables have an effect in combination that we do not see when we examine each independent variable on its own.

14-3 a. There are two factors: diet programs and exercise programs.

b. There are three factors: diet programs, exercise programs, and metabolism type.

c. There is one factor: gift certificate value.

d. There are two factors: gift certificate value and store quality.

14-4 a. The participants are the stocks themselves.

b. One independent variable is the type of ticker-code name, with two levels: pronounceable and unpronounceable. The second independent variable is time lapsed since the stock was initially offered, with four levels: 1 day, 1 week, 6 months, and 1 year.

c. The dependent variable is the stock's selling price.

d. This would be a two-way mixed-design ANOVA.

e. This would be a 2×4 mixed-design ANOVA.

f. This study would have eight cells: $2 \times 4 = 8$. We multiplied the numbers of levels of each of the two independent variables.

14-5 A *quantitative interaction* is an interaction in which one independent variable exhibits a strengthening or weakening of its effect at one or more levels of the other independent variable, but the direction of the initial effect does not change. More specifically, the effect of one independent variable is modified in the presence of another independent variable. A *qualitative interaction* is a particular type of quantitative interaction of two (or more) independent variables in which one independent variable reverses its effect depending on the level of the other independent variable. In a qualitative interaction, the effect of one variable doesn't just become stronger or weaker; it actually reverses direction in the presence of another variable.

14-6 An interaction indicates that the effect of one independent variable depends on the level of the other independent variable(s). The main effect alone cannot be interpreted because the effect of that one variable depends on another.

14-7 a. There are four cells.

		IV 2	
		Level A	Level B
IV 1	Level A		
	Level B		

b.

		IV 2	
		Level A	Level B
IV 1	Level A	$M = (2+1+1+3)/4$ $= 1.75$	$M = (2+3+3+3)/4$ $= 2.75$
	Level B	$M = (5+4+3+4)/4$ $= 4$	$M = (3+2+2+3)/4$ $= 2.5$

c. Because the sample size is the same for each cell, we can compute the marginal means as simply the average of the cell means.

		IV 2		Marginal means
		Level A	Level B	
IV 1	Level A	1.75	2.75	2.25
	Level B	4	2.5	3.25
	Marginal means	2.875	2.625	

d.

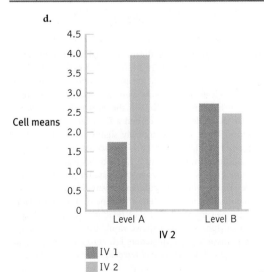

14-8 a. The independent variables are gender and attractiveness. For gender, there are two levels: male and female. For attractiveness, there are three levels: below average, average, and above average.

b. The dependent variable is GPA. GPA is a scale variable.

c. There are two independent variables and one dependent variable for these data. The two independent variables are nominal (or, in the case of attractiveness, ordinal, but can be interpreted as nominal) and the dependent variable is continuous. A two-way between-groups ANOVA would be the appropriate hypothesis test because it allows us to compare the levels from two independent variables. Additionally, a two-way between-groups ANOVA allows us to compare the combined effects of these two variables on the dependent variable. In this example, a two-way between-groups ANOVA allows us to compare the combined effect of gender and attractiveness on GPA instead of simply looking at each independent variable separately.

d. The results indicate that there is a significant interaction because the effect of attractiveness holds true only for female students. Female students who were more attractive had higher GPA scores. However, this pattern did not hold true for male students. For men, there were not statistically significant differences in their GPAs, on average, based on ratings of attractiveness.

e. Here is one possible solution.

	Level of attractiveness		
	Below average	Average	Above average
Men	3.3	3.2	3.35
Women	3.0	3.25	3.55

f. The results suggest that this is a quantitative interaction: Among women, grades became higher as they had increasingly higher levels of attractiveness, whereas there were not significant differences among the men at different levels of attractiveness. If the reverse had happened among male students—a decrease in grades associated with higher levels of attractiveness—this would be considered a qualitative interaction.

g. We don't necessarily know why attractive women receive better grades. It is possible that attractive women receive better grades because of professor bias. But it also is possible that prettier women are simply brighter. This second possibility has the potential to be a confound in the study—an alternative explanation for the finding. The second study eliminated the potential for professors to see a student's physical appearance because the study included online courses, so professors likely could not see a student's physical appearance. However, students were still ranked as below average, average, and above average as in the original study. When this potential confound (attractiveness bias from professors) was eliminated, the attractiveness effect on GPA for women was no longer statistically significant. The second study eliminated the possible confounding variable of intelligence. Attractive women are not necessarily smarter, but they do tend to receive higher grades as a result of their attractiveness. So, it seems as if there is professor bias toward attractive female students.

14-9 Hypothesis testing for a one-way between-groups ANOVA evaluates only one idea. However, hypothesis testing for a two-way between-groups ANOVA evaluates three ideas: two main effects and an interaction. So, the two-way ANOVA requires three hypotheses, three comparison distributions, three critical F values, three F statistics, and three conclusions.

14-10 Variability is associated with the two main effects, the interaction, and the within-groups component.

14-11 $df_{IV1} = df_{rows} = N_{rows} - 1 = 2 - 1 = 1$

$df_{IV2} = df_{columns} = N_{columns} - 1 = 2 - 1 = 1$

$df_{interaction} = (df_{rows})(df_{columns}) = (1)(1) = 1$

$df_{within} = df_{1A,2A} + df_{1A,2B} + df_{1B,2A} + df_{1B,2B} = 3 + 3 + 3 + 3 = 12$

$df_{total} = N_{total} - 1 = 16 - 1 = 15$

We can also verify that this calculation is correct by adding all of the other degrees of freedom together: $1 + 1 + 1 + 12 = 15$.

14-12 The critical value for the main effect of the first independent variable, based on a between-groups degrees of freedom of 1 and a within-groups degrees of freedom of 12, is 4.75. The critical value for the main effect of the second independent variable, based on 1 and 12 degrees of freedom, is 4.75. The critical value for the interaction, based on 1 and 12 degrees of freedom, is 4.75.

14-13 a. Population 1 is students who received an initial grade of C and received email messages aimed at bolstering self-esteem. Population 2 is students who received an initial grade of C and received email messages aimed at helping students take responsibility for their grades. Population 3 is students who received an initial grade of C and received emails with just review questions. Population 4 is students who received an initial grade of D or F and received email messages aimed at bolstering self-esteem. Population 5 is students who received an initial grade of D or F and received email messages aimed at helping students take responsibility for their grades. Population 6 is students who received an initial grade of D or F and received emails with just review questions.

b. *Step 2:* Main effect of first independent variable—initial grade:

Null hypothesis: The mean final exam grade of students with an initial grade of C is the same as that of students with an initial grade of D or F. H_0: $\mu_C = \mu_{D/F}$.

Research hypothesis: The mean final exam grade of students with an initial grade of C is not the same as that of students with an initial grade of D or F. H_1: $\mu_C \neq \mu_{D/F}$.

Main effect of second independent variable—type of email:

Null hypothesis: On average, the mean exam grades among those receiving different types of emails are the same— H_0: $\mu_{SE} = \mu_{CG} = \mu_{TR}$.

Research hypothesis: On average, the mean exam grades among those receiving different types of emails are not the same.

Interaction: Initial grade × type of email.

Null hypothesis: The effect of type of email is not dependent on the levels of initial grade.

Research hypothesis: The effect of type of email depends on the levels of initial grade.

c. *Step 3:* $df_{between/grade} = N_{groups} - 1 = 2 - 1 = 1$

$df_{between/email} = N_{groups} - 1 = 3 - 1 = 2$

$df_{interaction} = (df_{between/grade})(df_{between/email}) = (1)(2) = 2$

$df_{C,SE} = N - 1 = 14 - 1 = 13$

$df_{C,C} = N - 1 = 14 - 1 = 13$

$df_{C,TR} = N - 1 = 14 - 1 = 13$

$df_{D/F,SE} = N - 1 = 14 - 1 = 13$

$df_{D/F,C} = N - 1 = 14 - 1 = 13$

$df_{D/F,TR} = N - 1 = 14 - 1 = 13$

$df_{within} = df_{C,SE} + df_{C,C} + df_{C,TR} + df_{D/F,SE} + df_{D/F,C} + df_{D/F,TR} = 13 + 13 + 13 + 13 + 13 + 13 = 78$

Main effect of initial grade: F distribution with 1 and 78 degrees of freedom

Main effect of type of email: F distribution with 2 and 78 degrees of freedom

Main effect of interaction of initial grade and type of email: F distribution with 2 and 78 degrees of freedom

d. *Step 4:* Note that when the specific degrees of freedom is not in the F table, you should choose the more conservative— that is, larger—cutoff. In this case, go with the cutoffs for a within-groups degrees of freedom of 75 rather than 80. The three cutoffs are:

Main effect of initial grade: 3.97

Main effect of type of email: 3.12

Interaction of initial grade and type of email: 3.12

e. *Step 6:* There is a significant main effect of initial grade because the F statistic, 20.84, is larger than the critical value of 3.97. The marginal means, seen in the accompanying table, tell us that students who earned a C on the initial exam have higher scores on the final exam, on average, than do students who earned a D or an F on the initial exam. There is no statistically significant main effect of type of email, however. The F statistic of 1.69 is not larger than the critical value of 3.12. Had this main effect been significant, we would have conducted a post hoc test to determine where the differences were. There also is not a significant interaction. The F statistic of 3.02 is not larger than the critical value of 3.12. (Had we used a cutoff based on an alpha level of 0.10, we would have rejected the null hypothesis for the interaction. The cutoff for an alpha level of 0.10 is 2.38.) If we had rejected the null hypothesis for the interaction, we would have examined the cell means in tabular and graph form.

	Self-esteem	Take responsibility	Control group	Marginal means
C	67.31	69.83	71.12	69.42
D/F	47.83	60.98	62.13	56.98
Marginal means	57.57	65.41	66.63	

Chapter 15

15-1 (1) The correlation coefficient can be either positive or negative. (2) The correlation coefficient always falls between −1.00 and 1.00. (3) It is the strength, also called the *magnitude*, of the coefficient, not its sign, that indicates how large it is.

15-2 When two variables are correlated, there can be multiple explanations for that association. The first variable can cause the second variable; the second variable can cause the first variable; or a third variable can cause both the first and second variables. In fact, there may be more than one "third" variable causing both the first and second variables.

15-3 a. According to Cohen, this is a large (strong) correlation. Note that the sign (negative in this case) is not related to the assessment of strength.

b. This is just above a medium correlation.

c. This is lower than the guideline for a small correlation, 0.10.

15-4 Students will draw a variety of different scatterplots. The important thing to note is the closeness of data points to an imaginary line drawn through the data.

a. A scatterplot for a correlation coefficient of −0.60 might look like this:

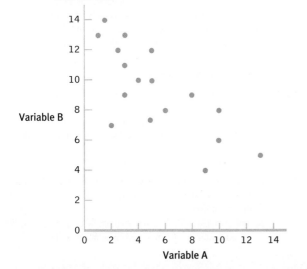

b. A scatterplot for a correlation coefficient of 0.35 might look like this:

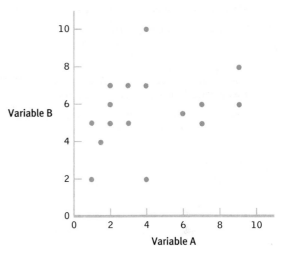

c. A scatterplot for a correlation coefficient of 0.04 might look like this:

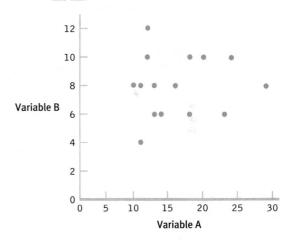

15-5 It is possible that training while listening to music (A) causes an increase in a country's average finishing time (B), perhaps because music decreases one's focus on running. It is also possible that high average finishing times (B) cause an increase in the percentage of marathon runners in a country who train while listening to music (A), perhaps because slow runners tend to get bored and need music to get through their runs. It also is possible that a third variable, such as a country's level of wealth (C), causes a higher percentage of runners who train while listening to music (because of the higher presence of technology in wealthy countries) (A) and also causes higher (slower) finishing times (perhaps because long-distance running is a less popular sport in wealthy countries with access to so many sport and entertainment options) (B). Without a true experiment, we cannot know the direction of causality.

15-6 The Pearson correlation coefficient is a statistic that quantifies a linear relation between two scale variables. Specifically, it describes the direction and strength of the relation between the variables.

15-7 The two issues are variability and sample size.

15-8

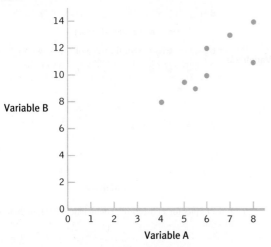

15-9 Step 1 is calculating the numerator:

Variable A (X)	$(X - M_X)$	Variable B (Y)	$(Y - M_Y)$	$(X - M_X)(Y - M_Y)$
8	1.812	14	3.187	5.775
7	0.812	13	2.187	1.776
6	−0.188	10	−0.813	0.153
5	−1.188	9.5	−1.313	1.56
4	−2.188	8	−2.813	6.155
5.5	−0.688	9	−1.813	1.247
6	−0.188	12	1.187	−0.223
8	1.812	11	0.187	0.339

$M_X = 6.118$ $M_Y = 10.813$ $\Sigma[(X - M_X)(Y - M_Y)] = 16.782$

Step 2 is calculating the denominator:

Variable A (X)	$(X - M_X)$	$(X - M_X)^2$	Variable B (Y)	$(Y - M_Y)$	$(Y - M_Y)^2$
8	1.812	3.283	14	3.187	10.157
7	0.812	0.659	13	2.187	4.783
6	−0.188	0.035	10	−0.813	0.661
5	−1.188	1.411	9.5	−1.313	1.724
4	−2.188	4.787	8	−2.813	7.913
5.5	−0.688	0.473	9	−1.813	3.287
6	−0.188	0.035	12	1.187	1.409
8	1.812	3.283	11	0.187	0.035

$\Sigma(X - M_X)^2 = 13.966$ $\Sigma(Y - M_Y)^2 = 29.969$

$$\sqrt{(SS_X)(SS_Y)} = \sqrt{(13.966)(29.969)} = \sqrt{418.547} = 20.458$$

Step 3 is computing r:

$$r = \frac{\Sigma[(X - M_X)(Y - M_Y)]}{\sqrt{(SS_X)(SS_Y)}} = \frac{16.782}{20.458} = 0.82$$

15-10 *Step 1:* Population 1: Children like those we studied. Population 2: Children for whom there is no relation between observed and performed acts of aggression. The comparison distribution is made up of correlations based on samples of this size, 8 people, selected from the population.

We do not know if the data were randomly selected (the first assumption), so we must be cautious when generalizing the findings. We also do not know if the underlying population distributions for witnessed aggression and performed acts of aggression by children are normally distributed. The sample size is too small to draw any conclusions about this assumption, so we should proceed with caution. The third assumption, unique to correlation, is that the variability of one variable is equal across the levels of the other variable. Because we have such a small data set, it is difficult to evaluate this. However, we can see from the scatterplot that the data are somewhat consistently variable.

Step 2: Null hypothesis: There is no correlation between the levels of witnessed and performed acts of aggression among children—H_0: $\rho = 0$. Research hypothesis: There is a correlation between the levels of witnessed and performed acts of aggression among children—H_1: $\rho \neq 0$.

Step 3: The comparison distribution is a distribution of Pearson correlations, r, with the following degrees of freedom: $df_r = N - 2 = 8 - 2 = 6$.

Step 4: The critical values for an r distribution with 6 degrees of freedom for a two-tailed test with an alpha level of 0.05 are −0.707 and 0.707.

Step 5: This was computed in the previous exercise.

Step 6: The test statistic, $r = 0.82$, is larger in magnitude than the critical value of 0.707. We can reject the null hypothesis and conclude that a strong positive correlation exists between the number of witnessed acts of aggression and the number of acts of aggression performed by children.

15-11 Psychometricians calculate correlations when assessing the reliability and validity of measures and tests.

15-12 Coefficient alpha is a measure of reliability. To calculate coefficient alpha, we take, in essence, the average of all split-half correlations. That is, the items on a test are split in half and the correlation of those two halves is calculated. This process is done repeatedly for all possible "halves" of the test, and then the average of those correlations is obtained.

15-13 a. The researchers is assessing validity by trying to see if her new measure of extraversion correlates with an existing measure of extraversion.

b. The correlation coefficient of −0.032 is very close to zero, an indication that her new scale may not be valid.

15-14 a. The psychometrician could assess test–retest reliability by administering the quiz to 100 readers who have boyfriends, and then one week later readministering the test to the same 100 readers. If their scores at the two times are highly correlated, the test would have high test–retest reliability. She also could calculate a coefficient alpha using computer software. The computer would essentially calculate correlations for every possible two groups of five items and then calculate the average of all of these split-half correlations.

b. The psychometrician could assess validity by choosing criteria that she believed assessed the underlying construct of interest, a boyfriend's devotion to his partner. There are many possible criteria. For example, she could correlate the quiz scores with the amount of money each participant's boyfriend spent on his partner's most recent birthday, the number of minutes the participant spent on the phone with the boyfriend today, or with the number of months the relationship ends up lasting.

c. Of course, we assume that these other measures actually assess the underlying construct of a boyfriend's devotion, which may or may not be true! For example, the amount of money that the boyfriend spent on the participant's last birthday might be a measure of his income, not his devotion.

Chapter 16

16-1 Simple linear regression is a statistical tool that lets statisticians predict the score on a scale dependent variable from the score on a scale independent variable.

16-2 The regression line allows us to make predictions about one variable based on what we know about another variable. It gives us a visual representation of what we believe is the underlying relation between the variables, based on the data we have available to us.

16-3 a. $z_X = \dfrac{X - M_X}{SD_X} = \dfrac{67 - 64}{2} = 1.5$

b. $z_{\hat{Y}} = (r_{XY})(z_X) = (0.28)(1.5) = 0.42$

c. $\hat{Y} = z_{\hat{Y}}(SD_Y) + M_Y = (0.42)(15) + 155 = 161.3$ pounds

16-4 a. $\hat{Y} = 12 + 0.67(X) = 12 + 0.67(78) = 64.26$

b. $\hat{Y} = 12 + 0.67(-14) = 2.62$

c. $\hat{Y} = 12 + 0.67(52) = 46.84$

16-5 a. $z_X = \dfrac{(X - M_X)}{SD_X} = \dfrac{(0 - 9.5)}{3.304} = -2.875$

$z_{\hat{Y}} = (r_{XY})(z_X) = 0.353(-2.875) = -1.015$

$\hat{Y} = z_{\hat{Y}}(SD_Y) + M_Y = -1.015(3.752) + 21.083 = 17.275$

b. $z_X = \dfrac{(X - M_X)}{SD_X} = \dfrac{(1 - 9.5)}{3.304} = -2.573$

$z_{\hat{Y}} = (r_{XY})(z_X) = 0.353(-2.573) = -0.908$

$\hat{Y} = z_{\hat{Y}}(SD_Y) + M_Y = -0.908(3.752) + 21.083 = 17.676$

$b = 17.676 - 17.275 = 0.401$

c. The regression equation for these data is:

$$\hat{Y} = 17.28 + 0.40(X)$$

d. The y intercept tells us what the value of $\hat{Y}$ is when X is 0. In this example, when X is 0, $\hat{Y}$ is 17.28. This means that when someone says zero taboo words in one minute, that person will, on average, say 17.28 animal words in one minute.

The slope tells us how much $\hat{Y}$ changes with every one-unit increase in X. In this example, for each additional taboo word a person says, we would expect that individual to say about 0.4 more animal words.

e. $\beta = (b)\dfrac{\sqrt{SS_X}}{\sqrt{SS_Y}} = 0.4 \dfrac{\sqrt{131}}{\sqrt{168.918}} = 0.353$

f. A stronger correlation means that the predictions made from the regression line will be more accurate.

g. The steps for a hypothesis test of a standardized regression coefficient are the same for a correlation coefficient. In Exercise 15.57, we failed to reject the null hypothesis: the test statistic, $r = .35$, is not larger in magnitude than the critical value of .576. We can conclude the same if we were to complete a hypothesis test for the standardized regression coefficient.

16-6 The standard error of the estimate is a statistic that indicates the typical distance between a regression line and the actual data points. When we do not have enough information to compute a regression equation, we often use the mean as the "best guess." The error of prediction when the mean is used is typically greater than the standard error of the estimate.

16-7 Strong correlations mean highly accurate predictions with regression. This translates into a large proportionate reduction in error.

16-8 a.

X	Y	Mean For Y (M_Y)	Error ($Y - M_Y$)	Squared Error $(Y - M_Y)^2$
5	6	5.333	0.667	0.445
6	5	5.333	−0.333	0.111
4	6	5.333	0.667	0.445
5	6	5.333	0.667	0.445
7	4	5.333	−1.333	1.777
8	5	5.333	−0.333	0.111

$$SS_{total} = \Sigma(Y - M_Y)^2 = 3.334$$

b.

X	Y	Regression Equation	$\hat{Y}$	Error $(Y - \hat{Y})$	Squared Error
5	6	$\hat{Y} = 7.846 - 0.431\,(5) =$	5.691	0.309	0.095
6	5	$\hat{Y} = 7.846 - 0.431\,(6) =$	5.260	−0.260	0.068
4	6	$\hat{Y} = 7.846 - 0.431\,(4) =$	6.122	−0.122	0.015
5	6	$\hat{Y} = 7.846 - 0.431\,(5) =$	5.691	0.309	0.095
7	4	$\hat{Y} = 7.846 - 0.431\,(7) =$	4.829	−0.829	0.687
8	5	$\hat{Y} = 7.846 - 0.431\,(8) =$	4.398	0.602	0.362

$$SS_{error} = \Sigma(Y - \hat{Y})^2 = 1.322$$

c. We have reduced error from 3.334 to 1.322, which is a reduction of 2.012. Now we calculate this reduction as a proportion of the total error:

$$\frac{2.012}{3.334} = 0.603$$

This can also be written as:

$$r^2 = \frac{(SS_{total} - SS_{error})}{SS_{total}} = \frac{(3.334 - 1.322)}{3.334} = 0.603$$

We have reduced 0.603, or 60.3%, of error using the regression equation as an improvement over the use of the mean as our predictor.

d. $r^2 = (-0.77)(-0.77) = 0.593$, which closely matches our calculation of r^2, 0.603. These numbers are slightly different due to rounding decisions.

16-9 Tell Coach Parcells that prediction suffers from the same limitations as correlation. First, just because two variables are associated, that doesn't mean one causes the other. This is not a true experiment, and if we didn't randomly assign athletes to appear on a *Sports Illustrated* cover or not, then we cannot determine whether a cover appearance causes sporting failure. Moreover, we have a limited range; by definition, those lauded on the cover are the best in sports. Would the association be different among those with a wider range of athletic ability? Finally, and most importantly, there is the very strong possibility of regression to the mean. Those chosen for a cover appearance are at the very top of their game. There is nowhere to go but down, so it is not surprising that those who merit a cover appearance would soon thereafter experience a decline. There's likely no need to avoid that cover, Coach.

16-10 Multiple regression is a statistical tool that predicts an outcome variable by using two or more predictor variables. It is an improvement over simple linear regression, which allows only one predictor variable to inform predictions.

16-11 $\hat{Y} = 5.251 + 0.06(X_1) + 1.105(X_2)$

16-12
a. $\hat{Y} = 5.251 + 0.06(40) + 1.105(14) = 23.12$
b. $\hat{Y} = 5.251 + 0.06(101) + 1.105(39) = 54.41$
c. $\hat{Y} = 5.251 + 0.06(76) + 1.105(20) = 31.91$

16-13
a. The predictor variable is how far a customer lives from an office supply store that is a competitor to Staples. The outcome variable is the price of various items at Staples. Distance to a store predicts the price of a product, such that people who live farther from a competitor are being charged higher prices at Staples. This is an example of a simple linear regression because there is only one predictor variable.

b. There are several predictor variables in this example: criminal record, age, job history, and patterns of crime within the person's family. The outcome variable is the likelihood that an individual would become a repeat offender. This is an example of a multiple regression because there are several predictor variables predicting the outcome variable, likelihood that an individual would become a repeat offender.

Chapter 17

17-1 A parametric test is based on a set of assumptions about the population, whereas a nonparametric test is a statistical analysis that is not based on assumptions about the population.

17-2 We use nonparametric tests when the data violate the assumptions about the population that parametric tests make. The three most common situations that call for nonparametric tests are (1) having a nominal dependent variable, (2) having an ordinal dependent variable, and (3) having a small sample size with possible skew.

17-3
a. The independent variable is the ranking of each destination, an ordinal variable. The dependent variable is the destinations' ranking on travel cost, also an ordinal variable.

b. The independent variable is continent; it is a nominal variable with two levels, Asia and South America. The dependent variable is how interesting each destination is, assessed on a scale of 1–10. This is a scale variable.

c. The independent variable is a traveler's typical cost per day for each destination, a scale variable. The dependent variable is how interesting a destination is on a scale of 1–10, also a scale variable.

d. The independent variable is continent with three levels: Europe, Africa, and North America. This is a nominal variable. The dependent variable is number of recommendations on the Facebook post for each destination, a scale variable.

17-4
a. We would choose a hypothesis test from category III because both the independent and dependent variables are ordinal. We would not meet the assumption of having a normal distribution of the dependent variable, even if we had a large sample.

b. We would choose a test from category II because the independent variable is nominal and the dependent variable is scale. (In fact, we would choose an independent-samples *t* test.)

c. We would choose a hypothesis test from category I because we have a scale independent variable and a scale dependent variable. (If we were assessing the relation between these variables, we would use the Pearson correlation coefficient. If we wondered whether the typical cost for a traveler predicted how interesting a destination is, we would use simple linear regression.)

d. We would choose a test from category II because the independent variable is nominal and the dependent variable is scale. (In fact, we would use a one-way between-groups ANOVA because there is only one independent variable and it has more than two levels.)

17-5 We use chi-square tests when all variables are nominal.

17-6 Observed frequencies indicate how often something actually happens in a given category based on the data we collected. Expected frequencies indicate how often we expect something to happen in a given category based on what is known about the population according to the null hypothesis.

17-7 a. $df_{\chi^2} = k - 1 = 2 - 1 = 1$

b. Observed:

Clear Blue Skies	Gray Skies
59 days	19 days

Expected:

Clear Blue Skies	Gray Skies
$(78)(0.80) = 62.4$ days	$(78)(0.20) = 15.6$ days

c.

Category	Observed (O)	Expected (E)	O − E	(O − E)²	$\frac{(O-E)^2}{E}$
Clear blue skies	59	62.4	−3.4	11.56	0.185
Gray skies	19	15.6	3.4	11.56	0.741

$$\chi^2 = \Sigma \left[\frac{(O-E)^2}{E} \right] = 0.185 + 0.741 = 0.93$$

17-8 a. The participants are the lineups. The independent variable is type of lineup (simultaneous, sequential), and the dependent variable is outcome of the lineup (suspect identification, other identification, no identification).

b. *Step 1:* Population 1 is police lineups like those we observed. Population 2 is police lineups for which type of lineup and outcome are independent. The comparison distribution is a chi-square distribution. The hypothesis test is a chi-square test for independence because there are two nominal variables. This study meets three of the four assumptions. The two variables are nominal; every participant (lineup) is in

only one cell; and there are more than five times as many participants as cells (8 participants and 6 cells).

Step 2: Null hypothesis: Lineup outcome is independent of type of lineup.

Research hypothesis: Lineup outcome depends on type of lineup.

Step 3: The comparison distribution is a chi-square distribution with 2 degrees of freedom:

$$df_{\chi^2} = (k_{row} - 1)(k_{column} - 1) = (2-1)(3-1) = (1)(2) = 2$$

Step 4: The cutoff chi-square statistic, based on an alpha level of 0.05 and 2 degrees of freedom, is 5.992. (*Note:* It is helpful to include a drawing of the chi-square distribution with the cutoff.)

Step 5:

	Observed			
	Suspect ID	Other ID	No ID	
Simultaneous	191	8	120	319
Sequential	102	20	107	229
	293	28	227	548

We can calculate the expected frequencies in one of two ways. First, we can think about it. Out of the total of 548 lineups, 293 led to identification of the suspect, an identification rate of 293/548 = 0.535, or 53.5%. If identification were independent of type of lineup, we would expect the same rate for each type of lineup. For example, for the 319 simultaneous lineups, we would expect: $(0.535)(319) = 170.665$. For the 229 sequential lineups, we would expect: $(0.535)(229) = 122.515$. Or we can use the formula; for these same two cells (the column labeled "Suspect ID"), we calculate:

$$\frac{Total_{column}}{N}(Total_{row}) = \frac{293}{548}(319) = (0.535)(319) = 170.665$$

$$\frac{Total_{column}}{N}(Total_{row}) = \frac{293}{548}(229) = (0.535)(229) = 122.515$$

For the column labeled "Other ID":

$$\frac{Total_{column}}{N}(Total_{row}) = \frac{28}{548}(319) = (0.051)(319) = 16.269$$

$$\frac{Total_{column}}{N}(Total_{row}) = \frac{28}{548}(229) = (0.051)(229) = 11.679$$

For the column labeled "No ID":

$$\frac{Total_{column}}{N}(Total_{row}) = \frac{227}{548}(319) = (0.414)(319) = 132.066$$

$$\frac{Total_{column}}{N}(Total_{row}) = \frac{227}{548}(229) = (0.414)(229) = 94.806$$

	Expected			
	Suspect ID	Other ID	No ID	
Simultaneous	170.665	16.269	132.066	319
Sequential	122.515	11.679	94.806	229
	293	28	227	548

Category	Observed (O)	Expected (E)	O − E	(O − E)²	$\frac{(O-E)^2}{E}$
Sim; suspect	191	170.665	20.335	413.512	2.423
Sim; other	8	16.269	−8.269	68.376	4.203
Sim; no	120	132.066	−12.066	145.588	1.102
Seq; suspect	102	122.515	−20.515	420.865	3.435
Seq; other	20	11.679	8.321	69.239	5.929
Seq; no	107	94.806	12.194	148.694	1.568

$$\chi^2 = \left(\frac{(O-E)^2}{E}\right) = (2.423 + 4.203 + 1.102 + 3.435 + 5.929 + 1.568)$$

$$= 18.660$$

Step 6: Reject the null hypothesis. It appears that the outcome of a lineup depends on the type of lineup. In general, simultaneous lineups tend to lead to a higher than expected rate of suspect identification, lower than expected rates of identification of other members of the lineup, and lower than expected rates of no identification at all, as compared with sequential lineups. (*Note:* It is helpful to add the test statistic to the drawing that included the cutoff.)

c. $\chi^2(1, N = 548) = 18.66$, $p < 0.05$

d. The findings of this study were the opposite of what had been expected by the investigators; the report of results noted that, prior to this study, police departments believed that the sequential lineup led to more accurate identification of suspects. This situation occurs frequently in behavioral research, a reminder of the importance of conducting two-tailed hypothesis tests. (Of course, the fact that this study produced different results doesn't end the debate. Future researchers should explore why there are different findings in different contexts in an effort to target the best lineup procedures for specific situations.)

17-9 The measure of effect size for chi square is Cramér's *V*. It is calculated by first multiplying the total *N* by the degrees of freedom for either the rows or columns (whichever is smaller) and then dividing the calculated chi-square value by this number. We then take the square root, which is Cramér's *V*.

17-10 To calculate the relative likelihood, we first need to calculate two conditional probabilities: the conditional probability of showing a "kissing pout" or duckface in a selfie for women, which is

$\frac{29}{250} = 0.116$, and the conditional probability of showing a "kissing pout" or duckface in a selfie for men, which is $\frac{6}{250} = 0.024$. Now we divide the conditional probability of showing a duckface given that one is a woman by the conditional probability of showing a duckface given that one is a man: $\frac{0.116}{0.024} = 4.833$. The relative likelihood of showing a duckface in a selfie for a woman as opposed to a man is 4.83.

17-11 a. Cramér's $V = \sqrt{\dfrac{\chi^2}{(N)(df_{row/column})}} = \sqrt{\dfrac{18.660}{(548)(1)}} = 0.185$.

This is a small-to-medium effect.

b. For simultaneous lineups:

Suspect identified: 191/319 = 0.599

Other person identified: 8/319 = 0.025

No person identified: 120/319 = 0.376

For sequential lineups:

Suspect identified: 102/229 = 0.445

Other person identified: 20/229 = 0.087

No person identified: 107/229 = 0.467

Conditional Proportions

	Suspect ID	Other ID	No ID	
Simultaneous	0.599	0.025	0.376	1.000
Sequential	0.445	0.087	0.467	0.999

Note: The bottom row adds up to 0.999 instead of 1.000 due to rounding.

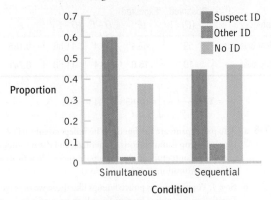

c. For simultaneous lineups:

Suspect identified: 191/319 = 0.599

For sequential lineups:

Suspect identified: 102/229 = 0.445

0.599/0.445 = 1.346

Based on this relative likelihood calculation, the chance of a suspect being accurately identified in a simultaneous lineup is 1.35 times that of a suspect being identified in a sequential lineup.

Chapter 18

18-1 It is important to identify the appropriate statistical test before beginning a study for two reasons: A data-analysis plan ensures that researchers are collecting data they can analyze, and it cuts down on unethical behaviors. If researchers have a plan, they are less likely, for example, to later analyze their data in multiple ways until they achieve a statistically significant result, a behavior known as *p*-hacking.

18-2 a. Chi-square test for goodness of fit

b. Regression

c. One-way within-groups ANOVA

d. *z* test

18-3 a. The nominal independent variable is type of traveler with two levels: those who had used Airbnb and those who had not. This is a between-groups design because no traveler can be in both groups. The scale dependent variable is ratings of various features of lodgings, such as the importance of security, on a scale of 1–5. Because there is one independent variable with two levels, one scale dependent variable, and a between-groups design, the appropriate test is an independent-samples *t* test.

b. Time is a scale variable, as is price. Because both are scale variables, we know that this hypothesis will be analyzed with either a Pearson correlation coefficient or a regression analysis. Because the question focuses on prediction rather than association, these data would be analyzed with a regression analysis.

c. There are two variables. One variable is type of travel companions, which is the more obvious independent variable and is nominal; it has two levels (friends and family). The second variable is type of lodging, which has two levels (vacation rental and hotel); it is the more obvious dependent variable and also is nominal. Because both variables are nominal, we know that the most appropriate statistical test is one of the two chi-square tests. Because there are two nominal variables, the most appropriate test is a chi-square test for independence.

18-4 It is important for researchers to report how they determined the size of the sample they used, which rules they planned to follow to eliminate any data points, and which statistical analyses they planned to use—before they even began collecting data. Many scientists preregister these details of their study, posting them online to demonstrate that they had a plan before they began.

18-5 Researchers should include summary statistics, the results of traditional statistical analyses, any relevant new statistics, and tables or graphs as necessary to highlight or clarify findings

18-6 a. Methods

b. Methods

c. Results

d. Results

e. Methods

f. Results

18-7 a. The researchers likely chose statistical power of 80% because it is the standard in the field. They may have chosen a Cohen's *d* of 0.4 because it is close to a medium effect or because it is based on previous research. (In this case, it was based on previous research.) It is important to include a power analysis in the research report for two reasons: (1) It ensures that the study will have sufficient power to detect the effect that the researchers hypothesize and (2) especially when preregistered, it prevents the researchers from checking the results after each batch of new participants, then stopping when statistical significance is achieved.

b. The researchers likely preregistered details from their power analysis that determined their sample size, any decision rules about how they would decide to delete data, and their statistical analysis plans.

c. These authors could earn the Open Materials badge because they are providing researchers with the materials and information necessary to replicate this study.

d. The *d* refers to Cohen's *d*, the effect size. It indicates a small-to-medium negative effect, which means that participants who used their phones had somewhat lower average well-being than those who did not, assuming that this result was statistically significant. *CI* refers to the 95% confidence interval around this effect size. It is plausible that an actual effect size that falls between −0.43 and −0.12. 0 is in the confidence interval, so it is not plausible that there is no effect. This information would be reported in the Results section of the manuscript.

GLOSSARY

A

adjusted standardized residual The difference between the observed frequency and the expected frequency for a cell in a chi-square research design, divided by the standard error. Also called *adjusted residual*.

adjusted r^2 A less biased and more conservative estimate of effect size for the regression equation than is *r*.

alpha level The probability used to determine the critical values, or cutoffs, in hypothesis testing; often called *p* level.

analysis of covariance (ANCOVA) A type of ANOVA in which a covariate is included so that statistical findings reflect effects after a scale variable has been statistically removed.

analysis of variance (ANOVA) A hypothesis test typically used with one or more nominal and sometimes ordinal independent variables (with at least three groups overall) and a scale dependent variable.

assumption A characteristic that we ideally require the population from which we are sampling to have so that we can make accurate inferences.

B

bar graph A visual depiction of data when the independent variable is nominal or ordinal and the dependent variable is scale. The height of each bar typically represents the average value of the dependent variable for each category.

base rate The underlying probability of a particular occurrence.

between-groups ANOVA A hypothesis test in which there are more than two samples, and each sample is composed of different participants.

between-groups research design An experimental design in which participants experience one, and only one, level of the independent variable.

between-groups variance An estimate of the population variance based on the differences among the means.

big data Very large data sets on which researchers harness computer technology to perform large numbers of statistical analyses, often without hypotheses guiding which analyses are conducted.

bimodal A term describing a distribution that has two modes, or most common scores.

Bonferroni test A post hoc test that provides a more strict critical value for every comparison of means; sometimes called the *Bonferroni correction, Bonferroni adjustment,* or *Dunn Multiple Comparison test.*

bubble graph A graph that resembles a scatterplot, but the dots are replaced by bubbles that can represent additional variables through their color and size.

C

ceiling effect A situation in which a constraint prevents a variable from taking on values above a given number.

cell A box that depicts one unique combination of levels of the independent variables in a factorial design.

central limit theorem The idea that a distribution of sample means is a more normal distribution than a distribution of scores, even when the population distribution is not normal.

central tendency A descriptive statistic that best represents the center of a data set, the particular value that all the other data seem to be gathering around.

chartjunk Any unnecessary information or feature in a graph that distracts from a viewer's ability to understand the data.

chi-square test for goodness-of-fit A nonparametric hypothesis test used when there is one nominal variable.

chi-square test for independence A nonparametric hypothesis test used when there are two nominal variables.

coefficient alpha A commonly used estimate of a test's or measure's reliability, or internal consistency, calculated by taking the average of all possible split-half correlations; symbolized as α; sometimes called *Cronbach's alpha.*

Cohen's *d* A measure of effect size that expresses the difference between two means in terms of standard deviation.

confidence interval An interval estimate, based on the sample statistic, that includes the population mean a certain percentage of the time if we sampled from the same population repeatedly.

confirmation bias Our usually unintentional tendency to pay attention to evidence that confirms what we already believe and to ignore evidence that would disconfirm our beliefs. Confirmation biases closely follow illusory correlations.

confounding variable A variable that systematically varies with the independent variable so that we cannot logically determine which variable is at work; also called a *confound.*

constraints on generality (COG) statement A statement about the target population to which the study results are expected to generalize.

continuous observation Observed data point that can take on a full range of values (i.e., numbers out to many decimal points); an infinite number of potential values exists.

control group A level of the independent variable that is designed to match the experimental group in all ways but the experimental manipulation itself.

convenience sample A subset of a population whose members are chosen strictly because they are readily available.

correlation An association between two or more variables.

correlation coefficient A statistic that quantifies a relation between two variables.

counterbalancing The minimization of order effects by varying the order of presentation of different levels of the independent variable from one participant to the next.

covariate A scale variable that we suspect associates, or covaries, with the independent variable of interest.

Cramér's *V* The standard effect size used with the chi-square test for independence; also called *Cramer's phi*, symbolized as *Φ*.

critical region The area in the tails of the comparison distribution in which we reject the null hypothesis if our test statistic falls there.

critical value A test statistic value beyond which we reject the null hypothesis; often called a *cutoff*.

crowdsourcing When a researcher solicits input from a very large group of people, usually recruited online.

D

data ethics A set of principles related to all stages of working with data—research design, data collection, statistical analyses, interpretation of analyses, and reporting of outcomes.

defaults The options that a software designer has preselected. They are the built-in decisions that the software will implement if you do not instruct it otherwise.

degrees of freedom The number of scores that are free to vary when estimating a population parameter from a sample.

dependent variable The outcome variable that we hypothesize to be related to, or caused by, changes in the independent variable.

descriptive statistic Statistical technique used to organize, summarize, and communicate a group of numerical observations.

deviation from the mean The amount that a score in a sample differs from the mean of the sample; also called *deviation*.

discrete observation Observed data point that can take on only specific values (e.g., whole numbers); no other values can exist between these numbers.

distribution of means A distribution composed of many means that are calculated from all possible samples of a given size, all taken from the same population.

dot plot A graph that displays each data point in a sample, with the range of scores along the *x*-axis and a dot for each data point above the appropriate value.

duck A form of chartjunk in which a feature of the data has been dressed up in a graph to be something other than merely data.

E

effect size A standardized value that indicates the size of a difference and is unaffected by sample size.

error bars Vertical lines added to bars or dots on a graph that represent the variability of those data and give us a sense of how precise an estimate a summary statistic is.

expected relative-frequency probability The likelihood of an event occurring based on the actual outcome of many, many trials.

experiment A study in which participants are randomly assigned to a condition or level of one or more independent variables.

experimental group A level of the independent variable that receives the treatment or intervention of interest in an experiment.

F

F statistic A ratio of two measures of variance: (1) between-groups variance, which indicates differences among sample means, and (2) within-groups variance, which is essentially an average of the sample variances.

factor A term used to describe an independent variable in a study with more than one independent variable.

factorial ANOVA A statistical analysis used with one scale dependent variable and at least two nominal independent variables (also called *factors*); also called a *multifactorial ANOVA*.

file drawer analysis A statistical calculation, following a meta-analysis, of the number of studies with null results that would have to exist so that a mean effect size would no longer be statistically significant.

first quartile The 25th percentile of a data set.

floor effect A situation in which a constraint prevents a variable from taking on values below a certain point.

forest plot This shows the confidence interval for the effect size of every study.

frequency distribution A distribution that describes the pattern of a set of numbers by displaying a count or proportion for each possible value of a variable.

frequency table A visual depiction of data that shows how often each value occurred—that is, how many scores were at each value. Values are listed in the first column, and the numbers of individuals with scores at that value are listed in the second column.

G

generalizability Researchers' ability to apply findings from one sample or in one context to other samples or contexts; also called *external validity*.

grand mean The mean of every score in a study, regardless of which sample the score came from.

grid A form of chartjunk that takes the form of a background pattern, almost like graph paper, on which the data representations, such as bars, are superimposed.

grouped frequency table A visual depiction of data that reports the frequencies within a given interval rather than the frequencies for a specific value.

H

HARKing, or "(H)ypothesizing (A)fter the (R)esults are (K)nown," is an unethical practice in which researchers change their hypotheses to match their findings.

heteroscedastic A term given to populations that have different variances.

histogram A graph that looks like a bar graph but depicts just one variable, usually based on scale data, with the values of the variable on the x-axis and the frequencies on the y-axis.

homoscedastic A term given to populations that have the same variance; also called *homogeneity of variance*.

hypothesis testing The process of drawing conclusions about whether a particular relation between variables is supported by the evidence.

I

illusory correlation The phenomenon of believing that one sees an association between variables when no such association exists.

independent variable A variable that we either manipulate or observe to determine its effects on the dependent variable.

independent-samples t test A hypothesis test used to compare two means for a between-groups design, a situation in which each participant is assigned to only one condition.

inferential statistic Statistical technique that uses sample data to make estimates about the larger population.

interaction The statistical result achieved in a factorial design when two or more independent variables have an effect on the dependent variable in combination that neither independent variable has on its own.

intercept The predicted value for Y when X is equal to 0, the point at which the line crosses, or intercepts, the y-axis.

interquartile range A measure of the difference between the first and third quartiles of a data set.

interval estimate An estimate based on a sample statistic, providing a range of plausible values for the population parameter.

interval variable A variable used for observations that have numbers as their values; the distance (or interval) between pairs of consecutive numbers is assumed to be equal.

K

Kruskal–Wallis H test A nonparametric hypothesis test used when there are more than two groups, a between-groups design, and an ordinal dependent variable.

L

level A discrete value or condition that a variable can take on.

line graph A graph used to illustrate the relation between two scale variables; sometimes the line represents the predicted y scores for each x value, and sometimes the line represents change in a variable over time.

linear relation A relation between two variables best described by a straight line.

M

main effect A result occurring in a factorial design when one of the independent variables has an influence on the dependent variable.

Mann–Whitney U test A nonparametric hypothesis test used when there are two groups, a between-groups design, and an ordinal dependent variable.

marginal mean The mean of a row or a column in a table that shows the cells of a study with a two-way ANOVA design.

mean The arithmetic average of a group of scores. It is calculated by summing all the scores and dividing by the total number of scores.

median The middle score of all the scores in a sample when the scores are arranged in ascending order. If there is no single middle score, the median is the mean of the two middle scores.

meta-analysis A study that involves the calculation of a mean effect size from the individual effect sizes of more than one study.

mixed-design ANOVA A hypothesis test used to analyze the data from a study with at least two independent variables; at least one variable must be within-groups and at least one variable must be between-groups.

mode The most common score of all the scores in a sample.

moiré vibrations Any patterns in a graph that create a distracting impression of vibration and movement; a form of chartjunk.

multimodal A term for a distribution that has more than two modes, or most common scores.

multiple regression A statistical technique that includes two or more predictor variables in a prediction equation.

multivariate analysis of covariance (MANCOVA) An ANOVA with multiple dependent variables and the inclusion of a covariate.

multivariate analysis of variance (MANOVA) A form of ANOVA in which there is more than one dependent variable.

N

negative correlation An association between two variables in which participants with high scores on one variable tend to have low scores on the other variable.

negatively skewed data An asymmetric distribution whose tail extends to the left, in a negative direction.

nominal variable A variable used for observations that have categories, or names, as their values.

nonlinear relation A relation between variables best described by a line that breaks or curves in some way.

nonparametric test An inferential statistical analysis that is not based on a set of assumptions about the population.

normal curve A specific bell-shaped curve that is unimodal, symmetric, and defined mathematically.

normal distribution A specific frequency distribution in the shape of a bell-shaped, symmetric, unimodal curve.

null hypothesis A statement that postulates that there is no difference between populations or that the difference is in a direction opposite of that anticipated by the researcher.

O

omega squared (ω^2) An estimate of the proportion of variance in the dependent variable that is accounted for by the independent variable; it is less biased than other estimates of effect size.

one-tailed test A hypothesis test in which the research hypothesis is directional, positing either a mean decrease or a mean increase in the dependent variable, but not both, as a result of the independent variable.

one-way ANOVA A hypothesis test that includes one nominal independent variable with more than two levels and a scale dependent variable.

open science An approach to research that encourages collaboration and includes the sharing of research methodology, data, and statistical analyses in ways that allow others to question and even to try to recreate findings.

operational definition The operations or procedures used to measure or manipulate a variable.

order effects The effects produced when a participant's behavior changes when the dependent variable is presented for a second time; also called *practice effects*.

ordinal variable A variable used for observations that have rankings (i.e., 1st, 2nd, 3rd, . . .) as their values.

orthogonal variable A predictor variable that makes a separate and distinct contribution to the prediction of an outcome variable, as compared with the contributions of another variable.

outcome In reference to probability, the result of a trial.

outlier An extreme score that is either very high or very low in comparison with the rest of the scores in a sample.

P

***p* value** The probability of finding this particular test statistic, or one even larger, if the null hypothesis is true—that is, if there is no difference between means.

***p*-hacking** The use of questionable research practices to increase the chances of achieving a statistically significant result.

paired-samples *t* test A test used to compare two means for a within-groups design, a situation in which every participant is in both samples; also called a *dependent-samples* t *test*.

parameter A number based on the whole population; it is usually symbolized by a Greek letter.

parametric test An inferential statistical analysis based on a set of assumptions about the population.

Pareto chart A type of bar graph in which the categories along the *x*-axis are ordered from highest bar on the left to lowest bar on the right.

partial correlation A technique that quantifies the degree of association between two variables that remains when the correlations of these two variables with a third variable are mathematically eliminated.

Pearson correlation coefficient A statistic that quantifies a linear relation between two scale variables.

personal probability A person's own judgment about the likelihood that an event will occur; also called *subjective probability*.

pictorial graph A visual depiction of data typically used for an independent variable with very few levels (categories) and a scale dependent variable. Each level uses a picture or symbol to represent its value on the scale dependent variable.

pie chart A graph in the shape of a circle with a slice for every level (category). The size of each slice represents the proportion (or percentage) of each level.

point estimate A summary statistic from a sample that is just one number used as an estimate of the population parameter.

pooled variance A weighted average of the two estimates of variance—one from each sample—that are calculated when conducting an independent-samples *t* test.

population All possible observations about which we would like to know something.

positive correlation An association between two variables such that participants with high scores on one variable tend to have high scores on the other variable as well, and those with low scores on one variable tend to have low scores on the other variable.

positively skewed data An asymmetric data distribution whose tail extends to the right, in a positive direction.

post hoc test A statistical procedure frequently carried out after the null hypothesis has been rejected in an analysis of variance; it allows us to make multiple comparisons among several means; often referred to as a *follow-up test*.

posterior The redistribution of belief after collecting the data.

preregistration A recommended open science practice in which researchers outline their research design and analysis plan before conducting a study.

prior A distribution that reflects the credibility or likelihood of the various values along the x-axis before we collect data.

probability The likelihood that a certain outcome will occur out of all possible outcomes.

proportionate reduction in error A statistic that quantifies how much more accurate predictions are when we use the regression line instead of the mean as a prediction tool; also called *coefficient of determination*.

psychometricians The statisticians and psychologists who develop tests and measures.

psychometrics The branch of statistics used in the development of tests and measures.

Q

qualitative interaction An interaction of two (or more) independent variables in which one independent variable reverses its effect depending on the level of the other independent variable.

quantitative interaction An interaction in which the effect of one independent variable is strengthened or weakened at one or more levels of the other independent variable, but the direction of the initial effect does not change.

R

R^2 The proportion of variance in the dependent variable that is accounted for by the independent variable.

random assignment The protocol established for an experiment whereby every participant in a study has an equal chance of being assigned to any of the groups, or experimental conditions, in the study.

random sample A subset of a population selected using a method that ensures that every member of the population has an equal chance of being selected into the study.

range A measure of variability calculated by subtracting the lowest score (the minimum) from the highest score (the maximum).

ratio variable A variable that meets the criteria for an interval variable but also has a meaningful zero point.

raw score A data point that has not yet been transformed or analyzed.

regression to the mean The tendency of scores that are particularly high or low to drift toward the mean over time.

relative risk A measure created by making a ratio of two conditional proportions; also called *relative likelihood* or *relative chance*.

reliability The consistency of a measure.

replication The duplication of scientific results, ideally in a different context or with a sample that has different characteristics.

research hypothesis A statement that postulates that there is a difference between populations or sometimes, more specifically, that there is a difference in a certain direction, positive or negative; also called an *alternative hypothesis*.

robust A term given to a hypothesis test that produces fairly accurate results even when the data suggest that the population might not meet some of the assumptions.

S

sample A set of observations drawn from the population of interest.

scale variable A variable that meets the criteria for an interval variable or a ratio variable.

scatterplot A graph that depicts the relation between two scale variables. The values of each variable are marked along the two axes, and a mark is made to indicate the intersection of the two scores for each participant.

simple linear regression A statistical tool that lets us predict a person's score on an outcome variable from his or her score on one predictor variable.

single-sample t test A hypothesis test in which we compare a sample from which we collect data to a population for which we know the mean but not the standard deviation.

skewed distribution A distribution in which one of the tails of the distribution is pulled away from the center.

slope The amount that Y is predicted to increase for an increase of one unit in X.

source table A table that presents the important calculations and final results of an ANOVA in a consistent and easy-to-read format.

Spearman rank-order correlation coefficient A nonparametric statistic that quantifies the association between two ordinal variables.

spurious correlation A correlation in which two variables vary together, but there is no connection between the variables; their quantitative association being due purely to chance.

square root transformation A transformation that reduces skew by compressing both the negative and positive sides of a skewed distribution.

standard deviation The square root of the average of the squared deviations from the mean; the typical amount that each score varies, or deviates, from the mean.

standard error The name for the standard deviation of a distribution of means.

standard error of the estimate A statistic indicating the average vertical distance between a regression line and the actual data points.

standard normal distribution A normal distribution of z scores.

standardization A way to convert individual scores from different normal distributions to a shared normal distribution with a known mean, standard deviation, and percentiles.

standardized regression coefficient A standardized version of the slope in a regression equation, it is the predicted change in the outcome variable in terms of standard deviations for an increase of 1 standard deviation in the dependent variable; symbolized by β and often called the *beta weight*.

statistic A number based on a sample taken from a population; it is usually symbolized by a Latin letter.

statistically significant A term for a finding in which the data differ from what we would expect by chance if there were, in fact, no actual difference.

statistical power A measure of the likelihood that we will reject the null hypothesis given that the null hypothesis is false.

success In reference to probability, the outcome for which we're trying to determine the probability.

sum of squares The sum of each score's squared deviation from the mean. Symbolized as *SS*.

T

t **statistic** A statistic that indicates the distance of a sample mean from a population mean in terms of the standard error.

test–retest reliability A term that refers to whether the scale being used provides consistent information every time the test is taken.

third quartile The 75th percentile of a data set.

time plot or time series plot A graph that plots a scale variable on the y-axis as it changes over an increment of time (e.g., second, day, century) labeled on the x-axis.

trial In reference to probability, each occasion that a given procedure is carried out.

Tukey *HSD* test A widely used post hoc test that determines the differences between means in terms of standard error; the *HSD* is compared to a critical value; sometimes called the *q test*.

two-tailed test A hypothesis test in which the research hypothesis does not indicate a direction of the mean difference or change in the dependent variable, but merely indicates that there will be a mean difference.

two-way ANOVA A hypothesis test that includes two nominal independent variables, regardless of their numbers of levels, and a scale dependent variable.

Type I error The result of rejecting the null hypothesis when the null hypothesis is correct.

Type II error The result of failing to reject the null hypothesis when the null hypothesis is false.

U

unimodal A term for a distribution that has one mode, or most common score.

V

validity The extent to which a test actually measures what it was intended to measure.

variability A numerical way of describing how much spread there is in a distribution.

variable Any observation of a physical, attitudinal, or behavioral characteristic that can take on different values.

variance The average of the squared deviations from the mean.

violin plot A graph shaped like a violin that includes information about a distribution's middle score and overall variability.

volunteer sample A special kind of convenience sample in which participants actively choose to participate in a study; also called a *self-selected sample*.

W

WEIRD samples Samples of participants from countries that represent a small portion of the world's population, countries that are Western, Educated, Industrialized, Rich, and Democratic.

Wilcoxon signed-rank test A nonparametric hypothesis test for matched pairs used when there are two groups, a within-groups design, and an ordinal dependent variable.

within-groups ANOVA A hypothesis test in which there are more than two samples, and each sample is composed of the same participants; also called a *repeated-measures ANOVA*.

within-groups research design An experimental design in which all participants in the study experience the different levels of the independent variable; also called a *repeated-measures design*.

within-groups variance An estimate of the population variance based on the differences within each of the three (or more) sample distributions.

Z

z **distribution** A normal distribution of standardized scores.

z **score** The number of standard deviations a particular score is from the mean.

REFERENCES

Acerbi, A., Lampos, V., Garnett, P., & Bentley, R. A. (2013). The expression of emotions in 20th century books. *PLOS One, 8,* e59030.

Adams, C., Coffee, P., & Lavallee, D. (2015). Athletes' perceptions about the availability of social support during within-career transitions. *Sport and Exercise Psychology Review, 11,* 37–48.

Adams, J. (2012). Consideration of immediate and future consequences, smoking status, and body mass index. *Health Psychology, 31,* 260–263.

Agresti, A., & Franklin, C. (2006). *Statistics: The art and science of learning from data.* Upper Saddle River, NJ: Prentice Hall.

Akan, M., Stanley, S. E., & Benjamin, A. S. (2018). Testing enhances memory for context. *Journal of Memory and Language, 103,* 19–27. https://doi.org/10.1016/j.jml.2018.07.003

Albers, C., & Lakens, D. (2018). When power analyses based on pilot data are biased: Inaccurate effect size estimators and follow-up bias. *Journal of Experimental Social Psychology, 74,* 187–195. https://doi.org/10.1016/j.jesp.2017.09.004

Alter, A., & Oppenheimer, D. (2006). Predicting short-term stock fluctuations by using processing fluency. *Proceedings of the National Academy of Sciences of the United States of America, 103,* 9369–9372.

Ambrose, S. A., & Lovett, M. C. (2014). Prior knowledge is more important than content: Skills and beliefs also impact learning. In V. A. Benassi, C. E. Overson, & C. M. Hakala (Eds.), *Applying science of learning in education: Infusing psychological science into the curriculum.* Retrieved from http://teachpsych.org/ebooks/asle2014/index.php.

American Academy of Physician Assistants. (2005). Income reported by PAs who graduated in 2004. Retrieved from http://www.aapa.org/research/05newgrad-income.pdf

American Civil Liberties Union. (2013). Report: The war on marijuana in black and white. Retrieved from https://www.aclu.org/report/report-war-marijuana-black-and-white?redirect=criminal-law-reform/war-marijuana-black-and-white

American Psychological Association (APA). (2010). *Publication manual of the American Psychological Association* (6th ed.). Washington, DC: Author.

Anderson, C. (2008). The end of theory: The data deluge makes the scientific method obsolete. Retrieved from https://www.wired.com/2008/06/pb-theory/

Anderson, C. J., Bahník, Š., Barnett-Cowan, M., Bosco, F. A., Chandler, J., Chartier, C. R., . . . Zuni, K. (2016). Response to Comment on "Estimating the reproducibility of psychological science." *Science, 351,* 1037-c.

Anderson, S. F., Kelley, K., & Maxwell, S. E. (2017). Sample-size planning for more accurate statistical power: A method adjusting sample effect sizes for publication bias and uncertainty. *Psychological Science, 28,* 1547–1562.

Andrews, I., & Kasy, M. (2017). *Identification of and correction for publication bias* (No. w23298). Cambridge, MA: National Bureau of Economic Research.

Andrews, M., & Baguley, T. (2013). Prior approval: The growth of Bayesian methods in psychology. *British Journal of Mathematical and Statistical Psychology, 66*(1), 1–7. https://doi.org/10.1111/bmsp.12004

Angwin, J., Larson, J., Mattu, S., & Kirchner, L. (2016, May 23). Machine bias. *ProPublica.* Retrieved from https://www.propublica.org/article/machine-bias-risk-assessments-in-criminal-sentencing

Apfel, L. (2019, February 1). Want lasting love? First, take this test. *The New York Times.* Retrieved from https://www.nytimes.com/2019/02/01/style/modern-love-myers-briggs-personality-test.html

Appelbaum, M., Cooper, H., Kline, R. B., Mayo-Wilson, E., Nezu, A. M., & Rao, S. M. (2018). Journal article reporting standards for quantitative research in psychology: The APA Publications and Communications Board task force report. *American Psychologist, 73,* 3–25. doi: 10.1037/amp0000191

Arnett, J. J. (2008). The neglected 95%: Why American psychology needs to become less American. *American Psychologist, 63,* 602–614. https://doi.org/10.1037/0003-066X.63.7.602

Arcidiacono, P., Bayer, P., & Hizmo, A. (2008). *Beyond signaling and human capital* (NBER Working Paper No. 13591). Cambridge, MA: National Bureau of Economic Research. Retrieved from http://www.nber.org/papers/w13951.

Aron, A., & Aron, E. N. (2002). *Statistics for psychology* (3rd ed.). Upper Saddle River, NJ: Pearson Education.

Aron, A., Fisher, H., Mashek, D. J., Strong, G., Li, H., & Brown, L. L. (2005). Reward, motivation, and emotion systems associated with early-stage intense romantic love. *Journal of Neurophysiology, 94,* 327–337.

Asano, E. (2017, January 4). How much time do people spend on social media? [Infographic]. *Social Media Today.* Retrieved from https://www.socialmediatoday.com/marketing/how-much-time-do-people-spend-social-media-infographic

Asher, J. (2018, September 21). A rise in murder? Let's talk about the weather. *The New York Times.* Retrieved from https://www.nytimes.com/2018/09/21/upshot/a-rise-in-murder-lets-talk-about-the-weather.html

Association for Psychological Science (APS). (2017, September 19). "A genius in the art of living": Industrial psychology pioneer Lillian Gilbreth. Retrieved from https://www.psychologicalscience.org/publications/observer/obsonline/a-genius-in-the-art-of-living-lillian-moller-gilbreth-industrial-psychology-pioneer.html

Atkinson, R. K., Derry, S. J., Renkl, A., & Wortham, D. (2000). Learning from examples: Instructional principles from the worked examples research. *Review of Educational Research, 70,* 181–214. https://doi-org.ezproxy.shu.edu/10.3102/00346543070002181

Ayaz, H., Shewokis, P. A., Bunce, S., Izzetoglu, K., Willems, B., & Onaral, B. (2012). Optical brain monitoring for operator training and mental workload assessment. *Neuroimage, 59,* 36–47.

Azim, E., Mobbs, D., Jo, B., Menon, V., & Reiss, A. L. (2005). Sex differences in brain activation elicited by humor. *Proceedings of the National Academy of Sciences, 102,* 16496–16501. Retrieved from http://www.pnas.org/cgi/doi/10.1073/pnas.0408456102

Badenes-Ribera, L., Frias-Navarro, D., Iotti, N. O., Bonilla-Campos, A., & Longobardi, C. (2018, June). Perceived statistical knowledge level and self-reported statistical practice among academic psychologists. *Frontiers in Psychology, 9*. https://doi.org/10.3389/fpsyg.2018.00996

Bai, H. (2018). Evidence that a large amount of low quality responses on MTurk can be detected with repeated GPS coordinates. Retrieved from https://www.maxhuibai.com/blog/evidence-that-responses-from-repeating-gps-are-random

Baker, D. A., & Algorta, G. P. (2016). The relationship between online social networking and depression: A systematic review of quantitative studies. *Cyberpsychology, Behavior, and Social Networking, 19*(11), 638–648. https://doi.org/10.1089/cyber.2016.0206

Banks, J., Marmot, M., Oldfield, Z., & Smith, J. P. (2006). Disease and disadvantage in the United States and England. *Journal of the American Medical Association, 295,* 2037–2045.

Barac, R., & Bialystok, E. (2012). Bilingual effects on cognitive and linguistic development: Role of language, cultural background, and education. *Child Development, 83,* 413–422.

Baranski, E. (2015, January 22). It's all happening: The future of crowdsourcing science. *Open Science Collaboration.* Retrieved from http://osc.centerforopenscience.org/2015/01/22/crowdsourcing-science/

Bardwell, W. A., Ensign, W. Y., & Mills, P. J. (2005). Negative mood endures after completion of high-altitude military training. *Annals of Behavioral Medicine, 29,* 64–69.

Barkhorn, E. (2012). The word that gets women negotiating their salaries: Negotiate. *The Atlantic.* Retrieved from http://www.theatlantic.com/sexes/archive/2012/11/the-word-that-gets-women-negotiating-their-salaries-negotiate/264567/

Barrett, L. F. (2015, September 1). Psychology is not in crisis. *The New York Times.* Retrieved from https://www.nytimes.com/2015/09/01/opinion/psychology-is-not-in-crisis.html

Barron, J. (2016, March 31). Letter of recommendation: Segmented sleep. *The New York Times.* Retrieved from https://www.nytimes.com/2016/04/03/magazine/letter-of-recommendation-segmented-sleep.html

Barry-Jester, A. M., Casselman, B., & Goldstein, D. (2015, August 4). The new science of sentencing: Should prison sentences be based on crimes that haven't been committed yet? *The Marshall Project.* Retrieved from https://www.themarshallproject.org/2015/08/04/the-new-science-of-sentencing

Bartlett, T. (2014, June 23). Replication crisis in psychology research turns ugly and odd. *The Chronicle of Higher Education.* Retrieved from https://www.chronicle.com/article/Replication-Crisis-in/147301

Becker, E. S., Barth, A., Smits, J. A. J., Beisel, S., Lindenmeyer, J., & Rinck, M. (2019). Positivity-approach training for depressive symptoms: A randomized controlled trial. *Journal of Affective Disorders, 245,* 297–304. https://doi.org/10.1016/j.jad.2018.11.042

Begg, C. B. (1994). Publication bias. In H. Cooper & L. V. Hedges (Eds.), *The handbook of research synthesis* (pp. 399–409). New York, NY: Russell Sage Foundation.

Begley, C. G., & Ellis, L. M. (2012). Drug development: Raise standards for preclinical cancer research. *Nature, 483*(7391), 531–533. https://doi.org/10.1038/485041e

Behenam, M., & Pooya, O. (2006). Factors affecting patients cooperation during orthodontic treatment. *The Orthodontic Cyber Journal.* Retrieved from http://www.oc-j.com/nov06/cooperation.htm

Bem, D. J. (2011). Feeling the future: Experimental evidence for anomalous retroactive influences on cognition and affect. *Journal of Personality and Social Psychology, 100*(3), 407–425. https://doi.org/10.1037/a0021524

Ben. (2018, January 3). Which is better, the IELTS or the TOEFL test? *Peterson's.* Retrieved from https://www.petersons.com/blog/which-is-better-the-ielts-or-the-toefl-test/

Benassi, V. A., Overson, C. E., & Hakala, C. M. (2014). *Applying the science of learning in education: Infusing psychological science into the curriculum.* Retrieved from http://teachpsych.org/ebooks/asle2014/index.php.

Benbow, C. P., & Stanley, J. C. (1980). Sex differences in math ability: Fact or artifact? *Science, 210,* 1262–1264.

Benefits Canada. (2018, July 30). 71% of global employers offer wellness programs: Survey. Retrieved from https://www.benefitscanada.com/

Bennhold, K. (2015, October 9). London police "super recognizer" walks beat with a Facebook of the mind. *The New York Times.* Retrieved from https://www.nytimes.com/2015/10/10/world/europe/london-police-super-recognizer-walks-beat-with-a-facebook-of-the-mind.html

Bensinger, G. (2014). Amazon wants to ship your package before you buy it. *The Wall Street Journal.* Retrieved from https://blogs.wsj.com/digits/2014/01/17/amazon-wants-to-ship-your-package-before-you-buy-it/

Bernasek, A. (2014, November 6). Disc connect: In this visual age, vinyl records are making more noise [Infographic]. *Newsweek.* Retrieved from https://www.newsweek.com/2014/11/14/two-numbers-vinyl-records-are-back-282604.html

Bernstein, P. L. (1996). *Against the gods: The remarkable story of risk.* New York, NY: Wiley.

Bilton, N. (2013) Disruptions: Data without context tells a misleading story. *The New York Times.* Retrieved from http://bits.blogs.nytimes.com/2013/02/24/disruptions-google-flu-trends-shows-problems-of-big-data-without-context/

Bittman, M. (2013). It's the sugar, folks. *The New York Times.* Retrieved from https://opinionator.blogs.nytimes.com/2013/02/27/its-the-sugar-folks/

Bittner, J. (2011, August 16). How much to charge your roommate's girlfriend? *Forbes.* Retrieved from https://www.forbes.com/sites/jonbittner/2011/08/16/how-much-to-charge-your-roommates-girlfriend/

Bless, H., & Burger, A. M. (2016). A closer look at social psychologists' silver bullet: Inevitable and evitable side effects of the experimental approach. *Perspectives on Psychological Science, 11,* 296–308. https://doi.org/10.1177/1745691615621278

Bohannon, J. (2016). Mechanical Turk upends social sciences. *Science, 352,* 1263–1264. https://doi.org/10.1126/science.352.6291.1263

Bojo, A. (2017, February 16). Cat brothers separated for 2 years first find each other when their humans started dating... *Love Meow.* Retrieved from https://www.lovemeow.com/cat-brothers-separated-for-2-years-find-each-other-when-their-humans-s-2266388942.html

Bollinger, B., Leslie, P., & Sorensen, A. (2010). *Calorie posting in chain restaurants* (NBER Working Paper No. 15648). Cambridge, MA:

National Bureau of Economic Research. Retrieved from http://www.gsb.stanford.edu/news/StarbucksCaloriePostingStudy.pdf

Boone, D. E. (1992). WAIS-R scatter with psychiatric inpatients: I. Intrasubtest scatter. *Psychological Reports, 71,* 483–487.

Borsari, B., & Carey, K. B. (2005). Two brief alcohol interventions for mandated college students. *Psychology of Addictive Behaviors, 19,* 296–302.

Boydstun, A. E., Ledgerwood, A., & Sparks, J. (2019). A negativity bias in reframing shapes political preferences even in partisan contexts. *Social Psychological and Personality Science, 10,* 53–61. https://doi.org/10.1177/1948550617733520

Bressan, D. (2018, August 21). Lake Nyos and other "killer lakes" of Africa: A rare but dangerous volcanic phenomenon. *Forbes.* Retrieved from https://www.forbes.com/sites/davidbressan/2018/08/21/lake-nyos-and-other-killer-lakes-of-africa-a-rare-but-dangerous-volcanic-phenomenon/

Brinthaupt, T. M., & Ananth, P. (2018). Teaching students to speak fluent "research." *Scholarship of Teaching and Learning in Psychology, 4,* 258–270. http://dx.doi.org/10.1037/stl0000128

Buckley, C. (2013, February 6). Storm's toll creeps inland, 4 tiny feet at a time. *The New York Times.* Retrieved from http://www.nytimes.com/2013/02/07/nyregion/after-storm-rats-creep-inland.html.

Buekens, P., Xiong, X., & Harville, E. (2006). Hurricanes and pregnancy. *Birth, 33,* 91–93.

Buhrmester, M., Kwang, T., & Gosling, S. D. (2011). Amazon's Mechanical Turk a new source of inexpensive, yet high-quality, data. *Perspectives on Psychological Science, 6*(1), 3–5.

Buhrmester, M. D., Talaifar, S., & Gosling, S. D. (2018). An evaluation of Amazon's Mechanical Turk, its rapid rise, and its effective use. *Perspectives on Psychological Science, 13,* 149–154. https://doi.org/10.1177/1745691617706516

Busseri, M. A., Choma, B. L., & Sadava, S. W. (2009). "As good as it gets" or "the best is yet to come"? How optimists and pessimists view their past, present, and anticipated future life satisfaction. *Personality and Individual Differences, 47,* 352–356. doi:10.1016/j.paid.209.04.002

Button, K. S., Ioannidis, J. P. A., Mokrysz, C., Nosek, B. A., Flint, J., Robinson, E. S. J., & Munafò, M. R. (2013). Power failure: Why small sample size undermines the reliability of neuroscience. *Nature Reviews Neuroscience, 14*(5), 365–376. https://doi.org/10.1038/nrn3475

Calude, C. S., & Longo, G. (2017). The deluge of spurious correlations in big data. *Foundations of Science, 22*(3), 595–612.

Can Facebook predict your breakup? (2010). *The Week.* Retrieved from http://theweek.com/article/index/203122/can-facebook-predict-your-breakup

Caramanica, J. (2018, August 20). Nicki Minaj and Travis Scott fumble toward yesterday's prize: A no. 1 album. *The New York Times.* Retrieved from https://www.nytimes.com/2018/08/20/arts/music/nicki-minaj-travis-scott-queen-astroworld.html

Carey, B. (2015, August 29). Psychologists welcome analysis casting doubt on their work. *The New York Times.* Retrieved from http://www.nytimes.com/2015/08/29/science/psychologists-welcome-analysis-casting-doubt-on-their-work.html

Carey, B. (2018, July 16). Psychology itself is under scrutiny. *The New York Times.* Retrieved from https://www.nytimes.com/2018/07/16/health/psychology-studies-stanford-prison.html

Carey, S. (2015). Mapping the united swears of America [Blog post.]. Retrieved from https://stronglang.wordpress.com/2015/07/28/mapping-the-united-swears-of-america/

Carney, D. R., Cuddy, A. J. C., & Yap, A. J. (2010). Power posing: Brief nonverbal displays affect neuroendocrine levels and risk tolerance. *Psychological Science, 21,* 1363–1368. https://doi.org/10.1177/0956797610383437

Carroll, A. (2018, August 6). Workplace wellness programs don't work well: Why some studies show otherwise. *The New York Times.* Retrieved from https://www.nytimes.com/2018/08/06/upshot/employer-wellness-programs-randomized-trials.html

Carroll, A. E. (2018, August 18). Study causes splash, but here's why you should stay calm on alcohol's risks. *The New York Times.* Retrieved from https://www.nytimes.com/2018/08/28/upshot/alcohol-health-risks-study-worry.html

Carter, B. (2012, February 1). In networks' race for ratings, chicanery is on the schedule. *The New York Times.* Retrieved from http://www.nytimes.com/2012/02/02/business/media/networks-resort-to-trickery-in-an-attempt-to-lift-ratings.html.

Chambers, C. (2017). *The seven deadly sins of psychology: A manifesto for reforming the culture of scientific practice.* Princeton, NJ: Princeton University Press.

Chan, G., & Yanos, P. T. (2018). Media depictions and the priming of mental illness stigma. *Stigma and Health, 3,* 253–264. http://dx.doi.org/10.1037/sah0000095

Chang, A., Sandhofer, C. M., & Brown, C. S. (2011). Gender biases in early number exposure to preschool-aged children. *Journal of Language and Social Psychology, 30,* 440–450. doi:10.1177/0261927X11416207

Chen, Y., & Xie, K. (2017). Consumer valuation of Airbnb listings: A hedonic pricing approach. *International Journal of Contemporary Hospitality Management, 29,* 2405–2424. https://doi.org/10.1108/IJCHM-10-2016-0606

Chopik, W. J., Bremner, R. H., Defever, A. M., & Keller, V. N. (2018). How (and whether) to teach undergraduates about the replication crisis in psychological science. *Teaching of Psychology, 45,* 158–163. https://doi-org.ezproxy.shu.edu/10.1177/0098628318762900

Chou, E. Y. (2015). What's in a name? The toll e-signatures take on individual honesty. *Journal of Experimental Social Psychology, 61,* 84–95. https://doi.org/10.1016/j.jesp.2015.07.010

Christensen, J., Cusick, M., Villanes, A., Veryovka, O., Watson, B., & Rappa, M. (2013). Win, lose or cheat: The analytics of player behaviors in online games. North Carolina State University, Department of Computer Science.

City of Chicago Data Portal. (2017). Retrieved from https://data.cityofchicago.org/Public-Safety/Strategic-Subject-List/4aki-r3np

City of Santa Cruz. (2012, March). Predictive policing. Retrieved from http://www.cityofsantacruz.com/government/city-departments/city-manager/community-relations/city-annual-report/march-2012-newsletter/predictive-policing

Clark, C. M., & Bjork, R. A. (2014). When and why introducing difficulties and errors can enhance instruction. In V. A. Benassi, C. E. Overson, & C. M. Hakala (Eds.), *Applying science of learning in education: Infusing psychological science into the curriculum.* Retrieved from http://teachpsych.org/ebooks/asle2014/index.php.

Cohen, J. (1988). *Statistical power analysis for the behavioral sciences* (2nd ed.). Hillsdale, NJ: Erlbaum.

Cohen, J. (1990). Things I have learned (so far). *American Psychologist, 45,* 1304–1312.

Cohen, J. (1992). A power primer. *Psychological Bulletin, 112,* 155–159.

Common Sense Media. (2015, November 3). Landmark report: U.S. teens use an average of nine hours of media per day, tweens use six hours. Retrieved from https://www.commonsensemedia.org /about-us/news/press-releases/landmark-report-us-teens-use-an -average-of-nine-hours-of-media-per-day

Conn, V. S., Valentine, J. C., Cooper, H. M., & Rantz, M. J. (2003). Grey literature in meta-analyses. *Nursing Research, 52,* 256–261.

Convertino, A. D., Rodgers, R. F., Franko, D. L., & Jodoin, A. (2016). An evaluation of the Aerie Real campaign: Potential for promoting positive body image? *Journal of Health Psychology, 24,* 726–737. doi:10.1177/1359105316680022

Cooper, J. S. (2018). Election surprises: Truman's 1948 victory. Retrieved from https://worldhistory.us/american-history/presidential -history/election-surprises-trumans-1948-victory.php

Cooper, M. J., Gulen, H., & Ovtchinnikov, A. V. (2007). *Corporate political contributions and stock returns.* http://ssrn.com /abstract-940790

Cortina, J. M. (1993). What is coefficient alpha? An examination of theory and applications. *Journal of Applied Psychology, 78,* 98–104.

Coulson, M., Healey, M., Fidler, F., & Cumming, G. (2010). Confidence intervals permit, but do not guarantee, better inference than statistical significance testing. *Frontiers in Psychology: Quantitative Psychology and Measurement, 1,* 1–9. doi:10.3389/fpsyg.2010.00026

Cox, R. H., Thomas, T. R., Hinton, P. S., & Donahue, W. M. (2006). Effects of acute bouts of aerobic exercise of varied intensity on subjective mood experiences in women of different age groups across time. *Journal of Sport Behavior, 29,* 40–59.

Cresswell, J. (2015, October 17). A small Indiana town scarred by a trusted doctor. *The New York Times.* Retrieved from https://www .nytimes.com/2015/10/18/business/a-small-indiana-town-scarred -by-a-trusted-doctor.html

Crouse, K. (2018, February 8). Nathan Chen struggles in Olympic figure skating debut. *The New York Times.* Retrieved from https://www .nytimes.com/2018/02/08/sports/olympics/nathan-chen-figure -skating.html

Cuddy, A. J. (2012). Your body language may shape who you are. *TEDGlobal 2012.* Retrieved from https://www.ted.com/talks/amy _cuddy_your_body_language_shapes_who_you_are?language=en

Cuddy, A. J., Schultz, S. J., & Fosse, N. E. (2018). *P*-curving a more comprehensive body of research on postural feedback reveals clear evidential value for power-posing effects: Reply to Simmons and Simonsohn (2017). *Psychological Science, 29,* 656–666. https://doi .org/10.1177/0956797617746749

Cumming, G. (2012). *Understanding the new statistics: Effect sizes, confidence intervals, and meta-analysis.* New York, NY: Routledge.

Cunliffe, S. (1976). Interaction. *Journal of the Royal Statistical Society, A, 139,* 1–19.

Curran, J., & Takata, S. R. (2002). Getting a sample isn't always easy. Retrieved from http://www5.csudh.edu/dearhabermas/sampling01.htm

Czerwinski, M., Smith, G., Regan, T., Meyers, B., Robertson, G., & Starkweather, G. (2003). Toward characterizing the productivity benefits of very large displays. In M. Rauterberg et al. (Eds.), *Human–computer interaction: INTERACT '03* (pp. 9–16). Amsterdam, Netherlands: IOS Press.

Darlin, D. (2006, July 1). Air fare made easy (or easier). *The New York Times.* Retrieved from https://www.nytimes.com/2006/07/01 /business/01money.html

Dean, G., & Kelly, I. W. (2003). Is astrology relevant to consciousness and PSI? *Journal of Consciousness Studies, 10,* 175–198.

Desjardins, J. (2018, March 29). The relationship between money and happiness. *Visual Capitalist.* Retrieved from http://www.visualcapitalist .com/relationship-money-happiness/

DeSoto, K. A. (2016, February 19). Under the hood of Mechanical Turk. Association for Psychological Science. Retrieved from https:// www.psychologicalscience.org/observer/under-the-hood-of -mechanical-turk

DeVellis, R. F. (1991). *Scale development: Theory and applications.* Newbury Park, CA: Sage.

Diamond, M., & Stone, M. (1981). Nightingale on Quetelet. I: The passionate statistician, II: The marginalia, III. Essay in memoriam. *Journal of the Royal Statistical Society, A,* 144, 66–79, 176–213, 332–351.

Diener, E., & Diener-Biswas, R. (n.d.). The replication crisis in psychology. *Noba Project.* Retrieved from http://nobaproject.com /modules/the-replication-crisis-in-psychology

Dienes, Z., & McLatchie, N. (2018). Four reasons to prefer Bayesian analyses over significance testing. *Psychonomic Bulletin & Review, 25*(1), 207–218. https://doi.org/10.3758/s13423-017-1266-z

Dijksterhuis, A., Bos, M. W., Nordgren, L. F., & van Baaren, R. B. (2006). On making the right choice: The deliberation-without -attention effect. *Science, 311,* 1005–1007.

Ditto, P. H., & Lopez, D. L. (1992). Motivated skepticism: Use of differential decision criteria for preferred and nonpreferred conclusions. *Journal of Personality and Social Psychology, 63,* 568–584.

Domingos, P. (2015). An algorithm might save your life: How the Amazon and Netflix method might someday cure cancer. *Salon.* Retrieved from https://www.salon.com/2015/10/10/an_algorithm _might_save_your_life_how_the_amazon_and_netflix_method_might _someday_cure_cancer/

Djordjevic, J., Lundstrom, J. N., Clement, F., Boyle, J. A., Pouliot, S., & Jones-Gotman, M. (2007). A rose by any other name: Would it smell as sweet? *Journal of Neurophysiology, 99,* 386–393.

Dominus, S. (2017, October 18). When the revolution came for Amy Cuddy. *The New York Times.* Retrieved from https://www.nytimes .com/2017/10/18/magazine/when-the-revolution-came-for-amy -cuddy.html

Donnelly, G. E., Zatz, L. Y., Svirsky, D., & John, L. K. (2018). The effect of graphic warnings on sugary-drink purchasing. *Psychological Science, 29,* 1321–1333. https://doi.org/10.1177 /0956797618766361

Döring, N., Reif, A., & Poeschl, S. (2016). How gender-stereotypical are selfies? A content analysis and comparison with magazine adverts. *Computers in Human Behavior, 55,* 955–962.

Dressel, J., & Farid, H. (2018). The accuracy, fairness, and limits of predicting recidivism. *Science Advances, 4,* eaao5580. https://doi .org/10.1126/sciadv.aao5580

Douma, L., Steverink, N., Hutter, I., & Meijering, L. (2015). Exploring subjective well-being in older age by using participantgenerated word clouds. *The Gerontologist*, 1–11, gnv119. doi:10.1093/geront/gnv119.

Dubner, S. J., & Levitt, S. D. (2006a, May 7). A star is made: The birth-month soccer anomaly. *The New York Times*. Retrieved from https://www.nytimes.com/2006/05/07/magazine/07wwln _freak.html

Dubner, S. J., & Levitt, S. D. (2006b, November 5). The way we live now: Freakonomics; The price of climate change. *The New York Times*. Retrieved from https://www.nytimes.com/2005/12/11/magazine /the-economy-of-desire.html

Duff, A. (2017, October 30). Cat vs. dog popularity in U.S. *data.world*. Dataset id: datanerd/cat-vs-dog-popularity-in-u-s. Retrieved from https://data.world/datanerd/cat-vs-dog-popularity-in-u-s

Duggan, M., & Levitt, S. (2002). Winning isn't everything: Corruption in sumo wrestling. *American Economic Review, 92*, 1594–1605.

Dunn, C. (2013): As 'normal' as rabbits' weights and dragons' wings. *The New York Times*. Retrieved from https://www.nytimes .com/2013/09/24/science/as-normal-as-rabbits-weights-and-dragons -wings.html

Dwyer, R. J., Kushlev, K., & Dunn, E. W. (2018). Smartphone use undermines enjoyment of face-to-face social interactions. *Journal of Experimental Social Psychology, 78*, 233–239. https://doi.org/10.1016 /j.jesp.2017.10.007

Dziak, J. J., Dierker, L. C., & Abar, B. (2018). The interpretation of statistical power after the data have been gathered. *Current Psychology*. https://doi.org/10.1007/s12144-018-0018-1

Elgion, J. & Williams, T. (2015). Police program aims to pinpoint those most likely to commit crimes. *The New York Times*. Retrieved from https://www.nytimes.com/2015/09/25/us/police-program -aims-to-pinpoint-those-most-likely-to-commit-crimes.html

Engle-Friedman, M., Riela, S., Golan, R., Ventuneac, A. M., Davis, C. M., Jefferson, A. D., & Major, D. (2003). The effect of sleep loss on next day effort. *Journal of Sleep Research, 12*, 113–124.

Epskamp, S., & Nuijten, M. B. (2016). Statcheck: Extract statistics from articles and recompute *p* values (R package version 1.2.2). Retrieved from http://CRAN.R-project.org /package=statcheck

Ert, E., Fleischer, A., & Magen, N. (2016). Trust and reputation in the sharing economy: The role of personal photos in Airbnb. *Tourism Management, 55*, 62–73. https://doi.org/10.1016/j. tourman.2016.01.013

Eskreis-Winkler, L., Fishbach, A., & Duckworth, A. L. (2018). Dear Abby: Should I give advice or receive it? *Psychological Science, 29*, 1797–1806. https://doi.org/10.1177/0956797618795472

Fackler, M. (2012, January 21). Japanese struggle to protect their food supply. *The New York Times*. Retrieved from http://www.nytimes .com/2012/01/22/world/asia/wary-japanesetake-food-safety-into -their-own-hands.html

Fagerstrøm, A., Pawar, S., Sigurdsson, V., Foxall, G. R., & Yani-de-Soriano, M. (2017). That personal profile image might jeopardize your rental opportunity! On the relative impact of the seller's facial expressions upon buying behavior on Airbnb™. *Computers in Human Behavior, 72*, 123–131. https://doi.org/10.1016 /j.chb.2017.02.029

Fallon, M. (2018). Writing quantitative empirical manuscripts with rigor *and* flair (yes, it's possible). *Psi Chi Journal of Psychological Research, 23*, 184–198. https://doi.org/10.24839/2325-7342.JN23.3.184

Fallows, J. (1999). Booze you can use: Getting the best beer for your money. *Slate*. Retrieved from http://www.slate.com/33771/

Fanelli, D. (2018). Is science really facing a reproducibility crisis, and do we need it to? *PNAS, 115*, 2628–2631. www.pnas.org/cgi /doi/10.1073/pnas.1708272114

Faul, F., Erdfelder, E., Lang, A.-G., & Buchner, A. (2007). G★Power 3: A flexible statistical power analysis program for the social, behavioral, and biomedical sciences. *Behavior Research Methods, 39*, 175–191.

Finkelstein, S. R., & Fishbach, A. (2012). Tell me what I did wrong: Experts seek and respond to negative feedback. *Journal of Consumer Research, 39*, 22–38.

Fisher, A. V., Godwin, K. E., & Seltman, H. (2014). Visual environment, attention allocation, and learning in young children: When too much of a good thing may be bad.

Fitzpatrick, D. J., Gorr, W. L., & Neill, D. B. (2019). Keeping score: Predictive analytics in policing. *Annual Review of Criminology, 2*, 473–491. https://doi.org/10.1146/annurev -criminol-011518-024534

Forsyth, D. R., Lawrence, N. K., Burnette, J. L., & Baumeister, R. F. (2007). *Attempting to improve the academic performance of struggling college students by bolstering their self-esteem: An intervention that backfired*. Unpublished manuscript.

Fosse, E., Gross, N., & Ma, J. (2011). *Political bias in the graduate admissions process: A field experiment* (Working Paper). Retrieved from https://www10.arts.ubc.ca/fileadmin/template/main/images /departments/soci/faculty/gross/audit_paper_march_3.pdf

Frankenhuis, W. E., & Nettle, D. (2018). Open science is liberating and can foster creativity. *Perspectives on Psychological Science, 13*, 439–447. https://doi.org/10.1177/1745691618767878

Freeman, S., Eddy, S.L., McDonough, M., Smith, M.K., Okoroafor, N., Jordt, H., & Wenderoth, M.P. (2014). Active learning increases student performance in science, engineering and mathematics. *Proceeding of the National Academy of Sciences of the United States of America, 111*, 8410–8415.

Friedman, L., Daniels, M., & Blinderman, I. (2016, January). Hollywood's gender divide and its effect on films. *Polygraph*. Retrieved from http://polygraph.cool/bechdel/

Friedrich, J., Childress, J., & Cheng, D. (2018). Replicating a national survey on statistical training in undergraduate psychology programs: Are there "new statistics" in the new millennium? *Teaching of Psychology, 45*, 312–323. https://doi-org.ezproxy.shu .edu/10.1177/0098628318796414

Gallagher, R. P. (2009). National survey of counseling center directors. *Monographs of the International Association of Counseling Services, Inc.* (Monograph Series No. 8R). Alexandria, VA: International Association of Counseling Services.

Gallistel, C. R. (2015). Bayes for beginners: Probability and likelihood. *Observer*. Retrieved from http://www.psychologicalscience.org/index

.php/publications/observer/2015/september-15/bayes-for-beginners-probability-and-likelihood.html

Gammell, C. (2009, January 28). Cows with names produce more milk, scientists say. *The Telegraph*. Retrieved from https://www.telegraph.co.uk/news/earth/agriculture/farming/4358115/Cows-with-names-produce-more-milk-scientists-say.html

Garcia-Retamero, R., & Cokely, E. T. (2013). Communicating health risks with visual aids. *Current Directions in Psychological Science, 22*, 392–399. doi:10.1177/0963721413491570

Gaspar, J. G., Street, W. N., Windsor, M. B., Carbonari, R., Kaczmarski, H., Kramer, A. F., & Mathewson, K. E. (2014). Providing views of the driving scene to drivers' conversation partners mitigates cell-phone-related distraction. *Psychological Science, 25*, 2136–2146. doi:10.1177/0956797614549774

Geier, A. B., Rozin, P., & Doros, G. (2006). Unit bias: A new heuristic that helps explain the effect of portion size on food intake. *Psychological Science, 17*, 521–525.

Gelman, A. (2018). The failure of null hypothesis significance testing when studying incremental changes, and what to do about it. *Personality and Social Psychology Bulletin, 44*, 16–23.

Gelman, A., & Carlin, J. (2014). Beyond power calculations: assessing type S (sign) and type M (magnitude) errors. *Perspectives on Psychological Science, 9*, 641–651. doi:10.1177/1745691614551642

Georgiou, C. C., Betts, N. M., Hoerr, S. L., Keim, K., Peters, P. K., Stewart, B., & Voichick, J. (1997). Among young adults, college students and graduates practiced more healthful habits and made more healthful food choices than did nonstudents. *Journal of the American Dietetic Association, 97*, 754–759.

Gerber, A., & Malhotra, N. (2006). Can political science literatures be believed? A study of publication bias in the *APSR* and the *AJPS*. Retrieved from http://www.jspure.org/news2.htm

Gerdeman, D. (2018, February 27). The Airbnb effect: Cheaper rooms for travelers, less revenue for hotels. *Forbes*. Retrieved from https://www.forbes.com/sites/hbsworkingknowledge/2018/02/27/the-airbnb-effect-cheaper-rooms-for-travelers-less-revenue-for-hotels/

Gibbs, C., Guttentag, D., Gretzel, U., Yao, L., & Morton, J. (2018). Use of dynamic pricing strategies by Airbnb hosts. *International Journal of Contemporary Hospitality Management, 30*, 2–20. https://doi.org/10.1108/IJCHM-09-2016-0540

Gibbs, M., Nansen, B., Carter, M., & Kohn, T. (2014). Selfies at funerals: Remediating rituals of mourning. *Selected Papers of Internet Research, 4*. Retrieved from https://pdfs.semanticscholar.org/deb9/e3c805517203159973f6de05fb0b6e3e4f65.pdf

Gigerenzer, G. (2009). Making sense of health statistics. *Bulletin of the World Health Organization, 87*(8), 567. https://doi.org/10.2471/BLT.09.069872

Gigerenzer, G. (2018). Statistical rituals: The replication delusion and how we got there. *Advances in Methods and Practices in Psychological Science, 1*, 198–218. https://doi.org/10.1177/2515245918771329

Gilbert, D. T., King, G., Pettigrew, S., & Wilson, T. D. (2016). Comment on "Estimating the reproducibility of psychological science." *Science, 351*, 1037-b.

Gill, G. (2005). *Nightingales: The extraordinary upbringing and curious life of Miss Florence Nightingale*. New York, NY: Random House.

Gilovich, T., & Medvec, V. H. (1995). The experience of regret: What, when, and why. *Psychological Review, 102*, 379–395.

Ginsberg, J., Mohebbi, M. H., Patel, R. S., Brammer, L., Smolinski, M. S., & Brilliant, L. (2009). Detecting influenza epidemics using search engine query data. *Nature, 457*(7232), 1012–1014. https://doi.org/10.1038/nature07634

Glassdoor. (2018). 50 best jobs in American for 2019. Retrieved from https://www.glassdoor.com/List/Best-Jobs-in-America-LST_KQ0,20.htm

Goldacre, B. (2013). Health care's trick coin. *The New York Times*. Retrieved from http://www.nytimes.com/2013/02/02/opinion/health-cares-trick-coin.html.

Goldenburg, D. (2014). The story behind the worst movie on IMDB. *FiveThirtyEight*. Retrieved from https://fivethirtyeight.com/features/the-story-behind-the-worst-movie-on-imdb/

Golder, S. A., & Macy, M. W. (2011). Diurnal and seasonal mood vary with work, sleep, and daylength across diverse cultures. *Science, 333*, 1878–1881. doi:10.1126/science.1202775

Goodman, A., & Greaves, E. (2010). *Cohabitation, marriage and relationship stability* (IFS Briefing Note BN107). London, UK: Institute for Fiscal Studies.

Gossett, W. S. (1908). The probable error of a mean. *Biometrics, 6*, 1–24.

Gossett, W. S. (1942). *"Student's" collected papers* (E. S. Pearson & J. Wishart, Eds). Cambridge, UK: Cambridge University Press.

Graehler, M., Mucci, A., & Erhardt, G. D. (2019). *Understanding the recent transit ridership decline in major US cities: Service cuts or emerging modes?* Paper presented at the Transportation Research Board Annual Meeting, Washington, DC. Retrieved from https://www.researchgate.net/publication/330599129

Graham, L. (1999). Domesticating efficiency: Lillian Gilbreth's scientific management of homemakers. 1924-1930. *Signs, 24*, 633-675. http://www.jstor.org/stable/3175321

Greenfield, P. M. (2017). Cultural change over time: Why replicability should not be the gold standard in psychological science. *Perspectives on Psychological Science, 12*, 762–771. https://doi.org/10.1177/1745691617707314

Grimberg, A., Kutikov, J. K., & Cucchiara, A. J. (2005). Sex differences in patients referred for evaluation of poor growth. *Journal of Pediatrics, 146*, 212–216.

Griner, D., & Smith, T. B. (2006). Culturally adapted mental health intervention: A meta-analytic review. *Psychotherapy: Research, Practice, Training, 43*, 531–548.

Guéguen, N., Jacob, C., & Lamy, L. (2010). "Love is in the air": Effects of songs with romantic lyrics on compliance with a courtship request. *Psychology of Music, 38*, 303–307.

Guidelines for academic requesters. (n.d.). In *WeAreDynamo Wiki*. Retrieved from http://wiki.wearedynamo.org/index.php/Guidelines_for_Academic_Requesters

Hacker, A. (2016, February 27). The wrong way to teach math. *The New York Times*. Retrieved from https://www.nytimes.com/2016/02/28/opinion/sunday/the-wrong-way-to-teach-math.html

Hamby, T., Taylor, W., Snowden, A. K., & Peterson, R. A. (2016). A meta-analysis of the reliability of free and for-pay Big Five scales. *Journal of Psychology: Interdisciplinary and Applied, 150*(4), 422–430. https://doi.org/10.1080/00223980.2015.1060186.

Handley, I. M., Brown, E. R., Moss-Racusin, C. A., & Smith, J. L. (2015). Quality of evidence revealing subtle gender biases in science is in the eye of the beholder. *Proceedings of the National Academy of Sciences, 112*(43), 13201–13206.

Hanrahan, F., Field, A. P., Jones, F. W., & Davey, G. C. L. (2013). A meta-analysis of cognitive therapy for worry in generalized anxiety disorder. *Clinical Psychology Review, 33,* 120–132.

Harding, K. (2010). Dispelling Sandra Bullock's Oscar curse. *Salon.* Retrieved from https://www.salon.com/2010/03/19/best_actress_curse

Haque, R. (2018, September 6). Charities in the United States. *data .world.* Dataset id: rashedul-haque/charities-in-the-united-states

Hardyns, W., & Rummens, A. (2018). Predictive policing as a new tool for law enforcement? Recent developments and challenges. *European Journal on Criminal Policy and Research, 24,* 201–218. https://doi.org/10.1007/s10610-017-9361-2

Hatchett, G. T. (2003). Does psychopathology predict counseling duration? *Psychological Reports, 93,* 175–185.

Hatfield, E., & Sprecher, S. (1986). Measuring passionate love in intimate relationships. *Journal of Adolescence, 9,* 383–410.

Haug, T. T., Mykletun, A., & Dahl, A. A. (2002). Are anxiety and depression related to gastrointestinal symptoms in the general population? *Scandinavian Journal of Gastroenterology, 37,* 294–298.

Hawkins, R. X. D., Smith, E. N., Au, C., Arias, J. M., Catapano, R., Hermann, E., … Frank, M. C. (2018). Improving the replicability of psychological science through pedagogy. *Advances in Methods and Practices in Psychological Science, 1,* 7–18. https://doi.org/10.1177/2515245917740427

Hays, W. L. (1994). *Statistics* (5th ed.). Fort Worth, TX: Harcourt Brace College Publishers.

Head, M. L., Holman, L., Lanfear, R., Kahn, A. T., & Jennions, M. D. (2015). The extent and consequences of p-hacking in science. *PLOS Biology, 13,* e1002106. https://doi.org/10.1371/journal.pbio.1002106

Healey, J. R. (2006, October 13). Driving the hard(top) way. *USA Today,* 1B.

Held, L. (2010). Profile of Lillian Gilbreth. In A. Rutherford (Ed.), *Psychology's feminist voices multimedia internet archive.* Retrieved from http://www.feministvoices.com/lillian-gilbreth/

Helliwell, J., Layard, R., & Sachs, J. (2017). *World happiness report 2016, update (Vol. I).* New York, NY: Sustainable Development Solutions Network. Retrieved from http://worldhappiness.report/ed/2016/

Helliwell, J., Layard, R., & Sachs, J. (Eds.). (2018). The world happiness report. Retrieved from https://s3.amazonaws.com/happiness-report/2018/WHR_web.pdf

Henrich, J., Ensminger, J., McElreath, R., Barr, A., Barrett, C., Bolyanatz, A., . . . Ziker, J. (2010). Markets, religion, community size, and the evolution of fairness and punishment. *Science, 327,* 1480–1484. Supporting online material retrieved from http://www.sciencemag.org/content/327/5972/1480

Henrich, J., Heine, S. J., & Norenzayan, A. (2010). The weirdest people in the world? *Behavioral and Brain Sciences, 33,* 61–83. https://doi.org/10.1017/S0140525X0999152X

Hernández-Julián, R., & Peters, C. (2015). Student appearance and academic performance. Retrieved from https://www.aeaweb.org/aea/2016conference/program/retrieve.php?pdfid=280

Herszenhorn, D. M. (2006, May 5). As test-taking grows, test-makers grow rarer. *The New York Times.* Retrieved from https://www.nytimes.com/2006/05/05/education/05testers.html

Heyman, J., & Ariely, D. (2004). Effort for payment. *Psychological Science, 15,* 787– 793.

Hickey, W. (2015, November 18). The 20 most extreme cases of "the book was better than the movie." *FiveThirtyEight.* Retrieved from https://fivethirtyeight.com/features/the-20-most-extreme-cases-of-the-book-was-better-than-the-movie/

Hill, M. (2018, February 10). Everything to know about how Olympic figure skating gets scored. *Cosmopolitan.* Retrieved from https://www.cosmopolitan.com

Hintze, J. L., & Nelson, R. D. (1998). Violin plots: A box plot–density trace synergism. *The American Statistician, 52,* 181-184.

Hockenbury, D. H., & Hockenbury, S. E. (2013). *Psychology* (6th ed.). New York, NY: Worth.

Hoffman, J. (2017, July 31). Is this dog dangerous? Shelters struggle with live-or-die tests. *The New York Times.* Retrieved from https://www.nytimes.com/2017/07/31/science/dogs-shelters-adoption-behavior-tests.html

Holiday, A. (2007). *Perceptions of depression based on etiology and gender.* Unpublished manuscript.

Hollenbeck, J. R., & Wright, P. M. (2017). Harking, sharking, and tharking: Making the case for post hoc analysis of scientific data. *Journal of Management, 43,* 5–18. https://doi.org/10.1177/0149206316679487

Hollon, S. D., Thase, M. E., & Markowitz, J. C. (2002). Treatment and prevention of depression. *Psychological Science in the Public Interest, 3,* 39–77.

Holm-Denoma, J. M., Joiner, T. E., Vohs, K. D., & Heatherton, T. F. (2008). The "freshman fifteen" (the "freshman five" actually): Predictions and possible explanations. *Health Psychology, 27,* s3–s9.

Hoxby, C., & Turner, S. (2013). *Expanding college opportunities for high-achieving, low-income students* (SIEPR Discussion Paper No. 12-014.) Stanford, CA: Stanford Institute for Economic Policy Research.

Hristova, D., Williams, M. J., Musolesi, M., Panzarasa, P., & Mascolo, C. (2016). Measuring urban social diversity using interconnected geo-social networks. *WWW '16 Proceedings of the 25th International Conference on World Wide Web, 21*–30. https://doi.org/10.1145/2872427.2883065

Hsiehchen, D., Espinoza, M., & Hsieh, A. (2015). Multinational teams and diseconomies of scale in collaborative research. *Science Advances, 1*(8), e1500211.

Hugenberg, K., Miller, J., & Claypool, H. (2007). Categorization and individuation in the cross-race recognition deficit: Toward a solution to an insidious problem. *Journal of Experimental Social Psychology, 43,* 334–340.

Hughes, S. M., & Miller, N. E. (2015, October 23). What sounds beautiful looks beautiful stereotype: The matching of attractiveness of voices and faces. *Journal of Social and Personal Relationships, 33,* 984–996.

Hull, H. R., Radley, D., Dinger, M. K., & Fields, D. A. (2006). The effect of the Thanksgiving holiday on weight gain. *Nutrition Journal, 21,* 29–34.

Hunsley, J., Lee, C. M., Wood, J. M., & Taylor, W. (2015). Controversial and questionable assessment technique. In S. Lilienfeld, S. Lynn, J. Lohr, & C. Tarvis (Eds.), *Science and pseudoscience in clinical psychology* (2nd ed., pp. 42–82). New York, NY: Guilford.

Hyde, J. S. (2005). The gender similarities hypothesis. *American Psychologist, 60,* 581–592.

Hyde, J. S., Fennema, E., & Lamon, S. J. (1990). Gender differences in mathematics performance: A meta-analysis. *Psychological Bulletin, 107,* 139–155.

Indiana University Media Relations. (2006). It's no joke: IU study finds *The Daily Show* with Jon Stewart to be as substantive as network news. Retrieved from http://newsinfo.iu.edu/news/page/normal/4159.html

Ingraham, C. (2017, March 9). Utah's drunken driving law is about to become the country's strictest. *The Washington Post.* Retrieved from https://www.washingtonpost.com/news/wonk/wp/2017/03/09/utahs-drunken-driving-law-is-about-to-become-the-countrys-strictest/

Ioannidis, J. P. A. (2008). Why most discovered true associations are inflated. *Epidemiology (Cambridge, MA), 19*(5), 640–648. https://doi.org/10.1097/EDE.0b013e31818131e7

Ioannidis, J. P. (2018). The proposal to lower *p* value thresholds to .005. *Journal of the American Medical Association, 319*, 1429–1430. https://doi.org/10.1001/jama.2018.1536

Irwin, M. L., Tworoger, S. S., Yasui, Y., Rajan, B., McVarish, L., LaCroix, K., . . . McTiernan, A. (2004). Influence of demographic, physiologic, and psychosocial variables on adherence to a year-long moderate-intensity exercise trial in postmenopausal women. *Preventive Medicine, 39,* 1080–1086.

Jacob, J. E., & Eccles, J. (1982). Science and the media: Benbow and Stanley revisited. Report funded by the National Institute of Education, Washington, DC. ERIC #ED235925.

Jacob, J. E., & Eccles, J. (1986). Social forces shape math attitudes and performance. *Signs, 11,* 367–380.

Jacobs, T. (2010). Ink on skin doesn't necessarily indicate sin. *PS Magazine.* Retrieved from http://www.psmag.com/navigation/books-and-culture/ink-on-skin-doesn-t-necessarily-indicate-sin-7068/.

Jaeger, B., Sleegers, W. W., Evans, A. M., Stel, M., & van Beest, I. (2018). The effects of facial attractiveness and trustworthiness in online peer-to-peer markets. *Journal of Economic Psychology.* https://doi.org/10.1016/j.joep.2018.11.004

Jakovcevic, A., Steg, L., Mazzeo, N., Caballero, R., Franco, P., Putrino, N., & Favara, J. (2014). Charges for plastic bags: Motivational and behavioral effects. *Journal of Environmental Psychology, 40,* 372–380. doi: 10.1016/j.jenvp.2014.09.004.

Jay, K. L., & Jay, T. B. (2015). Taboo word fluency and knowledge of slurs and general pejoratives: Deconstructing the poverty-of-vocabulary myth. *Language Sciences, 52,* 251–259.

John, L. K., Donnelly, G. E., & Roberto, C. A. (2017). Psychologically informed implementations of sugary-drink portion limits. *Psychological Science, 28,* 620–629. https://doi-org.ezproxy.shu.edu/10.1177/0956797617692041

Johnson, D. J., Cheung, F., & Donnellan, M. B. (2014a). Does cleanliness influence moral judgments? A direct replication of Schnall, Benton, and Harvey (2008). *Social Psychology, 45,* 209–215.

Johnson, D. J., Cheung, F., & Donnellan, M. B. (2014b). Hunting for artifacts: The perils of dismissing inconsistent replication results. *Social Psychology, 45,* 318–320.

Johnson, L. F., Mossong, J., Dorrington, R. E., Schomaker, M., Hoffmann, C. J., Keiser, O., . . . Boulle, A. (2013). Life expectancies of South African adults starting antiretroviral treatment: Collaborative analysis of cohort studies. *PLOS Medicine, 10*(4), 1–11. doi:10.1371/journal.pmed.1001418

Johnson, W. B., Koch, C., Fallow, G. O., & Huwe, J. M. (2000). Prevalence of mentoring in clinical versus experimental doctoral programs: Survey findings, implications, and recommendations. *Psychotherapy: Theory, Research, Practice, Training, 37,* 325–334.

Jones, D., Molitor, D., & Reif, J. (2018). *What do workplace wellness programs do? Evidence from the Illinois workplace wellness study.* NBER Working Paper No. 24229. Cambridge, MA: The National Bureau of Economic Research.

Kemp, S. (2018, January 30). Digital in 2018: World's Internet users pass the 4 billion mark. *We Are Social.* Retrieved from https://wearesocial.com/blog/2018/01/global-digital-report-2018

Kemp, S. (2018, April 18). Social media for travel marketers [LinkedIn SlideShare slides]. Retrieved from https://de.slideshare.net/wearesocialsg/social-media-for-travel-brands

Kerr, N. L. (1998). HARKing: Hypothesizing after the results are known. *Personality and Social Psychology Review, 2,* 196–217. https://doi.org/10.1207/s15327957pspr0203_4

Kim, K., & Morawski, S. (2012). Quantifying the impact of going trayless in a university dining hall. *Journal of Hunger and Environmental Nutrition, 7,* 482–486. http://dx.doi.org/10.1080/19320248.2012.732918

Kindley, E. (2016). *Questionnaire.* New York, NY: Bloomsbury Academic.

Kirchner, L. (2015, November 3). What we know about the computer formulas making decisions in your life. *Pacific Standard.* Retrieved from https://psmag.com/environment/what-we-know-about-the-computer-formulas-making-decisions-in-your-life

Kitayama, S., Park, J., Boylan, J. M., Miyamoto, Y., Levine, C. S., Markus, H. R., . . . Ryff, C. D. (2015). Expression of anger and ill health in two cultures: An examination of inflammation and cardiovascular risk. *Psychological Science, 26*(2), 211–220.

Kniffin, K. M., Sigirci, O., & Wansink, B. (2016). Eating heavily: Men eat more in the company of women. *Evolutionary Psychological Science, 2,* 38–46.

Koch, J. R., Roberts, A. E., Armstrong, M. L., & Owens, D. C. (2010). Body art, deviance, and American college students. *The Social Science Journal, 47,* 151–161.

Kolata, G. (2016, August 11). We're so confused: The problems with food and exercise studies. *The New York Times.* Retrieved from https://www.nytimes.com/2016/08/11/upshot/were-so-confused-the-problems-with-food-and-exercise-studies.html

Kornell, N., & Metcalfe, J. (2014). The effects of memory retrieval, errors, and feedback on learning. In V. A. Benassi, C. E. Overson, & C. M. Hakala (Eds.), *Applying science of learning in education: Infusing psychological science into the curriculum.* Retrieved from http://teachpsych.org/ebooks/asle2014/index.php.

Kosinski, M., Stillwell, D., & Graepel, T. (2013). Private traits and attributes are predictable from digital records of human behavior. *Proceedings of the National Academy of Sciences, 110,* 5802–5805.

Krugman, P. (2006, May 5). Our sick society. *The New York Times.* Retrieved from https://www.nytimes.com/2006/05/05/opinion/05krugman.html

Kruschke, J. K. (2010). An open letter to editors of journals, chairs of departments, directors of funding programs, directors of graduate training, reviewers of grants and manuscripts, researchers, teachers, and students. Retrieved from http://www.indiana.edu/~kruschke/AnOpenLetter.htm

Kruschke, J. K. (2011). *Doing Bayesian data analysis: A tutorial with R and BUGS.* Burlington, MA: Academic Press, Elsevier.

Kruschke, J. K., & Liddell, T. M. (2018a). Bayesian data analysis for newcomers. *Psychonomic Bulletin & Review, 25*(1), 155–177. https://doi.org/10.3758/s13423-017-1272-1

Kruschke, J. K., & Liddell, T. M. (2018b). The Bayesian new statistics: Hypothesis testing, estimation, meta-analysis, and power analysis from a Bayesian perspective. *Psychonomic Bulletin & Review, 25*(1), 178–206. https://doi.org/10.3758/s13423-016-1221-4

Kushlev, K., & Dunn, E. W. (2015). Checking email less frequently reduces stress. *Computers in Human Behavior, 43,* 220–228.

Lam, R. W., & Kennedy, S. H. (2005). Using meta-analysis to evaluate evidence: Practical tips and traps. *Canadian Journal of Psychiatry, 50,* 167–174.

Lambert, J. & Usher, A. (2013. The pros and cons of internalization: How domestic students experience the globalizing campus. *Higher Education Strategy Associates Intelligence Brief* 7. Retrieved from http://www.queensu.ca/sgs/sites/webpublish.queensu.ca.sgswww/files/files/Faculty-Internationalisation/HESA%20report%20pros_cons%20internationalization.pdf

Landrum, E. (2005). Core terms in undergraduate statistics. *Teaching of Psychology, 32,* 249–251.

Larzelere, R. E., Cox, R. B., & Swindle, T. M. (2015). Many replications do not causal inferences make: The need for critical replications to test competing explanations of nonrandomized studies. *Perspectives on Psychological Science, 10*(3), 380–389.

Lavner, J. A., Karney, B. R., & Bradbury, T. N. (2012). Do cold feet warn of trouble ahead? Premarital uncertainty and 4-year marital outcomes. *Journal of Family Psychology, 26,* 1012–1017.

Leggett, A., Burgard, S., & Zivin, K. (2016). The impact of sleep disturbance on the association between stressful life events and depressive symptoms. *Journals of Gerontology Series B: Psychological Sciences and Social Sciences, 71*(1), 118–128. https://doi.org/10.1093/geronb/gbv072

Leibbrandt, A., & List, J. A. (2012). *Do women avoid salary negotiations? Evidence from a large scale natural field experiment* (NBER Working Paper No. 18511). Cambridge, MA: National Bureau of Economic Research.

Leong, D. P., Teo, K. K., Rangarajan, S., Lopez-Jaramillo, P., Avezum, A., Orlandini, A., . . . Yufus, S. (2015). Prognostic value of grip strength: Findings from the Prospective Urban Rural Epidemiology (PURE) study. *Lancet, 386*(9990), 266–273.

Letzter, R. (2016, September 26). We talked to the scientist at the center of a brutal firestorm in the field of psychology. *Business Insider.* Retrieved from https://www.businessinsider.com/susan-fiske-methodological-terrorism-qa-2016-9

Levitt, S. D., & Dubner, S. J. (2005). *Freakonomics: A rogue economist explores the hidden side of everything* (1st ed.). New York, NY: William Morrow.

Levitt, S. D., & Dubner, S. J. (2009). *Freakonomics: A rogue economist explores the hidden side of everything.* New York, NY: Morrow.

Lindberg, S. M., Hyde, J. S., Petersen, J. L., & Linn, M. C. (2010). New trends in gender and mathematics performance: A metaanalysis. *Psychological Bulletin, 136,* 1123–1135.

Lindsay, S. (2017, October 16). Nineteen things editors of experimental psychology journals can do to increase the replicability of the research they publish. Retrieved from http://web.uvic.ca/~dslind/?q=node/209

Lloyd, C. (2006, December 14). Saved, or sacrificed? *Salon.com.* Retrieved from http://www.salon.com/mwt/broadsheet/2006/12/14/selection/index.html

Loschelder, D. D., Swaab, R. I., Trötschel, R., & Galinsky, A. D. (2014). The first-mover disadvantage: The folly of revealing compatible preferences. *Psychological Science, 25,* 954–962. doi:10.1177/0956797613520168

Lovett, M. C. & Greenhouse, J. B. (2000). *Applying cognitive theory to statistics instruction.* Department of Psychology. Paper 341. Retrieved from http://repository.cmu.edu/psychology/341

Lucas, M. E. S., Deen, J. L., von Seidlein, L., Wang, X., Ampuero, J., Puri, M., … Clemens, J. D. (2005). Effectiveness of mass oral cholera vaccination in Beira, Mozambique. *New England Journal of Medicine, 352,* 757–767.

Lull, R. B., & Bushman, B. J. (2015). Do sex and violence sell? A meta-analytic review of the effects of sexual and violent media and ad content on memory, attitudes, and buying intentions. *Psychological Bulletin, 141,* 1022–1048. http://dx.doi.org/10.1037/bul0000018

Luo, L., Hendriks, T., & Craik, F. (2007). Age differences in recollection: Three patterns of enhanced encoding. *Psychology and Aging, 22,* 269–280.

Lutz, G. M., Cornish, D. L., Gonnerman Jr., M. E., Ralston, M., & Baker, P. (2009). *Impacts of participation in high school extracurricular activities on early adult life experiences: A study of Iowa graduates.* Cedar Falls, IA: University of Northern Iowa, Center for Social and Behavioral Research.

Macnamara, B. N., Moreau, D., & Hambrick, D. Z. (2016). The relationship between deliberate practice and performance in sports: A meta-analysis. *Perspectives on Psychological Science, 11,* 333–350. https://doi.org/10.1177/1745691616635591

Maisel, M., & Smart, L. (1997). Women in science: A selection of 16 contributors. San Diego Supercomputer Center. Retrieved from https://www.sdsc.edu/ScienceWomen/GWIS.pdf

Mark, G., Gonzalez, V. M., & Harris, J. (2005, April). No task left behind? Examining the nature of fragmented work. *Proceedings of the Association for Computing Machinery Conference on Human Factors in Computing Systems* (ACM CHI 2005), Portland, OR, 321–330. New York, NY: ACM Press.

Mattke, S., Liu, H., Caloyeras, J., Huang, C. Y., Van Busum, K. R., Khodyakov, D., & Shier, V. (2013). Workplace wellness programs study: Final report. *Rand Health Quarterly, 3*(2), 7.

Matz, S. C., Gladstone, J. J., & Stillwell, D. (2017). In a world of big data, small effects can still matter: A reply to Boyce, Daly, Hounkpatin, and Wood (2017). *Psychological Science, 28*(4), 547–550. https://doi.org/10.1177/0956797617697445

Maxwell, S. E., & Kelley, K. (2011). Ethics and sample size planning. In A. T. Panter & S. K. Serba (Eds.), *Handbook of ethics in quantitative methodology* (pp. 159–184). New York, NY: Routledge/Taylor & Francis Group.

Mayer-Schönberger, V., & Cukier, K. (2013). *Big data: A revolution that will transform how we live, work, and think.* New York, NY: Eamon Dolan/Houghton Mifflin Harcourt.

Markoff, J. (2005, July 18). Marrying maps to data for a new web service. *The New York Times.* Retrieved from http://www.nytimes.com.

Mayo, D. G. (2018). *Statistical inference as severe testing: How to get beyond the statistics wars.* Cambridge, UK: Cambridge University Press.

Mazer, J. P., Murphy, R. E., & Simonds, C. J. (2007). I'll see you on "Facebook": The effects of computer-mediated teacher self-disclosure on student motivation, affective learning, and classroom climate. *Communication Education, 56*(1), 1–17.

McCabe, C. J., Kim, D. S., & King, K. M. (2018). Improving present practices in the visual display of interactions. *Advances in Methods and Practices in Psychological Science, 1,* 147–165. https://doi.org/10.1177/2515245917746792

McKee, S. (2014). Using word clouds to present your qualitative data. *SurveyGizmo blog.* Retrieved from https://www.surveygizmo.com/survey-blog/what-you-need-to-know-when-using-word-clouds-to-present-your-qualitative-data/.

McNeish, D. (2018). Thanks coefficient alpha, we'll take it from here. *Psychological Methods, 23*(3), 412–433. https://doi.org/10.1037/met0000144.

McShane, B. B., & Böckenholt, U. (2014). You cannot step into the same river twice: When power analyses are optimistic. *Perspectives on Psychological Science, 9*, 612–625. doi:10.1177/1745691614548513

Mecklenburg, S. H., Malpass, R. S., & Ebbesen, E. (2006, March 17). Report to the legislature of the State of Illinois: The Illinois Pilot Program on Sequential Double-Blind Identification Procedures. Retrieved from http://eyewitness.utep.edu/Documents /Malpass06NotesonTheIllinoisPilotProgram.pdf

Mehl, M. R., Vazire, S., Ramirez-Esparza, N., Slatcher, R. B., & Pennebaker, J. W. (2007). Are women really more talkative than men? *Science, 317*, 82. doi:10.1126/science.1139940

Mervosh, S. (2019, January 10). Do floppy-eared dogs look friendlier? The T.S.A. thinks so. *The New York Times.* Retrieved from https://www .nytimes.com/2019/01/10/science/tsa-dog-ears-floppy.html

Mitroff, S. R., Biggs, A. T., Adamo, S. H., Dowd, E. W., Winkle, J., & Clark, K. (2015). What can 1 billion trials tell us about visual search? *Journal of Experimental Psychology: Human Perception and Performance, 41*, 1–5.

Moertel, T. (2006, January 17). Mining gold from the Internet Movie Database, part 1: Decoding user ratings. *Tom Moertel's Blog.* Retrieved from http://blog.moertel.com/posts/2006-01-17-mining-gold-from -the-internet-movie-database-part-1.html

Moss-Racusin, C. A., Dovidio, J. F., Brescoll, V. L., Graham, M. J., & Handelsman, J. (2012). Science faculty's subtle gender biases favor male students. *Proceedings of the National Academy of Sciences, 109*, 16474–16479.

Müller, K., & Schwarz, C. (2018). Fanning the flames of hate: Social media and hate crime. *SSRN Electronic Journal.* https://doi:10.2139 /ssrn.3082972

Mueller, P. A., & Oppenheimer, D. M. (2014). The pen is mightier than the keyboard: Advantages of longhand over laptop note taking. *Psychological Science, 25*, 1159–1168. doi:10.1177/0956797614524581

Munro, G. D., & Munro, J. E. (2000). Using daily horoscopes to demonstrate expectancy confirmation. *Teaching of Psychology, 27*, 114–116. doi:10.1207/S15328023TOP2702_08

Murphy, K. R., & Myors, B. (2004). *Statistical power analysis: A simple and general model for traditional and modern hypothesis tests.* Mahwah, NJ: Erlbaum.

Murphy, R. (2018, September 7). What are the ingredients of a successful wellness program? *Benefits Canada.* Retrieved from https://www.benefitscanada.com/news/what-are-the-ingredients -of-a-successful-wellness-program-118684

Nail, P. R., Harton, H. C., & Decker, B. P. (2003). Political orientation and modern versus aversive racism: Tests of Dovidio and Gaertner's (1998) integrated model. *Journal of Personality and Social Psychology, 84*, 754–770.

National Sleep Foundation. (2015). Teens and sleep. Retrieved from https://sleepfoundation.org/sleep-topics/teens-and-sleep

Neighbors, L., & Sobal, J. (2008). Weight and weddings: Women's weight ideals and weight management behaviors for their wedding day. *Appetite, 50*(2–3), 550–554.

Nelson, J. M., & Gregg, N. (2012). Depression and anxiety among transitioning adolescents and college students with ADHD, dyslexia, or comorbid ADHD/dyslexia. *Journal of Attention Disorders, 16*, 244–254.

Newman, A. (2006, November 11). Missed the train? Lost a wallet? Maybe it was all Mercury's fault. *The New York Times*, p. B3.

Newton, R. R., & Rudestam, K. E. (1999). *Your statistical consultant: Answers to your data analysis questions.* Thousand Oaks, CA: Sage.

Nielsen Company. (2018, July 31). The Nielsen total audience report: Q1 2018. Retrieved from https://www.nielsen.com/us/en/insights /reports/2018/q1-2018-total-audience-report.html#

Nolan, S. A., Flynn, C., & Garber, J. (2003). Prospective relations between rejection and depression in young adolescents. *Journal of Personality and Social Psychology, 85*, 745–755.

Norris, F. H., Stevens, S. P., Pfefferbaum, B., Wyche, K. F., & Pfefferbaum, R. L. (2008). Community resilience as a metaphor, theory, set of capacities, and strategy for disaster readiness. *American Journal of Community Psychology, 41*, 127–150.

Nosek, B. A., & Lindsay, D. S. (2018, February 18). Preregistration becoming the norm for psychological science. Association for Psychological Science. Retrieved from https://www.psychologicalscience.org/observer /preregistration-becoming-the-norm-in-psychological-science

Nosek, B. A., Spies, J. R., Cohn, M., Bartmess, E., Lakens, D., Holman, D., … Giner-Sorolla, R. (2015, June 12). *Open Science Collaboration.* Retrieved from osf.io/vmrgu

Novak, M. (2018, October 1). Did the release of the iPhone cause millennials to move back in with their parents? *Paleofuture.* Retrieved from https://paleofuture.gizmodo.com/did-the-release-of-the -iphone-cause-millennials-to-move-1829432492

Nuijten, M. B., Hartgerink, C. H., van Assen, M. A., Epskamp, S., & Wicherts, J. M. (2016). The prevalence of statistical reporting errors in psychology (1985–2013). *Behavior Research Methods, 48*, 1205–1226. https://doi/10.3758/s13428-015-0664-2

Nunnally, J. C., & Bernstein, I. H. (1994). *Psychometric theory* (3rd ed.). New York, NY: McGraw-Hill.

Nuzzo, R. (2014). Statistical errors. *Nature, 506*, 150–152.

O'Brien, E., & Kassirer, S. (2019). People are slow to adapt to the warm glow of giving. *Psychological Science, 30*, 193–204. doi:0956797618814145

O'Connor, A. (2018, September 29). More evidence that nutrition studies don't always add up. *The New York Times.* Retrieved from https://www.nytimes.com/2018/09/29/sunday-review/cornell-food -scientist-wansink-misconduct.html

Odgaard, E. C., & Fowler, R. L. (2010). Confidence intervals for effect sizes: Compliance and clinical significance in the *Journal of Consulting and Clinical Psychology. Journal of Consulting and Clinical Psychology, 78*, 287–297.

Ogbu, J. U. (1986). The consequences of the American caste system. In U. Neisser (Ed.), *The school achievement of minority children: New perspectives* (pp. 19–56). Hillsdale, NJ: Erlbaum.

O'Loughlin, K., & Arkoudis, S. (2009). Investigating IELTS exit score gains in higher education. *IELTS Research Report, 10*, 95–180. Retrieved from https://www.ielts.org/pdf/Vol10_Report3.pdf

Open Science Collaboration. (2015). Open science framework. Retrieved from https://osf.io/vmrgu/wiki/home/

Palazzo, D. J., Lee, Y-J, Warnakulasooriya, R., & Pritchard, D. E. (2010). Patterns, correlates, and reduction of homework copying. *Physical Review Special Topics—Physics Education Research, 6.* Retrieved from http://prst-per.aps.org/pdf/PRSTPER/v6/i1/e010104. doi:10.1103/PhysRevSTPER.6.010104

Pastore, M., Lionetti, F., & Altoè, G. (2017). When one shape does not fit all: A commentary essay on the use of graphs in psychological research. *Frontiers in Psychology, 8.* https://doi.org/10.3389 /fpsyg.2017.01666

Pennycook, G., Cannon, T. D., & Rand, D. G. (2018). Prior exposure increases perceived accuracy of fake news. *Journal of Experimental Psychology: General, 147,* 1865–1880. https://doi.org/10.1037/xge0000465.supp

Pescosolido, B. A., Martin, J. K., Long, J. S., Medina, T. R., Phelan, J. C., & Link, B. G. (2010). "A disease like any other"? A decade of change in public reactions to schizophrenia, depression, and alcohol dependence. *American Journal of Psychiatry, 167,* 1321–1330. http://dx.doi.org/10.1176/appi.ajp.2010.09121743

Petrocelli, J. V. (2003). Factor validation of the Consideration of Future Consequences Scale: Evidence for a shorter version. *Journal of Social Psychology, 143,* 405–413.

Phillips, N. (2017). YaRrr! The pirate's guide to R. *Association for Psychological Science.* Retrieved from https://www.psychologicalscience.org/observer/yarrr-the-pirates-guide-to-r

Pittenger, D. J. (2005). Cautionary comments regarding the Myers–Briggs Type Indicator. *Consulting Psychology Journal: Practice and Research, 57,* 210–221. doi:10.1037/1065-9293.57.3.210

Plassmann, H., O'Doherty, J., Shiv, B., & Rangel, A. (2008). Marketing actions can modulate neural representations of experienced pleasantness. *Proceedings of the National Academy of Sciences, 105,* 1050–1054. doi:10.1073/pnas.0706929105

Poon, K. Y., & Huang, W. J. (2017). Past experience, traveler personality and tripographics on intention to use Airbnb. *International Journal of Contemporary Hospitality Management, 29,* 2425–2443. https://doi.org/10.1108/IJCHM-10-2016-0599

Popkin, S. J., & Woodley, W. (2002). *Hope VI panel study.* Washington, DC: Urban Institute.

Postman, N. (1985). *Amusing ourselves to death.* New York, NY: Penguin Books.

Poulton, A., Pan, J., Bruns, L. R. Jr., Sinnott, R. O., & Hester, R. (2018). Assessment of alcohol intake: Retrospective measures versus a smartphone application. *Addictive Behaviors, 83,* 35–41. https://doi.org/10.1016/j.addbeh.2017.11.003

Press, E. (2006, December 3). Do immigrants make us safer? *The New York Times Magazine,* pp. 20–24.

Pressman, S. D., Gallagher, M. W., & Lopez, S. J. (2013). Is the emotion–health connection a "first-world problem"? *Psychological Science, 24,* 544–549. doi:10.1177/0956797612457382

Primack, B. A., Shensa, A., Escobar-Viera, C. G., Barrett, E. L., Sidani, J. E., Colditz, J. B., & James, A. E. (2017). Use of multiple social media platforms and symptoms of depression and anxiety: A nationally-representative study among US young adults. *Computers in Human Behavior, 69,* 1–9. https://doi.org/10.1016/j.chb.2016.11.013

Prinz, F., Schlange, T., & Asadullah, K. (2011). Believe it or not: How much can we rely on published data on potential drug targets? *Nature Reviews: Drug Discovery, 10,* 712–713. https://doi.org/10.1038/nrd3439-c1

Psi Chi. (2015). The reproducibility project: A national project for Psi Chi in partnership with the Open Science Collaboration. Retrieved from http://c.ymcdn.com/sites/www.psichi.org/resource/resmgr/pdfs/psichiprojectosc.pdf

Public vs. private schools [Editorial]. (2006, July 19). *The New York Times.* Retrieved from https://www.nytimes.com/2006/07/19/opinion/public-vs-private-schools.html

Quaranta, A., Siniscalchi, M., & Vallortigara, G. (2007). Asymmetric tail-wagging responses by dogs to different emotive stimuli. *Current Biology, 17,* 199–201.

Rad, M. S., Martingano, A. J., & Ginges, J. (2018). Toward a psychology of *Homo sapiens:* Making psychological science more representative of the human population. *Proceedings of the National Academy of Sciences of the United States of America, 115,* 11401–11405. https://doi.org/10.1073/pnas.1721165115

Ratner, R. K., & Miller, D. T. (2001). The norm of self-interest and its effects on social action. *Journal of Personality and Social Psychology, 81,* 5–16.

Raz, A., Fan, J., & Posner, M. I. (2005). Hypnotic suggestion reduces conflict in the human brain. *Proceedings of the National Academy of Sciences, 102,* 9978–9983.

Renkl, A. (2014). Learning from worked examples: How to prepare students for meaningful problem solving. In V. A. Benassi, C. E. Overson, & C. M. Hakala (Eds.), *Applying science of learning in education: Infusing psychological science into the curriculum* (pp. 118–130). Washington, DC: American Psychological Association.

Resnick, B. (2016, September 30). A bot crawled thousands of studies looking for simple math errors: The results are concerning. *Vox.* Retrieved from https://www.vox.com/science-and-health/2016/9/30/13077658/statcheck-psychology-replication

Reynolds, G. (2015, March 26). An upbeat emotion that's surprisingly good for you. *The New York Times.* Retrieved from https://well.blogs.nytimes.com/2015/03/26/an-upbeat-emotion-thats-surprisingly-good-for-you/

Rhue, H. (2018, November 30). How Payless tricked influencers into paying $600+ for their $20 shoes. *Elle.* Retrieved from https://www.elle.com/fashion/accessories/a25361265/payless-trick-fake-luxury-shoe-store-palessi/

Richards, S. E. (2006, March 22). Women silent on abortion on NYT op-ed page. *Salon.com.* Retrieved from https://www.salon.com/2006/03/22/times_20/

Richardson, D. C., Griffin, N. K., Zaki, L., Stephenson, A., Yan, J., Hogan, J., Skipper, J. I., & Devlin, J. T. (2018). Measuring narrative engagement: The heart tells the story. https://doi.org/10.1101/351148

Roberts, P. M. (2003). Performance of Canadian adults on the Graded Naming Test. *Aphasiology, 17,* 933–946.

Roberts, S. B., & Mayer, J. (2000). Holiday weight gain: Fact or fiction? *Nutrition Review, 58,* 378–379.

Rodriguez, S. D., Drake, L. L., Price, D. P., Hammond, J. I., & Hansen, I. A. (2015). The efficacy of some commercially available insect repellents for *Aedes aegypti* (Diptera: Culicidae) and *Aedes albopictus* (Diptera: Culicidae). *Journal of Insect Science, 15,* 140–144.

Rogers, S. (2013, February 1). Car, bike, train, or walk: How people get to work mapped. *The Guardian: Data Blog.* Retrieved from http://www.guardian.co.uk/news/datablog/interactive/2013/feb/01/cycle-drive-work-map-census-2011.

Rohrer, J. M., Egloff, B., & Schmukle, S. C. (2015). Examining the effects of birth order on personality. *Proceedings of the National Academy of Sciences, 112,* 14224–14229.

Rosario, F. & Sutherland, A. (2014, March 6). Woman wins $2M playing fortune cookie lotto numbers. *New York Post.* Retrieved from https://nypost.com/2014/03/06/woman-plays-fortune-cookie-lottery-numbers-wins-2m/

Rosenblat, A. (2015, September 10). The future of work: For Uber drivers, data is the boss. *Pacific Standard.* Retrieved from http://www.psmag.com/business-economics/the-future-of-work-for-uber-drivers-data-is-the-boss

Rosenthal, R. (1991). *Meta-analytic procedures for social research.* Newbury Park, CA: Sage.

Rosenthal, R. (1995). Writing meta-analytic reviews. *Psychological Bulletin, 118,* 183–192.

Rosenthal, R., & DiMatteo, M. R. (2001). Meta-analysis: Recent developments in quantitative methods for literature reviews. *Annual Review of Psychology, 52,* 59–82. https://doi.org/10.1146/annurev.psych.52.1.59

Rothenberg, B., & Glanz, J. (2016, January 24). Match-fixing suspicions raised at Australian Open after site stops bets on match. *The New York Times.* Retrieved from https://www.nytimes.com/2016/01/25/sports/tennis/match-fixing-australian-open-mixed-doubles-betting.html

Rubin, M. (2017). When does HARKing hurt? Identifying when different types of undisclosed post hoc hypothesizing harm scientific progress. *Review of General Psychology, 21,* 308–320. doi:10.1037/gpr0000128

Ruby, C. (2006). *Coming to America: An examination of the factors that influence international students' graduate school choices.* Draft of dissertation.

Rudder, C. (2009, November 17). Your looks and your inbox. *Oktrends.* Retrieved from http://blog.okcupid.com/index.php/your-looks-and-online-dating/

Ruhm, C. J. (2000). Are recessions good for your health? *Quarterly Journal of Economics, 115,* 617–650.

Ruhm, C. J. (2006). *Healthy living in hard times* (NBER Working Paper No. 9468). Cambridge, MA: National Bureau of Economic Research. Retrieved from http://www.nber.org/papers/w9468

Sabeti, P. (2018, January 21). For better science, call off the revolutionaries. *Boston Globe.* Retrieved from https://www.bostonglobe.com/ideas/2018/01/21/for-better-science-call-off-revolutionaries/8FFEmBAPCDW3IWYJwKF31L/

Samarrai, F. (2015, August 28). Massive collaboration testing reproducibility of psychology studies publishes findings. University of Virginia. Retrieved from http://as.virginia.edu/news/massive-collaboration-testing-reproducibility-psychology-studies-publishes-findings

Sandberg, D. E., Bukowski, W. M., Fung, C. M., & Noll, R. B. (2004). Height and social adjustment: Are extremes a cause for concern and action? *Pediatrics, 114,* 744–750.

Sandhu, S. (2015, September 22). Selfies are killing more people than shark attacks. *Independent.* Retrieved from http://www.independent.co.uk/arts-entertainment/photography/selfies-are-killing-more-people-than-shark-attacks-10512449.html

Schnall, S. (2014). Commentary and rejoinder on Johnson, Cheung, and Donnellan (2014a): Clean data: Statistical artifacts wash out replication efforts. *Social Psychology, 45,* 315–318.

Schnall, S., Benton, J., & Harvey, S. (2008). With a clean conscience cleanliness reduces the severity of moral judgments. *Psychological Science, 19*(12), 1219–1222.

Schnohr, P., O'Keefe, J. H., Holtermann, A., Lavie, C. J., Lange, P., Jensen, G. B., Marott, J. L. (2018). Various leisure-time physical activities associated with widely divergent life expectancies: The Copenhagen City Heart Study. *Mayo Clinic Proceedings, 93*(12), 1775–1785.

Schulz, K. (2015, July 20). The really big one: An earthquake will destroy a sizable portion of the coastal Northwest. The question is when. *The New Yorker.* Retrieved from http://www.newyorker.com/.

Scientific American. (2018). E-cigs and second-hand vaping. Retrieved from https://www.scientificamerican.com/article/e-cigs-and-second-hand-vaping/

Seymour, C. (2006). Listen while you run. *Runner's World.* Retrieved from https://www.runnersworld.com/gear/a20799208/should-you-listen-to-music-while-running/

Shaikh, A. (2018, October 10). Why does Psychology of Human Sexuality have the lowest average grade of any class in LSA? *Michigan Daily.* Retrieved from https://www.michigandaily.com/section/academics/why-does-psychology-human-sexuality-have-lowest-average-grade-any-class-lsa

Shechet, E. (2015, December 7). Average age of the new *Bachelor* cast is 25, median name is "Lauren." *Jezebel.* Retrieved from https://jezebel.com/average-age-of-the-new-bachelor-cast-is-25-median-name-1746691678

Sherman, J. D., Honegger, S. D., & McGivern, J. L. (2003). *Comparative indicators of education in the United States and other G-8 countries: 2002,* NCES 2003-026. Washington, DC: U.S. Department of Education, National Center for Health Statistics. Retrieved from http://scsvt.org/resource/global_ed_compare2002.pdf.

Sigelman, M. (2018, April 30). Skills, not jobs: How higher ed can capitalize on big data's disruptive moment. Burning Glass Technologies Keynote at New Jersey Big Data Alliance.

Silberzahn, R., & Uhlmann, E. L. (2015). Many hands make tight work. *Nature, 526,* 189–191.

Silberzahn, R., Uhlmann, E. L., Martin, D. P., Anselmi, P., Aust, F., Awtrey, E., … Nosek, B. A. (2018). Many analysts, one data set: Making transparent how variations in analytic choices affect results. *Advances in Methods and Practices in Psychological Science, 1,* 337–356. https://doi.org/10.1177/2515245917747646

Simmons, J. P., Nelson, L. D., & Simonsohn, U. (2011). False-positive psychology: Undisclosed flexibility in data collection and analysis allows presenting anything as significant. *Psychological Science, 22,* 1359–1366. https://doi.org/10.1177/0956797611417632

Simmons, J. P., & Simonsohn, U. (2017). Power posing: *P*-curving the evidence. *Psychological Science, 28,* 687–693. https://doi.org/10.1177/0956797616658563

Simons, D. J., Shoda, Y., & Lindsay, D. S. (2017). Constraints on generality (COG): A proposed addition to all empirical papers. *Perspectives on Psychological Science, 12,* 1123–1128. https://doi.org/10.1177/1745691617708630

Simonsohn, U. (2014). *Posterior-hacking: Selective reporting invalidates Bayesian Results also* (SSRN Scholarly Paper No. ID 2374040). Rochester, NY: Social Science Research Network. Retrieved from https://papers.ssrn.com/abstract=2374040

Singh, R. K., & Göritz, A. S. (2018). Ego depletion does not interfere with working memory performance. *Frontiers in Psychology, 9.* https://doi.org/10.3389/fpsyg.2018.00538

Silver, N. (2012). Oct. 21: Uncertainty clouds polling, but Obama remains Electoral College favorite. *The New York Times.* Retrieved from http://fivethirtyeight.blogs.nytimes.com/2012/10/22/oct-21-uncertainty-clouds-polling-but-obama-remains-electoral-college-favorite/.

Silver, N. & McCann, A. (2014). How to tell someone's age when all you know is her name. *FiveThirtyEight*. Retrieved from https://fivethirtyeight.com/features/how-to-tell-someones-age-when-all-you-know-is-her-name/

Skurnik, I., Yoon, C., Park, D. C., & Schwarz, N. (2005). How warnings about false claims become recommendations. *Journal of Consumer Research, 31,* 713–724.

Spellman, B. A. (2015). A short (personal) future history of revolution 20. *Perspectives on Psychological Science, 10,* 886–899. doi:10.1177/1745691615609918

Stanford, E. (2015, October 30). Music to cats' ears. *The New York Times.* Retrieved from https://www.nytimes.com/2015/11/01/style/cat-music-for-cats-david-teie.html

Steele, J. P., & Pinto, J. N. (2006). Influences of leader trust on policy agreement. *Psi Chi Journal of Undergraduate Research, 11,* 21–26.

Stellar, J. E., John-Henderson, N., Anderson, C. L., Gordon, A. M., McNeil, G. D., & Keltner, D. (2015). Positive affect and markers of inflammation: Discrete positive emotions predict lower levels of inflammatory cytokines. *Emotion, 15,* 129–133. doi:10.1037/emo0000033

Sterne, J. A. C., & Smith, G. D. (2001). Sifting the evidence: What's wrong with significance tests? *British Medical Journal, 322,* 226–231.

Stevenson, S. (2014, April 30). Why YKK? The mysterious Japanese company behind the world's best zippers. *Slate.* Retrieved from www.slate.com/articles/business/branded/2012/04/ykk_zippers_why_so_many_designers_use_them_.html

Stigler, S. M. (1999). *Statistics on the table: The history of statistical concepts and methods.* Cambridge, MA: Harvard University Press.

Strauss, A. (2016, February 4). With this tattoo, I thee wed. *The New York Times.* Retrieved from https://www.nytimes.com/2016/02/07/fashion/weddings/tattoo-wedding-rings.html

Stromberg, J., & Caswell, E. (2015, October 8). Why the Myers–Briggs test is totally meaningless. *Vox.* Retrieved from https://www.vox.com/2014/7/15/5881947/myers-briggs-personality-test-meaningless

Swank, E. (2018). Sexual identities and participation in liberal and conservative social movements. *Social Science Research, 74,* 176–186. https://doi.org/10.1016/j.ssresearch.2018.04.002

Tal, A., & Wansink, B. (2016). Blinded with science: Trivial graphs and formulas increase ad persuasiveness and belief in product efficacy. *Public Understanding of Science, 25,* 117–125. doi:10.1177/0963662514549688

Talarico, J. M., & Rubin, D. C. (2003). Confidence, not consistency, characterizes flashbulb memories. *Psychological Science, 14,* 455–461.

Taylor, G. M., & Ste-Marie, D. M. (2001). Eating disorders symptoms in Canadian female pair and dance figure skaters. *International Journal of Sports Psychology, 32,* 21–28.

Tierney, J. (2008a). Health halo can hide the calories. *The New York Times.* Retrieved from http://www.nytimes.com/2008/12/02/science/02tier.html.

Tierney, J. (2008b). The perils of "healthy" food. *The New York Times.* Retrieved from http://tierneylab.blogs.nytimes.com.

Teubner, T., Saade, N., Hawlitschek, F., & Weinhardt, C. (2016, August). *It's only pixels, badges, and stars: On the economic value of reputation on Airbnb.* Paper presented at Australian Conference on Information Systems, Wollongong, Australia.

Trafimow, D., & Marks, M. (2015). Editorial. *Basic and Applied Social Psychology, 37,* 1–2.

Trudel, R., Argo, J. J., & Meng, M. D. (2016). The recycled self: Consumers' disposal decisions of identity-linked products. *Journal of Consumer Research, 43,* 246–264. https://doi.org/10.1093/jcr/ucw014

Tucker, K. L., Morita, K., Qiao, N., Hannan, M. T., Cupples, A., & Kiel, D. P. (2006). Colas, but not other carbonated beverages, are associated with low bone mineral density in older women: The Framingham Osteoporosis Study. *American Journal of Clinical Nutrition, 84,* 936–942.

Tuckel, P. & Milczarski, W. (2014). Bike lanes + bike program = bike safety: An observational study of biking behavior in lower and central Manhattan. *Hunter College, the City University of New York.* Retrieved from http://silo-public.hunter.cuny.edu/62eaab1fad6c75d37293d2f2f6504a15adacd5c6/Cycling_Study_January_2014.pdf

Tufte, E. R. (2001). *The Visual Display of Quantitative Information* (2nd ed.). Cheshire, CT: Graphics Press.

Turner, L. (2015, September 23). Is Lake Kivu set to explode? *Pacific Standard.* Retrieved from http://www.psmag.com/.

Upton, P., & Eiser, C. (2006). School experiences after treatment for a brain tumour. *Child: Care, Health and Development, 32,* 9–17.

Urbaniak, G. C., & Plous, S. (2013). Research Randomizer (Version 4.0) [Computer software]. Retrieved from http://www.randomizer.org/

Valentino-Devries, J., Singer-Vine, J., & Soltani, A. (2012, December 24). Websites vary prices, deals based on users' information. *The Wall Street Journal.* Retrieved from https://www.wsj.com/articles/SB10001424127887323777204578189391813881534

van der Zee, R. (2016, October 6). The "Airbnb effect": Is it real, and what is it doing to a city like Amsterdam? *The Guardian.* Retrieved from https://www.theguardian.com/cities/2016/oct/06/the-airbnb-effect-amsterdam-fairbnb-property-prices-communities

VanderStoep, S. W., Fagerlin, A., & Feenstra, J. S. (2000). What Do Students Remember from Introductory Psychology? *Teaching of Psychology, 27*(2), 89–92.

Vanman, E. J., Baker, R., & Tobin, S. J. (2018). The burden of online friends: The effects of giving up Facebook on stress and well-being. *Journal of Social Psychology, 158,* 496–507. https://doi.org/10.1080/00224545.2018.1453467

van Toorenburg, M., Oostrom, J. K., & Pollet, T. V. (2015). What a difference your e-mail makes: Effects of informal e-mail addresses in online résumé screening. *Cyberpsychology, Behavior, and Social Networking, 18,* 135–140.

Varma, A., Jukic, N., Pestek, A., Shultz, C. J., & Nestorov, S. (2016). Airbnb: Exciting innovation or passing fad? *Tourism Management Perspectives, 20,* 228–237. https://doi.org/10.1016/j.tmp.2016.09.002

Vasishth, S., Mertzen, D., Jäger, L. A., & Gelman, A. (2018). The statistical significance filter leads to overoptimistic expectations of replicability. *Journal of Memory and Language, 103,* 151–175. https://doi.org/10.1016/j.jml.2018.07.004

Vazire, S. (2018). Implications of the credibility revolution for productivity, creativity, and progress. *Perspectives on Psychological Science, 13,* 411–417. https://doi.org/10.1177/1745691617751884

Vevea, J. L., & Woods, C. M. (2005). Publication bias in research synthesis: Sensitivity analysis using a priori weight functions. *Psychological Methods, 10,* 428–443.

Vigen, T. (2015). Spurious correlations. Retrieved from http://www.tylervigen.com/spurious-correlations

Vinten-Johansen, P., Brody, H., Paneth, N., Rachman, S., & Rip, M. (2003). *Cholera, chloroform, and the science of medicine: A life of John Snow.* New York, NY: Oxford University Press.

Vogel, C. (2011, December 14). Art world star doesn't change his spots. *The New York Times.* Retrieved from https://www.nytimes.com/2011/12/14/arts/design/damien-hirsts-spot-paintings-will-fill-all-11-gagosians.html

von Hippel, W., Ronay, R., Baker, E., Kjelsaas, K., & Murphy, S. C. (2016). Quick thinkers are smooth talkers mental speed facilitates charisma. *Psychological Science, 27,* 119–122.

Volcanoes by country (2016). Retrieved from http://volcano.oregonstate.edu/volcanoes_by_country.

Wagenmakers, E. J., Dutilh, G., & Sarafoglou, A. (2018). The creativity–verification cycle in psychological science: New methods to combat old idols. *Perspectives on Psychological Science, 13,* 418–427. doi: 10.1177/1745691618771357.

Wagenmakers, E.-J., Marsman, M., Jamil, T., Ly, A., Verhagen, J., Love, J., … Morey, R. D. (2018). Bayesian inference for psychology. Part I: Theoretical advantages and practical ramifications. *Psychonomic Bulletin & Review, 25*(1), 35–57. https://doi.org/10.3758/s13423-017-1343-3

Walker, S. (2006). *Fantasyland: A season on baseball's lunatic fringe.* New York, NY: Penguin.

Ward, M. (2013). The gentle art of cracking passwords. *BBC News.* Retrieved from: http://www.bbc.com/news/technology-24519306

Wasserstein, R. L. (Ed.) (2016). ASA Statement on Statistical Significance and *p*-values. *The American Statistician.*

Wasserstein, R. L., & Lazar, N. A. (2016). The ASA's statement on *p*-values: Context, process, and purpose, *The American Statistician, 70*(2), 129–133. doi:10.1080/00031305.2016.1154108

Waters, A. (2006, February 24). Eating for credit. *The New York Times.* Retrieved from https://www.nytimes.com/2006/02/24/opinion/eating-for-credit.html

Weinberg, B. A., Fleisher, B. M., & Hashimoto, M. (2007). *Evaluating methods for evaluating instruction: The case of higher education* (NBER Working Paper No. 12844). Cambridge, MA: The National Bureau of Economic Research.

Weissgerber, T. L., Milic, N. M., Winham, S. J., & Garovic, V. D. (2015). Beyond bar and line graphs: Time for a new data presentation paradigm. *PLoS Biology, 13*(4), e1002128. https://doi.org/10.1371/journal.pbio.1002128

Westfall, J., Judd, C. M., & Kenny, D. A. (2015). Replicating studies in which samples of participants respond to samples of stimuli. *Perspectives on Psychological Science, 10*(3), 390–399.

White, B., Driver, S., & Warren, A. (2010). Resilience and indicators of adjustment during rehabilitation from a spinal cord injury. *Rehabilitation Psychology, 55*(1), 23–32. doi:10.1037/a0018451

White, M. (2014, July 11). Is social media saving science? *Pacific Standard.* Retrieved from http://www.psmag.com/nature-and-technology/academic-publishing-social-media-saving-science-85733

Wiley, J. (2005). A fair and balanced look at the news: What affects memory for controversial arguments. *Journal of Memory and Language, 53,* 95–109.

Wingfield, N. (2017, April 24). Video games help model brain's neurons. *The New York Times.* Retrieved from https://www.nytimes.com/2017/04/24/science/citizen-science-video-game-neurons.html

Wolff, A. (2002, January 21). Is the *SI* jinx for real? *Sports Illustrated.*

Woolley, K., & Fishbach, A. (2017). A recipe for friendship: Similar food consumption promotes trust and cooperation. *Journal of Consumer Psychology, 27,* 1–10. https://doi.org/10.1016/j.jcps.2016.06.003

Word, D. L., Coleman, C. D., Nunziata, R., & Kominski, R. (2008). Demographic aspects of surnames from census 2000. Unpublished manuscript, Retrieved from http://citeseerx.ist.psu.edu/viewdoc/download?doi=10.1.1.192.3093&rep=rep1&type=pdf

World Health Organization. (2018, March 22). Depression. Retrieved from https://www.who.int/news-room/fact-sheets/detail/depression

Wu, J. (2011). Improving the writing of research papers: IMRAD and beyond. *Landscale Ecology, 26,* 1345–1349. https://doi.org/10.1007/s10980-011-9674-3

Yanovski, J. A., Yanovski, S. Z., Sovik, K. N., Nouven, T. T., O'Neil, P. M., & Sebring, N. G. A. (2000). A prospective study of holiday weight gain. *New England Journal of Medicine, 23,* 861–867.

Yilmaz, A., Baran, R., Bayramgürler, B., Karahalli, E., Unutmaz, S., & Üskül, T. B. (2000). Lung cancer in non-smokers. *Turkish Respiratory Journal, 2,* 13–15.

York, B. N. & Loeb, S. (2014). One step at a time: The effects of early literacy text messaging program for parents and preschoolers. *National Bureau of Economic Research.* Retrieved from http://www.nber.org/papers/w20659

Yong, E. (2012, May). Replication studies: Bad copy. *Nature.* Retrieved from http://www.nature.com/news/replication-studies-bad-copy-1.10634

Zacks, J., & Tversky, B. (1997). *Bars and lines: A study of graphic communication.* Palo Alto, CA: AAAI Technical Report FS-97-03.

Zarate, C. A. (2006). A randomized trial of an *N*-methyl-d-aspartate antagonist in treatment-resistant major depression. *Archives of General Psychiatry, 63,* 856–864.

Zaringhalam, M. (2019, January 24). To groom better scientists, harness the power of narrative. *UNDARK.* Retrieved from https://undark.org/2019/01/24/to-groom-better-scientists-harness-the-power-of-narrative/

Zarsky, T. Z. (2018). Correlation versus causation in health-related big data analysis. In E. Vayena, H. F. Lynch, I. G. Cohen, & U. Gasser (Eds.), *Big data, health law, and bioethics* (pp. 42–55). Cambridge, UK: Cambridge University Press. https://doi.org/10.1017/9781108147972.005

INDEX

FORMULAS

CHAPTER 4

Mean of a Sample

$$M = \frac{\Sigma X}{N}$$

Range

$$\text{range} = X_{highest} - X_{lowest}$$

Variance

$$SD^2 = \frac{\Sigma(X - M)^2}{N}$$

Standard Deviation

$$SD = \sqrt{SD^2}$$

Standard Deviation (when we don't already have variance)

$$SD = \sqrt{\frac{\Sigma(X - M)^2}{N}}$$

Interquartile Range

$$IQR = Q3 - Q1$$

CHAPTER 6

z Score

$$z = \frac{(X - \mu)}{\sigma}$$

Raw Score from a z Score

$$X = z(\sigma) + \mu$$

Standard Error

$$\sigma_M = \frac{\sigma}{\sqrt{N}}$$

z Statistic for a Distribution of Means

$$z = \frac{(M - \mu_M)}{\sigma_M}$$

CHAPTER 8

Confidence Interval for a z Test

$$M_{lower} = -z(\sigma_M) + M_{sample}$$

$$M_{upper} = z(\sigma_M) + M_{sample}$$

Effect Size for a z Test

$$\text{Cohen's } d = \frac{(M - \mu)}{\sigma}$$

CHAPTER 9 and 10

Standard Deviation of a Sample

$$s = \sqrt{\frac{\Sigma(X - M)^2}{(N - 1)}}$$

Standard Error of a Sample

$$s_M = \frac{s}{\sqrt{N}}$$

t Statistic for a Single-Sample t Test

$$t = \frac{(M - \mu_M)}{s_M}$$

Degrees of Freedom for a Single-Sample t Test or a Paired-Samples t Test

$$df = N - 1$$

Confidence Interval for a Single-Sample t Test

$$M_{lower} = -t(s_M) + M_{sample}$$

$$M_{upper} = t(s_M) + M_{sample}$$

Effect Size for a Single-Sample t Test or a Paired-Samples t Test

$$\text{Cohen's } d = \frac{(M - \mu)}{s}$$

CHAPTER 11

Degrees of Freedom for an Independent-Samples t Test

$$df_{total} = df_X + df_Y$$

Pooled Variance

$$s_{pooled}^2 = \left(\frac{df_X}{df_{total}}\right)s_X^2 + \left(\frac{df_Y}{df_{total}}\right)s_Y^2$$

Variance for a Distribution of Means for an Independent-Samples t Test

$$s_{M_X}^2 = \frac{s_{pooled}^2}{N_X} \qquad s_{M_Y}^2 = \frac{s_{pooled}^2}{N_Y}$$

Variance for a Distribution of Differences Between Means

$$s_{difference}^2 = s_{M_X}^2 + s_{M_Y}^2$$

Standard Deviation of the Distribution of Differences Between Means

$$s_{difference} = \sqrt{s_{difference}^2}$$

t Statistic for an Independent-Samples t Test

$$t = \frac{(M_X - M_Y) - (\mu_X - \mu_Y)}{s_{difference}}$$

Often abbreviated as: $t = \dfrac{(M_X - M_Y)}{s_{difference}}$

Confidence Interval for an Independent-Samples t Test

$$(M_X - M_Y)_{lower} = -t(s_{difference}) + (M_X - M_Y)_{sample}$$
$$(M_X - M_Y)_{upper} = t(s_{difference}) + (M_X - M_Y)_{sample}$$

Pooled Standard Deviation

$$s_{pooled} = \sqrt{s_{pooled}^2}$$

Effect Size for an Independent-Samples t Test

$$\text{Cohen's } d = \frac{(M_X - M_Y) - (\mu_X - \mu_Y)}{s_{pooled}}$$

CHAPTER 12

One-Way Between-Groups ANOVA

$$df_{between} = N_{groups} - 1$$
$$df_{within} = df_1 + df_2 + \cdots + df_{last} \text{ (in which } df_1\text{, etc., are the}$$
degrees of freedom, $N - 1$, for each sample)
$$df_{total} = df_{between} + df_{within} \text{ or } df_{total} = N_{total} - 1$$

$$GM = \frac{\Sigma(X)}{N_{total}}$$

$$SS_{total} = \Sigma(X - GM)^2 \text{ for each score}$$
$$SS_{within} = \Sigma(X - M)^2 \text{ for each score}$$
$$SS_{between} = \Sigma(M - GM)^2 \text{ for each score}$$
$$SS_{total} = SS_{within} + SS_{between}$$

$$MS_{between} = \frac{SS_{between}}{df_{between}}$$

$$MS_{within} = \frac{SS_{within}}{df_{within}}$$

$$F = \frac{MS_{between}}{MS_{within}}$$

Effect Sizes for a One-Way Between-Groups ANOVA

$$R^2 = \frac{SS_{between}}{SS_{total}}$$

$$\omega^2 = \frac{SS_{between} - ((df_{between})(MS_{within}))}{SS_{total} + MS_{within}}$$

Tukey HSD Post Hoc Test

$$s_M = \sqrt{\frac{MS_{within}}{N}}, \text{ if equal sample sizes}$$

$$N' = \frac{N_{groups}}{\Sigma(1/N)}$$

$$s_M = \sqrt{\frac{MS_{within}}{N'}}, \text{ if unequal sample sizes}$$

$$HSD = \frac{(M_1 - M_2)}{s_M}, \text{ for any two sample means}$$

(Formulas continued on inside back cover.)

FORMULAS

CHAPTER 13 (Formulas continued from inside front cover.)

One-Way Within-Groups ANOVA

$df_{subjects} = n - 1$

$df_{within} = (df_{between})(df_{subjects})$

$df_{total} = df_{between} + df_{subjects} + df_{within}$

$SS_{subjects} = \Sigma(M_{participant} - GM)^2$ for each score

$SS_{within} = SS_{total} - SS_{between} - SS_{subjects}$

$MS_{subjects} = \dfrac{SS_{subjects}}{df_{subjects}}$

$F_{subjects} = \dfrac{MS_{subjects}}{MS_{within}}$

Effect Size for a One-Way Within-Groups ANOVA

$R^2 = \dfrac{SS_{between}}{(SS_{total} - SS_{subjects})}$

CHAPTER 14

Two-Way Between-Groups ANOVA

$df_{rows} = N_{rows} - 1$

$df_{columns} = N_{columns} - 1$

$df_{interaction} = (df_{rows})(df_{columns})$

$SS_{total} = \Sigma(X - GM)^2$ for each score

$SS_{between(rows)} = \Sigma(M_{row} - GM)^2$ for each score

$SS_{between(columns)} = \Sigma(M_{column} - GM)^2$ for each score

$SS_{within} = \Sigma(X - M_{cell})^2$ for each score

$SS_{between(interaction)} = SS_{total} - (SS_{between(rows)} + SS_{between(columns)} + SS_{within})$

Effect Sizes for a Two-Way Between-Groups ANOVA

$R^2_{rows} = \dfrac{SS_{rows}}{(SS_{total} - SS_{columns} - SS_{interaction})}$

$R^2_{columns} = \dfrac{SS_{columns}}{(SS_{total} - SS_{rows} - SS_{interaction})}$

$R^2_{interaction} = \dfrac{SS_{interaction}}{(SS_{total} - SS_{rows} - SS_{columns})}$

CHAPTER 15

Pearson Correlation Coefficient

$r = \dfrac{\Sigma\left[(X - M_X)(Y - M_Y)\right]}{\sqrt{(SS_X)(SS_Y)}}$

$df_r = N - 2$

CHAPTER 16

Standardized Regression Equation

$z_{\hat{Y}} = (r_{XY})(z_X)$

Simple Linear Regression Equation

$\hat{Y} = a + b(X)$

Standardized Regression Coefficient

$\beta = (b)\dfrac{\sqrt{SS_X}}{\sqrt{SS_Y}}$

Proportionate Reduction in Error

$r^2 = \dfrac{(SS_{total} - SS_{error})}{SS_{total}}$

CHAPTER 17

Chi-Square Statistic

$df_{\chi^2} = k - 1$ (for chi-square test for goodness of fit)

$$\chi^2 = \Sigma\left[\frac{(O-E)^2}{E}\right]$$

$df_{\chi^2} = (k_{row} - 1)(k_{column} - 1)$ (for chi-square test for independence)

Expected frequency for each cell $= \dfrac{total_{column}}{N}(total_{row})$,

where we use the overall number of participants, N, along with the totals for the rows and columns for each particular cell.

Effect Size for the Chi-Square Statistic

Cramér's $V = \sqrt{\dfrac{\chi^2}{(N)(df_{row/column})}}$, where we use the

smaller of the row and column degrees of freedom.